Contents

Preface

Teachers and students of economics are critical groups of people. Constantly dissatisfied with the materials that they use, they face the problems of limited resources, a wide variety of needs and a constantly changing world. This book is intended to go some way to resolving this example of the basic economic problem.

The book has a number of distinctive features.

Comprehensive The book contains sufficient material to satisfy the demands of students taking a wide range of examinations including 'A' level, 'AS' level and Higher Grade economics.

Flexible unit structure The material is organised not into chapters but into shorter units. This reflects the organisation of a number of GCSE textbooks, and therefore students should be familiar with this style of presentation. The unit structure also allows the teacher greater freedom to devise a course. Economics teachers have a long tradition of using their main textbooks in a different order to that in which they are presented. So whilst there is a logical order to the book, it has been written on the assumption that teachers and students will piece the units together to suit their own teaching and learning needs. Cross referencing has been used on occasions to further aid flexibility. This approach also means that it is relatively easy to use the book for a growing number of courses which encompass part of a traditional 'A' level syllabus, such as modular 'A' level syllabuses, 'AS' syllabuses and professional courses with an economics input.

Accessibility The book has been written in a clear and logical style which should make it accessible to all readers. Each unit is divided into short, easily manageable sections. Diagrams contain concise explanations which summarise or support the text.

A workbook The text is interspersed with a large number of questions. These are relatively short for the most part, and whilst some could be used for extended writing work, most require relatively simple answers. They have been included to help teachers and students assess whether learning and understanding has taken place by providing immediate application of content and skills to given situations. I hope that many will be used as a basis for class discussion as well as being answered in written form.

Applied economics as well as economic theory Many economics courses require teachers and students to have a book covering economic theory **and** an applied economic text. In this book, a systematic approach to applied economics has been included alongside economic theory. Each unit has an applied economics section and some units deal only with applied economics. It should be noted that many of the questions also contain applied economics material and where sufficiently significant, this has been referred to in the index.

Use of data Modern technology has allowed much of the book to proceed from manuscript to book in a very short period. This has meant that we have been able to use statistics which were available in mid-1995. Most statistical series therefore go up to 1994/5, although some were only available to earlier years. At the same time, experience has shown that too many current stories quickly date a book. Materials therefore been chosen, particularly for the macro-economic section of the book, from throughout the post-war era, with particular emphasis on the turbulent times of the 1970s, 1980s and 1990s. This approach will help candidates to answer questions which require knowledge of what has happened 'in recent years' or 'over the past decade'.

Investigations/coursework Coursework is increasingly being used as a method of learning and assessment. It is already a feature of some syllabuses. 8 sets of coursework investigations have been included in the book which should give candidates help with how to choose, research and present a piece of coursework even if they do not make full use of a particular suggestion in the book. If some of the comments in the coursework seem repetitive, they have been included because it has been assumed that students will only complete a few of the 16 core suggestions given.

Key terms Many units contain a key terms section. Each section defines new concepts, which appear in capitals in the text of the unit. Taken together, they provide a comprehensive dictionary of economics.

The basic economic problem

Summary

1. Nearly all resources are scarce.
2. Human wants are infinite.
3. Scarce resources and infinite wants give rise to the basic economic problem - resources have to be allocated between competing uses.
4. Allocation involves choice and each choice has an opportunity cost.
5. The production possibility frontier (PPF) shows the maximum potential output of an economy.
6. Production at a point inside the PPF indicates an inefficient use of resources.
7. Growth in the economy will shift the PPF outwards.

Scarcity

It is often said that we live in a global village. The world's resources are finite; there are only limited amounts of land, water, oil, food and other resources on this planet. Economists therefore say that resources are SCARCE.

Scarcity means that economic agents, such as individuals, firms, governments and international agencies, can only obtain a limited amount of resources at any moment in time. For instance, a family has to live on a fixed budget; it cannot have everything it wants. A firm might want to build a new factory but not have the resources to be able to do so. A government might wish to build new hospitals or devote more resources to its foreign aid programme but not have the finance to make this possible. Resources which are scarce are called ECONOMIC GOODS.

Not all resources are scarce. There is more than enough air on this planet for everyone to be able to breathe as much as they want. Resources which are not scarce are called FREE GOODS. In the past many goods such as food, water and shelter have been free, but as the population of the planet has expanded and as production has increased, so the number of free goods has diminished. Recently, for instance, clean beaches in many parts of the UK have ceased to be a free good to society. Pollution has forced water companies and seaside local authorities to spend resources cleaning up their local environment. With the destruction of the world's rain forests and increasing atmospheric pollution, the air we breathe may no longer remain a free good. Factories may have to purify the air they take from the atmosphere for instance. This air would then become an economic good.

QUESTION 1 Few experienced political observers could have been surprised by the recent highly critical report produced by the Commons' transport select committee on government plans to introduce tolls for UK motorway users. For the average MP, any suggestion that millions of car-owning voters should be compelled to pay for using roads that were hitherto 'free', has long been regarded as electoral dynamite. Both Tory and Labour MPs, therefore, have joined forces to chorus disapproval for a scheme which they fear could eclipse rail privatisation as the ultimate 'poll tax on wheels'. Even the government itself has decided that any decision to introduce tolls should be delayed until 1998, well after the next general election.

Meanwhile, in the real world, congestion continues to grow on motorways which are breaking up under the pressure of traffic; vehicles emit gases that pose an increasing threat to public health and public transport usage declines for lack of sufficient investment.

Source: the *Financial Times*, 14.12.1994.

Explain whether roads are, in any sense, a 'free good' from an economic viewpoint.

Infinite wants

People have a limited number of NEEDS which must be satisfied if they are to survive as human beings. Some are material needs, such as food, liquid, heat, shelter and clothing. Others are psychological and emotional needs such as self-esteem and being loved. People's needs are finite. However, no one would choose to live at the level of basic human needs if they could enjoy a higher standard of living.

This is because human WANTS are unlimited. It doesn't matter whether the person is a peasant in China, a mystic in India, a manager in the UK or the richest individual in the world, there is always something which he or she wants more of. This can include more food, a bigger house, a longer holiday, a cleaner environment, more love, more friendship, better relationships, more self-esteem, greater fairness or justice, peace, or more time to listen to music, meditate or cultivate the arts.

The basic economic problem

Resources are scarce but wants are infinite. It is this which gives rise to the BASIC ECONOMIC PROBLEM and which forces economic agents to make choices. They have to allocate their scarce resources between competing uses.

QUESTION 2 Draw up a list of minimum human needs for a teenager living in the UK today. How would this list differ from the needs of a teenager living in Bangladesh or sub-Saharan Africa?

QUESTION 3 The Secretary of State for Education has received a letter from students at Stakis Tertiary College. The letter argues that all 16-19 year olds staying on in education after the compulsory school leaving age should receive a grant of £2 000 per year. The students point out that this would provide a strong incentive for 16 year olds to stay in full time education. This would benefit the economy enormously, increasing the skills of the future labour force and providing jobs in education at a time of high unemployment.

Write a reply to the students pointing out the opportunity cost(s) of giving the grant.

Economics is the study of this allocation of resources - the choices that are made by economic agents. Every CHOICE involves a range of alternatives. For instance, should the government spend £10 billion in tax revenues on nuclear weapons, better schools or greater care for the elderly? Will you choose to become an accountant, an engineer or a vicar?

These choices can be graded in terms of the benefits to be gained from each alternative. One choice will be the 'best' one and a rational economic agent will take that alternative. But all the other choices will then have to be given up. The benefit lost from the next best alternative is called the OPPORTUNITY COST of the choice. For instance, economics may have been your third choice at 'A' level. Your fourth choice, one which you didn't take up, might have been history. Then the opportunity cost of studying economics at 'A' level is studying history at 'A' level. Alternatively, you might have enough money to buy just one of your two favourite magazines - *Melody Maker* or the *New Musical Express*. If you choose to buy the *Melody Maker*, then its opportunity cost is the benefit which would have been gained from consuming the *New Musical Express*.

Free goods have no opportunity cost. No resources need be sacrificed when someone, say, breathes air or swims in the sea.

Production possibility frontiers

Over a period of time, resources are scarce and therefore only a finite amount can be produced. For example, an economy might have enough resources at its disposal to be able to produce 30 units of manufactured goods and 30 units of non-manufactures. If it were now to produce more manufactured goods, it would have to give up some of its production of non-manufactured items. This is because the production of a manufactured item has an opportunity cost - in this case the production of non-manufactures. The more manufactures that are produced, the less non-manufactures can be produced.

This can be shown in Figure 1.1. The curved line is called the PRODUCTION POSSIBILITY FRONTIER (PPF) - other names for it include PRODUCTION POSSIBILITY CURVE or BOUNDARY, and TRANSFORMATION CURVE. The PPF shows the different combinations of economic goods which an economy is able to produce if all resources in the economy are fully and efficiently employed. The economy therefore could be:

- at the point C on its PPF, producing 30 units of manufactured goods and 30 units of non-manufactures;
- at the point D, producing 35 units of manufactured goods and 20 units of non-manufactures;
- at the point A, devoting all of its resources to the production of non-manufactured goods;
- at the points B or E or anywhere else along the line.

The production possibility frontier illustrates clearly the principle of opportunity cost. Assume that the economy is producing at the point C in Figure 1.1 and it is desired to move to the point D. This means that the output of manufactured goods will increase from 30 to 35 units. However, the opportunity cost of that (i.e. what has to be given up because of that choice) is the lost output of non-manufactures, falling from 30 to 20 units. The opportunity cost at C of increasing manufacturing production by 5 units is 10 units of non-manufactures.

The production possibility frontier for an economy is drawn on the assumption that all resources in the economy are fully and efficiently employed. If there are unemployed workers or idle factories, or if production is inefficiently organised, then the economy cannot be producing on its PPF. It will produce within the

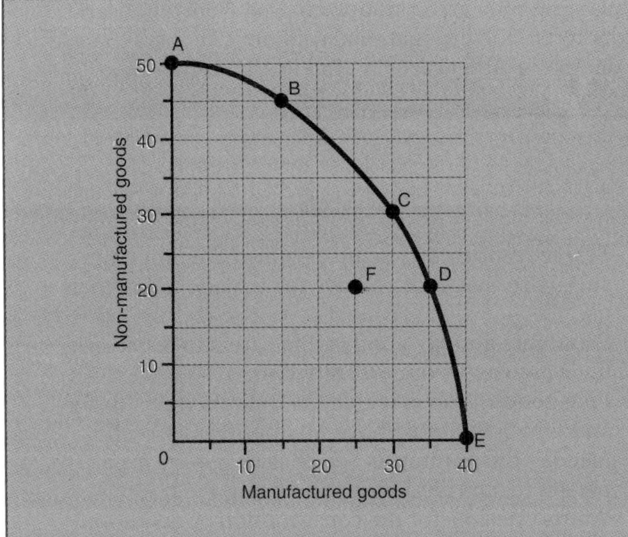

Figure 1.1 *The production possibility frontier*
ABCDE is a production possibility frontier. It shows the different combinations of goods which can be produced if all resources are fully and efficiently utilised. For instance, the economy can produce no manufactured goods and 50 units of non-manufactures, 30 units of manufactured goods and 30 units of non-manufactures, or 40 units of manufactured goods but no non-manufactures.

boundary. In Figure 1.1 the economy could produce anywhere along the line AE. But because there is unemployment in the economy, production is at point F.

The economy cannot be at any point outside its existing PPF because the PPF, by definition, shows the maximum production level of the economy. However, it might be able to move to the right of its PPF in the future if there is **economic growth**. An increase in the productive potential of an economy is shown by a shift outwards of the PPF. In Figure 1.2 economic growth pushes the PPF from PP to QQ, allowing the economy to increase its maximum level

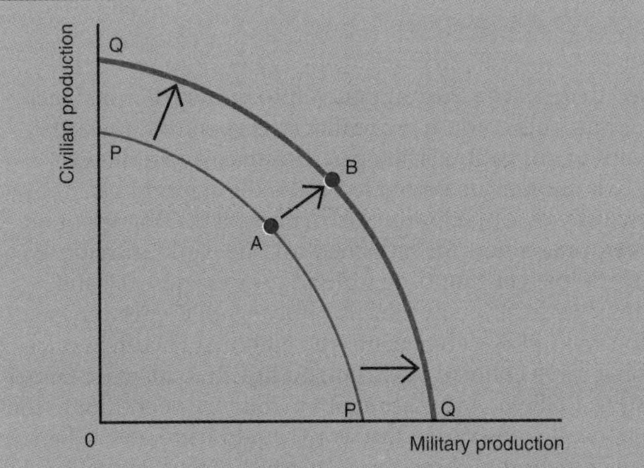

Figure 1.2 *Economic growth*
Economic growth in the quantity or quality of the inputs to the production process means that an economy has increased its productive potential. This is shown by a shift to the right of the production possibility frontier from PP to QQ. It would enable the economy to move production, for instance, from point A to point B.

of production say from A to B. Growth in the economy can happen if:

- the quantity of resources available for production increases; for instance there might be an increase in the number of workers in the economy, or new factories and offices might be built;
- there is an increase in the quality of resources; education will make workers more productive whilst technical progress will allow machines and production processes to produce more with the same amount of resources.

The production possibility frontiers in Figures 1.1. to 1.2 have been drawn concave to the origin (bowing outwards) rather than as straight lines or as convex lines. This is because it has been assumed that not all resources in the economy are as productive in one use compared to another.

Take, for instance, the production of wheat in the UK. Comparatively little wheat is grown in Wales because the soil and the climate are less suited to wheat production than in an area like East Anglia. Let us start from a position where no wheat is grown at all in the UK. Some farmers then decide to grow wheat. If production in the economy is to be maximised it should be grown on the land which is most suited to wheat production (i.e. where its opportunity cost is lowest). This will be in an area of the country like East Anglia. As wheat production expands, land has to be used which is less productive because land is a finite resource. More and more marginal land, such as that found in Wales, is used and output per acre falls. The land could have been used for another form of production, for instance sheep rearing. The more wheat is grown, the less is the output per acre and therefore the greater the cost in terms of sheep production.

In Figure 1.3 only sheep and wheat are produced in the economy. If no wheat is produced the economy could produce OC of sheep. If there is one unit of wheat production only OB of sheep can be produced. Therefore the opportunity cost of the first unit of wheat is BC of sheep. The second unit of wheat has a much higher

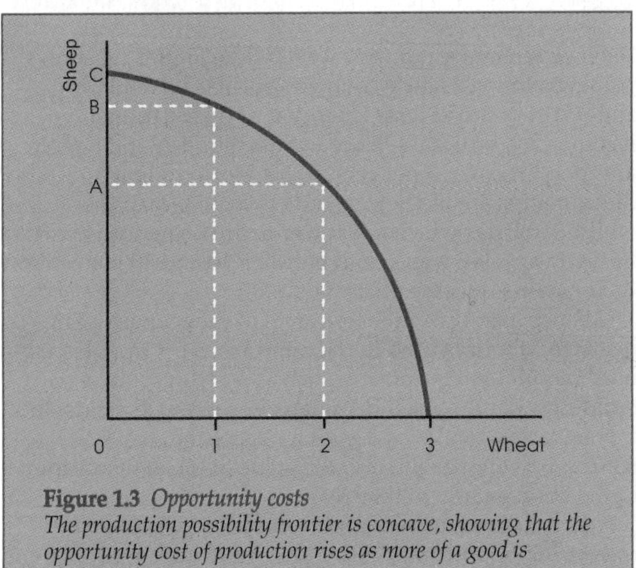

Figure 1.3 *Opportunity costs*
The production possibility frontier is concave, showing that the opportunity cost of production rises as more of a good is produced.

opportunity cost - AB. But if the economy produces wheat only, then the opportunity cost of the third unit of wheat rises to OA of sheep.

The PPF by itself gives no indication of which combination of goods will be produced in an economy. All it shows is the combination of goods which an economy could produce if output were maximised from a given fixed amount of resources. It shows a range of possibilities and much of economics is concerned with explaining why an economy, ranging from a household economy to the international economy, chooses to produce at one point either on or within its PPF rather than another.

QUESTION 4 Draw a production possibility frontier. The scale on both axes is the same. The economy is currently producing at point A on the frontier which is at the mid point between the vertical axis (showing public sector goods) and the horizontal axis (showing private sector goods). Mark the following points on your drawing.
Point B - a point which shows production following the election of a government which privatises many public sector services but maintains full and efficient employment.
Point C - where unemployment is present in the economy.
Point D - where the state takes over production of all goods and services in the economy.
Now draw two new production possibility frontiers.
PP - which shows the position after a devastating war has hit the economy.
QQ - where there is an increase in productivity in the economy such that output from the same amount of resources increases by 50 per cent in the public sector but twice that amount in the private sector.

Key terms

Scarce resources - resources which are limited in supply so that choices have to be made about their use.
Economic goods - goods which are scarce because their use has an opportunity cost.
Free goods - goods which are unlimited in supply and which therefore have no opportunity cost.
Needs - the minimum which is necessary for a person to survive as a human being.
Wants - desires for the consumption of goods and services.
The economic problem - resources have to be allocated between competing uses because wants are infinite whilst resources are scarce.
Choice - economic choices involve the alternative uses of scarce resources.
Opportunity cost - the benefits foregone of the next best alternative.
Production possibility frontier - (also known as the production possibility curve or the production possibility boundary or the transformation curve) - a curve which shows the maximum potential level of output of one good given a level of output for all other goods in the economy.

Applied economics

The opportunity cost of defence

Defence is a major industry worldwide. Figure 1.4 shows that even low spending countries such as Luxembourg and Spain spend at least 1 per cent of their national income each year on defence, whilst the USA and Greece are spending over 5 per cent. Third World military dictatorships are likely to spend even more than this, whilst countries which are at war or are being torn apart by civil war may well spend between 10 and 20 per cent of their national income on arms.

Defence uses up scarce resources in the economy. For instance, labour is used in the armed forces. Capital is used in military equipment, such as warships, tanks or buildings. Land is used in military bases and airfields. In money terms, total world military spending in 1992 of $662bn was almost equal to the value of the entire output of the US economy in that year.

Hence, defence has an opportunity cost. One way of measuring opportunity cost would be to look at the alternative civilian uses of the resources currently being used in defence - 'turning guns into butter'. For instance, governments could have reallocated spending towards health or education. The opportunity cost of a diesel-electric submarine priced at £250 million might be a brand new fully equipped large district hospital. £3bn spent on developing a new air-launched missile could provide an extra 30 per cent funding for one year for nursery and primary education in the UK. Putting all the resources allocated to UK defence into the National Health Service would have enabled spènding on health to increase 66 per cent in 1995-96. A donation of US military spending to the 20 poorest countries in the world could have given them a gift equivalent to three times their estimated annual national income.

Military spending can also be seen to have a further opportunity cost. Consider what might happen if resources used for defence were put into investment goods - 'turning swords into ploughshares'. Investment goods are goods like factories, offices, roads and machines. They are used to make other goods and services. Higher investment is likely to lead to higher growth in national income over time. Resources allocated today to roads and offices will increase national income in the future. If cuts in defence lead to a rise in investment, then it is likely that the capacity of the economy to produce goods and services would grow.

This logic is at the heart of what is called the 'peace dividend'. In 1989-90, the Soviet Union and Eastern Europe turned from being hostile nations to the West into neutral or friendly ones. This ending of the 'Cold War' allowed both the Eastern bloc countries and the West to begin a rundown in defence spending. UK defence spending for instance, has fallen from over 4 per cent of UK national income in the late 1980s to a little over 3 per cent in 1995. Similar deep cuts have been made elsewhere in the world. An International Monetary Fund study has predicted that a 20 per cent cut in military spending on world 1992 levels spread over five years would lead to a significant improvement in the performance of the world economy. By the end of the 11th year of such cuts, they predict that national income in the rich industrialised countries of the world would be $60bn higher than it would have been with no military spending reductions. However, not only would the national cake be larger than otherwise, the amount available for consumption and investment would be much higher. There would an extra $144bn available for increased consumer spending whilst investment spending would be up by $83bn, most of this financed directly from defence spending cuts in those years.

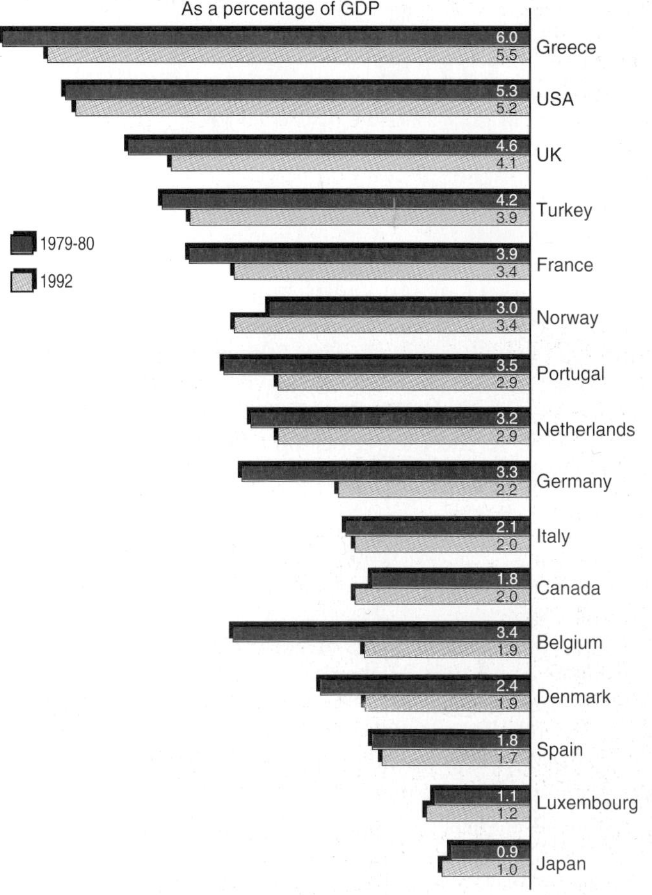

Source: adapted from OECD, *Economic Outlook*.

Figure 1.4 *Defence spending as a percentage of national income (GDP)*

Production possibility frontiers

Ethiopia

In the second half of the 1980s, Ethiopia and much of the rest of sub-Saharan Africa suffered a severe drought over a number of years. Ethiopia was already one of the poorest countries in the world with an income per person of less than $100 per year. Over the period 1980-92, income per person fell on average by 1.9 per cent per year. Average life expectancy was only 49 years.

The oil crises of the 1970s

In 1973-4 and 1978-80, there were substantial increases in the price of oil. In 1973-4, oil prices quadrupled whilst in 1978-80 they more than doubled. The initial cause of the oil price increase in both cases was political, but the members of OPEC, the Organisation of Petroleum Exporting Countries, contrived to maintain high prices by restricting oil supplies. These enormous increases in price had a substantial impact on economies throughout the world. In the industrialised countries of the world it made a considerable amount of equipment obsolete. For instance, a large new oil fired electricity power station on the Isle of Grain near London, built in 1972 and 1973, has never been used except as a reserve power station because the electricity it generates is so expensive. Oil fired heating systems were scrapped at an earlier date than they would otherwise have been, with gas or electric heating systems installed in their place. Scarce resources were used to develop engines which would use less petrol.

Former Yugoslavia

The collapse of communism in Eastern Europe was a mixed blessing for some. In Yugoslavia, it led to the break-up of the federation of states which formed the country. Serbia, which considered itself the most important part of the federation, strongly resisted the process. Slovenia, the state nearest to Austria and furthest from Serbia, was allowed to become independent but Serbia, which effectively inherited most of the armed forces of the former Yugoslavia, fought a war with Croatia in 1992 and over-ran part of the country, which today still remains in Serbian hands. The Serbs also prevented Bosnia-Herzegovina from gaining independence by starting a civil war in the state. The war in Croatia and Bosnia has been marked by ethnic cleansing, atrocities committed against civilian populations and a breakdown in economic links within the countries and with outside countries. Much of the infrastructure, such as houses and factories, in war zones has been destroyed. In the meantime, an embargo on trade with Serbia, imposed by the United Nations, has led to severe shortages.

The break-up of Eastern Europe

When communism in Eastern Europe was replaced by more democratic systems of government in the early 1990s, there was a move away from state control of the economy towards a market-led economy. Before, the state had often decided which factories were to produce what products, and would issue instructions about who was to buy the resulting output. In the new market-led system, factories had to find buyers for their products. The result was that many factories closed down. Consumers often preferred to buy foreign made goods, or were unable to carry on buying because they had been made redundant from closing enterprises. Factories making goods for the defence industry were particularly badly affected as governments cut their spending on defence. Some attempted to transfer their skills to making civilian goods, but it often proved impossible to make the jump from making fighter jets to making washing machines.

1. What is a production possibility frontier for an economy?
2. Explain, illustrating your answer with examples from the data, why a production possibility frontier might shift inwards.
3. A peace group has put forward a proposal that the UK should halve its spending on defence, including giving up its nuclear capability. Using production possibility frontiers, evaluate the possible economic implications of this proposal.

The function of an economy

Summary

1. An economy is a social organisation through which decisions about what, how and for whom to produce are made.
2. The factors of production - land, labour, capital and entrepreneurship - are combined together to create goods and services for consumption.
3. Specialisation and the division of labour give rise to large gains in productivity.
4. Markets exist for buyers and sellers to exchange goods and services using barter or money.

What is an economy?

Economic resources are scarce whilst human wants are infinite. An economy is a system which attempts to solve this basic economic problem. There are many different levels and types of economy. There is the household economy, the local economy, the national economy and the international economy. There are free market economies which attempt to solve the economic problem with the minimum intervention of government and command economies where the state makes most resource allocation decisions. Although these economies are different, they all face the same problem.

Economists distinguish three parts to the economic problem.

- **What** is to be produced? An economy can choose the mix of goods to produce. For instance, what proportion of total output should be spent on defence? What proportion should be spent on protecting the environment? What proportion should be invested for the future? What proportion should be manufactured goods and what proportion services?
- **How** is production to be organised? For instance, are hi-fi systems to be made in the UK, Japan or Taiwan? Should car bodies be made out of steel or fibreglass? Would it better to automate a production line or carry on using unskilled workers?
- **For whom** is production to take place? What proportion of output should go to workers? How much should pensioners get? What should be the balance between incomes in the UK and those in Bangladesh?

An economic system needs to provide answers to all these questions.

QUESTION 1 Consider your household economy.

(a) What is produced by your household (e.g. cooking services, cleaning services, accommodation, products outside the home)?
(b) How is production organised (e.g. who does the cooking, what equipment is used, when is the cooking done)?
(c) For whom does production take place (e.g. for mother, for father)?
(d) Do you think your household economy should be organised in a different way? Justify your answer.

Economic resources

Economists commonly distinguish three types of resources available for use in the production process. They call these resources the FACTORS OF PRODUCTION.

LAND is not only land itself but all natural resources below the earth, on the earth, in the atmosphere and in the sea. Everything from gold deposits to rainwater and natural forests are examples of land.

NON-RENEWABLE RESOURCES, such as coal, oil, gold and copper, are land resources which once used will never be replaced. If we use them today, they are not available for use by our children or our children's children. RENEWABLE RESOURCES on the other hand can be used and replaced. Examples are fish stocks, forests, or water. Renewable resources can sometimes be over-exploited by man leading to their destruction.

LABOUR is the workforce of an economy - everybody from housepersons to doctors, vicars and cabinet ministers. Not all workers are the same. Each worker has a unique set of inherent characteristics including intelligence, manual dexterity and emotional stability. But workers are also the products of education and training. The value of a worker is called his or her HUMAN CAPITAL. Education and training will increase the value of that human capital, enabling the worker to be more productive.

CAPITAL is the manufactured stock of tools, machines, factories, offices, roads and other resources which is used in the production of goods and services. Capital is of two types. WORKING or CIRCULATING CAPITAL is stocks of raw materials, semi-manufactured and finished goods which are waiting to be sold. These stocks circulate through the production process till they are finally sold to a consumer. FIXED CAPITAL is the stock of factories, offices, plant and machinery. Fixed capital is fixed in the sense that it will not be transformed into a final product as working capital will. It is used to transform working capital into finished products.

Sometimes a fourth factor of production is distinguished. This is ENTREPRENEURSHIP. Entrepreneurs are individuals who:

- organise production - organise land, labour and capital in the production of goods and services;
- take risks - with their own money and the financial capital of others, they buy factors of production to produce goods and services in the hope that they will be able to make a profit but in the knowledge that at worst they could lose all their money and go bankrupt.

It is this element of risk taking which distinguishes entrepreneurs from ordinary workers. There is much controversy today about the role and importance of entrepreneurs in a modern developed economy (☞ unit 57).

QUESTION 2

Table 2.1 *Composition of UK national wealth*

	Per cent 1957	Per cent 1987
Residential buildings	26.1	41.7
Agricultural land and buildings and forestry	2.2	1.8
Other building and civil engineering works	23.7	26.7
Plant and machinery	18.6	13.4
Vehicles including ships and aircraft	2.5	1.5
Stocks and work in progress	11.8	4.7
All tangible assets	85.0	89.7
Intangible non-financial assets	14.8	6.5
Net claims overseas	0.1	3.9
National wealth[1]	100.0	100.0

1. Totals may not add up to the sum of components due to rounding.

Source: adapted from CSO, *Economic Trends* May 1987; National Income Blue Book.

(a) Give examples of fixed and working capital from the data.
(b) Give two examples of goods or services produced by each of the six categories of capital distinguished in the data.
(c) Describe how the composition of wealth has changed over time and suggest some reasons as to why this might have occurred.

Specialisation

When he was alone on his desert island, Robinson Crusoe found that he had to perform all economic tasks by himself. When Man Friday came along he quickly abandoned this mode of production and specialised. SPECIALISATION is the production of a limited range of goods by an individual or firm or country in co-operation with others so that together a complete range of goods is produced.

Specialisation can occur between nations (☞ unit 84). For instance, a country like Honduras produces bananas and trades those for cars produced in the United States. Specialisation also occurs within economies. Regional economies specialise. In the UK, Stoke-on-Trent specialises in pottery whilst London specialises in services.

Specialisation by individuals is called THE DIVISION OF LABOUR. Adam Smith, in a passage in his famous book *An Enquiry into the Nature and Causes of the Wealth of Nations* (1776), described the division of labour amongst pin workers. He wrote:

> *A workman not educated to this business ... could scarce ... make one pin in a day, and certainly could not make twenty. But in the way in which this business is now carried on, ... it is divided into a number of branches ... One man draws out the wire, another straightens it, a third cuts it, a fourth points, a fifth grinds it at the top for receiving the head; to make the head requires two or three distinct operations; to put it on is a peculiar business, to whiten the pins is another; it is even a trade by itself to put them into the paper.*

He pointed out that one worker might be able to make 20 pins a day if he were to complete all the processes himself. But ten workers together specialising in a variety of tasks could, he estimated, make 48 000 pins.

This enormous increase in LABOUR PRODUCTIVITY (output per worker) arises from a variety of sources.

- Specialisation enables workers to gain skills in a narrow range of tasks. These skills enable individual workers to be far more productive than if they were jacks-of-all-trades. In a modern economy a person could not possibly hope to be able to take on every job which society requires.
- The division of labour makes it cost-effective to provide workers with specialist tools. For instance, it would not be profitable to provide every farm worker with a tractor. But it is possible to provide a group of workers with a tractor which they can then share.
- Time is saved because a worker is not constantly changing tasks, moving around from place to place and using different machinery and tools.
- Workers can specialise in those tasks to which they are best suited.

The division of labour has its limits. If jobs are divided up too much, the work can become tedious and monotonous. Workers feel alienated from their work. This will result in poorer workmanship and less output per person. Workers will do everything possible to avoid work - going to the toilet, lingering over breaks and reporting sick for instance. The size of the market too will limit the division of labour. A shop owner in a village might want to specialise in selling health foods but finds that in order to survive she has to sell other products as well.

Over-specialisation also has its disadvantages. In the colonial period, Britain and France allocated crops between different colonies. Ghana, for example, was forced to grow cocoa whilst Kenya grew tea and coffee. Today these countries are over-dependent on one cash crop. Low international prices or a poor harvest will lower incomes, create unemployment and play havoc with long term planning. Similarly in the UK, the North,

Wales, Scotland and Northern Ireland have paid a heavy price in terms of income and unemployment for their over-dependence on heavy manufacturing industry. Shipyard, steel and textile workers have all found that the division of labour can exact a heavy price if their skills are no longer wanted. Another problem with specialisation is that a breakdown in part of the chain of production can cause chaos within the system. Small falls in the supply of oil on world markets in the mid-1970s resulted in a major shock to the world economy. Equally, anyone dependent upon rail transport knows that a rail strike can cause chaos.

QUESTION 3

Factory workers manufacturing components.

(a) Explain with the help of the photograph what is meant by 'specialisation'.
(b) What might be some of the disadvantages of the division of labour for the workers shown in the photograph?

Money and exchange

Specialisation has enabled people to enjoy a standard of living which would be impossible to achieve through self-sufficiency. Specialisation, however, necessitates exchange. Workers can only specialise in refuse collecting, for instance, if they know that they will be able to exchange their services for other goods and services such as food, housing and transport.

Exchange for most of history has meant **barter** - swopping one good for another (☞ unit 70). But barter has many disadvantages and it would be impossible to run a modern sophisticated economy using barter as a means of exchange. It was the development of **money** that enabled trade and specialisation to transform economies into what we know today. Money is anything which is widely accepted as payment for goods received, services performed, or repayment of past debt. In a modern economy, it ranges from notes and coins to money in bank accounts and deposits in building society accounts.

Markets

There must be a buyer and a seller for exchange to take place. Buyers and sellers meet in the market place. For economists, markets are not just street markets. Buying and selling can take place in newspapers and magazines, through mail order or over the telephone in financial deals in the City of London, or on industrial estates as well as in high street shopping centres. A MARKET is any convenient set of arrangements by which buyers and sellers communicate to exchange goods and services.

Economists group buyers and sellers together. For instance, there is an international market for oil where large companies and governments buy and sell oil. There are also national markets for oil. Not every company or government involved in the buying and selling of oil in the UK, say, will be involved in the US or the Malaysian oil markets. There are also regional and local markets for oil. In your area there will be a small number of petrol filling stations (sellers of petrol) where you (the buyers) are able to buy petrol. All these markets are inter-linked but they are also separate. A worldwide increase in the price of oil may or may not filter down to an increase in the price of petrol at the pumps in your local area. Equally, petrol prices in your area may increase when

QUESTION 4

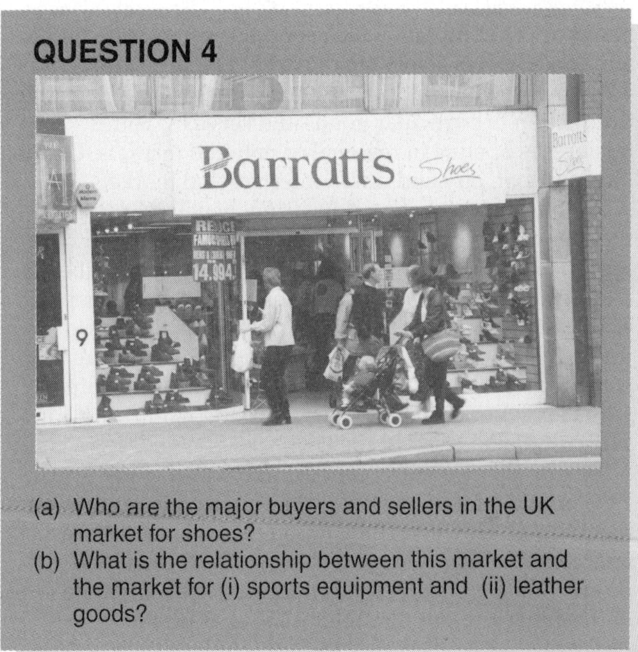

(a) Who are the major buyers and sellers in the UK market for shoes?
(b) What is the relationship between this market and the market for (i) sports equipment and (ii) leather goods?

prices at a national and international level remain constant.

How buyers and sellers are grouped together and therefore how markets are defined depends upon what is being studied. We could study the tyre industry or we could consider the market for cars and car components which includes part but not all of the tyre industry. Alternatively, we might want to analyse the market for rubber, which would necessitate a study of rubber purchased by tyre producers.

Many Western economists argue that specialisation, exchange and the market lie at the heart of today's economic prosperity in the industrial world. Whilst it is likely that the market system is a powerful engine of prosperity (☞ unit 111), we shall see that it does not always lead to the most efficient allocation of resources (☞ units 34-47).

Key terms

The factors of production - the inputs to the production process: land, which is all natural resources; labour, which is the workforce; capital, which is the stock of man-made resources used in the production of goods and services; entrepreneurs, individuals who seek out profitable opportunities for production and take risks in attempting to exploit these.
Non-renewable resources - resources, such as coal or oil, which once exploited cannot be replaced.
Renewable resources - resources, such as fish stocks or forests, which can be exploited over and over again because they have the potential to renew themselves.
Working or circulating capital - resources which are in the production system waiting to be transformed into goods or other materials before being finally sold to the consumer.
Fixed capital - economic resources such as factories and hospitals which are used to transform working capital into goods and services.
Specialisation - a system of organisation where economic units such as households or nations are not self-sufficient but concentrate on producing certain goods and services and trading the surplus with others.
The division of labour - specialisation by workers.
Labour productivity - output per worker.
Market - any convenient set of arrangements by which buyers and sellers communicate to exchange goods and services.

Applied economics

Norfloat

Norfloat is a company which specialises in marine buoys and fenders. It is a very small part of the large global economy in which millions of businesses specialise in the production of particular goods and services. Some businesses operate in regional or national markets. Others, like Norfloat, buy and sell in international markets.

The business was started in 1986 when Trevor Rogers, the founder of the company, secured an agreement to import and distribute buoys in the UK which were being manufactured by a Norwegian company called Norfloat. The Norwegian company almost immediately ceased trading, leaving the market. It was poorly run, using old, inefficient methods of production. Trevor Rogers joined with Gerry Row, who had been working in oilfields, to carry on the business in the UK.

Initially the two entrepreneurs attempted to get British PVC moulders to manufacture the buoys and fenders for them to sell. However, they found that the quality was unacceptable. They decided to set up their own production facilities. Fixed capital was needed, in the form of machinery, to put into their 2 250 sq ft unit on a business park off the M5. They obtained this by buying the moulds from the owners of the Norwegian company. Other equipment was bought and workers were trained.

This investment in human and physical capital paid off. Their products quickly established a high reputation in the market place. Unfortunately for them, by 1988-89 when they were beginning to get into full production, recession hit the UK economy. Undaunted, they turned to overseas markets and by 1994 were exporting 80 per cent of their production.

Ten workers are now employed. They specialise in manufacturing the products or in office work. Working capital is minimised by ensuring a tight turnaround of orders. There is 24 hour production. Consignments are sent out through the Parcel line delivery service every day. The buoys are used in a variety of ways, from marking crab and lobster pots, to dividing sections of sea between bathers, boats, windsurfers and water-skiers by local councils, to markers in the oil industry.

Source: adapted from *The Times*, 5.7.1994.

DATA QUESTION

The oil industry

Oil production in the North Sea

A petrol station and a plastics plant.

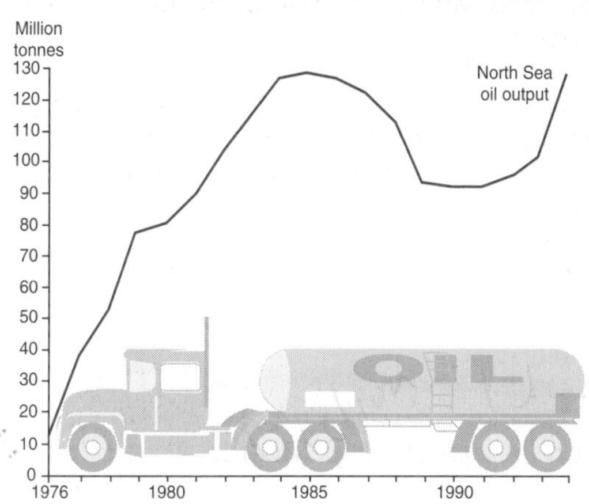

Source: adapted from CSO, *Annual Abstract of Statistics.*

Figure 2.1 *North Sea oil output*

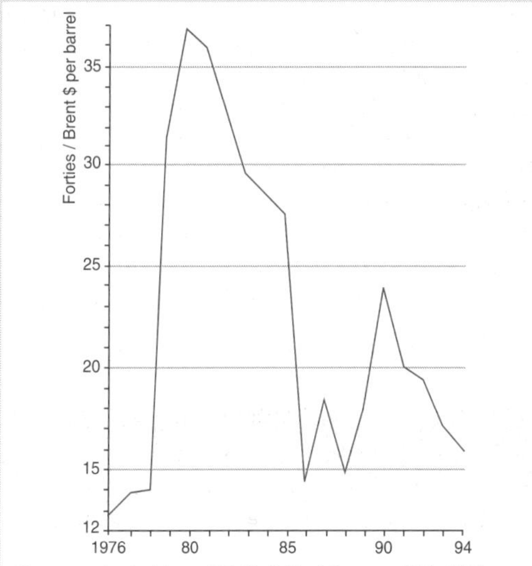

Source: adapted from *BP Statistical Survey of World Energy.*

Figure 2.2 *Oil prices, Forties/Brent $ per barrel*

Table 2.2 *Petroleum products by end use, 1994* — Thousand tonnes

	Butane and propane	Naphtha (LDF) and Middle Distillate Feedstock	Motor spirit	Kerosene: Aviation turbine fuel	Kerosene: Burning oil	Gas/diesel oil: Derv fuel	Gas/diesel oil: Other	Fuel oil	Orimul-sion	Bitumen	Lubric-ating oils	Total
1994	2 395	3 512	22 835	7 207	2 032	12 878	7 526	8 018	1 227	2 581	793	74 658

Source: adapted from DTI.

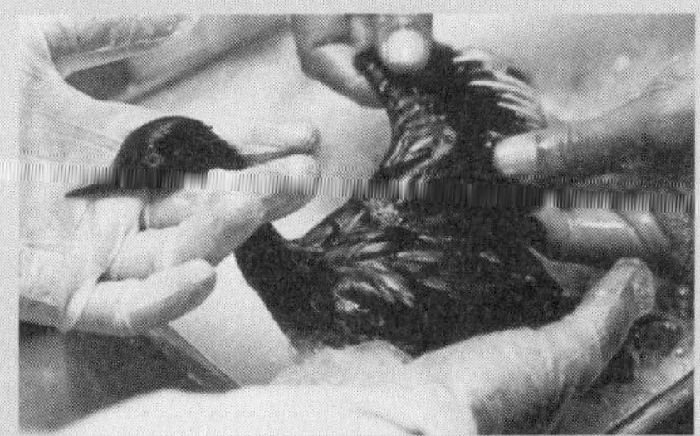

1. Explain the following economic concepts in the context of the UK oil industry:
(a) economic resources; (b) specialisation; (c) money and exchange; (d) markets.
2. North Sea oil companies face a problem about how to dispose of redundant oil rigs. Environmental groups are concerned that companies will either leave then to rot where they stand or sink them, rather than dismantle them on land. What criteria do you think should be used to decide whether scarce resources should be used to dismantle redundant oil rigs?

unit 3

Economic data

Summary

1. Economic data are collected not only to verify or refute economic models but to provide a basis for economic decision making.
2. Data may be expressed at nominal (or current) prices or at real (or constant) prices. Data expressed in real terms take into account the effects of inflation.
3. Indices are used to simplify statistics and to express averages.
4. Data can be presented in a variety of forms such as tables or graphs.
5. All data should be interpreted with care given that data can be selected and presented in a wide variety of ways.

The collection and reliability of data

Economists collect data for two main reasons.

- The scientific method requires that theories be tested. Data may be used to refute or support a theory. For instance, an economist might gather data to support or refute the hypothesis that 'Cuts in the marginal rate of income will increase the incentive to work', or that 'An increase in the real value of unemployment benefit will lead to an increase in the number of people unemployed'.
- Economists are often required to provide support for particular policies. Without economic data it is often difficult, if not impossible, to make policy recommendations. For instance, in his Budget each year the Chancellor of the Exchequer has to make a statement to the House of Commons outlining the state of the economy and the economic outlook for the next 12 months. Without a clear knowledge of where the economy is at the moment it is impossible to forecast how it might change in the future and to recommend policy changes to steer the economy in a more desirable direction.

Collecting economic data is usually very difficult and sometimes impossible. Some macro-economic data - such as the balance of payments figures or the value of national income - are collected from a wide variety of sources. The figures for the balance of payments on current account are compiled from returns made by every exporter and importer on every item exported and imported. Not surprisingly the information is not totally accurate. Some exporters and importers will conceal transactions to avoid tax. Others will not want to be bothered with the paper work.

Other macro-economic data such as the Index of Retail Prices (used to measure inflation) are based on surveys. Surveys are only reliable if there is accurate sampling and measuring and are rarely as accurate as a complete count.

Some macro-economic data are very accurate statistically but do not necessarily provide a good measure of the relevant economic variable. In the UK the unemployment level is calculated each month at benefit offices throughout the country. It is extremely accurate but no economist would argue that the figure produced is an accurate measure of unemployment. There is general agreement that some people who claim benefit for being unemployed are not unemployed and conversely there are many unemployed people who are not claiming benefit.

In micro-economics use is again made of survey data, with the limitations that this implies. Economists also make use of more experimental data, gathering evidence for case studies. For instance, an economist might want to look at the impact of different pricing policies on entry to sports centres. He or she might study a small number of sports centres in a local area. The evidence gathered would be unlikely to decisively refute or support a general hypothesis such as 'Cheap entry increases sports centre use'. But it would be possible to conclude that the evidence **tended** to support or refute the hypothesis.

In economics it is difficult to gather accurate data and for that reason academic economists mostly qualify their conclusions.

QUESTION 1

Table 3.1 *Selected balance of payments statistics for second quarter 1980 to 1994*

Date of estimate	Visible balance	Invisible balance	Current balance
		£ millions	
October 1980	-378	+85	-293
October 1981	-321	+159	-162
October 1982	-317	+67	-250
October 1983	-273	+109	-164
October 1985	-308	+51	-257
October 1987	-308	-2	-310
October 1991	-310	-48	-358
October 1994	-309	-46	-355

Source: adapted from CSO, *Economic Trends.*

(a) Comment on how the published estimate of the three current balances for the 2nd quarter of 1980 has changed over the period 1980 to 1994.
(b) Suggest reasons why there might have been these changes.

Real and nominal values

There are many different **measures** in use today such as tonnes, litres, kilograms and kilometres. Often, we want to be able to compare these different measures. For instance, an industrialist might wish to compare oil measured in litres, and coal measured in kilograms. One way of doing this is to convert oil and coal into therms using gross calorific values. In economics, by far the most important measure used is the value of an item measured in **monetary terms**, such as pounds sterling, US dollars or French francs. One problem in using money as a measure is that inflation (the general change in prices in an economy) erodes the purchasing power of money.

For instance, in 1948 the value of output of the UK economy (measured by gross domestic product at factor cost) was £10 398 million. Forty six years later in 1994 it was £578 300 million. It would seem that output had increased about 56 times - an enormous increase. In fact, output increased by only a fraction of that amount. This is because most of the measured increase was an increase not in output but in prices. Prices over the period rose about 18 times. Stripping the inflation element out of the increase leaves us with an increase in output of 3 times.

Values unadjusted for inflation are called NOMINAL VALUES. These values are expressed AT CURRENT PRICES (i.e. at the level of prices existing during the time period being measured).

If data are adjusted for inflation, then they are said to be at REAL VALUES or at CONSTANT PRICES. To do this in practice involves taking one period of time as the BASE PERIOD. Data are then adjusted assuming that prices were the same throughout as in the base period.

For instance, a basket of goods costs £100 in year 1 and £200 in year 10. Prices have therefore doubled. If you had £1 000 to spend in year 10, then that would have been equivalent to £500 at year 1 prices because both amounts would have bought 5 baskets of goods. On the other hand, if you had £1 000 to spend in year 1, that would be equivalent to £2 000 in year 10 prices because both would have bought you 10 baskets of goods.

Taking another example, the real value of UK output in 1948 at 1948 prices was the same as its nominal value (i.e. £10 398 million). The real value of output in 1994 at 1948 prices was £31 896 million. It is much lower than the nominal 1994 value because prices were much higher in 1994.

Table 3.2 *Nominal and real values*

Nominal value	Inflation between year 1 and 2	Real values: Value at year 1 prices	Real values: Value at year 2 prices
Example 1 £100 in year 1	10%	£100	£110
Example 2 £500 in year 1	50%	£500	£750
Example 3 £200 in year 2	20%	£166.66	£200
Example 4 £400 in year 2	5%	£380.95	£400

Note: £100 at year 1 prices is worth £100 x 1.1 (i.e. 1+10%) in year 2 prices. £200 at year 2 prices is worth £200 ÷ 1.2 in year 1 prices.

On the other hand, at 1994 prices, the real value of output in 1948 was £188 526 million, much higher than the nominal value because prices in 1994 were much higher than in 1948. Further examples are given in Table 3.2.

Prices can be adjusted to any base year. UK government statistics expressed in real terms are adjusted every 5 years. In 1994, figures are expressed at 1990 prices. In the late 1990s figures will be readjusted at 1995 prices.

QUESTION 2

Table 3.3 *Components of final demand at current prices*

	1990 = 100					£ million
	Index of prices	Consumers' expenditure	Government consumption	Investment	Exports	Imports
1988	87.8	299 449	93 641	91 530	107 273	124 796
1989	94.0	327 363	101 796	105 443	121 486	142 808
1990	100.0	347 527	112 934	107 577	133 165	148 285
1991	106.5	364 972	124 105	97 747	134 234	140 810
1992	111.1	382 240	131 886	93 942	140 477	149 492
1993	114.8	406 488	138 710	94 715	158 332	166 513
1994	117.1	427 521	144 393	99 011	173 857	179 625

Source: adapted from CSO, *Monthly Digest of Statistics.*

Using a calculator, work out for the period 1988 to 1994 the values of (i) consumers' expenditure, (ii) government consumption, (iii) investment, (iv) exports and (v) imports: (a) at constant 1988 prices; (b) at constant 1991 prices; (c) at constant 1994 prices.

Present your calculations in the form of three tables, one for each set of real prices.

Indices

It is often more important in economics to compare values than to know absolute values. For instance, we might want to compare the real value of output in the economy in 1988 and 1994. Knowing that the real value of output (GDP at factor cost at 1990 prices) in 1988 was £465 746 million and in 1994 was £495 066 million is helpful, but the very large numbers make it difficult to see at a glance what, for instance, was the approximate percentage increase. Equally, many series of statistics are averages. The Retail Price Index (the measure of the cost of living) is calculated by working out what it would cost to buy a typical cross-section or 'basket' of goods. Comparing say £458.92 in one month with £475.13 the next is not easy.

So, many series are converted into INDEX NUMBER form. One time period is chosen as the base period and the rest of the statistics in the series are compared to the

Table 3.4 *Converting a series into index number form*

Year	Consumption: £ millions	Index number if base year is: year 1	year 2	year 3
1	500	100.0	83.3	62.5
2	600	120.0	100.0	75.0
3	800	160.0	133.3	100.0

Note: The index number for consumption in year 2, if year 1 is the base year, is (600 ÷ 500) x 100.

value in that base period. The value in the base period is usually 100. The figure 100 is chosen because it is easy to work with mathematically. Taking the example of output again, if 1948 were taken as the base year, then the value of real output in 1948 would be 100, and in 1994 would be 306.8. Alternatively if 1994 were taken as the base year, the value of output would be 100 in 1994 and 32.6 in 1948. Or with 1990 as the base year, the value of output in 1948 would be 34.3 whilst in 1994 it would be 103.4. Further examples are given in Table 3.4.

The construction of one weighted index, the Retail Price Index, is explained in greater detail in unit 93.

The interpretation of data

Data can be presented in many forms and be used both to inform and mislead the reader. To illustrate these points, let us consider the unemployment figures in recent years in the UK economy. One way in which these figures can be presented is in **tabular form** as in Table 3.6. It shows that unemployment fell from 1988 to 1990, after which it rose before falling back again in 1994.

The data could also be presented in the form of a graph as in Figure 3.1(a). Graphs must be interpreted with some care. Figure 3.1(b) gives a pessimistic picture of unemployment. By excluding 1988-89 and 1994, the reader is left with the impression that unemployment has been rising for some years. By not starting the axis at zero but making the scale discontinuous between zero and 5.5 per cent, the rise in unemployment can be effectively exaggerated. On the other hand, Figure 3.1(c) would deceive the casual observer about changes in unemployment. It uses a log scale of the number of unemployed in millions. This compresses values as they increase. Without careful reading of the scale, it could look as if the fall in unemployment between 1988 and 1990 was larger than the rise in unemployment between 1991 and 1993. Data can be also be expressed in verbal form. To present a complete series in words would be tedious and difficult to take in. However, in verbal form we can note that unemployment was nearly twice as high in 1993 as in 1990, that unemployment fell 25 per cent between 1988 and 1990 and that unemployment fell at a faster rate in 1989 than in 1990.

Table 3.6 *UK unemployment.*

Year	% of workforce
1988	8.0
1989	6.2
1990	5.8
1991	8.0
1992	9.7
1993	10.3
1994	9.4

Source: adapted from CSO, *Economic Trends.*

QUESTION 3

Table 3.5 *Consumers' expenditure*

£ million

	Food	Alcohol & tobacco	Clothing & footwear	Energy	Vehicles	Catering
1988	36 491	26 308	19 023	19 291	17 456	23 879
1989	39 143	27 408	19 847	20 460	20 035	27 542
1990	41 816	29 583	20 876	22 422	19 034	30 249
1991	44 061	32 306	21 412	24 955	16 449	30 744
1992	45 476	33 765	22 085	25 399	16 121	32 184
1993	46 499	35 259	23 328	26 136	18 164	34 826
1994	47 346	36 124	24 715	26 718	21 650	37 033

Source: adapted from CSO, *Monthly Digest of Statistics.*

Using a calculator, convert each category of expenditure into index number form using as the base year: (a) 1988; (b) 1991; (c) 1994.

Present your calculations in the form of three tables, one for each base year.

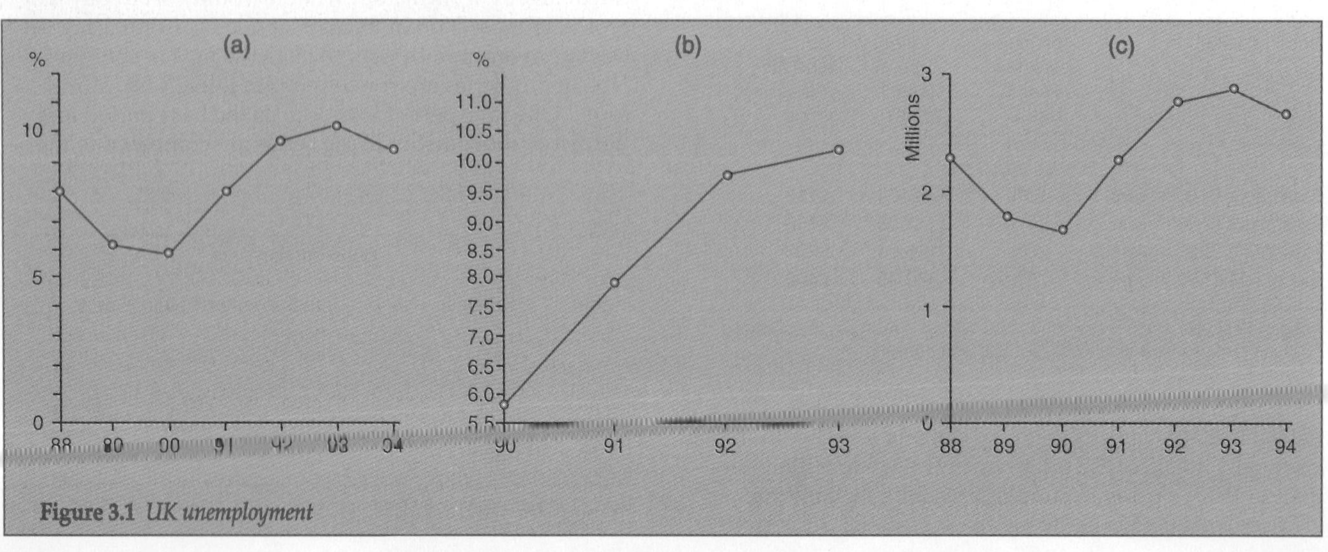

Figure 3.1 *UK unemployment*

QUESTION 4

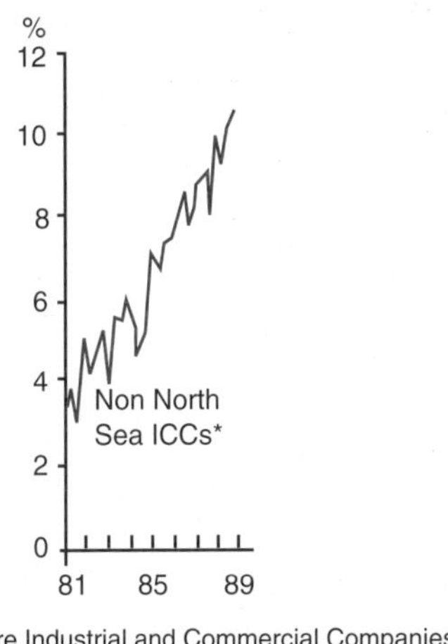

*ICCs are Industrial and Commercial Companies

Figure 3.2 *Return on capital (%)*

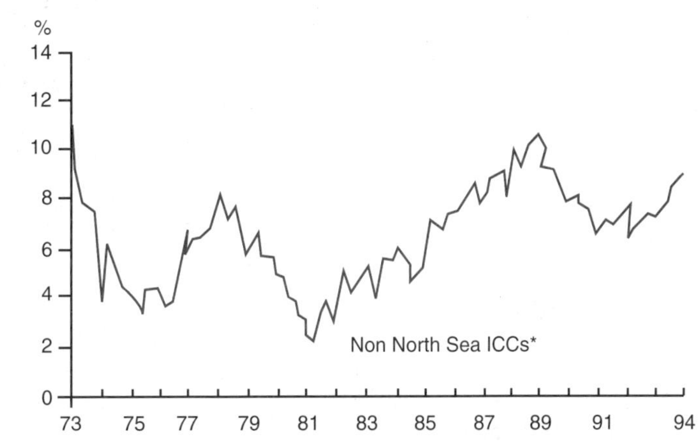

Figure 3.3 *Return on Capital (%)*

Source: adapted from *Bank of England Quarterly Bulletin*, August 1994.

Consider each graph in turn. What does each show? Explain why each seems to give a different picture of UK company profitability.

Key terms

Nominal values - values unadjusted for the effects of inflation (i.e. values **at current prices**).
Real values - values adjusted for inflation (i.e. values **at constant prices**).
Base period - the period, such as a year or a month, from which all other values in a series are compared. In an index number series, the base period is given the value of 100.
Index number - an indicator showing the relative value of one number to another from a base of 100. It is often used to present an average of a number of statistics.

Applied economics

Better or worse off?

Are Britain's pensioners becoming better or worse off? Pensioners receive income from a variety of sources including private occupational pensions and income from savings. However, half of pensioners' income is accounted for by state pensions and other social security benefits. Has their lot improved between 1971 and 1995?

Table 3.7 shows how the state old age pension for a single person has increased over time. A cursory glance at the table would seem to indicate that single pensioners were £53.15 a week better off in 1995 than in 1971. Using the index numbers for easy calculation, pensioners were 885 per cent better off in 1995 than in 1971.

However, these figures are expressed at **current prices**. No allowance has been made for the fact that prices too increased over the period. Table 3.8 shows how pensioners' **real incomes** have changed over the period (i.e. how their pensions adjusted for inflation have changed).

This gives a very different story. The real value of pensions rose markedly between 1971 and 1988. However, since 1980 the government has only increased pensions in line with inflation. Because of the way this increase is calculated (this year's increase in pension being based upon last year's inflation rate), it can mean that pensioners are either slightly better off or slightly worse off from one year to the next.

Indexing the value of retirement pensions might seem a reasonable arrangement. However, we know that the

Table 3.7 *State retirement pension for a single person under 80*

	£ per week at current prices	September 1971=100
September 1971	6.00	100
November 1976	15.30	255
November 1981	29.60	493
November 1983	34.05	568
November 1985	38.30	638
April 1987	39.50	658
April 1989	43.60	727
April 1991	52.00	867
April 1993	56.10	935
April 1994	57.60	960
April 1995	59.15	985

Source: adapted from CSO, *Annual Abstract of Statistics.*

Table 3.8 *State retirement pension for a single person under 80 at constant prices*

	£ per week at April 1995 prices	April 1995 = 100
September 1971	43.55	73.6
November 1976	54.27	91.7
November 1981	56.78	96.0
November 1983	58.61	99.1
November 1985	59.55	100.7
April 1987	57.76	97.7
April 1989	56.52	95.6
April 1991	59.21	100.1
April 1993	60.27	101.9
April 1994	60.44	102.2
April 1995	59.15	100.0

Source: adapted from CSO, *Annual Abstract of Statistics.*

nation's income has increased, on average, about 2½% per year over the past 25 years. Indexing state retirement pensions to the rate of inflation means that those pensioners whose sole income is the state pension will receive no share of Britain's ever increasing prosperity.

This can be seen by comparing the value of the retirement pension to average earnings in Figure 3.4. Since the mid-1970s, pensioners whose only income has been the state pension have been getting progressively worse off compared to the average male worker in the UK. Only linking retirement pensions to average earnings can prevent the steady erosion of the relative standard of living of pensioners. If a significant proportion of pensioners are poor today, they will be relatively much poorer in 10 years' time.

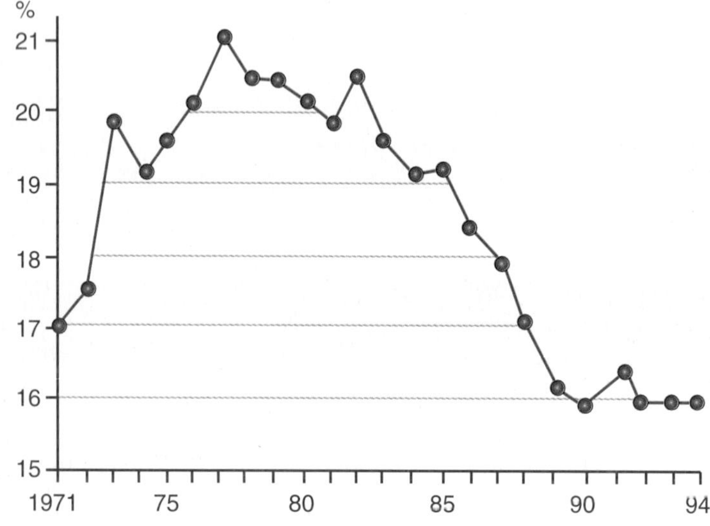

Source: adapted from CSO, *Annual Abstract of Statistics.*

Figure 3.4 ***Single person state retirement pension as a percentage of average male earnings***

DATA QUESTION

Food trends

A food manufacturer, making a wide range of canned meat and dairy products, is struggling to increase its sales. It has commissioned you, as a private consultant, to write a report, from an economic perspective, on trends in sales of food in the UK. In your report:

1. **describe the trends in sales of food since 1971 shown by the data;**
2. **assess which trends are the most important in explaining why the food manufacturer is struggling to increase quantities sold of its products;**
3. **suggest whether there are any strategies the firm could pursue to increase its sales.**

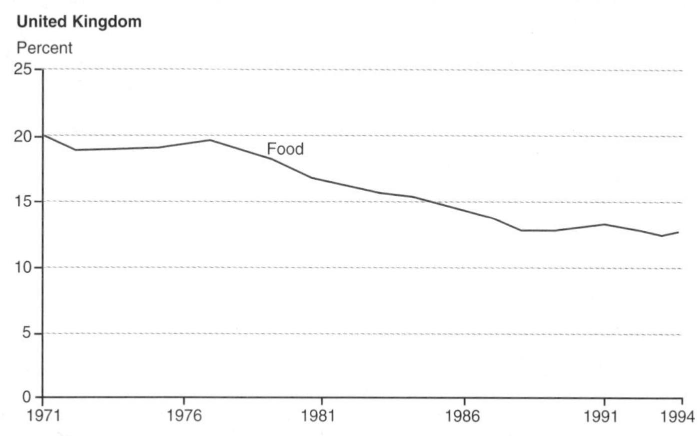

Source: adapted from CSO, *Social Trends.*

Figure 3.5 *Food as a percentage of total household expenditure*

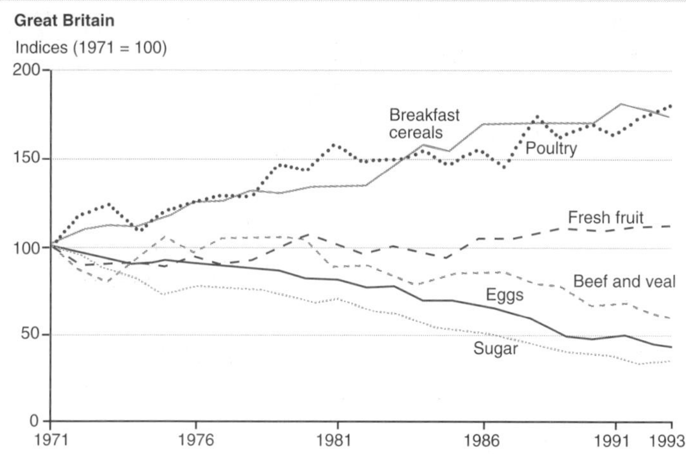

Source: adapted from Ministry of Agriculture, Fishing and Food.

Figure 3.6 *Changing patterns in the physical amount of foods consumed*

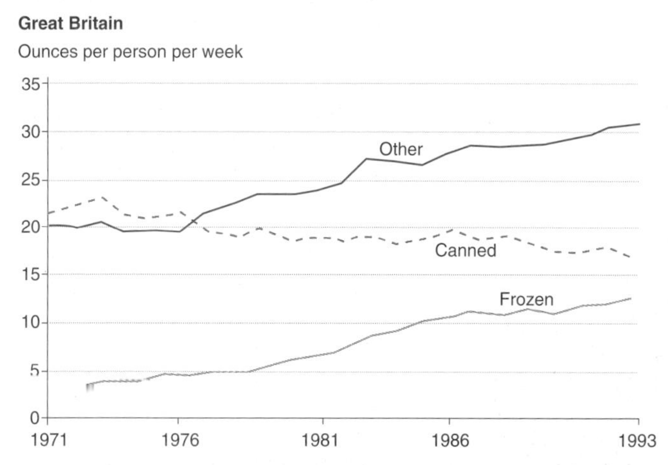

Source: adapted from Ministry of Agriculture, Fishing and Food.

Figure 3.7 *Consumption of convenience foods at home*

Table 3.9 *Household expenditure on food*

£ million

	At current prices	At constant (1990) prices
1971	7 105	36 312
1972	7 614	36 248
1973	8 751	37 120
1974	10 028	36 470
1975	12 313	36 480
1976	14 459	36 886
1977	16 596	36 547
1978	18 373	37 217
1979	20 988	38 046
1980	23 655	38 095
1981	24 946	37 849
1982	26 490	37 942
1983	28 061	38 582
1984	29 274	37 925
1985	30 657	38 402
1986	32 574	39 610
1987	34 402	40 621
1988	36 491	41 542
1989	39 143	42 249
1990	41 816	41 816
1991	44 061	41 880
1992	45 476	42 581
1993	46 449	42 957
1994	47 346	43 658

Source: adapted from CSO, *Economic Trends Annual Supplement.*

The demand curve

Summary

1. **Demand for a good is the quantity of goods or services that will be bought over a period of time at any given price.**
2. **Demand for a good will rise or fall if there are changes in factors such as incomes, the price of other goods, tastes, and the size of the population.**
3. **A change in price is shown by a movement along the demand curve.**
4. **A change in any other variable affecting demand, such as income, is shown by a shift in the demand curve.**
5. **The market demand curve can be derived by horizontally summing all the individual demand curves in the market.**

Demand

A market exists wherever there are buyers and sellers of a particular good (☞ unit 2). Buyers **demand** goods from the market whilst sellers **supply** goods on to the market.

DEMAND has a particular meaning in economics. Demand is the quantity of goods or services that will be bought at any given price over a period of time. For instance, approximately 2 million new cars are bought each year in the UK today at an average price of, say, £7 000. Economists would say that the annual demand for cars at £7 000 would be 2 million units.

Demand and price

If everything else were to remain the same (this is known as the **ceteris paribus** condition ☞ unit 115), what would happen to the quantity demanded of a product as its price changed? If the average price of a car were to fall from £7 000 to £3 500, then it is not difficult to guess that the quantity demanded of cars would rise. On the other hand, if the average price were £35 000 very few cars would be sold.

This is shown in Table 4.1. As the price of cars rises, then ceteris paribus, the quantity of cars demanded will fall. Another way of expressing this is shown in Figure 4.1. Price is on the vertical axis and quantity demanded over time is on the horizontal axis. The curve is downward sloping showing that as price falls, quantity demanded rises. This DEMAND CURVE shows the quantity that is demanded at any given price. When price changes there is said to be a **movement along** the curve. For instance, there is a movement along the curve from the point A to the point B, a fall of 1 million cars a year, when the price of cars rises from £7 000 to £14 000.

Table 4.1 *The demand schedule for cars*

Price (£)	Demand (million per year)
3 500	4.0
7 000	2.0
14 000	1.0
35 000	0.4

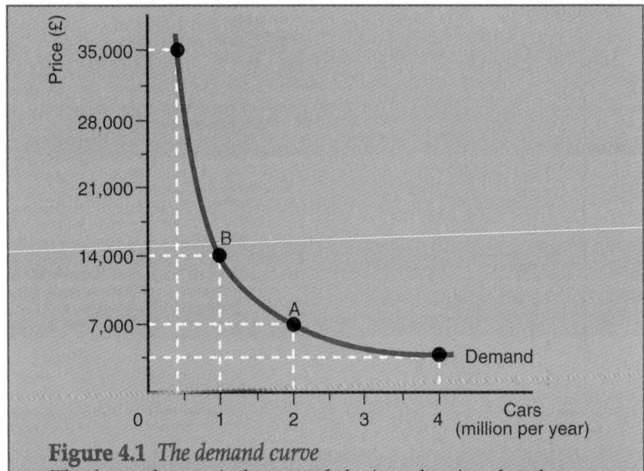

Figure 4.1 *The demand curve*
The demand curve is downward sloping, showing that the lower the price, the higher will be the quantity demanded of a good. In this example, only 0.4 million cars per year are demanded at a price of £35 000 each, but a reduction in price to £3 500 increases quantity demanded to 4 million units per year.

It is important to remember that the demand curve shows EFFECTIVE DEMAND. It shows how much would be bought (i.e. how much consumers can afford to buy and would buy) at any given price and not how much buyers would like to buy if they had unlimited resources.

Economists have found that the inverse relationship between price and quantity demanded - that as price rises, the quantity demanded falls - is true of nearly all goods. In unit 10 we shall consider the few examples of goods which might have upward sloping demand curves.

QUESTION 1 National water metering trials were conducted in 11 areas of the UK between 1989 and 1992. The trials were designed to provide evidence on different patterns of water consumption with a view to installing meters in every home. A variety of different tariff structures were used to see the effect on demand of charging different prices. Using a demand curve diagram, explain what would happen to demand for water per hour:

(a) during the afternoon if water prices were higher in the morning period;

(b) during the winter if water prices were higher in the summer;

(c) in area A where the price per cubic metre of water was 40p compared to area B where price declined the more water a household used, with the highest price charged set at 40p per cubic metre.

Demand and income

Price is not the only factor which determines the level of demand for a good. Another important factor is income. Demand for a normal good rises when income rises. For instance, a rise in income leads consumers to buy more cars. A few goods, known as inferior goods, fall in demand when incomes rise (☞ unit 10).

The effect of a rise in income on demand is shown in Figure 4.2. Buyers are purchasing OA of clothes at a price of OE. Incomes rise and buyers react by purchasing more clothes at the same price. At the higher level of income they buy, say, OB of clothes. A new demand curve now exists passing through the point S. It will be to the right of the original demand curve because at any given price more will be demanded at the new higher level of income.

Economists say that a rise in income will lead to an **increase in demand** for a normal good such as clothes. An increase in demand is shown by a SHIFT IN THE DEMAND CURVE. (Note that an **increase in quantity demanded** would refer to a change in quantity demanded resulting from a change in price and would be shown by a movement along the curve.) In Figure 4.2, the original demand curve D_1 shifts to the right to its new position D_2. Similarly, a fall in income will lead to a **fall in demand** for a normal good. This is shown by a **shift** to the left of the demand curve from D_1 to D_3. For instance, at a price of OE, demand will fall from OA to OC.

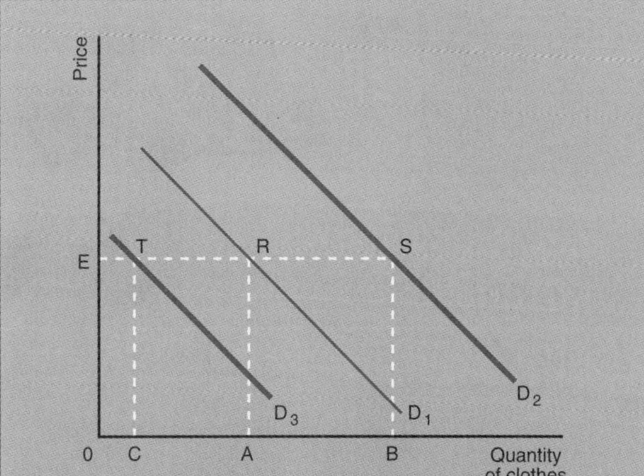

Figure 4.2 *A change in income*
An increase in income will raise demand for a normal good. At a price of OE, for instance, demand will rise from OA to OB. Similarly, at all other prices, an increase in income will result in a level of demand to the right of the existing demand curve. So the demand curve will shift from D_1 to D_2. A fall in income will result in less being demanded at any given price. Hence the demand curve will shift to the left, from D_1 to D_3.

Two points need to be made. First, the demand curves in Figure 4.2 have been drawn as straight lines. These demand curves drawn show a hypothetical (or imaginary) position. They are drawn straight purely for convenience and do not imply that actual demand curves for real products are straight. Second, the shifts in the demand curves are drawn as parallel shifts. Again this is done for convenience and neatness but it is most unlikely that a rise or fall in income for an actual product would produce a parallel shift in its demand curve.

QUESTION 2
Table 4.2

Quantity demanded (million units)	Price (£)
10	20
20	16
30	12
40	8
50	4

(a) Draw a demand curve from the above data.

(b) An increase in income results in the quantity demanded changing by the following amounts at every price level. For each, draw the new demand curve on your diagram: (i) 5 million units; (ii) 10 million units; (iii) 15 million units; (iv) 25 million units.

(c) Draw a demand curve which would show the effect of a fall in incomes on the original demand for the good.

(d) Draw a demand curve which would show that no products were demanded when price was £8.

The price of other goods

Another important factor which influences the demand for a good is the price of other goods. For instance, in the great drought of 1976 in the UK, the price of potatoes soared. Consumers reacted by buying fewer potatoes and replacing them in their diet by eating more bread, pasta and rice.

This can be shown on a demand diagram. The demand curve for pasta in Figure 4.3 is D_1. A rise in the price of potatoes leads to a rise in the demand for pasta. This means that at any given price a greater quantity of pasta will be demanded. The new demand curve D_2 will

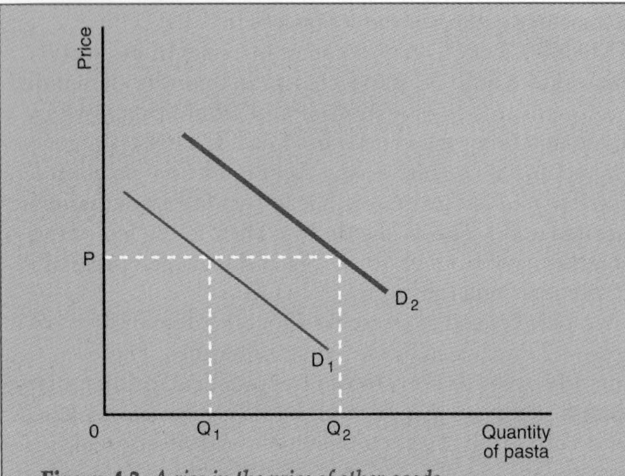

Figure 4.3 *A rise in the price of other goods*
A rise in the price of potatoes will lead to a rise in the demand for substitute goods. So the demand for pasta will increase, shown by a shift to the right in the demand curve for pasta from D_1 to D_2.

therefore be to the right of the original demand curve.

Not all changes in prices will affect the demand for a particular good. A rise in the price of tennis balls is unlikely to have much impact on the demand for carrots for instance. Changes in the price of other goods as well may have either a positive or negative impact on demand for a good. A rise in the price of tennis rackets is likely to reduce the demand for tennis balls as some buyers decide that tennis is too expensive a sport. On the other hand, the demand for cinema places, alcoholic drink or whatever other form of entertainment consumers choose to buy instead of tennis equipment, will increase. The effect on the demand for one good of changes in price of other goods is considered in more detail in unit 7.

QUESTION 3 Between 1973 and 1975, the US dollar price of crude oil quadrupled from approximately $3 to $12 a barrel provoking what came to be called 'the energy crisis'. Businesses and consumers expected oil prices to remain high after 1975. Explain, using demand diagrams, what effect you would expect this to have had on the demand in the UK for:
(a) oil tankers;
(b) coal;
(c) ice cream;
(d) gas-fired central heating systems;
(e) luxury cars with low-mileage petrol consumption;
(f) rail travel.

Other factors

There is a wide variety of other factors which affect the demand for a good apart from price, income and the prices of other goods. These include:

- changes in population - an increase in population is likely to increase demand for goods;
- changes in fashion - the demand for items such as wigs or flared trousers or black kitchen units changes as these items go in or out of fashion;
- changes in legislation - the demand for seat belts, anti-pollution equipment or places in old-people's homes has been affected in the past by changes in government legislation;
- advertising - a very powerful influence on consumer demand which seeks to influence consumer choice.

QUESTION 4

Explain the likely effect on demand for Nescafé of each of the four factors shown in the data. Use a separate demand diagram for each factor to illustrate your answer.

A summary

It is possible to express demand in the form of a **functional** relationship. The quantity demanded of good

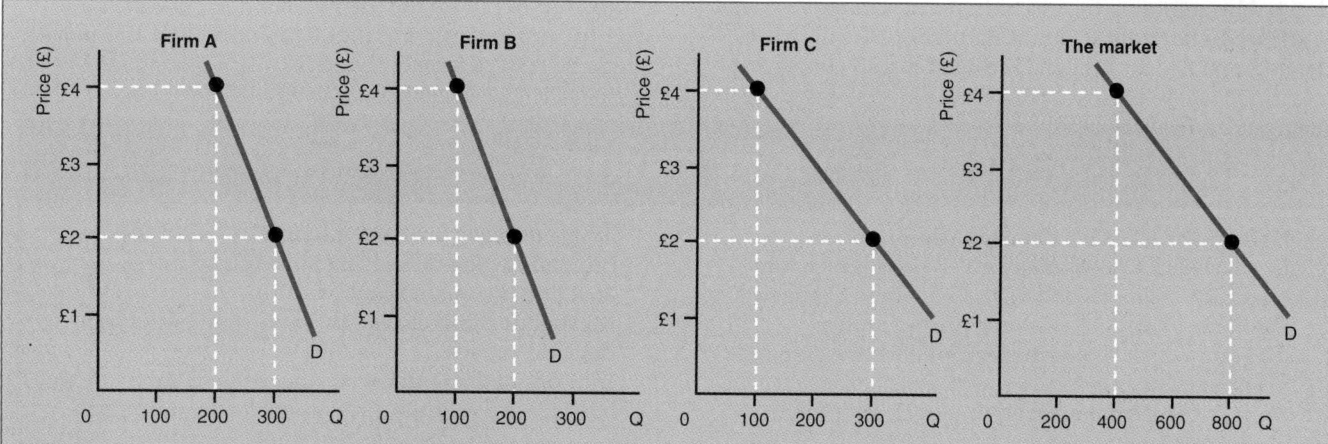

Figure 4.4 *Individual and market demand curves*
The market demand curve can be derived from the individual demand curves by adding up individual demand at each single price. In this example, for instance, the market demand at a price of £2 is calculated by adding the demand of firm A, B and C at this price.

N (Q_n) varies according to (i.e. is a function of) the price of good N (P_n), income (Y), the price of all other goods (P_1,... P_{n-1}) and all other factors (T). Mathematically, this is:

$$Q_n = f\,[P_n, Y, (Pl, \ldots P_{n-1}), T]$$

At this stage, this mathematical form of expressing the determinants of demand is a convenient shorthand but little else. The major tools for dealing with demand at this level are either the written word or graphs. At a far more advanced level, the algebraic formula for demand is often the most powerful and useful tool in analysing demand.

QUESTION 5

$$Q_D = 20 - \tfrac{1}{2}P$$

where Q_D is the monthly quantity demanded of compact discs (CDs) in millions and P is their price.

(a) Draw the demand curve given by this equation between CD prices of £1 and £20.
(b) A new format results in a fall in demand of CDs of 5 million per month at any given price. (i) What is the new formula for quantity demanded of CDs. (ii) Plot the new demand curve on your diagram.
(c) A rise in consumer incomes results in consumers being less price sensitive than before when buying CDs. As a result, instead of monthly demand falling by half a million when price is increased by £1, monthly demand now falls only by 400 000. Assume that the original equation for demand is as in (a). (i) What is the new formula for quantity demanded of CDs? (ii) Plot the new demand curve on your diagram.

Individual and market demand curves

So far, it has been assumed that demand refers to demand for a product in a whole market (i.e. MARKET DEMAND). However, it is possible to construct individual demand curves and derive market demand curves from them. An INDIVIDUAL DEMAND CURVE is the demand curve of an individual buyer. This could be a consumer, a firm or government.

The determinants of demand for an individual are no different from those of the market as a whole. When price rises, there is a fall in the quantity demanded of the product; when income rises, assuming that the product is a normal good, demand will increase, etc.

Figure 4.4 shows a situation where there are three and only three buyers in a market, firms A, B and C. At a price of £2, firm A will buy 300 units, firm B 200 units and firm C 300 units. So the total market demand at a price of £2 is 300 + 200 + 300 or 800 units. At a price of £4, total market demand will be 200 + 100 + 100 or 400 units. Similarly, all the other points on the market demand curve can be

QUESTION 6

Table 4.3

Price (£)	Quantity demanded of good X (000 units)		
	Firm A	Firm B	Firm C
100	500	250	750
200	400	230	700
300	300	210	650
400	200	190	600
500	100	170	550

There are only three buyers of good X, firms A, B and C.

(a) Draw the individual demand curves for each firm.
(b) Draw the market demand curve for good X.
(c) A fourth business, firm D, enters the market. It will buy 500 at any price between £100 and £500. Show the effect of this by drawing a new market demand curve for good X.
(d) Firm B goes out of business. Draw the new market demand curve with firms A, C and D buying in the market.

derived by summing the individual demand curves. This is known as **horizontal summing** because the figures on the horizontal axis of the individual demand curves are added up to put on the market demand curve. But the figures on the vertical axis of both individual and market demand curves remain the same.

Key terms

Demand or effective demand - the quantity purchased of a good at any given price, given that other determinants of demand remain unchanged.
Demand curve - the line on a price-quantity diagram which shows the level of effective demand at any given price.
Shift in the demand curve - a movement of the whole demand curve to the right or left of the original caused by a change in any variable affecting demand except price.
Market demand curve - the sum of all individual demand curves.
Individual demand curve - the demand curve for an individual consumer, firm or other economic unit.

Applied economics

The housing market

The demand for housing has changed over the past 30-40 years. There has been a significant increase in the number of houses and other types of dwelling in the UK from 16m to 24m between 1961 and 1993. Most of this increase can be explained by an increasing population and, more importantly, by an increase in the number of households within the population. As can be seen from Table 4.4, the total size of the population has increased by 10.2 per cent over the period, whilst the number of households has increased by 41.4 per cent.

Table 4.4

Millions

	Population	Number of households
1961	52.8	16.2
1971	55.9	18.2
1981	56.1	19.5
1991	57.8	21.9
1993	58.2	22.9

Source: adapted from CSO, *Social Trends.*

The greater than proportionate increase in households compared to population is due to an increasing number of small pensioner households, one parent families and divorces which split up family units. These population or **demographic** trends have shifted the demand curve for housing to the right.

Figure 4.5 shows that there has been a significant change in the **tenure** or ownership of houses. The number of people owning their own house has more than doubled since 1961 whilst renting has become less popular. One reason for the increase in demand for owner occupied dwellings was rising income. As workers' disposable income rose, shown in Figure 4.6, increasingly they wanted to own their own houses rather than rent them. This trend towards home ownership was given a boost by government in the 1980s. Margaret Thatcher's government made home ownership a political target and the climate of opinion persuaded many low income households to buy rather than rent. This was backed up by changes in the law which allowed council tenants to buy the houses they lived in. All these factors shifted the demand curve for owner-occupied houses to the right.

On the other hand, the number of households renting houses has declined. However, it is not possible to say that demand for rented housing has necessarily fallen. Throughout the period, there have been long waiting lists for council and housing association rented properties. Demand has therefore been greater than the number of houses available (a situation of **excess demand** ☞ unit 6). The fall in the number of local authority houses rented after 1980 says far more about the sale of council houses and central government refusal to allow councils to build new houses for rent than it does about demand for this type of accommodation.

The 1990s may well be different from the previous three decades with an increased demand for rented houses and a fall in demand for owner occupied houses. This is because of a variety of factors.

- The cost of mortgages has increased because the government has reduced tax incentives to people buying their own homes. The cost of the monthly repayment on the mortgage is the main way in which people judge the cost of buying a house.
- The number of households aged 18-30 is set to decline because of a decline in the number of 18-30 year olds in the population. These households are very active in the housing market.
- Many people suffered large losses on houses they bought in the late 1980s. This has frightened many people from buying a house.
- Hundreds of thousands of people had the houses they were buying repossessed by building societies from 1990 onwards because they couldn't keep up with the mortgage repayments. There were 271 000 repossessions alone between 1990 and 1994. These households are now in the rented sector and are most unlikely to return to the owner-occupied sector.
- Government has been actively encouraging the private rented sector through changes in the law. Far more people, particularly young people, now consider rented housing a better arrangement than in the 1980s.

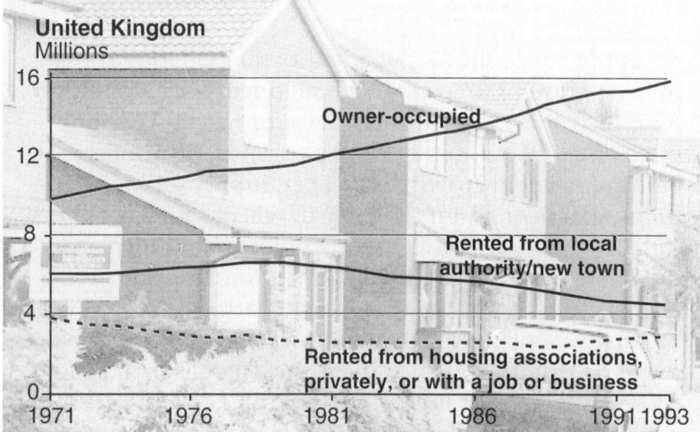

Source: adapted from Department of the Environment.
Figure 4.5 *Stock of dwellings by tenure*

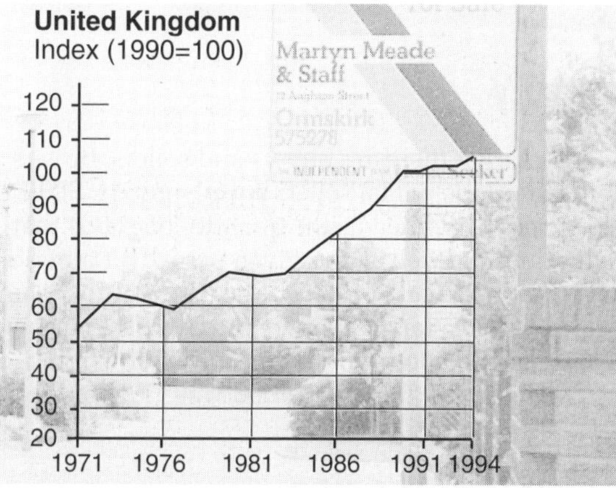

Source: adapted from CSO, *Social Trends.*
Figure 4.6 *Real personal disposable income per head (1990=100)*

DATA QUESTION

Private education

Table 4.5 *Number of pupils in schools*

Thousands

	1970-71	1980-81	1985-86	1990-91	1992-93
Private schools	621	619	607	613	607
of which boarding	na	131	117	117	94
All schools	10 230	10 633	9 545	9 260	9 513

Source: adapted from CSO, *Social Trends.*

Table 4.6 *Pupil/teacher ratios*

	1970-71	1980-81	1985-86	1990-91	1992-93
Private schools	14.0	13.1	13.2	10.7	10.4
State sector schools	22.6	19.0	18.5	18.2	18.6

Source: adapted from CSO, *Social Trends.*

Table 4.7 *School fees and disposable income per head*

	1971	1981	1986	1991	1993
School fees per term					
Day pupils	-	-	692	1 119	1 373
Boarding pupils	-	-	1 340	2 585	3 141
Personal disposable income per head of the population at current prices	690	3 134	4 661	7 044	7 890

Source: adapted from CSO, *Economic Trends Annual Supplement*; Independent Schools Information Service.

Table 4.8 *How prices have changed*

1985=100

	1971	1981	1986	1991	1993
Retail Price Index	21.4	79.1	103.4	141.1	148.7

1. **Analyse the trends in numbers attending independent schools since 1970.**
2. **Using diagrams, suggest what determines the demand for independent school places. Use the data to illustrate your answer.**
3. **What factors might determine whether independent schools in the UK survive in the next century?**

The supply curve

Summary

1. A rise in price leads to a rise in quantity supplied, shown by a movement along the supply curve.
2. A change in supply can be caused by factors such as a change in costs of production, technology and the price of other goods. This results in a shift in the supply curve.
3. The market supply curve in a perfectly competitive market is the sum of each firm's individual supply curves.

Supply

In any market there are buyers and sellers. Buyers **demand** goods whilst sellers **supply** goods. SUPPLY in economics is defined as the quantity of goods that sellers are prepared to sell at any given price over a period of time. For instance, in 1987 UK farmers sold 11.94 million tonnes of wheat at an average price of £111 per tonne so economists would say that the supply of wheat at £111 per tonne, over the 12 month period was 11.94 million tonnes.

Supply and price

If the price of a good increases, how will producers react? Assuming that no other factors have changed, they are likely to expand production to take advantage of the higher prices and the higher profits that they can now make. In general, quantity supplied will rise if the price of the good also rises, all other things being equal.

This can be shown on a diagram using a **supply curve**.

Figure 5.1 *The supply curve*
The supply curve is upward sloping, showing that firms increase production of a good as its price increases. This is because a higher price enables firms to make profit on the increased output whereas at the lower price they would have made a loss on it. Here, an increase in the price of wheat from £110 to £140 per tonne increases quantity supplied from 110 million tonnes to 150 million tonnes per year.

A supply curve shows the quantity that will be supplied over a period of time at any given price. Consider Figure 5.1 which shows the supply curve for wheat. Wheat is priced at £110 per tonne. At this price only the most efficient farmers grow wheat. They supply 110 million tonnes per year. But if the price of wheat rose to £140 per tonne, farmers already growing wheat might increase their acreage of wheat, whilst other non-wheat growing farmers might start to grow wheat. Farmers would do this because at a price of £140 per tonne it is possible to make a profit on production even if costs are higher than at a production level of 110 million units.

A fall in price will lead to a **fall in quantity supplied**, shown by a **movement along** the supply curve. At a lower price, some firms will cut back on relatively unprofitable production whilst others will stop producing altogether. Some of the latter firms may even go bankrupt, unable to cover their costs of production from the price received.

An upward sloping supply curve assumes that:

- firms are motivated to produce by profit - so this model does not apply, for instance, to much of what is produced by government;
- the cost of producing a unit increases as output increases (a situation known as rising marginal cost ☞ unit 18) - this is not always true but it is likely that the prices of factors of production to the firm will increase as firms bid for more land, labour and capital to increase their output, thus pushing up costs.

QUESTION 1

Table 5.1

Price (£)	Quantity supplied (million units per year)
5	5
10	8
15	11
20	14
25	17

(a) Draw a supply curve from the above data.
(b) Draw new supply curves assuming that quantity supplied at any given price:
(i) increased by 10 units; (ii) increased by 50 per cent; (iii) fell by 5 units; (iv) halved.

Costs of production

The supply curve is drawn on the assumption that the general costs of production in the economy remain constant (part of the **ceteris paribus** condition). If other things change, then the supply curve will shift. If the costs of production increase at any given level of output, firms will attempt to pass on these increases in the form of higher prices. If they cannot charge higher prices then profits will fall and firms will produce less of the good or might even stop producing it altogether. A rise in the costs of production will therefore lead to a decrease in supply.

This can be seen in Figure 5.3. The original supply curve is S_1. A rise in the costs of production means that at any given level of output firms will charge higher prices. At an output level of OA, firms will increase their prices from OB to OC. This increase in prices will be true for all points on the supply curve. So the supply curve will **shift** upwards and to the left to S_2 in Figure 5.3. There will have been a **fall in supply**. (Note that a fall in **quantity supplied** refers to a change in quantity supplied due to a change in price and would be shown by a movement along the supply curve.) Conversely a fall in the costs of production will lead to an increase in supply of a good. This is shown by a shift to the right in the supply curve.

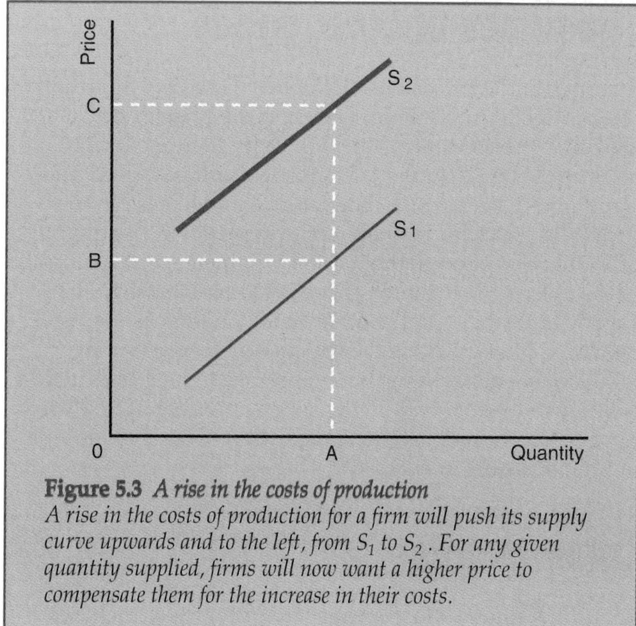

Figure 5.3 *A rise in the costs of production*
A rise in the costs of production for a firm will push its supply curve upwards and to the left, from S_1 to S_2. For any given quantity supplied, firms will now want a higher price to compensate them for the increase in their costs.

QUESTION 2

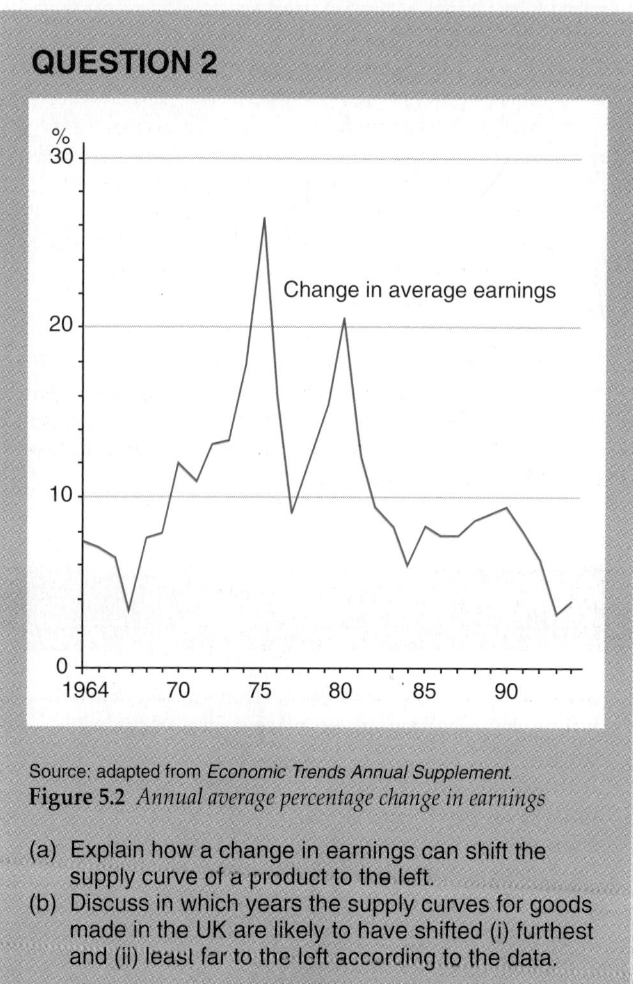

Source: adapted from *Economic Trends Annual Supplement.*
Figure 5.2 *Annual average percentage change in earnings*

(a) Explain how a change in earnings can shift the supply curve of a product to the left.
(b) Discuss in which years the supply curves for goods made in the UK are likely to have shifted (i) furthest and (ii) least far to the left according to the data.

Technology

Another factor which affects supply of a particular good is the state of technology. The supply curve is drawn on the assumption that the state of technology remains unchanged. If new technology is introduced to the production process it should lead to a fall in the costs of production. This greater **productive efficiency** will encourage firms to produce more at the same price or produce the same amount at a lower price or some combination of the two. The supply curve will shift downwards and to the right. It would be unusual for firms to replace more efficient technology with less efficient technology. However, this can occur at times of war or natural disasters. If new technical equipment is destroyed, firms may have to fall back on less efficient means of production, reducing supply at any given price, resulting in a shift in the supply curve to the left.

QUESTION 3

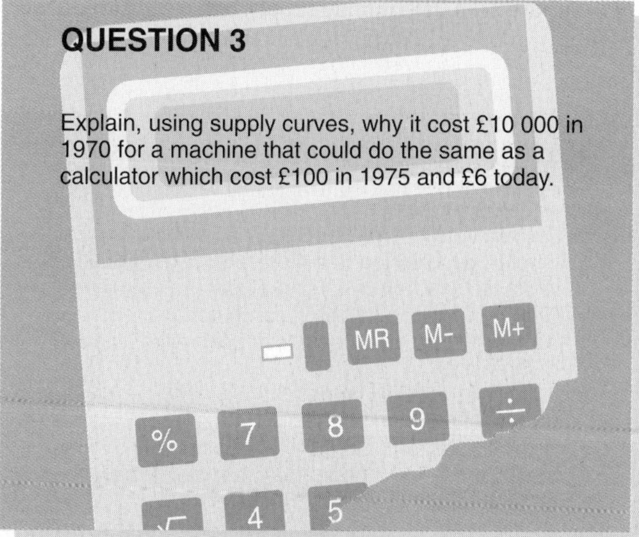

Explain, using supply curves, why it cost £10 000 in 1970 for a machine that could do the same as a calculator which cost £100 in 1975 and £6 today.

The prices of other goods

Changes in the prices of some goods can affect the supply of a particular good. For instance, if the price of beef increases substantially there will be an increase in the quantity of beef supplied. More cows will be reared and slaughtered. As a result there will be an increase in the supply of hides for leather. At the same price, the quantity of leather supplied to the market will increase. An increase in the price of beef therefore leads to an increase in the supply of leather. On the other hand, an increase in cattle rearing is likely to be at the expense of production of wheat or sheep farming. So an increase in beef production is likely to lead to a fall in the supply of other agricultural products as farmers switch production to take advantage of higher profits in beef.

Other factors

A number of other factors affect supply. These include:

- the goals of sellers - if for some reason there is a change in the profit levels which a seller expects to receive as a reward for production, then there will be a change in supply; for instance, if an industry such as the book retailing industry went from one made up of many small sellers more interested in selling books than making a profit to one where the industry was dominated by a few large profit-seeking companies, then supply would fall;
- government legislation - anti-pollution controls which raise the costs of production, the abolition of legal barriers to setting up business in an industry, or tax changes, are some examples of how government can change the level of supply in an industry;
- expectations of future events - if firms expect future prices to be much higher, they may restrict supplies and stockpile goods; if they expect disruptions to their future production because of a strike they may stockpile raw materials, paying for them with borrowed money, thus increasing their costs and reducing supply;
- the weather - in agricultural markets, the weather plays a crucial role in determining supply, bad weather reducing supply, good weather producing bumper yields.

QUESTION 4 Explain how you would expect supply to be affected by the following events, all other things being equal.

(a) Electricity, 1990. The privatisation of the electricity industry in 1990 led to the creation of an industry which sought to maximise profits for shareholders. Before, when the industry was in government ownership, the industry was not expected to make high profits.

(b) Gas, April 1993. In April 1993, VAT of 8 per cent was imposed on domestic gas supplies.

(c) UK Potatoes, summer 1994. Unfavourable weather conditions led to a poor potato harvest in the UK and the rest of northern Europe in 1994.

Individual and market supply curves

The MARKET SUPPLY CURVE can be derived from the INDIVIDUAL SUPPLY CURVES of sellers in the market (this assumes that supply is not affected by changes in the demand curve as would happen under monopoly or oligopoly; ☞ unit 28 for an explanation of why this is so). Consider Figure 5.4. For the sake of simplicity we will assume that there are only three sellers in the market. At a price of £10 per unit, Firm X is unwilling to supply any goods. Firm Y supplies 3 units whilst Firm Z supplies 2 units. So the market supply at a price of £10 is 5 units. At a price of £20, Firm X will supply 1 unit, Firm Y 5 units and Firm Z 9 units. So the market supply at a price of £20 is 15 units. The rest of the market supply curve can be derived by **horizontally summing** the level of output at all other price levels.

QUESTION 5

Table 5.2

Quantity supplied (million units)			Price (£)
Firms in area A	Firms in area B	Firms in area C	
10	2	0	1
12	5	3	2
14	8	6	3
16	11	9	4
18	14	12	5

Firms in areas A, B and C are the sole suppliers in the market and the market is perfectly competitive.

(a) Draw the market supply curve.

(b) What is supply at a price of (i) £1 and (ii) £3.50?

(c) One firm in area A decides to increase production by 5 units at every given price. Draw the new market supply curve on your diagram.

(d) Explain what would happen to the market supply curve if new technology in the industry led to greater productive efficiency amongst individual firms.

Key terms

Supply - the quantity of goods that suppliers are willing to sell at any given price over a period of time.

Individual supply curve - the supply curve of an individual producer.

Market supply curve - the supply curve of all producers within the market. In a perfectly competitive market it can be calculated by summing the supply curves of individual producers.

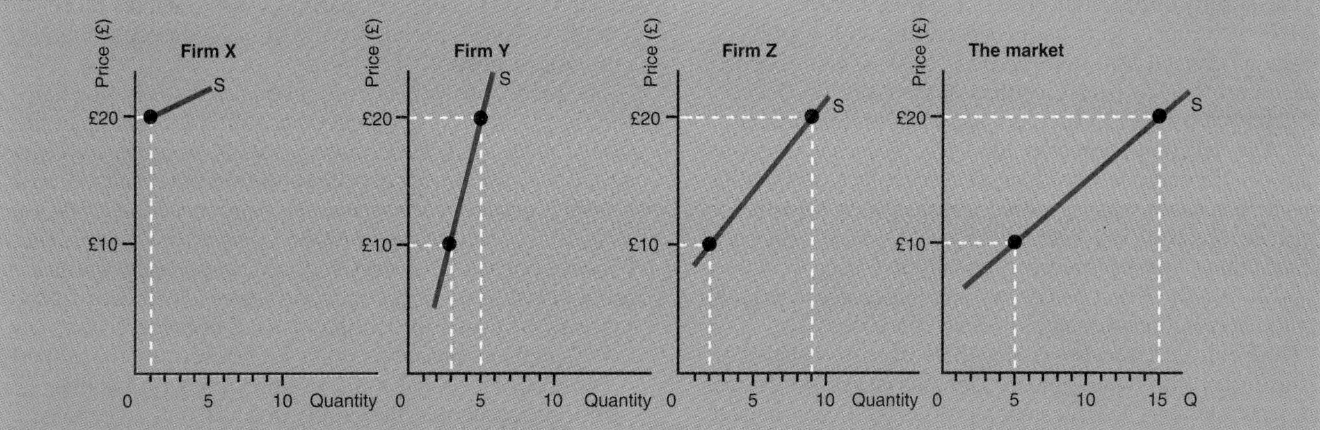

Figure 5.4 *Individual and market supply curves*
The market supply curve is calculated by summing the individual supply curves of producers in the market. Here the market supply at £20, for instance, is calculated by adding the supply of each individual firm at a price of £20.

Applied economics

The supply of rented accommodation

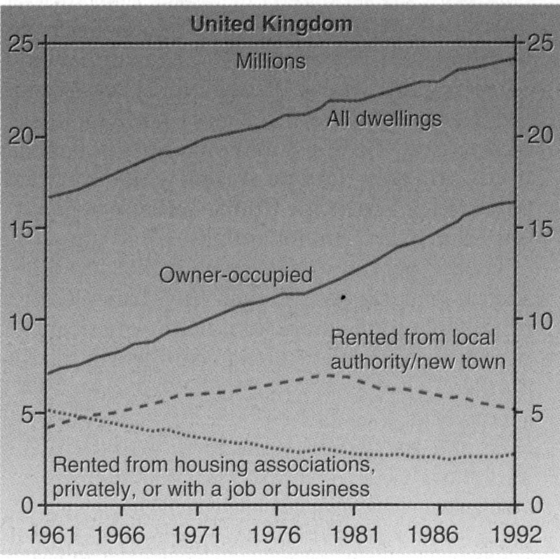

Source: adapted from Department of the Environment.
Figure 5.5 *Stock of dwellings by tenure*

The supply of rented accommodation in the UK remained broadly constant in the 1960s and 1970s but fell during the 1980s before beginning to pick up again. The supply of rented accommodation, shown in Figure 5.5, comes from three major sources:

- local councils renting out property (**council housing**);
- housing associations which are non-profit making organisations aiming to provide affordable housing for rent and which receive substantial government grants to build new houses;
- private landlords, which may be companies specialising in renting property or individuals renting out houses.

The supply of council houses and housing association dwellings is not dependent on the price of accommodation, the rent. Changes in rents will not lead to changes in the number of dwellings available for rent from either of these two sources. This is because central government controls the ability of both to build new housing through grants and permits. The supply curve for both is therefore vertical. Supply remains the same whatever the price (the rent).

The supply of privately rented accommodation, however, has proved to be price sensitive with supply halving between 1961 and the early 1990s. One important reason for this has been the effect of the Rent Act 1965 which established a system of 'fair rents' enforceable in law. The 'fair rent', however, tended to be be set at too low a level with many landlords unable to make a reasonable profit. The result was a gradual contraction in supply. In contrast, the Housing Act of 1988 gave landlords the right to set higher 'market' rents under certain letting conditions. The result has been a small increase in private rented accommodation supplied to the market.

The Rent Act 1965 also gave tenants right of occupancy. Landlords could no longer evict tenants easily. Whilst this protected tenants against unscrupulous landlords, as was intended, it also reduced the value of any house with a sitting tenant should the landlord want to sell the house. This discouraged people from letting out houses, thus reducing supply.

The price of owner-occupied housing had an effect on the supply of privately rented accommodation too. In the 1960s, 1970s and 1980s, house prices boomed. Forty years ago, it was not uncommon for children inheriting a house to rent it out and earn an income from it. By the 1980s, the attraction of selling any inherited property was far greater because house prices were so high. Property companies too had found it increasingly attractive to sell their rented houses and invest the capital realised elsewhere.

With higher rents, lower prices for houses after the property collapse of 1988-93 and a greater unwillingness of young people to buy houses, the supply of houses onto the rented market could well increase during the rest of the 1990s.

Jamaican bananas

Jamaica has traditionally sold its bananas to Europe and particularly the UK. In the 1960s, the island's exports averaged 150 000 tonnes a year with the UK preventing the import of lower priced bananas from Latin American countries and giving preference to higher priced bananas imported from its former colonies in the Caribbean. Entry to the European Community in 1973 cut the strength of these links and the UK began to allow greater imports from Latin American countries whilst still maintaining some preferential access for Caribbean bananas. The result was that higher priced Jamaican exports of bananas in the 1970s averaged only half the levels of the 1960s. A hurricane in 1980 and another in 1988 which devastated the banana plantations further depressed exports in the 1980s to an average of 35 000 tonnes. By 1993, production had recovered enough for exports to grow to 77 000 tonnes.

Traditional suppliers of bananas to the UK and France from the Caribbean and Africa have long had preferential access to these two markets. Bananas from Latin American countries have been kept out by high import taxes or outright bans on imports. The creation of a single market in the European Union in 1993 and the signing of the GATT world trade talks in 1994 have created strains for the arrangement. A new deal struck in 1994 was for 1.5 million tonnes of bananas from traditional Caribbean and African suppliers to come into the EU free of any import tax, of which 105 000 tonnes were allocated to Jamaica. In comparison, the first 2 million tonnes of bananas from Latin American producers would have to pay a tax of Ecu100 per tonne and any bananas imported over 2 million tonnes would attract a tax of Ecu850 per tonne. The result is that suppliers such as Jamaica can sell their their bananas at Ecu100 per tonne more than Latin American producers and still be able to compete in the EU market.

However, the Germans are objecting. They want to be able to continue to import cheap Latin American bananas untaxed because their consumers have traditionally bought these bananas at world prices. The Latin American producers are saying that the deal is unfair to them. They ought to be able to compete on the same terms as African and Caribbean producers in EU markets.

Costs of production of Jamaican bananas are falling as productivity rises. Over the past 40 years, there has been a consolidation of farms on the island. By the early 1990s, three farms accounted for 70 per cent of bananas exported. Crop yields have increased from an average of three export tonnes per acre in the 1970s to nine export tonnes in the early 1990s.

Source: adapted from the *Financial Times*, 28.2.1994.

The Jamaican government is concerned about the situation. It wants its banana industry to survive and if possible expand.

1. **Explain what would be likely to happen to the supply of Jamaican bananas if import taxes on Latin American bananas into the EU were taken away.**
2. **(a) Suggest a package of measures which the Jamaican government could implement to help its banana growers shift their supply curves to the right.**
   (b) Explain what might be the opportunity costs of your suggestions.
3. **(a) How might the world supply of bananas change if higher cost producers like Jamaica were forced out of the market and abandoned banana production for export?**
   (b) Is it in the interests of the UK to see Jamaica forced out of the market?

Price determination

Summary

1. The equilibrium or market clearing price is set where demand equals supply.
2. Changes in demand and supply will lead to new equilibrium prices being set.
3. A change in demand will lead to a shift in the demand curve, a movement along the supply curve and a new equilibrium price.
4. A change in supply will lead to a shift in the supply curve, a movement along the demand curve and a new equilibrium price.
5. Markets do not necessarily tend towards the equilibrium price.
6. The equilibrium price is not necessarily the price which will lead to the greatest economic efficiency or the greatest equity.

Equilibrium price

Buyers and sellers come together in a market. A price (sometimes called the **market price**) is struck and goods or services are exchanged. Consider Table 6.1. It shows the demand and supply schedule for a good at prices between £2 and £10.

Table 6.1

Price (£)	Quantity demanded (million units per month)	Quantity supplied (million units per month)
2	12	2
4	9	4
6	6	6
8	3	8
10	0	10

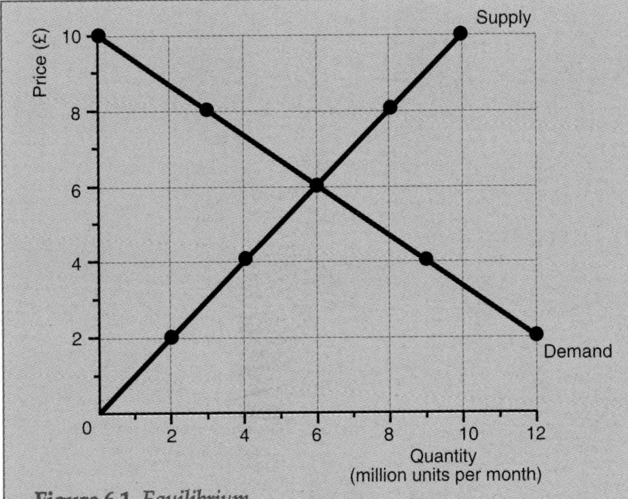

Figure 6.1 *Equilibrium*
At £6, the quantity demanded is equal to the quantity supplied. The market is said to be in equilibrium at this price.

- If the price is £2, demand will be 12 million units but only 2 million units will be supplied. Demand is greater than supply and there is therefore EXCESS DEMAND (i.e. too much demand in relation to supply) in the market. There will be a **shortage** of products on the market. Some buyers will be lucky and they will snap up the 2 million units being sold. But there will be a 10 million unit shortfall in supply for the rest of the unlucky buyers in the market. For instance, it is not possible to buy some luxury cars without being on a waiting list for several years because current demand is too great.
- If the price is £10, buyers will not buy any goods. Sellers on the other hand will wish to supply 10 million units. Supply is greater than demand and therefore there will be EXCESS SUPPLY. There will be a **glut** or surplus of products on the market. 10 million units will remain unsold. A sale in a shop is often evidence of excess supply in the past. Firms tried to sell the goods at a higher price and failed.
- There is only one price where demand equals supply. This is at a price of £6 where demand and supply are both 6 million units. This price is known as the EQUILIBRIUM PRICE. This is the only price where the planned demand of buyers equals the planned supply of sellers in the market. It is also known as the MARKET-CLEARING price because all the products supplied to the market are bought or cleared from the market, but no buyer is left frustrated in his or her wishes to buy goods.

An alternative way of expressing the data in Table 6.1 is shown in Figure 6.1. The equilibrium price is where demand equals supply. This happens where the two curves cross, at a price of £6 and a quantity of 6 million units. If the price is above £6, supply will be greater than demand and therefore excess supply will exist. If the price is below £6, demand is greater than supply and therefore there will be excess demand.

QUESTION 1

Table 6.2

Price (£)	Quantity demanded (million units)	Quantity supplied (million units)
30	20	70
20	50	50
10	80	30

(a) Plot the demand and supply curves shown in Table 6.2 on a diagram.
(b) What is the equilibrium price?
(c) In what price range is there (i) excess demand and (ii) excess supply?
(d) Will there be a glut or a shortage in the market if the price is: (i) £10; (ii) £40; (iii) £22; (iv) £18; (v) £20?

Changes in demand and supply

It was explained in units 4 and 5 that a change in price would lead to a change in quantity demanded or supplied, shown by a movement along the demand or supply curve. A change in any other variable, such as income or the costs of production, would lead to:

- an **increase** or **decrease** in demand or supply and therefore
- a **shift** in the demand or supply curve.

Demand and supply diagrams provide a powerful and simple tool for analysing the effects of changes in demand and supply on equilibrium price and quantity.

Consider the effect of a rise in consumer incomes. This will lead to an increase in the demand for a normal good. In Figure 6.2 (a) this will push the demand curve from D_1 to D_2. As can be seen from the diagram, the equilibrium price rises from P_1 to P_2. The quantity bought and sold in equilibrium rises from Q_1 to Q_2. The model of demand and supply predicts that an increase in incomes, all other things being equal (the **ceteris paribus** condition) will lead to an increase both in the price of the product and in the quantity sold. Note that the increase in income **shifts**

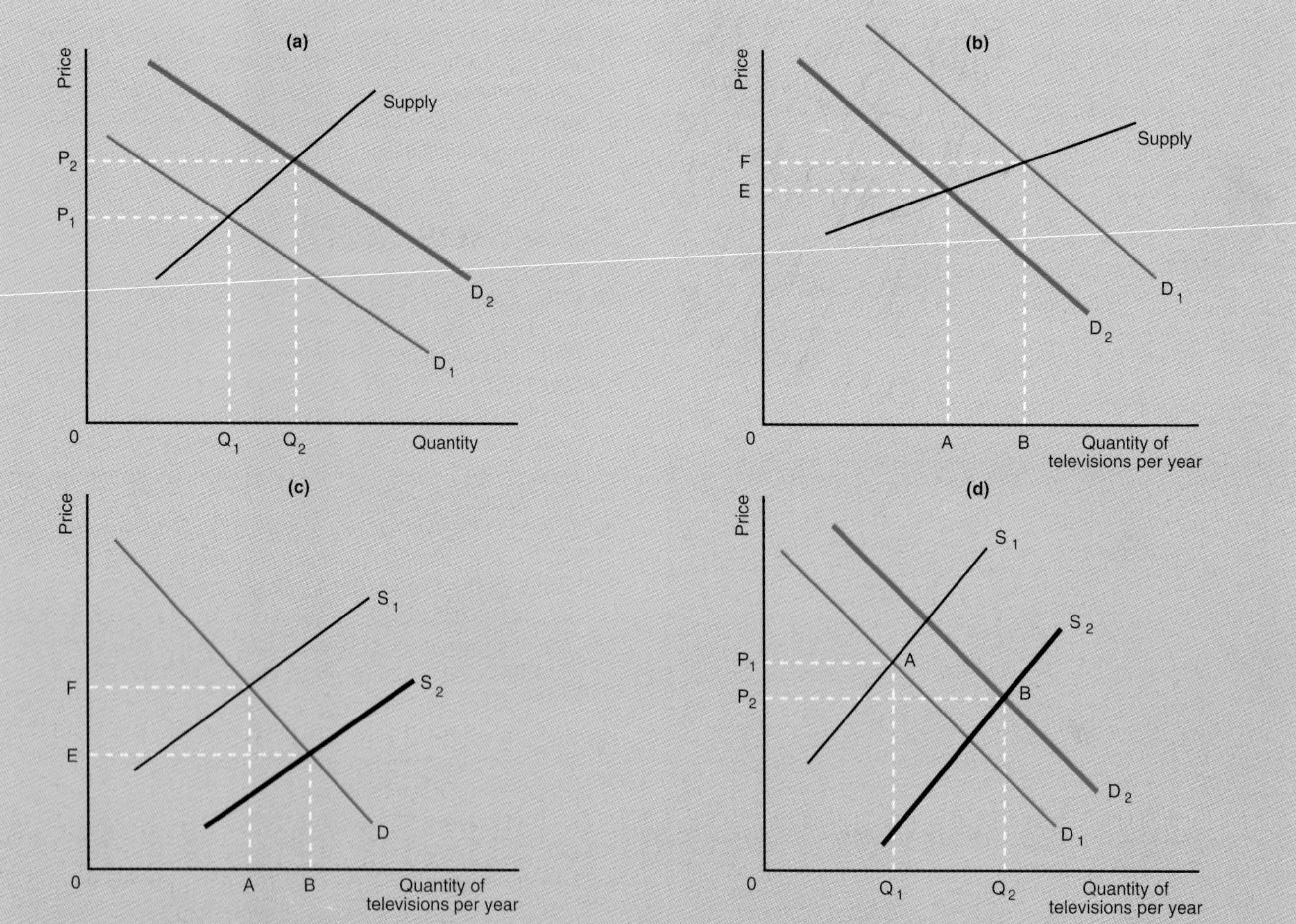

Figure 6.2 *Shifts in demand and supply curves*
Shifts in the demand or supply curves for a product will change the equilibrium price and the equilibrium quantity bought and sold.

the demand curve and this then leads to a **movement along** the supply curve.

Figure 6.2 (b) shows the market for black and white televisions. In the early 1970s, both the BBC and Independent Television started to broadcast programmes in colour for the first time. Not surprisingly there was a boom in sales of colour television sets and a slump in sales of black and white ones. In economic terms the demand for black and white sets fell. This is shown by a shift to the left in the demand curve. The equilibrium level of sales in Figure 6.2 (b) falls from OB to OA whilst equilibrium price falls from OF to OE. Note again that a shift in the demand curve leads to a movement along the supply curve.

Prices of both black and white and colour television sets tended to fall in the 1970s and 1980s. The main reason for this was an increase in productive efficiency (☞ unit 34) due to the introduction of new technology, enabling costs of production to fall. A fall in costs of production is shown by the shift to the right in the supply curve in Figure 6.2 (c). At any given quantity of output, firms will be prepared to supply more television sets to the market. The result is an increase in quantity bought and sold from OA to OB and a fall in price from OF to OE. Note that there is a shift in the supply curve which leads to a movement along the demand curve.

So far we have assumed that only one variable changes and that all other variables remain constant. But in the real world, it is likely that several factors affecting demand and supply will change at the same time. Demand and supply diagrams can be used to some extent to analyse several changes. For instance, in the 1970s and 1980s the demand for colour television sets increased due to rising real incomes (☞ unit 3 for a definition of 'real' values). At the same time, supply increased too because of an increase in productive efficiency. Overall, the price of television sets fell slightly. This is shown in Figure 6.2 (d). Both the demand and supply curves shift to the right. This will lead to an increase in quantity bought and sold. In theory, depending upon the extent of the shifts in the two curves, there could be an increase in price, a fall in price or no change in the price. Figure 6.2 (d) shows the middle of these three possibilities.

QUESTION 2 During the 1970s the price of metals such as nickel was historically high. This prompted nickel producers to invest in new production facilities which came on stream during the late 1970s and early 1980s. But the world economy went into deep recession during the early 1980s, prompting a collapse in the world price of nickel. Producers reacted by closing facilities. Between 1980 and 1986, the industry lost about 32 500 tonnes of annual capacity compared with an annual demand of between 400 000 and 500 000 tonnes.

The world economy started to recover from 1982 but it wasn't until 1987 that a sharp increase in demand from Japanese stainless steel producers, one of the major buyers in the industry, made prices rise. In the last quarter of 1987, nickel could be bought for $1.87 a lb. By March 1988, it had soared to over $9 per lb.This price proved unsustainable. Both the US and UK economies began to go into recession in 1989 and nickel prices fell to below $3 per lb by the end of 1989.

The invasion of Kuwait by Iraq in 1990 and the subsequent large military involvement of the USA and other countries in defeating Iraq led to a rise in most metal prices. The markets feared a long drawn out war with a possible increase in demand from armaments manufacturers and a possible fall in supply if any nickel producing countries decided to side with Iraq and suspend nickel sales onto the world market. However, the swift defeat of Iraq led to a sharp fall back in price. Recession in Europe and Japan produced further falls in price between 1991 and 1993 despite the beginning of recovery in the US economy, with the price falling below $2 per lb in the last quarter of 1993. The price would have been even lower but for cutbacks in output by major nickel producers over the period.

1994 saw a sharp rise in demand as all the major industrialised countries showed economic growth. By the start of 1995, nickel prices had risen to over $3 per lb.

Using demand and supply diagrams, explain why the price of nickel changed when:

(a) new production facilities came on stream in the late 1970s;
(b) there was a world recession in the early 1980s;
(c) the industry closed capacity during the early 1980s;
(d) Japanese stainless steel producers increased purchases in 1987;
(e) Iraq invaded Kuwait in 1990;
(f) all the major industrialised countries showed economic growth in 1994.

Do markets clear?

It is very easy to assume that the equilibrium price is either the current market price or the price towards which the market moves. Neither is correct. The market price could be at any level. There could be excess demand or excess supply at any point in time.

Nor will market prices necessarily tend to change to

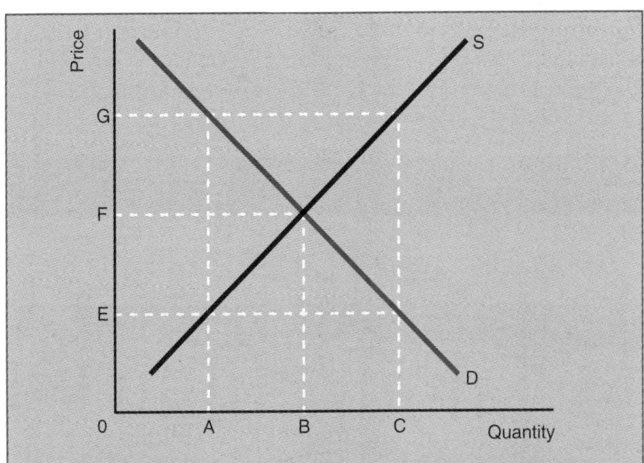

Figure 6.3 *The operation of market forces in the coffee market*
Market pressure will tend to force down coffee prices when there is excess supply, such as at price OG, but force up coffee prices when there is excess demand such as at price OE.

equilibrium prices over time. One of the most important controversies in economics today is the extent to which markets tend towards market-clearing prices.

The argument put forward by neo-classical free market economists is that markets do tend to clear. Let us take the example of the coffee market. In this market, there are many producers (farmers, manufacturers, wholesalers and retailers) that are motivated by the desire to make as large a profit as possible. When there is excess demand for coffee (demand is greater than supply), coffee producers will be able to increase their prices and therefore their profits and still sell all they produce. If there is excess supply (supply is greater than demand), some coffee will remain unsold. Producers then have a choice. Either they can offer coffee for sale at the existing price and risk not selling it or they can lower their price to the level where they will sell everything offered. If all producers choose not to lower their prices, there is likely to be even greater pressure to reduce prices in the future because there will be unsold stocks of coffee overhanging the market. Therefore when there is excess demand, prices will be driven upwards whilst prices will fall if there is excess supply.

This can be shown diagrammatically. In Figure 6.3, there is excess demand at a price of OE. Buyers want to purchase AC more of coffee than is being supplied. Shops, manufacturers and coffee growers will be able to increase their prices and their production and still sell everything they produce. If they wish to sell all their output, they can increase their prices to a maximum of OF and their output to a maximum OB, the market-clearing prices and production levels. This they will do because at higher prices and production levels they will be able to make more profit. If there is excess supply, coffee producers will be left with unsold stocks. At a price of OG, output left unsold will be AC. Producers in a free market cannot afford to build up stocks forever. Some producers will lower prices and the rest will be forced to follow. Production and prices will go on falling until equilibrium output and price is reached. This is usually referred to as a **stable equilibrium** position.

These pressures which force the market towards an equilibrium point are often called FREE MARKET FORCES. But critics of the market mechanism argue that free market forces can lead away from the equilibrium point in many cases. One example of **unstable equilibrium**, the Cobweb theory, is explained in unit 11. In other markets, it is argued that market forces are too weak to restore equilibrium. Many Keynesian economists cite the labour market as an example of this. In other markets, there are many forces such as government legislation, trade unions and multi-national monopolies which more than negate the power of the market.

QUESTION 3

$$Q_D = 20 - 1/2\,P$$
$$Q_S = 10 + 3/4\,P$$

where Q_D is quantity demanded, Q_S is quantity supplied and P is price (in £).

The current price is £12.

(a) Is there excess demand or excess supply in the market?

(b) Will free market forces tend to lead to a fall or rise in price?

Points to note

Equilibrium is a very powerful concept in economics but it is essential to remember that the equilibrium price is unlikely to be the most desirable price or 'right' price in the market. The most desirable price in the market will depend upon how one defines 'desirable'. It may be, for instance, the one which leads to the greatest economic efficiency, or it may be the one which leads to greatest equity. Alternatively it may be the one which best supports the defence of the country.

Demand can also equal supply without there being equilibrium. At any point in time, what is actually bought must equal what is actually sold. There can be no sellers without buyers. So actual demand (more often referred to as **realised** or **ex post** demand in economics) must always equal actual (or realised or ex post) supply. Equilibrium occurs at a price where there is no tendency to change. Price will not change if, at the current price, the quantity that consumers wish to buy (called **planned** or **desired** or **ex ante** demand) is equal to the quantity that suppliers wish to sell (called planned or desired or ex ante supply).

Therefore only in equilibrium will planned demand equal planned supply.

Key terms

Excess demand - where demand is greater than supply.
Excess supply - where supply is greater than demand.
Equilibrium price - the price at which there is no tendency to change because planned (or desired or ex ante) purchases (i.e. demand) are equal to planned sales (i.e. supply).
Market clearing price - the price at which there is neither excess demand nor excess supply but where everything offered for sale is purchased.
Free market forces - forces in free markets which act to reduce prices when there is excess supply and raise prices when there is excess demand.

Applied economics

Demand and supply in the passenger transport market

The quantity demanded and supplied of passenger transport in the UK over the past 30 years has more than trebled, as Figure 6.4 shows. However, almost all of this growth is accounted for by a rise in demand for car travel. Rail travel has remained broadly constant, whilst bus and coach travel have declined. Air travel has grown enormously but only accounts for a fraction of the total passenger miles travelled in the UK.

The main reason for the growth in demand for passenger transport has been rising incomes. As Table 6.3 shows, real personal disposable income (income after income tax and inflation have been accounted for) roughly doubled between 1965 and 1991. Consumers have tended to spend a relatively high proportion of increases in income on transport. As a result, spending on transport as a proportion of household expenditure has risen from 9.7 per cent in 1965 to 15.3 per cent in 1991. Spending on car transport has risen faster than spending on other types of passenger transport. In 1965, there were 6.2 million cars and light vans on the road, with three quarters of all household spending on transport being on cars and their running costs. By 1991, this has risen to 85.9 per cent. Rising income has enabled many households to buy a car, with the number of cars and light vans on British roads rising from 6.2 million in 1961 to 22.7 million in 1994.

Notice that in the recession of 1990-91, when incomes fell, spending on transport fell as did the proportion of household spending on transport.

The average price of transport has risen broadly in line with the average increase in all prices in the economy, as

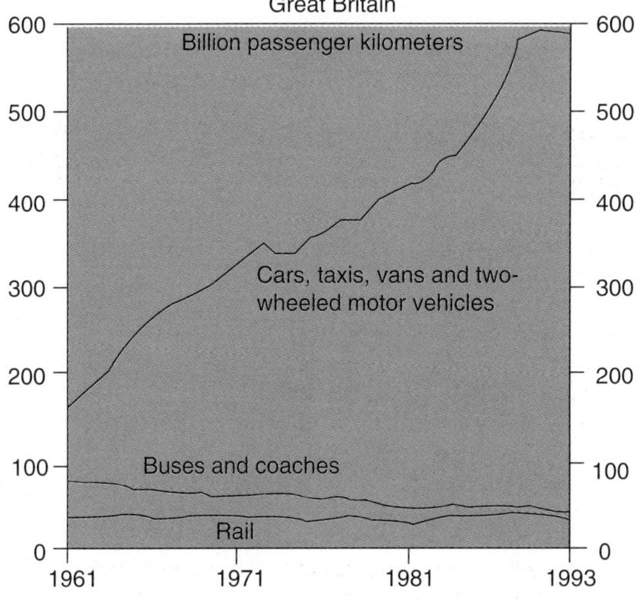

Source: adapted from *Department of Transport.*

Figure 6.4 *Road and rail passenger transport use*

Table 6.3 *Household expenditure on passenger transport*

	Personal disposable income	Household expenditure on transport	Household expenditure on transport as a percentage of total household expenditure	Motoring expenditure as a percentage of all household expenditure on transport
	£bn at 1990 prices	£ average per week per household at 1990 prices	%	%
1965	197	22.48	9.7	74.5
1970	218	26.41	10.2	77.2
1975	254	27.50	13.8	80.0
1980	285	29.50	14.6	81.2
1985	310	32.20	15.2	84.4
1990	380	40.02	16.2	84.5
1991	380	35.70	15.3	85.9
1992	390	38.37	15.8	83.2

Source: adapted from Department of Transport, *Transport Statistics.*

can be seen from Table 6.4. However, the price of travelling by rail, bus and coach has risen faster than that of travelling by car. This has been particularly so since 1979. The Conservative governments of Margaret Thatcher and John Major have cut subsidies to both British Rail and bus and coach companies, who have reacted by charging higher prices. The fall in price of motoring relative to bus and train travel is one factor accounting for the relative decline in demand for bus and train services.

Since 1990, the government has been increasing taxes on petrol. This is reflected in the sharp rise in the cost of motoring compared to the average increase in prices for the whole economy. The government has a double objective. Firstly, it wishes to reduce atmospheric pollution from cars by encouraging motorists to drive fewer miles and use more fuel-efficient cars. Secondly, it wishes to reduce traffic congestion, again by discouraging driving.

Demand for transport has also grown for a number of other reasons. The population of the UK has increased. Planning policies have led to a greater separation of housing and places of work, necessitating more commuting to work. Faster and more reliable cars, together with faster roads, have also encouraged more workers to commute longer distances.

There is no 'supply curve' for motor vehicle transport because no single firm or industry provides this service. There are, of course, supply curves for the components of the service, such as petrol and servicing of cars. Nor is there a supply curve for rail travel. Until 1995, British Rail has been a monopoly (i.e. only) supplier and there is no supply curve under monopoly (☞ unit 28).

However, there has arguably been a supply curve for bus and coach travel since 1980 (for coaches) and 1985 (for buses) when the industry was deregulated. Before deregulation, the government issued licences and in general only one licence was offered on a route, establishing monopolies. After deregulation, any firm could set up and offer regular bus services in the UK. Table 6.5 shows that there was an increase in the number of buses on the roads during the 1980s, travelling more kilometres. This was despite a fall in the number of kilometres travelled by passengers. This suggests that the demand curve for bus transport has been shifting to the left as more people switch to cars. The supply curve, however, has shifted to the right with new companies coming into the market and existing companies expanding their services. Opposing this rightward shift has been a fall in government subsidies to bus companies, which all other things being equal would have shifted the supply curve to the left.

Overall, the price of bus and coach travel has increased more than the general increase in prices in the economy. This would suggest that the cut in subsidies has more than outweighed the effect of the increase in supply due to deregulation and the effect of the fall in demand.

Table 6.4 *Passenger transport: consumer price indices (1990=100)*

	Motor vehicles		Rail	Bus and coach	All transport	All consumer expenditure (RPI)
	Total	*of which* net purchase				
1965	11.9	13.2	9.2	7.7	10.8	12
1970	15.1	15.5	11.8	10.8	13.8	15
1975	28.5	27.1	24.1	20.7	26.0	27
1980	59.4	63.1	54.8	49.4	54.1	75
1985	82.0	80.7	70.1	71.6	74.1	82
1990	100.0	100.0	100.0	100.0	100.0	100
1993	119.6	109.2	126.7	127.4	122.1	112

Source: adapted from Department of Transport, *Transport Statistics.*

Table 6.5 *Bus and coach travel*

	Number of kilometres travelled by passengers on buses and coaches (bn)	Number of buses and coaches on UK roads	Number of kilometres travelled by buses and coaches (bn)	Index of prices (1990 = 100) Bus and coach fares	All prices (RPI)
1980	52	69.9	3.5	-	53
1981	49	69.1	3.5	-	59
1982	48	70.7	3.5	-	64
1983	48	70.2	3.7	67	67
1984	48	68.8	3.9	69	71
1985	49	67.9	3.7	75	75
1986	47	69.6	3.7	78	78
1987	47	71.7	4.1	82	81
1988	46	72.0	4.3	88	85
1989	47	72.5	4.5	95	91
1990	46	71.9	4.6	100	100
1991	45	71.4	4.8	114	106
1992	43	72.6	4.6	122	110
1993	42	74.9	4.6	127	112

Source: adapted from CSO, *Annual Abstract of Statistics;* Department of Transport, *Transport Statistics.*

Aluminium

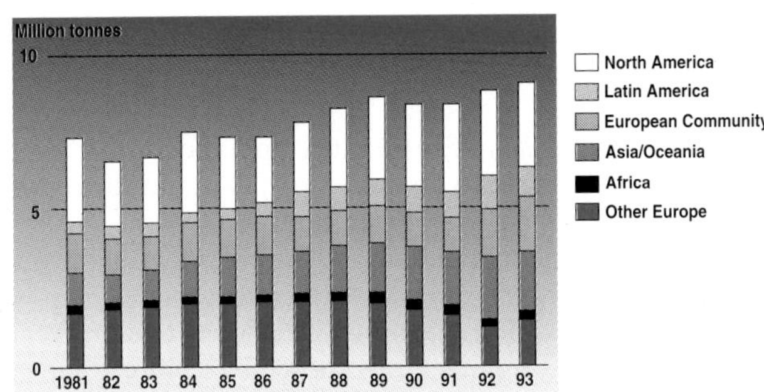

Source: adapted from US Bureau of Mines.

Figure 6.5 *World primary production of aluminium*

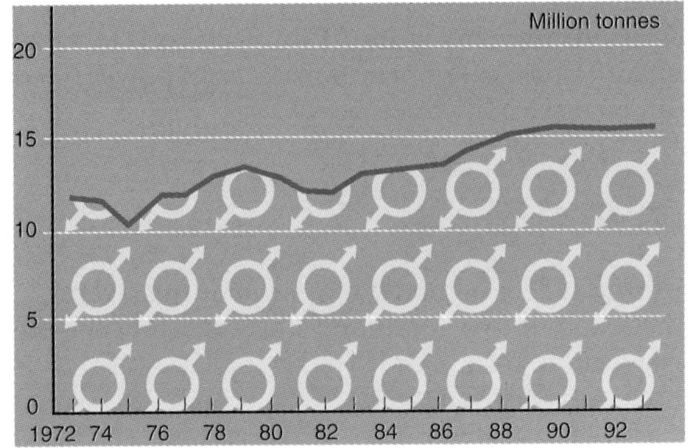

Source: adapted from *International Mining Monthly.*

Figure 6.6 *Western world consumption of aluminium*

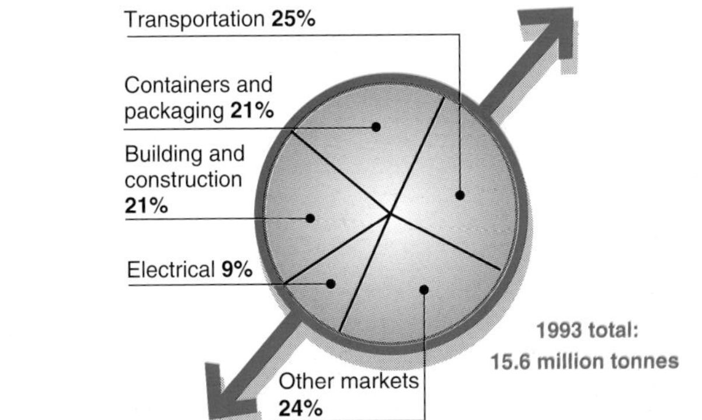

Figure 6.7 *Western world use of aluminium*

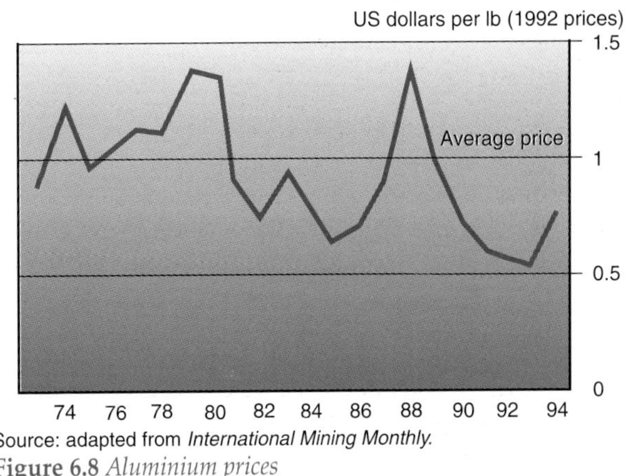

Source: adapted from *International Mining Monthly.*

Figure 6.8 *Aluminium prices*

Demand

Demand for aluminium has been growing since the early 1980s. The recessions in the world economies in the late 1980s and early 1990s served only to dent that growth, not stop it. This is because aluminium producers have been very successful in expanding the markets for the product. Aluminium has been steadily displacing steel and glass in packaging such as beverage cans. The car industry has been using increasing amounts of aluminium to replace steel in order to keep the weight of cars down and thus improve fuel efficiency. The building industry too uses aluminium to keep weight down when a metal is needed. In the electrical market, aluminium is increasingly being used in cable.

Recycling

Aluminium claims to be 'green'. Although very energy intensive to produce, its high value makes it worthwhile to recycle. In the USA, for instance, over 60 per cent of all aluminium beverage cans are recycled, collected typically by schools and charities. The industry has been keen to promote recycling. It gives its product a marketing edge over what are perceived to be less environmentally friendly substitutes such as steel. It also lowers costs of production since it is far cheaper to produce 1 tonne of aluminium from recycled material than it is from the raw material, bauxite.

Supply

The supply of aluminium tends to be far more unstable than demand. When prices rise and stocks of aluminium held fall, aluminium producers tend to increase capacity. When these new plants come on stream, prices fall. As a result, further planned increases in capacity are shelved and older plants mothballed or closed. Prices then begin to rise again and investment begins. The early 1990s saw a further problem. The collapse of the Soviet Union led to Russian smelters suddenly switching output to their export market, attracted by the opportunity to earn dollars. There was a surge in supply and world aluminium prices fell further. Prices did not begin to rise again until 1994.

Write a report for a company thinking of setting up in the aluminium manufacturing business.

In the report:

1. **outline the trends in demand for and supply of aluminium since the early 1980s and explain the changes in price experienced;**
2. **discuss the likely future demand for aluminium and the effect this will have on price, all other things being equal;**
3. **discuss what is likely to happen to supply in the future;**
4. **evaluate whether long term trends are likely to result in long term price falls or rises.**

Interrelationships between markets

Summary

1. Some goods are complements, in joint demand.
2. Other goods are substitutes for each other, in competitive demand.
3. Derived demand occurs when one good is demanded because it is needed for the production of other goods or services.
4. Composite demand and joint supply are two other ways in which markets are linked.

Partial and general models

A model of price determination was outlined in unit 6. It was explained that the price of a good was determined by the forces of demand and supply. This is an example of a **partial model**. A partial model is an explanation of reality which has relatively few variables (☞ unit 115). But a more **general model** or wider model of the market system can be constructed which shows how events in one market can lead to changes in other markets. In this unit we will consider how some markets are interrelated.

Complements

Some goods, known as COMPLEMENTS, are in JOINT DEMAND. This means that, in demanding one good, a consumer will also be likely to demand another good. Examples of complements are:

- tennis rackets and tennis balls;
- washing machines and soap powder;
- strawberries and cream;
- video tapes and video recorders.

Economic theory suggests that a rise in the quantity demanded of one complement will lead to an increase in the demand for another, resulting in an increase in the price and quantity bought of the other complement. For instance, an increase in the quantity demanded of strawberries will lead to an increase in demand for cream too, pushing up the price of cream.

This can be shown on a demand and supply diagram. Assume that new technology reduces the cost of production of washing machines. This leads to an increase in supply of washing machines shown by a shift to the right of the supply curve in Figure 7.1 (a). As a result there is a fall in price and a rise in the quantity demanded of washing machines, shown by a movement along the demand curve. This in turn will increase the demand for automatic soap powder, shown by a shift to the right in the demand curve in Figure 7.1 (b). This leads to a rise in the quantity purchased of automatic soap powder and also an increase in its price.

Substitutes

A SUBSTITUTE is a good which can be replaced by another good. If two goods are substitutes for each other, they are said to be in COMPETITIVE DEMAND. Examples of substitutes are:

- beef and pork;
- Coca-cola and Pepsi-cola;
- fountain pens and biros;
- gas and oil (in the long term but not particularly in the short term).

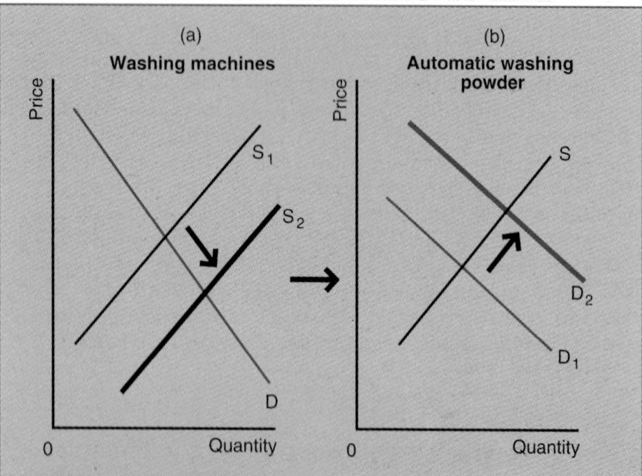

Figure 7.1 *Complements*
An increase in supply and the consequent fall in price of washing machines will lead to a rise in the quantity of washing machines and a rise in demand (shown by a shift in the demand curve) for a complementary good such as automatic washing powder.

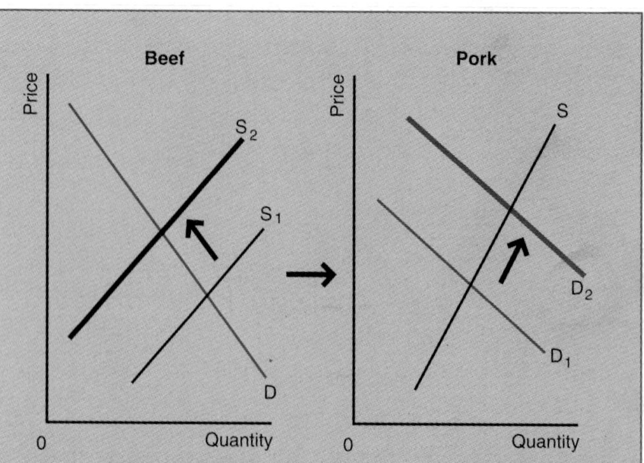

Figure 7.2 *Substitutes*
A fall in the supply of beef leading to a rise in its price will lead to a fall in the quantity demanded of beef and an increase in the demand for a substitute product such as pork.

Economic theory predicts that a rise in the price of one good will lead to an increase in demand and a rise in price of a substitute good.

Figure 7.2 shows a rise in the price of beef, due to a fall in its supply. This leads to a fall in the quantity demanded of beef as the price of beef rises. In turn, there will be an increase in the demand for pork as consumers substitute pork for beef. The demand for pork will increase, shown by a shift to the right in the demand curve for pork. This leads to a rise in the price of pork and a rise in quantity purchased.

Many substitute goods are not clearly linked. For instance, a rise in the price of foreign holidays will lead some consumers to abandon taking a foreign holiday. They may substitute a UK holiday for it, but they may also decide to buy new curtains or a new carpet for their house, or buy a larger car than they had originally planned.

QUESTION 1

(a) It could be argued that the following pairs of products are both complements **and** substitutes. Explain why.
- (i) Electricity and gas.
- (ii) Tea and milk.
- (iii) Bus journeys and train journeys.
- (iv) Chocolate bars and crisps.

(b) (i) For each pair of products, explain whether you think they are more likely to be complements or substitutes.
(ii) Show on a demand and supply diagram the effect on the price of the first product of a rise in price of the second product.

Derived demand

Many goods are demanded only because they are needed for the production of other goods. The demand for these goods is said to be a DERIVED DEMAND.

For instance, the demand for steel is derived in part from the demand for cars and ships. The demand for flour is derived in part from the demand for cakes and bread. The demand for sugar is in part derived from demand for some beverages, confectionery and chocolate.

Figure 7.3 shows an increase in the demand for cars. This leads to an increase in quantity bought and sold. Car manufacturers will increase their demand for steel, shown by a rightward shift of the demand curve for steel. The price of steel will then increase as will the quantity bought and sold. Economic theory therefore predicts that an increase in demand for a good will lead to an increase in price and quantity purchased of goods which are in derived demand from it.

QUESTION 2 The world tungsten market was severely depressed between 1989 and 1993. Traditional uses for the metal have been in decline for many years. Cermets and ceramics have been increasingly used in place of tungsten carbide and the longer life of cutting tools has reduced replacement demand. Tungsten was also widely used in the defence industry, spending on which has been cut in the major industrialised countries since the ending of the cold war in the late 1980s. The recession experienced by most industrialised countries between 1989-1993 further cut demand.

The economic recovery of many countries in 1994 saw a doubling in price of the metal as demand increased. Future prices are likely to depend on the extent to which tungsten can be put to new uses, such as in electronics, medical equipment and new generations of armaments.

Source: adapted from the *Financial Times*, 11.11.1994.

(a) Explain with the help of a diagram and the concept of derived demand what is likely to have happened to the price of tungsten between 1989 and 1993.

(b) Why do future prices 'depend on the extent to which tungsten can be put to new uses'?

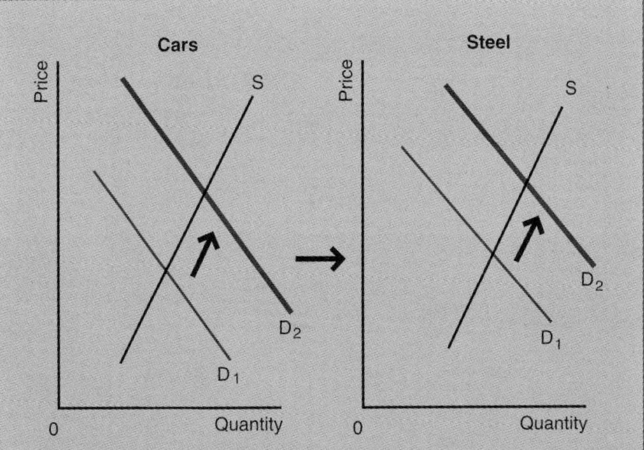

Figure 7.3 *Derived demand*
An increase in the demand for cars will lead to an increase in demand for steel. Steel is said to be in derived demand from cars.

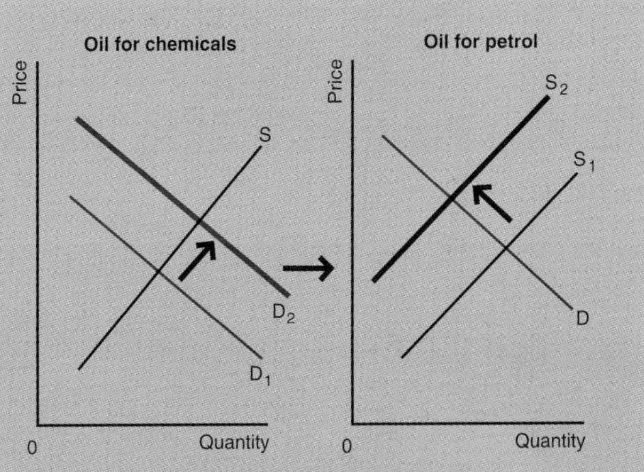

Figure 7.4 *Composite demand*
An increase in the demand for oil from chemical producers will result in a fall in the supply of oil to the petrol market because oil is in composite demand.

Composite demand

A good is said to be in COMPOSITE DEMAND when it is demanded for two or more distinct uses. For instance, milk may be used for yoghurt, for cheese making, for butter or for drinking. Land may be demanded for residential, industrial or commercial use. Steel is demanded for car manufacturing and for shipbuilding.

Economic theory predicts that an increase in demand for one composite good will lead to a fall in supply for another. Figure 7.4 shows that an increase in the demand by the chemical industry for oil will push the demand curve to the right, increasing both the quantity sold and the price of oil. With an upward sloping supply for oil as a whole, an increase in supply of oil to the chemical industry will reduce the supply of oil for petrol. This is shown by a shift upwards in the supply curve in Figure 7.4. The price of oil for petrol will rise and the quantity demanded will fall.

Economic theory therefore predicts that an increase in demand for a good will lead to a rise in price and a fall in quantity demanded for a good with which it is in composite demand.

Joint supply

A good is in JOINT SUPPLY with another good when one good is supplied for two different purposes. For instance, cows are supplied for both beef and leather. An oil well may give both oil and gas.

Economic theory suggests that an increase in demand for one good in joint supply will lead to an increase in its price. This leads to an increase in the quality supplied. The supply of the other good therefore increases, leading to a fall in its price. Figure 7.5 shows that an increase in demand for beef leads to an increase in both price and quantity bought and sold of beef. More beef production will lead, as a by-product, to greater supply of leather. This is shown by a shift to the right in the supply curve for leather. The price of leather will then fall and quantity demanded, bought and sold will increase.

QUESTION 3 Market forces could end the old tradition of kissing under the mistletoe. The price of mistletoe has been rising in recent years as supply falls. This has occurred because of what has been happening in the apple market. Mistletoe grows on apple trees, feeding off the sap of the tree. The past twenty years have not been good for British apple growers. Fierce competition from foreign producers has resulted in many traditional apple orchards being 'grubbed out,' with half of British apple trees disappearing since 1973. What's more, parasitic mistletoe is not allowed to grow on trees in new orchards. As old orchards disappear, so too will the mistletoe.

Source: adapted from the *Financial Times*, 20.12.1994.

With the help of a diagram and the concept of joint supply, explain why the price of mistletoe has been rising in recent years.

Key terms

Complement - a good which is purchased with other goods to satisfy a want.
Joint demand - when two or more complements are bought together.
Substitute - a good which can be replaced by another to satisfy a want.
Competitive demand - when two or more goods are substitutes for each other.
Derived demand - when the demand for one good is the result of or derived from the demand for another good.
Composite demand - when a good is demanded for two or more distinct uses.
Joint supply - when two or more goods are produced together, so that a change in supply of one good will necessarily change the supply of the other goods with which it is in joint supply.

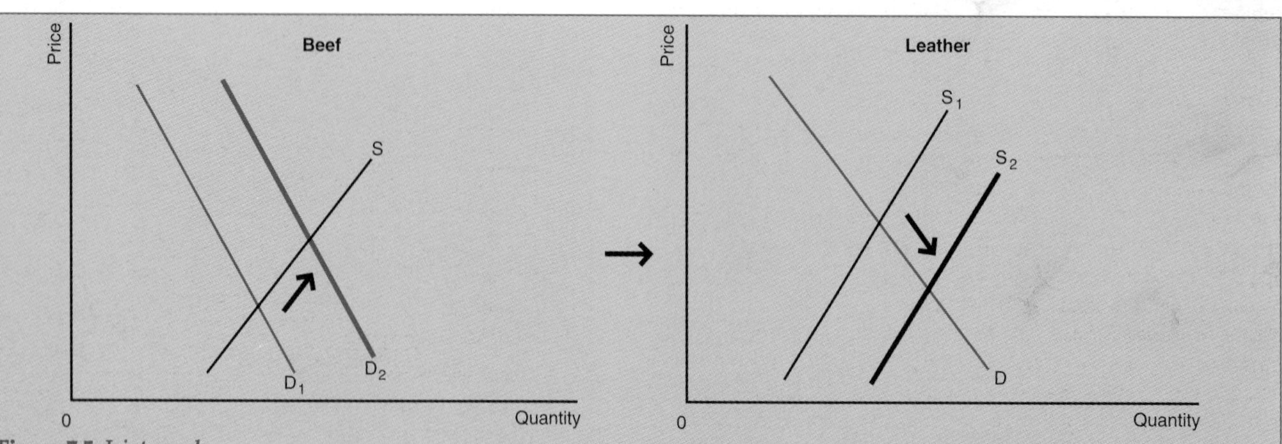

Figure 7.5 *Joint supply*
An increase in the demand for beef, which leads to more beef being produced, results in an increase in the supply of leather. Beef and leather are said to be in joint supply.

Applied economics

Commercial transport

Commercial transport, the transporting of goods in the UK, from factory to shop for instance, is a derived demand. It is ultimately derived from the purchase of consumer goods and services. The movement of coal from a coal pit to an electricity power station is part of the long chain of production in the eventual consumption of, say, a packet of cornflakes.

Demand for commercial transport has grown over time as consumer incomes have risen and more goods and services have been consumed. Table 7.1 shows, however, that the growth in tonnage of goods moved has been relatively small since the 1960s. Much of this is due to the fact that goods have got lighter and less bulky. Far more plastic and far less metal are used today, for instance. So whilst more consumer goods are purchased, the total weight and volume have only increased a little. In contrast, Table 7.2 shows that there has been a significant growth over the same period in the number of tonne kilometres travelled. Each tonne is travelling a longer distance today than 30 years ago. This is the result of greater specialisation between regions and firms. In part, this has happened because of the growth of the motorway network in the UK which has allowed much faster journey times.

Different modes of transport are substitutes for each other. Both tables indicate that, over time, there has been a substitution of road for rail transport. As Figure 7.6 indicates, in the early 1950s railways carried slightly more freight than the roads. By the 1960s, rail had already lost much of its market share to road haulage. There has been a steady growth in pipeline traffic associated with the growth of gas consumption and North Sea oil production. The sudden increase in the share of water transport between 1976 and 1985 was entirely due to the growth of the North Sea oil industry.

The future of rail transport lies as a complement to road transport. Lorries and vans will take goods to railway collection depots. The goods will then be transported by rail before being taken away again by lorry. Loading and unloading from one mode of transport to another is relatively expensive. Therefore, rail transport has proved to be economic mainly when journeys of over 300-400 miles are made by rail or when a dedicated rail link can take goods door to door, for instance, from a pit head to a power station. The number of dedicated rail links is, if anything, likely to decrease in the immediate future with the electricity industry burning more gas and imported coal and less domestic coal. The Channel Tunnel, on the other hand, provides the rail industry with a unique opportunity to encourage exporting firms to transfer long distance haulage from road to rail.

Roads are in composite demand with commercial transport and passenger transport. At present, there is no pricing mechanism for the road system. Most roads are free at all times of day. A minority of roads suffer from congestion at certain times of the day. Then, journey times tend to lead to an allocation of resources. Some potential road users prefer either not to travel or travel by an alternative mode of transport like rail because the extra journey time represents too high an opportunityy cost. Other road users accept that their road journey times will be longer in the rush hour than at other times of the day. Proposed road pricing (☞ unit 37), where vehicles will have to pay tolls on roads, means that cars and commercial vehicles might begin to compete for limited road space. An increase in demand by commercial vehicles could lead to higher road prices which would then reduce quantity demanded by private vehicles.

Table 7.1 *Goods: total transported in millions of tonnes*

	Road	Rail	Water: coastwise oil	Water: other	Pipelines	Total
1961	1,295	249	57		6	1,607
1965	1,634	239	64		27	1,964
1970	1,610	209	58		39	1,916
1975	1,602	176	48		52	1,878
1980	1,383	154	54	83	83	1,757
1985	1,452	122	50	92	89	1,805
1990	1,749	140	44	108	121	2,163
1992	1,555	125	43	97	106	1,923

Table 7.2 *Goods: distance transported: total tonne kilometres (billions)*

	Road	Rail	Water: coastwise oil	Water: other	Pipelines	Total
1961	85.6	16.4	3.2	0.6	0.4	106.2
1965	108.0	15.8	3.7	0.6	1.8	129.8
1970	85.0	26.8	23.2	0.1	3.0	138.1
1975	95.3	23.5	18.3	0.1	5.9	143.1
1980	92.4	17.6	38.2	15.9	10.1	174.2
1985	103.2	15.3	38.9	18.7	11.2	187.3
1990	136.3	15.8	32.1	23.6	11.0	218.8
1992	126.5	15.3	30.1	25.0	11.2	208.3

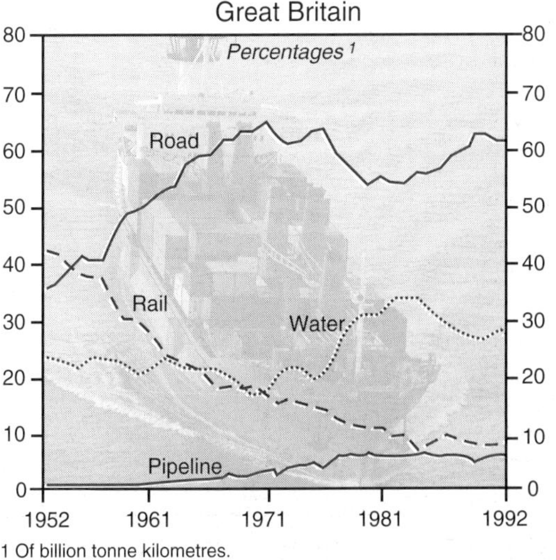

Source: adapted from *Department of Transport.*

Figure 7.6 *Commercial transport: by mode*

Land usage

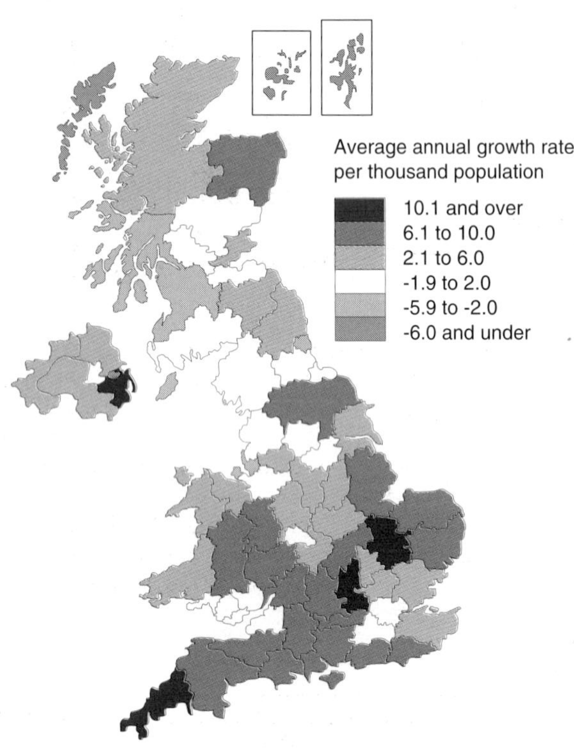

Source: adapted from OPCS; General Register Offices (Scotland and N. Ireland).

Figure 7.7 *Population change: by area, mid 1981-1991*

Table 7.3 *Changing population and number of households, Great Britain*[1]

Millions

	1961	1971	1981	1991
Population	51.4	54.4	54.8	56.2
Number of households	16.2	18.2	19.5	21.9

1. England, Wales and Scotland but not Northern Ireland.

Source: adapted from CSO, *Social Trends*, 1994.

Nimbyism

A 'Nimby' is someone who says 'not in my backyard'. The word came into fashion in the 1980s to describe people who were all in favour of economic growth and housing development in general, but were fiercely opposed to it in their own vicinity.

It has often been justified by high-sounding references to preserving rural England, maintaining local amenities and protecting areas of natural beauty. But in practice, Nimbys are often motivated by a desire to keep up the price of their properties by suppressing new building which could increase supply.

A study commissioned by the Department of the Environment gives some estimates of the cost of Nimbyism. It rejects the view that the planning system, which includes Greenbelt policies, puts a straitjacket on the amount of land for development. New land for building houses can be found by small scale easing of greenbelt and other restrictions, usually amounting to just a few tens of acres in a specific locality. Second, 'windfall sites' become available as large houses are knocked down and replaced by an estate of smaller houses or as homeowners sell part of their back garden for development. Third, there are 'brownfield sites' which consist of land already used for commercial or other urban purposes, but which becomes profitable to transfer to residential use as housing land prices rise.

Even so, planning restrictions have increased the price of housing land. The price of farming land, for instance, is often one-thirtieth or one-fortieth of what it is when housebuilding is allowed. Hence, there would be plenty of farmers willing to sell off their land for residential use. The study points out, however, that this is misleading because the cost of preparing farming land for housing or industrial purposes is high. Instead, they estimated the opportunity cost of housing land by looking at the price in Barnsley, where there is no shortage of housing land available for sale. The cost of planning restrictions could then be calculated. For instance, in Reigate, prime commuter country in Surrey in the South of England, land prices were 3.6 times their opportunity cost. Even in Beverley in Yorkshire, the ratio was 2.2.

Planning restrictions equally apply to land for industrial use. Greenbelt policies have pushed up factory, warehouse and office prices. Firms from furniture manufacturers to supermarket giants have often faced fierce local opposition to proposed developments when they have not been in designated industrial areas. At the same time, an easing on planning permission for industry could simply reduce availability of housing land, pushing up house prices further.

Overall, the planning system has had a significant effect on housing and industrial development in the UK. It has preserved rural areas, but it is not always clear that the cost is properly understood.

Source: adapted from the *Financial Times*, 7.7.1994.

1. Explain the following.
(a) The demand for land is a derived demand.
(b) Land is in composite demand.
(c) Land is in joint supply.
(d) Land is in joint demand with buildings.

2. Explain the economic relationships in the UK between between land use and
(a) a growing population,
(b) a shifting population geographically,
(c) increasing affluence.

3. Do you think greenbelt regulations should be loosened to allow more house building in the UK? In your answer, consider the costs and benefits of such a change in policy. This will include an analysis of the effects on the price of houses, industrial property and agricultural land.

Price elasticity of demand

Summary

1. Elasticity is a measure of the extent to which quantity responds to a change in a variable which affects it, such as price or income.
2. Price elasticity of demand measures the responsiveness of quantity demanded to a change in price.
3. Price elasticity of demand varies from zero, or infinitely inelastic, to infinitely elastic.
4. The value of price elasticity of demand is determined by the availability of substitutes and by time.

The meaning of demand elasticity

The quantity demanded of a good is affected by changes in the price of the good, changes in price of other goods, changes in income and changes in other relevant factors. Elasticity is a measure of just how much the quantity demanded will be affected by a change in price or income etc.

Assume that the price of gas increases by 1 per cent. If quantity demanded consequently falls by 20 per cent, then there is a very large drop in quantity demanded in comparison to the change in price. The price elasticity of gas would be said to be very high. If quantity demanded falls by 0.01 per cent, then the change in quantity demanded is relatively insignificant compared to the large change in price and the price elasticity of gas would be said to be low.

Different elasticities of demand measure the responsiveness of quantity demanded to changes in the variables which affect demand. So price elasticity of demand measures the responsiveness of quantity demanded to changes in the price of the good. Income elasticity measures the responsiveness of quantity demanded to changes in consumer incomes. Cross elasticity measures the responsiveness of quantity demanded to changes in the price of another good. Economists could also measure population elasticity, tastes elasticity or elasticity for any other variable which might affect quantity demanded, although these measures are rarely calculated.

Price elasticity of demand

Economists choose to measure responsiveness in terms of percentage changes. So PRICE ELASTICITY OF DEMAND - the responsiveness of changes in quantity demanded to changes in price - is calculated by using the formula:

$$\frac{\text{percentage change in quantity demanded}}{\text{percentage change in price}}$$

Table 8.1 shows a number of calculations of price elasticity. For instance, if an increase in price of 10 per cent leads to a fall in quantity demanded of 20 per cent, then the price elasticity of demand is 2. If an increase in price of 50 per cent leads to a fall in quantity demanded of 25 per cent then price elasticity of demand is ½.

Elasticity is sometimes difficult to understand at first. It is essential to memorise the formulae for elasticity. Only then can they be used with ease and an appreciation gained of their significance.

Table 8.1

Change in price (%)	Change in quantity demanded (%)	Elasticity
10	20	2
50	25	1/2
7	28	4
9	3	1/3

QUESTION 1

Table 8.2

	Percentage change in quantity demanded	Percentage change in price
(a)	10	5
(b)	60	20
(c)	4	8
(d)	1	9
(e)	5	7
(f)	8	11

Calculate the price elasticity of demand from the data in Table 8.2.

Alternative formulae

Data to calculate price elasticities are often not presented in the form of percentage changes. These have to be worked out. Calculating the percentage change is relatively easy. For instance, if a consumer has 10 apples and buys another 5, the percentage change in the total number of apples is of course 50 per cent. This answer is worked out by dividing the change in the number of apples she has (i.e. 5) by the original number of apples she possessed (i.e. 10) and multiplying by 100 to get a percentage figure. So the formula is:

$$\text{percentage change} = \frac{\text{absolute change}}{\text{original value}} \times 100\%$$

Price elasticity of demand is measured by dividing the percentage change in quantity demanded by the percentage change in price. Therefore an alternative way of expressing this is $\Delta Q/Q \times 100$ (the percentage change in quantity demanded Q) divided by $\Delta P/P \times 100$ (the percentage change in price P). The 100s cancel each other out, leaving a formula of:

$$\frac{\Delta Q}{Q} \div \frac{\Delta P}{P} \quad \textbf{or} \quad \frac{\Delta Q}{Q} \times \frac{P}{\Delta P}$$

This is mathematically equivalent to:

$$\frac{P}{Q} \times \frac{\Delta Q}{\Delta P}$$

Examples of calculations of elasticity using the above two formulae are given in Figure 8.1.

QUESTION 2

Table 8.3

	Original values		New values	
	Quantity demanded	Price (£)	Quantity demanded	Price (£)
(a)	100	5	120	3
(b)	20	8	25	7
(c)	12	3	16	0
(d)	150	12	200	10
(e)	45	6	45	8
(f)	32	24	40	2

Calculate the price elasticity of demand for the data in Table 8.3.

Elastic and inelastic demand

Different values of price elasticity of demand are given special names.

- Demand is price ELASTIC if the value of elasticity is greater than one. If demand for a good is price elastic then a percentage change in price will bring about an even larger percentage change in quantity demanded. For instance, if a 10 per cent rise in the price of tomatoes leads to a 20 per cent fall in the quantity demanded of tomatoes, then price elasticity is 20÷10 or 2 and therefore the demand for tomatoes is elastic. Demand is said to be **infinitely elastic** if the value of elasticity is infinity (i.e. a fall in price would lead to an infinite increase in quantity demanded whilst a rise in price would lead to the quantity demanded becoming zero).
- Demand is price INELASTIC if the value of elasticity is less than one. If demand for a good is price inelastic then a percentage change in price will bring about a smaller percentage change in quantity demanded. For instance, if a 10 per cent rise in the price of commuter fares on British Rail Southern Region resulted in a 1 per cent fall in rail journeys made, then price elasticity is 1÷10 or 0.1 and therefore the demand for BR commuter traffic is inelastic. Demand is said to be **infinitely inelastic** if the value of elasticity is zero (i.e. a change in price would have no effect on quantity demanded).
- Demand is of UNITARY ELASTICITY if the value of elasticity is exactly 1. This means that a percentage change in price will lead to an exact and opposite change in quantity demanded. For instance, a good would have unitary elasticity if a 10 per cent rise in price led to a 10 per cent fall in quantity demanded. (It will be shown in unit 9 that total revenue will remain constant at all quantities demanded if elasticity of demand is unity.)

This terminology is summarised in Table 8.4.

Example 1

Quantity demanded originally is 100 at a price of £2. There is a rise in price to £3 resulting in a fall in demand to 75.

Therefore the change in quantity demanded is 25 and the change in price is £1.

The price elasticity of demand is:

$$\frac{\Delta Q}{Q} \div \frac{\Delta P}{P} = \frac{25}{100} \div \frac{1}{2} = {}^1/_2$$

Example 2

Quantity demanded originally is 20 units at a price of £5 000. There is a fall in price to £4 000 resulting in a rise in demand to 32 units.

Therefore the change in quantity demanded is 12 units resulting from the change in price of £1 000.

The price elasticity of demand is:

$$\frac{P}{Q} \times \frac{\Delta Q}{\Delta P} = \frac{5000}{20} \times \frac{12}{1000} = 3$$

Figure 8.1 *Calculations of elasticity of demand*

QUESTION 3 Explain whether you think that the following goods would be elastic or inelastic in demand if their price increased by 10 per cent whilst all other factors remained constant: (a) petrol; (b) fresh tomatoes; (c) holidays offered by a major tour operator; (d) a Ford car; (e) a Mars Bar; (f) the music magazine, *Melody Maker*.

Table 8.4 *Elasticity: summary of key terms*

	Verbal description of response to a change in price	Numerical measure of elasticity	Change in total outlay as price rises[1]
Perfectly inelastic	Quantity demanded does not change at all as price changes	Zero	Increases
Inelastic	Quantity demanded changes by a smaller percentage than does price	Between 0 and 1	Increases
Unitary elasticity	Quantity demanded changes by exactly the same percentage as does price	1	Constant
Elastic	Quantity demanded changes by a larger percentage than does price	Between 1 and infinity	Decreases
Perfectly elastic	Buyers are prepared to purchase all they can obtain at some given price but none at all at a higher price	Infinity	Decreases to zero

1. This is explained in unit 9.

Graphical representations

Figure 8.2 shows a straight line graph. It is a common mistake to conclude that elasticity of a straight line demand curve is constant all along its length. In fact nearly all straight line demand curves vary in elasticity along the line.

- At the point A, price elasticity of demand is infinity. Here quantity demanded is zero. Putting Q = 0 into the formula for elasticity:

$$\frac{\Delta Q}{Q} \div \frac{\Delta P}{P}$$

we see that zero is divided into ΔQ. Mathematically there is an infinite number of zeros in any number.

- At the point C, price elasticity of demand is zero. Here price is zero. Putting P = 0 into the formula for elasticity, we see that P is divided into ΔP giving an answer of infinity. Infinity is then divided into the fraction ΔQ÷Q. Infinity is so large that the answer will approximate to zero.
- At the point B exactly half way along the line, price elasticity of demand is 1.

Worth noting is that the elasticity of demand at a point can be measured by dividing the distance from the point to the quantity axis by the distance from the point to the price axis, BC ÷ AB. In Figure 8.2, B is half way along the line AC and so BC = AB and the elasticity at the point B is 1.

Two straight line demand curves discussed earlier do not have the same elasticity all along their length.

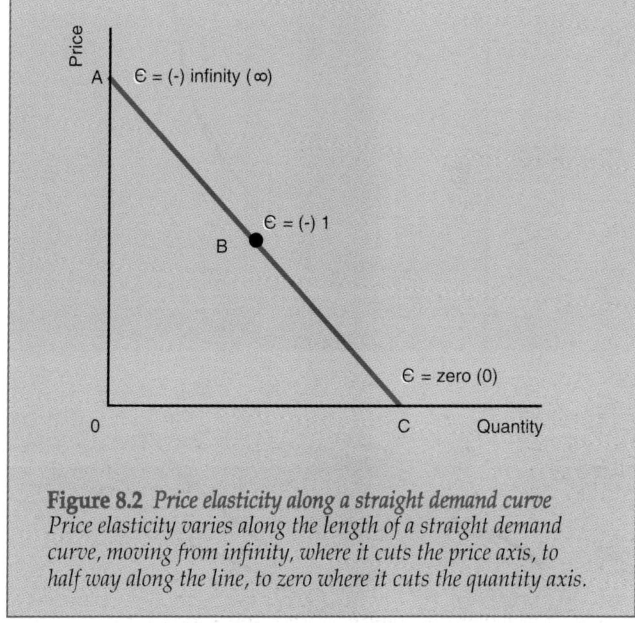

Figure 8.2 *Price elasticity along a straight demand curve*
Price elasticity varies along the length of a straight demand curve, moving from infinity, where it cuts the price axis, to half way along the line, to zero where it cuts the quantity axis.

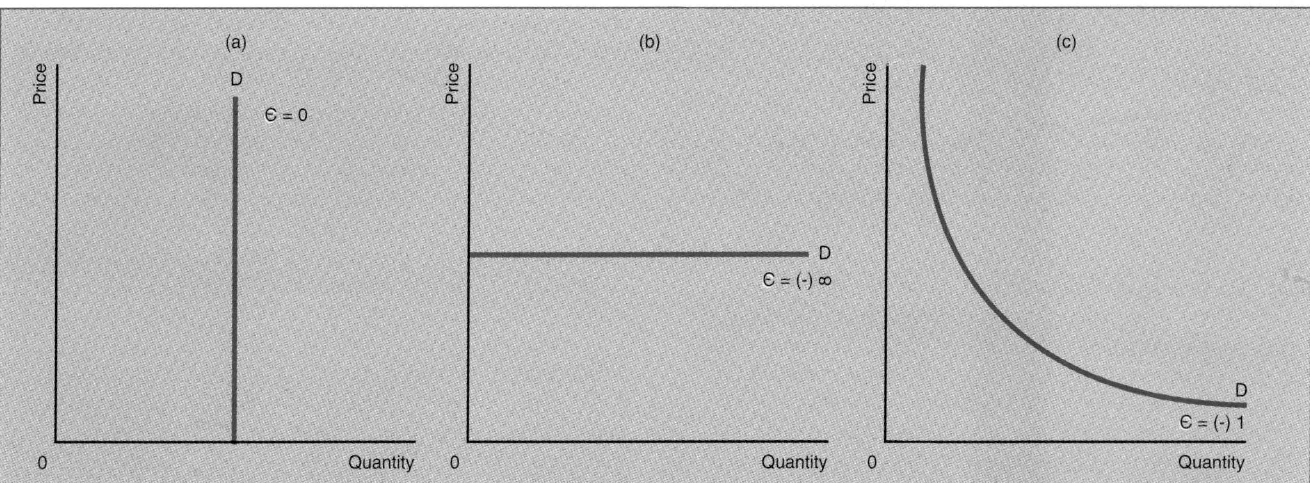

Figure 8.3 *Perfectly elastic and inelastic demand curves and unitary elasticity*
A vertical demand curve (a) is perfectly inelastic, whilst a horizontal demand curve (b) is perfectly elastic. A curve with unitary elasticity (c) is a rectangular hyperbola with the formula PQ = k where P is price, Q is quantity demanded and k is a constant value.

Figure 8.3(a) shows a demand curve which is perfectly inelastic. Whatever the price, the same quantity will be demanded.

Figure 8.3(b) shows a perfectly elastic demand curve. Any amount can be demanded at one price or below it whilst nothing will be demanded at a higher price.

Figure 8.3(c) shows a demand curve with unitary elasticity. Mathematically it is a rectangular hyperbola. This means that any percentage change in price is offset by an equal and opposite change in quantity demanded.

QUESTION 4

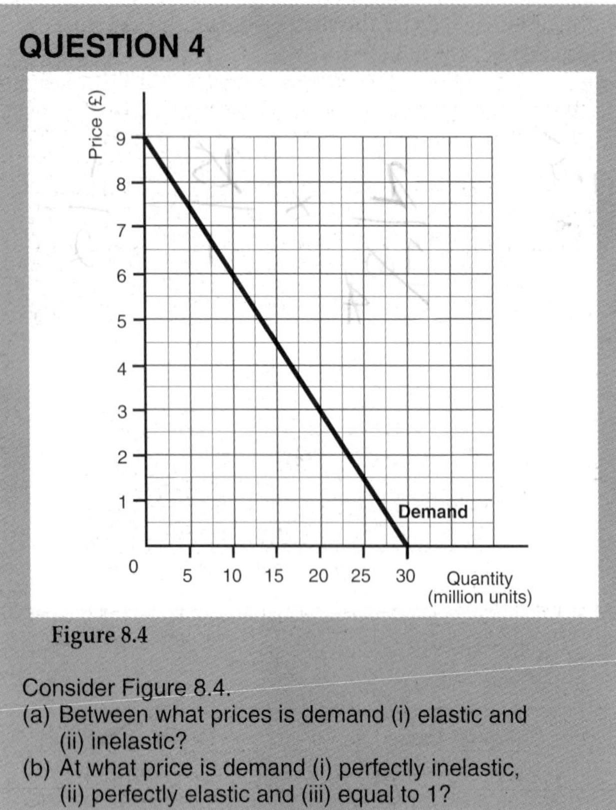

Figure 8.4

Consider Figure 8.4.
(a) Between what prices is demand (i) elastic and (ii) inelastic?
(b) At what price is demand (i) perfectly inelastic, (ii) perfectly elastic and (iii) equal to 1?

Two technical points

So far we have written of price elasticity of demand as always being a positive number. In fact any downward sloping demand curve always has a negative elasticity. This is because a rise in one variable (price or quantity) is always matched by a fall in the other variable. A rise is positive but a fall is negative and a positive number divided by a negative one (or vice versa) is always negative. However, economists find it convenient to omit the minus sign in price elasticity of demand because it is easier to deal in positive numbers whilst accepting that the value is really negative.

A second point relates to the fact that elasticities over the same price range can differ. For example, at a price of £2, demand for a good is 20 units. At a price of £3, demand is 18 units. Price elasticity of demand for a rise in price from £2 to £3 is:

$$\frac{P}{Q} \times \frac{\Delta Q}{\Delta P} = \frac{2}{20} \times \frac{2}{1} = \frac{1}{5}$$

But price elasticity of demand for a fall in price from £3 to £2 is:

$$\frac{P}{Q} \times \frac{\Delta Q}{\Delta P} = \frac{3}{18} \times \frac{2}{1} = \frac{1}{3}$$

The price elasticity for a rise in price is therefore less than for a fall in price over the same range. This is not necessarily a problem so long as one is aware of it. One way of resolving this is to average out price and quantity. In the formulae, P becomes not the original price but the average price (i.e. the original price plus the new price divided by 2) and Q becomes the average quantity demanded (i.e. the original quantity demanded plus the new quantity demanded divided by 2). In the above example, the average price is £(2+3)/2 or £2½ The average quantity demanded is (20+18)/2 or 19. Price elasticity of demand is then:

$$\frac{P}{Q} \times \frac{\Delta Q}{\Delta P} = \frac{2\frac{1}{2}}{19} \times \frac{2}{1} = \frac{5}{19}$$

As you would expect, this value is in between the two price elasticities of ⅕ and ⅓.

The determinants of price elasticity of demand

The exact value of price elasticity of demand for a good is determined by a wide variety of factors. Economists, however, argue that two factors in particular can be singled out: the availability of substitutes and time.

The availability of substitutes The better the substitutes for a product, the higher the price elasticity of demand will tend to be. For instance, salt has few good substitutes. When the price of salt increases, the demand for salt will change little and therefore the price elasticity of salt is low. On the other hand, spaghetti has many good substitutes, from other types of pasta, to rice, potatoes, bread, and other foods. A rise in the price of spaghetti, all other food prices remaining constant, is likely to have a significant effect on the demand for spaghetti. Hence the elasticity of demand for spaghetti is likely to be higher than that for salt.

The more widely the product is defined, the fewer substitutes it is likely to have. Spaghetti has many substitutes, but food in general has none. Therefore the elasticity of demand for spaghetti is likely to be higher than that for food. Similarly the elasticity of demand for boiled sweets is likely to be higher than for confectionery in general. A 5 per cent increase in the price of boiled sweets, all other prices remaining constant, is likely to lead to a much larger fall in demand for boiled sweets than a 5 per cent increase in the price of all confectionery.

Time The longer the period of time, the more price elastic is the demand for a product. For instance, in 1973/74 when the price of oil quadrupled the demand for oil was initially little affected. In the short term the demand for oil was price inelastic. This is hardly surprising. People still needed to travel to work in cars and heat their houses whilst industry still needed to operate. Oil had few good substitutes. Motorists couldn't put gas into their petrol tanks whilst businesses could not change oil-fired systems to run on gas, electricity or coal. However, in the longer term motorists were able to and did buy cars which were more fuel efficient. Oil-fired central heating systems were replaced by gas and electric systems. Businesses converted or did not replace oil-fired equipment. The demand for oil fell from what it would otherwise have been. In the longer run, the demand for oil proved to be price elastic. It is argued that in the short term, buyers are often locked into spending patterns through habit, lack of information or because of durable goods that have already been purchased. In the longer term, they have the time and opportunity to change those patterns.

It is sometimes argued that **necessities** have lower price elasticities than **luxuries.** Necessities by definition have to be bought whatever their price in order to stay alive. So an increase in the price of necessities will barely reduce the quantity demanded. Luxuries on the other hand are by definition goods which are not essential to existence. A rise in the price of luxuries should therefore produce a proportionately large fall in demand. There is no evidence, however, to suggest that this is true. Food, arguably a necessity, does not seem to have a lower elasticity than holidays or large cars, both arguably luxuries. Part of the reason for this is that it is very difficult to define necessities and luxuries empirically. Some food is a necessity but a significant proportion of what we eat is unnecessary for survival. It is not possible to distinguish between what food is consumed out of necessity and what is a luxury.

It is also sometimes argued that goods which form a relatively low proportion of total expenditure have lower elasticities than those which form a more significant proportion. A large car manufacturer, for instance, would continue to buy the same amount of paper clips even if the price of paper clips doubled because it is not worth its while to bother changing to an alternative. On the other hand, its demand for steel would be far more price elastic. There is no evidence to suggest that this is true. Examples given in textbooks, such as salt and matches, have low price elasticities because they have few good substitutes. In the case of paper clips, manufacturers would long ago have raised price substantially if they believed that price had little impact on the demand for their product.

QUESTION 5 Changes in the price of cigarettes do have an effect on smoking. In France, when the real price of cigarettes halved between 1964 and 1974, the number of cigarettes smoked doubled. In Canada, a doubling of prices between 1983 and 1993 led to a fall in consumption of one-third. The Tax Foundation of the United States estimated in 1993 that adding 75 cents to a packet of $1.75 would cut smoking by 13 per cent. Figure 8.5 shows the UK experience mirrors that found internationally.

Source: adapted from *The Guardian*, 28.10.1993.

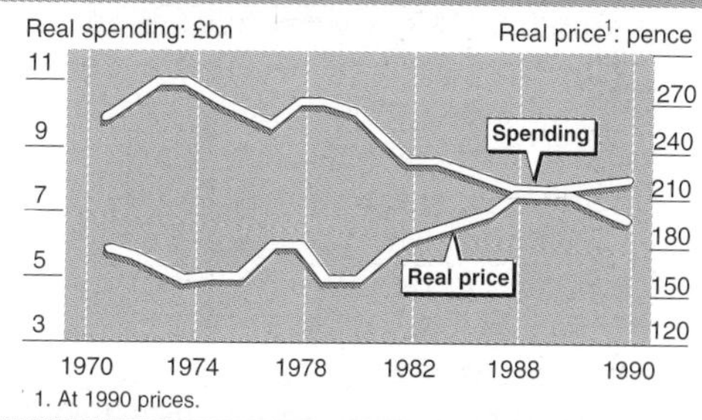

Source: adapted from Medical Research Council.

Figure 8.5 *The effect of price rises on smoking: the British Experience*

(a) Assuming all other things are equal, calculate the price elasticity of demand for cigarettes for:
(i) France between 1964 and 1974; (ii) Canada between 1983 and 1993; (iii) the United States in 1993.

(b) Estimate the price elasticity of demand for cigarettes in the UK between:
(i) 1978 and 1980; (ii) 1980 and 1988.

(c) Would you expect the demand for cigarettes to be price inelastic?

Key terms

Price elasticity of demand - the responsiveness of changes in quantity demanded to changes in price, measured by the formula:

$$\frac{P}{Q} \times \frac{\Delta Q}{\Delta P}$$

Elastic demand - where the price elasticity of demand is greater than 1. The responsiveness of demand is proportionally greater than the change in price. Demand is infinitely elastic if price elasticity of demand is infinity.

Inelastic demand - where the price elasticity of demand is less than 1. The responsiveness of demand is proportionally less than the change in price. Demand is infinitely inelastic if price elasticity of demand is zero.

Unitary elasticity - where the value of price elasticity of demand is 1. The responsiveness of demand is proportionally equal to the change in price.

Applied economics

The elasticity of demand for oil

Throughout the 1950s and 1960s oil was a cheap fuel. Indeed, the price of oil fell from approximately $1.70 a barrel in 1950 to $1.30 a barrel in 1970 as supply increased at a faster rate than demand. The early 1970s saw a reversal of this trend. Demand increased more rapidly than supply as the world economy boomed and policy makers became increasingly convinced that oil would remain a cheap and an efficient energy source. By 1973, the price of a barrel of oil had risen to approximately $3.

In November 1973, politics in the Middle East was to catapult the oil market into the world headlines. The Egyptians launched an attack on Israel on the day of Yom Kippur, the Jewish equivalent to Christmas. Other Middle Eastern states, such as Saudi Arabia, gave support to their Arab neighbours by threatening to cut off oil supplies to any country which gave support to Israel. With an existing tight market, the result was an explosion in the price of oil. The war was soon over but its economic fall-out was not lost on OPEC, the Organisation for Petroleum Exporting Countries. OPEC, whose members at the time supplied over 60 per cent of world demand for oil, organised a system of quotas amongst themselves, fixing limits on how much each member could produce. By slightly cutting back on pre-1973 production levels, they were able to increase the average price of oil to $10.41 a barrel in 1974, as shown in Figure 8.6.

The reason why OPEC could engineer this massive price rise was because the demand for oil was price inelastic in the short run. Oil consumers had invested heavily in capital equipment such as oil-fired heating systems and petrol-driven cars. In the short term, there were no cheap alternative substitutes. Car owners, for instance, did not suddenly change their cars for more fuel efficient models because the price of petrol at the pumps increased. Hence the near quadrupling of the price of oil (a 300 per cent increase) only led to a 5 per cent fall in world demand for oil (i.e. the price elasticity of demand for oil in the short term was 0.016).

In the longer term, consumers were able to replace oil-powered equipment. Cars became far more fuel-efficient. Homeowners insulated their houses. In the UK, the bottom dropped out of the market for oil-fired heating systems. As a consequence, when the demand for oil began to grow again in 1976, it was at a slower rate than in the early 1970s.

In 1978, the Shah of Iran was toppled and was replaced by an Islamic fundamentalist government led by the Ayatollah Khomeini. Iran was a major oil producer and the Islamic revolution and subsequent war between Iran and Iraq severely disrupted supplies from these two countries. OPEC used this opportunity to tighten supply again. With highly inelastic demand, the price rose from $13.03 a barrel in 1978 to $35.69 a barrel in 1980. Total world demand, which peaked in 1979 at approximately 63 million barrels per day, fell to a low of 58 million barrels per day in 1982 before resuming its growth.

In August 1990, political events in the Middle East yet again rocked the world price of oil. Iraq invaded Kuwait and oil sanctions were immediately applied to the output of both countries by oil consuming countries. Other oil producing countries quickly increased production to fill the gap but the fear of a major shortage had driven oil prices up from $18 a barrel to $40. Prices fell back as it became clear that overall supply had not fallen. The successful counter attack by US and other forces in 1991 to retake Kuwait saw the price drop back to below $20 a

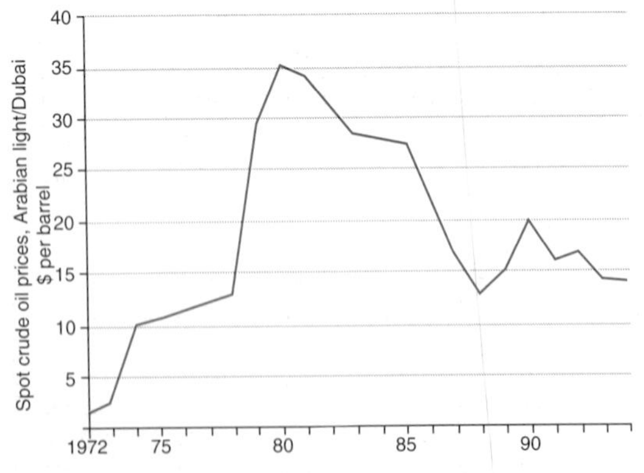

Source: adapted from *BP Statistical Review of World Energy*.

Figure 8.6 Oil prices

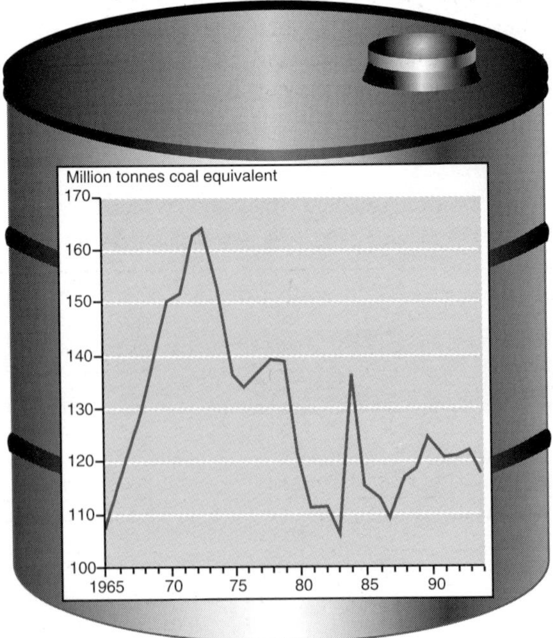

1. Demand for oil in the UK was artificially increased in 1984 and 1985 by the miners' strike when oil was burnt instead of coal in power stations.

Source: adapted from Department of Trade and Industry.

Figure 8.7 *Oil consumption, UK*

barrel, since when there has been a steady drift downward in the price. It is difficult to calculate the long term elasticity of demand for oil because there are so many other variables affecting the demand for oil, many of which change over time.

Figure 8.7 shows what has happened to the UK demand for oil since 1965. The longer term rises and falls in demand follow the sharp changes in the price of oil in the 1970s and 1980s.

The impact of rising incomes on demand can be excluded by calculating the amount of oil used per £1 000 of income of the UK. This rose from 0.39 tonnes of coal equivalent in 1965 to 0.5 tonnes in 1972, reflecting the fall in the price of oil over the period. Demand then fell sharply and by 1987 was just 0.25 tonnes, a fall of 50 per cent in response to an approximate 900 per cent rise in price. Since 1987, demand has risen slightly in response to an approximate 15 per cent cut in prices to 1994. The evidence would suggest that, whilst demand is extremely inelastic over a 12 month period, in the longer term, over a 5-10 year period, price elasticity is higher, although still inelastic.

Newspaper wars

1. **Analyse what happened to circulation and prices between August 1993 and April 1995. In your analysis calculate and discuss the significance of the price elasticity of demand for:**
   (a) *The Times* between; (i) August 1993 and December 1993; (ii) August 1993 and May 1994; (iii) June 1994 and September 1994; (iv) June 1994 and April 1995;
   (b) the *Daily Telegraph* between May 1994 and April 1995.
2. **Discuss whether, on the basis of the evidence to April 1995, *The Times* is likely to reach a circulation figure of 800 000-900 000.**
3. **Evaluate whether or not it would be in the interests of all quality newspapers if each cut its price to match the cover price of *The Times*.**

Price war in Fleet Street

Newspapers have traditionally competed on the quality of their product and their editorial line. However, in 1993, the Murdoch group which included both *The Sun*, a tabloid paper, and *The Times*, a quality newspaper, decided to launch a price war to increase circulation. In July 1993, the cover price of *The Sun* was cut from 25p to 20p and in September 1993 *The Times* was cut in price from 45p to 30p. The result was a rise in demand for *The Sun* and *The Times*. The management at the *Daily Telegraph* eventually decided that they could not continue to see their circulation eroded. On 23 June 1994, they dropped their cover price from 48p to 30p. *The Times* responded immediately, dropping its cover price from 30p to 20p on 24 June. *The Independent* felt forced to follow, cutting its price from 50p to 30p on 1 August 1994.

Cutting the cover price obviously had implications for profits at *The Times*. On the one hand, considerably more copies had to be sold to make up for the revenue lost from the one-third drop in price. Also, printing and distributing extra copies of *The Times* cost money. On the other hand, advertising revenues should go up as *The Times* could charge more for advertising in a larger circulation paper. More advertisers would also be attracted to the newspaper. Also, if circulation increased sufficiently, revenues from the cover price of the newspaper would actually increase, higher sales more than offsetting lower prices.

Table 8.5 *Circulation figures of the quality press (Average daily net sales)*

	JULY 93	AUG 93	SEPT 93	OCT 93	NOV 93	DEC 93	JAN 94	FEB 94	MAR 94	APR 94	MAY 94
Daily Telegraph	1,017,483	1,027,656	1,007,687	1,011,172	1,032,389	1,008,480	1,032,944	1,014,833	1,000,671	998,621	993,395
Financial Times	288,339	275,316	287,493	287,881	294,083	293,872	283,640	300,305	304,096	298,971	300,135
The Guardian	402,517	391,526	403,937	403,124	401,609	389,327	406,463	405,129	403,061	397,172	401,831
The Independent	336,925	325,856	332,435	328,562	313,504	301,987	291,072	292,397	276,837	271,372	276,660
The Times	359,822	354,280	442,106	444,503	445,343	439,327	455,628	468,174	470,742	478,419	517,575
TOTAL AVERAGE DAILY NET SALES	2,405,086	2,374,634	2,473,658	2,475,242	2,486,928	2,432,993	2,469,747	2,480,338	2,455,407	2,444,855	2,489,596

	JUN 94	JUL 94	AUG 94	SEP 94	OCT 94	NOV 94	DEC 94	JAN 95	FEB 95	MAR 95	APR 95
Daily Telegraph	1,006,961	1,070,908	1,091,658	1,091,622	1,078,945	1,071,172	1,052,963	1,069,818	1,057,777	1,061,230	1,064,229
Financial Times	296,894	282,659	272,151	290,284	286,944	293,182	297,395	279,253	291,204	305,928	290,954
The Guardian	404,225	394,862	378,987	410,786	406,390	403,773	396,491	410,836	403,405	400,921	397,139
The Independent	277,377	257,812	289,403	290,031	290,481	290,129	275,980	290,804	290,118	290,360	291,369
The Times	524,270	599,358	597,636	607,143	614,477	606,147	598,611	631,449	630,690	631,638	630,277
TOTAL AVERAGE DAILY NET SALES	2,509,727	2,605,599	2,629,835	2,689,866	2,677,237	2,644,403	2,621,440	2,682,160	2,673,194	2,690,077	2,673,968

Source: adapted from Brad Newspapers; ABC.

unit 9 Elasticities

Summary

1. Income elasticity of demand measures the responsiveness of quantity demanded to changes in income.
2. Cross elasticity of demand measures the responsiveness of quantity demanded of one good to the change in price of another good.
3. Price elasticity of supply measures the responsiveness of quantity supplied to changes in price.
4. The value of elasticity of supply is determined by the availability of substitutes and by time factors.
5. The price elasticity of demand for a good will determine whether a change in the price of a good results in a change in expenditure on the good.

Income elasticity of demand

The demand for a good will change if consumers' incomes change. INCOME ELASTICITY OF DEMAND is a measure of that change. If the demand for housing increased by 20 per cent when incomes increased by 5 per cent, then the income elasticity of demand would be said to be positive and relatively high. If the demand for food were unchanged when income rose, then income elasticity would be zero. A fall in demand for a good when income rises gives a negative value to income elasticity of demand.

The formula for measuring income elasticity of demand is:

$$\frac{\text{percentage change in quantity demanded}}{\text{percentage change in income}}$$

So the numerical value of income elasticity of a 20 per cent rise in demand for housing when incomes rise by 5 per cent is +20/+5 or +4. The number is positive because both the 20 per cent and the 5 per cent are positive. On the other hand, a rise in income of 10 per cent which led to a fall in quantity demanded of a product of 5 per cent would have an income elasticity of -5/+10 or -½. The minus sign in -5 shows the fall in quantity demanded of the product. Examples of items with a high income elasticity of demand are holidays and recreational activities, whereas washing up liquid tends to have a low income elasticity of demand.

Just as with price elasticity, it is sometimes easier to use alternative formulae to calculate income elasticity of demand. The above formula is equivalent to:

$$\frac{\Delta Q}{Q} \div \frac{\Delta Y}{Y}$$

where Δ is change, Q is quantity demanded and Y is income. Rearranging the formula gives another two alternatives:

$$\frac{Y}{Q} \times \frac{\Delta Q}{\Delta Y} \quad \text{or} \quad \frac{\Delta Q}{Q} \times \frac{Y}{\Delta Y}$$

Examples of the calculation of income elasticity of demand are given in Table 9.1.

Table 9.1 *Calculation of income elasticity of demand*

Original quantity demanded	New quantity demanded	Original income (£)	New income (£)	Income elasticity of demand: $\frac{\Delta Q}{Q} \div \frac{\Delta Y}{Y}$	Income elasticity of demand: Numerical value
20	25	16	18	5/20 ÷ 2/16	+2
100	200	20	25	100/100 ÷ 5/20	+4
50	40	25	30	-10/50 ÷ 5/25	-1
60	60	80	75	0/60 ÷ -5/80	0
60	40	27	30	-20/60 ÷ 3/27	-3

QUESTION 1

Table 9.2

£

	Original: Quantity demanded	Original: Income	New: Quantity demanded	New: Income
(a)	100	10	120	14
(b)	15	6	20	7
(c)	50	25	40	35
(d)	12	100	15	125
(e)	200	10	250	11
(f)	25	20	30	18

Calculate the income elasticity of demand from the data in Table 9.2.

Cross elasticity of demand

The quantity demanded of a particular good varies according to the price of other goods. In unit 7 it was argued that a rise in price of a good such as beef would increase the quantity demanded of a substitute such as pork. On the other hand, a rise in price of a good such as cheese would lead to a fall in the quantity demanded of a complement such as macaroni. CROSS ELASTICITY OF DEMAND measures the responsiveness of the quantity demanded of one good to changes in the price of another. For instance, it is a measure of the extent to which demand for pork increases when the price of beef goes up; or the extent to which the demand for macaroni falls when the price of cheese increases.

The formula for measuring cross elasticity of demand for good X is:

$$\frac{\text{percentage change in quantity demanded of good X}}{\text{percentage change in price of another good Y}}$$

Two goods which are substitutes will have a positive cross elasticity. An increase (positive) in the price of one good, such as gas, leads to an increase (positive) in the quantity demanded of a substitute such as electricity. Two goods which are complements will have a negative cross elasticity. An increase (positive) in the price of one good such as sand leads to a fall (negative) in demand of a complement such as cement. The cross elasticity of two goods which have little relationship to each other would be zero. For instance, a rise in the price of cars of 10 per cent is likely to have no effect (i.e. 0 per cent change) on the demand for Tipp-Ex.

As with price and income elasticity, it is sometimes more convenient to use alternative formulae for cross elasticity of demand. These are:

$$\text{Cross elasticity of good X} = \frac{\Delta Q_X}{Q_X} \div \frac{\Delta P_Y}{P_Y}$$

or

$$\frac{P_Y}{Q_X} \times \frac{\Delta Q_X}{\Delta P_Y}$$

QUESTION 2 Explain what value you would put on the cross elasticity of demand of: (a) gas for electricity; (b) tennis shorts for tennis rackets; (c) luxury cars for petrol; (d) paper for tights; (e) compact discs for audio cassettes; (f) Sainsbury's own brand baked beans for Tesco's own brand baked beans; (g) Virgin Cola for Coca Cola.

Price elasticity of supply

Price elasticity of demand measures the responsiveness of changes in quantity demanded to changes in price. Equally, the responsiveness of quantity supplied to changes in price can also be measured - this is called PRICE ELASTICITY OF SUPPLY. The formula for measuring the price elasticity of supply is:

$$\frac{\text{percentage change in quantity supplied}}{\text{percentage change in price}}$$

This is equivalent to:

$$\frac{\Delta Q}{Q} \div \frac{\Delta P}{P}$$

or

$$\frac{P}{Q} \times \frac{\Delta Q}{\Delta P}$$

where Q is quantity supplied and P is price.

The supply curve is upward sloping (i.e. an increase in price leads to an increase in quantity supplied and vice versa). Therefore price elasticity of supply will be positive because the top and bottom of the formula will be either both positive or both negative.

As with price elasticity of demand, different ranges of elasticity are given different names. Price elasticity of supply is:

- **perfectly inelastic** (zero) if there is no response in supply to a change in price;
- **inelastic** (between zero and one) if there is a less than proportionate response in supply to a change in price;
- **unitary** (one) if the percentage change in quantity supplied equals the percentage change in price;
- **elastic** (between one and infinity) if there is a more than proportionate response in supply to a change in price;
- **perfectly elastic** (infinite) if producers are prepared to supply any amount at a given price.

These various elasticities are shown in Figure 9.1.

It should be noted that any straight line supply curve passing through the origin has an elasticity of supply equal to 1. This is best understood if we take the formula:

$$\frac{P}{Q} \times \frac{\Delta Q}{\Delta P}$$

$\Delta Q/\Delta P$ is the inverse of (i.e. 1 divided by) the slope of the line, whilst P/Q, assuming that the line passes through the origin, is the slope of the line. The two multiplied together must always equal 1.

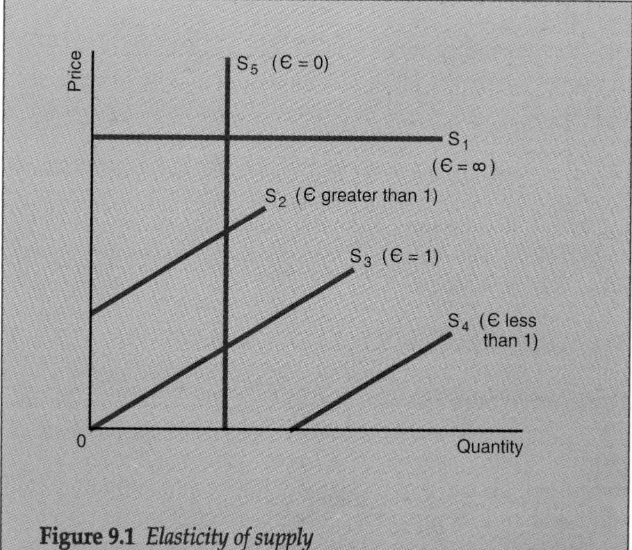

Figure 9.1 *Elasticity of supply*
The elasticity of supply of a straight line supply curve varies depending upon the gradient of the line and whether it passes through the origin.

QUESTION 3

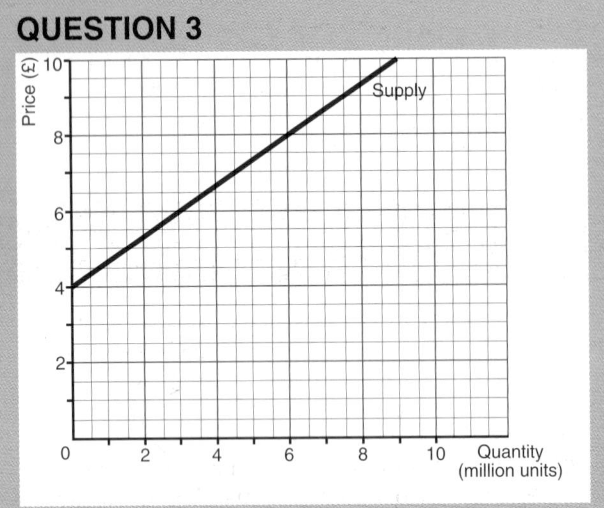

Figure 9.2
Calculate from Figure 9.2 the elasticity of supply of a change in price from: (a) £4 to £6; (b) £6 to £8; (c) £8 to £10; (d) £9 to £7; (e) £7 to £5.

Determinants of elasticity of supply

As with price elasticity of demand, there are two factors which determine supply elasticity across a wide range of products.

Availability of substitutes Substitutes here are not consumer substitutes but producer substitutes. These are goods which a producer can easily produce as alternatives. For instance, one model of a car is a good producer substitute for another model in the same range because the car manufacturer can easily switch resources on its production line. On the other hand, carrots are not substitutes for cars. The farmer cannot easily switch from the production of carrots to the production of cars. If a product has many substitutes then producers can quickly and easily alter the pattern of production if its price rises or falls. Hence its elasticity will be relatively high. But if a product has few or no substitutes, then producers will find it difficult to respond flexibly to variations in price. If there is a fall in price, a producer may have no alternative but either to carry on producing much the same quantity as before or withdrawing from the market. Price elasticity of supply is therefore low.

Time The shorter the time period, the more difficult firms find it to switch from making one product to another. During the late 1970s when skateboarding first became a craze, the supply of skateboards was relatively inelastic. Suppliers were overwhelmed with orders and were initially unable to expand production sufficiently to cope with demand. Supply elasticity was therefore low. In the longer term new firms came into the market, existing firms expanded their production facilities and price elasticity of supply rose. This has also been the case with videos, personal stereos and CD players.

QUESTION 4

Table 9.3 *Estimates of price elasticities of demand for selected household foods, 1984-89*

	Estimated price elasticity
Milk and cream	-0.19
of which:	
liquid wholemilk and low fat milks, full price	-0.29
Cheese	-1.20
Carcase meat	-1.37
Other meat and meat products	-0.49
of which:	
bacon and ham, uncooked	-0.70
broiler chicken, uncooked	-0.13
other poultry, uncooked	-0.85
frozen convenience meat and meat products	-0.94
Sugar and preserves	-0.24
Fresh potatoes	-0.21
Fresh green vegetables	-0.58
Other fresh vegetables	-0.27
Processed vegetables	-0.54
of which:	
Frozen peas	-1.12
Frozen chips and other frozen convenience potato products	-0.29
Processed fruit and fruit products	-1.05
of which:	
fruit juices	-0.80
Bread	-0.09
Other cereals and cereal products	-0.94
of which:	
cakes and pastries	-0.37
frozen convenience cereal foods	-0.07

Source: adapted from HMSO, *Household Food Consumption and Expenditure.*

(a) Suggest reasons why the demand for some foods in Table 9.3 is more price elastic than the demand for others.
(b) An increase in the price of which foods would be most likely to lead to
  (i) the greatest and
  (ii) the least change in household expenditure?
Explain your answer.

Price elasticity of demand and total expenditure

Price elasticity of demand and changes in total expenditure on a product are linked. Total expenditure can be calculated by multiplying price and quantity:

Total expenditure = quantity purchased x price

For instance, if you bought 5 apples at 10 pence each, your total expenditure would be 50 pence. If the price of apples went up, you might spend more, less, or the same on apples depending upon your price elasticity of demand for apples. Assume that the price of apples went up 40 per cent to 14p each. You might react by buying fewer apples. If you now buy 4 apples (i.e. a fall in demand of 20 per cent), the price elasticity of demand is 20 ÷ 40 or ½. Your expenditure on apples will also rise (from 50 pence to 56 pence). If you buy two apples (i.e. a fall in quantity demanded of 60 per cent), your elasticity of demand is 60 ÷ 40 or 1½ and your expenditure on apples will fall (from 50 pence to 28 pence).

These relationships are what should be expected. If the percentage change in price is larger than the percentage change in quantity demanded (i.e. elasticity is less than 1, or inelastic), then expenditure will rise when prices rise. If the percentage change in price is smaller than the percentage change in quantity demanded (i.e. elasticity is greater than 1 or elastic), then spending will fall as prices rise. If the percentage change in price is the same as the change in quantity demanded (i.e. elasticity is unity), expenditure will remain unchanged because the percentage rise in price will be equal and opposite to the percentage fall in demand.

Key terms

Income elasticity of demand - a measure of the responsiveness of quantity demanded to a change in income. It is measured by dividing the percentage change in quantity demanded by the percentage change in income.
Cross elasticity of demand - a measure of the responsiveness of quantity demanded of one good to a change in price of another good. It is measured by dividing the percentage change in quantity demanded of one good by the percentage change in price of the other good.
Price elasticity of supply - a measure of the responsiveness of quantity supplied to a change in price. It is measured by dividing the percentage change in quantity supplied by the percentage change in price.

Applied economics

Cross elasticities of demand for food

Many foods are substitutes for each other. Tea is a substitute for coffee; oranges are substitutes for apples; butter is a substitute for margarine. Economic theory would suggest that these goods would therefore have a positive cross elasticity of demand. An increase in the price of one good would lead to an increase in demand of the substitute good, whilst a fall in price of one good would lead to a fall in demand of another.

Evidence from the General Household Survey gives some support for this. Table 9.4 shows estimates of the cross elasticity of demand for 10 foods, grouped into four categories. The estimates are based on UK data for 1981-88. The cross elasticities are shown in black.

The cross elasticities of demand of butter for margarine and margarine for butter are 0.06 and 0.08 respectively. So a 10 per cent increase in the price of margarine will lead to a 0.6 per cent increase in the demand for butter, whilst a 10 per cent increase in the price of butter will lead to a 0.8 per cent increase in the demand for margarine.

Of the three fruits in Table 9.4, apples and pears have a relatively high cross elasticity. Pears seem to be a good substitute for apples. A 10 per cent increase in the price of apples leads to a 2.8 per cent rise in the quantity demanded of pears. Interestingly though, apples are less good a substitute for pears since a 10 per cent increase in the price of pears results in only a 0.5 per cent increase in the demand for apples. The data would suggest that apples and oranges are not substitutes at all since their cross elasticities are negative at - 0.22 and - 0.09. Similarly pears and oranges have negative cross elasticities.

One explanation of the negative cross elasticities in Table 9.4 would be in terms of income and substitution effects. For instance, a rise in the price of coffee will lead to more tea being demanded because tea is now relatively cheaper (the substitution effect of the price rise). However, the real income of consumers (what they can buy with their money income) will have declined. Hence they buy less coffee (a drop of 1.4 per cent for every 10 per cent rise in price) but also less tea (the income effect). The data would suggest that this income effect is more significant than the substitution effect in the case of tea when the price of coffee increases.

Table 9.4 also shows (in red) the price elasticities of demand for the 10 food products. The demand for butter, margarine, tea, instant coffee and apples is price inelastic, whilst the demand for beef and veal, mutton and lamb, pork, oranges and pears is price elastic.

Table 9.4 *Estimates of price and cross-price elasticities of demand for certain foods, 1981-1988*

	Elasticity with respect to the price of	
	Tea	Instant coffee
Tea	-0.33	-0.01
Instant coffee	-0.01	-0.14

	Elasticity with respect to the price of		
	Beef and veal	Mutton and lamb	Pork
Beef and veal	-1.23	0.04	0.02
Mutton and lamb	0.10	-1.75	-0.11
Pork	0.05	-0.11	-1.57

	Elasticity with respect to the price of	
	Butter	Margarine
Butter	-0.38	0.06
Margarine	0.08	-0.29

	Elasticity with respect to the price of		
	Oranges	Apples	Pears
Oranges	-1.44	-0.22	-0.11
Apples	-0.09	-0.19	0.05
Pears	-0.28	0.28	-1.70

Source: adapted from HMSO, *Household Food Consumption and Expenditure.*

Euro Disney

Prepare a report for a bank which has given a loan to Euro Disney.

1. **Write an introduction, outlining the problems that Euro Disney faced in November 1994.**
2. **Analyse whether or not the December 1994 price cut will help Euro Disney. In this section (a) calculate and use the range of price elasticities of demand quoted by the company and (b) explain the significance of these for revenues from (i) admissions, (ii) sales of merchandise and (iii) overall revenues from both admissions and sales.**
3. **Discuss whether Euro Disney's problems are just short term problems. In this section (a) consider the possible value of income elasticity of demand for Euro Disney and (b) evaluate the threat posed by other theme parks and suggest a value for the cross elasticity of demand for Euro Disney if other theme parks cut their prices.**
4. **In a conclusion, evaluate whether Euro Disney could increase admission levels to the 13 or 14 million per year it needs to secure its long term future at current prices.**

When Euro Disney opened near Paris in 1992, there was a confident expectation that the theme park would be an instant success. The US Disney theme parks, such as the one in Florida which is so popular with tourists from Europe, were highly profitable. Bringing the US formula to a location which was more convenient for Europeans to visit should attract the millions needed to make Euro Disney profitable too.

Euro Disney did attract millions of visitors. In the year to September 1994, there were 8.8 million attendances. Unfortunately, this wasn't enough to generate sufficient revenues from admission and other associated receipts such as meals and merchandise sales, to cover costs. A large financial restructuring in early 1994 saved the company from bankruptcy. However, Euro Disney desperately needed to increase attendances if it was to have a long term future.

In December 1994, it announced that it was cutting admission prices by about 20 per cent. The company estimated that it could expect a 1 to 2 per cent increase in visitors for every one per cent cut in the price of entry. It would need to attract an extra 700 000 visitors a year to generate enough profit from extra admissions and other sales to compensate for lower priced tickets.

Euro Disney has been far more ambitious than most of its rivals. Its financial problems stem partly from the very high cost of building the theme park. Less costly theme parks, offering perhaps fewer facilities but also lower prices, have prospered. The Asterix theme park, also just north of Paris, has made profits on lower entry numbers and lower admission prices. Other operators are being attracted into the business. 1995 saw the opening of Port Aventura near Barcelona which expects to pull in at least 2.5 million visitors a year from all over Europe. Warner Brothers is building a film-studio theme park near Dusseldorf with an even greater capacity. There is no doubt that theme parks are increasingly popular with more and more Europeans enjoying an income large enough to visit one in a foreign country. But it could be that Euro Disney was just too ambitious in wanting to take such a large share of the European market for a single site.

Source: adapted from the *Financial Times*, 15.12.1994; *The Sunday Times*, 18.12.1994.

Normal, inferior and Giffen goods

Summary

1. An increase in income will lead to an increase in demand for normal goods but a fall in demand for inferior goods.
2. Normal goods have a positive income elasticity whilst inferior goods have a negative elasticity.
3. A Giffen good is one where a rise in price leads to a rise in quantity demanded. This occurs because the positive substitution effect of the price change is outweighed by the negative income effect.
4. Upward sloping demand curves may occur if the good is a Giffen good, if it has snob or speculative appeal or if consumers judge quality by the price of a product.

Normal and inferior goods

The pattern of demand is likely to change when income changes. It would be reasonable to assume that consumers will increase their demand for most goods when their income increases. Goods for which this is the case are called NORMAL GOODS.

However, an increase in income will result in a fall in demand for other goods. These goods are called INFERIOR GOODS. There will be a fall in demand because consumers will react to an increase in their income by purchasing products which are perceived to be of better quality. Commonly quoted examples of inferior goods are:

- bread - consumers switch from this cheap, filling food to more expensive meat or convenience foods as their incomes increase;
- margarine - consumers switch from margarine to butter, although this has become less true recently with greater health awareness;
- bus transport - consumers switch from buses to their own cars when they can afford to buy their own car.

A good can be both a normal and an inferior good depending upon the level of income. Bread may be a normal good for people on low incomes (i.e. they buy more bread when their income increases). But it may be an inferior good for higher income earners.

Normal and inferior goods are shown on Figure 10.1. D_1 is the demand curve for a normal good. It is upward sloping because demand increases as income increases. D_2 is the demand curve for an inferior good. It is downward sloping, showing that demand falls as income increases. D_3 is the demand curve for a good which is normal at low levels of income, but is inferior at higher levels of income.

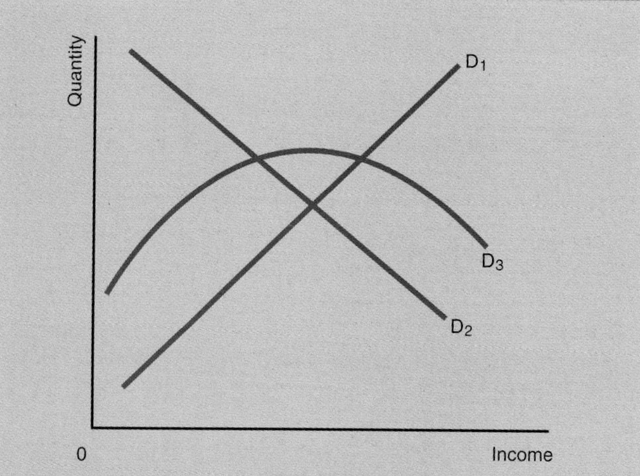

Figure 10.1 *Normal and inferior goods*
On the quantity-income diagram, a normal good such as D_1, has an upward sloping curve, whilst an inferior good such as D_2 has a downward sloping curve. D_3 shows a good which is normal at low levels of income but is inferior at higher levels of income.

QUESTION 1

Table 10.1 *Estimated household food consumption in Great Britain*

	Ounces per person per week			
	1976	1981	1986	1993
Liquid milk	5.05	4.43	4.12	3.80
Sugar	12.2	11.08	8.04	5.33
Chicken	6.00	7.3	7.3	8.42
Canned beans	3.99	4.12	4.79	3.95
Bread	33.17	31.23	30.79	26.70
Pickles and sauces	1.66	2.01	2.18	2.70

Source: CSO, *Annual Abstract of Statistics.*

Household incomes rose between each of the years 1976, 1981, 1986 and 1993. Assuming that all other factors remained constant, which of the goods shown in Table 10.1 are normal goods and which are inferior?

Inferior goods and income elasticity

Inferior goods can be distinguished from normal goods by their income elasticity of demand. The formula for measuring income elasticity is:

$$\frac{\text{percentage change in quantity demanded}}{\text{percentage change in income}}$$

A normal good will always have a positive income elasticity because quantity demanded and income either both increase (giving a plus divided by a plus) or both decrease (giving a minus divided by a minus). An inferior good, however, will always have a negative elasticity because the signs on the top and bottom of the formula will always be opposite (a plus divided by a minus or a minus divided by a plus giving a minus answer in both cases).

For instance, if the demand for bread falls by 2 per cent when incomes rise by 10 per cent then it is an inferior good. Its income elasticity is -2/+10 or -0.2.

Giffen goods

A GIFFEN GOOD is a special sort of inferior good. Alfred Marshall (1842-1924), an eminent economist and author of a best selling textbook of his day, claimed that another eminent economist, Sir Robert Giffen (1837-1910), had observed that the consumption of bread increased as its price increased. The argument was that bread was a staple food for low income consumers. A rise in its price would not deter people from buying as much as before. But 'poor' people would now have so little extra money to spend on meat or other luxury foods that they would abandon their demand for these and instead buy more bread to fill up their stomachs. The result was that a rise in the price of bread led to a rise in the demand for bread.

Another way of explaining this phenomenon is to use the concepts of income and substitution effects (☞ unit 15 for a more detailed discussion). When a good changes in price, the quantity demanded will be changed by the sum of the substitution effect and the income effect.

- **Substitution effect.** If the price of a good rises, consumers will buy less of that good and more of others because it is now relatively more expensive than other goods. If the price of a good falls, consumers will buy more of that good and less of others. These changes in quantity demanded are known as the substitution effect of a price change.
- **Income effect.** If the price of a good rises, the real income of consumers will fall. They will not be able to buy the same basket of goods and services as before. Consumers can react to this fall in real income in one of two ways. If the good is a normal good, they will buy less of the good. If the good is an inferior good, they will buy more of the good. These changes in quantity demanded caused by a change in real income are known as the income effect of the price change.

For a normal good the substitution effect and the income effect both work in the same direction. A rise in price leads to a fall in quantity demanded because the relative price of the good has risen. It also leads to a fall in quantity demanded because consumers' real incomes have now fallen. So a rise in price will always lead to a fall in quantity demanded, and vice versa.

For an inferior good, the substitution effect and income effect work in opposite directions. A rise in price leads to a fall in quantity demanded because the relative price of the good has risen. But it leads to a rise in quantity demanded because consumers' real incomes have fallen. However, the substitution effect outweighs the income effect because overall it is still true for an inferior good that a rise in price leads to an overall fall in quantity demanded.

A Giffen good is a special type of inferior good. A rise in price leads to a fall in quantity demanded because of the substitution effect but a rise in quantity demanded because of the income effect. However, the income effect outweighs the substitution effect, leading to rises in quantity demanded. For instance, if a 10p rise in the price of a standard loaf leads to a 4 per cent fall in the demand for bread because of the substitution effect, but a 10 per cent rise in demand because of the income effect, then the net effect will be a 6 per cent rise in the demand for bread.

The relationship between normal, inferior and Giffen goods and their income and substitution effects is summarised in Figure 10.2.

Giffen goods are an economic curiosity. In theory they could exist, but no economist has ever found an example of such a good in practice. There is no evidence even that Sir Robert Giffen ever claimed that bread had an upward sloping demand curve - it crept into textbooks via Alfred Marshall and has remained there ever since!

Type of good	Effect on quantity demanded of a rise in price		
	Substitution effect	Income effect	Total effect
Normal good	Fall	Fall	Fall
Inferior good	Fall	Rise	Fall because substitution effect > income effect
Giffen good	Fall	Rise	Rise because substitution effect < income effect

Figure 10.2 *Substitution and income effects on quantity demanded of a rise in price for normal, inferior and Giffen goods*

QUESTION 2

Table 10.2

Good	Change in price (pence per unit)	Change in quantity demanded as a result of	
		income effect	substitution effect
Bacon	+10	+5%	-8%
Bus rides	+15	+7%	-5%
Jeans	-100	+1%	+5%
Baked beans	-2	-1%	+4%
Compact discs	-150	+4%	+3%

An economist claims that she has observed the effects detailed in Table 10.2 resulting solely from a change in price of a product. Which of these products are normal goods, which are inferior and which are Giffen goods?

Upward sloping demand curves

Demand curves are usually downward sloping. However, there are possible reasons why the demand curve for some goods may be upward sloping.

Giffen goods Giffen goods, a type of inferior good, have been discussed above.

Goods with snob appeal Some goods are bought mainly because they confer status on the buyer. Examples might be diamonds, fur coats or large cars. The argument is that these goods are demanded because few people can afford to buy them because their price is high. If large numbers of people could afford to buy them, then the demand (the quantity buyers would buy) would be low. This might be true for some individual consumers, but economists have not found any proof that it is true for markets as a whole. Whilst some might buy diamonds only because they are expensive, the majority of consumers would buy more diamonds if their price fell because they like diamonds. So there must be some doubt as to whether snob appeal does give rise to upward sloping demand curves.

Speculative goods Throughout most of 1987, stock markets worldwide boomed. Share prices were at an all time high and the demand for shares was high too. But in October 1987 share prices slumped on average between 20 and 30 per cent. Overnight the demand for shares fell. This could be taken as evidence of an upward sloping demand curve. The higher the price of shares, the higher the demand because buyers associate high share prices with large speculative gains in the future. However, most economists would argue that what is being seen is a shift in the demand curve. The demand curve is drawn on the assumption that expectations of future gain are constant. When share prices or the price of any speculative good fall, buyers revise their expectations downwards. At any given share price they are willing to buy fewer shares, which pushes the demand curve backwards to the left.

Quality goods Some consumers judge quality by price. They automatically assume that a higher priced good must be of better quality than a similar lower priced good. Hence, the higher the price the greater the quantity demanded. As with snob appeal goods, this may be true for some individuals but there is no evidence to suggest that this is true for consumers as a whole. There have been examples where goods that have been re-packaged, heavily advertised and increased in price have increased their sales. But this is an example of a shift to the right in the demand curve caused by advertising and repackaging rather than of an upward sloping demand curve.

In conclusion, it can be seen that there are various reasons why in theory demand curves might be upward sloping. But few, if any, such goods have been found in reality. The downward sloping demand curve seems to be true of nearly all goods.

QUESTION 3

Stock market analysts made redundant after the crash.

Before the Stock Market crash of October 1987 which wiped out approximately 25 per cent of the value of shares on the London Stock Exchange, the number of shares traded was considerably more than after the crash. For instance, on 29 September 1987, the FT ordinary share index (a measure of the average price of shares listed on the Stock Exchange) stood at 1853.7 and 731.7 million shares were bought and sold. On 27 September 1990, the Ordinary Share Index had fallen to 1535.7 whilst the number of shares traded was 376.7 million.

To what extent can this data be used as evidence to support the existence of an upward sloping demand curve for shares?

Key terms

Normal good - a good where demand increases when income increases (i.e. it has a positive income elasticity of demand).
Inferior good - a good where demand falls when income increases (i.e. it has a negative income elasticity of demand).
Giffen good - a special type of inferior good where demand increases when price increases.

Applied economics

Income elasticities and inferior goods

Table 10.3 gives estimates of the income elasticity of demand for food in the UK. Food has an income elasticity of -0.01 and therefore could be seen as a necessity. This compares with many other goods or services which have higher income elasticities and could be classed as luxuries. For instance, Deaton (1975) estimated that the income elasticity of demand for wines and spirits was 2.59, for recreational goods was 1.98 and for expenditure abroad was 1.14.

Ten of the foods in Table 10.3 are inferior goods (i.e. have a negative income elasticity).

- Margarine is a traditional textbook example of an inferior good. As incomes rise, households buy less margarine. Interestingly, though, butter too is an inferior good according to the data. This is likely to be due to recent awareness of the dangers of eating too much fat.
- Rising incomes enable poorer households to switch from cheap filling foods such as bread, potatoes and liquid milk to a more varied diet of more expensive food products.
- Processed cheese is likely to be replaced by natural cheese products as incomes rise.
- Tea has a surprisingly large negative income elasticity. As incomes rise, households substitute a greater variety of drinks for tea which, per cup, is very cheap. One very good substitute is coffee, which has a positive income elasticity.
- It is more difficult to explain why eggs and bacon should be inferior goods. However, it could be that eggs and bacon are cheap substitutes for more expensive meats, or that the traditional British breakfast is more common in low income households.

The category of food with the highest income elasticity is fruit juices, an expensive but increasingly popular item of expenditure amongst the more affluent households in the economy.

Table 10.3 *Income elasticities of demand for household foods, 1989*

	Elasticity
Milk and cream	- 0.02
of which	
Liquid wholemilk	- 0.40
Cheese	0.19
of which	
Natural	0.22
Processed	- 0.12
Chicken, uncooked	- 0.08
Other poultry, uncooked	0.24
Bacon and ham, uncooked	- 0.28
Eggs	- 0.41
Butter	- 0.04
Margarine	- 0.44
Fresh potatoes	- 0.48
Fresh fruit	0.48
Fruit juices	0.94
Bread	- 0.25
Tea	- 0.56
Coffee (instant)	0.23
All foods	- 0.01

Source: adapted from HMSO, *Household Food Consumption and Expenditure*, 1989.

Alcoholic drink and tobacco

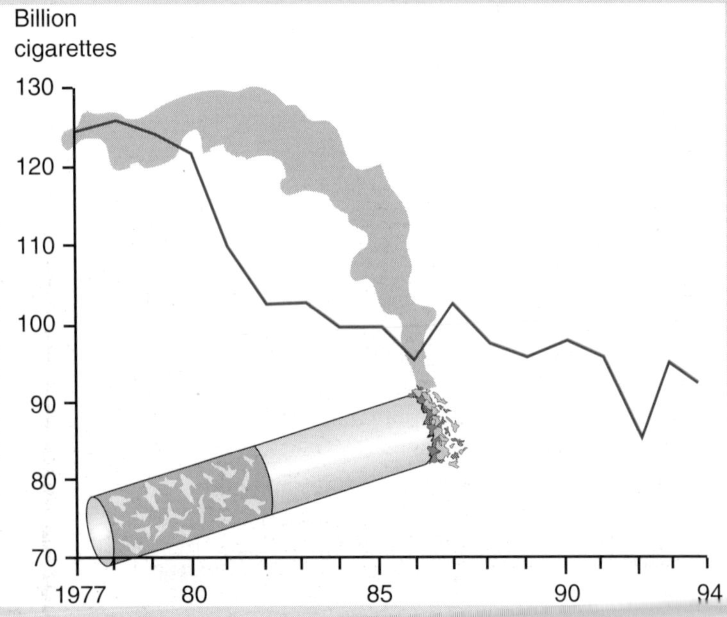

Source: adapted from CSO, *Annual Abstract of Statistics.*

Figure 10.3 *Tobacco sales, UK*

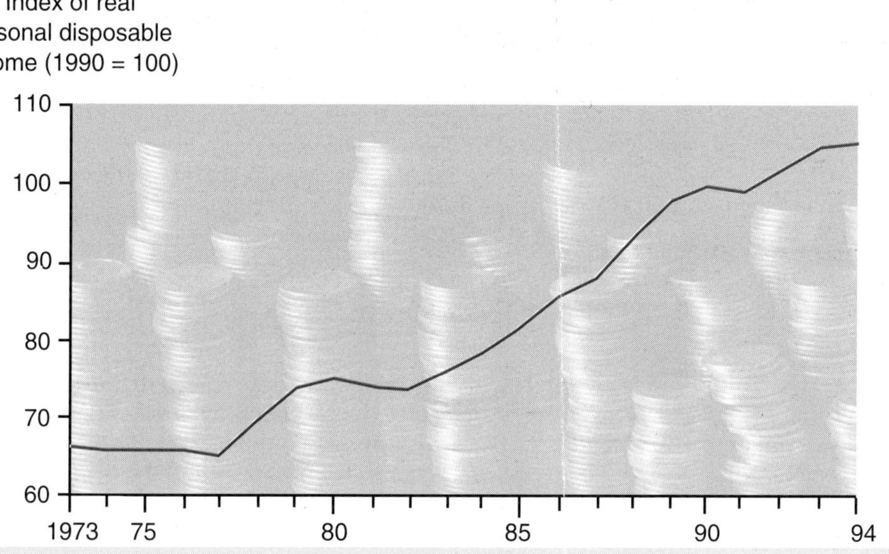

Source: adapted from CSO, *Annual Abstract of Statistics.*

Figure 10.4 *Personal disposable income*

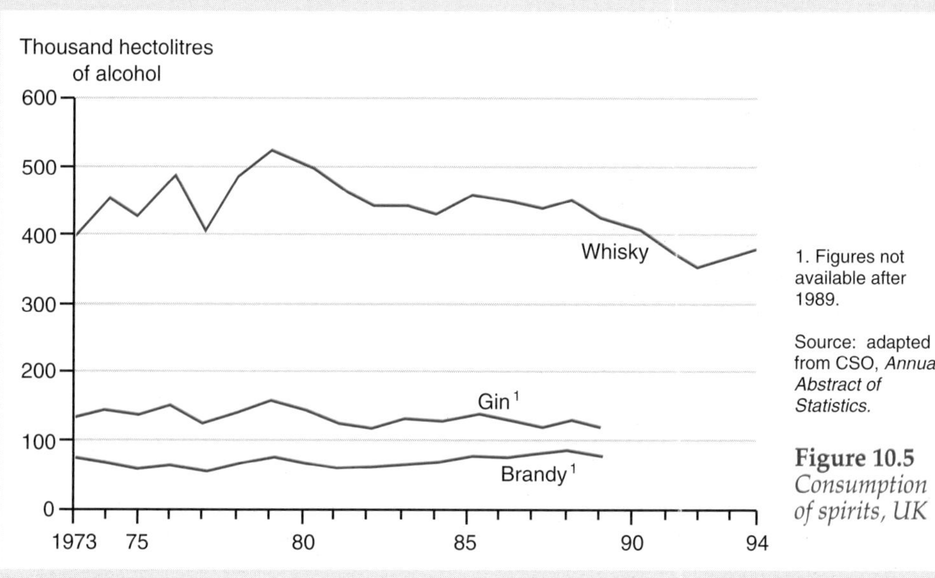

1. Figures not available after 1989.

Source: adapted from CSO, *Annual Abstract of Statistics.*

Figure 10.5 *Consumption of spirits, UK*

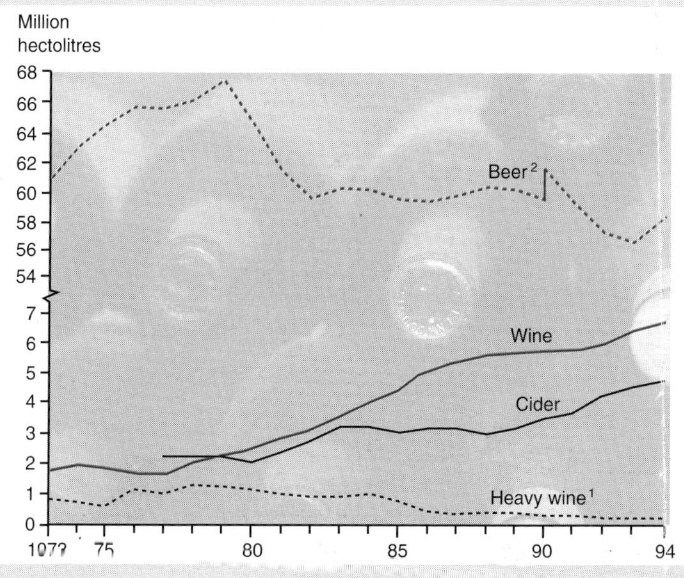

1. Such as sherry and port.
2. Discontinuity in 1990 due to revision of system for beer duties.

Source: adapted from CSO, *Annual Abstract of Statistics.*

Figure 10.6 *Consumption of beer, cider and wine, UK*

Write a report for a nationwide chain of supermarkets discussing future trends in demand for alcohol and tobacco. The chain is considering opening on the high street and in local shopping parades.

1. **Describe and explain past trends in sales of alcohol and tobacco. In particular, state whether you think these particular products are normal or inferior goods.**

2. **How might the alcohol and tobacco industry change in the future? Explain whether you think a supermarket chain could expand the whole market for alcohol and tobacco or whether it could only capture a larger share of sales in a given market.**

Static and dynamic market models

Summary

1. The cobweb theorem is a dynamic model of price and output determination.
2. It assumes that suppliers base their output decisions on the price received in the previous time period.
3. Cobwebs can be divergent, convergent or stable.
4. The cobweb theorem predicts that markets do not necessarily converge to their long term equilibrium position.

Static market models

A static model is one where time is not a variable. Time is said to be an **exogenous variable**, a variable which is not determined within the model. The theory of demand, supply and price outlined in unit 6 is an example of a static model.

However it was pointed out that there is a tendency for people who use this model to make a hidden assumption: that there are market forces at work which will move the market from a point where demand does not equal supply to an equilibrium position where the two are equal. To make this assumption explicit would require a more complicated **dynamic** model of price determination, one where time was an **endogenous variable** (i.e. included in the model).

Economists have devised many dynamic models of the market, but in this unit we will consider only one such model, called the COBWEB THEORY.

The assumptions of the cobweb model

The cobweb theory was devised by an American economist, Mordecai Ezekial, in the 1930s. He used it to try to explain why there were price oscillations in the pig market in Chicago.

He postulated that farmers based their supply decisions upon the price they received in the previous time period. Mathematically this can be expressed as:

$$Qt = f(P_t\text{-}1)$$

This says that the quantity supplied in time period t (Q_t) is a function of (i.e. varies with) the price received in the previous time period t-1 (P_{t-1}).

> **QUESTION 1** Supply is given by the following equation:
>
> $$Q_t = 0.5\, P_{t-1} - 10$$
>
> where Q_t is quantity supplied in time period t, and P_{t-1} is price in time period t-1.
>
> What would be the level of quantity supplied in 1995 if price in 1994 were:
> (a) £60; (b) £100; (c) £300; (d) £250?

The cobweb diagram

The market for carrots can be used to illustrate the workings of the cobweb model. It takes time to plant and grow carrots for sale on the market. Because of this time lag, farmers are assumed within the model to base their decision as to how many carrots to grow this season on the price they received last season. So the supply in 1998 would be dependent upon the prices received by farmers in 1997.

In Figure 11.1, the market is in long run equilibrium at a price of P_0 and quantity Q_0. Assume that in year 1 a severe attack of carrot fly destroys much of the crop such that only Q_1 is available for sale. Consumers will pay a price of P_1 for Q_1 of carrots (remember the demand curve shows how much buyers will purchase at any given price). At the beginning of year 2 farmers have to decide how many carrots to grow. According to the cobweb theorem, they will base their decision on last year's prices. Hence, given that the price was P_1 last year and given that the supply curve S remains unchanged, farmers in year 2 will decide to grow Q_2 of carrots. But when they come to sell them they will find that buyers are not prepared to buy Q_2 of carrots at a price of P_1. Farmers cannot store carrots for several years. They have to sell them within 12 months or destroy them. Therefore the price of carrots will have to fall to P_2 to clear the market of Q_2 carrots. At the beginning of year 3, farmers will base their planting decision on the very low price of P_2 obtained the previous

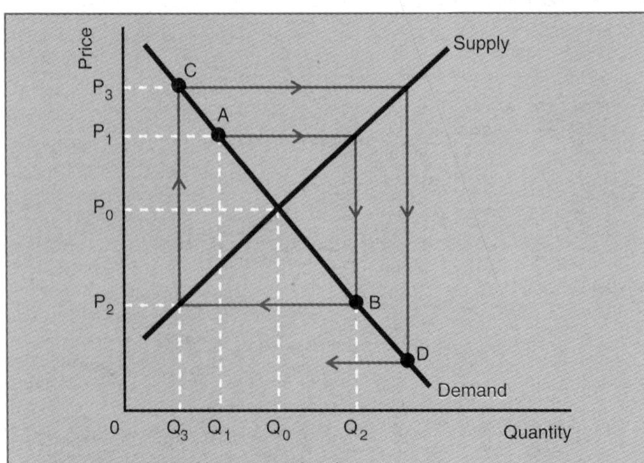

Figure 11.1 *A divergent cobweb*
Output is based upon price received in the previous time period. So short term equilibrium, starting at the point A, moves to B, then to C and then to D, steadily moving away from the stable equilibrium price of P_0.

year. They will therefore only plant Q_3 of carrots and be pleasantly surprised at the end of the year to receive a price of P_3 for them. In year 4, carrot planting will be higher than in any of the previous years and consequently prices will plummet at harvest time.

The path shown in Figure 11.1, from point A through to point D, shows a market which is moving further and further away from the long term equilibrium price of P_0 and quantity Q_0. This is called a **divergent cobweb**. However, cobwebs can also be either **convergent** or **stable**. A convergent cobweb is shown in Figure 11.2.

Here market forces do act to restore a market to its long run equilibrium position where demand and supply are equal. Figure 11.3 shows a stable cobweb. The market has regular cycles of high prices followed by low prices and there is no tendency for the market either to move nearer the point where demand and supply are equal or to move away from it.

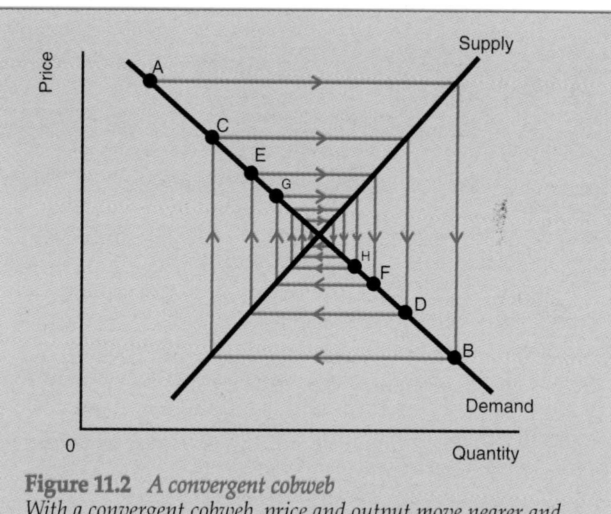

Figure 11.2 *A convergent cobweb*
With a convergent cobweb, price and output move nearer and nearer to the long term equilibrium where demand equals supply. Starting at A, the market moves from B to C and so on.

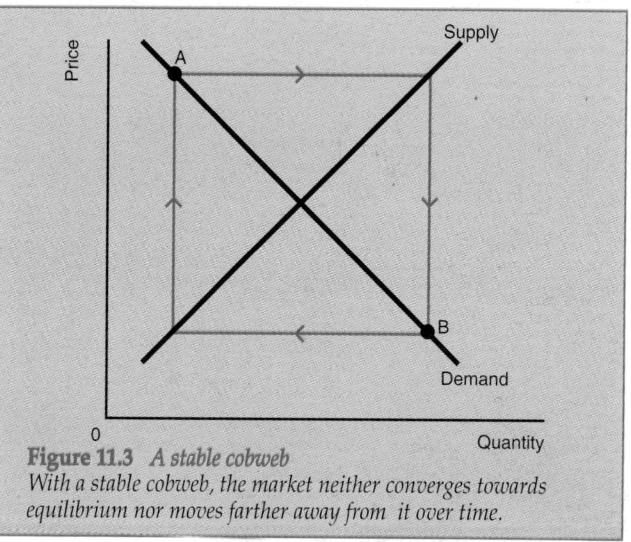

Figure 11.3 *A stable cobweb*
With a stable cobweb, the market neither converges towards equilibrium nor moves farther away from it over time.

QUESTION 2 Demand and supply are given by the equations:

$$D = 30 - 0.75\,P_t$$
$$S = P_{t-1} - 10$$

where D is quantity demanded, S is quantity supplied, P is price and t is time period t.

(a) Draw the demand and supply curves within the quantity range 0 to 30 and the price range 0 to 40.
(b) Will these equations produce a convergent, divergent or stable cobweb?
(c) (i) Draw two new supply curves which would make the cobweb different to your answer in (b).
(ii) What would be the equation for each of the new supply curves?

Realism of the model

The theory does not suggest that a convergent cobweb is any more likely to occur than a divergent or stable cobweb. However, empirical evidence suggests that divergent cobwebs are not common. Farmers operating in free markets do not base their planting decisions solely on the basis of last year's price. If they did, they would soon learn that it was an inaccurate predictor of current prices. They use more sophisticated techniques, using both past prices and estimates of future supplies from other farmers. Even so, these techniques are unlikely to lead to accurate predictions, especially given the vagaries of the weather and other factors which affect output. Cycles do seem to exist but they are for the most part either stable or convergent. Anyway, many agricultural product markets are regulated by the state in industrialised countries, from rice in Japan to wheat in the USA to beef in the European Union. Such regulation destroys any cobweb-type relationship that might have existed in these markets.

Apart from farming, the cobweb theory is likely to be less relevant since most products are capable of being stored from one time period to the next. If prices fall too low, businesses can within limits refuse to supply to the market, store production and sell in some future time period. Therefore price cycles are more likely to be more convergent in other industries than in an industry such as farming where the possibilities of storage are more limited.

Key terms

Cobweb theorem - a dynamic model of price determination which assumes that output decisions are based upon price received in the previous time period.

Applied economics

The commercial property cycle

Property prices have twice gone from boom to bust in the past 25 years. In the first half of the 1970s, property prices rose sharply before falling in 1975. Prices then remained depressed until the early 1980s when they began to increase again. Then, during the 'Lawson Boom', property prices rocketed only to collapse again in the recession which started in 1990.

This cycle is shown in Figure 11.4. The total return on all property reflects what is happening to rents and prices. When rents are increasing, the percentage return on property is likely to rise and vice versa.

Figure 11.5 shows the value of commercial property construction deflated by the RPI. The rate of inflation in commercial property prices is different from the RPI, so the statistics don't give an exact measure of the change in volume of construction work. However, it is reasonable to assume that the volume of construction increased when the real value increased and vice versa.

What Figures 11.4 and 11.5 show is that at the time of the two property booms, when commercial property prices were rising sharply, property companies increased their construction activity. They based their decisions on what had recently been happening to property prices and commercial rents. So when property prices and rents had been rising in the immediate past, they built more commercial property. On the other hand, in the price slumps of 1975-78 and 1990-93, commercial building was sharply curtailed.

It could then be argued that there is a cobweb-type cycle in the commercial property market. Overbuilding in a boom leads to excess supply. Prices fall sharply. Property developers then cut back on new building.

Eventually, at the new low prices, demand equals supply again. But there is overcompensation as developers then fail to increase their building rate. Property prices therefore begin to rise. Only after a time lag does property construction begin to pick up again. Eventually there is oversupply, prices crash and construction activity falls in consequence.

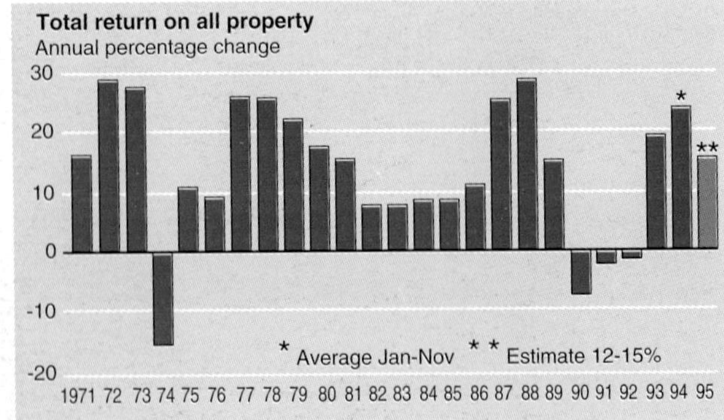

Source: adapted from Datastream.

Figure 11.4 *Total return on all property*

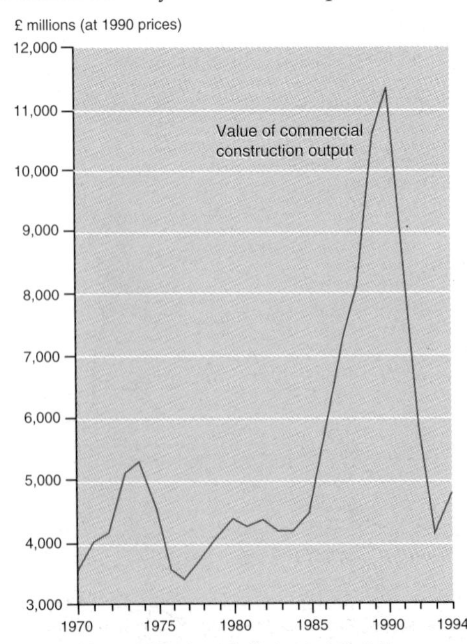

Source: adapted from CSO, *Annual Abstract of Statistics.*

Figure 11.5 *Value of commercial construction output at constant (January 1990) prices*

The pig cycle

Too many little piggies come to market

Most pigs to be slaughtered in the UK this week will be sold at a loss of about £3.40 per animal as the pig industry remains in the deep trough of a year-old recession. Even for an industry used to the ups and downs of the production cycle, the latest downturn has hit producers hard.

Pig producers have been operating below break-even for most of the past year except for a brief respite in May when prices rose above the cost of production for four to six weeks. Pigs operate in a typical farm commodity cycle whereby high prices encourage over-production which leads to a slump in the market. But the National Farmers' Union complains that the pig cycle - the period between the peaks and lows in price - used to take five years, but has recently speeded up to two. Added to that, the current downturn has lasted longer than usual.

Source: adapted from the *Financial Times*, 1.9.1994.

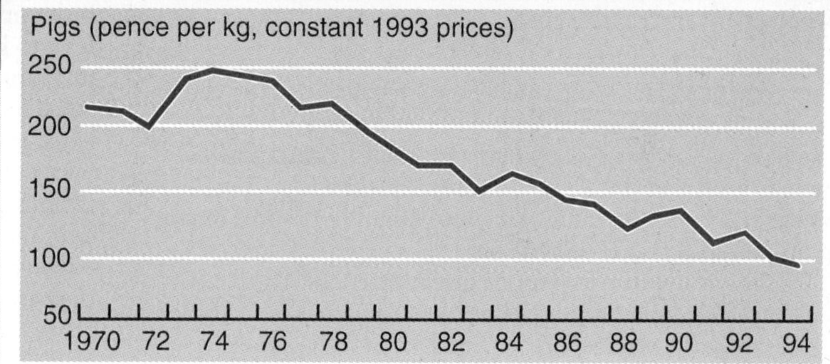

Source: adapted from Ridgeon: *The Economics of Pig Production*, Meat and Livestock Commission.

Figure 11.6 *Pig prices in real terms*

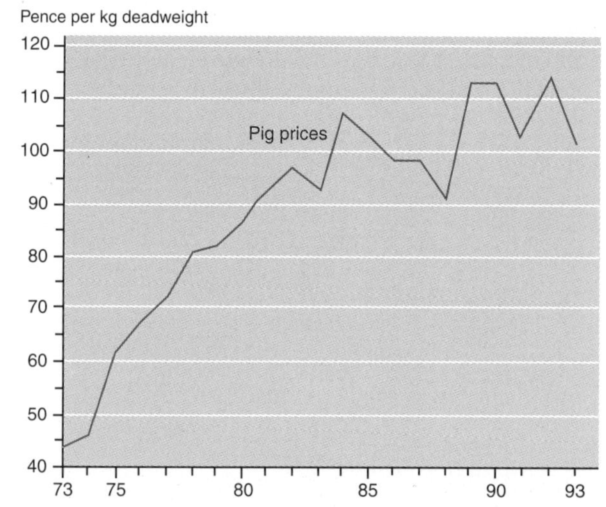

Source: adapted from CSO, *Annual Abstract of Statistics.*

Figure 11.7 *Pig prices in current terms*

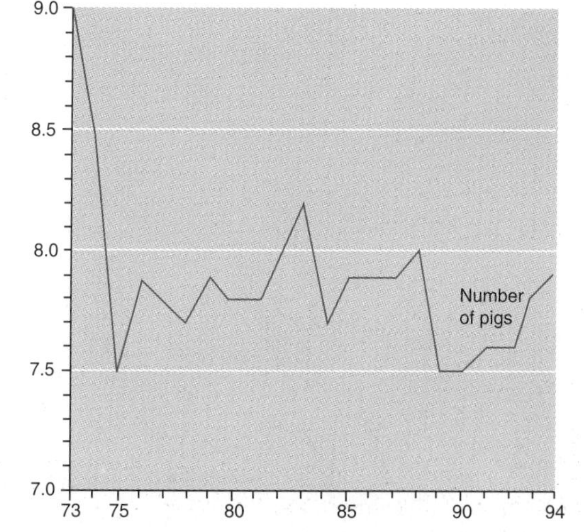

Source: adapted from CSO, *Annual Abstract of Statistics.*

Figure 11.8 *Total number of pigs on UK farms*

1. **Explain (a) what is meant by 'the pig cycle' and (b) using diagrams, what might cause the cycle.**
2. **To what extent does the evidence in Figures 11.6 to 11.8 support the view expressed by the National Farmers' Union that a pig cycle exists in the UK?**
3. **As a farmer, how might a knowledge of the pig cycle affect your decisions about pig rearing?**

Market stabilisation

Summary

1. Prices of commodities and agricultural products tend to fluctuate more widely than the prices of manufactured goods and services.
2. Governments may impose maximum or minimum prices to regulate a market.
3. Maximum prices can create shortages and black markets.
4. Minimum prices can lead to excess supply and tend to be maintained only at the expense of the taxpayer.
5. Cartels raise prices by restricting output.
6. Buffer stock schemes attempt to even out fluctuations in price by buying produce when prices are low and selling when prices are high.

Price fluctuations

The price of a can of tomatoes fluctuates far less than the price of fresh tomatoes. This illustrates a general point. The free market price of primary products (commodities such as gold and tin, and agricultural products such as wheat and beef) fluctuates far more than the price of either manufactured goods or services.

This is mainly due to supply side influences. The demand for canned tomatoes or fresh tomatoes is likely to remain broadly constant over a twelve month period. However, the supply of these two products will differ. Canned tomatoes can be stored. Therefore the supply too will remain broadly the same over a twelve month period. But the supply of fresh tomatoes varies greatly. In the summer months, supply is plentiful and the price of tomatoes is therefore low. In winter, supply is low and prices are high.

On a year to year basis, the supply of raw agricultural commodities can vary greatly according to crop yields. A bumper crop will depress prices whilst crop failure will lead to high prices. Bumper crops can be disastrous for farmers. In Figure 12.1, if the demand for a product is price inelastic, a large fall in price is needed to sell a little extra produce. This will greatly reduce farmers' revenues.

Equally, a poor crop can be disastrous for individual farmers. Although farm income overall will be higher than average, only farmers who have crops to sell will benefit. Farmers whose crops have been mostly or completely destroyed will receive little or no income.

Manufactures and services also contain greater value added than primary products. The cost of a can of tomatoes is made up not only of the cost of tomatoes themselves but also of the canning process and the can. If fresh tomatoes only account for 20 per cent of the cost of a can of tomatoes, then a doubling in the price of fresh tomatoes will only increase the price of a can by just over 7 per cent.

Demand side influences can, however, also be a source of price fluctuations for commodities. In manufacturing

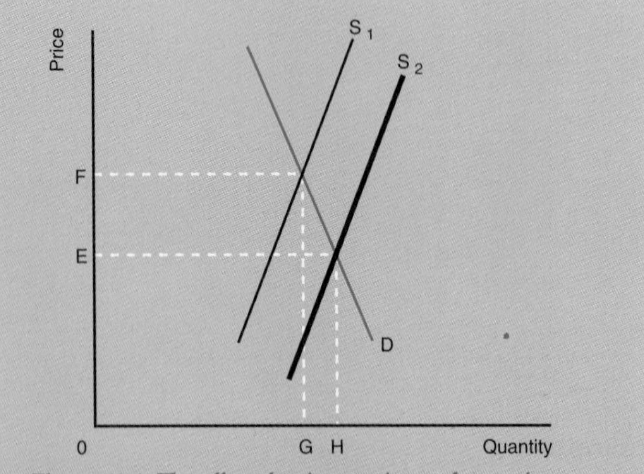

Figure 12.1 *The effect of an increase in supply on price*
If demand and supply are both relatively inelastic, then a small increase in supply from S_1 to S_2 will lead to a large fall in price of FE. Incomes will therefore be greatly reduced.

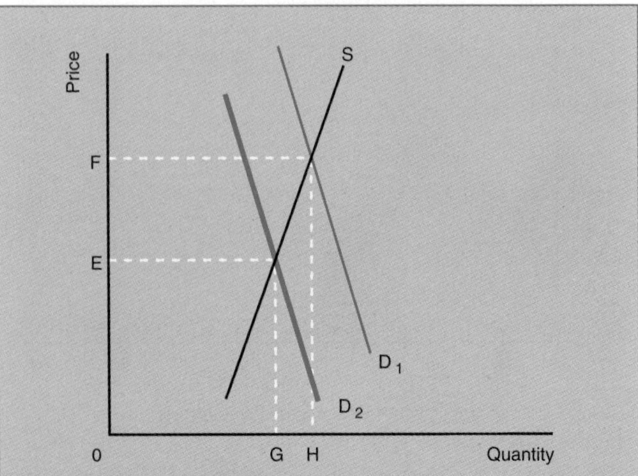

Figure 12.2 *The effect of a fall in demand on price*
If demand and supply are both relatively inelastic, then a small fall in demand from D_1 to D_2 will lead to a large fall in price of FE.

and services, producers devote much effort and money to stabilising demand through branding, advertising and other marketing techniques. However, Zambian copper is little different from Chilean copper. Buyers are free to buy from the cheapest source so demand fluctuates more greatly. In the short term, supply is relatively inelastic. Countries have invested in mines, oil wells and other commodity producing plant and need, often for foreign exchange purposes, to maximise output and sales. Small changes in demand, as shown in Figure 12.2, can produce large changes in price. Any slowdown in the world economy is likely to have a larger impact on commodities than on manufactured goods. Manufacturers may react to a small fall in their sales by cutting their stock levels and perhaps delaying the buying of stock by a few months. This results in a large, if temporary, fall in the price of raw materials. Whilst the slowdown persists, prices are likely to remain low. (The converse is also true - in a boom, commodity prices go up far faster than those of manufactures or services.)

Demand and supply influences combine to bring about large fluctuations in the price of commodities. Governments and other bodies have often reacted to this situation by intervening in the market place. Producers also attempt to manipulate prices, and the quantity demanded and supplied for their own benefit.

QUESTION 1

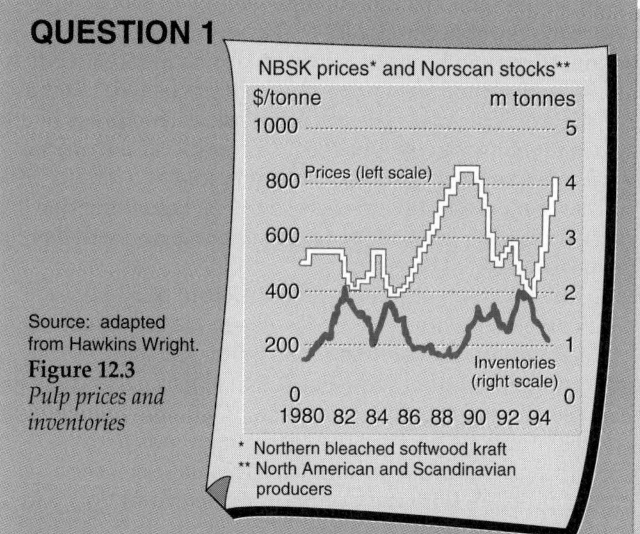

Source: adapted from Hawkins Wright.

Figure 12.3
Pulp prices and inventories

Newsprint is a commodity product. Newsprint, the paper on which newspapers are printed, is manufactured worldwide in large paper mills. In 1993, an upturn in the world economy led to a rise in demand for newsprint after three years of severely depressed prices. The paper mill firms forced through a 15 per cent rise in prices on 1st January 1995 and intended to increase prices by another 10 to 15 per cent in June 1995. The average cover price of newspapers in the UK, on the other hand, hardly changed.

Use demand and supply diagrams to explain why:
(a) there was a large increase in price of newsprint in 1994-95;
(b) the price of newsprint fluctuated more than the price of newspapers.

Government intervention in the market

Governments may intervene in markets by setting minimum prices or maximum prices. Minimum prices may be set to guarantee incomes to producers. For instance, a minimum wage (the wage rate is the price employers have to pay to obtain labour) is designed to prevent employers from paying their workers too low a wage. Minimum prices for wheat or beef, offered by the European Union to farmers, are designed to give farmers minimum returns on their crops. Maximum prices on the other hand may be used to set limits on the returns that producers can make. Or they may be intended to help consumers afford products, often staple necessities such as bread, rice or housing.

Maximum prices

The workings of maximum prices can be illustrated using a demand and supply diagram. In Figure 12.4, the free market price is P_1 and Q_1 is bought and sold. Assume that this is the market for rented accommodation. At a price of P_1 the poorest in society are unable to afford to rent houses and there is therefore a problem of homelessness. The government intervenes by fixing a maximum price for accommodation of P_2. In the very short term, this may well seem to alleviate the problem. Landlords will continue to offer Q_1 of housing whilst the poorest in society will be more able to afford the new lower cost housing. But in the longer term, economic theory predicts that new problems will arise. At a price of P_2, demand will be higher than at P_1, whilst supply will be lower. There will in fact be an excess demand of Q_2Q_3. At the lower price, consumers will demand more housing. On the other hand, landlords will reduce their supply, for instance by selling off their properties for owner occupation, not buying new properties to rent out, or living in their own

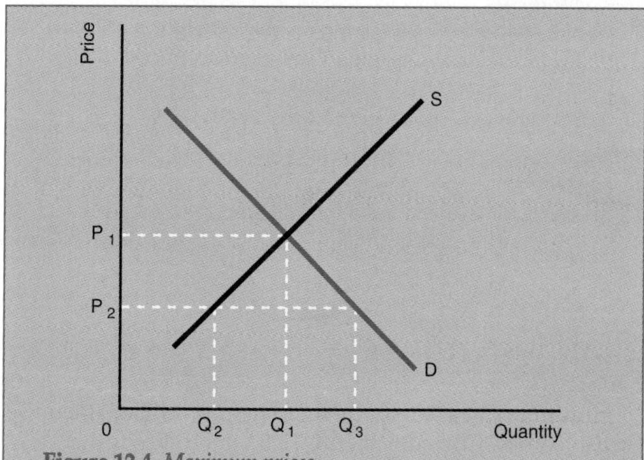

Figure 12.4 *Maximum prices*
OP_1 is the free market price. If the government sets a maximum price of OP_2 in the market, demand will increase to OQ_3 whilst supply will fall to OQ_2. The result will be excess demand in the market of Q_2Q_3.

properties instead of renting them out.

Permanent rent controls will thus reduce the supply of privately rented accommodation to the market whilst increasing its demand. The market may react in a number of ways. In a law abiding society, queues or waiting lists may develop. It may be a matter of luck rather than money whether one is able to get rented accommodation. The state may devise systems to allocate rented accommodation on the basis of greatest need. Landlords may develop a variety of ways in which they can get round the price controls. A black market may develop, illegal and uncontrolled, where rents are fixed at, or greater than, the free market price of P_1. Economic theory therefore predicts that maximum prices may benefit some consumers - those able to obtain the goods which are controlled in price - but will disadvantage those who are prepared to pay a higher price for the good but are unable to obtain it because of a shortage of supply.

If the maximum price were set at P_3, there would be no effect on the market. P_1, the free market price, is below the maximum price and therefore nothing will happen following the introduction of maximum price controls.

QUESTION 2 In 1992, the Indian government partially liberalised the Indian coffee market. Prior to this, Indian coffee growers had to sell all their coffee to the Coffee Board, a state monopoly buyer of coffee. Prices paid were relatively low. Equally, however, the price of coffee sold to Indian consumers by the Coffee Board was low. The Coffee Board sold the balance of the crop for export.

From 1992, coffee growers were allowed to sell half their coffee on the free market and only had to sell half to the Coffee Board. The free market price quickly rose above the Coffee Board price with Indian consumers complaining about 'runaway' inflation in coffee prices. Coffee farmers began to invest more money in their plantations, creating new irrigation systems and planting more bushes. The 1993-94 crop was 180 000 tonnes compared to 169 000 tonnes in 1992-93 and was forecast to grow in subsequent years. Farmers want to be able to sell all their crops on the open market in order to be able to sell at world prices rather than the lower Coffee Board prices.

Source: adapted from the *Financial Times*, 26.7.1994.

Using a diagram and the concept of maximum price, explain why Indian coffee prices and output rose following the partial liberalisation of the Indian coffee market.

Minimum prices

Minimum prices are usually set to help producers increase their incomes. Consider Figure 12.5 which shows the market for wheat. The free market price is P_1. The government decides that this is too low a price for farmers to receive and sets a minimum price of P_2. As a result, farmers will now grow Q_1Q_3 more wheat. Consumers will react to the new higher prices by reducing their demand

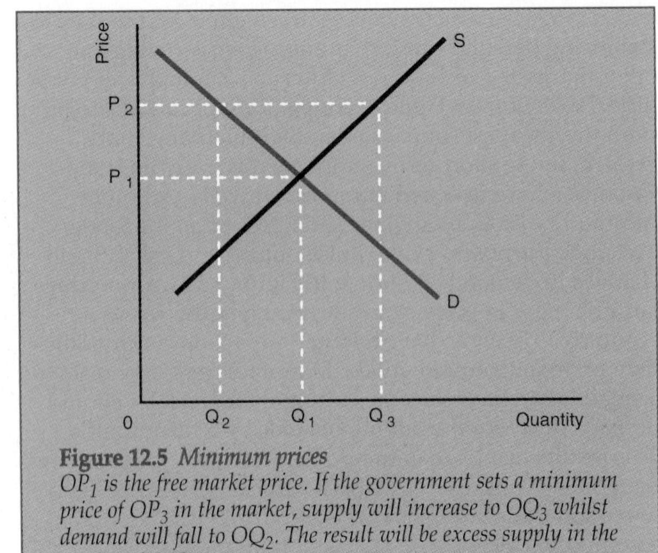

Figure 12.5 *Minimum prices*
OP_1 is the free market price. If the government sets a minimum price of OP_3 in the market, supply will increase to OQ_3 whilst demand will fall to OQ_2. The result will be excess supply in the market of Q_2Q_3.

by Q_1Q_2. Total excess supply of Q_2Q_3 will result.

This poses a problem for the government. With maximum prices, the government did not need to intervene when excess demand appeared. The excess demand could remain in the market forever if need be. But this is not true of excess supply. If consumers only buy Q_2 of wheat then farmers can only sell Q_2 of wheat. Q_2Q_3 will remain unbought. Unless the government takes action, there will be strong pressure for farmers to sell this at below the minimum price. Average prices will fall until the market is cleared. The resulting price structure is likely to be very complex, some wheat being sold at the official minimum price of P_2 whilst the rest is sold at a variety of prices, the lowest of which is likely to be below the free market clearing price of P_1. Government action will have been frustrated.

So an effective minimum price structure must be accompanied by other measures. There are two main ways of dealing with this problem. The first is for the government to buy up the wheat that consumers refuse to buy (i.e. buy up the excess supply Q_2Q_3). This in turn creates problems because the government has to do something with the wheat it buys. This has been the classic problem with the Common Agricultural Policy in the European Union. A variety of solutions, from selling wheat mountains to Third World countries at rock bottom prices, selling it back to farmers to feed to animals, or offering it at reduced prices to those in need in the EU, or simply destroying the produce, have been adopted. All have one drawback - they cost the taxpayer money because the price paid to farmers is inevitably higher than the price received from the sale of the surplus.

The second solution to the problem of excess supply is to restrict production. Governments can either force, or pay, farmers to reduce the size of their herds or leave part of their land uncultivated. At a price of P_2, the government ensures that only Q_2 is supplied to the market. If farmers are paid to set aside land, the taxpayer will have to subsidise the farmer. If farmers receive no compensation, the scheme may defeat its own purposes.

As was pointed out in unit 9, whether a farmer receives a higher income by selling a smaller quantity at a higher price depends upon the price elasticity of demand. Only if the demand is price inelastic will higher prices give farmers higher revenues.

QUESTION 3 In 1994, the European Union (EU) spent £1.08bn buying up beef from farmers. Despite this, stocks of beef held from intervention fell from 1.1m tonnes in 1993 to 430 000 tonnes in 1994 mainly due to less beef being bought in and greater exports to countries outside the EU. The EU plans to reduce the amount of beef bought from farmers at intervention prices from 650 00 tonnes in 1994 to 350 000 in 1997.

Price support mechanisms for cereal crops such as wheat were even greater than for beef at £5.5bn in 1994. However, subsidies paid might have been even higher had it not been for the introduction of set-aside in 1992. Under this scheme, farmers are paid not to use 15 per cent of their land in a given year. The result has been a drop in annual wheat production from 185m tonnes before 1992 to an estimated 162m tonnes in 1994.

With fruit and vegetables, the EU pays farmers to destroy crops which are bought at intervention prices. 600 000 tonnes of fruit and vegetables are destroyed in a typical year. The 430 000 tonnes of peaches trashed in 1992 as a result of a record harvest was headline news. Despite the lack of possibility of resale, as exists with beef or wine bought into storage, the fruit and vegetable regime is relatively cheap to run at £1.16bn spent in 1993.

Source: adapted from the *Financial Times*, 13.4.1994, and 26.10.1994.

Using demand and supply diagrams, explain how the EU maintains minimum prices in (a) beef, (b) wheat and (c) fruit and vegetables.

Cartels

A CARTEL is an organisation of producers grouped together for their own benefit. The most well known cartel in existence today is OPEC, the Organisation of Petroleum Exporting Countries. Its members are some (but not all) of the most important oil producing countries including Saudi Arabia and Mexico. Most cartels try to raise prices at the expense of consumers.

As was shown above, any attempt to raise prices above the free market price produces problems of excess supply. A cartel must deal with these problems if it is to survive. Unlike in the agricultural sector, governments are not likely to be willing to buy up any excess supply. So cartels have to devise arrangements to restrict supply. Members are likely to be given production **quotas** (i.e. maximum output figures). There is a great incentive for individual members to sell more than their quota. By increasing their supply, which is likely to be only a fraction of total supply to the market, they can sell more at a price which is likely to be close to the high cartel price. They get the benefits of higher output and higher prices. But if all members cheat in this way, the price will fall. If there is no effective discipline, the price will revert to the free market price.

QUESTION 4 In 1994, 19 companies across Europe were fined a record £104.27m for operating a cartel. The 19 companies made carton-board, the material which is then used by carton printers and manufacturers to make the packaging on products from toothpaste to cosmetics and frozen foods.

From 1986 onwards, top officials from the carton-board manufacturers had met monthly for 'social' meetings, usually in Zurich. They would agree on prices to be charged. When price rises were to be enforced, companies would take it in turns to announce the price rise and then the other companies would follow shortly afterwards. Companies agreed to sharing out the market. If there was oversupply, the big producers would agree to temporary plant stoppages. Not all the 19 companies co-operated fully. Sometimes a company would delay announcing a price rise, presumably hoping to increase its sales. Sometimes a company would sell more than its market share. When this happened, the guilty companies would be forced to explain their actions to the other companies and brought back into line.

The cartel was illegal under European competition law. Hence, official minutes which were kept at the 'social' meetings were falsified so that no trace could be found later of what had actually gone on. Evidence to convict the companies had been gained in dawn raids in 1991 by 40 officials from the European Commission.

Source: adapted from the *Financial Times*, 5.7.1994.

(a) Using a diagram, explain how the 19 carton-board companies kept prices at levels higher than the free market price.
(b) Why did some companies attempt to delay price rises?
(c) To what extent would the cartel have been able to operate if two of the major European producers had not been part of the cartel?

Buffer stock schemes

A BUFFER STOCK SCHEME is a cartel arrangement which combines the elements of both minimum and maximum pricing. In theory it is designed to even out price fluctuations for producers. An intervention price is set. If the free market price is below this, the buffer stock agency will buy in the market until the price is at the intervention price. (It may, as the Common Agricultural Policy does, offer to buy any amount at the intervention price.) If the free market price is above the intervention price, the buffer stock will sell, forcing down the price towards the intervention price.

Buffer stock schemes are not common. One major reason for this is that a considerable amount of capital is needed to set them up. Money is required to buy produce when prices are too low. There are also the costs of administration and storage of produce purchased. But in theory, the overall running costs of the scheme should be low. Indeed, with skilful buying and selling the scheme may make an operational profit. This is because the scheme buys produce at or below the intervention price but sells at a price above the intervention price.

Buffer stock schemes also have a mixed record of success. Pressure to set up these schemes tends to come from producers who have a vested interest in setting the intervention price above the average market price. If they succeed in doing this, their revenues in the short term are likely to be larger than they would otherwise have been. But the buffer stock scheme will have been buying more produce than it sold. Eventually it will run out of money, the scheme will collapse, and prices will plummet because the accumulated stocks will be sold to pay the debts of the scheme. The glut of produce on the market will result in producers receiving below average prices for some time to come. Successful buffer stock schemes are those which correctly guess the average price and resist attempts by producers to set the intervention price above it.

Key terms

Cartel - an organisation of producers which exists to further the interests of its members, often by restricting output through the imposition of quotas leading to a rise in prices.
Buffer stock scheme - a scheme whereby an organisation buys and sells in the open market so as to maintain a minimum price in the market for a product.

QUESTION 5 In 1985 the International Tin Council's (ITC) price support scheme collapsed. Countries like the UK, which had agreed to support the Council's purchase of tin when tin prices fell below the intervention price, refused to provide any more money to buy tin to put into stock. Tin prices collapsed and remained weak between 1985 and 1988 as tin stocks, totalling 120 000 tonnes and equivalent to nine months of tin demand, were gradually sold. The main tin producing countries formed themselves into a cartel and agreed production quotas. By 1989, the ITC's stocks were down to 25 000 tonnes and tin prices had risen from $7 200 a lb at the end of 1988 to a peak of $10 000 a lb in 1989.

The recession in the world economy, which began in the USA and the UK in the late 1980s and which only ended in 1993, depressed tin prices despite cutbacks in output by tin producers. Tin prices surged in 1994 as the world recovery got under way.

Using diagrams, explain why:

(a) the ITC's price support scheme collapsed in 1985;
(b) the price of tin was weak between 1986 and 1988;
(c) the price of tin rose in 1989;
(d) the price of tin fell between 1989 and 1993, whilst rising in 1994.

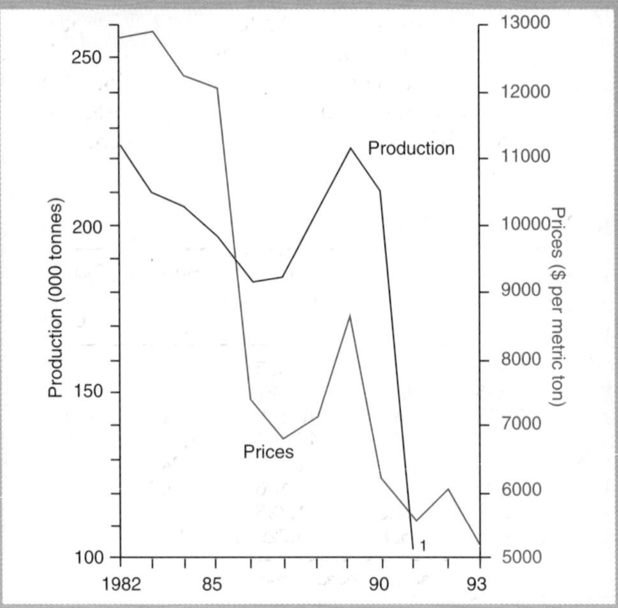

1 Excluding former communist countries.
Figure 12.6 *Prices and production of tin*

Applied economics

The Common Agricultural Policy (CAP)

One of the most important steps taken by the European Union (formerly the European Community) in its early years was to create the Common Agricultural Policy in 1958. Article 39 of the Treaty of Rome cites 5 objectives of agricultural policy:

- to increase agricultural productivity;
- to ensure a fair standard of living for farmers;
- to stabilise markets;
- to guarantee availability of supplies;
- to ensure fair prices for consumers.

It was hoped that CAP would achieve this through regulation of the agricultural industry in the Union. For many products, an **intervention price** was established. Farmers could then choose to sell their produce on the open market or to the EU at this minimum fixed price. The EU guaranteed to buy up any amount at the intervention price. Farmers were protected from overseas competition through a complex system of tariffs and quotas.

CAP proved to be far more favourable to farmers than to consumers. The farming community in the EU became very good at lobbying their individual governments to vote for high intervention prices at the annual price fixing negotiations in Brussels. Consumers lost out in two ways.

First, they had to pay directly for food which was much higher in price than it would otherwise have been if it had been bought on world markets. Second, as taxpayers, they had to pay for the heavy costs of running the CAP.

In theory, the CAP should have been fairly inexpensive to run. If there was a glut of produce on the market in one season, the EU would buy some of it at the intervention price and store it. The next season, when there was perhaps a shortage, the EU could take the produce out of storage and sell it. Prices would not fluctuate by as much as under a market system and the sale of produce would ensure that the major cost of the system would be administration and storage.

In practice, the cost of the CAP rose year after year. High intervention prices led to increased production, as economic theory would predict. Supply then began to outstrip demand. Instead of selling produce taken into storage to European consumers at a later date, mountains and lakes of produce developed, as shown in Table 12.1. This produce then had to be sold, often at a fraction of the cost of production, to the former USSR, Third World countries, and to EU farmers for use as animal feed. Some was even destroyed.

Table 12.1 *EU intervention stocks (1 000 tonnes)*

Marketing year	Common wheat	Barley	All cereals	Butter	Skimmed milk powder
1983/84	3,318	222	4,335		
1984/85	10,256	2,013	13,927		
1985/86	10,312	5,296	18,502	1,122	646
1986/87	7,319	4,235	14,271	1,188	765
1987/88	4,567	3,916	11,748	640	240
1988/89	2,906	3,242	9,146	64	7
1989/90	5,521	3,320	11,795	820	21
1990/91	8,520	5,538	18,729	324	354

Source: European Commission, *European Economy, EC Agricultural Policy for the 21st Century*, Number 4, 1994.

Reform of CAP has been a long standing issue. As early as 1968, the Mansholt Plan recommended that farm size should increase to enable farmers to enjoy economies of scale and thus be better able to provide food at world market prices. By the early 1980s, political pressure was building to limit the growth of the CAP budget shown in Figure 12.7. By 1985, spending on CAP was threatening to exceed the maximum amount permitted in the EU budget. At a summit meeting at Fontainebleau in that year, the first measures which would begin to tackle the CAP problem were announced. In particular, a quota system for milk was imposed. Each farm in the EU was given a milk quota based on existing production levels minus a given percentage to reduce the milk surplus which had developed. Farmers were not allowed to produce more than their quota. In 1986, these quotas became tradeable, with farmers able to buy and sell quotas amongst themselves.

The financial crisis worsened despite this and in 1987 CAP was forced to transfer some spending over into 1988 because it had run out of money in its budget. This led to the member countries agreeing to an increase in spending on CAP, but fixing any future growth in spending on CAP to three-quarters of the average growth rate in national income of the European Union. A start was also made on tackling the structural overproduction of cereal crops. Intervention prices were cut by about 3 per cent. A limit was also set on total wheat production in the European Union of 160 million tonnes. If production exceeded that limit, the intervention price paid would automatically fall. Pressure for reform continued and in 1992 the commissioner for agriculture, Raymond MacSharry, secured agreement for a further tightening of CAP. An important element in this was a set aside scheme for cereal crops. Cereal farmers would be paid for setting aside (i.e. not using) 15 per cent of their land in a single year. The MacSharry proposals formed the basis of the EU's negotiations with other countries in the GATT world trade talks (☞ unit 85). The USA and other countries wanted subsidies to EC farmers cut drastically or removed altogether. The final 1993 agreement saw the EU agreeing to cut income support to farmers by 20 per cent, to reduce the levels of tariffs (taxes on imports) by 36 per cent and cut the value of subsidised exports by 36 per cent by the year 2000.

The reforms since 1985 have tended to tackle the outcomes rather than the root cause of the problem. The root cause of the problem is that agricultural prices have been set too high in relation to the world market clearing price. Figure 12.8 shows that EU producer prices, whilst falling in real terms in the 1980s, were at times more than double those of world market prices. Too high prices encourage farmers to produce too much and discourage consumption. Surpluses have to be disposed of, sometimes onto world markets at knock down prices which angers farmers in other countries who complain of 'unfair competition'. The reforms have concentrated on restricting supply rather than reducing price.

A radically different solution would be completely to dismantle the price support mechanisms and replace them with an income support scheme. If the main political objective of CAP is to guarantee farmers a minimum income, it would be more efficient to pay them a yearly benefit and not link this to how much they produce as at present. In some reform proposals, this benefit has been linked to other issues such as rural depopulation or the environment. Paying workers to look after the land in Wales or central France might prevent depopulation and preserve the continuation of a farming culture in these areas. Alternatively, farmers could be paid for keeping the countryside tidy or for adopting land management policies which would be environmentally friendly. Given that each person working in agriculture in the EU currently receives a subsidy of £2 500 per annum and that the average farm receives a subsidy of £13 000, there is plenty of scope to offer generous income benefits if price support schemes were abolished.

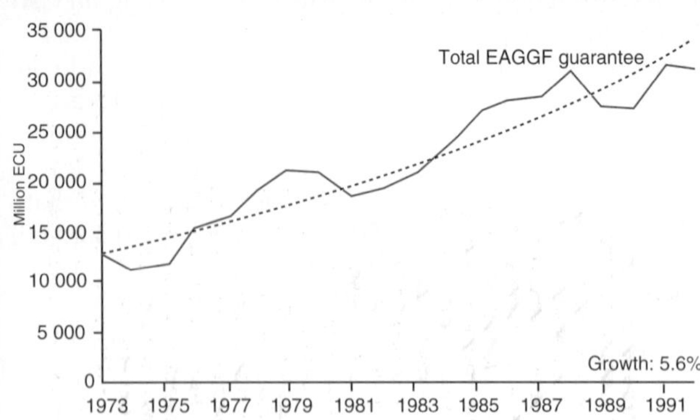

Source: adapted from European Commission, *European Economy, EC Agricultural Policy for the 21st Century*, Number 4, 1994.

Figure 12.7 *Trends in EU agricultural budget expenditures in real terms (1992 values), 1973-1992*

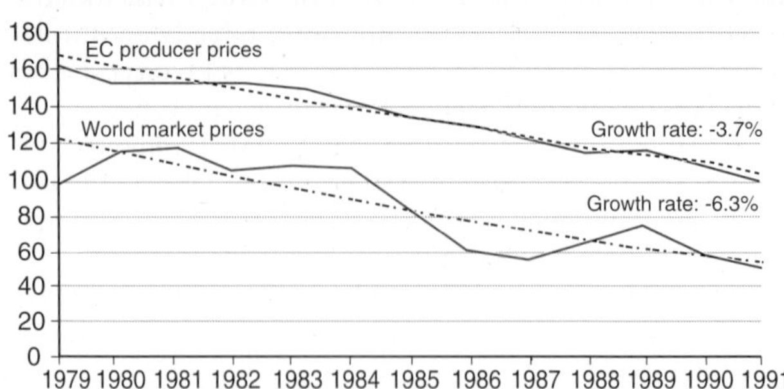

1. Both series weighted by value of EU production at domestic producer prices and deflated by ECU deflator. World market price index in 1979=100. (EU domkestic producer prices/world market prices).

Source: adapted from European Commission, *European Economy, EC Agricultural Policy for the 21st Century*, Number 4, 1994.

Figure 12.8 *Evolution of EU domestic producer prices and world market prices for agricultural products in real terms, 1979-1991*[1]

OPEC

The strengths of OPEC

There are a number of reasons why OPEC has been one of the few international cartels which has survived over a long period of time.

- There is no need for any buffer stocks or large amounts of financial capital. If OPEC wishes to reduce supply, member countries simply produce less and leave their oil in the ground.
- There are a relatively small number of members of OPEC. Member countries are able to exert a high degree of control over the volume of oil lifted within their countries. This contrasts, for instance, with coffee where governments wishing to limit production have to control tens of thousands of small farmers.
- Oil production is not particularly affected by the vagaries of weather. Hence supply need not fluctuate wildly and randomly from year to year as it does in many agricultural markets.
- OPEC countries supply a significant proportion of total world output and control an even larger proportion of known oil reserves. Because non-OPEC producers tend to produce at maximum capacity, countries such as the USA and the UK are unable to exert downward pressure on oil prices even if they wanted to.

The cartel

OPEC, the Organisation of Petroleum Exporting Countries, was founded in 1960. For the first 13 years of its existence, it remained an obscure and relatively unimportant organisation, but in 1973, with the Arab-Israeli Yom Kippur War, it leapt to world prominence. The members of the organisation realised that they could form an effective cartel if they agreed production quotas amongst themselves. By slightly reducing supply in 1974, they were able to quadruple the world price of oil.

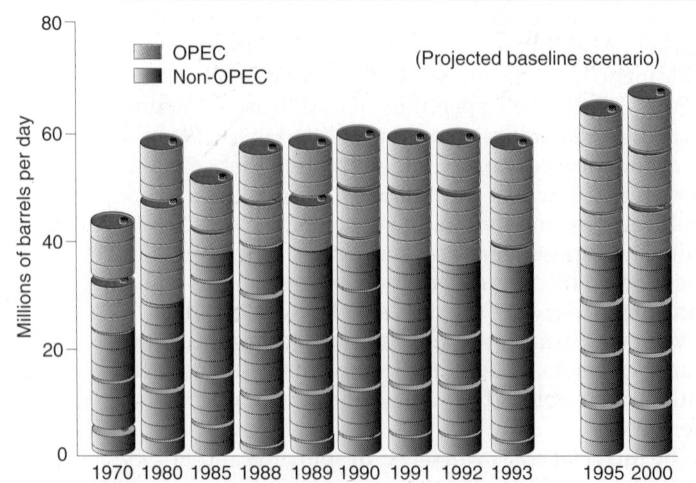

Source: adapted from UN/DESIPA.

Figure 12.9 *World crude oil production*

Weaknesses

In real terms, oil prices today are little different from those at the start of 1973. OPEC countries increased their revenues substantially in the mid-1970s and again in 1979-80 but these were short lived gains. OPEC suffers from three fundamental weaknesses.

- The large increases in oil prices in the 1970s led to stagnant demand for oil until the mid-1980s. Consumers substituted other types of energy for oil and there was a shift towards much greater energy conservation.
- Large increases in oil prices also led to a large increase in supply from non-OPEC countries. Known oil reserves are higher today than they were at the time of the 'energy crisis' in the 1970s. The operation of market forces led to a substantial increase in exploration and subsequent output from non-OPEC countries. This increase in supply has depressed world prices since the start of the 1980s.
- The increase in non-OPEC supply has led to strains amongst OPEC members. In any cartel, there is an incentive to cheat. If one country can increase its production above its allocated quota, it can sell this extra output at a price almost equal that of the cartel price. However, if countries cheat, then the price will fall rapidly. In the mid-1980s, many OPEC countries exceeded their quotas, driving down the price of oil. Saudi Arabia, the OPEC member with by far the largest oil reserves and OPEC's largest producer, was prepared for some time to reduce its liftings in order to prevent too rapid a fall in price. In 1986, its patience ran out and it began to supply as much oil as buyers would purchase at the market price. World oil prices tumbled to $8 a barrel and analysts estimated that the free market price was below $5 a barrel. Other OPEC members, realising they had everything to lose if OPEC broke up, agreed to new quotas and the price rose rapidly to above $15 a barrel. It has broadly stayed in the $15-$20 a barrel range since then, apart from during the Gulf War when prices reached $40 a barrel.

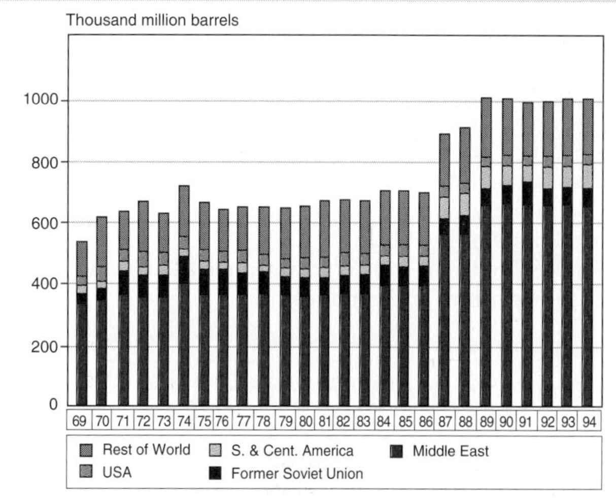

Source: adapted from *BP Statistical Review of World Energy.*
Figure 12.10 *World proven oil reserves, 1969-94*

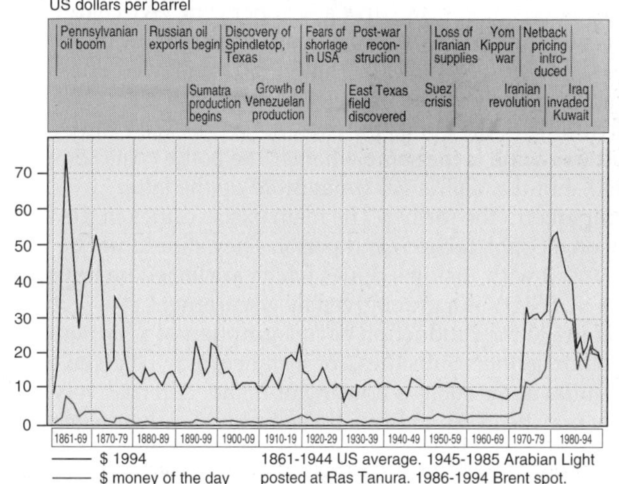

Source: adapted from *BP Statistical Review of World Energy.*
Figure 12.11 *Crude oil prices since 1861*

Write a report outlining possible future trends in the world oil market for the government of a small OPEC producer. Your report needs to cover the following.

1. **A summary of past trends in oil production, prices and proven reserves since 1970.**
2. **An economic analysis using demand and supply diagrams of (a) why oil prices have changed and (b) why the market share of OPEC countries has shifted since 1970.**
3. **Future trends in the world oil market. In your analysis, use the evidence of what has happened over the past 20 years to predict the future. Consider too the implications of oil being a non-renewable energy source.**
4. **Suggestions of the best course of action over the next ten years for a small OPEC producer given your predictions in 3. Assume the producer wishes to maximise revenues from its oil exports.**

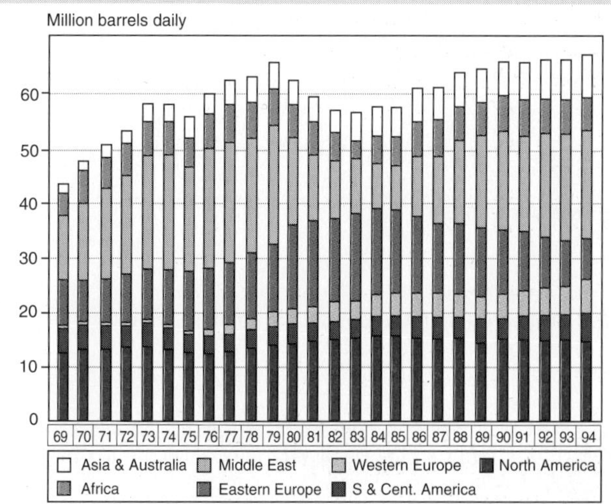

Source: adapted from *BP Statistical Review of World Energy.*
Figure 12.12 *Supply of oil, production by area*

unit 13 Indirect taxes and subsidies

Summary

1. **Indirect taxes can be either ad valorem taxes or specific taxes.**
2. **The imposition of an indirect tax is likely to lead to a rise in the unit price of a good which is less than the unit value of the tax.**
3. **The incidence of indirect taxation is likely to fall on both consumer and producer.**
4. **The incidence of tax will fall wholly on the consumer if demand is perfectly inelastic or supply is perfectly elastic.**
5. **The incidence of tax will fall wholly on the producer if demand is perfectly elastic or supply is perfectly inelastic.**

Indirect taxes and subsidies

An indirect tax (discussed in greater detail in unit 47) is a tax on expenditure. The two major indirect taxes in the UK are VAT and excise duties.

VAT is an example of an AD VALOREM tax. The tax levied increases in proportion to the value of the tax base. In the case of VAT, the tax base is the price of the good. Most goods in the UK carry a 17½ per cent VAT charge. Excise duties on the other hand are an example of a SPECIFIC or UNIT tax. The amount of tax levied does not change with the value of the goods but with the amount or volume of the goods purchased. So the excise duty on a bottle of wine is the same whether the bottle costs £5 or £500, but the VAT is 100 times more on the latter compared to the former. The main excise duties in the UK are on alcohol, tobacco and petrol. They should not be confused with customs duties which are levied on imports.

A SUBSIDY is a grant given by government to encourage the production or consumption of a particular good or service. Subsidies, for instance, may be given on essential items such as housing or bread. Alternatively they may be given to firms that employ disadvantaged workers such as the long term unemployed or handicapped people. Or they may be given to firms manufacturing domestically produced goods to help them be more competitive than imported goods.

QUESTION 1 The price of a litre of 4 star petrol at the pumps is made up as follows:

	pence
Petrol cost before tax	15.0
Excise duty	35.2
	50.2
VAT @ 17½%	8.8
Price at the pumps	59.0

Calculate the new price of petrol if:

(a) an increase in the cost of crude oil pushed up the cost of petrol before tax from 15.0p to 24.8p;

(b) the government increased excise duty from 35.2p to 40p;

(c) VAT was reduced from 17½ per cent to 15 per cent;

(d) the government subsidised the cost before tax by 2p a litre.

(For each part, assume that the price at the pumps is initially 59p.)

The incidence of tax

Price theory can be used to analyse the impact of the imposition of an indirect tax on a good. Assume that a specific tax of £1 per bottle is imposed upon wine. This has the effect of reducing supply. Sellers of wine will now want to charge £1 extra per bottle sold. In Figure 13.1, this is shown by a vertical shift of £1 in the supply curve at every level of output. However many bottles are produced, sellers will want to charge £1 more per bottle and therefore there is a parallel shift upwards of the whole supply curve from S_1 to S_2.

The old equilibrium price was £3.30, at which price 60 million bottles were bought and sold. The introduction of the £1 tax will raise price and reduce quantity demanded. The new equilibrium price is £4, at which price quantity demanded falls to 40 million bottles.

This result might seem surprising. The imposition of a

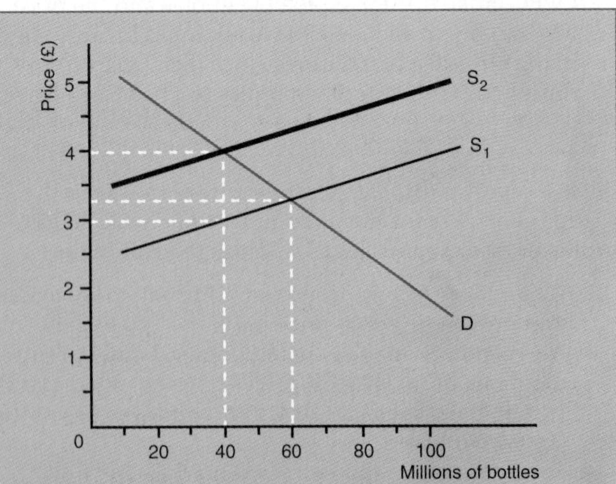

Figure 13.1 *The incidence of a specific tax*
The imposition of an indirect tax of £1 per unit on wine will push up the supply curve from S_1 to S_2. The vertical distance between the two supply curves at any given output is £1. As a consequence equilibrium price will rise from £3.30 to £4. The consumer therefore pays an extra 70p per bottle of wine. The other 30p of the tax is paid by the producer because the price it receives per bottle before tax falls from £3.30 to £3.

£1 per bottle tax has only raised the price of a bottle by 70p and not the full £1 of the tax. This is because the INCIDENCE OF TAX is unlikely to fall totally on consumers. The incidence of tax measures the burden of tax upon the taxpayer. In this case the consumer has paid 70p of the tax. Therefore the other 30p which the government receives must have been paid by producers.

QUESTION 2 In October 1994, a new indirect tax came into operation. It was a 2.5 per cent tax on insurance premiums. A motor insurance policy priced at £100, for instance, would now cost the motorist £102.50. Most insurance companies simply passed on the cost to the consumer in high premiums. Some. though, chose to absorb some or all of the cost themselves. The Prudential and the Pearl, for instance, announced that their premium rates would remain unchanged. The result has been that insurance rates on average rose less than the 2.5 per cent that might have been expected.

Source: adapted from the *Financial Times*, 1.10.1994.

Using a demand and supply diagram, explain why 'insurance rates on average rose less than 2.5 per cent' in October 1994.

Tax revenues

Using Figure 13.1 we can also show the change in total expenditure before and after imposition of the tax as well as the amount of tax revenue gained by the government. The government will receive total tax revenue of £1 x 40 million (the tax per unit x the quantity sold); hence tax revenues will be £40 million. Consumers will pay 70p x 40 million of this, whilst producers will pay 30p x 40 million. Consumers will therefore pay £28 million of tax whilst producers will pay £12 million. Total spending on wine will fall from £198 million (£3.30 x 60 million) to £160 million (£4 x 40 million). Revenues received by producers will fall from £198 million (£3.30 x 60 million) to £120 million (£3 x 40 million).

Ad valorem taxes

The above analysis can be extended to deal with ad valorem taxes. The imposition of an ad valorem tax will lead to an upwards shift in the supply curve. However, the higher the price, the greater will be the amount of the tax. Hence the shift will look as in Figure 13.2. Consumers will pay FG tax per unit whilst the incidence of tax on producers per unit will be HG.

Subsidies

A subsidy on a good will lead to an increase in supply, shifting the supply curve downwards and to the right.

QUESTION 3

Table 13.1

Price (£)	Quantity demanded	Quantity supplied
4	16	4
6	12	6
8	8	8
10	4	10
12	0	12

(a) Draw the demand and supply curves from the data in Table 13.1.
(b) What is the equilibrium quantity demanded and supplied?

The government now imposes Value Added Tax of 50 per cent.

(c) Show the effect of this on the diagram.
(d) What is the new equilibrium quantity demanded and supplied?
(e) What is the new equilibrium price?
(f) What is the incidence of tax per unit on (i) the consumer and (ii) the producer?
(g) What is (i) the tax per unit and (ii) total government revenue from the tax?
(h) By how much will the before tax revenue of producers change?

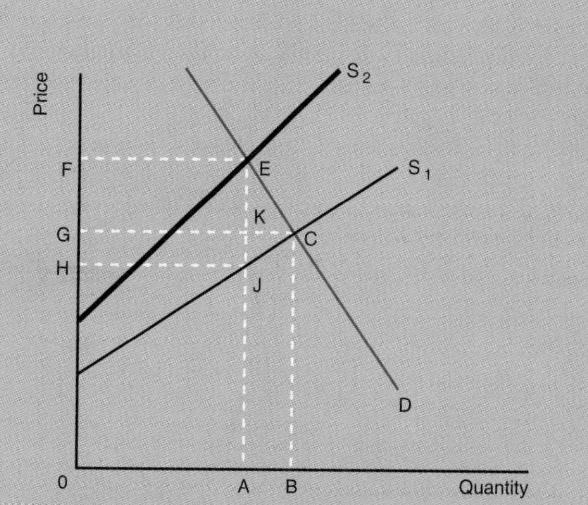

Figure 13.2 *The incidence of an ad valorem tax*
The imposition of an ad valorem tax will push the supply curve upwards from S_1 to S_2. The following gives the key facts about the change:
(a) original equilibrium price and quantity, OG and OB;
(b) new equilibrium price and quantity, OF and OA;
(c) incidence of tax per unit on consumers, GF;
(d) incidence of tax per unit on producers, HG;
(e) tax per unit in equilibrium, HF;
(f) total tax paid by consumers, GKEF;
(g) total tax paid by producers, GHJK;
(h) total tax revenue of government, FHJE;
(i) change in producers' revenue, OBCG - OAJH;
(j) change in consumers' expenditure, OBCG - OAEF.

This is shown in Figure 13.3. It should be noted that a subsidy of AC will not lead to a fall in price of AC. Part of the subsidy, AB, will be appropriated by producers because of the higher unit cost of production of higher levels of output (shown by the upward sloping supply curve). Prices to consumers will only fall by BC.

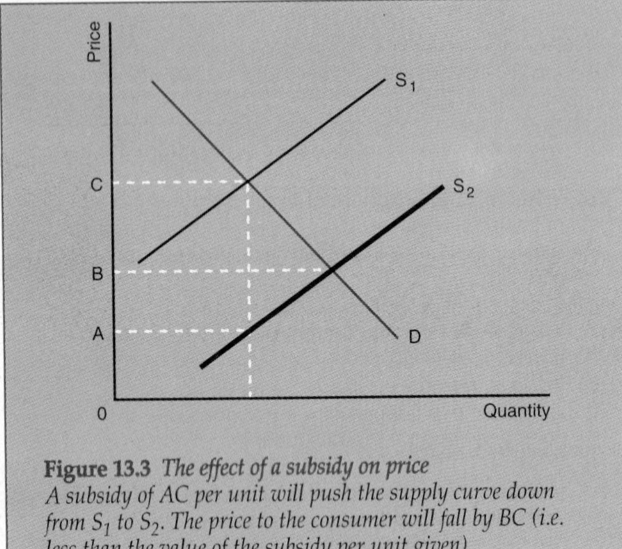

Figure 13.3 *The effect of a subsidy on price*
A subsidy of AC per unit will push the supply curve down from S_1 to S_2. The price to the consumer will fall by BC (i.e. less than the value of the subsidy per unit given).

Taxes and elasticity

The extent to which the tax incidence falls on consumers rather than producers depends upon the elasticities of demand and supply. Figure 13.4 shows a situation where either the supply curve is perfectly elastic or the demand curve is perfectly inelastic. In both cases, the vertical shift in the supply curve, which shows the value of the tax per unit, is identical to the final price rise. Therefore, all of the tax will be paid by consumers.

Figure 13.5, on the other hand, shows two cases where

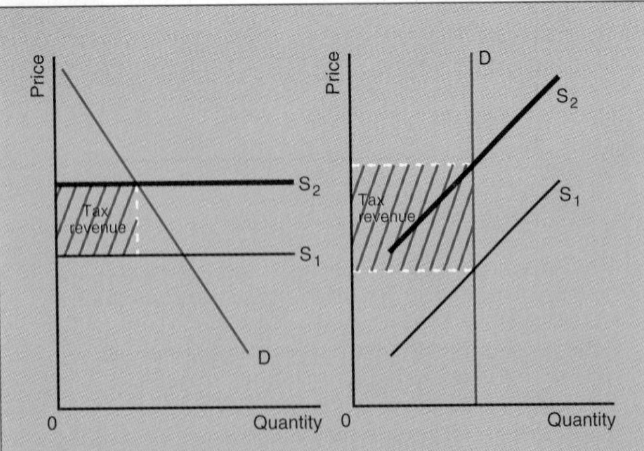

Figure 13.4 *Where the incidence of tax falls wholly on the consumer*
If supply is perfectly elastic or demand perfectly inelastic, then it can be seen from the graphs that the incidence of tax will fall wholly on consumers.

the incidence of tax falls totally on the producer. Producers will find it impossible to shift any of the tax onto consumers if the demand curve is perfectly elastic. Consumers are not prepared to buy at any higher price than the existing price. If the supply curve is perfectly inelastic, then the supply curve after imposition of the tax will be the same as the one before. Equilibrium price will therefore remain the same and producers will have to bear the full burden of the tax.

Generalising from these extreme situations, we can conclude that the more elastic the demand curve or the more inelastic the supply curve, the greater will be the incidence of tax on producers and the less will be the incidence of tax on consumers. So far as the government is concerned, taxation revenue will be greater, all other things being equal, the more inelastic the demand for the

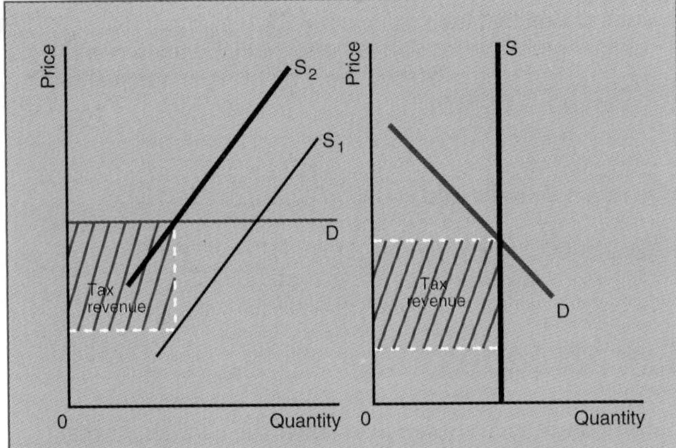

Figure 13.5 *Where the incidence of tax falls wholly on the producer*
If supply is perfectly inelastic or demand perfectly elastic, then it can be seen from the graphs that the incidence of tax will fall wholly on producers.

QUESTION 4

Table 13.2

	Price elasticity of demand
Food	- 0.52
Durables	- 0.89
Fuel and light	- 0.47
Services	- 1.02

Source: John Muellbauer, 'Testing the Barten Model of Household Composition Effects and the Cost of Children', *Economic Journal*, September 1977.

The government wishes to raise VAT on selected goods, all these goods and services being zero-rated at present. Which categories of goods does the data suggest would yield (a) the most and (b) the least revenues? (Assume that at present the average price and the quantity demanded of goods in each category is identical.) Explain your reasoning carefully.

product taxed. For instance, if demand were perfectly elastic, the imposition of an indirect tax would lead to quantity demanded falling to zero and tax revenue being zero. At the opposite extreme, if demand were perfectly inelastic, consumers would buy the same quantity after imposition of the tax as before. Hence revenue will be equal to the tax per unit times the quantity demanded before imposition. If the price elasticity of demand lies between these two extremes, the imposition of a tax will lead to a fall in quantity demanded. The higher the elasticity, the larger will be the fall in quantity demanded and hence the lower will be the tax revenue received by government. Hence, it is no coincidence that in the UK excise duties are placed on alcohol, tobacco and petrol, all of which are relatively price inelastic.

Key terms

Ad valorem tax - tax levied as a percentage of the value of the good.
Specific or unit tax - tax levied on volume.
Subsidy - a grant given which lowers the price of a good, usually designed to encourage production or consumption of a good.
Incidence of tax - the tax burden on the taxpayer.

Applied economics

Taxes on petrol

In its April 1993 Budget, the government committed itself to raising taxes on petrol by 3 per cent per year in real terms for the foreseeable future, a figure which it increased to 5 per cent in its December 1993 Budget. It justified this by pointing out that petrol was cheaper in real terms in 1993 than it was in the early 1980s as can be seen in Figure 13.6. This was because the cost of oil had fallen sharply over the period. More importantly, the government is committed to reducing the level of carbon dioxide emissions by the year 2000 to the level that they were at in 1990. Fuel is a major source of carbon dioxide emissions in the UK. Hence, discouraging fuel use could help the UK achieve its internationally agreed target.

The extent to which the government will achieve its objective depends, in part, upon the price elasticity of demand for petrol. If it is perfectly inelastic, then the shift to the left in the supply curve of 5 per cent per year in real terms will result in a movement up a vertical demand curve. The government will collect 5 per cent more revenue but there will be no change in demand for fuel. If demand is relatively inelastic, as is probably the case, the percentage fall in demand will be less than 5 per cent per year, with most of the increase in tax being paid by the consumer rather than absorbed by the producer.

This does not take into account the likely increase in demand for fuel. As Figure 13.7 shows, the number of kilometres travelled by cars increased by 68 per cent between 1980 and 1989. This stagnated between 1989 and 1993, mostly because of the severe recession at the time. A continuation of zero growth in vehicle mileage would be one way in which the government's environmental target might be met. The other would be if there was a significant increase in the fuel efficiency of car engines. The 5 per cent per annum increase gives a considerable incentive for motorists to buy more fuel-efficient cars.

Raising fuel taxes by 5 per cent per annum also allows the government to achieve two other objectives. First, the revenue from the tax will rise over time in real terms given inelastic demand for petrol. This will enable the government either to reduce its borrowing or cut income tax. Second, reducing the growth of vehicle mileage will freeze congestion on British roads and reduce demands for further roadbuilding, both of which can be seen as environmentally friendly.

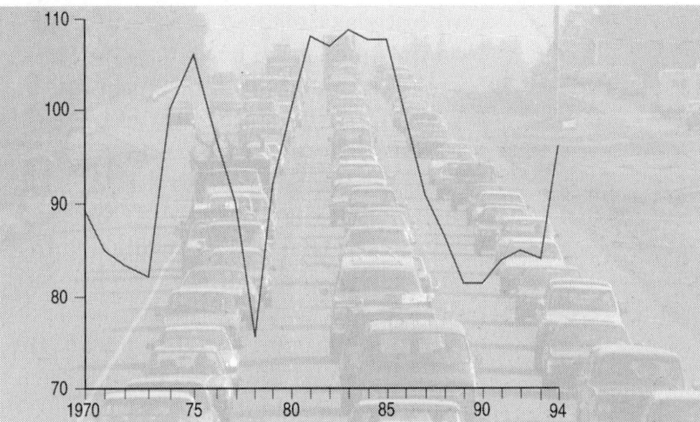

Source: adapted from HMSO, *Transport Statistics.*
Figure 13.6 *Real cost of petrol and oil, UK, 1980 = 100*

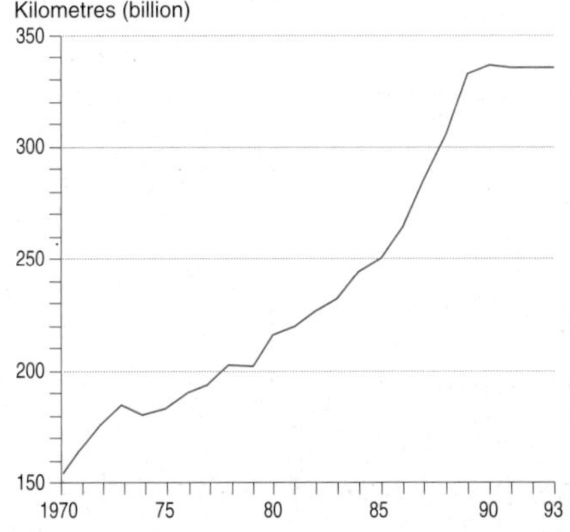

Source: adapted from CSO, *Annual Abstract of Statistics.*
Figure 13.7 *Estimated number of kilometres (billion) travelled by cars and taxis, UK, 1970-1993*

VAT on domestic fuel

VAT imposed on domestic fuel

VAT at 8 per cent has been imposed for the first time on domestic fuels* - gas, electricity, coal and oil - used to heat and light homes. The move has been very controversial. Consumer groups have warned that it will bring hardship to many, with more old people dying of hypothermia. The Chancellor defended his decision, saying that it would encourage consumers to use fuel more efficiently and thus contribute towards environmental targets the government has set.

* In April 1994

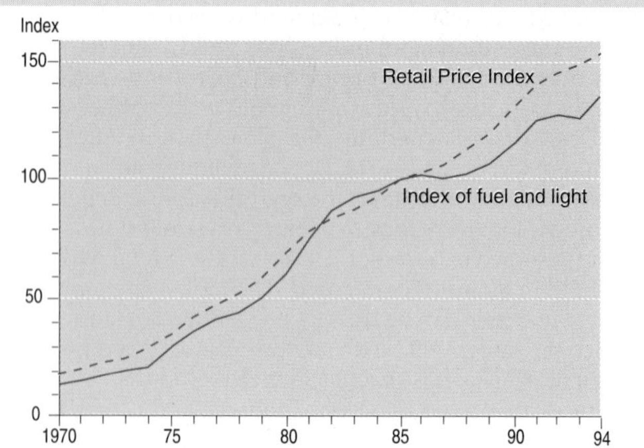

Source: adapted from Department of Employment, *Employment Gazette.*

Figure 13.8 *Index of fuel and light, and the Retail Price Index, 1985 = 100*

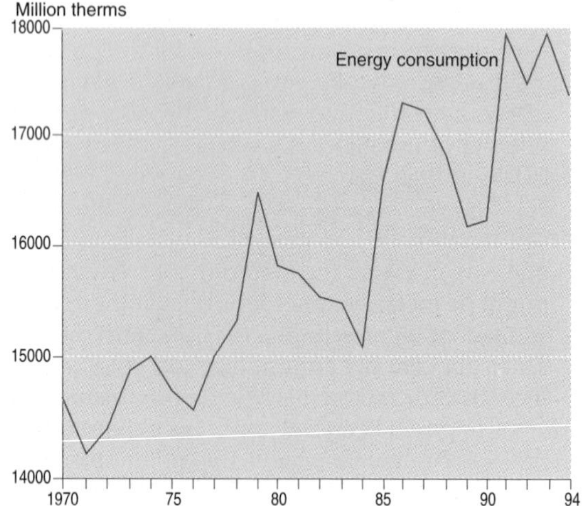

Source: adapted from CSO, *Annual Abstract of Statistics.*

Figure 13.9 *Energy consumption of households*

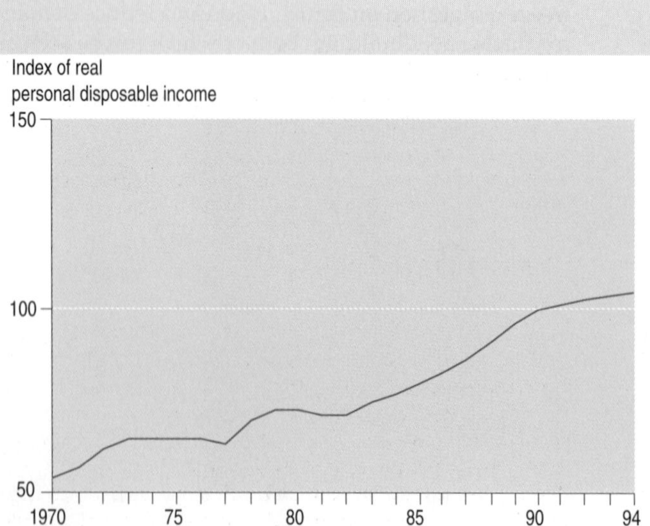

Source: adapted from CSO, *Annual Abstract of Statistics.*

Figure 13.10 *Personal disposable income, 1970-1994; 1990 = 100*

You work as an economist for a consumer organisation. You have been asked to write a report assessing the likely impact of the imposition of VAT on domestic fuel. In your report:

1. **Outline trends in prices, incomes and consumption of domestic fuels from the data given above.**
2. **Using diagrams, explain what economic theory would predict would happen to consumption as price and income change. Discuss whether the data over the period 1987-93 support the economic theory.**
3. **Again using a diagram, explain what economic theory would predict would happen in the domestic fuel market following the imposition of 8 per cent VAT. Analyse who is likely to bear the burden of the tax and suggest what is likely to happen to overall consumption of domestic fuels, all other things being equal.**
4. **In its November 1994 Budget, the government had hoped to increase the rate of VAT on domestic fuel to 17.5 per cent but was defeated in this attempt by a group of rebel back-benchers. Instead, it raised the same amount of tax by increasing excise duties on tobacco, alcoholic drink and petrol. Would it have been better for consumers if the original VAT increase on domestic fuel had gone ahead? In your answer, consider: (a) who might pay either set of taxes; (b) the environmental and social impact of the alternatives; (c) the effect on businesses and their workers supplying goods in different markets; (d) any other points which you consider important.**

INVESTIGATIONS 1

A. Price fluctuations

Aims

- To compare the causes of price fluctuations in two commodity markets, one which is a free market, the other where either a cartel or a buffer stock scheme influence price.
- To evaluate the extent to which a cartel or buffer stock scheme may reduce price fluctuations.
- To judge whether the introduction of a cartel or buffer stock scheme would stabilise prices in a previously free market.
- To predict whether the abandonment of a price-fixing arrangement would lead to greater price instability.

Research activity

Choose two goods. Both should be internationally traded commodities such as tin, wheat, coffee or rubber. One should be traded in a free market (such as copper or zinc), the other in a market in which there is one or several cartels or buffer stock schemes which regulate prices (such as oil or wheat).

Find out as much as you can about demand and supply conditions in the markets you have decided to investigate. For instance, which countries are the main producers and consumers? Are there any firms of significant size which either buy or sell in the market? Where are the main markets for buying and selling of the commodity? Do prices fluctuate freely or are prices fixed? Do cartels or buffer stock schemes operate in the market? If so, how? What are the aims of the cartel or buffer stock scheme? What has been its recent history?

Follow the price movements of the two commodities over a period of time. This could be a historical analysis, for instance investigating broad price movements over the past ten years, or investigating detailed price movements over the previous twelve months. Alternatively it could be an ongoing investigation, recording and analysing price movements for a three month period. Record how prices change. Note any factors which might cause either demand for or supply of the commodity to change.

Sources

The *Financial Times* publishes an excellent section on commodity prices every day. There are regular reviews of commodity markets as well. The dates of recent articles can be found using the index to the newspaper published by the *Financial Times*. Other quality newspapers, such as the *Independent*, also have the occasional article, as do quality magazines such as the *Economist*. *The Guardian* and *The Times* both publish indexes too. Alternatively, the *Research Index*, published by Business Surveys Ltd. may be available in the reference library which you intend to use. It covers articles of financial interest in 100 newspapers and periodicals on a monthly basis. The library may also construct its own indexes.

The Central Statistical Office publish statistics relating to agricultural prices in the UK. *The Annual Abstract of Statistics* gives annual prices for selected commodities over a ten year period whilst the *Annual Review of Agriculture* (White Paper) gives prices over the previous 4 years. Monthly figures for the previous twelve months are given in *Agricultural Statistics, England and Wales*. *Agricultural Market Report*, a weekly publication, gives prices and quantities bought and sold for grains such as wheat for the previous week. For the latest details of sources, consult the *Guide to Official Statistics*.

The EU *Index of Producer Prices of Agricultural Products*, a Eurostat publication, gives agricultural prices across the EU. UNCTAD, the UN and the World Development Bank also publish commodity prices in a number of their publications.

Structuring your report

Introduction Outline the aim of your investigation. The aim should be put in the form of a hypothesis or question which will allow you to come to some conclusions.
Techniques used to collect your data Outline how you collected your data.
Economic theory Outline briefly a theory of price determination in a free market and in one covered by a cartel or buffer stock scheme (whichever applies to the market you have chosen). Suggest the most likely factors which economic theory might suggest would influence either demand for or supply of the product.
Market background Describe the characteristics of the two markets which you have investigated taking into account those factors described above.
Analysis of price movements Describe the price movements which you have observed over time. To what extent have prices in the market covered by a cartel or buffer stock arrangement fluctuated less than those in the free market? Using the concepts of demand and supply, put forward possible reasons why prices have changed in the two markets. Compare the importance of different factors which influence price between the two markets, and in particular analyse the reasons why the cartel or buffer stock scheme has succeeded or failed in providing greater price stability than in the free market.
Evaluation of alternatives Suggest what would happen to prices if the cartel or buffer stock scheme were abandoned and the market became a free market. Would it be possible for producers in the free market to form a cartel or organise a buffer stock scheme? Would the price-fixing arrangement be durable? What effect might it have on prices in your opinion?
Sources Outline the sources of information you used. What problems did you encounter in gathering relevant data? What data would you have liked to have obtained but could not? To what extent was the data reliable?
Bibliography Write down a list of your sources in alphabetical order.

When presenting your report, use appropriate diagrams whenever possible. For instance, you could use charts showing price movements over time, or demand and supply diagrams showing shifts in the demand and supply curves which cause changes in price.

Other suggestions

Instead of investigating two commodities, investigate a range of commodities. For instance, agricultural commodities within the EC could be chosen to analyse the effects of the Common Agricultural Policy.

Primary research could be undertaken by recording the price of fresh foods such as tomatoes or potatoes in the shops over a period of time. It would then be important to distinguish the extent to which price movements are the result of changes in commodity prices and which are the result of price changes by retailers and wholesalers. More difficult would be to attempt to calculate elasticities of demand and supply for commodities. Not only would you need to collect data over a period of time relating to price, quantities bought and sold, incomes, etc., but you would also need to assume when making one calculation (e.g. price elasticity of demand) that all other factors remained constant. Since this will not be so in the real world, your estimates of elasticity will only be approximations at best.

Investigate house prices in your area. Remember that houses are non-homogeneous (i.e. no two houses are likely to be the same). Therefore, when explaining how house prices change over time, it is important to compare the prices of similar houses. The Halifax Building Society publishes regularly a house price index giving changes in house prices by region.

B. School or college - provision of a service

Aims

- To investigate the nature of resource allocation within an educational establishment.
- To evaluate whether resources could be used more effectively to provide educational services.

Research activity

All economic systems, such as a school or college, have to resolve three basic questions.

What? Identify the range of educational services which your school or college provides. For instance, what courses are offered to what age of client? What, if any, qualifications are available on each course? What else, apart from qualifications, could be seen to be the outcome of attendance at school or college (for example the development of personal skills such as politeness, ability to work in a group, initiative and confidence)? What recreational services are offered to students (e.g. swimming or squash)? What other services, such as meals or shopping facilities, are offered by the school or college? How could the services offered be improved?

How? How is production organised and what factors of production are used? Find out what division of labour there is within the organisation. Having established a broad outline, select certain areas of the school or college to investigate in detail. For instance, how are GCSE courses organised, what is the structure of the social science faculty, or how are meals organised? Why is production organised in this way rather than another? Which services are sold in a market and which are supplied free at the point of sale (within a **command** structure ☞ unit 110). Who pays for services provided free at the point of consumption? How is payment organised? How could the production of services in the school or college be better organised?

For whom? Who receives the services that the school or college provides? There is some controversy over this. For instance, is it individual students, their parents, government, or employers and industry? Would there be any benefits if production of services were switched to suit the needs of one group more than another?

Sources

The school or college is likely to produce a variety of documents which will give some of the information you need to collect. For instance, it may produce a brochure which it sends to prospective students or their parents. By law, schools have to produce an Annual Report giving such information as levels of staffing. There will also be a large number of confidential documents which you **may** be able to obtain, such as organisation of teaching by faculty, the staff handbook and financial budgets.

You will need to interview a number of staff. This is likely to include your economics teachers or lecturers, as well as more senior members of staff such as a deputy head or vice principal. Interview some non-teaching staff as well, such as caretaking staff or kitchen staff. You may also wish to interview an industrialist and a parent to seek their views on what ought to be produced by the school or college. Interviewing a governor may also give valuable information. A questionnaire drawn up before hand is likely to be useful in these interviews. Think what questions you wish to ask, and what form of question is more likely to give you the information you need. Alternatively, you could get an individual to fill in a questionnaire instead of interviewing them. Note though that many people don't bother to fill in questionnaires even if they say they will.

Newspaper articles, from national newspapers such as *The Guardian* and specialist newspapers such as the *Times Educational Supplement*, may give useful background material on a wide range of issues arising from the assignment.

Structuring your report

Introduction Outline the aim of your investigation. The aim should be put in the form of a hypothesis or question which will allow you to come to some conclusions.

Economic theory Outline the economic concepts such as scarcity, resource allocation and the division of labour which you will use in your report for the purpose of analysis.

Techniques used to collect your data Outline how you collected your data.

What is produced Present your findings on what services are produced by the school or college.

How it is produced Analyse how production takes place. What factors of production are used and what contribution do they make to the production process?

For whom production takes place Discuss who are the recipients of the education service and how they benefit.

How resource allocation could be changed Evaluate how resource allocation could be altered, either to provide the same services but at lower cost, or provide improved services. You must outline how you would judge whether there had been an improvement in services.

Sources Explain how you collected your data for the report. What problems did you encounter in obtaining relevant data? How reliable was the evidence gathered. In particular, how reliable was the evidence from interviews and questionnaires? What data would you have liked to obtain but were unable to?

Bibliography Write down a list of your sources in alphabetical order.

Use appropriate diagrams and graphs throughout. For instance, you may want to use diagrams showing the hierarchy within the organisation. Or you may want to show spending on a block graph.

Other suggestions

Instead of studying an educational establishment, it would be possible to study one of the following. The aim would remain to find out what, how and for whom production takes place and how, if at all, the allocation of resources could be improved: a small local firm such as a hairdressers; a local hospital; a youth club, or society; an aspect of local authority service provision such as a swimming baths or sports centre; a local cinema.

Marginal utility theory

Summary

1. A consumer gains utility when he or she consumes a good.
2. The law of diminishing marginal utility states that marginal utility will decline as consumption of a good increases.
3. The consumer is in equilibrium when the marginal utility per £ spent is the same for all goods.
4. The paradox of value is explained by the fact that consumers base their spending decisions not on total utility gained but on marginal utility.
5. Consumer surplus is the difference between the total utility (measured by the maximum amount that a consumer would be prepared to pay for a number of units of a good) and the actual amount paid.

Total and marginal utility

UTILITY is the satisfaction derived from consuming a good. That good could be anything from a pint of beer, to a night out at the cinema or a donation to charity. Consumption may also yield negative utility - **disutility** as it is sometimes called. A spell in prison or a pint of beer which makes you sick would yield disutility.

The TOTAL UTILITY of consuming a good is the utility derived from consuming a given quantity of the good. So we can talk about the total utility of consuming 5 pints of beer, 2 holidays or 6 records. MARGINAL UTILITY is the utility gained from consuming an **extra** unit of the good. So we can talk about the marginal utility of consuming the fifth pint of beer, or the second holiday or the sixth CD.

Table 14.1 shows an example of utility gained from consuming beer by an individual. Utility is measured in terms of units of utility (or UUs). As can be seen, the greater the consumption of beer, the greater the total utility. However, total utility peaks when 5 pints are consumed and actually falls when 6 pints are consumed. This is because the marginal utility at this level (the utility gained by consuming the extra sixth unit which makes you feel sick) is negative.

Table 14.1 *Total and marginal utility*

Pints of beer consumed	Total utility (in UUs)	Marginal utility (in UUs)
1	10	10
2	19	9
3	27	8
4	34	7
5	37	3
6	35	-2

Total utility can be derived from marginal utility and vice versa. Marginal utility is the utility gained from consuming one extra unit of a good and is found by measuring the difference between two levels of total utility. The marginal utility of the fifth pint of beer is the difference in the total utility gained from consuming 5 pints and that gained by consuming 4 pints. The marginal utility gained from consuming the second pint is the difference between the total utility gained by 2 pints and the total utility gained by 1 pint. Conversely total utility is the sum of marginal utilities. The total utility gained by consuming 4 pints is the sum of the marginal utility of the first pint, added to the second pint, added to the third pint, added to the fourth pint.

The law of diminishing marginal utility

Economists argue that marginal utility declines as consumption of a good increases. Each unit consumed gives less and less additional utility (although total utility will continue to rise until the marginal unit gives disutility). For instance, it is likely that a second car gives less utility than a first car to a two car family. Equally, consumption of the fifth packet of crisps of the day is likely to yield less utility than consumption of the first. This proposition, known as the **law of diminishing marginal utility**, can be illustrated diagrammatically in Figure 14.1. As consumption rises between O and A, total utility rises but marginal utility per unit falls. If consumption is pushed beyond OA, marginal utility is negative and total utility falls.

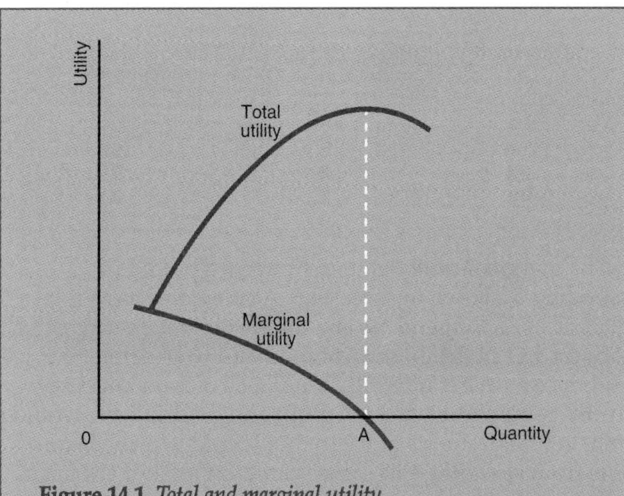

Figure 14.1 *Total and marginal utility*
Marginal utility falls as consumption increases because of the law of diminishing marginal utility. Total utility is at a maximum when marginal utility is zero.

QUESTION 1

Table 14.2

Number of cars	Total utility		
	Family A	Family B	Family C
1	100	150	200
2	180	280	320
3	230	350	330
4	240	370	300

Table 14.2 shows the total utility gained by three families from the ownership of cars.

(a) Calculate the marginal utility gained from each car by each family.
(b) What is the maximum marginal utility which family A could gain from the ownership of a fifth car assuming that the law of diminishing marginal utility applies?
(c) Comment on the value to Family C of owning a fourth car.

Consumer equilibrium

The law of diminishing marginal utility can be used to explain how a consumer will allocate resources. Three assumptions will be made.

- Consumers seek to maximise their total utility (i.e. consumers will allocate their resources in such a way as to maximise the satisfaction derived from it).
- Their resources are defined as the goods and services that could be bought with their income. They have other resources available to them, such as their time, but these will be ignored.
- Food and drink are the only two goods available for purchase.

Table 14.3

Expenditure £	Utility gained from £1 of income spent on Food	Drink
1st	10	20
2nd	6	10
3rd	3	6
4th	1	2

The marginal utility gained from each pound of spending is shown in Table 14.3. A consumer has a total income of £5 to spend. So she could spend it on, say, £4 of food and £1 of drink, or £2 of food and £3 of drink. She will maximise her utility by buying £2 of food and £3 of drink. For if she spent a fourth pound on drink she would only get 2 extra units of utility but would lose the 6 she gets from spending this same pound on food. If she spent a third pound on food, she would get 3 extra units of utility but would lose the 6 units of utility gained from consuming the third pound of drink.

Generalising this argument, a consumer will maximise total utility when the marginal utility per £1 spent is equal for all goods. If the marginal utility per £1 spent were higher on good X than on good Y, the consumer could increase utility by buying more X and less Y. As more X is bought, the marginal utility will fall whilst the marginal utility of good Y will rise as less is bought. When the two are equal per £1 spent, the consumer will not be able to increase utility by switching from one good to another.

Mathematically this is expressed as:

$$\frac{\text{marginal utility of good X}}{\text{price of good X}} = \frac{\text{marginal utility of good Y}}{\text{price of good Y}}$$

Dividing the marginal utility by the price gives the marginal utility per £ or pence or per whatever unit of money in which the price is denominated. In Table 14.3, the consumer will maximise total utility where the marginal utility of the last pound spent is 6.

Deriving the demand curve

Demand theory states that an increase in the price of a good will lead to a reduction in demand. Marginal utility theory can be used to prove this. Assume that the price of good X increases. The value of the marginal utility of good X ÷ the price of good X will now fall because the figure on the bottom of the fraction (the price) has increased. The marginal utility of good X per £1 spent will now be less than on other goods. The consumer can therefore increase total utility by spending less on good X (which will

QUESTION 2

Table 14.4

Numberof cassette tapes purchased	Total utility	Number of jackets purchased	Total utility
0	0	0	0
1	50	1	150
2	90	2	230
3	120	3	300
4	140	4	360
5	150	5	410
6	150	6	410

Table 14.4 shows the total utility gained from consumption of tapes and jackets. Assuming she spends all her income, what combination of tapes and jackets will a utility-maximising consumer buy if:

(a) the price of a tape is £5, the price of a jacket is £20 and her income is £60;
(b) the price of a tape is £10, the price of a jacket is £20 and her income is £110;
(c) the price of a tape is £15, the price of a jacket is £30 and her income is £90?

increase the value of the marginal utility of good X per £1 spent) and spending more on other goods (reducing the value of their marginal utility per £1 spent). In other words, as the price of X rises, the consumer only maximises total utility by buying less of good X. The demand curve for a good is therefore downward sloping.

The paradox of value

We are now in a position to understand one of the problems which perplexed economists for a long time. Adam Smith, for instance, was puzzled as to why consumers paid high prices for goods such as diamonds, which were unnecessary to human existence, whilst the price of necessities such as water was very low. These economists failed to make the distinction between total and marginal utility.

Consumer decisions are made at the margin. The total utility from consuming water will be very high compared to diamonds. But water and diamonds will be consumed to the point where their marginal utilities per pound spent are equal. An ordinary person may consume thousands of gallons of water per year but only buy a diamond once every 20 years. So it is not surprising that the marginal utility of that one diamond is relatively high compared to the marginal utility of, say, the sixty thousandth gallon of water consumed, and that today's consumers are therefore prepared to pay a much higher price for an extra diamond than for an extra gallon of water.

Consumer surplus

CONSUMER SURPLUS is generated when a consumer pays less for a good than he or she would be prepared to pay for it. Consider the demand curve shown in Figure 14.2. A consumer buys 3 cassette tapes at a price of £6 each. The demand curve shows that she would have been prepared to pay £10 for the first tape purchased. This means that she values the marginal utility of the first tape at £10. Therefore she has gained £4 of utility free on her first purchase. This is part of her consumer surplus. On the second tape, she valued the tape at £8 but only paid £6 for it. Her consumer surplus on this was therefore £2. On the third tape she paid exactly the price at which she valued the tape. There was no consumer surplus on the third tape. Her total consumer surplus is therefore £4 + £2 or £6.

Consumer surplus is the shaded area under the demand curve above the horizontal price line of £6. It is the difference between the total expenditure on the good (price x quantity) and the value of the total utility that the consumer placed on purchase of the good.

If tapes were banned from sale, how much would the consumer need to be compensated if her utility were to remain the same? She values the 3 tapes she buys at £24 (£10 + £8 + £6). If she could no longer buy tapes, she would have £18 (£6 x 3) available to spend on other goods. However, she would need to be compensated by an extra £6 (£24 - £18), the consumer surplus on her purchases, if she is not to lose utility as a result of the ban.

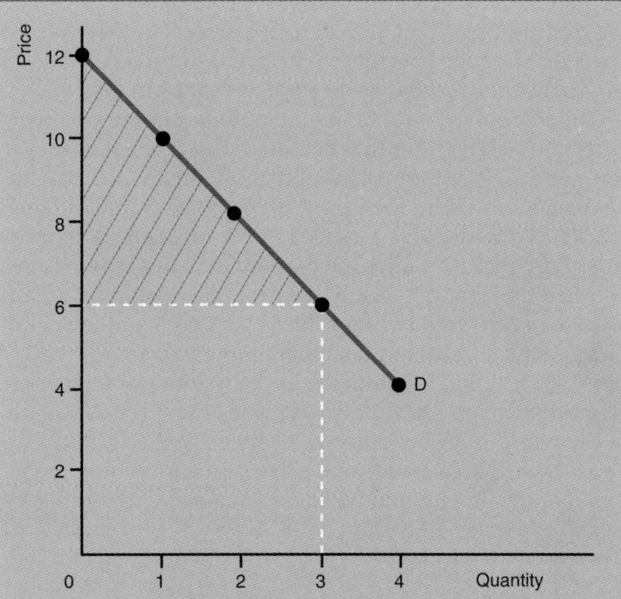

Figure 14.2 *Consumer surplus*
The demand curve shows the price that the consumer would be prepared to pay for each unit. Except on the marginal unit purchased, the price that the consumer is prepared to pay is above the market price that is paid. The difference between these two values is the consumer surplus. It is represented by the shaded area under the demand curve.

QUESTION 3 A demand curve is given by the equation:

$$Q_D = 100 - 0.5P$$

where Q_D is quantity demanded and P is price.

(a) Draw the demand curve for prices between 0 and £200.
(b) Shade the area of consumer surplus at a price of £60.
(c) Is consumer surplus larger or smaller at a price of £40 compared to £60? Explain your answer.
(d) Demand changes such that the constant in the equation increases by 50. Using a diagram, show how consumer surplus will change.

Key terms

Utility - the satisfaction derived from consuming a good.
Total utility - the utility derived from consuming a given quantity of the good.
Marginal utility - the utility gained from consuming an extra good.
Consumer surplus - the difference between what consumers are prepared to pay for a good and what they actually pay.

Applied economics

The economics of altruism

The process of giving, asserts Dr. Barry Bracewell-Milnes in a recent pamphlet* for the Institute for Economic Affairs, 'at least doubles the value of the gift'. This is a rather startling claim. Suppose, out of the goodness of my heart, I give you a crisp £5 note. You are £5 better off; I am £5 worse off. Wealth has been redistributed, but surely not created. After all, there is still only one £5 note.

Dr. Bracewell-Milnes says this accurately describes what happens when money is redistributed through the tax system. In effect, assets are seized and allocated to other individuals. But voluntary giving, he claims, is something else. If I am rational, I will donate a gift only if its value to me in the hands of the recipient exceeds its value to me in my own hands. In other words, I will give you £5 only if the monetary value of the psychic satisfaction I derive exceeds £5.

After my act of giving, you possess a physical act worth £5. I possess psychic satisfaction or 'utility' worth more than £5. Hence wealth has been more than doubled. This form of wealth creation, moreover, is both environmentally clean and virtually costless. It is also, the author claims, of considerable economic significance. The annual sum passing by gift and bequest is of the order of £50bn; the wealth created by these transfers therefore exceeds £50bn, possibly by a large margin.

Tax relief for charitable giving is usually justified either on the grounds that charities perform socially useful functions or that they supply services which would otherwise have to be provided by the public sector at taxpayers' expense. The wealth-creating potential of giving, suggests Dr. Bracewell-Milnes, provides a further powerful justification for tax relief. Governments have long accepted the maximisation of incomes (or living standards) as a goal of public policy: why not also encourage personal wealth creation through giving?

In fact, he goes further and argues that if tax rates are low, tax relief should be allowed at a rate in excess of an individual's marginal tax rate.

There is an ingenious reason for this: the extra relief can turn virtuous thoughts into actual deeds. If I do not give £5 to Save the Children it is because the value of the £5 in my hands is greater than its value to me in the hands of the charity. But if I am well disposed to Save the Children, the difference may be quite small. The value to me of £5 in their hands might be, say, £4.90. If tax relief in excess of my marginal rate reduced the cost to me of the gift below £4.90, ineffective altruism would become effective and I would make the donation. Benign thoughts would be translated into possible action: and a little tax relief would have triggered the creation of a much larger amount of psychic wealth.

At this stage, readers may be wondering whether Dr. Bracewell-Milnes is either demented or perpetrating an elaborate hoax. He admits that the wealth created by giving exists only in the minds of givers. How can he expect us to pay attention to anything so nebulous? But wait a moment. The only reason we consume or possess anything is because it 'makes us feel good'. In the last analysis, the utility we derive from consumption or ownership is every bit as cerebral as that from giving.

The problem lies not in the intangibility of the wealth created by giving, but in whether giving actually makes us feel good. The author assumes that all human actions can be explained within the utility-maximising framework of market economics. He assumes that I donate £5 only if this use of my money makes me happier than any alternative use. But this is surely rarely the case. We often give out of a sense of duty, not because this is how we want to spend our money: charities appeal to an aspect of our personalities that is irrelevant to the workings of a market economy. This is sad because it means there is less wealth in the world than Dr. Bracewell-Milnes suspects, but encouraging because it implies we care about more than merely our own happiness.

*The Wealth of Giving. 2 Lord North Street. London SW1.

Source: the *Financial Times*, 16.1.90.

Water meter trials

In April 1989, 11 areas of the UK became subject to an economic experiment. By the year 2000, the privatised water boards will have to find a way of charging households for water which is not based on the rating system. Under the rating system, a tax system last used by local authorities in 1989 in England and Wales, households are charged a fixed amount per year, however much water they consume. In 1989, the water boards favoured moving away from a fixed fee system to one where water bills were directly related to water consumed.

As a step towards this change, 11 areas were chosen to take part in the National Water Metering Trials. The largest area was the whole of the Isle of Wight, covering 53 000 households. There were about 1 000 households in each of the other 10 areas. All houses in these areas were fitted with a water meter and water consumption was closely monitored.

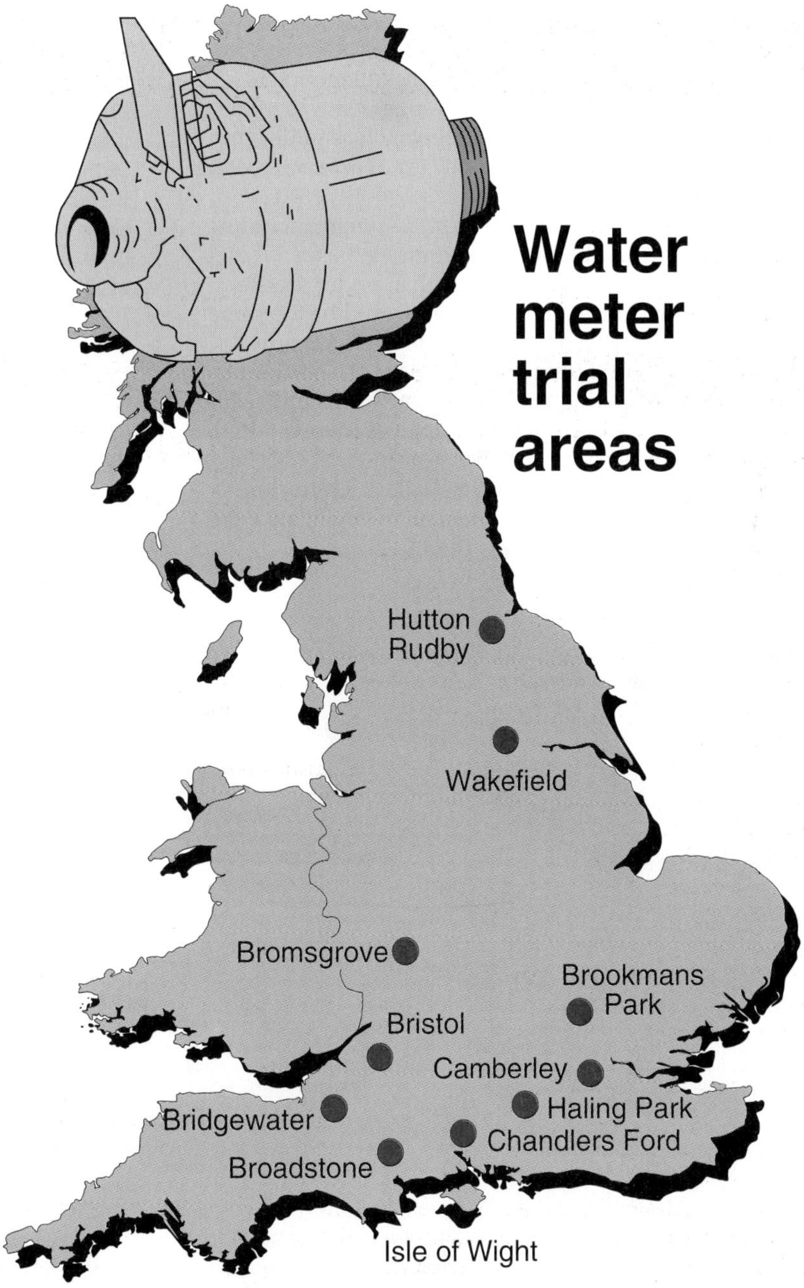

Figure 14.3 *Water meter trial areas*

Tariff structures

Five different tariff structures were tested.

- A flat rate tariff - each unit of water cost the same regardless of the amount consumed.
- A rising block tariff - the more water consumed, the higher the tariff per unit. This was intended to discourage consumption and was of interest to water boards in areas such as the South East and the South West which had difficulty meeting demand in times of drought.
- A declining block tariff - the more water consumed, the lower the tariff per unit. This was predicted to encourage consumption and was of interest to Northumbrian Water which had excess supplies of water.
- A seasonal tariff - charges were set at a lower level in winter when water was plentiful and a higher level in summer when water was scarcer. Again, this would be of interest to water boards facing scarcity problems in summer.
- Peak demand tariff - tariffs were higher in the morning and afternoon when demand was high than in the evening when demand was lower.

The cost of installing and operating meters and meter based systems

The water boards found the cost of installing meters higher than they expected. The average cost was £165 per household for an internal meter (such as under the stairs or in a garage). The average cost of external meters was £200.

The cost of operating a meter based system, including reading meters and billings, was found to be on average £19.08 more per property per year than under a system using rateable values. The extra cost would be the same compared to any system which made a fixed charge irrespective of the amount of water used. These figures should be compared with average yearly bills under the rateable value system. For the companies involved in the trials these ranged from £145 per year in Northumberland to £289 in Three Valleys. Of the ten companies taking part in the trials on the mainland, six had average yearly bills of less than £235.

Water saving

Metering allows the water companies to identify much more clearly where leaks are occurring in pipes outside houses in the water carrying system. In the Isle of Wight, where effective monitoring took place because of the size of the trial, it was found that savings in the amount of water put into the system from fixing leaking pipes was nearly as much as the drop in consumption by households over the period of the trial. Over one quarter of all water put into the supply on the Isle of Wight in 1988-89 was being lost. There was a 44 per cent saving in this amount over the three years of the trial, saving 4.16 million litres per day. Consumption by households, in comparison, fell 27 per cent, saving 5.61 million litres per day. Overall, given a 0.28 million litre per day increase in demand by businesses, the amount of water put into the supply fell 22 per cent, a reduction of 9.49 million litres per day.

Source: The National Metering Trials Working Group, *Water Metering Trials Final Report* (1993).

Table 14.5 *Average household consumption in the year before the trials and during the three years of the trials*

Litres/property/day

	Flat rate				Declining	Rising		Seasonal		Peak rate	
	Bristol	Mid Southern	Three Valleys (Chorley Wood)	Wessex (Turlin Moor)	Northumbrian	Thames	York-shire	East Worcs	Southern	Three Valleys (Brookmans Park)	Wessex (Broadstone)
Before	261	444	455	365	372	387	289	385	500	434	472
Year 1	245	458	422	333	342	365	277	341	468	406	399
Year 2	236	419	417	346	337	373	279	357	454	404	423
Year 3	231	395	398	342	347	356	247	337	425	410	440

After the ending of the trials, the government has received representations from the water companies to keep the present rateable value system of payment for an indefinite time. As an economist working for the government write a report arguing the advantages and disadvantages of this. In your report:

1. **explain, using utility theory, what happened to the demand for water when metering was imposed during the National Water Trials;**
2. **discuss, using demand analysis, what you would have expected to happen to water consumption under different types of tariffs. Analyse the extent to which your predictions are born out by the evidence from the trials;**
3. **analyse the possible advantages of a metering system compared to a lump sum annual payment for water;**
4. **analyse the possible disadvantages of a metering system;**
5. **briefly summarise whether you think the water boards should impose metering on households.**

unit 15

Indifference theory

Summary

1. A consumer will maximise utility when he or she consumes at the point where the budget line is tangential to his or her highest indifference curve.
2. An increase in price results in a rotation of the budget line. As a consequence, there is a fall in consumption shown on the indifference curve map. This can be used to explain why the demand curve slopes downward from left to right.
3. Indifference curve analysis can be used to distinguish between the income and substitution effects of a price change.

Indifference curves

One of the fundamental assumptions of economics is that consumers have unlimited wants (☞ unit 1). They would always prefer to consume more rather than less. A consumer would prefer to have 4 pairs of jeans and 6 jumpers rather than 2 pairs of jeans and 3 jumpers, for instance. However, what if the consumer were offered either 2 pairs of jeans and 3 jumpers **or** 3 pairs of jeans and 2 jumpers? It is not immediately obvious which she would prefer. Indeed, she might be **indifferent** between the two bundles of goods. She doesn't mind which she has.

An INDIFFERENCE CURVE is a line which links bundles or combinations of goods between which a consumer is indifferent. In Figure 15.1, the consumer is indifferent between the following bundles of goods - 8 ties and 1 shirt, 6 ties and 2 shirts, 4 ties and 4 shirts, and 2 ties and 7 shirts.

The consumer would prefer to have more goods rather than less goods. Hence he would prefer to be to the right of the existing indifference curve. In Figure 15.1, he would prefer to have 8 ties and 2 shirts at B to 8 ties and 1 shirt at A. Similarly, he would prefer to have 6 ties and 4 shirts at D to 4 ties and 4 shirts at C. Indeed, if he prefers B to A, and is indifferent between A and C, he must logically prefer B to C. He must prefer to consume 8 ties and 2 shirts to 4 ties and 4 shirts.

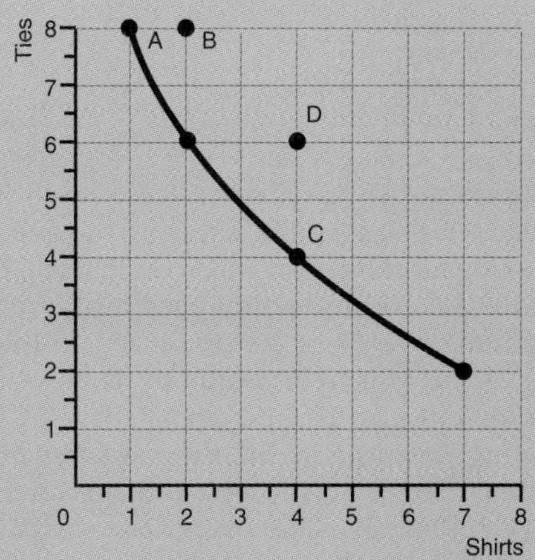

Figure 15.1 *Indifference curves*
The indifference curve shows the combination of ties and shirts between which the consumer is indifferent.

Similarly, if he consumed any combination of goods to the left of the indifference curve, he would be worse off than if he consumed on the indifference curve shown.

Note that an indifference curve is drawn on the assumption that a consumer can rank alternative combinations or bundles of goods in order of preference, stating which give the highest utility, which the second highest and so on (although he does not need to place a value on utility as he must in marginal utility theory ☞ unit 14).

QUESTION 1 A student is indifferent between the following combinations of chocolate bars and packets of crisps - 1 chocolate bar and 14 packets of crisps, 2 chocolate bars and 6 packets of crisps, and 5 chocolate bars and 1 packet of crisps.

(a) Draw her indifference curve for these combinations putting chocolate bars on the vertical axis and crisps on the horizontal axis..

(b) Explain whether she would prefer to consume:
- (i) 14 packets of crisps and 3 chocolate bars rather than any of the combinations on her indifference curve;
- (ii) 3 chocolate bars and 4 packets of crisps, or 1 chocolate bar and 8 packets of crisps.
- (iii) 4 chocolate bars and 3 packets of crisps, or 2 chocolate bars and 5 packets of crisps;
- (iv) 2 chocolate bars and 4 packets of crisps or 1 chocolate bar and 20 packets of crisps.

The marginal rate of substitution

Indifference curves slope downward (i.e. they have a negative slope). If the indifference curve were upward sloping it would indicate that the consumer was indifferent between more and fewer goods.

They are also drawn convex to the origin. This is because of the hypothesis of the diminishing marginal rate of substitution. The MARGINAL RATE OF SUBSTITUTION is the amount a consumer has to give up of a good to get one unit of another good and leave the level of utility or satisfaction unchanged. For instance, between points B and C in Figure 15.2, the consumer has to give up 3 lipsticks to gain 2 ribbons if utility is to remain unchanged. Therefore the marginal rate of substitution is 3/2.

The hypothesis of the diminishing marginal rate of

substitution states that the more is consumed of a good, the larger the quantities needed to compensate for the loss of consumption of another good to hold utility constant. In Figure 15.2, the consumer with a large number of lipsticks is prepared to give up a relatively large number of them to gain one ribbon. But if she has few lipsticks and a large number of ribbons she will want a large number of ribbons to compensate her for the loss of just one lipstick. Hence the marginal rate of substitution of lipsticks for ribbons falls as consumption of lipsticks falls and this is what produces the convex shape of the indifference curve.

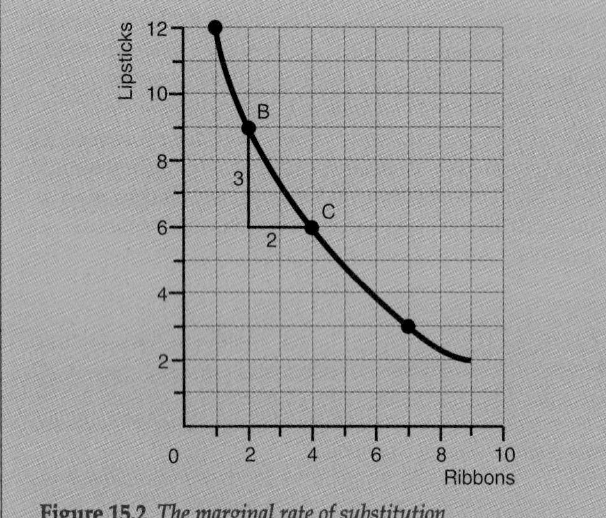

Figure 15.2 *The marginal rate of substitution*
The marginal rate of substitution is given by the slope of the line - the number of lipsticks which have to be given up to gain more ribbons to give the same level of utility.

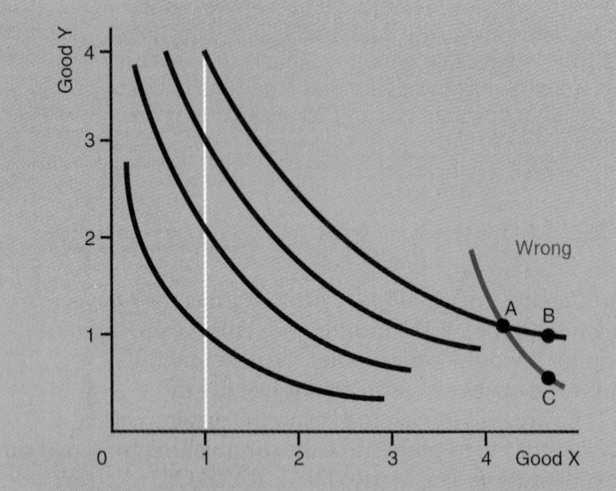

Figure 15.3 *A family or map of indifference curves*
Each indifference curve on the map shows bundles of goods between which the consumer is indifferent. The bundles of goods get larger the further out from the origin is the indifference curve. Note that two indifference curves can never cross. If they did it would mean the consumer was indifferent between points C, A and B, but also preferred B to C.

Indifference maps

The tastes of an individual consumer are represented by a family or set of indifference curves shown on an indifference map. In Figure 15.3, a consumer has an indifference curve associated with the consumption of 1 unit of good X and 1 unit of good Y. She also has a higher indifference curve associated with the consumption of 1 unit of good X and two units of good Y and so on.

Two indifference curves can never cross. In Figure 15.3, the two indifference curves AB and AC show that the consumer is indifferent between consumption at the points A and B, and A and C. Therefore we know that the consumer must be indifferent between points B and C. But we also know that the consumer would prefer B to C because at B the consumer can have more of both goods X and Y. The consumer cannot be indifferent between B and C and prefer B to C. Therefore it is logically impossible for indifference curves to cross.

Budget lines

A student on a fixed budget is able to buy different bundles of goods. But each bundle has an **opportunity cost**. For instance, buying more clothes leaves less to spend on books. This can be shown on a BUDGET LINE.

A budget line shows combinations of goods which a consumer is able to buy. Consider a consumer who has £100 to spend. Suppose she can spend it on only two goods: cassette tapes costing £5 each, or boxes of chocolates costing £2.50. Table 15.1 shows combinations of tapes and boxes of chocolates which she could purchase. For instance, she could buy 20 tapes and no chocolates, or 10 tapes and 20 boxes of chocolates.

Table 15.1 *Combinations of tapes priced at £5 and boxes of chocolates priced at £2.50 which a consumer could buy with a budget of £100*

Tapes		Boxes of chocolates
20	AND	0
15	AND	10
10	AND	20
5	AND	30
0	AND	40

These figures are shown graphically in Figure 15.4. The line is the consumer's budget line, showing the different combinations of tapes and chocolate boxes that can be bought with £100. Like a **production possibility frontier** (☞ unit 1), consumers can only consume on or within the line. For instance, the consumer could buy 40 boxes of chocolates and no tapes, or 10 tapes and 10 boxes of chocolates leaving £25 unspent. But the consumer cannot purchase combinations of goods beyond the frontier. She cannot buy 20 tapes and 10 boxes of chocolates because that would cost £125, which is more than her budget.

The slope of the budget line indicates the relative prices of goods. In Figure 15.4, the slope of the line is given by the change in consumption of boxes of chocolates divided by the change in tapes (i.e. the vertical change divided by the horizontal change). For every 2 boxes of chocolates purchased, 1 tape has to be foregone. The price ratio of chocolates to tapes is therefore 2:1.

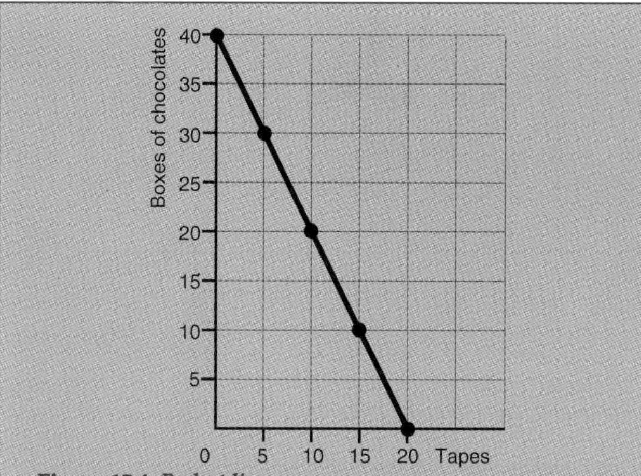

Figure 15.4 *Budget lines*
The budget line shows the combinations of tapes and boxes of chocolates which a consumer can buy with £100 assuming that the price of a tape is £5 and the price of a box of chocolates is £2.50. The consumer does not have enough income to buy combinations to the right of the line, but can choose to buy within the boundary if she chooses to save part of her money.

A change in income If income changes, there will be a parallel outward shift in the budget line. For instance, if the consumer in our example is given an income increase of £50, she can buy more of both tapes and boxes of chocolates. How much more is shown in Figure 15.5 (a). Relative prices have not changed and therefore the slope of the budget line remains the same.

A change in price If prices change, the budget line again will shift but the shift will not be a parallel one. Assume that the price of tapes increases from £5 to £10 but that the price of a box of chocolates remains unchanged. Common sense says that the consumer will now be able to buy less with her unchanged income of £100. How much less is shown in Figure 15.5 (b). The budget line has pivoted round its point on the horizontal axis. This shows that the same number of chocolate boxes can be bought if no tapes are consumed, but that fewer tapes can be bought at every level of chocolate box consumption. If no boxes of chocolates are purchased, only half the number of tapes can be bought compared to previously. Points to the right of the new budget line become unobtainable. The steeper slope of the line gives the new relative prices of 4:1.

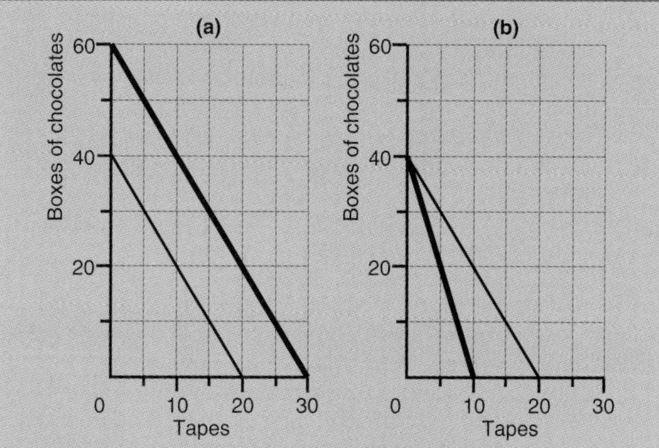

Figure 15.5 *A movement in the budget line*
An increase in income, in (a) from £100 to £150, will push the budget line to the right in a parallel shift. An increase in the price of tapes from £5 to £10 in (b), with the price of chocolates and income remaining unchanged, will swing the budget line round the point where it cuts the vertical axis.

QUESTION 2 A pair of tights and a pair of socks both cost £1.
(a) Draw the budget line for tights and socks for a consumer with an income of £12, putting tights on the vertical axis and socks on the horizontal axis.
Now show the effect on the budget line if:
(b) the price of a pair of tights now increases to £1.50;
(c) the price of a pair of socks decreases to 75p when tights are £1;
(d) the price of both tights and socks increases to £2 per pair.

Utility maximisation

Indifference curve analysis can be used to explain what combination of goods a consumer will choose to consume. The budget line shows the combination of goods which a consumer is able to purchase. An indifference map shows the different combinations of goods between which a consumer would choose. Assuming that the consumer will seek to maximise utility, it is true that the consumer will seek to consume on the highest indifference curve possible within the budget line constraint.

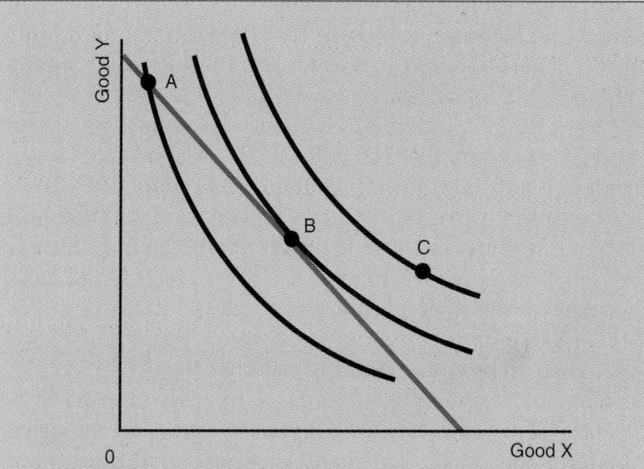

Figure 15.6 *Utility maximisation*
A consumer will maximise utility by consuming on the highest indifference curve possible, subject to the constraint of his or her budget line. This will be at point B where the indifference curve is tangential to the budget line.

In Figure 15.6, the consumer is unable to consume at point C. This is because he does not have the resources shown by his budget line to do so.

On the other hand, he would prefer to consume at B rather than A because at B he is on a higher indifference curve. B, where the indifference curve just touches or is **tangential** to the budget line, is the highest possible indifference curve that the consumer can afford to be on.

The consumer will therefore maximise utility where the slopes of the two lines are equal. The slope of the budget line is the relative price of good Y compared to good X. The slope of the indifference curve is the marginal rate of substitution of Y for X. Therefore the consumer will be in equilibrium, maximising utility where relative prices are equal to the marginal rates of substitution.

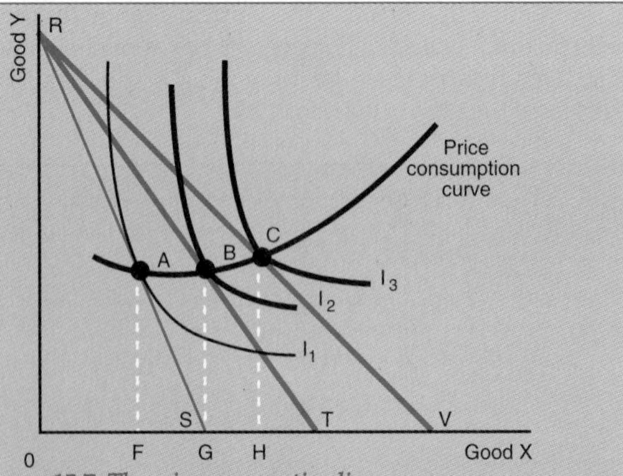

Figure 15.7 *The price consumption line*
A fall in the price of good X, shown by a shift in the budget line from RS to RT and then to RV, will change equilibrium consumption patterns from A to B and then to C. Consumption of good X will consequently increase from OF to OG and then to OH. The line joining the points A, B and C is called the price consumption line, and shows how quantity demanded changes as price changes.

QUESTION 3

(a) On a diagram, draw a budget line for a consumer and the indifference curve on which she will consume if she maximises her utility. Label the vertical axis 'apples' and the horizontal axis 'crisps'.
(b) Mark points on the diagram which show each of the following:
(i) A, where the consumer buys only apples;
(ii) B, the utility maximising point of consumption;
(iii) C, an unattainable level of consumption;
(iv) D, an attainable level of consumption but one which does not maximise the consumer's utility;
(v) E, where the consumer is indifferent between that level of consumption and the utility maximising level of consumption;
(vi) F, where the consumer might prefer to be if she had a higher income.

QUESTION 4

Table 15.2

Indifference curve I_1		Indifference curve I_2		Indifference curve I_3	
Skirts	Dresses	Skirts	Dresses	Skirts	Dresses
16	3	16	5	16	7
8	4	8	6	12	8
6	5	4	8	7	10
1	12	2	12	5	12

Table 15.2 shows three different bundles of goods which form convex indifference curves, I_1 to I_3, for a consumer.
(a) Draw the three indifference curves, putting skirts on the vertical axis and dresses on the horizontal axis.
(b) On which indifference curve would the consumer prefer to be?
(c) Which indifference curve shows the lowest level of utility?
(d) What is the marginal rate of substitution on each indifference curve when consumption of skirts falls from 16 to 8?

A consumer has an income of £360. Skirts are priced at £30 whilst dresses are priced at £36.
(e) Draw the consumer's budget line.
(f) What is the utility maximising combination of consumption of skirts and dresses for the consumer?

The price of a dress now falls to £30.
(g) Draw the consumer's new budget line.
(h) What will be the new optimum point of consumption for the consumer?

The price of a dress now falls again to £17.50.
(i) What will be the new optimum point of consumption for the consumer?
(j) Draw the price consumption curve for the consumer.

The downward sloping demand curve

It is now possible to show that the demand curve is downward sloping. In Figure 15.7, the price of good X is falling. This changes the budget line from RS to RT and then to RV. The consumer was initially in equilibrium at the point A, consuming OF of good X. The fall in price of good X, shown by the change in the budget line to RT, will result in a new equilibrium consumption point of B. At this point the consumer will buy OG of good X. When the budget line shifts to RV, consumption will again change to the point C where OH of good X will be bought. We have therefore shown that a fall in price will increase quantity demanded.

A line can be drawn joining together the different equilibrium consumption points as the price of good X changes. This line, ABC on Figure 15.7, is called the **price consumption curve.** Tracing these points onto the demand curve shows that as the price of good X falls, the quantity demanded increases.

Note that if I_2 were drawn such that the point B lies above but to the left of point A, then a fall in price would lead to a fall in quantity demanded. Good X would then be a **Giffen good** (☞ unit 10).

It is also possible to draw an **income consumption curve**. If income rises, budget lines shift outwards. The income consumption curve then links all the associated equilibrium points. From Figure 15.7, it is not difficult to imagine how parallel shifts of the budget line out from RS would lead to increased equilibrium consumption of good X. Hence good X would be a normal good. For good X to be an inferior good (i.e. one where an increase in income led to a fall in consumption), the income consumption curve would have to slope upwards and to the left from the point A. Indifference curves I_2 and I_3 would then have to be drawn much higher up and further to the left of their existing positions.

Income and substitution effects

Indifference curves can be used to analyse more deeply the concepts of income and substitution effects first introduced in unit 14. A consumer will buy more or less of a product when its price changes for two reasons.

- The price of the good relative to all other goods has changed. If price increases, demand will fall because other goods will become relatively cheaper. This is known as the SUBSTITUTION EFFECT of a price change.
- The real income of a consumer has changed. If price has increased, the consumer will be able to buy a smaller number of goods than before and therefore his or her real income will have fallen. The consumer will react by buying less of the good if the good is **normal**, but more of the good if the good is **inferior**. This is known as the INCOME EFFECT.

Consider Figure 15.8. TR is the original budget line.

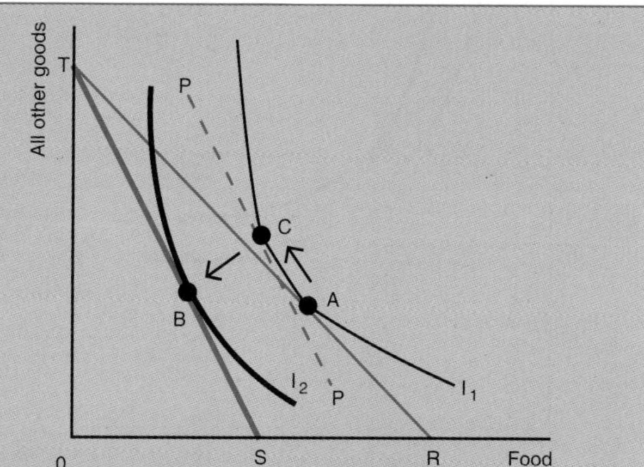

Figure 15.8 *Income and substitution effects for a normal good*
The consumer is originally at point A. The price of food increases so that the budget line shifts from TR to TS. The substitution effect of the price change is found by drawing a line PP showing the new price relativities tangential to a point on the original indifference curve I_1. At point C, the consumer is no better or worse off than before but consumes as if food had increased in price. The movement from A to C is therefore the substitution effect of the price change. The movement from C to B is then the income effect of the price change.

The consumer is in equilibrium at the point A where he is on his highest indifference curve. The price of food now increases so that the budget line shifts to TS. The new equilibrium consumption point is B. But we can disaggregate the income and substitution effects of the change.

- To find the **substitution effect**, we must find a point where the new level of prices is effective but the consumer is no better or no worse off than before. To do this, we draw a line PP which is parallel to the new budget line TS and therefore has the same slope. This line then gives the same relative prices as implied by TS. The consumer will be no better or worse off if he is consuming on his original indifference curve I_1. So drawing the line PP tangential to the indifference curve I_1, we see that the consumer would consume at the point C if prices had changed but income had not. The movement from the point A to the point C is therefore the substitution effect of the price change.
- To find the **income effect**, we must find the movement between two points where income has changed but the same relative prices are effective. So the movement from C to B is the income effect of the price change.

The good in Figure 15.8 is a normal good because a rise in price leads to a fall in demand both from the substitution effect and from the income effect. Figure 15.9 shows the income and substitution effects of a price rise for an inferior good. The movement from A to C, the substitution effect, shows a decline in demand for food when the price of food increases. The movement from C to B shows an increase in demand for food due to the fall in income. The substitution effect is greater than the income effect and therefore a rise in price leads to an overall fall in demand for food. If the income effect had been greater than the substitution effect (i.e. the indifference curves had been drawn such that B was to the right of A), then food would have been a Giffen good.

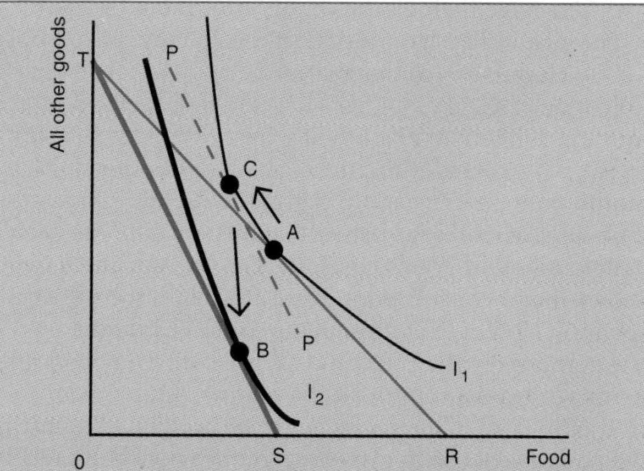

Figure 15.9 *Income and substitution effects for an inferior good*
Food in this diagram is assumed to be an inferior good. A rise in the price of food, shown by a shift in the budget line from TR to TS, produces a fall in quantity demanded due to the substitution effect (from A to C) but a rise in quantity demanded due to the income effect (from C to B). The overall effect will still be a fall in quantity demanded because the substitution effect outweighs the income effect.

QUESTION 5 Show on a diagram the income and substitution effects of the change in price resulting from the situation in the photograph. Assume all other prices remain constant.

Key terms

Indifference curve - a line which links combinations of goods between which a consumer is indifferent to consuming.
Marginal rate of substitution - the amount of a good a consumer has to give up to obtain one unit of another good and leave total utility unchanged.
Budget line - a line showing the combinations of goods which a consumer is able to purchase with a given budget.
Substitution effect - that part of the change in quantity demanded of a good when price changes which is caused by the consequent change in relative prices.
Income effect - that part of the change in quantity demanded of a good when price changes which is caused by the consequent change in real income.

Applied economics

Benefits in kind or in cash

Clothing allowances

Who pays for your clothes? Most students aged 16-18 are funded in one of two ways:

- some are given an allowance by their parents (which they may top up with earnings from a part time job) out of which they have to pay for everything from clothes to bus fares to cassettes;
- others have their clothes bought for them by their parents; if they have a part time job, they may choose to buy clothes out of that as well.

Economic theory suggests that the first method of funding is likely to yield the highest utility for the student. To see why, consider Figure 15.10. Parents spend £50 a month on their 17 year old daughter Sophie. On average, each item of clothing costs £10, whilst on average each item of all other goods costs £1. The budget line XY shows that if consumption were at X, with the £50 all spent on clothes, 5 clothes items could be bought.

Alternatively the £50 could all be spent on non-clothes items with consumption at the point Y. Or a mix of clothes and all other goods could be bought. Assume that the parents choose to give £20 a month pocket money to Sophie to spend on all other goods and use the remaining £30 a month to purchase clothes for her. Sophie therefore consumes at the point A on her indifference curve I_1. But she would be better off if she were given all of the £50 and were free to spend it as she wished. She would prefer to consume at B, on the highest indifference curve available to her, I_2. Sophie would choose, if left to herself, to spend less on clothes and more on all other goods.

Hence, Sophie's utility could well not be maximised if spending choices are made for her by her parents. Sophie's spending patterns will reflect the utility maximising choices of her parents more than her own.

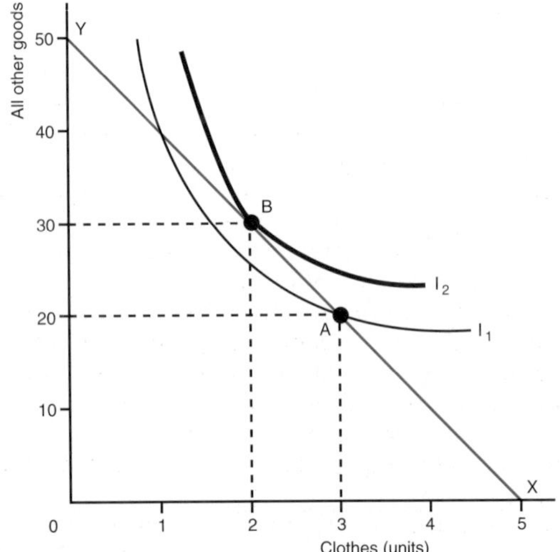

Figure 15.10

Public policy

Indifference curves can be used to analyse public policy issues too. For instance, it is sometimes argued that old age pensioners should be able to travel on public transport at a reduced rate or even free of charge. Figure 15.11 shows possible policy alternatives. With no subsidy, a pensioner's budget line is AB and she consumes at the point P on her highest indifference curve I_1. Government then introduces a subsidy scheme which changes her budget line to AC. She is now better off, consuming on a higher indifference curve I_2 at Q. However, the government could have used the money to increase the state old age pension instead. Whether the pensioner would be better off or worse off than with the alternative of cheap public transport depends on the shape of her indifference curves and the size of the shift in her budget line. In Figure 15.11, the pensioner would be better off with an increase in pension rather than subsidised public transport if her budget line had shifted to DE. She could have consumed on the higher indifference curve I_3 at the point R. On the other hand, if the increase in her old age pension had been relatively small with her budget line shifting only a little to the right from AB, she would have been better off with the subsidy on public transport.

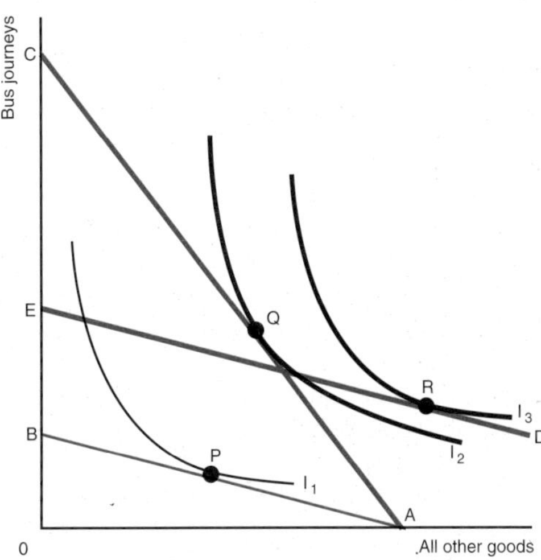

Figure 15.11

Value added tax

Mr Deputy Speaker, in recent years there has been much debate on the subject of global warming and the role tax measures can play in combating it. This has led to the European Commission to propose a Community-wide carbon tax. There may indeed be a case for further co-ordinated international action on global warming. But I remain unpersuaded of the need for a new European Community tax. Tax policy should continue to be decided here in this House - not in Brussels.

Individual countries should, of course, take their own measures to give people the right signals to encourage the efficient use of energy. Today, I shall propose measures designed to do just that and to raise revenue at the same time.

Last June, my Rt Hon friend the Prime Minister signed the UN Convention on Climate Change at Rio. This was a milestone in international efforts to halt global warming.

When Britain and other countries have ratified the Convention, the government will be committed to bring forward measures aimed at returning greenhouse gas emissions from this country to 1990 levels by the year 2000. My Rt Hon friend the Secretary of State for the Environment published last December a consultation paper which set out the various options.

The largest contribution to the growth in UK carbon dioxide emissions in the coming years is expected to come from the transport sector. I therefore propose to raise road fuel duties on average by at least 3 per cent a year in real terms in future Budgets, in addition to the increase I have already announced for this year.

But, Mr Deputy Speaker, in order to meet the commitment we entered into at Rio, action will be required not just in the transport sector, but across the whole economy. And in deciding how best to meet our carbon emissions target we will need to ensure that the right incentives are in place throughout the economy - encouraging people to consume less and conserve more. Above all, it is crucial to avoid taking measures that will have a disproportionate impact on the competitiveness of British industry.

Against this background, Mr Deputy Speaker, I have one further measure to propose that will not only encourage greater energy efficiency in every household in the country; but will also raise a considerable amount of revenue for the Exchequer over the years ahead. Fuel and energy supplies to industry pay VAT in Britain. Those to the home do not. In this respect, we are unique in the European Community.

I therefore propose, over the next two years, to end the zero rate of VAT on domestic fuel and power. Again, this change will not come into effect immediately, but in 1994. VAT will be charged at 8 per cent from1 April 1994 and at $17^1/_2$ per cent from 1 April 1995.

Mr Deputy Speaker, this measure will raise some £950 million in 1994-95, £2.3bn in 1995-96 and around £3bn a year thereafter. For the first time the rate of VAT on domestic fuel and power will be the same as that charged on goods like loft insulation material, which improve energy efficiency. This will bring an end to the current anomaly which makes a nonsense of any attempt to use the tax system to improve the environment. My intention is to legislate for this proposal this year.

Mr Deputy Speaker, social security benefits will, of course, rise automatically to reflect the price effect of this change. But I recognise that this will cause particular problems for those on low incomes. My Rt Hon friend, the Secretary of State for Social Security, will take this into account when the income related benefits are updated next year. Together with measures which have already been announced, these tax proposals should take Britain two-thirds of the way to meeting the Rio target.

Source: The Chancellor's Budget Speech, 17.3.1993

VAT to be 'handed back'

More than 40 per cent of the money raised through VAT on fuel is to be handed back to pensioners and other vulnerable people under elaborate compensation terms drawn up by ministers.

Fifteen million people, including all pensioners regardless of their means, will get special help with the tax. The total bill for compensation will be £1.29 billion in 1996-97, at least 43 per cent of the 'nearly £3 billion' the Chancellor said fuel VAT would eventually yield.

However, critics said the compensation package did little for poorer families and was inadequate even for pensioners. The package has three elements. First, the Government is bringing forward the updating of income-related benefits in respect of fuel VAT at 8 per cent from next April, and 17.5 per cent from April 1995. The increase will be reflected in the benefits next spring instead of 12 months later under the index-linked system.

Second, there will be increases in cold weather payments for those on income support benefit during sustained freezing weather. The present rate of £6 a week will rise to £7 next year and £7.50 in 1995.

The third element is the most significant, however. All pensioners, together with younger disabled people receiving income-related benefits, will get extra increases of 50p a week for a single person and 70p for a couple next April, and £1 and £1.40 respectively in 1995. In 1996, those on income-related benefits, including some pensioners will get an extra £1.40 for a single person and £2 for a couple, while other pensioners will get £1.30 and £1.85 respectively.

Kenneth Clarke said the measures were the first break since 1980 with the Government's policy of updating pensions strictly in line with prices. Next April, a retired couple on income support would get a total pension increase of £4, compromising a £1.60 index-linked rise, an extra £1.70 advance indexation in respect of fuel VAT and 70p more special help. Under the same heading of help for pensioners and disabled people, Mr Clarke announced an increase of £35 million a year over the next three years in funding for the home energy efficiency scheme, enabling people to improve home insulation.

Sally Greengross, director of Age Concern, said the package as a whole was 'something, but not enough'. Paul Goggins, national co-ordinator of Church Action on Poverty, said: 'We are dismayed that the Chancellor is pressing on with the introduction of VAT on fuel.

'Nothing he is proposing will prevent this tax hitting those on low income very hard - particularly families with children. Even so, he is proposing to give back 40 per cent of the revenue raised in higher benefits and pensions.'

Donald Dewar, the shadow social security secretary, said: 'The compensation package on VAT is complex but inadequate. It won't do. No pensioner will believe that 50 pence a week will meet the bill.'

Source: *The Guardian*, 1 12 1993.

Table 15.3 *Estimated effects of 17.5% VAT on fuel*

Based on 1991 data

Groups of net equivalent household income	Additional indirect tax payments (£ per week)	Additional indirect tax payments as a % of total spending	Change in energy consumption
1 (poorest)	£1.56	2.0	-9.2%
2	£1.83	1.3	-8.3%
3	£2.11	0.9	-6.2%
4	£2.18	0.7	-4.2%
5 (richest)	£2.63	0.6	-1.1%
All households	£2.06	1.1	-5.8%

Source: adapted from IFS Paper 39, September 1993.

The table does not show the impact of the government's proposed compensation package for low income households. The Chancellor of the Exchequer claimed that low income households would be fully compensated for any increase in their fuel bills because of the imposition of VAT.

Changes in VAT on fuel

In his 1993 Budget, the Chancellor of the Exchequer, Kenneth Clarke, announced that he was going to impose VAT on domestic fuel - gas, electricity, etc. used to heat and light houses. The imposition was to be phased. There would an 8 per cent tax imposed from April 1994 rising to the full standard rate of VAT of 17.5 per cent in April 1995. Because income elasticity of demand for fuel is low, the measures would particularly hit poor households. The Chancellor therefore announced a series of measures in his December 1993 Budget speech which he claimed would leave low income households no worse off from April 1994. These measures were mainly in the form of an increase in state benefits to pensioners and non-pensioner low income households. **Most of the data in this question assume that the 17.5 per cent increase would have gone ahead.**

In December 1994, however, there was a back bench revolt in the House of Commons which meant that the Chancellor had to abandon his plans to impose the second stage of the increase from 8 per cent to 17.5 per cent. He subsequently cut the planned increases in state benefits from April 1995 which had been designed to cushion low income households against the second increase in VAT.

1. **Explain the arguments which could be put forward (a) in favour of and (b) against the imposition of VAT on domestic fuel.**
2. **Using indifference curves and budget lines, explain how (a) a low income household receiving benefits and (b) a high income household might have been affected by the imposition of VAT on domestic fuel.**
3. **How does indifference curve analysis support the Chancellor's claim that the imposition of VAT on domestic fuel would help reduce the emission of greenhouse gases?**

unit 16 Business structure
Applied economics

Business organisation

From a legal point of view, there are a number of different ways in which a UK business may be structured.

Sole proprietorships A SOLE PROPRIETORSHIP is a business organisation with only one owner. For tax purposes he or she would be classed as self employed. It is the most common form of business organisation in the UK by number, although sole proprietorships produce comparatively little of total UK output.

The typical sole proprietor is a shopkeeper who owns his or her own shop. Family might be employed to help run the shop. Sole proprietorship is also common in agriculture and in manual trades such as plumbing.

Owners of a sole proprietorship have **unlimited liability**. This means that no distinction is made between the assets of the business and the private assets of the owner. If the business goes bankrupt and the assets of the business do not cover the debts, then the owner will be forced to sell his or her own private assets as well.

Sole proprietorships are common because they are very easy to establish or wind down. There are no particular legal formalities to setting up the business apart from those which would apply to any business in the particular industry chosen. Income tax and national insurance contributions have to be paid on profits of the business, but the total tax liability is likely to be far less than if the owner established a limited company. The owner is also likely to be in full control of the company. Sole proprietorships may employ workers, but it would be quite exceptional for a sole proprietor to employ a manager to be in charge of a considerable number of personnel.

The great disadvantage of sole proprietorships is their inability to attract finance. As will be explained in unit 22 it is often difficult for small businesses to raise finance in order to expand.

Figure 16.1 shows the breakdown by industry of VAT registered sole proprietorships in 1993. Comparing them with the average for all businesses, sole proprietorships are more common in agriculture, 'all other services', motor trades (garages etc.), finance and property, retailing, transport and construction. These are all industries where it is relatively cheap and easy to set up a firm in the industry and where small firms can establish a competitive niche for themselves.

Partnerships In a PARTNERSHIP, there are usually (though not always) between 2 and 20 shareholders. It is in a far stronger position than a sole proprietorship to raise money to invest in the business. The partners can also work together allowing their complementary skills to benefit the firm.

However, each partner has unlimited liability (except in a limited liability partnership where partners who do not work for the partnership - 'sleeping partners' - are allowed limited liability). If the partnership breaks up or goes bankrupt, this can expose individual partners to the risk of paying for another partner's mistakes. This is one reason why partnerships are common in family firms, where family members are seen as more trustworthy than outsiders.

Partnerships are also particularly common in certain professions, such as accountancy, the law, medical practices and architectural consultancies, where professional associations advise or insist that professionals should be exposed to unlimited liability as a form of professional discipline.

Figure 16.2 shows the breakdown by industry of VAT registered partnerships in 1993. Compared to the average for all businesses, shown in Figure 16.1, partnerships are

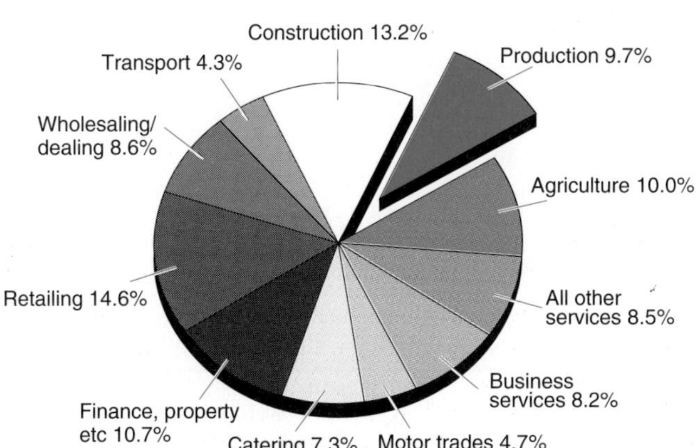

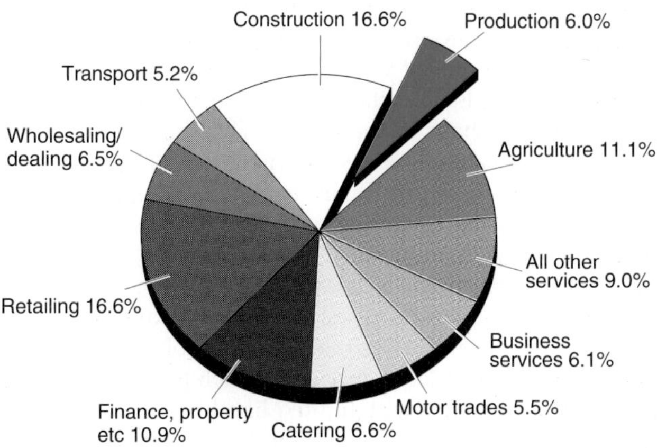

Source: adapted from CSO, 'Size analysis of United Kingdom businesses, 1993', *Business Monitor, PA* 1003.

Figure 16.1 *VAT registered sole proprietorships compared to the average for all businesses, 1993*

particularly common in agriculture, motor trades, catering, and retailing. Of these, agriculture and retailing are particularly important for partnerships, with nearly 40 per cent of partnerships being in these industries. Like sole proprietorships, partnerships are common in industries where it is relatively cheap and easy to set up in the industry and where small firms are competitive against larger firms.

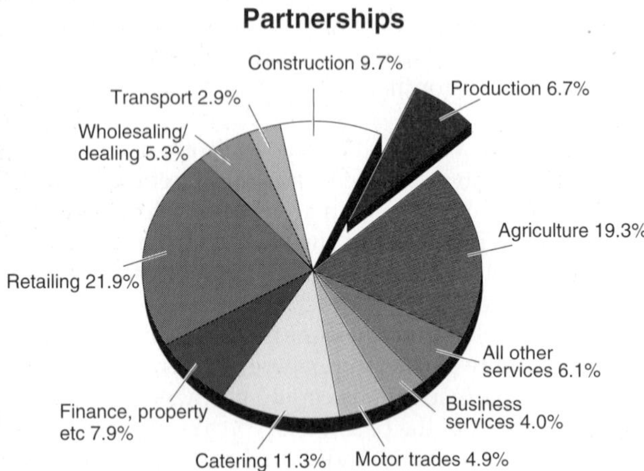

Source: adapted from CSO, 'Size analysis of United Kingdom businesses, 1993', *Business Monitor, PA* 1003.

Figure 16.2 *VAT registered partnerships*

Joint stock companies A JOINT STOCK COMPANY is one where a number of shareholders own a company and enjoy the benefit of **limited liability**. A joint stock company is a legal entity in itself and can, for instance, be sued.

The great advantage of a joint stock company is that it can attract money for investment in the form of new shares. Shareholders know that if the firm goes bankrupt, the most they stand to lose is the value of their shareholding. This advantage is so great that almost all privately owned large companies and most medium sized companies in the UK are joint stock companies.

There are two types of joint stock company. **A private limited** company is one where shares are not freely available for purchase by the public. This limits their attractiveness to shareholders and therefore larger companies tend to be **public limited companies** (plcs). A plc will have its shares quoted on a stock exchange, such as the London or Birmingham Stock Exchanges. These stock exchanges provide a cheap and efficient way in which owners of shares can sell them. This makes these types of shares far more desirable to shareholders than shares in private limited companies which have no open market. This, together with limited liability, explains why plcs find it easier to attract new shareholder capital than other forms of business organisation.

There are about half a million joint stock companies in the UK with only about 3 per cent being public limited companies. However, nearly all the largest companies in the private sector are plcs.

Various Companies Acts lay down regulations about the information which plcs have to disclose to the public about their operations. For instance, they have to present accounts and name directors of the company and their salaries. Private limited companies do not have to disclose this information. Some owners prefer to keep their companies small to retain control and keep secret the financial affairs of their company. But C&A is the only company of any size in the UK that is not a plc. It is owned by a family originating in Holland who have chosen to keep their financial affairs completely secret by establishing a partnership.

Neo-classical economic theory suggests that firms are motivated by a desire to maximise profits. This may well be true when the owners of a firm also have day to day control of the business. However, in a plc power is often more diffuse. Shareholders elect directors at an Annual General Meeting. Directors then appoint a chairman of the company and a managing director from amongst themselves, who may be one and the same person. The directors are appointed to look after the interests of shareholders. In a plc, the directors must be shareholders themselves. The managing director is responsible for the day to day running of the company and is responsible for appointing all other staff.

In theory, this chain ensures that shareholders remain in overall control of the company. In practice, the shareholding in a company may be very widespread, with no single shareholder owning more than a few per cent of the shares. Many shareholders may know little or nothing about the company apart from its name and share price. Directors are often part time and are likely to know less about the company than its managers. In consequence,

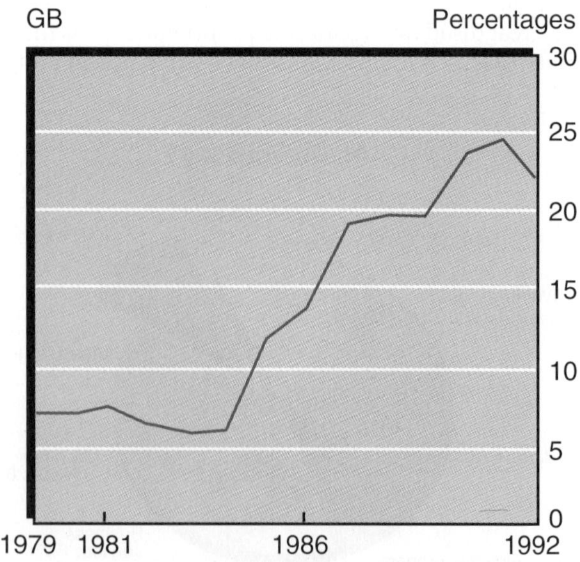

Source: adapted from HM Treasury.

Figure 16.3 *Shareholders as a percentage of the adult population*

managers have far more power in deciding how the company should be run than the theory would suggest. Couple this with the fact that relatively few shareholders bother to vote at, let alone attend, AGMs and it can be understood why many economists believe that ownership of a plc is often very different from control. Where shareholders do play a key role is when directors are major shareholders themselves. This tends to occur either when a member or members of the original family which started the company are still involved in its day to day running, such as John Sainsbury or Cadbury or when another company has built up a minority stake and is then represented on the board of the company.

Traditionally shareholders have been relatively wealthy private individuals who have owned shares to gain a private income. However, in the post-war period, the pattern of shareholding has been changed. The percentage of shares owned by individuals has declined from over 50 per cent in the 1950s to less than 20 per cent in the mid-1990s. The percentage owned by institutions has correspondingly increased. These institutions are assurance companies, pensions funds and other savings businesses which take money from the individual and use it to invest on their behalf in a variety of assets including shares. Since 1979, the government has actively promoted the idea of 'wider share ownership' and 'a share owning democracy'. It has been government policy to encourage individuals to buy shares in order to own a part of the industrial and commercial wealth of the country. Figure 16.3 shows that the government has achieved some success in this, although most new shareholders are owners of just one or two privatised share issues. Given that shares are a risky form of investment, it is perhaps not surprising that individuals prefer to reduce that risk by saving indirectly in shares through assurance companies, pension funds and unit trusts rather than building up their own portfolios of shares.

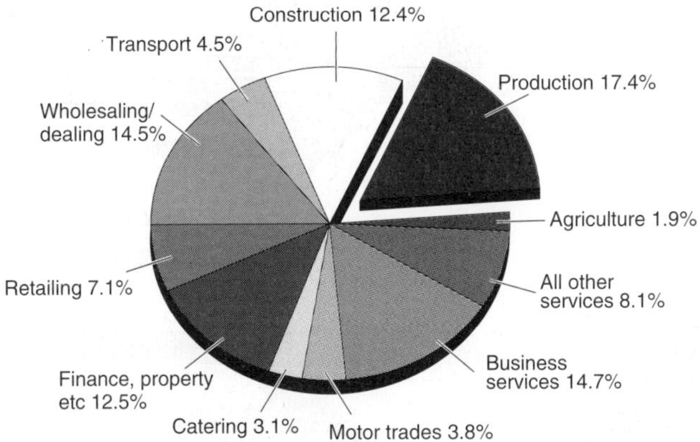

Source: adapted from CSO, '*Size analysis of United Kingdom businesses, 1993*', *Business Monitor, PA* 1003.

Figure 16.4 *VAT registered companies and public corporations*

Figure 16.4 shows the breakdown by industry of VAT registered companies and public corporations in 1993. Compared to the average for all businesses, shown in Figure 16.1, companies are particularly common in production (including manufacturing), business services, finance and property, wholesaling and dealing and transport. Manufacturing, finance and wholesaling in particular are industries where size can give cost advantages to firms and where it is often expensive to set up in the industry.

Co-operatives There are two main types of co-operatives. Consumer co-operatives, the familiar Co-op shops and superstores, are limited liability businesses which exist to further the interests of their customers. Shareholders each have one vote and are entitled to a fixed dividend on their shares (rather like preference shares in a plc). The remainder of the profits, after tax and investment, is distributed to customers in the form of a purchase dividend which today usually takes the form of stamps.

Worker co-operatives are owned by some or all of the workers of a limited liability business. They may be created by workers to prevent redundancies or create employment. Alternatively they may be set up to produce some good or service which the workers believe should be provided to society, such as religious books or health foods.

Neither form has been particularly successful in the UK over the past 40 years. Consumer co-operatives have suffered a crisis because more and more consumers have preferred to shop at plcs such as Sainsbury's and Tesco's rather than at the Co-op store which should be providing best value for money. Worker co-operatives, on the other hand, have not proved particularly popular amongst workers. It needs a great deal of initiative and trust amongst a group of workers to set up a co-operative. If it is successful, problems arise because some workers will want to sell their shareholding to non-workers and make a capital gain. Others will want to see the firm expand by introducing new shareholders who may not be workers.

Public corporations Public corporations (or nationalised industries) are a fast-disappearing type of limited liability company owned by the state.

Legal units by location

Figure 16.5 shows the total number of VAT registered businesses per square kilometre in the UK. It shows that the South East and the North West have the highest number of businesses per square kilometre. This reflects population density. It should be remembered that 30 per cent of the UK's population lives in the South East whilst 10 per cent lives in the North West. The areas with the lowest density of legal units are Scotland, Wales and Northern Ireland, areas which account for less than 20 per cent of the country's population.

Establishments, businesses, enterprises and firms

'Business' can be defined in a number of different ways. The Central Statistical Office (CSO) distinguishes between three of these.

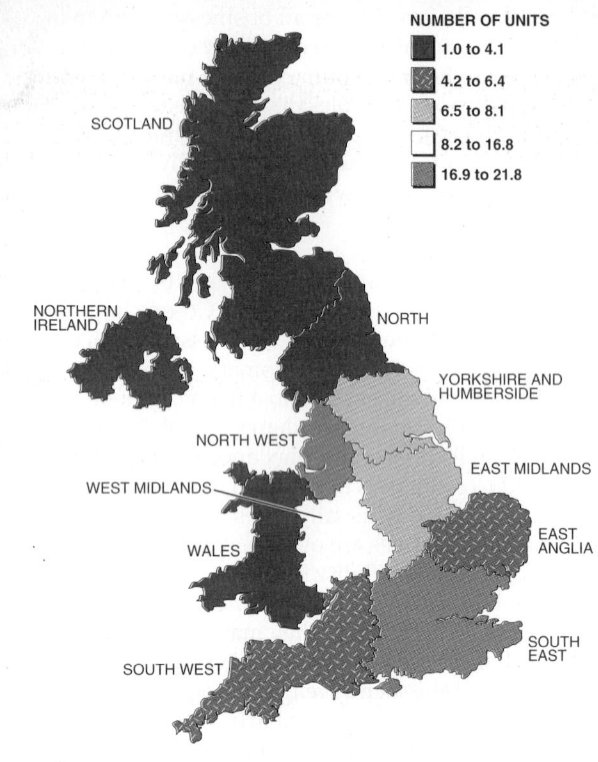

Source: adapted from CSO, '*Size analysis of United Kingdom businesses, 1993*', *Business Monitor, PA* 1003.

Figure 16.5 *Total VAT registered firms per square kilometre*

- **Establishments** are individual factories or plants.
- **Businesses** are firms which could be considered to be a single unit. They could be sole proprietorships or companies. A business may operate several establishments, for instance in different areas of the country or manufacturing different products.
- **Enterprises** are one or more businesses under common ownership. For instance, in a very large company, there may well be a complicated legal structure. There may be a **parent company** (often called a **holding company**) in which shareholders will own shares. This parent company would be classified as an enterprise. The parent company will then own **subsidiary companies**, which would be classified as 'businesses' by CSO. There is likely to be a **head office** which will supervise and set targets for the subsidiary companies in the **group**. Head office may also provide financial services and bulk buying facilities so that individual subsidiary companies can enjoy greater **economies of scale** (☞ unit 20).

From an economic viewpoint, a firm is an organisation which makes decisions about prices and outputs. This is likely to be equivalent to what CSO defines as a 'business'. For small firms, there is likely to be only one establishment in the business. The business itself is directly owned by an individual, partners or shareholders. In a very large firm, there will be many subsidiary companies, each of which may run a number of establishments. However, decision making about price and output will have been 'pushed down the line' from head office to the subsidiary company or business level. So long as the subsidiary is meeting profit targets, the parent company may be less concerned about individual pricing and production decisions.

The size of firms

The Central Statistical Office publishes information about the size of manufacturing firms in the UK. In 1991, as Table 16.1 shows, nearly all enterprises, and 91 per cent of businesses, employed fewer than 100 workers. So nearly all manufacturing firms in the UK are small firms. Only a fraction of small enterprises own more than two businesses, not surprising given the administrative cost of running two businesses owned by one set of shareholders. However, these small firms only employ approximately one-quarter of all workers in manufacturing and produce only 20 per cent of the output.

Table 16.1 *Size of enterprise by employment and output, 1991*

Number of employees	Total enterprises		Total businesses		Total employment		Total net output	
	Number	% of total	Number	% of total	Millions	% of total	£ billions	% of total
1-99	123 208	96.3	124 788	90.8	1.16	25.7	26.9	19.9
100-999	4 138	3.2	7 029	5.1	1.11	24.6	30.7	22.7
1000-7499	497	0.4	3 632	2.6	1.13	25.0	39.3	29.1
7500+	64	-	1 966	1.4	1.11	24.7	38.3	28.3

Source: adapted from CSO, *Business Monitor*, PA 1002.

The other 3.7 per cent of enterprises employs three-quarters of the workers and produce 80 per cent of the output. The 64 largest manufacturing enterprises employ one-quarter of the workers and produce a little over a quarter of the total output. These 64 enterprises are sub-divided into nearly 2 000 businesses. On average, each

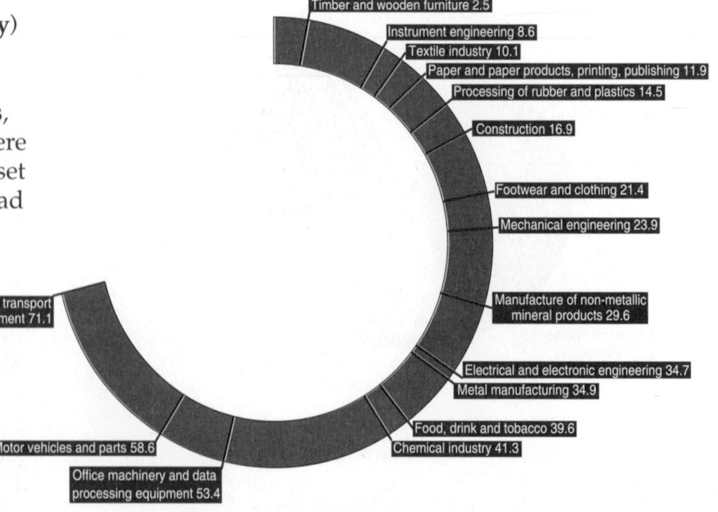

Source: adapted from CSO, *Business Monitor.*

Figure 16.6 *Percentage of total employment in selected industries in businesses with 1 000 or more workers*

parent company (the enterprise) owns 31 subsidiary companies (the businesses). Figure 16.6 indicates that there are greater economies of scale to be gained in some industries than in others. Nearly 60 per cent of workers in the motor vehicles and parts manufacturing industry work in businesses which employ more than 1 000 workers. This is likely to be because of the need for large amounts of capital for cost effective production and because of the possibilities of exploiting the division of labour. In the timber and wood furniture industry, on the other hand, only 2.5 per cent of workers are employed in businesses with 1 000 or more workers. Nearly all timber and wood furniture firms are likely to be relatively small. Much of the higher quality output will be manufactured using traditional craft techniques not suited to mass production.

Key terms

Sole proprietorship - a business with one owner who has unlimited liability.
Partnership - a business with usually between 2 and 20 partners or owners with unlimited liability.
Joint stock company - a company with at least two shareholders who have limited liability.

The motor manufacturing industry

Table 16.2 *Motor vehicles and their engines, 1991*

Number of employees	Number of enterprises	Number of businesses	Total employment	Total net output £ millions
1-99	135	137	2 800	36.0
100-199	12	12	1 500	71.2
200-1 999	14	17	9 200	302.0
2 000+	8	13	118 500	3 628.6

Source: adapted from CSO, *Business Monitor*, PA 1002.

Table 16.3 *Motor vehicle bodies, trailers and caravans, 1991*

Number of employees	Number of enterprises	Number of businesses	Total employment	Total net output £ millions
1-99	505	505	9 600	175.0
100-199	33	33	4 600	94.1
200+	46	46	11 300	251.4

Source: adapted from CSO, *Business Monitor*, PA 1002.

Table 16.4 *Motor vehicles parts, 1991*

Number of employees	Number of enterprises	Number of businesses	Total employment	Total net output £ millions
1-99	1 099	1 101	10 200	284.5
100-199	44	47	4 800	135.5
200-1 999	82	109	32 200	1 034.1
2 000+	5	30	17 100	533.1

Source: adapted from CSO, *Business Monitor*, PA 1002.

Table 16.5 *Share of five largest enterprises in the industry, 1991 (%)*

	Employment	Net output
Motor vehicles and their engines	82.3	82.3
Motor vehicle bodies, trailers and caravans	14.5	13.2
Motor vehicle parts	27.4	26.8

Source: adapted from CSO, *Business Monitor*, PA 1002.

The motor vehicle and parts industry is split into three sub-sections by the Central Statistical Office: motor vehicles and their engines; motor vehicle bodies and caravans; and motor vehicle parts. Some firms produce in all three industries but the majority do not.

1. **To what extent do large firms dominate production of motor vehicles and parts?**
2. **Suggest why there are differences in the average size of firms in the motor vehicles and their engines industry compared to the motor vehicle parts industry.**
3. **The majority of output in the motor vehicle and parts industry is produced by companies rather than sole proprietorships and partnerships. Discuss why this might be the case.**

Production

Summary

1. A production function shows the relationship between output and different levels and combinations of factor inputs.
2. The short run is defined as that period of time when at least one factor of production cannot be varied. In the long run, all factors can be varied, but the state of technology remains constant. In the very long run, the state of technology may change.
3. If a firm increases its variable inputs in the short run, eventually diminishing marginal returns and diminishing average returns will set in.
4. Constant returns to scale, increasing returns to scale or decreasing returns to scale may occur in the long run when all factors are changed in the same proportion.

The production function

A farmer decides to grow wheat. In economic terms, wheat is then an output of the production process. To grow wheat, the farmer will have to use different factors of production (☞ unit 2).

- She will grow the wheat on land.
- It will be planted and harvested using labour.
- She will also use capital. If she is a Third World farmer, the capital may be some simple spades, hoes, irrigation ditches and sacks. If she is a First World farmer, she may use tractors, combine harvesters, fertilizers and pesticides.

The land, labour and capital used to produce wheat are the factor inputs to the production process.

A PRODUCTION FUNCTION shows the relationship between output and different levels and combinations of factor inputs. For example, if it needs 50 cows and 1 worker to produce 50 pints of milk a day, then the production function could be expressed as:

$$50Q = L + 50\,C$$

QUESTION 1 C W Cobb and P H Douglas, two American economists estimated, in an article published in 1938, that the production function for US manufacturing industry between 1900 and 1922 was:

$$x = 1.10\ L^{0.75}\ C^{0.25}$$

where x is an index of total production per year, L is an index of labour input and C an index of capital input.

Using a calculator with a power function, calculate the increase in the index of production if:

(a) the quantity of labour inputs were increased by (i) 10% and (ii) 20%;

(b) the quantity of capital inputs were increased by (i) 20% and (ii) 30%;

(c) the quantity of both labour and capital inputs were increased by (i) 30% and (ii) 50%.

where Q is the number of pints of milk, L is the number of workers and C is the capital input, the number of cows.

A production function assumes that the state of technology is fixed or given. A change in the state of technology will change the production function. For instance, the microchip revolution has enabled goods (the outputs) to be produced with fewer workers and less capital (the inputs).

The short run and long run

Economists make a distinction between the short run and the long run. In the SHORT RUN, producers are faced with the problem that some of their factor inputs are fixed in supply. For instance, a factory might want to expand production. It can get its workers to work longer hours through overtime or shift work, and can also buy in more raw materials. Labour and raw materials are then variable inputs. But it only has a fixed amount of space on the factory floor and a fixed number of machines to work with. This fixed capital places a constraint on how much more can be produced by the firm.

In the LONG RUN, all factor inputs are variable. A producer can vary the amount of land, labour and capital if it so chooses. For instance, in the long run, the firm in the above example could move into a larger factory and buy more machines, as well as employ more labour and use more raw materials.

In the long run, existing technologies do not change. In the VERY LONG RUN, the state of technology can change. For instance, a bank would be able to move from a paper-based system with cheques, bank statements and paper memos to a completely electronic paperless system with cards, computer terminal statements and memos.

The way that the short run and the long run are defined in the theory of production means that there is no standard length of time for the short run. In the chemical industry, a plant may last 20 years before it needs replacing and so the short run might last 20 years. In an industry with little or no permanent physical capital, the short run may be measured in months or even weeks. The short run for a market trader, who hires everything from the stall to a van and keeps no stock, may be as short as one day, the day of the market when she is committed to hiring equipment and selling stock.

QUESTION 2 In late December 1994, Pentos, the company which owned Dillons, the bookstore, and Ryman, the office stationary group, forced another of its subsidiary companies, Athena, into receivership. Athena sold prints, posters and cards. In the first half of 1994, it had made a loss of £5m on sales of £16.2m. Pentos argued that it would take between £9 million and £12 million to get Athena back into profit. It was simply unwilling to invest this amount of money into the business. Critics of Pentos argued that this was another example of the company making the wrong decision. The former owner of Dillons, Mr Terry Maher, who was removed from the Board in 1993, has criticised the new management for understocking and understaffing the bookshops compared to when he was in charge.

Explain carefully what would be the time scale (short run, long run or very long run) for:

(a) Athena ordering new stock;
(b) Dillons reducing staff and stock levels in their bookshops;
(c) Pentos closing down Athena;
(d) At some future date, Pentos possibly being forced to close Dillons because CD Rom technology had reduced demand for printed books.

The short run: diminishing returns

In the short run at least one factor is fixed. Assume for example that a firm uses only two factors of production - capital, in the form of buildings and machines, which is fixed and labour which can be varied. What will happen to output as more and more labour is used?

Initially, output per worker is likely to rise. A factory designed for 500 workers, for instance, is unlikely to be very productive if only one worker is employed. But there will come a point when output per worker will start to fall. There is an optimum level of production which is most productively efficient (☞ unit 3). Eventually, if enough workers are employed, total output will fall. Imagine 10 000 workers trying to work in a factory designed for 500. The workers will get in each other's way and result in less output than with a smaller number of workers. This general pattern is known as the LAW OF DIMINISHING RETURNS or LAW OF VARIABLE PROPORTIONS.

QUESTION 3 You wish to employ cleaners to clean your house. They will use your own cleaning equipment (brooms, mops, dusters, polish etc.). Using the law of diminishing returns, explain what would happen if you employed 1 cleaner,5 cleaners, 20 cleaners or 1 000 cleaners, to clean at one time.

Total, average and marginal products

The law of diminishing returns can be explained more formally using the concepts of total, average and marginal products.

- TOTAL PRODUCT is the quantity of output produced by a given number of inputs over a period of time. It is expressed in physical terms and not money terms. (Indeed, economists often refer to total physical product, average physical product and marginal physical product to emphasise this point.) The total product of 1 000 workers in the car industry over a year might be 30 000 cars.
- AVERAGE PRODUCT is the quantity of output per unit of input. In the above example, output per worker would be 30 cars per year (the total product divided by the quantity of inputs).
- MARGINAL PRODUCT is the addition to output produced by an extra unit of input. If the addition of an extra car worker raised output to 30 004 cars in our example, then the marginal product would be 4 cars.

Now consider Table 17.1. In this example capital is fixed at 10 units whilst labour is a variable input.

- If no workers are employed, total output will be zero.
- The first worker produces 20 units of output. So the marginal product of the first worker is 20 units.
- The second worker produces an extra 34 units of output. So the marginal product of the second worker is 34 units. Total output with two workers is 54 units (20 units plus 34 units). Average output is 54 ÷ 2 or 27 units per worker.
- The third worker produces an extra 46 units of output. So total output with three workers is 100 units (20 plus 34 plus 46). Average output is 100÷3 or approximately 33 units per worker.

Table 17.1 *Total, average and marginal products*

Units

Capital	Labour	Physical product as labour is varied		
		Marginal	Total	Average[1]
10	0		0	0
		20		
10	1		20	20
		34		
10	2		54	27
		46		
10	3		100	33
		51		
10	4		151	38
		46		
10	5		197	39
		33		
10	6		230	38
		20		
10	7		251	36
		-17		
10	8		234	29

1. Rounded to the nearest whole number.

Initially, marginal product rises, but the fifth worker produces less than the fourth. **Diminishing marginal returns** therefore set in between the fourth and fifth worker. Average product rises too at first and then falls, but the turning point is later than for marginal product. **Diminishing average returns** set in between 5 and 6 workers.

The law of diminishing returns states that if increasing quantities of a variable input are combined with a fixed input, eventually the marginal product and then the average product of that variable input will decline.

It is possible to draw total, average and marginal product curves. The curves in Figure 17.1 are derived from the data in Table 17.1. All three curves first rise and then fall. Marginal product falls first, then average product and finally total product.

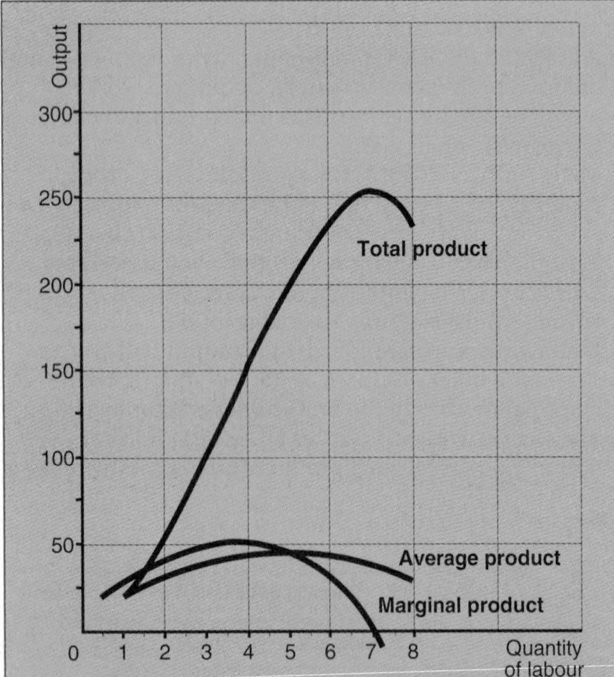

Figure 17.1 *Total, average and marginal product*
The curves are derived from the data in Table 17.1. Note that diminishing marginal returns set in before diminishing average returns. Note too that the marginal product curve cuts the average product curve at its highest point, whilst the total product curve falls when the marginal product curve cuts the horizontal axis.

The long run: returns to scale

The law of diminishing returns assumes that firms operate in the short run. In the long run, firms can vary all their factor inputs. What would happen to the output of a firm if, for instance, it were to increase all its inputs by the same proportion? There are only three possibilities.

- INCREASING RETURNS TO SCALE occur if an equal percentage increase in inputs to production leads to a more than proportional increase in output. If a firm doubles its land, labour and capital inputs, but as a consequence trebles its output, then increasing returns to scale have occurred. For instance, if as in Table 17.3, 1 unit of capital and 1 unit of all other factors of production are used, then 20 units of output are produced. Doubling the inputs to 2 units of capital and 2 units of all other factors more than doubles output to 50 units. An increase in inputs by 50 per cent from 2 to 3 units of all factors increases output by more than 50 per cent from 50 units to 80 units. Therefore the firm is operating under conditions of increasing returns to scale.
- CONSTANT RETURNS TO SCALE occur if an equal percentage increase in inputs to production leads to the same percentage increase in output. For example, if a firm doubles its inputs and this leads to a doubling of output, then constant returns to scale occur.
- DECREASING RETURNS TO SCALE occur if an equal percentage increase in inputs to production leads to a less than proportional increase in output. So decreasing returns to scale occur if a firm trebles its inputs but only doubles its output.

Table 17.3 *Increasing returns to scale*

		Units of capital		
		1	2	3
Units of all other factors of production	1	**20**	35	45
	2	30	**50**	65
	3	35	63	**80**

QUESTION 4

Table 17.2 Units

Capital	Labour	Total product
10	1	8
10	2	24
10	3	42
10	4	60
10	5	70
10	6	72

Table 17.2 shows the change in total product as the quantity of labour increases and all other factor inputs remain constant.

(a) Calculate the average and marginal product at each level of labour input.
(b) Draw the total, average and marginal product curves on a graph.
(c) At what level of output do (i) diminishing marginal returns and (ii) diminishing average returns set in?

QUESTION 5

Table 17.4

		Units of labour				
		1	2	3	4	5
Units of all other factors of production	1	1	2	4	5	6
	2	2	3	6	8	10
	3	3	5	9	11	12
	4	5	7	10	12	13
	5	7	9	11	13	14

The table shows the output of a firm given different levels of factor inputs over the long run. Over what range does the firm experience:
(a) increasing returns;
(b) constant returns;
(c) decreasing returns to scale?

Key terms

Production function - the relationship between output and different levels and combinations of inputs.

The short run - the period of time when at least one factor input to the production process cannot be varied.

The long run - the period of time when all factor inputs can be varied, but the state of technology remains constant.

The very long run - the period of time when the state of technology may change.

Law of diminishing returns or variable proportions - if increasing quantities of a variable input are combined with a fixed input, eventually the marginal product and then the average product of that variable input will decline. Diminishing returns are said to exist when this decline occurs.

Total product - the quantity of output measured in physical units produced by a given number of inputs over a period of time.

Average product - the quantity of output per unit of factor input. It is the total product divided by the level of output.

Marginal product - the addition to output produced by an extra unit of input. It is the change in total output divided by the change in the level of inputs.

Returns to scale - the change in percentage output resulting from a percentage change in all the factors of production. There are increasing returns to scale if the percentage increase in output is greater than the percentage increase in factors employed, constant returns to scale if it is the same and decreasing returns to scale if it is less.

Applied economics

Increasing returns at petrol stations

Petrol stations provide a service to their customers. They buy in fuel and other merchandise in large quantities, store it and then sell it in smaller quantities to customers when they want to make their purchases. Other inputs apart from stock to this production process include the land on which the petrol station is built, capital in the form of buildings and equipment, and labour.

Petrol stations were originally usually attached to garages which repaired and perhaps also sold cars. Garages aimed to provide a complete service to the motorist. Increasingly, however, petrol stations were built without the provision of other garage services. This enabled them to benefit from specialisation. By the 1970s, petrol stations started to undergo another change. New petrol stations began to be built by the supermarket chains. They were able to undercut existing petrol station prices by selling large volumes of petrol and by buying at lowest prices on the world oil markets. Whilst there were few supermarket petrol stations in a region, this posed little threat to traditional suppliers. By the late 1980s, however, supermarket petrol stations could be found in most localities. Traditional petrol stations started to close under the fierce price competition.

The survival of petrol stations may be dependent on two trends. One, which has been developing for some time, is for petrol stations to broaden their product range and become convenience stores. What they are doing is increasing their stock, an example of capital, whilst keeping other factors of production broadly constant. For instance, it takes up no extra land for a petrol station to begin to sell flowers, bread and pizzas alongside petrol. The result is that petrol stations which successfully adopt this strategy can probably enjoy constant physical returns: a 50 per cent increase in stock can result in a 50 per cent increase in physical sales. Profit on the site increases because every extra sale generates extra profit. Petrol stations can then generate the profits needed for survival.

An alternative strategy for survival takes an opposite route. If an existing petrol station is not profitable, why not cut factor inputs if petrol sales can be maintained? Less land and less capital can be used by getting rid of the petrol station kiosk. It is replaced by automatic payment machines attached to petrol pumps where customers can feed cash or cards in machines to pay. Elf has just started to introduce these petrol stations into the UK on sites where it is not possible to build the size of kiosk demanded by the new convenience store petrol station format. If Elf can, say, sell 90 per cent of petrol compared to an average petrol station with only 80 per cent of its land and capital, then it would tend to show that many petrol stations suffer from diminishing returns.

Source: adapted from the *Financial Times*, 12.1.1995.

Overfishing

Law of diminishing returns hits world fish catch

The world fish catch declined in 1992 for the third consecutive year and fisheries experts say that gross over-fishing is wrecking chances of increasing output. According to recent figures from the United Nations Food and Agriculture Organisation, the 1992 catch was just under 97m tonnes compared with a record 100m tonnes in 1989. Until then, the world fish catch had risen steadily from little over 20m tonnes in the early 1950s. The overall figures hide the even steeper decline in fish caught at sea. In 1992, the marine catch totalled about 80m tonnes, down from about 86m tonnes in 1989.

The FAO says that fish has been harvested under the misconception that natural stocks are an unlimited natural resource, 'incapable of being affected by fishing pressure' according to FAO fisheries specialist Mr Robin Welcomme. The drop in sea catches is due to a large over-capacity in fisheries equipment around the world. 'This makes for overfishing and means that fishing grounds are exploited long after they should be.' The northern Mediterranean, the Gulf of Thailand, the southern part of the North Sea and the seas of South-East Asia are the most overfished.

Source: adapted from the *Financial Times*, 17.6.1994.

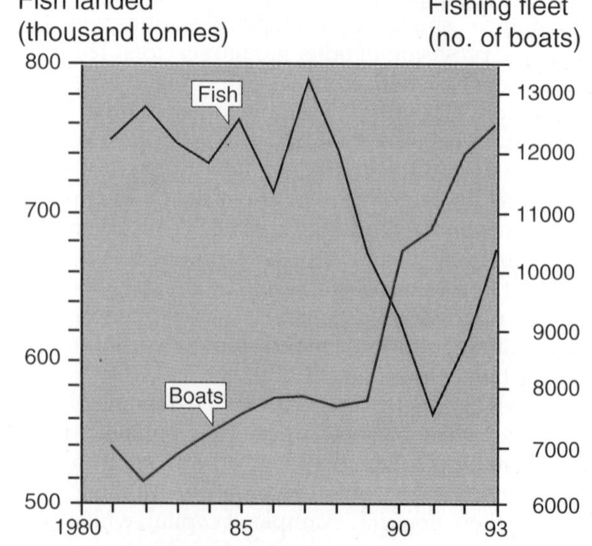

Source: adapted from CSO, *Annual Abstract of Statistics*.

Figure 17.2 *British fishing (fish landed and number of boats)*

The British government has commissioned you to write a report on the fishing problem. Write a report as follows.

1. **Outline the problem of overfishing.**
2. **Explain why it is an example of diminishing returns.**
3. **Suggest why there was an incentive for more UK boats to enter the fishing industry in the 1980s and early 1990s despite falling total catches.**
4. **Discuss THREE different measures which the UK government could press the European Union to implement to help resolve the crisis. In your discussion, evaluate who would be the main winners and losers of each of your proposals. Take into account any knowledge you may have of existing restrictions on fishing in EU waters.**

Costs, revenue and profits

Summary

1. Economists use the word 'cost' of production in a way different to its general usage. Economic cost is the opportunity cost of production.
2. Many costs are imputed - that is they form part of the cost of production but the producer does not directly pay for them.
3. Fixed costs (or indirect or overhead costs) are costs of production which do not vary directly with the level of output. Variable costs (or direct costs) are costs which increase as the level of output increases.
4. Economists distinguish between the total, average and marginal costs of production.
5. Total, average and marginal revenues can be distinguished too.
6. Economic or abnormal profit is the difference between total revenue and total cost. Normal profit is an economic (i.e. opportunity) cost of production.

The economic definition of cost

Economists use the word 'cost' in a very specific sense. The ECONOMIC COST of production for a firm is the opportunity cost of production. It is the value that could have been generated had the resources been employed in their next best use.

For instance, a market trader has some very obvious costs, such as the cost of buying stock to sell, the rent for her pitch in the market and the petrol to get her to and from the market. Money will be paid for these and this will be an accurate reflection of opportunity cost. But there are a number of costs which are hidden. Resources which have an opportunity cost but for which no payment is made must have an IMPUTED COST. There are a number of examples that can be used to illustrate imputed cost.

Labour A market trader working on her own account may calculate that she has made £50 'profit' on a day's trading. But this may not include the value of her own time. If she could have earned £40 working in another job for the day, then her economic profit is only £10. Hence, the opportunity cost of her labour must be included as an economic cost of production.

Financial capital A small businessman may start a company with his own money investing, say, £50 000. The economic cost of production must include the opportunity cost of that start-up capital. If he could have earned 10 per cent per annum in an alternative investment, then the economic cost (the opportunity cost) is £5 000 per year.

Depreciation The **physical capital** of a company will deteriorate over time. Machines wear out, buildings need repairs, etc. Moreover, some capital will become obsolete before the end of its physical life. The economic cost of depreciation is the difference between the purchase price and the second hand value of a good. A car, for instance, which lasts for 8 years does not depreciate at 12½ per cent each year. In the first year, cars depreciate on average by 40 per cent. So a company paying £10 000 for a new car which depreciates by 40 per cent over its first year only has an asset worth £6 000 at the end of the year. £6 000 is the monetary value of the opportunity cost of keeping the car rather than selling it at the end of that year.

Goodwill A firm trading over a number of years may acquire a good reputation. It may produce branded goods which become household names. The goodwill of these brands has an opportunity cost. They could be sold to a rival company. Therefore the interest foregone on the potential sale value of these must be included as an economic cost. For instance, Nestlé bought Rowntree Mackintosh in 1988 for £2.3bn. It paid £1.9bn over and above the value of buildings, machinery, etc. This was effectively a payment for the brand names of Rowntree Mackintosh products such as KitKat, Smarties, Polo and After Eight as well as the relationships which the company had with its suppliers and customers. The opportunity cost of this sum (e.g. the interest that could have been received had the money been lent) should have been included as an economic cost for Rowntree Mackintosh.

It can be seen from this discussion that economists differ in their use of the word 'cost' from accountants, tax inspectors, businesses and others. Accountants have developed specific conventions about what is and what is not a cost and what should and should not be included on a balance sheet and an accountant's balance sheet may be very different from that of an economist's.

QUESTION 1 A business person runs her own business. Over the past twelve months, she has paid £12 000 for materials and £6 000 in wages to a worker whom she employs. She runs the business from premises which her parents own. These premises could be rented out for £4 000 a year if she were not occupying them. She has £20 000 worth of her own capital tied up in the business. She is a trained teacher and at present works exactly half time in a school earning £10 000. She could work full time as a teacher (earning £20 000) if she didn't run the business. The current rate of interest is 10 per cent. The total revenue of her business over the past 12 months was £36 000.

On the basis of these figures, what were her accounting costs and what were her economic costs? Did she make a profit last year?

Fixed and variable costs

Economists distinguish between two types of cost: fixed and variable cost.

A FIXED COST (also called an INDIRECT or OVERHEAD COST) is a cost which does not vary directly with output. As production levels change, the value of a fixed cost will remain constant. For instance, a company may rent premises. The rent on the premises will remain the same whether the company produces nothing or produces at full capacity. If a firm pays for an advertising campaign, the cost will be the same whether sales remain constant or increase. Costs commonly given as examples of fixed costs are capital goods (e.g. factories, offices, plant and machinery), rent and rates, office staff and advertising and promotion.

A VARIABLE (or DIRECT or PRIME) COST is a cost which varies directly with output. As production increases, so does variable cost. For instance, a steel maker will use iron ore. The more steel produced, the more iron ore will be needed, so the cost of iron ore is a variable cost. Raw materials for production are the clearest example of variable costs for most firms. It is not always easy to categorise a cost as either fixed or variable. Many costs are SEMI-VARIABLE COSTS. Labour is a good example. Some firms employ a permanent staff, which could be classified as a fixed cost. They might ask the permanent staff to do overtime when necessary, or employ temporary labour. These costs would be classified as variable. But permanent staff could be seen as a variable cost if a firm were willing to hire and fire staff as its output changed. In practice, firms do adjust staff numbers with output, but the adjustment is sluggish and therefore the cost of labour is neither variable nor fixed - it is semi-variable.

In the **short run** (☞ unit 17), at least one factor input of production cannot be changed. So in the short run, some costs are fixed costs whilst others will be variable. In the long run, all factor inputs can vary. So in the long run, all costs will be variable costs.

QUESTION 2 Rachel Hughes owns a whole food vegetarian restaurant. Explain which of the following costs would be most likely to be fixed costs, variable costs or semi-variable costs for her business: rice; rent; wages of casual staff; interest payments on a loan; electricity; cooking oil; pots and pans; her own wage; VAT.

Total, average and marginal cost

It is important to distinguish between the total, average and marginal costs of production. The TOTAL COST (TC) of production is the cost of producing a given level of output. For instance, if a manufacturer produces 100 units a week and its weekly costs come to £1 million, then £1 million is the total cost of production. Increased production will almost certainly lead to a rise in total costs. If the manufacturer increased output to 200 units a week, it would need to buy more raw materials, increase the number of workers, and generally increase its factor inputs.

Table 18.1 *Total costs of production*

(1)	(2)	(3)	(4)
Output (per week)	Total variable cost (£)	Total fixed cost (£)	Total cost (columns 2+3) (£)
0	0	200	200
1	200	200	400
2	300	200	500
3	600	200	800
4	1200	200	1400
5	2000	200	2200

This is illustrated in Table 18.1. At an output level of 1 unit per week, the total cost of production is £400. If output were 2 units per week, total costs would rise to £500.

The total cost of production is made up of two components:

- TOTAL VARIABLE COST (TVC) which varies with output;
- TOTAL FIXED COST (TFC) which remains constant whatever the level of output.

So in Table 18.1, total variable cost increases from zero to £2 000 as output increases from zero to 5 units per week, whilst total fixed costs remain constant at £200 whatever the level of output. Total variable costs when added to total fixed costs are equal to total cost. Mathematically:

$$TVC + TFC = TC$$

The AVERAGE COST OF PRODUCTION is the total cost divided by the level of output. For instance, if a firm makes 100 items at a total cost of £1 000, then the average cost per item would be £10. If a firm made 15 items at a cost of £30, then the average cost of production would be £2. Mathematically:

$$AC = \frac{TC}{Q}$$

where AC is average cost, TC is total cost and Q is quantity or the level of output.

Average cost, like total cost, is made up of two components.

- AVERAGE VARIABLE COST (AVC) is total variable cost divided by the level of output.
- AVERAGE FIXED COST (AFC) is total fixed cost divided by the level of output.

The average costs of production for the example given in Table 18.1 are given in Table 18.2.

MARGINAL COST is the cost of producing an extra unit of output. For instance, if it costs £100 to produce 10 items and £105 to produce 11 items, then the marginal cost of the eleventh item is £5. If it costs £4 to produce 2 items but £10 to produce 3 items, then the marginal cost of the third unit is £6. Mathematically, marginal cost (MC) is calculated by dividing the change in total cost (ΔTC) by the change in total output (ΔQ).

$$MC = \frac{\Delta TC}{\Delta Q}$$

The marginal costs of production for the figures in Tables 18.1 and 18.2 are given in Table 18.3.

Table 18.2 *Average costs of production*[1]

(1)	(2)	(3)	(4)
Output (per week)	Average variable cost (£)	Average fixed cost (£)	Average total cost (columns 2+3) (£)
1	200	200	400
2	150	100	250
3	200	67	267
4	300	50	350
5	400	40	440

1. Rounded to the nearest pound.

Table 18.3 *Marginal costs of production*

(1)	(2)	(3)
Output (per week)	Total cost (£)	Marginal cost per unit of output (£)
1	400	400
2	500	100
3	800	300
4	1400	600
5	2200	800

QUESTION 3

Table 18.4

£

Output	Total fixed cost	Total variable cost	Total cost	Average fixed cost	Average variable cost	Average cost	Marginal cost
0	40						
1		6					
2		11					
3		15					
4			60				
5			66				

Complete Table 18.4, calculating the missing figures.

Total, average and marginal revenues

A firm's revenues are its receipts of money from the sale of goods and services over a time period such as a week or a year. The relationships between total, average and marginal revenue are the same as between total, average and marginal cost.

- TOTAL REVENUE (TR) is the total amount of money received from the sale of any given level of output. It is the total quantity sold times the average price received.
- AVERAGE REVENUE (AR) is the average receipt per unit sold. It can be calculated by dividing total revenue by the quantity sold. If all output is sold at the same price, then average revenue must equal the price of the product sold.
- MARGINAL REVENUE (MR) is the receipts from selling an extra unit of output. It is the difference between total revenue at different levels of output. Mathematically:

$$MR = TR_n - TR_{n-1}$$

where n and n-1 are the last and last but one goods sold respectively. For instance, if a firm sold 9 units for a total of £200 and 10 units for £220, then the marginal revenue from the tenth unit sold would be £20.

QUESTION 4

Table 18.5

Sales (million units)	Average revenue (£)	Marginal revenue (£)
1	20	
2	18	
3	16	
4	14	
5	12	
6	10	
7	8	
8	6	
9	4	
10	2	

Calculate (a) total revenue and (b) marginal revenue at each level of sales from 1 million to 10 million.

Profit

The PROFIT of a company can be calculated by taking away its total cost from its total revenue:

$$\text{Profit} = TR - TC$$

It can also be calculated by finding the average profit per unit, which is average revenue minus average cost, and multiplying that by the quantity sold.

It should be remembered that cost for an economist is different from that for an accountant or business person. As explained above, the economic cost of production is its **opportunity cost**. It is measured by the benefit that could have been gained if the resources employed in the production process had been used in their next most profitable use. If a firm could have made £1 million profit by using its resources in the next best manner, then the £1 million profit is an opportunity cost for the firm. In economics this profit, which is counted as an economic cost, is called NORMAL PROFIT.

If the firm failed to earn normal profit, it would cease to produce in the long run. The firm's resources would be put to better use producing other goods and services where a normal profit could be earned. Hence, normal profit must be earned if factors of production are to be kept in their present use.

ECONOMIC PROFIT (also called PURE PROFIT, or ABNORMAL PROFIT or SUPERNORMAL PROFIT) is the profit over and above normal profit (i.e. the profit over and above the opportunity cost of the resources used in production by the firm). It is important to remember that the firm earns normal profit when total revenue equals total cost. But total revenue must be greater than total cost if it is to earn abnormal profit.

QUESTION 5 A business person leaves her £70 000 a year job to set up a company from which she draws a salary of £30 000 in its first year, £50 000 in its second year and £70 000 in its third year. She puts £50 000 of her own savings into the company as start up capital which previously had been invested and could earn a rate of return of 10 per cent per annum. Accountants declare that the costs of the firm over the first twelve months were £250 000, £280 000 in the next twelve months and £350 000 in the third year. Revenues were £270 000 in the first year, £310 000 in the second year and £450 000 in the third year.

For each year, calculate the firm's:
(a) accounting profit;
(b) economic profit;
(c) normal profit.

Key terms

Economic cost - the opportunity cost of an input to the production process.
Imputed cost - an economic cost which a firm does not pay for with money to another firm but is the opportunity cost of factors of production which the firm itself owns.
Fixed or indirect or overhead costs - costs which do not vary as the level of production increases or decreases.
Variable or direct or prime costs - costs which vary directly in proportion to the level of output of a firm.
Total cost - the cost of producing any given level of output. It is equal to total variable cost + total fixed cost.
Average cost - the average cost of production per unit, calculated by dividing the total cost by the quantity produced. It is equal to average variable cost + average fixed cost.
Marginal cost - the cost of producing an extra unit of output.
Total revenue - the total money received from the sale of any given quantity of output.
Average revenue - the average receipts per unit sold. It is equal to total revenue divided by quantity sold.
Marginal revenue - the addition to total revenue of an extra unit sold.
Profit - the difference between total revenue and total cost.
Normal profit - the profit that the firm could make by using its resources in their next best use. Normal profit is an economic cost.
Economic profit (or pure profit or abnormal profit or supernormal profit) - the profit over and above normal profit (i.e. the profit over and above the opportunity cost of the resources used in production by the firm).

Applied economics

Stagecoach

Stagecoach was founded in 1980 by Brian Souter and his sister Ann Cloag. In 1993, the company was floated on the Stock Exchange. Revenues in that year were £191 million and profits were £18.9 million. Stagecoach has grown through a series of takeovers. In the 1990s, it actively sought to buy smaller regional bus companies which it felt were underperforming. Costs in these companies were too high, whilst they might not have fully exploited all the potential for increasing revenues.

Stagecoach has a standard formula for reorganising a company once it has been bought, which focuses on four key areas. First, it cuts fixed overhead costs. It reduces layers in the organisation to just five:

- the bus driver or fitter;
- a depot manager;
- the four person management team in charge of the day-to-day running of the company;
- the board of the subsidiary which has been taken over;
- the main board of Stagecoach.

For instance, at Western Travel, bought in 1993, 12 separate companies in the Gloucestershire, Warwickshire and South Wales area were merged into three.

Second, variable costs are cut. Stagecoach can achieve cost savings of 1.5 per cent on spare parts, tyres and engine components. The company also tends to replace ageing buses. The average age of a Stagecoach fleet is 7.6 years compared with the industry average of 11. The new buses have lower running costs because they are more reliable and need fewer spare parts.

Third, the company reduces its semi-variable costs by negotiating new contracts with workers and their trade unions. These new contracts aim to eliminate inefficient working practices, thus increasing labour productivity.

Finally, it tackles the revenue side of the profit equation by improving the transport network. It aims to provide a stable, reliable service which will win customer loyalty. It also encourages managers to develop new services. For instance, Fife Scottish introduced a hub and spoke system on its links between Fife and Edinburgh, Glasgow and Dundee allowing it to achieve 40 per cent revenue growth.

Source: adapted from the *Financial Times.*

Princely touch in the East End

A combination of the Prince's Youth Business Trust and the British arm of Lehman Brothers, the US investment bank, has over the past 12 months got ten new businesses up and running in London's Tower Hamlets, one of the capital's more disadvantaged areas.

The trust, of which the Prince of Wales is president, usually gives financial as well as advisory assistance to entrepreneurs up to the age of 29. In this case, it provided counselling and other advice while Lehman injected £25,000 a year for three years.

The Trust targets people who are out of work and finding life tough, with no chance of raising money from the usual sources for a business idea. A survey has found that among those helped by the trust, two-thirds were still trading after two to three years, a much greater proportion that the national average for young businesses.

One with a thriving business in virtually a year is Heath Phillips who does events catering, mainly at football stadiums but also at horse racing meetings. Mr Phillips, 26, played for Tottenham Hotspur but at 18 turned down a professional contract as a footballer to become one of the youngest dealers on the London financial futures exchange.

He learned more about business when 2 ½ years later he became commercial manager of Leyton Orient Football Club. He was there more than four years, seeing them prosper commercially, but it also made him aware of a gap in the market for good catering facilities at some football stadiums. He said: 'I took a 12-week business course, did market research on the catering idea while I was out of a job and thought I was ready to go - except I was drawing a blank with the banks on raising cash.' This was when he secured a £5,000 Lehman-PYBT loan and another for the same amount from the East London Small Business Centre.

He found the business adviser assigned to him, the finance director of a large trust organisation, was invaluable in showing him how to present cost estimates to clients. He added: 'Without his help, I would have had to learn from my mistakes, and in my position I couldn't afford to do that.'

With the help of some other cash available from family sources, Mr Phillips now has £27,000 worth of equipment, mainly kitchen items but also two vans. He employs a full-time chef and 50 part-timers ranging from chefs and waitresses to sales and office staff. His Royal House Catering company now has contracts at Colchester and Leyton Orient Football Clubs and is negotiating with other clubs. He has already won the award of Division III caterer of the year.

First year turnover is set to reach £87,000. He expects one more football club contract almost to double that, so his second year sales target is £155,000. To fund the expansion, he has applied for a further £5,000 from Lehman-PYBT and £3,000 from the centre. He said: 'In five years, I would like to think we would have three to four football club contracts at third division level plus one premier division club.' He is eyeing other sports events including more race meetings. But he wants to expand at a pace which will allow him to meet what he sees as the most crucial criterion for the business: keeping the personal touch with clients.

Source: Derek Harris, *The Times*, 28 June 1994, ©Times Newspapers Limited, 1994.

1. **Explain the different types of costs faced by Heath Phillips' business.**
2. **Analyse what might happen to**
   (a) total revenue and
   (b) average revenue
   of the business over the next few years.
3. **A firm offers Heath Phillips a £50 000 a year employment contract if he will give up his own business and come and run their catering subsidiary. Using the concept of economic cost, discuss whether or not he should take up the offer.**

Short run costs - diminishing returns

Summary

1. **The short run average cost is U-shaped because of the law of diminishing marginal returns.**
2. **Diminishing average returns set in when average variable cost begins to increase.**
3. **Diminishing marginal returns set in when marginal cost begins to increase.**
4. **If factor input prices are constant, the average and marginal product curves are the mirror image of short run average and marginal cost curves.**
5. **The marginal cost curve cuts the average variable cost and average cost curves at their lowest point.**

Diminishing returns

It was explained in unit 17 that in the short run a firm was faced with employing at least one factor input which could not be varied. For instance, it might have a given number of machines or a fixed quantity of office space. If it were to increase output by using more of the variable factor inputs, diminishing marginal returns and then diminishing average returns would set in eventually.

Diminishing returns are a technical concept. Therefore, they were expressed in terms of physical inputs and physical product (the output of the firm). But it is possible to express physical inputs in terms of costs. For example, a firm which employed 5 workers at a wage of £200 per week, and had no other costs, would have total weekly costs of £1 000. If each worker produced 200 units of output, then the average cost per unit of output would be £1 [£1 000 ÷ (5 x 200)]. The marginal cost of the 200 units produced by the fifth worker would be her wage (£200), and so the marginal cost per unit of output would be £1 (£200 ÷ 200).

Short run cost schedules

Having looked at inputs, it is now possible to see how the law of diminishing returns affects short run costs. Table 19.1 is an example of how this can be done. It is assumed that the firm can employ up to 8 workers at identical wage rates (i.e. the supply of workers over the range 1 to 8 is **perfectly elastic**). The price of capital per unit is £100 and the price of labour is £200 per unit.

Capital is the fixed factor of production. Therefore whatever the level of production, total fixed cost will be £1 000 (10 units x £100). Total variable cost will increase as more and more labour is added. So the total variable cost of producing 20 units is £200 (1 unit of labour x £200), of 54 units it is £400 (2 units of labour x £200), and so on.

Total cost is total fixed cost plus total variable cost. Once the three measures of total cost have been worked out, it is possible to calculate average and marginal costs (☞ unit 18). Alternatively, it is possible to calculate marginal cost per unit by finding the cost of the additional

Table 19.1

Units			£						
Capital	Labour	Total physical product (output)	Total cost[1] TVC	TFC	TC	Average cost[2] AVC	AFC	ATC	Marginal cost MC
10	0	0	0	1000	1000	0	-	-	
									10.0
10	1	20	200	1000	1200	10	50	60	
									5.9
10	2	54	400	1000	1400	7.4	18.5	25.9	
									4.3
10	3	100	600	1000	1600	6.0	10.0	16.0	
									3.9
10	4	151	800	1000	1800	5.3	6.6	11.9	
									4.3
10	5	197	1000	1000	2000	5.1	5.1	10.2	
									6.1
10	6	230	1200	1000	2200	5.2	4.3	9.6	
									9.5
10	7	251	1400	1000	2400	5.6	4.0	9.6	
									22.2
10	8	260	1600	1000	2600	6.8	3.8	10.0	

1. Assuming that capital costs £100 per unit and labour costs £200 per unit.
2. The three measures of average cost have been calculated to the nearest decimal from total figures. ATC therefore does not always equal AVC+ATC because of rounding.

labour and dividing it by the marginal physical product. In our example, the cost of hiring an extra worker is a constant £200. So the marginal cost of producing, say, an extra 34 units once 20 have been made is £200 (the cost of the second worker). The marginal cost per unit is then £200 ÷ 34. Average variable cost can be calculated in a similar manner.

QUESTION 1

Table 19.2

	Units
Labour	Total physical product
1	20
2	45
3	60
4	70

Table 19.2 shows how total physical product changes as the number of units of labour changes with a fixed quantity of capital. The cost of the capital employed is £200. The firm can employ any number of workers at a constant wage rate per unit of labour of £50. What is the value of the following if: (a) 1 unit of labour (b) 2 units of labour; (c) 3 units of labour; (d) 4 units of labour are employed?
(i) Total fixed costs (ii) Total variable costs (iii) Total costs (iv) Average fixed costs (v) Average variable costs (vi) Total average cost (vii) Marginal cost.

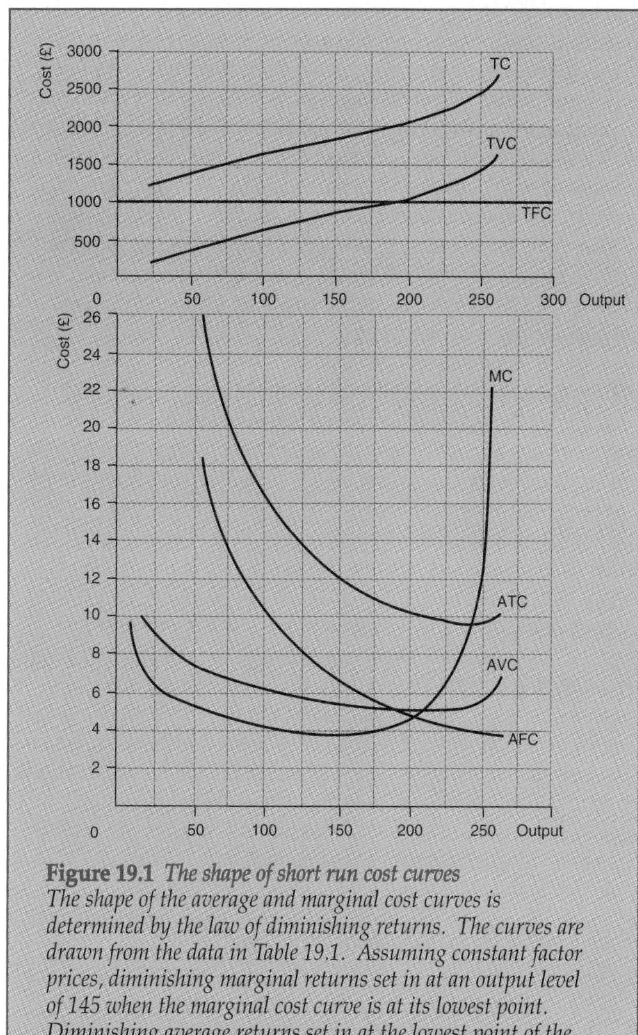

Figure 19.1 *The shape of short run cost curves*
The shape of the average and marginal cost curves is determined by the law of diminishing returns. The curves are drawn from the data in Table 19.1. Assuming constant factor prices, diminishing marginal returns set in at an output level of 145 when the marginal cost curve is at its lowest point. Diminishing average returns set in at the lowest point of the average variable cost curve at an output of 210 units.

Short run cost curves

The cost schedules in Table 19.1 can be plotted on a graph (Figure 19.1) to produce cost curves.

Total cost curves The total fixed cost (TFC) curve is a horizontal straight line, showing that TFC is constant whatever the level of output. The total cost (TC) and total variable cost (TVC) curves are parallel because the vertical distance between the two (the difference between TC and TVC) is the constant total fixed cost. The inflections in the TC and TVC curves are caused by the change from increasing returns to diminishing returns.

Average cost curves The average fixed cost (AFC) curve falls as output increases because fixed costs represent an ever decreasing proportion of total cost as output increases. The average cost (AC) curve and average variable cost (AVC) curve fall at first and then rise. They rise because diminishing average returns set in. The vertical distance between the AC and AVC curves is the value of average fixed cost. This must be true because average cost minus average variable cost is equal to average fixed cost.

Marginal cost curve The marginal cost (MC) curve at first falls and then rises as diminishing marginal returns set in.

Points to note

U-shaped AC and MC curves The MC and AC curves in Figure 19.1 are 'U-shaped'. This is a characteristic not just of the sample figures in Table 19.1, but of all short run MC and AC curves. They are U-shaped because of the law of diminishing returns. The lowest point on the MC and the AVC curves shows the point where diminishing marginal returns and diminishing average returns set in respectively.

Product and cost curves The marginal and average cost curves shown in Figure 19.1 are mirror images of the marginal and average product curves that could be drawn from the same data in Table 19.1. Marginal and average physical product rise when marginal and average cost fall, and vice versa. This is what should be expected. If marginal physical product is rising, then the extra cost of producing a unit of output must fall, and similarly with average physical product and average variable cost. For instance, when the second worker produces 34 units, the third worker 46 units and the fourth worker 51 units, the marginal cost of production must be falling because the increase in output is rising faster than the increase in cost. When marginal physical product is falling, the extra cost of producing a unit output must rise for the same reason. However, the cost and product curves will only be mirror images of each other if there are constant factor costs per unit. If, for instance, we assumed that the unit cost of labour rose as more workers were employed, so that the average wage of three workers was higher than the average wage of two, then the product and cost curves would not be mirror images.

MC curve cuts AC curve at its lowest point In Figure 19.1, the marginal cost curve cuts the average cost curve and average variable cost curve at their lowest points. To understand why this must be so, consider the example of a group of students whose average height is 6 feet. A new student (the marginal student) arrives in the group. If the student is above 6 feet then the average height of the group will now rise. If the student is less than 6 feet, the average height of the group will fall. If the student is exactly 6 feet herself, then the average height of the group will stay the same. Now apply this to average and marginal cost. If the average cost curve is falling, then the cost of an extra unit of output (the marginal cost) must be less than the average cost. If average cost is rising, it must be true that the cost of an extra unit of output is even higher than the average cost. When average cost is neither rising or falling, marginal cost must be the same as average cost. Hence we know that:

- the average cost curve is above the marginal cost curve when average cost is falling;
- the average cost curve is below the marginal cost curve when average cost is rising;
- average cost and marginal cost are equal for all levels of output when average cost is constant; if the average cost curve is U-shaped, this means that marginal cost will be equal to and will cut the average cost curve at its lowest point.

The same chain of reasoning applies to the relationship between the average variable cost curve and the marginal cost curve.

QUESTION 2

Table 19.3

Units

Capital	Labour	Total product
10	0	0
10	1	8
10	2	24
10	3	42
10	4	60
10	5	70
10	6	72

Table 19.3 shows the change in total product as more labour is added to production and all other factor products remain constant. The price of capital is £1 per unit whilst labour is £2 per unit.

(a) Calculate the following over the range of output from zero to 72 units: (i) total fixed cost; (ii) total variable cost; (iii) total cost; (iv) average fixed cost; (v) average variable cost; (vi) average total cost; (vii) marginal cost.
(b) Plot each of these cost schedules on graph paper, putting the total cost curves on one graph and the average and marginal cost curves on another.
(c) Mark on the graph the point where (i) diminishing marginal returns and (ii) diminishing average returns set in.

Applied economics

Diminishing returns in agriculture

In agriculture, farmers combine land, labour and capital to produce their crops. Land could be said to be a fixed factor of production. Labour and capital, however, are variable. Therefore, in theory, farmers could face diminishing returns. Is there any evidence to suggest that this is the case?

Table 19.4 shows growth rates of total food production across the world by area during the period 1961 to 1992. The annual rate of growth of food production fell from 3.1 per cent in the 1960s to 1.9 per cent in the 1980s and early 1990s. This might suggest the existence of diminishing returns, but any such conclusion would, in fact, be very debatable for a number of reasons.

- Whilst regions have seen a fall in the annual rate of growth of production, some increased their rate of growth between decades. The socialist countries of Asia, which includes China, had a higher growth rate of output in the 1980s and early 1990s than they did in the 1970s. The 1980s were also difficult times for agriculture in certain parts of the world due to drought. Sub-Saharan Africa was badly affected throughout the decade, whilst, for instance, the US drought of 1988 saw an overall 7 per cent fall in US food production in that year.
- The figures say nothing about factor inputs. The proportion of the world's labour force working in agriculture fell from 71 per cent in 1960 to 59 per cent in 1980 in the developing world, whilst in the developed world it fell from 28 per cent in 1960 to 12 per cent in 1980. This meant that the agricultural labour force increased in the Third World but decreased in the First World. In the First World, where diminishing returns

Table 19.4 *Annual average growth rate of food production*

	Total food production		
	1961-70	1970-80	1980-92
World	3.1	2.4	1.9
Developed market economies	2.3	2.0	0.6
of which			
US	2.2	2.3	0.8
Canada	2.4	2.4	0.9
UK	1.5	1.6	0.5
Developing countries	2.9	2.9	2.8
Eastern European countries	3.6	1.4	0.4
Socialist countries of Asia	5.4	3.3	4.2

Source: adapted from UNCTAD, *Handbook of International Trade and Development Statistics.*

should have been found to be greatest because land is being used most intensively, increases in output per worker throughout the period 1961-92 averaged 3 per cent per annum. Fewer workers produced more food.

- Both in the USA and in the EC, the 1980s and 1990s saw an attempt by government to restrict the growth of food output. Supply was far outstripping demand in domestic markets where farmers were receiving large subsidies. So the fall in the growth of output in these regions probably had far more to do with government policy than with the law of diminishing returns.

Why is there little clear evidence of diminishing returns in agriculture? Part of the reason must be that land itself is in one sense not a fixed factor of production. Although the total quantity of land is in fixed supply, its productive potential has a great deal to do with the quality of land. The productivity of land can be greatly improved, for instance through drainage, irrigation and the use of fertilizers. Many economists in the past, including Malthus, an early 19th century British economist, have predicted that agricultural production could not keep up with the growth in population. However, so far they have been proved wrong. The average world increase in food production per capita was 0.54 per cent per annum between 1961 and 1992, and in the developed world, the main problem in agriculture is not under-production but over-production.

Holiday cottages

Jim and Mavis Edwards run a holiday accommodation business in the Lake District. Jim retired in 1985, earning a large golden handshake. He used the money to buy his first four cottages. Having found them immediately profitable, he bought up another six in quick succession, using all the cottages as collateral for mortgages on the new properties.

Jim and Mavis didn't take anything out of the business in its first four years. With hindsight, this was possibly the wisest decision they made. They were able to make large inroads into their mortgages in the first few years. By the time mortgage interest rates had climbed to astronomical levels in 1989, much of their debt was repaid and they were able to survive the recession of the early 1990s despite falls in occupancy rates.

Jim and Mavis aimed up market. They refurbished the properties to create the atmosphere and quality they themselves would want out of a holiday cottage. Fees were pitched slightly higher than others in local villages. 'You must charge a decent rental or you can't pay to keep it up. Then the place goes downhill and visitors don't return.' Today, they have a repeat booking rate of 65 per cent.

Initially, they hired all the help they needed locally, but changed that policy in 1989 because the standard was variable. Now they sub-contract the cleaning to a company in Barrow-in-Furness. 'It's worked very well. We now spend £6 500 per year on cleaning.'

All other labour continues to be local. The Edwards have built up a reliable army of builders and plumbers, who will come out at short notice at inconvenient times. This reliability matters in a remote rural area. 'If the plumbing fails in one cottage, it's important that clients see us dealing with a problem straight away.'

They advertise in a range of publications. However, they found that increasing their advertising budget substantially brought in few extra bookings. On the other hand, the year they cut back their advertising by 25 per cent saw a near disastrous 25 per cent fall in bookings. The most effective advertising they do is simply placing a stand outside their home with free leaflets which are taken by passing tourists. 'The cheapest publicity brings in the most enquiries.'

1. Identify the fixed and variable costs involved in running the Edwards' estate of 10 holiday cottages.

2. To what extent would the Edwards suffer increasing or diminishing returns if: (a) they increased their advertising; (b) their occupancy rates went up from 65 per cent to 75 per cent?

3. (a) What might happen to costs if the Edwards bought another 5 cottages, but didn't increase advertising, their own time spent working for the business or their drawings (their income taken) from the business?

(b) Suggest what the Edwards should consider in making a decision about whether or not to buy an extra 5 cottages.

unit 20 Economies of scale

Summary

1. Economic theory suggests that the long run average cost curve is U-shaped.
2. Production is at an optimal level when average cost is lowest.
3. Sources of economies of scale are technical, managerial, purchasing and marketing and financial.
4. Diseconomies of scale may arise due to the inability of management to control large organisations.
5. External economies will shift the average cost curve downwards.
6. The long run average cost curve of a firm is an envelope for the firm's short run average cost curves.

Economies of scale and average cost

In the long run, all factors of production are variable. This has an effect on costs as output changes. To start with, long run costs fall as output increases. ECONOMIES OF SCALE are then said to exist. For instance, a firm doubles its output from 10 million units to 40 million units. However, total costs of production only increase from £10 million to £20 million. The average cost of production consequently falls from £1 per unit (£10m ÷ 10m) to 50p per unit (£20m ÷ 40m).

Empirically (i.e. from studying real examples of the costs of firms), economists have found that firms do experience economies of scale. As firms expand in size and output, their long run average costs tend to fall. At some point, which varies from industry to industry, long run average costs become constant. However, some firms become too large and their average costs begin to rise. They are then said to experience DISECONOMIES OF SCALE. For instance, if a firm doubled its output, but as a result its costs were four times as high, then the average cost of production would double.

This pattern of falling and the rising long run average costs is shown in Figure 20.1. At output levels up to OA, the firm will enjoy falling long run average costs and therefore experience economies of scale. Between output levels of OA and OB, long run average costs are constant. To the right of OB, long run average costs rise and the firm faces diseconomies of scale.

LRAC in Figure 20.1 is drawn given a set of input prices for costs. If the cost of all raw materials in the economy rose by 20 per cent, then there would be a shift upward in the LRAC curve. Similarly, a fall in the wage rates in the industry would lead to a downward shift in the LRAC curve.

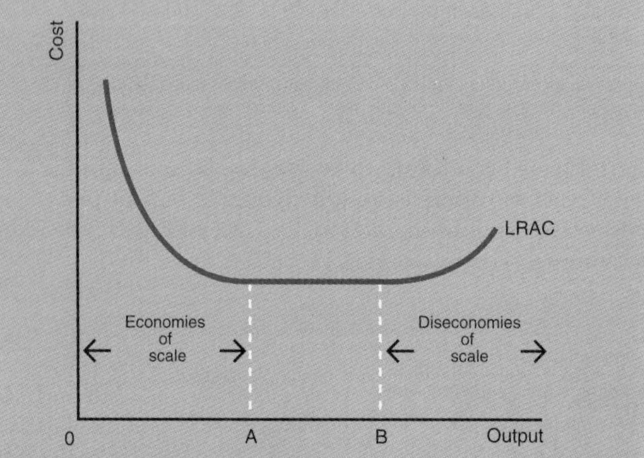

Figure 20.1 *Economies of scale.*
The long run average cost curve is U-shaped because long run average costs:
- *at first fall over the output range OA showing economies of scale;*
- *then are constant over the output range AB;*
- *then rise when output exceeds OB showing diseconomies of scale.*

Over the output range AB, the minimum cost level of production, the firm is said to be at its optimum level of production.

The optimum level of production

Productive efficiency is said to exist when production takes place at lowest cost (☞ unit 34). If the long run average cost curve is U-shaped, then this will occur at the bottom of the curve when constant returns to scale exist. The output range over which average costs are at a minimum is said to be the OPTIMAL LEVEL OF PRODUCTION. In Figure 20.1 the optimal level of production occurs over the range AB.

The output level at which lowest cost production starts is

QUESTION 1

Table 20.1

Output (million units)	Long run average cost (£) Firm A	Firm B	Firm C	Firm D	Firm E
1	10	20	16	19	20
2	8	18	14	18	17
3	5	16	15	17	15
4	5	11	17	16	14
5	5	10	20	15	14
6	5	10	24	14	14
7	6	11	30	13	14

For each firm, A to E, give:

(a) the range of output over which there are:
(i) economies of scale; (ii) diseconomies of scale;
(b) the optimum level or range of output;
(c) the minimum efficient scale of production.

called the MINIMUM EFFICIENT SCALE (MES) of production. In Figure 20.1, the MES is at point A. If a firm is producing to the left of the MES, then long run average costs will be higher. To the right, they will either be the same (if there are constant returns) or will be increasing (if there are diseconomies of scale).

Sources of economies of scale

Economies of scale occur for a number of reasons.

Technical economies Economies and diseconomies of scale can exist because of **increasing** and **decreasing** returns returns to scale (☞ unit 17). These economies and diseconomies are known as **technical economies**. They arise from what happens in the production process. For instance, many firms find that they need equipment but are unable to make maximum use of it. For instance, a small builder may use a cement mixer on average only 3 days a week. If he were able to take on more work he might be able to use it 5 days a week. The total cost of the cement mixer is the same whether used for 3 days or 5 days a week (apart from possible depreciation) but the average cost per job done will be lower the more it is used. This is an example of an **indivisibility**. The larger the level of output, the less likely that indivisibilities will occur.

Technical economies arise too because larger plant size is often more productively efficient. For instance, because an oil tanker is essentially a cylinder, doubling the surface area of the tanker (and therefore doubling the approximate cost of construction) of an oil tanker leads to an approximate three-fold increase in its carrying capacity. It is generally cheaper to generate electricity in large power stations than in small ones. The average cost of production of a car plant making 50 000 cars a year will be less than one making 5 000 cars a year.

So far, it has been assumed that unit costs are constant. However, unit costs may change as a firm changes in size. Other factors, apart from technical economies, can then lead to economies and diseconomies of scale.

Managerial economies Specialisation (☞ unit 2), is an important source of greater efficiency. In a small firm, the owner might be part time salesman, accountant, receptionist and manager. Employing specialist staff is likely to lead to greater efficiency and therefore lower costs. The reason why small firms don't employ specialist staff is because staff often represent an indivisibility.

Purchasing and marketing economies The larger the firm the more likely it is to be able to buy raw materials in bulk. Bulk buying often enables these firms to secure lower prices for their factor inputs. Large firms are also able to enjoy lower average costs from their marketing operations. The cost of a sales force selling 40 different lines of merchandise is very much the same as one selling 35 lines. A 30 second TV commercial for a product which has sales of £10 million per annum costs the same as a 30 second TV commercial for one which has sales of only £5 million per annum.

Financial economies Small firms often find it difficult and expensive to raise finance for new investment. When loans are given, small firms are charged at relatively high rates of interest because banks know that small firms are far more at risk from bankruptcy than large firms. Large firms have a much greater choice of finance and it is likely to be much cheaper than for small firms.

QUESTION 2 Whirlpool, the large US producer of white goods such as freezers and washing machines, bought the Philips white goods business in 1991 from the Philips Group. It set about cutting costs and exploiting the potential economies of scale in the business. Traditionally, the business had been organised on a national basis. Whirlpool wanted to exploit the new Single Market in the European Union by selling products on a European scale. Fewer suppliers were used, but each supplying more components, lowering cost and increasing ability to control quality. Production and models were rationalised, with fewer production centres and fewer basic models but higher production levels of each model. In 1995, the company rationalised its sales organisation. Instead of a country by country structure, it set up a pan-European organisation concentrating on free standing equipment, typically sold through shops, and built-in equipment, typically sold through the trade to builders and kitchen fitters.

Source: adapted from the *Financial Times*, 29.12.1994.

Discuss what economies of scale Whirlpool achieved through reorganising the old Philips business it bought in 1991 on European rather than national lines.

Diseconomies of scale

Diseconomies of scale arise mainly due to management problems. As a firm grows in size it becomes more and more difficult for management to keep control of the activities of the organisation. There are a variety of ways of dealing with this problem. Some companies choose to centralise operations with a small, tightly-knit team controlling all activities. Sometimes a single charismatic figure, often the founder of the company, will keep tight control of all major decisions. In other companies, management is decentralised with many small subsidiary companies making decisions about their part of the business and head office only making those decisions which affect the whole group. However, controlling an organisation which might employ hundreds of thousands of workers is not easy and there may come a point where no management team could prevent average costs from rising.

Geography too may lead to higher average costs. If a firm has to transport goods (whether finished goods or raw materials) over long distances because it is so large, then average costs may rise. Head office may also find it far more difficult to control costs in an organisation 1 000 miles away than in one on its door step.

Movements along and shifts in the long run average cost curve

The long run average cost curve is a boundary. It represents the minimum level of average costs attainable at any given level of output. In Figure 20.2, points below the LRAC curve are unattainable. A firm could produce above the LRAC boundary, but if it were to do this it would not use the most efficient method to produce any given level of output. So a firm could, for instance, produce at the point A, but it would be less efficient than a firm producing the same quantity at the point B.

An increase in output which leads to a fall in costs would be shown by a **movement along** the LRAC curve. However, there are a variety of reasons why the LRAC might **shift**.

External economies of scale The economies of scale discussed so far in this unit have been INTERNAL ECONOMIES OF SCALE. Internal economies arise because of the growth in output of the firm. EXTERNAL ECONOMIES OF SCALE arise when there is a growth in the size of the industry in which the firm operates. For instance, the growth of a particular industry in an area might lead to the construction of a better local road network, which in turn reduces costs to individual firms. Or a firm might experience lower training costs because other firms are training workers which it can then poach. The local authority might provide training facilities free of charge geared to the needs of a particular industry. The government might assist with export contracts for a large industry but not a small industry. External economies of scale will shift the LRAC curve of an individual firm downwards. At any given level of output, its costs will be lower because the industry as a whole has grown.

Taxation If the government imposes a tax upon industry, costs will rise, shifting the LRAC curve of each firm upwards. For instance, if the government increased employers' National Insurance contributions, a tax upon the wage bill of a company, the total cost of labour would rise, pushing up average costs.

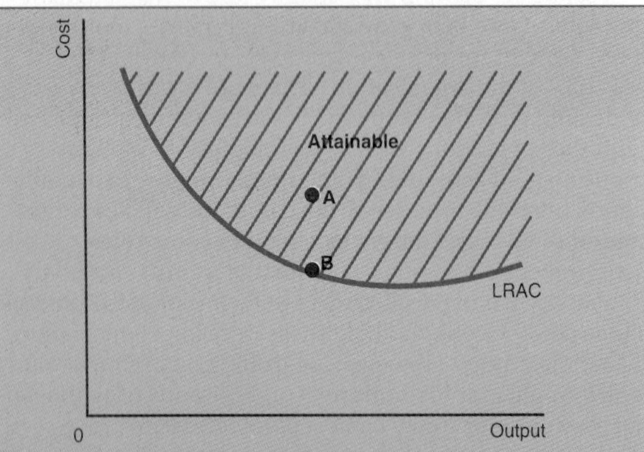

Figure 20.2 *The LRAC as a boundary*
The LRAC curve is a boundary between levels of costs which are attainable and those which are unattainable. If a firm is producing on the LRAC curve, then it is producing at long run minimum cost for any given level of output, such as at point B. If long run production is inefficient, cost will be within the LRAC boundary such as at point A.

Technology The LRAC curve is drawn on the assumption that the state of technology remains constant. The introduction of new technology which is more efficient than the old will reduce average costs and push the LRAC curve downwards.

External diseconomies of scale These will shift the long run average cost curve of individual firms in the industry upwards. They occur when an industry expands quickly. Individual firms are then forced to compete with each other and bid up the prices of factor inputs like wages and raw materials.

QUESTION 3 In 1989, the government announced a £12 billion road building programme over the following 10 years. The Road Hauliers' Association, representing firms in the road transport business, welcomed the announcement and claimed that if the programme were not implemented the costs of road haulage in the UK would continue to rise due to increased congestion.

Explain, using a diagram, the argument of the Road Hauliers' Association.

The relationship between the short run average cost curve and the long run average cost curve.

In the short run, at least one factor is fixed. Short run average costs at first fall, and then begin to rise because of diminishing returns. In the long run, all factors are variable. Long run average costs change because of economies and diseconomies of scale.

In the long run, a company is able to choose a scale of production which will maximise its profits. Assume in Figure 20.3 that it decides to produce in the long run at point A. It buys factors of production such as plant and machinery to operate at this level. Later it wishes to expand production by PQ but in the short run it has fixed factors of production. Expanding production may well lead to lower average costs as it does in Figure 20.3. Diminishing average returns have not set in at point A. But production must be less cost efficient at B compared to the long run situation where the firm could have varied all its factors of production and produced at C. At B the firm is working with plant and machinery designed to work at optimum efficiency at a lower output level OP. At C, the firm is working with plant and machinery designed to produce at C.

Similarly, if D and F are long run cost positions, a firm producing at E with plant and machinery designed to produce at D must be less cost effective than a firm operating at F with a factory designed to produce OS of output.

A, C, D, F, G and J are least cost points in the long run. Combining these, as in Figure 20.4, we get a long run average cost curve. For each point on this curve there is an associated short run average cost curve, such as AB. If the firm operates in the short run at the point where the short run cost curve just touches (is tangential to) the long run cost curve, then it is operating where the company thought it would operate when it was able to vary all its factor inputs. If short run output is different from this position, then its short run costs will be higher than if it could have varied all its factors of production. But it could be higher or lower than the tangency point depending upon whether diminishing returns have or have not set in.

The long run average cost curve is said to be the envelope for the short run average cost curves because it contains them all.

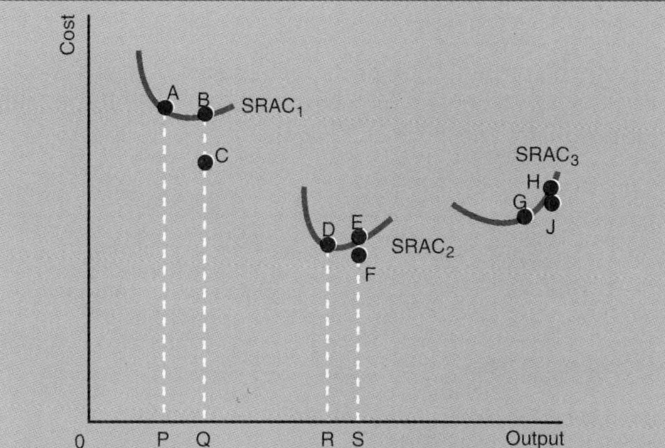

Figure 20.3 *The long run average cost curve*
In the long run, all factors are variable. Points A, D and G show long run cost levels at different levels of production. If the firm in the short run then expands production, average costs may fall or rise to B, E or H respectively. But they will be above the long run costs, C, F and J, for those levels of output because the cost of production with at least one fixed factor is likely to be higher than the cost if all factors were variable.

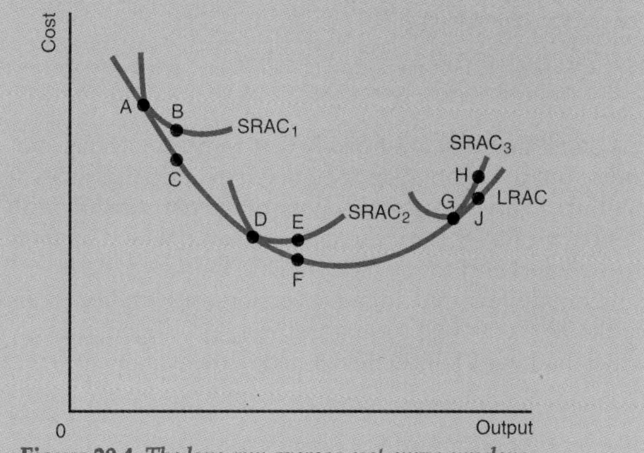

Figure 20.4 *The long run average cost curve envelope*
The long run average cost curve is an envelope for all the associated short run average cost curves because long run average cost is either equal to or below the relevant short run average cost.

QUESTION 4 In 1989, Ford announced that it was to transfer part of the production of its (now discontinued) Sierra model from Dagenham in the UK to Genk in Belgium. Dagenham in future would only make the Fiesta model. It blamed the move on high costs of production at Dagenham. Part of the problem lay in the inefficient physical layout of the 50 year old Dagenham plant. At the same time, Toyota was announcing the building of a green field motor manufacturing plant near Derby.

Using a diagram, explain why you might expect Toyota to enjoy lower average costs of production at its Derby plant than Ford at its Dagenham plant.

Key terms

Economies of scale - a fall in the long run average costs of production as output rises.
Diseconomies of scale - a rise in the long run average costs of production as output rises.
Optimal level of production - the range of output over which long run average cost is lowest.
Minimum efficient scale of production - the lowest level of output at which long run average cost is minimised.
Internal economies of scale - economies of scale which arise because of the growth in the scale of production within a firm.
External economies of scale - falling average costs of production, shown by a downward shift in the average cost curve, which result from a growth in the size of the industry within which a firm operates.

Applied economics

Economies of scale

Economic theory suggests that, in the long run, a firm will experience first economies of scale, but eventually diseconomies of scale will set in. The long run average cost curve is therefore U-shaped. However, research in this area tends to support the view that long run average cost curves in practice are not U-shaped but L-shaped. Firms experience economies of scale, but when output reaches the minimum efficient scale of production, average costs do not start to climb but remain constant. For instance, CF Pratten (1971) studied 25 industries, including newspapers, soap, oil, bread and steel and found L-shaped rather than U-shaped long run average cost curves.

Figure 20.5 shows an estimate of economies of scale in three areas of vehicle production: diesel engine production, commercial vehicles and cars. Economies of scale are largest in car production and smallest in diesel engine production. This is what would be expected given the much greater complexity of car production than engine production. Note, however, that the evidence suggests that for cars most economies of scale have been gained with an annual production of 2 million. But the market for commercial vehicles and diesel engines is much smaller and it was not possible to estimate data for production levels over 100 000 units a year. The data would suggest that economies of scale had not been exhausted at these production levels for these two products and that therefore existing producers had not reached the minimum efficient scale of production.

The sources of economies of scale in car manufacturing are shown in Table 20.2. For instance, the minimum efficient scale of production for the casting of an engine block is 1 million units a year whilst in final assembly it is 250 000 units a year. Economies of scale are greatest in research and development at 5 million units a year. This explains the proliferation of mergers, takeovers and co-operation agreements which have characterised the world motor industry for the past 20 years.

Table 20.2 *Economies of scale in car production*

	Minimum efficient scale of production volume output per year (millions)
Technical economies	
Casting of engine block	1
Casting of various other parts	0.1-0.75
Power train (engine, transmission, etc.) machining and assembly	0.6
Pressing of various panels	1-2
Paint shop	0.25
Final assembly	0.25
Non-technical economies	
Advertising	1
Sales	2
Risks	1
Finance	2
Research and development	5

Source: Garel Rhys, 'Economics of the Motor Industry', *Economics*, Journal of the Economics Association, Volume XXIV, Part 4, no.104, Winter 1988, p.161.

A small manufacturer like Rover, for instance, had no choice but to collaborate or be taken over. In the 1980s, it built up a very successful collaborative partnership with Honda, a smaller Japanese manufacturer, which seemed the way forward for the company in the 1990s. At first Rover manufactured adapted versions of Honda cars and by the 1990s the two companies were producing cars which had been jointly developed. However, in 1994

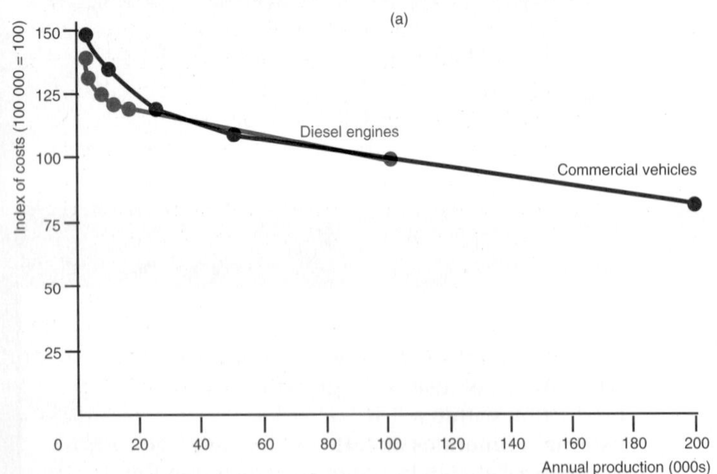

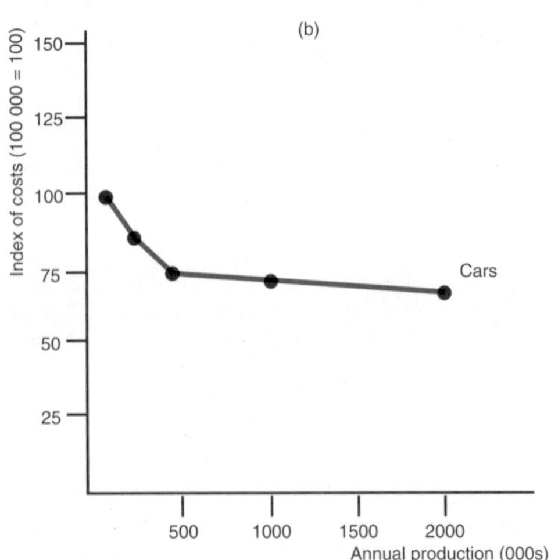

Source: adapted from Garel Rhys, 'Heavy Commercial Vehicles: a decade of change', *National Westminster Bank Quarterly Review* August 1984; Garel Rhys, 'Economics of the Motor Industry', *Economics*, Volume XXIV, Part 4, no.104, Winter 1988.

Figure 20.5 *Economies of scale in vehicle manufacture*

Rover's owner, British Aerospace, sold the company to BMW, another small European car manufacturer also looking for economies of scale. The Honda partnership looked at risk, but BMW wanted the link to continue and Honda decided that it was in its own best interest to keep the relationship going at least for the time being. BMW wanted to buy another manufacturer to spread development and production costs across a much larger number of cars sold. Rover was a good fit. It was a relatively small manufacturer and therefore affordable to buy. It had a full range of cars in markets which would not compete with BMW's existing output. It had also benefited enormously in terms of eliminating production inefficiencies and improving quality and reliability of cars from working with Honda.

Joint ventures, mergers and takeovers will continue in the future. With the opening up of markets in Eastern Europe and in Asia, the major car companies will also seek to gain longer production runs by establishing manufacturing facilities in these countries and 'exporting' the fruits of research and development in which there are very large economies of scale to be gained.

The Scottish & Newcastle and Courage merger

Scottish & Newcastle bid for Courage

In May 1995, Scottish & Newcastle (S&N) breweries made a £425m bid for Courage, owned by Foster's Brewing Group of Australia. S&N is particularly strong in the North and in Scotland whilst Courage is particularly strong in the South of England. The deal is likely to herald further restructuring and intensified competition in the UK brewing industry beset by over-capacity and thin profit margins. 'It's going to be a man's game out there', said Mr Mike Foster, chairman of Courage.

Table 20.2 *Main brands*

Scotish & Newcastle	Courage
Newcastle Brown	Courage
Theakston's	John Smith's
McEwan's	Webster's
Younger's	Beamish
Matthew Brown	Hofmeister
Home	Watney's
Gillespie's	Truman
	Wilson's

Brewing

NatWest Securities, the stockbrokers, believes that the combined group could save £35 million a year on its brewing operations. Courage has breweries in Tadcaster and Halifax in Northern England, its main brewery at Reading, west of London, and smaller breweries in London, Bristol and Cork, Ireland. S&N's breweries are mainly in the North of England and in Scotland. Brewing is highly capital intensive. The marginal cost of brewing an extra pint for the large brewers is only 2p. So pushing more orders through a brewery will reduce costs.

Administration

Courage and S&N will not need the administration staff that is needed by two individual companies. Almost certainly, Courage's head office in West London will be closed. Whilst some staff will find jobs elsewhere in the new organisation, many will face redundancy. NatWest Securities estimates that the annual saving on administration of the merger will be £10 million.

Distribution

Distribution costs are an important element in costs for a brewer. Courage, for instance, has 23 sales and distribution depots, mainly in the South of England and the Midlands. S&N will be able to close some of its own distribution depots in the South and push S&N deliveries through Courage depots. Equally, it will be able to rationalise Courage depots in the North. The new group will continue to sell the existing range of brands of beer of the existing two groups. Hence, individual brands will continue to need supporting in terms of advertising and other forms of promotion.

However, there should be scope for rationalising the sales force of the two companies. A growing number of pubs in the UK are independent, rather than being owned by a brewer and forced to stock its beers. Hence, there is a growing need for a salesforce to sell beers to pubs. NatWest Securities estimate that S&N can save £35 million annually on distribution through the merger with Courage.

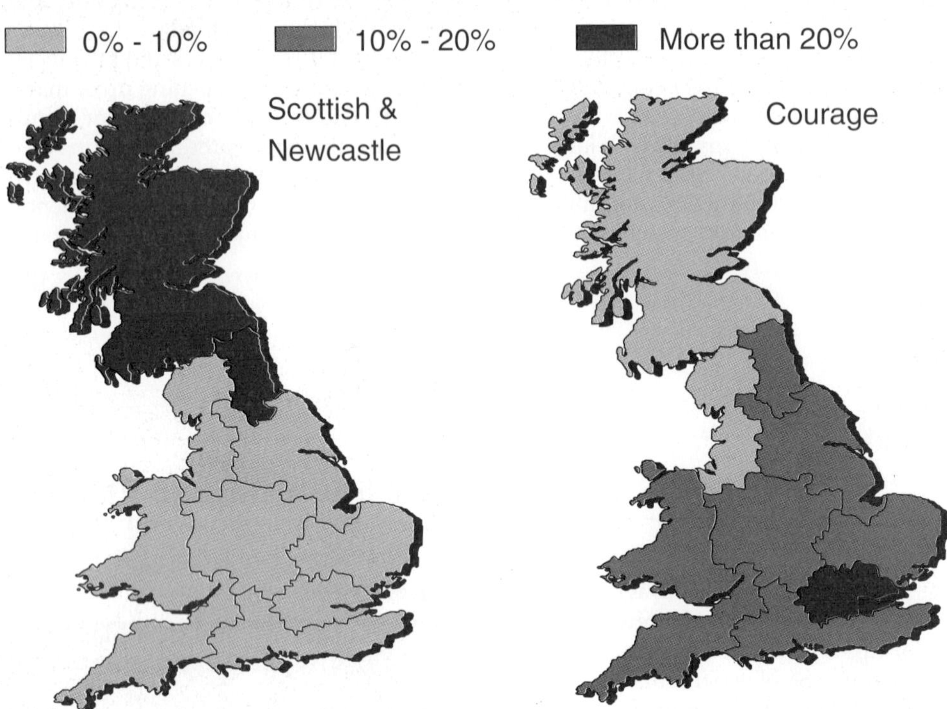

Source: adapted from Scottish & Newcastle.

Figure 20.6 *Share of British beer consumption*

1. What economies of scale might be achieved by the merger?
2. To what extent are the cost reductions arising from the merger reductions in short run rather than long run costs?
3. (a) Who might benefit and who might lose from the merger?
   (b) Discuss whether the government should allow the merger to go ahead.

Isoquants and isocost lines

Summary

1. An isoquant shows different combinations of inputs which can be used to produce a given level of output.
2. An isocost line shows the combination of factor inputs which a firm can buy with a given budget.
3. The firm will minimise cost where the isoquant curve is tangential to its isocost line.
4. A rise in the price of one factor of production will lead to the substitution of that factor by other factors in the production process.

How to produce

It was argued in unit 2 that the function of an economy was to resolve three fundamental economic questions: what to produce, how to produce it and how to distribute it. This unit considers why a firm might decide to use one production technique rather than another, and why firms might change their production techniques over time as, for instance, the cost of labour increases, or the cost of capital decreases. Much of what follows is very similar to indifference curve analysis (☞ unit 15), and just as in indifference curve analysis the economist is interested in how a consumer can maximise utility, so below it will be explained how a firm can minimise its costs through the efficient allocation of factor inputs.

Isoquants

There is a variety of production techniques which a firm could use to produce 1 million chocolate bars a year. Assume that its land or raw material inputs are constant (so it is producing in the short run), but it can vary the amount of labour and capital it uses. As the firm employs more and more labour, economists would predict that it would need to use less and less capital to produce 1 million chocolate bars. Labour can be **substituted** for capital in the production process.

However, the more labour is used, the greater the amount that needs to be substituted to replace 1 unit of capital. Adding an extra 10 workers to a firm which already has many workers but little capital is unlikely to be as productive as adding 10 workers to a firm producing the same good which has few workers but a great deal of capital.

This is shown in Table 21.1. The chocolate firm can use a lot of labour and little capital (such as 100 units of labour and 20 units of capital), or little labour and a lot of capital (such as 12 units of labour and 100 units of capital), or choose some combination in between. Figure 21.1 shows these input combinations in graphical form.

Table 21.1 *Units needed to produce 1 million chocolate bars*

Labour	Capital
100	20
70	30
40	44
20	70
12	100

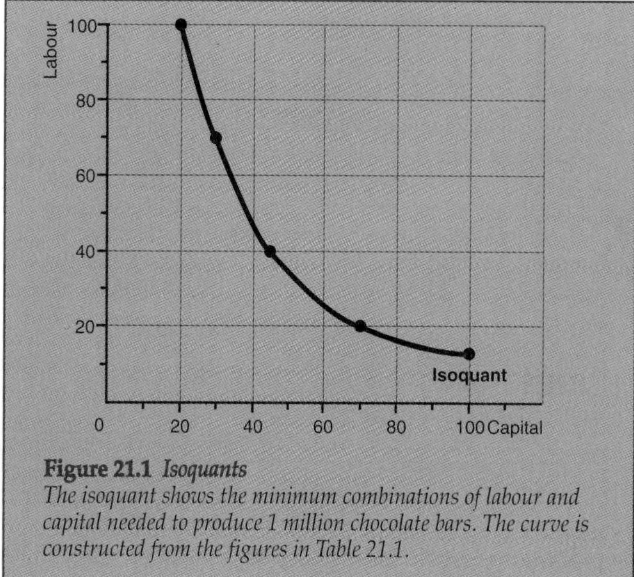

Figure 21.1 *Isoquants*
The isoquant shows the minimum combinations of labour and capital needed to produce 1 million chocolate bars. The curve is constructed from the figures in Table 21.1.

The curve joining the four points shown in Figure 21.1 is known as an ISOQUANT. An isoquant is a line which shows different combinations of inputs needed to produce a given level of output efficiently. Reading off the graph, it would also be possible to produce 1 million chocolate bars a year by using 80 units of labour and 25 units of capital in addition to the points noted in Table 21.1.

The isoquant shows the most efficient form of production possible. It would not be possible to produce 1 million chocolate bars with input combinations below the curve. On the other hand, it is possible to produce above the curve. For instance, 100 units of labour could be combined with 40 units of capital instead of 20, but this input combination would be less **productively efficient** than an input combination on the isoquant.

The isoquant drawn in Figure 21.1 is part of a family of isoquants. Isoquants can be drawn for every production level of chocolate bars. In Figure 21.2, three isoquants are drawn for production levels of 500 000, 1 million and 1.5 million chocolate bars. It takes more inputs to produce 1 million than ½ million chocolate bars, so the isoquant for the former will be farther out from the origin than the latter.

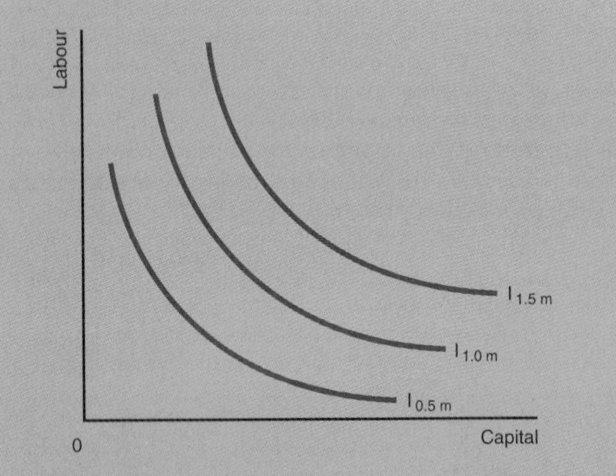

Figure 21.2 *A family of isoquants*
There is an isoquant associated with each level of output. The greater the output, the greater will be the number of inputs needed in the production process. Therefore the isoquant for the production of 1.5 million chocolate bars, $I_{1.5m}$, is farther out from the origin than the isoquants for the production of 1 million or 1/2 million chocolate bars.

QUESTION 1

Table 21.2

Inputs, units per month					
100 units of output		200 units of output		300 units of output	
Labour	Capital	Labour	Capital	Labour	Capital
12	1	12	2	12	4
3	3	6	4	8	6
1	5	2	9	6	10

(a) Draw the three isoquant curves for output levels of 100 units, 200 units and 300 units per month on graph paper.
(b) A firm wishes to produce 100 units per month. State whether the following input combinations are possible but productively inefficient **or** possible and efficient **or** insufficient to produce that level of output: (i) 5 units of labour and 5 units of capital; (ii) 2 units of labour and 2 units of capital; (iii) 8 units of labour and 2 units of capital; (iv) 4 units of labour and 2 units of capital.

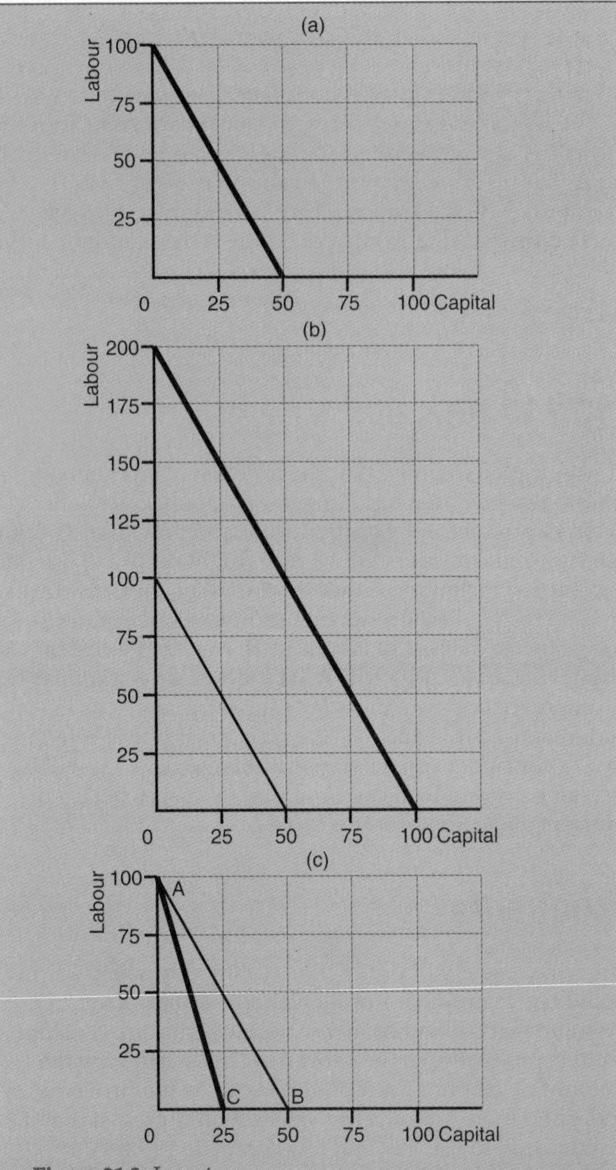

Figure 21.3 *Isocosts*
An isocost line shows the combination of inputs which can be purchased with a fixed budget. Figure 21.3(a) shows the combination of inputs that could be bought with £100 if the price of labour were £1 per unit and the price of capital were £2 per unit. If relative input prices remain unchanged at £1 per unit for labour and £2 per unit for capital, but a firm's budget increases from £100 to £200, then twice the number of inputs can be bought, as in Figure 21.3(b). A doubling in the price of capital from £2 to £4 per unit with the price of labour remaining unchanged, given a budget of £100, will result in a swing of the isocost line from AB to AC as in Figure 21.3(c).

Isocost lines

An ISOCOST LINE shows the combination of factor inputs which a firm can buy with a given budget. For instance, if a firm has a budget of £100 and the price of labour per unit is £1 whilst the price of capital is £2, then the firm can buy 100 units of labour and no units of capital, or no units of labour and 50 units of capital or some combination in between. The isocost line based upon these numbers is shown in Figure 21.3(a).

The slope of the isocost line reflects the relative prices of inputs. The slope of the line in Figure 21.3(a) is 2, showing that 2 units of labour can be bought for every 1 unit of capital not purchased.

If the firm is able to increase its budget, it will be able to buy more labour and capital as in Figure 21.3(b). The budget has increased from £100 to £200, allowing the firm to buy 200 units of labour and no capital **or** no units of labour and 100 units of capital **or** some combination in between. The new line is parallel to the original line because relative prices of labour and capital have not changed. 2 units of labour still cost the same as 1 unit of capital despite the increased budget.

If the relative price of inputs does change, then the slope of the isocost curve will change too. Assume that a firm has a budget of £100, the price of labour is £1 per unit but the cost of capital increases from £2 per unit to £4 per unit. The isocost curve will then shift from AB to AC as in Figure 21.3(c). AB is the same isocost line as drawn in Figure 21.3(a). AC shows the new isocost curve with the higher price of capital. At any given level of input usage, the firm can only buy half the amount of capital because the price of capital has doubled.

QUESTION 2

(a) Draw an isocost line for a firm spending £2 400 per month on factor inputs when labour costs £200 per unit per month and capital £300 per unit per month.
(b) Show how the isocost line changes if: (i) the price of capital now increases to £600 per month; (ii) the firm's budget for the purchase of factor inputs increases to £3 000 per month when the cost of capital is £300 per unit per month.

Cost minimisation

By combining isoquants and isocost lines, it is possible to explain which combination of factors a firm will use in its production process. In Figure 21.4, a firm wishes to produce at an output level associated with the isoquant I. AB, CD and EF are three isocost lines. Production on EF is the most costly, AB the least costly. All three show the same relative cost of labour to capital because the lines are parallel with each other. If the firm chooses to produce at P or R, it will be more costly than if it produces at Q because Q is on a lower isocost line. It cannot produce on the isocost line AB if it wishes to secure an output level associated with the isoquant I. Q is the least cost point of production because CD is the lowest isocost line on which the firm can be.

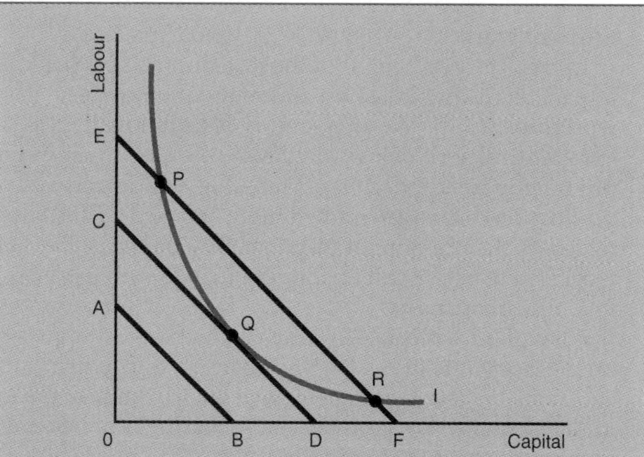

Figure 21.4 Minimum cost of production
A firm wishes to produce a level of output given by the isoquant I. It faces relative input prices shown by the identical slopes of the three isocost lines, AB, CD and EF. It is unable to produce on the line AB because the isoquant I does not cut or touch it. It could produce on the isocost curve EF, but it would be cheaper to produce at the point Q on the isocost curve CD. CD is the lowest isocost curve on which the firm can produce.

A firm will therefore minimise its production costs by choosing that point where the isocost curve is tangential to (just touches) the isoquant. This is the same as saying that cost minimisation will occur where the slope of the isocost line (the relative price of factor inputs) is equal to the slope of the isoquant.

QUESTION 3 Combining the solutions to the previous two sets of questions in this unit,
(a) what is the lowest cost combination of factor inputs if:
(i) output of the firm is 200 units when its budget is £2400 per month, labour costs £200 per unit per month and capital costs £300 per unit per month;
(ii) output of the firm is 100 units when its budget is £2400 per month, labour costs £200 per unit per month and capital costs £600 per unit per month;
(b) what is the minimum budget needed to produce 200 units of output per month when labour costs are £220 per unit and capital costs are £170 per unit per month?

Factor substitution

Common sense tells us that if the price of labour increases when the price of capital remains the same, a firm will react by using less labour and more capital. In other words, capital will be **substituted** for labour.

This can be shown using isoquants and isocost lines. In Figure 21.5, an increase in the price of labour pivots the isocost line round from AB to AC. As a result the firm will no longer be able to produce on the isoquant I_1. With a fixed budget, it will be forced to reduce output to the level given by the isoquant I_2. Production will change from the point P to the point Q.

This change is made up of two components, a **substitution effect** and an **output effect**. The substitution effect occurs because the price of labour has become higher relative to capital. The output effect occurs because the firm now has a smaller real budget to spend on inputs. The size of the substitution effect can be seen by assuming that the company is able to produce the same amount as before (i.e. it can still produce on the isoquant I_1) but that it faces the new relative prices. DE is an isocost line which, being parallel to AC, shows the new relative prices but is also the minimum isocost curve which will allow the company to produce on I_1. At the new prices and the old output level, the firm will produce at R. Hence the movement from P to R is the substitution effect of the

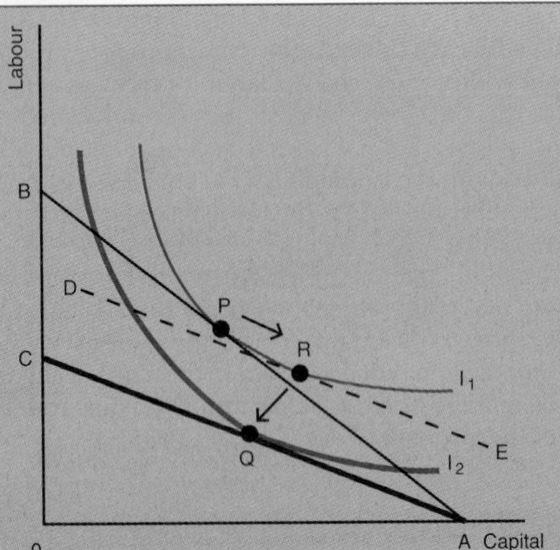

Figure 21.5 *Substitution and output effects.*
A firm producing at the point P on an isocost I_1 is faced with an increase in the cost of labour. As a result, its isocost line pivots round A from AB to AC. It will as a result use less labour as production shifts from the point P to the point Q. Part of the reduced demand for labour occurs because of the substitution effect of the price change. If the firm was in a position to produce the same output as before, but faced new relative prices, then it would have shifted production from P to R: this is the substitution effect of the price change. The output effect is shown by the shift from R to Q when, at the new relative prices, the firm suffers a fall in the real value of its budget.

price change. The movement from R to Q is the output effect. This represents the fall in demand for both labour and capital because the firm is now able to produce less due to the fall in the real value of its budget. Figure 21.5 shows that a firm will buy less labour when the cost of labour rises because labour becomes relatively more expensive to other inputs and because the firm suffers a real fall in its budget.

QUESTION 4 Modern industrial development has been characterised by a rise in the cost of labour relative to capital. What does economic theory predict would happen to the quantity of labour employed in the production process compared to the quantity of capital? Giving examples, discuss whether this prediction is supported by recent economic history.

Key terms

Isoquant - shows different combinations of inputs needed to produce a given level of output efficiently.
Isocost line - shows the combination of factor inputs which a firm can buy with a given budget.

Applied economics

'Just-in-time' production systems

It can be argued that the most important innovation in the manufacturing process since Henry Ford began building cars on a production line has been 'just-in-time' production systems. Pioneered by Toyota in the 1950s and 1960s, it has become standard practice amongst large Japanese manufacturers and has increasingly been adopted by European and American companies in the 1980s. The concept is simple. Instead of holding stocks of goods at every stage of the manufacturing process, firms reduce or eliminate stocks by telling their suppliers to deliver parts only when they are needed. For a car manufacturer this may mean deliveries of parts three or four times a day.

The advantages are numerous. As Clive Wolman, writing in the *Financial Times*, argued: 'Most obviously, just-in-time production leads to a drastic reduction of inventory. This means less working capital, no double handling of components, no laborious checking of materials into and out of storage, and less warehousing space. Just-in-time production allows machines to be placed close to each other - with no work in progress piling up between - which in turn makes it easier for teams of workers to supervise groups of machines'.

'In fact, the key benefit of the just-in-time approach is its impact on the organisation and motivation of the workforce. In the West, inventory is traditionally used as a buffer to absorb delays - and also mistakes. Just-in-time production is supposed to ensure that any defects and any production delays are immediately exposed. This in turn increases the pressure of responsibility on the individual workers; he or she can no longer bury defective products in a pile of inventory.'

What effect have just-in-time production techniques had on the isoquant curves facing a manufacturing firm such as Toyota? These techniques have led to a shift to the left in the isoquant curves as shown in Figure 21.6. Assume that before the introduction of just-in-time production, a firm produces at the point A on the isoquant I_1. The new techniques allow the firm to produce the same amount using fewer factors of production. The isoquant shifts to I_2 and the firm now produces at B. It has been able to make a substantial reduction in its use of inventories of PQ, but the other advantages of just-in-time production also enable a reduction in the use of all other factors of RS.

In general, technical progress in production will lead to a shift to the left of isoquant curves facing a firm. With a constant budget and no change in the relative prices of factors, this means that firms will be able to produce more, shown by a movement to a higher isoquant curve. This in turn is likely to lead to lower prices, the outcome that would be expected from technical progress.

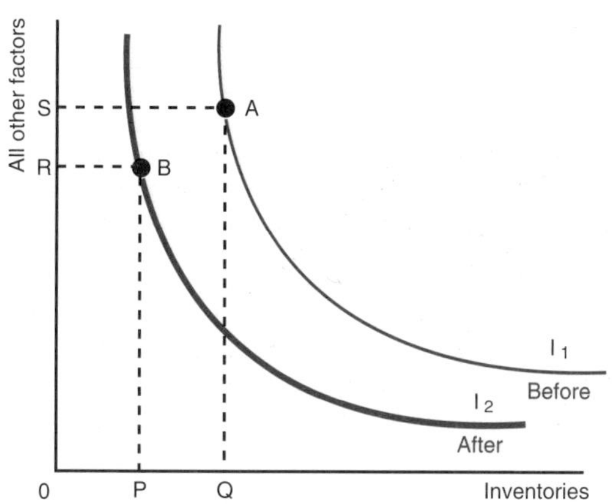

Figure 21.6

Grasshopper Babywear

Grasshopper Babywear, based in Wolverhampton, has a customer list which reads like a Who's Who of the High Street. Debenhams, Littlewoods, Boots, Mothercare, Safeway, Asda, Childrens World, BhS and Woolworths are among its customers. The group is now Europe's biggest producer of clothes for the under-twos. Grasshopper's Chair, Mr John Matto, today unveiled the sophisticated computer-controlled cutting and planning machines which have been installed at the group's production divisions in Wolverhampton and Cumbria. Traditionally, the new technology destroys jobs but in Grasshopper's case, the opposite has happened.

Customers like Mothercare have been impressed by the investment - and the £4.5m creation of a dyehouse subsidiary in Nottingham - and upped their orders.

Fabric waste has halved to around five per cent, efficiency standards have improved by between five and ten per cent and quality is also up, with work now done to tolerances of just a centimetre.

Instead of laboriously producing templates by hand, it is a simple task to use the computer to 'lift' the design from its data bank. It is also far easier to ask the CAD-CAM equipment to work long hours.

Mr Matto says the machine can be left overnight with a series of shapes to fit onto fabric and will have produced the optimum solution by morning.

The hi-tech investment also helps destroy the sweat shop image of the clothing industry.

Staff training is a key focus for the Wolverhampton division's general manager Mike Henshaw. 'We are determined to persuade people that we do not see them as production line fodder and we encourage machinists and supervisors to reach NVQ2 level to try to develop a career in textiles.'

'They really are enthusiastic about it because most have not received any education since they left school.'

Source: *Express and Star*, 19.6.1995.

1. **Explain, giving examples, what factors of production are likely to be used by Grasshopper Babywear to manufacture clothes.**
2. **Using the concept of isocost and isoquant lines, discuss why Grasshopper has changed its production techniques.**
3. **Grasshopper is committed to increasing the skills of its staff. What economic benefits would the company gain from an increase in skill level?**

Business finance in the UK

Applied economics

Cost, revenue and cash flow

A company's finances can be split into two types. A company, operating on a day to day basis, receives money from sales of goods (its sales **turnover**) and pays out money (its **costs**), for instance to its workers in wages and to its suppliers. The difference between the monies received by a company and its outgoings over a period of time is known as the CASH FLOW of the company. Table 22.1 shows the cash flow for a new company over its first six months of operation.

Table 22.1

Month	1	2	3	4	5	6
Receipts(£)	10	20	30	40	50	60
Payments(£)	50	30	10	10	10	10
Cash flow(£)	-40	-10	20	30	40	50

The cash flow is negative for the first two months. Far more is paid out than is received. However, the cash flow for the next four months is positive. Overall, the company is in a strong position, but without financial reserves or an ability to borrow money it would go out of business at the end of the first month.

A company needs financial capital to cope with negative cash flows. In a company starting up, or a company which is growing, negative cash flows are often associated with investment by the company - the purchase of equipment, premises, stock, etc. The rest of this unit will consider ways in which companies can obtain funds for investment.

Sources of funds for companies

Table 22.2 shows how companies in the UK raise funds to finance investment (e.g. additions to their stock of capital).

Table 22.2 *Sources of capital funds for industrial and commercial companies, 1981-1994*

£ million

	1981	1983	1985	1987	1989	1991	1993	1994
Retained profit	20 569	26 771	29 894	33 810	25 758	36 241	51 702	66 349
Bank borrowing	6 340	1 552	7 454	12 142	33 386	-922	-11 284	-5 289
Ordinary shares	900	1 872	3 407	13 410	2 340	9 761	14 372	8 775
Debenture and preference shares	523	608	1 586	2 935	7 034	5 673	2 900	1 564
Other	2 590	3 733	1 946	6 899	22 503	18 241	19 026	-455
Total	28 971	34 536	44 287	69 196	91 021	68 994	76 716	70 944

Source: adapted from CSO, *Financial Statistics*.

Retained profit RETAINED PROFIT is by far the most important source of company finance in the UK. Companies split the profits they make three ways. They give some to their shareholders in the form of **dividends**. Some is taken by the government in tax (mainly corporation tax). The rest, **retained profit**, is kept by companies to plough back into the business.

Bank borrowing Bank borrowing is the second most important source of company finance. Essentially there are only two types of bank borrowing. An **overdraft** facility allows a company to borrow and repay money at will within a specified limit. A **loan** is where money is lent to the company on a certain date and it has to be repaid in regular instalments on specified dates. There are many variations on these two basic forms of borrowing, and the bigger the sum borrowed the more hybrid might be the borrowing package offered by a bank or group of banks. The largest companies in the world are able to borrow hundreds of millions of pounds at a time to finance their capital needs.

Ordinary shares An **ordinary share** or **equity stake** signifies ownership of a part of a company. Shareholders buy shares because they thus become entitled to a share of the profits (company dividends). Also, they hope that the company will grow in value and this will be reflected in an increased share price. They will then be able to make a **capital gain** by selling their shares for more than they bought them. When a company issues new shares, it creates new part owners of the company, diluting the percentage of the company owned by existing shareholders. Ordinary shareholders carry the greatest risk in a company. All bills, including interest on bank loans, will be paid before shareholders receive a dividend. If the company makes a loss no dividend will be paid, but the interest on a loan or overdraft will still need to be paid.

Preference shares and debentures A **preference share** is a share which carries a fixed rate of dividend (such as 5 per cent), but is less risky than an ordinary share because preference shareholders must be paid in full before ordinary shareholders can receive any dividend. However, as in the case of ordinary shares, a company making a loss or insufficient profit need make no dividend payment to preference shareholders. A **debenture or stock** is a long term loan which, like a share certificate, can be traded on a stock exchange. A company might issue 20 million £1 stock certificates at a fixed rate of interest to be repaid in 20 years' time. During the 20 year lifetime of the stock, individual certificates might be bought and sold. In effect, it is a loan which the lenders can sell to another party in order to regain their money. In unit 72 it will be explained that stocks can fluctuate in price according to the prevailing rate of interest. Large stocks, denominated in a different currency from the domestic currency of the issuing company, are called Eurobonds. If ICI, for instance, issued stock in French francs, then this would be a Eurobond issue.

Other means of finance Companies may get grants from government or the European Union for locating in a particular area, training workers (such as Youth Training), or investing in new technology. They may use **hire purchase** rather than bank loans to finance investment.

Leasing (i.e. renting) equipment is popular. Some companies sell their debt collection to a specialist finance company - this is called **factoring**. The company is given, for instance, 95 per cent of the value of invoices to be collected. This improves the cash flow of the company, saves on wages of staff who would have to chase up payment and reduces risk because the factoring firm takes on any consequent bad debts. A company may also choose to mortgage its property, or sell buildings to a property company which then leases it back. In the latter case, the company is receiving a large lump sum now but the opportunity cost is that it will have to pay rent on the property in the future.

Choice of finance

Firms seem to have a wide range of finance available to them. In practice their choice is more limited.

Small firms often find it difficult to raise money. They are seen as risky ventures; approximately one-third of companies which register for VAT cease trading within three years of starting up. They are too small to be able to tap sources of money in the City of London which have a large minimum start-up fee attached to them. So new share money usually comes either from the people wanting to set up the company or their close relatives and friends. Banks will provide loans at high rates of interest but only after the company has put forward a convincing business plan detailing, amongst other things, how it plans to repay the loan.

Larger firms, (almost all public limited companies in the UK), have a greater choice. Retained profit is important for two reasons. First, the UK taxation system makes it very attractive for companies to retain profit for investment, and for shareholders to receive benefits in the form of rising share prices rather than high dividends. Second, retained profit is a low risk form of capital acquisition. If the investment proves unprofitable, the firm will not have the burden of bank interest charges to pay, or have disappointed shareholders wanting their dividends maintained. However, it is important to remember that retained profit has an opportunity cost. The company could have used it, for instance, to repay existing debts or build up a cushion of financial capital which would earn interest. A company which fails to make effective use of its retained profit is likely to see its share price slide, making it a takeover target.

Bank loans are attractive because, although they are often an expensive form of raising finance, they are flexible. It is far easier to arrange a bank loan than to issue new shares for instance. Bank loans can be repaid and the interest burden removed, whilst share capital is unlikely ever to be redeemed and therefore dividends will have to be paid forever. Shareholders in small companies may not wish to see their control over the firm diluted, whilst new share issues in large companies are often unpopular with their existing shareholders because the share price tends to go down after a new share issue.

Stock exchanges

The media in the UK give a great deal of coverage to stock exchange prices. Most news bulletins on national radio or television, for instance, will give the latest figure for the *Financial Times* Ordinary Share Index, an index which measures changes in the average value of shares quoted on the exchange. However, it can be argued that day to day share price movements have little economic significance and that stock exchanges, such as the London Stock Exchange, are marginal to the workings of the UK economy.

A stock exchange is a market for second hand securities, such as shares issued by companies or stocks issued by governments. A company which wishes to issue new share capital to expand its business is unlikely to sell these new shares on a stock exchange (and is not allowed to on the London Stock Exchange). The shares are offered for sale directly to the public or to investing institutions such as assurance or pension fund companies. Once the sale has been completed, the company may be able to get the shares quoted on a stock exchange. This means that these shares may be bought and sold through the exchange. Quoted companies have to accept the rules and regulations of the stock exchange and be accepted as a suitable company by the exchange.

A stock exchange has two main economic functions. First, it makes it easier for companies to issue new shares because savers who buy the shares know that they can sell the shares through the exchange when they want to. They might have to sell them for a lower price than they bought them at, or they might lose all their money because the firm goes bankrupt. But it is far easier to sell shares in a quoted company than to try to find buyers for shares in an unquoted company. Because it is easier to sell second hand shares which are quoted, companies as a whole can raise more money through share issues than they would otherwise have been able to do. However, it should be remembered that, in the UK, only a few per cent of money raised to finance the expansion of firms each year is raised from share issues. Therefore it is debatable as to how important a stock exchange is in the financing of industry.

Second, a stock exchange provides a clear mechanism for mergers and takeovers. The argument is that profit is an indicator of economic efficiency. Companies which fail to make the profits expected of them will see their share price fall. A low share price will attract predator firms who will buy up the company and use its assets more efficiently. So an economic system with stock exchanges, where it is easy to buy shares and to obtain important information about the performance of companies, leads to greater economic efficiency than one where it is difficult to buy shares in companies and where firms are able to keep their finances secret. The validity of this argument turns on whether takeovers and mergers are seen as beneficial or harmful to an economy (☞ unit 40).

Many companies see stock exchanges as harmful to their

Key terms

Cash flow - the difference between money received and money paid out over a period of time.
Retained profit - profit kept back by the company to pay for investment.

business. Pressure to make large profits in the short term to satisfy shareholders and to keep predator companies at bay leads to the long term interests of the company being sacrificed. The short term interests of a company may coincide with its long term interests. But sometimes an investment which may be excellent in the long term has high short term costs. The desire to please shareholders today may lead to the investment not going ahead, resulting in a loss of economic efficiency both for the company and the economy as a whole.

Businesses complain of bank pains

Frederick Warren is hopping mad. He runs a kitchens business in Rayleigh, Essex, with a turnover of £500,000 a year. Having held an account at National Westminster Bank for 40 years, he has been incensed by the bank's attitude to his effort to agree a £7,500 loan to expand his business. Mr Warren has spent five days this month preparing financial information for his local bank manager, only to be told that the bank still wants more details about his seven employee company, European Kitchens, before agreeing to lend. 'It's a joke for banks to say that are trying to help small businesses,' says Mr Warren. He is meeting his bank manager this week for yet more discussions.

Anecdotes like this have fuelled concern that clearing banks may be adopting over-rigorous procedures for small businesses. Mr Eddie George, governor of the Bank of England, is examining these worries in a probe of small business finance that started during the summer.

The health of small businesses will be vital to the recovery. Businesses with sales of £1m or less account for more than 95 per cent of all UK enterprises and a third of the non-government workforce. The big four clearers - NatWest, Barclays, Midland and Lloyds - are especially important to the fortunes of Britain's 3m or so small businesses as 80 per cent of them rely on banks for short-term finance.

In recent months the nature of the complaints about banks has changed. During the recession small-business lobby groups criticised them for increasing charges and reducing credit lines.The grouses now are that banks are instituting much tougher criteria when deciding on small-business loans, making the decisions in regional offices on the basis of financial information rather than on the judgement of local bank managers who have dealt with clients over many years.

Mr Stephen Alambritis of the 58,000 -member Federation of Private Businesses says: 'Many local bank branches won't talk to people running small businesses, even when they've got good ideas.'

Mr Charles Burton, partner in the Bradford office of accountants Haines Watts, specialising in small businesses, says: 'If you have a newish business or are looking to expand, then the banks are being extremely sceptical. 'It's a waste of time putting some ideas to the bank.'

Mr Hikmet Ozkutan runs a petrol station and shop in east London with annual sales of £2.2m. Having built up the business tenfold in the past seven years, Mr Ozkutan has spent two months putting his case to four separate bank branches for a £750,000 loan to buy the freehold on his property and expand his shop. I'm depressed that so far I've failed to get a fair hearing,' he says.

These complaints are supported by at least one branch manager of one of the big four banks in the north of England who says that head-office controls on lending have intensified and that 'some of the local managers' discretion has been eroded'.

Professor David Storey, director of the small and medium-sized enterprise centre at Warwick University, says that banks have 'a bloody good case' for tightening controls after large losses in recent years.

But not all small businesses agree that lending conditions have worsened. Some say the relationship between banks and small companies has eased after the tension bred by the recession, when the government launched two separate studies to determine whether banks were failing to pass on interest-rate cuts and were being too tough with their small-business customers. 'Banks had a strike against lending, but that seems over now,' said Mr Peter Folkman, managing director of North of England Ventures, a Manchester-based venture-capital fund.

One explanation for banks reluctance to lend may be a lack of staff trained to assess small-business risk. Mr Graham Elliott, a partner at the Manchester office of accountants Stoy Hayward, says banks in general are becoming more co-operative towards small businesses. 'The real problem now is that they don't have enough personnel to understand widely enough how to assess risk.'

Another problem, according to Mr Richard Brucciani, the Leicester-based chairman of the Confederation of British Industry's small-firms council, is that banks largely offer loans secured against fixed assets such as property rather than against the strength of the business.

He says: 'Reliance on security encourages provision of short-term finance rather than long-term debt or equity, compounding balance-sheet problems and overgearing.'

One idea proposed by many in both the banking and small-business communities is to build better relationships through such measures as enrolling more local branch managers as company directors. Mr Sean Henry, administrative director of Lastolite, a photographic equipment company based in Coalville, Leicestershire, said: 'In Germany it's quite common for a bank manager to be on the board. I would welcome that in Britain.'

Source: the *Financial Times*, 27.9.1993.

1. What problems are faced by small businesses when dealing with banks, according to the article?

2. Suggest what might be the advantages and disadvantages of using loans for the two businesses described in the article.

3. How do you think Mr Hikmet Ozkutan might react if a friend, hearing of his problems with the bank, approaches him with an offer to take a share in the business. Draw up a case (a) for and (b) against Mr Ozkutan accepting the offer.

The location of industry

Summary

1. In a pure free market, there would be perfect factor mobility and no unemployment.
2. In reality, firms choose to site themselves according to criteria such as closeness to the market, transport costs, the presence of external economies, government policy, the quality of the local environment and historical links with a locality.

A factory needs space for manufacturing (F), offices (O), car parking (C), materials (M), and loading (L). It also needs access to markets via road transport (R), rail trains (T), and if possible room for expansion (E).

Location in a pure free market

Arguably the UK has had a North-South divide since the end of the First World War. Unemployment has been higher and wages lower in the North than in the South of the UK. The UK is not alone in having regional divides. In what was West Germany, the South was more prosperous than the North whilst in Italy it is the North which is the more prosperous.

In a pure free market, this situation would be an impossibility. Firms would locate where the costs of production were lowest. In a region of high unemployment, such as the North of England or Northern Ireland, average wage rates would, in theory, be lower than in a full employment region such as the South East. Land and factory values too will be lower. Firms from the South East would therefore migrate to the North and to Ireland. They would invest in these regions, reducing unemployment, pushing up wage rates and property prices. At the same time, workers would migrate from high unemployment regions to low unemployment regions. By increasing the supply of labour in the South East, wages in that region would tend to fall. But there would be upward pressure on wage rates in the high unemployment regions because their supply of labour had fallen. This process would carry on till the costs of production were equal in all these regions.

QUESTION 1

Table 23.1 *Selected regional statistics*

	South East (excluding Greater London)	North
Average weekly wage rate (April 1994)	£339.10	£297.00
Unemployment (Nov 1994)	7.1%	11.0%
Vacancies at Jobcentres (Nov 1994)	35 800	7 600
Average house price (1994)	£77 700	£49 400
Average weekly household disposable income (1993)	£335.40	£246.67
Annual consumers' expenditure per head (1992)	£7 393.00	£5 825.00

Source: adapted from CSO, *Economic Trends*, December 1994, and CSO, *Regional Trends.*

Discuss whether the data indicate that there are economic incentives
(a) for workers in the North to move to the South East and
(b) for firms to move from the South East to the North.

Barriers to mobility

In practice, free market forces have been too weak to solve the problems of the higher unemployment regions of the UK. In part this is because there are many other influences apart from the cost of labour and capital which influence the location of industry.

Nearness to the market Many industries need to be located near to their market if they are to minimise costs and maximise revenues. At one extreme, many service industries have to be located in the middle of their market. A company selling petrol will not open a new petrol service station in Glasgow, however cheap the land, if it wants to sell petrol to Londoners. Many industries prefer to be sited near to their markets so that they can keep in touch with their customers. Selling parts in London to a firm two miles down the road, all other things being equal, is likely to be easier than selling parts to Scotland or Northern Ireland.

Transport costs No mention was made of transport costs in the pure free market described above. However, transport costs can be a major component of final costs. In general, firms should locate near to their markets if the cost of transport of the finished product is higher than the cost of transport of raw materials. Conversely, firms should locate near to their raw materials if the transport of raw materials is more costly than the transport of finished products. Steel production is an example of an industry which is located near to its raw materials because the cost of transporting iron ore and coal is much higher than the cost of transporting steel itself. Coal fired electricity power generation plants have been located next to coal fields because they need to be near their source of power to minimise transport costs. The early cotton mills in Lancashire and Yorkshire were located in the Pennines with machinery driven by water power.

External economies of scale External economies of scale (☞ unit 20) arise when an increase in the size of the industry results in a reduction in average costs for a firm in the industry. Many external economies arise within a small geographical area. Stoke on Trent, for instance, has a large pool of workers experienced in working for the pottery industry. Local education colleges run special courses for the industry. There are many firms supplying the industry in the local area. Therefore the average costs of pottery in the Stoke area are likely to be lower than in a city such as Swansea. This helps to account for the fact that Stoke on Trent continues to be the centre of the UK pottery industry.

Industrial inertia Industries may locate initally in an area for a sound economic reason. Over a period of time, these factors may lose their importance but firms stay in the same location. This is known as industrial inertia. For instance, the Lancashire textile industry was initially based there because of cheap power, first from water and then coal. Lancashire also has a damp climate which prevented threads from drying out and breaking easily in manufacture. It was also on the west coast facing America and the colonies, the main sources of imports of raw cotton and of exports. Today, these factors are unimportant commercially. A textile company could as well set up in Glasgow or Bath as in Lancashire. However, the textile industry is still strongly represented in Lancashire because there are no economic reasons why most companies should move from their traditional base in Lancashire to another part of the country.

The local environment Decisions to set up or move a medium sized or large business are made by managers and directors. The quality of their lives and the lives of their families will be an important factor in deciding where to locate. Advertisements for particular locations often place great stress on the availability of golf courses, access to the countryside or to a big city, or quality of the housing. One reason why firms don't relocate even when there are big savings to be made from doing so is that the staff of the company are likely to be very antagonistic to moving away from their locality. A firm which loses too many key staff in a move could find itself in serious trouble.

Government policy Both local and central government play an important role in determining the location of industry. Everything from giving grants to firms that locate in unemployment blackspots to advertising campaigns for a local area, or building a new motorway, will change the attractiveness to businesses of a particular location.

QUESTION 2 One Monday morning, a US manager arrived back from holiday to a memo from the chief executive telling him to find a European outlet. No problem, he thought. Another memo to the research department, and within a week the manager had a neat table of local salaries, rents and transport costs. He picked out two or three similarly attractive locations for the board 'just so they could think that they were making the decision'. Northern Spain, southern Italy and Bulgaria went into the meeting. 'They all had the cheapest all-round costs. I figured we would cover expenses within two years', says the manager. The board chose France.

Source: adapted from the *Financial Times*, 27.9. 1994.

(a) What criteria did the manager use to assess the potential location of a European outlet?
(b) Explain the criteria the Board might have used which outweighed in importance the ones chosen by the manager.

Applied economics

Location of industry by region in the UK

Each region of the UK has a different industrial base. Figure 23.1 shows in outline the relative importance of different primary, secondary and tertiary industries throughout the UK in 1994. A region is shown to specialise in the production of a particular type of good or service if a greater percentage of its total employees are employed compared to the national average in that industry. For instance, 4.1% of workers in the West Midlands are employed in the metals, minerals and chemical industries compared to a national average of 2.7%. Because the West Midlands percentage is above the national percentage, the region can be said to specialise in these products. The fact that the West Midlands does not specialise in any service industries does not mean that no services are produced in the region - just that local service employment is below the national average.

A clear pattern emerges from the map. The South East of England is predominantly a service economy. The three other administrative areas of the UK apart from England - Northern Ireland, Wales and Scotland - have a considerable number of public administration jobs which in England tend to be concentrated in London (part of the South East region). But apart from this, the UK outside of the South East specialises mainly in primary and secondary industries. The West Midlands, for instance, specialising only in the metal and motor industries, has a very narrow industrial base. The North West of England specialises in manufacturing, transport and communication.

The reasons for geographical specialisation

The pattern of a service-rich South, and a more impoverished North relying on primary and secondary industries, has arisen from the economic history of the UK over the past two hundred years. Service industries associated with government have traditionally been located in regional capitals. London, Edinburgh and Belfast, for instance, have been the centre of civil service jobs and employment in the legal profession. These centres have also attracted companies in the financial sector such as banks and insurance companies, both because of the presence of government and because of good transport links with the rest of the country. Headquarters of companies have also come to be centred in these capitals for the same reasons.

Primary industry needs to be located where there are raw materials. The South East, apart from its farm land, has not been a rich source of raw materials. It has been the other areas of the UK which have developed concentrations of coal mining, clay workings, offshore oil, etc.

Secondary industry after the Industrial Revolution sited itself near to its raw material sources, such as coal or iron ore. Therefore, in the main it tended to site itself in the 'North' where such raw materials were relatively abundant. The West of England also developed more industrially than the East because of the pattern of trade in the 19th century. Britain's colonies and the United States of America were our major trading partners. It was cheaper to send goods to these destinations from west coast ports such as Glasgow, Belfast, Liverpool and Bristol than from east coast ports.

In the 19th century, London was a thriving commercial centre but so too were the industrial towns of the Midlands, the North of England, Scotland, Wales and Northern Ireland.

Since the end of the First World War, three important changes have occurred to create the North-South divide. First, as the UK has become more affluent, it has moved progressively to a more service sector based economy. The South East, which specialised throughout the 19th century in the provision of services, has been able to reinforce its comparative advantage. Second, the direction

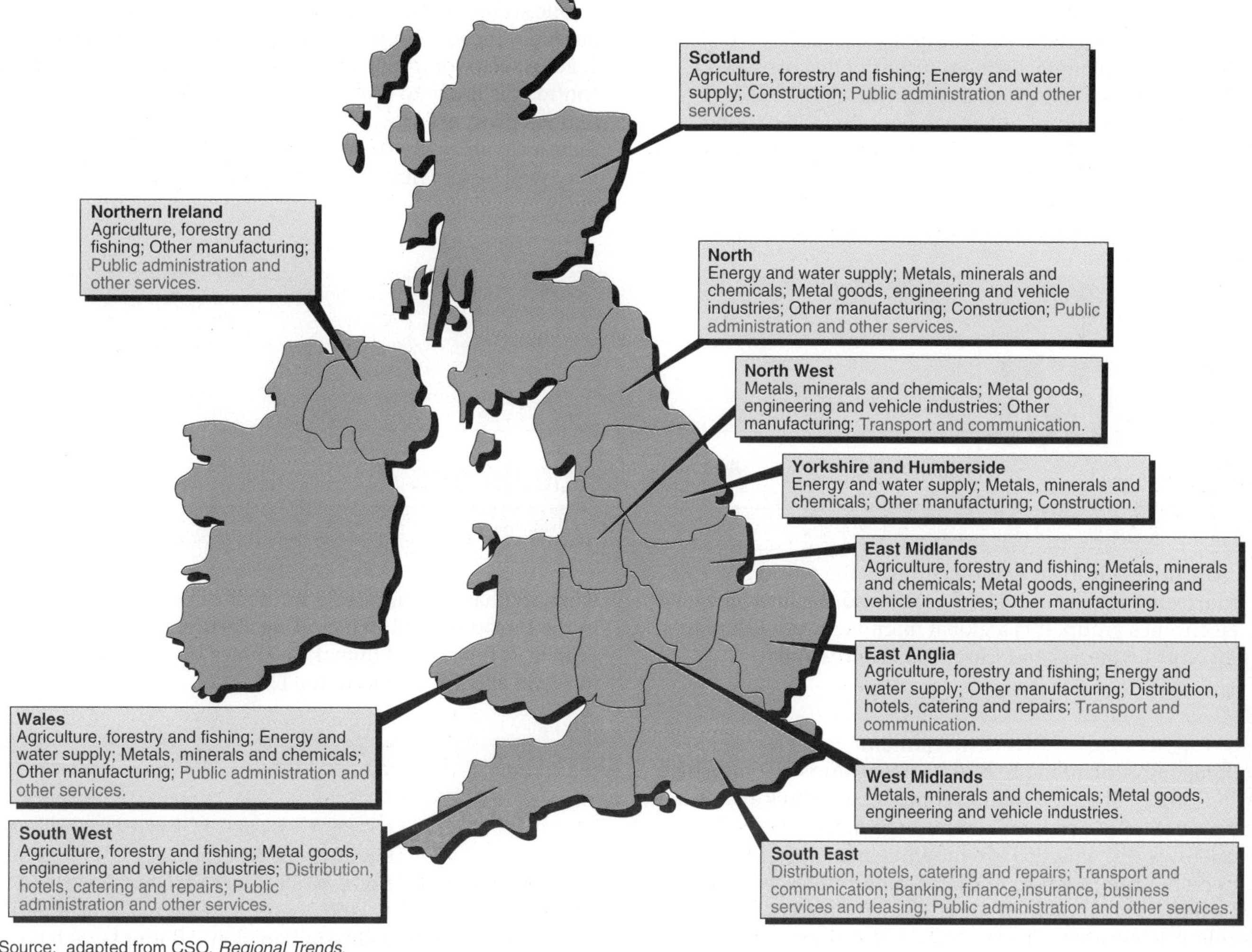

Source: adapted from CSO, *Regional Trends.*

Figure 23.1 *Specialisation by region in the UK*

of trade has altered. Today Europe is our major trading partner. Therefore the regions of the UK closest to Europe, and particularly the South East, have a transport cost advantage over the rest of the UK. The west of the UK has had to cope with a relative decline in trade. Most of the west coast's docks, for instance, have long since closed to commercial freight traffic and have been converted to service sector use such as yachting marinas, housing or leisure centres.

Third, and perhaps most important, the UK has lost much of its comparative advantage in the production of manufactured goods relative to the rest of the world (☞ unit 61). Industry after industry has been hit by foreign competition, from textiles to shipbuilding to car manufacturing. Countries such as Japan, Korea or Germany have taken away British markets and devastated British industry. Manufacturing industry was heavily concentrated in the 'North' of England and hence the North has declined relative to the South.

The decline in manufacturing was at its most intense in the early 1980s. In the recession of 1980-1982, manufacturing output fell 15 per cent whilst employment in the sector fell 19 per cent. Employment in manufacturing has continued to decline since then because labour productivity (the amount each worker produces) has increased faster than any growth in output in manufacturing. However, output itself has grown since 1982. In 1988, manufacturing output finally surpassed its 1973 level. In the following recession of 1990-1992, manufacturing output fell only 6 per cent, a very good result for an industry which in the previous two major recessions had savagely contracted.

Today, the prospects for manufacturing and those regions which depend heavily upon it are now relatively good. The international competitiveness of UK manufacturing industry seems to have stabilised. In some industries, such as car manufacture, there has even been an increase in competitiveness. This has mainly come from inward investment, for instance by Japanese companies like Toyota, Nissan and Honda. Their plants are 'world-class' plants, i.e. they are as efficient as the best internationally. Their presence in the UK has gone on to stimulate UK manufacturers to strive for world-class status, particularly so if they are to be suppliers to Japanese companies based in the UK.

In contrast, the outlook for service industries is mixed. In the recession of 1990-1992, the worst hit regions and industries were not the 'North' with its reliance upon manufacturing, but the South with its reliance on market traded service industries. The fall in employment between 1990 and 1992 in the South East was 8.1 per cent, whilst the unemployment rate trebled between 1990 and 1993. In contrast, the fall in employment in the Midlands, the north of England, Scotland, Wales and Northern Ireland was only 3.8 per cent.

Over the next ten years, there is predicted to be a sharp fall in employment in financial services such as banking and insurance as automation increases labour productivity. The government is committed to controlling public sector employment, which again limits any potential increase in public sector service employment. Service sector employment in areas outside the South, in contrast, is likely to grow if manufacturing in these regions prospers and gives workers incomes to spend in their local areas. By the year 2000, regional specialisation may well be less marked than it has been over the past 100 years.

A time for decisions

Samsung, a Korean manufacturer, is the world's fourteenth largest industrial group and the fifth biggest electronics group. It is a global manufacturer with plants in North America and Europe, as well as Asia.

New investment

Samsung is planning to build a new complex somewhere in Europe. The £450 million complex will have an annual production of 1 million computer monitors, 1.3 million microwave ovens, 250 000 facsimile machines, 250 000 personal computers, 3 million monitor tubes as well as facilities to make 8 inch semiconductor wafers and colour televisions. The facilities will generate an estimated annual turnover of $2bn.

Possible locations

Samsung has investigated a number of possible locations in the European Union including Portugal, Germany and France. It finally had to make a choice between Barcelona in Spain and Cleveland in the UK.

Existing facilities

Samsung has a plant which manufactures television sets at Billingham in Cleveland already. It also has a VCR and TV manufacturing facility in Barcelona. Both plants have been successful.

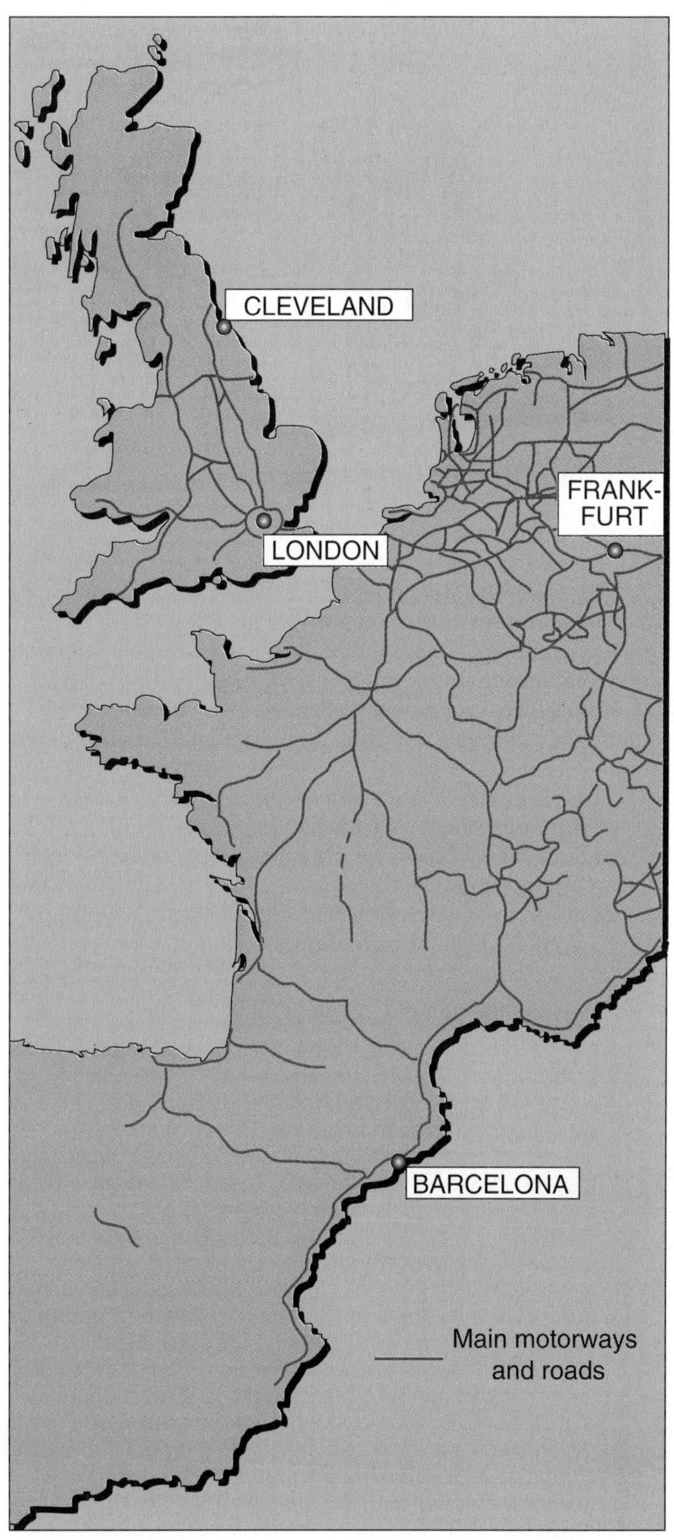

Figure 23.2 *Main motorway and road links in Europe*

Regional grants

The UK government has offered Samsung £58 million in regional grants and loans together with another £32 million in indirect aid such as infrastructure development. The offer is conditional on Samsung also agreeing to move its European headquarters to London from Frankfurt. The Spanish government has offered Samsung an undisclosed sum which is reportedly higher than the UK bid.

Markets

Samsung has chosen to come to Europe as part of a global strategy of establishing regional manufacturing centres round the globe. It wants to be able to manufacture within a trading area free of trade barriers between countries. The UK is already a major market for the company. Sales have grown 100 per cent since 1989. Cleveland is near to Scotland's Silicon Valley where there are a large number of computer companies which could become customers for Samsung's products. Spain too is an important customer for Samsung. It offers greater potential for sales since ownership of many Samsung products, such as microwave ovens, is lower in Spain than in the UK. Barcelona is nearer Southern European markets than Cleveland.

Table 23.2 *Hourly labour costs in industry for manual and non-manual workers, UK=100*

	1988	1991
UK	100.0	100.0
Spain	82.7	90.9
France	138.2	-
Germany	167.4	158.3
Portugal	26.5	29.3

Source: adapted from Eurostat, *Basic Statistics of the Community*, 1994.

Source: adapted from the *Financial Times*, 18.10.1994.

You are an economist working for Samsung. The Board has requested a report from you outlining your recommendation for the siting of their new facility in Europe.

1. **Outline the decision that has to be made.**
2. **Explain the factors that need to be taken into account when making the decision.**
3. **Make a recommendation based on the evidence given above.**

The goals of firms

Summary

1. Shareholders, managers, workers, government, consumers and others influence decision making in a firm.
2. Neo-classical theory assumes that firms are short run profit maximisers. In the short run, such firms will operate so long as their revenue is greater than their variable cost.
3. The neo-Keynesian theory of the firm assumes that firms are long run profit maximisers.
4. Managerial theories assume that managers maximise their own utility subject to a profit satisficing constraint.
5. Behavioural theories assume that decision making within a firm is not controlled by any one group, such as shareholders, but by all parties involved with the firm.

The main participants

The question of what motivates a firm in its actions can only be answered if there is a clear understanding of who controls the decision making processes. There are a number of possible answers to this in a UK context.

The owners or shareholders It might seem obvious to state that it is the owners or shareholders of a company who control it. This is perhaps true for small businesses where the owner is also the director or manager of the business. The owner of a small local corner shop, for instance, who also runs the shop will make the decisions about the business. However, it is less obvious that owners control the business they own when there are a very large number of shareholders.

Directors and managers Shareholders in a public limited company elect directors to look after their interests. Directors in turn appoint managers who are responsible for the day to day running of the business. Therefore there may be a divorce between ownership and control. The only way in which owners can influence decision making directly is by sacking directors at the Annual General Meeting (AGM) of the company. In practice the company needs to be going bankrupt to stir sufficient shareholders for this to happen. Shareholders can also sell their shares, forcing the share price down and making the company more vulnerable to a takeover bid. If there is a takeover the directors and managers may well lose their jobs and hence there is pressure on managers to perform well.

The workers The workers, particularly through their trade unions, may be able to exert strong pressure on a company. They do not have the power to run the company in the way that shareholders or managers might be able to do. However, they can have an important influence on matters such as wages (and therefore costs), health and safety at work and location or relocation of premises.

The state The state provides an underlying framework for the operation of the company. Legislation on taxation, the environment, consumer protection, health and safety at work, employment practices, solvency and many other issues force companies to behave in a way which they might otherwise not do in an unregulated environment.

The consumer The consumer, through organisations such as the Consumers' Association or various trade organisations, can bring pressure to bear on companies in an attempt to make them change their policies. This form of influence is often rather weak; **consumer sovereignty** (☞ unit 42) is more important. In a free market, consumers

QUESTION 1 In 1988, the Swiss multinational company Nestlé made a bid to take over Rowntree Mackintosh, a British company based in York which produced brands such as KitKat and After Eight. There was strong opposition to the bid. Directors advised shareholders not to sell their shares to Nestlé because they felt that the price offered by the multinational was too low. Managers and workers opposed the bid because they feared that Nestlé would move production and research facilities away from York, and would close down some plants completely in order to rationalise production across Europe. They lobbied Parliament because the Department of Industry had the power to refer the bid to the Monopolies and Mergers Commission. This body would have investigated the bid and could have recommended that the merger was not in the public interest. The government, however, decided not to refer the bid. Nestlé increased its share price offer. Consumers stood by helpless. The Board of Directors of Rowntree Mackintosh recommended that shareholders accept because the new price offered was very good. Enough shareholders sold to ensure that Rowntree Mackintosh passed into Swiss hands.

Which interest groups controlled decision making at Rowntree Mackintosh during the bid by Nestlé?

cast their spending votes amongst companies. Companies which do not provide the products that consumers wish to buy will go out of business whilst companies which are responsive to consumers' needs may make large profits. According to this argument, it is the consumer who ultimately controls the company. This assumes that consumer sovereignty exists. In practice, firms attempt to manipulate consumer preferences by marketing devices such as advertising. Firms are therefore not the powerless servants which theory implies.

Short run profit maximisation

In neo-classical economics it is assumed that the interests of owners or shareholders are the most important. Just as consumers attempt to maximise utility and workers attempt to maximise their rewards from working, so shareholders will be motivated solely by maximising their gain from the company. Therefore it is argued that the goal of firms is to maximise profits.

Firms are not always able to operate at a profit. They may be faced with operating at a loss. Neo-classical economics predicts that firms will continue in production in the short run so long as they cover their variable costs.

Consider Table 24.1. The company would lose £20 million in any period in which it shut down its plant and produced nothing. This is because it still has to pay its fixed costs of £20 million even if output is zero. Total fixed costs represent the maximum loss per period the company need face.

Table 24.1

£ million

Period	Total variable cost	Total fixed cost	Total cost	Total revenue	Profit or loss	
					If production takes place	If plant is shut down
1	30	20	50	60	+10	-20
2	30	20	50	50	0	-20
3	30	20	50	40	-10	-20
4	30	20	50	30	-20	-20
5	30	20	50	20	-30	-20

The table shows that the firm is facing a steadily worsening trading situation. Its costs remain the same throughout, but each period its revenue declines. In period 1, total revenue exceeds total costs. The firm makes a profit of £10 million if production takes place. In period 2, it makes no profit by operating its plant (although it should be remembered that cost includes an allowance for normal profit ☞ unit 18).

However, this is better than the alternative of shutting down and making a £20 million loss. So too is producing in period 3. Although the company makes a loss of £10 million, it will continue to produce because the alternative to not producing is a loss of £20 million. In period 4 the company is on the dividing line between whether to produce or not. In period 5, the company will clearly not produce. Its operating losses would be greater than if the plant were shut down.

So short run profit maximisation implies that a firm will continue to produce even if it is not fully covering its total costs. It will only shut down production when its total revenue fails to cover its total variable cost.

QUESTION 2 A company has fixed costs of £10 million. Its variable costs increase at a constant rate with output. The variable cost of production of each unit is £1 million. Explain whether it will produce:
(a) 10 units if total revenue is £30 million;
(b) 15 units if total revenue is £25 million;
(c) 20 units if total revenue is £22 million;
(d) 25 units if total revenue is £20 million.

Long run profit maximisation

Neo-Keynesian economists believe that firms maximise their long run rather than their short run profit. This is based upon the belief that firms use COST PLUS PRICING techniques. The price of a product is worked out by calculating the average total cost of operating at full capacity and adding a profit mark-up. The price set and therefore the profit aimed for is based upon the long run costs of the firm.

Short run profit maximisation implies that firms will adjust both price and output in response to changes in market conditions. However, according to neo-Keynesians, rapid price adjustments may well damage the firm's position in a market. Consumers dislike frequent price changes. Price cuts may be seen as a sign of distress selling and large buyers may respond by trying to negotiate even larger price reductions. Price increases may be interpreted as a sign of profiteering, with consumers switching to other brands or makes in the belief that they will get better value for money. Price changes also involve costs to the company because price lists need to be changed, sales staff informed, advertising material changed, etc. Therefore it is argued that firms attempt to maintain stable prices whilst adjusting output to changes in market conditions.

This may mean that a firm will produce in the short run even if it fails to cover its variable cost. If it takes the view that in the long run it may make a profit on production of

QUESTION 3 A firm has total fixed costs of £900 and variable costs of £1 per unit.
(a) What will be the price per unit if it sets out to manufacture 300 units a week and make a 25 per cent profit over costs?
(b) Demand is not as great as the company hoped. If it maintains its price, what is the minimum number of units that must be sold per week if the company is to break-even?
(c) Demand is 150 units per week. The company is offered an order for an extra 350 units a week if it drops its price on all units sold to £3 per unit. But it believes that demand will slowly increase in the future to the planned 300 units a week if the original price is maintained. Should the firm accept the order?

a particular good, it may prefer to produce at a loss rather than disrupt supplies to the market. Equally, it may cease production in the short run even if it can cover its variable costs. It may prefer to keep prices above the market price in the short run and sell nothing if it believes that price cutting in the short run would lead to a permanent effect on prices and therefore profits in the long run.

Managerial theories

Managerial theories of the firm start from the assumption that there is some divorce between ownership and control of companies. The shareholders are assumed to be a different group of people from the managers of the company. Shareholders will wish to see profits maximised. However, it is far from obvious that managers will share this goal. As workers they will attempt to maximise their own rewards. These may include their own pay and fringe benefits, their working conditions, their power within the organisation, their ability to appropriate resources, and the amount of effort they have to make. For instance, a manager may be more interested in which company car he or she will get, whether there is time to play golf on a Wednesday afternoon, or whether there is an extra £1 million available for the budget, than whether the company has maximised its profits at the end of the financial year.

This does not mean to say that making a profit is not important. Managers have to be seen to be efficient enough to justify their salaries. A shareholders' revolt is always a possibility. Some directors may take it upon themselves to promote actively the interests of the owners of the company. There is always the threat of takeover or bankruptcy leading to a loss of jobs, so managers have to make enough profit to satisfy the demands of their shareholders. This is known as PROFIT SATISFICING. But once a satisfactory level of profits has been made, the managers are free to maximise their own rewards from the company.

One theory put forward in the 1950s by William Baumol was that firms would attempt to maximise sales rather than profits. Increased sales and increased salaries for top managers and directors tend to go hand in hand. Another more complicated theory put forward by O. Williamson postulates that managers have a utility function consisting of factors such as salary, size of the workforce directed by the manager, the amount of money under his or her control and the number of perks, such as company cars, that the manager receives (☞ unit 33).

Behavioural theories

Behavioural theories of the firm, pioneered by the American economist Herbert Simon, argue that decision making within a company is made not by any one group but by all groups involved in the firm. It is only by studying the relative power of each group and the power structures within the organisation that the way in which a firm behaves can be understood.

QUESTION 4

From Mr Edward Leigh MP.

Sir, The problems surrounding shareholder control of executive salaries were accurately and extensively reflected in your leader ('Can pay, will pay', December 6).

I am glad to hear that the government intends to act, as this was an issue which I addressed in a policy pamphlet which I published on November 28. I said there that the way forward was to empower shareholders. Two days later the prime minister told the House of Commons that he was prepared to consider a similar solution.

In my pamphlet, *Responsible Individualism*, I wrote that the public is justifiably suspicious when executives raise each other's salaries in a round of mutual pocket-lining. Especially since many of them perform roles more akin to ministers presiding over large bureaucracies than to genuine entrepreneurs who innovate and create wealth and jobs.

It is indisputable that capitalism and the market are the most effective systems to generate wealth and improve the material well-being of the nation. But man cannot live by those alone; a sense of right and justice must also be part of the equation. Politicians should give a lead.

The issue cannot be dismissed by the simple argument that British companies must be free to offer world-class salaries. There has been a real public outrage and that is something companies and government ignore at their peril. There is an important moral dimension and it is this which has been missing on recent economic policy. A sense of duty and service on the part of executives and a sensitivity to the feeling of those on low wages would not go amiss.

I do not advocate the Labour remedies of intervention and state regulation. We should empower shareholders - who, after all, own the companies and employ the managers - to enable checks to be placed on what the public suspects are unnecessarily large pay packages.

This can be achieved, first by fiscal measures to encourage direct share ownership - something lacking at present; and, second, by legislation to ensure that City institutions take due note of the views of the beneficial owners of the shares they nominally hold.

I recognise there are difficulties in devising a mechanism by which the latter could be achieved, but it should be possible to introduce a legal system, however rough and ready, which would make fund managers respond to the opinions of the millions of investors whom they represent.

We should trust the people in this respect. The public is bright enough to know when they need adequately to reward an entrepreneur who boosts their dividends, asset values and pensions, but jaundiced enough to recognise blind greed.

Edward Leigh
House of Commons,
London SW1A 0AA

Source: Edward Leigh, MP.

(a) Explain what evidence the writer of the letter, Edward Leigh, puts forward to argue that managers and not shareholders control large companies in the UK.

(b) Discuss the benefits and problems to businesses of implementing his suggested solutions.

For instance, it could be argued that in the 1960s and the 1970s, trade unions were very powerful in large companies. They were influential in increasing the share of revenues allocated to wages and reducing the share that went to shareholders. During the 1980s and 1990s, government legislation and mass unemployment has seriously weakened the power of unions in the UK. At the same time, shareholders have become more conscious of their right to make profits. The result has been a large increase in the returns to shareholders, which could be seen as being financed by a reduction in the returns to the workers of the firm. Shareholders are more important today in company board rooms and workers less important than they were 20 years ago.

Behavioural theories assume that each group has a minimum level of demands. Shareholders demand that the firm makes a satisfactory level of profits. The government demands that laws be obeyed and taxes paid. Workers will require a minimum level of pay and work satisfaction if they are to stay with the company. Consumers demand a minimum level of quality for the price they pay for goods purchased. Local environmentalists may be able to exert enough moral pressure on the company to prevent gross over-pollution.

Other goals

Some firms have clearly distinct aims apart from those mentioned above. Consumer co-operatives aim to help consumers (although there is considerable debate in the UK as to whether they do not, in practice, serve the interests of their workers and management more). Worker co-operatives are often motivated by a desire either to maintain jobs or to produce a particular product, such as health foods. There have been examples of philanthropic owners in the past, such as Rowntree or Cadbury, who have placed great priority on improving the living conditions of their workers. Nationalised industries in the UK prior to 1979 had a whole range of goals from avoiding a loss to maintaining employment to providing a high quality service.

So it is simplistic to argue that all firms aim to maximise profit. However, there is much evidence to suggest that large firms whose shares are freely traded on stock exchanges, and which are vulnerable to takeover, place the making of profit very high on their list of priorities. Therefore it is not unreasonable to make an assumption that, in general, firms are profit maximisers.

QUESTION 5 During the 1960s and 1970s, it was difficult to see who controlled the Fleet Street newspaper industry. Owners of the newspapers were often rich entrepreneurial-type figures who allowed their titles to make little or no profit in return for the prestige and influence over the UK public that ownership gave them. Trade unions had a virtual veto on changes in working practices. Trade unions, not management, controlled shop floor appointments. The ability to call wildcat strikes which would lose a paper its entire production run for a day ensured that shop floor workers earned wages which bore no resemblance to the wages of workers in other comparable occupations.

Consumers rewarded with more sales those newspapers which included more page 3 pin-ups and less serious political news. Governments, meanwhile, made public noises about deteriorating press standards whilst in private attempting to get the press to toe the current party line. Management were caught in the middle, attempting to balance all the conflicting demands made of them.

New technology and soaring property prices put paid to all this. In the 1980s it became apparent that newspapers could make large profits for their owners. The key to success was to sack as many shop floor workers as possible and replace them with machines. Those kept on would be paid reduced rates. Fleet Street offices could be sold off at vast profit on a soaring property market, the proceeds more than paying for a move to new technology premises elsewhere. The unions resisted but not even continual mass pickets and what came to be called the 'Wapping riots' in 1986 could prevent change.

Today, union power is much reduced and, in some newspaper jobs, unions are not recognised by management for negotiating purposes. Newspapers are more profit orientated although most of the British press arguably can still be relied upon to support the Conservative Party.

To what extent can behavioural theories of the firm explain the recent history of the Fleet Street newspaper industry?

Key terms

Cost-plus pricing - the technique adopted by firms of fixing a price for their products by adding a fixed percentage profit margin to the long run average cost of production.

Profit satisficing - making sufficient profit to satisfy the demands of shareholders.

Applied economics

The role of the shareholder

Shareholder power

In both the UK and the USA, large companies tend to claim that shareholders are powerful. Company chairs make referrals to 'serving the interest of shareholders' or 'maximising shareholder value'. However, the power of the shareholders tends to be an indirect one. Annual general meetings (AGMs) of quoted companies are poorly attended, annual shareholder reports are not understood (even when read) by many shareholders, and directors rely on getting blocks of proxy votes before AGMs from key investors to push through any resolutions they recommend, including their own election to the board.

On the whole, shareholders' power lies not in being able to influence decisions directly, but in their ability to sell their shares freely. If enough shareholders are disappointed with a company's performance and sell their shares, then the share price will fall and make the company an attractive takeover target. The directors and management of a company taken over could, at worst, face immediate redundancy. So in the UK and the USA, shareholder power is vitally dependent upon free and open stock markets.

There has been some revival of direct shareholder power in the USA. Individual speculators wanting to make money have bought blocks of shares in companies which they consider are performing poorly. They have then used their voting rights to agitate for reform. Sometimes they have secured a seat on the board of directors. Once changes of policy have been implemented and monetary benefits have accrued to shareholders, perhaps in the form of higher dividends, a much higher share price or the issue of free shares in companies which have been split off from the main company, the speculator sells out and turns his or her attention to another company. Despite a trend towards more aggressive individual shareholders in the USA, most US companies and UK companies can still ride out shareholder dissatisfaction without necessarily implementing change.

In continental Europe and Japan, shareholder power is exercised in a different way. It is far more difficult for companies to be taken over. In Italy, for instance, hardly any of the approximately 200 companies listed on the stock market are open to a British-style takeover bid. This is because hardly any have more than half their shares in public hands, the rest being held by families or other companies.

In Spain, shareholdings are not even disclosed but bank, family and corporate cross shareholdings tie up control of most companies. In France, it is estimated that more than half of the 200 largest quoted or unquoted companies are family controlled and many of the rest have key blocks of shares held either by the government or by single private shareholders. In Germany, three large banks, which for more than a century have financed German industry, have huge stakes. In Japan, companies prevent individual shareholders from becoming too powerful by buying them out or diluting their shareholding by the issue of more shares. There is also a strong tradition of corporate cross holdings.

Short-termism

For many years now, there has been a debate in the UK about whether or not the system of shareholding has a major influence on the behaviour of firms. There are those who argue that the UK system leads to 'short-termism'. Companies are forced to pursue the goal of maximising short term profit for fear that they will otherwise be taken over. This makes it difficult for them to pursue other objectives, particularly investment both in capital equipment and in their workers which have long pay-back periods.

In contrast, on the Continent and in Japan, companies can afford to take a long term view. Ultimately the company will only survive if it makes a profit. But profit should increase if the company grows over time. Hence it is the interests of the company which are paramount. The company is not just the shareholders, but also the workers, the management, the customers, the local citizens etc. Because shareholders do not expect their companies to maximise short term profits, management is free to invest in a way which will maximise the long term growth of the company. Maximising the long term growth of the company, as a by-product, is also likely to maximise the long term gain for the shareholder. It is also likely to maximise long term growth in the economy. It is interesting to note that continental European countries and Japan have enjoyed higher economic growth in the post-war period on average than either the UK or the USA.

If the 'short-termist' view is correct, then it could be argued that firms are short run profit maximisers in the UK and in the USA. In contrast, on the Continent and in Japan firms are long run profit maximisers. However, long run profit maximisation is an incidental outcome of a process of decision making which is perhaps best explained by behavioural theories of the firm.

Priorities and purpose at the heart of capitalism

What is a company for? The question sits uneasily at the heart of capitalism. Until recently, with communism and centrally planned economies as our common opponents, we were not pressed to provide an answer. To many reared in the traditions of Anglo-American business, the answer anyway was clear - 'to enhance shareholder value', with all that implied for efficiency, customer service, shrewd investment and personnel policies.

The capitalist world, however, has lost its common enemy, and must now look more closely at itself. The countries newly emerging from socialism are not entirely happy with all they see of capitalism. To them it is not self-evident that what is good for some shareholders is necessarily good for the rest of society. They also see there are different versions of capitalism: Japanese, American, German, British.

As the world of business becomes more and more global, these different traditions of capitalism bump up against each other. We not only have to learn about them, we need to learn from them because they begin to close towards each other as companies compete and combine. Working on different assumptions will be untenable in the long term.

Akio Morita, the chairman of Sony, has taken the point. In an article in the January edition of *Bungei Shinju*, the political and economic journal, he suggests that Japan's competitiveness has been achieved by keeping margins and prices low over a long time in a constant search for volume to provide the cash-flow. This has, however, meant skimping the other stakeholders in favour of the customer.

The average pay-out ratio, for instance, was 30 per cent in Japan in 1990 compared with 66 per cent for the average British company and 54 per cent for US ones. Japanese employees worked 2,159 hours on average in 1989 compared with 1,638 in France and only 1,546 in Germany. Mr Morita argues that neither the world nor Japanese society will tolerate these differences much longer. Japan, he says, must fashion a new corporate attitude, rebalancing stakeholder interests and going some way to meet the west.

We, on our part, may have to do the same but in the other direction. If we don't, we may lose competitively. More of the earned surplus needs to go back to the customer by way of lower margins and lower return on projects. An open and tempting share market will also lure new owners for Anglo-Saxon assets from overseas without any corresponding opportunities in their more closed markets. A change to foreign ownership can often be beneficial in the short term, but if too much of Britain ends up as an offshore manufacturing subsidiary subject to the whims of outside owners, the risks are obvious.

We may, therefore, start to look at our shareholder rather differently, and more as other countries do, as financiers rather than as owners. Satisfying these financiers then becomes a requirement not a purpose. To turn shareholders' needs into a purpose runs the risk of confusing means with ends. But this is a risk we seek to avoid by saying that shareholders' needs are actually a yardstick for all other purposes.

The danger in doing this is that we undersell the real purpose of the business, which is to provide quality goods and services to customers and quality lives and work to its people. One cannot continue to do that without keeping one's financiers happy at the same time. If they are not happy they will blow the whistle, warn and then, if necessary, move the management before the marketplace removes the business. Whistle-blowing is their function, not the indirect management of the business.

Ownership is a misleading concept in other ways too. It suggests that a company is a commodity to be traded and that its people are commodities too. Too often that is exactly what happens, because in the Anglo-American stockmarkets financiers have that power.

Should they have that power? They do not, after all, have the balancing responsibilities of ownership. Because of the different ownership patterns of Japanese and Continental companies the casual investor does not have the same power as his counterparts in New York or London. The financiers in Japan and on the Continent, therefore, are more like guardians, keeping a watchful eye, but not jumping ship just because there is a torn sail.

Akio Morita called for a change in Japan's corporate attitude and suggested that the big companies should lead the way. There are encouraging signs that that is happening in Britain. More and more companies are formally listing their priorities, often putting customers and employees ahead of shareholders in the pecking order of stakeholders and taking pains to educate the stockmarket about their long-term strengths and plans.

Now, too, that the investing institutions own two-thirds of the equity of British businesses, they are effectively locked in and must become guardians (though not owners) rather than traders. Some company chairmen are cautiously lowering their real long term dividends without upsetting their share price in a more sophisticated market. Share option schemes are beginning to be designed to reward long-term performance by managers rather than acting as short-term cash bonuses.

We need to go farther faster. We need ways to put numbers on people's skills, which are an increasingly important element in companies' wealth-creating capacity, and on other forms of intellectual property. Intangible assets already outweigh the tangible assets on the balance sheets of many advertising agencies, consultants, publishers and architects. They probably do so in most businesses, although this fact usually only shows up during contested takeovers. Accountants, in other words, need to turn their gaze on the future and measure it. If they will not do so, management should.

We can no longer shelter behind shareholder value as a synonym for corporate purpose. In business, as in life, we all need 'a purpose beyond ourselves' to feel useful, worthwhile and good about ourselves.

Companies today are not like they were in Victorian times - properties with tangible assets worked by hands whose time owners bought. Business today depends largely on intellectual property, which resides inalienably in the hearts and hands of individuals. Companies have to be re-conceptualised. They are communities with members, communities which need customers, suppliers, financiers and community support if they are to survive and prosper in the interests of all.

We do not need to change company law to create this new idea of the company, but we do need to change the way we count. That way we will start to change the way we think and then the way we act.

Source: Charles Handy (Visiting Professor at the London Business School) published in the *Financial Times*, 12.5.1992.

1. **Contrast the goals, as outlined in the article, of a typical UK company with those of a Japanese company.**
2. **A UK firm is considering whether to shut down a loss making plant in the North East of England, a high unemployment area. The plant makes low cost organic fertilizers. Discuss whether there might be any difference between the final decision of the UK company and that of a Japanese or German company faced with similar circumstances.**
3. **A politician argues that any firm which makes large profits is bound to be supplying products which consumers want to buy and maintaining jobs in the economy. Therefore high profits are a sign that the firm is serving the interests of consumers and its workers. To what extent do you think that this is true?**

Right: A 'traditional' view of the capitalist. More and more firms are moving away from the traditional approach and are often putting customers ahead of shareholders.

Market structure

Summary

1. Market structures are the characteristics of a market which determine firms' behaviour within the market.
2. The number of firms within a market may vary from one (as in monopoly), to several (as in oligopoly), to a large number (as in monopolistic competition or perfect competition).
3. Barriers to entry prevent potential competitors from entering a market.
4. Industries may produce homogeneous or differentiated (branded) goods.
5. Perfect knowledge or imperfect knowledge may exist in an industry.
6. Firms may be independent or interdependent.

Market structure

MARKET STRUCTURES are the characteristics of a market which determine firms' behaviour. Economists single out a small number of key characteristics:

- the number of firms in the market and their relative size;
- the number of firms which might enter the market;
- the ease or difficulty with which these new entrants might come in;
- the extent to which goods in the market are similar;
- the extent to which all firms in the market share the same knowledge;
- the extent to which the actions of one firm will affect another firm.

The number of firms in an industry

The number of firms in an industry may vary from one to many. In the UK market for letter deliveries, the Post Office is essentially the sole supplier. In agriculture, on the other hand, there are tens of thousands of farms supplying potatoes and carrots to the market in the UK.

- A **monopoly** is said to exist where there is only one supplier in the market.
- In a market dominated by a few large producers, the market structure is **oligopolistic**. In an oligopolistic market there may be a large number of firms, but the key characteristic is that most are small and relatively unimportant, whilst a small number of large firms produces, most of the output of the industry.
- In **perfect competition** or in **monopolistic** competition there is a large number of small suppliers, none of which is large enough to dominate the market.

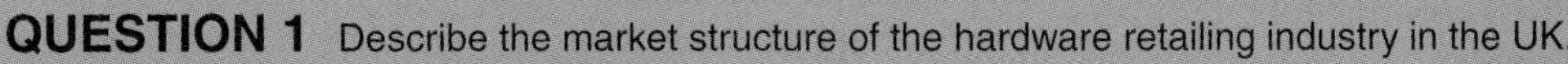

QUESTION 1 Describe the market structure of the hardware retailing industry in the UK.

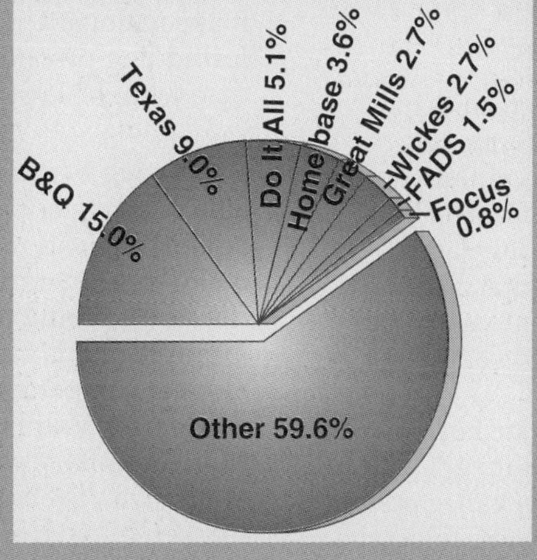

Source: adapted from Verdict.

Figure 25.1 *DIY spending, top eight percentage share, 1993*

QUESTION 2

(a) How many firms are there in each of the industries in which these particular firms operate?
(b) In which of these industries do a few large firms dominate output?

Barriers to entry

Market structures are not only affected by the number of firms in an industry and their relative output, but also by the potential number of new entrants to the market. Firms in an industry where there are unlikely to be any new entrants may behave differently from firms in an industry where there are many strong potential competitors.

There are a number of BARRIERS TO ENTRY which prevent potential competitors from entering an industry.

Capital costs Buying a local corner shop is relatively cheap and therefore the entry cost to most forms of retailing is low. Buying a car plant or an aluminium smelter, on the other hand, is extremely expensive. Entry costs to these industries are very high and only large companies on the whole can pay them. Capital costs therefore represent a very important barrier to entry and vary from industry to industry.

Sunk costs SUNK COSTS are costs which are not recoverable. For instance, a woman may set up a gardening business, buying a lawnmower, a van, garden tools and paying for advertising. If the business folds, she will be able to get some money back by selling the van, the tools, and mower, but she won't be able to get any of the money back from the advertising. The cost of advertising and the difference between the purchase price and resale price of the capital equipment would be her sunk costs. High sunk costs will act as a barrier to entry because the cost of failure for firms entering the industry will be high. Low sunk costs, on the other hand, will encourage firms to enter an industry because they have little to lose from failure (☞ unit 32, the theory of contestable markets).

Scale economies In some industries, economies of scale are very large. A few firms operating at lowest average cost (the **optimum level of production** ☞ unit 20) can satisfy all the demand of buyers. This will act as a barrier to entry because any new firm entering the market is likely to produce less and therefore have much higher average costs than the few established producers. In some industries, it could be that a few firms supplying the whole industry are still unable to exploit fully the potential economies of scale. A **natural monopoly** is then likely to result, with just one firm surviving in the industry, able to beat off any new entrants because it can produce at lowest costs.

Natural cost advantages Some producers possess advantages because they own factors which are superior to others and which are unique (i.e. have no close substitutes). For instance, a petrol station site on a busy main road is likely to be superior to one in a sleepy country village. A stretch of desert in Saudi Arabia with oil underneath may be superior for oil production to the most beautiful of the Derbyshire Dales. The Victoria and Albert Museum should be able to attract more visitors because of its wide collection than a small provincial town museum. As a result, they will either be able to produce at lower cost or be able to generate higher revenues than their potential competitors.

Legal barriers The law may give firms particular privileges. Patent laws can prevent competitor firms from making a product for a given number of years after its invention. The government may give a firm exclusive rights to production. For instance, it may give broadcast licences to commercial television companies or it may make nationalised industries into monopolies by legally forbidding private firms to set up in the industry, as is the case with the Post Office in the UK.

Marketing barriers Existing firms in an industry may be able to erect very high barriers through high spending on advertising and marketing. The purpose of these is to make consumers associate a particular type of good with the firm's product, creating a powerful brand image. One example of this from 50 years ago was the success of the Hoover company with its vacuum cleaner. Even today, many people still refer to vacuum cleaners as 'hoovers'. More recently, a personal stereo is often called a 'Walkman', the brand name of Sony who first put it on the market. In the UK detergent industry, a national launch of a new brand of soap or washing powder will cost in excess of £10 million. Soap and washing powders are low technology products whose costs of production are relatively low. Marketing barriers, however, make the industry almost impossible to enter.

Restrictive practices Firms may deliberately restrict competition through restrictive practices (☞ unit 41). For instance, a manufacturer may refuse to sell goods to a retailer which stocks the products of a competitor firm. A manufacturer may refuse to sell a good, when it has a monopoly in production, unless the buyer purchases its whole range of goods. Firms may be prepared to lower prices for long enough to drive out a new entrant to the business.

These barriers to entry may be divided into two groups. Some occur inevitably. These are known as innocent **entry barriers**. Most cost advantages fall into this category. However, other barriers are created by firms in the industry **deliberately** to keep out potential competitors. Marketing barriers and restrictive practices are examples of these.

QUESTION 3

Compare and contrast the barriers to entry to the UK food retailing industry, the international oil industry and the UK banking industry.

The extent to which there is freedom of entry to a market varies enormously. Manufacturing industries, with high capital costs and with extensive marketing power, tend to have higher barriers than service industries. But many service industries have high barriers too. Banking, for instance, has a high capital cost of entry, legal permission is required, and marketing barriers are high. In the professions, like law, architecture and accountancy, new entrants are kept out by enforcement of minimum qualification levels, qualifications which are impossible to obtain except through working in the profession itself.

Product homogeneity and branding

In some industries products are essentially identical whichever firm produces them. Coal, steel and potatoes are examples. This does not mean to say that there are not different grades of coal or types of steel, but no producer has a monopoly on the production of any such grade or type. Goods which are identical are called HOMOGENEOUS goods.

Firms find it much easier to control their markets if they can produce goods which are non-homogeneous.

QUESTION 4 Nothing demonstrates the value of brands more clearly than the frequency which which they are copied and counterfeited around the world by fly-by-night operators in search of a quick profit. International Distillers and Vintners (IDV), the drinks subsidiary of Grand Metropolitan, has taken action against about 50 pirate brands during the past year.

'A brand is costly to create and establish, but can be very easy and profitable to copy', says Michael Leathes, legal director of IDV. 'Brands are our most important assets. Through them we communicate the quality of our products to consumers. They represent a huge investment of time, effort and money, that can be diluted, weakened, even destroyed by those who copy them. Counterfeits or imitations can be sold cheaply. Their producers do not have to spend on advertising and marketing. Nor do they have to bother about the quality of the drink or the packaging. We have to be rigorous in the protection of our brands against the damage that copies can do to them.'

Brand counterfeiting is a criminal offence in most countries in which the drinks groups operate, and, once the counterfeiters are identified, it is relatively easy to stop. The main problems arise from imitations which deliberately seek to deceive consumers by suggesting an affinity with a leading brand: using a similar name, or similar designs and colours in their bottles and labels. IDV's Bailey's Irish Cream liqueur, for instance, has encouraged the illegal production of a host of copies, including Bailes, Teleys and Raylas, all in squat brown bottles with pastoral scenes incorporated into the labels.

Source: adapted from the *Financial Times*, 14.10.1993.

(a) What are the costs and benefits to a firm of developing a brand?
(b) To what extent do consumers benefit from being offered branded rather than non-branded goods to purchase?

Differentiating their product from their competitors, and creating BRANDS allows them to build up brand loyalty. This in turn leads to a reduction in the elasticity of demand for their product. A branded good may be physically no different from its competitors, or it may be slightly different. But branding has value for the firm because consumers think that the product is very different, so different that rival products are a very poor substitute for it. This perception is built up through advertising and marketing and enables firms to charge higher prices without losing very much custom (i.e. demand is relatively inelastic).

Knowledge

Buyers and sellers are said to have PERFECT INFORMATION or PERFECT KNOWLEDGE if they are fully informed of prices and output in the industry. So if one firm were to put up its prices, it would lose all its customers because they would go and buy from elsewhere in the industry. Hence, there can only be one price in the market.

Perfect knowledge also implies that a firm has access to all information which is available to other firms in its industry. In UK agriculture, for instance, knowledge is widely available. Farmers can obtain information about different strains of seeds, the most effective combinations of fertilizers and pesticides and when it is best to plant and reap crops.

Perfect knowledge does not imply that all firms in an industry **will** possess all information. An inefficient farmer might not bother to gather relevant information which is readily available. In the short term, the farmer might survive, although in the longer term the farm will be driven out of business by more efficient competitors. Equally, perfect information does not imply that all firms know everything about their industry and its future. Farmers do not know if in 6 months' time a drought will destroy their crops. They have to work on the basis of probability. Perfect knowledge only means that all firms have the same access to information.

Firms have imperfect knowledge where, for instance, there are industrial secrets. Individual firms may not know the market share of their competitors or they may be unaware of new technology or new products to be launched by rival companies. Information could then act as a barrier to entry, preventing or discouraging new firms from entering the industry.

Interrelationships within markets

There are two possible relationships between firms in an industry. Firms may be **independent** of each other. This means that the actions of any one firm will have no significant impact on any other single firm in the industry. In agriculture, for instance, the decision of one farmer to grow more wheat this season will have no direct impact on any other farmer. It will not affect his next door neighbour. This independence is one reason why perfect knowledge exists to some degree in agriculture. There is no point in keeping secrets if your actions will not benefit you at the expense of your competitors.

If firms are **interdependent** then the actions of one firm will have an impact on other firms. An advertising campaign for one brand of soap bar, for instance, is designed mainly to attract customers away from other brands. Firms are more likely to be interdependent if there are few firms in the industry.

Competition and market structure

The neo-classical theory of the firm recognises a number of market structures derived from the characteristics above. In units 27 to 32 these market structures will be considered in greater detail. Here, however, the key features are summarised. In neo-classical theory, there are three main types of market structure.

- **Perfect competition**. A large number of firms, each producing a homogeneous good, compete in the industry. None of the firms is large enough to have a direct impact on any other firm or on the market price of the good. There is freedom of exit and entry to the industry.
- **Monopoly**. There is only one firm in the industry. Barriers to entry make it impossible for new firms to enter.
- **Imperfect competition**. Exists where there are at least two firms in the industry, and the industry is not perfectly competitive. For instance, non-homogeneous goods may be produced, there may be imperfect knowledge or firms may be interdependent, or some combination of these.

Firms in imperfectly competitive industries can compete in a number of ways. For instance, they can compete on:

- **price** - offering a lower price should attract more orders;
- **quality** - consumers are likely to prefer a better quality good;
- **after-sales service**;
- **delivery date** - a buyer may look elsewhere if a firm cannot deliver quickly and on time;
- **image** - building a strong brand image through advertising and other forms of marketing is likely to be a major factor in determining demand for the product.

In perfect competition, firms are not in direct competition with each other. One firm can expand output without affecting either the price received by or the sales of another firm. Each firm is a price taker, facing a perfectly elastic demand curve. However, competition is 'perfect' because any firm which charges a higher price than its competitors, or sells an inferior product, will lose all its sales as perfectly informed consumers buy elsewhere in the market. The discipline of the market is so strong in a perfectly competitive industry that, in the long run, productive inefficiency (production at above minimum cost) cannot exist.

QUESTION 5 Producers in the 1.5 billion Christmas card market face a variety of different types of competition. At one end of the market are mainly Eastern European producers who compete on price. If you buy a large box of budget Christmas cards in your local supermarket, the likelihood is that it will have been made in an Eastern European country. Slightly more expensive are cards from the large UK producers such as Hallmark Cards and Rust Craft Greetings Cards. They produce better quality cards and market them along with their range of birthday and other greetings cards through a wide range of newsagents. At the top end of the price range are cards produced by a large number of small independent card publishers, exploiting market niches such as joke Christmas cards, fine art cards and pop-art cards. They too are sold mainly through newsagents. Finally, charities offer a wide range of designs, selling at medium prices mainly through mail order.

To what extent do firms in the Christmas card market compete on price?

Key terms

Market structures - the characteristics of a market which determine the behaviour of firms within the market.
Barriers to entry - factors which make it difficult or impossible for firms to enter an industry and compete with existing producers.
Sunk costs - costs of production which are not recoverable if a firm leaves the industry.
Homogeneous goods - goods which are identical.
Brand - a named good which in the perception of its buyers is different from other similar goods on the market.
Perfect knowledge or information - exists if all buyers in a market are fully informed of prices and quantities for sale, whilst producers have equal access to information about production techniques.

Applied economics

Market structures in the UK

What is an industry or market?

How many firms are there in an industry or market (here we will assume that the two terms can be used interchangeably)? The answer to this question will depend on how we define the market or industry. For instance, the economy could be split up into three very broad market classifications, - the market for primary goods, the market for secondary goods and the market for tertiary goods. There are a large number of firms operating in each of these markets. At the other extreme, one could ask how many UK firms produce balls for use in professional cricket. This is an extremely narrow market in which there are only two producers.

It should be obvious that the more narrowly a market is defined, the more likely it is that there will be relatively few producers. In the transport market, there are bus companies, rail companies, airlines, etc. In the air transport market, there will be fewer companies. In the market for air travel to the Isle of Skye there is only one company.

The Standard Industrial Classification

The Central Statistical Office (CSO) conducts regular censuses of production in the UK. The statistics record production levels in different industries using the Standard Industrial Classification 1992. This is a classification system which subdivides industry into broad divisions. For instance, Section C comprises mining and quarrying. Section D is manufacturing, whilst Section E is electricity, gas and water. Each section is then divided into sub-sections. Sub-section DA, for instance, is food, drink and tobacco. DB is textiles and textile products. The CSO classification is one way of grouping firms into individual industries, each sub-section representing an industry or group of industries.

Concentration ratios

Having classified firms into industries, it is possible to see how many producers there are in the industry. The number of producers is likely to be less important in studying the behaviour of the industry than the economic power of individual producers within the industry. One way of measuring this potential power is to calculate how important are the top few companies in the market. It can be done by looking at their importance in terms of market share in the industry, how many workers they employ or some other measure. This measure is then called a CONCENTRATION RATIO.

A three-firm concentration ratio would be the total share of the market (by output, employment or some other measure) held by the three largest producers in the industry; a four-firm concentration ratio would be the total share of the market held by the four largest producers; etc.

Market concentration in the UK

Table 25.1 shows the five-firm concentration ratios for UK manufacturing industry in 1992. On average the largest five firms in an industry accounted for approximately 40 per cent of net output. However, an industry can be widely defined. For instance, one of the 103 industries included in Table 25.1 is passenger car production (Class 351 under the 1980 Standard Industrial Classification). A revised 1992 Standard Industrial Classification is currently being used for figures later than those shown in Table 25.1. Within that industry, it could be argued that there are a number of different markets, for instance the small car market, the family-size saloon car market and the luxury car market. The concentration ratio is likely to be higher in each of these markets than in the market for passenger car production as a whole because there will be fewer producers in each market segment. In general, the narrower the definition of the market, the higher the concentration ratio is likely to be.

Figure 25.2 shows concentration ratios for selected industries in the UK. This ranges from 6.8 per cent in the metal working machine tool industry to 99.5 per cent in the tobacco industry.

Table 25.1 *Five-firm concentration ratios[1]: manufacturing industries, 1992*

Percentage of net output of the five largest firms in the industry	Number of industries
0-9	4
10-19	17
20-29	12
30-39	13
40-49	19
50-59	11
60-69	11
70-79	5
80-89	2
90-99	5

1. Percentage of total sales and work done by the five largest enterprises.
Source: adapted from Census of Production, Summary Tables, *Business Monitor*, PA 1002.

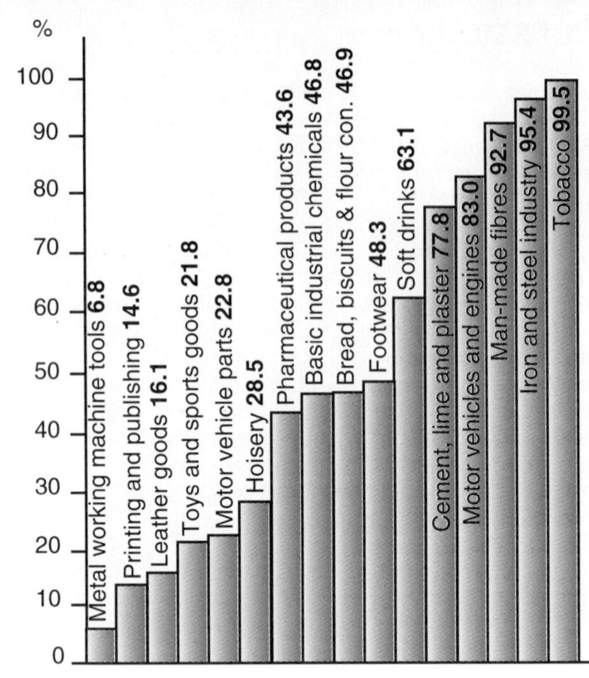

1. Percentage of total sales and work done by the five largest enterprises.
Source: adapted from Census of Production, Summary Tables, *Business Monitor*, PA 1002.

Figure 25.2 *Five-firm concentration ratios[1] for selected UK industries, 1992*

In manufacturing, there has been increasing concentration this century. A slight fall in concentration during the 1970s can be partially explained by the decline in manufacturing industry at the time due to severe international competitive pressure. Many large manufacturers cut back production or left the market altogether, reducing their power within the market place. The take-over boom in the 1980s and continued European economic integration post-1992 is likely to see an upward trend in industrial concentration once again.

UK car registrations 1994

'The Toyota plant near Derby, first announced in 1989, became operational in 1994, costing £700 million. It represents a significant attempt by Toyota to gain a major share of the UK and European markets.

New entrants to the UK car market, Proton and Daewoo.

Table 25.2 *UK vehicle production and registrations, 1994*

Manufacturer	Production 1994	Sales* 1994
Total	**1 466 823**	**1 353 632**
Rover (BMW)	**462 614**	**290 814**
- cars	390 856	266 954
- Land Rover	71 758	23 860
Ford group	**300 614**	**425 381**
- Ford	269 058	418 657
- Jaguar	31 429	6 659
- Aston Martin	127	65
General Motors group	**289 859**	**310 619**
-Vauxhall	250 439	-
- IBC Vehicles (GM/Isuzu)	39 420	-
Nissan	204 944	91 995
Toyota	85 467	49 943
Peugeot	74 440	146 551
Honda	42 805	38 187
Rolls-Royce (Vickers)	1 357	142

* If sales are greater than production this indicates that the firm is importing more cars from its factories abroad than it is selling into its foreign export markets.
Source: Society of Motor Manufacturers and Traders Ltd.

Malaysia launches 'people's car'

Malaysia has launched its second national car a decade after it began manufacturing the Proton. Now the small 660cc Kancil is appearing in the country's showrooms. The Kancil's success is by no means assured. Analysts forecast a rough ride before the second car project becomes profitable. The car is manufactured by Perodua, a consortium of local companies with strong government interests, together with Daihatsu and Mitsui of Japan. The four-seat sub-compact is modelled on the Daihatsu Mira and the Japanese company has a 25 per cent stake in the project.

Annual production is expected to reach 45 000 within two years. At least 50 per cent of the content of the car will initially be sourced from Daihatsu. The Japanese partner has pledged to transfer technology as fast as possible. Perodua says that the level of local content in the Kancil will rise to 75 per cent within three years.

Perodua, like all producers of mass market cars, needs economies of scale if it is to achieve profitability. This is a tough proposition. With a population of only 19 million, Malaysia is too small a market to achieve these without exports. Proton, considered to be a success, exported 17 000 cars, mainly to the UK, out of total production of 117 000 cars in 1993.

Source: adapted from the *Financial Times*, 28.9.1994.

The Vietnamese government is considering establishing a domestic motor manufacturing industry in the country. It would be export orientated. The UK has traditionally been an excellent market for new world producers of motor cars seeking export markets. Produce a report describing the structure of the UK market and analyse the barriers to entry that would be present for a Third World producer in setting up a motor manufacturing business. In your report:

1. **Write an introduction briefly outlining what is meant by 'market structure'.**
2. **Analyse the market structure of the world motor car manufacturing industry and consider the market structure of the car industry in the UK. In your analysis, give examples from the experience of other car manufacturers.**
3. **Evaluate under what conditions Vietnam is likely to be successful in establishing a domestic car manufacturing operation.**

Short run profit maximisation

Summary

1. Profit is maximised at a level of output where the difference between total revenue and total cost is greatest.
2. At this profit maximising level of output, marginal cost = marginal revenue.
3. An increase in costs will lower the profit maximising level of output.
4. An increase in revenues will raise the profit maximising level of output.

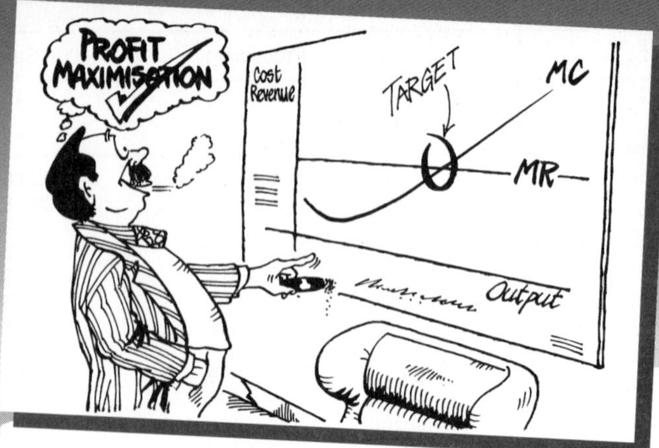

Total cost and total revenue

Profit is the difference between **revenue** (the receipts of the firm) and **costs** (the monies paid out by the firm). A firm will make the most profit (or **maximum** profit) when the difference between total revenue and total cost is greatest.

This is shown in Table 26.1. Total revenue is shown in the second column whilst total cost is in the third column. Profit is the difference between the two. At low levels of production, the firm will make a loss. The BREAK-EVEN point, where total revenue equals total cost, is reached at an output level of 3 units. Thereafter the profit made increases as output increases.

There are two levels of output where profit is highest at £27. But it should be remembered that the difference between revenue and cost here is **abnormal** or **economic profit**. Normal profit is included as a cost of production (☞ unit 18). So profit, both normal and abnormal, is at a maximum at an output level of 7 units rather than 6 units because the cost of the seventh unit includes an allowance for normal profit.

Table 26.1

Output	Total revenue (£)	Total cost (£)	Profit (£)
1	25	35	-10
2	50	61	-11
3	75	75	0
4	100	90	10
5	125	106	19
6	150	123	27
7	175	148	27
8	200	182	18
9	225	229	-4

Marginal cost and marginal revenue

Marginal cost and marginal revenue can also be used to find the profit maximising level of output. Marginal cost is the addition to total cost of one extra unit of output. Marginal revenue is the increase in total revenue resulting from an extra unit of sales.

Table 26.2

Output	Marginal revenue (£)	Marginal cost (£)	Addition to total profit (£)
1	25	35	-10
2	25	26	-1
3	25	14	11
4	25	15	10
5	25	16	9
6	25	18	8
7	25	25	0
8	25	34	-9
9	25	47	-22

Table 26.2 shows the marginal cost and marginal revenue figures derived from Table 26.1. Marginal revenue minus marginal cost gives the extra profit to be made from producing one more unit of output. The firm makes a loss of £10 on the first unit, and £1 on the second. But the third unit of output yields a profit of £11, the fourth £10 and so on. So long as the firm can make

QUESTION 1

Table 26.3

Output (million units)	Total revenue (£ million)	Total cost (£ million)
1	10	8
2	20	14
3	30	20
4	40	30
5	50	50
6	60	80

(a) Calculate the total profit at each level of output.
(b) What is the profit maximising level of output?
(c) Calculate the marginal revenue and marginal cost of production at each level of output.
(d) Explain, using the data, why MC = MR at the profit maximising level of output.

additional profit by producing an extra unit of output, it will carry on expanding production. But it will cease extra production when the extra unit yields a loss (i.e. where marginal profit moves from positive to negative). In Table 26.2, this happens at an output level of 7 units. The seventh unit contributes nothing to **abnormal** profit.

However, as explained above, cost includes an allowance for normal profit and therefore the firm will actually produce the seventh unit. The eighth unit yields a loss of profit of £9. The firm will therefore not produce the eighth unit if it wishes to maximise its profit.

Economic theory thus predicts that profits will be maximised at the output level where marginal cost equals marginal revenue.

Cost and revenue curves

These same points can be made using cost and revenue **curves.** The revenue curves in Figure 26.1 are drawn on the assumption that the firm receives the same price for its product however much it sells (i.e. demand is perfectly price elastic) So the total revenue curve increases at a constant rate.The marginal revenue curve is horizontal, showing that the price received for the last unit of output is exactly the same as the price received for all the other units sold before (☞ unit 28 for a discussion of the alternative assumption that a firm has to lower its price if it wishes to increase sales). The shape of the cost curves are as described in units 19 and 20.

The total revenue and total cost curves show that the firm will make a loss if it produces between O and B. Total cost is higher than total revenue. B is the break-even point. Between B and D the firm is in profit because total revenue is greater than total cost. However, profit is maximised at the output level C where the difference between total revenue and total cost is at a maximum. If the firm produces more than D, it will start making a loss again. D, the second break-even point on the diagram, is the maximum level of output which a firm can produce without making a loss. So D is the sales maximisation point subject to the constraint that the firm should not make a loss.

Now consider the marginal cost and marginal revenue curves. It can be seen that the profit maximising level of output, OC, is the point where marginal cost equals marginal revenue. If the firm produces an extra unit of output above OC, then the marginal cost of production is above the marginal revenue received from selling the extra unit. The firm will make a loss on that extra unit and total profit will fall. On the other hand, if the firm is producing to the left of OC the cost of an extra unit of output is less than its marginal revenue. Therefore the firm will make a profit on the extra unit if it is produced. Generalising this, we can say that the firm will expand production if marginal revenue is above marginal cost. The firm will reduce output if marginal revenue is below marginal cost.

It should be noted that there is another point in Figure 26.1 where MC = MR. This is at the point A. It isn't always the case that the marginal cost curve will start

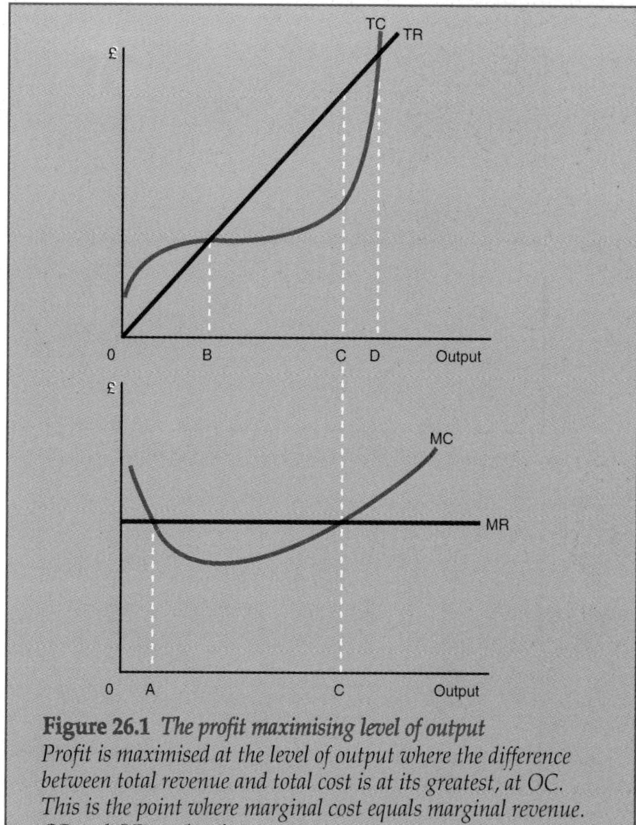

Figure 26.1 *The profit maximising level of output*
Profit is maximised at the level of output where the difference between total revenue and total cost is at its greatest, at OC. This is the point where marginal cost equals marginal revenue. OB and OD are break-even points.

above the marginal revenue curve at the lowest level of output. However, if it does, then the first intersection point of the two curves, when marginal cost is falling, is not the profit maximising point. The MC = MR rule is therefore a **necessary** but not **sufficient** condition for profit maximisation. A second condition has to be attached, namely that marginal cost must be rising as well.

QUESTION 2

(a) From the data in Table 26.3, draw two graphs showing (i) total revenue and total cost curves and (ii) marginal revenue and marginal cost curves. Draw the graphs one underneath the other using the same scale on the output axis.

(b) Mark on each of the graphs (i) the break-even levels of output and (ii) the profit maximising level of output.

Shifts in cost and revenue curves

It is now possible to analyse in greater depth the effects of changes in costs or revenues on output. Assume that costs, such as the price of raw materials, increase. This will mean that the marginal cost of production at every level of output will be higher. The marginal cost curve will shift upwards as shown in Figure 26.2. The profit maximising level of output will fall from OQ_1 to OQ_2.

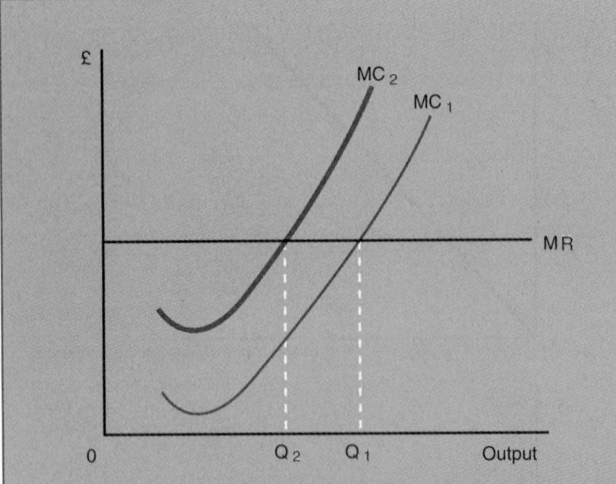

Figure 26.2 *An increase in costs*
An increase in costs of production which pushes up the marginal cost curve from MC_1 to MC_2 will lead to a fall in the profit maximising level of output from OQ_1 to OQ_2.

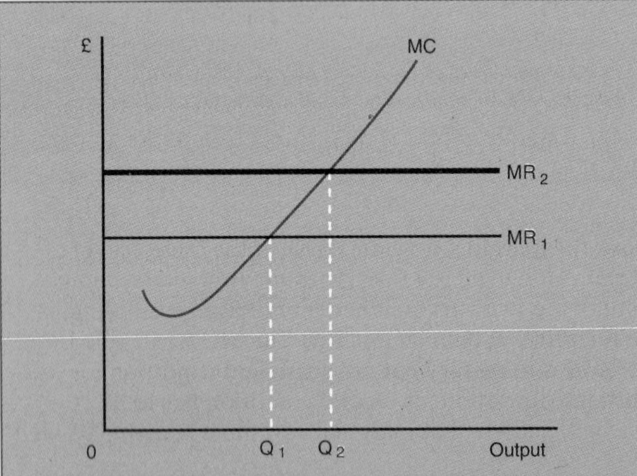

Figure 26.3 *An increase in revenue*
An increase in revenue at any given level of output will push the marginal revenue curve upwards from MR_1 to MR_2. This will lead to a rise in the profit maximising level of output from OQ_1 to OQ_2.

QUESTION 3 Consider the data in Table 26.3.
What is the new profit maximising level of output if:
(a) marginal revenue falls to £6 million at each level of output;
(b) marginal revenue increases to £20 million at each level of output;
(c) marginal cost increases by £4 million at each level of output;
(d) total cost increases by £5 million at each level of output;
(e) total revenue doubles at each level of output?

Hence a rise in costs will lead to a fall in output.

On the other hand a rise in revenue will lead to an increase in output. Assume that revenue increases at every given level of output. Perhaps consumers are prepared to pay higher prices because their incomes have increased, or the good has become more fashionable to purchase. This will push the marginal revenue curve upwards as shown in Figure 26.3. The profit maximising level of output will then rise from OQ_1 to OQ_2.

Good models

The MC = MR condition is one which is very important in the neo-classical theory of the firm. However, economists know from studies made that most businessmen are not familiar with the economic concepts of marginal cost and marginal revenue, and even fewer could state their current marginal cost of production.

In one sense this is very damning for the neo-classical theory of the firm. It will be explained in unit 115 that one criterion for judging a good model or theory is whether the model is realistic.

However, neo-classical economists would not claim that businessmen decide on their output levels by equating marginal cost and marginal revenue. They would start from the premise that firms attempt to maximise profits. If they don't, then in the real world they tend either to be forced out of business by more efficient firms which are maximising profit or they are taken over and made more efficient. So there are strong pressures forcing businesses towards their profit maximising levels of output. Economists then find it helpful to analyse the profit maximising level of output in terms of marginal cost and marginal revenue.

The MC = MR rule then is not an attempt by economists to explain how businesses arrive at their level of output. Rather, it is a rule which says that if businesses have maximised profit, it must logically be true that marginal cost equals marginal revenue. Parallels can be found in the physical sciences. A cricketer throwing a ball to another player will not analyse the throw in terms of velocity, friction, wind speed etc. But a physicist, using these concepts, could work out the optimum trajectory for the ball. The theory is not worthless because it fails to describe accurately how the player thinks and acts about the throw. Rather the theory helps us to understand the science behind everyday reality.

Key terms

Break-even point - the levels of output where total revenue equals total cost.

Applied economics

Insurance

Insurance companies have a variety of different costs. One important cost is the administration of the system - the physical selling of policies and the administration of the collection of premiums and payment of claims. Insurance companies need personnel, buildings and equipment to meet this requirement. On the whole, it could be argued that average administration costs fall as output increases.

A larger cost is the payment of claims. Insurance is, after all, bought because individuals and firms want to cover themselves if things go wrong. Average claims should tend to increase the greater the number of policy holders. This is because not every customer is identical. Some customers are riskier than others. In selecting which customers to offer policies to, insurance companies take account of risks. If they wish to underwrite 100 000 policies in a year, they will select those 100 000 customers with the lowest risk. Taking on an extra 10 000 customers could well lead to average claims payments increasing. Hence, the marginal cost associated with premium payments increases. The shape of the marginal and average cost curves for an insurance company is therefore arguably U-shaped. Marginal and average costs fall to start with because of the falling average costs associated with administration. However, attracting too much business leads to a rise in marginal and average costs because average claims payments increase.

In the late 1980s many UK insurance companies attempted to increase market share. They thought that the marginal revenue to be gained from selling extra policies was greater than the marginal cost of providing that policy. Competition in the insurance industry brought about a fall in premiums. The insurance companies, however, misjudged the situation. The early 1990s saw a rapid increase in crime, particularly against property. Cars were more likely to be stolen or broken into. The number of house burglaries increased. There was also an increase in difficult to detect fraudulent crimes. The early 1990s was a period of deep recession and some households and firms found that one way to realise some cash from their assets was to destroy them (or pretend to destroy them) and claim on the insurance. Natural disasters, such as drought or high winds, also increased in frequency. The result was that claims payouts soared.

The insurance companies responded by increasing insurance premiums and being more selective about which customers they were prepared to offer policies to. Some customers found that they were refused cover from their traditional insurance company and could only get themselves covered with another company at an exorbitant premium. One car, the Ford Cosworth, a variant of the Ford Granada, even had to be taken off the market by its manufacturers because so many insurers weren't prepared to offer insurance for the car, and those that did wanted thousands of pounds for a year's insurance.

Increased premiums meant higher marginal revenue, whilst a more selective approach to customers meant lower marginal costs. By 1994, it became apparent that insurance companies had over-corrected their mistakes of the late 1980s. Profits soared. Competition then put downward pressure on premiums. Individual firms were forced to cut rates in order to prevent their customers from switching to another company. The result was a fall in marginal revenue and a fall in profits. However, profits remained healthy and by 1995, the downward pressure on premiums seemed to have largely disappeared.

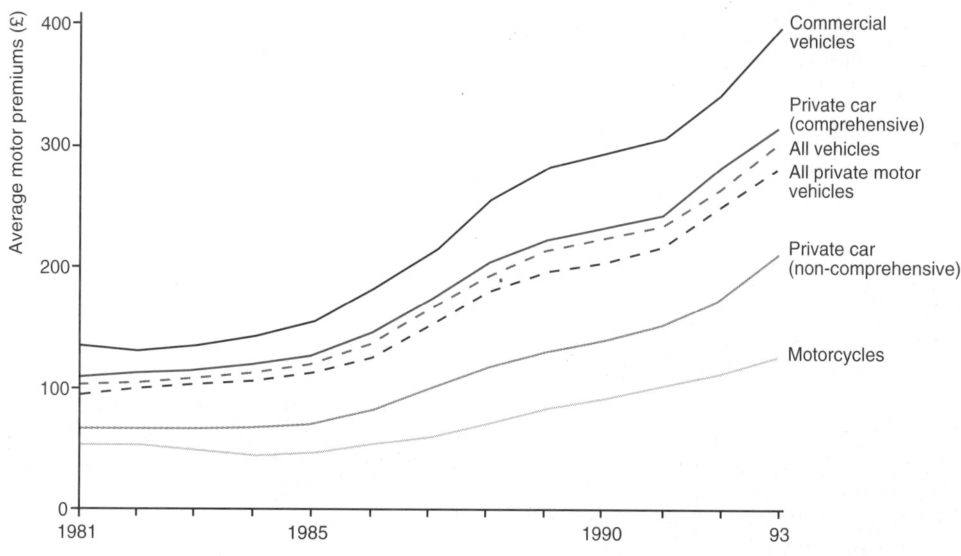

Source: adapted from Association of British Insurers.

Figure 26.4 *Average motor vehicle premiums*

DATA QUESTION

Sandwiches

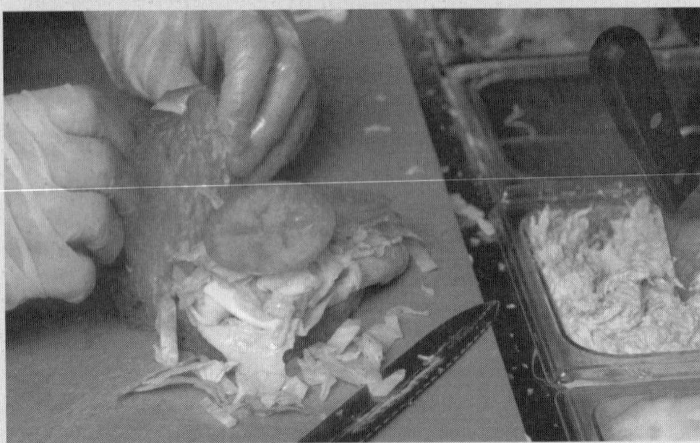

The sandwich market in the UK is big business. It has been growing at an annual rate of 10 per cent per annum over the past 10 years, with a current turnover of £2bn. One quarter of the UK fast food market is now accounted for by the not-so-humble sandwich.

The typical sandwich is still made of white bread and filled with ham, beef, bacon, prawn, cheese or tomato. But growth in the market is very much coming from more exotic products. Some of the more successful large new entrants to the market are meeting the demand for sophisticated ingredients, such as Mediterranean breads, roasted walnuts and herb loaves. Fillings include chicken breast and avocado pear, roast red peppers, courgettes and mozzarella, and asparagus and mayonnaise.

The market leader is Marks and Spencer with 7 per cent of total sales. However, the large supermarkets such as Tesco and Sainsbury's, and retailers like Boots, are big players too. All these retailers buy their sandwiches ready made from specialist suppliers such as Hillsdown Chilled Foods, United Biscuits and Derbyshire Chilled Foods. Each is capable of making up to 1 million sandwiches per week. Even so, these top players only account for 17 per cent of all sandwiches sold in the UK.

Below them are hundreds of companies producing 1 000 to 100 000 sandwiches a week, usually distributing them to retailers locally or regionally. Many began their businesses with basket deliveries to shops and offices; closeness to the point of sale is an advantage in a business where the product's shelf-life is no more than two days. However, smaller producers can face cost problems. They can lack the financial and management resources of the larger manufacturers. They are also being forced to comply with increasingly stringent fresh food legislation which necessitates them purchasing vans with chilled compartments as well as equipping their production plants with chill facilities at the point of assembly of the sandwich.

At the bottom of the pyramid are the smallest manufacturers, making no more than 1 000 sandwiches a week. Many of these are individuals or couples, tempted by the low cost of entry into sandwich-making. Some have come into the industry in recent years after losing more conventional jobs, supported by redundancy payments.

Pressure on profit margins and prices will intensify in the future. The largest manufacturers expect to take a bigger share of the market, cashing in on their investment in production methods that keep costs down. They will squeeze out medium-sized competitors such as Holme Maid Foods of Scunthorpe, which in 1995 went into receivership despite having opened a new factory capable of producing 45 000 sandwiches a week. At the same time, the market is expected to carry on growing. In particular, the growth of the petrol forecourt supermarket could well add a whole dimension to sandwich sales. Instead of popping down to the local shops for sandwiches for lunch, the local petrol station might be far more convenient. And an increasing number of evening snackers may choose to buy a herb loaf sandwich rather than a packet of greasy fish and chips.

Source: adapted from the *Financial Times*, 1.4.1995.

1. **(a) What might be the costs faced by a sandwich manufacturer? (b) How might the costs of a large 1 million sandwich a week manufacturer differ from that of one making 500 sandwiches a week?**
2. **Explain why a sandwich manufacturer will maximise its profit at the point where marginal cost equals marginal revenue.**
3. **What would you expect to happen to the output of producers who manage to reduce their marginal cost of production of sandwiches in the future?**
4. **Using diagrams, explain why a sandwich maker, producing speciality sandwiches such as avocado pear and mayonnaise, can survive in business when its costs are higher than a standard sandwich maker manufacturing, say, ham sandwiches.**
5. **Discuss what would happen to sandwich prices if demand continued to grow but costs increased too.**

Perfect competition

Summary

1. In a perfectly competitive market it is assumed that there are a large number of small firms that produce a homogeneous product. Firms are price-takers. There are no barriers to entry or exit and there is perfect knowledge.
2. The demand curve facing an individual firm is perfectly elastic because the firm is a price taker. This means that price = AR = MR.
3. The short run supply curve of the firm is its marginal cost curve above its average variable cost curve.
4. If firms in the short run are making abnormal profits, new firms will enter the industry, increasing market supply and thus reducing price. This will continue until only normal profits are being made.
5. If production is unprofitable, firms will leave the industry, reducing market supply and increasing price. This will continue until only normal profits are being made.
6. In long run equilibrium, AR = AC because no abnormal profits are made.

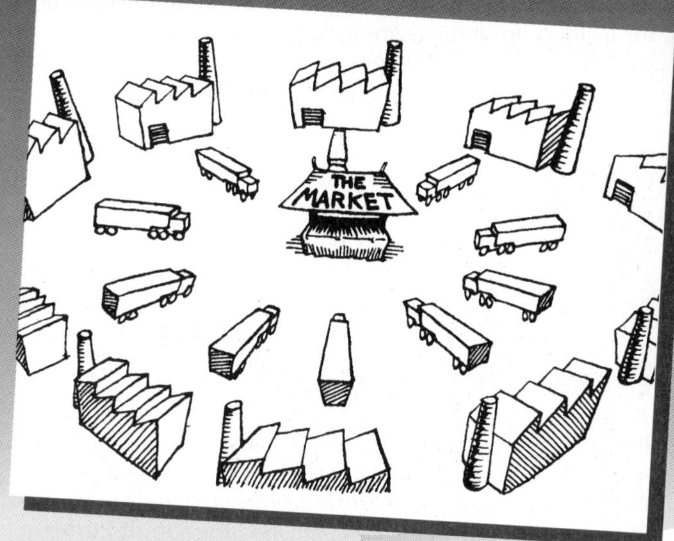

Assumptions

The model of PERFECT COMPETITION describes a market where there is a high degree of competition. The word 'perfect' does not mean that this form of competition produces ideal results or maximises economic welfare; in other words, the word 'perfect' should not have any **normative** overtones (☞ unit 115).

A perfectly competitive market must possess four characteristics.

- There must be **many buyers and sellers** in the market, none of whom is large enough to influence price. Buyers and sellers are said to be PRICE TAKERS. This type of market has many relatively small firms that supply goods to a large number of small buyers.
- There is **freedom of entry and exit** to the industry. Firms must be able to establish themselves in the industry easily and quickly. Barriers to entry must therefore be low. If a firm wishes to cease production and leave the market, it must be free to do so.
- Buyers and sellers possess **perfect knowledge** of prices. If one firm charges a higher price than the market price, the demand for its product will be zero as buyers buy elsewhere in the market. Hence the firm has to accept the market price if it wishes to sell into the market (i.e. it must be a price taker).
- All firms produce a **homogeneous** product. There is no branding of products and products are identical.

There are relatively few industries in the world which approximate to this type of market structure. One which might is agriculture. In agriculture there are a large number of farmers supplying the market, none of whom is large enough to influence price. It is easy to buy a farm

QUESTION 1 The basic chemicals industry produces the building blocks for many consumer products. Ethylene, for instance, is the most important ingredient in plastic manufacture. Like oil or coal, basic chemicals are standard products produced and sold in a worldwide market. Differences in prices between national markets tend to reflect transport costs and delivery times. Whilst it costs millions of pounds to build a chemicals factory, there is never any shortage of firms, either already in the chemicals industry or wanting to diversify their range of products, which are prepared to build new plants when profits are high enough.

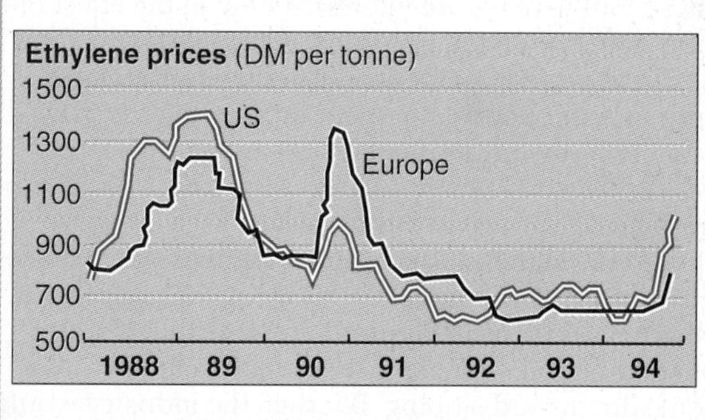

Source: adapted from Goldman Sachs.

Figure 27.1 *Ethylene prices*

Discuss why firms in the basic chemicals industry might be described as operating in a perfectly competitive market.

and set up in business. Equally it is easy to sell a farm and leave the industry. Farmers on the whole possess perfect knowledge. They know what prices prevail in the market, for instance from the farming press. Finally, farmers produce a range of homogeneous products. King Edwards potatoes from one farm are indistinguishable from King Edwards potatoes from another. In Europe and in many countries round the world, farming is in certain instances not a perfectly competitive market. This is because governments may interfere in the market, buying and selling to fix a price (☞ unit 12).

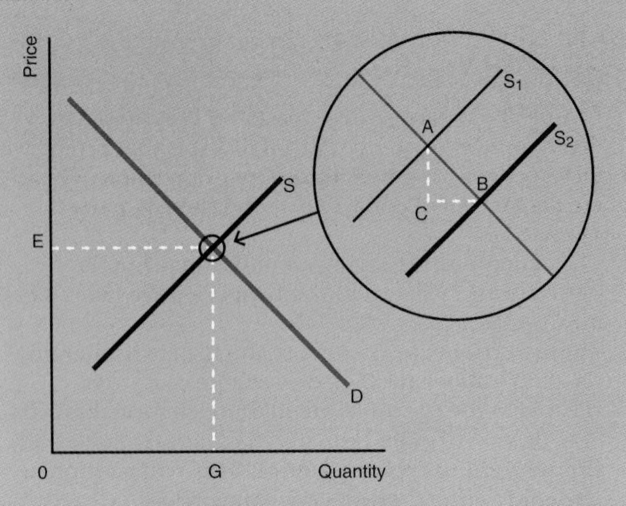

Figure 27.2 *The effect of an increase in supply by one firm in a perfectly competitive industry*
An increase in supply by one firm from S_1 to S_2 will have such a small effect on total supply that equilibrium price will remain at OE.

Demand and revenue

It is an assumption of the model of perfect competition that there is a large number of sellers in the market. Assume that one of these firms decides to double output. Industry supply will increase, pushing the supply curve to the right. However, the increase in supply is necessarily very small because the firm is small. In fact it will be so small that the resulting movement along the demand curve will be impossible to distinguish and the price will not change.

This can be seen in Figure 27.2. The area round the existing equilibrium point has been enlarged. An increase in supply by one firm has shifted the supply curve from S_1 to S_2, reducing equilibrium price by AC and increasing equilibrium quantity demanded and supplied by CB. However, AC is so small that it has no effect on the overall equilibrium price of OE and it is impossible to draw two supply curves thinly enough to show this shift in supply.

In agriculture, for instance, it would be surprising if the decision of one farmer to double wheat output were to have any perceptible influence on equilibrium price. His or her extra output is so insignificant that it cannot affect the market price for wheat. Of course, if all farmers were to double their wheat output, the price of wheat would collapse. But here we are interested only in the effect on price of the production decisions of a single farm.

A firm in perfect competition can therefore expand output or reduce output without influencing the price. Put another way, the firm cannot choose to raise price and expect to sell more of its product. It can lower its price but there is no advantage in this since it can sell its entire output at the higher market price. The demand curve for an individual firm is therefore horizontal (i.e. **perfectly elastic** ☞ unit 18) as in Figure 27.3. (Note that if a firm expanded output sufficiently its demand curve would become downward sloping. But then the industry would be made up of one large firm and many small firms and would no longer be perfectly competitive.)

This demand curve is also the firm's average and marginal revenue curve. If a firm sells all its output at one price, then this price must be the average price or average revenue received. If a firm sells an extra or marginal unit, it will receive the same price as on preceding units and therefore the marginal price or revenue will be the same as the average price or revenue.

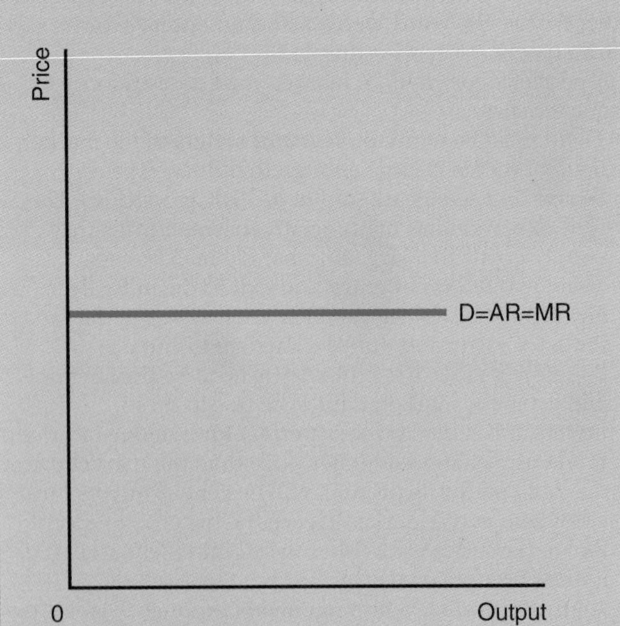

Figure 27.3 *The demand curve facing a firm in perfect competition*
A change in output by the firm will have no effect on the market price of the product. Therefore the firm faces a perfectly elastic demand curve. This is also the firm's average and marginal revenue curve.

QUESTION 2

Table 27.1 *Market demand and supply*

Quantity demanded (million units)	Quantity supplied (million units)	Price (£)
1000	6000	10
3000	4000	8
5000	2000	6

(a) Draw the market demand and supply curves on graph paper.
(b) There are 1000 firms in the industry each producing the same quantity. One firm now doubles its output.
 (i) Show the effect of this on market demand and supply.
 (ii) On a separate graph draw the demand curve facing the firm.
(c) All firms in the industry now double their output.
 (i) Show the effect of this on market demand and supply.
 (ii) What will be the effect on the demand curve for the individual firm?

Cost and supply curves

In a perfectly competitive market, the supply curve of the firm will be its marginal cost curve.

- The marginal cost of production is the lowest price at which a firm would be prepared to supply an extra unit of output. For instance, if the marginal cost were £3 when price received was £5, then the firm would be able to make £2 **abnormal profit** (profit over and above the **normal profit** included in cost on that unit). The firm would definitely produce this marginal unit. If marginal cost were £3 when price were £3 it would still produce this marginal unit because it would earn normal profit on it. However, if marginal cost were £3 when price was £2 it would not produce the extra unit because it would make a £1 loss on it.
- In the short run, a firm will not necessarily shut down production if it makes a loss (☞ unit 24). A firm has fixed costs which it has to pay whether it closes down and produces nothing or whether it continues to operate. Any revenue over and above variable cost will make some contribution towards paying its fixed costs. Therefore it will only close down (i.e. cease to supply) if average revenue or price is below average variable cost.

The firm's short run supply curve will therefore be that part of the marginal cost curve above its average variable cost curve - the thick portion of the marginal cost curve in Figure 27.4 (a).

In the long run there are no fixed costs and the average total cost and average variable cost curves are one and the same. The firm will not produce unless it can cover all its costs. Therefore in the long run, the firm's supply curve is the marginal cost curve above its average cost curve as shown in Figure 27.4 (b).

The supply curve for the industry can be constructed by horizontally summing the individual supply curves of each firm (☞ unit 5).

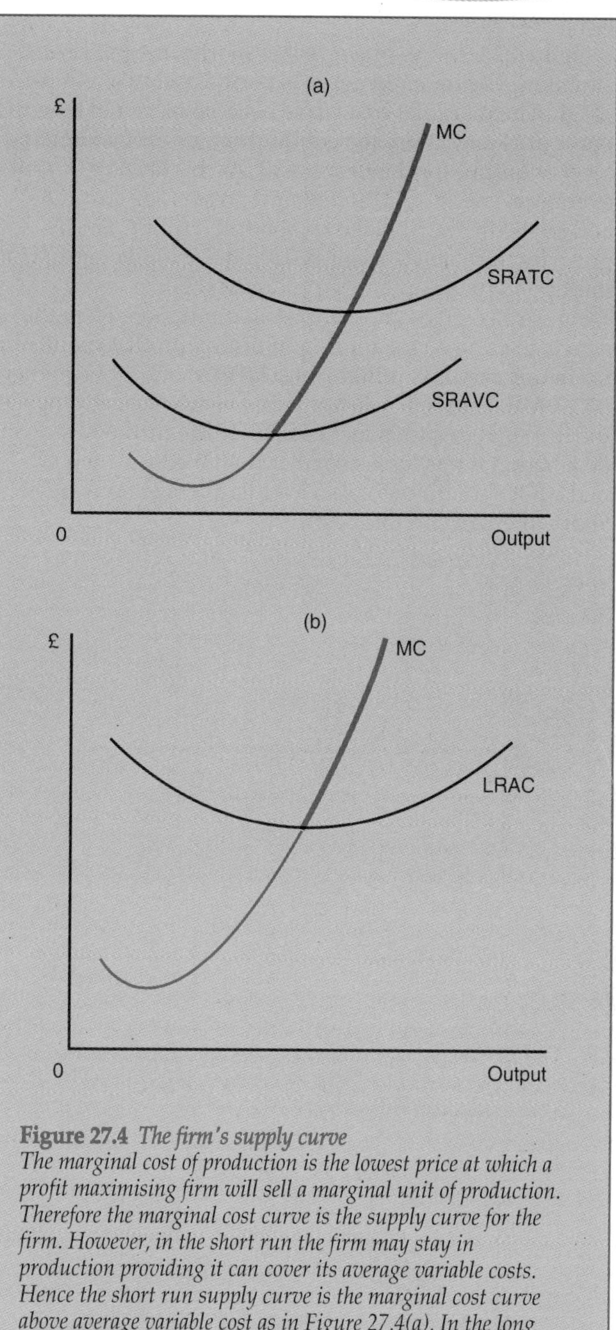

Figure 27.4 *The firm's supply curve*
The marginal cost of production is the lowest price at which a profit maximising firm will sell a marginal unit of production. Therefore the marginal cost curve is the supply curve for the firm. However, in the short run the firm may stay in production providing it can cover its average variable costs. Hence the short run supply curve is the marginal cost curve above average variable cost as in Figure 27.4(a). In the long run a firm will leave the industry if it makes a loss. Hence, the supply curve in the long run is the marginal cost curve above the average cost curve as in Figure 27.4 (b).

Short run equilibrium

In perfect competition it is assumed that firms are short run profit maximisers. So the firm will produce at that level of output where marginal cost equals marginal revenue (the MC= MR rule ☞ unit 26). The price it charges is fixed by the market because the individual firm is a price-taker.

Figure 27.5 shows one possible short run equilibrium situation. The demand curve is perfectly elastic at a price of OE. The marginal cost curve cuts the marginal revenue curve at H and hence the equilibrium, profit maximising level of output for the firm is OQ. At this level of output, average revenue (QH) is higher than average cost (QG) and so the firm will make an abnormal profit. This is given by the shaded area EFGH and is average profit (EF) multiplied by the quantity produced (FG).

Figure 27.6 gives another possible situation. Here the firm is making a loss at its equilibrium, profit maximising (or in this case loss minimising) level of output OQ where MC = MR. Price OF is lower than average cost and hence the firm makes a total loss of EFGH. The firm will stay in production if this loss is smaller than the loss it would make if it shut down (i.e. so long as average revenue is above average variable cost).

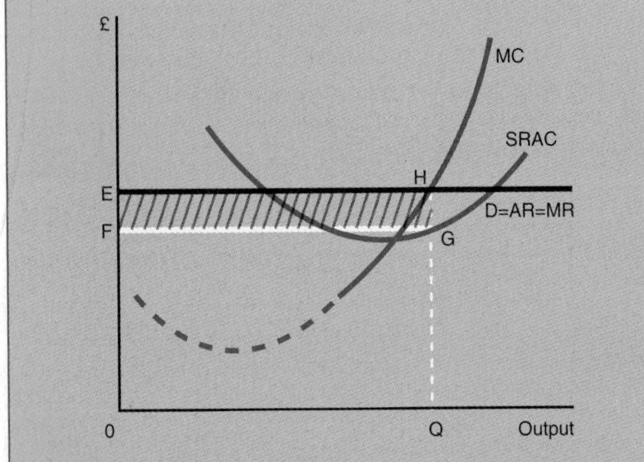

Figure 27.5 *Short run profit maximisation*
The firm produces at its profit maximising equilibrium level of output OQ where MC = MR. Because AR is greater than AC, it makes an abnormal profit of EFGH.

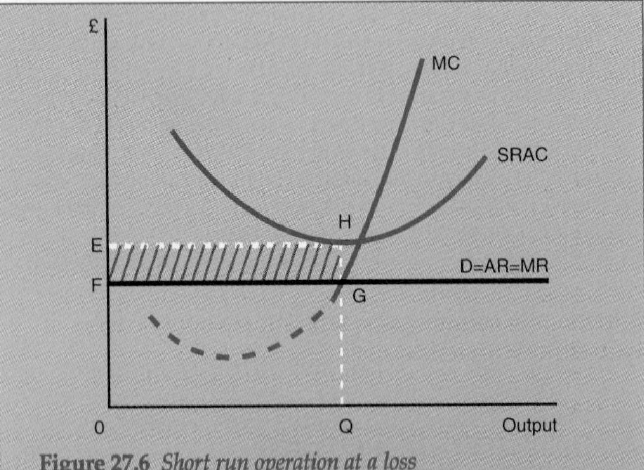

Figure 27.6 *Short run operation at a loss*
The firm produces at its profit maximising equilibrium level of output OQ where MC = MR. In this case, because AR is less than AC, it will make a loss shown by the shaded area EFGH. This is the minimum loss it will make if AR is greater than AVC.

QUESTION 3

Table 27.2

£

Output	Marginal cost (£)	Total fixed cost	Total variable cost	Total cost	Average variable cost	Average total cost
2		100	100			
	40					
3						
	30					
4						
	40					
5						
	60					
6						
	100					
7						

Table 27.2 shows the costs of production of a firm.

(a) Calculate for levels of output from 2 to 7 units: (i) total fixed cost (ii) total variable cost; (iii) total cost; (iv) average variable cost; (v) average total cost.

(b) Plot the firm's short run supply curve on a graph.

(c) Would a firm cease production (1) in the short run and (2) in the long run if the sales price per unit were: (i) £80; (ii) £70; (iii) £60; (iv) £50; (v) £40; (vi) £30?

Long run equilibrium

In the long run, a perfectly competitive firm will neither make losses nor abnormal profits.

Consider a situation where firms were making losses. In the long term, some firms would leave the industry. It is pointless carrying on production in the long term at a loss. If firms leave the industry, total supply will fall. The more firms that leave the industry, the greater will be the fall in supply and the greater will be the rise in price of the product. Firms will continue to leave the industry until the industry as a whole returns to profitability. This is shown in Figure 27.7. When the supply curve is S_1 the firm is making a loss. Firms leave the industry, pushing the supply curve to the left. With S_2, the price is just high enough for firms to make **normal profit**. If on the other hand a firm were making abnormal profit in the short run, other firms would enter the industry eager to gain high profits. This is shown in Figure 27.8. At a price of P, firms are making abnormal profit. This encourages new entrants to the industry, increasing supply from S_1 until with S_2 the price is just low enough for firms to make a normal profit.

In the long run, then, competitive pressures ensure equilibrium is established where the firm neither makes abnormal profits or losses. This means that in equilibrium, average revenue equals average cost (AR = AC). It should also be remembered that MC = MR because the firm is profit maximising and that AR = MR because the demand curve is horizontal. Putting these three conditions

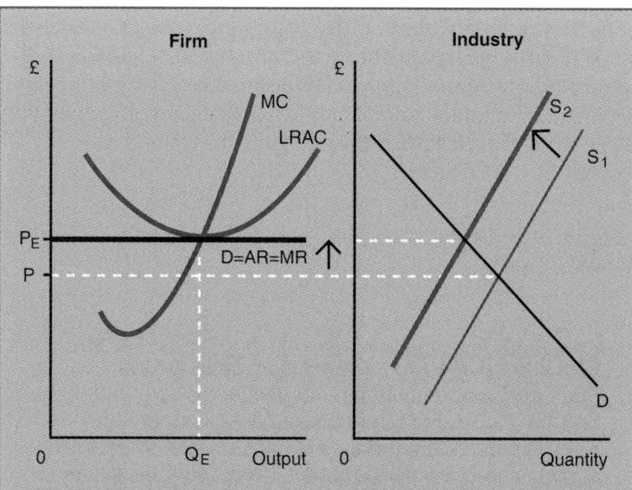

Figure 27.7 *Long run equilibrium following short run losses*
If losses are being made in the short run firms will leave the industry, pushing the supply curve from S1 to S2. At S2 there will no longer be any pressure for firms to leave because they will be able to make normal profits on their operations.

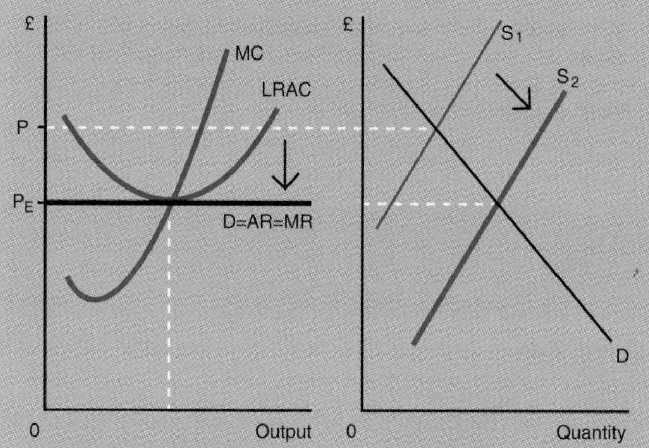

Figure 27.8 *Long run equilibrium following short run abnormal profit*
If abnormal profits are being made in the short run, firms will enter the industry, pushing the supply curve from S_1 to S_2. At S_2 firms will no longer be attracted into the industry because they will only be able to make normal profits on their operations.

together, it must be true that for a firm in long run equilibrium in a perfectly competitive market:

$$AC = AR = MR = MC$$

Long run cost curves

One interesting point to note is that the model of perfect competition predicts that all perfectly competitive firms will have identical costs in the long run. Assume a firm discovers some new technique of production which enables it to reduce costs and increase profits in the short run. Other firms will respond by copying this technique.

QUESTION 4

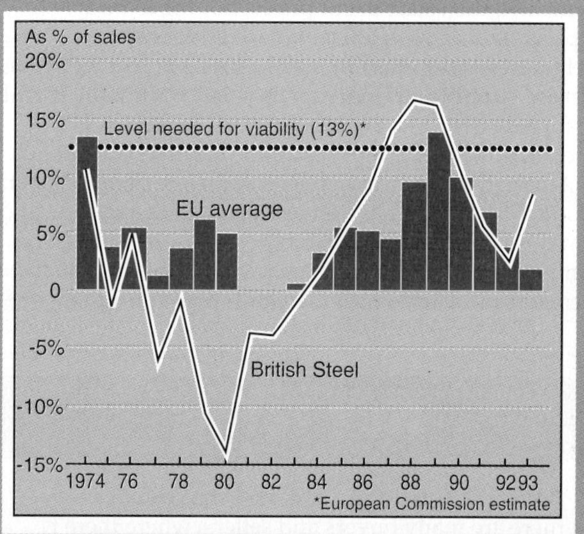

Source: adapted from British Steel.
Figure 27.9 *Operating profit before interest and depreciation*

The international steel market can be seen as a perfectly competitive market. There are a large number of steel producers worldwide manufacturing a large number of homogeneous products.

During the early 1970s, profits were high and new steel producers, particularly in the newly industrialised countries such as South Korea, entered the market. The first oil crisis of 1973-4, however, had a disastrous impact on steel producers. Demand for steel fell as economies went into recession. For the next ten years, many steel companies made little if any profit and many made large losses. In Europe and the USA, plants were closed and firms merged or went out of business.

Slowly, however, demand began to increase again in the 1980s. By the mid-1980s, with rising demand and falling capacity, much of the European and US steel industry began to be profitable again. British Steel, in evidence to a House of Commons committee in 1994, cited a European Commission estimate that steel producers needed to make 13 per cent profit as a percentage of sales if capacity was not to fall further in the long term. In the late 1980s, steel producers were able to make this and more.

The world recession of the early 1990s once again severely hit steel producers, reducing demand and profits. There were some closures of steel plants, but the process was halted when demand began to pick up again as the world economy recovered from 1992-93.

In its 1994 evidence to the House of Commons, British Steel argued that there was still too much capacity in Europe for steel producers to earn a sufficient rate of return. Equally, British Steel was considering expanding into the Far East where very fast economic growth might allow better rates of return on investment in new plant.

How can the model of perfect competition explain the behaviour of steel firms from 1970 onwards?

They can do this because there is perfect knowledge in the industry and therefore there can be no industrial secrets. Firms will then start to cut prices, hoping to be able to expand their sales. If a firm fails to adopt the new techniques, it will start to make a loss when other firms expand supply and undercut its price. Eventually it will be forced either to leave the industry because it is uncompetitive, or adopt the latest production techniques.

Alternatively, a firm may possess some unique factor of production. It may have an exceptional manager, or find that it is far better sited than other firms. In a perfectly competitive world the manager will be able to demand increases in salary which match the extra profit that she is generating for the firm. If the firm fails to pay this, she will be headhunted by another firm which realises the potential of the manager to create profits. As for the better site, the firm could sell it to another firm in the industry for a much higher price than those sites owned by competitors. Therefore the opportunity cost of the site is much higher than other sites and it is the opportunity cost, not the accounting cost, that is shown in economists' cost curves.

Key terms

Perfect competition - a market structure where there are many buyers and sellers, where there is freedom of entry and exit to the market, where there is perfect knowledge and where all firms produce a homogeneous product.
Price-taker - a firm or other economic agent which is forced to accept the ruling market price for the sale of its product.

QUESTION 5 In 1988, it was reported that Pompes Funébres Générales (PFG), the largest firm of French undertakers, had bought a 29 per cent stake in Kenyon Securities, the third largest quoted undertaking business in Britain. In France a declining mortality rate had hit undertakers hard and PFG was looking for new markets. One reason why the UK was attractive was because there were more cremations in the UK than in France. 70 per cent of the UK market was accounted for by cremations whereas in France the figure was only 4 per cent. Profit margins on cremations are much higher than on burials.

Why might PFG have been prepared to pay more for its stake in Kenyon Securities than it would have had to pay if it attempted to set up a rival undertaking business from scratch in the UK?

Applied economics

Lloyds of London

Lloyds of London has a long history dating back to the eighteenth century. It is a provider of insurance and reinsurance. Lloyds differs from a typical insurance company in that it is made up of a large number of different firms operating under the Lloyds umbrella. These firms are called 'syndicates'. Each syndicate is run by a set of professional brokers. They transact the day to day business, arranging new contracts, fixing prices ('insurance premiums') and paying out claims.

In a typical year, the insurance premiums being paid in will equal the economic costs of running the firm. The economic costs include the claims paid, the salaries of the brokers and other staff, other costs such as rent on the floor space occupied in the Lloyds building in London, and finally a payment to the Names of the syndicate. The Names put up the financial capital of the business. These are the reserves which can be used to pay claims in years when a syndicate makes a loss. For instance, taking a simplified example, if a syndicate's claims and other costs were £20m but its insurance premiums were only £18m, then the Names of the syndicate would have to pay a 'call' of £2m. On the other hand, if costs were £20m and premiums were £22m, the Names would receive a payment of £2m. The Names have unlimited liability, which means that they risk all their personal wealth in the market. If a Name received a 'call' for £1m but only had assets worth £750 000, then he or she would be forced to sell everything to pay the call. A central reserve held by Lloyds might then pay the remaining £250 000. Payments to Names in profitable years can be seen as representing the reward for the risks Names face in putting their financial capital at the disposal of Lloyds' syndicates.

Throughout most of the post-war period, Names made money. In the first half of the 1980s, it could even be argued that syndicates were making abnormal profits. This is because there was an expansion of business in what is arguably a perfectly competitive market. It is perfectly competitive because there are a large number of firms in the market - there were over 400 syndicates in the 1980s - facing a large number of customers. There is no branding, insurance at Lloyds being a homogeneous good. There was freedom of entry and exit whilst knowledge in the market was easily available.

The expansion of the market in the 1980s led to major problems. Expansion led to more syndicates chasing the same amount of business. Premiums fell, and with them profits. Expansion also meant that more people had to be found to become Names. Previously, Names had tended to be very affluent individuals who could afford to lose substantial sums of money in a single year. However, syndicates started to target individuals who were less affluent and for whom losing a few hundred thousand pounds in a year would almost bankrupt them. A third problem emerged. Some syndicates, such as Gooder-Walker syndicates, were run by brokers who mismanaged the affairs of the syndicates. They took on business which gave high short term profits but which proved disastrous in the longer term. The syndicates which were particularly mis-managed were those which took on old policies which had been written for industrial disease insurance or pollution insurance.

By the late 1980s, as Figure 27.10 shows, Lloyds began to make losses. Between 1988 and 1992, Lloyds syndicates made an estimated net loss of £8bn. This should be seen in the context of the estimated profit for Lloyds in 1993, a good year for the market, of £800m. Between 1988 and 1992, some syndicates were profitable. So the loss to other syndicates was even greater than the net £8bn loss. Many Names were bankrupted. Other Names pulled out of the market, frightened by the losses they had incurred as Figure 27.11 shows. The number of syndicates fell from 401 in 1990 to 179 in 1994. This is what would be predicted by the theory of perfect competition. Losses lead to some firms leaving the industry. Syndicates also began turning away more business. Rather than accept the going price, on which they judged they would make a loss, they didn't sell a policy - exactly what is implied by the horizontal demand curve facing an individual firm in perfect competition. This reduction in supply then led to a rise in price. Insurance premiums increased sharply in the early 1990s. This led to a shift upward in the individual demand curve facing each firm, and allowed the gradual return to profitability of the market by 1993.

Lloyds is currently radically changing direction. In 1994, it allowed firms with limited liability for the first time to provide capital for the market. It had to because unlimited liability Names were no longer prepared to supply enough capital to allow for the amount of business that syndicates wanted to write. Some predict that within ten years unlimited liability Names will be marginalised and capital will, for the most part, by provided by institutional limited liability investors.

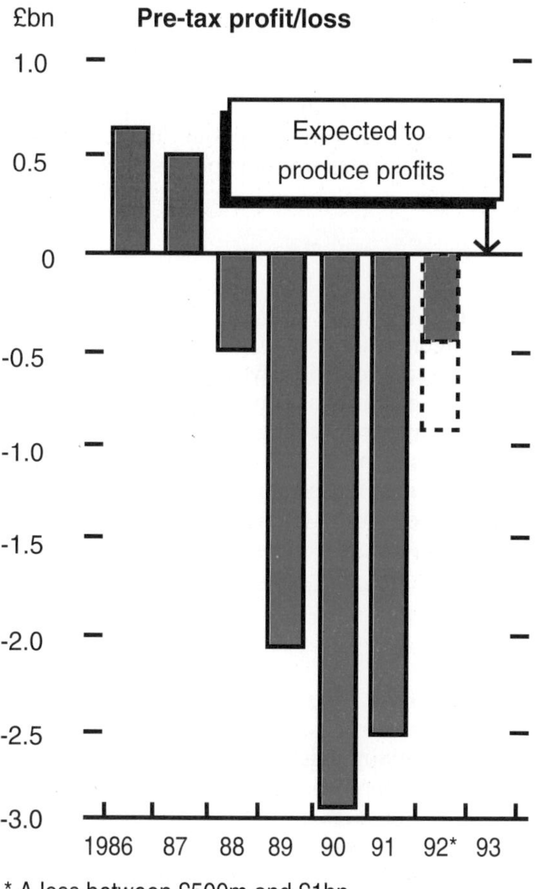

Source: adapted from Lloyds.
Figure 27.10 *Lloyds: pre-tax profit/loss*

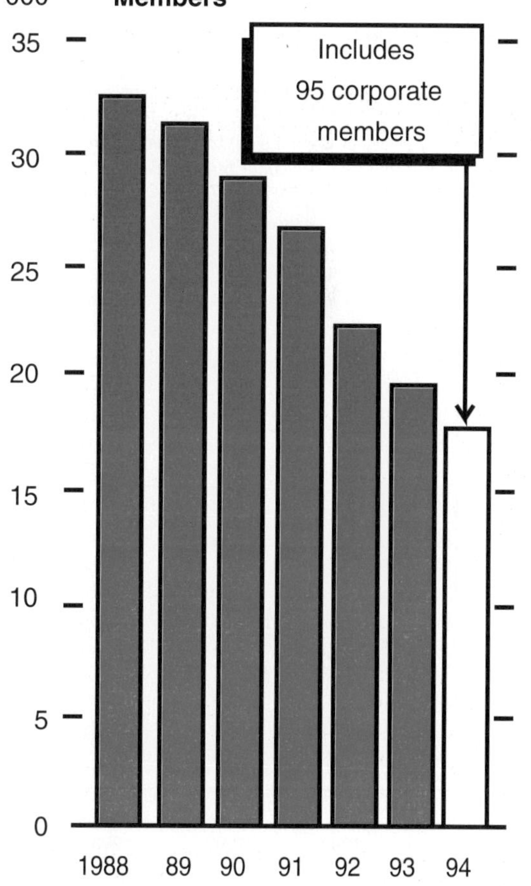

Source: adapted from Lloyds.
Figure 27.11 *Lloyds: members*

Pig production

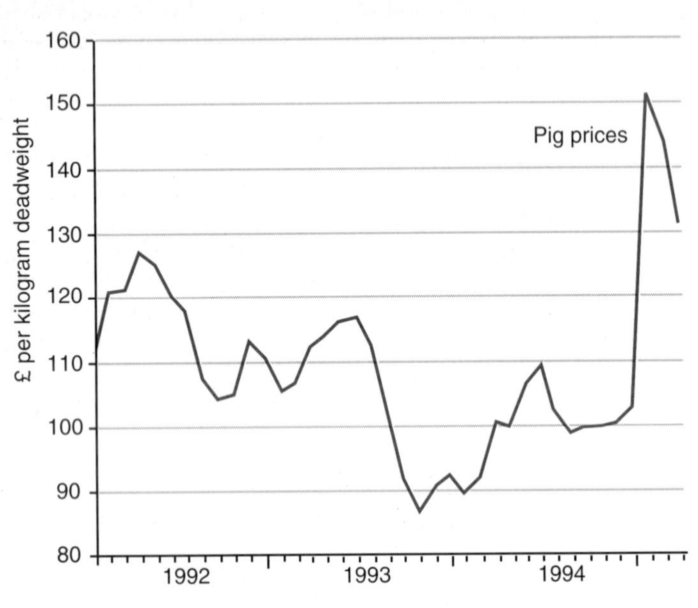

Source: Meat and Livestock Commission, *Meat Demand Trends.*

Figure 27.12 *Pig prices (£ per kilogram deadweight)*

The plight of British pig farmers

Pig farmers are used to swings in the market. The UK pig cycle has meant that over the past 20 years, pig farmers have regularly moved from periods when pig farming was highly profitable to ones where they were making losses. The period of losses which started in mid-1993 was particularly long compared to previous loss-making periods. Pig farmers did not start to make profits again till over 18 months later in early 1995. Normally, the loss making period lasts only 6 months. Not surprisingly, the number of pig herds declined in 1994. However, the fall in number was less than might have been expected from previous cycles. One reason is that the pig farmers that have remained after previous shake-outs have bigger herds and have invested money in specialised buildings. They are more committed to long term pig farming. Another factor has been the good returns made in 1994 on arable farming. Farm incomes rose sharply in 1994, allowing farmers to bail out their loss making pig operations from the profits made on arable crops.

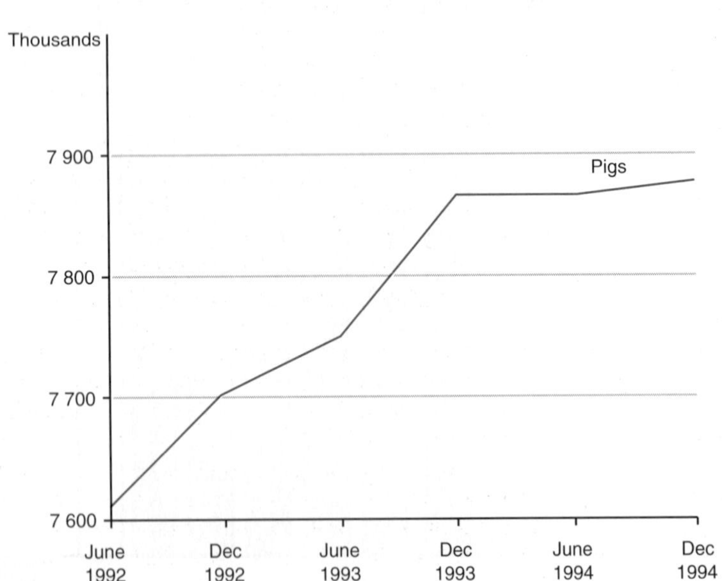

Source: adapted from Agricultural Departments.

Figure 27.13 *Pigs on UK farms*

New regulations

From 1 January 1999, pigs in the UK will no longer be allowed to be kept in stalls or tethers. Instead, they will have to be kept in open strawed yards or similar. This move is in response to lobbying by animal welfare activists. In 1995, an estimated 38 per cent of pig farmers still used stalls and tethers. Open strawed yards will require capital investment and are more expensive to operate than stalls.

Source: adapted from the *Financial Times*, 14.3.1995.

1. **Why is pig farming a perfectly competitive industry?**
2. **Explain, using diagrams, why:**
   (a) there was a fall in the number of UK pig farmers between the middle of 1993 and the start of 1995;
   (b) pig farmers continued to produce in 1994 even when they were making losses.
3. **What do you think is likely to happen to the number of pig farmers between 1995 and 2000? Use a diagram to illustrate your answer.**

unit 28 Monopoly

Summary

1. A monopolist is the sole producer in an industry.
2. The demand curve faced by the monopolist is the market demand curve.
3. The monopolist's demand curve is also its average revenue curve.
4. The marginal revenue falls twice as steeply as the average revenue curve.
5. The profit maximising monopolist will produce where MC = MR and price on its demand curve.
6. The monopolist is likely to be able to earn abnormal profit because average revenue will be above average cost at the equilibrium level of output.
7. A monopolist may be able to price discriminate and further increase abnormal profit.

Assumptions

The neo-classical theory of monopoly assumes that a MONOPOLY market structure has the following characteristics:

- there is only one firm in the industry - the monopolist;
- barriers to entry prevent new firms from entering the market;
- the monopolist is a short run profit maximiser.

There are many industries in the world economy which possess most or all of these characteristics. In the UK, for instance, gas, electricity, telecommunications, rail transport and water supply are monopolies. Some of these monopolies are state owned whilst others were state monopolies which have since been privatised without the creation of genuine new competition (☞ unit 45).

Some monopolies, such as the UK water companies, possess considerable market power because there are no good substitutes for their products. The Post Office too is a monopolist, but its monopoly position is weaker because it faces competition from other forms of communication service. In fact the existence of monopoly depends upon how an industry is defined. For instance, The Post Office is a monopolist in letter delivery, but not in communication services. Shell is not a monopoly supplier of petrol to the UK market, but it may have a monopoly in a rural area if it owns the only garage for miles around.

Monopolies can only remain as monopolies if there are high barriers to entry to the industry (☞ unit 25). In the case of a natural monopoly(☞ unit 39), economies of scale are so large that any new entrant would find it impossible to match the costs and prices of the established firm in the industry. Other barriers to entry include legal barriers such as patents, natural cost advantages such as ownership of all key sites in an industry, marketing barriers such as advertising, and restrictive practices designed to force any competitor to leave the market.

QUESTION 1 In 1994 British Gas was a company in transition. When it was privatised in 1986, it was decided not to break up the company, but to allow it to be the sole supplier of natural gas in the UK. Subsequently, the government decided that there would be considerable efficiency gains if the gas market were to become competitive. In 1988, the company was forced to allow other gas companies to supply gas to industrial customers using British Gas pipelines. In 1994, the government announced that other gas companies could begin to compete in the domestic market within the next four years. British Gas, whilst remaining as a single company, would have to create a subsidiary which would own the gas pipeline infrastructure. This subsidiary would have to publish open tariffs for carrying gas. Another British Gas subsidiary would be free to supply the gas, but would have to pay a pipeline fee like any other gas company to the transport subsidiary.

(a) To what extent was British Gas a monopoly supplier of gas in the UK: (i) in 1986; (ii) in 1990?
(b) To what extent was British Gas a monopoly supplier of energy in the UK: (i) in 1986; (ii) in 1990?
(c) Discuss whether British Gas will retain any monopoly powers in the year 2000.

Revenue curves

A monopoly firm is itself the industry. Because the industry faces a downward sloping demand curve, so too must the monopolist. It can therefore only increase sales by reducing price, or increase price by reducing sales. It can set either price or output but not both.

The demand curve shows the quantity bought at any given price. For instance, a water company might sell 2 billion gallons of water at 1p per gallon. This price is the same as its average revenue; on average it will receive 1p per gallon. So the downward sloping demand curve facing the firm is also the average revenue curve of the firm.

If average revenue is falling, marginal revenue must be falling too and at a faster rate. For example, assume a firm sells 10 units at £20 each. To sell an eleventh unit, it needs to lower its price, say to £19. Not only will it have to lower its price on the eleventh unit, but it will also have to lower its price on the other 10 units. This is because it cannot charge a higher price to some consumers than others (although we will see later on in this unit that it is possible in limited cases). There is a loss of revenue not just of £1 on the sale of the eleventh unit but of a further £10 on the first 10 units. Total revenue increases from £200 (£20 x 10 units) to £209 (£19 x 11 units). So marginal revenue on the eleventh unit is £9 (£209 - £200) whilst the average revenue on selling 11 units is £19 (£209 ÷ 11 which is, of course, the price).

Table 28.1 gives a further example of falling marginal and average revenues. Note that the fall in marginal revenue is twice as large over any given change in quantity as the fall in average revenue. This is true of all straight line average revenue curves. Plotting these figures

Table 28.1

Quantity	Average revenue or price £	Total revenue £	Marginal revenue £
0			
			8
1	8	8	
			4
2	6	12	
			0
3	4	12	
			-4
4	2	8	
			-8
5	0	0	

on a diagram, we arrive at Figure 28.1. The marginal revenue figures, as with all marginal figures, are plotted half way between 'whole' output figures. So the marginal revenue of the second unit is plotted half way between 1 and 2 units. It can be seen that at any given level of output, average revenue is twice marginal revenue. Total revenue is maximised when marginal revenue is zero. If marginal revenue (the addition to total revenue) becomes negative then total revenue will automatically fall. Total revenue is zero if average revenue, the price received per unit of output, is zero too.

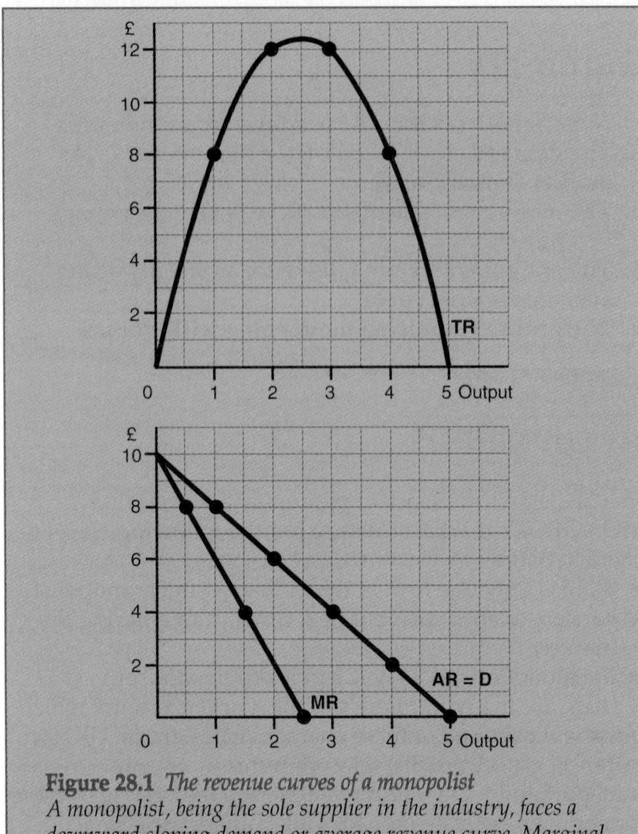

Figure 28.1 *The revenue curves of a monopolist*
A monopolist, being the sole supplier in the industry, faces a downward sloping demand or average revenue curve. Marginal revenue falls at twice the rate of average revenue and becomes zero when total revenue is maximised.

QUESTION 2

Table 28.2

Output (units per week)	Marginal revenue (£)
0	
	10
1	
	7
2	
	4
3	
	1
4	
	-2
5	

(a) Calculate (i) total revenue and (ii) average revenue at output levels 0 to 5 units.

(b) (i) Draw the axes of a graph with revenue from £0 to £10 and output from 0 to 10. (ii) Plot the marginal and average revenue curves. (iii) Extend the average revenue curve to the output axis assuming that average revenue continues to fall at the same rate as in the table.

(c) What is the value of marginal revenue when total revenue is at a maximum?

Equilibrium output

The neo-classical theory of the firm assumes that a monopolist will be a short run profit maximiser. This means that it will produce where MC = MR.

Figure 28.2 adds the traditional U-shaped average and marginal cost curves (☞ units 19 and 20) to the average and marginal revenue curves outlined above.

- **The equilibrium profit maximising level of output** is OA where MC = MR.
- **The price** will be OE. Buyers are prepared to pay OE for this output. We know this because the average revenue curve is also the demand curve and the demand curve shows the maximum price buyers will pay for any given level of ouput.
- **Abnormal profit** of EFGC will be made. The abnormal profit per unit (GF) is the difference between the average revenue received (AF) and the average cost incurred (AG). OA units are sold. Therefore total abnormal profit is OA x FG, or the area EFGC. Note that this is abnormal profit because economic cost includes an allowance for normal profit.

Note also that price is not equal to the intersection of the MC and MR curves (i.e. price is not AB). This is because the firm, although deciding on the level of output by the MC = MR condition, fixes its price on the average revenue or demand curve. Also abnormal profit is not the area EF x

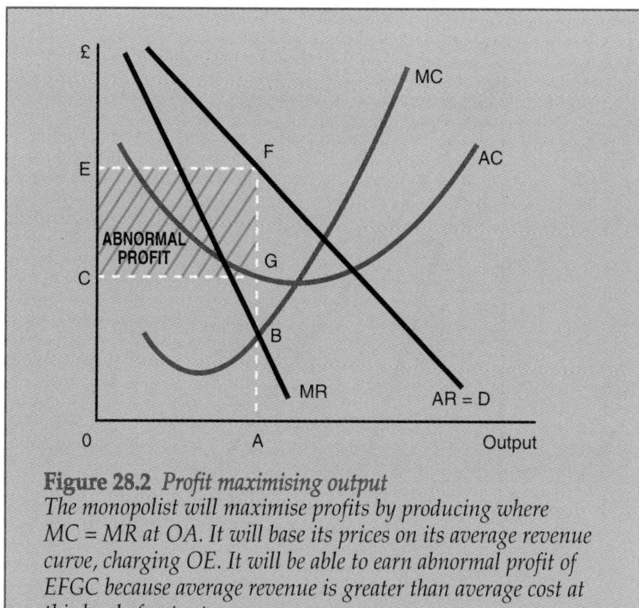

Figure 28.2 *Profit maximising output*
The monopolist will maximise profits by producing where MC = MR at OA. It will base its prices on its average revenue curve, charging OE. It will be able to earn abnormal profit of EFGC because average revenue is greater than average cost at this level of output.

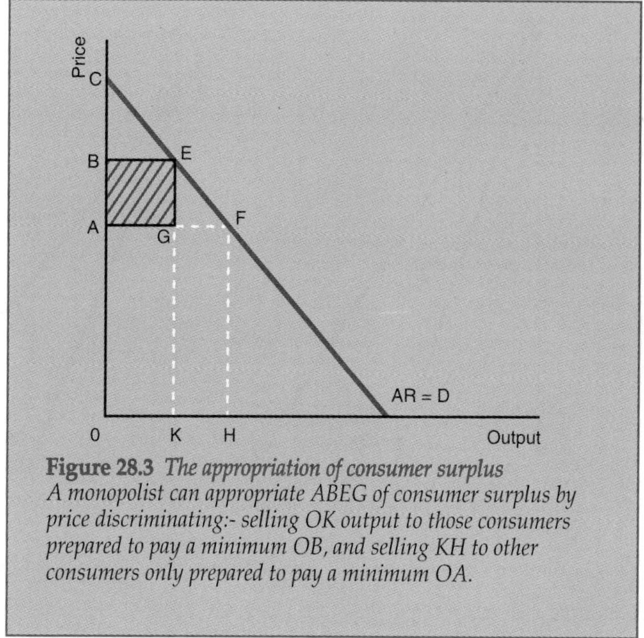

Figure 28.3 *The appropriation of consumer surplus*
A monopolist can appropriate ABEG of consumer surplus by price discriminating:- selling OK output to those consumers prepared to pay a minimum OB, and selling KH to other consumers only prepared to pay a minimum OA.

FB (i.e. it is not the area between the average revenue curve and the marginal revenue and cost curves). Profit per unit is the difference between average revenue and average cost.

Discriminating monopoly

Some buyers in the market will almost certainly be prepared to pay a higher price for a product than other buyers. In Figure 28.3, the profit maximising output for a monopolist is assumed to be OH and the profit maximising price is therefore OA. OA represents the maximum price that the marginal consumer is prepared to pay. Other consumers are prepared to pay a higher price. For instance, if output were only OK, the marginal consumer would be prepared to pay OB. The area ACF represents the area of consumer surplus (☞ unit 14), the difference between what consumers are prepared to pay in total for a good and what they actually pay. For instance, a rail commuter is likely to be prepared to pay more for a journey at 8 o'clock in the morning to take her to work than would a shopper. A millionaire faced with the need for heart surgery will pay more than a poor person with the same complaint.

A monopolist may be able to split the market and PRICE DISCRIMINATE between different buyers. For instance, in Figure 28.3, the monopolist may be able to charge OB for OK of output, and then charge a lower price of OA for KH of output. In this way, the monopolist appropriates ABEG of consumer surplus in the form of higher profit.

There are a number of different ways in which a monopolist may choose to discriminate.

- Time. It may charge a different price at different times of the day or week, as do the electricity distribution companies or rail companies.
- Place. It may vary price according to the location of the buyer. The same car can be bought at different prices in different countries of the EU for instance.
- Income. It may be able to split up consumers into income groups, charging a high price to those with high incomes, and a low price to those with lower incomes. Examples of this can be found in medical practice and amongst lawyers. Hairdressers (who may be local monopolists) offering reduced rates to pensioners are likely to be price discriminating according to income too.

Three conditions must hold if a monopolist is to be able to price discriminate effectively.

- The monopolist must face different demand curves from separate groups of buyers (i.e. the elasticity of demand of buyers must differ). If all buyers had the same demand curve, then the monopolist could not charge different prices to buyers.
- The monopolist must be able to split the market into distinct groups of buyers, otherwise it will be unable to distinguish between those consumers prepared to pay a higher price and those prepared to a pay a lower price.
- The monopolist must be able to keep the markets separate at relatively low cost. For instance, it must be able to prevent buyers in the high priced market from buying in the low price market. If a German car company sells its cars at 25 per cent less in Belgium than in the UK, then it must be able to prevent UK motorists and UK retailers from taking a day trip to Belgium to buy those cars. Equally, it must be able to prevent traders from buying in the low price market and selling into the high price market at a price which undercuts that of the monopolist.

Price discrimination can be analysed using the concepts of marginal cost and marginal revenue. Assume that the monopolist is able to divide its market into two and that the costs of production are identical for both markets.

The firm needs to allocate production between the two markets so that the marginal revenue is identical for each

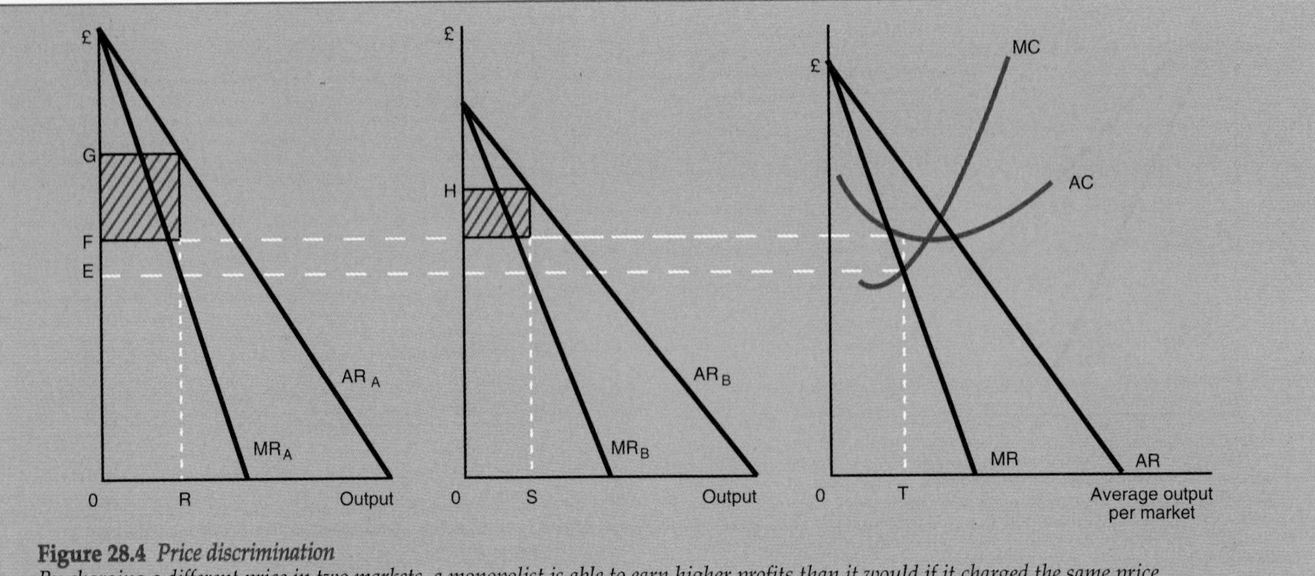

Figure 28.4 *Price discrimination*
By charging a different price in two markets, a monopolist is able to earn higher profits than it would if it charged the same price.

market if it is to maximise profit. To understand why, take a situation where marginal revenue in one market, A, is higher than in another market, B. The firm could increase its total revenue from a given output by switching goods from B to A. Marginal revenue in market B will now rise because it can charge a higher price if it sells less. Marginal revenue in market A will fall because it has to lower price to sell more. For instance, if marginal revenue in market A were £10 when it was £6 in market B, then the firm could gain an extra £4 of revenue by switching the marginal unit of production from market B to market A. It will carry on switching from market B to A until there is no more advantage in doing so, which occurs when the marginal revenues are the same.

In Figure 28.4, the demand curves in markets A and B are drawn first. From these demand or average revenue curves, the marginal revenue curves in each market can then be calculated. The average and marginal revenue curves for the total market can be calculated by summing horizontally the average and marginal revenue curves in each market. The profit maximising monopolist will produce where MC = MR across the whole market, at output level OT. This output (OT) is then split between the two markets (OR and OS) so that the marginal revenue is equal in both individual markets (OE). In each market, a firm's price will be based on the average revenue curve. A price of OG can be charged in market A, and a price of OH can be charged in market B. Average cost of production is OF and the abnormal profit earned in each market is shown by the shaded areas on the diagram. This will be higher than the abnormal profit the firm would have made if it had not discriminated.

QUESTION 3

Table 28.3 *InterCity fares Wolverhampton-London and London-Wolverhampton*

	Wolverhampton-London return	London-Wolverhampton return
First class	82.00	82.00
Standard class	57.00	57.00
Saver	27.50	33.00
Cheap day return	19.50	25.00
Shuttle advance	15.00	15.00

InterCity operate a complicated system of fares on their Wolverhampton to London route. First class and Standard Class passengers are entitled to catch any scheduled train during the day. Saver ticket and Cheap Day Return travellers cannot travel outwards from Wolverhampton before 9.30 in the morning. They also cannot return from London or travel outwards from London between 4 and 6 o'clock in the evening. Shuttle Advance passengers must book their tickets at least 7 days in advance and are only allowed to start their journey between 11 a.m and 3 p.m. or after 7 p.m.

Using diagrams, explain why InterCity has such a complicated fare structure on its Wolverhampton to London and London to Wolverhampton services.

Three technical points

Absence of a supply curve in monopoly In perfect competition, the supply curve of the firm is its marginal cost curve above average cost in the long run (☞ unit 27). In monopoly, there is no supply curve which is determined independently of demand.

Look back at Figure 28.2. The firm will produce at output OA because that is the output where MC = MR. Now assume that demand changes in such a way that the marginal revenue curve is much steeper but still passes through the point B. If the MR curve is steeper, so too will be the AR curve. The firm will now be able to charge a much higher price than OE for its product. For each differently sloped MR curve that passes through the point B, the firm will charge a different price to the consumer. The firm is prepared to supply OA output at a variety of different prices, depending upon demand conditions. So no supply curve for the monopolist can be drawn. (Contrast this with the firm in perfect competition. Falls in demand which reduce prices received by the firm will result in a fall in quantity supplied as the firm moves down its supply curve.)

A monopolist will produce only where demand is elastic Look back to Figure 28.1. It should be obvious that the firm will not produce more than 2½ units of output. If it produces 3 units, it will almost certainly have higher costs than if it produces 2½ units but total revenue will fall. Profit therefore is bound to fall. 2½ units is the output where marginal revenue is zero. It is also the point where price elasticity of demand is unity because we are now half way along the demand or average revenue curve (☞ unit 8). To the left, elasticity is greater than 1, to the right less than 1. Since the firm will only produce to the left of 2½ units, it must produce where demand is elastic. An alternative explanation is to remember that a fall in price (needed to increase quantity sold) will only increase revenue if demand is elastic. Therefore a monopolist would not increase sales to the point where demand became inelastic.

Short run and long run operation So far no distinction has been made between the short run and the long run. A firm will produce in the short run if total revenue is greater than total variable cost (☞ unit 24). In the short run, a monopolist may therefore operate at a loss but it will close down if it cannot cover its variable costs. In the long run, a monopolist will not operate if it cannot cover all costs of production. Such a situation is shown in Figure 28.5. To maximise profits or minimise losses, it will produce where MC = MR, but at this level of output average cost is greater than average revenue. Hence this is a loss minimising point of production which will not attract any firms to the industry.

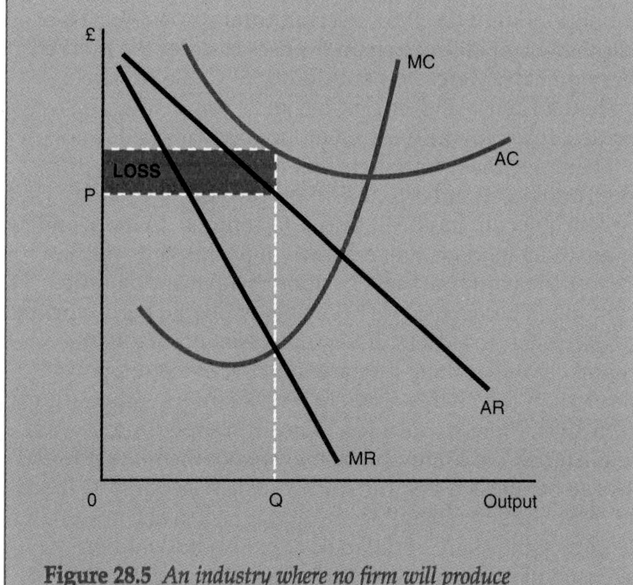

Figure 28.5 *An industry where no firm will produce*
The figure shows an industry in the long run. Because AC is greater than AR, no firm will be prepared to operate and therefore no goods will be produced.

QUESTION 4 Draw two diagrams showing the change in equilibrium output of a profit maximising monopolist if: (a) its marginal revenue increases; (b) its marginal cost increases.

Key terms

Monopoly - a market structure where one firm supplies all output in the industry without facing competition because of high barriers to entry to the industry.

Price discrimination - charging a different price for the same good or service in different markets.

Applied economics

British Telecom

The telecommunications industry in the UK was a monopoly until the 1981 Telecommunications Act. This allowed competitors to gain licences to enter the market. Very quickly, Mercury, a subsidiary of Cable & Wireless, gained a licence and in 1984 began to compete against British Telecom, the existing monopoly supplier.

Economic theory predicts that a monopolist will price discriminate in order to maximise profits. Since 1984, British Telecom has been forced to compete in more and more of its markets, but arguably it has used its market power to favour business customers against domestic customers because it has been able to charge higher prices to domestic customers. It has also been increasing line rental charges, where it retains an effective monopoly, more than call charges, where it now suffers competition.

In 1984, Mercury decided to begin competition in what was arguably a highly profitable area of the market for BT - large business users. Initially, British Telecom, privatised in 1986, did not react. It knew that it had to allow Mercury to gain some share of the market or else it would be accused of engaging in unfair competitive practices by its regulator, Oftel (☞ unit 45). However, by 1989, Mercury had gained a significant share of the large business market. British Telecom felt able then to engage in a price war. It began to cut its charges to large business users at a faster rate than it was cutting them to small businesses and domestic users where, on the whole, it still had a monopoly. Mercury then began to compete aggressively, first for small business users, and then by 1993-94 for domestic customers. British Telecom again reacted by cutting tariffs where it faced competition but increasing them where it remained a monopoly provider.

Figure 28.6, for instance, shows how the average cost per line has fallen both for large users and domestic users since 1983. The percentage fall between 1983 and 1993 for business users where there was more competition was approximately 30 per cent, whilst that for domestic users where there was less competition was 20 per cent. Another example of British Telecom's ability to price discriminate has been its recent policy of increasing line rentals whilst at the same time reducing the cost of phone calls. In 1994, for instance, British Telecom announced line rental increases of 3 per cent but cut phone call charges by over 7 per cent.

In October 1994, Mercury pulled out of marketing its services to domestic users - an admission, perhaps, of defeat in its battle with BT. However, the 1990s has seen some growth in line rental business from cable companies. In the long term British Telecom is likely to lose all its monopoly powers. Cable will be available to all users as an alternative to BT lines. At the same time, BT, Mercury, the cable companies and other companies will be battling it out for a share of the call market. British Telecom will then have lost its powers to price discriminate and so force through price increases in some markets where it has a monopoly whilst cutting prices where it faces competition.

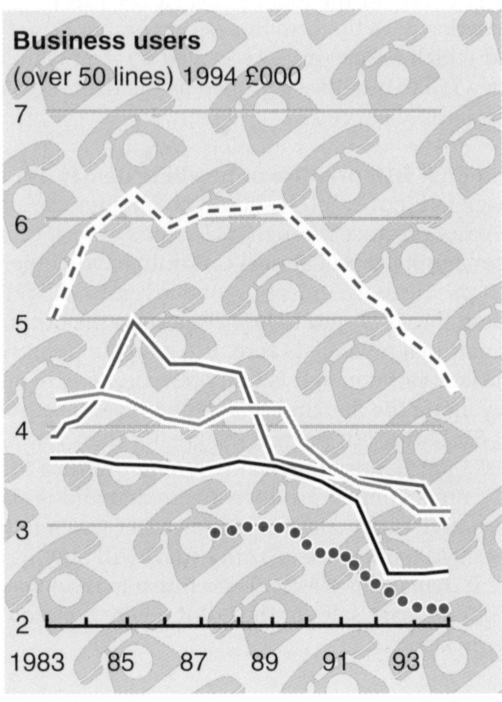

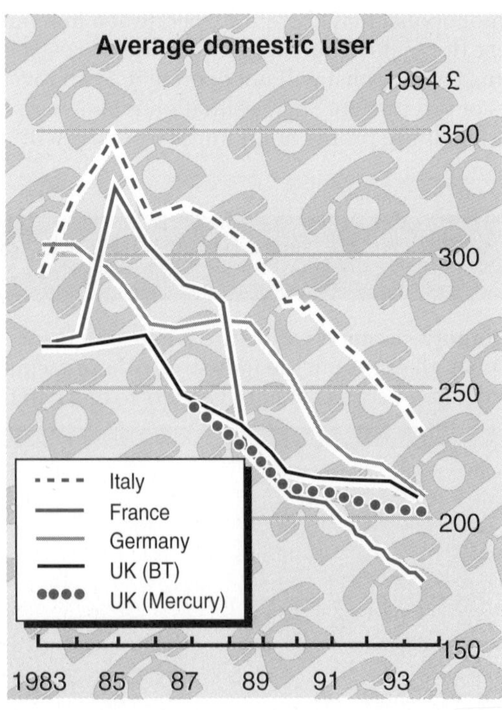

Source: adapted from Analysys.

Figure 28.6 *Average annual cost per line*

Sega and Nintendo

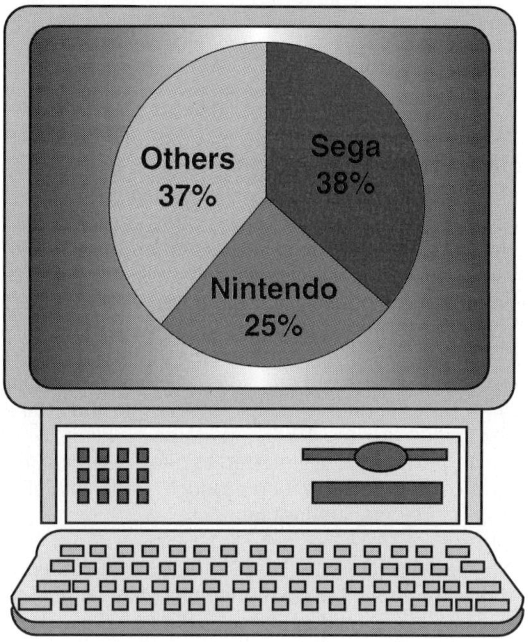

Figure 28.7 *Console and games software sales, UK 1994*

Sega and Nintendo

Sega and Nintendo, both Japanese companies, dominate the UK market for consoles and software sales. Sega is best known for its 'Sonic the Hedgehog' games whilst Nintendo's most popular characters are the 'Super Mario Brothers'. In 1994, the technology for the games was based on 16-bit consoles. To play, consumers had to buy a dedicated console which could only be used with games cartridges compatible with the console. Games cartridges for both Sega and Nintendo were protected by patent. Hence, a Nintendo game cartridge could not be used on a Sega machine. Equally, a company would find it difficult to design a game and cartridge which would fit on, say, a Nintendo console without breaking the patent of Nintendo.

Source: adapted from *Financial Times*, 15.1.1994, 17.1.1994, 16.3.1995

Sega Mega Drive console with software

- £82.82 in the USA
- £132.39 in the UK
- £116.62 in Germany
- £112.64 in France

Rental

Sega and Nintendo control carefully the rental market for their games. Any retailer wanting to rent out games has to pay a fixed £550 fee and then pay a £5 surcharge on each game it buys to rent out. Sega and Nintendo argued that the fees and surcharges covered them for the cost of lost royalties on games which were copied and of policing the system to prevent pirate copies appearing on the market.

Source: adapted from *Financial Times'* reports on the findings of the Monopolies and Mergers Commission, 10.3.1995.

Pricing policy

Both Sega and Nintendo sell consoles at low profit margins. However, games are sold at high profit margins. Some games are produced by Sega and Nintendo. Others are produced by other independent software companies. To avoid infringing patents, the independent companies are forced to seek licences to produce from Sega and Nintendo. They have to pay a royalty to Sega and Nintendo for each game sold. In addition they pay a manufacturing charge. Finally, they are forced to buy their blank cartridges from Sega and Nintendo. Sega's gross margin on cartridges supplied to third parties is 45 per cent, or about £7 for a 16-bit Mega Drive game.

Source: adapted from *Financial Times*, 15.1.1994, 17.1.1994, 16.3.1995

'We conclude that discriminatory pricing is a step taken by Nintendo UK and Sega Europe for the purpose of maintaining and exploiting the complex monopoly situation. We further conclude that this operates against the public interest with the particular adverse effects of raising the price of software to consumers and thus over time the total costs of games, and of impeding the entry of new games systems.'

Monopolies and Mergers Commission, 1995.

1. (a) What is meant by a 'monopoly'?
(b) In what sense might Sega and Nintendo be called 'monopolists'?

2. Using diagrams, explain how Sega and Nintendo exploited their monopoly position to earn higher profits, according to the Monopolies and Mergers Commission.

3. The Monopolies and Mergers Commission suggested that Sega and Nintendo should be forced to allow other companies to manufacture and sell blank games cartridges without having to pay any royalty or fee. Why might this lessen the monopoly power of the two companies?

4. Sega and Nintendo argued that their markets were fiercely competitive and that the new 32-bit games which were to come onto the market in 1995 and which could not be played on 16-bit consoles would completely open up the market to competition. To what extent do you think this is true?

Monopolistic competition

Summary

1. **Most industries operate in imperfectly competitive markets.**
2. **The monopolistic competition model makes the same assumptions as that of perfect competition except it is assumed that each firm produces a differentiated product and is therefore a price-maker.**
3. **In long run equilibrium, each firm will only earn normal profit and therefore AC = AR. Each firm will produce at its profit maximising output where MC = MR.**

Imperfect competition

Perfect competition and monopoly are at either end of a spectrum of market structures. There are relatively few industries which conform to the strict characteristics of these two models. Most industries fall somewhere in between. In most industries:

- competition exists because there are at least two firms in the industry;
- competition is imperfect because firms sell products which are not identical to the products of rival firms.

The neo-classical theories of perfect competition and monopoly were first developed during the latter half of the 19th century. At the time, it was not unreasonable to suggest that many industries were made up of a large number of small firms producing identical or homogeneous products. In the 20th century fewer and fewer industries can be said to be perfectly competitive. So a number of theories of IMPERFECT COMPETITION have been advanced to explain the behaviour of firms. One important model, the model of MONOPOLISTIC COMPETITION, was developed by Edward Chamberlain, an American economist, in the 1930s, and his work was mirrored by an English economist, Joan Robinson, at the same time.

Assumptions

The theory of monopolistic competition makes almost the same assumptions as that of perfect competition, namely:

- there are a large number of buyers and sellers in the market, each of which is relatively small and acts independently;
- there are no barriers to entry or exit;
- firms are short run profit maximisers;
- there is perfect knowledge in the market.

However, one assumption is different:

- firms produce differentiated or non-homogeneous goods.

It can be argued that relatively few industries possess these characteristics. One possible example would be retailing in the UK. It has traditionally been fragmented. Even in areas where there are large national chains such as groceries (Sainsbury's, Tesco, Waitrose, Co-op) or DIY (Do-it-all, B&Q, Texas Homecare), **concentration ratios** (☞ unit 25) are relatively low. Firms possess a certain amount of market power because of the location of stores or brand images, but this power is relatively weak in most cases.

QUESTION 1 The large assurance and pension fund companies have in recent years taken to advertising their products heavily on television. Previously, they had relied very much on their sales forces to deliver new business from millions of potential customers. The industry is fragmented with hundreds of different firms offering products in the market for long term savings. Although firms need a licence to operate, to ensure their financial credit-worthiness, it is relatively easy for other financial institutions to enter the industry. Indeed, since the late 1980s, the large building societies have gradually started to offer their own life assurance and pension fund products rather than sell those of traditional companies.

To what extent could the life assurance and pension fund market be said to be monopolistically competitive?

The downward sloping demand curve

If a firm produces a product which is slightly different from that of its competitors, then it has a certain amount of market power. It will be able to raise price, for instance, without losing all its customers to firms which have kept their prices stable. So it is not a **price-taker** like a perfectly competitive firm. However, because there are a large number of firms in the industry producing relatively close substitutes, its market power is likely to be relatively weak. Small changes in price are likely to result in relatively large changes in quantity demanded as consumers switch to close substitutes (i.e. demand is likely to be relatively elastic).

The demand curve facing the firm is therefore downward sloping but elastic (i.e. it will operate on the upper portion of its demand curve). The firm's marginal revenue curve will fall twice as steeply as the average revenue curve (or demand curve), as shown in Figure 29.1.

Long run equilibrium

The firm will produce where MC = MR because it is a profit maximiser. In Figure 29.1, this means that it will produce at an output level of OA. It will charge a price based on its demand or average revenue curve, in this case OB.

The firm in the long run will not be able to earn

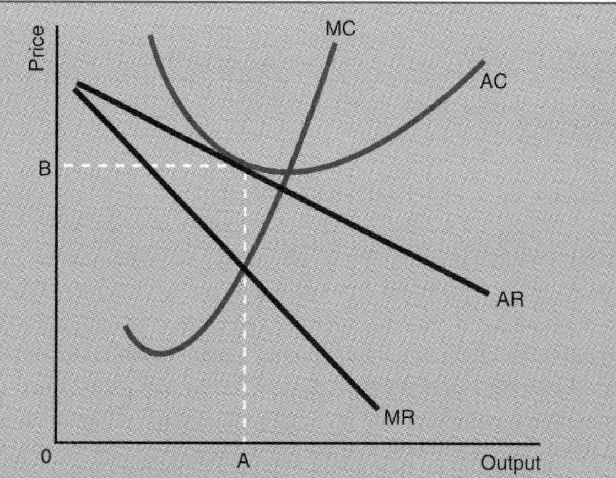

Figure 29.1 *Long run equilibrium for a monopolistically competitive firm*
A firm will produce where MC=MR. Because there are no barriers to entry, the firm will be unable to earn abnormal profits in the long run. Therefore it must also be true that AC=AR at the equilibrium level of output. This occurs when the AC curve is tangential to the AR curve.

QUESTION 2
Table 29.2

Sales	Average revenue (£)
100	10
200	9
300	8
400	7
500	6

The table shows the average revenue curve for a firm operating under conditions of monopolistic competition.
(a) On graph paper, draw
(i) the demand curve facing the firm and
(ii) the firm's marginal revenue curve.
(b) How do these curves differ to those of a monopolist and a firm operating in a perfectly competitive industry?

abnormal profit. This is because there is freedom of entry to the market. If the firm is making abnormal profit in the short run (which would be shown on the diagram by average cost falling below average revenue at output OA), then firms will come into the industry attracted by the high level of profits. This will increase supply, shifting the average revenue curve downwards to the point where average revenue is just equal to average cost. If firms in the industry are making losses in the short run, then firms will leave the industry, reducing supply and shifting the average revenue curve upwards to the point where average revenue is just equal to average cost.

So in monopolistic competition two conditions must hold in long run equilibrium:

- MC = MR because the firm is a profit maximiser;
- AC = AR because competitive pressures mean that a firm cannot either make a loss or earn abnormal profit.

This means that at the profit maximising output, the average cost curve is tangential to the average revenue curve.

QUESTION 3 Next, the fashion retailer, had grown rapidly in the 1980s, first expanding its chain of women's and men's clothing shops, and then diversifying into mail order, jewellery, childrenswear and household furnishings, as well as buying a chain of newsagents. In late 1988, the bottom began to fall out of the clothing market. Next's young customers had been hard hit by the large rises in mortgage interest rates since June 1988. Sales revenues fell, whilst rising interest rates added to Next's costs since it had borrowed heavily to finance expansion. The company moved from being highly profitable to showing large losses.

Slowly the economy moved into recession, adding to Next's problems. The company responded by contracting. It sold most of its non-core businesses like its newsagent chain, a carpet wholesaling business called Mercado and Grattan, the mail order catalogue. It closed down over 60 of its Next stores. By 1993, it was back in profit but in a very much slimmed down form.

(a)(i) What evidence is there that Next earned abnormal profits before 1988? (ii) Draw a diagram showing the short run equilibrium of Next during this period.
(b)(i) Use the theory of monopolistic competition to explain why Next contracted after 1988. (ii) Using a diagram, analyse the long run equilibrium position of the company.

Key terms

Imperfect competition - a market structure where there are several firms in industry, each of which has some ability to control the price they set for their product.
Monopolistic competition - a market structure where a large number of small firms produces non-homogeneous products and where there are no barriers to entry or exit.

Applied economics

Grocery retailing

The grocery retailing market in the UK is arguably monopolistically competitive. As Figure 29.2 shows, the five firm concentration ratio in 1993 was 41.7 per cent whilst the top 11 companies only took 53.9 per cent of the market. The 46.1 per cent of the market taken by 'other' grocery retailers is very fragmented. In 1991, there were 62 000 food retailing businesses. Of the 82 572 food stores run by the businesses, only 8 309 were run by the large grocery retailers shown in Figure 29.2. The rest were run by small to medium sized businesses.

The large retailers attempt to develop a brand image for themselves. For instance, Sainsbury's has, through advertising, portrayed itself as being good value for money, selling a large range of high quality products. Kwik Save, on the other hand, has developed a brand image of very low prices on leading branded goods from food manufacturers. However, the branding is not particularly strong. The leading supermarkets, such as Sainsbury's and Tesco, have found that a significant proportion of their customers will switch shops, either when a new supermarket is built nearer to where the shopper lives, or when a chain offers significantly lower prices. In 1994, for instance, the leading supermarkets were forced to cut prices on essential products in response to a perceived threat from new discount chains such as Netto and Aldi, and from warehouse clubs (which are large no-frills retailers from the USA).

Freedom of entry and exit exists in the industry. Grocery retailing has low barriers to entry. It is relatively cheap to rent premises to set up in business. The large grocery chains have typically been built up from an initial single outlet by entrepreneurs able to see the potential for growth in the industry. On the other hand, some large chains have been established by large companies wanting to break into the UK market. Safeway, now owned by the Argyll group, was built from scratch by a large overseas company exporting its retail formula to the UK. The existence of freedom of exit can be seen by the significant numbers of grocery retailers which cease trading each year. Large chains, too, can get into financial difficulties and may contract or be bought out. Gateway, for instance, has closed many outlets which have proved unprofitable, whilst Argyll bought Safeway from its American parent when the American parent ran into financial difficulties.

Perfect knowledge can be said to exist in the industry. Information is relatively easy to come by. There are no patents or secret success stories. As to short run profit maximisation, this seems to be the most likely objective of firms in the industry. Most firms are small, owned and run by an individual or family. The owners will be likely to measure success in terms of the profit made by the firm. Large firms have either succeeded in making large profits, or have attracted heavy criticism from the financial press and the City of London when their profit performance has been poor. This would imply that there is considerable pressure on firms to earn large profits.

The theory of monopolistic competition could help explain events in the 1990s. The large supermarkets ambitiously expanded over the preceding two decades. It could be argued that their low cost bases, resulting from an ability to exploit economies of scale, enabled them to earn abnormal profit. This abnormal profit gave them the incentive to increase the average size of existing stores whilst at the same time opening new stores. However, by the mid-1990s, they had come to the point where nearly all local areas were well served by large supermarkets. Till then, they had been able to open new stores and take local market share from largely small, high cost independent traders. In the mid-1990s, new store openings were more likely to result in a downturn in trade for other large supermarkets in the local area. This led many commentators to predict that there would be a tailing off of growth in sales per sq ft in supermarkets and a fall in profit margins as supermarkets cut prices to attract customers. Indeed, in 1994 both Sainsbury's and Tesco announced plans to cut back on future store openings.

In 1995, Sainsbury's took over Texas Homecare, another signal that it thought that investment outside grocery retailing might prove more attractive than continued expansion of its supermarkets. This is what the theory of monopolistic competition would predict. Firms will enter the industry or expand whilst abnormal profits can be made. Industry equilibrium will be reached when only normal profits are made. Supermarket competition in a mature grocery retailing industry is likely to benefit the customers, but the large gains made by shareholders in the 1970s and 1980s could well come to an end in the 1990s.

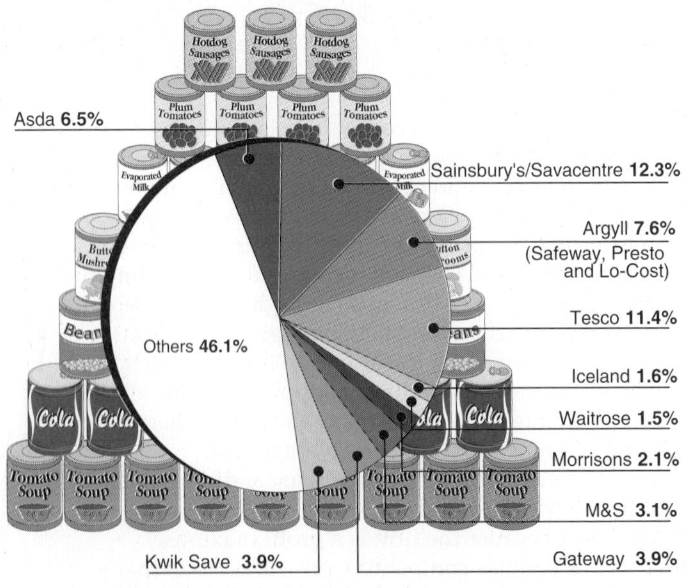

Source: adapted from Verdict Analysis.

Figure 29.2 *How the leading supermarkets stack up*

The package tour industry

International Leisure Group

In March 1991, International Leisure Tours, at the time the second largest package tour operator, collapsed. It had lost out from the fierce price wars that characterise the industry. Forced to sell many holidays below cost in 1990, it didn't have the financial reserves to ride out the storm.

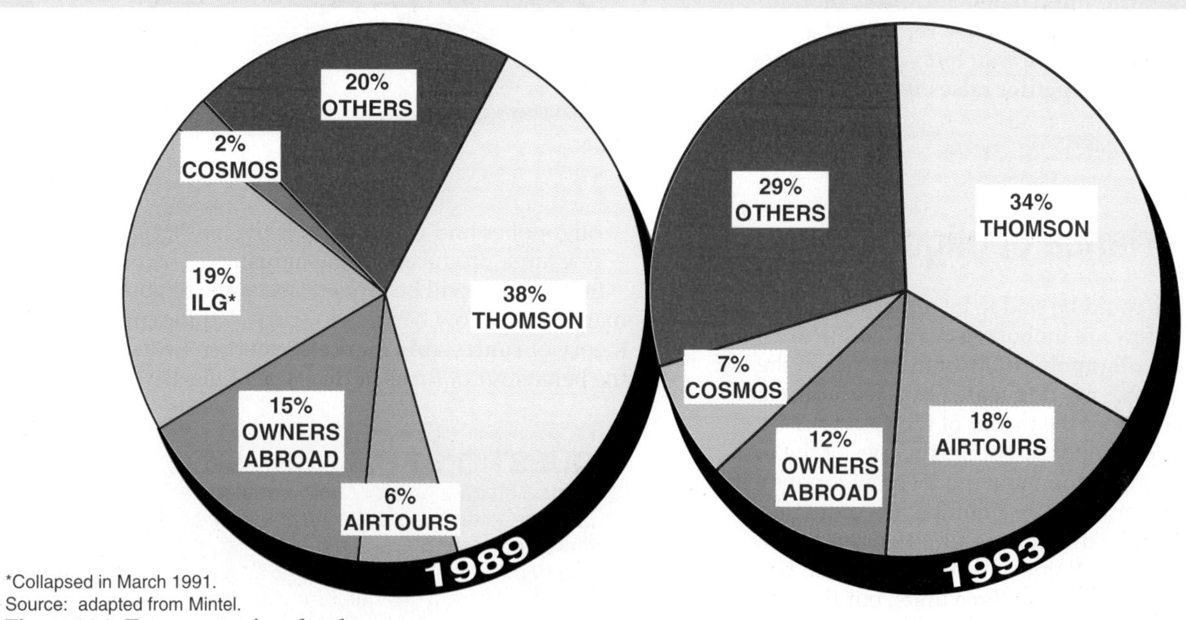

*Collapsed in March 1991.
Source: adapted from Mintel.

Figure 29.3 *Tour operators' market share*

You have been asked to prepare a report from an economist's viewpoint on the package tour industry. The client, who has commissioned a number of reports, is considering setting up in the industry.

1. Discuss the market characteristics of the package tour industry.
2. Use the theory of monopolistic competition to explain
   (a) why there is such intense price competition in the industry and
   (b) what happens to businesses which fail to price above cost.
3. (a) Evaluate how easy it would be for a firm considering setting up in the market (i) to enter and (ii) to survive.
   (b) What are the prospects for profits for the new firm?

unit 30 Oligopoly

Summary

1. **Most markets are oligopolistic.**
2. **An oligopolistic market is one where a small number of interdependent firms compete with each other.**
3. **Non-price competition is an important feature of oligopolistic markets.**
4. **The neo-classical kinked demand curve model assumes that a firm will reduce its price if a competitor starts a price war, but will leave price unchanged if a competitor raises its price.**

The importance of oligopoly

Most industries could be said to be imperfectly competitive. A few are monopolistically competitive but the majority are **oligopolistic**. Most industries in the UK, the EC and the USA are dominated by a few suppliers (☞ unit 25). Therefore the theory of OLIGOPOLY is arguably the most important of the theories of the firm. Yet there is no single dominant model of oligopoly within economics. Rather there are a number of competing models which make different assumptions and draw different conclusions. Some of these models will be outlined in this and the next three units, but first the characteristics of an oligopolistic market will be described.

Characteristics of oligopoly

For a market to be called 'oligopolistic', it must possess two characteristics.

- Supply in the industry must be concentrated in the hands of relatively few firms. For instance, an industry where the three largest firms produce 80 per cent of output would be oligopolistic. Note that alongside a few very large producers there may also be a much larger number of very small firms. So an industry with 100 firms, where the three largest firms produced 80 per cent of the output, would still be classed as oligopolistic.
- Firms must be interdependent. The actions of one large firm will directly affect another large firm. In perfect competition, firms are independent. If one farmer decides, for instance, to grow more wheat, that will have no impact on price or sales of other farmers in the industry. In oligopoly, if one large firm decides to pursue policies to increase sales, this is likely to be at the expense of other firms in the industry. One firm is likely to sell more only by taking away sales from other firms.

In addition, the neo-classical theory of oligopoly assumes that:

- there are barriers to entry to the industry. If there were no barriers, firms would enter the industry to take advantage of the abnormal profits characteristic of oligopolies and would reduce the market share of the few large producers in the industry.

In unit 32, it will be argued that some oligopolistic markets have low barriers to entry. A different theory, the theory of **contestable markets**, can then be used to explain the behaviour of firms in this type of market.

QUESTION 1 The mobile phone market in the UK started off as a duopoly, with Vodafone and Cellnet being granted licences to establish networks. By 1995, there were four players in the market, the two original companies and Mercury One-2-One and Hutchinson Orange. The government is committed to establishing a competitive market. At the same time, it has limited the number of licences to run mobile phone networks in order to allow existing firms in the industry to recoup the very substantial cost of setting up the physical infrastructure needed to operate a network. The capital cost of creating a nationwide network runs into billions of pounds. The two newcomers are attempting to compete on price. However, none of the operators wants a price war which would savage profits. Vodafone and Cellnet accept that Mercury One-2-One and Hutchinson Orange will eat into their market share. However, they hope that growth in the market will outweigh any losses to the two new entrants.

Using information from the passage, explain why the market for mobile phone calls could be said to be oligopolistic.

Features of oligopolistic markets

Studies of oligopolistic markets have shown that individual firms can exhibit a wide number of different behaviour patterns. However, there are some features which are common to most oligopolistic markets. It is these features which an economic model of oligopoly must be able to incorporate or explain.

Non-price competition In a perfectly competitive market, firms producing homogeneous goods compete solely on price. In the short run, factors such as delivery dates might assume some importance, but in the long term price is all that matters. In an imperfectly competitive market, price is often not the most important factor in the competitive process. Firms decide upon a MARKETING MIX - a mixture of elements which form a coherent strategy designed to sell their products to their market. The marketing mix is often summarised in the '4 Ps'. Firms produce a **product** which appeals to their customers. The product may or may not be differentiated from rivals' products. A **price** needs to be set but this could be above or below the price of competing products depending upon the pricing strategy to be used. For instance, a high price will be set if the product is sold in a quality market. A low price will be set if the firm wishes to sell large quantities of a standard product. **Promotion** (advertising and sales promotion) is essential to inform buyers in the market that the good is on sale and to change their perceptions of a product in a favourable manner. A good distribution system is essential to get the product to the right **place** at the right time for the customer.

Many markets are dominated by **brands**. A branded good is one which is produced by a particular firm and which appears to possess unique characteristics. These may be real characteristics, such as a unique formulation or a unique design. A Mars Bar or a Rolls Royce car, for instance, are unique products. But often more important than the real characteristics are the imagined characteristics of the product in the mind of the buyer. This image is likely to have been created by advertising and promotion. So it is possible for the same baked beans or the same breakfast cereal to be packaged differently and sold on the same supermarket shelves at different prices. Often the higher priced branded product will sell far better than the lower priced unbranded product despite the fact that the product itself is the same.

Price rigidity Prices in oligopolistic markets seem to change far less than in perfectly competitive markets. Despite changes in underlying costs of production, firms are often observed to maintain prices at a constant level.

L-shaped average cost curves Economic studies (☞ unit 20) have established that in the real world average variable cost curves are often more L-shaped than U-shaped. Over a wide range of output, large firms face the same average variable costs whether they increase or decrease output, as shown in Figure 30.1.

Collusion Oligopolistic firms will often benefit if they collude. This means that they make agreements amongst themselves so as to restrict competition and maximise their own benefits. Before such **restrictive trade practices** (☞ unit 41) were made illegal in the UK by the 1956 Restrictive Trade Practices Act, most large UK manufacturing companies had entered into agreements with other firms.

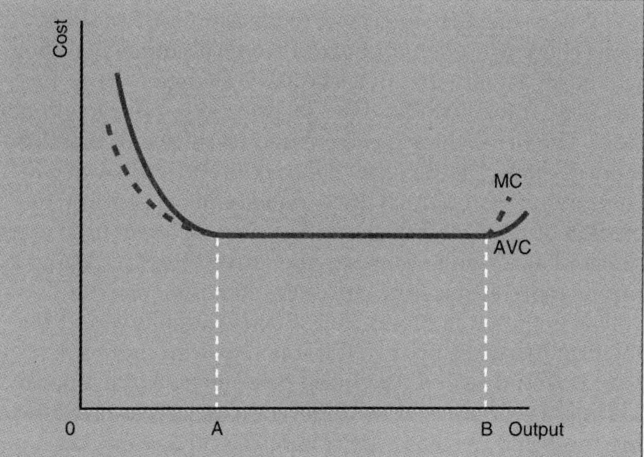

Figure 30.1 *L-shaped average cost curve*
Many firms in practice seem to face an L-shaped average cost curve. The minimum efficient scale of production extends over a wide range of output, from OA to OB in this diagram.

QUESTION 2 The National Lottery was launched in November 1994. Camelot, the company which obtained the licence to run the lottery, exceeded its forecasts about the number of players willing to gamble from the start. The Lottery operates in a gambling market dominated by a few large players. Its most obvious rivals are the pools companies, Littlewoods and Vernons. However, it is also in competition with bingo clubs such as those owned by Rank and betting shops such as Ladbrokes. Smaller competitors include casinos and amusement arcades.

None of these rivals has altered its products or prices much following the advent of the Lottery. It is not in the interests of any firm in the industry to increase substantially the cost of gambling to the consumer or raise the prize money. Instead, each will continue to attempt to segment its area of the market, trying to make consumers feel that its product is different from those of others. Rank, for instance, is typical of bingo clubs in wanting to make its gambling experience to be seen more and more as a night out by its customers rather than as a cold chance draw for money. The betting shops have won their battle to be able to open seven days a week for twelve weeks of the year and be open on summer evenings. They can also now have clear windows, allowing passers by to see inside the shops, hopefully attracting them in. The major players in the gambling industry hope that the National Lottery will expand the market, with a smaller market share being more than compensated for by higher betting. The pools operators are the most likely firms to suffer directly from the increased competition.

Explain, using examples from the gambling industry, how firms in an oligopolistic market compete.

The neo-classical kinked demand curve model

One model of oligopoly was developed in the late 1930s by Paul Sweezy in the USA and R Hall and C Hitch in the UK. Any theory of oligopoly must make an assumption about how one firm will react to the actions of another firm. The kinked demand curve model assumes that there will be an asymmetrical reaction to a change in price by one firm. If the firm increases its price, other firms will not react. The firm which has increased its price will then lose market share. On the other hand, if it reduces its price its competitors will reduce price too in order to prevent an erosion of their market share. The firm will gain little extra demand as a result. The demand curve therefore facing a firm is more elastic for a price rise than for a price fall.

This is shown in Figure 30.2. Price is initially at OP. If the firm increases price to OR it will lose far more sales than it would gain if it reduced price by an equal amount. This occurs because of the different reactions to price increases and decreases by competitors. Therefore the demand curve is kinked around the original price. If the demand curve (i.e. the average revenue curve) is kinked, then this produces a discontinuous marginal revenue curve. At output level OQ, there will be a jump in marginal revenue between a small increase in price and a small decrease in price (an example of this is given in Question 3).

The firm is assumed to be a short run profit maximiser. Therefore if the price is OP and the firm is producing OQ, the marginal cost curve must cut the marginal revenue at output OQ, somewhere between price OV and OW. This means that there are a number of possible marginal cost curves which would produce a price of OP. It could, for instance, be MC_1 or MC_2. Assume that it is MC_1 then a rise in costs to MC_2 would result in no change in price.

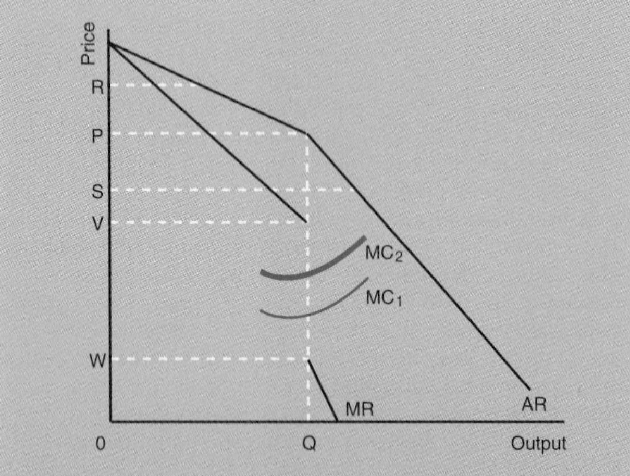

Figure 30.2 *The kinked demand curve model*
With a demand curve kinked round the prevailing price OP, a rise or fall in marginal cost will not affect the profit maximising level of output or price. Hence this model can be used to explain relative price stability in oligopolistic markets.

The oligopolist would absorb the whole of the cost increase by reducing its profit.

This theory provides one explanation of why prices in oligopoly are relatively stable. Changes in costs which shift the marginal cost curve will not change either the profit maximising level of output or the profit maximising price.

However, there are a number of weaknesses in the theory. First there is no explanation of how the original price, P, was arrived at. Second, the theory only deals with price competition and ignores the effects of non-price competition. Third, the model assumes a particular reaction by other firms to a change in price of a firm's product. It is unlikely that firms will react in exactly this way all the time. A much wider range of possible reactions needs to be explored.

QUESTION 3

Table 30.1

			£
Output	Average revenue	Total revenue	Marginal revenue
1	49	49	
			45
2	47		
3	45		
3	45		
			25
4	40		
5	35		
6	30		

(a) Complete Table 30.1, filling in the missing figures.
(b) Plot the average and marginal revenue curves on a graph. Remember that marginal revenue for the second unit of output should be plotted at output level 1½, the third at 2½, etc. Also mark on the graph a vertical line at output level 3 and draw the marginal revenue curves up to the line on either side of it as in Figure 30.2.
(c) Why is the marginal revenue curve discontinuous?
(d) **Table 30.2**

Output	Marginal cost (£)
	40
2	
	32
3	
	36
4	

Draw the marginal cost curve in Table 30.2 onto your graph.

(e) Why is the firm in equilibrium at an output of 3 units?
(f) Explain what would happen to equilibrium output and price if marginal cost (i) rose by £4 and (ii) fell by £2 at every level of output.

Key terms

Oligopoly - a market structure where there is a small number of firms in the industry and where each firm is interdependent with other firms. Barriers to entry are likely to exist.

Marketing mix - different elements within a strategy designed to create demand for a product.

Applied economics

The UK detergent market

Two firms dominate the UK detergent industry: the US giant, Proctor and Gamble (P&G), and the Anglo-Dutch company, Unilever. They have been in competition with each other since the 1920s, battling for supremacy of the market. In the mid-1980s, each had a market share of approximately 43 per cent, making the industry a virtual duopoly. By 1994, P&G had overtaken Unilever, securing a 53 per cent market share against Unilever's 31 per cent.

Detergents are not a particularly high technology product. There are plenty of small manufacturers supplying supermarket own brand products and commercial buyers such as laundries. Whilst P&G and Unilever tend to lead the field in product development, small manufacturers are easily able to imitate the products and supply acceptable quality goods to customers who are buying on price. Neither product nor the cost of purchase of equipment is a barrier to entry.

The major barrier to entry is the promotion costs of a brand. P&G and Unilever are the two highest spenders on advertising in the UK. Combined advertising budgets exceeded £120 million in 1994. Typically, one-quarter of the shop price of a packet of P&G or Unilever detergent is accounted for by promotion costs, the equivalent of 5p per wash. Advertising spending on Persil and Ariel, the two leading brands, accounted for over £40 million. No small entrant to the market can in any way match these expenditures. Even large potential entrants are deterred. Advertising by itself cannot establish a new brand in the market place. To gain a significant foothold in the market, a new entrant would probably have to sell a product which was superior to existing P&G or Unilever products and spend large amounts on advertising.

The two detergent giants do not compete on price. On the supermarket shelves, own brands or unadvertised brands can sell for less than half the price of a P&G or Unilever product and yet still fail to capture more than a few per cent of the market. This indicates that the two firms have had considerable success in making demand for their products relatively price inelastic. Instead of competing on price, they fight it out through the establishment and maintenance of strong brands. Each company sells a range of brands. In the UK, the main Unilever brand is Persil which had 26 per cent of the market in 1994. The other Unilever brands, such as Surf and Radion, only have 5 per cent of the market. P&G's brands have proved more successful in recent years, mainly because they were quicker into the market to produce concentrate powders and liquids than Unilever in the late 1980s. Ariel is P&Gs main brand, and it produces other brands such as Daz.

In the early 1990s, Unilever successfully launched a new brand onto the market called Radion. With very heavy advertising, it quickly managed to take over 6 per cent of the UK market before falling back. Launching new brands is a high risk exercise. If they fail, it will have cost the company millions of pounds in product development, market research and promotion. One estimate put the spending on developing, manufacturing and marketing the unsuccessful Power products launched by Unilever in 1994 at £200m. On the other hand, establishing a successful new brand will take market share away from existing brands. Radion took away some market share from other Unilever brands. But it also took away market share from P&G brands and was one factor in helping Unilever stem its loss of market share relative to P&G in the late 1980s and early 1990s. This shows the interdependence of the two firms.

It is difficult to find direct evidence as to whether a change in marginal cost would have any effect on price or output. However, it is interesting to note that soap powders tend to be 'positioned' in the market in pricing terms. The marginal cost of producing a packet of Ariel is almost certainly little different for P&G than the marginal cost of Daz. Yet Daz is sold at a slightly cheaper price to appeal to cost conscious customers. This would tend to indicate that small falls and rises in marginal cost are unlikely to affect the pricing strategies of P&G and Unilever.

The importance of brands

Even before the great soap war erupted this summer between Unilever and Procter & Gamble, the two companies were together expected to spend more than £75m in 1994 advertising and promoting their Persil and Ariel brands in the UK.

That is more than last year's total annual sales of Britain's 28th biggest grocery brand, Felix catfood. On its own, Persil's 1993 marketing and advertising expenditure of around £38m was equivalent to the total supermarket and high street grocery sales of Cadbury's Dairy Milk chocolate, and Ariel's £35m to the total grocery sales of Schweppes mixers.

Such can be the cost of maintaining and refreshing a top grocery brand - a cost which is making it prohibitive even for many household names to sustain their special place in consumers' hearts by using traditional marketing strategies.

Economies of scale are making life hard even for medium-sized brands. The average cost of maintaining a top 10 brand last year was £15m, about 7 per cent of sales. But for the top 70 as a whole it was £8m, more than 10 per cent of sales, according to a new study by Added Value, a marketing consultancy. For the first time, its research estimates both advertising and normally hidden 'below the line' expenditure figures. The latter covers direct marketing, sales promotion, trade promotions and public relations.

'Many brands have an uphill struggle to enter the mainstream,' comments Rahul Sen, a manager at Added Value. 'If they can create critical mass then the ratio of advertising and promotion expenditure to sales falls rapidly. But if the marketing is not quite working, the ratio becomes very high.'

Sen suggests that marketers in many categories of product are too influenced by competitors' expenditures and advertising patterns, rather than concentrating on what is needed to build a credible overall presence. Only a few can afford to create that presence on television.

He adds: 'The question is what happens to the rest. A lot of small brands will die.'

Sen's gloomy predictions are backed by as yet unpublished research conducted by OC&C Strategy Consultants earlier this year.

For one of the top 10 food companies, the marketing costs of a typical food product launch - currently running at an average £2m - will take 2 per cent of operating profits, says Michael Jary, OC&C director. But for a company ranking 31-40 they will account for 27 per cent of profits. For one between 51 and 60 they will gobble up 84 per cent.

'Escalating marketing costs suggest that fewer products are getting sufficient support during launch to create a defensible franchise,' says Jary. 'You don't have to be too far down the league before you can't launch a new product.'

Source: the *Financial Times*, 1.9.1994.

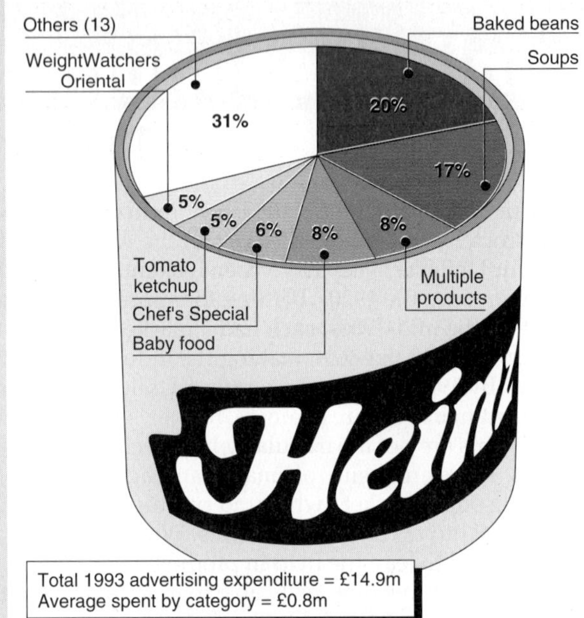

Source: adapted from Added Value, Register Meal, December 1993.

Figure 30.3 *Heinz's problem: too thinly spread*

The dilemma facing Heinz

The research by Added Value highlights the problems facing Heinz. It has an advertising budget of just £0.8m to support each of its leading categories, such as baked beans, baby foods and ketchup. With 350 separate variants within each of those categories, it would be a Herculean task for Heinz to support them on television. It has decided that it needs a radical new approach to its promotional spending.

Source: the *Financial Times*, 1.9.1994.

Produce a report for Heinz outlining the problems that it faces suggesting possible solutions.

1. **Explain why the markets into which Heinz sells could be called 'oligopolistic'.**
2. **Suggest why Heinz needs to maintain brand loyalty if it is to stay in these markets.**
3. **(a) Discuss a range of strategies which Heinz could adopt to tackle the problems it faces, pointing out their advantages and disadvantages.**
   (b) Which strategy do you think is the most promising for Heinz and why?

Game theory

Summary

1. **Game theory explores the reactions of one player to changes in strategy by another player.**
2. **Oligopoly is characterised by price stability. One explanation of this is that changing price is a very risky strategy for one firm because it will provoke a reaction by other firms.**
3. **Non-price competition is common in oligopolistic markets. It is a less risky strategy than price competition.**
4. **Successful branding enables producers to charge a premium price and earn abnormal profit on a product.**
5. **Collusion enables oligopolistic firms to move to their most profitable output level.**
6. **The large number of different market strategies available to oligopolistic firms may result in permanent disequilibrium in the market.**

Game theory

Central to any understanding of oligopoly is interdependence. The actions of one large firm in the industry will directly affect all other firms in the industry. It is therefore essential, in any theory of oligopoly, to understand the nature and consequences of those reactions.

One very powerful tool for analysing oligopolistic behaviour is the theory of games. GAME THEORY has a wide variety of applications, from playing cards through to nuclear deterrence. In a game the players are interdependent. The best move for a player depends upon how the other players will react.

Price stability

One commonly observed feature of oligopoly is price stability. Firms maintain stable prices over a pricing season which may last from 6 months to several years. Price stability may be a rational strategy for oligopolists.

If an oligopolistic firm raises price, it risks losing market share if its competitors do not follow suit. Lower market share could lead to lower profits and, if investment and research and development budgets are cut, a reduced ability to compete in the long run.

If it lowers its price, it risks starting a price war. It could be that the size of the market will expand as consumers buy more of the industry's products. But the benefits in the form of larger sales could well be more than offset by losses in revenue due to lower prices. All firms in the industry could see sharp falls in profits as they battle it out. Eventually, prices will have to rise again to restore profitability and the firm which started the price war could have lost market share.

So changing prices is a risky strategy. When prices do change, all firms tend to change their prices by the same percentage. For instance, a rise in the interest rate by one large building society tends to lead to a rise in all building society interest rates. A rise in petrol prices by one company is usually matched by the other petrol suppliers.

Game theory can be used to explain this. Consider Table 31.1. There are just two firms in the industry (it is a DUOPOLY). Each firm has two strategies. It can either raise the price of its product or leave it unchanged. The figures in the box represent the change in profits for firm A which would result from each strategy. We will assume that each firm has the same expectations of what would happen to profits as a result of each strategy. We will further assume that the game is a ZERO SUM GAME. This means that any gain by one player is exactly offset by a loss by the other player. For instance, if firm A raises its price and firm B reacts to this by raising price too, then firm A will be the winner. Its profits will increase by £10 million whilst firms B's profits will fall by £10 million. If on the other hand firm B were to react by keeping its price unchanged, firm A would see its profits fall by £2 million whilst firm B would see its profits rise by £2 million.

The game in Table 31.1 has an equilibrium solution. Firm A will decide to leave its price unchanged. This is because if it raises its price, it could gain an extra £10 million in profits if firm B also raised its price. But it knows that firm B would be most unlikely to react in this

Table 31.1

		Firm B	
		Raise price	Leave price unchanged
Firm A	Raise price	£10 million	-£2 million
	Leave price unchanged	-£1 million	0

way because firm B would stand to lose £10 million by adopting that strategy. So firm B would adopt the strategy of leaving its price unchanged. This would result in losses of £2 million for firm A if it raised price. If, on the other hand, firm A kept its price unchanged, the most it would stand to lose is £1 million.

As for firm B, raising price would be a very dangerous strategy because it would lose £10 million in profit if firm A raised price too. Leaving price unchanged would either result in no change in profits or a gain in profits of £2 million.

So both firms will choose to leave their prices unchanged. This is the safest strategy for both firms. The alternative for each firm would lead to losses because of the rival firm's reactions.

Now consider Table 31.2 which shows a game where firms cut prices. The game here is not a zero sum game. The change in profits of firm A of a particular combination of strategies is shown in black, whilst the change in profits for firm B is shown in red. For instance, if both firms cut prices, firm A will lose £10 million in profits whilst firm B will lose £20 million.

Table 31.2

		Firm B	
		Lower price	Leave price unchanged
Firm A	Lower price	-£10m/-£20m	+£5m/-£27m
	Leave price unchanged	-£13m/+£5m	0

It is clear from the table that it is in both firms' interests to leave prices unchanged. If one firm decides to lower its price in order to gain market share, the other firm would suffer a large drop in profits. For instance, firm A would lose £13 million in profits if it left its price unchanged when firm B lowered its price. It would prefer to lower its price too and limit the loss in profits to £10 million. The same is true for firm B. If it dropped its price and firm A did not react, it would increase its profit. But if firm A reacted by dropping its price too, the resulting price war would have disastrous consequences for both sides.

Many economists have argued that firms avoid risk (they are said to be 'risk averse'). Competition is always risky and strategies which aim to reduce market share and profits of competitors especially so. 'The best of all monopoly profits is a quiet life', argued J R Hicks (1935).

QUESTION 1 The major building societies tend to move their saving and mortgage interest rates at the same time, usually following a change in bank base rates, the rate of interest around which banks structure their saving and borrowing rates. Occasionally, building societies have responded to government concern and not raised interest rates to mortgage borrowers when banks have increased their rates. The result has been a flow of funds from building societies to banks as savers have switched their money to take advantage of higher interest rates. Equally, at such times, building societies have tended to increase their share of the mortgage market at the expense of the banks. Before too long, the building societies have been forced to raise their interest rates in order to attract back the savings to meet the demand for mortgage loans.

Use game theory to explain why building societies tend to move their interest rates in line with each other and with those of the banks.

Non-price competition

A characteristic of oligopoly is the lack of price competition. Price wars can be very damaging for firms in an oligopolistic industry. So firms choose to compete in other ways apart from price. An advertising campaign, for instance, by firm A is likely to be limited in cost and may increase market share. Other firms in the industry may react by launching their own advertising campaign, but there is a reasonable chance that the advertising campaign of the competitors may not be as good, plus the fact that advertising may expand the market as a whole. The reward for firm A will be a small increase in market share and, presumably, profits. Other firms, however, will not be hit too hard and so will not take drastic measures which might affect the profitability of all firms in the industry. On the other hand, firm A's campaign may back-fire if another firm launches a more successful advertising campaign. But the potential loss is unlikely to be very great.

This suggests that, in oligopoly, firms might not attempt to drive their main rivals out of the market. This would be an extremely risky strategy which might lead to themselves being the victim of such a move. Rather, oligopolists limit competition in order to limit the risks to their own market shares and profits.

Non-price competition is also a very powerful means of deterring potential competitors - firms which might enter the industry. This is discussed further below.

Branding

Interdependence limits the ability of oligopolistic firms to exploit markets to their own benefit. Ideally oligopolistic firms would like to turn themselves into monopolists with full control of their markets. One way of doing this is by the creation of strong brands. A strong brand has two major advantages for a producer.

- A strong brand has few good substitutes so far as the buyer is concerned. The firm is therefore able to charge a premium price (a relatively high price for the good) and earn monopoly profit on the good without seeing too great a fall in demand for it.
- It is very difficult for competitors to challenge the supremacy of the brand. For instance, Kellogg's Corn Flakes, Mars Bars, and Jaguar cars all have stable demands at premium prices in the short run. In the long run, tastes may change or new strong brands may appear. But even then old brands, such as Ovaltine,

QUESTION 2 American comic books represent a small niche market in the much larger market for magazines in the UK. In 1994, three companies dominated the niche market. Marvel Comics, which publishes Spider-man, The Fantastic Four and The X-Men, held 40 per cent of the market. DC comics, which publishes comics featuring Superman and Batman, held 30 per cent of the market. Finally, Image Comics, publishers of Spawn and Youngblood, held 24 per cent of the market.

There is no real price competition. Prices of comics are fixed in comparison with prices of rival comics. Instead, comics compete on the strength of their story lines and characters. Free gifts, special editions and graphic novels help keep existing customers loyal or attract new customers.

Until 1992, the market had been essentially a duopoly, with DC Comics and Marvel Comics carving up sales between them. Many others had tried to establish themselves, but lacked knowledge and money to create a range of comics which could compete with the two large companies. However, in 1992 a group of artists left Marvel Comics to set up the successful Image Comics. They were able to establish themselves for two reasons. The Image artists had gained considerable reputations through their work at Marvel. This 'core group' of artists attracted a large number of consumers to purchase the new Image comics and were able to create new characters which instantly appealed to consumers. Heavy promotion of the products by the company was also an important factor in generating sales.

(a) How do American comic book publishers establish a brand image?
(b) Use game theory to suggest why Marvel Comics and DC did not engage in a price war to drive Image Comics out of the market in 1992 and 1993.
(c) Why might game theory suggest that it is worthwhile to a company to pay key employees more than the going rate for the job?

Horlicks or Ambrosia rice pudding may continue to be highly profitable to their owners, still commanding premium prices at lower sales volumes but with little or no development costs.

Strong brands are difficult to create, which is why many firms prefer to take over other companies and their brands at very high prices rather than attempt to establish new brands. For instance, Nestlé paid £1.9 bn for the brands of

QUESTION 3

In 1995, Sainsbury's launched Indulgence, a new own-brand of ice-cream. It was aimed at the luxury end of the market, competing with brands such as Haagen-Dazs and Ben & Jerry's. Even five years before, supermarkets were not in the business of putting separate names on their own brands. Sainsbury's cola drink was marketed as 'Sainsbury's Cola'. Own brands were cheaper than manufacturers' branded products and were often perceived as being at best equal in quality to, but often slightly inferior to the main brands.

The market has now changed, however. Supermarkets have become much more confident about their abilities to take on nationally known manufacturers of branded products such as Coca-Cola or Procter & Gamble. Sainsbury's Classic Cola, brought out in 1994, has been a runaway success. Sainsbury's Novon, a washing powder and liquid, has managed to carve a substantial niche in its market. These supermarket products are advertised separately from the store's general advertising. Whilst still considerably cheaper than the manufacturers' brands, they are marketed as being equal in quality to, if not better than, the traditional brands.

For Sainsbury's, the advantage of these quality own-brands is that they raise sales of own-brands and the items can be sold at higher profit margins than either the manufacturer's brands or Sainsbury's cheaper own-label products. They can also pull in customers through the door who specifically want to buy a Sainsbury own-brand. However, there might be a down-side. Tesco has concentrated on promoting 'value for money', through schemes such as Club Card (a loyalty card) and Value Lines (very cheap essential products). Early indications are that this strategy has increased Tesco's share of the market slightly at the expense of Sainsbury's.

Source: adapted from *The Times*, 7.6.1995.

Use game theory to explain why Sainsbury's might:
(a) find it easier to establish a new brand than manufacturers like Heinz or Proctor & Gamble;
(b) choose to compete by launching own brands rather than engaging in a price war with Tesco.

Rowntree Mackintosh, a recognition of how much it would possibly cost to establish rival brands from scratch. To establish a new brand, a company usually has to produce an innovative product (innovative could mean anything from changing the colour or smell of a product to a radically new technological breakthrough) and then market it effectively. The failure rate of new brands in some markets such as food and confectionery can be as high as nearly 100 per cent. With this in mind, it is hardly surprising that a firm would be prepared to pay millions of pounds for an established brand rather than employ research workers to devise new products.

Collusion

Another way in which an oligopolist can turn itself into a monopoly is by colluding with other firms. In markets which are unregulated by government, there is a strong tendency for firms to collude (i.e. to join together and act as if they were one firm). Cartels and restrictive trade practices (☞ unit 41) were the norm in British manufacturing industry before such practices were made illegal in the 1950s.

Game theory can help us understand why this is the case. Consider Table 31.3. The figures show the profits to be gained by two firms, A and B, depending upon whether they adopt a high or low price strategy. Firm A, whose profit figures are in black, would like to adopt a low price strategy in opposition to a high price strategy by its rival. That would result in profits of £25m. But it can see that firm B would not allow such a situation because its profits would only be £5m. However, a high price strategy for firm A would be worse because it would face making the lowest possible profit, £10m, should firm B choose to adopt a low price strategy. So firm A will choose a low price strategy, hoping that firm B will adopt a high price strategy, but more realistically knowing that it too will adopt a low price strategy. Firm A will then make a profit of £15m - the highest minimum profit it can make.

Firm B will adopt a low price strategy too. Although it stands to gain £25m in profit by a high price strategy if firm A too goes for a high price stategy, it risks only making £5m if firm A were to go for a low price. So it will maximise its minimum profit of £10m and go for a low price strategy.

Table 31.3

		Firm B	
		Low price	High price
Firm A	Low price	£15m/**£10m**	£25m/**£5m**
	High price	£10m/**£20m**	£20m/**£25m**

The result is that both firms adopt low price strategies because they fear the reactions of their competitor. They would have been considerably better off if they had both adopted high price strategies. The only way to get into the high price 'box' is for the two firms to come to some form of understanding that they will not adopt low price strategies (i.e. they must collude).

The figures shown in Table 31.3 are an example of what is often called the 'Prisoner's Dilemma'. Substitute profits for prison sentences and prices for pleading guilty or not guilty. If both prisoners kept apart in different cells plead not guilty, then they will be released through lack of evidence. But if one prisoner pleads guilty, then he will get a reduced sentence and the other will get a heavier sentence. If both plead guilty they will get heavy sentences. If they could get together (i.e. collude) they would choose to plead not guilty. But in isolation they cannot trust the other prisoner. So each chooses to plead guilty and they both suffer!

QUESTION 4 In 1992, fifteen shipping companies signed an agreement to fix prices and limit competition on cargo shipping between the United States and Europe. The Trans-Atlantic Agreement (TAA) came into existence in response to heavy losses in the industry. Lines involved in the TAA had lost a total of $650m between 1989 and 1992. Exporters have complained that TAA has reduced capacity and forced them to pay more for exporting goods to the USA. Lord Sterling, chairman of P&O, the British transport and shipping group, speaking on behalf of the TAA, said: 'The whole point is that there's no way we can give them (the exporters) the service they expect or want, without getting a realistic return on the capital investment employed.'

Source: adapted from the *Financial Times*, 9.12.1993.

Use game theory to suggest why shipping companies in the TAA found it in their interests to collude.

Disequilibrium

So far the game considered have had a definite solution. An equilibrium set of strategies has been arrived at which leads to stability within the market. However, there are many games which lead to disequilibrium, where the players are unable to pursue stable strategies. A move by one firm will lead to a change in strategy of the other firm and so on.

Moreover, only two-firm, two-option situations have been discussed. In reality there are likely to be more than two firms in the industry each with more than two policy options. For instance, a six policy zero-sum game for two firms is shown in Table 31.4. There are 36 (6x6) different possible solutions to this game. If there were 3 firms in the industry, the number of possible solutions would rise to 216 (6x6x6)..

Game theory predicts, then, that there are a large number of different possible outcomes in an oligopolistic setting. Given this very large number, it is perhaps not surprising that economic theory has found it difficult to provide one unified model which would explain price and output decisions in the industry.

Table 31.4

			Firm B					
			Price			Advertising expenditure		
			Raise	Lower	Leave unchanged	Raise	Lower	Leave unchanged
Firm A	Price	Raise	£10m	-£5m	-£10m	£2m	-£1m	-£2m
		Lower	£2m	-£1m	-£4m	-£1m	£2m	£1m
		Leave unchanged	£3m	-£5m	0	£2m	-£4m	0
	Adv. exp.	Raise	-£1m	£7m	£5m	£3m	-£5m	-£1m
		Lower	£2m	-£3m	-£5m	£4m	-£2m	-£1m
		Leave unchanged	£2m	-£2m	0	£3m	-£1m	0

Key terms

Game theory - the analysis of situations in which players are interdependent.
Duopoly - an industry where there are only two firms.
Zero sum game - a game in which the gain of one player is exactly offset by the loss by other players.

Applied economics

The micro-chip market

Intel is the dominant world supplier of microprocessors, with an estimated 80 per cent of $10bn market in 1995. Its nearest rival is Micro Devices with estimated sales of $700 million in 1994. Over the past few years, it has pursued a number of business strategies which suggest that it realises only a careful playing of the market will prevent its current market power disappearing.

One problem it faces is that its chips are bought wholesale by computer manufacturers such as Compaq and IBM. They are sophisticated enough to shop around for the cheapest prices. Other chip manufacturers can, within a few years of a chip being put onto the market by Intel, produce a chip which will perform the same functions. Clone chips tend to be cheaper. In 1993-94, Intel attempted to get around this problem by advertising its latest mass market chip, the Pentium, directly to the final customer with the slogan 'Intel inside'. The computer manufacturers were furious. Sales of non-Pentium computers slowed down and manufacturers were left with more stocks of these products than they had anticipated. It also limited their ability to shop around for the cheapest chips. In terms of games theory, Intel realised that pursuing a strategy which increased customer awareness of its product would lead to larger revenues and profits than a strategy which left customers thinking that the only branded product they were buying was the computer itself. Intel's gain was a loss for other chip manufacturers.

In the longer term, Intel realises that it needs to pursue an aggressive strategy of product development if it is to stay as the dominant producer in the market (Schumpeter's process of creative destruction ☞ unit 39). In games theory terms, a failure to launch new products will allow other manufacturers to gain a technological lead. This would reduce revenue, market share and profit for Intel whilst allowing other chip manufacturers to gain these. Intel already faces a potential threat from Reduced Instruction Set Computing (RISC) chips. These chips work in a different way to Intel's microprocessors and out-perform them. Intel's response has been to develop a new chip, the P6 which performs almost as well as the RISC chips. Its great advantage is that, unlike the RISC chip, it is compatible with the millions of PC computers that have been sold worldwide to date and with their software.

In 1995, Intel needed to decide when to launch the chip. A games theory approach again would help its decision making. If it launched it immediately, it might lead to a fall in sales of PC computers. This is because consumers might think that if Intel could produce a new generation chip so quickly after its Pentium chip, then it would be worthwhile delaying the purchase of a new computer until the successor to the P6 came onto the market. Consumers avoid buying products which rapidly become obsolete. On the other hand, if it allowed, say, a four year gap between the introduction of the Pentium and the P6 into the mass PC market, it could face losing market share to RISC technology and the manufacturers such as Hewlett-Packard which are promoting RISC micro-processors. The lowest risk solution could be to launch the P6 as soon as possible.

DATA QUESTION

Europe reaches for its cereal

The French are abandoning their croissants, Belgians their rolls and Italians their habit of nothing but espresso. Across Europe, people are swapping their traditional breakfasts for a bowl of processed grain and cold milk. The European market for breakfast cereals has grown in recent years to be worth some £1bn annually.

Even during recession, most countries have increased consumption. For example, sales in France, the second largest European market for the cereal after the UK, increased by 21 per cent in the year to May 1993.

Europe has become an increasingly competitive market for cereal manufacturers. The recent acquisition of two cereal companies by the Dutch food and drinks company BolsWessanen, giving it almost 10 per cent of the European cereal market overnight, has brought into the open what industry insiders have known for some time.

To compete seriously, companies must have the market share and financial muscle to back new products with heavy advertising. This year Kellogg is estimated to be spending £5m in the UK alone to support its Corn Pops brand.

Harrison & Crosfield, the UK conglomerate which sold the companies to BolsWessanen, admitted it would not compete in this league by shedding what had been for it a successful, but peripheral, business.

The European breakfast cereals market is controlled by a few large companies. According to the Food Industry Bulletin, Kellogg dominates with more than 50 per cent, followed by Weetabix at 9.5 per cent and Cereal Partners Worldwide (CP), a joint venture between Nestlé and General Mills, with 6 per cent.

The arrival of CP in 1989 is widely credited with setting off the real explosion in the market. Within three years, through aggressive marketing and new product launches, it has won sales of some $348m (£225m). Naturally, Kellogg fought back. When CP launched its Golden Grahams, Kellogg came back a few weeks later with its own Golden Crackers. When CP introduced Clusters, Kellogg responded with Nutfeast.

The battle even threatened a veteran campaigner, Tony the Tiger, of Frosties fame. CP lit upon Huey, Dewey and Louie, Donald Duck's nephews, as the cartoon warriors for its Trio cereal in France.

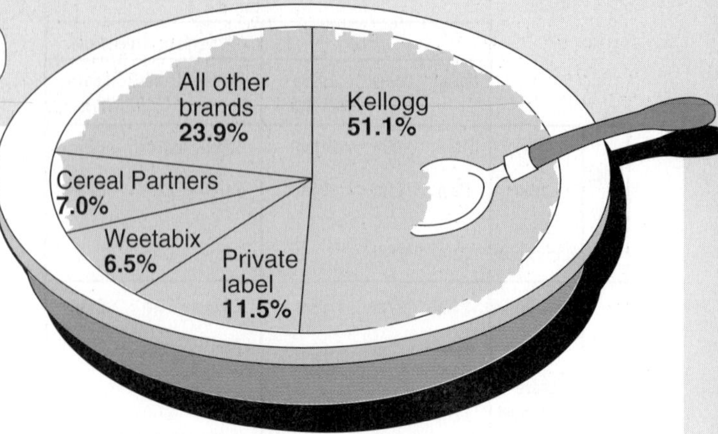

Source: adapted from Goldman Sachs.

Figure 31.1 *Cereal market shares in Europe and other countries outside North America, April/May 1994*

But the biggest beneficiaries of the battle between the cereal giants appear to have been the manufacturers own label products. Own label products claim 11.5 per cent of total European cereal sales, second only to Kellogg. The European market for private label products is widely acknowledged to be growing at a faster rate than the branded sector.

It is partly due to the increasing number of adults who are turning to cereal as a healthier breakfast option. In the UK, for example, the own label market is largely an adult market, focusing on mueslis and bran products.

'Staples deliver more steady virtues,' says Mr Mike Batten, marketing manager of the UK private label manufacturer. Telford Foods. 'They may have shown a dip in the market share at times, but have stable volumes.' And with the prospect of an ageing population, 'staples and bran are good bets for the future.' In the UK, own label sales are estimated to be outperforming the overall breakfast cereal market's growth of 2 per cent a year.

'Private labels need size to compete,' says Ms Nomi Ghez, an analyst with Goldman Sachs in the US. 'Who wants to fight for a share of a market which only has sales of about $40m?'

But BolsWessanen, now with 50 per cent of the European private label market, and the financial muscle to back this up, could force Tony the Tiger and his rivals, Huey, Dewey and Louie, to sing even louder for their breakfast.

Source: the *Financial Times*, 4.10.1994.

1. Use game theory to suggest why:
(a) Kellogg launched similar products when Cereal Partners Worldwide (CP) entered the European market in 1989;
(b) Kellogg and CP have tended not to compete on price;
(c) BolsWessanen bought two cereal companies from Harrison & Crosfield.

2. Use game theory to discuss whether BolsWessanen should now EITHER concentrate on remaining an own label (i.e. private label) producer OR attempt to establish branded products in the way that CP has done. Assume that the corporate goal of BolsWessanen is long run profit maximisation.

The theory of contestable markets

Summary

1. In a contestable market, there are one or a number of firms which profit maximise. The key assumption is that barriers to entry to the industry are relatively low, as is the cost of exit from the industry.
2. Firms in a contestable market will only earn normal profit in the long run. If they earn abnormal profit in the short run, then new firms will enter the industry and drive prices and profits down.
3. The existence of potential entrants to the industry will tend to keep profits to their normal level even in the short run because existing firms will want to deter new entrants from coming into the market.
4. Contestable markets are both productively and allocatively efficient in the long run and are likely to be efficient in the short run as well.
5. It is not necessarily possible to predict the exact output of an individual firm in a contestable market if average cost curves are L shaped.

Contestable market theory vs neo-classical theory

Many, if not most, markets in the UK and in other industrialised economies are dominated by a few producers. The **neo-classical theory of oligopoly** (☞ unit 30) assumes that oligopolistic markets feature high **barriers to entry** (☞ unit 25). However, there is also evidence to suggest that many oligopolistic markets have low barriers to entry. Therefore, firms in the industry are likely to behave in a different way to that predicted by neo-classical theory. The theory of contestable markets explores the implications of low barrier to entry markets.

Assumptions

The theory of contestable markets makes a number of assumptions.

- The number of firms in the industry may vary from one (a monopolist) having complete control of the market, to many, with no single firm having a significant share of the market.
- In a CONTESTABLE MARKET, there is both freedom of entry to and exit from the market. This is a key assumption of the model. Its implications are discussed below.
- Firms compete with each other and do not collude to fix prices.
- Firms are short run profit maximisers, producing where MC = MR.
- Firms may produce homogeneous goods or they may produce branded goods.
- There is perfect knowledge in the industry.

Normal and abnormal profit

The theory of contestable markets shows that in a contestable market:

- abnormal profits can be earned in the short run;
- only normal profit can be earned in the long run.

Assume that firms in a contestable market were making abnormal profit in the short run. Then new firms would be attracted into the industry by the abnormal profit. Supply would increase and prices would be driven down to the point where only normal profit was being made. This is the same argument that is used in the theory of perfect competition (☞ unit 27). Equally, if a firm is making losses, it will eventually leave the industry because in the long run it cannot operate as a loss making concern.

QUESTION 1

To what extent do (a) clothing manufacturers and (b) clothing retailers operate in contestable markets?

Entry to and exit from the industry

The ability of firms to enter and leave the industry is crucial in a contestable market and is not necessarily linked to the number of firms in the industry as in neo-classical theories of the firm. In neo-classical theory, low barriers to entry are linked with a large number of firms in an industry (perfect competition and monopolistic competition ☞ units 27 and 29) whilst high barriers are linked with few firms in the industry (oligopoly or monopoly ☞ units 28 and 30). Perfectly competitive and monopolistically competitive industries are contestable because an assumption of both these models is that there are low barriers to industry. But what of oligopolies and monopolies?

Some barriers to entry are natural (sometimes called **innocent entry barriers**). For instance, the industry may be a natural monopoly (☞ unit 39) as in Railtrack. Alternatively, there may be very high capital entry costs to the industry, as in car manufacturing. Neo-classical theory would predict that firms in these industries would earn abnormal profits. Contestable market theory suggests that this depends to a large extent on the costs of **exit** from the industry.

For instance, assume that the natural monopolist is charging high prices and earning abnormal profit. A competitor then enters the industry and takes market share by charging lower prices. The natural monopolist reacts by cutting prices and the competitor leaves the industry, unable to compete on these new lower prices because its costs are too high. So long as the cost of leaving the industry is small, it still makes sense for the competitor to have earned profit in the short run by entering the industry. The costs of exit are the **sunk costs** of operating in the industry (i.e. the fixed costs of production which cannot be recovered if the firm leaves the industry). Money spent on advertising would be an example of a sunk cost. So too would capital equipment which had no alternative use. If the sunk costs are low - the firm has done little advertising and capital equipment has been leased on a short term basis for instance - then the firm has lost little by entering and then leaving the industry. But in the meantime, it has earned profit at the expense of the existing firm in the industry.

Some barriers to entry, however, are erected by existing firms in the industry. In the soap powder market, soap powder producers spend large amounts of money advertising and branding their products. It may still be worth a firm entering this industry if the new entrant can charge a high enough price to cover the cost of entering and then possibly being forced to leave the industry. For instance, a firm might seek to earn £10m profit over 12 months. It is then forced to leave the industry because existing firms drive down prices or increase their advertising budget. If it earned £15m operating profit but lost £5m in leaving the industry, it would still be worthwhile for the firm to have entered and operated for a year.

QUESTION 2 Explain whether the following would make it more likely or less likely that there would be potential entrants to an industry.

(a) The inability of firms in the industry to lease capital equipment for short periods of time.
(b) Very high second hand prices for capital equipment.
(c) Heavy advertising by existing firms in the industry.
(d) The existence of a natural monopolist which was highly inefficient and had high costs of production.
(e) Patents held by an existing firm in the industry which were crucial to the manufacture of the product.
(f) Government legislation which gave monopoly rights to a single producer in the industry.

Potential competition

In a contestable market, firms are able to enter and leave the industry at relatively little cost. So far, we have implied that, in the short run, existing firms in a contestable market may well be earning abnormal profit. However, contestable market theory suggests that, in practice, established firms in a contestable market earn only normal profit even in the short run (i.e. they behave as if they operated in a perfectly competitive market).

Assume that a monopolist is the established firm in an industry. If it charges prices which would lead to it earning abnormal profit, then another firm may enter the industry charging lower prices. The new entrant will remain so long as the existing firm is earning abnormal profit, taking market share away from it and reducing its overall profits. To force the new entrant out, the monopolist would have to lower its prices. If it did this, and the new entrant left, and then the monopolist put up its prices again, all that will happen is that another firm will enter the industry. The only way to prevent new entrants constantly coming into the industry is for the existing firm to price at a level where it only earns normal profit.

Hence, the ability of firms to earn abnormal profit is dependent on the barriers to entry and exit to the industry, not on the number of firms in the industry as neo-classical theory would imply. With low barriers, existing firms will price such that AR = AC (i.e. no abnormal profits are being earned) because they are afraid that otherwise hit-and-run entrants to the industry will come in and damage the market for them. They are also afraid that new entrants may stay on a permanent basis, reducing the market share of existing firms in the industry.

Efficiency

In the long run, firms (apart from those which are natural monopolies) in a contestable market will operate at the bottom of their average cost curve (i.e. at the **optimal level of output** where MC = AC ☞ unit 20). To understand why, assume that they didn't operate at this level. Then a new entrant would be able to establish itself, producing at the bottom of its average cost curve and charging at this level too, undercutting other firms' prices. Existing firms would then be forced to cut costs if they wanted to stay in the industry. Hence, firms in the long run in a contestable market must be **productively efficient** (☞ unit 34).

They must also be **allocatively efficient** (☞ unit 34). It has already been argued that firms in a contestable market can only earn normal profits in the long run (i.e. AR = AC). It has just been argued that firms will be productively efficient, producing where MC = AC. Hence, since AR = AC and MC = AC, firms must produce where AR = MC. This is the condition for allocative efficiency.

Stability of contestable markets

It is not always possible to predict the level of output of a firm in a contestable market. To understand why, assume that total market demand is 300 units at a price of £10 whilst lowest average cost for a single producer is £10 at an output of 100 units. Three firms will therefore find it profitable to produce in the industry, but each firm will only earn normal profits because AC=AR. With only normal profits being earned, the industry is in long run equilibrium because there is no incentive for other firms to enter.

However, a problem arises if market demand is, for instance, 300 units but the optimal level of production for each firm is 120 units. If there were only two firms in the industry, each firm would be producing under conditions of diseconomies of scale if each produced 150 units. There would be an incentive for a new firm to enter the industry and produce the optimum lowest cost level of output of 120 units. It would be difficult to believe that the two existing firms would not react by reducing output, moving towards the optimal level. But if there were three firms each producing the same output of 100 units, then one firm could expand output and experience greater economies of scale. The other firms in the industry would then be likely to react by expanding their own output. Market price would fall below the minimum average cost of production and firms would make losses, sending back signals that firms should cut their production. There is in fact no level of output which would produce an equilibrium situation.

This is likely to be less of a problem if average cost curves are L-shaped rather than U-shaped. If demand is 300 units, and the minimum efficient scale of production is 120 units, then two firms could produce 150 units each at lowest cost. The theory does not, however, predict whether one firm will produce 120 units and the other 180, or both produce 150 units, or some other combination, subject to a minimum of 120 units.

Key terms

Contestable market - a market where there is freedom of entry to the industry and where costs of exit are low.

Applied economics

The breakfast cereal market

Kellogg invented the cornflake in 1891. Since then, the Kellogg company has expanded from its base in Battle Creek, Michigan, across the breakfast tables of 50 countries around the world. It has created the market for ready-to-eat cereals, changing the breakfast eating habits first of Anglo-Saxons in the USA, the UK, Canada and Australia, and more recently of continental Europeans, Latin Americans and the Japanese. Its worldwide market share is approximately 40 per cent.

There are other major companies in the market, but none approach Kellogg in terms of size. Outside of North America, for instance, Weetabix had 6.5 per cent of the market in 1994, mainly with its cereal biscuit and Alpen brand muesli. Cereal Partners, makers of Golden Grahams and Clusters, had a 1994 market share in the same area of 7.0 per cent. Many cereal producers are particularly strong in one country but have little or no presence elsewhere. Rank Hovis McDougal (RHM), for instance, had 6 per cent of the UK market in 1994 with its Shredded Wheat brand but no market share in France or Germany. General Mills, one of the partners in Cereal Partners, had approximately one-quarter of the US market in 1994, but had no separate operations in Europe.

Kellogg's formidable market power has been created and sustained through the introduction of new brands and through advertising. In 1994, Kellogg had over 50 brands in the UK, from its original Cornflakes, through the children's suite of sugary brands such as Frosties, to brands aimed at the adult health and fitness market such as Fruit 'N' Fibre. Brands are sustained through heavy advertising. In 1994, it is estimated that Kellogg spent £6 million alone supporting its Corn Pops brand.

From the evidence so far presented, it could be argued that the breakfast cereal market worldwide is not contestable. However, recent evidence suggests that it is possible to enter the cereal market at relatively low cost.

For instance, Kellogg's dominance in the European market was challenged in 1989 when Cereal Partners (CP) was formed. This was an alliance between General Mills, the US producer with a great deal of experience of manufacturing and selling branded cereals in the USA, and Nestlé, the European food producer with little experience in the cereal market but with considerable knowledge of promotion and the channels of distribution of food in Europe. Initially, CP produced cereals based on already successful General Mills' cereals produced in the USA. Hence, development costs of the new venture were small. For production, CP used spare capacity in existing Nestlé plants, again keeping entry costs to a minimum.

CP has proved remarkably successful. By 1994, it had taken 6 per cent of the European cereal market. Kellogg certainly saw it as a strong competitor. When CP launched its Golden Grahams, Kellogg retaliated within weeks by launching Golden Crackers. When CP introduced Clusters, Kellogg responded with Nutfeast.

In a quieter way, the market has also proved contestable for own label manufacturers. Own labels make up 11.5 per cent of the total European market but their share of the market has grown over time. In the early 1990s, own label sales were estimated to be outperforming the overall breakfast cereal market's growth of 2 per cent a year. With no advertising costs, it is relatively easy to enter the own label market and compete on price. Capital costs of entry are not particularly large.

Kellogg remains the dominant producer in the industry. However, it has seen no growth in its share of a rapidly expanding market in Europe. CP and own label manufacturers have been remarkably successful at entering the industry. In the long term, with own labels growing at a faster rate than the branded cereal market, Kellogg may be forced to enter a price war to retain market share, leading to a fall in the abnormal profits it arguably earns today from its strong brands.

The financial services market

Virgin launches retail financial services group

Virgin, Richard Branson's airline and leisure group, has launched a retail financial services group in conjunction with Norwich Union, one of the country's largest insurers. The new company, called Virgin Direct Personal Financial Services, will initially sell Personal Equity Plans (PEPs). These are tax free savings plans based on investment in companies on the stock market. Virgin will not use traditional means of selling these products. Rather, it has set up a direct-line operation to sell its PEPs over the telephone. It is imitating the highly successful direct-line motor insurance companies, such as Direct-Line and Churchill, which have captured a significant share of their markets.

The direct-line service will enable Virgin to cut costs radically because it won't be paying commission to agents. Initially, 60 to 70 staff working in Norwich will provide a telephone-based service five days a week with the plan to expand to a 24 hour service later based in north-east or central England.

Source: adapted from the *Financial Times*, 2.2.1995.

GM launches card

GM, the world's largest car manufacturer and owner of Vauxhall, have launched a new credit card. It has a below average interest rate and there is no annual fee. Users of the card can accumulate points towards gaining a rebate if they buy a new Vauxhall car. GM, who operate a large credit card operation in the United States, are confident that their card will quickly establish itself in the market place. It aims to attract customers through television and press advertising, posters and direct mail shots.

Source: various, 1993.

Nationwide delays financial services launch

Nationwide Building Society has traditionally offered its customers a variety of financial service products, such as life insurance, through Guardian, the financial services group. In 1994, it announced that it was breaking its ties with Guardian and setting up its own financial services operation selling life insurance and unit trusts. Nationwide hoped that it would be able to offer a more attractive service to its customers if it owned its own life insurance and unit trust operations than acting as a broker for Guardian. However, in 1995 Nationwide announced that it was delaying the launch of its new operations till the start of the next year because it wanted more time to test its systems and train staff.

Source: adapted from the *Financial Times*, 1.2.1995.

1. **What is meant by a 'contestable market'?**
2. **Suggest why the financial services market is a contestable market.**
3. **The government could increase regulation of the industry. For example, it could increase the amount of capital (i.e. money) that a new entrant to the industry had to hold as a reserve, or increase the amount of information that had to be supplied to government regulators. Why might this increased regulation make the market less contestable?**

Other theories of the firm

Summary

1. The neo-Keynesian theory of the firm assumes that firms are long run profit maximisers which determine prices according to cost-plus pricing principles. Price stability is a feature of this model.
2. Baumol's sales maximisation model assumes that firms aim to maximise sales subject to a profit satisficing constraint.
3. Managerial theories predict that costs and output are likely to be higher than neo-classical theory would suggest.
4. Both managerial and behavioural theories predict that organisational slack is likely to be present.
5. Limit pricing occurs when firms don't attempt to maximise short run profits for fear that this will attract competitors into the market, resulting in overall smaller long run profits. Instead, they set prices which are low enough to deter new entrants from entering the market, and which result in maximum long run profits given the potential competition in the market.

The neo-Keynesian model

R Hall and C Hitch in the 1930s outlined a radically different model of the firm from existing neo-classical models. Their research indicated that firms did not equate marginal cost and marginal revenue in an attempt to maximise short run profits. Rather, firms maximised profits in the long run (☞ unit 24). Firms then determined prices by calculating costs and adding a profit mark-up (hence the term **cost-plus pricing**). Prices are stable because firms take a long term view of the market.

In the model, it is argued that firms respond to changes in demand and cost not by changing price but by changing output. A large inflow of orders will not lead to a rise in price but to an increase in production. If a manufacturer is already producing at normal full capacity, it may attempt to produce at over-full capacity by encouraging its employees to work overtime or extra shifts. In the service sector, a booming supermarket will not increase prices if it proves far more popular than expected. Rather it will allow overcrowding in the short term and in the longer term may open longer hours, open an extension or build a new supermarket close by. Alternatively, a firm may allow waiting lists to develop. (A waiting list may be helpful in some cases to the image of a product because it is a sign that there are customers who think the product is so good that they are prepared to wait to buy it.)

If demand falls or costs rise, a firm will not necessarily respond by reducing price. Rather it will reduce output. If losses threaten to become too high, it will close down production rather than reduce price which may be seen to be damaging to the longer term prospects for the product.

Prices may not change on a daily basis (as for instance for carrots or tomatoes in the agricultural market) but, equally, firms' prices are not permanently fixed. The frequency of price changes will vary from industry to industry, but a yearly review of prices is not uncommon in British manufacturing industry.

The size of the profit mark-up will vary too. However, the mark up will tend to be higher where:

- firms in the industry are able to collude, acting as if they were a monopolist;
- there are only a few large firms in the industry, which results in less price competition;
- barriers to entry are high, limiting the possibility of new firms entering the industry;
- there are a large number of small buyers in the market, rather than a few significant buyers who are able to use their buying power to exert downward pressure on prices.

QUESTION 1 In 1994, the cola market in the UK was thrown into turmoil by the arrival of a new producer, Cott Corporation of Canada. It signed deals both with Sainsbury's and Virgin to produce cola drinks to be sold under the Sainsbury's and Virgin names. Following the launch of Classic Cola by Sainsbury's in June 1994, the own brand rapidly gained 11 per cent of the cola market in the UK. Virgin Cola, launched in November 1994, had gained 7 per cent of the cola market within three months. The attraction of both Classic Cola and Virgin Cola to consumers is that they are both much cheaper than Coca Cola and Pepsi Cola, and yet most customers see the product as being of equal quality to the two major international brands.

Coca Cola and Pepsi Cola have both seen their market shares decline. Coca Cola, the dominant brand, saw its market share decline from 55 per cent to 42 per cent since June 1994. However, it intends to fight back through a doubling of its advertising budget. Gavin Derby, the head of Coca Cola in the UK and Ireland, stated that: 'We have not communicated with the consumer at the same level as we have in other countries in the past few years.' He added that he had just instigated the most serious 'ratcheting-up of consumer communication in recent times'.

Source: adapted from *The Sunday Times*, 5.3.1995.

(a) Demand for Coca Cola and Pepsi Cola fell as a result of new competition in the market. Why did Coca Cola and Pepsi Cola not respond by cutting prices?

(b) Virgin wants its cola product to be sold throughout the world. To what extent should it lower the price of the product to achieve its sales objectives?

The neo-Keynesian theory of the firm is able to explain relative price stability in the market. However, it is pointed out by neo-classical economists that traditional cost curves should include an allowance for the cost of changing price - in other words, the insight that price changes can be costly can be incorporated within a neo-classical model.

Revenue maximisation model

Neo-classical theory assumes that firms are short run profit maximisers. In the early 1950s an American economist, W Baumol, put forward an alternative model suggesting that firms might maximise sales revenue rather than profits. He recognised that firms cannot make a loss if they are to survive in the long term, so at least some profit must be made. Managers also need to make enough profit to satisfy their shareholders (☞ unit 24).

In Figure 33.1, total cost and total revenue curves are drawn. The difference between the two is profit, shown by the curve at the bottom of the graph. The firm can operate anywhere between output levels OA and OD without making a loss. It will maximise profit at OB. If shareholders are content to earn just normal profit and managers wish to maximise sales, then the firm will operate at OD. On the other hand, if the minimum acceptable level of profit for shareholders is OE, then output will be at OC. As can be seen from the diagram, the higher the profit satisficing level of output, the lower will be the level of output and the nearer it will be to the profit maximising level of output.

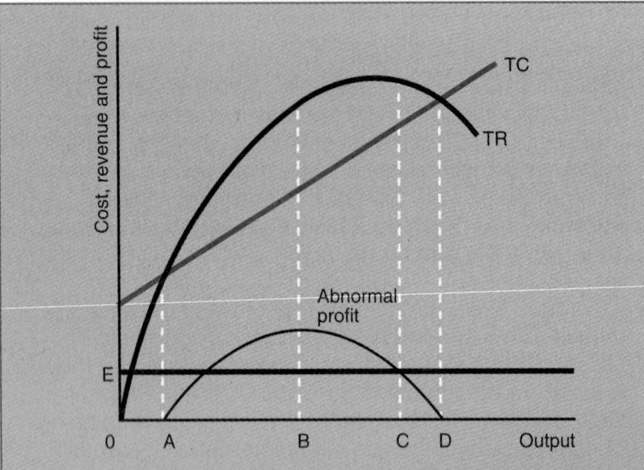

Figure 33.1 *Sales maximisation*
A firm maximising sales will earn normal profit at an output level of OD. If shareholders demand a minimum level of profit of OE, then it will maximise sales by producing at OC. Both output levels will be above the profit maximising level of output OB.

QUESTION 2

(a) A monopolist is a revenue maximiser subject to the constraint that it needs to make normal profits to satisfy its shareholders. Draw a standard neo-classical monopoly diagram (☞ unit 28). Mark on it:
  (i) the profit maximising level of output;
  (ii) the firm's revenue maximising level of output subject to its profit constraint.

(b) Compare the effect on output and price if a monopolist moves from being a profit maximiser to being a sales maximiser.

Managerial and behavioural theories of the firm

In both managerial and behavioural theories of the firm (☞ unit 24), it is argued that there is a divorce of ownership and control. In managerial theories, it is assumed that managers control the firm subject to a profit satisficing constraint.

Managerial models tend to make three clear predictions.

- Costs will be higher than neo-classical theory would predict. Higher salaries, expensive company cars and unnecessary levels of staffing have to be paid for.
- Firms will produce at higher levels of output than neo-classical theory would predict. This is because higher output and higher sales will lead to more staff being employed, which is beneficial to the utility of managers. Moreover, higher output levels may be more important in determining salary levels than increased profitability.
- In a recession, management may suffer disproportionately. In the attempt be to prevent the company from sliding into loss and possible take over or bankruptcy, managers may be sacked as administration is streamlined and their salaries and perks reduced. In an economic boom, managers may benefit more than most as they are able to increase their own salaries and perks whilst increasing profits too. Shareholders find it difficult to prevent this because they are unable to gauge how much more profit the company could have made if managers had not increased costs unnecessarily.

In behavioural theories, it is argued that it is not just shareholders and managers who determine the behaviour of firms. Other interested parties, such as government, trade unions and other pressure groups like environmentalists, can have an important say too. The eventual outcome will depend upon the relative strength of the various competing parties. In the UK newspaper industry in the 1970s, for instance, it could be argued that trade unions played an unusually dominant role in decision making, which led to exceptionally high wages being paid to their members. In the 1980s, shareholder power became more fashionable. The 1990s might be the decade when environmentalists substantially increase their power within corporate structures. The main supermarket chains in the UK, for instance, now carry a wide range of 'environmentally friendly' products which were not on the shelves ten years ago. A profit maximising assumption is then seen to be simplistic and will necessarily lead to misunderstanding about how firms behave.

QUESTION 3 According to a letter by K P McCann in the *Financial Times*, 14.12.1989, 'the maximisation of shareholders' wealth (is not) necessarily regarded as an overriding objective in many countries outside the UK. This is especially true in Germany where ... the relative lack of importance attached to the stock markets, social and employment legislation, tax regulations and the approach to financing industry all point to an economic culture which believes that a business is important in many different ways to a country, its economy and its society. The idea that shareholders' interests alone should prevail is not widely accepted.'

Explain why this letter supports a behavioural view of the firm.

Organisational slack

Both managerial and behavioural theories predict that ORGANISATIONAL SLACK is likely to be present. Organisational slack or X-INEFFICIENCY were terms used by Professor Harvey Leibenstein to describe the tendency of firms in non-competitive markets to produce at higher than minimum cost. So when a manager receives a Jaguar when she would have been content with a Carlton, or when a trade union member receives £500 a week when he would have worked for £300, or when a chargehand chooses to organise production in a traditional way when a far more efficient modern method is available, then organisational slack is present.

Organisational slack exists partly because of a lack of knowledge. Decision makers don't know the exact minimum amount for which a worker might be prepared to work for instance. Perhaps more importantly, organisations are often very conservative. They might order components from a firm they have always dealt with even if they know that the components could be purchased more cheaply elsewhere. Or they might be reluctant to invest in new machinery because all investment is a risk, despite the fact that potentially there are considerable cost savings to be made.

Different interest groups in the firm might be able to exploit their potential power to their advantage, thus increasing organisational slack. Environmental groups, for instance, might force a firm to adopt stricter environmental standards than cost-minimisation would dictate by threatening a media campaign against the firm. Trade unions might threaten to strike, causing short term chaos, unless their demands are met.

In a recession, organisational slack tends to decline. Firms are forced to concentrate on safeguarding profits and, as a result, unnecessary costs tend to be pruned first. Everything, from the size of the company director's car to working practices on the shop floor to the provision of food in the company canteen, is likely to be affected.

QUESTION 4 Business people are returning to air travel after being grounded by their companies during the recession. British Airways reported a 6.6 per cent increase in its passenger numbers in 1994-95. Moreover, passengers whose companies insisted on their flying economy class during the recession are now moving back into business class.

Frequent flyer points are proving a bone of contention between some employers and their workers. These points are gained by individuals every time they fly with a particular airline, rather like petrol coupons with petrol purchases. But like petrol coupons, points gained with one airline can't be added to points gained with another airline. So individual business people have an incentive to travel all the time by the same airline if they want to collect points. Most companies turn a blind eye to employees accumulating points, but worry about it all the same. It does not matter too much when the employees are flying the company's preferred airline on a particular route. The problems arise when individual employees start making their own travel arrangements using airlines which may not be the cheapest in order to gain points.

Source: adapted from the *Financial Times*, 20.4.1995.

(a) What examples of organisational slack are given in the data?
(b) Using air travel as an example, explain why organisational slack might be reduced in a recession.

Limit pricing

Limit pricing is when firms in an oligopolistic industry set a low enough price (the 'limit price') to deter new entrants from coming into the market. Limit pricing theories assume that firms look beyond maximising short run profits. For instance, assume that firms in an industry can earn £50 million in abnormal profit this year by

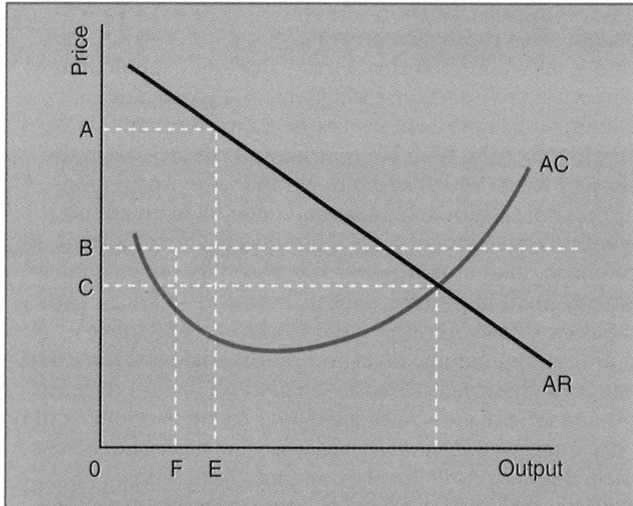

Figure 33.2 *Limit pricing*
If a new entrant proposes to come into a market charging a price of OB, then it might be deterred from doing so if existing firms in the industry are charging less than this price.

charging an average price of £10 for each product sold. However, at £10, new firms would be prepared to enter the market, driving down both price and market share of existing firms in the future. It might pay existing firms to charge a lower price than £10 now and lessen the risk of new entrants coming into the market.

Consider Figure 33.2. Assume that existing firms in the industry all have identical cost and revenue curves. Company X, shown in the figure, produces at a short run profit maximising level of output of OE where MC = MR. A new entrant is considering coming into the market. Initially, it proposes to produce OF. Because it is a new entrant, it will not be able to price on the same demand curve as Company X. It will have to sell at a discount. However, so long as it receives a price equal to OB, it will at least make normal profit. How might Company X and other firms in the industry react to the new entrant? Assuming that the new entrant could potentially take away large parts of the market, they should lower their price to below OB. If they do this, they will force the new entrant to make a loss. So long as their price is above OC, revenues will exceed costs and they will continue to earn some abnormal profit.

This assumes that all existing firms in the industry will lower their prices below the short run profit maximising price. This would be easier to achieve if firms openly **colluded** - getting together to fix prices and output to maximise profit (☞ unit 41). However, firms may achieve the same result through custom and practice, prices settling down at a level where there is some stability in the market and where no firm believes that it is in its long term interests to change price.

The limit price will be greater, the higher the barriers to entry to the industry. This is because the higher the barriers to entry, the less likely it is that a new entrant will come into the industry. For instance, if there were large financial barriers to entry because setting up would be highly costly, then new entrants would be worried that they would lose large amounts of money if the venture proved unprofitable and they had to withdraw. A relatively small reduction from the short run profit maximising price might therefore be enough to completely deter a potential new entrant.

Key terms

Organisational slack or X-inefficiency - inefficiency arising because a firm or other productive organisation fails to minimise its costs of production.

Applied economics

Japanese companies

The behaviour of large Japanese companies arguably differs from that of large US and UK companies. In the Anglo-Saxon world, shareholders are supposed to be the most important economic agents in a company. They are the owners and the company should be run for their benefit. This means maximising shareholder value. This comes in two main forms. First, companies should aim to maximise their dividend payments, which means maximising short term profits. Second, companies should aim to maximise their share price and the growth in the share price so that shareholders can make capital gains. A number of fashionable business concepts, such as Total Quality Management (TQM) emphasise the important of providing high quality products or services to customers. Government initiatives, such as Investors In People, stress the importance of training the workforce. However, building up a happy, loyal and productive workforce and ensuring that customers are satisfied with what they are buying are not ends in themselves. A hard working staff is only important ultimately because that staff is likely to make higher profits for the company than if it is demotivated and unhappy. Happy customers are only important because if they were unhappy they might take their custom to another company.

In continental Europe and Japan, attitudes differ. Shareholders are important, but they are only one group amongst many which influence decision making in the company. Partly this is because shareholders are unable to exert as much power. In Anglo-Saxon countries, direct shareholder involvement in the running of large companies is rare. Shareholders exert power through the buying and selling of shares on stock exchanges. A poorly performing company tends to see its share price slide as shareholders sell their stock in the face of poor dividend and share price growth. The company then becomes easy prey to a take-over bid from another company. In continental Europe and Japan, few companies are open to be taken over in this way because the majority of their voting shares are not tradeable on the stock exchange - they are owned by family members or by other large companies.

Shareholders in continental Europe and Japan are also far less likely to be short run maximisers than in Anglo-Saxon countries because of who owns shares. In the UK and the USA, banks are not allowed to hold company shares as part of their reserves. In Germany and Japan, in contrast, banks have always been encouraged to invest capital in company shares. As a consequence, bankers sit on the boards of companies in these countries. Banks are not particularly interested in short term profits. They wish to see the companies in which they own shares prosper over a long period of time. A company which produces shoddy goods might make a fast profit initially, but is unlikely to grow and prosper in the long term. Equally, shareholders in family controlled businesses are likely to be in business to secure the long term growth and prosperity of the company rather than pursuing the highest profit in the next month.

The importance of workers in a company is emphasised in the European Union through the Social Charter. Under the Charter, all large companies must have works councils, comprising representatives of workers and management, which have some power to influence long term decision making in a company. In contrast, the UK has opted out of the Social Charter and has declared that it will not encourage UK firms to organise works councils. In Japan, workers are seen as one of the key stake holders in a company. Large companies have a policy of providing jobs for life whilst trade unions see it as their role to safeguard the prosperity of the company to ensure that jobs can be for life.

European and Japanese governments have a history of being more interventionist than in the UK or the USA. In Japan, for instance, the government heavily influenced the development of individual industries in the post-war period. In France, national plans in the 1950s, 1960s and 1970s directed the growth of different sectors in the economy. Whilst direct government intervention in industry has diminished in the 1980s and 1990s, no European or Japanese government has gone down the road pursued by Margaret Thatcher and Ronald Reagan in the 1980s of minimising the role of government in the economy as much as possible.

Anglo-Saxon firms, then, can be seen broadly as short term profit maximisers. Continental European and Japanese firms, in contrast, tend to pursue long term profit objectives. The way they work is perhaps best described by behavioural theories of the firm, where a number of competing interest groups in a business come to a consensus about the direction the firm should pursue. The superior growth performance of continental Europe and Japan might suggest that short term profit maximisation is perhaps not the best way to maximise long term welfare in an economy.

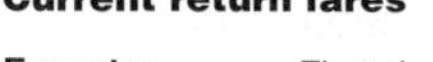

Travel services

In October 1994, the three railway companies of Britain, France and Belgium launched Eurostar, the high speed train service from London to Paris and London to Brussels using the Channel Tunnel. The service is in competition with two other main means of transport.

First, the airlines provide services to and from these capital cities. Journey times are short although for those wishing to go from city centre to city centre, the time to get from the centre to the airport must be included. Some food is provided on the flights.

Second, there are services which use bus and boat or bus and hovercraft. These travel from city centre to city centre but the journey time is much longer than with Eurostar or the airlines. No food is provided free on the services. Inability to move around for most of the long journey and the length of the journey makes it tiring for passengers.

Eurostar offers free food on its first class service. Although longer than the air flight, the service goes from city centre to city centre. The journey is exceptionally comfortable and business people can work throughout the journey on trains which run so smoothly that letters and reports can be written.

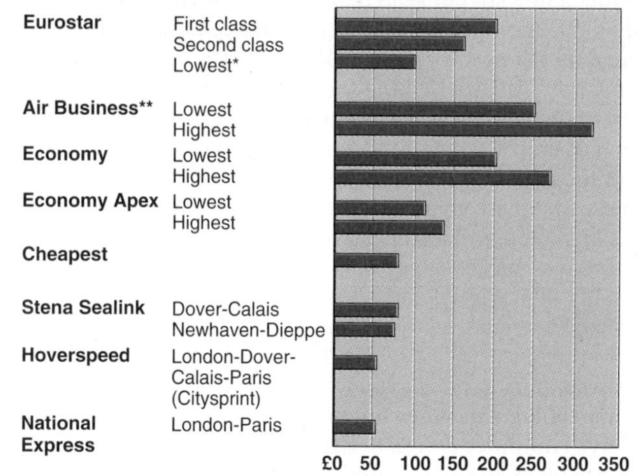

Source: adapted from the *Financial Times*, 18.10.1994.

Figure 33.3 *Return fares from London to Paris*

1. **(a) What is meant by 'competition'? (b) How do the different companies offering London to Paris services compete?**
2. **If the airlines are long run profit maximisers, discuss how they might react to the entry of Eurostar into the market.**
3. **In the late 1980s and early 1990s, the cross-Channel shipping companies, knowing that the Channel Tunnel was going to be operational by the mid-1990s, cut costs ruthlessly by introducing larger ships, reducing manning and reducing wages. Why might this be an indication that there was organisational slack in cross-Channel ferry operations in the 1980s?**

INVESTIGATIONS 2

A. Business finance

Aims

- To analyse how a large firm has financed expansion in recent years.
- To evaluate the extent to which this has enabled it to secure its goals.
- To evaluate alternative means of financing for the firm.

Research activity

Choose a large company which either has grown very fast in recent years or one which has got into difficulties over its finances.

Write to the company explaining that you are undertaking an economics 'A' level investigation into its financing. Request its latest Annual Report and Accounts, together with any other material they might think is appropriate for the study. (The company which has got into difficulties is unlikely to be very co-operative to any request greater than that for a copy of the Annual Report.)

Conduct a newspaper search. Using whatever indexes are available in your nearest large reference library, find and read all the newspaper articles about the company in recent years. You are looking for material about the history of the company, its products and the markets in which it operates. More importantly, you will find out the aims of the firm in financing expansion, and how the company obtained finance (for example issuing shares or bank loans). You will also need to evaluate whether the financing was successful or not. The library may have its own index of newspaper articles. It may have indexes published by the newspapers themselves, such as the index to the *Financial Times*, *The Times* and *The Guardian*. The newspapers may be available on CD Rom, in which case there will be an index on the computer. The library may have computer access to Extel or Datastream, both of which are likely to carry material about the company or the industry in which it operates. Alternatively, it may have the Research Index, a monthly index of financial interest covering 100 newspapers and periodicals and published by Business Surveys Ltd.

Structuring your report

Introduction Outline the aim of your investigation. The aim should be put in the form of a hypothesis or question which will allow you to come to some conclusions.
Economic theory Outline the economic concepts such as profit, shares, stocks, rates of interest, and markets which you will use in your report for the purpose of analysis.
Techniques used to collect your data Outline how you collected your data.
Company background Describe the company you have chosen to investigate, the products it sells and the markets in which it operates. Write a brief history of the company.
Analysis of company finance Describe how the company has financed its expansion. Explain the company's aims in obtaining finance for expansion. Discuss the extent to which the chosen means of finance have enabled the firm to achieve its goals.
Evaluation of alternative strategies Outline alternative strategies that the firm could have pursued. Compare and contrast the merits of each for the particular firm in question. Would these have resulted in a more profitable outcome for the firm? What methods did you use to evaluate the success of alternative strategies (e.g. profitability or security)?
Sources Outline the sources of information you used. What problems did you encounter in gathering relevant data? What data would you have liked to have obtained but could not? To what extent was the data reliable?
Bibliography Write down a list of your sources in alphabetical order.

Other suggestions

Instead of investigating the financing of expansion by one company, you could compare:

- the growth of a number of companies, perhaps contrasting a successful company with one which has failed;
- companies which have adopted similar financial strategies; for instance, you could compare two or more companies who issued additional share capital at roughly the same time, or you could compare two management buy-outs;
- a small company with a large company; what different sources of finance are available and what problems would they face in financing expansion?

Alternatively, you could investigate the financing of a single small company and examine the problems and successes that it has had in financing itself. Small companies are usually very reluctant to give details of their finances. Therefore a personal contact in the firm, such as a parent or relative, is often the best form of introduction to a potential source of information. Outline its current sources of finance. Discuss how it has financed itself in the past. For instance, how did it find the start-up capital for the company? What are its likely future financing needs and how best could it obtain that finance?

B. Market structure

Aims

- To investigate the market structure of a particular industry and the resultant behaviour of firms within the market.

- To discuss the extent to which the structure of the industry and the behaviour of firms within it conforms to an economic model of the firm.

Research activity

Choose an industry which you wish to investigate (e.g. the airline industry, bus transport, crisps and other snacks, telecommunications, soap powders or grocery retailing). Find out about the market structure of the industry. For instance, how many firms are there in the industry? What barriers to entry and exit exist? Do firms produce homogeneous or branded products and what range of products are sold? Is there perfect knowledge in the industry? Are firms interdependent? Is the aim of firms to maximise profits?

At the same time, make observations about the nature and outcome of competition within the industry. For instance, are firms price takers? Can a firm price discriminate between different consumers? Are prices similar? Is competition mainly price competition or is it based on other factors such as advertising or branding? Do firms earn abnormal profits? Do price movements within the industry appear to be co-ordinated? Are there recent examples of firms entering or leaving the industry and, if so, why did this occur? This information should allow you to identify the type of market structure within which the firm operates.

Sources

You are likely to start your research in one of three ways.

- You might read an interesting newspaper or magazine article about a particular industry.
- You might have a personal interest in and knowledge of the products of a particular industry, for instance through a part time job or a hobby (e.g. skateboard production, cinemas, grocery retailing, or chocolate manufacture!).
- You may have a contact, such as a relative, working in the industry from whom you can gather preliminary information.

To acquire further information, you will need to undertake a newspaper search. Using indexes for the *Financial Times* and other quality newspapers such as *The Times*, as well as magazines such as the *Economist*, find and read all recent articles about the industry and the activities of firms within the industry.

Materials may be available on CD Rom or on-line via Extel or Datastream services. If the firms in the industry are plcs, write to as many as possible outlining your investigation and requesting any relevant information. Ask specifically for the firm's Annual Report and Accounts and samples of advertising literature. There could well be a trade magazine/journal/ newspaper for the industry. Individual firms may be able to indentify its name and send you past copies or give you a contact address. Alternatively your nearest large public reference library may be able to help. There may be a controlling or regulatory body (such as OFTEL or ABTA) to which you could write for information.

Information about output, employment levels and imports and exports of different industries can be obtained from the *Annual Abstract of Statistics* published by the Central Statistical Office. A more detailed analysis can be found in the relevent *Business Monitor* for the industry, published by the Department of Industry. You may be able to gather primary evidence by obtaining an interview with a company in the industry, or by making direct observations about sales and marketing techniques.

Structuring the report

Introduction Outline the aim of your investigation. The aim should be put in the form of a hypothesis or question which will allow you to come to some conclusions.
Economic theory Outline briefly what economists mean by 'market structure' and put forward a model of behaviour of the firm which you judge is applicable to the industry you have chosen to investigate.
Techniques used to collect your data Outline how you collected your data.
Analysis of market structure Outline the main features of the market structure of the industry you have chosen to investigate. Discuss the extent to which the structure conforms to the model of the firm you have already described.
Evaluation To what extent does the behaviour of firms conform to your chosen model of the firm?
Sources Outline the sources of information you used. What problems did you encounter in gathering relevant data? What data would you have liked to have obtained but could not? To what extent was the data reliable?
Bibliography Write down a list of your sources in alphabetical order.

Other suggestions

Instead of investigating one industry, you could investigate contrasting industries, such as a monopoly (e.g. the water industry) and a perfectly competitive industry (e.g. parts of agriculture).

Alternatively, you could concentrate on particular characteristics of industries and test a variety of hypotheses. For instance:

- does the opening of competition to a previously monopolised industry lead to (a) greater choice and (b) lower prices?
- do prices in oligopolistic markets tend to be stable when compared to competitive industries?
- do more firms enter and leave competitive industries than imperfectly competitive industries?
- do restrictive practices lead to fewer firms going bankrupt?

Unit 34 Economic efficiency

Summary

1. **Productive efficiency exists when production is achieved at lowest cost.**
2. **Static efficiency refers to efficiency at a point in time. Dynamic efficiency concerns how resources are allocated over time so as to promote technical progress and economic growth.**
3. **Allocative efficiency is present if the marginal cost of production equals price in all markets in an economy.**
4. **To judge whether there is an optimal allocation of resources in an economy, it is necessary to make value judgements about the allocation of resources.**

Efficiency

The market mechanism allocates resources, but how well does it do this? One way of judging this is to consider how **efficiently** it resolves the three fundamental questions in economics of how, what and for whom production should take place (☞ unit 1). Efficiency is concerned with how well resources, such as time, talents or materials, are used to produce an end result. In economic terms, it is concerned with the relationship between scarce inputs and outputs. There are a number of different forms of efficiency which need to be considered.

Static vs dynamic efficiency

STATIC EFFICIENCY exists at a point in time. An example of static efficiency would be whether a firm could produce 1 million cars a year more cheaply by using more labour and less capital. Another example would be whether a country could produce more if it cut its unemployment rate. Productive and allocative efficiency (discussed below) are static concepts of efficiency. Economists use them to discuss whether more could be produced **now** if resources were allocated in a different way. These concepts can be used, for instance, to discuss whether industries dominated by a monopoly producer might produce at lower cost if competition were introduced into the industry (☞ unit 39). Or they might be used to discuss whether a firm should be allowed to pollute the environment (☞ unit 36).

DYNAMIC EFFICIENCY is concerned with how resources are allocated **over a period of time**. For instance, would there be greater efficiency if a firm distributed less profit over time to its shareholders and used the money to finance more investment? Would there be greater efficiency in the economy if more resources were devoted to investment rather than consumption over time (☞ unit 99). Would an industry invest more and create more new products over time if it were oligopolistic or a monopoly than if there were perfect competition (☞ unit 39)?

Productive efficiency

PRODUCTIVE EFFICIENCY exists when production is achieved at lowest cost. There is productive inefficiency when the cost of production is above the minimum possible given the state of knowledge. For instance, a firm which produces 1 million units at a cost of £10 000 would be productively inefficient if it could have produced that output at a cost of £8 000.

Productive efficiency will only exist if there is TECHNICAL EFFICIENCY. Technical efficiency exists if a given quantity of output is produced with the minimum number of inputs (or alternatively, if the maximum output is produced with a given number of units). For instance, if a firm produces 1 000 units of output using 10 workers when it could have used 9 workers, then it would be technically inefficient. However, not all technically efficient outputs are productively efficient. For instance, it

QUESTION 1

Table 34.1

Output	Minimum input levels	Units
	Labour	Capital
10	4	1
20	8	2
30	11	3
40	14	4
50	16	5

(a) Firm A uses 21 units of labour and 6 units of capital to produce 60 units of output. A competing firm uses 19 units of labour and 6 units of capital to produce the same output. Explain whether Firm A is more technically efficient than the competing firm.

(b) Firm B uses 24 units of labour and 7 units of capital to produce 70 units of output. Firm B pays £10 000 to employ these factors. A competing firm employs the same number of factors to produce the same level of output but only pays £8 000 for them. Explain whether Firm B is more productively efficient.

(c) Now look at Table 34.1.
From the table, which of the following combinations are: (i) technically efficient and (ii) productively efficient if the minimum cost of a unit of labour is £100 and of a unit of capital is £500?
(1) 8 units of labour and 2 units of capital to produce 20 units of output at a cost of £1 800.
(2) 15 units of labour and 4 units of capital to produce an output of 40 units at a cost of £3 500.
(3) 4 units of labour and 1 unit of capital to produce 10 units of output at a cost of £1 000.

might be possible to produce 1 000 units of output using 9 workers. But it might be cheaper to buy a machine and employ only 2 workers.

Equally, Firm A might be using a machine and two workers to produce a given output. However, if it is paying £100 0000 a year for this, whilst a competing business is paying only £80 000 a year for the same factor inputs, then Firm A is productively inefficient.

Allocative efficiency

ALLOCATIVE or ECONOMIC EFFICIENCY is concerned with whether resources are used to produce the goods and services that consumers wish to buy. For instance, assume that consumers place equal value on consumption of shoes and jumpers. However, the last 1 million pairs of shoes produced in the economy cost 10 times as much to manufacture as an extra 1 million jumpers would have done (i.e. the economy could have produced either 1 million pairs of shoes or 10 million jumpers). It would have been more allocatively efficient if 1 million jumpers had been produced rather than the 1 million pairs of shoes because:

- consumers value the jumpers as much as the shoes;
- either an extra 9 million jumpers or 900 000 pairs of shoes or some combination of the two could have been produced **as well as** the 1 million jumpers (assuming constant costs of production).

This argument can be developed using demand and cost curves. Demand and marginal cost have a particular significance in WELFARE ECONOMICS, the study of how an economy can best allocate resources to maximise the utility or economic welfare of its citizens.

- The demand curve shows the value that consumers place on the last unit bought of a product. For instance, if a utility maximising consumer bought a pair of tights at £2, then the pair of tights must have given at least £2 worth of value (or **satisfaction** or **utility** ☞ 14 unit). If total demand for a product is 100 units at a price of £10, then the value placed by consumers on the hundredth unit must have been £10. The value placed on each of the other 99 units bought is likely to be above £10 because the demand curve slopes back upwards from that point. The marginal (or extra) value of a good to the consumer (i.e. the marginal utility) is given by the price shown on the demand curve at that level of output.
- The marginal cost curve shows the cost to firms of producing an extra unit of the good. 'Cost', we will assume here, is the cost of production to society as well as to firms. (We will see in unit 36 that the **private cost** of production of the firm may differ from the **social cost** because of **externalities**, and that this has important implications for allocative efficiency.)

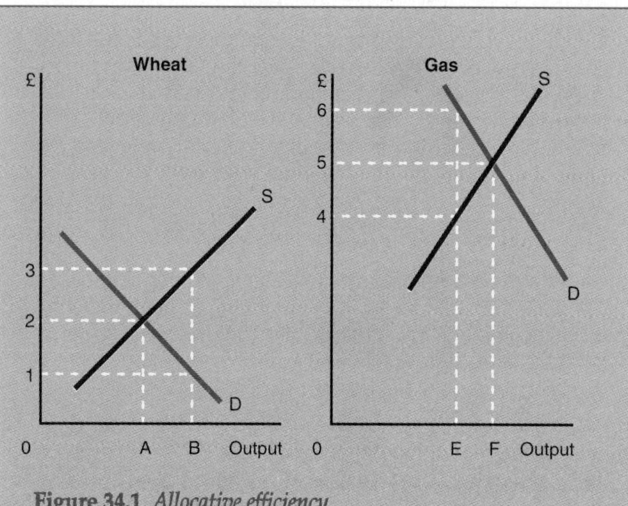

Figure 34.1 *Allocative efficiency*
Transferring resources from the wheat market where price is below marginal cost to the gas market where price is above marginal cost will be efficient.

In Figure 34.1, two markets are shown. In the wheat market, current output is OB. The market price is £1 per unit, but farmers receive £3 per unit, for instance because the government subsidises production. In the gas market, output is OE. Price is £6 but gas suppliers receive only £4, for instance because the government imposes a £2 tax per unit.

In the wheat industry, price is below marginal cost (P < MC). This means that the value that consumers place on the product is less than the cost to society of producing the product. Consumers value the last unit produced at OB at £1 (shown on the demand curve). The cost to society of producing the last unit is £3 (shown on the marginal cost curve). Therefore consumers value the last unit of wheat purchased at £2 less than it cost to produce.

In the gas market, price is above marginal cost (P > MC). This means that the value consumers place on the last unit produced is more than the cost to society of its production. Consumers value the last unit produced at OE at £6 whilst its cost to society is only £4. Hence consumers value the last unit of gas purchased at £2 more than it cost to produce.

This suggests that scarce resources would be more efficiently allocated if less wheat and more gas were produced in the economy, but how much wheat and gas should be produced? If price is equal to marginal cost in both markets (P = MC), then consumers value the last unit consumed of both wheat and gas as much as it costs to produce those commodities. If the price of wheat in Figure 34.1 were £2 and gas £5, then it would be impossible to reallocate resources between the two industries to the advantage of consumers.

Hence allocative efficiency will exist if price is equal to marginal cost in each industry in the economy. This is a very important conclusion but we shall see in unit 35 that this conclusion needs to be very heavily qualified.

If P=MC in all industries (such as wheat and gas in the above example), it is impossible to make any one better off without making someone else worse off. The allocation of resources is then said to be PARETO EFFICIENT (after Vilfredo Pareto, an Italian economist, who first put forward this condition in 1909 in a book entitled *Manuel D'Economie Politique*). If an allocation of resources is said to be Pareto inefficient, then it must be possible to make some or all people better off without making anybody worse off.

QUESTION 2

Table 34.2

Millions	£ per unit			
	Goods		Services	
Quantity	Price	Marginal cost	Price	Marginal cost
1	10	2	10	4
2	8	4	9	5
3	6	6	8	6
4	4	8	7	7
5	2	10	6	8

The table shows the relationship between quantity demanded and price and between output and marginal cost for the only two commodities produced in an economy. Producing 1 million units of goods and 5 million units of services would not be allocatively efficient. This is because, at this level of output, the price of goods (£10 per unit) is above marginal cost (£2 per unit) whilst the price of services is below the marginal cost of production (£6 compared to £8). Consumers would be better off if resources were transferred from the production of services, where the marginal cost of production is greater than the marginal, value placed on them by consumers, to the production of goods where the opposite is the case.

(a) The economy produces 3 million units of goods and 4 million units of services. Why is this an allocatively efficient level of production?

(b) Explain, using a diagram, why there would be a loss of economic efficiency if the allocation of resources changed such that:
(i) only 2 million units of goods were produced and the resources released were switched to the production of services;
(ii) only 2 million units of services were produced and the resources released were switched to the production of goods.

Efficiency and the production possibility frontier

The various concepts of efficiency can be illustrated using a **production possibility frontier - PPF** (☞ unit 1). A production possibility frontier shows combinations of goods which could be produced if all resources were fully used (i.e. the economy were at full employment). If there were productive inefficiency in the economy, production would take place within the boundary, for instance at points A, B or C in Figure 34.2. With all resources fully employed, it would be possible to move, for instance, from A to D if costs were minimised.

A, B and C are also Pareto inefficient. This is because it is possible to increase output for both John and all other people without making anyone worse off by moving to a point north east of these combinations. So production at D is more efficient than at A, production at E is more

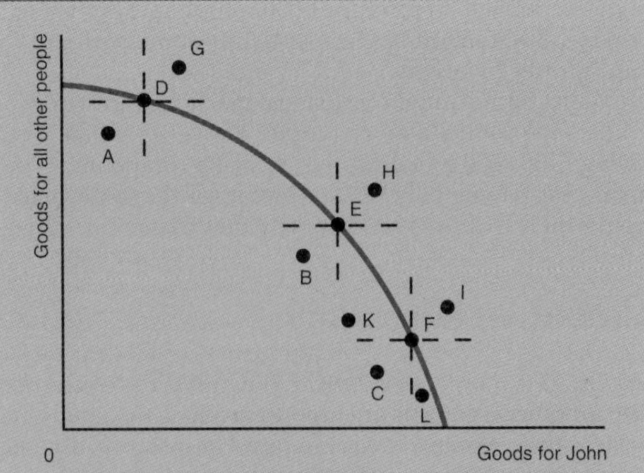

Figure 34.2 *Pareto efficient points of production*
Points on the production possibility frontier, such as D, E and F are Pareto efficient because it is not possible to produce more goods for John without reducing the production of goods for other people. Points G, H and I are unattainable whilst points A, B and C are Pareto inefficient because it is possible to increase production and produce more goods for both John and all others.

efficient than at B etc.

On the other hand, D, E and F are Pareto efficient. At any of these points it is not possible to produce more for John without reducing production for all other people. This is true for all points on the production possibility frontier. Hence, all points on the PPF are Pareto efficient.

All points on the PPF also satisfy the P=MC condition. So points on the frontier are both productively and allocatively efficient.

Note that it is only possible to make Pareto efficiency statements about points which are north east and south west of each other. For instance, F is Pareto efficient whilst C is not. But K cannot be compared with F because at K all other people are better off than at F but John is worse off.

QUESTION 3 Many scientists have predicted that the destruction of the Brazilian rain forests will add to the 'greenhouse effect', in turn leading to a rise in world temperatures and a rise in sea levels. Much of the destruction is being carried out by ranchers who wish to clear land to rear cattle. They can then earn a profit by selling the beef to First World countries such as the USA and the UK.

Using a production possibility frontier (putting 'beef' on one axis and 'rain forest' on the other), discuss whether a ban on the felling of trees in the Brazilian rain forests would lead to Pareto efficiency.

The optimal allocation of resources

All points on the production possibility frontier are productively and allocatively (i.e. Pareto) efficient. Therefore in one sense all points on the frontier represent an OPTIMAL ALLOCATION OF RESOURCES. It is not possible to make one person better off without making another worse off. In making this judgement, we are implicitely assuming that it is not possible to say that one distribution of resources is better than another.

However, this gives little help to policy makers who believe that one distribution of resources is superior to another. For instance, in Figure 34.3, points A and B are both Pareto efficient and therefore in one sense represent an optimal allocation of resources. However, the government may believe that society would be better off if there were less rather than more defence spending so that the economy would be better off at B rather A. It is making a value judgement about what constitutes economic welfare.

This value judgement can be expressed in terms of **social welfare** functions. These are the equivalent of indifference curves (☞ unit 15) for society as a whole, giving relative welfare values of different combinations of output. A social welfare function (called here a **community indifference curve**) is shown in Figure 34.3. An optimal allocation of resources exists when the highest level of social welfare is achieved on the production possibility frontier of the economy, where the community indifference curve is tangential to the production possibility frontier at B. But a social welfare function necessarily reflects the value judgements of the economist or politician who constructs it.

Efficiency and equity

When making decisions, efficiency may be only one of many considerations to be taken into account. Governments in particular need to consider what impact a decision might have on the standard of living of different groups in society. It could be argued, for instance, that government policy since 1979 has increased the efficiency of British industry and the economy as a whole. However, it has increased inequalities in society, with evidence that the poorest 10 per cent of the population have seen no increase in income over the period when the top 10 per cent saw their incomes rise by over 50 per cent in real terms (☞ unit 43).

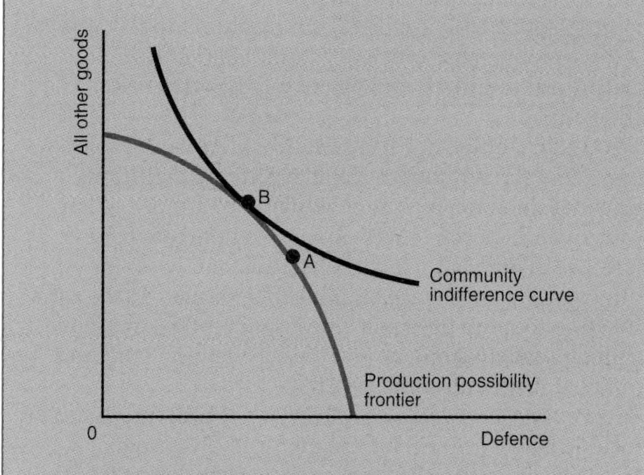

Figure 34.3 *The optimal allocation of resources*
If it is assumed that it is not possible to make comparisons about welfare between individuals, then all points on the production possibility frontier give an optimal allocation of resources. However, if value judgements are made, then a community indifference curve can be constructed and a single optimal allocation of resources, B, can be found.

Key terms

Static efficiency - occurs when resources are allocated efficiently at a point in time.
Dynamic efficiency - occurs when resources are allocated efficiently over time.
Productive efficiency - is achieved when production is at lowest cost.
Technical efficiency - is achieved when a given quantity of output is produced with the minimum number of inputs.
Allocative or economic or Pareto efficiency - occurs when no one can be made better off by transferring resources from one industry to another without making someone else worse off. Allocative efficiency will exist in an economy if price = marginal cost in all industries.
Welfare economics - the study of how an economy can best allocate resources to maximise the utility or economic welfare of its citizens.
Optimal allocation of resources - occurs when resources are efficiently used in such a way as to maximise the welfare or utility of consumers.

Applied economics

The Common Agricultural Policy (CAP)

When the European Union (EU), formerly the European Community, was first formed there was a commitment to free trade between member countries. This found its first major expression in 1962 in the Common Agricultural Policy, a Community-wide policy which aimed to harmonise the agricultural policies of the original six member countries (☞ unit 12). One of the implicit aims of CAP was to increase efficiency in the market for agricultural products. To what extent has this been achieved?

Productive efficiency has certainly increased. Table 34.3 shows that the number of small, relatively inefficient, farms has declined over time whilst the number of large farms over 50 hectares with lower overall costs has increased. There has been a substantial fall in employment in the agricultural sector as Table 34.4 shows. At the same time, due to more intensive farming methods, more use fertilizers and machinery and higher yielding crop and animal strains, output has risen.

However, European agriculture is not fully productively efficient. There are still far too many small farmers producing on marginal land, such as in Wales or the French Alps. In 1991, the average size of a farm ranged from 5.3 hectares in Greece, to 16.0 hectares in Spain, 30.7 hectares in France and 68.9 hectares in the UK. Small farmers are unable to exploit the economies of scale enjoyed by large farms and consequently their costs of production are much higher.

But it could be argued that the difference in productivity between farms in Europe is not as important an issue as the difference in the cost of production between the EU and the rest of the world. World prices for many agricultural commodities, such as wheat or butter, are considerably below those maintained by the complex system of tariffs, quotas and intervention prices in the EU. In the EU, wheat prices were 3.4 times the world price in 1988, for instance. Japan has been particularly protectionist, with domestic wheat, coarse grains and rice prices being between 8 and 11.65 times world prices.

Consumers lose out because of these high domestic prices. Their loss can be calculated by multiplying the amount they purchase by the difference between domestic and world farm gate prices. In 1990, three-quarters of all subsidies to EU farmers came from consumers.

However, farmers worldwide also tend to be supported by the taxpayer. In the EU, this comes from the Community's budget, figures for which can be found in unit 12. The EU operates a variety of agricultural support schemes. A small amount is structural aid, helping farmers leave the land or improve their productivity. Most is spent on intervention buying, purchasing produce to support prices. Much of this produce is put into store and sold at knock down prices outside the EU.

Table 34.5 shows the total transfers of money to agriculture from both consumers and producers in major agricultural producing countries between 1987 and 1991. The total amount spent in 1991 was $320.7bn, roughly equivalent to the total output of the Australian economy in that year. This represents an enormous cost to citizens in developed countries. Table 34.6 shows that the cost per head of the population in the EU of supporting farmers was 350 ecus, roughly equal to £270. For a family of four, this means paying £1 080 a year in higher taxes and higher food prices than would be needed if all subsidies were abolished and it was able to buy food at world prices. Each farmer, on the other hand, was receiving an £11 000 subsidy for farming from the EU.

The agricultural market is not just productively inefficient. It is arguably allocatively inefficient in terms of the MC = price criterion. The fact that taxpayers throughout the developed world are having to subsidise farmers means that the marginal cost of production far exceeds the price consumers are prepared to pay. Allocative efficiency could therefore be increased by shifting resources out of agriculture into other industries.

Over the past ten years, there has been an increasing awareness of the costs of CAP and other agricultural support systems. In the Uruguay Round of trade talks completed in 1994, the USA, Australia and New Zealand pressed for a complete abolition of all subsidies. The EU resisted and in the end only agreed to reduce but not eliminate farm subsidies. This was because the abolition of CAP would produce losers as well as gainers. EU land owning farmers would be the main losers. Land prices would plummet because prices for produce would fall substantially. Marginal farmers too would lose because their land would not be productive enough to support them in business. The experience of New Zealand, which almost abolished farm subsidies in the 1980s, suggests, however, that farm profits would remain roughly constant. There would be lower prices and less state handouts. But equally, the costs of production, particularly rents on farms, would fall too leaving most farmers on good farming land with broadly similar incomes.

Table 34.3 *Number of holdings by size (in 1 000s) 1970-1987*

	Total	<1 ha	1-5ha	5-10ha	10-20ha	20-50ha	>50ha
EUR-10							
1970	7 667		3 087	1 244	1 115	850	201
1975	7 100	703	2 728	1 044	938	867	325
1977	6 802		2 632	1 012	895	865	330
1979	6 820	1 362	2 494	923	847	852	338
1983	6 515	1 338	2 342	866	762	830	355
1985	6 359	1 321	2 275	826	751	816	367
1987	5 005		2 312	813	719	780	373
EUR-12							
1987	6 920		3 411	1 163	936	946	473

Source: European Commission, *European Economy, EC Agricultural Policy for the 21st Century*, Number 4, 1994.

Table 34.4 *Changes in the agricultural labour force, 1970-90*

Country	Agricultural labour force				Share of agricultural employment in total civilian employment		
	Equivalent full-time workers (AWU)		Average annual change		Shares		Average annual change
	1970	1990	1970 to 1990	1980 to 1990	1970	1988	1970 to 1988
	in 1 000	in 1 000	in %	in %	in %	in %	%/year
B	181.2	93.2	-3.27	-2.10	4.8	2.7	-3.15
DK	216.1	96.1	-3.97	-3.49	11.5	6.3	-3.29
D	1 527.0	762.5	-3.41	-2.54	8.6	4.3	-3.78
GR	1 192.4	781.8	-2.09	-2.00	40.8	26.1	-2.45
E	3 566.5	1 400.7	-4.57	-4.94	29.5	14.4	-3.91
F	2 369.0	1 473.8	-2.35	-2.16	13.5	6.8	-3.74
IRL	365.2	238.4	-2.11	-1.92	27.1	15.4	-3.09
I	3 653.8	2 156.7	-2.60	-3.04	20.2	9.9	-3.88
L	14.6	6.0	-4.37	-3.97	9.4	3.4	-5.49
NL	303.3	235.1	-1.26	-0.77	6.3	4.8	-1.50
P	1 630.5	867.6	-3.11	-3.21	30.0	20.7	-2.04
UK	615 0	456.4	-1.48	-1.47	3.2	2.2	-2.06
EUR -12	15 634.6	8 532.3	-2.98	-3.00	13.8	7.4	-3.40

Source: European Commission, *European Economy, EC Agricultural Policy for the 21st Century*, Number 4, 1994.

Table 34.5 *Total transfers associated with agricultural policies*

	Billion US dollars					
	1987	1988	1989	1990	1991	Change (%)
Australia	0.6	0.6	0.7	1.1	1.2	7.3
Austria	3.8	3.5	2.9	4.1	4.1	-0.4
Canada	8.6	8.7	8.3	9.8	9.5	-2.9
EURO-12	119.4	120.8	101.2	138.3	141.8	2.6
Finland	4.4	4.9	4.9	6.0	5.9	-2.5
Japan	65.5	70.7	65.8	60.4	63.2	4.6
New Zealand	0.1	0.2	0.1	0.1	0.1	-24.3
Norway	3.3	3.5	3.3	4.2	4.2	-0.2
Sweden	3.2	3.0	3.1	3.5	3.6	3.7
Switzerland	5.3	5.6	5.0	6.2	6.4	2.1
United States	80.9	69.2	70.8	73.0	80.8	10.6
TOTAL	**295.2**	**290.7**	**266.1**	**306.8**	**320.7**	**4.5**

Source: OECD, *Agricultural Policies: Market and Trade*, 1992.

Table 34.6 *Total agricultural policy transfers, EC, 1990-92 (billion ECU)*

	1990	1991	1992	OECD average 1992
From taxpayers	39.3	47.5	51.8	
From consumers	66.1	71.4	69.3	
Budget revenues	0.7	0.5	0.6	
Total transfers	104.8	118.4	120.5	
share in total GDP (%)	1.9	2.0	2.0	2.1
per head of population (ecu/hd)	300	340	350	340
per full-time farmer equivalent (ecu/FFE)	11 900	13 400	13 700	16 900
per hectare of farmland (ecu/ha)	750	850	870	240

Source: European Commission, *European Economy, EC Agricultural Policy for the 21st Century*, Number 4, 1994.

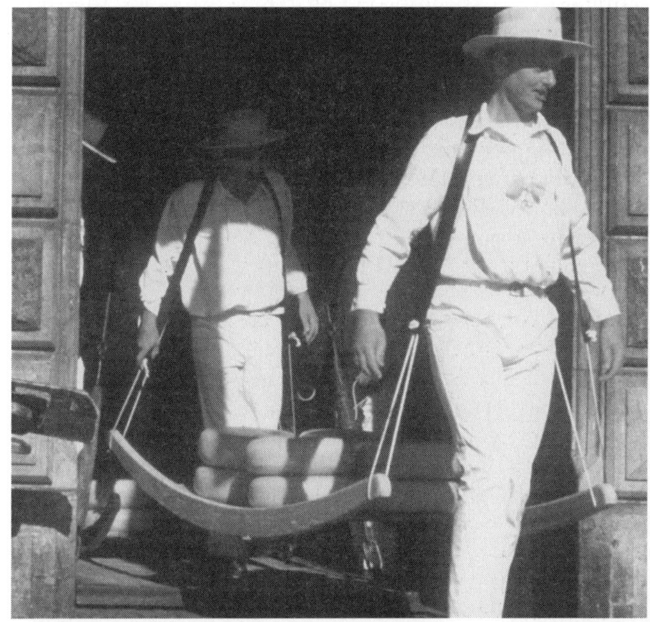

DATA QUESTION

Education spending

Real expenditure on education, taking account of inflation in education costs, gradually fell from the mid-1970s to the late 1980s, after 30 years of almost continuous growth after the 1944 Education Act. In 1975-6, just before the cuts in public spending imposed on the Labour government by the International Monetary Fund, 6.4 per cent of the gross domestic product (total output of the country) was being spent on education. By 1979-80, this had fallen to 5.1 per cent. In spite of ups and downs, this pattern continued in this trough until 1987-88, since when it has slightly risen.

A look at what has been happening to expenditure on the average young person between the ages of 18 and 24 makes gloomy reading. Real higher education spending on that age group fell by a quarter from the mid-1970s to the mid-1980s. In the polytechnics (now the 'new' universities), spending per head fell sharply in 1977-78 as a result of the IMF cuts; a further fall came in 1981-82, as polytechnics packed in students as a result of the Conservative cuts in universities. Spending per head in universities fell steadily between 1981-2 and 1985-86. The price of this disinvestment will be paid in decades to come.

Household spending on private education and training - ranging from shorthand to music classes to top private schools - rose steadily in the 1970s and 1980s. As people's incomes rose, they chose to spend more on education out of their own pockets. For every 1 per cent increase in their income, households spent 1.05 per cent more on education in 1960-65, 1.06 in 1970-75, and 1.07 in 1975-80. In the 1980s, this figure reached 1.16 and it rose most in local education authorities that cut their spending most.

During the same period, state spending on education fell, relative to rising incomes. For every extra 1 per cent growth in the economy in the 1960s, the state increased education expenditure by 1.5 per cent. In the period 1980-86, this figure fell to below 0.9 per cent. In other words, education's share of national spending fell. Yet individuals were still showing their consumer preferences for education in the market place.

Source: adapted from *The Times Educational Supplement*, 5.10.1990.

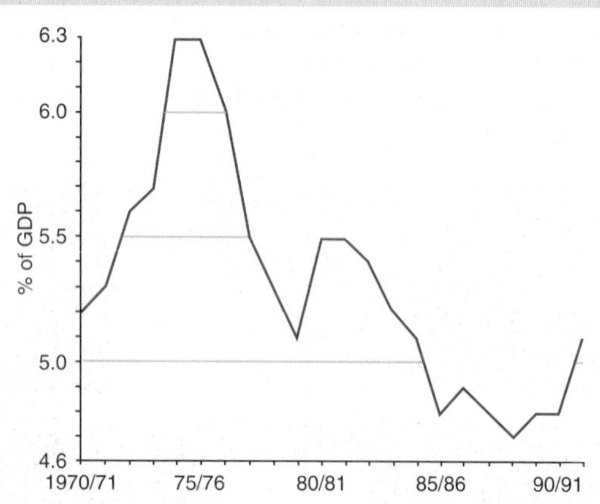

Figure 34.4 *Education spending as a percentage of GDP*

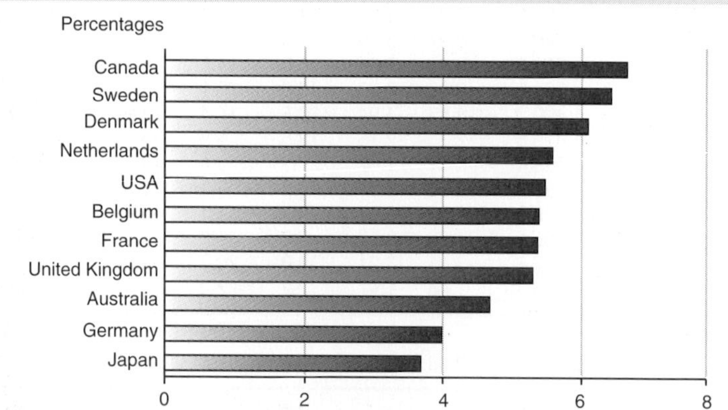

Source: adapted from Department of Employement.

Figure 34.5 *Public expenditure on education as a percentage of GNP: international comparison, 1991*

Produce a report arguing for greater state spending on education.

1. **Describe the trends in state spending on education since the 1960s.**
2. **Discuss whether the state is spending in such a way as to give rise to allocative efficiency in the economy. In your report, you will need to consider how consumers are choosing to allocate resources when given a free choice in their spending.**
3. **Evaluate whether the state is ensuring dynamic efficiency in the economy through its spending on education. In particular, you will need to consider the benefits of education for the long term growth of the economy and whether current levels of spending on education are sufficient.**

The market: efficiency and market failure

Summary

1. The market is a mechanism for allocating resources.
2. In a free market, consumers, producers and owners of the factors of production interact, each seeking to maximise its returns.
3. Prices and profits play a key role, signalling how resources should be allocated or reallocated within the market.
4. In the absence of market failure, a free market will achieve an optimal allocation of resources.
5. There are many examples of market failure, including imperfect competition and monopoly, externalities and missing markets.
6. The General Theory of the Second Best shows that, in an imperfect market economy, a move towards marginal cost pricing in one industry may not lead to a Pareto improvement.

The role of the market

Adam Smith, in his book *An Enquiry into the Nature and Causes of the Wealth of Nations*, attacked the economic system of his day. It was a system founded upon protectionism, economic restrictions and numerous legal barriers. He presented a powerful case for a free market system in which the 'invisible hand' of the market would allocate resources to everyone's advantage. There are three main types of actor or agent in the market system. Consumers and producers interact in the **goods markets** of the economy. Producers and the owners of the factors of production (land, labour and capital) interact in the **factor markets** of the economy.

The main actors in the market

The consumer In a pure free market system it is the consumer who is all powerful. Consumers are free to spend their money however they want and the market offers a wide choice of products. It is assumed that consumers will allocate their scarce resources so as to maximise utility (☞ units 14 and 15).

The firm In a pure free market, firms are servants of the consumer. They are motivated by making as high a profit as possible. This means maximising the difference between revenues and costs.

- **Revenues.** If they fail to produce goods which consumers wish to buy, they won't be able to sell them. Consumers will buy from companies which produce the goods they want. Successful companies will have high revenues; unsuccessful ones will have low or zero revenues.
- **Costs**. If firms fail to minimise costs, then they will fail to make a profit. Other more efficient firms will be able to take their market away from them by selling at a lower price.

The price of failure - making insufficient profit to retain resources and prevent factor owners from allocating their resources in more profitable ways - will be the exit of the firm from its industry. On the other hand, in the long run firms cannot make abnormal profit. If they did, new competitors would enter the industry attracted by the high profits, driving down prices and profits and increasing output.

Owners of the factors of production Owners of land, labour and capital - rentiers, workers and capitalists - are motivated by the desire to maximise their returns. A landowner wishes to rent her land at the highest possible price. A worker wishes to hire himself out at the highest possible wage, all other things being equal. A capitalist wishes to receive the highest rate of return on capital. These owners will search in the market place for the highest possible reward and only when they have found it will they offer their factor for employment. Firms, on the other hand, will be seeking to minimise cost. They will only be prepared to pay the owner the value of the factor in the production process.

QUESTION 1

(a) How does this photograph illustrate the workings of the market system?

(b) Explain what is likely to happen in a market system if:

(i) a brand of biscuits fails to sell in sufficient quantities;

(ii) the rent on the premises of the supermarket shown in the photograph increases five fold whilst rents in general are only increasing by a few per cent;

(iii) the shopper in the photograph loses her job.

The allocation of resources

In the market mechanism, everyone is assumed to be motivated by pure self interest. Consumers are motivated by the desire to maximise their utility.

Producers wish to maximise profits. Workers, rentiers and capitalists seek to maximise the returns from the factors that they own. What Adam Smith argued was that this apparently chaotic system of billions of separate transactions would not only allocate resources, but it would allocate resources in an efficient way. It wasn't necessary for government or any other body to order that resources should go in this way or that. The hidden hand of the market would do the job, and it would do it far better. The following three examples show how the market can reallocate resources when market conditions change.

Example 1 Assume that lobbying from animal welfare groups changes consumers' tastes. In the market for fur coats, fewer fur coats will be purchased. In the short run, companies in the fur trade are likely to cut prices to boost demand but this will depress profits. In the long run, some firms will leave the fur industry, reducing supply. This in turn will affect the factor markets. For instance, the demand by firms in the fur industry for workers, equipment and animals will fall. So wages of fur workers may fall. The price of hunting permits or of land for fur farms may fall too. Some workers will leave the industry attracted by higher wages elsewhere whilst land will be put to other uses. Meanwhile, consumers will have increased their spending on other goods, for instance on imitation furs. In the short term the price of imitation furs will rise. Increased profits will attract new firms into the industry, thus boosting supply. This will increase the demand for factors of production used in the making of imitation furs. Their prices will tend to rise.

Example 2 A new production process is invented which reduces the cost of manufacturing shoes. Initially, firms will be able to make abnormal profit - revenues will be the same but costs will be lower. However, new firms will be attracted to the industry by high profits. Extra supply will lead to price reductions. The price of shoes will go on falling until no abnormal profit can be made. Competition has forced firms to offer the lowest price possible to consumers. Meanwhile the new low prices will have increased the demand for shoes. So more factors of production will be demanded by the shoe industry and their price will tend to rise.

Example 3 There is a large increase in the number of young workers in the population. This increased supply of young workers will force their wages down. Firms will employ more young workers at lower wages. This should reduce the costs of firms, which in turn will be passed on to the consumer in the form of lower prices. The market mechanism has once again ensured that the consumer benefits from this change.

QUESTION 2 In February 1995, Thorn EMI, the music and rentals group, announced that it was closing its Rumbelows electricals chain. By 1995, the group had 300 shops which had failed to make a profit for more than 10 years. Thorn had been attempting to turn Rumbelows round for a long time. Originally, Rumbelows rented equipment as well as selling it. By the mid-1980s, this formula was proving unprofitable, and in 1986 television rental accounts were transferred to Radio Rentals, another chain owned by Thorn. In 1992, it reverted back to renting as well as selling after it had lost £50m over three years. Thorn experimented with new formats but nothing seemed to bring enough customers in to cut the estimated £12m loss a year it was still making.

Shops will be sold or leased to new tenants. 2 500 workers lost their jobs. The electricals retailing market at the time was generally suffering low profits, with too many stores and too many chains chasing too little business.

Source: adapted from the *Financial Times*, 6 .2.1995.

Explain how resources have been reallocated by the market mechanism according to the article.

Prices and profits

Prices and profits play a key role in the market mechanism. They are the signals which allocate resources within the market. When prices rise, buyers react by buying less, whilst sellers react by wanting to sell more. Profits too act as signals for firms. Abnormal profits will lead to increased supply as firms move into the industry. Losses will lead to firms leaving the industry. If governments or other agencies intervene to control prices and profits, distorted signals will be sent out. The result will be the misallocation of resources to the detriment of the consumer.

The market and economic efficiency

It would seem from what has been said above that the market is likely to promote **economic efficiency** (☞ unit 34). Indeed, it is possible to show that if all markets are **perfectly competitive** (☞ unit 27), resources in the economy will be efficiently allocated.

- In long run equilibrium in a perfectly competitive market, firms will produce at the bottom of their average cost curves. Therefore there will be productive efficiency.
- For there to be allocative efficiency, the cost to society of producing an extra unit of output must equal the value placed on consumption of that good by the individual (the price = marginal cost condition outlined in unit 34). In a perfectly competitive market, firms maximise profits by producing where marginal cost = marginal

revenue. Marginal revenue is equal to price because the perfectly competitive firm is a price taker. Therefore marginal cost = price. On the other hand consumers maximise their utility by equating the marginal utility of each good consumed per £1 spent. Hence price is an accurate reflection of the value of the good (the marginal utility) to the individual.

It is also true that allocative efficiency in the sense of Pareto efficiency will exist in an economy where all markets are perfectly competitive. Because firms are producing at least cost, the economy must be on its production possibility frontier and therefore the allocation of resources must be Pareto efficient.

Market failure

If all markets in an economy are perfectly competitive, then two conditions must hold.

- There must be perfect competition in all goods markets. Consumers must be able to allocate their resources in a way which will maximise their utility. They must possess perfect knowledge, for instance. There must be enough consumers in any market to prevent undue pressure being exerted on producers to their advantage. Production too must be organised under conditions of perfect competition. Each industry must comprise a large number of small producers, all of whom are price takers. There must be freedom of entry and exit to every industry and all firms must possess perfect knowledge.
- All factor markets must be perfectly competitive. There must be perfect mobility of labour for instance. There must be no trade unions which act as monopoly suppliers of labour. Neither must there be any monopoly employers, such as the UK government with teachers and nurses. Capital must flow freely between industries and regions according to the levels of profit being made.

No real economy is like this. Imperfections exist in all sectors of modern industrialised economies as they do in developing economies which **prevent** the efficient allocation of resources through the market mechanism. This MARKET FAILURE is the subject of units 36 to 47. Here we will provide a summary of the different types of market failure.

- **Imperfect competition** (☞ units 39-42 and 45). The free market model assumes that there are a large number of buyers and sellers in all markets and that there is therefore no concentration of market power. The reality is often very different. Power is often very concentrated in market economies. Most goods markets are oligopolistic, dominated by a few large firms. Consumers, far from being all powerful, can often be seen as pawns in the games that firms play to maximise their own gains. In factor markets, monopoly suppliers such as trade unions are often present. So too are monopoly buyers such as governments. This can (but does not necessarily) lead to inefficiency.
- **Externalities** (☞ unit 36-38). Prices and profits should be accurate signals, allowing the actors in the market mechanism to allocate resources efficiently. In reality, prices and profits can be very misleading. This is because actual prices and profits do not reflect the true prices and profits to society of different economic activities. For instance, in Brazil it makes commercial sense to cut down huge areas of rain forest to provide grazing land for cattle sold to the West as meat for hamburgers. This could lead to global economic catastrophe in the long run. The market is putting out the wrong signals.
- **Missing markets** (☞ unit 42 and 44). The market, for a variety of reasons, fails to provide certain goods and services. Some goods, called **public goods**, such as defence, will not be provided by a market. Other goods, called **merit goods**, will be underprovided by the market. Health care and education are two examples of merit goods. Part of the reason for underprovision is because the market mechanism is often poor at dealing with risk and with providing information to agents in the market.

QUESTION 3

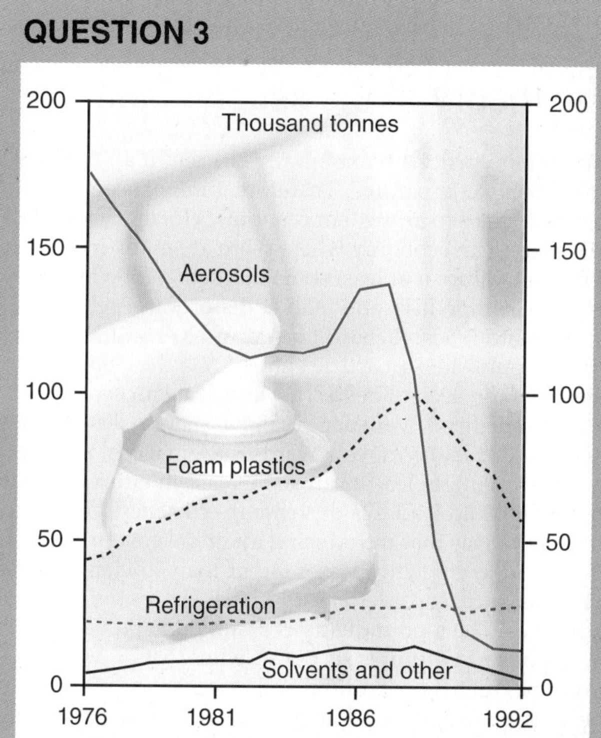

Source: adapted from Eurostat.

Figure 35.1 *EU sales of CFCs by use*

During the 1970s and early 1980s, increasing use was made of aerosol cans containing CFCs (chlorofluorocarbons). The cans were cheap to manufacture and technically efficient. But scientists showed that CFCs were causing damage to the ozone layer. This led most aerosol cans to be withdrawn from sale.

(a) Explain why the cost to society of aerosol cans containing CFCs was different from the market cost and price.

(b) Why did this difference in costs lead the market mechanism to overproduce such aerosol cans?

Efficiency vs equity

Even if a market were efficient, it would not necessarily lead to a socially desirable distribution of resources between individuals. Both **efficiency** and **equity** (☞ units 43 and 47) contribute to the level of economic welfare. For instance, Pareto efficiency exists when an economy operates on its production possibility frontier. But there are an infinite number of points on the frontier. Which is the one which is most desirable? That question cannot be answered without some view about the distribution of resources within an economy (i.e. without a **social welfare function** ☞ unit 34). Most would agree that an economy where one person enjoyed 99 per cent of the resources whilst the other 100 million people were left with 1 per cent would be unlikely to provide a higher level of welfare than one where the distribution of resources was more equal. Most (but not all) would agree that it is unacceptable in today's Britain to allow people to die of hunger on our streets. The question of what distribution is desirable or is judged to maximise total welfare is a value judgement.

The theory of the second best

An economy will be economically efficient if all markets are perfectly competitive. Therefore it might seem like common sense to argue that economic efficiency will be increased in an economy where there are many instances of market failure if at least some markets can be made perfectly competitive and market distortions removed.

In the late 1950s, Richard Lipsey and Kelvin Lancaster (1956-7) published an article entitled 'On the General Theory of the Second Best'. They assumed an economy where some firms were not pricing at marginal cost. They then showed that a move towards marginal cost pricing by one firm might lead to an an increase in efficiency, but equally it could lead to a decrease in efficiency. The radical conclusion was that introducing marginal cost pricing could lead to efficiency losses rather than efficiency gains.

For instance, consider Figure 35.2. It shows two industries. The food industry is assumed to be monopolistic. Output is set at OA where MC = MR (the profit maximising condition) and price is then set at OP on the average revenue or demand curve. The entertainment industry is perfectly competitive. Output is at OF where marginal cost equals price. Assume that resources were transferred from the entertainment industry to the food industry such that output in the food industry rose to OB whilst output in the entertainment industry fell to OE. The welfare gain in the food industry, shown by the difference between demand and marginal cost, is the shaded area on the graph. This is larger than the welfare loss in the entertainment industry, shown by the shaded triangle. Hence in this case there is a net welfare gain if there is a move away from perfect competition in the entertainment industry.

It can be shown that, in general, efficiency can be increased by transferring resources to industries where price is far in excess of marginal cost from industries where it is less so or where demand is less than marginal cost. Efficiency is likely to be achieved where the difference between price and marginal cost is the same throughout an economy.

This is a very important conclusion. Every economy suffers from market failure. It will never be the case that marginal cost can equal price across all sectors of the economy. Therefore simple rules or slogans such as 'competition good, monopoly bad' are unlikely to lead to good economic policy making. What the theory of the second best suggests is that distortions within an economy need to be evened out as far as possible. Eliminating them in some markets but allowing them to remain high in others could well lead to less efficiency overall than decreasing them in markets where they are high but actually increasing them in markets where distortions are low.

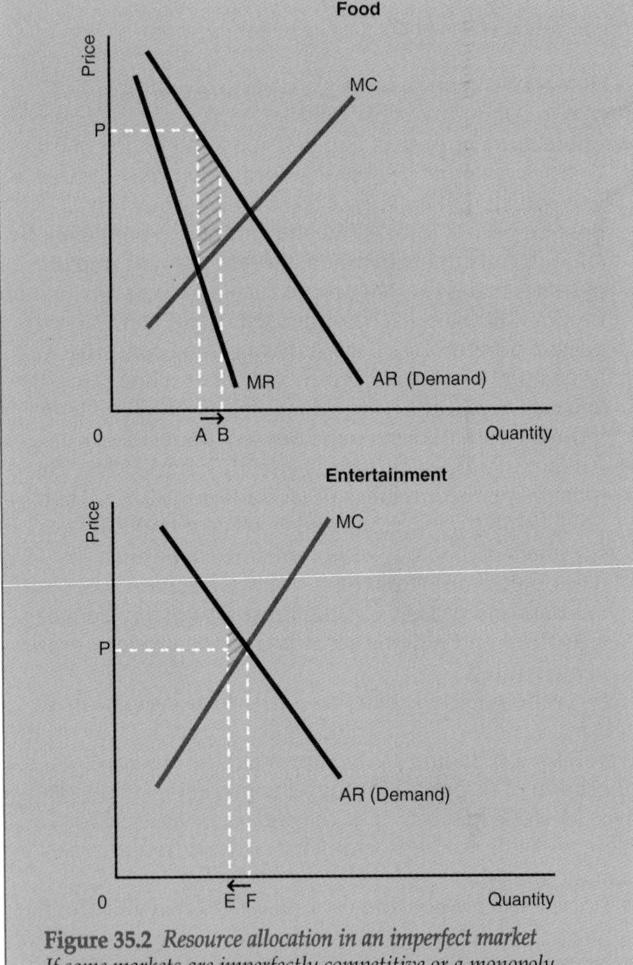

Figure 35.2 *Resource allocation in an imperfect market*
If some markets are imperfectly competitive or a monopoly, there could be efficiency gains if resources are transferred from a perfectly competitive market to the imperfectly competitve market or the monopoly. The loss of efficiency in the entertainment market, shown by the shaded area, is less than the gain in welfare in the food market in this example.

Key terms

Market failure - where resources are inefficiently allocated due to imperfections in the working of the market mechanism.

Applied economics

Motor cars

Table 35.1 *Annual production, exports and sales of cars, UK (millions)*

	Production	Exports	UK domestic sales	Imports
1964	1.9	0.71	1.2	0.1
1965	1.7	0.65	1.1	0.1
1966	1.6	0.63	1.1	0.1
1967	1.6	0.56	1.1	0.1
1968	1.8	0.80	1.1	0.1
1969	1.7	0.82	1.4	0.5
1970	1.6	0.72	1.0	0.1
1971	1.7	0.71	1.1	0.1
1972	1.9	0.61	2.1	0.8
1973	1.7	0.60	1.6	0.5
1974	1.5	0.60	1.2	0.3
1975	1.3	0.53	1.2	0.4
1976	1.3	0.57	1.3	0.6
1977	1.3	0.56	1.3	0.6
1978	1.7	0.49	1.6	0.6
1979	1.1	0.39	1.7	1.0
1980	0.9	0.35	1.5	1.0
1981	1.0	0.30	1.5	0.8
1982	0.9	0.23	1.6	0.9
1983	1.0	0.24	1.8	1.0
1984	0.9	0.19	1.8	1.1
1985	1.0	0.21	1.8	1.0
1986	1.0	0.19	1.9	1.1
1987	1.1	0.23	2.0	1.1
1988	1.2	0.21	2.2	1.2
1989	1.3	0.28	2.3	1.3
1990	1.3	0.41	2.0	1.1
1991	1.2	0.60	1.6	1.0
1992	1.3	0.59	1.6	0.9
1993	1.4	0.53	1.8	0.9
1994	1.5	0.62	1.9	1.0

Source: adapted from CSO, *Economic Trends Annual Supplement.*

The UK motor car industry has been typical of the rest of UK manufacturing since the 1960s. The UK has had a long history of being a manufacturing nation stretching back to the nineteenth century when it was described as the 'workshop of the world'. However, since the beginning of this century, it has become apparent that consumers both in the UK and abroad have been increasingly dissatisfied with British made goods. The late 1980s, however, may have proved to be a turning point.

In the 1950s and early 1960s, for instance, imports of cars into the UK were negligible whilst UK manufacturers exported hundreds of thousands of cars per year. In 1964, UK car production peaked at 1.9m, a figure which has yet to be surpassed. From then on, car production figures fell. By 1980, they had fallen to a low of 0.9 million, a figure which was maintained throughout the first half of the 1980s. In the second half of the 1980s, there was a significant revival in car production. Production rose. More significantly, exports began to increase from 1989 whilst imports fell from a high of 1.3 million cars in 1989 to 1.0m in 1994.

The UK car industry faced two major problems over the period. First, domestic manufacturers, particularly what is now Rover cars, failed to design and manufacture cars which appealed to consumers. Imported cars increasingly represented better value, in terms of specification, performance, reliability or price. Second, as car manufacturing became increasingly global, the three large US companies which owned significant parts of the UK motor industry reduced their output of cars in the UK and switched production to European plants. British plants proved uneconomic. Quality and reliability were poor whilst car production costs were higher than on the continent. In particular, UK car workers proved to have significantly lower productivity than European car workers.

The result was that profits on UK plant were low. As economic theory would predict, manufacturers closed plants and cut their labour forces. The number of workers fell from 852 000 in 1964 to 218 000 in 1993. Resources were moved out of car manufacturing into other sectors of the economy, particularly service industries. Some of the labour resources also became part of the long term unemployed, with unemployment in the whole economy rising from 0.3 million in 1964 to a peak of 3.1 million in 1992. The second half of the 1980s, however, saw the beginning of a revival in UK manufacturing. The Conservative government from 1979 had transformed industrial relations law. Poor industrial relations had bedevilled the car industry in the 1960s and 1970s, with hardly a week going by without at least one car plant being on strike. In the 1980s, strikes and other forms of industrial unrest became a thing of the past. The UK had also become a relatively low wage economy.

The poor performance of the whole economy relative to other European countries and to Japan in the 1960s and 1970s meant that UK wages rose more slowly in real terms than those in competitor countries. Tax and social security payments paid by employers were also relatively low. Lower productivity could be more than offset by paying lower wages and associated taxes to workers.

A third important factor was improved management. Ford and General Motors, US owners of car plants in the UK, became determined to bring their UK plants up to world class standards. UK managers knew that if they failed, the plants would be starved of investment and eventually closed. They were spurred on by aggressive Japanese competition. The Japanese had already taken a significant share of the US car market and were only being kept out of the European market by quotas (limits) on the amount they could import. In the 1980s they began to develop strategies for taking a larger share of the market. Honda established a partnership with Rover, sharing development costs on cars and, as a by-product, helping Rover transform itself into a world-class manufacturing company. Nissan and then Toyota decided to establish car plants in Europe to beat the protectionist barriers. They chose to locate in the UK, attracted by cheap labour costs and availability of labour. Resources flowed in from abroad. Other UK car manufacturers could see at first hand that high productivity plants could be operated successfully in Britain.

The result in the 1990s has been a fall in imports and a rise in exports of cars. Admittedly, car production in the UK is not back to its mid-1960s levels. However, if Japanese producers' plans are realised, UK car production should be nearly half a million cars more by the year 2000, with most of that being exported to the rest of the European Union.

In all of this, market forces have allocated resources. Consumers rejected British-made cars in the 1960s and 1970s and so production fell. During the same period, manufacturers shifted production from the UK to Europe in response to low profits. In the second half of the 1980s, low wages, improving industrial relations and higher quality work saw an expansion of manufacturing capacity again in the UK. It is true that governments have played some part in these events. The Japanese decision to locate in Europe, for instance, was in part a response to a fear that they would be kept out of the European market by the European Union. However, Adam Smith's hidden hand can easily be seen at work.

Unleaded petrol

Leaded petrol gives rise to externalities. The users of leaded petrol, the motorists, create pollution in the environment. Other people, particularly children, suffer as a result. Reducing the amount of leaded petrol consumed reduces the externality created by its use.

The Chancellor announced a cut in the duty on unleaded petrol of 5p a gallon (1.1p a litre), including VAT. It previously bore excise duty at the same rate as leaded petrol. The reduction applied to all unleaded petrol cleared at import or from bonded warehouse from 6 pm yesterday.

Under European Community* law (Directive 85/210/EEC), as a result of a United Kingdom initiative, unleaded petrol is to be generally available throughout the Community by October 1 1989. Member States are to take appropriate steps to ensure its balanced distribution and to encourage its use.

In his Budget Statement last year the Chancellor announced his intention of assisting the introduction of unleaded petrol by creating a duty differential in its favour to offset its higher production costs.

* Now the European Union.
Source: Treasury Statement following the 1987 Budget, 17.3.1987.

Lead is absorbed by people via food, air, water and solid or dust. Once inhaled or ingested it can accumulate in the body and can lead eventually to health problems, particularly in children. Lead gets into the atmosphere from burning leaded petrol and coal, or as a result of industrial processes, such as metal smelting. The largest single source of lead in the air originates from burning leaded petrol. Directives by the EC have progressively reduced the amount of lead in petrol, and since 1986 unleaded petrol has been available in the United Kingdom. The relative reduction of fuel duty on unleaded, compared with leaded, petrol since 1987 has boosted sales and in February 1993 the amount of unleaded petrol delivered to petrol stations in the United Kingdom exceeded leaded petrol for the first time.

Source: CSO, *Social Trends* 1994.

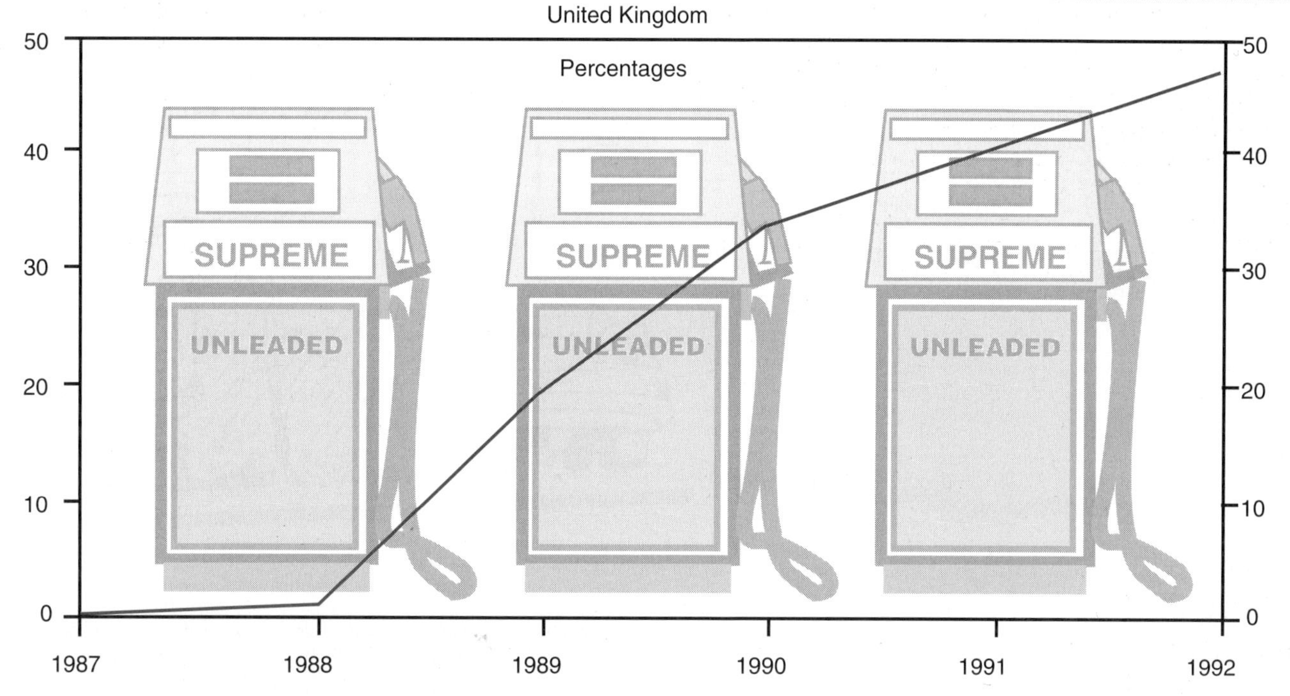

Source: adapted from Department of Trade and Industry.
Figure 35.3 *Consumption of unleaded petrol as a percentage of total petrol consumption*

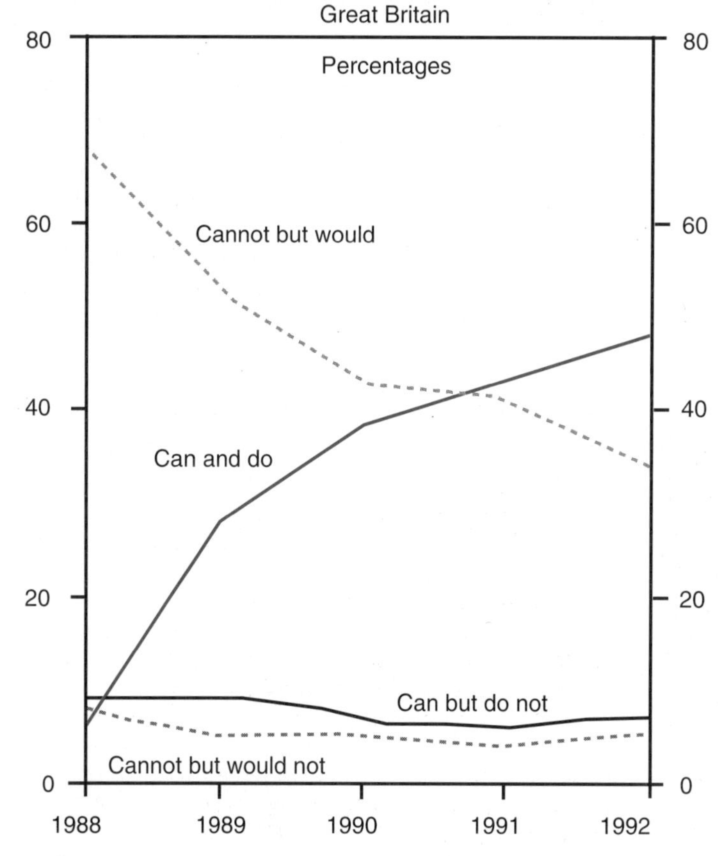

Source: adapted from *MORI/Lex Report on Motoring.*
Figure 35.4 *Use of unleaded petrol*

1. Explain why the government reduced excise duties on unleaded petrol.
2. Analyse, using diagrams, how buyers and sellers in the petrol market responded to the change in duties on petrol.
3. Discuss whether the government should increase the incentive to use unleaded petrol by further widening the price differential between leaded and unleaded petrol. Amongst other issues, your answer needs to take into account:
   (i) what impact an increase in the differential might have on purchases of petrol in the market;
   (ii) whether the way in which the increased price differential was achieved (i.e. increasing the current price of leaded petrol OR reducing the price of unleaded petrol OR some combination of the two) would produce different effects;
   (iii) whether an increased differential would have an effect on other environmental issues such as carbon monoxide emissions;
   (iv) what impact the measure might have on the distribution of income in the UK.

Externalities and the environment

Summary

1. Externalities are created when social costs and benefits differ from private costs and benefits.
2. Externalities can lead to economic inefficiency if the marginal social cost of production is not equal to price.
3. Externalities can also redistribute real income within the economy.

Private and social costs and benefits

A chemical plant may dump waste into a river in order to minimise its costs. Further down the river, a water company has to treat the water to remove dangerous chemicals before supplying drinking water to its customers. Its customers have to pay higher prices because of the pollution.

This is a classic example of EXTERNALITIES or SPILLOVER EFFECTS. Externalities arise when private costs and benefits are different from social costs and benefits. A PRIVATE COST is the cost of an activity to an individual economic unit, such as a consumer or a firm. For instance, a chemical company will have to pay for workers, raw materials and plant and machinery when it produces chemicals. A SOCIAL COST is the cost of an activity not just to the individual economic unit which creates the cost, but to the rest of society as well. It therefore includes all private costs, but may also include other costs. The chemical manufacturer may make little or no payment for the pollution it generates. The difference between private cost and social cost is the externality or spillover effect. If social cost is greater than private cost, then a NEGATIVE EXTERNALITY or EXTERNAL COST is said to exist.

However, not all externalities are negative. A company may put up a building which is not just functional but also beautiful. The value of the pleasure which the building gives to society over its lifetime (the SOCIAL BENEFIT) may well far exceed the benefit of the building received by the company (the PRIVATE BENEFIT). Hence, if social benefit is greater than private benefit, a POSITIVE EXTERNALITY or EXTERNAL BENEFIT is said to exist.

This is often the case with health care provision (an example of a merit good ☞ unit 44). Although one individual will benefit from inoculation against illness, the social benefit resulting from the reduced risk of other members of society contracting the illness will be even greater. Positive externalities could also result from

QUESTION 1 Why might each of the examples in the photographs give rise to positive and negative externalities?

education and training. An individual may benefit in the form of a better job and a higher salary but society may gain even more from the benefits of a better trained workforce.

Activities where social benefit exceeds private benefit are often inadequately provided by a market system. In many cases this results in either state provision or a government subsidy to encourage private provision.

Market failure

The price mechanism allocates resources. Prices and profits are the signals which determine this allocation. However, a misallocation of resources will occur if market prices and profits do not accurately reflect the costs and benefits to society of economic activities.

For instance, in the case of the chemical plant above, the price of chemicals does not accurately reflect their true cost to society. The private cost of production to the manufacturer is lower than the social cost to society as a whole. Because the price of chemicals is lower than that which reflects social cost, the quantity demanded of chemicals and therefore consumption of chemicals will be greater than if the full social cost were charged. On the other hand, if the water company is pricing water to consumers, it will have to charge higher prices to consumers than would have been the case without the chemical pollution. Demand for water and consumption of water will therefore be less than it would otherwise have been without the externality.

The greater the externality, the greater the market failure and the less market prices and profits provide accurate signals for the optimal allocation of resources.

The efficient allocation of resources

Externalities imply that there is an inefficient or sub-optimal allocation of resources. Consider Figure 36.1. Assume that all other markets in the economy are producing at a point where marginal social cost equals marginal social benefit. Marginal cost and benefit curves are drawn on the diagram.

- Marginal cost curves are U-shaped (☞ units 19 and 20). The cost of producing an extra unit of output is assumed to fall to start with, and then to rise according to the principles of diminishing marginal returns, if this is a short run position, or economies and diseconomies of scale if this is the long run.
- Marginal benefit curves are downward sloping. This is because the benefit from consuming an extra unit of output is assumed to decline the more is consumed (the law of diminishing marginal utility ☞ unit 14). The marginal benefit curve is also the demand curve for the product since the demand curve shows the value that consumers place on consuming an extra unit of the good (☞ unit 34).

Figure 36.1 shows that the marginal social cost of production is above the marginal private cost. Therefore, there are external costs of production in this market. The vertical distance between the two lines shows the external

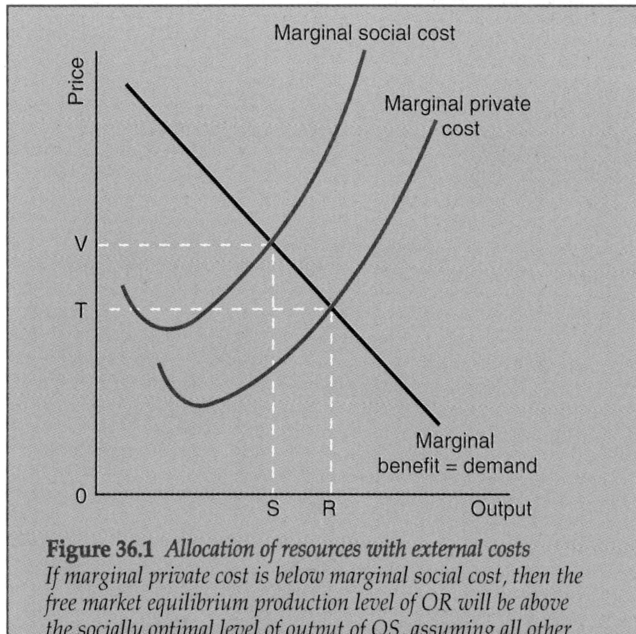

Figure 36.1 *Allocation of resources with external costs*
If marginal private cost is below marginal social cost, then the free market equilibrium production level of OR will be above the socially optimal level of output of OS, assuming all other markets in the economy produce where price equals marginal social cost.

cost at any given level of output. The equilibrium quantity demanded and supplied in a free market would be where marginal private cost equalled marginal benefit. Market signals are such that OR will be produced and sold at a price of OT. However, resources could be allocated more efficiently if marginal benefit were equated with the full cost of production shown by the marginal social cost line. If all costs were taken into consideration, equilibrium quantity produced and consumed would fall to OS whilst price would have to rise to OV. This is what one would expect. Society needs, for instance, to consume less

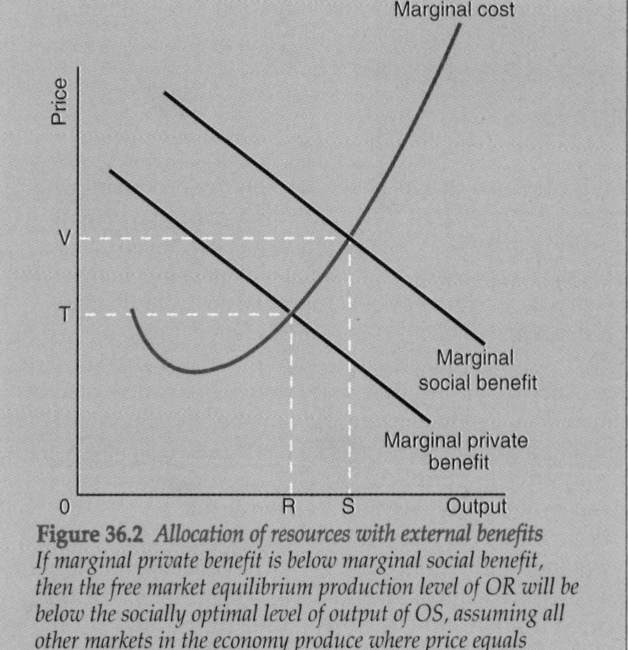

Figure 36.2 *Allocation of resources with external benefits*
If marginal private benefit is below marginal social benefit, then the free market equilibrium production level of OR will be below the socially optimal level of output of OS, assuming all other markets in the economy produce where price equals marginal social cost.

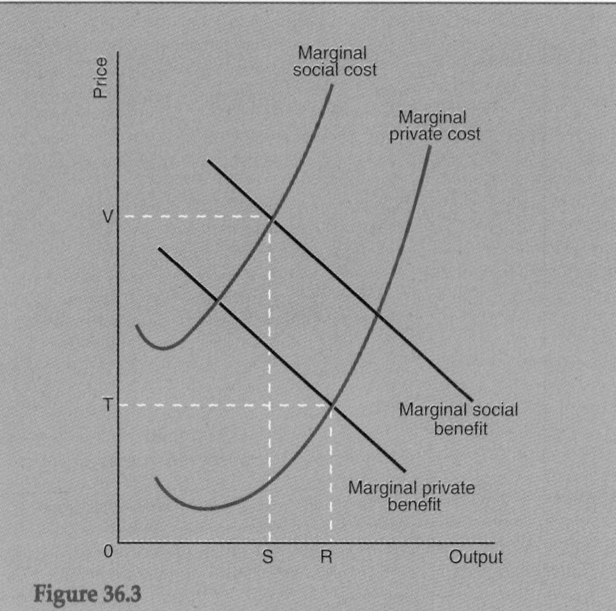

Figure 36.3
If marginal private costs and benefits are below marginal social costs and benefits, then the free market equilibrium production level of OR will be above the socially optimal level of output of OS, assuming all other markets in the economy produce where price equals marginal social cost.

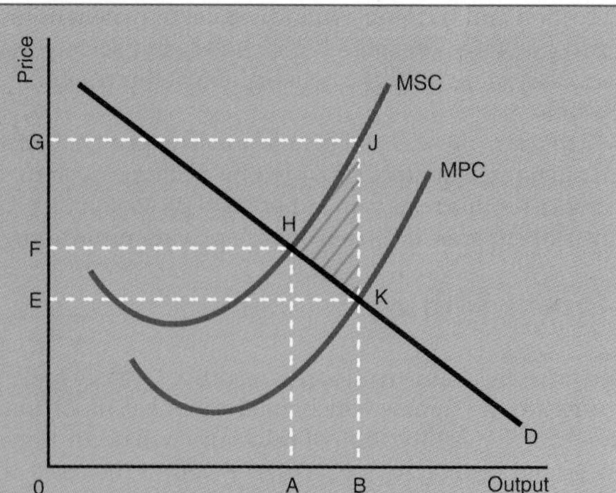

Figure 36.4 *Social cost arising from an externality*
If an industry is perfectly competitive, long run production will take place where price = marginal private cost (MPC) at output OB. This, assuming that all other markets produce where P=MC and that private and social costs and benefits are the same, is also the allocatively efficient level of production. But if there is a negative externality leading to marginal social cost being higher than MPC in this one market, then output should be lower to maximise efficiency. The externality causes overproduction of AB.

chemicals and pay a higher price for them if their production leads to pollution of the environment.

The same analysis can be applied to external benefits. Figure 36.2 shows a situation where marginal private benefits are lower than marginal social benefits. The free market would lead to an underconsumption of the product. Production and consumption of OS should lead to a more efficient allocation of resources than the free market equilibrium point of OR.

Combining these two, Figure 36.3 shows a market where there are both external costs and external benefits. The free market equilibrium output point is OR. The socially optimal point is OS.

Welfare losses

If it is assumed that all other markets are producing where price = marginal cost (the demand or marginal benefit equalling marginal cost condition just discussed), then **allocative efficiency** (☞ unit 34) will exist in a market if it too produces where price = marginal cost. On the other hand, there will be allocative inefficiency if private cost or benefit differs from social cost or benefit and markets are free. The size of this allocative inefficiency can be seen in Figure 36.4. Production should only be at OA if price is set equal to marginal social costs. Overproduction of AB leads to allocative inefficiency. The efficiency loss to society is given by the difference between the cost to society of production of AB (shown by the marginal social cost curve) and the value placed by society on consumption of AB (shown by the demand curve). The difference is the shaded triangle HJK. The greater the difference between marginal social cost and marginal private cost, the greater will be the net social cost shown by the area of the triangle.

It is interesting to note that the welfare loss arising from an external cost is likely to be less under conditions of imperfect competition than under perfect competition. If the market shown in Figure 36.4 were perfectly competitive, then the supply curve of the industry would be the marginal private cost curve and production would take place where demand equalled supply, at the point K

QUESTION 2 According to Professor James Cooper, director of the Cranfield Centre for Logistics and Transportation, manufacturers in Europe are now transporting goods twice as far as they did 30 years ago. Partly this is because of changes in production techniques. Factories and companies have become increasingly specialised. Moreover, the development of just-in-time production techniques leads to more frequent deliveries of smaller consignments, keeping stock levels to a minimum but leading to more journeys.

Greater distances have also come about because of a demand for greater variety of goods by customers. British consumers are no longer satisfied with just being able to buy UK made goods. They want to be able to choose from European, American or Asian products as well.

This growth in transport has led to a large increase in environmental pollution.

Source: adapted from the *Financial Times*, 31.1.1995.

(a) Using a demand curve diagram, explain why there has been a growth in transport in recent years.
(b) Using the same diagram, but now including marginal private and social cost curves, analyse why this growth has probably led to an increase in allocative inefficiency in the economy.

as has already been argued above. There would be a net welfare loss of HJK.

If, on the other hand, the market were supplied by a monopolist, then production would be lower than under perfect competition (☞ unit 39). Monopolists charge a higher price than an industry with competition. Therefore, in Figure 36.4, the free market price under a monopolist would be higher than OE and production would have to be lower than OB. Hence, the welfare loss will be less than HJK. It could be the case that the monopolist will so reduce output that production is to the left of OA. Then, there will be a welfare loss not due to overproduction but to underproduction by the monopolist. Given that there is no supply curve under monopoly (☞ unit 28), it is impossible to say whether the free market equilibrium point will result in overproduction or underproduction.

Distributional effects

Externalities don't just create potential inefficiencies. There are also distributional implications. For instance, in the example under Market Failure above, there is a redistribution of income from consumers of water, who pay too high a price for water, to consumers of chemicals who pay less than the social cost of production.

Assume that the price of chemicals is raised by a tax on output to reflect the marginal social cost of production. This should correct the market failure present in the market for chemicals. However, the water company downstream is still having to pay to clean up the pollution created by the chemical company. Only if the chemical company pays the water company will there also be efficiency in the market for water. In this case it would seem to be relatively simple for an arrangement to be made for the water company to charge the chemical company for the latter's dumping of chemical waste in the river.

But there is likely to be no such simple remedy for local residents and local anglers. Their welfare may be diminished by the polluted river. How do you decide who to compensate in the local community and how much compensation should you give? One answer which economists have suggested involves local residents and local anglers and the chemical company paying the other party an amount which is equal to the welfare loss. If citizen A is willing to pay £5 a year, and citizen B £10 a year and all other citizens £9 985, then the value of a clean river to the local community is £10 000. That is how much:

- either the chemical company should give in compensation to the local community;
- or the local community should pay to the chemical company to stop them polluting the river.

In this example, it might **seem** clear that the chemical company should pay the local community. However, to show that it is not quite as obvious as it first seems, take another example. Assume that the chemical company is making an anti-malaria drug for use in Third World countries. These drugs are cheap to produce and are widely used. If the chemical company compensates local residents for polluting the river, its costs will double and so too will the price of the drug. This will make the drug too expensive for many in the Third World and an extra 50 000 people a year will die. In this case, if might **seem** clear that local residents should pay the chemical company to reduce its pollution.

This shows that there is no simple answer to the question of 'who should compensate whom'. Should it be the customer of the polluting company paying through higher prices for its product, or should it be the individual, group or firm which bribes the company to stop polluting? What is more, it is often impossible to find out who exactly loses how much as a result of an externality. Therefore, taxes or other methods of reducing externalities may lead to over-compensation or under-compensation. These are issues about the distribution of income and resources more than the efficient allocation of resources.

QUESTION 3 In 1994, 30 000 households in the Worcester area were affected by a pollution alert. People complained that their tap water smelled and tasted of paraffin. Severn Trent, the local water company, immediately advised the 100 000 people in the area to stop drinking the water. As it turned out, there was no serious risk from the organic industrial solvent that contaminated the water. However, the alert, during which households were advised not to drink the water, lasted several days. Severn Trent paid compensation of £10 a day to each household for the period of the alert. The final cost would be over £1m. The source of the pollution was traced to a firm on an industrial estate in Wem in Shropshire.

(a) How did the Shropshire firm create a negative externality?
(b) What distributional impact did the spillage have?

Key terms

Externality or spillover effect - the difference between social costs and benefits and private costs and benefits. If net social cost (social cost minus social benefit) is greater than net private cost (private cost minus private benefit), then a **negative externality** or **external cost** exists. If net social benefit is greater than net private benefit, a **positive externality** or **external benefit** exists.
Private cost and benefit - the cost or benefit of an activity to an individual economic unit such as a consumer or a firm.
Social cost and benefit - the cost or benefit of an activity to society as a whole.

Applied economics

Road transport

Britain's roads are becoming increasingly congested. Figure 36.5 shows the explosion of car ownership in the UK since 1951. The motor car has revolutionised the way we live. It has brought immense benefits. At the same time, there have been significant costs.

The private benefits have been so significant that households have been prepared to spend an increasing proportion of household income on motoring (☞ unit 6). Cars are used for work. Some mileage is accounted for by people who use the car as a work tool, such as electricians or sales representatives. Others use it as a quick, convenient and relatively comfortable way to travel to and from work. Public transport is a second best solution for most, involving longer journey times and uncomfortable walks to and waits at bus stops or train stations, followed by a journey on a crowded bus or train. Cars are also in derived demand from other expenditures of the household. The car is used to get the weekly shopping, get the family to a leisure centre or take a relative to catch a train. The car's advantages over public transport include door to door travel, privacy during a journey and, on most journeys made, faster journey times.

The private costs of a motor car differ significantly from those of public transport for the user. As Table 36.1 shows, the single largest cost for most motorists is the purchase of the car, a fixed cost. Road tax, insurance and maintenance, fixed or semi-variable costs, are large too. Petrol, a variable cost, accounts for only approximately one-quarter of the total cost of running a car. When considering whether to make an individual journey, a motorist only considers his or her marginal cost, the cost of the petrol. On public transport, however, the user will almost certainly have to pay part or all of the average fixed cost of the journey. Hence, a single journey by public transport is usually more expensive than a single journey by car.

Cars give rise to significant externalities. First, they cause noise pollution. When new roads are built, such as motorways, houses near the new road are sometimes offered double glazing to cut down the noise pollution they now have to suffer. Second, cars emit harmful gases and particles. Carbon monoxide, for instance, is a greenhouse gas. Lead in leaded petrol can damage the brain, particularly in children. Petrol fumes are blamed by many doctors for a significant rise in asthma in recent years in the UK. Third, cars kill and injure people. It could be argued that this cost is accounted for in the cost of compulsory insurance. However, insurance companies have an incentive to undercompensate victims of road accidents. Lastly, one car can lead to longer journey times for other cars. On a congested road, the marginal car slows down the speed of other cars. At its most extreme, you get 'gridlock' - a situation where there are so many cars on the road that nothing moves. On an uncongested road, one extra car will not give rise to lower speeds for other cars and there is no externality.

It could be argued that motorists already pay others for the externalities they create. Motoring is heavily taxed. Nearly one-third of the annual cost of running a car to the motorist is accounted for by tax, including the tax on petrol. These tax revenues, however, are not used to compensate systematically those who lose out from the negative externalities caused by the motor car. For instance, those who suffer from noise pollution are not compensated by regular payments. No compensation is given to asthma sufferers who might suffer as a result of car fumes. Some individuals are therefore major losers.

It could also be argued that, whilst motorists pay taxes, these payments are only a fraction of the external costs which arise from car use. On this argument, motorists would have to be far more heavily taxed if their contribution to, say, global warming were to be quantified in money terms. Organisations like Friends of the Earth would say that the private motor car is a luxury which society cannot afford. Only public transport can allow travellers to travel at a cost which includes both private and external costs.

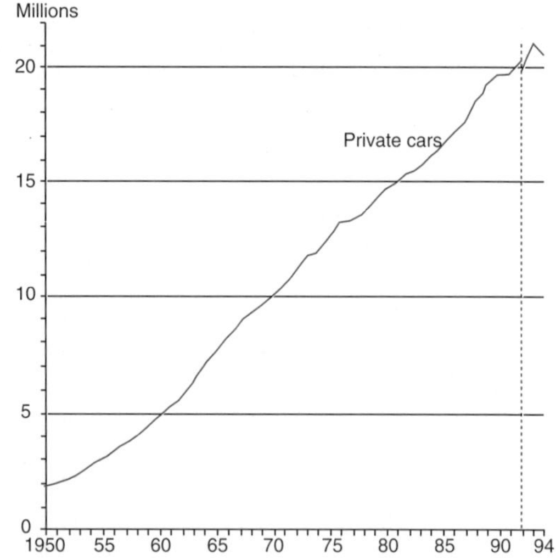

*Discontinuity at 1992 due to a change in the way statistics were calculated.
Source: adapted from CSO, *Transport Statistics*.

Figure 36.5 *Number of private cars licenced: 1950-94*

Table 36.1 *Average household weekly expenditure on motoring (£), 1991*

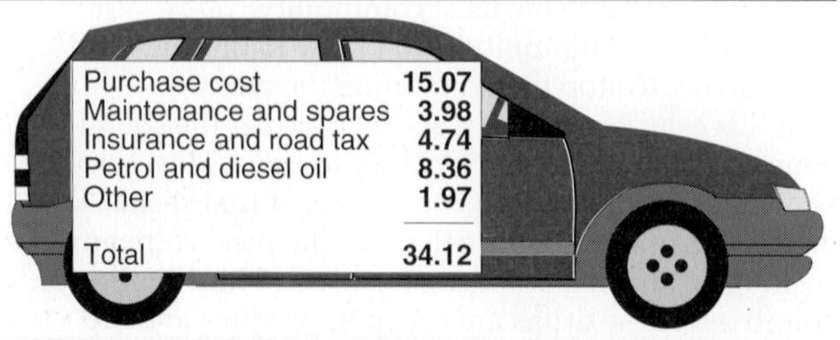

Purchase cost	15.07
Maintenance and spares	3.98
Insurance and road tax	4.74
Petrol and diesel oil	8.36
Other	1.97
Total	34.12

Source: adapted from CSO, Transport Statistics.

The ozone layer

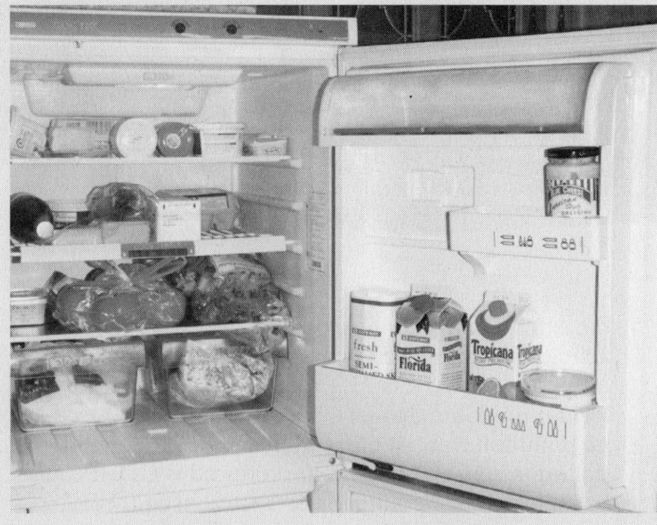

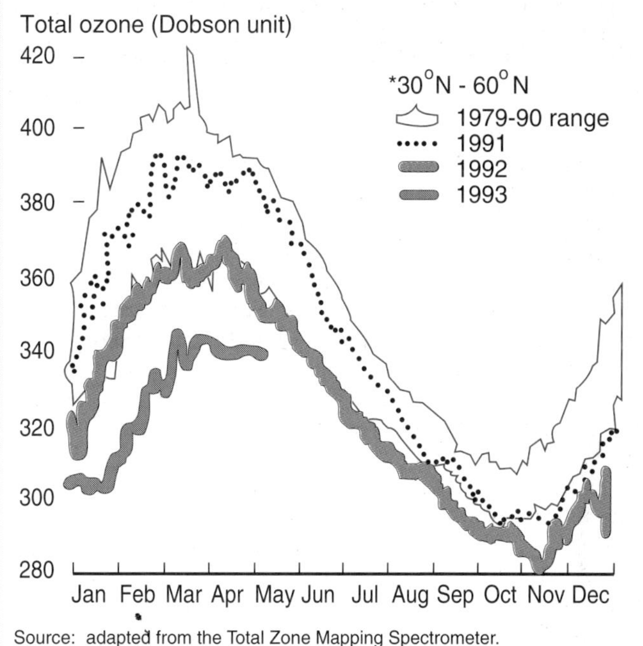

Source: adapted from the Total Zone Mapping Spectrometer.

Figure 36.6 *Declining ozone in the upper atmosphere*

In 1987, the developed countries of the world signed the Montreal Protocol which committed them to phasing out the production of CFCs by the year 2000. Five years later they renegotiated the agreement and promised to phase them out by 1996. By 1992, there had already been a halving of the ozone depletion potential of CFCs since their peak in 1987. CFCs used in aerosols have been virtually eliminated. Production of foam plastic using CFCs has fallen considerably, as has their use in solvents.

However, till 1992, use of CFCs in coolant systems in refrigerators and air conditioning systems in cars had remained constant. This is now changing rapidly. Production of CFCs is being wound down by the major producers. CFC based coolant systems are being replaced by coolant systems using HFCs (hydroflurocarbons). Unfortunately, HFCs contribute to global warming. It is likely that HFCs will be phased out too in the medium term to be replaced by coolant systems based on other gases, such as hydrocarbons. The problem with hydrocarbons is that they are a fire hazard and potentially explosive.

CFC's and the ozone layer

The ozone layer protects the earth from harmful ultraviolet-B radiation by reducing the amount which reaches the earth's surface. This radiation may cause skin cancer in people and have harmful effects on plant and animal life. Chlorofluorocarbons (CFCs) damage the ozone layer, making it thinner. CFCs are typically found in aerosols, foam plastics, coolants used in refrigeration systems and solvents.

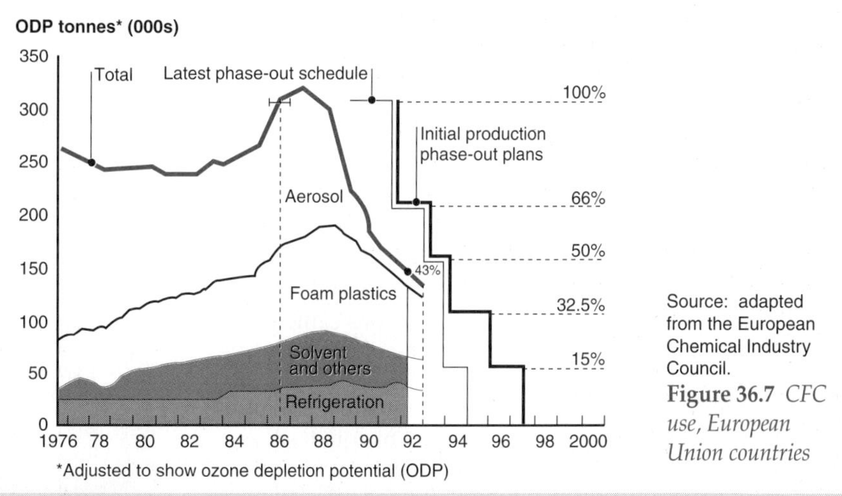

Source: adapted from the European Chemical Industry Council.

Figure 36.7 *CFC use, European Union countries*

1. (a) Explain from the data why the purchasers of certain refridgerators, solvents, foam plastics and aerosols might be paying less than the full social cost for these products.
   (b) Using a diagram, explain why this results in allocative inefficiency.
2. To what extent have intergovernmental actions resolved the problem of negative externalities being created by the production and consumption of aerosols etc.?
3. Discuss whether production of refrigerators should be banned because they give rise to negative externalities.

Externalities and government policy

Summary

1. The problem of externalities can be tackled by government in a number of different ways.
2. One method of control is to impose regulations limiting pollution.
3. Another method is to internalise the externality by extending property rights.
4. A third method is to impose taxes on pollution.
5. A fourth method is to impose regulations but to allow companies to trade permits to pollute amongst themselves.

Market failure revisited

Externalities, or **external costs and benefits**, are one source of **market failure** (☞ unit 36). The free market fails to allocate resources in an optimal way because social costs and benefits differ from private costs and benefits. Market signals lead to a misallocation of resources with too much or too little being produced. Economists argue that governments might have a role in intervening in the market when this occurs. A number of different forms of intervention, and their relative merits, will be discussed in this unit.

Regulation

Regulation is a method which is widely used in the UK and throughout the world to control externalities. The government could lay down maximum pollution levels or might even ban the pollution-creating activities altogether. For instance, in the UK, the Environmental Protection Act 1989 laid down minimum environmental standards for emissions from over 3 500 factories involved in chemical processes, waste incineration and oil refining. The system is policed by HM Inspectorate of Pollution. There are limits on harmful emissions from car exhausts. Cars can be failed on their MOT if exhausts do not meet the standard. 40 years before the MOT regulations came into force, the government banned the burning of ordinary coal in urban areas.

Regulation will only result in an efficient allocation of resources in the economy if the government equates the pollution cost to society of producing an extra unit with the benefit to society of consuming that good after all non-pollution costs have been taken into account. This can be expressed using a diagram, as in Figure 37.1.

- The marginal pollution cost (MPC) line shows the damage done to the environment when output is increased by an extra unit. Cost here is defined as external cost. It is the cost which producers don't pay in the production process but impose on society. The MPC line is drawn upward sloping on the assumption that the extra damage to the environment caused by the activity increases the more is produced. For instance, at output level OA, there is production but pollution levels are so low that an extra unit can be produced at no pollution cost. At output OB, on the other hand, the pollution cost of the last unit produced is OD. It could be that marginal pollution costs are constant. For instance, if the pollution cost of producing an extra barrel of oil from the North Sea were exactly the same whether 1bn were being produced per year or 100bn barrels of oil were being produced per year, then the MPC line would be horizontal.
- The marginal net private benefit line (MNPB) shows the value to society of producing an extra unit of output. It is defined as the difference between the marginal revenue of a firm and its marginal private cost of production (i.e. the profit it makes on the last unit). The firm will want to produce at OC because at this point its profit is maximised. If it produces less than OC, it could

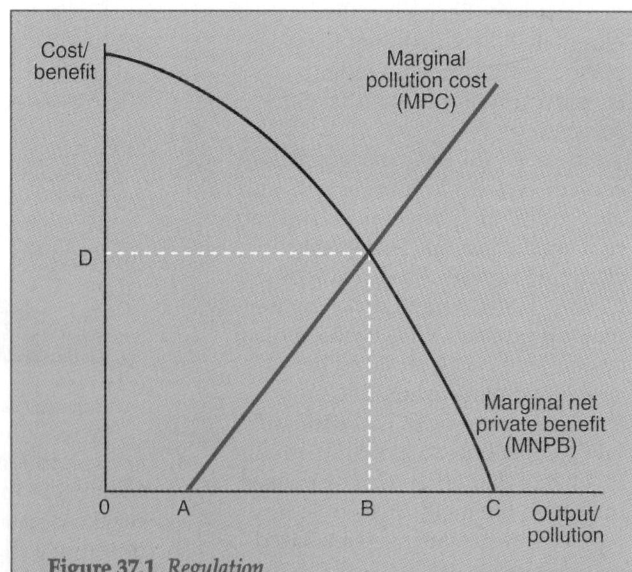

Figure 37.1 *Regulation*
Governments should impose regulations to reduce pollution to OB because this is where the marginal pollution cost (MPC) is equal to the marginal net private benefit (MNPB) for the firm and therefore society.

expand output and gain extra profit. If it produced more than OC, it would make a loss on its last unit of output.

For society, the optimal level of output and pollution is OB. The government should then set limits of OB on the amount of pollution that a firm can create. A ban on pollution would only be economically justifiable if the marginal pollution cost were greater than marginal net private benefit at all levels of output. This situation is shown in Figure 37.2. The marginal pollution cost of producing even one unit of output is OC whereas the benefit to the firm of production is lower at OB. There is no level of output where the MNPB is greater than the MPC.

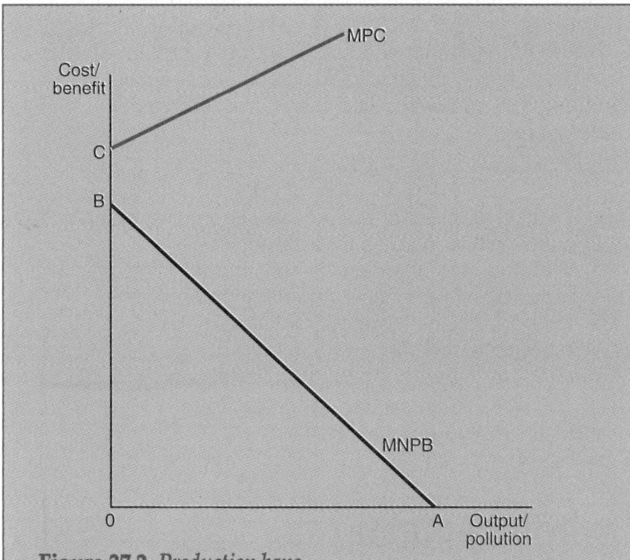

Figure 37.2 *Production bans*
If the marginal pollution cost MPC is higher at all levels of output than any benefit to be gained from production, shown by MNPB, then the government should impose a ban on the pollutant.

QUESTION 1 In 1993, checks on carbon monoxide and other emissions became a compulsory part of the MOT test. Cars failing to meet the standard would fail their MOT. It also became illegal to drive cars exceeding the emission limit. In February 1995, the Minister for Transport, Mr Brian Mawhinney, announced that there would now be regular curbside checks on cars and lorries which were suspected of grossly polluting the environment, particularly in city centres. The checks would be nationwide and would include fines for drivers. Vehicle inspectors would be able to issue a prohibition notice requiring drivers to take their vehicles off the road, or give drivers a specified time to repair the vehicle.

Source: adapted from the *Financial Times*, 27.2.1995.

(a) How, according to the article, is the government intending to tighten up on fuel emissions?

(b) With the help of a diagram, discuss how you might decide whether or not the emission levels for motor vehicles set by the Department of Transport are too lax or too tight.

If physical regulations are to be used to achieve an optimal allocation of resources, the government must be able to assess accurately costs and benefits and act accordingly. If pollution controls are too lax, permitting production above OB in Figure 37.1, then there will be a misallocation of resources. Firms will produce above OB and will have no incentive to reduce pollution levels below the minimum legal requirement. On the other hand, pollution controls might be too strict. If pollution levels were fixed below OB in Figure 37.1, society would make a net gain by an increase in output and the associated increase in pollution.

Extending property rights

If a chemical company lorry destroyed your home, you would expect the chemical company to pay compensation. If the chemical company polluted the atmosphere so that the trees in your garden died, it would be unlikely that you would gain compensation, particularly if the chemical plant were in the UK and the dead trees were in Germany.

Externalities often arise because property rights are not fully allocated. Nobody owns the atmosphere or the oceans, for instance. An alternative to regulation is for government to extend property rights. They can give water companies the right to charge companies which dump waste into rivers or the sea. They can give workers the right to sue for compensation if they have suffered injury or death as a result of working for a company. They can give local residents the right to claim compensation if pollution levels are more than a certain level.

Extending property rights is a way of **internalising the externality** - eliminating the externality by bringing it back into the framework of the market mechanism. Fifty years ago, asbestos was not seen as a dangerous material. Today, asbestos companies around the world are having to pay compensation to workers suffering from asbestosis. They have also had to tighten up considerably on safety in the workplace where asbestos is used. Workers have been given property rights, which enable them to sue asbestos companies for compensation. This has resulted in a fall in the production of asbestos. The marginal net private benefit to the firm of producing asbestos has fallen from $MNPB_1$ to $MNPB_2$ in Figure 37.3 because it has had to pay compensation to victims. The new marginal pollution cost line MPC_2 is horizontal, running along the horizontal axis. This shows that the industry is no longer imposing any external costs on society. The result is that the industry reduces its free market production from OA to OB. An optimal allocation of resources has been achieved.

In some cases, the owner of property rights may have no other option than to pay a polluter to stop polluting rather than the other way round. As explained in unit 36, it would be rational for property owners in a local community to offer to pay a chemical company to stop polluting the local environment if the government was failing to do anything about it. There have been suggestions, for instance, that First World countries should pay Third World countries to stop chopping down tropical rainforests, or to reduce emissions of greenhouse gases.

One advantage of extending property rights is that the government does not have to assess the cost of pollution. It is generally assumed that property owners will have a far better knowledge of the value of property than the government. There should also be a direct transfer of resources from those who create pollution to those who suffer. With regulation, on the other hand, the losers are not compensated whilst polluters are free to pollute up to the limit despite the fact that the pollution is imposing costs on society. One problem is that it is very difficult to extend property rights in many cases. Who, for instance, should pay and who should be compensated for the depletion of the ozone layer or the increase in greenhouse gases in the atmosphere? A second problem is that transfers from polluters to sufferers can be highly imperfect. Asbestos companies, for instance, will not pay claims to asbestos workers unless it can definitely be proved that their medical condition was caused by working with asbestos. The compensation process can take years, and many ex-workers die before their cases are settled. They receive no compensation and the asbestos company has not had to include payment in its costs. This would tend to lead to a continuing overproduction of asbestos. A final problem is that it is often very difficult even for the owners of property rights to assess the value of those rights. For instance, one homeowner might put a far higher value on trees in his or her garden than another homeowner. If a cable company lays cable in the road, cutting the roots of trees in front gardens, should the homeowner who places a high value on trees be compensated more than the homeowner who is fairly indifferent when trees die?

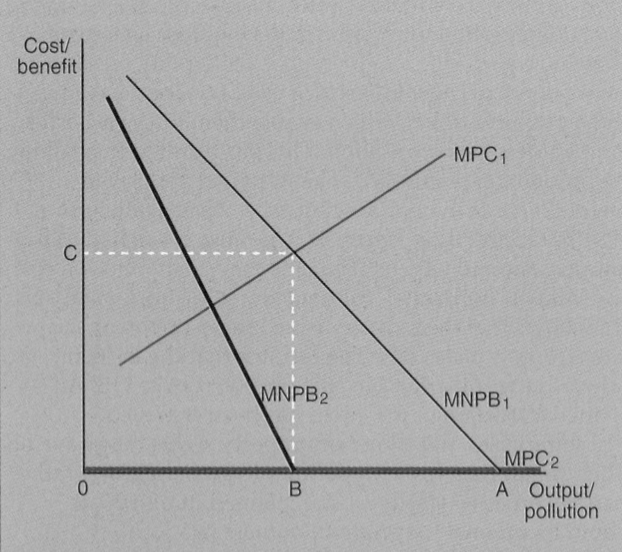

Figure 37.3 *Extending property rights*
If property rights are fully extended, the polluter will have to pay what was before an external cost. The new external cost is therefore zero at all levels of output, shown by the horizontal MPC_2 line running along the bottom axis.

QUESTION 2 The government wants between 50 per cent and 75 per cent of packaging waste to be recycled by the year 2000. In 1993, the UK recycled less than a third of its 7.3m tonnes of household and commercial waste packaging. Rather than impose a statutory scheme, the government asked companies involved to draw up proposals for a voluntary scheme. Industry has pointed out that recycling would be costly. The National Association of Waste Disposal Contractors believes that 'recycling makes people feel good' but recycling most types of domestic waste would use more energy and chemicals than it saves, and is therefore expensive. The Packaging and Industrial Films Association called for a levy on retailers to help pay for recycling proposals. This would add 1p to every £10 food shopping bill with ambitious recycling targets costing £100m to implement. The Confederation of British Industry called for a levy to finance recycling schemes to be raised 'as close as possible to the consumer'.

Source: adapted from the *Financial Times*, 14.4.1994 and 25.4.1994.

(a) Explain whether or not industry is arguing that an externality should be internalised.
(b) With the help of a diagram, discuss whether greater recycling of household and commercial waste would lead to a more optimal allocation of resources.

Environmental taxes

Another solution, much favoured by economists, is the use of environmental taxes. Government needs to assess the cost to society of pollution. It then sets tax rates on polluters so that the tax is equal to the value of the externality. Because costs of production then increase, firms reduce their output and thus reduce their pollution emissions.

In Figure 37.3, the marginal tax rate would be set equal to the marginal pollution cost, MPC_1. The optimal point of production for the firm would be OB. At OB, the firm would have to pay a marginal tax of OC. This would mean that all of the profit from the last unit produced would be paid in pollution tax. The firm would have no incentive to produce a higher output because the extra pollution tax would then outweigh any extra profit made. Firms which were polluting above OB before the imposition of a pollution tax would now have an economic incentive to reduce their pollution levels.

Environmental taxes, like extending property rights, have the advantage that they allow the market mechanism to decide how resources should best be allocated given that pollution is included as a cost of production. Heavy polluters have an incentive to reduce pollution emissions, whilst light polluters, who might have had to cut production under a system of government pollution regulations, can now expand production and pollution but to the benefit of society as a whole.

However, it is difficult for government to place a monetary value on pollution and therefore decide what should be the optimal tax rate. Production of some goods might still have to be banned because their environmental costs were so high that no level of taxes could adequately compensate society for their production.

QUESTION 3 Economic growth fails to take account of the ecological costs of production. 'This could leave us with a world where there's lots of money but dirty air and water and environmental degradation', says Alan Thein Durning, author of *Saving the Forests: What Will it Take?* from the Worldwatch Institute, an environmental group. 'What is needed is a system of 'full-cost pricing' that includes environmental costs in costs of production', he says. This would radically alter cost structures.

A mature forest tree in India would then be worth \$50 000 (£34 000), according to the Centre for Science and Environment in New Delhi. A hamburger produced on pasture cleared from rain forests would cost \$200. One hectare of a Malaysian forest, providing carbon storage services and helping to prevent climate change, would be worth more than \$3 000 over the long term, according to Durning. Environmentalists fear the costs of not moving towards ecological pricing will only become clear after it is too late. Deforestation is accelerating; two-thirds of the planet's original forests have already disappeared. Durning would like full-cost pricing phased in over 10-20 years through user fees (such as charging people to enter national parks), green taxes and tariffs (taxes on imported goods).

Source: adapted from the *Financial Times*, 12.1.1994

(a) Explain why a hamburger costs \$200 according to environmentalists.
(b) With the help of a diagram, explain how Durning's proposed solutions would help bring about an optimal allocation of resources.

Pollution permits

A variation on regulating pollution through direct controls is the idea of pollution permits. Here, the government sets a limit on the amount of pollution permitted. In Figure 37.3, this would be at OB. The government then allocates permits to individual firms or other polluters. These permits can then be traded for money between polluters. For instance, one electricity generating company might have relatively modern power plants which in total let out fewer emissions than its permits allows. It could then sell surplus permits to another electricity company which had older plants which, if allowed to run, would exceed its permits given by the government.

The main advantage of permits over simple regulation is that costs in the industry and therefore to society should be lower than with regulation. Each firm in the industry will consider whether it is possible to reduce emissions and at what cost. Assume that Firm A, with just enough permits to meet its emissions, can reduce emissions by 500 tonnes at a cost of £10m. Firm B is a high polluter and needs 500 tonnes worth of permits to meet regulations. It calculates that it would need to spend £25m to cut emissions by this amount.

- If there was simple regulation, the anti-pollution costs to the industry, and therefore to society, would be £25m. Firm B would have to conform to its pollution limit whilst there would be no incentive for Firm A to cut pollution.
- With permits, Firm A could sell 500 tonnes of permits to Firm B. The cost to society of then reducing pollution would only be £10m, the cost that Firm A would incur. It might cost Firm B more than £10m to buy the permits. It would be prepared to spend anything up to £25m to acquire them. Say Firm A drove a hard bargain and sold the permits to Firm B for £22m. Society would save £15m, distributed between a paper profit of £12m for Firm A and a fall in costs from what otherwise would have been the case for Firm B of £3m.

QUESTION 4 The United Nations Conference on Trade and Development (UNCTAD) has backed the idea of a worldwide market in carbon dioxide emission permits as the most cost-effective way of tackling global warming and transferring resources to poorer nations.

UNCTAD has called for a start to be made by the USA, Japan and the EU, the three largest world emitters of greenhouse gases. Between them, they account for almost 40 per cent of global carbon dioxide emissions. Under the proposal, an overall emissions target would be set. Tradeable carbon dioxide permits would then be issued to these three countries and to developing countries. The three industrialised countries would be issued with fewer permits than they would be expected to hold whilst developing countries would be issued with a surplus of permits. Heavy polluters in the rich countries would then have to buy permits in the open market, expected to be worth more than \$8bn per year. Because of the initial issue of permits, some of those permits would have to bought from developing countries holding a surplus of permits. Thus, in addition to an efficient fall in emissions, there would also be a net transfer of resources from the rich to the poor countries of the world.

US experience of sulphur dioxide emission permits, traded since 1992 shows that the system would let global warming targets be reached more cheaply than through legal regulation or emission charges such as carbon taxes, UNCTAD argues.

Source: adapted from the *Financial Times*, 12.1.1995.

(a) What is a 'pollution permit'?
(b) Using a diagram, explain why pollution permits might 'let global warming targets be reached more cheaply than through legal regulation or emission charges'.
(c) What distributional effects would the UNCTAD proposal have?

Applied economics

Global warming

The environmental problem

During the 1980s, there was a growing awareness that levels of greenhouse gases in the atmosphere were rising, and that this might pose a serious problem for the future of the planet. Global warming, a rise in world temperatures, comes about because greenhouse gases act as a blanket, trapping heat within the Earth's atmosphere.

Figure 37.4 shows the main sources of greenhouse gas emissions in the UK. Three-quarters of the emissions are of carbon dioxide. Industries, particularly coal fired power stations, are the main polluters. Households are relatively unimportant in producing greenhouse gases directly, although they are the ultimate source of the problem because they consume the products that industry produces.

A rise of a few degrees in world temperatures sounds very little. However, it would be enough to cause major shifts in the desert zones of the world. Many of the major wheat producing areas, such as the American plains, would become deserts. Old deserts, such as the Sahara, would become fertile in time. However, the transition costs to the world economy would be substantial. A second problem would be that there would be some melting of the polar icecaps, with a consequent rise in sea levels. With a 3 degree centigrade rise in world temperatures, a rise at the bottom end of recent predictions, there would be an increase in sea levels of 30cm. This would be enough to flood areas such as the east coast of England, the Bangladesh delta and the Maldive Islands. Sea defences and dykes could and probably would be built, but the cost to the world economy could run to tens of billions of pounds.

Progress to date

It is easy to assume that there is a direct link between growth in the economy and pollution; the higher the income of a country, for instance, the higher its pollution levels. However, the evidence does not bear this out. Figure 37.5 shows how certain emissions have fallen as incomes have increased in the rich industrialised nations of the world. Figure 37.6 shows how carbon dioxide emissions have fallen between 1971 and 1992 in the UK.

There are two main reasons why higher growth may lead to less rather than more pollution. First, industry may, by itself, move over to less polluting forms of technology. For instance, over time, coal fired power stations have become more efficient, producing more electricity from a tonne of coal. If efficiency gains are faster than the rate of growth in the economy, economies can enjoy both higher incomes and lower pollution.

Second, governments have been implementing policies to reduce the amount of pollution. Some of these policies have come about because of agreed action on an international scale. For instance, the Montreal Protocol signed in 1987 committed 93 countries, including the major industrialised nations of the world, to phasing out the use of CFCs. The Rio Summit of 1992 led to the industrialised nations committing themselves to reducing greenhouse gas emissions by the year 2000 to their 1990 levels.

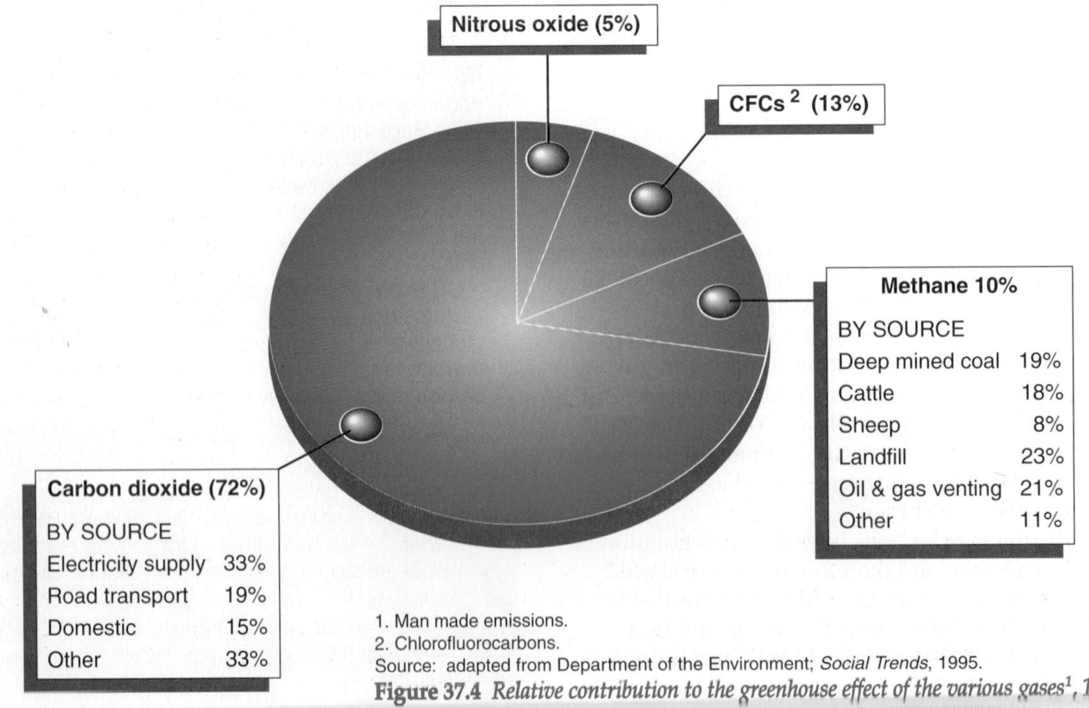

1. Man made emissions.
2. Chlorofluorocarbons.
Source: adapted from Department of the Environment; *Social Trends*, 1995.

Figure 37.4 *Relative contribution to the greenhouse effect of the various gases[1], 1992*

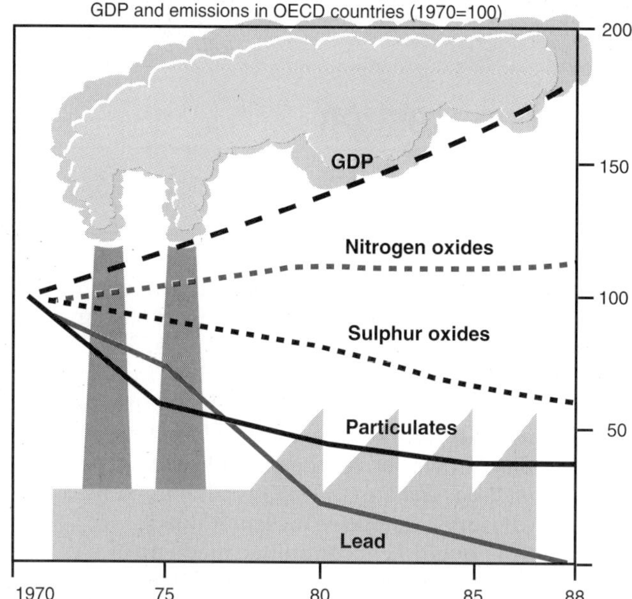

Source: adapted from OECD 1991; US Environmental Protection Agency.

Figure 37.5 *GDP and emissions in OECD countries (1970=100)*

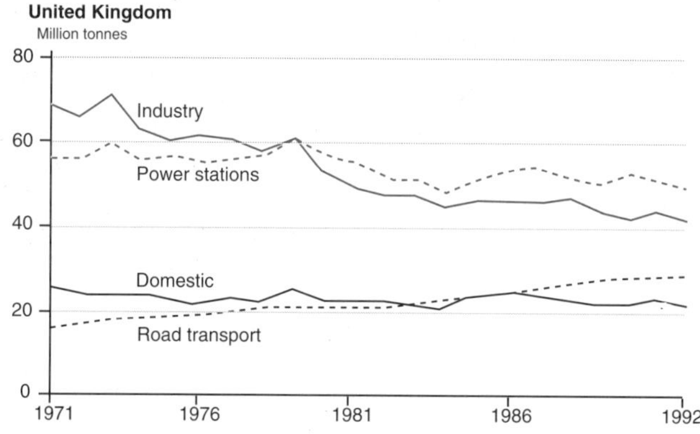

Source: adapted from National Environmental Technology Centre.

Figure 37.6 *Carbon dioxide emissions, UK: by source*

UK policies

The UK government has adopted a piecemeal approach to ensuring that it meets its greenhouse gas emission targets. Figure 37.6 shows that the single most important contributors to emissions in the UK are power stations, including power stations using deep-mined coal. Since the early 1990s, the government has done nothing to discourage a major shift in electricity power generation from older coal fired power stations to new, highly efficient gas-fired power stations. In the 1970s and 1980s, with the coal, gas and electricity industries owned by the state, the electricity industry was not allowed to burn gas. This was because the government needed a market for the coal being produced. In the early 1990s, government policy changed. British Coal was forced to close a large number of pits, reducing output, in order to meet government profit targets. One justification for this was the need for the UK to move to more environmentally friendly fuels.

The second most important contributor to carbon dioxide emissions is the motor car. The government is faced with the major problem of congestion on British roads. The solution of the 1960s, 1970s and 1980s was to build more roads. In the 1990s, there has been a major switch in policy with government realising that an alternative solution to congestion, which would also help the UK achieve its CO_2 target, is to stabilise or even reduce the number of cars on British roads. In his April 1993 Budget, the Chancellor announced that he would increase the tax on fuel by 3 per cent more than the rate of inflation for the foreseeable future. This will increase the real cost of motoring, all other things being equal, and hence should reduce car use. It should also be an economic incentive for motorists to buy more fuel efficient cars, again helping to reduce CO_2 emissions. The government has also cut its proposed road building programme.

A third policy which the government has implemented is to impose VAT on domestic fuel in 1994. Although demand for domestic fuel is relatively price inelastic, it will discourage some consumption of gas, oil and electricity and increase the incentive for households to insulate their homes to a higher standard.

There are a number of other policies which the government could implement. It could, for instance, regulate emissions from major producers of greenhouse gases. This would tend to impose heavier costs on the few larger easily regulated polluters than on thousands or even millions of smaller polluters who would probably escape regulation.

The government could impose a system of tradeable permits, as has already happened in the United States. Again, this would tend to cover only some of the contributors to the problem, imposing higher costs on them.

Another alternative, which has been put forward by the European Union, is the introduction of a carbon tax. This tax would be be imposed on all users of fossil fuels. The amount of the tax would differ from fuel to fuel depending upon how much carbon each releases into the atmosphere. Coal, for instance, would be taxed more heavily than gas because coal releases more carbon per unit of energy. The EU also proposes another tax on the energy content of all non-renewable energy forms. Hence, wind power would pay no tax. Nuclear energy would pay the energy part of the tax. Coal would pay both the carbon tax and the energy tax. This is designed to reflect the differing environmental costs of all forms of energy.

A final alternative is to introduce road pricing, with prices at a level which would reduce the number of miles travelled on British roads. This would then indirectly cut down greenhouse gas emissions from cars. From an economic viewpoint, the government's pragmatic mix of policies is unlikely to achieve the optimal solution for the reduction of emissions. That would require a carefully thought out strategy for reducing emissions from polluters who could cut emissions at lowest cost per tonne. However, such a solution might be difficult to implement politically.

Solving the problem of congestion

Building new roads

The UK government has a long term programme of improving existing roads and building new roads. In 1994, for instance, the Department of Transport had 270 road schemes which were at the planning stage, including the widening of the M25 and M6, and the building of two new motorways around Birmingham, as well as many bypass schemes for villages or towns.

The transport lobby in the UK, including motoring organisations such as the AA and the RAC, as well as commercial organisations like the British Road Federation, believes that building or improving roads is the best long term solution to problems of congestion. Bypass schemes and motorways take traffic away from urban areas, reducing pollution. Better roads also lead to shorter journey times, resulting in a massive saving for the economy as transport costs fall.

The environmental lobby, such as Transport 2000, argues that building new roads simply helps to create problems. It argues that shorter journey times encourage businesses and people to make more journeys. Some switch from other forms of transport, such as from rail to car. Others increase the number or length of journeys made. For instance, workers have tended to move away from their place of work over the past 40 years. A 1994 report, *Trunk Roads and the Generation of Traffic*, by the Standing Advisory Committee on Trunk Road Assessment, a government committee made up of independent transport experts, concluded that additional or 'induced traffic can and does occur, probably quite extensively, though its size and significance is likely to vary widely in different circumstances' when new roads were built.

Toll motorways

A Conservative government is committed to the privatisation of as much of the public sector as possible. Privatising roads can be achieved in limited circumstances. The main proposal at the moment is to invite private construction companies to bid for contracts to build motorways which they themselves would pay for, and then allow them to charge tolls to motorway users. Motorway tolls, such as are found in France and Italy, have the additional advantage that they can be set at levels which allow the free flow of traffic on the motorway. The higher the potential congestion, the higher the toll charged. More sophisticated tolls can be used. If a particular stretch of motorway is too congested on a particular day or at a particular time of day, the motorway owners could charge a higher toll to relieve the congestion.

Proponents of the scheme argue that toll motorways will relieve congestion of existing roads. Critics argue that motorway tolls will discourage people from using the motorways and encourage them to continue using the existing untolled road network. They will also create new traffic, further blocking up existing roads as motorway traffic leaves the tolled motorway to complete its journey.

The first tolled motorway, the Northern Orbital round Birmingham, was at planning permission stage in 1995, to be built by the end of the century.

Road pricing

The government is aiming to begin implementing a system of road pricing by 1998. There are many possible systems for road pricing. The favoured solution is for cars to be fitted with some sort of meter. This would either be fed with pre-paid cards, like telephone cards, with points which would be used up as the car went along. Or the meter would be read on a regular basis, say once a year when a car was given its MOT. The motorist would be billed after the mileage had been done. The meters would be activated by beacons on the road side or gantries over the road. Motorways would initially be targeted, with the government stating in 1994 that cars might be charged 1.5p a mile with trucks being charged 4.5p a mile. In theory, the system could be very sophisticated. The beacons could measure the amount of road congestion at any point in time and charge more the greater the congestion. Charges would then be set to discourage motorists from driving along congested roads. There are three major problems with road pricing. First, there are doubts about the technology. Will a system be found which could start working in 1998? Second, the technology would be expensive to introduce and the system would have running costs. Third, there could be an enormous political backlash for any government which imposed the measure. Motorists regard roads as 'free' and would bitterly resent having to pay for their use.

Motorway charges

The government has suggested that it might impose a motorway tax of, say, £15 a year for any car wishing to use the motorway system. The Swiss have used this system for a number of years now. Motorway users would have to display a tax disc. Although the move would be mainly aimed at raising tax revenues to pay for the government's road building programme, it would also have the effect of discouraging the occasional motorway user from using already congested motorways.

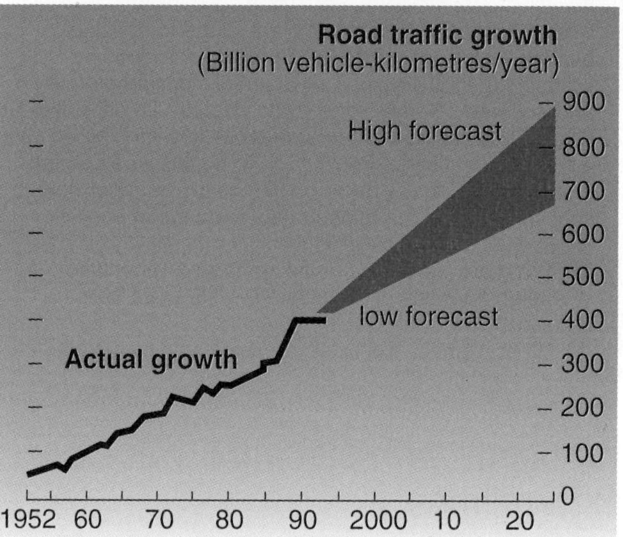

Source: adapted from HMSO, *Transport and the Environment*. Cmnd 2674, 1994.

Figure 37.7 *Road traffic growth*

Such insight could re-write history

From Mr Colin S Jones

Sir, The standing advisory committee on trunk road assessment (Sactra) offers us a valuable insight in suggesting that new roads generate new traffic. It is a pity that the railway builders a century and a half ago did not refrain from laying down new railway lines for fear that they might generate new economic activity. Or indeed, the canal builders in the 18th century.

Come to think of it, it is a pity that the same insight was not shared by electronic engineers, chemists, pharmaceutical scientists, steel makers, oil prospectors, or indeed the explorers of the 15th, 16th and 17th centuries.

Source: the *Financial Times*, 22.12.1994.

Increasing fuel duties

The government is committed to raising duties on petrol and other fuels by 5 per cent a year in real terms for the foreseeable future. The price of petrol could double in ten years. This would increase the cost of motoring, discouraging motorists from travelling by car.

The advantages of increasing duties include the fact that there would be no extra cost of collecting the taxes since duties are already being paid. The increased tax is politically acceptable since it is being phased in gradually and most motorists have little understanding of how little of the cost of a litre of petrol is actually the cost of petrol, and how much is tax. It would also encourage the development and purchase of more fuel efficient cars, helping the UK meet its greenhouse gas emission targets. The main disadvantage is that fuel taxes fail to distinguish between use of cars on congested roads and on empty roads. They work by discouraging all travel.

A new government has just been elected and has commissioned a report on the problem of congestion on UK roads. The government wants to maintain freedom of movement in the UK. It wishes to reduce congestion rather than limiting the number of journeys being made by motorists. At the same time, it is committed to reducing carbon emissions by the year 2000 to their 1990 levels. It wants to consider measures which would help it achieve this target. The government is also interested in finding ways of funding its expenditure. Write a report outlining possible solutions to the problem.

1. **(a) Outline briefly the nature of the problem. You may want to use material in units 6 and 7 as well as the information in this unit to help you do this.**
   (b) What might be the optimal level of road traffic?
2. **Summarise the main possible solutions, explaining briefly in one or two sentences how each would achieve its objectives.**
3. **Which solution or combination of solutions would you recommend? In your answer, you need to consider:**
   (a) how far each solution would enable an optimal level of road traffic to be achieved;
   (b) the economic cost of implementing differing solution(s);
   (c) the distributional effects of differing solution(s), e.g. the different impact it would have on high and low income households.

unit 38 Cost-benefit analysis

Summary

1. Cost-benefit analysis is a technique which attempts to evaluate the social costs and benefits of an economic decision.
2. Social costs and benefits may differ from private costs and benefits.
3. It is often difficult and sometimes impossible to place a price on externalities.
4. Cost-benefit analysis is often used to assess public sector investment projects.

Market failure

In a free market, decisions are based upon the calculation of **private costs and benefits**. However, there are many markets where significant **externalities** exist (☞ unit 36). This means that there are significant costs or benefits which are unlikely to be taken account of by the private economic decision maker.

COST-BENEFIT ANALYSIS is a procedure which takes into account all costs and all benefits (i.e **social costs and benefits**). Its purpose is to give guidance in economic decision making. It is used particularly by governments to evaluate important investment projects.

Costs and benefits

It is relatively easy to place a value on private costs and benefits. For instance, the government may want a toll motorway to be built round Birmingham. The company which builds and operates the motorway will be able to calculate the financial cost of constructing the road. This is the private cost to the operating company. It will also be able to calculate the revenues to be earned from tolls. These will be its private benefits. If the private benefits exceed private costs the motorway will be profitable and the operating company will be prepared to build the road.

However, there will be other costs and benefits associated with the project. These are the externalities of the road. For instance, residents near the motorway will suffer from pollution, including noise pollution. The motorway may generate more traffic on some roads joining the motorway, again increasing pollution to local residents. The motorway may go through areas of outstanding natural beauty or take away areas which have been used by local people for recreational activities such as walking. Habitats of rare species may be destroyed. Sites of historical interest may be lost. On the other hand, jobs and wealth may be created locally as industry is attracted to the area by the new motorway. Car and lorry drivers may save time using the new motorway. Traffic may be taken off some local roads, relieving congestion.

These externalities are very important costs and benefits which could be completely ignored by the operating company if it operated in a pure free market. In a cost-benefit analysis the company would attempt to place a value on these externalities in order to calculate the social cost and social benefit of the project and proceed only if social benefit exceeded social cost.

QUESTION 1 Leigh Interests is currently Britain's largest waste treatment group. Its headquarters at Walsall in the West Midlands has been the subject of much controversy in recent years. The local council and local residents would like to see the treatment plant and a large landfill site for industrial (including solid toxic) waste closed down. The treatment plant, close to housing estates, deals with some of the most hazardous by-products of industry such as arsenic, cyanide, mercury and antimony. Some of the liquid waste most difficult to deal with is blended together in tanks and then piped into a disused coal mine. Permission to do this was granted after a public inquiry back in 1978 because impermeable clay surrounding the mine makes seepage impossible.

(a) What are the likely private costs and benefits to Leigh Interests of processing waste at its Walsall plant?
(b) What might be the externalities caused by the plant?

Problems with placing a value on externalities

The value of many externalities is difficult to estimate. For instance, assume that, as a result of the building of the motorway, 5 million travellers every year save on average 30 minutes each on their journey times around Birmingham. In a cost-benefit analysis, a value would need to be placed on the 2½ million hours saved. However, it is unclear what value should be given to each hour since there is no obvious market in which a price is set for the time. A high cost estimate would assume that the time should be valued as if the travellers could have earned money during that time. This might give an estimate of £10 per hour at an average annual wage for the typical motorway user of £20 000. On the other hand, it could be assumed that the traveller places almost no value on the time saved. It could be just 50p per hour. Comparing these two estimates, we get a high estimate of £25 million and a low estimate of £1.25 million.

Even more difficult is how to place a value on a human life. Assume that the motorway takes traffic off other roads and as a result 5 fewer people are killed in road accidents each year. The value of a life today in a court case involving accidents is mainly determined by the expected earnings of the deceased. For instance, if a company director earning £500 000 per annum were killed in a road crash, together with her chauffeur earning

£10 000 per year, then all other things being equal (age, family circumstances etc.) the family of the company director would receive far more compensation than the family of the chauffeur. These values, however, are open to much debate.

Other intangibles, such as pollution and illness, are very difficult to value in money terms. Even the values placed on private costs and benefits may be difficult to estimate. For instance, the operating company may charge £2 for a journey from one end of the motorway to the other. But that may not necessarily reflect the cost to the operating company of the journey. It may include a large element of monopoly profit, or it may be subsidised by the government to encourage people to use the motorway. It may therefore be necessary for the cost-benefit analysis to estimate a **shadow price** for the journey - a price which more accurately reflects the cost to the operating company of providing the service.

QUESTION 2 The Department of Transport plans to build an 11-mile stretch of dual carriageway close to the existing A27 north of Lewes in East Sussex. The current A27 is a travellers' nightmare. Mr Robert Caffyn, a local industrialist, said: 'Tourists enjoy Eastbourne when they arrive but complain bitterly about the last part of the journey. Large employers have left the town largely because of poor access.' The county council, which supports the scheme, wants the extension because it will help the local tourist industry, the county's main industry, to help fill the small industrial estates in Hastings, Lewes, Newhaven and Polegate, and to boost the only port, Newhaven.

There is fierce local opposition, however. Mr Nick Davies, secretary of the A27 Action Group, said the road would cost £70m and be the biggest construction project ever in the area. He said the road 'would be polluting in terms of noise and atmospheric discharge. It would cause considerable damage to our homes, our countryside and our health. Above all, the road is unnecessary. Recent research suggests that motorways do not reduce congestion but create new traffic. This road would pull traffic through our villages.'

Source: adapted from the *Financial Times*.

(a) Explain the external costs and benefits of the proposed A27 road scheme.
(b) How might you estimate a shadow price for each of these costs and benefits?

Benefit across time

Calculations are further complicated by the fact that costs and benefits will occur at different points in time. A Channel Tunnel rail link, for instance, could still be carrying passengers in the year 2100 and beyond. Many of our major rail links today in the UK were first built over 100 years ago.

A value has to be given to future costs and benefits. Economic theory suggests that £1 of benefit in 20 years' time is worth considerably less than £1 of benefit today (☞ unit 55). This is because £1 today could be saved or invested. Each year that passes it should be worth more. For instance, if the rate of interest (or rate of return, or rate of discount) is 10 per cent per annum then £1 today is worth £1.10 in one year's time, £1.21 in two years' time, £1.33 in three years' time, £10.83 in 25 years' time and £117.39 in 50 years' time (these figures are calculated using compound interest). It must therefore be true that a benefit of £117.39 available in 50 years' time is only worth £1 today if the rate of return is 10 per cent per annum.

So in cost-benefit analysis, all future costs and benefits need to be revalued using a rate of discount. There are two ways of doing this (☞ unit 55). Either a rate of discount is assumed and all costs and benefits are calculated as if they occurred today. This is known as calculating present values. Saying that £117.39 available in 50 years' time is worth £1 today is an example of this technique. Alternatively the internal rate of return on the project can be calculated. So if we knew that £1 had been invested today and the one and only benefit were £117.39 which would be paid in 50 years' time, then we would know that the rate of return on the project would be 10 per cent per annum.

QUESTION 3 A rail link could be built to last either 25 years or 50 years. It has been estimated that it would cost £100 million to build it for 25 years and £200 million for 50 years. In 25 years' time the cost of upgrading it to make it last another 25 years would be £900 million.

(a) If the rate of discount (or rate of interest or rate of return) were 10 per cent, would it be cheaper to build it to last for 25 years and repair it, or build it to last for 50 years?
(b) Would your answer would be different if the rate of discount were 5 per cent? Explain why.

Note: you might find it helpful to read unit 55 if you have difficulty with this question.

A critique of cost-benefit analysis

Cost-benefit analysis is a procedure where:
- all costs and benefits, both private and social, are identified;
- then a value is placed on those costs and benefits, wherever possible in monetary terms.

The technique is used mainly where it is assumed that market failure is present. Calculating all costs and benefits would seem to be a more rational way of evaluating an important investment project than relying upon projections of private profit or even having no facts and figures to consider.

However, cost-benefit analysis can be a very imprecise procedure. It is difficult to place a value on certain important costs and benefits and the results depend crucially upon the rate of discount of future costs and benefits used.

So the results of cost-benefit analysis should be used with caution. The assumptions made in the analysis should be explicit. Ideally a range of results should be calculated showing what would happen to costs and benefits if different assumptions were made. Social costs and benefits which cannot be valued in monetary terms should be clearly stated.

If this is done, cost-benefit analysis can be a useful tool in the evaluation of investment projects. But it should be recognised that it is only one piece of evidence amongst many and it could well be that other considerations, such as political considerations, prove ultimately to be more important.

Key terms

Cost-benefit analysis - a procedure, particularly used by governments to evaluate investment projects, which takes into account social cost and benefits.

Applied economics

The Channel Rail link

The French had finished building a dedicated railway line from Paris to the Channel Tunnel a year before the Eurostar trains first began making the journey from London to Paris. At the same time, the British had not yet even decided on a route for their new dedicated line from the Channel Tunnel to London, let alone decided who should build it or when. In January 1995, the government finally announced what is likely to be the actual route, shown in Figure 38.1, which skirts the east of London before finishing at St Pancras. In 1988, the government had announced a different route which went through the south east of London. Many in Kent had argued that no link at all should be built. Should the link be built and which is the right route? Cost-benefit analysis can help answer these questions.

The private costs and benefits of building a Channel Rail link are relatively easy to list. A private consortium would build the rail link at an estimated cost of £2.6bn, in January 1994. The consortium would then charge railways companies to run trains along the track. The operators of the Eurostar trains would only be one amongst many train companies who might want to use the track. If the London to Paris or London to other continental destinations train services were to become very popular, other companies such as Virgin might well want to run their own train services along these routes. It will certainly be the case that local train companies running trains into London from the south east will want to use the track because the existing network is often overcrowded. So the private costs include the construction of the line, maintenance of the line once built and the cost of running trains along the line. The private benefits are best measured by adding up the total fare revenue paid by passengers. Some of this money will be kept by the train companies. The rest will go to the consortium which has built the track. There may also be increased **consumer surplus** (☞ unit 14). The extra 30 minutes travel time saved by the new route will be a benefit to travellers on which they will place a value. Busy, highly-paid business travellers will increase their consumer surplus more than tourist day trippers. In the cost-benefit study, a value should be placed on this time saved which equates to increased consumer surplus.

However, there are many external costs and benefits. One external cost is the environmental damage caused by the line. Inevitably, the line will go through unspoilt areas of countryside which local residents value. On a long term basis, there will be noise pollution from passing trains and vibration to local buildings. Houses very near the line will probably be offered free double glazing. Putting a price on such pollution is very difficult. Some houses will be demolished and homeowners will receive compensation for the market value of their house. However, some people place a higher value on their house than the market value. They may, for instance, have lived there all their lives and have an attachment to the property. The consortium building the line will not compensate them for this. Another external cost is 'planning blight'. Homeowners near the line find that they cannot sell their houses because of the fear of any potential purchaser of the noise pollution which will be generated. Equally, homeowners along the route suffer from stress and anxiety, not knowing what will happen and how the line and its construction will eventually affect them.

There are many external benefits though. The route should cut the number of passengers travelling by road and particularly by air to Paris and other destinations. Reduced road and air traffic will lead to less congestion and pollution costs associated with these modes of transport. Residents around Heathrow in London or Orly in Paris will receive a benefit as a result which should be included in the cost-benefit appraisal of the Channel Link.

All these costs and benefits need to be valued across time. The main economic reason given by the British government for refusing to build the Channel Link by 1995 was that the rate of return on the project was too low. The original plan, with the link running into Kings Cross from the south, would have cost anything up to £5bn to build. This was because the line would have demolished many houses and there would have been a large section of expensive to build underground line from the south of London up to a terminal at Kings Cross. It

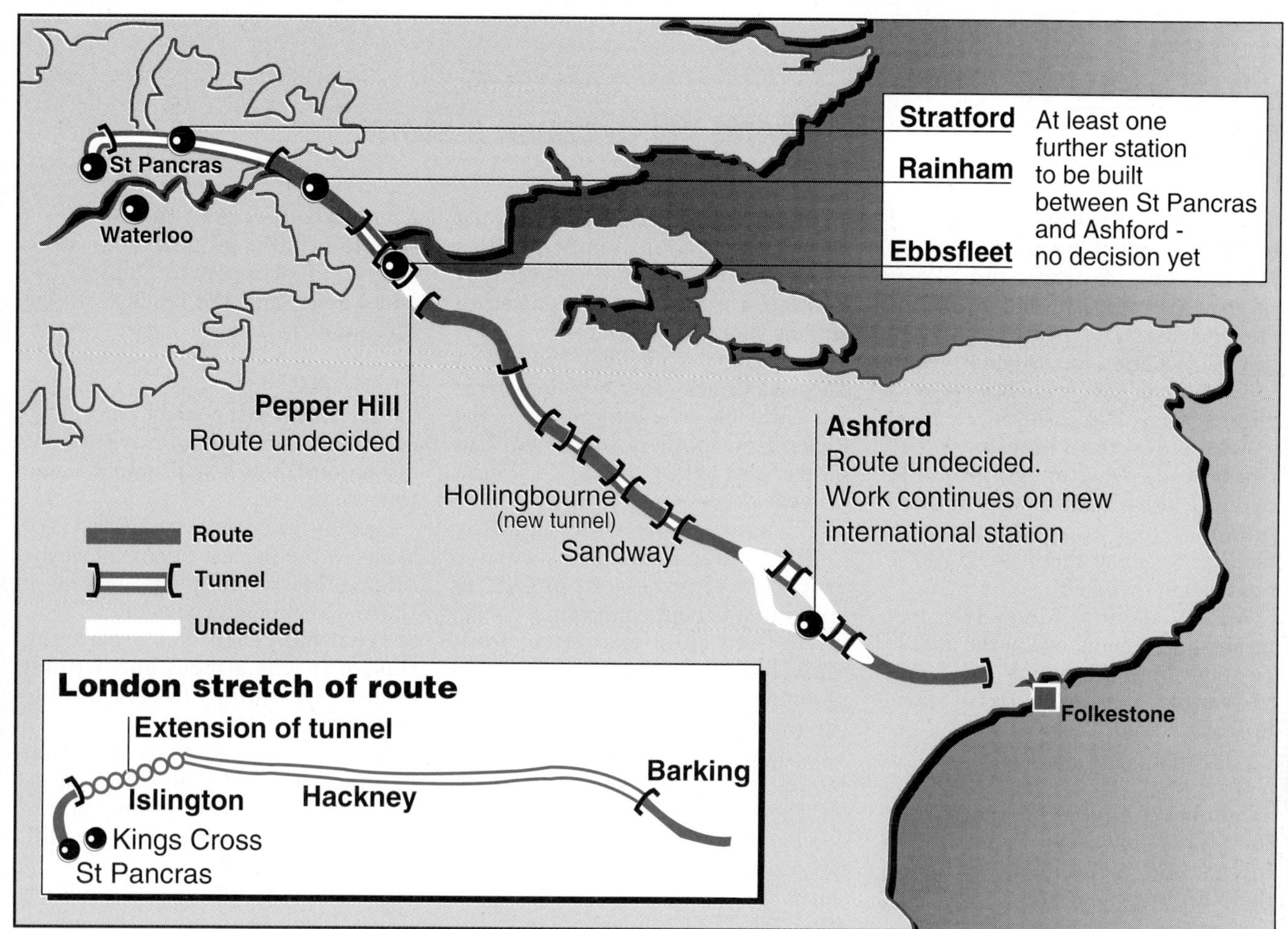

Figure 38.1 *Final route for fast rail link between London and the Channel Tunnel*

would then have been built in the mid-1990s. The rate of return on this proposal was very low. There were substantial start up costs of at least £5bn. The revenues from charging for trains to be run over the tracks would have only built up slowly as the Eurostar service built up its business. The prediction was that there would be far more passengers and far more trains being run in 2005 than in 1995.

The new plan has a much higher rate of return. There are now predicted to be much more substantial revenues in the early years of the project because Eurostar will have already had 7 years to build up a clientele. The initial capital cost is much lower. Even so, the government will have to provide some form of subsidy for the construction because the rate of return is still below what could be earned by a company in a normal investment project.

The French built their link in the first half of the 1990s. Were they wrong to do so? Certainly, the private rate of return on the project will be very low. In 1994-95 when the line first began to be used, it was vastly underutilised. But the French prefer to take a much longer term view. So many infrastructure projects in the past have proved to be commercially unviable to begin with. Everything from the M1 motorway to the Victoria line on the London underground to the Suez canal would never have been built if the private commercial rate of return in the first years of the project had been the most important criterion. The French instead point out that decisions made today can have enormous implications for the economy in 25 or 50 years. In particular, the French want to attract industry to the high unemployment northern France. The Channel Tunnel and the Rail Link could be the catalyst for attracting much needed investment by British or, say, German companies wanting to sell into the British market from a low cost base in northern France. Assume that each unemployed worker costs the French state £5 000 per year in benefits and lost taxes and that 100 000 jobs are created in ten years time in northern France as a result of the rail link. The saving to the French government would then be £500 million per year. The French believe that too narrow a concentration of private costs and benefits results in gross underinvestment in infrastructure in the economy. Many external costs and benefits are difficult to quantify. The French are much more prepared than their English counterparts to place a high value on these potential external benefits.

Growing pains cause a storm

Retired Robert Sawtell has shopped in Black Country towns like Dudley, Halesowen, Tipton and West Bromwich for nearly half a century. He and his wife Phyllis went to different centres for different goods long before Merry Hill was a glimmer in a planner's eye.

And news that London based Chelsfield developers want to expand the complex by a third prompted him to pen a warning to the *Express & Star* that it could be the final nail in their coffins.

'Money spent at Merry Hell just means profit going out of the area to be spent on millionaires' row', says 85-year-old Mr Sawtell, of Glynfarm Road, Quinton.

Destroying

'If you haven't got a car you can't get there. It's just destroying life in towns, and the majority of shops there are big multiples so the local community gets nothing out of it.'

They are familiar criticisms levelled at the centre since it was given planning permission in 1986.

It's doubtful if the 2,000 people due to gets jobs at a larger Merry Hill would agree with them.

But Stourbridge Chamber of Trade has already joined with Birmingham City Council planners and Halesowen Township Council chairman Jack Deeley in saying they will object to the expansion.

They fear the £100 million application to build 650,000 square feet of extra shopping space will mean shop closures, job losses and increased traffic chaos on already swamped roads.

Dudley market traders also fear the development could tempt Beatties away from the town, leaving it without a major department store and the shoppers it attracts.

The giant complex has been dogged by such bleak warnings from the start, when building tycoons the Richardson brothers suggested it to fill the void left by the closed Round Oak steelworks.

It was supported by Dudley Council's then ruling Conservative group, but fiercely opposed by opposition Labour councillors.

The then chief executive, John Mulvehill, quit his job after issuing planning consent on instructions of the outgoing Tories the day after Labour won control of the council. Since then, Labour have been charged with managing the consequences of a development it never wanted.

But the success of Merry Hill - attracting 25 million shoppers a year - and Chelsfield's inclusion of £6.75 million of private money for other centres in the borough - means expansion is unlikely to be resisted. It would make the centre reputedly the largest in Britain and many say the prestige could only benefit the borough.

Chairman of Dudley Retail Business Watch Stephen Schwartz, who might be expected to oppose further expansion of Merry Hill, say he is thrilled by the idea.

'Dudley is on the way up and nothing at Merry Hill can change that. The extra people it attracts can only help us,' he says.

And Dudley Chamber of Commerce president Richard Tesh says the challenge now is to bring Merry Hill shoppers to Dudley Zoo and Castle, and the Black Country Museum.

Attractions

'If we can get just a small percentage of them coming to our tourist attractions then it will help Dudley town centre.'

Dudley Labour councillor Gary Willets - the fiercest opponent of the original Merry Hill plans - is one of the few to oppose expansion.

'What happened was a planning fiasco. It was a mess and I don't believe we should have a double mess,' he says.

Councillor Willets warns that expansion would be doomed to failure unless money is pumped into road improvements in Brierley Hill, Quarry Bank and Lye.

Chelsfield has pledged £1.5 million to a scheme to improve the A4036 Pedmore Road. But Councillor Willets says the Government might want a larger contribution of private cash if it is to finance a wholesale package of improvements.

Councillor Willets says Chelsfield's application is so major that Environment Secretary John Gummer would have to 'call it in' for his consideration.

Source: *Express & Star*, 27.10.1994.

1. Assess the costs and benefits of the proposed Merry Hill shopping centre expansion. In your answer:

(a) make a clear distinction between the private costs and benefits to the developers and the potential users of the project, and the associated external costs and benefits;

(b) discuss what other information apart from that contained in the article you would need to make the assessment

2. Discuss whether or not, in your opinion, the expansion should be given planning permission.

Competition and efficiency

Summary

1. Neo-classical theory suggests that monopoly has higher prices and lower output than perfect competition.
2. This is only likely to be true for a multi-plant monopolist. A natural monopolist may have far lower costs than if the industry were split up into competing units.
3. A monopolist might have higher costs because it needs to maintain barriers to entry. It may also suffer from X-inefficiency.
4. On the other hand, monopolies may be far more innovative than perfectly competitive firms.
5. Government may attempt to correct market failure caused by monopoly. It could tax abnormal profit away, subsidise production, set maximum prices, nationalise the industry, break it up or reduce entry barriers.

Perfect competition vs monopoly

Traditional neo-classical economic analysis has tended to support the view that competition increases efficiency. One argument used is that allocative efficiency will be reduced if a perfectly competitive industry becomes a monopoly.

Multi-plant monopolists In a perfectly competitive industry there is a large number of small producers each operating at the bottom of the average cost curve. Each firm has therefore exploited all potential economies of scale. If new firms enter the industry because of price increases, their cost curves will be identical to the cost curves of existing firms. Equally, firms leaving the industry will have the same cost curves as those firms remaining.

If the industry became a monopoly, the new firm would be made up of a large number of small factories or plants. The monopolist would not attempt to merge these plants because they were already at their most efficient size under perfect competition. Hence the monopolist will become a MULTI-PLANT MONOPOLIST.

If, in the long run, the multi-plant monopolist wished to expand output, it would do so not by expanding an existing plant but by building a new one. It would operate the plant at its most efficient scale, at the bottom of the plant's average cost curve. If it wanted to contract output in the long run it would close down a plant rather than maintain the same number of plants each producing at less than the most efficient scale of production. Hence, the long run average cost curve for a multi-plant monopolist is horizontal. It can increase or reduce output in the long run at the same minimum average cost.

Allocative efficiency The demand curve for the monopolist is downward sloping (☞ unit 28). The marginal cost curve will be the same as the average cost curve if the AC curve is horizontal (for the same reasons that AR = MR if average revenue is constant ☞ unit 27). Hence, the cost and revenue curves facing the multi-plant monopolist are as shown in Figure 39.1.

If the industry were perfectly competitive, it would produce where demand equals supply (i.e. where price is equal to marginal cost). If it is a monopoly, the firm will produce at its profit maximising position where MC = MR, and price on its demand or average revenue curve. Hence, under perfect competition output will be at OB whilst

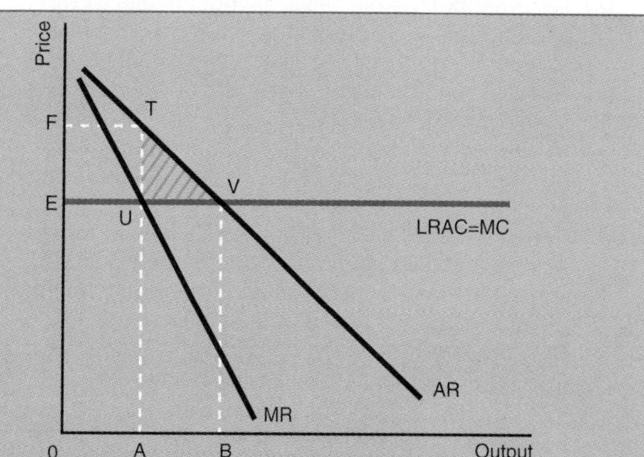

Figure 39.1 *Net social cost if a perfectly competitive industry becomes a monopoly*
If the industry were producing under conditions of perfect competition, price and output would occur where price = MC, at output OB and price OE. If the industry were a monopoly, output would be where MC = MR at OA whilst price would be on the demand curve at OF. Price is higher and output lower in the monopoly industry. The welfare loss is the shaded triangle.

price will be at OE. If the industry were a monopoly, long run output would fall to OA and price would rise to OF. This leads to the conclusion that output will be lower and price will be higher in monopoly than under perfect competition. The multi-plant monopolist is **allocatively inefficient.**

The net social cost (or welfare cost) can be shown on the diagram. It is assumed that there are no externalities. The demand curve shows the marginal social benefit received by consumers of the product (☞ unit 34). The marginal cost curve is the marginal social cost curve, the cost to society of producing an extra unit of output. Consumers were prepared to pay OF for the extra unit at OA whilst it would only have cost OE to produce. Therefore the net social cost (the difference between social benefit and social cost) on the last unit of output is EF. Similarly the vertical distance between the demand curve and the average cost curve shows the net social cost of each unit not produced between OA, the monopoly output, and OB, the output under perfect competition. Hence the net social cost to society of multi-plant monopoly production compared to production under conditions of perfect competition is the shaded triangle TUV.

The net social cost might be even greater than this triangle for two reasons.

- The monopolist might have to create and maintain barriers to entry to keep potential competitors out of the industry. For instance, it might have to spend large sums of money on advertising or other promotions. This will increase its average and marginal cost in the long run. Output will then be even lower and price even higher than if it operated under the same cost conditions as perfect competition.
- The firm may be able to shelter behind barriers to entry and as a consequence inefficiency may result. **X-inefficiency** is the term used to describe inefficiencies which occur in large organisations which are not under pressure to minimise cost. Average costs will therefore be higher than under perfect competition, resulting in even lower output and even higher prices.

QUESTION 1 In 1991, the government privatised the electricity generation industry. When the industry had been owned by the government, it had operated as a single corporation. When the government sold it off, it was split into a considerable number of different companies including area companies selling electricity to local consumers and a single company which owned the national grid. Electricity generation - making electricity from fuels such as coal or nuclear power - was a multi-plant monopolist when it was a state owned business. It was split at privatisation. Nuclear power remained in government control as did the Scottish generating company. However, the mainly coal fired electricity power stations in England and Wales were split between two new companies, PowerGen and National Power.

After privatisation, the profits of the two generating companies soared as shown in Table 39.1.

Table 39.1 *Profits of PowerGen and National Power*

£m

	PowerGen	National Power
1991	267	427
1992	326	525
1993	449	599
1994	477	734
1995	531	769

(a) Assume that, before privatisation, the electricity industry priced its product as if it were a perfectly competitive industry, earning only normal profits. Assume too that it was X-efficient (producing at the lowest cost possible). Using a diagram, explain (i) where the industry would have produced and (ii) whether this would have resulted in an efficient allocation of resources.

(b) Assume that after privatisation, costs in the industry remain constant. (i) What do the figures in Table 39.1 indicate about normal and abnormal profit? (ii) Are resources now efficiently allocated?

(c) Assume that PowerGen and National Power were making abnormal profits in 1994 but that the industry had been X-inefficient when it was government owned before 1991. Assume also that PowerGen and National Power had succeeded in reducing costs considerably between 1991 and 1994. Would the industry have been more or less efficient in 1991 compared to 1994?

(d) In the long run, any company can become an electricity producer in the UK and sell into the market. If abnormal profits were being earned in 1994, (i) what would economic theory predict will happen in the next years and (ii) is this likely to lead to a more or less efficient allocation of resources?

Natural monopoly

So far it has been assumed that the monopolist is a multi-plant monopolist. However, many monopolies are

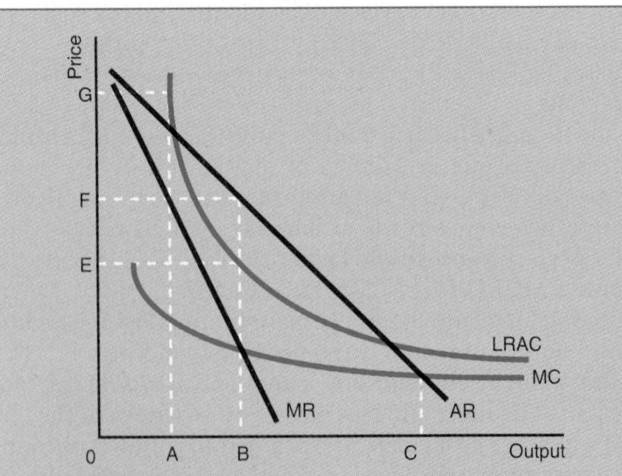

Figure 39. 2 *Natural monopoly*
In a natural monopoly, economies of scale are so large that not even a single producer could fully exploit them. Competition would be highly inefficient, raising the average cost of production. The profit maximising level of output for the monopolist is OB, but output where price = MC would be greater at OC.

NATURAL MONOPOLIES. Natural monopolies occur in industries where not even a single producer is able to exploit fully the potential economies of scale. Hence, the dominant firm in the industry, the firm with the largest output and the lowest cost, is always able to undercut competitors in price and force them out of the industry if it so chooses.

This is shown in Figure 39.2. The monopolist will produce where MC = MR at output OB and earn abnormal profit by pricing at OF. However, it would be a nonsense to talk about making the industry more competitive. Splitting the industry into two, for instance, with each firm producing OA (half of OB), would increase the average cost of production from OE to OG. More competition in the industry would result in a loss of welfare, not a gain. It should also be noted that producing at the Pareto-efficient level of output where price = MC would result in a loss for the firm. At output OC, average revenue is less than average cost.

Natural monopolies tend to occur in industries where fixed costs are very large. For instance, it would be inefficient to have two railway companies with two sets of tracks in the same area running between two towns. In gas, electricity, water and telephones, it would be inefficient to have two or more sets of lines or pipes to every household so that they had the choice of which company to buy from. The Channel Tunnel is a natural monopoly too. It would make no economic sense to build a second tunnel until the first is being used to full capacity.

QUESTION 2 BAA, the British Airports Authority, was privatised in 1987. It was given the monopoly right to operate the three London airports at Heathrow, Gatwick and Stansted. BAA is highly profitable. Its share price increased fourfold between 1987 and 1994, reflecting its attractiveness to shareholders. The prices it can charge airlines for using the landing and taking off facilities are regulated under a formula agreed with the Monopolies and Mergers Commission. However, it can be argued that the price cap is extremely generous in BAA's favour at the expense of the airlines. Airports also earn high profits if they are crowded because they earn money from rents and royalties on sales of duty-free goods.

Heathrow is operating very much at full capacity. Indeed, BAA would like to extend the airport by building a new terminal and a new runway. However, Gatwick and Stansted are operating below full capacity. Both could take more planes.

(a) Using a diagram, suggest why BAA is highly profitable.
(b) Assume that a competitor wanted to build a new London airport. Would average costs and prices be higher or lower in the industry if it built a new airport next to (i) Heathrow and (ii) Gatwick or Stansted?

Innovation

So far, the analysis has been **static**. Perfect competition and monopoly have been compared at a point in time. However, there are also important **dynamic** considerations. The Austrian economist, Joseph Schumpeter (1883-1950), argued that monopoly might be far more efficient over time than perfect competition.

In perfect competition, there are a large number of small firms operating in the market. No one firm will have large enough funds available for research and development. Small firms in general find it more difficult to raise finance for growth and expansion than large firms (☞ unit 22), and banks are likely to be unsympathetic if borrowed money is to be used on risky research projects. Moreover, perfect knowledge is assumed to exist in the market. The invention of one firm will quickly be adopted by other firms, so there is little or no incentive to undertake research and development.

Patent laws and copyright laws can protect the inventions of small firms, providing some encouragement to innovate. However, it is noticeable that in the few perfectly competitive industries which might be argued to exist, innovation is often provided not by individual firms but by government funded or government organised research institutions. In agriculture, for instance, major advances in crop strains in the Third World have been developed by state-funded universities and research institutes. This is an example of government correcting **market failure**.

A monopolist, safe behind high entry barriers, can react in two ways. It may choose to take the easy life. Sleepy and inefficient, it exploits the market and earns enough profits to satisfy shareholders. Research and development, which imply potential change, are unlikely to be a high priority for this type of firm.

Schumpeter, however, argued that the reverse was likely. The monopolist would have the resources from its abnormal profits to spend on research and development. Remember that in the UK, for instance, about 70 per cent of all investment is funded from retained profit (☞ unit 22). The monopolist would also have the incentive so to spend. It would be able to exploit any new products or new techniques of production to its own advantage, safe from competitors behind its high entry barriers. Productive efficiency would increase because costs would fall. Allocative efficiency would increase because the monopolist would bring new products to the market.

Moreover, a monopolist is never safe from competition. In the 18th century, the canal seemed unassailable as a form of industrial transport. Yet during the 19th century, the monopoly of canals, and the monopoly profits of canal owners, were destroyed by the coming of railways. In the 20th century, the same process turned railways into loss making concerns as railway monopolists saw their markets taken away by the motor car and lorry. Schumpeter called this 'the process of creative destruction'. High barriers mean that potential competitors have to produce a substitute product which is radically better than the old. It is not good enough to add some fancy packaging or change the colour of the product or add a few gadgets. Therefore monopoly encourages fundamental rather than superficial progress. So Schumpeter argued that a system of monopoly markets was far more likely to produce efficiency over a period of time than perfect competition.

QUESTION 3 The world's large pharmaceutical companies are big spenders on research and development. Successful companies are ones which can produce new wonderdrugs. Protected by patents and sold at high prices, these drugs generate enormous profits for the companies for the duration of the patent. Risks in the industry are considerable. A company can spend hundreds of millions of pounds developing a drug only for it to fail in the final clinical trials, usually because the drug is found to have significant side effects.

Once the patent expires, the price of the drug falls to a fraction of its previous price as other companies copy the drug and sell it at a price based almost solely on the cost of manufacture and distribution. Figure 39.3 shows what happened to ICI's Tenormin, a highly successful heart treatment drug, when its patent expired in June 1991. It is interesting to note that pharmaceutical companies in countries which have traditionally had very little or no patent protection for drugs such as Italy have tended to devote themselves almost entirely to copying and marketing drugs invented by other companies worldwide. The major pharmaceutical companies, like Hoffman-La Roche, SmithKline and Glaxo, have on the whole decided that their strength lies in bringing to market new patented drugs. Drugs whose patents have expired will tend to be produced by generic drug companies specialising in this field.

Source: adapted from the *Financial Times*, 18.5.1994

(a) Why could drug development be seen as an example of 'creative destruction'?
(b) Would there be an increase in efficiency if drug patent protection laws worldwide were completely abolished?

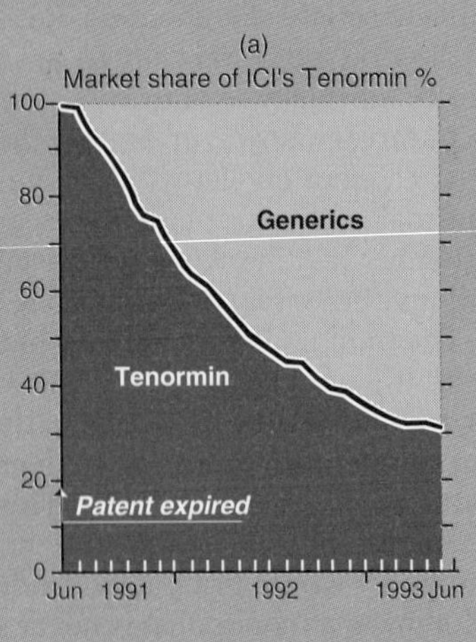

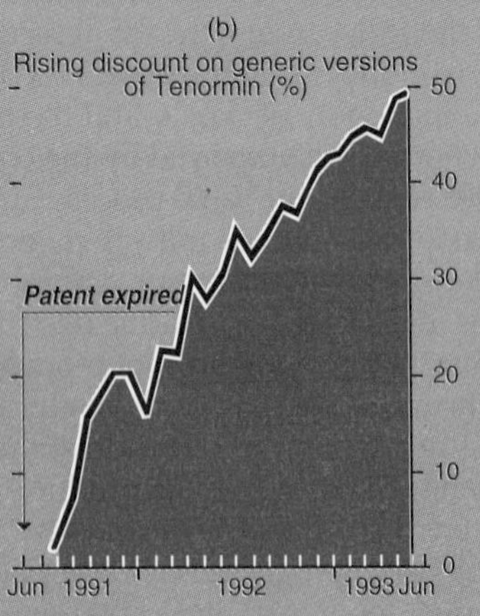

Source: adapted from Lehman Brothers.

Figure 39.3

Imperfect competition

So far, monopoly has been contrasted with perfect competition. The same arguments can be used to consider the social costs or benefits of imperfect competition. In imperfect competition output is likely to be lower and price higher than in perfect competition and hence there is a net social cost. Abnormal profits are likely to be made, again imposing net social costs.

In perfect competition and in many cases of monopoly, the consumer is offered only a homogeneous product. On the other hand, imperfect competition is characterised by the selling of a large number of different branded goods. Welfare is likely to be increased if consumers can choose between many, if fairly similar, products rather than being faced with no choice at all.

Schumpeter's arguments about innovation apply to imperfect competition too. Oligopolists, for instance, are more likely to innovate than perfectly competitive firms.

The verdict?

It can now be seen that it is not possible to come to any simple conclusions about the desirability of competition in the market. Competition is by no means always 'best'. On the one hand, multi-plant monopolists and many imperfectly competitive firms may exploit the market, earning abnormal profits at the expense of consumers, reducing output and increasing price. This leads to a welfare loss. On the other hand, natural monopolies are far more efficient than any alternative competitive market structures. There may or may not be a link between monopoly and innovation.

Government policy

Governments have a range of possible COMPETITION POLICIES which can be used to improve economic efficiency.

Taxes and subsidies Abnormal profit can simply be taxed away. This may improve equity within the economic system, transferring the resources which the monopolist has expropriated from consumers back to taxpayers. Unfortunately, this will not improve allocative efficiency. A tax on profits will not affect either marginal cost or marginal revenue. Therefore the monopolist will continue to produce at less than the efficient level of output.

However, it is possible to shift the marginal cost curve downwards by providing a **subsidy**. At any given level of output, the government could subsidise production, reducing marginal cost. If the government wishes the monopolist to produce where MC = price, it will need to find out the level of output where the marginal cost curve cuts the average revenue curve before a subsidy is given. In Figure 39.4, this occurs at output level OB where MC_1 = AR. The size of the subsidy required on the last unit of output is EF. This shifts the marginal cost curve to MC_2. The monopolist produces OB because this is now the

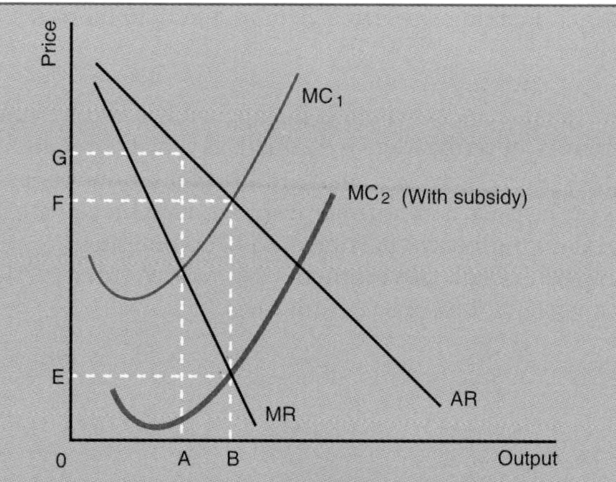

Figure 39.4 *Subsidising a monopolist to improve efficiency*
A profit maximising monopolist will produce at OA where MC = MR and price is OG. Output under perfect competition would be at OB, where price = MC. A subsidy of EF on the last unit of output would shift the marginal cost curve downwards from MC_1 to MC_2. The monopolist would now produce at the perfect competition level of output. The government could recoup the subsidy by a tax on profits.

level of production where MC = MR, and society benefits because production is at a level where the true cost to society, MC_1, is equal to price. The government can recoup that subsidy by taxing away the profits made by the monopolist.

This seems an ideal solution. Unfortunately there are a number of practical problems. First, giving subsidies to private sector monopolists is likely to be politically impossible for any government. It is difficult enough for governments to subsidise nationalised industries. Second, the policy requires an accurate knowledge of cost and revenue curves. When the policy is first imposed there is some chance that a reasonable guess can be made. However, taxes and subsidies distort the market so that in the long term it becomes very difficult to guess where hypothetical points on the curves might be. Third, it has already been discussed in detail whether allocative efficiency would increase by moving to a price = MC level of output in one industry (☞ unit 35). Imposing taxes and subsidies assumes that there is clear understanding of what the efficiency maximising level of output and price might be.

Price controls An obvious method of controlling monopolists would be to impose price controls on their goods. The maximum price that a monopolist could charge would be set equal to the marginal social cost; in Figure 39.5 where MC = price. To the left of output OA, the average revenue curve is horizontal because the government has imposed a maximum price of OB. To the right, the free market average revenue curve reappears. If the monopolist wishes to sell more than OA, it has to lower its price. Marginal revenue is equal to average revenue if average revenue is constant (☞ unit 27). There is then a discontinuity at OA for the marginal revenue curve. The monopolist will produce at OA because that is now the level of output where MC = MR. The policy works because the government has effectively turned the marginal revenue curve from being downward sloping to being horizontal up to the efficiency maximising level of output.

This type of policy is being used to control privatised industries in the UK (☞ unit 45). However, it suffers from the same defects as subsidies. It is difficult to know where the cost and revenue curves lie and what is the allocatively efficient level of output.

Nationalisation The private monopolist is assumed to maximise profit. This leads to an inefficient level of output. Another way of controlling monopoly is to change the goals of the firm. This could be achieved by nationalising the industry. The industry is then charged with maximising social welfare and not private profit.

Privatisation and deregulation Many monopolists in the past have been government owned monopolies such as gas or telephones. Their monopolies have been protected by laws preventing private firms setting up in the industry. It is difficult for state owned companies to compete on the same terms as private sector firms. Governments judge investment in a different way from a private firm. They can also always pay any debts if the firm runs up large losses. So to create a 'level playing field' where all firms are competing on the same terms, it is argued that state monopolies should be privatised. At the point of privatisation, they can either be split up into competing firms or barriers to entry can be lowered so that competitors can come into the market (an example of **deregulation** ☞ unit 69), both of which are discussed below.

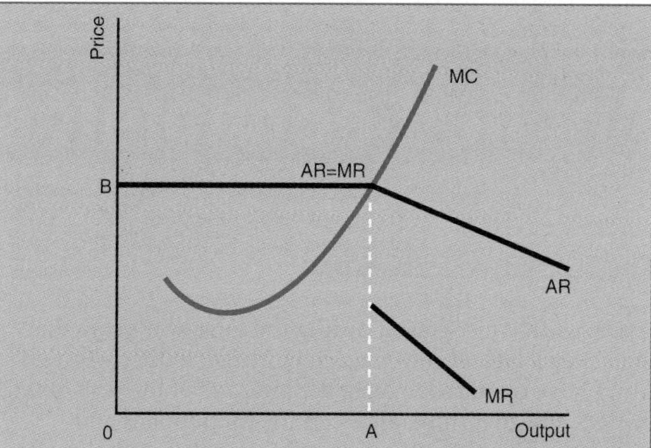

Figure 39.5 *Price controls in a monopoly industry*
Price controls change the shape of the average and marginal revenue curves. A maximum price of OB will produce a kinked average revenue or demand curve. To the left of OA, the average revenue curve is horizontal, showing the maximum price of OB that the firm is allowed to charge. To the right the average revenue falls because the free market price is below the maximum price. The monopolist will now produce at OA, the output level of a perfectly competitive industry where MC = price. This is because OA is now the profit maximising level of output (i.e. where MC = MR for the monopolist).

Breaking up the monopolist The monopolist can be broken up into competing units by government. This might be an effective solution for a multi-plant monopolist with a large number of plants where the **minimum efficient scale of production** (☞ unit 20) is very low. But most monopolists or oligopolists have relatively high minimum efficient scales. The welfare gain from splitting a monopolist into a duopoly, for instance, might be negligible. In the case of natural monopolies, breaking up a monopolist would almost certainly lead to welfare losses. Breaking up cartels is more likely to increase welfare.

Reducing entry barriers It is impossible for governments to reduce entry barriers to industries which are natural monopolies. However, many multi-plant monopolists and oligopolists earn abnormal profit because they artificially maintain high entry barriers and keep potential competitors out. Governments can reduce entry barriers by a variety of means (☞ unit 41).

QUESTION 4 In 1981, the Monopolies and Mergers Commission recommended that British Posters Ltd be broken up. At the time, British Posters controlled 80 per cent of Britain's 170 000 roadside poster sites, hiring the sites from their owners and then marketing them to potential advertisers. The Commission found that British Posters' monopolies 'have led to a higher level of prices than would have obtained in a more competitive market'. Advertisers also complained that British Posters was inflexible. They were not offered a choice of sites. Sites next to each other were differently priced. Clients were forced to accept lengthy contracts which sometimes meant that a product was being advertised long after it had been withdrawn from the market.

(a) How did British Posters exploit its monopoly position?
(b) To what extent would the break up of British Posters into several competing companies lead to greater economic efficiency?

Key terms

Multi - plant monopolist - a monopoly producer working with a number of factories, offices or plants.
Natural monopoly - where economies of scale are so large relative to market demand that the dominant producer in the industry will always enjoy lower costs of production than any other potential competitor.
Competition policy - government policy to influence the degree of competition in individual markets within the economy.

Applied economics

Competition policy

The legislative framework

It was widely recognised during the inter-war years that there was a lack of competition in British industry which could have operated against the interests of the consumer. In 1948, the government passed the Monopolies and Restrictive Practices (Inquiry and Control) Act designed to curb anti-competitive practices. It set up what is now the Monopolies and Mergers Commission. In 1956, the restrictive practices part of its work was given over to the Restrictive Practices Court (☞ unit 41). The 1973 Fair Trading Act established the present day structure of referrals for handling anti-competitive practices.

- A Director General of Fair Trading is appointed by the government. He or she is responsible for co-ordinating competition and consumer protection policy and advising the Secretary of State for Trade and Industry. Either the Director General or the Secretary of State has the power to refer monopolies for investigation to the Monopolies and Mergers Commission.
- The Monopolies and Mergers Commission is an administrative tribunal which investigates potential monopoly situations. A firm is defined as possessing a monopoly if it has at least 25 per cent of the market. This could be either a national market or a local market. The result of an inquiry by the Commission is given in a Report. This explains the Commission's findings and lists its policy recommendations.
- The Secretary of State for Trade and Industry is the minister responsible for competition policy. He or she receives reports of the Monopolies and Mergers Commission. The Secretary of State may decide not to act, effectively rejecting the Commission's recommendations. Most likely the Secretary of State

will ask the Director General of Fair Trading to negotiate a voluntary agreement with the firms concerned. This is designed to curb the malpractices found by the Commission. If the firms refuse to co-operate, he or she has the power to issue an order forcing them to comply.

The 1948 Act only covered firms in the private sector of the economy. The 1980 Competition Act made it possible for the Monopolies and Mergers Commission to investigate public sector monopolies too. The Act also gave the Director General of Fair Trading powers to curb anti-competitive practices such as refusal to supply without the need for a full referral to the Commission.

The EU has the power to investigate monopolies under Article 86 of the Treaty of Rome. The European Commission is responsible for investigating and applying policies. To date, the Commission has been more concerned with mergers and restrictive trade practices than monopolies.

The effectiveness of policy

In the USA, monopolies are illegal because it is presumed that monopoly will always act against the public interest. The basis of UK law is different. Monopoly is permissible unless government is convinced that it acts against the public interest.

The 1973 Fair Trading Act defined the public interest as 'the desirability (a) of maintaining and promoting effective competition between persons supplying goods and services; (b) of promoting the interests of consumers ... in respect of the prices charged and ... the quality and the variety of goods and services supplied; (c) of promoting, through competition, the reduction of costs and the development and use of new techniques and new products, and of facilitating the entry of new competitors into existing markets; (d) of maintaining and promoting the balanced distribution of industry and employment; (e) of maintaining and promoting activity in markets outside the United Kingdom.'

This definition, and the similar one in the 1948 Act, whilst comprehensive, has frequently been criticised as being too vague. Moreover, it has been difficult to ensure continuity of interpretation of the criteria. The Monopolies and Mergers Commission is made up of a constantly changing pool of members who sit on the Commission in a part time capacity. No two reports are compiled by the same group of people. Hence it has not been difficult to detect differences in emphasis and interpretation between different investigations.

When clear recommendations have been made by the Commission, the government has favoured a voluntary approach to their enforcement. Critics argue that this can lead to firms negotiating very favourable terms with governments anxious to avoid upsetting the industrial lobby. In major cases, such as the breweries, political considerations can be seen to be more important than economic ones. Where changes are enforced, firms lobby over time for the release of the undertakings they have made. Governments can prove weak in the face of this type of pressure.

The whole process of investigation by the Monopolies and Mergers Commission has been accused of being unwieldy and time consuming. Since 1948, the Commission has produced around 320, of which slightly more than 25 per cent have related to monopoly supply situations. Most of the latter have found evidence of anti-competitive practices. During the 1980s much of the energy of the Commission was devoted to investigating industries which were under government control and ownership. One part of government had been appointed watchdog over another part. Some see this as an admission that government cannot control its own activities. It also diverted resources away from investigations of the private sector of the economy.

Since the early1990s, there has been a distinct softening of policy towards possible monopoly supply situations. Secretaries of State for Trade and Industry have shown a reluctance to act on Office of Fair Trading recommendations that a situation should be investigated by the Monopolies and Mergers Commission. MMC reports have shown a reluctance to condemn what are apparently clear cut instances of anti-competitive practices. Part of the reason for this could be that there is a much greater awareness of contestable market theory (☞ unit 32). For instance, the MMC investigated ice cream distribution in the UK. Birds Eye Wall's has a technical monopoly, with over 25 per cent of the market. It could be argued that part of the reason for this is that Birds Eye Wall's supplies free freezer cabinets to shops which stock Birds Eye Wall's ice creams. But they only do this on condition that no other ice creams are stocked in the freezer. Mars complained, saying that this was a major barrier to entry. The MMC disagreed, pointing out that Mars had been extremely successful in entering the ice cream market from 1989 onwards. Exclusive use of freezer cabinets is anti-competitive, but it is relatively unimportant and therefore not worth condemning.

So the experience of the past 50 years is that an industry is unlucky if it finds itself being investigated and even unluckier if it has to change its competitive practices in any serious way. More frequent investigations, regular monitoring of industries found to be operating against the public interest, and more serious penalties for offending firms, are seen by some to be essential if monopoly control is to have teeth.

Others argue that many alleged instances of monopoly are not against the public interest because markets are contestable. Firms should therefore be subject to less interference and control than is currently the case.

DATA QUESTION

Competition in the rail industry

Railtrack

Railtrack owns the railway infrastructure in the UK. This includes 10 270 miles of train route, 2 482 railway stations, 1 160 signal boxes and control centres, 984 tunnels and 90 000 bridges. It is responsible for maintaining and improving the existing network. It won't do any of the physical work itself. It will put this out to contract. Equally, it won't run trains. Operating companies will do this and will be charged rent for running trains over the tracks. The railway stations will be leased to the operating companies who will be responsible for minor repairs. Railtrack will be responsible for major repairs and alterations.

Infrastructure companies

14 infrastructure companies have been created. They will be responsible for doing the maintenance and repair work on the infrastructure owned by Railtrack, such as renewing sections of track and maintaining signalling equipment. They will have to compete amongst themselves for the work.

Train operating companies

25 train operating companies have been created. Some companies, such as Gatwick Express, will run on a single route. At the opposite extreme, ScotRail will operate a complete network of trains in Scotland. They will rent track and stations from Railtrack, running trains which have been leased from the three rolling stock leasing companies. The government hopes that private companies like Virgin will want to enter the market and establish their own operating companies. On some lines, an operating company will be the only company to offer a train service to passengers. This is almost bound to be true on lines which make a loss and where the government will offer a subsidy to the company which offers to provide a service on the line for the lowest price. These are likely to be local commuter or rural lines. On other lines, particularly the main lines between city centres, several railway companies are likely to compete for providing services between the same cities.

Freight

The freight business of British Rail has been organised into three separate regional companies. They will pay Railtrack rent for running freight trains along the tracks. Freightliner, the domestic container business which moves container wagons from seaports to inland terminals, and Haulmark, the international container business, will be sold as separate companies. Any of the three companies will be able to move freight anywhere on the network. The regional companies will not have a monopoly in their area.

Rolling stock leasing companies

The 11 000 locomotives, carriages and freight wagons owned by British Rail have been split between three leasing companies. They will lease the rolling stock to the train operators. They will buy new rolling stock to replace existing stock.

Parcels

Red Star Parcels, the railway express parcels business, will be sold off as one single company. It could become an independent company or it might be sold to an existing courier business.

*The statistics were correct at April 1994 when British Rail was completely reorganised.

In 1994, the government reorganised British Rail prior to privatising the industry. It believed that introducing competition into the railway industry in the UK will increase efficiency. Produce a report which includes diagrams discussing whether or not this is likely to be the case. In particular, you need to discuss:

(a) the extent to which there is now competition in the railway industry;

(b) how competition following the break up of the monopolist, British Rail, might increase efficiency;

(c) whether efficiency would have been further increased if Railtrack had been broken up into competing companies.

Mergers and the growth of firms

Summary

1. Small firms in an industry exist because economies of scale may be limited, barriers to entry low and the size of the market may be very small.
2. A healthy small firm sector in the economy may lead to increased economic efficiency if it increases competition, reduces prices and increases future efficiency.
3. Firms may grow internally or through mergers, amalgamation or takeover.
4. Mergers may be horizontal, vertical or conglomerate.
5. Firms grow in order to exploit potential economies of scale, control their markets or reduce risk through diversification.
6. Firms may choose to grow by amalgamation, for instance, because it is cheaper to buy a firm than grow internally.
7. Evidence suggests that many mergers fail to increase economic efficiency.

The size of firms

Although production in the UK is dominated by large firms (☞ unit 16), there are many industries where small and medium sized enterprises play a significant role.

Large firms exist for two main reasons.

- Economies of scale in the industry may be significant. Only a small number of firms, producing at the minimum efficient scale of production, may be needed to satisfy total demand. The industry may be a natural monopoly where not even one firm can fully exploit potential economies of scale.
- Barriers to entry may exist which protect large firms from potential competitors.

Conversely, small firms survive for the opposite reasons.

Economies of scale may be very small relative to the market size A large number of firms in an industry may be able to operate at the minimum efficient scale of production. Small firms may also be able to take advantage of the higher costs of larger firms in the industry caused by diseconomies of scale.

The costs of production for a large scale producer may be higher than for a small company In part, this may be due to productive inefficiency - a large firm operating within its average cost curve boundary. For instance, larger firms may be poorly organised in what they see as small unimportant segments of the market (called market **niches**). Or X-inefficiency may be present (☞ unit 33). Equally, the average cost curve of a large producer may be higher in certain markets than for a small producer. For instance, a large firm may be forced to pay its workers high wages because it operates in formal labour markets (☞ unit 52). A small firm may be able to pay relatively low wages in informal labour markets. Indeed owners of small companies can work exceptionally long hours at effective rates of pay which they would find totally unacceptable if in a normal job. Or a small producer, like a corner shop sole proprietorship, may be prepared to accept a much lower rate of return on its capital employed than a large company.

Barriers to entry may be low The cost of setting up in an industry, such as the grocery industry or the newsagents market, may be small. Products may be simple to produce or sell. Finance to set up in the industry may be readily available. The product sold may be relatively homogeneous. It may be easy for a small firm to produce a new product and establish itself in the market.

Small firms can be monopolists A monopolist offers a product for sale which is available from no other company. Many small firms survive because they offer a local, flexible and personal service. For instance, a newsagent may have a monopoly on the sale of newspapers, magazines, greetings cards, toys and stationery in a local area. Consumers may be unwilling to walk half a mile extra to buy greetings cards at a 10 per cent discount or travel 10 miles by car to a local superstore to buy a £2 toy at a 25 per cent reduction. Or the newsagent may double up as a grocery store and off-licence, opening till 10 o'clock at night and all day Sunday, again offering a service which is not offered anywhere else in the locality. A small shop could be the only place locally where informal credit is offered, or where it is possible to buy a single item instead of a pack of six. Equally in the case of some products, such as cricket balls or croquet mallets, the size of the market is so small that one or two very small firms can satisfy total demand.

QUESTION 1

(a) Why can small firms survive successfully in the hotel industry?
(b) What economic forces might favour hotel chains in the future?

Efficiency and size

There is no direct correlation between the size of a firm and economic efficiency. Some economists argue that small firms are a major source of economic efficiency in the economy.

- The small firms of today are the large firms of tomorrow. Historically in the UK and the USA, today's top largest 100 firms bear little relation to the list of the largest 100 firms 50 years ago. It is important to have as large a number of small firms as possible so that a few can become the large firms of tomorrow.
- Small firms provide the necessary competition to prevent large firms from exploiting their markets. Large firms would be less efficient and their prices higher if they were not aware that small firms could enter the market and take away parts of their market. In some markets, economies of scale are small relative to market size. The alternative to a large number of small firms would be multi-plant oligopolists or monopolists which would erect barriers to entry to the industry and then make abnormal profit. Prices would then be higher and output lower, leading to a loss of efficiency.

There are, however, a number of arguments which suggest that large firms can be more efficient. Large firms may be necessary to exploit economies of scale. They are more likely to be in a position to undertake research and development. Moreover, the size of firms and the number of firms in an industry is not necessarily an indication of competition or the lack of it. As the **theory of contestable markets** (☞ unit 32) shows, what is important is not size or number of firms operating in the industry but the degree of potential competition. Barriers to entry are the key indicator of likely inefficiency, not size of the firm.

QUESTION 2 Anita Roddick's Body Shop has been one of the success stories of the 1980s and 1990s. Providing a range of environmentally sound products, it grew steadily in the face of competition from established multiples such as Boots and from the large scale advertising and promotion of giants such as Revlon and Unilever.

In what sense might it be said that Body Shop contributed to greater economic efficiency in the UK economy in recent years?

The growth of firms

Firms may grow in size in two ways:

- by **internal growth**;
- through MERGER, AMALGAMATION or TAKEOVER.

Internal growth simply refers to firms increasing their output, for instance through increased investment or an increased labour force. A merger or amalgamation is the joining together of two or more firms under common ownership. The boards of directors of the two companies, with the agreement of shareholders, agree to merge their two companies together. A takeover implies that one company wishes to buy another company. The takeover may be amicable. Company X makes a bid for company Y. The board of directors considers the bid and finds that the price offered is a good price for the shareholders of the company. It then recommends the shareholders to accept the offer terms. However, the takeover may be contested. In a hostile takeover the board of directors of company Y recommends to its shareholders to reject the terms of the bid. A takeover battle is then likely to ensue. Company X needs to get promises to sell at the offer price of just over 50 per cent of the shares to win and take control.

Types of merger

Economists distinguish between three types of merger.

- A HORIZONTAL MERGER is a merger between two firms in the same industry at the same stage of production, for instance, the merger of two building societies, or two car manufacturers or two bakeries.
- A VERTICAL MERGER is a merger between two firms at different production stages in the same industry. **Forward integration** involves a supplier merging with one of its buyers, such as a car manufacturer buying a car dealership, or a newspaper buying newsagents. **Backward integration** involves a purchaser buying one of its suppliers, such as a drinks manufacturer buying a bottling manufacturer, or a car manufacturer buying a tyre company.
- A CONGLOMERATE MERGER is the merging of two firms with no common interest. A tobacco company buying an insurance company, or a food company buying a clothing chain would be conglomerate mergers.

QUESTION 3 Explain whether each of the following is a horizontal, vertical or conglomerate merger.

(a) Nestlé with Rowntree Mackintosh (1988);
(b) MCA (the US film and entertainment company) with Matshita (the consumer electronic company which includes the Panasonic and Technics brand names) (1990);
(c) Severn Trent (a water company) with Biffa (a waste disposal company) (1991);
(d) Ever Ready with Ralston Purina (the world's largest manufacturer of dry cell batteries) (1992);
(e) Viacom (a US cable company) with Paramount (the US TV and film producer) (1994);
(f) British American Tobacco with Farmers Group (a US insurance group) (1988);
(g) the Cheltenham and Gloucester Building Society with Lloyds Bank (1995).

The reasons for growth

It is suggested that profit maximising companies are motivated to grow in size for three main reasons.

- A larger company may be able to exploit economies of scale more fully. The merger of two medium sized car manufacturers, for instance, is likely to result in potential economies in all fields, from production to marketing to finance. Vertical and conglomerate mergers are less likely to yield scale economies because there are unlikely to be any technical economies. There may be some marketing economies and more likely there may be some financial economies.
- A larger company may be more able to control its markets. It may therefore reduce competition in the market place in order to be better able to exploit the market.
- A larger company may be able to reduce risk. Many conglomerate companies have grown for this reason. Some markets are fragile. They are subject to large changes in demand when economies go into boom or recession. A steel manufacturer, for instance, will do exceptionally well in a boom, but will be hard hit in a recession. So it might decide to **diversify** by buying a company with a product which does not have a cyclical demand pattern, like a supermarket chain. Other industries face a very uncertain future. It became fashionable in the 1970s and early 1980s for tobacco companies to buy anything which seemed to have a secure future, from grocery stores to insurance companies.

Reasons for amalgamation

Why do profit maximising companies choose to grow through amalgamation rather than through internal growth?

Cost One answer is that it is often cheaper to merge than to grow internally. For instance, a company may wish to expand and calculates that it will cost £50 million if it does so internally. It then looks to the stock markets and sees that a firm which already has the capabilities required is valued at £25 million. Even after paying the likely premium on the share price involved in takeover bids, it would be cheaper to buy the existing firm than undertake new investment. The ratio between the value of assets of a firm and its stock market price is called the **valuation ratio**. In theory, the larger the difference between asset values and stock market prices, the greater the incentive for firms to grow through takeovers rather than grow internally.

The position is often complicated because it is very difficult to place a value on the assets of a firm. In particular, it has become clear in recent years that intangible assets, particularly brands, can be more valuable than all the factories, offices, stock and other physical assets put together. A strong brand represents a guaranteed income for the foreseeable future. It is also a block on which to build. However large the company, it cannot guarantee to establish a new brand in the market place. Companies can invest money for years in the attempt to build a brand, and fail.

Asset stripping Not all companies in the merger market are necessarily interested in growing in size. Some companies specialise in asset stripping. The predator company will look for companies which have high asset values but low stock market prices. Companies being stalked may well have inefficient management who are unable to manage the company to earn the profit expected by shareholders and the stock market in general. Once a company is taken over, it will be broken up in the most profitable manner to the asset stripper. For instance, parts of the company may be sold as going concerns to other companies. Parts may be closed down. A factory site may be far more profitable sold off as building land than as a working factory. The predator company will then keep the rest to add to its portfolio of companies. A successful asset stripper will often aim to sell off some of the parts of the company for more than it paid for the whole. The part of the company which the predator might keep is then a useful addition to the profit made on the whole deal.

Rewards to management So far, it has been assumed that companies are motivated to grow because of profit. But there is much evidence to suggest that profits of merged companies are often no more and sometimes less than the combined profits of the two individual firms would have been. **Managerial and behavioural theories** of the firm (☞ units 24 and 32) can explain this by pointing out that the goal of a firm is not necessarily to maximise profit. The managers of the firm have a vested interest in seeing a firm grow because their rewards (their pay, bonuses, company cars, prestige and influence) tend to increase with the size of the firm. The managing director of a company which doubles its size overnight is likely to receive a substantial pay rise in the not-too-distant future.

Moreover, the financial markets have a strong incentive to encourage takeovers and mergers. Banks, merchant banks and other financial institutions can make very large profits from organising takeovers.

QUESTION 4 In 1994, Service Corporation International, the biggest funeral company in the USA, offered to buy two of the largest funeral companies in the UK. The first, Great Southern Group, ran 150 funeral homes, 12 crematoria and two cemeteries, mainly in the south of England. Its taxable profits in 1993 were £6.2m. The second, Plantsbrook, buries one in ten people in the UK, mainly in the north of England. Its profits in 1993 were £12m. Service Corporation International will have paid £306m to buy the two UK companies. It is a highly acquisitive group. In the USA, it spent $250m in 1994 financing acquisitions and expansion. It operates Australia's largest funeral business and has a substantial presence in Canada. Bill Heiligbrodt, president and chief operating officer of Service Corporation International said, when it made a bid for Great Southern Group, that the UK was 'a large mature market in terms of population'.

Source: adapted from *The Times* 10.6.1994 and the *Financial Times* 3.9.1994.

Suggest why Service Corporation International wanted to buy the two UK companies.

Mergers and efficiency

There is much controversy as to whether mergers increase economic efficiency. Productive efficiency will increase if average costs of production after the merger fall because of economies of scale. Allocative efficiency will increase if the merged company provides a wider range of goods, better quality products, etc.

On the other hand, mergers tend to reduce competition in the market. The loss of efficiency which might arise was discussed in detail in unit 39.

Moreover, asset stripping is very controversial. Its supporters argue that the asset stripper performs a useful economic function. The value to society of a company can be calculated by the sum of its component parts. If greater profit can be made by demolishing a factory, sacking the workforce and selling the land for shops, houses or offices than by keeping the factory operational, then the asset stripper is performing a useful social role by doing so. The asset stripper is reallocating resources according to the signals of the market. The problem is that market prices may not be an accurate reflection of true social value. Short run profit maximisation by one company may well not lead to an economically efficient outcome for society.

Key terms

Merger, amalgamation, integration or takeover - the joining together of two or more firms under common ownership.
Horizontal merger or integration - a merger between two firms in the same industry at the same stage of production.
Vertical merger or integration - a merger between two firms at different production stages in the same industry.
Conglomerate merger - a merger between two firms producing unrelated products.

Applied economics

Mergers and efficiency

Merger activity

This century, there has been a significant growth in the importance of large firms in the UK economy. For instance, in 1949 the share of the 100 largest private enterprises in manufacturing net output was 22 per cent. By 1975, this had risen to 42 per cent. Since then it has fallen back to 37 per cent as manufacturing industry has shrunk under competitive pressures. Most of this increase in concentration (☞ unit 25) has come about through mergers, particularly horizontal mergers. There has been a similar trend in both primary and tertiary industry.

Merger activity has tended to be relatively uneven over time. Figure 40.1 shows there were waves of merger activity in the 1960s and early 1970s, and then again in the 1980s. The mergers in the 1960s were often motivated by a desire to increase in size in order to gain market power or to cut costs. The abolition of restrictive trade practices by the 1956 Act (☞ unit 41) in particular increased mergers. Unable to collude to rig the market in their favour, firms resorted to taking over other firms to gain sufficient control of the market to gain monopoly profits. The mergers of the 1980s were often more concerned with buying market share in what could be difficult to enter oligopolistic markets. By the late 1980s, there was also a growing realisation that only large firms would survive in many markets when a Single Market was created in the European Union in 1993 (☞ unit 88).

The recession of the early 1990s led to a fall in merger activity. There were even some de-mergers, such as the split of ICI into two companies, ICI and Zeneca. This reflected a new business awareness that two smaller companies might be more efficient than a single larger company. Better economic conditions by the second half of the 1990s are likely to see a return to high merger activity.

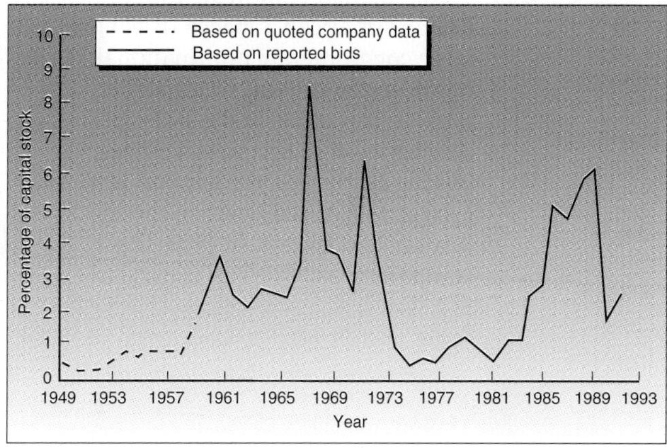

Source: adapted from J Fairburn and J Kay, *Mergers and Merger Policy*, OUP, 1989.

Figure 40.1 *Merger and takeover activity in the UK, 1949-1993*

The legislative background

The 1948 Monopolies Act did not cover merger activity. However, it came to be recognised that monopolies against the public interest could be created by merger activity. The Monopolies and Mergers Act (1965) gave the Monopolies and Mergers Commission (MMC) the duty to investigate mergers referred to it by the Secretary of State for Trade and Industry. It had to produce a report with recommendations within 6 months. The Secretary of State could then accept or reject the advice of the Commission. The Secretary of State could refer any merger where the assets acquired are more than £30 million.

In 1984, the government stated that the main consideration for referral would be whether the merger would potentially affect competition. In a major review of merger policy in 1988, the government confirmed this. The 1988 review also said that 'the vast majority of mergers raise no competition or other objections, and are rightly left free to be decided by the market' (DTI 1988)(i.e. that the government would intervene only rarely). This reflects the general pattern of intervention over time. Since 1965, approximately only 3 per cent of eligible UK mergers (mergers over the size limit) have been referred to the Monopolies and Mergers Commission and these mergers in turn represent only a fraction of all mergers in the economy.

By the mid-1990s the MMC investigated any merger which created a 25 per cent market share or £70 million of assets. It usually produced a report on any investigation within 9-12 months.

Mergers and economic efficiency

Evidence suggests [see, for instance, G Meekes (1977) or K G Cowling (1980)] that most mergers do not lead to any efficiency gains. Many in fact lead to losses of economic efficiency. There are a number of ways in which this could be measured.

- Profits of the combined company decline from what they might otherwise have been. This is often anticipated in the stock market where the share price of a company taking over another falls when the takeover is announced.
- Turnover falls. Mergers may well lead to 'rationalisation' of plant and other facilities. In the process the capacity of the firm falls, leading to a loss of turnover. This reduction of capacity may not be compensated for by an increase in capacity elsewhere in the economy, pushing the production possibility frontier backwards towards the origin.
- Employment falls. Rationalisation often involves reducing the workforce. These workers may then be added to a pool of long term unemployed people.

If mergers fail to improve efficiency, why do mergers take place? Is there any significance in the fact that merger activity increased during the 1980s but fell back sharply when the economy went into recession from 1989 onwards? It can be argued that the merger activity of the 1980s was dominated by firms increasing rapidly in size. It was relatively easy to borrow money to finance acquisitions. It was also relatively easy to issue new shares to pay for external growth because the stock market was booming during this period. The main gainers were managers and directors as well as City Institutions. The larger the firm, the larger is likely to be the remuneration of top managers and directors. Managerial theories of the firm (☞ unit 33) can then help to explain why mergers can be so attractive to decision makers in firms. City institutions encourage firms to merge because they earn large fees from takeovers. The recession of the late 1980s and 1990s brought much of this to an end. Stock market prices went nowhere, which meant that it was difficult to raise new equity capital. Interest rates went up to record real levels, making borrowing money very expensive. Some of the empires built up in the 1980s through acquisition, such as Next or Coloroll either were forced to sell off many of their purchased companies or went bust, discouraging new mergers. Many managers and directors also had to fight for the survival of their companies in very difficult trading conditions, leaving far less time to think about how they might grow through mergers.

The effectiveness of mergers control

Merger policy has done little to prevent the increased concentration of UK industry. Some have argued that:

- too few cases are referred to the Monopolies and Mergers Commission;
- there is little rationale behind the choice of which potential mergers are referred;
- this lottery is made worse by the inconsistency of the stance taken by a Monopolies and Mergers Commission staffed by different people at different times.

It can then be argued that a much tougher line needs to be taken. In particular, companies should need to prove more than just that a merger would not be against the public interest. Merging companies should be forced to prove that the merger is likely to be in the public interest.

Free marketeers take an opposite viewpoint. They would say that governments are ill placed to decide what would be in the public interest and what would not. This is because governments cannot predict what will happen after a merger with any certainty. More government intervention would be likely to lead to a series of mistakes with beneficial mergers being stopped because of government interference. Even if it were true that most mergers lead to no increase in economic efficiency, letting the market decide is unlikely to lead to wrong decisions being made. Whatever happens, free market forces lead to better decision making than anything government could achieve.

The tobacco industry

Prepare a report discussing whether BAT should (1) take over American Tobacco OR (2) take over the tobacco interests of RJR Nabisco OR (3) stay at its present size. In your report:

(a) outline the reasons why a firm might want to take over another firm;

(b) discuss, using the reasons you have outlined in (a), the advantages and disadvantages of BAT taking over either American Tobacco OR the tobacco interests of RJR Nabisco;

(c) discuss the possible advantages to BAT of staying at its present size and not taking over either business;

(d) make a recommendation on which of the three courses of action BAT should take on the basis of the existing evidence, but also explain what further information you would like to have to come to a more informed decision.

British American Tobacco

British American Tobacco (BAT) is a large conglomerate multinational. As its name implies, it was originally a tobacco company. In the 1980s, it diversified into financial services, buying Eagle Star, the general insurance group, and Allied Dunbar, the life insurance business. In 1993, the company was worth an estimated $21.7bn.

Source: adapted from *The Sunday Times*, 1.5.1994.

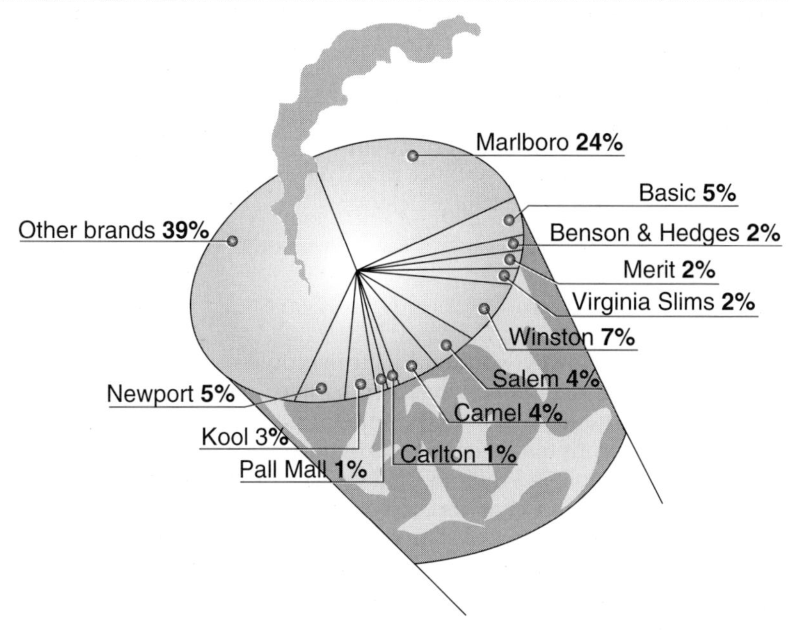

Figure 40.2 *US cigarette market by brand, 1993*

RJR Nabisco

RJR Nabisco is a large US food multinational. In the 1980s, it became 'highly leveraged', which meant that it borrowed a great deal of money relative to its share capital and size. It then wanted to reduce its borrowing by selling parts of its business. For sale in 1993 was its $10bn tobacco business with 30 per cent of the US market and with brands such as Winston and Camel. If BAT bought RJR Nabisco's tobacco business, there would be a possibility that the US government might intervene to stop the merger, arguing under anti-trust laws (the US equivalent of anti-monopoly legislation) that the move would reduce competition in the market to the disadvantage of consumers. The likelyhood would be that BAT would be forced to sell Brown & Williamson, its US cigarette business. Analysts predict that BAT would face an immense challenge integrating another tobacco business into its own organisation.

Source: adapted from *The Sunday Times*, 1.5.1994.

American Tobacco

American Tobacco is owned by the US conglomerate American Brands. It wants to sell American Tobacco given its lacklustre performance. In the 1930s, its brands, such as Lucky Strike and Pall Mall, held 35 per cent of the US market. By 1993, this had fallen to just 7 per cent. In 1993, it made disappointing profits of $188m with a further fall forecast to $150m in 1994. Analysts predict that BAT could rationalise American Tobacco with its operations if purchased. Combining the two firms' marketing and production operations could save BAT up to $150m. American Brands is prepared to sell American Tobacco for $1bn.

Source: adapted from *The Sunday Times*, 1.5.1994.

The US cigarette market

The US cigarette market is a large market, but it is in decline. In 1977, Americans smoked 617 billion cigarettes per year. By 1993, this had fallen to 485 billion. The US cigarette manufacturers have been caught out by a number of factors. There is now a much greater awareness of the health risks associated with cigarette smoking. Many states have passed laws restricting smoking in public spaces, whilst most large firms have banned smoking from places of work. Taxes on cigarettes have increased. The future is uncertain. The US government wants to impose higher taxes on smoking. The US cigarette companies are also facing a barrage of law suits claiming damages. This is nothing new, and cigarettes companies in the past have always won any court action because they have been able to prove that smokers were aware of the risks they faced when smoking. However, a number of new suits, including two from states claiming damages against medical costs of treating smokers, might just win. If they did, the damages resulting from these and further copycat suits would run into billions if not tens of billions of dollars.

Source: adapted from *The Sunday Times*, 1.5.1994.

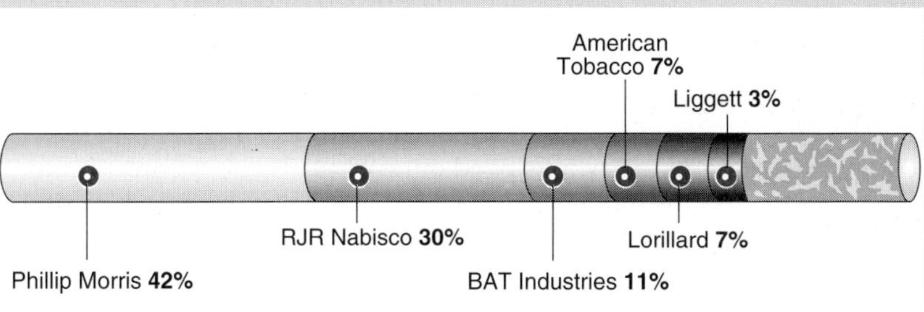

Figure 40.3 *US cigarette market by manufacturer, 1993*

Price fixing and collusion

Summary

1. **Collusion enables individual producers to share monopoly profits with other producers.**
2. **Cartels may collapse. Individual members have an incentive to cheat on the agreement. Non-cartel members may increase their market share at the expense of cartel members.**
3. **Restrictive trade practices are likely to lead to a loss of economic efficiency.**

Collusion

During the 19th century and for most of the 20th century, British industry was dominated by collective agreements. Firms COLLUDED to restrict competition. By colluding, firms could gain some monopoly power over their markets. As a result, they became price-makers rather than price-takers.

Consider Table 41.1. It shows the cost and revenues for an industry. If the market were perfectly competitive, then long run output would be 6 million units. This is because no firm in the industry could earn abnormal profit. If it did, competitor firms would be attracted into the industry, increasing supply and driving down prices and profits until abnormal profit was eliminated.

Table 41.1

Million units			£ millions
Output (a)	Average revenue (b)	Average cost (including normal profit) (c)	Total abnormal profit (b - c) x a
1	10	5	5
2	9	5	8
3	8	5	9
4	7	5	8
5	6	5	5
6	5	5	0

QUESTION 1 A firm operates in a perfectly competitive market with another 9999 firms in the market. A cartel is now formed in the industry, with all firms agreeing to join the cartel. The cartel is successful in erecting barriers to entry to the industry. The new cartel price is double the old free market price but all members of the cartel have had to reduce their output by 20 per cent.

(a) Draw a diagram for an individual firm in perfect competition marking on it the long run equilibrium output of the firm.
(b) Show what happens to the firm's equilibrium output and price after it has joined the cartel.
(c) Explain why the firm benefits from the cartel.

However, individual firms could earn abnormal profit if they combined together to force up price, restrict output and keep potential competitors out of the industry. The profit maximising level of output for the industry as a whole is 3 million units. If each firm in the industry agreed to half its current output, £9 million of abnormal profit could be shared between the colluding firms.

The problems facing cartels

A **cartel** is a group of producers which has agreed to restrict competition in the market. Possibly the most famous cartel today is OPEC, the Organisation of Petroleum Exporting Countries. Restricting competition is not necessarily easy.

- An agreement has to be reached. This is likely to be easiest in oligopolistic industries where only a few firms dominate the market; the larger the number of firms, the greater the possibility that at least one key participant will refuse to collude. It is also likely to be easiest in stable mature industries where no single firm has recently been able to gain advantage by pursuing aggressive competitive strategies. For instance, collusion is far more likely in a mature industry like steel manufacturing or cement making than in a rapidly changing industry like the computer industry.
- Cheating has to be prevented. Once an agreement is made and profitability in the industry is raised, it would pay an individual firm to cheat so long as no other firms do the same. For instance, it would pay a small cartel producer with 10 per cent of the market to expand production to 12 per cent by slightly undercutting the cartel price. The profit it would lose by the small cut in price on the 10 per cent is more than offset by the gain in profit on the sale of the extra 2 per cent. However, if every producer does this, the market price will quickly fall to the free market level and all firms will lose the privilege of earning abnormal profit.
- Potential competition must be restricted. Abnormal profits will encourage not only existing firms in the industry to expand output but also new firms to enter the industry. Firms already in the industry which don't join the cartel may be happy to follow the policies of the cartel in order to earn abnormal profits themselves. To prevent this, cartel firms could agree to drive other firms which compete too aggressively out of the market. Cartel firms could also agree to increase barriers to entry to the industry.

QUESTION 2

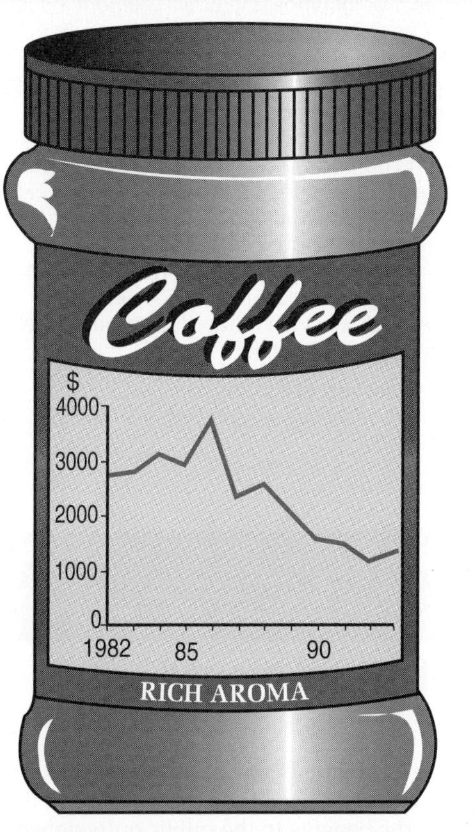

Source: adapted from UNCTAD, *Commodity Year Book 1994.*

Figure 41.1 *Coffee prices (ICA composite indicator price), $ per metric tonne*

Between 1962 and 1989, the International Coffee Agreement (ICA) created a cartel in the international coffee industry. Prices were kept artificially high as individual countries were given quotas restricting their sales of coffee onto world markets. The cartel broke down in 1989 because of the opposition of Brazil and Columbia. Brazil had seen its world market share decline from 40 per cent in 1962 to 24 per cent in 1988 as less efficient producers, particularly African countries, entered the market or increased production as a result of high prices. Prices fell sharply with Brazil vowing to drive high cost producers out of the market.

By the early 1990s, Brazil began to realise that it had made a mistake. Many Brazilian farmers went bankrupt, unable to survive with the new low prices. The value of Brazilian exports had fallen because any small increase in volumes sold was completely outweighed by the fall in price. Brazil then began to lobby to recreate the cartel. However, the coffee producers have not managed to agree on the terms on which a cartel could be recreated.

(a) Suggest reasons why Brazil took steps to break up the ICA.
(b) What problems about cartels does the breakdown of the ICA illustrate?

Restrictive trade practices and efficiency

RESTRICTIVE TRADE PRACTICES are strategies used by producers to restrict competition in the market. Cartels use them to enforce their collective agreements and to deter competitors. Individual firms use them to establish or reinforce monopoly positions. A wide variety of practices could have been and have been used, including minimum prices, market sharing agreements, resale price maintenance, refusal to supply firms which stock competitors' products, discriminatory pricing and sharing information. Examples are given in the applied section below.

The arguments for and against the restriction of competition have already been given in units 34, 35, 39 and 40. Restrictive trade practices tend to raise price and reduce output. There is therefore a loss of economic efficiency. There is also a redistribution of income from consumers to shareholders of companies because of abnormal profit. Choice may also be restricted. On the other hand, restrictive trade practices may enable companies to earn sufficient profit to engage in research and development to the benefit of consumers. They may also encourage potential competitors to bring new products to the market which are so attractive that the monopoly of an established producer is competed away.

Key terms

Collusion - collective agreements between producers which restrict competition.
Restrictive trade practices - strategies used by producers to restrict competition in the market.

QUESTION 3 In 1994, the European Commission imposed record fines totalling £193m on 33 European cement producers. The 33 companies, all members of the European Cement Association, had established what was known as the 'Cembureau agreement'. This prevented national producers from selling to other European countries. A French cement manufacturer was not allowed to sell into Germany, for instance. In return, German manufacturers agreed not to sell into the French market. All the EU countries were thus separated into distinct markets serviced solely by their own national producers. The cartel was enforced through an exchange of information on prices. Different producers fixed prices so that there was no incentive for a firm in one country to buy cement from a cement manufacturer in another country.

The Cembureau agreement came under pressure when firms in countries outside the EU decided to export into the EU. Eastern Europe posed a particular threat in the early 1990s. European cement manufacturers have tended to respond by buying up the cement companies in those countries. For instance, the Czech cement industry has effectively been bought up by French, German and Italian cement manufacturers.

The problem for the cement manufacturers is that open competition could be ruinous. Cement manufacture is very capital intensive. Cement is a low value good. What's more, the demand for cement is highly cyclical, varying with demand for construction goods in general. There would be a great temptation for cement companies with spare capacity in a period of low demand to sell below cost price. If all companies then tried to undercut each other, huge losses would result. The cement companies obviously decided that collusion was far more in their interests than competition.

(a) How did the cement manufacturers collude?
(b) Suggest what effect this collusion might have had on economic efficiency.

Applied economics

Restrictive trade prices - the legislative background

The Monopolies Commission, set up in 1948, quickly found that British industry was riddled with restrictive trade practices. In 1955 the Commission published a report on collective discrimination which detailed many such practices. The government of the day responded by passing the Restrictive Trade Practices Act in 1956.

The 1948 Monopolies Act made the fundamental assumption that monopolies were against the public interest only if this could be proved by the state. The 1956 Act took the opposite route. Restrictive trade practices would be illegal unless the companies involved could prove that the practices were in the public interest.

A court of law, the Restrictive Practices Court, was established. All firms which engaged in restrictive practices had to register these with the Registrar of Restrictive Trading Agreements. The agreements would then be brought before the Court which would either uphold them or order their abandonment.

The Act laid down eight 'gateways' through which companies could attempt to uphold their restrictive practices. Companies had to show the agreement was necessary:

- to protect the public against injury;
- because its abandonment would deny to the public specific and substantial benefits;
- to counter anti-competitive practices by other producers;
- to negotiate 'fair terms' with others;
- because otherwise there would be 'serious and persistent' effects on unemployment;
- to prevent a fall in exports;
- to uphold another agreement accepted by the Court.

Finally, an agreement would be allowed if it was not anti-competitive.

Even if the agreement met one of these criteria, then it would still be declared illegal (or 'struck down') if it was not shown that the benefits to the public outweighed the costs.

Subsequent acts widened the net of the 1956 Act. In 1964, the Resale Prices Act 1964 made it illegal for firms to enforce resale price maintenance (RPM) unless it could be shown to be in the public interest. RPM was a practice whereby a manufacturer could force a retailer to sell its product at a particular price, usually a minimum price. It meant that goods such as television sets or cigarettes from one manufacturer were sold at identical prices in all shops in the UK. Information agreements, where firms agreed to circulate price lists or market share figures amongst themselves, were made illegal in 1968. The 1976 Restrictive Practices Act included service industries as well as goods industries. The 1980 Competition Act gave powers to the Monopolies and Mergers Commission to investigate uncompetitive practices in monopoly situations.

Articles 85 and 86 of the Treaty of Rome cover restrictive practices. Price-fixing and market-sharing agreements are illegal unless it can be proved that they are of benefit to the public. The European Commission is responsible for investigating illegal EU-wide practices.

Three examples of restrictive trade practices

In many industries, the 1956 Restrictive Trade Practices Act brought to an end a tradition of collusive agreements. But there is evidence to suggest that they continued, illegally, in the the UK building trade. For instance, in

February 1989 the Office of Fair Trading took four ready-mixed concrete companies to the Court, alleging that the companies concluded price-fixing and market-sharing agreements in parts of Oxfordshire during 1983 and 1984. This was after the Office of Fair Trading had uncovered 146 price fixing and market-sharing agreements involving a large part of the ready-mixed concrete industry in the mid-1970s.

Until 1995 the book trade was covered by one of the few restrictive practices which the Restrictive Trade Practices Court upheld (i.e. made legal). Under the Net Book Agreement, publishers were allowed to set a minimum price for which a book may be sold. In effect, the prices of most books were the same whether bought in a small local booksellers, a supermarket or a large book chain. Publishers and small booksellers were, for the most part, in favour of the agreement. They argued that without the agreement consumers would buy from the cheapest source. These would be large book chains like W H Smith, or non-traditional booksellers like supermarkets or garage shops which had the financial power to buy cheaply in bulk. The small local bookseller would be forced out of business and many communities would be left without a bookshop. Consumers would also suffer from a smaller choice of books. Publishers would concentrate on producing fewer books which would be marketed more heavily, for instance by cutting their price. Opponents of the agreement argued that the small local bookseller would survive because most books are bought on impulse or as a present and convenience of purchase is therefore very important. Equally, the number of books sold would increase if the prices of some books were cut because the demand curve for books is downward sloping. The ending of the Net Book Agreement in 1995 provided an opportunity for ecnomists to study which of these arguments were correct.

At an EU level, the European Commission investigated the steel industry in the 1990s. In 1994, it imposed fines of ECU 104.4m (£79m) on 16 companies which were found to have been guilty of infringing all the provisions of Article 65 of the European Coal and Steel Treaty. This outlaws price-fixing, market-sharing and exchanging confidential information. British Steel was fined £24.3m. The steel producers had been faced with considerable over-capacity in the industry. Restricting output to raise price was too tempting to resist for the 16 companies involved.

The effectiveness of UK policy

There is general agreement that restrictive practices legislation has been effective in changing the climate of competition in the UK. Before 1956, most of manufacturing and much of the service sector contained restrictive practice agreements which operated to the advantage of the producer and to the detriment of the consumer. Since 1956, about 5 000 agreements have been registered with the Court. These represent a fraction of the number of agreements that were in operation. Almost all of the 5 000 were abandoned voluntarily before being brought before the Court.

However, the Office of Fair Trading and the European Commission continue to unearth agreements made in secret. Illegal restrictive trade practices are still present within some sectors of the economy.

Perhaps more importantly, there is much evidence to suggest that the merger boom in UK industry which started in the 1960s is a direct response to restrictive practices legislation. After 1956, firms could not collude to give themselves monopoly profits. There followed a period of intense competition. Some companies went out of business. Others were taken over. The result was increased concentration ratios throughout much of British industry. This process continued to the point where industry, as a whole, was able once again to enjoy the level of monopoly profits it earned before the abolition of restrictive agreements. For instance, P E Hart and R Clarke (1980 and 1984) estimated the average three firm concentration ratio in a sample of 42 industries increased from 29 per cent in 1951 to 32 per cent in 1958 but jumped to 41 per cent in 1968. Since then there has been little change. If this is true, restrictive practices legislation will have had little impact on efficiency in UK industry because collusion has been replaced by monopoly.

On the other hand, the creation of the **Single Market** (☞ unit 88) has considerably increased competition in markets where goods are traded internationally. This will have reduced concentration ratios and made domestic restrictive agreements more difficult to implement effectively. It is true though that industries which have been most reluctant to give up illegal restrictive practices in the UK, such as the cement industry or the chemicals industry, have also been the ones which have created European illegal cartels, precisely to counter the threat of increased competition from abroad. It is difficult to assess the extent to which illegal Europe-wide cartels exist.

The book trade until 1995 was covered by the Net Book Agreement, which had been upheld by the Restrictive Trade Practices Court.

The European car market

Car selling in the European Union: the 1985 block exemption

Car sales in the European Union are exempt from normal EU rules governing the sale of goods under a 1985 agreement. Car manufacturers have chosen to restrict competition in the market. Each car manufacturer appoints dealers in a local area to sell and service its cars. These dealers are given a 'territory' and manufacturers agree not to establish another dealership in this area. In return, dealers agree not to sell other makes of cars. They also agree only to stock spare parts provided by the manufacturer. Consumers in one country have been discouraged from buying the same car in other countries even when prices have been lower. They have been denied access to manufacturers' warranties and have been faced with different model specifications.

Table 41.2 *EU car prices*

Lowest=100 (May 1, 1994)	**Executive:** Volvo 850 GLE 2.5L	**Large:** GM Opel Vectra 1.6GL	**Medium:** VW Golf CL 60 PS	**Small:** Ford Fiesta 1.1CLX
Belgium	**124.6**	**119.4**	**117.2**	**116.7**
Germany	**117.3**	**129.0**	**117.0**	**125.6**
Spain	**104.3**	**114.1**	**100.0**	**108.6**
France	**117.0**	**118.9**	**113.3**	**114.7**
Ireland	**105.8**	**117.0**	**115.3**	**116.6**
Italy	**106.6**	**115.7**	**106.2**	**100.0**
Luxembourg	**124.6**	**119.4**	**112.1**	**116.7**
Netherlands	**116.9**	**118.8**	**110.8**	**125.0**
Portugal	**110.0**	**100.0**	**106.1**	**102.7**
UK	**100.0**	**116.9**	**116.8**	**121.1**

Source: adapted from European Commission.

Prices of the same car differ from country to country in the EU. Table 41.2 shows that in 1994, after allowing for differences in tax etc., prices could vary by over 20 per cent between one country and another.

The manufacturers' case

The motor manufacturers have argued that the block exemption is vital to the interests of consumers. Cars are complex products which need expert sale, repair and maintenance. Exclusive dealerships give consumers the certainty that they are buying a high quality product which will be safely maintained. They point out that there is fierce competition between manufacturers. Differences in car prices between countries are far less than for many consumer products such as washing machines or CDs which are not exempt from competition rules. Dealers also face severe competition in repairs from independent chains such as Kwik-Fit.

The block exemption 1995

In 1994, the European Commission published new regulations governing sales of cars in the EU. The 1985 block exemption was to stay in force apart from a number of minor alterations.

- Dealers could sell more than one make of vehicle. However, they could only do this if they sold each make of vehicle in a different building with a different sales force.
- Spare parts could be obtained by dealers from sources other than those of the manufacturer but only if they were of the same quality.
- Independent garages should be given access to the technical knowledge required for repairing vehicles.
- Practices which discouraged consumers from one country in the EU buying cars in another country would be banned.

The view of consumer organisations

Consumer organisations argue that the block exemption raises the prices of cars, maintenance and spares to the consumer because competition is restricted. They argue that safety issues can be addressed through a system of regulation for any garage wishing to carry out repair work. Consumers would be better off if they could choose from a variety of makes in the same showroom and be able to shop around from country to country for the cheapest prices.

1. **Explain how motor manufacturers in the EU restrict competition in the market.**
2. **Discuss whether the changes made in 1994 to the block exemption are likely to increase competition in the market.**
3. **Evaluate the extent to which the block exemption increases or reduces efficiency in the market.**

Consumer sovereignty

Summary

1. Consumer sovereignty exists when consumer choices determine the allocation of resources in the economy.
2. Consumer sovereignty can only fully exist if there is perfect information in the market.
3. Consumers are less likely to possess perfect information if they make infrequent purchases, if goods are technically complex, if time and risk are elements of the purchase and if the product is heavily advertised.
4. Advertising can be informative or persuasive. The former increases knowledge in the market. The latter is intended to manipulate consumer preferences.
5. Governments can increase consumer sovereignty by passing laws and increasing the availability of information in the market.

Consumer sovereignty

CONSUMER SOVEREIGNTY exists when resources are allocated according to the wishes of consumers (☞ unit 35). This will occur in a perfectly free market. Consumer spending is comparable to votes in an election. The companies which receive the most votes will be able to purchase the factors of production needed to produce the goods demanded by consumers. Firms which receive no votes will go out of business.

QUESTION 1 Many consumers are prepared to use their purchasing power to campaign for a cleaner environment, according to a survey by Leo Burnett, the advertising agency.

The survey of 2 000 adults showed that 72 per cent believed individuals can make a difference to environmental problems while 70 per cent said they would discriminate in favour of 'green' products. A total of 42 per cent were prepared to pay a premium for 'environmentally friendly' goods whilst 20 per cent were willing to boycott products they believed to be environmentally harmful, and 40 per cent were prepared to boycott products tested on animals.

Asked which retailers were actively helping to protect the environment, 32 per cent said The Body Shop, 25 per cent J Sainsbury and 25 per cent Boots The Chemists.

Source: the *Financial Times*, 15.11.1989.

(a) How can consumers 'campaign for a cleaner environment'?
(b) How does this illustrate the concept of consumer sovereignty?

Perfect information

Total consumer sovereignty only exists if there is perfect knowledge or perfect information in the market place (☞ unit 25). If consumers are to allocate their resources in a way which will maximise their utility, they need to know about the products they are buying. In many cases, consumers are well placed to make consumption decisions. For instance, a consumer is likely to be the best judge of whether to buy bananas or apples. However, there are markets where consumers have less than perfect knowledge.

In many markets, like those for cars, television sets or solicitors, consumers make infrequent purchases. If they buy, and find for whatever reason that they don't like the product, then it is very expensive to make a fresh choice. When they come to replace an item the product range may have changed completely. This is different from markets like food where consumers are making frequent purchases. In the food market, consumers can experiment at little cost and find the products they prefer. So in general, the less frequent the purchase, the less likely it is that consumers will have built up sufficient knowledge of the product to make a optimal choice.

Consumers may not be capable of making rational choices because of the technical nature of the product. For instance, consumers for the most part are unable to tell which make of freezer has the best insulation, which television set has the most durable components, or which solicitor might do the best conveyancing job on a house purchase.

Time and risk too pose problems. Consumers often find it difficult to project forward. Healthy 25 year olds may see little point in providing for health care or paying into a pension scheme. Yet when they have a serious accident or come to retire they may think that their utility would have been greater over time if they had made different spending decisions.

There are other reasons why consumers are sometimes not the best judge of what they should buy. Some goods, such as drugs (including alcohol and tobacco), are addictive, so the consumer is unable to make a rational choice about present and future consumption. Often these same goods also create externalities, such as increased crime or road accidents, not to mention the cost of medical treatment. Society, through government, may choose to limit or ban the sale of these goods because it does not wish to pay the cost of the externality.

Finally, consumer choices are deliberately manipulated by producers through advertising and other forms of marketing.

QUESTION 2

Why might consumers find it difficult to make rational choices about each of these products?

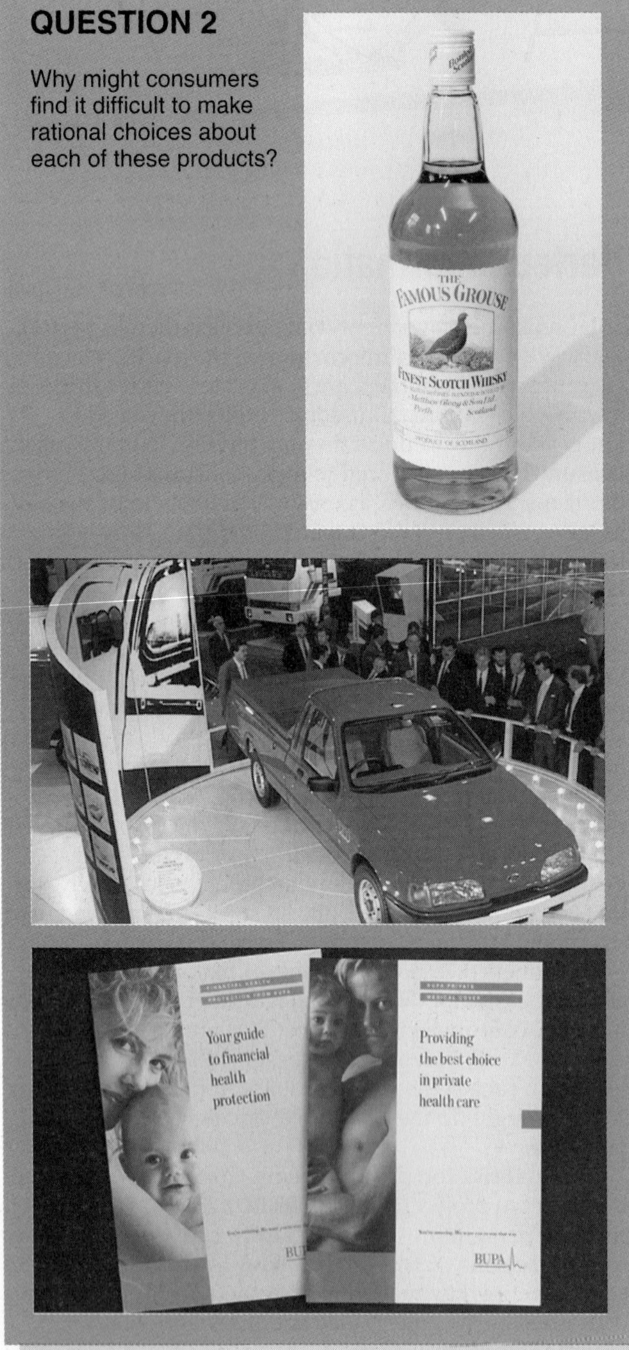

Informative and persuasive advertising

Between 1 and 2 per cent of UK national income is spent each year on advertising. On some products, such as some brands of soap powder, 25 per cent of the cost to the consumer is advertising cost. Advertising is a cost to the producer (a cost which of course will ultimately be borne by the consumer). Therefore producers must be convinced that advertising increases demand for their products if such large sums are spent on advertising each year.

Neo-classical economic theory predicts that advertising could be beneficial for a firm. Figure 42.1 shows the cost and revenue curves for a profit maximising monopolist. Before advertising, it faces a demand or average revenue curve of AR_1 and average and marginal cost curves of AC_1 and MC. A successful advertising campaign will push the firm's demand curve to the right to AR_2. The advertising campaign will cost money. It is debatable as to whether advertising is a fixed or variable cost, but here we will assume that it is a fixed cost. Hence the marginal cost curve will stay the same but average total cost will rise to AC_2. (The analysis is fundamentally no different if advertising is treated as a variable cost which consequently raises marginal cost too.) It can be seen that monopoly profits rise from ABCD to EFGH. The extra revenue generated as a result of the advertising campaign has been greater than the cost of the advertising campaign and the extra costs of production.

Two types of advertising can be distinguished. INFORMATIVE ADVERTISING is advertising which increases consumer knowledge about a product. Small ads in local newspapers, for instance, inform potential buyers that a product is for sale. Consumers may need to be made aware that a new product has come onto the market through a national advertising campaign. Firms may wish to inform consumers in local telephone directories that they supply services. In general, economists would argue that this type of advertising increases consumer

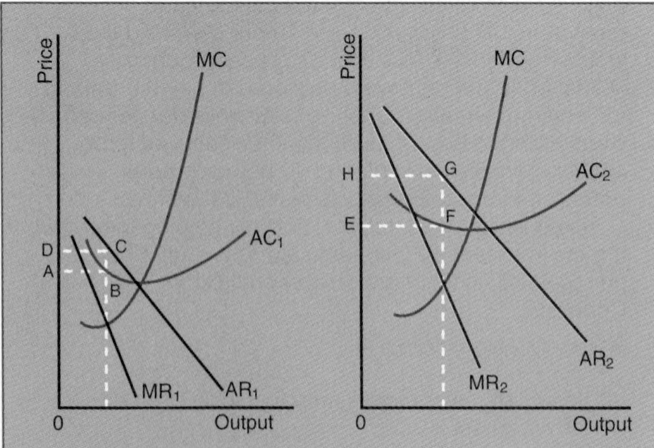

Figure 42.1 *The gains from advertising for a monopolist*
An advertising campaign which increases demand will increase abnormal profit from ABCD to EFGH despite an increase in average costs.

sovereignty because it enables consumers to make a more rational choice of what to buy. It gives them more information about what is available in the market place.

PERSUASIVE ADVERTISING is advertising intended to manipulate consumer preferences. Most television advertisements or large advertisements in magazines and newspapers are persuasive. These advertisements may contain some information, but the main aim is to persuade consumers that a particular product is more desirable than competitors' products. At best, persuasive advertising may tip the balance for a consumer who is undecided between alternative products. At worst, persuasive advertising makes consumers buy products they would otherwise not have bought.

QUESTION 3

To what extent do these advertisements increase consumer sovereignty?

Government policy

It is difficult to assess the extent to which consumer sovereignty exists in a modern industrialised economy. J K Galbraith, in his book *The New Industrial State*, argued that consumer sovereignty was largely lacking in markets dominated by oligopolistic and monopoly industries (i.e. most of manufacturing industry and much of the service industry). Producers were able through advertising and promotion to channel consumer spending. Of course consumers won't buy just any product because it is advertised. But they will buy product X rather than product Y if the producer can find the right combination of jingle, story, sex symbol or other image to associate with the product.

On the other hand free market economists argue that even if consumer knowledge is imperfect, the alternatives which involve the state deciding what is desirable or undesirable leads to a far less efficient allocation of resources.

Governments have a wide range of choice of policies to correct possible market failure arising from imperfect consumer knowledge.

Governments can try to prevent sellers from misinforming the consumer. Much of consumer protection legislation is designed to protect the consumer from unfair practices on the part of sellers. For instance, the Trade Descriptions Act 1968 made it illegal for retailers to sell goods with misleading descriptions. Government can also encourage or force sellers to provide information which

QUESTION 4

To what extent does this advertisement extend or limit consumer sovereignty?

they might otherwise prefer not to give. Contents of manufactured food, or 'best before' dates, are two such examples.

The government can help consumers fight more effectively for redress against often better financed sellers. Making it cheaper to take a firm to court, for instance through a Small Claims Court system, makes consumers far more powerful.

The government can also provide information itself to the consumer, or encourage independent bodies to do so. Bodies such as the British Standards Institution and local Trading Standards Departments help in this area.

More controversial are bans on advertising. Alcohol and tobacco advertising is already limited in the UK. It would be possible to introduce much wider controls on advertising, particularly to control persuasive advertising. However, governments have chosen not to, partly because of a scepticism (not shared by industry) about the effectiveness of such advertising. Moreover, advertising creates tax revenue and pays for commodities such as television services which otherwise might have to be paid for by government or by consumers. The consumer lobby is also far weaker than industrial lobbies because consumers are fragmented whilst large firms may spend considerable sums of money persuading government of their case. As Galbraith pointed out, governments can be 'captured' by industry and manipulated to serve the interests of business against the interests of the consumer.

Ultimately it may be felt that consumers are not in the best position to decide how resources should be allocated and that collective provision is necessary. Health care, education and pension provision are some of the markets where governments have decided that free markets can lead to market failure. This will be explored in more detail in unit 44.

Key terms

Consumer sovereignty - exists when the economic system permits resources to be allocated according to the wishes of consumers.
Informative advertising - advertising which increases consumer knowledge about a product.
Persuasive advertising - advertising intended to manipulate consumer preferences.

Applied economics

Advertising in the UK

Advertising is big business in the UK. As Figures 42.2 shows, advertising expenditure has risen broadly over time, with spending averaging over 1.5 per cent of national income (measured by GDP) in the 1990s. In 1994, it represented a spending of approximately £156 per head, or £624 for a family of four per year. If advertising were banned, consumers would have to pay for commercial television, for instance through decoder systems as with satellite and cable television. They would also have to pay much higher prices for newspapers and many magazines. Even so, the advertising industry uses up a significant proportion of resources in the economy, resources which have an opportunity cost.

Producers use advertising because they know that it influences consumer preferences and therefore, arguably, reduces consumer sovereignty and increases producer sovereignty. For instance, BMW, in a winning case study written for the 1994 Advertising Effectiveness Awards, argued that advertising expenditure of £91m between 1979 and 1993 created extra sales of £3bn. BMW was a small marque in the UK with sales of 13 000 cars a year when BMW(UK) was created in 1979 to take over the franchise to sell the luxury cars in the UK. It set itself the twin objectives of maintaining high profit margins whilst trebling sales to 40 000 by 1990. It more than achieved these objectives through a long term advertising campaign which emphasised the technical superiority of the car. With a theme of the 'ultimate driving machine', BMWs were shown as 'precise, cold, technical icons with jewel-like perfection'.

Another 1994 winner of the Advertising Effectiveness Awards was Whitbread the brewers. In 1989 it bought Boddingtons brewery in Manchester and decided to turn the bitter produced at the brewery into a national brand without alienating its existing regional drinkers. Whitbread gradually built up its advertising spending on Boddingtons from £1.8m in 1991 to £4.5m in 1993. The campaign emphasised the creamy appearance of the brand which was then linked to smooth taste when the beer was drunk. By 1994, it was the fourth largest bitter brand in the UK and had trebled its sales since 1989.

Not all advertising is successful of course. However, firms only advertise because they know that advertising has the potential to change consumer preferences. Consumers do buy products which are advertised in preference to ones which are not advertised.

Because advertising is widely recognised to change consumer behaviour, governments have been forced to regulate advertising. In the UK, the advertising industry regulates itself through the Advertising Standards Authority (ASA). This is an 'independent' body paid for by the advertising industry. It has the powers to request but not order a company to halt a particular advertising campaign if it is not legal, decent, honest and truthful. Consumers or other interested parties are free to complain to the ASA which will then look at the complaint and

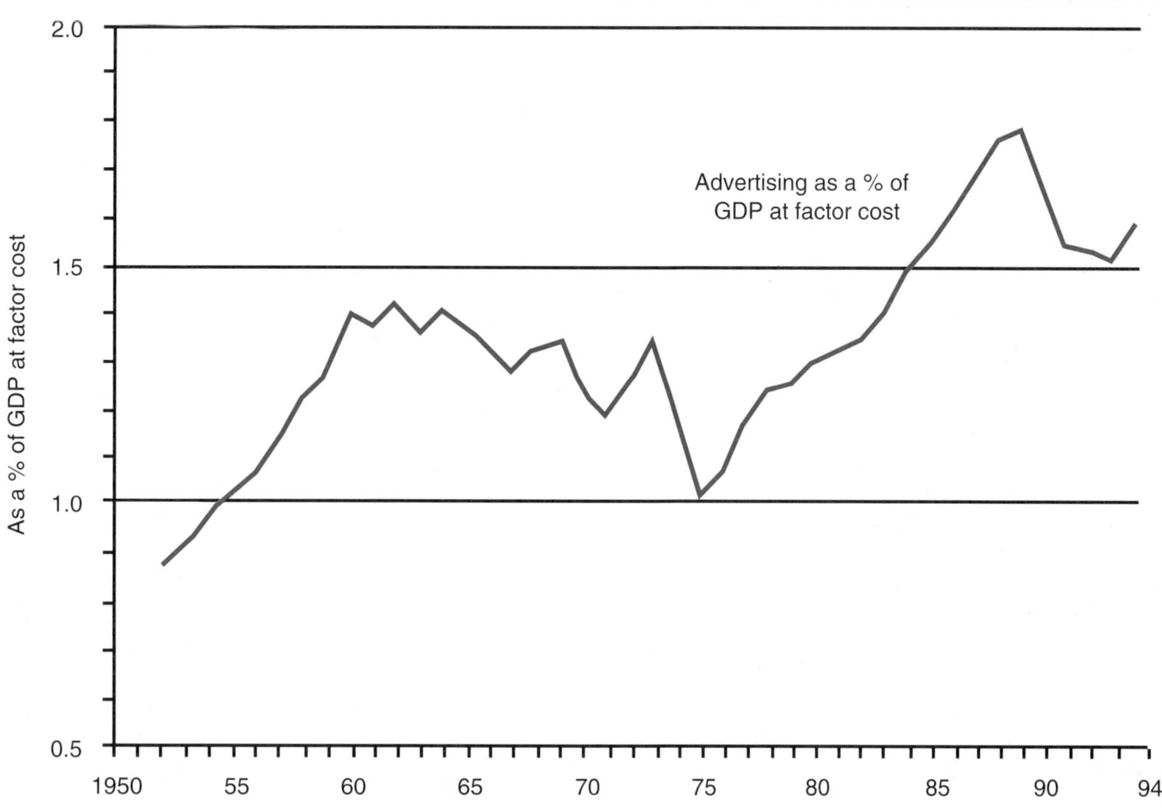

Source: The Advertising Association.

Figure 42.2 *Advertising expenditure as % of GDP at factor cost*

either uphold it or reject it. If the complaint is upheld, the company will be asked to withdraw the advertisement. If they refuse, the ASA will bring pressure to bear on the company to change its mind. It will make it known in the media that the company is being awkward. It will ask newspapers, magazines, television companies, etc. to refuse to carry any further advertisements. It will also ask the Post Office to refuse to carry any advertising literature through the post from the company.

Self-regulation is cheap for the industry and for anyone wishing to make a complaint. However, there are many situations where a much tougher line is needed. For instance, withdrawing an advert does not help dissatisfied customers see firms prosecuted and get their money back. In this case, there are consumer laws, such as the Trade Descriptions Act or the Sales of Goods Act which deter firms from making misleading claims and which allow consumers to claim compensation.

In other cases, the government has regulated advertising directly. For instance, in the UK tobacco manufacturers are not allowed to advertise on television, whilst any advert in a newspaper or magazine must carry a government health warning. The tobacco manufacturers argue that this is a restriction on liberty and free speech. It reduces consumer sovereignty because consumers are denied access to information about what brands are available on the market. They further argue that advertising cannot increase demand for a particular type of product, such as cars or cigarettes. Instead, advertising merely increases demand for a particular brand of product. Hence, bans on tobacco advertising have no effect on overall smoking levels but do affect which brand of cigarette is being smoked. Taking another example, a ban on advertising of alcoholic drink would not reduce sales of alcohol but it would affect what type of alcohol was being consumed.

Economists would argue that economic efficiency would be increased if informative advertising were encouraged whilst persuasive advertising were discouraged. However, because it is almost impossible to draw a dividing line between the two types of advertising, it is difficult to lay down practical policy guidelines. What's more, heavy advertisers tend to be precisely the firms which maintain close links with those in power, such as MPs and government departments. 'Capture' by firms of government (☞ unit 45) maintains economic inefficiency.

Tobacco

Table 42.1 *Tobacco advertising in the EU*

(TV advertising is banned throughout EU)		Cigarettes per capita per annum (1991)
France	Banned	1,714
Portugal	Banned	1,503
Italy	Banned - widely circumvented by indirect advertising	1,691
Belgium	Severe restrictions; total ban in the pipeline	1,681*
Denmark	Local radio ban; other controls through voluntary agreement	1,556
Germany	Banned on radio. Other legal controls and voluntary agreements	1,821
Greece	Banned on radio. Other controls	3,012
Ireland	Detailed regulations	1,714
Luxembourg	Major legal restrictions	1,681*
Netherlands	Banned on radio; press and posters voluntary agreements	1,222
Spain	Radio and poster banned; additional voluntary restrictions	2,140
UK	Voluntary agreements	1,641

* For Belgium and Luxembourg combined.
Source: adapted from *Action Smoking and Health* and *Euromonitor.*

From Mr A.D.C. Turner.

Sir, Lucy Kellaway, in her article ('Fighting to the last gasp', February 8) about tobacco advertising ban proposals emanating from Brussels, asks why, if there is no link between advertising and consumption of tobacco, would the tobacco industry wish to advertise?

The answer remains as it has been over many years of a declining UK market; namely that the 300 brands of cigarettes currently on sale must advertise to retain, or gain, market share. A total ban would simply see an immediate freezing of the brand share picture with total consumption not necessarily being related.

European Commission officials appear to have little or no understanding of the role of advertising as it pertains to a mature product category.

A.D.C. Turner,
Deputy Chief Executive,
Tobacco Advisory Council,*
Glen House, Stag Place, SW1.

* 1995 - The Tobacco Manufacturers Association.
Source: *Financial Times*, 13.2.1990.

Promotion in the USA

Tobacco companies in the USA continue to promote cigarettes with some success. In 1994, RJ Reynolds was accused by the Federal government of being so successful at appealing to young people with its Camel brand advertising that it wanted to see the advertising campaign banned. However, advertising is declining in relative importance in the total promotion mix. In the late 1980s, advertising represented one-third of the typical promotion budget. By 1994, this had fallen to 20 per cent. The companies, instead, have been spending more on such things as direct mail and free gifts. Large databases on smokers have been compiled and used to target potential clients by sending free packs through the post. Marlboro, the single largest company and brand in the US market, operates a free gift scheme with smokers collecting stamps to receive anything from binoculars to lighters. RJ Reynolds has introduced a 'flavour seal' in its Winston brand of cigarettes. Made of polyester film, the seals have boosted market share of the brand by capitalising on the cigarettes' freshness. Advertising is still important though. The Marlboro man, a macho image smoking a cigarette, is one of the most widely recognised advertising symbols in the USA. RJ Reynolds has been very successful with its cartoon Joe Camel advertisements. In 1992, the Medical College of Georgia found in research that children between the ages of three and five were as familiar with Joe Camel as they were with Mickey Mouse. Bans on direct television advertising are widely flouted by sponsoring sports events and purchasing billboard space at televised events.

In 1994, the World Health Organisation (WHO) and the Imperial Cancer Research Fund published a study entitled 'Mortality from Smoking in Developed Countries 1950-2000'. It concluded that 3m people each year are dying from smoking related diseases. The main victims at the moment are males in developed countries who started smoking in the mid-1940s. However, falls in the number of male smokers in developed countries should lead to a fall in smoking-related deaths in this group. The number of female deaths in developing countries is rising though because of an increase in smoking by this group over the past 50 years. The number of deaths worldwide will almost certainly increase in the future because of the large increase in smoking and an increase in life expectancy in the Third World. Smokers in developing countries are now living long enough to be killed by their habit.

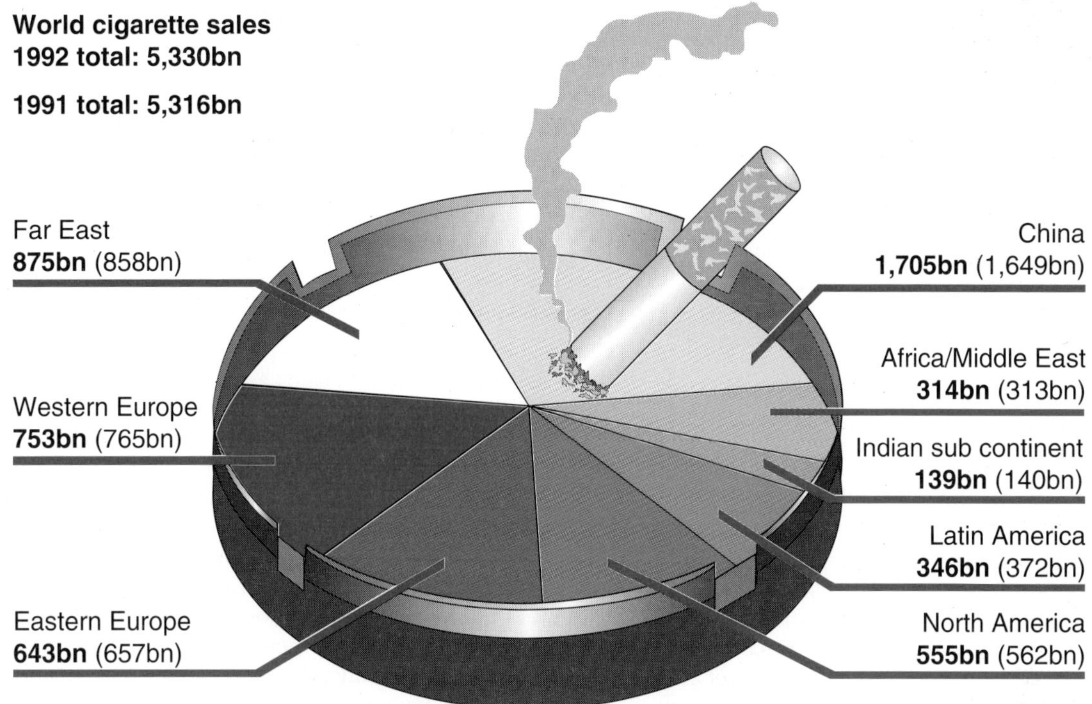

Figure 42.4 *World cigarette sales, 1992*

In 1994, the tobacco industry was investigated by a congressional committee in the United States. It maintained firmly throughout the proceedings that, in its opinion, nicotine was not addictive and that smoking did not cause lung cancer.

The committee did force Brown and Williamson, the US tobacco company owned by the UK BAT industries, to concede that it had used high-nicotine tobacco in some of its brands in 1993. The tobacco contained twice the amount of nicotine normally found in tobacco plants and came from genetically engineered plants grown in Brazil. Brown and Williamson said that the tobacco had been withdrawn from use by 1994 because it had proved unpopular with smokers.

It is well known that tobacco companies use a variety of techniques to increase the nicotine intake of cigarettes. For instance, ammonia is used in cigarettes as an 'impact booster', doubling the amount of nicotine a smoker inhales.

Source: adapted from the *Financial Times*, 23.10.1993, 22.6.1995, 25.6.1994, 22.9.1994, 14.10.1994.

1. **Outline patterns of world cigarette consumption and explain how cigarette manufacturers promote their products.**
2. **Discuss to what extent (a) advertising and other forms of promotion of cigarettes and (b) cigarettes themselves reduce consumer sovereignty in the market.**
3. **Evaluate from an economic perspective whether there should be a complete ban on (a) advertising of cigarettes; (b) all forms of promotion of cigarettes; (c) the sale of cigarettes.**

unit 43 Equality and equity

Summary

1. In a market economy, there is a variety of reasons why the incomes of individuals and households differ, including differences in wage rates, economic activity and financial wealth.
2. A Lorenz curve can be used to show the degree of inequality in income in society.
3. Two types of equity or fairness can be distinguished - horizontal equity and vertical equity.
4. There can be a conflict between efficiency and equity, although redistributive government policies need not necessarily result in greater inefficiency.

Resource allocation, equality and equity

The chairperson of a large company may earn hundreds of thousands of pounds per year. A pensioner might exist on a few thousand pounds per year. This distribution of income in the economy is the result of the complex interaction between the workings of the market and government intervention in the market. Markets are impersonal. They produce a particular allocation of resources which may or may not be efficient but is almost certainly not equal. In this unit, we will consider how the market allocates resources and then consider how the market may be judged on grounds of equality and EQUITY (or fairness).

The distribution of resources in a market economy

Individuals receive different incomes in a market economy. This is because it is based on the ownership of property. Individuals, for instance, are not slaves. They are able to hire themselves out to producers and earn income. They might own shares in a company and receive dividends, a share of the profits. They might own a house from which they receive rent. How much they receive depends upon the forces of demand and supply.

Workers with scarce skills in high demand, such as chairpersons of companies, can receive large salaries. Workers with few skills and in competition with a large number of other unskilled workers are likely to receive low wages. Workers who fail to find a job will receive no wage income through the market mechanism. These workers might be highly capable and choose not to take a job. On the other hand, they might be disabled or live in a very high unemployment region. Similarly, the market decides upon the value of physical assets and the income that can be earned from them through the market mechanism. If an individual inherits a house, all other things being equal, the house will be worth more if it is in Central London than if it is in Doncaster. The rent on the house will be higher in Central London. Shares in one company will be differently priced to shares in another company, and the dividends will be different.

The owners of assets which have a high value are likely to earn a high income. The **human capital** (☞ unit 2) of the chairperson of ICI is likely to be very high and therefore he or she will be able to command a high salary. The Duke of Westminster, the largest individual landowner in London, owns large amounts of physical capital. This too generates large incomes. Some individuals own large amounts of financial capital, such as stocks and shares. Again, they will receive a far larger income than the majority of the population who own little or no financial capital.

In a pure free market economy, where the government plays only a small role in providing services, such as defence, those with no wealth would die unless they could persuade other individuals to help them. Usually, non-workers are supported by others in the family. In many societies, the family network provides the social security net. Charities too may play a small role.

In the UK, the government has made some provision for the poor since medieval times. In Victorian England, the destitute were sent to workhouses where conditions were made so unpleasant that it was meant to encourage people to work to stay out of these institutions. Since 1945, a welfare state has been created which goes some way towards altering the distribution of income to ensure greater equality (☞ unit 102). In other words, government has decided that the market mechanism produces an allocation of resources which is sub-optimal from an equality viewpoint and attempts to correct this situation.

Causes of inequality in income

There are a number of reasons why the PERSONAL DISTRIBUTION OF INCOME is unequal in a market economy.

Earned income Some workers earn more than others. The reasons for this are explored in units 48-54.

Unemployment and retirement Not all people work. Non-workers are likely to receive lower incomes than those in work. The increase in the numbers of unemployed and the retired in recent years in the UK, for instance, is likely to have been a cause of increases in poverty.

Physical and financial wealth Those in society who own a great deal of physical or financial wealth will be able to generate a higher income from their assets than those who own little or nothing. Wealth is accumulated in two main ways. First, a significant proportion of wealthy individuals has inherited that wealth. Second, wealthy individuals may have built up their wealth over their life time from working or from multiplying their existing assets, for instance through playing the Stock Exchange or simply holding onto an asset which grows in value at a particularly fast rate.

Household composition How income is measured can be important in determining inequalities. An individual may earn a high salary. However, if he or she has to support a large family, then the income per person in the household may be quite low. On the other hand, a household where there are two parent wage earners and four child wage earners may have a high income despite the fact that all six adults are individually 'low paid'. So inequalities differ according to whether they are being measured per individual or per household.

Government policy The extent to which government redistributes income through taxes and benefits will affect the distribution of income. This is explored in unit 102.

The degree of competition in product markets Imperfectly competitive markets will result in a different distribution of income and wealth than perfectly competitive markets. Consider Figure 43.1. It shows the cost and revenue curves for an industry (☞ unit 39). If the industry were perfectly competitive, production would take place where price = MC at output level OB. If the industry now became a multi-plant monopolist, output would be at OA where MC = MR. EFG is the allocative loss to society. It is sometimes called a **deadweight loss** because the loss is not recoverable. However, there is also a transfer of income from consumers to the monopoly producer represented by the rectangle CDEF. Under perfect competition, the consumer would only have paid OCFA for the output OA. Under monopoly, consumers are forced to pay ODEA.

In a free market system, monopolies are owned by private shareholders. In the nineteenth century, these private shareholders would, for the most part, have been private individuals. Undoubtedly some, such as the Rockefellers and the Vanderbilts, grew extremely rich from monopoly profits. Today, monopolies are more likely to be owned by pension funds, assurance companies and a host of other financial institutions which channel savings through the money and capital markets on behalf of wealthy and not so wealthy individuals. In the nineteenth century, elections particularly in the USA could be won or lost on this monopoly profit issue. Today, it is a less important issue because monopoly profits are distributed more widely through the economic system. However, it should still be remembered that monopolies effectively

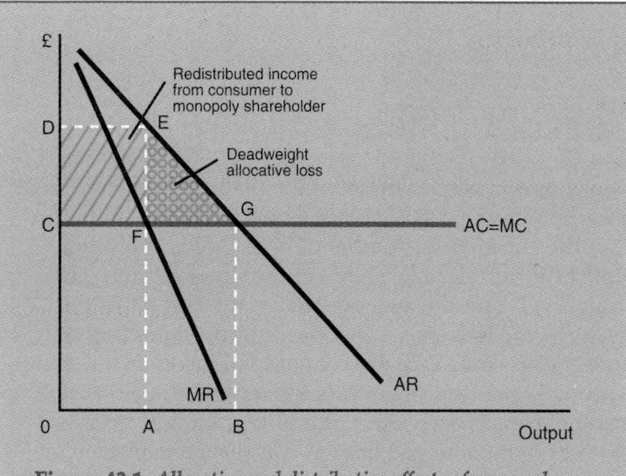

Figure 43.1 *Allocative and distributive effects of monopoly*
If the industry is perfectly competitive, it will produce at OB where price = MC. If it were a multi-plant monopolist, it would produce at OA where MC = MR. EFG is the deadweight allocative loss to society. CDEF is the total 'tax' of the monopolist on the consumer. It results in a redistribution of income from consumer to shareholder.

QUESTION 1

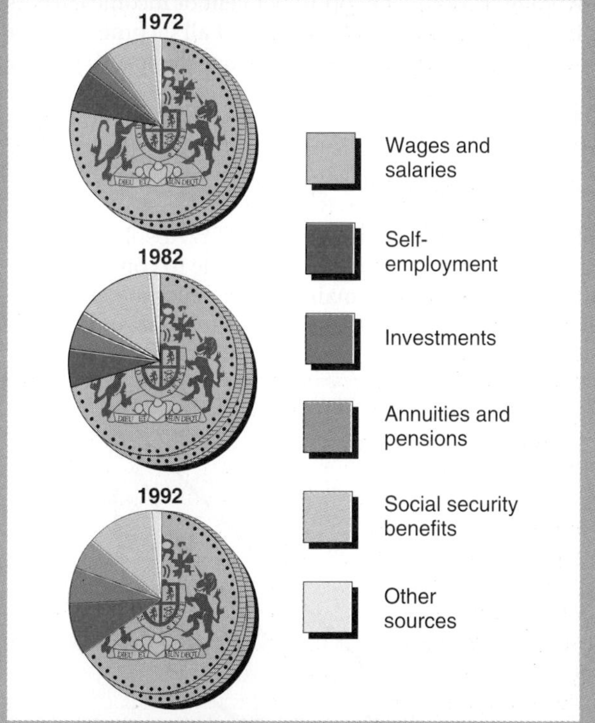

Source: adapted from Family Expenditure Surveys.

Figure 43.2 *How sources of income have changed*

(a) How have the sources of income for UK households changed between 1972 and 1992?
(b) Inequalities have increased over the twenty year period. Using the data, suggest why this has occurred.

impose a 'tax' on consumers, the revenue being received by shareholders.

Measuring inequality

One common way to measure inequalities in income is to use a LORENZ CURVE. On the horizontal axis in Figure 43.3, the cumulative number of households is plotted, whilst the vertical axis shows cumulative income. The straight 45° line shows a position of total equality. For instance, the line shows that the bottom 20 per cent of households receive 20 per cent of total income whilst the bottom 80 per cent of households receive 80 per cent of income. Hence, each 1 per cent of households receives 1 per cent of income and there is complete equality of income.

Line 1 shows an income distribution which is relatively equal. The bottom 20 per cent of households receive 10 per cent of income. This means that they receive half the average income. The top 10 per cent of households (between 90 and 100 on the horizontal axis) receive 20 per cent of income (from 80 to 100 on the vertical axis). So they receive twice the average income.

Line 2 shows a very unequal society. The bottom 50 per cent of the population receive only 10 per cent of income. Therefore half of all households receive one-fifth (10 ÷ 50) of average income. The top 10 per cent of income earners, on the other hand, earn 60 per cent of all income (from 40 to 100 on the vertical axis). That means the top 10 per cent earn 6 times the average income.

These two examples taken together show that the farther the Lorenz curve is from the 45° line, the greater the income inequality in society.

Inequality is sometimes discussed in terms of ABSOLUTE and RELATIVE POVERTY. Absolute poverty occurs when human beings are not able to consume sufficient **necessities** to maintain life. Human beings who are homeless or malnourished suffer from absolute poverty. Absolute poverty can be eradicated from society. In the UK today there are some suffering from absolute poverty, such as homeless young people, but the vast majority of the population have a sufficiently high income not to be poor in this sense. The largest concentrations of absolute poverty today are to be found in the Third World.

Relative poverty is always present in society. The poor in this sense are those at the bottom end of the income scale. There is no exact measure of this, like the poorest 10 per cent or 20 per cent of society. But Adam Smith gave one measuring rod of relative poverty when he wrote that necessities were 'whatever the custom of the country renders it indecent for creditable people, even of the lower order, to be without.'

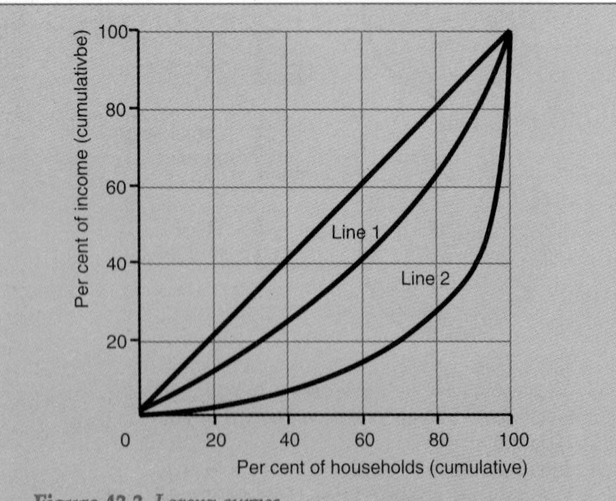

Figure 43.3 *Lorenz curves*
A Lorenz curve shows the degree of inequality of income in a society. The farther from the 45° line is the curve, the greater the degree of inequality.

QUESTION 2

Table 43.1 *Distribution of disposable household income*[1]

	Quintile groups of households				
	Bottom fifth	Next fifth	Middle fifth	Next fifth	Top fifth
1979	10	14	18	23	35
1991-92	7	12	17	23	41

1. After direct taxes and benefits.
Source: adapted from CSO, *Social Trends.*

(a) Construct two Lorenz curves from the data above.
(b) Has the distribution of income become more or less equal between 1979 and 1991-92?

Horizontal and vertical equity

Inequalities are not necessarily unfair. For instance, assume one worker worked 60 hours per week and another in an identical job worked 30 hours per week. It would seem fair that the 60 hour per week worker should receive roughly twice the pay even though this would then lead to inequality in pay between the two workers. Similarly, many poor pensioners today are poor because they failed to make adequate pension provision for themselves whilst they were working. It seems only fair that a worker who has saved hard all her life through a pension scheme should enjoy a higher pension than one who has decided to spend all her money as she earned it. Nevertheless, there is an inequality in this situation. In economics, EQUITY or fairness is defined in a very precise way in order to distinguish it from inequality.

Horizontal equity HORIZONTAL EQUITY is the identical treatment of identical individuals in identical situations. Inequitable treatment can occur in a number of different situations in our society today. An Asian applicant for a job may be turned down in preference to a white applicant even though they are the same in all other respects. A woman may apply to a bank for a business loan and be refused when a male applicant for exactly the same project may have been successful. A 55 year old may be refused a job in preference to a 25 year old despite identical employment characteristics. An 18 year old may gain a place at university in preference to another solely because her father is much richer.

Vertical equity Everybody is different, from the colour of their hair to the size of their toes and from their intellectual capacities to their social background. VERTICAL EQUITY is the different treatment of people with different characteristics in order to promote greater equity. For instance, if equity were defined in terms of equality, vertical equity would imply that everybody should have the opportunity to receive the same standard of education and the same standard of health care whatever their job, race, income or social background.

QUESTION 3

Table 43.2 *Gross weekly earnings, gross hourly earnings and hours worked per week, male and female UK*[1]

	Average gross weekly earnings (£)		Hours worked per week		Average gross hourly earnings (£)		Retail Price Index (1985=100)
	Males	Females	Males	Females	Males	Females	
1971	32.9	18.3	42.9	37.4	0.74	0.47	21.4
1981	140.5	91.4	41.7	37.2	3.32	2.42	79.1
1991	318.9	222.4	41.5	37.4	7.55	5.91	141.1
1994	362.1	261.5	41.6	37.6	8.61	6.89	152.3

1. Full time employees on adult rates whose pay was not affected by absence.
Source: adapted from Department of Employment, *Employment Gazette.*

(a) To what extent has horizontal equity between males and females increased over time in the UK?
(b) Suggest reasons why there has been this change.

Equity vs efficiency

Governments intervene in the market to redistribute income because it is widely accepted that the distribution of income thrown up by the workings of free market forces is unacceptable. In a pure free market, efficiency is maximised because all production takes place where price = MC (☞ unit 34). If a government then intervenes in the market, say by subsidising food for the poor, imposing taxes of any kind to pay for government expenditure, subsidising housing or providing welfare benefits, it introduces a distortion in the market. Hence, government intervention leads to allocative inefficiency.

In practice there are no pure free market economies. Economies are riddled with market imperfections, such as oligopolistic and monopoly industries, monopoly unions and externalities. The theory of the second best shows that introducing another distortion, such as welfare payments to the poor, may in fact lead to greater economic efficiency. The theory suggests that efficiency will be greatest if the distortion is spread thinly across many markets rather than concentrated on a few markets. For instance, it is likely that large housing subsidies combined with no subsidies to any other goods would lead to less economic efficiency than small subsidies spread across all goods in the economy. Equally, low levels of unemployment benefit available to all unemployed workers in the economy are likely to lead to greater economic efficiency than high levels of unemployment benefit available only to male manual employees.

QUESTION 4 In 1976, the government replaced a scheme whereby a few per cent of handicapped people received specially adapted small cars, by Mobility Allowance, a benefit which all handicapped people with mobility problems would receive. Those who used to receive a car complained bitterly because the new Mobility Allowance was only a fraction of what a car cost to buy and run.

To what extent did the change described lead to (a) greater equity and (b) greater efficiency?

Key terms

Equity - fairness.
Personal distribution of income - the distribution of the total income of all individuals.
Lorenz curve - shows the extent of inequality of income in society.
Absolute poverty - absolute poverty exists when individuals do not have the resources to be able to consume sufficient necessities to survive.
Relative poverty - poverty which is defined relative to existing living standards for the average individual.
Horizontal equity - the identical treatment of identical individuals or groups in society in identical situations.
Vertical equity - the different treatment of individuals or groups which are dissimilar in characteristics.

Applied economics

The distribution of income and wealth in the UK

The distribution of income

Income is distributed unevenly in the UK. Table 43.3 gives three measures of distribution of income between households. Original income is the gross income of households from sources such as wages and salaries, private pensions and investment income. Disposable income is gross income after income tax and National Insurance contributions have been paid but including state welfare benefits such as unemployment benefit, family credit and the state old age pension. Final income is disposable income minus indirect taxes such as VAT, but including the value of state services such as education and the National Health Service.

Table 43.3 *Distribution of income*[1]

	Percentage of total					
	Bottom fifth	Next fifth	Middle fifth	Next fifth	Top fifth	Total
Original income						
1976	4	10	18	26	43	100
1993	2	6	16	26	49	100
Disposable income						
1976	10	14	18	23	36	100
1993	7	11	17	24	41	100
Final income						
1976	10	14	18	23	36	100
1993	10	12	18	23	38	100

1. Figures may not add up to 100 due to rounding.
Source: adapted from CSO, *Social Trends*.

The statistics give an indication of the extent of inequality in income. For instance, in 1993, the bottom 20 per cent of households (mostly pensioner households and those with unemployed adults) received only 2 per cent of total original income generated in the UK. That means that each household received just 0.1 (2 ÷ 20) of average income in the UK. In comparison, the top 20 per cent of households received 49 per cent of total UK original income. On average each of these households received 2.45 times (49 ÷ 20) the average income.

In a welfare state, it should be expected that the distribution of disposable income and final income would show less inequality than original income. Taxes should fall most heavily on the better off whilst benefits should be received mainly by the poorer sections of society. Table 43.3 shows that to some extent this is true in the UK. The share of disposable income of the bottom 20 per cent of households was 7 per cent in 1993 (compared to 2 per cent of original income). That means that the average household in the bottom 20 per cent received 0.35 (7 ÷ 20) of the average income. The share of the top 20 per cent of households was 41 per cent giving the average household 2.05 times the average income in the UK. Figures for final income (disposable income minus indirect taxes such as VAT plus the value of benefits in kind such as education and the NHS) differ little compared to disposable income although the bottom 20 per cent of households show some increase in their share of income under this measure.

It should be remembered that there will be considerable variation in income within each of the quintile groups (groups of 20 per cent). For instance, in the bottom quintile there will be some households whose final income will be markedly less than the average for the group. On the other hand in the top quintile there will be a few who will earn hundreds of times the national average income. Equally, the statistics say nothing about how many people live in a household. A one person household in the bottom quintile may have a higher income per person than a six person household in the middle quartile.

Trends in the distribution of income

For most of this century, the long term trend has been for income differentials to narrow. Since 1979, this trend has been reversed. Figure 43.4 shows that in the 1980s the poorest 10 per cent of the population saw their annual incomes after housing costs have been taken into account fall by nearly 20 per cent. In contrast, average incomes after housing costs rose by around 35 per cent whilst the top 10 per cent increased their incomes by 61 per cent. The majority of the population over the period received an increase in income which was below the average, whilst the top 30 per cent received increases above the average.

There are a number of reasons why this occurred. First, wage inequalities have widened. In 1994, the real hourly wage rate for men in the bottom tenth of the earnings league was lower than their 1975 level. In contrast, the wages of the top 10 per cent had increased by over 50 per cent of the same period. Why wage inequalities have increased is debatable. However, it is likely to have something to do with the fall in demand for unskilled labour in an economy which is becoming more and more capital intensive, the decrease in trade union power which previously had helped lift the wages of the low paid, and the increased internationalisation of the UK economy which puts unskilled labour in direct competition with unskilled labour in the third world.

Second, there has been a growth in occupational pension income. These are incomes paid by pension schemes to former employers. High income earners tend to be part of occupational pension schemes. When they retire, they tend to be relatively well off. Low income earners, on the other hand, are often not offered membership of such schemes. When they retire, they have to rely almost entirely on the state pension scheme. Since 1981, this has only grown in line with inflation. Hence there is a growing inequality between pensioners who rely on the flat rate state pension which is not growing at all in real terms, and those who retire on occupational schemes which are linked to rises in earnings.

Third, high income earners tend to have more financial wealth. As discussed below, the distribution of wealth is highly uneven. The bottom 20 per cent of income earners will receive almost nothing from investment and other income. They receive little benefit from, say, the growth of firms which is reflected in increasing dividend payments on shares over time. In contrast, the top 20 per cent earned 11 per cent of their total income from investment income likely to be increasing in line with the real growth of the economy.

Fourth, since 1979, the government has limited increases in state benefits, the most important source of income to the bottom 20 per cent of income earners. Broadly, benefits have not been increased in real terms at all, whilst some benefit rates have been cut or even abolished. In contrast, income tax rates have fallen. The cuts in income tax have mainly benefited high income earners who pay higher rates of tax.

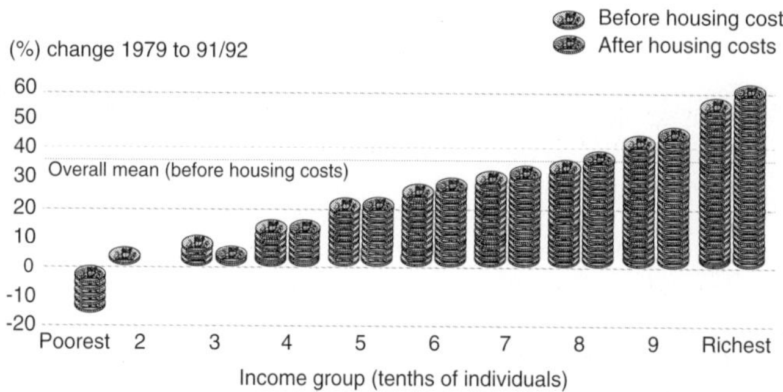

Source: adapted from Joseph Rowntree Foundation, *Income and Wealth*, 1995.

Figure 43.4 *Changes in real net income, 1979-1991/2*

The distribution of wealth

The distribution of wealth in the UK is far less equitable than the distribution of income. Table 43.4 shows that in 1992 the top 1 per cent owned 18 per cent of marketable wealth in the UK. That meant that the richest 1 per cent of the population owned 18 times the national average.

Table 43.4 *Distribution of wealth*

Percentage of marketable wealth owned by:	1911	1954	1971	1981	1986	1992
Most wealthy 1%	69	43	31	21	18	18
Most wealthy 5%	-	-	52	40	36	37
Most wealthy 10%	92	79	65	54	50	49
Most wealthy 25%	-	-	86	77	73	72
Most wealthy 50%	-	-	97	94	90	92
Least wealthy 50%	-	-	3	6	10	8

Source: adapted from CSO, *Social Trends*.

Perhaps even more surprising is that half the population owned just 7 per cent of the nation's wealth. Each person on average in the bottom 50 per cent owned a mere 0.14 of the average wealth per person in the UK.The single most important divide today between 'rich' and 'poor' is home ownership. Approximately one-third of marketable wealth according to *Social Trends* is now made up of the value of owner occupied houses.

Horizontal equity

Horizontal inequity exists in the UK in a number of different ways. One measure is the relative earnings of males and females. As Table 43.2 showed, there is a wide disparity between the relative earnings of males and females. Part of this can be explained by factors such as different education and training experiences, different age compositions of the male and female workforce and the loss of work experience by women during the crucial years when they might leave the workforce to raise children. However, despite equal pay legislation, it is unlikely that all of the difference in pay between males and females can be explained in this way and therefore horizontal inequity can be said to exist between males and females.

Table 43.5 *Distribution of household income by region, 1993*

	Average gross income per week per household (£)
South East	423.6
UK	353.0
East Anglia	346.9
East Midlands	341.7
North West	335.2
Scotland	334.1
South West	330.5
Wales	306.1
Northern Ireland	302.7
West Midlands	301.0
Yorkshire and Humberside	291.1
North	291.1

Source: adapted from CSO, *Regional Trends*.

Another measure of horizontal inequity is the North-South divide in the UK. Table 43.5 shows average income per week per household in the UK in 1993. The South East had the highest income whilst the North of England had the lowest. The difference in real income is likely to be less than that implied by Table 43.5 because of lower prices, for instance for houses in areas outside the South.

Absolute and relative poverty

Absolute poverty is rare in the UK, although evidence suggests that it has been growing since 1979. The main indicator of absolute poverty in the UK is homelessness. There are no reliable estimates of the numbers of people who live 'rough' on the streets of our cities, but at the end of 1993 there were 58 400 people according to government figures who were living in temporary accommodation such as hostels and refuges. If there is little absolute poverty in the UK, there is, by the definition of the term, relative poverty. The extent of relative poverty is difficult to gauge. One common measure is to see how many people are living at or below the minimum income set by government for the receipt of means tested benefits. Table 43.6 shows numbers claiming a variety of different benefits. Income support is paid to those out of work (including retired people). Family credit is paid to those in low paid jobs. Housing benefit is paid to any household on a low income. Each claimant of benefit is likely to have dependants, so the total number of people in poverty is much higher than the number receiving benefit. Many benefits also have low take-up rates. In 1991 for instance, the take-up rate of Family credit was only 62 per cent. The result is that on the government's own estimates produced by the DSS, there were 6 million people in relative poverty in 1979, 8.8 million in 1983 and over 11 million today.

There are those who point out that using benefit levels to define poverty has the perverse effect of increasing poverty when benefits are raised whilst reducing poverty when benefits are lowered. It is also pointed out that relative to our Victorian ancestors, nearly all in society today enjoy a very high standard of living. However, relative poverty is most commonly defined in terms of poverty relative to the average in the society of the day. The evidence shows that there has been an increase in relative poverty since 1979.

Table 43.6 *Number of people in receipt of selected social security benefits*

Millions

	1979-80	1988-89	1993-94
Supplementary pensions and supplementary benefit/income support[1]	2.92	4.22	5.79
Family income supplement/ family credit[1]	0.08	0.29	0.51
Housing benefit	1.43	4.03	4.70

1. Major reforms of the benefit system in April 1988 saw supplementary pensions and supplementary benefits replaced by income support whilst family income supplement was replaced by family credit.

Source: adapted from CSO, *Social Trends.*

The distribution of income

Table 43.7 *Composition of quintile groups of household income: by occupation group of head of household*

United Kingdom — Percentages

	Quintile groups of households ranked by equivalised disposable income[1]					
	Bottom fifth	Next fifth	Middle fifth	Next fifth	Top fifth	All households
Occupational group of head of household						
Professional	-	1	4	7	14	5
Employers and managers	3	4	9	17	34	13
Intermediate and junior non-manual	3	7	14	21	22	13
Skilled manual	10	17	27	26	15	19
Semi-skilled manual	6	10	12	9	2	8
Unskilled manual	3	3	3	2	-	2
Retired	49	44	22	12	7	27
Unoccupied	25	15	9	6	4	12
Other[2]	-	-	1	1	1	1
All occupational groups	100	100	100	100	100	100

1. Equivalised disposable income has been used for ranking the households into quintile groups.
2. Mainly armed forces.
Source: *CSO, Social Trends No25, 1995.*

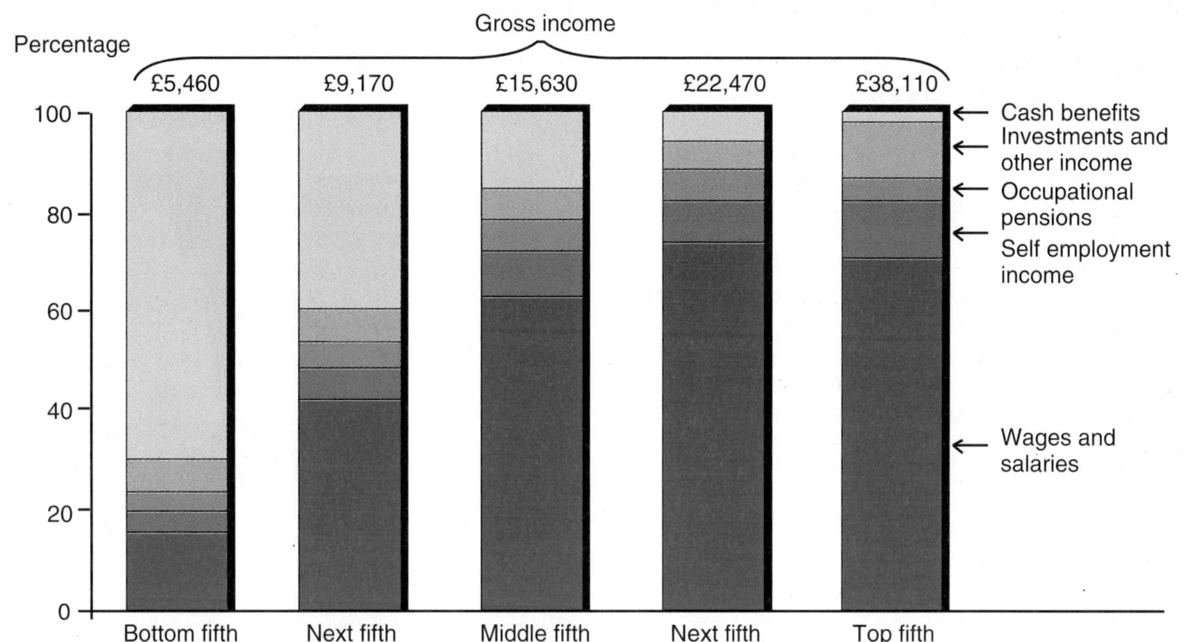

Source: adapted from CSO, *Social Trends*.

Figure 43.5 *Sources of gross household income: by income grouping, 1991, UK*

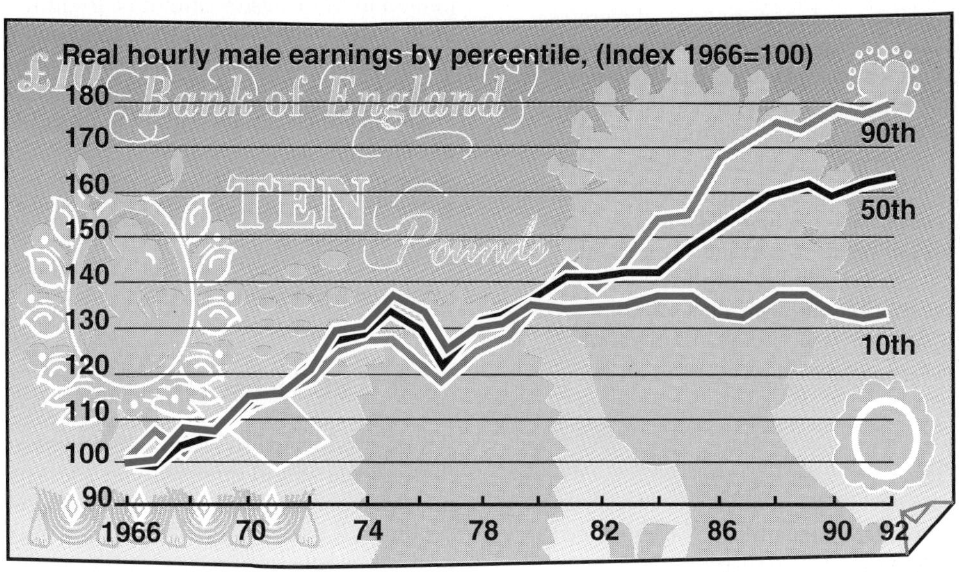

Source: adapted from Institute of Fiscal Studies.

Figure 43.6 *Real hourly male earnings by percentile (Index 1966=100)*

1. (a) From Table 43.7, analyse who are the poor and the rich in the UK.
   (b) Explain, using the data, why the same individual may go from one quintile group to another quintile ranked by income as he or she grows older.
2. Using the data here suggest why inequalities in income occur.
3. To what extent would inequalities be reduced if the government:
   (a) introduced a national minimum wage (a minimum wage which an employer must pay a worker) of £3.50 an hour;
   (b) increased the state old age pension by 50 per cent;
   (c) guaranteed work to any person unemployed for more than 12 months on state work schemes for £3.50 an hour.

Government spending

Summary

1. There will inevitably be market failure in a pure free market economy because it will fail to provide public goods.
2. Public goods must be provided by the state because of the free rider problem.
3. Merit goods are goods which are underprovided by the market mechanism. Demerit goods, such as drugs, are overprovided.
4. Part of public expenditure is devoted to achieving a more equitable distribution of income.
5. The desirability of state provision of goods and services can be judged using the criteria of productive and allocative efficiency and of equity.
6. Public choice theory suggests that governments may not always act to maximise the welfare of society because politicians may act to maximise their own welfare.

Market failure

A pure free market system is most unlikely to produce an efficient and equitable distribution of resources. In theory, a free market system would be Pareto-efficient only if every market were perfectly competitive, (☞ unit 35). However, modern industrialised economies are dominated by oligopolistic and monopoly producers; externalities are widespread in many markets, and the free market system produces instability, seen in fluctuations in the level of economic activity. Equally, there are goods which the market system is unlikely to produce at all, or which it is likely to underproduce or overproduce. The market system may also lead to an inequitable distribution of resources in the economy (☞ unit 43). Therefore it is argued that government needs to regulate the private market system, to take responsibility for the production of goods which the free market underproduces and to redistribute income in a way that will result in a more equitable distribution of income.

Public goods

Nearly all goods are **private goods** (not to be confused with goods produced in the private sector of the economy). A private good is one where consumption by one person results in the good not being available for consumption by another. For instance, if you eat a bowl of muesli, then your friend can't eat it; if ICI build a plant on a piece of land, that land is not available for use by local farmers.

A few goods, however, are PUBLIC GOODS. These are goods which possesses two characteristics:

- **non-rivalry**- consumption of the good by one person does not reduce the amount available for consumption by another person;
- **non-excludability** - once provided, no person can be excluded from benefiting (or indeed suffering in the case of a public good like pollution).

There are relatively few examples of pure public goods, although many goods contain a public good element. Clean air is a public good. If you breathe clean air, it does not diminish the ability of others to breathe clean air. Moreover, others cannot prevent you from breathing clean air. Defence is another example. An increase in the population of the UK does not lead to a reduction in the defence protection accorded to the existing population. A person in Manchester cannot be excluded from benefiting even if she were to object to current defence policy, prefer to see all defence abolished, and refuse to pay to finance defence.

Goods which can be argued to be public goods are:

- defence;
- the judiciary and prison service;
- the police service;
- street lighting.

Many other goods, such as education and health, contain a small public good element.

The free rider problem

Public goods need to be provided by the state because these goods would otherwise be underprovided in a pure market economy. This is because of the FREE RIDER problem. A public good is one where it is impossible to prevent people from receiving the benefits of the good once it has been provided. So there is very little incentive for people to pay for consumption of the good. A free rider is someone who receives the benefit but allows others to pay for it. For instance, citizens receive benefits from defence expenditure. But individual citizens could increase their economic welfare by not paying for it.

In a free market, national defence is unlikely to be provided. A firm attempting to provide defence services would have difficulty charging for the product since it could not be sold to benefit individual citizens. The result would be that no one would pay for defence and therefore the market would not provide it. The only way around this problem is for the state to provide defence and force everyone to contribute to its cost through taxation.

QUESTION 1

Explain why lighthouses might be classed as a public good.

Merit and demerit goods

Even the most fervent advocates of free market economics agree that public goods are an example of market failure and that the government should provide these public goods. However, more controversial are merit and demerit goods.

A MERIT GOOD is one which is underprovided by the market mechanism (i.e. one which some people think should be provided in greater quantities). One reason for underprovision is that individuals lack perfect information and find it difficult to make rational decisions when costs occur today but the benefits received only come in, say, thirty years time. Another reason is because there are significant positive externalities (☞ unit 36) present.

Health, education and insurance are the main merit goods provided today by government in the UK. Health and insurance are two examples where consumers find it difficult to make rational choices because of time. If left totally to market forces, the evidence suggests that individuals would not give themselves sufficient health cover or cover against sickness, unemployment and old age. Young people tend to be healthy and in work. Many find it difficult to appreciate that one day they will be ill and out of work. However, the cost of health care and pensions etc. is so great that young people can only afford them if they save for the future. If they don't, they find when they are older that they do not have sufficient resources to pay for medical services, or the insurance needed to cover them against loss of earnings due to illness or retirement. Therefore it makes sense for the state to intervene and to force young people in particular to make provision against sickness, unemployment and old age.

In the case of education, the main beneficiary (the child or student) is unlikely to be the person paying for the education. Therefore there could be a conflict of interest. It could be in the interest of the parents to pay as little as possible for the child's education but in the interest of the child to receive as high quality an education as possible. Others in society also have an interest. A child who, for instance, cannot read or write is an economic liability in the UK of the 1990s. He or she is more likely than not to have to receive support from others rather than contribute to the nation's welfare. There are many other examples of goods with a merit good element. Lack of industrial training, for instance, is seen as a major problem in the UK. Individual firms have an incentive not to train workers not only because it is so costly but also because their trained workers can then be poached by competitors. Rather, they go into the market place and recruit workers who have been trained at other firms' expense. This is an example again of the free rider problem. It would perhaps be more desirable if the state were to organise industrial training and levy a tax on all firms to pay for this.

QUESTION 2 Suggest reasons why education might be considered a merit good.

A DEMERIT GOOD is one which is overprovided by the market mechanism. The clearest examples of demerit goods are drugs - everything from hard drugs such as LSD to alcohol and tobacco. Consumption of these goods produces large negative **externalities**. Crime increases, health costs rise, valuable human economic resources are destroyed, and friends and relatives suffer distress. Moreover, individuals themselves suffer and are unable to stop consuming because drugs are addictive. Therefore it can be argued that consumers of drugs are not the best judges of their own interests.

Governments intervene to correct this market failure. They have three main weapons at their disposal: they can ban consumption as with hard drugs; they can use the price system to reduce demand by placing taxes on drugs; or they can try to persuade consumers to stop using drugs, for instance through advertising campaigns.

Equity

It would be extremely improbable that a free market system would lead to a distribution of resources which every individual would see as equitable. It is therefore argued by some economists that the state has a duty to reallocate resources.

It could be argued that, in the UK today, there is some consensus that citizens should not die for lack of food, or be refused urgent medical treatment for lack of money.

In the UK, over 30 per cent of all public spending is devoted to social security payments. Some of these payments come from the National Insurance fund and therefore could be seen as merit goods. But benefits such as family credit are an explicit attempt to redistribute income to those in need. It could also be argued that the free provision of services such as health and education leads to a more equitable distribution of resources.

The effectiveness of government attempts to redistribute income are evaluated in more detail in unit 102.

QUESTION 3

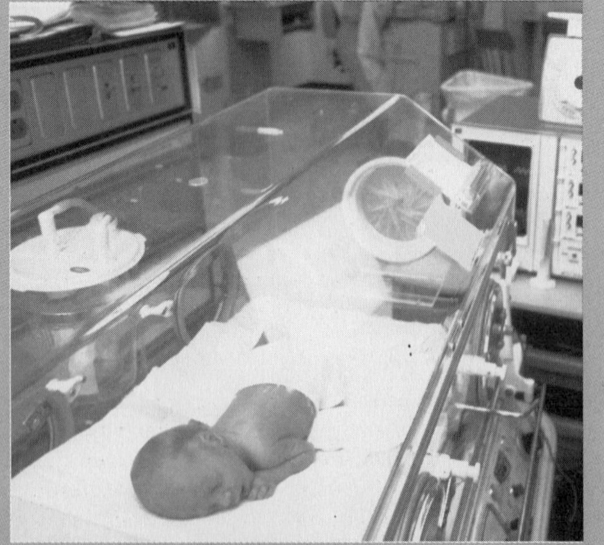

(a) Distinguish between horizontal and vertical equity.
(b) Discuss the ways in which the provision of free health care in the NHS (i) increases equity and (ii) leads to greater inequity in society.

State provision of goods and services

The amount of state spending in the economy has increased in industrialised nations over the past 100 years. Since 1979, however, the UK government has been committed to rolling back the frontiers of the state. Figure 44.1 illustrates some of the changes that have taken place in state funding and provision of services.

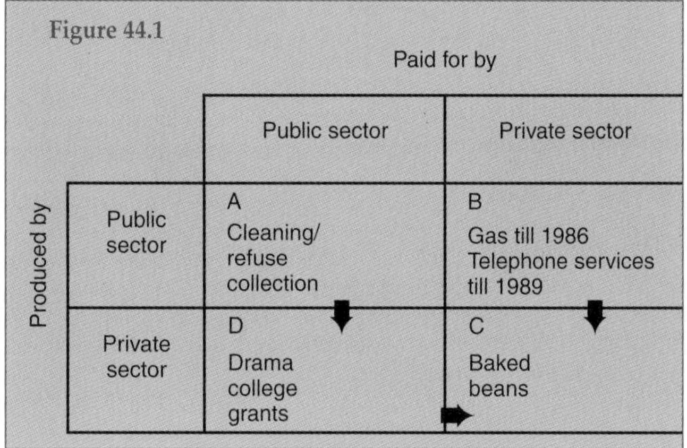

Privatisation Some goods and services, such as gas, telecommunications or coal, are private goods. In many countries, including the UK up until the 1980s, these goods were produced by the public sector and then sold to (i.e. paid for) by individual private sector customers. However, these industries can be **privatised** (i.e. state owned companies can be sold into the private sector ☞ unit 45). Gas etc. are then no different from other goods produced by the private sector and sold to the private sector like bread or holidays. In Figure 44.1, privatisation of, say, gas has to led to a move from Box B to Box C.

Tendering Some goods and services, such as hospital cleaning, refuse collection and legal services have, in the UK at least, traditionally been produced and paid for by the public sector. However, these sorts of services are also provided by the private sector and sold to private sector customers. For instance, a local authority might have its own legal department. But there is also a large number of private lawyers serving private sector clients. Government may decide that it needs to continue to provide and pay for these services, but that it no longer wishes to produce them. Instead, it will buy in the services from the private sector. In Figure 44.1, tendering leads to a move from Box A to Box D.

Internal markets In some cases, the government has decided that only the state can both pay for and produce goods and services, such as education or health care. However, rather than have a single monopoly producer, the government can deal with a considerable number of publicly owned producers. These producers compete amongst themselves in an **internal market** (☞ unit 46). Consumers may be given the spending power to choose between the providers. For instance, parents may have the right to choose which school their child is sent to. In Figure 44.1, introduction of an internal market leads to no change from Box A. However, competition has been introduced into the state sector.

Abandonment of provision The government may attempt to abandon paying for a service which it also produces. For instance, the government may have a state pension scheme paid for out of social security contributions - effectively taxes. It decides that it wishes to reduce taxes. So it encourages individuals to take out personal pensions. Private individuals then pay contributions to private pension companies, which in turn, on retirement, will pay a pension to their customers. In Figure 44.1, there has been a move from Box A to Box C. Alternatively, the public sector may have been buying in services from the private sector. It then decides to make the private sector pay for the service completely. For instance, local authorities may choose to stop giving discretionary grants to 18+ students attending drama schools or colleges. Students wanting to attend these colleges then have to pay for the courses completely themselves. In Figure 44.1, there has been a move from Box D to Box C.

Choosing between public sector and private sector provision

Whether state provision or private provision is more desirable depends on a number of factors.

Productive efficiency There can be large **economies of scale** available if a service is provided for the total population by one producer. For instance, it will almost certainly be more costly for two competing refuse collection companies to collect refuse from a housing estate than just one. Therefore, it may be more efficient for the state to organise household refuse collection rather than allow each household to employ different firms. The same might apply to the National Health Service (NHS). The amount spent on the NHS is about two-thirds of that in France and Germany and half that of the USA as a percentage of national income. It could be argued that this is because the NHS provides lower quality health care than in other countries. But there is evidence to suggest that there are significant economies of scale in the NHS which are not found in the private health care systems of continental Europe and the USA. For instance, bed utilisation in NHS hospitals is considerably higher than in Europe or the USA because the NHS has much greater control of when patients are to be treated. Equally, drug costs are lower because doctors in the NHS are encouraged to prescribe the minimum doses necessary of the cheapest drug available.

On the other hand, it is sometimes claimed that **diseconomies of scale** are present in organisations like the NHS. They are such large bureaucracies that management is unable to control costs and utilise resources efficiently. **X-inefficiency** (☞ unit 33) raises costs as workers within the organisation manipulate the system for their own advantage. Only the break-up of the organisation and the creation of strong competition in the market place can lower costs and eliminate inefficiency. This provides a strong argument for either breaking up a public sector monopoly and then selling the competing parts to the private sector, as for instance happened to the electricity generating industry in 1991, or the creation of strong internal markets, as in the NHS, where hospitals have to compete with other hospitals for patients.

Allocative efficiency State production or tendering systems are unlikely to create much consumer choice. Households, for instance, are unlikely to have any choice about who collects their refuse or who polices their neighbourhood. Moreover, they are unable to influence the amount spent on services except perhaps indirectly through the ballot box.

Choice is much greater in the private sector. UK consumers now, for instance, have a choice about which telephone company to use. By the late 1990s, households will be able to choose which company supplies them with gas. Already they can shop around for gas appliances or gas repair services. State provision, however, can involve an element of choice. Parents in the UK have the right to choose which school they wish to send their child to. Patients can choose their doctor. Choice may be not as great as it might seem though. Consumers of education or health care likely to want to buy from their nearest supplier. Therefore, weak local monopolies are likely to emerge, particularly in rural areas. The 'best' schools in an area might be oversubscribed and turn applicants away. Hospitals are likely to be full and so patients are unlikely to be able to exercise much choice about when to have an operation.

Choice also implies that consumers are able to make rational choices. But there may be little **consumer sovereignty** (☞ unit 42) in the market. Producers may use their market power to distort information supplied to customers. Consumers may also have extremely limited understanding of the services they are asked to buy themselves.

Distribution of resources The transfer of resources from the public sector to the private sector can have important implications for the distribution of income. For instance, when the state ceases to pay for certain activities through the tax system, individuals have to pay the full cost themselves. A student wanting to study at a drama school might before have been financed by collecting a fraction of a penny per year from local taxpayers. If the local authority ceases to pay a grant, then the student or the student's family has to pay the full cost of thousands of pounds.

The attempt by the UK government to reduce its future pension commitments through encouraging people to take out personal pensions will almost certainly lead to poorer pensioners in the future. This is because the state scheme (SERPS) was compulsory and workers had to make regular payments into the scheme. Personal pensions, however, tend to be underfunded, with many making few or no regular contributions into their scheme. Their pension entitlement in the future will therefore be very low.

QUESTION 4 It has been suggested that local authorities should no longer provide public libraries. Instead, they could either contract out, getting a private company to run the service in return for a fee from the local authority, or the local authority could stop offering a service at all and leave the market mechanism to decide whether library services should be offered to consumers and in what form. Libraries are used by all age and income groups but are disproportionately used by females and older people.

Discuss the impact of both contracting out and completely privatising the library service on efficiency and equity.

Public choice theory

PUBLIC CHOICE THEORY analyses how and why public spending and taxation decisions are made. 'Consumers' or 'customers' are voters in the system. They vote for politicians and political parties who are the 'producers' in the system. Producers make decisions about how public money should be spent, about taxes and about laws. The decisions have to be 'sold' by politicians to voters.

The voters want to maximise the net benefits they get from the state. For instance, all other things being equal, voters would like the state to provide large quantities of goods and services but with minimal levels of taxation.

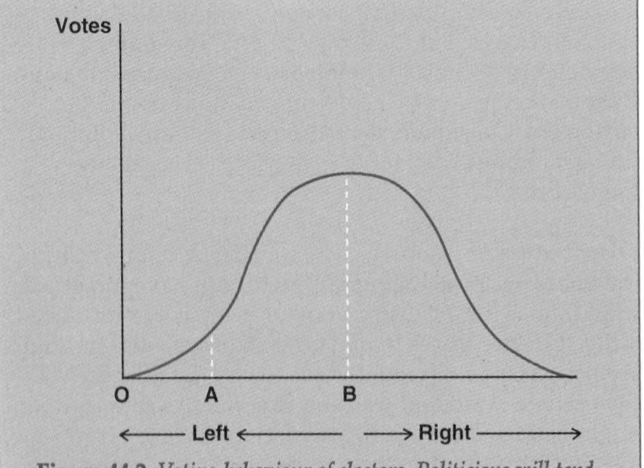

Figure 44.2 *Voting behaviour of electors. Politicians will tend to maximise their votes by moving to the centre ground in politics.*

Politicians want to maximise their welfare too. In the simplest models, politicians are assumed to want to maximise their votes, so that they can get into power and remain in power. In more complicated models, more sophisticated assumptions can be made, such as that politicians want to get posts in government, or use their political connections to maximise their own earnings.

If politicians want to maximise their votes, then the most obvious thing to do is to appeal to the centre ground. Consider Figure 44.2 which shows a normal distribution of votes. A right wing politician is facing a left wing politician who has pitched his policies so that they will attract votes to the left of OA. The obvious stance to take is for the right wing politician to pitch his policies just to the right of B, as near as possible to the middle ground whilst remaining to the right of the political spectrum. On the other hand, if the left wing politician were rational, he too would move to the centre ground to try and maximise his vote.

In practice, democracies tend to throw up governments which do veer towards the centre. It is for this reason that governments like those of Margaret Thatcher's in the 1980s were so unusual. Due to Britain's first past the post voting system, a UK party can get a majority in Parliament with as little as 40 per cent of the votes cast. With a 75 per cent turnout on polling day (i.e. 25 per cent of eligible voters don't vote), this means that a British government only has to gain the vote of 30 per cent of all voters. Not surprisingly, this allows a right wing party which itself has voted in a right wing leader to gain office. The same would of course be true for a left wing party in the UK which had a left wing leader.

In much of economic theory, there is a hidden assumption that governments act so as to maximise the welfare of society as a whole. Public choice theory can help explain why governments often fail to do this.

Local interests Assume that an MP has a large textile mill in her constituency which employs 1 000 workers. The company owning the mill lobbies the MP to support the imposition of higher tariffs (taxes on imports) on textiles, arguing that the mill will have to close unless foreign competition is reduced. Economic theory would probably suggest that the mill should be allowed to close and the resources released be used to produce something which the UK is better at producing (the **theory of comparative advantage**). However, the MP may be frightened that losing 1 000 jobs could mean losing 1 000 votes. Therefore, she could well put pressure on the government to impose higher tariffs even if she knows that the nation's welfare would be lessened as a result.

Favouring minorities Assume that a political party can get elected with considerably less than 50 per cent of the votes, because of the nature of the voting system and because not all voters turn out on polling day. In UK national elections, as argued above, a party could get a majority with the support of just 30 per cent of voters. In a local election, where the turnout is often only 30-50 per cent, a party can get a majority with far less. Assume that those who do vote tend to possess similar characteristics. For instance, in the UK, middle class voters are more likely to vote than working class voters. In a local election, voters from one ethnic group may be far more likely to vote than voters from another ethnic group. In these situations, it is clear that politicians wishing to maximise their share of the vote will want to appeal to a minority, not the majority, because it is the minority who cast votes. A government might, for instance, introduce government spending and tax changes which leave 30 per cent of the population better off and 70 per cent worse off. This would be rational behaviour if the 30 per cent of the population better off tended to vote for that party in a first past the post system with a 75 per cent turnout. However, it is arguable as to whether the nation's welfare would be maximised as a result.

Conflicting personal interests Politicians, parties and governments may be prone to corruption. Assume that politicians are not just interested in winning votes and retaining power, but also in gaining personal economic wealth. There may then be a conflict of interest between maximising the nation's welfare and maximising the welfare of the individual politician. Assume, for instance, that a Third World political leader can remain in power by giving massive bribes to electors at election time. Between elections, he accepts bribes from electors for granting political favours. In the process, the country fails to develop because decisions are made on the basis of maximising the wealth of the individual politician rather than that of the country. The individual politician is far better off as a rich head of a poor country than as a leader who has lost power in a fast growing country.

Short-termism In the UK, there has to be a general election at least every five years. Assume that a government wants a high growth, low inflation economy. Unfortunately, the current state of the economy at the time is one of high inflation and low growth. If the government pursues anti-inflationary policies, these will need to be long term policies if they are to be successful. But they are also likely to push up unemployment and lead to a tough tax and low government spending regime. A government coming up to re-election has two choices. It can cut taxes, increase public spending, and cut interest rates to stimulate spending and make voters 'feel good'. Or it can pursue austere policies which might keep the economy on course but leave voters feeling they are not particularly well off. Assume that the austere policies are the ones which will maximise welfare in the long term, but would mean the government losing the election. It is obvious that the government will go for the reflationary policies if that means it can win the election, even though it knows this will damage welfare. This political cycle is discussed further in unit 67.

Regulatory capture Governments are responsible for regulating many areas, such as monopolies or the environment. 'Regulatory capture' means that groups such as monopolists earning abnormal profit or polluters damaging the environment can strongly influence the way they are being regulated to their own advantage. Take, for instance, a utility which is about to be privatised. The board of the utility will want to make sure that it is as easy as possible after privatisation for it to make high profits to satisfy its shareholders and maximise the pay of members of the board. It will lobby hard to have as weak powers as possible given to the regulatory body which will supervise it after privatisation. National welfare would probably be maximised if the regulatory body were given strong powers to keep consumer prices as low as possible.

However, in the short term, the government is far more likely to be wanting to maximise its own short term electoral advantage from having a successful sale of the shares and by allowing small investors (probably its own voters) to make quick gains on the share price. This requires weak regulation. Once the company has been privatised, it will want to dominate the regulator. It will do this by supplying only the information which is favourable to its case. For instance, it will tend to underestimate revenues and overestimate costs in order to make it seem that future profits will be low. The regulator, with little evidence apart from that supplied by the utility, will constantly make decisions which are in the utility's interest.

Evidence from the UK since 1984, when the first regulator was appointed, suggests that the individual appointed to head the regulatory team can be crucial in determining whether or not the regulatory body is

QUESTION 5

Table 44.1 *Shares of disposable income*

Percentages

	Quintile groups of individuals				
	Bottom fifth	Next fifth	Middle fifth	Next fifth	Top fifth
Year 0	10	14	18	23	35
Year 5	8	12	17	23	36
Year 10	6	11	17	23	43

A right wing political party enjoys the support mainly of above average income voters. It faces a left wing party which gains a majority of its votes from below average income supporters. The electoral system is such that a party only needs 40 per cent of the vote to secure a majority in Parliament, whilst a 45 per cent vote would give it a massive majority. On average, 75 per cent of the electorate vote, but the higher the income of the individual, the more likely they are to turn out to vote. The top 20 per cent of income earners have a turnout rate of 90 per cent.

The right wing party wins an election in year 0 committed to 'increasing incentives for individuals to earn money and create wealth for the nation'. It wins two further elections in year 5 and year 10.

(a) (i) Would Table 44.1 suggest that the nation's welfare has been maximised?
(ii) What additional information would you need to support your conclusion?
(b) Explain why the party can win elections when the relative income position of most individuals is worsening over time.

captured. A regulator who wants to minimise confrontation with a utility (i.e. have a quiet life) will allow him or her self to be captured.

In economic theory, it is often assumed that market failure should be corrected by government. If a monopolist is exploiting the consumer, then the government should regulate or abolish the monopoly. If a polluter is damaging the environment, then the government should act to limit the actions of those responsible. Public choice theory suggests that government may fail to act in these cases because politicians are more interested in maximising their own rewards (such as votes to stay in power) than maximising the nation's welfare. Indeed, in some cases, politicians maximising their own rewards may lead to an even greater loss of economic welfare than if market failure had been left unregulated. At one extreme, some economists argue that governments should intervene as little as possible in the economy because their interventions are likely to be more damaging than the problems they are trying to solve. On the other hand, it is argued that politicians are not all out to maximise their own self-interest. Some politicians do act in the public interest even when this does not accord with their own self-interest. A left wing MP, for instance, who votes for higher income tax rates on higher income earners is likely to pay more in tax as a result. This doesn't mean to say that he or she won't vote in favour. The more a political system can encourage its politicians to act in the public interest, the more it will accord with the traditional view that government acts as an impartial actor in the economic system intervening to maximise national welfare.

Key terms

Public good - a good where consumption by one person does not reduce the amount available for consumption by another person and where once provided, all individuals benefit or suffer whether they wish to or not.
Free rider - a person or organisation which receives benefits that others have paid for without making any contribution themselves.
Merit good - a good which is underprovided by the market mechanism. A demerit good is one which is overprovided by the market mechanism.
Public choice theory - theories about how and why public spending and taxation decisions are made.

Applied economics

Public expenditure in the UK

Public expenditure totals

The public sector in the UK comprises central government, local government and government enterprises such as public corporations. Central government is responsible for approximately three-quarters of total public spending. Compared to other countries, the size of Britain's public sector is unexceptional. As shown in Table 44.2, it is greater as a proportion of GDP than the free market economies of the United States or Japan, broadly similar to our EU partners, but much lower than a mixed economy such as Sweden.

Public expenditure totals can be divided by function, as illustrated in Figure 44.3.

- The largest single item of public expenditure is social security. This covers **transfer payments** such as unemployment benefit and family credit from government to individuals. The largest single component of this is the state retirement pension.
- Spending on health and personal social services is the second largest category of expenditure. Most of this is accounted for by the cost of the National Health Service. Personal social services are mainly the social services departments of local authorities.

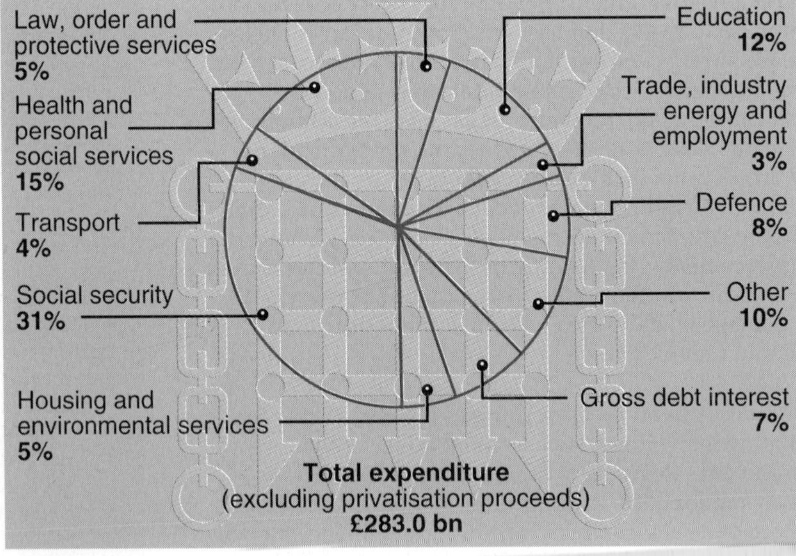

Source: adapted from The Red Book.

Figure 44.3 *General government expenditure, 1993-94*

- Education covers local government spending on primary and secondary schools, and colleges of further education. Central government pays for higher education and research grants.
- Defence spending is expenditure on the army, navy and airforce.
- Environmental services includes spending on street lighting, parks, refuse collection and sanitation.
- Transport is mainly spending on roads.
- Law, order and protective services covers spending on the police, the judiciary, prisons and the fire service.
- Other functions included are spending on housing, industry, energy and employment.
- General government debt interest is the interest that the government has to pay on the money it has borrowed in the past - the National Debt.
- Other expenditure includes expenditure on overseas aid, agriculture, forestry and fishing, the arts, libraries, and embassies abroad.

Table 44.2 *Government expenditure as percentage of GDP*

	1960 - 67	1968 - 73	1974 - 79	1989 - 94
Sweden	34.8	44.3	54.4	64.6
France	37.4	38.9	43.3	51.6
Italy	31.9	36.0	42.9	53.7
Germany	35.7	39.8	47.5	47.5
UK	34.7	39.5	44.6	41.3
Canada	29.3	34.7	39.2	47.6
US	28.3	31.0	32.6	33.8
Japan	18.7	20.5	28.4	32.7

Source: adapted from OECD, *Historical Statistics.*

Trends in public expenditure

Total government spending in real terms has tended to rise over time. Figure 44.4 shows that it has also risen as a percentage of GDP. Public expenditure, not unexpectedly, peaked on the latter measurement during both World Wars. Since 1979 it has been government policy to reduce public expenditure as a percentage of GDP. The Conservative government hoped that public expenditure in real terms would fall. However, commitments to higher spending on defence and law and order, together with the worst recession since the 1930s, initially led to a rise in public spending. Since the mid-1980s, government has found it politically impossible to reduce spending on the National Health Service or to cut pensions in real terms. Growing awareness that spending on roads, education and the environment was inadequate led to an increase in spending on these programmes from the late 1980s. The recession of 1990-92 led to a further rise in public spending as unemployment-related spending increased as it did in the early 1980s. By 1993, government spending, as a proportion of GDP, had risen back to approximately 45 per cent, its average for the period 1975-1995. The government is still committed to reducing expenditure and by the second half of the 1990s, with continued growth in the economy, the proportion of government spending to GDP should fall back to 40 per cent.

Changes in the components of public spending in recent years are shown in Figure 44.5. There have been large falls in real spending on industry and housing by the government. Health, social security and the police have been major gainers. Note that whilst overall government

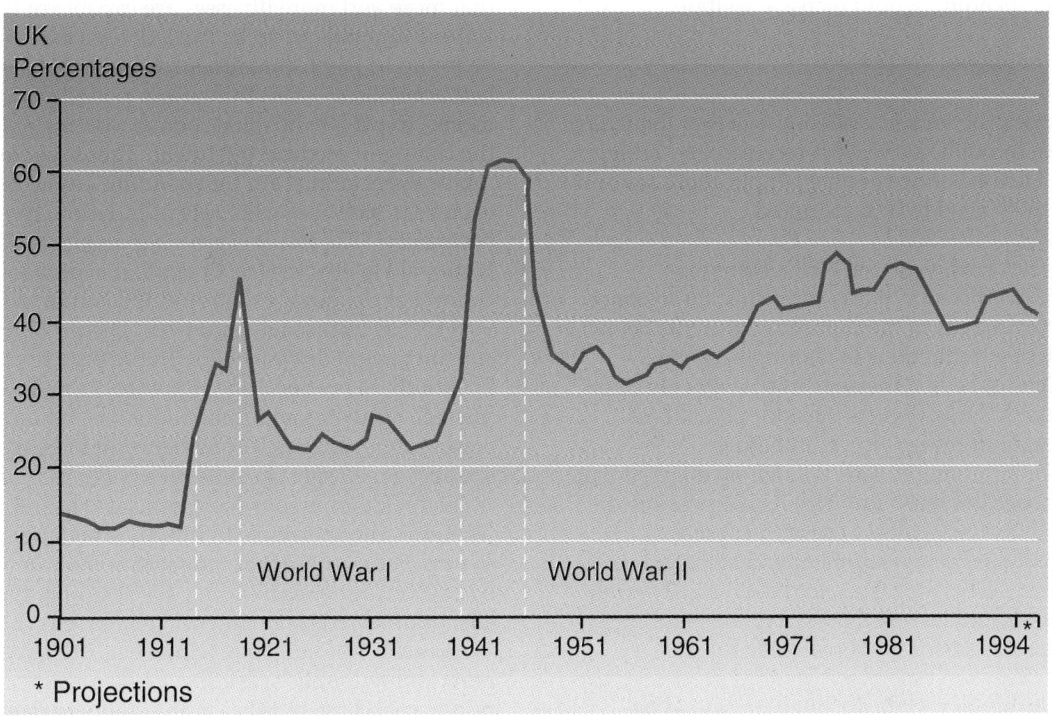

Source: adapted from CSO, *Social Trends.*

Figure 44.4 *General government expenditure as a percentage of GDP (UK)*

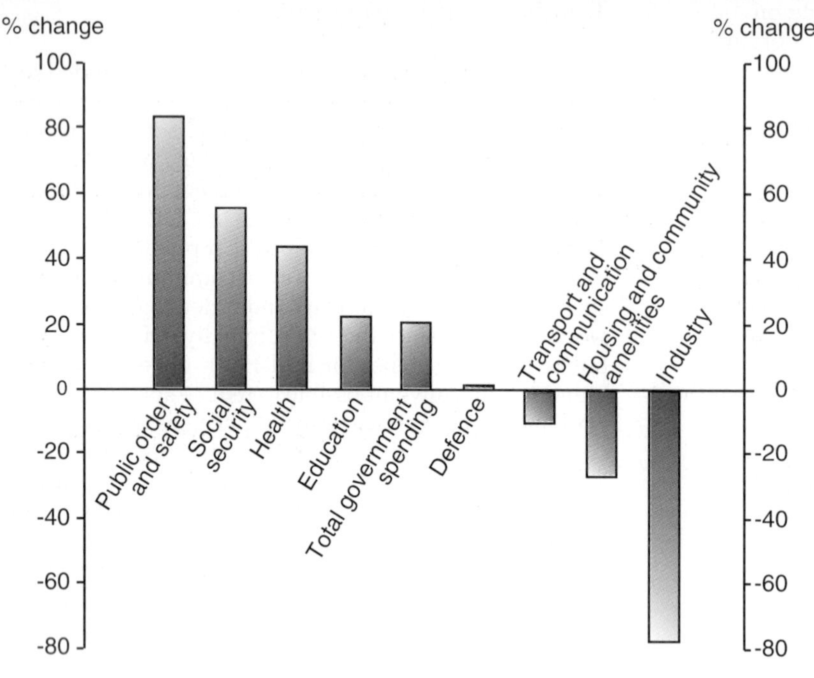

Source: adapted from CSO, *Social Trends.*

Figure 44.5 *Changes in government expenditure by function in real terms, 1981-93, % change*

spending between 1981 and 1993 increased by 21.9 per cent in real terms, real GDP grew by 30.8 per cent. Hence whilst real spending on education, for instance, grew over the period, as a proportion of GDP it fell. Critics would argue that the government is spending too little and that greater public spending would increase welfare.

Are public services improving?

There are major problems in assessing whether there has been a growth in public services in recent years. Taking the National Health Service as an example, there are four key factors which need to be considered.

Efficiency gains Each year, the NHS claims an improvement in efficiency. It measures this, for instance, through improvements in the number of patients being treated per doctor, reductions in waiting lists and occupancy rates of beds. Efficiency improvements come from two sources. First, there is the adoption of best practice throughout the service, eliminating **X-inefficiency** (☞ unit 33). This is a one-off effect in that once best practice has been adopted, it is impossible to make further efficiency gains. Second, advances in medical knowledge, new equipment and better trained staff can increase efficiency. This, in theory, is a dynamic process and it should be possible to generate efficiency gains from this source for the foreseeable future.

The cost of the service Data are often presented 'at constant prices'. This means that figures are adjusted for the general rate of inflation in the economy (measured by the GDP deflator rather than the Retail Price Index). However, increases in real expenditure on services do not necessarily mean that the volume of services has increased. This is because inflation in the public sector is likely to be higher than inflation in the economy as a whole. The public sector is far more labour intensive than the private sector. There is also far less scope for increases in productivity. Earnings on average increase about 2 per cent more than the increase in inflation each year. Hence the NHS has to pay more in real terms each year to buy the same number of doctors, nurses, etc.

The needs of the patients The population structure is slowly changing. In particular, there is a growth in the number of over 75 year olds. This age group is a particularly heavy user of NHS facilities. If public spending on the NHS is kept constant, the level of service to the average patient will inevitably decline.

Expectations and technology Each year, consumers expect to be able to buy better products. They expect to see more advanced cars, eat a wider range of foods and go to more exotic places for their holidays. They also expect to receive better health care. Advances in medicine mean that more and more illnesses are capable of treatment. But if these illnesses are to be treated, then extra money must be found to pay for treatment. Consumers also expect better facilities - everything from potted plants in waiting rooms, to private hospital rooms, to being able to choose the timing of medical treatment. These cost money.

Our expectations are for spending on the NHS to rise each year well above the rate of inflation. But this is not happening. The result is growing dissatisfaction with the National Health Service. Overall, it is probably right to claim that the quality of care in the National Health Service has improved since 1979. The problem is that consumers are dissatisfied with the pace of change. J K Galbraith, in his book *The Affluent Society*, talked about 'private affluence and public squalor'. Opinion polls consistently show that consumers and taxpayers wish to spend more of their income on a better National Health Service. Government policy which curbs public spending frustrates those desires. In this argument, there is market failure. Some argue that the same applies in areas such as education and road building. On the other hand, the electorate voted three times in general elections between 1979 and 1993 for a party which was perceived to be the party of low public spending. Consumers want more public spending, but they want others to pay for it - the free-rider problem. When it comes to the ballot box, people have voted to keep taxes low rather than spending high.

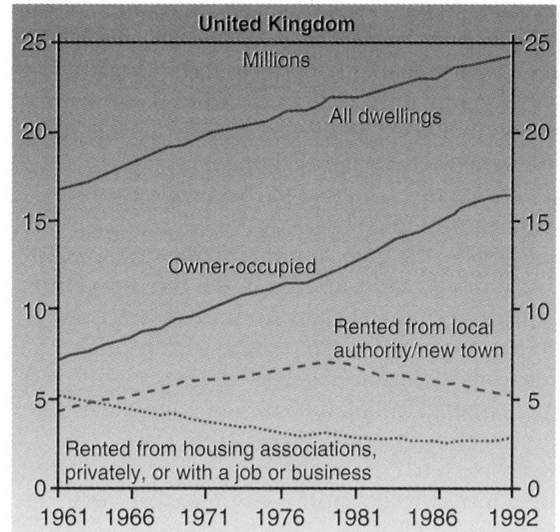

Source: adapted from Department of the Environment.

Figure 44.6 *Stock of dwellings: by tenure*

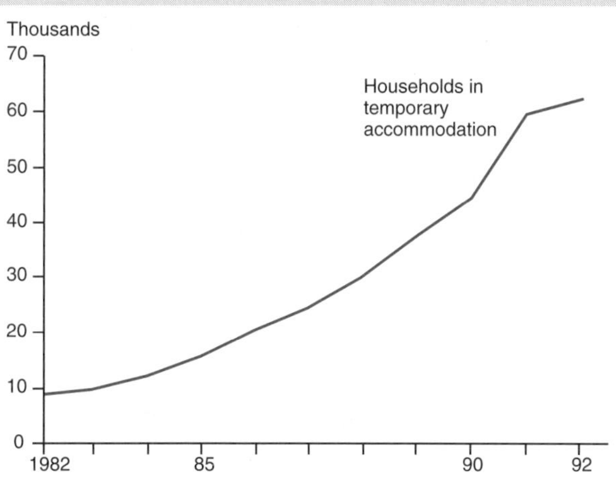

Source: adapted from Department of the Environment.

Figure 44.7 *Households living in temporary accommodation*

Table 44.3 *Tenure: by socio economic group*

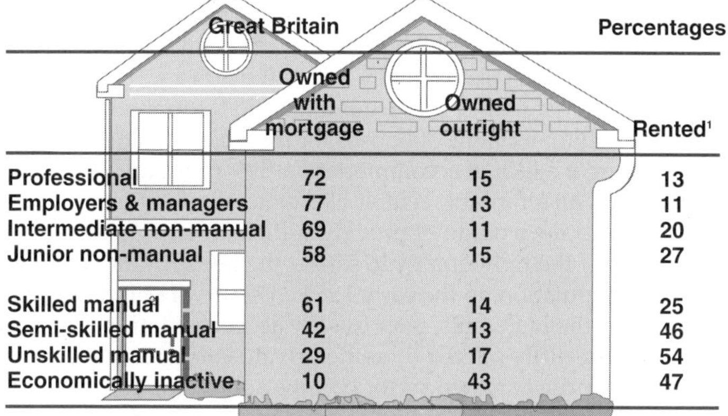

Great Britain			Percentages
	Owned with mortgage	Owned outright	Rented[1]
Professional	72	15	13
Employers & managers	77	13	11
Intermediate non-manual	69	11	20
Junior non-manual	58	15	27
Skilled manual	61	14	25
Semi-skilled manual	42	13	46
Unskilled manual	29	17	54
Economically inactive	10	43	47

Source: adapted from General Household Survey.

United Kingdom

Thousands

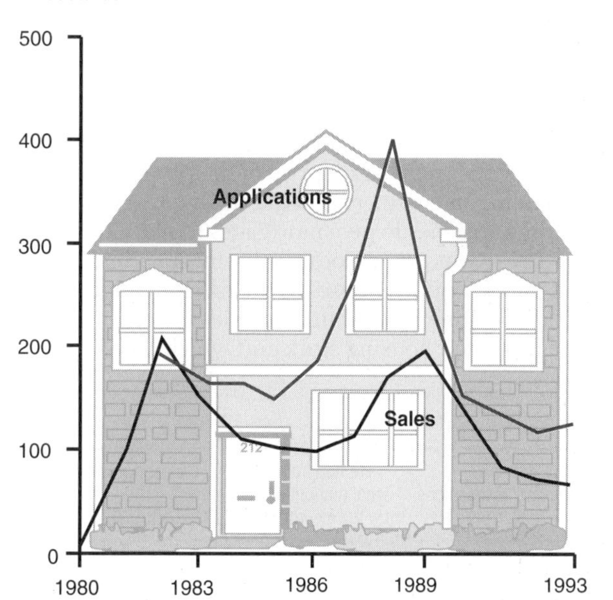

Source: adapted from Department of the Environment; Department of the Environment, Northern Ireland.

Figure 44.8 *Right to buy applications for, and sales of, dwellings owned by local authorities and new towns*

Table 44.4 *Housing benefit*

								£ million at 1992-93 prices and thousands
	Expenditure (£ million at 1992-93 prices)				Recipients (thousands)			
	1976-77	1981-82	1991-92	1992-93	1976-77	1981-82	1991-92	1992-93
Housing benefit - rent rebates and allowances	707	1 036	2 672	3 520	-	1 840	4 110	4 315

Source: adapted from DHSS.

Housing since 1945

Housing was identified as one of the key elements of a Welfare State in the Beveridge Report of 1942. Since 1945, the government has played a key role in the housing market. In the 1950s and 1960s, government, through local authorities, built millions of houses for rent to overcome the problem of a lack of accommodation fit for human habitation at an affordable rent. It was generally felt that the private sector would not provide sufficient new housing or of the right quality to satisfy the needs of the post-war population. In the early 1960s, a series of scandals highlighted the high rents, poor quality accommodation and lack of security offered by some private landlords. As a result, the private rented sector became subject to controls through the imposition of maximum rents and the introduction of strong rights of tenure for tenants. Again, from the 1960s, a strong financial incentive to buy houses was introduced through the scrapping of a tax on the notional rent on owner occupied houses and the introduction of tax relief on mortgage payments.

1979 saw the beginnings of a marked shift in government policy. Owner occupation was given a more important priority, with government talking of the creation of a 'property owning democracy'. Council tenants were given the right to buy their rented homes at a price below the true market price of the property. Financial deregulation increased the willingness of banks and building societies to give mortgages to individuals. A severe squeeze was put on local authority spending on building of new council houses in the belief that local authorities were inefficient bureaucracies which mismanaged their housing stock and which failed to give their tenants sufficient choice and control over their dwellings. At the same time, the government channelled much larger grants to Housing Associations, charity-type bodies which had a long history of building and renting out houses at affordable rents. Central government forced local authorities to increase rents, although much of the cost of this was born by central government which then had to give larger housing benefits to individuals whose income was too low to be able to afford to pay the rent. Homelessness increased as the stock of affordable rented property declined whilst social changes, such as increased divorce rates, increased the numbers of households needing to be housed.

In the late 1980s, the government further changed its policy. House prices had rocketed in the the 1980s, but exceptionally high interest rates from 1988 onwards resulted in a collapse in house purchases and prices. The government was also concerned about the growing bill for mortgage interest relief, the subsidy to home owners buying their houses through a mortgage. The government began to cut the mortgage subsidy. At the same time, it introduced a number of measures to encourage the revitalisation of the private rented sector, allowing landlords to charge much higher rents and offer short leases. Sales of council houses to their tenants fell sharply as high interest rates and then a collapse in confidence in the housing market made tenants very wary of taking on an expensive mortgage commitment. The government continued to see Housing Associations as the main providers of new cheap rented accommodation.

Table 44.4 *Changes in housing tenure since 1979*

	Rented from housing associations		Rented from local authorities or new town corporations		Owner occupied	
	Millions	% of all dwellings	Millions	% of all dwellings	Millions	% of all dwellings
1979	-	-	6.568	31.5	11.520	55.3
1980	-	-	6.550	31.1	11.791	56.1
1981	0.448	2.1	6.491	30.6	12.104	57.1
1982	0.459	2.2	6.300	29.5	12.247	58.7
1983	0.504	2.3	6.035	28.1	12.604	58.8
1984	0.525	2.4	5.924	27.4	12.913	59.6
1985	0.548	2.5	5.820	26.6	13.223	60.5
1986	0.565	2.6	5 723	25.9	13.575	61.5
1987	0.586	2.6	5 600	25.1	13.962	62.7
1988	0.614	2.7	5 412	24.0	14.418	64.0
1989	0.651	2.9	5 190	22.8	14.826	65.2
1990	0.706	3.1	5 015	21.9	15.094	65.8
1991	0.741	3.2	4 972	21.6	15.261	66.0
1992	0.806	3.5	4 830	20.7	15.408	66.1
1993	0.874	3.7	4 724	20.1	15.595	66.4

Source: adapted from Department of the Environment, *Housing and Construction Statistics*, Great Britain.

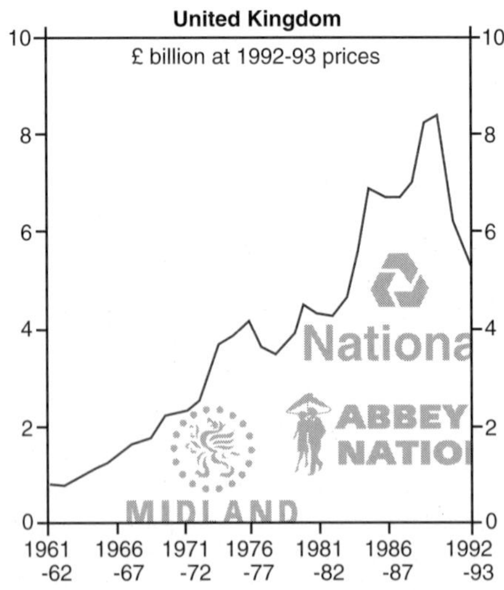

1. Series deflated by RPI.
2. Includes expenditure on option mortgage scheme.
Source: adapted from Inland Revenue.

Figure 44.9 *Total real[1] cost of mortgage interest tax relief[2]*

Write a report to be submitted by a housing charity to government arguing the case for more public spending on housing.

1. **Outline the main changes in the housing market shown in the data.**
2. **Discuss the extent to which housing could be seen as a merit good.**
3. **Suggest ways in which the government could change public spending on housing to increase both efficiency and equity in the sector.**

unit 45

Privatisation

Summary

1. State ownership of key industries in the economy was the norm in western Europe for most of the post-war era. Industries were taken into state ownership for a number of reasons including the desire to achieve economies of scale, improve management and run these industries for the benefit of the whole nation.
2. Privatisation is the sale of state owned assets to the private sector.
3. A number of arguments have been used to justify privatisation including lower costs of production, increased choice, quality and innovation, wider share ownership and a reduction in state borrowing and debt.
4. Arguments used against the privatisation process include concerns about monopoly pricing, increasing inequalities in society and increasing externalities.
5. Allocative efficiency can be increased in the privatised utilities if they are either subject to greater competition or if they are regulated.

State ownership

As western economies developed in the late nineteenth and twentieth centuries, the role of the state grew. Governments came to intervene more actively in the management of the economy. Also, they gradually acquired ownership of many industries and became producers and providers of a wide variety of goods and services. These included:

- public goods, such as defence, police and the judiciary;
- merit goods, such as education and health;
- other goods and services, such as telephones, gas, electricity and railways - key basic industries in the economy.

By the late 1970s, state or NATIONALISED INDUSTRIES (if organised as a separate firm, called PUBLIC CORPORATIONS in the UK) played a significant role in production in all western European countries. A number of arguments were put forward as to why the state should own and run firms.

Lower costs Nationalised industries could be more **productively efficient** than equivalent firms in the private sector. Most of the post-war nationalisation programme involved the purchase of a number of private firms in an industry. For instance, before 1947 there were a number of private railway companies operating throughout the UK. It was argued that **economies of scale** could be achieved by merging the competing firms into one, dispensing with duplication of production resources. Moreover, competition with expenditure on advertising and promotion was seen as wasteful. The elimination of such marketing costs would result in even lower total costs of production. To a great extent, these arguments rely upon the fact that industries which were nationalised were **natural monopolies** (☞ unit 39).

Better management Supporters of nationalisation often held a very poor view of private sector management. They argued that private firms were often run in a very amateurish way by managers or owners more interested either in enjoying a quiet life or short run profit than in the welfare of the company and the economy. Nationalisation was seen as a chance to appoint efficient modern management which would run the industries to maximise net social benefit. In some of the industries, particularly coal, there was an poor record of industrial disputes. It was hoped that nationalisation would make labour relations more harmonious because workers would see the industry as 'their' industry and management would no longer see workers as enemies.

Control of monopolies Many of the nationalised firms, such as railway companies and gas suppliers, were local monopolists. Nationalisation was seen as the easiest and most effective way of controlling these monopolies and preventing them from reducing social benefit by raising prices and lowering output.

Maximisation of net social benefit and not private profit Significant **externalities** were seen to be present in the industries which were nationalised. For instance, in the coal industry it was felt that private companies had too little regard for the welfare of their workers. The safety and lives of coalminers were sacrificed for the sake of private profit. Nationalised industries were given the task of maximising net social benefit even if this meant sacrificing private profit.

Greater control of the economy State ownership of some of the most important industries in the economy (sometimes called control of the **commanding heights** of the economy) was seen as essential if the government was to manage an unstable market economy. The 1930s, for instance, were seen as an example of the inability of free market forces to bring stability and prosperity to an economy. Nationalisation was effectively a move towards a more centrally planned type of economy. In the 1970s, a number of key UK companies, such as Rolls Royce and British Leyland (now the Rover Group), were taken into public ownership because they went bankrupt under private management. It was felt that the state had to intervene to prevent free market forces from destroying companies which played a key role in assuring the long term prosperity of the country.

A fairer distribution of resources Private firms are in business to make private profit for their owners. Before 1945 most firms were owned by the people who ran them. The family firm was the most typical business organisation. It was therefore easy for workers to see the difference in income of owners and workers. Coal miners, for instance, could compare the standard of living of their children, with barely enough to eat, badly clothed, perhaps not having a pair of shoes and sleeping several to a room, with the comparatively luxurious life-style of the mine owner's children. Capitalist profit was seen as expropriation of money which had been earned by the workers. Nationalisation was an opportunity to seize those profits and use them for the benefit of everybody in society, both workers and consumers, not just a few capitalists.

There are a number of assumptions made in these arguments which are of direct relevance to the current privatisation debate.

- The public sector is seen as more efficient than the private sector. In particular, public sector management is seen as better at allocating the economy's resources than private sector management.
- The private sector is seen as exploitative of workers and consumers. State control is needed to neutralise monopoly power and the pursuit of private profit at the expense of the public interest.
- Profit is seen more as an indication of monopoly power than as a signal which allocates resources efficiently within the economy.

Overall, there was a presumption that state allocation of resources was as good as if not better than private sector allocation - or to mimic George Orwell (in '*Animal Farm*'), 'public sector good, private sector bad'.

QUESTION 1 Amalgamation under public ownership will bring great economies in operation and make it possible to modernize production methods ... Public ownership ... will lower charges, prevent competitive waste, open the way for co-ordinated research and development... Only if public ownership replaces private monopoly can industry become efficient.'

Source: *Labour Party Manifesto*, 1945.

Explain the economic arguments which lie behind the views expressed in the *Labour Party Manifesto* of 1945.

Privatisation

PRIVATISATION has come to be associated with the sale of large nationalised industries to the private sector. British Steel, British Gas and British Telecom are examples of public corporations which have been sold off. Such sales are just one part of a wider programme aimed at transferring resources from the public sector to the private sector. Other aspects of privatisation include the following.

- Sales of parts of nationalised industries to the private sector. For instance, Jaguar cars (now part of the Ford Motor Company) was part of British Leyland (now owned by BMW) before it was sold off.
- Sales of individual assets of government bodies. For instance, local authorities are now forced to allow council house tenants to buy their own homes if they wish. Government departments have been encouraged to sell surplus land and buildings.
- The creation of private sector competition to state monopolies. Regulations, often created at the time of nationalisation, prevented effective competition in industries such as telecommunications, coal and gas. Abolishing these regulations has enabled competitors, such as Mercury and cable companies, to enter markets previously supplied exclusively by public sector concerns.
- Compulsory competitive tendering (☞ unit 46). Many services, often local authority services, have been provided by public sector employees in the past. Dustbins have been emptied by council refuse collectors, schools cleaned by council cleaners and hospital sheets washed by health service employees. The government has now forced its own departments, local authorities, and other government bodies to put these services out to tender. Workers who previously provided the services have been sacked, although most have regained their jobs working for the private sector companies which gained the contracts.

QUESTION 2 Explain what type of privatisation each of the following would be:
(a) staffing prisons with private security guards; (b) the sale of British Coal; (c) the sale of land owned by the Post Office; (d) allowing companies to set up rival services to those run by the Post Office.

Arguments in favour of privatisation

A number of arguments have been put forward in favour of privatisation.

Cost Publicly owned industries have no incentive to cut costs. The result is that there is likely to be X-inefficiency (☞ unit 33) in the industry. There is no incentive because there is little or no mechanism by which government can bear down on costs. There is also often little comparison with what costs might be if reduced to a minimum since the state owned firm is often a monopoly. State owned industries also tend to behave like bureaucracies, where the interests of the workers are as important as the interests of the owners (the state) and consumers. **Behavioural theories of the firm** (☞ unit 33) are more appropriate to understanding their decision making than traditional neo-classical profit maximising theories. A privatised profit maximising company does have an incentive to reduce cost because reduced cost is translated into higher profit. This is true whether the privatised company faces competition in the market place or whether it enjoys a monopoly. Hence privatisation leads to greater **productive efficiency** (☞ unit 34).

Choice and quality Public sector organisations have little incentive to produce goods which consumers want to buy. They tend to be 'product led' organisations, mass producing a limited range of goods and services which state employees feel is what consumers ought to be provided with. This is particularly true where the public sector organisations are monopoly or near-monopoly providers. In contrast, private sector firms have an incentive to provide both choice and quality. If they are in competitive markets, then a failure to provide choice and quality will result in consumers buying from other firms which do provide these. Even if they are monopolists, privatised firms can often raise prices and expand their market by providing quality services with choice. Higher prices and greater sales can then feed through to higher profits, the ultimate goal of private sector firms. Choice and quality are aspects of **allocative efficiency** (☞ unit 34).

Innovation As with choice and quality, state organisations have little incentive to innovate. Private sector organisations, however, can earn higher profit if they innovate and persuade consumers to buy more of their product. This increases **dynamic efficiency** in the economy.

The invisible hand of the market Market forces allocate resources so that they are used in the most efficient manner. Consumer spending decisions in a free market act like votes in a democratic election, indicating consumer preferences. Monopoly state organisations, on the other hand, lack the knowledge of consumer preferences to make efficient allocative decisions on their behalf. Moreover, governments interfere in the market place and misallocate resources for short term political objectives. Governments are the enemy of economic freedom because they have such overwhelming political power. Therefore, governments should have as little control over the economy as possible. Only the operation of free market forces will ensure the optimal allocation of resources.

QUESTION 3

'In privatising British Telecom, we stimulated competition by licencing Mercury as a competing network. We have also liberalised other aspects of telecommunications - permitting anyone to provide value added and data services and to run their own branch system; introducing competition in paging, cellular, other mobile radio and satellite services; allowing 'telepoint' services and personal communications networks to develop; and giving choice to the public over the telephone apparatus they buy. The result is a dramatic improvement in the variety and quality of services available to the public and of course a growing and flourishing telecommunications service sector able to compete in the international market place.'

Source: Nicholas Ridley, then Secretary of State for Trade and Industry writing in the *Financial Times*, 6 11 1989.

How, according to Nicholas Ridley, did privatisation increase economic efficiency?

Other considerations in favour of privatisation

The process of privatisation can also be used to achieve other goals.

Wider share ownership It has been argued that wider share ownership is desirable. In the past, share ownership has been too narrow. Only a few relatively rich people have chosen to invest their savings in shares. The result has been a divide between workers and capitalists, with some workers seeing share owners as parasites who skim off the profits which arise from the efforts of workers. In a wide share owning democracy, the distinction between worker and capitalist is not present because workers are also capitalists. Workers will be better able to appreciate the risks that capitalists take with their assets and will be able to see, for instance, that wage increases are not necessarily economically desirable. The wealth of the country will be more evenly spread and this too can be seen as desirable.

Reduction in public borrowing and state spending In the short term, the sale of state owned assets raises money for the government which can be used to reduce public borrowing for the year or even pay off part of the National Debt. There will also be an improvement in state finances in the long term if, as if often the case, state owned enterprises make losses and need to be subsidised. Less borrowing leads to lower interest repayments and hence less need for taxes, as do reduced subsidies to state industries.

QUESTION 4 Privatisation share issues have tended to favour the small investor. For instance, applicants for the minimum number of shares (often 100 shares) have often been allocated all of the shares they applied for. Shareholders applying for more than the minimum have had their applications scaled down - the larger the number of shares applied for, the larger the scaling down.

Why has the government chosen to allocate shares in privatisation issues in this way?

Potential problems with privatisation

There are a number of potential problems with privatisation.

Monopoly Some state owned industries operate in a competitive market place already. Before privatisation, British Steel, for instance, although a monopoly producer in the UK, faced fierce competition from overseas steel producers. However, some are privatised as monopolies and remain monopolies. Traditional neo-classical theory would suggest that they would then exploit that position, charging high prices and restricting output, leading to a loss of allocative efficiency (☞ unit 39). Two ways around this problem are discussed below - breaking up the monopoly and regulating the monopoly.

Equity Nationalised industries do not necessarily price in the same way that a privatised company would do. The process of privatisation is likely to lead to a change in the pricing structure. This will result in there being gainers and losers amongst consumers. There will be also be a change in equity arising from ownership of shares and payouts of dividends to private shareholders.

Externalities Nationalised industries may have given greater weighting to factors such as the impact of their operations on the environment than a privatised industry. Privatisation may then lead to greater negative externalities (☞ unit 36). On the other hand, nationalised industries may not have to conform to environmental or other legislation because the state has given them exemption. In this case, privatisation will lead to fewer negative externalities.

The control of privatised companies

As explained above, some companies or industries which were privatised already operated within a competitive environment. However, others, such as electricity, gas and water in the UK, were monopolies before privatisation. If left as monopolies, they could exploit their monopoly position, leading to allocative inefficiency. There are two main ways in which this can be prevented.

The creation of competition There are two ways of creating competition. The first is to privatise the company or industry as a whole, but encourage other private sector companies to set up in the industry. For instance, the UK government gave a licence to Mercury to set up in competition with British Telecom. In the gas industry, the government forced British Gas to allow other gas companies to supply to the industrial gas market. The second way of creating competition is to split the industry up into competing companies at the point of privatisation. For instance, electricity generation was split up into three parts at privatisation - PowerGen, National Power and Nuclear Electric.

Regulation of the industry A second route is to allow the monopoly to remain after privatisation but create a regulatory framework which prevents it from earning abnormal profit and creating allocative inefficiency. All the privatised utilities in the UK have regulators which act by limiting prices.

There are two main issues which arise from regulation. The first relates to the objective of regulation. The ultimate goal is to prevent the monopoly earning abnormal profit and to encourage it to be productively efficient (i.e. produce at lowest cost). In the USA,

QUESTION 5 In February 1994, National Power and PowerGen agreed with the industry regulator, Offer, that they would sell off some of their power stations. National Power agreed to dispose of between 3 000 and 4 000 MW of its generating plant within two years. PowerGen agreed to dispose of 2 000 MW of capacity. This is the equivalent to six large power stations or 10 to 15 per cent of the two companies' generating capacity. The agreement was part of a larger package of measures which also included a reduction in prices in the wholesale electricity pool of 7 per cent. The pool is a market for electricity where prices are set on a day-to-day basis, depending on the supply of electricity offered by the power generators and the demand for electricity from large industrial users and the regional electricity distribution companies.

The regulator, Professor Littlechild, wants to increase the amount of competition in the electricity generation market. At present, there are only three major suppliers of electricity, National Power, PowerGen and Nuclear Electric. By forcing two of the companies to sell off some of their power stations, he hopes that new companies will enter the market.

Source: adapted from the *Financial Times*, 12.2.1994.

(a) Explain what is meant by 'competition'. Illustrate your answer with examples from the electricity industry.
(b) What effect might the agreement described in the passage have on electricity prices?
(c) Why would a higher degree of competition in the electricity industry reduce the need for a regulator in the industry?

regulators have tended to focus on profits, limiting the amount of profit a regulated company can earn. This, it is argued, neither encourages the firm to reduce its costs nor be innovative by creating new products and new markets. In the UK, regulation has centred on prices. Privatised utilities have been set price limits but allowed to earn as much profit as they can within those limits. This, it is argued, leads to greater efficiency. If the firm cuts costs and thus becomes more productively efficient, it can retain part of or all of the gains in the form of higher profits. Equally, if the company is successful in gaining new sales and expanding its market, then it can share in this success by keeping the resulting higher profits.

A second issue arising from regulation is that of **regulatory capture** (☞ unit 44). It is argued that regulators of privatised companies can be 'captured' by the industries they are supposed to be regulating. The decisions of the regulator are often based on information which is given to them by the industry. The privatised company will obviously only want to pass on to the regulator information which supports the need to keep prices high. If the regulator assumes that the company is giving it full and impartial information, then the regulator can be said to have been 'captured' by the company because it is effectively acting in the best interests of the company, rather than the best interests of consumers. More worrying would be situations where a regulator benefited in some way from allowing weak regulation of the industry. Bribery would be one obvious way for the company to achieve this. However, an intimate association between regulator and the regulated company, where the company was paying the regulator large amounts of expenses, could well lead to the regulator failing to take an impartial approach to regulation.

Key terms

Nationalised industries and public corporations - state owned industries or companies.
Privatisation - a transfer of the organisation of production from the public sector to the private sector.

Applied economics

Nationalisation and privatisaton in the UK

History

The state is responsible for organising the production of many goods and services. Some, such as defence and education, have traditionally been financed through taxes and have been provided free at the point of sale. However, there has also been a long tradition of the state selling goods and services in the same way that a private company might. For instance, a public postal service was established in 1840 which has grown to be today's Post Office. In 1912, the Post Office first provided a national telephone service. During the 1920s and 1930s, successive UK governments established the British Broadcasting Corporation, the London Passenger Transport Board (now London Transport), the British Overseas Airways Corporation (now part of British Airways) and the Central Electricity Generating Board. Local authorities also provided many goods and services such as public baths, bus transport and gas.

Up to the Second World War, government enterprises were set up on an ad hoc basis where it was felt that state provision would be better than private provision in that particular case. However, the Labour government elected to office in 1945 believed strongly that nationalisation was in general likely to be beneficial. Clement Attlee's government nationalised coal, rail, steel, the Bank of England and road transport. It created the gas boards and electricity boards that existed for the next 40 years. The Labour Party after 1951 remained committed to further nationalisation but it was not a high priority. The two remaining firms which passed into public ownership were both firms which went bankrupt and were taken over in the national interest - Rolls Royce in 1971 by the Conservative government of Edward Heath and British Leyland cars in 1975 by Harold Wilson's Labour government.

Privatisation was not even specifically mentioned in the 1979 Conservative Party manifesto. Yet within 10 years, many public sector companies had been sold off to the private sector. Table 45.1 shows the timetable for the sale of state owned assets to the private sector from 1979.

Table 45.1 *Sale of state owned companies to the private sector*

Date begun			
1979	*British Petroleum	1986	British Gas
	*ICL	1987	British Airways
	*Ferranti		Rolls Royce
	Fairey		Leyland Bus
1981	British Aerospace		Leyland Truck
	*British Sugar		Royal Ordnance
	Cable and Wireless		British Airport Authority
	Amersham International	1988	British Steel
1982	National Freight Corporation		British Leyland
	Britoil	1989	British Water Authorities
1983	*Associated British Ports	1990	Electricity Area Boards
	British Rail Hotels	1991	Electricity Generation
1984	British Gas Onshore Oil	1994	British Coal
	Enterprise Oil	1995	British Rail
	Sealink Ferries		
	Jaguar Cars		
	British Telecom		
	British Technology Group		

*Partly owned by government at the time of sale.

Initially, relatively small companies with healthy profits were put up for sale. These were in markets where there was already competition. The first public monopoly to be privatised was British Telecom in 1984.

By 1995, the only substantial companies left in public hands were the Post Office and most of the former British Rail. The latter had been reorganised in 1994 to facilitate its sale.

Utilities - the regulatory regime

Each of the utilities privatised in the 1980s - British Telecom, British Gas, the electricity industry and the water industry - has a regulator. It is his or her job to ensure that the utility does not abuse its monopoly power to exploit its customers.

The main way in the short term in which this is achieved is through fixing prices. The regulator sets a pricing formula which allows the utility to change its prices by a formula linked to the inflation rate - an RPI plus or RPI minus formula.

When British Gas was privatised in 1986, its price formula was set at RPI minus 2 per cent. This meant that each year it had to reduce gas prices by at least 2 per cent. This reflected a belief that British Gas could improve efficiency, for instance by making its workforce more productive. In 1992, the formula was tightened to RPI minus 5 per cent. However, it was cut in 1994 to RPI minus 4 per cent. This was because British Gas had been forced to open its industrial market up to competition and had lost so much market share that investment at British Gas was being affected.

When British Telecom was privatised, its pricing formula was set at RPI minus 3 per cent. In 1989 this was tightened to RPI minus 4½ per cent and in 1991 to RPI minus 6½ per cent. It was further tightened in 1993 when it was set at RPI minus 7½ per cent. Moreover, BT is now not allowed to increase the price of any single service apart from line rental by more than the RPI. In part this is to discourage BT from increasing residential charges where it has little or no competition, and cutting charges where it does have competition from Mercury.

The electricity companies are covered by a variety of formulae. At privatisation between 1990 and 1991, the industry was split into three parts - electricity generation, the National Grid and the distribution companies. The electricity generation companies include Nuclear Power, National Power and PowerGen. They sell electricity into a 'pool' - effectively a market. Pool prices in the early 1990s were often higher than buyers had hoped. In 1994, the regulator agreed a limit with the power generators of a maximum average of 2.4p per Kwh on the pool price of electricity over the following two years. The distribution boards, which distribute electricity to domestic and industrial customers, were given a price formula in 1991 which allowed them to increase prices to domestic customers by the rate of inflation. The distribution companies have since made very large profits. In August 1994, a new price formula was agreed. The distribution companies agreed to cut distribution prices (part of the final cost of electricity to the customer) by between 11 and 18 per cent depending on the company. Annual price rises would be limited to the RPI minus 2 per cent.

However, Trafalgar House, a UK conglomerate company, subsequently made a bid for Northern Electric, which Northern Electric opposed. As part of its defence, it forecast large profits for the future and promised a large payout to shareholders if they refused Trafalgar's offer. The sums talked about made it clear to the regulator that he had been misled by the electricity industry about likely future profits. In March 1995, he announced that he would review his 1994 pricing formula, the results of the review were announced in July 1995. Charges would fall by between 10 and 13 per cent in real terms in 1996 on top of the 11-18 per cent fall announced in 1994. In addition, prices would fall by 3 per cent a year in real terms between 1996 and 2000 instead of the 2 per cent announced in 1994.

The water industry has seen the largest price rises allowed of all the privatised utilities. It needed to spend billions of pounds upgrading Britain's water and sewage disposal infrastructure in order to comply with EU regulations. By the year 2000, the privatised water companies will have spent an estimated £40bn in new investment. This has not come cheaply and the pricing formulae set at privatisation averaged RPI plus 5.4 per cent. In July 1994, the Ofwat regulator announced a new set of 'K' factors (K being the amount above the increase in the RPI by which water companies can increase their charges) which limited price rises to an average of 1 per cent plus the rate of inflation over the next 10 years. This recognises that the water boards have been successful in cutting their cost base and can, therefore, afford to bear much more of the cost of upgrading their infrastructure than before.

Advantages and disadvantages of privatisation

Privatisation by the mid-1990s was generally considered to be a success. Few now argue that companies such as Rover, British Steel or British Aerospace would have performed better if they had remained in state ownership. So far as the privatised utilities are concerned, the UK regulatory regime can be claimed to have been highly successful. Prices in real terms have tended to fall in the privatised utilities. Gas prices, for instance, fell 20 per cent in real terms between 1986 and 1994. Average British Telecom call prices fell 40 per cent between 1984 and 1994. In comparison with similar utilities in Europe, price falls have been far greater. The quality of service provided has not generally diminished and in many instances has improved. It would seem that moving these industries from the public sector into the private sector, even when no competition has been created, has been enough radically to improve productive efficiency through large reductions in costs.

However, there are a number of concerns still being raised about the privatisation process.

- The movement of share prices in most of the privatised companies would indicate that the government sold off the companies at too low a price. This has benefited new shareholders at the expense of the taxpayer.
- There were considerable productivity improvements in most privatised companies in the years before

privatisation as companies were told to adopt a more commercial approach before being sold off. If these gains could be achieved when the companies were still state-owned, why did they need to be privatised?

- The profits of the privatised utilities have been substantial, and far in excess of rates of return on capital in other comparable industries. This has been reflected in the high share prices of the companies. It must then be questioned whether the regulators have not been too lenient with the utilities and whether they have been **captured**. Critics would argue that shareholders have received far too much of the efficiency gains made by the utilities and that consumers have received too little. If dividends had been lower, prices could have been lower. The evidence would suggest that no regulator has as yet deliberately set out to collude with its industry to keep prices as high as possible. However, there is considerable evidence that companies have deliberately set out to be as 'economical with the truth' as possible, usually by providing highly pessimistic forecasts of future trends and by withholding as much data as possible. Sir James McKinnon, the first gas regulator, enjoyed a notoriously bad relationship with British Gas, as British Gas attempted to marginalise him in decision making processes. Professor Littlechild, the electricity regulator, reviewing a decision made only 8 months before, (discussed above), is another example of a regulator not being given all the facts and figures needed to make a decision.
- Whilst services have been maintained and in some cases improved, there have also been casualties of the new commercial approach of the utilities. There has been a dramatic increase in the number of households disconnected by the water companies for failure to pay bills, for instance. Disconnecting telephones is arguably fair practice in the case of BT, but water is an essential service. Households with no water face serious health risks. Equally, the number of disconnections for gas and electricity has increased, again giving cause for concern especially where there are children in the household. Fears that services would be cut in rural areas was arguably a major reason why the government was forced to abandon its plans to privatise the Post Office in 1994.

A model in need of overhaul

A decade after the flotation of British Telecom, Deutsche Telekom, the German state-owned monopoly, is lumbering towards the stock market. The DM15bn Telekom sale, one of the largest in the world, reflects the eagerness with which much of Europe and Asia is now embracing the UK model of privatisation.

The transfer of state companies to the private sector, widely regarded as the essence of Thatcherism, remains one of the UK's most popular exports. The collapse of communism, which shook faith in the virtues of state ownership, has helped its international propagation.

But in the UK, where sales of state-owned companies have raised nearly £60bn for the government since 1980, the philosophy is under attack. Customers of the privatised utilities feel that shareholders have been the real winners, with sharp rises in profits and dividends. That grievance has been deepened by steep hikes in directors' pay, notably the 75 per cent rise awarded last month to Mr Cedric Brown, British Gas Chief executive.

In the face of public and back-bench criticism of privatised utilities, the government has recently shelved proposed sales of the Forestry Commission, Scottish water, and the Post Office. It is under increasing pressure to demonstrate that past privatisations have delivered the promised benefits.

Some privatisations are now less controversial - including British Steel, British Airways, the Rover car maker and Cable & Wireless, the telecoms group. These all face competition in their markets, and have greatly improved their performance (while many of their international rivals are loss-making).

However it is on the performance of the utilities - telecommunications, gas, electricity and water - that privatisation is judged by the British public. With some or all of their businesses effectively monopolies, they have not faced competitive pressures in the private sector. The UK privatisation model relies on independent regulators to curb their monopoly power and encourage economic efficiency through price controls. These controls have taken the form of capping annual price rises according to a formula linked to the Retail Price Index (RPI); in most cases, these are 'RPI-X' formulae that hold rises below the rate of inflation.

Of the four, British Telecom provide the most convincing case that the UK model works. A decade ago, BT warned 250,000 customers waiting for new telephone lines that it would not even suggest an installation date; now it says it will install a new residential line within 48 hours. Before privatisation, telephones had to be rented from BT; now there are hundreds of models on sale in shops.

Since 1984, the price of calls has also dropped by an average 40 per cent in real terms. Meanwhile, turnover has doubled to £13.8bn in the year to March 1994; the 90,000 fall in staff numbers to 150,000 has allowed pre-tax profits to treble to £2.8bn.

The spur has been competition, largely from Mercury, the Cable & Wireless subsidiary, as well as technological change and price controls. But growth of competition was slower than expected, with some would-be rivals arguing that they were inhibited by the terms of access to BT's network.

Privatising electricity presented greater challenges, in the absence of competition in the industry. Radical structural reform during the sale separated transmission and generation. The 12 regional electricity companies (Recs) that supply power to consumers were allowed to compete in generation, to a limited degree.

That competition, together with price capping imposed by the regulator, has caused staff numbers and operating costs to fall sharply. But Mr Dieter Helm, director of Oxera, the forecasting group, argues that the savings should have been greater since the price of coal, gas, oil and uranium has fallen since privatisation. 'There is little evidence to show that customers are much better off,' he says.

Moreover, the industry's restructuring proved unexpectedly controversial when it triggered a 'dash for gas', as generators built power stations using cheaper gas to replace coal as fuel. Professor Stephen Littlechild, the electricity regulator, backed the switch on the grounds that it cut costs and increased competition in power generation. But it also hastened the decline of the coal industry, creating a row over pit closures that harmed the image of privatisation.

Despite those concerns, the restructuring of the electricity industry has spared its regulator many of the problems that have confronted his counterpart in gas. The government chose to privatise British Gas with an intact monopoly in transportation and supply of gas. The company was also the only UK buyer of gas from producers. While it has been forced to cut gas prices for smaller customers, initially it faced no price cap in the market for larger customers.

The light regulation and unchanged structure were heavily criticised at the time of privatisation. Professor John Vickers, an Oxford economist, says the price controls on British Gas required 'lower productivity gains than those British Gas had previously achieved while in public ownership'.

The government has since introduced curbs on British Gas, including limits on its market share and a requirement to sell gas to competitors to allow them to supply customers. But these fall short of the changes recommended by the Office of Fair Trading and the Monopolies and Mergers Commission, which have both criticised the terms on which competitors can gain access to the British Gas network to deliver their gas to customers.

The problems of gas regulation dwindle, however, when set beside those of water where it is impossible to introduce direct competition without creating competing networks of water pipes. The weight placed on the regulator to curb abuse of this monopoly is consequently higher.

A complication in his task is that companies have embarked on a £40bn capital spending programme, to modernise pipes and sewage plants after decades of under-investment and to enable the UK to comply with European environmental directives. Under the price formula set at privatisation, the costs are passed onto customers, and have pushed bills up by 5 per cent a year above inflation since 1989.

Mr Ian Byatt, the water regulator, has criticised the Brussels standards, particularly those on drinking water, for being unnecessarily tough. He has also attempted to lighten the consumer's burden by restraining real price increases for the next 10 years to an average of 1 per cent. But as Professor Colin Mayer, an Oxford economist, comments, it has 'been difficult' for the regulator to determine the industry's cost of capital and to compare companies' efficiency. 'There are no easy answers', he adds.

The mixed record of utility regulation indicates that insufficient ambition in creating competition when privatising utilities creates a troublesome legacy for the regulators - even if it helps sell the shares. As Professor Littlechild says: ' however well-intentioned and well-informed [is] price control, effective competition is better'.

Professor Littlechild originally believed that regulators would be able to introduce enough competition to allow regulation to wither away. However, as Professor Vickers argues, 'it is over-optimistic to view regulation as a stopgap until sufficient competition arrived'.

In his view, the regulatory framework and pricing formula have 'so far survived reasonably well'. In recent reviews, regulators have tightened the price curbs, helping customers, at shareholders' expense (although they have satisfied neither their customers nor companies).

But problems remain. In particular, the terms on which competitors use the telecommunications, gas and electricity networks are hotly disputed. As Professor John Kay of London Economics, the consultancy, says, in the context of telecoms, 'It has been evident since the first stirrings of competition ... that the terms on which entrants would be allowed access to the incumbent's network were critical'.

It is clear that inadequate attention to such problems at the time of privatisation is the cause of many of the complaints about the privatised utilities. The forthcoming privatisation of British Rail is the next chance for the government to show whether it has learned that lesson.

Source: the *Financial Times*, 22.12.1994.

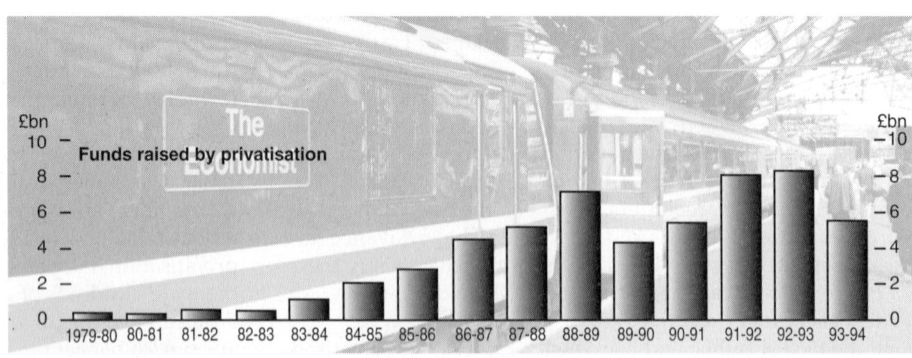

Source: adapted from HM Treasury.

Figure 45.1 *Funds raised by privatisation*

1. (a) What is meant by 'privatisation'?
   (b) Outline the arguments in favour of privatisation to be found in the passage.
2. (a) What are the likely goals of privatised companies?
   (b) Explain how regulation has limited the ability of privatised utilities to achieve those goals.
3. Discuss whether or not there would be both efficiency and equity gains for the economy if regulation of the privatised utilities were lightened or even abolished altogether.

Internal markets

Applied economics

Since 1979, the government has attempted to reduce the role of the state in the economy, and increase the role of the market in allocating resources. In unit 45, the part that privatisation has played in this process was discussed. In this unit, we will consider three other ways in which the government has sought to achieve its objectives.

Competitive tendering

The government has to provide certain goods and services because they are public or merit goods, or because state provision is more efficient or more equitable than private sector provision (☞ unit 44). However, this does not necessarily imply that the state has to be the producer of all or part of these goods and services. For instance, the state has never made the sheets that are used in NHS hospitals, or the tanks that are used in the British army. These are produced by private sector firms and sold to the public sector.

Since the 1980s, the government has attempted to increase the proportion of government spending which is CONTRACTED OUT to the private sector. Instead of the government producing a good or service, it invites private sector firms to bid for a contract to provide the good or service. A specification for the contract is drawn up. Failure to conform with the specification by the winning company can lead to fines or even loss of the contract. One of the groups likely to be bidding for the contract is the government department or agency which previously did the work. If they put in the lowest bid, then they will win the contract. They will then remain government employees. If they fail to win the contract, then many of the workers may be taken on by the winning private sector firm.

A number of areas of public spending have been targeted for this process of COMPETITIVE TENDERING. Local authority expenditure is one key area. In 1980, local authorities were forced to put construction and building maintenance work to tender. Since 1988, local authorities have had to put out to tender a large number of services, including catering, cleaning streets and buildings, maintenance of grounds and vehicles, the management of sport and leisure facilities and refuse collection. The government has also encouraged local authorities to contract out accountancy, architectural services, careers services, computer and data processing services, fire protection and housing sales. In the NHS, there is compulsory competitive tendering for catering and cleaning and laundry services. In defence, there is competitive tendering for catering and cleaning, refitting of warships, aircraft servicing and vehicle repair, air transport and the management of stores.

The main advantage claimed for contracting out services is that the government saves money. It is argued that public sector provision is bureaucratic and inefficient. There is no incentive for public sector providers to reduce costs or be innovative. Competition, on the other hand, whether the contract goes to a private sector firm or a government body, forces down prices, leading to greater productive efficiency. The buyer of the service, the government, is also able to concentrate on deciding the exact specification of what is to be bought, rather than having to worry about how the service will be provided.

On the other hand, there is concern that private sector providers might fail to meet the specifications of the contract. Whilst this might not be too important in the area of, say, ground maintenance, it is obviously a very serious issue if a private firm is contracted to run an old people's home or it is refitting a warship. There is also concern that only a relatively small number of firms will bid for any contract. If only two firms bid for a contract, there must be some doubt about whether either is bidding at the lowest price possible. There is also the danger of collusion (☞ unit 41), with private firms choosing to divide the market amongst themselves rather than compete. Finally, lower costs may only be achieved because private firms pay their workers less and work them harder than if those workers were public sector employees. The apparent increase in productive efficiency arising from the lower costs of the contract may have only been achieved at the expense of redistribution in society, with taxpayers gaining and the workers involved losing.

The evidence to date suggests that there have been substantial savings for government from compulsory competitive tendering. In health and local authority services, this has averaged 25 per cent (Hartley and Hooper). Whilst some of this has been achieved through giving workers less pay and worsening their conditions of service, most of it has been achieved through productivity improvements. There has been no evidence of collusion between private sector firms, although many local authorities have frustrated the competitive tendering process by adopting procedures which favour the in-house local authority department winning any contract. There have been isolated instances of very poor work being carried out, but then this was also true when government directly produced the goods or services. On average, however, services are no worse than before competitive tendering was introduced. Competitive tendering, then, seems to have achieved its objective of cutting costs.

Deregulation

DEREGULATION is the process of removing government controls from markets.

- The government may allow private firms to compete in a market which is currently being supplied by a state monopoly. An example of this would be if the government lifted the present regulation that private firms must charge at least £1 for the delivery of any letter or package, which effectively prevents the private sector from developing a rival letter service to the Post Office.

- The government may lift regulations which prevent competition between private firms. For instance, the Building Societies Act 1986 gave building societies the ability to compete with banks in the personal loan market. 'Big bang', the deregulation of the London financial markets, again in 1986, allowed banks to offer stock broking services.
- The government may lift regulations when an industry is privatised. For instance, when coal was privatised, the regulation that no private coal mine employing more than 10 workers could operate was abolished.

Deregulation attempts to improve economic efficiency through the promotion of competition. This, it is argued, will lower costs (leading to greater productive efficiency) whilst reducing prices and increasing output (increasing allocative efficiency). The major problem with deregulation to date is that it has encouraged 'creaming' of markets (firms only providing services in the most profitable areas of the market). For instance, in the bus industry, deregulated in the 1980s, bus firms have concentrated on providing bus services on profitable urban routes into town centres, arguably to the detriment of country passengers. It has been suggested that one of the reasons why the government backed down on privatisation of the Post Office in 1994 was that it was feared that privatisation would be accompanied by deregulation, with the Post Office losing its letter monopoly. New private firms would enter the industry, but they would concentrate on urban services. These would go down in price, but the privatised Post Office would be forced to put up the price for rural deliveries because it could no longer afford to cross-subsidise its these services.

Internal markets

In some industries, the government has been forced to accept that the state must not only provide a good or service, but also produce it. For instance, in education and health, there has been little support for the argument that private production would significantly reduce costs. Indeed, international evidence suggests that private production of health care is far more costly than state provision. In these markets, the government has chosen to create competition between different public sector providers - the INTERNAL MARKET solution.

In an internal market, one group must be given purchasing power. In the NHS, it is the general practitioners (GPs) who have become **fund holders**, buyers in the market with money (funds) provided by the government. With these funds, GPs have to run their own practices and buy in extra services needed by their patients. These extra services are mainly the services provided by hospitals, such as consultants' appointments and operations. Each hospital has to compete for monies from the general practitioners. If a hospital doesn't get enough patients and therefore enough money from GPs, the fund holders, then it has to reduce in size. If, on the other hand, it receives more patients than anticipated, then it can expand. To further encourage competition, hospitals have been allowed to break away from the control of the district authorities which used to run medical services in a local area. Instead, they have become Trusts, independent bodies which are still in the public sector, like a local authority, but which are now directly accountable to central government.

In education, there is a much weaker form of the internal market. Here, parents are free to choose which school their child should attend. Schools are financed mainly on the number of children on roll in a year. So a school which attracts children will receive extra cash. An unpopular school with declining rolls will see its budget fall. Schools therefore have to compete amongst themselves for pupils. Unpopular schools, which the government would argue would be the ones providing poor quality education, will eventually be forced to close or improve the quality of their provision. Government has also encouraged schools operated by local authorities to 'opt out' and become Grant Maintained Schools. These schools are directly funded by central government. They have been encouraged to compete with other local schools for pupils.

The government argues that internal markets increase efficiency in the market. In the NHS, there should be an increase in productive efficiency on the part of hospitals. GPs, anxious to make their budgets stretch as far as possible, will send patients to the cheapest hospital for operations, all other things being equal. There will therefore be an incentive for hospitals to cut costs to attract customers. However, GPs will also be looking at allocative efficiency. They will want to send their patients to hospitals which provide high quality care, or which have short waiting lists or which are locally convenient for their patients. In education, competition is designed to raise standards of service provided with 'bad' schools being forced to adopt good practices in order to survive.

Critics argue that any benefits from competition will be outweighed by extra administrative costs. There has had to be a considerable increase in the number of managers in the NHS since the internal market was introduced. They also point out that closing wards, hospitals or schools because of a supposed lack of demand is very wasteful since the buildings and the equipment represent scarce resources which could be used.

Key terms

Contracted out - getting private sector firms to produce the goods and services which are then provided by the state for its citizens.
Competitive tendering - introducing competition amongst private sector firms which put in bids for work which is contracted out by the public sector.
Deregulation - the process of removing government controls from markets.
Internal market - markets, with buyers and sellers, which are within a single organisation.

NHS league tables

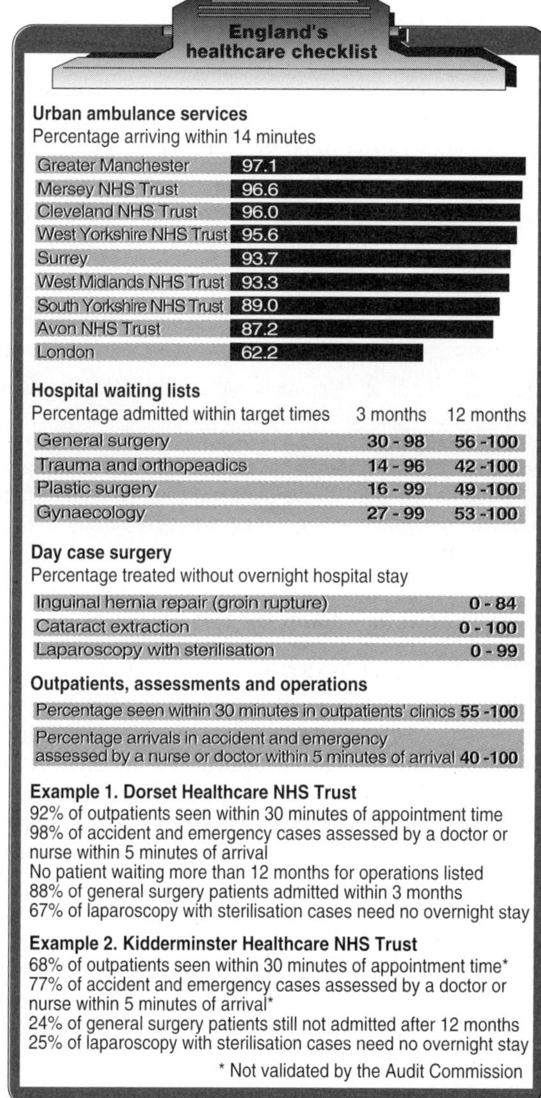

England's healthcare checklist

Urban ambulance services
Percentage arriving within 14 minutes

Greater Manchester	97.1
Mersey NHS Trust	96.6
Cleveland NHS Trust	96.0
West Yorkshire NHS Trust	95.6
Surrey	93.7
West Midlands NHS Trust	93.3
South Yorkshire NHS Trust	89.0
Avon NHS Trust	87.2
London	62.2

Hospital waiting lists

Percentage admitted within target times	3 months	12 months
General surgery	30 - 98	56 -100
Trauma and orthopeadics	14 - 96	42 -100
Plastic surgery	16 - 99	49 -100
Gynaecology	27 - 99	53 -100

Day case surgery
Percentage treated without overnight hospital stay

Inguinal hernia repair (groin rupture)	0 - 84
Cataract extraction	0 - 100
Laparoscopy with sterilisation	0 - 99

Outpatients, assessments and operations

Percentage seen within 30 minutes in outpatients' clinics	55 -100
Percentage arrivals in accident and emergency assessed by a nurse or doctor within 5 minutes of arrival	40 -100

Example 1. Dorset Healthcare NHS Trust
92% of outpatients seen within 30 minutes of appointment time
98% of accident and emergency cases assessed by a doctor or nurse within 5 minutes of arrival
No patient waiting more than 12 months for operations listed
88% of general surgery patients admitted within 3 months
67% of laparoscopy with sterilisation cases need no overnight stay

Example 2. Kidderminster Healthcare NHS Trust
68% of outpatients seen within 30 minutes of appointment time*
77% of accident and emergency cases assessed by a doctor or nurse within 5 minutes of arrival*
24% of general surgery patients still not admitted after 12 months
25% of laparoscopy with sterilisation cases need no overnight stay

* Not validated by the Audit Commission

Source: adapted from Department of Health

Figure 46.1

Hospital league tables

As part of the creation of an internal market in the National Health Service, the government is compiling league tables based upon statistics which hospitals are having to supply to the Department of Health. 23 performance indicators are given, from waiting times to the percentage having to stay overnight for certain operations. Hospitals which do particularly well are awarded stars.

Hospital league tables are 'a milestone in the information revolution sweeping the National Health Service. Information is a lever for change and a spur to improvement. Performance tables are an established way of identifying strengths and weaknesses and raising standards in our public services.'

Virginia Bottomley, Minister for Health, 29.6.1994.

'It (the league tables) is a bit like an Egon Ronay guide to restaurants, except it doesn't deal with the starter, it doesn't deal with the main course, and makes highly dubious judgements about the quality of the coffee.'

David Blunkett, Shadow Health Secretary, 29.6.1994.

'You can't pigeonhole the complexities of hospital treatment into crude, simplistic star ratings which mean little or nothing to patients. Giving hospitals stars and placing them in league order based purely on waiting times tells patients nothing about the quality of care they are likely to receive. I have grave doubts about a system which, for example, gives points for not allowing hernia patients to stay in hospital overnight.'

James Johnson, Deputy Chair of the British Medical Association's Consultants Committee, 29.6.1994.

1. **Explain how the internal market works in the health service in the UK.**
2. **Suggest what role hospital league tables might have in the efficient running of an internal market.**
3. **(a) What other information would GP fundholders need to have in order to make rational decisions about how to allocate their funds?**

   (b) Is it (i) possible or (ii) desirable for GPs to have all the information available to them that they need to make such decisions?

unit 47 Taxation

Summary

1. Governments need to raise taxes to pay for public spending. Taxes are also used to correct market failure, to redistribute income and wealth and to manage the economy.
2. Taxes can be direct or indirect, proportional, progressive or regressive.
3. The canons of taxation are a set of principles by which taxes can be evaluated.

The reasons for taxation

Governments use taxation for a number of purposes.

To pay for government expenditure Governments need to raise finance for their expenditure programmes (☞ unit 44). They can borrow a limited amount of money for this, but most of the finance must come from taxation if inflation is to be avoided.

To correct market failure such as externalities Governments can intervene in individual markets by changing taxes and thus changing demand. For instance, tobacco consumption can be reduced by raising taxes on cigarettes, pollution can be controlled by imposing pollution taxes, or sales of books can be increased by exempting them from VAT. Used in this way, taxation becomes a way of increasing economic efficiency.

To manage the economy as a whole Taxation can have an important influence on the **macro-economic** performance of the economy (☞ unit 68). Governments may change tax rates in order to influence variables such as inflation, unemployment and the balance of payments.

To redistribute income A government may judge that the distribution of resources is inequitable. To redistribute income, it may impose taxes which reduce the income and wealth of some groups in society and use the money collected to increase the income and wealth of other groups.

QUESTION 1 Each year in the Budget, the Chancellor of the Exchequer announces whether or not he will change the level of excise duties on tobacco. In most years, this is increased at least in line with inflation, although in some years, particularly election years, it is not increased at all. Why might the government change the level of excise duty on tobacco each year?

Direct and indirect taxes

Taxes are classified into two types. A DIRECT TAX is a tax levied directly on an individual or organisation. For instance, income tax is a direct tax because individual income earners are responsible for paying it. Corporation tax, a tax on company profits, is a direct tax too because companies have to pay it directly to the Inland Revenue.

An INDIRECT TAX is a tax on a good or service. For instance, value added tax is an indirect tax because it is a 17.5 per cent tax on most goods and services. Local Authority rates were an indirect tax on the notional rent of a property as is the new Uniform Business Rate for businesses.

QUESTION 2 Explain which of the following taxes are direct taxes and which are indirect:

(a) income tax; (b) National Insurance contributions; (c) inheritance tax; (d) corporation tax; (e) capital gains tax; (f) council tax; (g) VAT; (h) excise duties.

Progressive, regressive and proportional taxes

Another way of classifying taxes is to consider their **incidence** (☞ unit 13) as a proportion of income. A PROGRESSIVE TAX is a tax where the proportion of income paid in tax rises as the income of the taxpayer rises. For instance, income tax would be progressive if a worker earning £ 4 000 a year were to pay 5 per cent of income in tax, but 25 per cent on income of £ 40 000.

A REGRESSIVE TAX is a tax where the proportion of income paid in tax falls as the income of the taxpayer rises. An extreme example of a regressive tax was the poll tax in the UK between 1990 and 1992. The amount paid in poll tax was identical for most poll tax payers. A person earning £8 000 per year and paying £400 a year in poll tax paid exactly the same amount as a person earning £40 000. So the proportion of tax paid was different - 5 per cent of income for the person earning £8 000 a year (£400 ÷ £8 000), but only 1 per cent for the person earning £40 000 a year (£400 ÷ £40 000).

A PROPORTIONAL TAX is one where the proportion paid in tax remains the same as the income of the taxpayer changes (although the actual amount paid increases as income increases). VAT is an example of a broadly proportional tax. Whilst lower income earners spend a higher proportion of their income on zero-rated goods and services, higher income earners tend to save more of their income. Hence, the average rate of VAT paid by individuals tends to be a little less than 17.5 per cent.

The distinction between progressive, regressive and

proportional taxes is made because it is important in the study of the distribution of income and wealth. The more progressive the tax, the greater the link with ability to pay the tax and the more likely it is to result in a redistribution of resources from the better off in society to the less well off.

QUESTION 3 National Insurance contribution rates: employees, 1995-96 (from April).

- Those with earnings below £58 per week will continue to pay nothing.
- Those with earnings at or above £58 per week will pay 2 per cent on the first £58 (i.e. £1.16p) and 10 per cent on the rest up to the upper earnings limit of £440.

(a) Calculate the total amount of National Insurance contributions a worker would have to pay if her weekly earnings were: (i) £20; (ii) £57; (iii) £59; (iv) £158; (v) £258; (vi) £530.
(b) Are National Insurance contributions progressive, regressive or proportional over the weekly income range: (i) £20 to £56; (ii) £57 to £59; (iii) £59 to £158; (iv) £158 to £258; (v) £258 to £530?

The canons of taxation

Taxation has been a source of much controversy since the first tax was introduced. Adam Smith wrote at length on the subject of taxation in his book *An Enquiry into the Nature and Causes of the Wealth of Nations*, published in 1776. He argued that a good tax was one which had four characteristics:

- the cost of collection should be low relative to the yield of the tax;
- the timing of collection and the amount to be paid should be clear and certain;
- the means of payment and the timing of the payment should be convenient to the taxpayer;
- taxes should be levied according to the ability to pay of the individual taxpayer.

These canons relate to efficiency and equity. For instance, the cost of collection is about productive efficiency. Ability to pay is about equity.

There have been examples in history where taxes did not possess these canons. For instance, at certain periods in Roman history tax collecting was privatised. The Roman government sold the right to collect taxes in a province to the highest bidder. This individual would buy the right, hoping to charge more in taxes than he paid to the Roman authorities. With luck he might make 100 per cent profit on the contract - in this case the cost of collection would hardly be low. He would terrorise the province, forcing anyone and everyone to pay as much tax as he could exact from citizens. No attempt was made to make means of payment or timing suitable to the taxpayer. It was not clear on what basis citizens were being taxed, and there was no attempt to link taxes to ability to pay, since it was the poor who were the most easily terrorised whilst better off citizens were left alone for fear that they might complain to Rome!

Economists today have argued that in addition to Adam Smith's canons, a 'good' tax should be one which:

- leads to the least loss of economic efficiency, or even increases economic efficiency;
- is compatible with foreign tax systems, and in the case of the UK, particularly with EU tax regimes;
- automatically adjusts to changes in the price level - this is particularly important in a high inflation economy.

QUESTION 4

Table 47.1 *Revenue and cost of collection for selected taxes, 1986-87*

	Revenue	Administration costs		Compliance costs	
	£ bn	£m	%	£m	%
Income tax, capital gains tax & National Insurance contributions	65.1	997	1.53	2 212	3.4
VAT	21.4	220	1.03	791	3.69
Excise duties	16.5	42	0.25	33	0.20
Average central government	122.3	1 369	1.12	3 409	2.33

Source: adapted from the *Financial Times*, 20 .12.1989

Revenue is defined as the total revenue received by the government from the tax. Administrative costs are the costs to the government of collecting the tax (in £m and as a percentage of the revenue raised in tax). Compliance costs are an estimate of the cost of collection which is borne by private firms and individuals (again in £m and as a percentage of the revenue raised in tax). For instance, businesses have to spend time and therefore money accounting for the VAT they charge customers.

To what extent is VAT a 'good tax'?

Taxation, efficiency and equity

A tax is likely to lead to a fall in supply and a consequent reduction in the quantity demanded of the product or service being taxed. For instance:

- VAT and excise duties on a product push the supply curve to the left which in turn leads to a fall in the quantity demanded of the product (☞ unit 13);
- Income tax is likely to lead to a fall in the supply of labour to the market (☞ unit 69);
- Corporation tax is likely to lead to a fall in the supply of entrepreneurs to the market (☞ unit 57).

Taxes therefore distort markets. This may be beneficial in some markets, particularly if there are important negative externalities present and the tax brings private costs and benefits into line with social costs and benefits (☞ unit 37).

In other markets, taxes may lead to a loss of efficiency. For instance, if all markets were perfectly competitive, then the economy would be Pareto efficient (☞ unit 34). The introduction of a tax on one commodity, such as petrol, would then lead to a loss of efficiency in the economy because marginal cost would no longer equal price in that market. In practice, there are so many examples of market failure that it is impossible to come to any simple conclusions about whether a tax does or does not lead to efficiency losses. However, the **theory of the second best** suggests that taxes which are broadly based are less likely to lead to efficiency losses than narrow taxes. Low rates of tax spread as widely as possible are likely to be less damaging to economic welfare than high rates of tax on a small number of goods or individuals. For instance, a single rate VAT is likely to result in greater efficiency than a tax solely on petrol which raises the same revenue. Or an income tax which all earners pay is likely to lead to lower efficiency losses than an income tax paid solely by manufacturing workers.

It should be remembered that taxes are raised mainly to pay for government expenditure. Even if the imposition of taxes does lead to a loss of efficiency, this loss should be outweighed by the gain in economic efficiency resulting from the provision of **public** and **merit** goods by the government.

Taxes are also raised to ensure a redistribution of resources within the economy. There will be an increase in economic welfare if the welfare gains from a more desirable distribution of resources outweigh the welfare losses from the greater inefficiency arising from taxation.

QUESTION 5 In 1994, the Chancellor of the Exchequer imposed VAT on domestic fuel at 8 per cent. Previously, gas, electricity and coal used by households had been exempt from the standard rate of VAT of 17.5 per cent. The government wanted to increase the VAT rate on domestic fuel to 17.5 per cent from April 1995 but this was defeated by a back bench revolt in Parliament.

(a) Discuss the effect of the imposition of 8 per cent VAT on domestic fuel in terms of (i) efficiency and (ii) equity.
(b) Would efficiency have been increased if the VAT rate on domestic fuel had increased to 17.5 per cent?

Key terms

Direct tax - a tax levied directly on an individual or organisation, such as income tax.
Indirect tax - a tax levied on goods or services, such as value added tax or excise duties.
Progressive, regressive or proportional taxes - taxes where the proportion of income paid in tax rises, falls or remains the same respectively as income rises.

Applied economics

Taxation in the UK

The main taxes in the UK

Table 47.2 shows the breakdown of government revenue forecast for 1995-96. All but 5 per cent is gained from taxation (including social security receipts). The main UK taxes are as follows.

Income tax This is the single most important source of revenue for government. It is a tax on the income of individuals. Each person in the UK is allowed to earn a certain amount before paying tax. This amount is called a **tax allowance**. One tax allowance which everyone gets is the **personal allowance**. In 1995-96, a person could earn £3 525 a year 'tax free'. An additional allowance of £1 720 is also given to one person of a married couple or it can be split between them. The two other main allowances are payments to pension schemes and mortgage interest relief on mortgages up to £30 000 a year.

Income earned over the value of allowances (the tax **threshold**) is liable to tax (and is called **taxable income**). The first £3 200 of taxable income is taxed at the **lower rate** of tax of 20 per cent. Income earned from £3 201 to £24 300 is taxed at the **basic rate** of tax. Income over £24 300 is taxed at the **higher rate** of tax. Table 47.3 gives an example of how the income tax of an individual could be calculated.

For very low income earners, such as part-time workers, the **marginal rate of tax** is 0 per cent (i.e. they can earn an extra £1 without paying income tax). Slightly better paid workers will have a marginal rate of tax of 20 per cent. Most workers, though, earn more than their allowance plus the income charged at the lower rate of tax. The majority therefore pay tax at the basic rate of tax of 25 per cent. For high income earners (those earning more than £24 300 plus allowances), the marginal rate of tax is 40 per cent. However, their average rate of tax is less than this.

Look again at Table 47.3. This person is earning £60 000 before tax. She pays just £14 595 in tax. Therefore her average rate of tax is only 24.32 per cent. But her marginal rate is 40 per cent because she paid 40p in tax on the last £1 earned. **The average rate of tax is always less than the marginal rate for income taxpayers**. This is because all income earners can earn a portion of their income 'tax free'. Moreover, they pay lower rates of tax on their initial taxable earnings. It is only at a certain income level that they pay the top marginal rate of tax.

Income tax from employed workers is collected by employers through the PAYE (pay as you earn) system. Employers then pay it to the Inland Revenue.

Table 47.2 *1994 Budget forecast of government revenues in 1995-96 (£ billion)*

Inland Revenue:	
Income tax	70.1
Corporation tax	26.4
Petroleum revenue tax	0.7
Capital gains tax	0.8
Inheritance tax	1.5
Stamp duties	2.0
Total Inland Revenue	**101.5**
Customs and Excise:	
Value added tax	49.0
Fuel duties	15.6
Tobacco duties	7.0
Alcohol duties	7.5
Betting and gaming duties	1.2
Customs duties	2.1
Agricultural levies	0.2
Air passenger duty	0.3
Insurance premium tax	0.7
Total Customs and Excise	**81.5**
Vehicle excise duties	4.0
Oil royalties	0.5
Business rates	13.8
Other rates and royalties	5.8
Total taxes and royalty receipts	**207.2**
Social security receipts	44.5
Council tax and community charge	9.2
Interest and dividends	4.6
Gross trading surpluses and rent	5.7
Other receipts	7.6
General government receipts	**278.9**

Table 47.3

			£
Income before tax			60 000
Allowances			
Personal allowance	3 525		
Pension payments	9 000		
Other allowances	1 475		
Total	14 000		
Taxable income	46 000		
Tax			
3 200 at 20%		640	
21 100 at 25%		5 275	
21 700 at 40%		8 680	
Total tax paid		14 595	14 595
Income after tax			45 405

National Insurance contributions (NICs) All taxes apart from NICs are paid into one central fund (called the **Consolidated Fund**) and are used to pay for government spending. However, there is a separate National Insurance Fund out of which is paid National Insurance benefits such as state pensions and unemployment benefit. The National Insurance Fund is financed from National Insurance contributions. Strictly speaking, contributions are not taxes because they are a form of insurance premium. However, they have come to be seen, and used by, government as a form of tax. NICs are paid by workers. In 1995-96 employed workers paid contributions of 10 per cent of earnings between £58 and £440. In addition, employers have to pay employers' National Insurance contributions on a sliding scale from 0 to 10.2 per cent of earnings. For instance, they have to pay 10.2 per cent of the weekly earnings of any worker earning more than £200 per week.

Corporation tax Corporation tax is a tax on company profits. The top rate of tax is 33 per cent on profits over £1.5 million per annum. However, companies can claim numerous allowances, including investment allowances. As a result the average rate of tax on company profits is considerably less than the marginal rate for most companies.

Capital gains tax This is a tax on real capital gains - the difference between the buying price and selling price of an asset adjusted for inflation. Most goods and services are exempt, including the buying and selling of a person's main home. It is paid mainly on stocks and shares. Individuals can make capital gains of up to £6 000 per year free of tax. Thereafter capital gains are included with income and taxed at the appropriate marginal rate of income tax (i.e. either 20 per cent, 25 per cent or 40 per cent).

Inheritance tax This is a tax on the value of assets left on death by an individual. The first £154 000 (in 1995-96) of any inheritance is tax free. Thereafter, it is taxed at 40 per cent. There are numerous exemptions. For instance, any money left by one spouse to another is completely tax free. Also, there is no tax on gifts made during the lifetime of an individual provided that they are made 7 years before death.

Excise duties These are not to be confused with customs duties - taxes on imported goods. Excise duties are taxes levied on fuel, alcohol, tobacco and betting. They are calculated not on value (as with VAT) but on the volume sold. So excise duty is paid per litre of petrol or per bottle of wine for instance.

Value added tax (VAT) This is a tax on expenditure. There are different rates of tax. Essential commodities - food, water, children's clothing, books, newspapers, magazines and public transport - are tax exempt (i.e. there is a zero rate). Domestic fuel (gas, electricity, heating oil and coal) is taxed at 8 per cent. All other goods and services are taxed at 17.5 per cent. VAT is collected by business and is imposed on the value added to a product by that business.

Petroleum revenue tax and oil royalties These are taxes on the output of North Sea oil.

Council tax Council tax is a tax imposed on domestic property by local authorities. Each dwelling has been assessed for sale value in April 1992. The property has then been put into one of 7 bands, from band A for properties up to £40 000 to band H for properties over £320 000. For instance, a £130 000 property would be put in Band F, which covers properties between £120 000 and £160 000. The local authority then fixes a charge each year to each band. The differences in charges between bands are fixed by law. For instance, properties in Band H, the highest band, pay three times the Council Tax of properties in Band A, the lowest band in a local area.

Business rates Business rates are a local authority tax on business property. Each business property has been given a rateable value based on an estimate of the yearly rent at which property might reasonably have been let. The amount paid by the business is the rateable value multiplied by a 'factor'. This factor is called the 'Uniform Business Rate'. It is fixed by the government each year and is the same for all areas of the country.

Progressive, proportional and regressive taxes

Some taxes in the UK are progressive, i.e. the higher the income, the higher the proportion of income paid in tax. Income tax is progressive because there are personal allowances and because there are three rates of tax depending upon how much is earned. For instance, in Table 47.2, the £60 000 income earner paid an average rate of tax of 24.3 per cent. If the same individual had a gross income of £40 000, with the same allowances and pension payments, the amount of tax paid would have been £6 595 (i.e. £8 000 less). The average rate of tax paid would have been 16.5 per cent [(£6 595 ÷ £40 000) x 100%].

National Insurance contributions are mildly progressive up to the upper earnings limit. Again, this is because of the lower rate of tax on the first £57. However, they become regressive for individuals earning over the upper earnings limit. For instance, an £8 000 a year worker will pay a lower average rate of tax than a worker earning £20 000 a year and hence over this income range the tax is progressive. However, a £60 000 a year worker will pay a lower average rate of tax than the £20 000 a year worker and hence over this income range the tax is regressive.

Corporation tax could be argued to be progressive. Corporation tax leaves less profit to be distributed to shareholders. Given that shareholders tend to be higher income individuals, this means that higher income individuals tend to be more affected by corporation tax.

Capital gains tax is certainly progressive. It is paid only by those with enough (mainly) financial assets to make capital gains over £6 000 a year. Similarly, inheritance tax is in general progressive over much of the income range. Wealth and income tend to be correlated. So the larger the amount left, the larger tends to be the income of the deceased and indeed of those who inherit. Very high income earners, though, who are also very wealthy are likely to pay very little inheritance tax. This is because inheritance tax can be avoided, for instance by giving wealth away before death. The greater the wealth, the more incentive there is to avoid the tax and hence at the top of the income scale, inheritance tax might become regressive.

Indirect taxes tend to be regressive. A much larger proportion of low income households' budget is spent on alcohol, tobacco and betting than that of high income households and hence excise duties are regressive. It could be argued that VAT is progressive because items which form a disproportionate part of low income budgets, such as food and public transport, are zero rated. On the other hand, higher income earners tend to save a larger proportion of their income than low income earners, and hence the proportion of income paid in VAT declines as income rises - a regressive effect. Council tax is clearly regressive. Individuals living in the highest band houses with values over £320 000 are likely to have incomes more than three times greater than those of individuals living in the lowest band houses with values less than £40 000, yet they only pay three times the amount of council tax.

Table 47.4 shows that the overall tax system in 1993 was regressive if income is taken as income before state benefits and broadly proportional if income is taken as income after state benefits have been paid. Although income tax and National Insurance contributions (NICs) were progressive, council tax and other indirect taxes were regressive.

Table 47.4 *Taxes as a proportion of income (1993)*

	Bottom fifth	Next fifth	Middle fifth	Next fifth	Top fifth	All households
Income tax and NIC (£)	230	650	2 080	3 870	8 590	3 080
Council tax (£)	560	550	620	660	730	620
Indirect taxes (£)	1 710	1 950	3 100	3 790	4 900	3 090
Total taxes (£)	2 500	3 150	5 800	8 320	14 220	6 790
Income before state benefits (£)	1 920	5 020	12 860	20 850	39 370	16 000
Income after state benefits (£)	6 380	9 370	15 930	22 780	40 420	18 980
Proportion of income paid in tax						
Before state benefits (%)	130	63	45	40	36	42
After state benefits (%)	39	34	36	37	35	36

Source: adapted from CSO, *Social Trends*.

International comparisons

Figure 47.2 gives an international comparison of taxes. It has been argued in the past that Britain is highly taxed and that this has contributed to low economic growth rates. Certainly, in 1992, there is little evidence of this. Of the six countries in Figure 47.2, the UK has the third lowest overall rate of tax. Moreover, taxes paid by firms (direct taxes on corporations and social security contributions per worker employed) as a proportion of total taxes are the lowest of the six countries. Notice too that the UK has the highest proportion of indirect tax paid amongst the 6 countries. Conversely, taxes on household income (direct taxes on households plus employees' social security contributions) are relatively low.

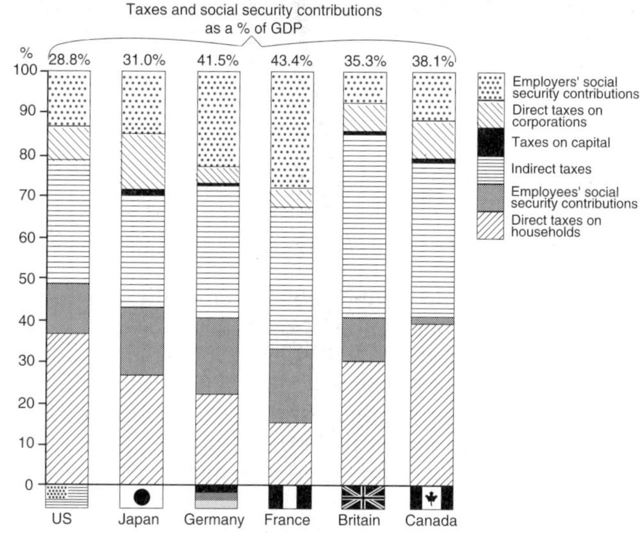

Source: adapted from *Economic Trends*, 1995.

Figure 47.2 *International tax comparisons; taxes as a percentage of GDP*

Changes in tax

Since 1979 there have been significant changes in the burden of tax, as Tables 47.5 and 47.6 show.

A shift from income tax to VAT In the 1979 Budget, the standard rate of VAT was increased from 8 per cent to 15 per cent. The extra revenue generated was used to finance cuts in income tax, in particular a cut in the top rate of income tax from 83 per cent to 60 per cent. Throughout the 1980s and 1990s, government has made its top priority cuts in income tax rather than indirect tax. In 1988 the top rate of tax was reduced again from 60 per cent to 40 per cent and over the period 1979 to 1989 the standard rate of income tax was cut from 33 per cent to 25 per cent. A new lower rate of 20 per cent tax was introduced in 1992, and some predict that in the long term the government would like to make this the new basic rate of tax. VAT was increased to 17½ per cent in 1991 to pay for a cut in local authority poll tax.

A reduction in the incidence of taxes on capital Capital gains tax has become progressively less of a burden. Possibly the two most important measures which accomplished this were the index linking of capital gains (where capital gains were calculated in real terms and not money terms for the purpose of tax) and the abolition of tax liabilities for all capital gains made before 1982. Inheritance tax, introduced in 1986, replaced capital transfer tax. The latter taxed not only transfers of money on death but also lifetime gifts. Anybody wishing to avoid inheritance tax is now able to give away their money during their lifetime.

A shift in the burden of National Insurance contributions National Insurance contributions paid by employees have increased as a percentage of tax revenue. It could be argued that part of the reduction in income tax has effectively been paid for by the overall increase in National Insurance contributions.

Increased local authority taxes As Table 47.5 shows, central government has increased its grants to local authorities between 1979 and 1993 as a percentage of total local authority income. There was a large shift upwards in grants in 1991 when government increased VAT from 15 per cent to 17½ per cent to pay for a halving in the highly unpopular, newly introduced, poll tax. However, in general, central government attempted to reduce grants in real terms over the period.

Table 47.5 *Central government income*

Per cent

	1979	1993
Taxes on income		
Paid by persons	31.0	26.0
Paid by corporations	7.5	8.1
Taxes on expenditure		
Customs and excise (including VAT)	27.9	33.3
Other indirect taxes	7.2	9.3
Social insurance contributions		
Paid by employees	6.9	7.4
Paid by employers	10.5	10.6
Rent, interest, dividends, royalties and other current income	7.4	4.4
Taxes on capital	1.5	1.1
Total[1]	100.0	100.0

1. Figures may not add up to 100 because of rounding.
Source: adapted from CSO, National Income and Accounts Blue Book.

Table 47.6 *Local authority income*

Per cent

	1979	1993
Grants from central government	51.6	57.4
Rates/community charge/Council tax }	29.4	10.6
Business rates		17.9
Other	19.0	14.1
Total	100.0	100.0

Source: adapted from CSO, National Income and Accounts Blue Book.

Has the tax system become more regressive ? The changes introduced since 1979 have served to shift the burden of taxation from the better off to those worse off. Cuts in higher rate income tax have made income tax less progressive. Increases in National Insurance rates have had the same effect. The increases in the rate of VAT from 8 to 15 per cent in 1979 and then to 17½ per cent in 1991 are likely to have made the tax system more regressive. Council tax is now more regressive than the rating system which was in place in 1979. Having said that, the council tax, introduced in 1993, was far less regressive than the poll tax which replaced the rating system in England and Wales in 1990.

Local authority finance

Four taxes in four years

Traditionally, local authorities have raised taxes through local authority rates. These were a tax on the notional rental value of both domestic property and commercial and industrial property. In theory, the notional rental values should have been reviewed every few years. However, because any rate review brings losers whose notional rents are increased, as well as gainers, and because governments didn't want to lose votes, rate reviews kept on being put off after 1973, the date of the last review. By the time of the general election in 1987, the government had decided that rates for domestic property should be abolished and replaced by a poll tax system. Business rates would continue, but in a modified form. The poll tax, a tax per head of the population, was introduced in Scotland in April 1989 and in England and Wales in April 1990. Within 8 months of its introduction into England and Wales, the government announced a fundamental review of local authority finance. In its March 1991 Budget, the government reduced poll tax bills by £140 per person and financed this by increasing VAT from 15 per cent to 17.5 per cent. A month later, it announced that the poll tax would be scrapped and replaced by a new council tax from April 1993. The council tax would be a tax on property values.

Local authority rates

Local authority rates were a long standing tax on the rental value of property in an area. Rates were relatively cheap to collect. A Price Waterhouse study, for instance, estimated that the average collection cost per authority was £560 000 in 1989-90. It was cheap because there were a limited number of properties in an area. There was little risk of default on payment because local authorities could secure a charge against any property if its owner failed to pay. Households on low income received rate rebates, and some as a result paid no rates at all. Rates were unpopular though. It was pointed out that a poor pensioner living on her own in a house would pay the same rates as an identical house next door where there were two parents and four children all working. It discouraged people from putting up extensions because the rateable value would be increased. It also meant that a property with a notional rent of £2 000 per year would pay 20 times as much in rates as a property with a notional rent of £200 per year.

Rates were also unpopular with businesses. They complained that some local authorities imposed high rates on businesses in order to reduce the bills faced by domestic rate payers.

The community charge or poll tax

The poll tax was a tax on each adult (over 18) living in a local authority. Low income adults paid 20 per cent of the full poll tax; otherwise, there was no linkage of the tax to income. This was justified on the grounds that local authority services should be paid for like cornflakes or soap. Just as everyone, whatever their income, pays the same for a packet of cornflakes, so it was only fair that everyone, whatever their income, should pay a fixed price for local authority services. Unlike the previous rating system, households were taxed according to the number of adults in the house. So a poor pensioner living on her own would only have paid one-sixth of the poll tax compared to a household with two parents and four adult children working.

The introduction of the poll tax brought substantial gainers and losers. On the whole, the gainers were households which before had above average rates. The losers, on the whole, were households which paid below average rates or the very large number of people who had never paid rates because they didn't own their own home. The cost of administering the poll tax was substantially greater than the rates - an estimated average £1 271 000 per local authority. The cost of collection was higher because there was approximately twice the number of taxpayers as under the old rating system. Costs also proved higher because there was widespread evasion. Many initially refused to pay the tax and had to be taken to court at considerable expense. For instance, 2.3 million court summonses were issued at the end of 1992 to non-payers. Others simply disappeared. Electoral registers shrank at the time. Local authorities are still owed millions of pounds today in unpaid poll tax.

The council tax

The council tax is a tax on the value of domestic property. Each property was valued at April 1992. Properties are then put into one of eight bands shown in Table 47.5. The local authority then fixes a rate. The amount paid by each homeowner is then determined by a fixed ratio shown in Table 47.5. Houses where there is only one adult occupant receive a 25 per cent rebate. Like the old rating system, there is also a sliding scale of council tax rebates for low income families. The council tax should be no more expensive to collect than the old rates since the tax base is identical. The transition to the council tax created winners and losers. On the whole, the winners were those living in rented accommodation and low income families who owned their own homes. The losers tended to be higher income home-owning families. Any extensions to the property are not assessed for tax.

Table 47.5 *Council tax valuation bands (England)*

Band	Range of values	Proportion Payable*
A	Up to £40 000	100
B	£40 000 - £52 000	117
C	£52 001 - £68 000	133
D	£68 001 - £88 000	150
E	£88 001 - £120 000	183
F	£120 001 - £160 000	217
G	£160 001 - £320 000	250
H	Above £320 000	300

*As a percentage of the tax payable in A

Uniform business rates

In 1990, local authorities in England and Wales lost the power to fix their own business rates. Under the new system, all businesses were assessed for rates in 1989. The government then imposed a single uniform rate across the whole country. Hence, a firm owning premises with a rateable value of £20 000 in London would pay exactly the same amount of rates as a firm owning £20 000 premises in Manchester. Business rates are not allowed by law to increase by more than the rate of inflation year on year. The new system meant that high spending local authorities could no longer charge much higher rates on similar property to a low spending authority next door.

A unique tax

All industrialised countries have some form of tax on property. No industrialised country has a poll tax. In fact, poll taxes are a rarity even in the developing world. They are associated with the introduction of a taxation system into a market economy when it is difficult to identify either levels of spending or income.

Local authority finances

Since 1979, central government had attempted to control local authority spending and borrowing. It felt that local authorities spent too much, providing unnecessary services inefficiently. The main way in which central government controlled local authority spending was through a system called **rate capping**. Central government placed a ceiling on the amount local authorities could spend. This was only partially successful. Local authorities which normally spent below their ceiling could increase their spending in any one year. One feature of the system was that only a minority of individuals felt the impact of any rate rise because only a minority of the population owned property. Local authorities which were at the ceiling found ways round the restrictions, for instance through selling assets and then leasing them back again.

The government hoped that the poll tax system would curb local authority spending. When the poll tax was introduced, the government deliberately cut grants to local authorities in real terms whilst leaving business rate revenue unchanged. This meant that local authorities either had to cut their real spending or increase their poll tax demands. What's more, because only approximately 25 per cent of local authority revenue came from the poll tax, a 1 per cent fall in other revenues would have to be made up by a 3 per cent rise in the poll tax. Alternatively, assume a local authority was told by central government that it should be spending £100 million. £50 million would come in central government grants, £25 million in business rates and £25 million in poll tax. If the local authority wanted to spend £110m, the extra £10 million would have to come from the poll tax. Local poll tax payers would have to pay £35 million in poll tax rather than just £25 million. A 10 per cent increase in spending would result in a 40 per cent extra poll tax bill.

The government assumed that local authorities would reduce spending. It was argued that large poll tax bills would be very unpopular and local voters would vote out councils which imposed these charges. Instead, local authorities didn't cut spending and set very high poll tax bills. The voters blamed central government for the bills and many refused to pay the tax.

When the poll tax was replaced, the government was forced to reintroduce a form of rate capping.

1. What were the main differences between the systems of local authority taxation described in the data?
2. To what extent was each system (a) efficient and (b) equitable?
3. Two alternative systems of local authority taxation that have been suggested are (a) a local income tax and (b) a local sales tax (similar to VAT). Discuss whether these would be better taxes than a property tax.

INVESTIGATIONS 3

A. Externalities

Aims

- To examine a local example of externalities.
- To investigate the private and social costs and benefits of an activity which gives rise to externalities.
- To identify the methods of internalising externalities and evaluate their costs and benefits.

Research activity

Choose a local example of an activity which results in externalities. For example, you could investigate the externalities resulting from the building of a new road or the repair or alteration of an existing road. Alternatively you could investigate a local airport or the building of a new factory in the area. In making your choice consider carefully how much information you will be able to obtain.

Identify the nature of the activity which leads to the occurrence of externalities. For instance, if you are investigating the location of a new factory, find out what is produced and the process which is used.

Identify the externalities which result and who suffers and who benefits. Quantify the externalities if possible.

If negative externalities result, find out what restrictions exist to control them. What suggestions have, if any, been put forward to limit further production of negative externalities?

Sources

Primary evidence can be gathered by direct observation. For instance, if you investigate noise pollution from a local road, it might be possible to measure noise levels at various distances from the road at various times of the day. You could also design a questionnaire for local residents, pedestrians, motorists and local business people. Question them about the externalities which result from the road. Further information could be found by interviewing business people who benefit or suffer as a result of the road and the traffic on it.

Some research into the scientific and technical causes of pollution resulting from road traffic and how it could be reduced is likely to be needed. Approach your science department for help with this.

Government publications, such as *Social Trends* and the *Digest of Environmental Protection and Water Statistics*, published by the Central Statistical Office, might give regional and national figures for road use and traffic pollution. The *CSO Guide to Official Statistics* will give you more detailed sources by type of pollution. The Environmental Department of your local council might be able to give figures or other information on a local basis. If the road has been built recently, then surveys may have been taken. Local meetings may have been held on the potential benefits and problems of the road. You may also be able to find articles in the local newspaper, back copies of which should be available either at your local public reference library or at the offices of the newspaper.

Environmental pressure groups such as Friends of the Earth and Greenpeace may have relevant data. They may also have policy documents on the reduction of negative externalities caused by road transport.

Structuring your report

Introduction Outline the aim of your investigation. The aim should be put in the form of a hypothesis or question which will allow you to come to some conclusions.
Economic theory Outline the economic theory which is relevant to your investigation. This likely to include concepts such as private and social costs and benefits and externalities.
Techniques used to collect your data Outline how you collected your data.
Analysis Present the results of your information in a suitable form. What, if any, controls exist on the negative externalities present? Explain what impact these controls may have had.
Evaluation Are negative externalities greater than positive externalities? Are social costs greater than social benefits? What criteria did you use to judge these? Justify your use of criteria. Would it be possible to increase positive externalities and reduce negative externalities? What would be the cost of this? What role should the government, either central or local, play in this issue?
Sources Outline your sources and evaluate your method of research.
Bibliography Write down a list of your sources in alphabetical order.

Other suggestions

Identify the private and social costs and benefits of a particular course of action. For instance:

- your decision to go to university or perhaps leave education after 'A' levels to get a job;
- the decision by your local authority to increase or reduce spending on education in the next financial year;
- a decision by your parents to buy you a car.

Evaluate the extent of the externalities created and suggest policies which could help reduce any negative externalities which arise.

B. Local authority finance

Aims

- To investigate different local authority financing systems.
- To compare the workings of the rating system with the community charge and then the council tax.

- To compare these three tax systems with alternative systems of local authority finance.
- To evaluate each system according to recognised economic criteria.

Research activity

Explore how the local authority rating system worked in England and Wales before 1989, and find out examples of rates and rateable values in **your** local authority and at least one other. Do the same for the poll tax or community charge and the uniform business rate introduced in 1989. Then investigate the current system of the council tax combined with uniform business rates. Find out what other tax systems could be used by local authorities, perhaps by considering the American experience. Find out what advantages and disadvantages are said to exist for each type of tax system and the arguments used to support those opinions.

Sources

Economics and tax textbooks will provide some background to the different local authority tax systems which have operated over the past ten years. For details of current or recent proposals for reform of local authority finance, conduct a newspaper and magazine search in a local large public reference library. Using indexes, or a CD-Rom, find and read recent articles in quality newspapers such as the *Financial Times* and the *Independent* as well as magazines such as the *Economist*. Photocopy anything which you find particularly useful. Local newspapers are also likely to have given wide coverage to local authority finance, but remember to take into account that there is considerable bias in both national and local newspapers.

By asking parents and friends, it should be possible to obtain a range of rateable values for differing properties. It should also be possible, again by interviewing relations and friends, to find out how much in rates was paid on a variety of properties before 1989 and the levels of community charge paid per person after April 1989.

By contacting the Treasurer's Department of your local authority, you may be able to find out a variety of figures which would help you to compare the rating system with the community charge system. For instance, how many taxpayers were there under each system? What was the cost of collection? What were the problems with taxpayers who either didn't pay or paid late? If you conduct a personal interview, you may also be able to find out the views of the interviewee about changes in the system of local authority finance. Do the same research for the latest council tax system.

Conduct a survey amongst adults. Find out their views about the previous rating system, the community charge and the council tax. The wider the range of people interviewed, the better. For instance, attempt to interview people who differ by income, age, the area in which they live and their known political views.

Structuring the report

Introduction Outline the aim of your investigation. The aim should be put in the form of a hypothesis or question which will allow you to come to some conclusions.
Economic theory Outline the economic theory to be used in this investigation. This is likely to include the concepts of progressive and regressive taxation and the canons of taxation.
Techniques used to collect your data Outline how you collected your data.
Local authority tax systems Describe, giving examples from your survey work, the operation of the rating system, the community charge system and any system which might replace the present system. Compare the basis on which people, households and firms were taxed. Identify the major problems claimed to be inherent in each system.
Analysis Using the concepts of progressive and regressive taxation, assess the incidence of tax on different groups. Analyse the extent to which each system in practice affects or affected incentives (e.g. incentives to work, incentives to save, incentives to improve property).
Evaluation Using the canons of taxation, evaluate alternative local authority financing systems. Give as evidence the results of any interviews you may have conducted.
Sources Outline the sources of information you used. What problems did you enounter in gathering relevant data? What data would you have liked to have obtained but could not? To what extent did the data gathered show evidence of bias? To what extent was the evidence gathered from interviews typical of the views of people in the UK as a whole?
Bibliography Write down a list of your sources in alphabetical order.

Other suggestions

It would be possible to evaluate any change in taxation. For instance:

- should National Insurance contributions become part of the income tax system;
- should there be an increase in VAT to finance a reduction in income tax rates;
- should excise duties on tobacco, alcohol and petrol be raised and the revenue gained be used to lower VAT;
- should the UK harmonize VAT rates with the rest of the European Union;
- should the UK introduce a wealth tax?

For each of these, it would be possible to research possible arguments and opinions by using newspapers, periodicals and books as well as through interviews. It is important to examine the arguments for and against the change, expose any bias in arguments used and come to an overall conclusion.

unit 48 The demand for labour

Summary

1. In the long run, the demand curve for labour is downward sloping because capital can be substituted for labour.
2. In the short run, the downward sloping demand curve for labour can be explained by the law of diminishing returns.
3. The marginal revenue product curve of labour is the demand curve for labour. This is true whether the firm operates in a perfectly competitive or imperfectly competitive market.
4. The elasticity of demand for labour is determined by time, the availability of substitutes, the elasticity of demand for the product and the proportion of labour costs to total costs.

The downward sloping demand curve

Firms need workers to produce goods and services. The demand curve for labour shows how many workers will be hired at any given wage rate over a particular time period. A firm, for instance, might want to hire 100 workers if the wage rate were £2 per hour but only 50 workers if it were £200 per hour.

Economic theory suggests that the higher the price of labour, the less labour firms will hire.

- In the long run, other things remaining equal, firms can vary all factors of production. The higher the wage rate, the more likely it is that firms will substitute machines for workers and hence the lower the demand for labour.
- In the short run, firms are likely to have an existing stock of capital. They will have to produce with a given amount of factory or office space and with a fixed amount of plant, machinery and equipment. The more workers that are added to this fixed stock of capital, the less likely it is that the last worker employed will be as productive as existing employees. Hence the wage rate would have to fall to encourage the employer to take on an extra worker.

So the demand curve for labour is likely to be downward sloping both in the long run and the short run. Why do the long run and short run demand curves slope downward and what determines the elasticity of demand for labour?

QUESTION 1

Table 48.1 *Real gross capital per employee in the UK (£ thousands at 1990 prices)*

	Real gross capital per employee 1979	1993
Agriculture, forestry and fishing	101	131
Energy and water supply	299	511
Manufacturing	45	92
Construction	16	26
Distribution, hotels and catering, repairs	21	36
Transport and communication	107	127
Banking, finance, insurance etc.	57	87

Source: adapted from CSO, *National Income Accounts; Annual Abstract of Statistics.*

(a) How has real capital per employee changed over the period 1979 to 1993?

(b) Real average earnings rose 34 per cent between 1979 and 1993. There was little difference in this rise between industries. Assuming that the real cost of capital did not increase over this period, would a firm setting up in 1993 be likely to have used a more or less capital intensive technique of production than if it had set up in 1979? Give reasons for your answer.

The long run demand for labour

In the long run, all factors of production are variable. A firm has complete freedom to choose its production techniques. In the Third World, where labour is cheap relative to capital, firms tend to choose labour intensive methods of production. In the First World, labour is relatively expensive and hence more capital intensive techniques of production are chosen. So in the First World, far more use is made of tractors and other machinery, whilst in the Third World, far more workers per acre are employed.

A full explanation of this using **isoquants** and **isocost lines** was developed in unit 21.

The short run demand for labour

In the short run, at least one of the factors of production is fixed. Assume that all factors are fixed except labour. The **law of diminishing returns** states that marginal output will start to decline if more and more units of one variable factor of production are combined with a given quantity of fixed factors. One common example is to imagine a plot of land with a fixed number of tools where extra workers are employed to cultivate the land. Diminishing returns will quickly set in and the eleventh worker, for instance, on a one acre plot of land will contribute less to total output than the tenth worker.

This is shown in Table 48.2. Labour is assumed to be a variable factor of production whilst all other factors are fixed. As extra workers are employed, total output, or TOTAL PHYSICAL PRODUCT increases. However, MARGINAL PHYSICAL PRODUCT, the number of extra units of output a worker produces, starts to decline after the employment of the second worker. So diminishing marginal returns set in with the third worker. Assume that the firm is in a perfectly competitive industry and therefore faces a horizontal, perfectly elastic demand curve. This means that the firm can sell any quantity of its product at the same price per unit. In Table 48.2, it is assumed that the price of the product is £10. MARGINAL REVENUE PRODUCT can then be calculated because it is the addition to revenue from the employment of an extra worker. For instance, the first worker produces 8 units and so, at a price per product unit of £10, her marginal revenue product is £80 (£10 x 8). The marginal revenue product of the second worker is £90 (£10 x the marginal physical product).

Table 48.2

Per week

1	2	3	4	5	6	7
Labour input	Total output	Marginal physical product	Price of product	Marginal revenue product (3 x 4)	Wage rate per worker	Contribution (5 - 6)
(workers)	(units)	(units)	£	£	£	£
1	8	8	10	80	70	10
2	17	9	10	90	70	20
3	25	8	10	80	70	10
4	32	7	10	70	70	0
5	38	6	10	60	70	-10
6	43	5	10	50	70	-20

It is now possible to calculate how many workers a firm will employ. The contribution to the payment of fixed costs and the earning of profit of each worker is the difference between the marginal revenue product of the firm and the cost to the firm of the worker. Assume that the firm is able to employ any number of workers at a wage rate of £70. The contribution of the first worker is £10, her marginal revenue product minus her wage (£80 - £70). The contribution of the second worker is £20 (£90 - £70). It can be seen from Table 48.2 that the first three workers each make a positive contribution. The fourth worker neither increases nor decreases total profit for the firm. The firm would definitely not employ a fifth worker because her employment would result in a loss of £10 to the firm. Her wage of £70 would exceed her marginal revenue product of £60. So marginal revenue product theory suggests that the firm will employ a maximum of 4 workers because this number maximises total profit (or minimises the loss) for the firm.

If the wage rate were to fall to £50, the firm would employ more workers. The fourth worker would now definitely be employed because her contribution would be £20. The fifth worker too would contribute a positive £10. The firm might also employ a sixth worker although her contribution is zero. Marginal revenue product theory therefore suggests that the lower the wage, the more workers will be employed.

QUESTION 2

Table 48.3

Number of workers employed	Total physical product per week	Total revenue product	Marginal revenue product
1	10		
2	24		
3	36		
4	44		
5	50		
6	53		

Table 48.3 shows the total physical product per week for a small firm as the number of workers employed varies. The price of the product sold is £10 per unit.

(a) Calculate total revenue product at each level of employment.

(b) Calculate marginal revenue product as employment increases.

(c) Explain how many workers the firm should employ if the weekly wage per worker were: (i) £60; (ii) £30; (iii) £120; (iv) £100.

The demand curve for labour

Figure 48.1 shows a firm's marginal revenue product curve for labour. It is downward sloping because marginal revenue product declines as output increases (as shown in Table 48.2). If the wage rate is OF, the firm will employ OB units of labour. If the wage rate rises, the firm will cut back employment to OA. If, on the other hand, wage rates fall to OE, then the firm will take on extra workers and increase the labour force to OC. The marginal revenue product curve therefore shows the number of workers the firm will employ at any given wage rate. But this is the definition of the firm's demand curve for labour. Therefore the marginal revenue product curve is also the firm's demand curve for labour.

This is true for all factors of production. Figure 48.1 shows the familiar price/quantity diagram. The price of labour is the wage rate. Quantity is the quantity of labour employed. The downward sloping marginal revenue product curve gives us the familiar downward sloping demand curve.

Perfect and imperfect competition

So far it has been assumed that the employer is supplying goods in a perfectly competitive market. This is because it has been assumed that the firm can supply any quantity of goods to the market at the same price per unit (i.e. the

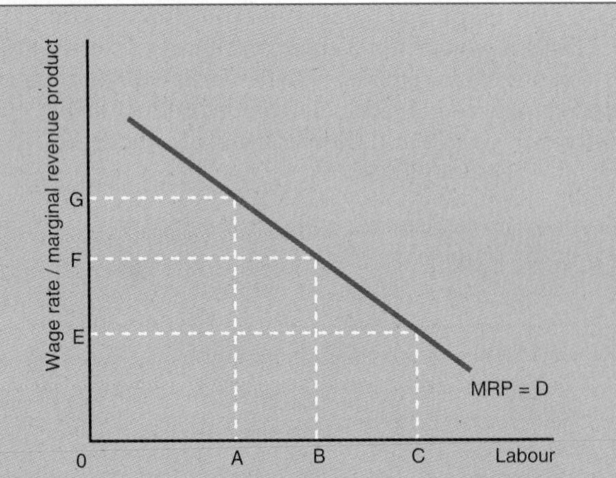

Figure 48.1 *The MRP curve is the demand curve for a factor*
The MRP curve shows the maximum price a firm would be prepared to pay for an extra unit of a factor of production and therefore it is the demand curve for that factor.

firm faces a horizontal demand curve). The marginal revenue product curve falls because of diminishing returns.

However, if the employer supplies goods in an imperfectly competitive market, then it faces a downward sloping demand curve for its product. If it expands output, price per unit sold will fall. Consider Table 48.2 again. The fall in marginal revenue product would be even greater than that shown if the price of the product did not remain at £10 per unit, but fell as output expanded. So the marginal revenue product curve for an imperfectly competitive firm falls not only because of diminishing returns but also because the price or average revenue of the product sold falls too as output expands.

Whether the firm is perfectly or imperfectly competitive, it is still true that the demand curve for labour is the marginal revenue product curve of labour.

QUESTION 3 The firm in Table 48.4 produces in an imperfectly competitive market. As output increases, the price falls.

Table 48.4

Number of workers employed	Number of units produced and sold per week	Price per unit £
1	10	£15
2	24	£14
3	36	£12
4	44	£11
5	50	£10
6	53	£9

(a) Calculate (i) the total revenue product and (ii) the marginal revenue product of labour as employment increases.
(b) How many workers would the firm employ if the weekly wage were: (i) £20; (ii) £40; (iii) £60; (iv) £80; (v) £100; (vi) £120?

Determinants of the elasticity of demand for labour

The elasticity of demand for labour is a measure of the responsiveness of the quantity demanded of labour to changes in the price of labour (i.e. the wage rate; ☞ units 8 and 9 for a full discussion of elasticity). For instance, if elasticity of demand for labour were 2 and wage rates increased 10 per cent then, all other things being equal, the demand for labour would fall by 20 per cent. If demand for labour fell by 1 per cent when wage rates rose by 100 per cent, all other things being equal, then elasticity of demand for labour would be 0.01 (i.e. highly inelastic).

Time The longer the time period for adjustment, the easier it is to substitute labour for other factors of production or vice versa. In the short term, a firm may have little choice but to employ the same number of workers even if wage rates increase rapidly. Workers will have contracts of employment. There may be severe financial penalties in the form of redundancy payments if workers are sacked. Or a firm may not wish to lose skilled staff because they would be difficult to replace. In the longer term, the firm can buy new labour saving machinery and carry out changes in its methods of work which will reduce the labour employed. Hence the longer the time period, the higher will tend to be the elasticity of demand for labour.

Availability of substitutes The easier it is to substitute other factors for labour, the greater will be the response by firms to a change in real wage rates. So the better the substitutes, the higher will tend to be the elasticity of demand for labour.

Elasticity of demand for the product Labour is a **derived demand** (☞ unit 7). It is only demanded because the goods that it produces are demanded. For instance, if there is a collapse in demand for coal, then there will also be a collapse in the demand for coal miners. This means that the elasticity of demand for labour in an industry is directly correlated with the elasticity of demand for the product made in the industry. If the elasticity of demand for the product is low, as for instance for gas or electricity, then a sudden rise in wages which pushes up gas or electricity prices will have little effect on demand for gas or electricity. There will be little effect on employment in the industry and hence the demand for labour will be low. If, on the other hand, elasticity of demand for the product is high, elasticity of demand for labour will be high. British Steel, for instance, faces highly elastic demand for many of its products. A rise in wages not matched elsewhere in the industry is likely to increase British Steel prices and lead to a loss of orders and therefore jobs.

The proportion of labour cost to total cost A rise in costs will reduce the supply of a product, shifting the supply curve upwards and to the left. This will lead to a reduction in quantity demanded. The bigger the shift, the larger the reduction in demand. If a group of workers gains a 50 per cent pay rise but these workers only account for one per cent of the total cost of production, then the supply curve of the product will hardly shift. There will be little fall in demand and hence little loss of employment in the firm. If however this group of workers accounted for 50 per cent of the costs of the firm, then a 50 per cent pay rise would have a dramatic effect on the supply curve and lead to a large decrease in quantity demanded of the product. This in turn would lead to a large fall in employment. Hence, the larger the proportion of labour cost to total cost, the higher the elasticity of demand for labour.

QUESTION 4

Explain whether you would expect the elasticity of demand for labour on North Sea oil rigs to be relatively high or low.

Key terms

Total physical product – the total output of a given quantity of factors of production.
Marginal physical product - the physical addition to output of an extra unit of a variable factor of production.
Marginal revenue product - the value of the physical addition to output of an extra unit of a variable factor of production. In a perfectly competitive product market where marginal revenue equals price, it is equal to marginal physical product times the price of the good produced.

Applied economics

Performance-related pay

Performance-related pay began to be a significant way of rewarding managers in the 1980s. Performance-related payment systems link the performance or output of an individual worker to his or her wages. It had been quite common on the shop floor for a long time. Many manual workers were on a piece-rate system. The more they produced, the higher their wages were at the end of the week. If they produced nothing, they received no pay. Equally, many sales people have been rewarded mainly on sales commission rather than basic pay.

Such systems can be seen as an attempt by employers to pay workers according to their revenue product. For instance, if one worker produces twice as many steel bars as another per week, it might seem logical to pay that worker twice as much. If one foreign exchange dealer generates a £300 000 surplus on foreign exchange dealings over the year for his bank, whilst another only generates £30 000, then the £300 000 dealer should be paid more than the other.

It also enables companies to decide whether or not to retain staff. For instance, if a foreign exchange dealer is paid £35 000 a year, but only generates £15 000 a year surplus for his bank, then he should be sacked. Equally, if a company has five workers, all equally productive, but the output of one worker is sold at a loss, then one worker should be sacked.

Piece rates became less common in the 1980s. It was felt that they encouraged individualism. The emphasis in manufacturing in the 1980s was on team work. Japanese production techniques, copied by many UK manufacturing companies, stressed the importance of co-operation. Just-in-time manufacturing techniques, for instance, demanded that workers act in the best interests of the group, not themselves.

At the same time, there was a move away from collectivism at management level. The **entrepreneur** (☞ unit 57) became a role model for many. Companies tried to identify the contribution of an individual manager or director to the business. This could then be used to set targets for future performance. It could also be used to set remuneration levels.

The 'performance' of the individual manager or director could be linked to a number of variables. At chief executive level, it could be linked to profit, share price or dividends paid. These variables are chosen because of the view that shareholders are the most important group in a company and they seek to maximise their returns on their shareholding. At a managerial level, it might be linked to factors such as costs, sales, labour productivity or customer satisfaction. All these variables ultimately affect profit, share price and dividends.

The 'pay' which is related to performance is varied. Managers and directors almost invariably are paid a basic salary. On top of this, though, they may receive cash bonuses in years when they achieve targets. Alternatively, the company may attempt to retain staff by offering rewards which can only be realised for cash in the longer term. A director may be offered shares if he or she is still with the company in three years time. Alternatively, they may be offered share options. These are opportunities given to buy shares at some point in the future at a price fixed now - usually the current share price. For instance, an executive might be given an option for 100 000 shares at a price of £3, which can be exercised in three years' time if the executive is still with the company. If the share price has risen to £5 over that period, the executive can buy the shares in three years' time and immediately sell them on the open market' making a profit of £2 per share or £200 000 overall. The justification for this is that a higher share price presumably indicates that the company has performed well over the period, in part because of the work of the executive.

Firms are willing to pay large salaries and bonuses to top staff because the demand for their labour is relatively inelastic. Whether a chief executive is paid £500 000 or £1 million is almost irrelevant to a company with a turnover of £1 000 million or £5 000 million. A new chief executive who increases profits from, say, £750 million per year to £1 000 million is well worth a few extra hundred thousand pounds in salary. There are also few good substitutes. A machine can replace a machine operator or a bank clerk but can't replace a chief executive.

There are two major problems with performance related pay. First, there seems to be little overall link between the performance of companies and bonuses paid to senior executives. Whilst it is clear why some executives receive large bonuses, outsiders are often baffled as to why an executive should be given a large bonus in a year when profits have fallen. Second, it is not clear that the revenue product of a senior executive can be clearly separated from the performance of the staff under him or her. Effective leadership is important, but so too is the reaction of staff willing to make the effort to change and adapt.

Firms may be willing to pay high salaries to managers because demand for their labour is relatively inelastic.

Banking

Banks have faced competition from building societies in the 1980s and 1990s.

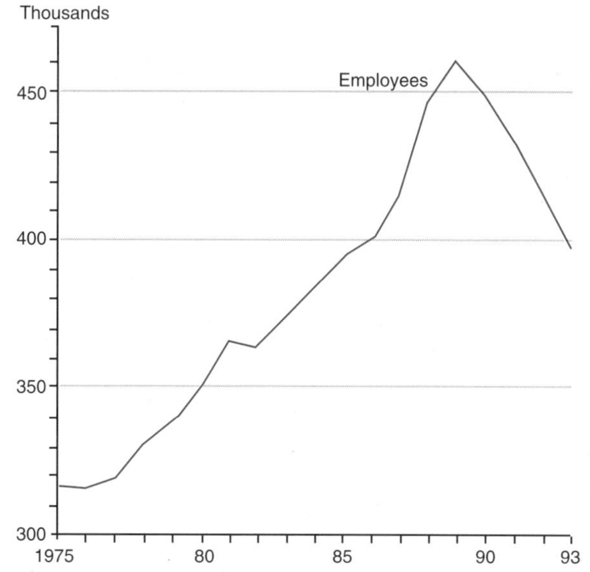

Source: adapted from CSO, *Annual Abstract of Statistics.*

Figure 48.2 *Employees in banking and discounting*

1. **Outline three factors which affected the demand for workers in banking in the post-war period.**
2. **To what extent is the demand for workers in banking inelastic?**
3. **Using economic theory, suggest why banks have increasingly changed over to paying bonuses to their workers.**

A changing climate

Banking used to be seen as a safe, stable if somewhat unexciting career. In the 1950s and 1960s, banks essentially provided a place for individuals and businesses to deposit their money. In return, they either got the use of a cheque book but no interest, or they received interest but no cheque book. Banks lent money of course. However, there was little effective competition. Other financial institutions offered different services. The major banks offered roughly the same terms and the same rates of interest. There was little point in competing because the government, through the Bank of England, controlled lending. There were restrictions on the total amount banks could lend, and for what they could lend. There were restrictions, for instance, on the amount a bank could lend to an individual if the person wanted to use the loan to buy a car.

In the 1970s, banking began to change, with many of the restrictions on lending being removed. This process was completed by the early 1980s. This decade saw a radical transformation in banking. Banks increased their market share in a number of markets. They built on experience in the 1970s to become major mortgage lenders to individuals, competing with building societies. They embraced government policies, encouraging wider share ownership by promoting their share dealing services and unit trust plans. They became significant providers of personal pensions and, to a lesser extent, insurance. The result was that, by the end of the 1980s, the banks liked to think of themselves as providers of a wide range of financial services, rather than just deposit takers and loan givers. With a booming economy, employment in the industry rose. Wages rose too, and many were attracted into the industry by the high wages and job security that seemed on offer.

However, at the same time, other financial institutions, such as building societies, began to offer services which traditionally had been offered mainly by banks. Banks faced competition in their markets. The boom years of the 1980s came to an end and, in the recession of 1990-92, the number of customers wanting loans or wanting to buy other types of financial products fell. Heavy investment in computers and automated equipment in the 1980s began to lead to sharp increases in labour productivity. Banks no longer needed so many workers. Wages rises were limited, with some banks giving virtually no increases in basic pay in some years.

But the 1990s saw the growth of performance related pay. Staff were increasingly awarded bonuses for the volume of financial products sold. Some staff were put on individual bonuses. Others were grouped, such as all the staff in a branch, and set targets for which, if reached, they shared a bonus. Many older staff regretted the passing of an era in which they felt banks had been in business to provide a service to clients. Now, they felt, they were in the business of selling financial products to customers.

The supply of labour

Summary

1. The supply curve for an individual worker is backward sloping at high levels of income.
2. Backward sloping supply curves result because the negative income effect of a wage increase outweighs the positive substitution effect.
3. The supply curve of labour to a firm, to an industry and to the economy as a whole is likely to be upward sloping.

The supply curve for an individual worker

A supply curve shows the quantity that will be supplied to the market at any given price. For an individual worker, the quantity supplied is the number of hours worked over a time period, such as a year. Neo-classical theory starts by assuming that a worker can decide how many hours to work per week and how many weeks' holiday to take per year. The price of labour is the wage per time period (i.e. the wage rate). The wage rate that determines supply is the **real wage rate** (the money or nominal wage rate divided by the price level). This is because the worker decides how many hours to work by relating it to what the wage will buy. For instance, a worker might take a job if a week's wages of £300 were to buy a television set, but she would be likely to turn it down if £300 were to only buy a newspaper.

Figure 49.1 shows a backward bending supply curve for labour. Between wages rates O and B a rise in real wage rates will lead to an increase in working hours supplied.

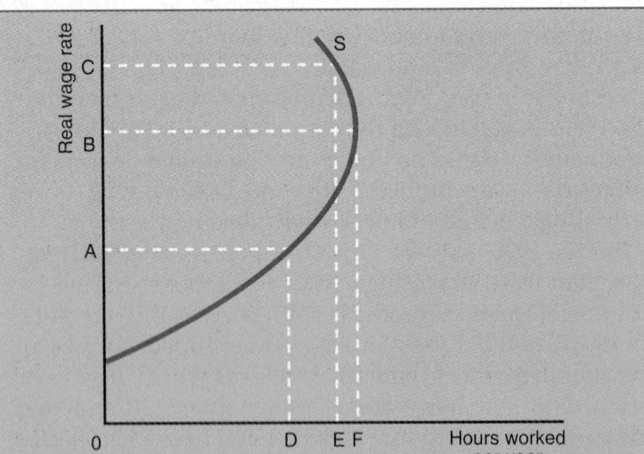

Figure 49.1 *The backward bending supply curve*
The supply curve for an individual worker is assumed to be this shape because at high levels of income the worker will prefer to work shorter hours rather than receive the extra income he or she could have earned.

For instance, the worker will offer to work DF extra hours if real wage rates increase from A to B . However, a rise in real wage rates above OB, for instance from B to C, will lead to a desire for shorter working hours.

To understand why this might be the case, consider a part time factory worker. Initially she is low paid, as are nearly all part time workers. The firm she works for then doubles her real wage rate. She is likely to respond to this by wanting to work longer hours and perhaps become a full time worker. Further increases in real wage rates might persuade her to work overtime. However, there are only 24 hours in a day and 365 days in a year. Eventually it is likely that increases in wage rates will make her want to reduce her working week or increase her holidays. She

QUESTION 1

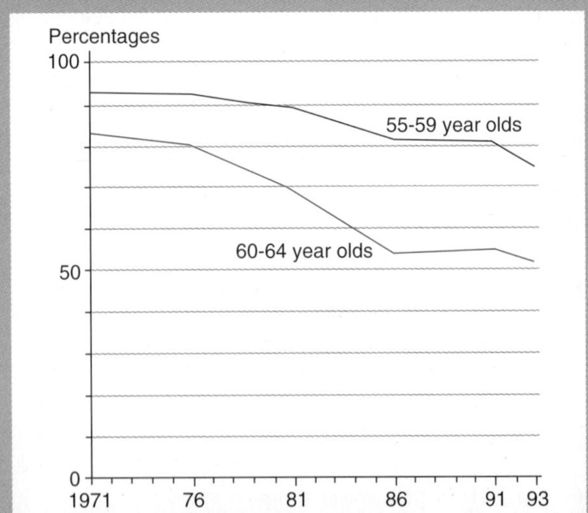

Source: adapted from Employment Department.

Figure 49.2 *Civilian labour force economic activity rates: males 55-59 and 60-64*

Real wage rates in the UK increased between 1971 and 1993. Does the data support the idea that the supply curve of labour for an individual worker is backward sloping?

will value increased leisure time more than extra money to spend. Put another way, she is choosing to buy leisure time by forgoing the wages she could otherwise have earned and the goods she could otherwise have bought. This is an example of the concept of opportunity cost.

This process can be seen at work over the past 100 years in the UK. Real wage rates have risen considerably but hours worked have fallen. The typical Victorian working week was 60 to 70 hours with few or no holidays. Today, average hours worked per week are down to about 40 hours with a typical holiday entitlement of 4 weeks per year. Workers have responded to increases in wage rates by supplying less labour.

Note that when wage rates increase, workers are likely to be able to both increase earnings **and** reduce hours worked. For instance, if real wage rates increase by 20 per cent from £10 per hour to £12 per hour, then workers can cut their hours worked by 10 per cent from 40 hours to 36 hours per week and still see an increase in earnings from £400 per week (40 x £10) to £432 per week (36 x £12). Real wage rate increases in the neo-classical model give workers a choice between increased earnings or increased leisure time or some combination of the two.

Income and substitution effects

The backward bending supply curve occurs because of the interaction of **income and substitution effects**. (A thorough understanding of unit 15 would be helpful for what follows.) If a consumer is in equilibrium, the utility gained from the goods bought with the money earned from the last hour worked will exactly match the utility gained from the last hour of leisure time. If leisure time were more valuable, the consumer could increase utility by working less and having more leisure time.

An increase in real wage rates is likely to lead to a positive substitution effect. The number of goods that can be bought with the money earned from the last hour worked will increase. The utility derived from the last hour worked will now be greater than the last hour of leisure. So the worker will substitute work for leisure until the two once again become equal.

However, work is arguably an **inferior good** (☞ unit 10). The higher the income, the fewer hours individuals will wish to work. For instance, it is pointless being able to buy tennis or squash equipment if you don't have the time to play. At low levels of income, the positive substitution effects outweighs the negative income effect. Hence, a rise in wage rates leads to an increase in the number of hours worked. For some workers, the positive substitution effect exactly offsets the negative income effect. For these workers, a rise in wages will have no effect on the number of hours worked. But at high levels of income, the positive substitution effect of a wage increase is more than offset by the negative income effect. Hence, the worker will choose to work fewer hours.

This can be shown in Figure 49.3. At wage rates up to OA, higher wage rates will lead increased hours of work. Between A and B, hours of work will remain the same. Above OB, the supply curve slopes backward showing

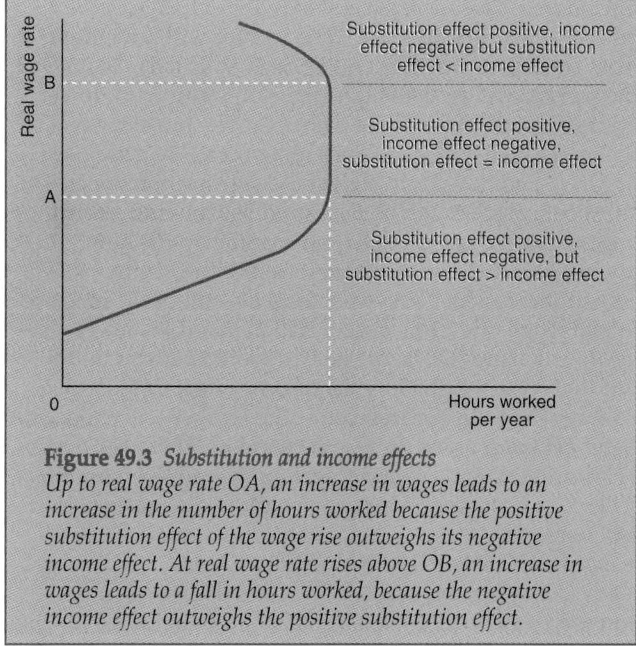

Figure 49.3 *Substitution and income effects*
Up to real wage rate OA, an increase in wages leads to an increase in the number of hours worked because the positive substitution effect of the wage rise outweighs its negative income effect. At real wage rate rises above OB, an increase in wages leads to a fall in hours worked, because the negative income effect outweighs the positive substitution effect.

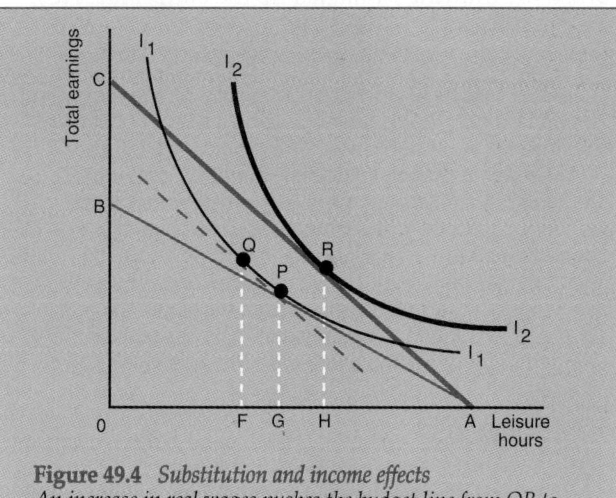

Figure 49.4 *Substitution and income effects*
An increase in real wages pushes the budget line from OB to OC. The worker 'moves' from P to R. The negative income effect of the rise in real wage rates from Q to R outweighs the positive substitution effect from P to Q.

that the negative income effect of a wage rise more than offsets its positive substitution effect.

In Figure 49.4, indifference curves are combined with budget lines to show the impact of a rise in real wages. Total earnings (i.e. the real wage rate x the number of hours worked) is on the vertical axis. The number of leisure hours available to the worker is on the horizontal axis. The budget lines AB and AC show the various combinations of earnings and leisure that the worker may enjoy. The greater the number of hours worked, the greater will be total earnings but the less will be time available for leisure. I_1I_1 and I_2I_2 are indifference curves showing the worker's indifference between earnings and leisure.

An increase in real wages will lead to an increase in total real earnings assuming that leisure time remains unchanged. This increase is shown by a change in the budget line from AB to AC. The worker will now move from equilibrium at P to equilibrium at R. This shows that the worker will receive higher earnings **and** work fewer hours because leisure time increases. The income effect of the increase in real wage rates must therefore have been negative and have outweighed the substitution effect. The substitution effect can be measured by drawing a third budget line tangential to I_1I_1 but parallel to the new budget line AC. The movement from P to Q is the substitution effect. It shows that as a result of the increase in real wage rates, the worker will demand FG fewer hours of leisure (i.e. he or she will work FG extra hours). But this is outweighed by the income effect from Q to R. As a result of the rise in income, the worker will choose to 'buy' FH extra hours of leisure (i.e. work FH fewer hours). FH is greater than FG and therefore overall the worker will work GH fewer hours as a result of the increase in real wages.

Figure 49.4 shows a situation where a rise in real wages leads to a reduction in working hours. However, it is equally possible to draw a diagram showing that a rise in real wages will lead to an increased number of hours worked (by drawing I_2I_2 higher up the budget line AC).

QUESTION 2 In 1986, the results of a government commissioned report on the incentive effects of cuts in income tax were published. The report, by Professor C V Brown of Stirling University, found no evidence that tax cuts encourage people in employment either to work harder or to work longer. Lower taxes did encourage women, particularly in part time jobs, to work longer because they would keep more of their earnings. But for males on average earnings, the boost to existing income provided by lower taxes tended to be more important than the incentive (i.e. substitution) effect of the tax cut.

Using indifference curve diagrams, explain the typical effects found by Professor Brown of income tax cuts on
(a) a male worker on average earnings and
(b) a female part time worker.

Supply of labour to a firm

In a perfectly competitive market there are many buyers and sellers (☞ unit 27). In a perfectly competitive factor market, there are many firms hiring many individual workers. This means that an individual firm will be able to hire an extra worker at the existing wage rate.

Figure 49.5 (a) shows the supply curve of labour facing the firm. The firm is small and wants to expand its workforce from 20 workers to 21 workers. Figure 49.5 (b) shows the supply curve of labour for the industry to be upward sloping, as will be argued below. 100 000 workers are currently employed in the industry. The movement up the industry supply curve from 100 000 workers to 100 001 workers is so small that the firm can employ the extra worker at the ruling industrial wage rate. Therefore the supply curve facing the firm is horizontal (i.e. perfectly elastic).

Many industries, however, are either oligopolies or monopolies. Firms in these industries are therefore likely to be significant employers of particular types of labour. For instance, the government employs over 90 per cent of all UK teachers. If a firm is a monopsonist (i.e. is the sole buyer) in its labour market, then the supply curve of labour to the firm will also be the supply curve of labour to the industry. It will be upward sloping, showing that the firm has to offer increased wages if it wishes to increase its labour force.

Table 49.1

Units of labour supplied	Cost per unit (£)	Total cost (£)	Marginal cost (£)
0	-	0	
			10
1	10	10	
			30
2	20	40	
			50
3	30	90	
			70
4	40	160	

The cost of employing an extra worker (the marginal cost) will be higher than the wage rate the firm has to pay the extra worker. This is because it not only has to pay a higher wage rate to the worker but it must also pay the higher wage rate to all its other workers. In Table 49.1, for instance, the firm has to increase the wage rate as extra workers are employed. The wage rate needed to attract 3 workers to the industry is £30 per worker. However, the marginal cost of the third worker is £50; £30 for the third worker plus an extra £10 paid to each of the first two workers.

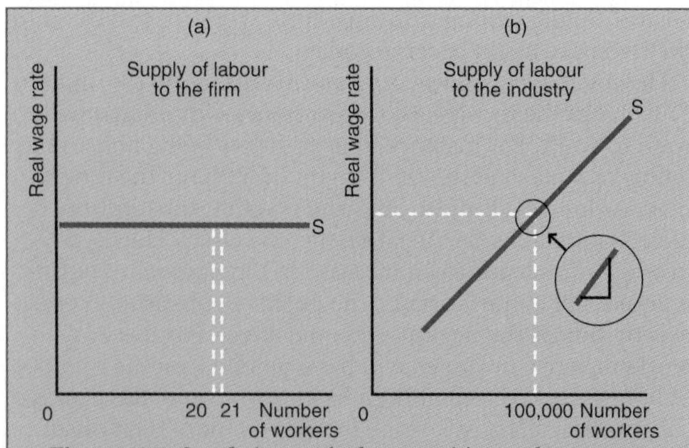

Figure 49.5 *Supply in a perfectly competitive market*
The supply curve of labour facing a firm in a perfectly competitive factor market is perfectly elastic. The firm can hire new workers at the existing wage rate because their employment has an insignificant impact on the total supply of labour in the market.

The supply curve of labour to the firm and the firm's marginal cost of labour derived from the data in Table 49.1 are shown in Figure 49.6. The marginal cost curve for labour for the monopsonist employer is higher than the supply curve of labour.

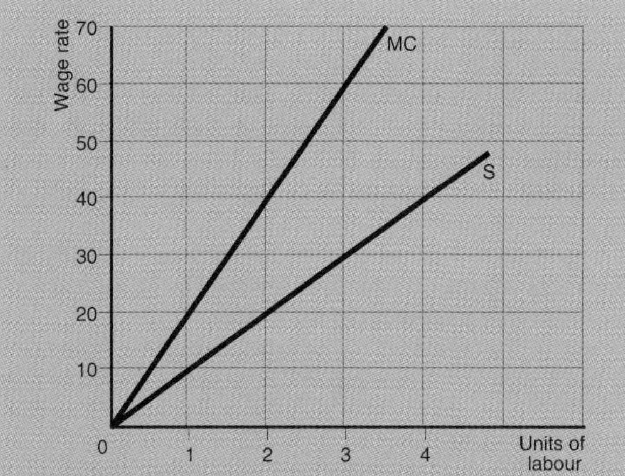

Figure 49.6 *Supply curve and marginal cost curve of labour facing a monopsonist employer*
The supply curve for labour facing a monopsonist employer is upward sloping. The marginal cost of hiring extra workers is more than the wage rate because the higher wage rate paid to the marginal worker needs to be paid to all existing workers.

QUESTION 3

Table 49.2

Number of workers employed	Wage per week per worker (£)
100	200
200	220
300	240
400	260

The table shows the wage rates per week a firm has to offer to recruit workers.

(a) Draw (i) the supply curve of labour and (ii) the marginal cost curve of labour facing the firm. (Remember that the marginal cost of, for instance, the 100 workers employed between 300 and 400 is drawn at the 350 point.)

(b) How would the supply curve and marginal cost curve differ if the firm could recruit any number of workers at a wage rate of £200 per week?

The supply curve of labour for an industry

An industry can increase the number of hours worked by its labour force in two ways:

- it can increase the number of hours worked by its existing labour force;
- it can recruit new workers.

As explained above, a rise in real wage rates all other things being equal may or may not increase the supply of labour by individual workers in the industry. However, it is likely to attract new workers into the industry. These new workers may be from other industries or they may be workers who previously did not hold a job, such as housepersons or the unemployed. Therefore the supply curve of labour for an industry is likely to be upward sloping, the ability of firms to recruit new workers outweighing any possible disincentive effect on existing workers. The higher the industry real wage rate, the more workers will want to enter that particular industry. The elasticity of supply of labour to an industry will depend upon a number of factors.

The availability of suitable labour in other industries An engineering company wanting to recruit unskilled workers will be able to 'poach' workers relatively easily from other industries because there is a large pool of unskilled workers spread throughout industry. The National Health Service will have more difficulty recruiting brain surgeons because nearly all brain surgeons in the UK are already employed by the NHS. So the elasticity of supply of a pool of workers spread across many industries is likely to be higher than that of a group of workers concentrated in the recruiting industry.

Time Elasticity of supply is likely to be lower in the short run than in the long run. For instance, the NHS might not be able to recruit large numbers of brain surgeons tomorrow. But it could expand supply considerably over a 20 year period by training more of them.

The extent of under-employment and unemployment The higher the level of unemployment, the higher is likely to be the elasticity of supply. With high unemployment, firms are more likely to be able to recruit workers at the existing real wage rate from the pool of the unemployed.

It could be that there is a **cobweb** effect (☞ unit 11) in a market. For instance, the large increase in numbers in the 5-16 age group in the 1960s and first half of the 1970s due to high birth rates led to a considerable increase in the number of workers entering the teaching profession. Pupil numbers then began to decline as the birth rate fell. The demand for teachers fell. It so happened that governments between 1975 and 1985 also wanted to cut public spending. An easy way of doing this was to cut public sector pay relative to the private sector. This cut recruitment onto teacher education courses. It also led to an increase in the number of students completing teacher training courses taking up non-teaching jobs. By the late 1980s, there was a crisis in teaching, with considerable shortages of suitable teachers. In other words, a move away from the equilibrium of the mid-1970s led to a fall in teachers' relative pay. This in turn led to a fall in supply of teachers after a period of time. Government reacted in the late 1980s by putting up teachers' relative pay. The result was an increase in the numbers of people wanting to become teachers by entering teacher training courses and taking first jobs in teaching. By the mid-1990s, it could be argued that there was over-supply. This may have encouraged government to cut relative pay for teachers again, leading at a later date, to excess demand for teachers.

This cobweb effect is the result of there being a delayed response in the market to current market conditions. In occupations where there are long training periods and where it is difficult for existing workers to change to another job, decisions about whether to supply labour today are based on decisions about whether to enter the occupation a year ago, five years ago or perhaps even thirty years ago.

QUESTION 4

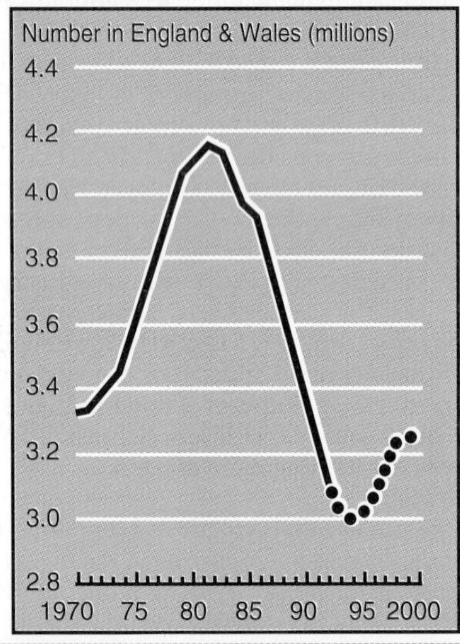

Source: adapted from Population Estimates Unit, OPCS.

Figure 49.7 *15 to 19 year-olds: number in England and Wales (millions)*

In the mid to late 1980s, it was widely predicted that there would be a severe shortage of young people in the labour force. The National Economic and Development Council published a report *Defusing the Demographic Time Bomb* which urged employers to diversify their recruitment patterns to meet the coming crisis. The report in particular suggested that employers take on more mature workers, people with disabilities and the unemployed.

(a) Using the concept of elasticity of supply, suggest why a supermarket is more likely to be able to fill jobs like shelf stackers or checkout assistants than managerial posts from people aged 50+.

(b) The predicted shortage failed to occur in the first half of the 1990s. This was mainly because the economy went through a deep recession in 1990-1992 which lead to a fall in the demand for labour by industry. Why should a recession, like that of 1990-92, lead to a rise in the elasticity of supply of labour to an industry?

Supply of labour to the economy

The supply of labour to the economy as a whole might seem to be fixed (i.e. perfectly inelastic). However, this is unlikely to be the case.

- In the UK, only about three-quarters of people aged 16-64 are in employment. The rest tend to be in education, at home looking after children, unemployed or have taken early retirement. This pool of people are potential workers and some would enter the workforce if real wages rose.
- Some of the retired could be brought back to work if there were sufficient incentives for them.
- Immigration too could expand the domestic supply of labour. Immigration was used by the UK to solve labour supply problems in the 1950s.

So the supply of labour to the economy as a whole is likely to be upward sloping too. There is some evidence to suggest that it might also be backward sloping. Over the past ten years there has been an increase in early retirement. This has been due to many factors, but one is that males particularly have been able to earn sufficiently high wages during their working life to make early retirement with a reduced pension attractive. Workers are choosing to reduce the number of hours worked over their lifetime.

QUESTION 5

Table 49.3 *Pay and employment of women*

	1971	1981	1994
Real average earnings of females (at 1994 prices)	£130.97	£177.17	£261.50
Total UK female employment (millions)	9.3	10.6	12.3

Source: adapted from Department of Employment, *Employment Gazette.*

(a) Do the data support the theory that the supply curve for labour in an economy is upward sloping?

(b) What other factors apart from earnings might affect the supply of female labour in an economy?

Key terms

Population of working age - defined in the UK as men aged 16 to 64 and women aged 16-59.
Labour force - those in work or officially counted as unemployed.
Workforce in employment - the numbers of workers with a job.
Activity or participation rates - the percentage or proportion of any given population in the labour force.
Net migration - immigration minus emigration.

Applied economics

The supply of labour in the UK

The UK labour force

In 1995, the population of the UK was approximately 58.3 million people. Not all were available for work. Those below the age of 16 were in full time education whilst women over 60 and men over 65 were officially counted as retired. The rest, those aged 16-60/65, are known as the POPULATION OF WORKING AGE. Figure 49.8 shows that the numbers in this age group have increased in recent decades from 31.7 million in 1971 to nearly 35 million in 1994.

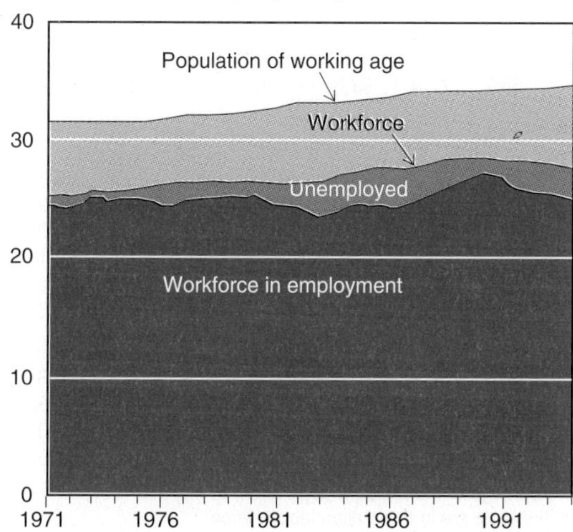

Source: adapted from *Employment Gazette Historical Supplement*, October 1994; *Employment Gazette*, April 1994.
Figure 49.8 *Population of working age, workforce and workforce in employment*

Not all those of working age are members of the LABOUR FORCE or WORKFORCE or WORKING POPULATION. Many women choose to leave employment to bring up children. Young people too may stay on in education after the age of 16. There is also a growing trend for the over-50s to take early retirement. So the workforce is smaller than the population of working age.

The labour force or workforce is made up of two groups. By far the largest group, the WORKFORCE IN EMPLOYMENT, consists of those workers with a job. Figure 49.9 gives a breakdown of the workforce in employment. Most are **employees**, who work for someone else, their **employer**. A minority work for themselves and are known as **self-employed**. The rest are in the armed forces or are on government training schemes. Note that the numbers in the armed forces has declined as a proportion of the workforce in employment over time, as has the number of employees. Self employment has grown whilst government training schemes were only introduced in the late 1970s. The rest of the labour force is made up of the unemployed.

Figure 49.8 shows that the workforce has tended to increase over time, from 25.3 million in 1971 to 27.9 million in 1994. The growth in the workforce in employment has been less smooth than that of the workforce itself. Three major recessions, 1975-1977, 1980-1982 and 1990-1992, resulted in large increases in unemployment and falls in the workforce in employment. The recessions of 1980-1982 and 1990-1992 were so deep that there was even a fall in the workforce. In the early 1980s, the workforce fell from 26.7 million in 1980 to 26.5 million in 1982, whilst in the early 1990s, the workforce fell from 28.7 million in 1990 to 27.9 million in 1994. Workers, particularly women, became discouraged from looking for work and disappeared from official counts of the unemployed.

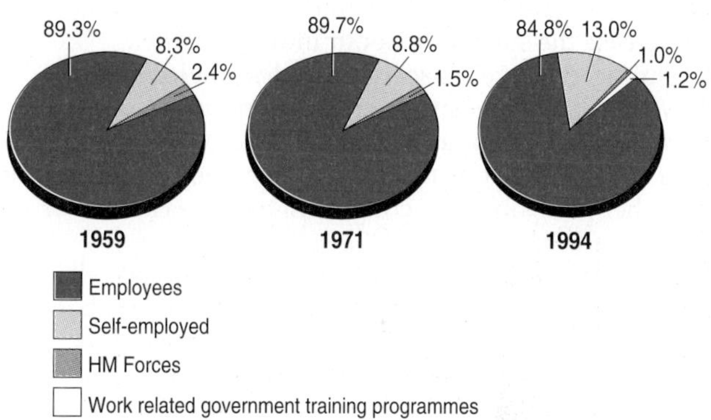

Source: adapted from Employment Gazette, October 1994.
Figure 49.9 *Components of the workforce in employment: United Kingdom*

Male and female employment

The labour force over the past 20 years has grown at a faster rate than the population of working age. Table 49.4 shows that whilst the total population of working age grew by 10 per cent over the period 1971 to 1994, the civilian labour force has grown by 12.5 per cent. The totals, however, mask a much larger change in the composition by sex of the labour force. There has been little change in the male force over the period. The growth has come from an increase in the number of women working, from 9.3 million in 1971 to 12.3 million in 1994.

Within the female total, there has been a substantial growth in employment of women aged 20-54 as indicated in Table 49.5. This table shows ACTIVITY or PARTICIPATION RATES. These are the percentages of any given population in the labour force (i.e. the percentages of an age group either in work or officially counted as unemployed). There are a number of reasons why a larger proportion of females have gone out to work.

Table 49.4 *Civilian labour force and population of working age*

Great Britain				Millions
	Civilian labour force			Population of working age
	Males[2]	Females[2]	Total[3]	
Estimates				
1971	15.6	9.3	24.9	31.7
1976	15.6	10.1	25.7	31.9
1981	15.6	10.6	26.2	32.9
1986	15.6	11.3	26.9	33.9
1991	16.0	12.2	28.1	34.5
1994	15.6	12.3	28.0	34.8
1996[1]	15.6	12.5	28.2	35.0
2001[1]	15.8	13.1	28.8	35.7
2006[1]	15.9	13.5	29.4	36.2

1. Projections.
2. Includes workers older than 65/60.
3. May not add up due to rounding.

Source: adapted from CSO, *Social Trends*; Department of Employment.

- Real wages have increased over the period. Economic theory would predict that an increase in real wages will increase the supply of labour into the market.
- Through changes in social attitudes and legislation, women now have much greater opportunities in employment than in 1971 and far more than say in 1931 or 1901. Again, this means that more women are getting higher paid jobs, attracting them to make careers for themselves.
- The opportunity cost of going out to work has fallen. A hundred years ago, women created a large number of household services, from cleaning the house, to baking bread to making clothes. They had to spend large amounts of time each week doing this. Today, cheap and efficient machines do much of this work. What's more, the real price of washing machines, microwaves etc. has tended to go down over time. Households have been able to afford to buy more and more of these gadgets. The result is that women have increasingly been able to combine a career with running a home. Moreover, changes in social attitudes over the past 20 years have meant that men have increasingly begun to share in domestic chores, again helping to create time for women to work in paid employment.
- Falls in the number of children in a family help explain why there was an increase in the number of women working over the period 1900 to 1970. However, family size has remained roughly constant since 1970. What has changed is an increase in nursery education and in pre-school and child-minding facilities. Women have found it easier to get their children looked after at an affordable cost since 1970.

Male activity rates, in contrast, have fallen. In 1971, virtually all males aged 25-59 were in the labour force. This is still broadly true for men aged 25-50. The small decline in activity rates for this group has come about mainly because more men now have the opportunity to retire through ill health or disability than in 1971. The sharp fall in activity rates for the over-50s comes from the trend towards early retirement. Increased staying on rates in education account for the fall in activity rates for the 16-25 age group.

Table 49.5 *Economic activity rates[1] by gender and age*

Great Britain								Percentages
	16-19	20-24	25-34	35-44	45-54	55-59	60-64	All aged 16 and over[2]
Males								
Estimates								
1971	69.4	87.7	94.6	96.2	95.7	93.0	82.9	80.5
1976	70.5	85.9	95.1	96.4	96.1	92.4	80.4	78.9
1981	72.4	85.1	95.4	96.0	94.8	89.4	69.3	76.5
1986	73.2	86.2	93.7	94.8	91.8	81.1	53.8	73.8
1991	70.4	85.6	94.0	94.7	91.0	80.3	54.1	73.7
1993	63.9	83.8	92.5	93.6	90.3	75.4	52.2	71.9
Projections								
1996	58.3	81.0	92.7	93.7	89.9	74.0	50.0	71.1
2001	56.7	78.0	92.6	93.9	89.5	74.0	46.9	70.1
2006	55.7	77.9	92.6	93.9	89.1	74.0	45.5	69.0
Females								
Estimates								
1971	65.0	60.2	45.5	59.7	62.0	50.9	28.8	43.9
1976	68.2	64.8	54.0	67.4	66.5	54.3	26.9	46.8
1981	70.4	68.8	56.4	68.0	68.0	53.4	23.3	47.6
1986	70.3	70.7	63.5	72.1	70.5	51.8	19.1	49.6
1991	69.1	72.7	69.7	76.7	72.7	54.5	24.1	52.4
1993	63.8	70.7	70.7	77.0	74.8	54.6	24.8	52.6
Projections								
1996	60.1	68.8	73.4	79.1	75.9	55.3	25.6	53.6
2001	59.8	68.1	77.4	82.1	77.2	56.0	25.8	55.2
2006	59.2	68.8	80.6	85.2	78.1	56.7	27.0	56.0

1. The percentage of the resident population, or any sub-group of the population who are in the civilian labour force.
2. Includes those aged 65 and over.

Source: CSO, *Social Trends*, No. 25, 1995.

Employment by age

Not only has the balance of the labour force changed between the sexes, it has also changed by age as Table 49.6 shows. Since 1971, there has been a significant increase in

Table 49.6 *Civilian labour force: by age*

Great Britain				Thousands
	16-24	25-44	45 and over	All aged 16 and over
Estimates				
1971	5,082	9,725	10,096	24,903
1976	5,095	10,824	9,782	25,700
1981	5,832	11,358	9,052	26,242
1986	6,173	12,455	8,310	26,938
1991	5,536	13,879	8,714	28,129
1993	4,932	13,863	9,094	27,890
Projections				
1996	4,339	14,346	9,477	28,162
2001	4,206	14,678	9,951	28,835
2006	4,434	14,389	10,587	29,409

Source: CSO, *Social Trends*, No.25, 1995.

the proportion of 25-44 year olds in the labour force. The numbers and percentages of workers over 45 declined between 1971 and 1986 because of increased early retirement. The numbers in this age group have only increased again since then because of a growth in numbers coming through from higher birth rates in the post-war period.

The numbers of 16-24 year old workers have fluctuated. Between 1971 and 1986, the numbers in this age group increased, again because of increasing birth rates in the post-war period. Some economists believe that this was a prime cause of the increase in unemployment over that period, and particularly the increase in youth unemployment. The economy was unable to provide jobs for a growing number of young workers entering the labour market for the first time. However, a fall in the birth rate from the mid-1960s led to falls in the 16-24 age group in the labour force from the mid-1980s. At the height of the Lawson boom, in 1986-88, many commentators predicted that there would be a crisis in recruitment of young people in the 1990s. Demand for young workers would be increasing at a time when their supply was falling. The crisis had not materialised by the mid-1990s. Probably the main reason for this was the recession of 1990-1992 which led to a sharp fall in the demand for labour. However, any moderate increase in demand for young workers in the second half of the decade is likely to lead to a shortage, with consequent increases in relative pay of young people.

Employment by ethnic group

Detailed statistics for the employment of different ethnic groups in the population can be found in the data question. In general, the employment patterns of those of non-white origin seem less favourable than those of the white population.

Employment by industry and by region

The supply of workers to different industries and different regions has changed considerably over the past 30 years. Broadly, there has been a major shift of workers from the primary and secondary sectors of the economy to the tertiary sector. Consequently, regions heavily dependent upon coal mining and heavy manufacturing have seen losses of jobs and population to regions which have traditionally specialised in light manufacturing and service industries. These trends are discussed in more detail in unit 61.

Other factors affecting the labour force

There are factors other than the increased participation of women and the growth of early retirement amongst men which affect the labour force.

Migration If immigration is larger than emigration, then the workforce is likely to increase. During the 1950s, the UK encouraged immigration from new Commonwealth countries to fill an acute labour shortage. In the 1960s and 1970s, following the 1961 Immigration Act, NET MIGRATION (immigration minus emigration) tended to be negative. More people left the country than entered. In the 1980s and 1990s, the trend has been reversed. However, net migration tends to account for only 25 per cent of the total population change in the UK. What is happening to the birth rate and to activity rates is a far more important determinant of the size of the labour force in the longer term.

Part-time work There has been almost a doubling in the proportion of part-time workers in the labour force since 1971, as Figure 49.10 shows. In 1994, there were nearly 6 million part-time workers in Great Britain, 86 per cent of whom were women. Table 49.7 shows that service industries have a particularly high proportion of workers as part-timers. In food retailing, for instance, 65 per cent of workers are part-timers. Primary and secondary industries have far lower proportions of

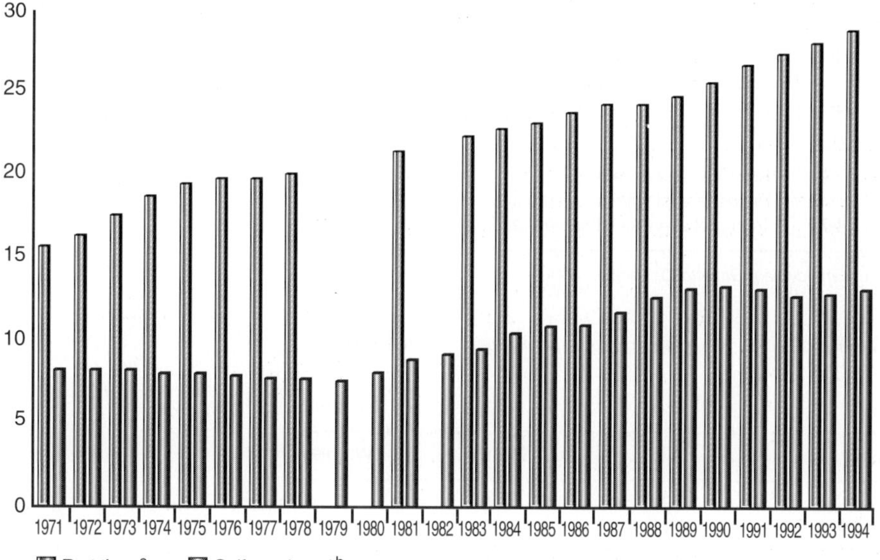

a Part-time employees as a percentage of all employees, June, seasonally adjusted.
b Self-employed as a percentage of the workforce in employment, June, seasonally adjusted.

Source: adapted from Labour Force Survey and ED Statistics.

Figure 49.10 *Part-time and self-employed workers as a percentage of all employees/workforce, Great Britain 1971-1994* part-time workers in their labour force. The move to increased part-time work in the economy has mainly been caused by the growth in female employment. In a 1994 survey, the results of which are shown in Table 49.8, 73 per cent of part-time workers asked stated that they were in part-time work because they didn't want a full-time job. Women still are expected to take the main responsibility for bringing up children and looking after the household. Part-time jobs enable them to fulfil these roles and hold a job. As society changes and men increasingly share in domestic responsibilities, it is likely that there will be a much greater proportion of males amongst part-time workers. Note too the increasing numbers of students in part-time work. Cuts in grants to students have forced more and more students to take on part-time work to survive at University.

Table 49.7 *Proportion of all jobs that are part-time by industry, June 1994*

Great Britain, unadjusted

	SIC	Industry	Per cent
Highest proportions			
1	**663**	Night clubs	77.3
2	**662**	Public houses and bars	77.3
3	**642**	Retail of confectionery and tobacco	71.6
4	**92**	Cleaning and refuse services	65.0
5	**641**	Food retail	64.8
6	**661**	Restaurants, snack bars, cafes	57.1
7	**643**	Dispensing chemists	56.9
8	**96**	Social and community services	52.2
9	**645-648**	Retail of clothing, textiles and household goods	46.7
10	**95**	Health	46.4
Lowest proportions			
1	**35-36**	Transport-related manufacturing	1.9
2	**2**	Extraction of minerals and ores other than fuels/ manufacture of metals, mineral products and chemicals	4.0
3	**32**	Mechanical engineering	4.4
4	**915**	National defence (exc HM Forces)	4.9
5	**1**	Energy and water supply	5.0
6	**33-34**	Electrical/electronic engineering and manufacture of office machinery	5.6
7	**31**	Manufacture of metal goods	6.6
8	**94**	Research and development	6.9
9	**48**	Rubber and plastic manufacturing	8.3
10	**71,74-77**	Transport services other than road transport	8.3

Source: *Employment Gazette*, December 1994.

Table 49.8 *Reasons why people take part-time work: United Kingdom, Spring 1994*

Per cent

Reason	All	Men	Women
Student	12	42	8
Ill/disabled	1	2	1
Couldn't find full-time job	13	26	11
Didn't want full-time job	73	29	80

Source: *Employment Gazette*, December 1994.

Self-employment As Figure 49.10 shows, there has been a considerable increase in self-employed workers in the labour force since 1971. This will be considered in greater detail in unit 57.

Hours of work and holidays Hours of work have changed little since the early 1970s. On average, full time workers have worked 41 hours per week in the 1970s, 1980s and 1990s. However, whilst weekly hours of work have remained broadly constant, yearly hours of work have decreased because holiday entitlements have significantly increased. In 1961, nearly all workers were only entitled to two weeks paid holiday per year. By 1994, nearly 10 per cent were entitled to 4 weeks paid holiday a year, a further 60 per cent approximately were entitled to between 4 and 5 weeks whilst over 30 per cent were entitled to over 5 weeks. Longer holidays and shorter working lives due to early retirement would tend to indicate that either workers prefer increases in leisure time to be in blocks of time rather than a few hours extra per week, or that employers see the 40 hour week as optimal for completing work efficiently and prefer to concede the desire for shorter hours in longer holidays or shorter working lives.

The quality of the labour force

Greater production can be achieved by using more labour. However, the size of the UK labour force is likely to change only slowly over the next 50 years. Of more significance are likely to be changes in the quality of the labour force. Rising educational standards, as shown for instance by greater numbers gaining high grades at GCSE, 'A' levels, GNVQs and degrees,would suggest that the labour force is becoming potentially more productive over time. However, many have argued that the UK has been left behind in international terms in the quality of its labour force. This has had significant implications for the the UK's rate of economic growth (☞ unit 99).

Ethnic groups in the labour force

Table 49.9 *Population of working age economic activity rates: by ethnic group, gender and age, Spring 1994*

Great Britain — Percentages

	Males			Females		
	16-24	25-44	45-64	16-24	25-44	45-59
White	77	95	79	67	75	70
Black[1]	62	86	77	51	71	72
Indian	55	93	76	51	69	53
Pakistani/ Bangladeshi	57	92	63	35	24	-
Other[2]	45	82	80	34	57	54
All ethnic groups[3]	75	94	79	65	74	70

1. Includes Caribbean, African and other Black people of non-mixed origin.
2. Includes Chinese, other ethnic minority groups of non-mixed origin and people of mixed origin.
3. Includes ethnic group not stated.

Source: CSO, *Social Trends*, No.25,1995.

Table 49.10 *Population: by ethnic group and age, 1991*

Great Britain — Percentages and thousands

	0-15	16-29	30-44	45-59	60 and over	All ages (=100%) (000s)
Ethnic group						
Ethnic minority group						
Black Caribbean	21.9	27.6	20.0	19.6	10.9	500
Black African	29.3	32.1	26.7	9.2	2.7	212
Black other	50.6	30.8	12.4	4.2	2.1	178
Indian	29.5	23.9	25.9	13.8	6.8	840
Pakistani	42.6	24.0	19.2	10.4	3.7	477
Bangladeshi	47.2	23.3	14.8	11.4	3.3	163
Chinese	23.3	29.7	29.4	12.0	5.7	157
Other Asian	24.4	25.2	33.0	13.3	4.1	198
Other	41.7	24.9	19.9	8.5	5.0	290
All ethnic minority groups	33.0	26.0	22.6	12.6	5.8	3,015
White	19.3	20.4	21.2	17.0	22.1	51,874
All ethnic groups	20.1	20.7	21.2	16.8	21.2	54,889

Source: CSO, *Social Trends*, 1994.

Table 49.11 *People in employment[1] by ethnic group, socio-economic group[2] and gender, Spring 1994*

Great Britain — Percentages

	Ethnic group						
	Black	Indian	Pakistani or Bangladeshi	Other ethnic minority groups	All ethnic minority groups	White	All persons
Males							
Professional	..	13.7	..	19.5	11.7	8.2	8.4
Intermediate	25.2	30.5	18.3	28.2	26.3	31.1	30.9
Skilled non-manual	13.7	13.5	15.7	16.8	14.7	11.6	11.8
Skilled manual	28.6	22.3	33.5	19.2	25.3	31.6	31.3
Partly skilled	17.2	17.0	22.9	11.1	16.9	13.4	13.5
Unskilled	9.4	..	..	..	5.1	4.1	4.1
All males (=100%) (thousands)[3]	144	190	110	126	571	12,887	13,458
Females							
Professional	..	7.0	..	..	4.8	2.6	2.6
Intermediate	35.1	23.2	28.7	30.9	29.4	30.3	30.3
Skilled non-manual	28.8	34.2	40.7	35.9	33.5	37.0	36.8
Skilled manual	9.6	..	..	..	8.1	8.1	8.1
Partly skilled	14.2	26.7	..	13.0	18.7	15.5	15.7
Unskilled	9.7	..	..	..	5.5	6.6	6.5
All females (=100%) (thousands)[3]	147	152	45	103	443	10,272	10,715

1. Males aged 16 to 64, females aged 16 to 59.
2. Based on occupation.
3. Includes members of the armed forces and those who did not give ethnic group or occupation.

Source: CSO, *Social Trends*, No.25, 1995.

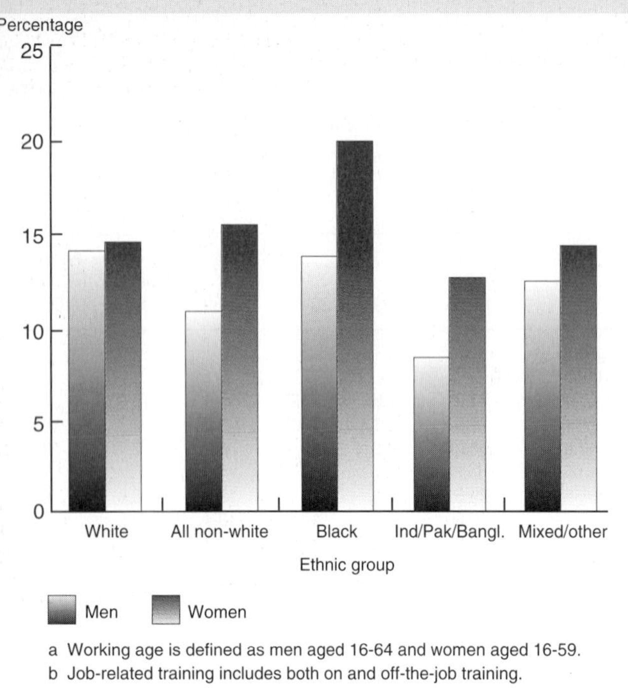

Source: adapted from *Employment Gazette*, November 1994.

Figure 49.11 *Employees of working age[a] receiving job-related training[b] during the previous four weeks by ethnic group and sex, Winter 1993-94, Great Britain*

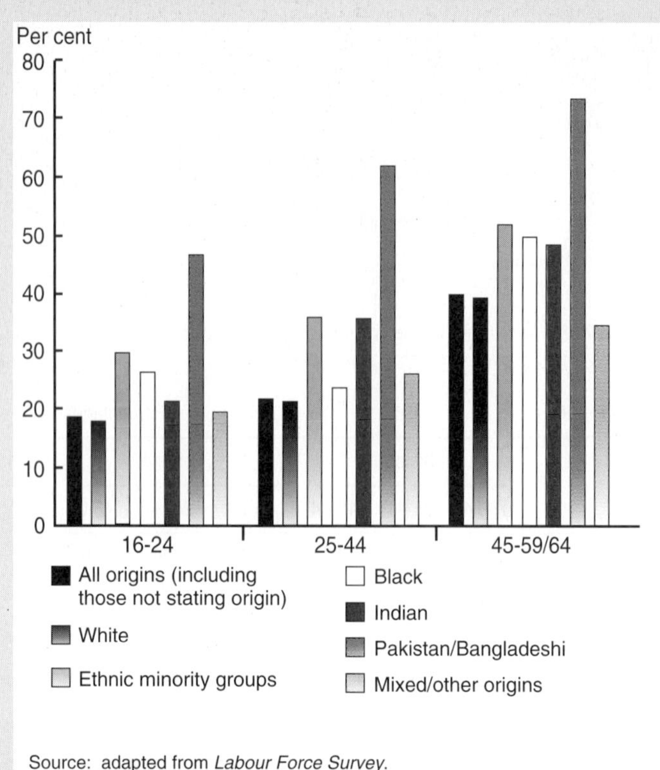

Source: adapted from *Labour Force Survey*.

Figure 49.12 *Percentage of population with no qualifications by ethnic origin and race: Great Britain, Spring 1993.*

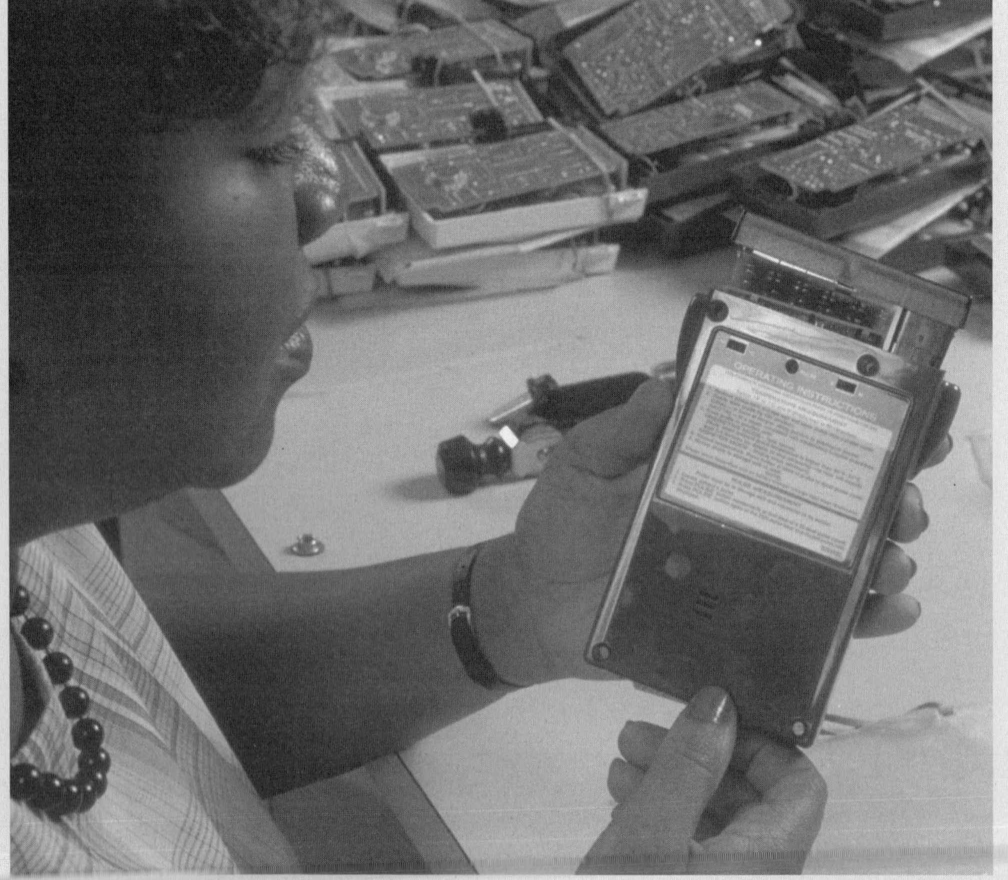

Write a report analysing future trends in the position of workers from ethnic minorities in the labour force. Use the data in Figures 49.11 and 49.12 and Tables 49.9 to 49.11, as well as any additional information that you may have available.

1. **Analyse the position of workers from ethnic minorities in the labour force in the early 1990s.**
2. **Discuss how the proportion of workers from ethnic minorities in the labour force is likely to change over the next 30 years.**
3. **Evaluate what economic measures could be taken to improve the position of workers from ethnic minorities relative to whites.**

Wage determination

Summary

1. **The wage rate of labour is determined by the demand for labour and the supply of labour.**
2. **In an economy where labour is homogeneous and all markets are perfect, wage rates would be identical for all workers.**
3. **Wage differentials are caused partly by market imperfections and partly by differences in individual labour characteristics.**
4. **In a perfectly competitive market, individual firms face a horizontal supply curve and will hire labour up to the point where the wage rate is equal to the marginal revenue product of labour.**
5. **In an imperfectly competitive market, either the firm is a monopsonist or there is a monopoly supplier of labour, such as a trade union, or both. A monopsonist drives down wage rates and employment levels, whilst a monopoly supplier increases wage rates.**

How wage rates are determined

Prices are determined by demand and supply. So the price of labour, the real wage rate, is determined by the demand for and the supply of labour.

The demand curve for labour in an industry is the marginal revenue product curve of labour (☞ unit 48). This is downward sloping, indicating that more labour will be demanded the lower the real wage rate. The supply curve of labour to an industry is upward sloping (☞ unit 49), indicating that more labour will be supplied if real wage rates increase. This gives an equilibrium real wage rate of OA in Figure 50.1. OB units of labour are demanded and supplied.

The demand and supply curves for labour can shift for a variety of reasons, giving new equilibrium real wage rates and levels of employment in the industry. The demand curve for labour will move to the right showing an increase in the demand for labour if the marginal revenue product of labour increases. This might occur if:

- productivity improves, perhaps due to changing technology or more flexible working practices, increasing output per worker;
- there is a rise in the selling price of the product, increasing the value of the output of each worker;
- the price of capital increases, leading to a substitution of labour for capital.

The supply curve might move to the right, showing an increase in supply, if:

- there is an increase in the number of workers in the population as a whole, perhaps because of changing demographic trends, or because government alters tax and benefit levels increasing incentives to work;
- wages or conditions of work deteriorate in other industries, making conditions relatively more attractive in this industry.

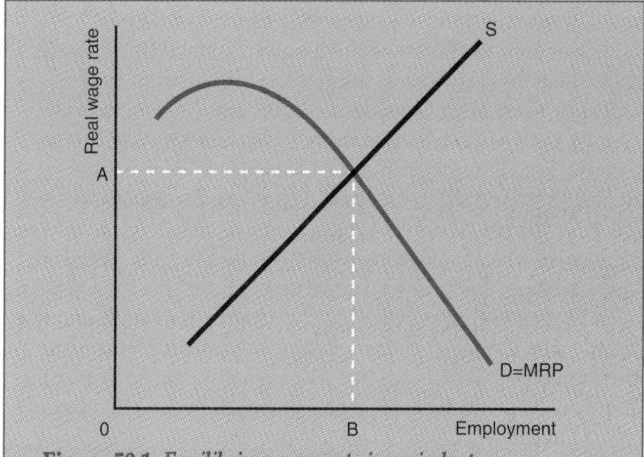

Figure 50.1 *Equilibrium wage rate in an industry*
The equilibrium real wage rate is OA whilst the level of employment in equilibrium is OB.

QUESTION 1

(a) On a diagram, draw a demand and supply curve for labour in the CD production industry.
(b) Mark on the diagram the equilibrium wage rate and the equilibrium level of employment.
(c) Show how the demand curve or the supply curve might shift if there is:
  (i) a fall in labour productivity;
  (ii) an increase in wage rates in all other labour markets in the economy;
  (iii) a fall in demand for CDs;
  (iv) an introduction of new labour saving technology;
  (v) a fall in the number of 16-25 year olds in the population as a whole.

A labour market where all workers are paid the same

Consider an economy which has the following labour market characteristics.

- Labour is homogeneous (i.e. all workers are identical, for instance in age, skill and sex).
- There is perfect knowledge in the labour market. A worker in Scotland is as aware of job opportunities in London as a Londoner.
- There is perfect mobility of labour. Workers can move at no cost between jobs in the same industry, between different industries and between geographical areas. Equally, there are no costs to firms in hiring and firing workers.
- All workers and employers are price takers. There are no trade unions or monopsonist employers.
- There are no barriers which prevent wages rising and falling to accommodate changes in the demand for and supply of labour.
- Firms aim to maximise profit and minimise costs of production, whilst workers aim to maximise their wages.

In this perfect labour market, all workers would be paid the same wage rate. To show that this must be true, consider two markets where wage rates are different. In the Welsh steel industry, wages are higher than in the catering market in London. London catering workers would know this because there is perfect knowledge in the market. They would apply for jobs in Welsh steel firms. They would be prepared to work for less than existing Welsh steel workers so long as the wage rate was higher than their existing wage rate as caterers. Welsh steel makers, seeking to minimise cost, would then either sack their existing workers and replace them with cheaper London catering workers, or offer to continue employing their existing workforce but at a lower wage. Meanwhile, London catering firms would be threatened with a loss of their workers. To retain them they would need to put up their wage rates. Only when the two wage rates are equal would there be no incentive for London catering workers to become Welsh steel workers.

QUESTION 2 The second half of the 1980s saw a construction boom in commercial property. Developers refurbished or built millions of square feet of office space in, for instance, the City of London and its surrounding areas. Canary Wharf came to be the symbol of what turned out to be a massive over expansion of property. There were insufficient construction workers at the time in London and the South East, so large numbers of workers from other areas of the country came to work in the capital. Friday early evening trains from London to Liverpool, for instance, were packed with construction workers returning home for the weekend. On Sunday nights, the workers would return to London, sleeping through the week in bed and breakfast accommodation or in vans or cars. Liverpool, even at the height of the Lawson boom, still faced high unemployment and relatively low wages,

Using diagrams, show how this flow of workers might have helped to equalise wage rates between Liverpool and London.

Why wage rates differ

In the real world, wage rates differ. One important reason is because labour is not homogeneous. Each worker is a unique factor of production, possessing a unique set of employment characteristics such as:

- age - whether young, middle aged or old;
- sex - whether male or female;
- ethnic background;

QUESTION 3

Name Judith Ashton
Age 29
Occupation Personnel assistant
Location Chester
Earnings £11,300 per year

Name Errol Grant
Age 49
Occupation Sales and marketing director
Location West Midlands
Earnings £35,000 per year

Name Mike Jones
Age 17
Occupation Receptionist
Location Tenby, West Wales
Earnings £5,500 per year

Name Geoff Pennington
Age 44
Occupation Civil engineer
Location Preston
Earnings £24,250 per year

Why do the earnings of these workers differ?

- education, training and work experience;
- ability to perform tasks - including how hard they are prepared to work, their strength and their manual or mental dexterity.

For instance, a manager of a company is likely to be paid more than a cleaner working for the same company. On the one hand, the marginal revenue product of the manager is likely to be higher. Her education, skills and work experience are likely to provide greater value to the company than the cleaner's. On the other hand, the supply of managers is lower than the supply of cleaners. Most workers in the workforce could be a cleaner, but only a few have sufficient qualities to be managers. Greater demand and less supply lead to higher wage rates for managers than cleaners.

Wage rates also differ because workers do not necessarily seek to maximise wages. Wages are only part of the net benefit workers gain from employment. Workers whose jobs are dangerous, unpleasant, tedious, where there is little chance of promotion, where earnings fluctuate and where there are few or no fringe benefits, may seek higher wages than workers whose jobs possess the opposite characteristics. Market forces will tend to lead not to equality of wage rates but to equality of net benefits to workers.

Labour is not perfectly mobile. Hence there can be unemployment and low wages in Scotland whilst employers offering much higher wages are crying out for labour in London. Part of the reason why there is a lack of mobility is the absence of perfect knowledge within the labour market. Workers in Scotland may be unaware of job opportunities in the South of England. There are also many other imperfections in the market which prevent wage rates rising or falling in response to market pressures (☞ unit 52).

Perfectly competitive labour markets

In a perfectly competitive factor market, there are a large number of small firms hiring a large number of individual workers. For the individual firm operating in such a market:

- the demand curve for labour, the marginal revenue product curve of labour, is downward sloping (☞ unit 48);
- the supply curve of labour is perfectly elastic and therefore horizontal (☞ unit 49); the firm can hire any number of workers at the existing industry wage rate.

How many workers should this type of firm employ? If a worker costs £200 per week, but increases revenue net of all other costs by only £150, then he should not be employed.

Putting this theoretically, the firm will hire workers up to the point where the marginal cost of labour is equal to the marginal revenue product of labour. If the marginal cost were higher than marginal revenue product, for instance at OC in Figure 50.2, the firm would make a loss on the output produced by the marginal worker and hence it would cut back on employment of labour. If the marginal revenue product of labour were higher than the marginal cost of labour, for instance at OA, then it would hire more workers because these workers would generate a profit for the firm.

Hence, in Figure 50.2 the equilibrium level of employment by the firm is OB. This is the point where the marginal cost of labour (the supply curve) is equal to the marginal revenue product of labour (the demand curve). The equilibrium real wage rate is OW. This is the ruling equilibrium wage rate in the industry as a whole.

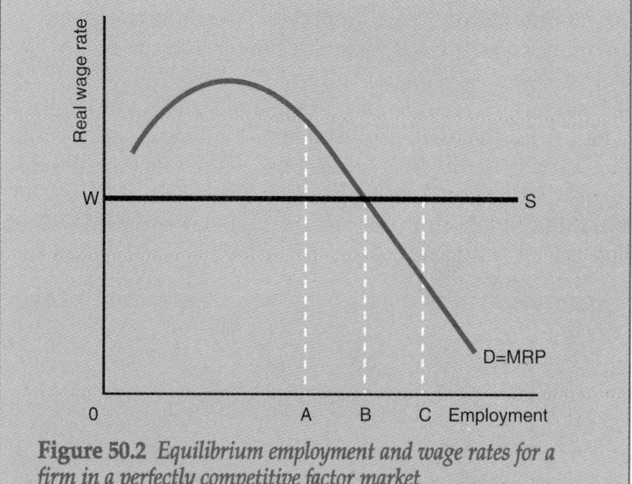

Figure 50.2 ***Equilibrium employment and wage rates for a firm in a perfectly competitive factor market***
In a perfectly competitive factor market, the supply curve for labour facing the firm is horizontal. The equilibrium real wage rate, OW, is set by the industry as a whole. The firm will then employ OB workers in equilibrium.

QUESTION 4

Table 50.1

Number of workers employed	Total revenue product (£ month)
1	700
2	1300
3	1800
4	2200

The data show the monthly total revenue product of a profit maximising manufacturing company in a perfectly competitive industry.

(a) Plot the marginal revenue product curve on graph paper (remembering to plot the MRP half way between whole numbers on the employment axis).

(b) What would be the maximum number of workers the firm would employ if the monthly wage per worker were:
(i) £600; (ii) £400; (iii) £425; (iv) £800; (v) £525?

Imperfectly competitive labour markets

An imperfectly competitive labour market is one where:
- either the firm is a dominant or monopoly buyer of labour;
- or the firm is faced by a monopoly supplier of labour, which is most likely to be a trade union.

If the firm is the sole buyer of labour, it is called a **monopsonist**. The state, for instance, employs over 90 per cent of teachers in the UK and therefore is essentially a monopsonist. A monopsonist is able to exploit market power and therefore common sense would suggest that the monopsonist would use this power to force down wage levels.

The marginal cost of employing an extra unit of labour is higher for the monopsonist than the average cost or wage. This is because the firm has to raise wage rates to attract extra labour into the industry. So the cost of employing an extra unit of labour is not just the higher wage paid to that unit but also the extra wages that now need to be paid to all the other workers in the industry (☞ unit 49).

In Figure 50.3, the demand and supply curves for labour are drawn. The firm will employ workers up to the point where the marginal cost of an extra worker is equal to the worker's marginal revenue product. Therefore the monopsonist will employ OA workers, the intersection of the marginal cost curve and the marginal revenue product or demand curve. The firm does not then need to pay a real wage rate of OG to each worker. It only needs to pay a real wage rate of OE to attract OA workers to the industry.

If the market were perfectly competitive, employment would be OB and the equilibrium wage rate would be OF. So economic theory suggests that a monopsonist drives down wages and reduces employment levels compared to a perfectly competitive factor market. Note that this is similar to the perfect competition/monopoly analysis in a goods market where it is argued that a monopolist reduces output and raises prices compared to a perfectly competitive market.

The effect of a monopoly supplier of labour will be considered in the next unit on trade unions.

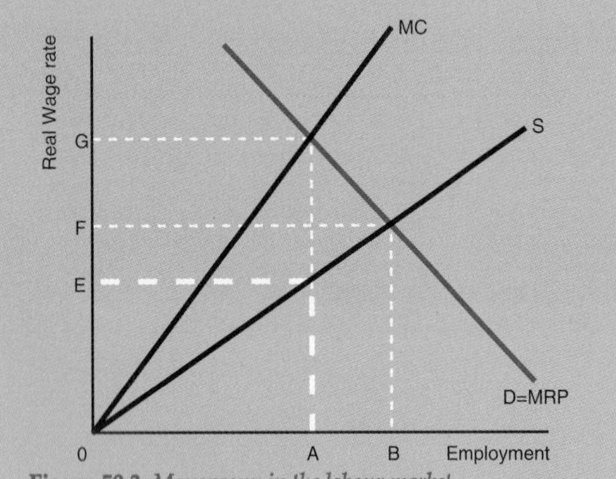

Figure 50.3 *Monopsony in the labour market*
A monopsonist will hire labour to the point where MC = MRP (i.e. up to the point OA). It will then pay labour the lowest wage rate possible which is OE. If the industry had been perfectly competitive then both the equilibrium wage rate OF and the equilibrium level of employment OB would be higher than under monopsony.

QUESTION 5 Teachers' pay in the UK is currently determined by the findings of a pay review board. This takes evidence from the government, which generally wishes to keep wage increases to a minimum, and from trade unions, which want to see high increases in wages. The government can choose either to accept the recommendations of the pay review board or to impose its own, invariably lower, pay deal. The government is effectively a monopsonist employer for teachers because only 9 per cent of teachers work in private sector schools.

(a) Draw a diagram to show the situation of the government facing trade unions in the market for teachers.

The government would like to see work place bargaining in teaching, with individual teachers negotiating with each school in which they are employed.

(b) Using a diagram, compare the wages and level of employment this system might create to the current system of national bargaining.

Applied economics

Wage determination

Wage structure by occupation

Economic theory would suggest that wage rates would be the same if all labour was homogeneous and all jobs possessed the same characteristics. In the real world workers are not identical. They differ, for instance, in where they are prepared to work, their hours of work and their levels of **human capital** (☞ unit 2). Jobs differ too. In particular, the marginal revenue product curve for each type of job is different.

For example, the average weekly earnings of a doctor in 1994 were £746. This compares with bar staff who earned on average £165 a week (Table 50.2). Neo-classical economic theory suggests that such differences are due to differences in the demand for and supply of different types of labour.

Table 50.2 *Real[1] gross weekly earnings[2] by selected occupation*

Great Britain					£ per week at April 1994 prices[1]	
	1971	1976	1981	1986	1991	1994
Waiter/waitress	105	150	138	151	161	157
Bar staff	116	143	143	160	153	165
Cleaner	110	174	169	179	181	180
Receptionist	113	128	135	153	173	182
Caretaker	159	191	179	196	213	220
Bricklayer/mason	198	244	225	235	248	252
Carpenter/joiner	203	236	223	236	260	261
Nurse	142	187	188	216	298	316
Social worker	202	228	246	264	303	332
Primary teacher	235	285	292	302	358	394
Secondary teacher	235	317	314	322	390	427
Mechanical engineer	322	365	375	423	493	511
Solicitor	347	379	367	418	590	569
Medical practitioner	499	488	550	592	669	746

1. Adjusted to April 1994 prices using the Retail Price Index.
2. At April each year. Full-time employees on adult rates whose pay was not affected in the survey period by absence.
Source: CSO, *Social Trends*, No.25, 1995.

On the supply side, there are potentially far more workers with the ability and training to become manual workers than non-manual workers. The manager could become the office cleaner, but the office cleaner could not necessarily become a successful manager. Not all workers are prepared to take on any particular job. Occupations which are unpleasant or dangerous, or where earnings can fluctuate greatly, are likely to attract fewer workers than others where the non-pecuniary (i.e. non-monetary) advantages are much greater. Hence, earnings in construction and mining are likely to be higher than average, all other things being equal, because of the danger of the job. In general, the larger the potential supply of labour to an occupation, the lower is likely to be the level of earnings.

On the demand side, non-manual jobs are likely to carry a higher marginal revenue product than manual jobs. Without an effective manager, a company may lose thousands and perhaps millions of pounds of potential revenue or suffer high costs of production. But the company could get by without an effective office cleaner. Hence professional workers in management and administration are paid more highly than workers in catering, cleaning and hairdressing because their revenue product is greater.

So far we have assumed that labour markets are perfectly competitive and that they are in equilibrium. In practice, many of the differences in wages between occupations may be accounted for by trade unions or monopsony employers. For instance, print workers in the 1980s saw their trade union power decline as employers, such as Times Newspapers, won a number of key industrial disputes.

Alternatively, the market may be in disequilibrium. In the 1980s, for instance, earnings in the shipbuilding industry were depressed as the industry declined. On the other hand, earnings in occupations related to computers have been buoyant over the past 15 years as the industry has expanded.

Changes in wage structure by occupation

Relative differences in wages between manual and non-manual workers have changed considerably since the late 1970s. Before then, the wages of manual and non-manual workers moved broadly in line with each other. In the 1980s and 1990s, however, the pay of manual workers has fallen behind those of non-manual workers as can be seen from Figure 50.4.

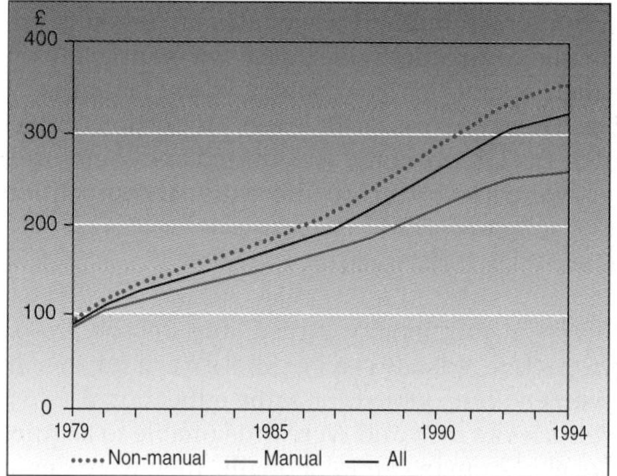

Source: adapted from *Employment Gazette*, December 1994.
Figure 50.4 *Average gross weekly earnings, full time employees on adult rates*

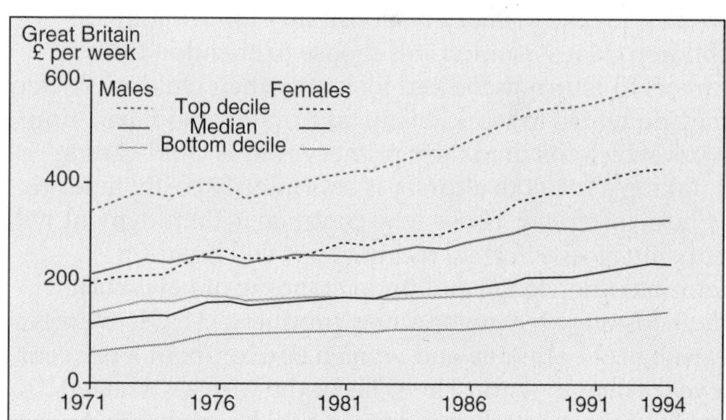

1. Adjusted to April 1994 prices using the Retail Price Index.
2. At April each year. Full time employees on adult rates whose pay was not affected in the survey period by absence.
Source: adapted from Employment Department.
Figure 50.5 *Real[1] gross weekly earnings[2]: by gender*

The same story is true of unskilled workers relative to skilled workers. Figure 50.5 shows that whilst the top 10 per cent of workers enjoyed wage increases of over 50 per cent between 1979 and 1994, the bottom 10 per cent of workers received almost no wage increases. In occupational terms, as Table 50.2 shows, whilst the pay of doctors went up 36 per cent and that of solicitors by 55 per cent between 1981 and 1994, that of a carpenter/joiner went up only 11 per cent and of bar staff by 15 per cent.

There are two likely reasons why the earnings of manual

workers and unskilled workers are lagging behind. First, automation has led to a sharp fall in demand for these workers. Whilst it is true that the supply of these workers has also fallen as the workforce becomes more skilled, supply and demand have remained broadly in balance leading to little or no changes in real wage rates. The demand for skilled workers, on the other hand, has grown at a faster rate than supply, pushing up their real wage rates as a consequence.

The second possible reason for the stagnation of real wage earnings of the low paid is that many of these workers are now in direct competition with workers from the Third World. In manufacturing, unskilled textile workers in Yorkshire have to compete with unskilled textile workers in India. If wage rates in Yorkshire are too high, textile companies will shut down completely or move their operations to a country where labour is cheaper. Twenty years ago, a lower proportion of the output of the UK economy was traded and therefore UK workers were less subject to international competition.

Wage structure by gender

Females have traditionally earned considerably less than men. Economic reasons can be put forward for this. In the past, women were denied the same educational opportunities as men and were thus unable to acquire the same level of human capital. Equally, they were denied access to all but a narrow range of jobs.

Today, possibly the most important factor causing inequality in earnings between the sexes in the UK is the unequal burden of child care. It is still almost universal for women to take primary responsibility for bringing up children. Many women still choose to abandon their careers to return home and look after their children. When they do return to work, many take up low paid, part time work which fits in to their primary role as child-carers.

Taking a break in a career is enormously costly in terms of human capital. Those who continue in employment will not only receive formal training, but will build up informal knowledge and understanding of new work methods, new technology, new products, etc. On average, earnings of both men and women rise by about 3 per cent a year when in work. The skills of the woman who left work 10 years ago in comparison will be outdated. A woman's earning potential drops by 3 per cent a year for every year a woman is out of the labour force (M J Artis, 1989). The time when women choose to leave their careers is also important. It is traditional for workers to make their most important career progressions between the ages of 20 and 40, precisely the time when many women are out of the workforce. Employers respond to the less stable work patterns of women by offering less training to female employees. There is also evidence to suggest that, despite legislation, women are passed over in promotion.

Table 50.3 shows the relative weekly earnings of men and women. During the 1970s, the gap between male and female earnings narrowed. This was mainly the result of the Equal Pay Act 1970 and the Sex Discrimination Act 1975. The 1970 Act made it illegal to pay women less than men if they were doing the same job. The 1975 Act

Table 50.3 *Wage relativities by gender: ratio of female to male gross weekly earnings, full time employees*

	1971	1976	1981	1986	1991	1994
Manual employees	.53	.62	.62	.62	.63	.65
Non-manual employees	.52	.61	.61	.60	.63	.65
All employees	.57	.66	.67	.67	.70	.72

Source: adapted from CSO, *Social Trends*.

guaranteed women equality of opportunity. Table 50.3 would suggest that this was a once and for all gain. Relative earnings then hardly changed for a decade. From the mid-1980s, however, there has been another substantial gain by women. It could be that the relatively tight labour market created by the Lawson boom of 1986-88 forced employers to increase the relative pay they offered to their female employees. This gain was then not lost when unemployment rose back to 3 million in the recession of 1990-92.

A number of other factors affect the pay of women. Earnings of women are lower than those of men simply because women work shorter hours. In 1994, women worked on average 37.6 hours per week compared to 41.6 hours for men. Even so, in 1994, hourly rates of pay averaged only 79 per cent those of men. Many occupations, such as secretarial work, are dominated by females, and it could be that the marginal revenue product of occupations traditionally filled by women is lower than that of occupations which are traditionally male dominated. Women are slightly less likely to be members of trade unions, and this could affect their relative pay. However, discrimination is still likely to play a part in the determination of female rates of pay.

Wages by ethnic group

Workers from ethnic minorities tend to earn less than white workers. Table 50.4 shows that the hourly rate of pay of ethnic workers is only 92 per cent that of white workers' pay. This figure, however, conceals large differentials. The average hourly rate of pay of black women workers, for instance, is 6 per cent more than that of white women workers, whilst males of mixed origin are paid 3 per cent more than white males per hour on average. On the other hand, the hourly rate of pay of workers of Pakistani or Bangladeshi origin is considerably less than that of white workers. Overall, women workers from ethnic minority groups earn almost the same hourly rates as those of white women workers. The difference in overall hourly earnings between white and ethnic minority groups comes almost entirely from differences in male earnings.

There are a number of factors which cause male workers from ethnic minority groups to earn less on average than white workers. First, workers from ethnic minorities, on average, tend to be less well qualified than white workers. This means workers from ethnic minorities are more likely to be in manual jobs than white workers, and also less likely to be in managerial posts. Second, workers from ethnic minorities are more likely to work in distribution (including shops), hotels, catering and repairs, and in the health services than white workers. In 1993, for instance, 29 per cent of all ethnic minority workers worked in the distribution, hotel, catering and repair industries compared to only 17 per cent of white workers. Some jobs in these industries are well paid, such as being a doctor, but there is an above average proportion of low paid jobs. So the choice of which sector to work in may account for some of the difference in earnings. Third, where workers live may affect their wage rates. A disproportionate number of workers from ethnic minorities compared to white workers live in the South East, particularly Greater London. Given that wages in the South East are higher than the average for the UK, this should reduce the differential between ethnic minority workers and white workers. However, to counter-balance this, a disproportionate number of jobs in distribution, hotels, catering and repairs are found in the South East. So workers from ethnic minorities are more likely to work in low paid jobs in this high pay region than white workers, helping to account for the wage differentials. Finally, there is evidence that pay discrimination against workers from ethnic minorities takes place, despite Equal Pay legislation. There is also discrimination against ethnic minority workers when it comes to recruitment, selection, promotion and training.

Table 50.4 *Average hourly pay rates of full time employees by ethnic groups and sex; Great Britain, average of Winter 1993-94 to Autumn 1994 (not seasonally adjusted)*

(£)

Ethnic origin	All	Men	Women
Average hourly pay			
All origins	7.42	7.97	6.39
White	7.44	8.00	6.40
Ethnic minority groups	6.82	7.15	6.31
Black	6.92	7.03	6.77
Indian	6.70	7.29	5.77
Pakistani/Bangladeshi	5.39	5.47	5.15
Mixed/Other origins	7.70	8.45	6.77
Average hourly pay of ethnic minority groups as a percentage of that of the white population			
Ethnic minority groups	92	89	99
Black	93	88	106
Indian	90	91	90
Pakistani/Bangladeshi	72	68	81
Mixed/Other origins	103	106	106

Source: Department of Employment, *Employment Gazette*, June 1995.

DATA QUESTION

Regional earnings and employment

Table 50.5 Average weekly earnings, April 1994

	All industries and services	
	Males	Females
United Kingdom	361.0	260.8
North	327.8	237.0
Yorkshire & Humberside	329.5	238.4
East Midlands	325.0	230.5
East Anglia	334.8	241.6
South East	419.4	301.1
Greater London	467.3	336.5
Rest of South East	380.0	268.0
South West	343.9	245.4
West Midlands	336.2	236.5
North West	343.9	243.6
England	367.0	264.6
Wales	320.9	239.0
Scotland	335.6	244.1
Northern Ireland	319.2	236.7

Source: adapted from CSO, *Regional Trends*, 1995.

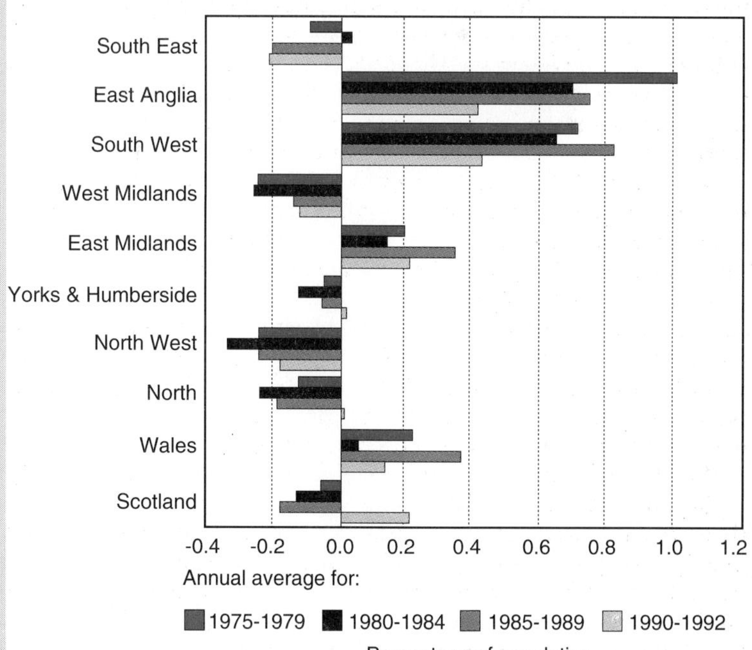

1. Net migration (immigrants minus emigrants) as a proportion of the mid-year population. Only migration flows *between* British regions are included.

Source: adapted from *Employment Gazette*, February 1995.

Figure 50.6 *Average net migration rates by standard region*[1]*: Great Britain*

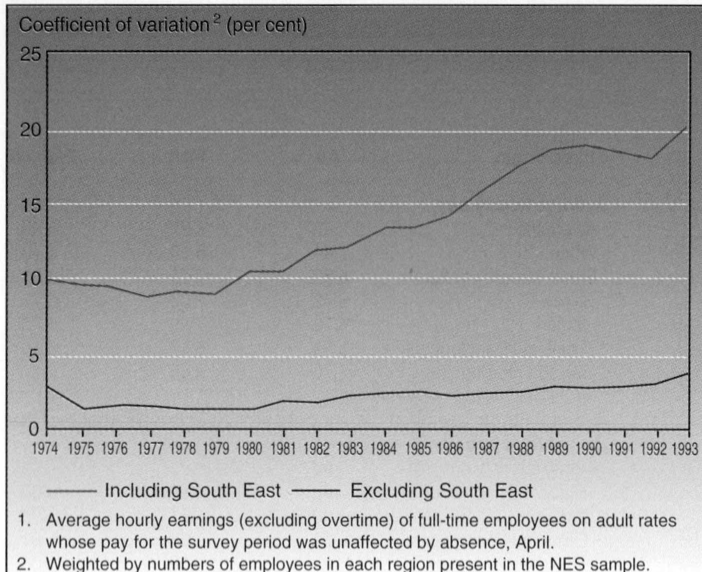

Source: adapted from *Employment Gazette*, February 1995.

Figure 50.7 *Regional dispersion of average hourly earnings of full-time employees[1]; Great Britain, 1974-1993*

Table 50.6 *Cost of living comparison between regions 1993: average weekly spending on housing and fuel, light and power*

	Housing	Fuel, light and power
£ per week		
United Kingdom	44.9	13.2
North	36.9	13.0
Yorkshire & Humberside	38.8	13.1
East Midlands	42.3	13.6
East Anglia	44.1	12.6
South East	58.6	13.2
Greater London	61.6	12.3
Rest of South East	57.0	13.7
South West	43.0	12.8
West Midlands	36.5	12.7
North West	41.1	13.2
Wales	39.2	13.9
Scotland	35.4	13.5
Northern Ireland[1]	25.1	16.3

1. Northern Ireland data are calculated from an enhanced sample, but the United Kingdom figures are calculated from the main Family Expenditure Survey sample.
Source: adapted from CSO, *Regional Trends*.

Table 50.7 *Employees in employment by industry and gender, 1994*

Percentages

	Agriculture Forestry, fishing (0)	Energy & water supply (1)	Metals minerals & chem-icals (2)	Metal goods, engineering & vehicles industries (3)	Other manufac-turing(4)	Total manufac-turing(2)-(4)	Const-ruction (5)	Distribution hotels & catering, repairs (6)	Transport & commun-icaton (7)	Banking, fina-nce, insurance, business servi-ces & leasing (8)	Public administr-ation & other services (9)	All industries, UK	All industries & services (thousands)
1994 Males													
United Kingdom	1.8	2.2	4.0	13.4	10.3	27.7	6.8	19.4	8.5	12.3	21.1	100	10,911
North	1.6	3.3	7.1	14.2	10.8	32.1	8.6	16.5	7.6	8.6	21.7	100	553
Yorkshire & Humberside	1.8	2.3	6.7	12.7	13.4	32.8	8.1	19.0	8.0	9.1	18.8	100	928
East Midlands	2.2	2.1	4.6	17.0	16.4	38.1	6.8	18.9	6.7	7.6	17.6	100	766
East Anglia	4.1	2.5	2.7	12.7	12.9	28.2	6.6	19.5	9.2	10.4	19.5	100	403
South East	0.9	1.8	2.1	10.0	7.6	19.7	5.5	20.7	10.5	18.5	22.5	100	3,504
South West	3.2	1.8	3.0	13.9	9.8	26.7	5.1	22.2	6.8	12.2	22.0	100	840
West Midlands	1.6	1.6	6.0	23.6	9.7	39.2	6.7	18.6	6.7	9.1	16.5	100	1,017
North West	0.9	2.0	4.8	15.2	12.4	32.4	6.8	19.1	8.7	10.1	20.1	100	1,139
Wales	2.9	2.7	8.2	13.0	10.9	32.0	7.1	17.1	7.1	8.3	22.6	100	487
Scotland	2.2	4.1	2.4	12.0	9.2	23.7	11.1	17.9	8.3	9.5	23.1	100	996
Northern Ireland	5.9	1.9	3.1	8.5	12.6	24.2	6.9	17.6	5.9	7.1	30.5	100	276
1994 Females													
United Kingdom	0.6	0.7	1.4	3.6	7.2	12.2	1.3	23.9	2.8	12.8	45.7	100	10,651
North	0.3	0.9	1.5	3.4	8.5	13.4	1.2	25.3	2.0	8.2	48.6	100	531
Yorkshire & Humberside	0.5	0.6	1.7	2.8	9.3	13.7	1.5	25.4	2.3	10.4	45.6	100	915
East Midlands	0.8	0.5	1.8	3.7	14.7	20.2	1.3	23.9	2.2	9.0	42.2	100	748
East Anglia	1.9	0.7	0.7	3.6	8.0	12.3	1.2	26.0	2.2	11.6	44.1	100	390
South East	0.5	0.7	1.2	3.1	4.8	9.2	1.4	22.1	3.8	17.8	44.5	100	3,389
South West	1.0	0.7	0.7	3.3	5.1	9.0	1.2	27.4	2.1	13.4	45.2	100	853
West Midlands	0.7	0.6	2.2	7.1	6.7	16.0	1.4	23.5	2.5	10.7	44.5	100	943
North West	0.4	0.7	1.8	3.4	7.8	13.0	1.2	25.0	2.8	10.6	46.3	100	1,140
Wales	0.7	0.8	1.4	4.9	7.4	13.7	1.1	24.3	1.9	8.4	49.2	100	478
Scotland	0.4	0.8	1.1	3.4	7.5	12.0	1.4	24.0	2.4	11.1	48.0	100	990
Northern Ireland	0.8	0.3	0.6	2.1	9.8	12.5	0.8	20.9	1.6	7.7	55.3	100	274

Source: adapted from CSO, *Regional Trends*.

Table 50.8 *School leavers' examination achievements[1]: by gender and region, 1991-92*

Percentages

	1 or more A levels[2] (or SCE highers)		GCSEs[3] or SCE O/standard (no A levels or SCE highers)		No graded results[4]		All leavers (=100%) (thousands)	
	Males	Females	Males	Females	Males	Females	Males	Females
United Kingdom	27.8	31.4	65.2	62.6	7.1	6.0	323.9	312.0
North	17.6	24.7	74.7	69.4	7.7	5.9	18.2	18.0
Yorkshire & Humberside	23.5	26.6	68.6	65.9	7.9	7.5	28.2	25.5
East Midlands	22.8	26.7	72.5	69.0	4.6	4.3	21.2	20.7
East Anglia	33.1	26.2	62.0	67.9	5.0	5.9	9.3	7.6
South East	31.5	35.5	63.3	59.5	5.3	5.0	92.7	89.5
South West	27.1	29.2	69.4	68.5	3.4	2.3	27.8	25.5
West Midlands	25.7	27.2	67.8	68.1	6.5	4.7	31.9	30.3
North West	24.8	24.4	68.2	68.5	7.0	7.0	35.0	37.8
England	27.0	29.6	67.1	65.1	5.8	5.3	264.3	254.8
Wales[5]	22.8	28.3	63.0	61.4	14.2	10.4	16.7	15.9
Scotland	36.9	47.2	51.9	44.2	11.2	8.7	30.8	29.8
Northern Ireland	28.0	36.7	57.2	54.9	14.7	8.5	12.0	11.4

1. Excludes results in further education.
2. Two AS levels are counted as equivalent to one A level.
3. Includes equivalent grades at GCE and CSE and leavers with 1 AS level.
4. Some of these pupils will have achieved passes in other examinations, eg BTEC, RSA, Certificate of Education (in Wales) and SCOTVEC (in Scotland).
5. Includes leavers from maintained and independent schools but not special schools.

Source: CSO, *Social Trends*, No.25, 1995.

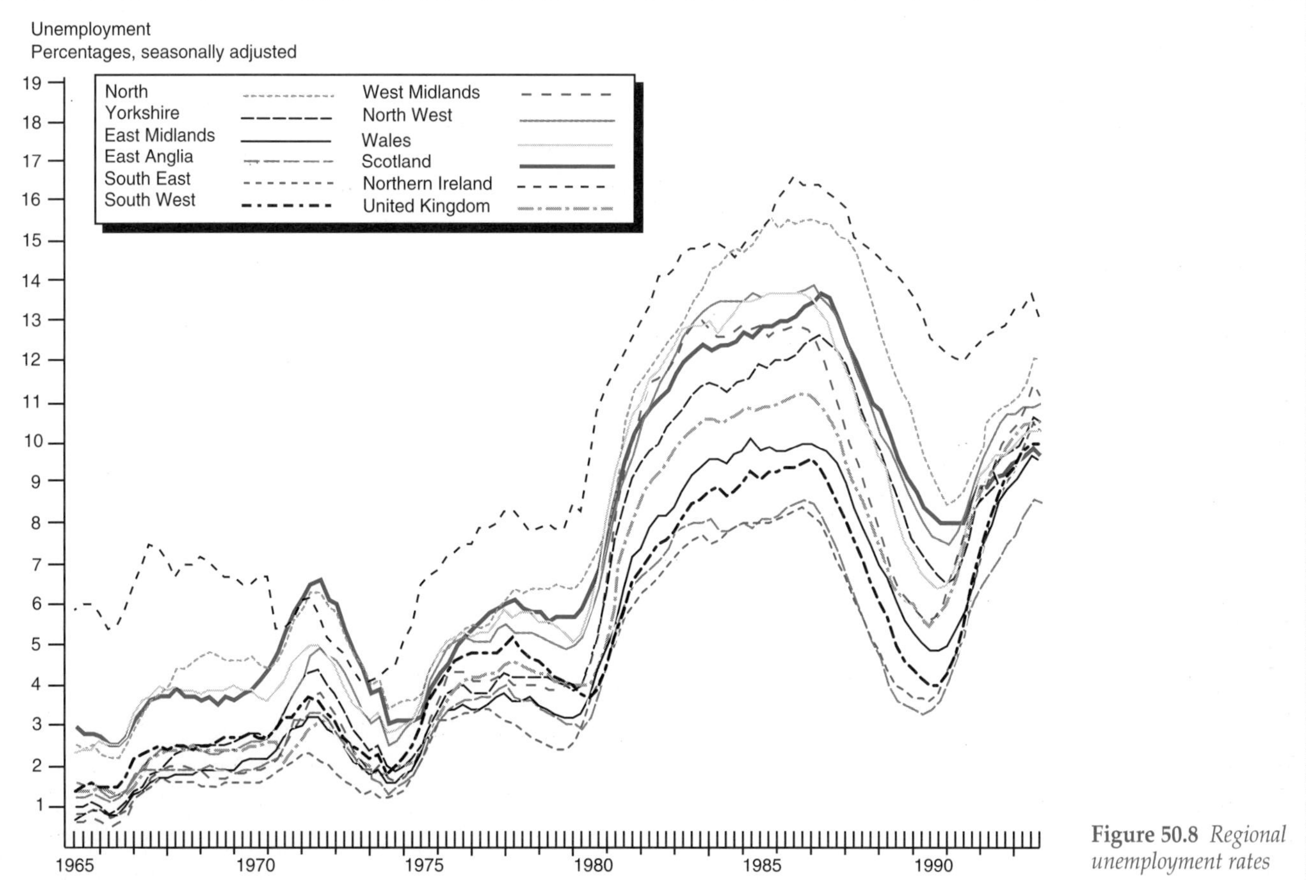

Figure 50.8 *Regional unemployment rates*

1. **Outline the main differences in wages and employment between the regions in the UK.**
2. **What economic factors might account for differences in average earnings between regions?**
3. **(a) Suggest what would have to happen in the future if regional earnings differentials were to be reduced.**
   (b) To what extent do the data suggest that regional earnings differentials will narrow?

Trade unions

Summary

1. Trade unions exist to further the interests of their own members.
2. Neo-classical economic theory predicts that trade unions increase wages but create unemployment in perfectly competitive industries.
3. Theory also predicts that a monopsonist buyer of labour will employ more workers and pay them a higher wage rate when bargaining with a union than in a situation where it is bargaining with a large number of individual employees.
4. Trade unions will be more powerful the larger the trade union membership, the less elastic the demand for labour and the greater the profitability of the employer.
5. Trade unions will reduce efficiency in a perfectly competitive economy, but they may increase efficiency if the economy is imperfectly competitive.
6. Trade unions may reduce costs of production for firms if they facilitate change and perform some of the tasks, such as personnel management, which management would otherwise have to undertake.

Collective bargaining

A trade union is an organisation of workers who combine together to further their own interests. Within a company organisation, an individual worker is likely to be in a relatively weak bargaining position compared to his or her employer. The employer possesses far greater knowledge about everything from safety standards to the profitability of the firm than an individual worker. Moreover, the loss of an individual worker to a firm is likely to be far less significant than the loss of his or her job to the employee.

So workers have organised themselves in unions to bargain collectively. Instead of each individual worker bargaining with the firm on a wide range of wage and employment issues, workers elect or appoint representatives to bargain on their behalf. From an economic viewpoint, trade unions act as monopoly suppliers of labour.

Trade unions play a very controversial role in the economy. Critics argue that trade unions, by forcing up wages and resisting changes in working practices, create unemployment. Neo-classical economic theory supports this view, assuming that factor markets are perfectly competitive. However, as will be argued below, it also suggests that trade unions increase employment if a trade union represents workers in a firm which is the sole buyer of labour.

Competitive industries

Trade unions act to further the interests of their members. One of the key ways in which they do this is to press for

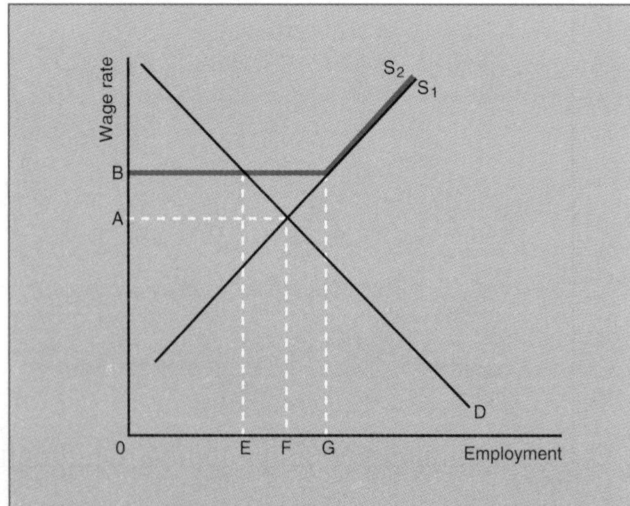

Figure 51.1 *Trade unions in a competitive market*
The entry of a trade union to a competitive factor market is likely to 'kink' the supply curve of labour. OB is the union negotiated wage rate in an industry. Employment will fall from OF to OE whilst wages rates will rise from OA to OB.

higher wages. In economic terms, they attempt to fix a minimum price for the supply of labour. This produces a kinked supply curve.

In Figure 51.1 the non-union demand and supply curves for labour in an industry are D and S_1 respectively. A union agreement to raise wages from the free market wage of OA to the unionised wage rate of OB means that employers in the industry cannot hire workers below a wage rate of OB. The supply curve therefore is perfectly elastic (i.e. horizontal) over the employment range OG. The union agreement does not prevent employers paying higher wages than the negotiated wage. Employers would need to pay higher wage rates if they wished to hire more workers than OG. Above OG the new supply curve S_2 is the same as the old supply curve S_1. The new equilibrium wage rate is OB, the wage rate that the union negotiated. However, employment in the industry falls from OF (the equilibrium in a non-unionised market) to OE.

Neo-classical micro-economic theory therefore suggests that trade unions increase wages for their members, but also cause unemployment in the industry. Wages would be lower and employment higher if the industry were non-unionised.

QUESTION 1 In early1993, Timex, whose core business is the manufacture of watches, decided that it had to stem the losses being made at its Dundee plant which manufactured circuit boards for computers. It cut staff, imposed a wage freeze and cut fringe benefits substantially. The workers came out on strike. The company responded by employing new workers, 'scab labour', who had to cross union picket lines. Several attempts at mediation between unions and management failed because the striking workers refused to accept the compromises negotiated on their behalf.

In June 1993, Timex announced that it was closing the plant. Although it had a full order book, and indeed had won new business since early 1993 which would have required almost doubling the workforce, the company said that it had been left 'financially exhausted' by the strike. Its employment of non-union labour with the old workers manning picket lines outside the factory had attracted worldwide negative publicity for Timex. With a pay freeze and reduced fringe benefits, estimated to amount to a 27 per cent pay cut by the unions, the factory was economically viable. But Timex was not prepared to run it on this basis if strikers were to continue to get publicity coverage. Neither was it prepared to give in to the strikers and allow the plant to be unprofitable.

'Trade unions raise wage levels in an industry but cause a loss of jobs.' Explain, using a diagram and the example of Timex, why this might be the case.

Trade unions vs monopsony employers

Many trade unions operate in factor markets where there are monopsony employers. A sole seller of labour (the trade union) faces a sole buyer of labour (the monopsonist).

Economic theory suggests that a trade union will increase both wages and employment compared to a factor market where a monopsony employer negotiates with a large number of individual employees. Figure 51.2 (a) shows the wage and employment levels in an industry with a monopsonist and many individual employees (☞ unit 50 for a full explanation of the graph). Employment is OA and the equilibrium wage rate is OE. Figure 51.2 (b) shows the entry of a trade union to the

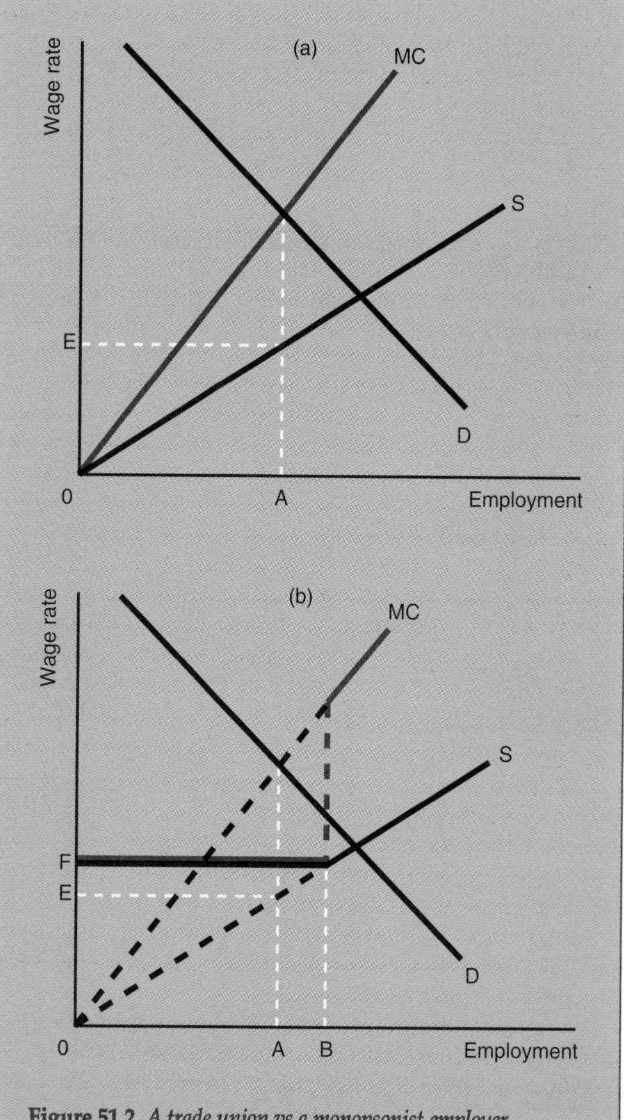

Figure 51.2 *A trade union vs a monopsonist employer*
A monopsonist facing a large number of employees in an industry will force wage rates down to OE and restrict employment to OA. The entry of a trade union to the industry which sets a minimum wage of OF will 'kink' the supply curve of labour and produce a discontinuity in the marginal cost curve for labour. The monopsonist has a profit incentive to hire extra workers so long as the marginal revenue product of labour, shown by the demand curve, is greater than the marginal cost of labour. Hence it will employ OB workers.

industry. Assume that the trade union forces the wage rate up to OF. This produces a kinked supply curve. The monopsonist cannot pay a wage rate lower than OF because of its union agreement. However, it is free to pay higher wage rates if it wishes to employ more than OB workers. This produces a kink in the marginal cost of labour to the firm. Up to OB, the marginal cost of labour is the same as the union negotiated wage rate. The employer can hire an extra unit of labour at that wage rate. If it employs more than OB workers, the wage rate will rise, resulting in a jump in marginal cost at OB. The monopsonist has a profit incentive to hire extra workers so long as the marginal revenue product of labour, shown by the demand curve, is greater than the marginal cost of labour. Hence it will employ OB workers.

Why should a monopsonist buy more labour at a higher wage rate from a union than it would otherwise? It should be remembered that a firm bases its decision on how much labour to hire not on the wage rate (the average cost of labour) but on the marginal cost of labour. It can be seen from Figure 51.2 that the marginal cost of unionised labour is lower between employment levels A and B than it would have been if labour had been non-unionised. In the former case it is flat at OF, whilst in the latter it is rising steeply above OF.

QUESTION 2

Table 51.1

£

Units of labour employed	Wage rate per worker		Marginal cost of employing 1 extra worker		Marginal revenue product of labour
	With no trade union	With a trade union	With no trade union	With a trade union	
2	4	8	4	8	16
3	5	8	6	8	14
4	6	8	8	8	12
5	7	8	10	8	10
6	8	8	12	8	8
7	9	9	14	14	6
8	10	10	16	16	4

The table shows wage rates, marginal employment costs and MRPs facing a monopsonist employer of labour.

(a) (i) What is the maximum number of workers the firm would employ if the labour force were non-unionised?
(ii) What would be the equilibrium wage rate?

(b) What is the maximum number of workers the firm would employ if workers belonged to a trade union and it had negotiated a minimum wage rate of £8?

(c) Explain why trade unions might increase rather than decrease the level of employment in an industry.

The power of trade unions

There are a variety of factors which make trade unions more or less powerful.

Trade union membership and militancy A union which has 100 per cent membership in an industry is likely to be stronger than a union which only represents 10 per cent of potential members. It could be argued that the RMT is far more powerful in the railway industry than the Transport and General Workers Union is in the hairdressing industry. Equally, unions are more likely to call for industrial action if union members are militant. The more militant the union membership, the more costly a dispute is likely to be for an employer.

The demand curve for labour is relatively inelastic A rise in wage rates will have far less impact upon employment in the industry if the demand for labour is

QUESTION 3

How would economic theory account for the strength and weakness of union power in these industries?

relatively inelastic than if it is elastic. Hence, there will be far less cost to the union of a wage rate increase in terms of lost membership and to its members in terms of lost employment (☞ unit 48 for a discussion of why the demand for labour might be inelastic).

Profitability of the employer A trade union is unlikely to be able to negotiate large wage increases with an employer on the verge of bankruptcy. It is likely to be in a stronger position with a highly profitable firm. This implies that trade unions will be stronger in monopolistic and oligopolistic industries, where firms are able to earn abnormal profit, than in perfectly competitive industries where only normal profit can be earned in the long run.

Efficiency

Neo-classical economic theory suggests that trade unions operating in competitive industries reduce employment levels and raise wage rates. If all industries but one were perfectly competitive then a trade union in that one industry would mean that the economy as a whole was not Pareto efficient (☞ unit 34).

However, most industries in the UK are imperfectly competitive. A trade union facing a monopsonist will redress the balance of power in the industry and lead to a level of employment and a wage rate which will be nearer to the free market price of labour. It could well be that the presence of a trade union increases economic efficiency in an imperfectly competitive market. Hence the effect of trade unions on economic efficiency depends on the structure of markets in an economy.

A further important argument needs to be considered. Some economists have suggested that trade unions raise economic efficiency because they lower costs of production to the firm. The trade union performs many of the functions of a personnel department within a firm. It deals with workers' problems and obviates the need for the firm to negotiate pay with each and every worker. More importantly, it can be a good vehicle for negotiating changes in working practices. A firm may wish to implement changes which will lead to less pleasant working conditions for its workers. Perhaps it wishes to increase the speed of the assembly line, or force workers to undertake a variety of tasks rather than just one. It may find it difficult to implement these changes on a non-unionised workforce because some workers may take unorganised industrial action or do their best to disrupt any changes being introduced. A union may help the firm to persuade workers that changes in working practices are in their own interest. The union will usually demand a price for this co-operation - higher wage rates for its members. But it still leads to an increase in economic efficiency because the firm is able to make higher profits whilst workers receive higher wage rates. According to this view, trade unions increase productivity in the economy.

QUESTION 4 It could be argued that there has been a revolution in working practices in the UK during the1980s. Many companies have reorganised the way in which workers perform tasks. One way of increasing flexibility is to organise the workforce into multi-skilled work groups, or 'hit squads' able to carry out a range of tasks as required. Examples include a deal made in 1988 at Ind Coope Burton Brewery, Burton-on-Trent which provided for the formation of teams within which allocation of work is based on competence. In return, team members were awarded higher pay. Also in 1988 an agreement was signed at an industry level between the British Printing Industry Federation and the National Graphical Association (NGA) trade union which provided for workers to 'carry out any of the duties within and between origination and printing room departments in accordance with the needs of production'. Another way of increasing flexibility is to make production line workers responsible for their own quality control instead of employing supervisors . For example, at Cameron Iron Works welders have been given theoretical and practical training and now do their own inspection.

Source: adapted from the *Employment Gazette*, August 1989.

(a) How might the changes described in the data increase efficiency?

(b) What are the possible advantages and disadvantages to workers of the changes outlined?

Key terms

Trade union mark-up - the difference between wage rates in a unionised place of work and the wage rate which would otherwise prevail in the absence of trade unions.

Closed shop - a place of work where workers must belong to a recognised trade union.

Applied economics

Trade unions

Trade unions in the UK have existed for over 200 years. In the early 19th century, trade unions were outlawed for being anti-competitive. By the early 20th century there were 2 million trade union members and, as Figure 51.3 shows, this rose to a peak of over 13 million in 1979.

Since 1979, there has been a sharp fall in the number of trade union members. By 1992 membership had fallen to 9 million. There are a number of possible explanations for this radical change in union membership.

- The recessions of 1980-82 and 1990-92 both created over one and half million unemployed. The unemployed tend to allow their union membership to lapse. So it is not surprising that the drop in union membership was highest in both of these periods. The lowest fall in membership over the period 1979-1992 occurred in the boom year of 1987.
- The 1980s and 1990s saw a radical restructuring of British industry. Employment in primary industries and manufacturing, both sectors which were very highly unionised, fell significantly. The new jobs that were created tended to be in the service sector of the economy, traditionally far less unionised than manufacturing. Moreover, most of the lost jobs were full-time whilst many of the new jobs were part-time. In autumn 1993, 39 per cent of all full-time workers were union members compared to only 21 per cent of part-time workers. Important too was that many jobs lost were traditionally male jobs and the new jobs created were traditionally female jobs. In Autumn 1993, 38 per cent of male workers were union members compared to 31 per cent for female workers.
- Since 1979, the government has shown a marked hostility to trade unions. This has affected the willingness of workers to join unions and increased the confidence of those employers attempting to reduce or eliminate trade union activity in their workplaces.
- A perceived loss of power of trade unions has made workers less willing to join.

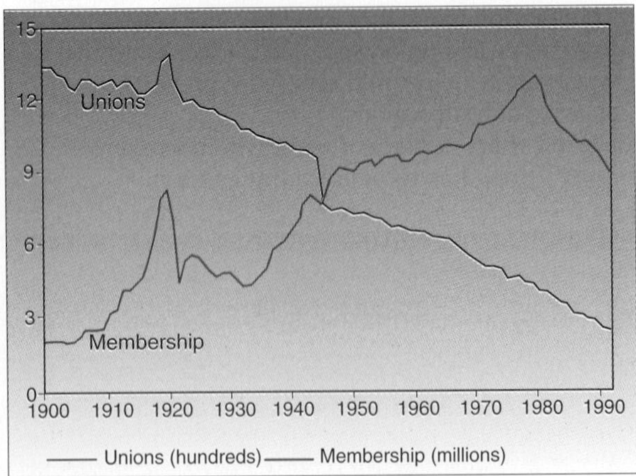

Source: adapted from *Employment Gazette*, June 1994.

Figure 51.3 *Trade union membership and number of unions*

The trade union mark-up

Economic theory suggests that trade unions will increase wage rates for their members by shifting the supply curve of labour upwards. Studies of the UK economy tend to confirm that such a MARK-UP, the difference between actual wage rates in unionised labour markets and the wage rate which would otherwise prevail in the absence of trade unions, is indeed present. Figure 51.4 is one estimate of the union mark-up over time. The trend suggests that the size of the mark-up is **cyclical** (☞ unit 67). When the economy is in boom and unemployment is falling, non-union wages tend to rise faster than union wages. Hence the mark-up falls. When the economy is in recession and unemployment is rising, non-union wages tend to rise more slowly than union wages. Hence the mark-up tends to rise.

The union mark-up varies from industry to industry. M Stewart (1983) found that the mark-up ranged from 18 per cent in shipbuilding to 2 per cent in electrical engineering. The results are shown in Table 51.2.

Table 51.2 *Estimate of the trade union mark-up by industry 1975*

Industry	Mark-up (%)
Shipbuilding and marine engineering	18.2
Paper, printing and publishing	11.4
Other manufacturing industries	10.9
Metal goods not elsewhere specified	10.7
Clothing and footwear	10.1
Chemicals and allied industries	9.6
Vehicles	9.6
Timber and furniture	9.1
Instrument engineering	8.6
Food, drink and tobacco	6.6
Metal manufacture	5.4
Mechanical engineering	4.1
Bricks, pottery, glass and cement	2.4
Electrical engineering	2.0

Source: M. Stewart (1983).

In another study, Blanchflower (1984) found that the mark-up for skilled workers was only 1 per cent but was 10 per cent for semi-skilled manual workers. Given that trade union power has declined since the study was made, and that fewer semi-skilled workers are now union members, this mark up for semi-skilled manual workers may well be less today. This might then be one cause of the relative decline in the earnings of low paid workers (☞ unit 50).

Sources of trade union power

It can be seen from Figure 51.4 that the mark-up rose from about 3.5 to 4 per cent in the early 1950s to between 5 and 6 per cent in the 1970s. The union mark up then broadly fell in the 1980s. What factors might determine the size of this union mark-up and why does the union mark-up vary from industry to industry?

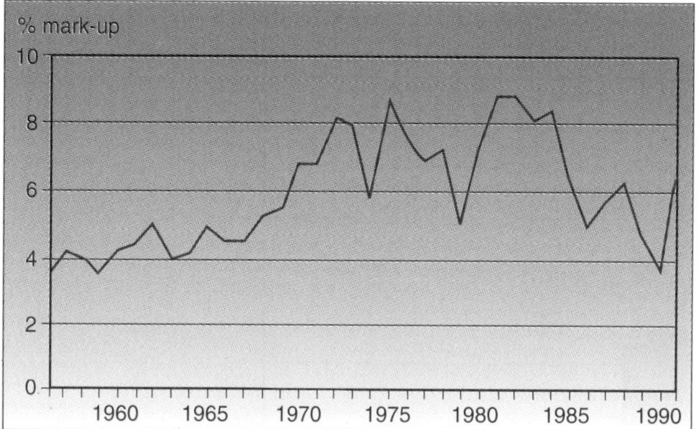

Source: adapted from Layard and Nickell (1986) and G Jones and G Taylor, *The UK Economy*, Weidenfeld and Nicolson, 1992.

Figure 51.4 *Estimated mark-up of union over non-union wages, 1956-91*

Union density Union density refers to the proportion of the workforce which belongs to a trade union. Figures 51.3 and 51.4 show that over the 1950s, 1960s and 1970s trade union membership has risen at the same time as the union mark-up. So the size of the mark-up may be linked to the percentage of workers belonging to a trade union. Indeed, the industries with a high union mark-up shown in Table 51.2, such as shipbuilding and printing, have traditionally been highly unionised. Many firms within these industries are CLOSED SHOPS. In a closed shop, all workers have to belong to a recognised trade union. Closed shops are commonly assumed to increase trade union power at the expense of the employer.

The decline of union membership in the 1980s may help to account for a decline in the union mark-up in the 1980s. The power of closed shops was also weakened in the 1980s. Legislation between 1980 and 1990 limited the power of trade unions to enforce closed shop agreements. Moreover, the decline in union membership directly led to a decline in the number of informal closed shops. Millward found that the number of manual workers covered by closed shop agreements fell from 3.7 million in 1984 to 0.5 million in 1990.

Union militancy The willingness of trade unions to take industrial action may be another factor influencing the size of the union mark-up. Industrial action may take a variety of forms, including strikes, work-to-rules, and overtime bans. The greater the willingness of unions to strike, the more costly industrial action will be to employers and therefore the more likely it is that they will concede high pay rises. In practice, it is difficult to measure the degree of union militancy and therefore it is difficult to gauge the degree of correlation between such militancy and the change in the union mark-up.

However, Figure 51.5 shows that there has been a broad fall in the number of working days lost in industrial disputes since the 1970s. Workers in the 1980s and 1990s have been less willing to take industrial action than in the 1970s. Again, this may help explain a fall in the union mark-up in the 1980s.

Collective bargaining Collective bargaining involves trade unions negotiating with employers. In the 1970s, large numbers of workers were covered by national agreements. Trade unions would negotiate with groups of employers representing a whole industry. In some cases, this would then be followed up by local bargaining at plant level where workers in an individual place of work would negotiate a deal based on the national agreement. In the 1980s and 1990s, the government has, through its policies, put pressure on employers to cease national collective bargaining. In fact, the government has encouraged firms to stop any form of collective bargaining. Trade union reforms have led to a number of firms de-recognising trade unions, i.e. ceasing to recognise their right to negotiate on behalf of their members. Instead, the government has encouraged individual bargaining. Performance related pay (☞ unit 48), for instance, is often linked to individual bargaining by an employee with an employer over salary levels. The ability to bargain collectively is at the heart of the power of a trade union to gain a mark-up for its members. With individual bargaining, the rate of pay should be set at the market clearing level, i.e. the mark-up should be zero. As a half-way house, the government has encouraged firms to negotiate on a local basis, plant by plant or region by region, for instance. This considerably reduces the ability of trade unions to carry out damaging industrial action.

The legislative background Unions have to work within a legal framework. Unions in the UK gained the right to organise in 1824 with the repeal of the Combination Acts. Their right to strike without being sued for damages by an employer was enshrined in the Industrial Disputes Act of 1906. During the 1960s, however, there was a growing feeling that trade unions and their members were using their power in a way which was damaging to the economy as a whole. The Labour government of 1964-1970 shelved plans to introduce trade union reforms in the face of trade union opposition, but Edward Heath's Conservative government of 1970-1974 did take action. The Industrial Relations Act (1971) was highly controversial, met substantial opposition from the trade union movement and failed to reduce their power effectively. It was repealed in 1974 when a new Labour government came into office and trade union rights were extended by various pieces of legislation in the following two years. The 1980s, arguably, saw a transformation in the climate of industrial relations in the UK. The Conservative government, instead of introducing large scale legislative reform, passed a number of acts each of which restricted union power at the margin. By the mid-1990s:

- secondary picketing (picketing by workers not involved in a dispute, e.g. miners picketing a school where the teachers are on strike in 'solidarity' with the teachers) had been made illegal;
- trade unions had to hold a secret ballot and gain a

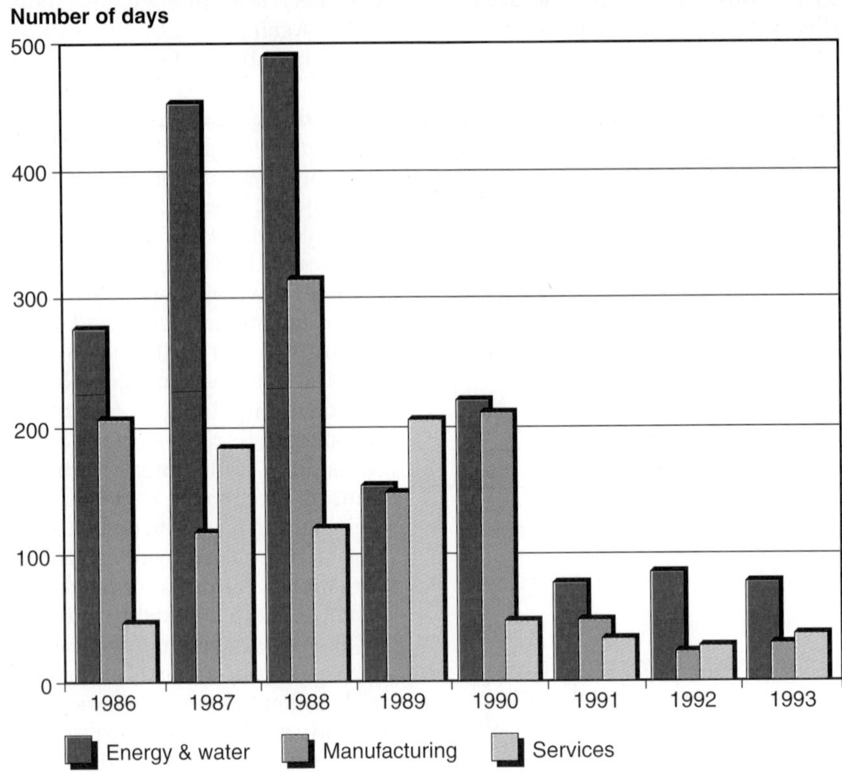

Source: adapted from *Employment Gazette*, June 1994.

Figure 51.5 *Working days lost per 1000 employees; broad industrial sectors (1986-93)*

majority of the votes cast to call an official strike;

- social security benefits were withdrawn from the dependants of striking workers;
- union officers had to be elected by secret ballots;
- closed shop agreements were restricted and greater opportunities were given for employees to opt out of closed shops.

Power within the union movement shifted. Before 1979, small groups of workers who were willing to take unofficial strike action and certain militant trade union leaders tended to dominate at least the newspaper headlines. The reforms of the 1980s and 1990s made it more costly and more difficult for workers to take widespread unofficial action. The power of trade union leaders to call strikes was curbed because workers now had to be balloted on strike action. Moreover, the democratisation of union voting procedures made it much more difficult for militant trade union leaders to get elected to key posts within trade unions.

The government also shrewdly distanced itself from the prosecution of trade unions. Previous legislation had concentrated on criminal law, where offenders were prosecuted by the state and could be fined or imprisoned. Government always risked creating trade union 'martyrs'. Much of the union legislation of the 1980s and 1990s concentrated on civil law. Employers were given powers to sue trade unions for breaches of the law. For instance, if a trade union calls a strike without holding a secret ballot, it is the employer affected which sues the trade union for damages. The government has no power to prosecute the union.

This means that trade unions risk losing considerable sums of money if they do not comply with the law, but individual trade union members cannot gain public sympathy by being sent to prison as they could in theory under the 1971 Industrial Relations Act.

Not only has the government considerably reduced the ability of trade unions and their members to take industrial action, it also, during the 1980s and 1990s, took a strong stance with public sector trade unions. The most important trade union defeat in the public sector was the breaking of the miners' strike in 1984-5.

Furthermore, the government completely cut off the trade union movement from decision making at a national level. This contrasted with the 1960s and 1970s when governments, both Labour and Conservative, would often consult trade union leaders before making important decisions.

It is perhaps not surprising then that the trade union mark-up declined in the 1980s. Some groups of workers, such as miners and print workers, saw substantial cuts in their mark-up as a result of employers winning bitter strikes in the mid-1980s. In the 1990s, the government is continuing to implement policies designed to produced a **flexible market** (☞ unit 52). In this flexible market, trade unions have little or no place. The whole emphasis is on workers moving from job to job as demand requires, negotiating individually, not collectively with employers. Trade unions are likely to continue to lose membership for some time to come.

Banks talk tough over pay as profits improve

Pay negotiations in Britain's banks are turning out to be as tough as any held in recent years, in spite of improving bank profits.

Recent pay offers suggest many banking staff can expect wage increases below the current 2.9 per cent rate of inflation.

Mr Ed Sweeney, deputy general secretary of Bifu, the banking union, said yesterday: 'It is monstrous that employers in the banking sector should be proposing to pay their staff such small rises given what is likely to be the size of their profits for 1994.'

Five years of drastic upheaval in the sector have seen staff numbers cut by nearly a quarter and led to the closure of hundreds of branch offices. The spread of cash machines and widespread automation inside banks has made an enormous impact on the organisation of work.

But most banking staff cannot expect either a respite in the pace of change or higher pay deals. The British Bankers' Association said: 'Many banks may have gone through most of their restructuring but they are still under competitive pressures to cut their costs.'

Improvements in bank profits are unlikely to be sufficient to allow banks to meet the pay expectations of their surviving staff.

The mood of some of those staff will be clear today when the results of dispute ballots are announced at two of the country's smaller banks.

Clydesdale Bank yesterday imposed a performance-related pay offer on its 4,000 staff, who are demanding 6.75 per cent. The move will add an estimated 3.13 per cent to the bank's pay bill and bring increases of 3 per cent to 7 per cent for an estimated 90 per cent of staff.

Mr Keith Brookes, the union's assistant secretary, said: 'These contemptuous tactics are typical of the way they treat their staff - with utter contempt.'

Bifu has urged its members at Clydesdale - just over half the staff - to take part in one-day strikes.

Last-minute negotiations in Leeds at Yorkshire Bank were adjourned yesterday, on the eve of a ballot of staff who have also been called on to take industrial action.

They have rejected a 4.4 per cent pay and performance package. But if the ballot shows a majority favour industrial action, it seems possible the deal will be improved.

Wage negotiations are also likely to prove difficult at the main clearing banks this year. Barclays has offered a 2.75 per cent performance-related rise for most of its 50,000 non-managerial staff with an added £200 for 4,000 staff on the lowest grades as a way of improving recruitment.

Barclays says more money for staff will be coming from individual bonuses and profit sharing. The bank's profits for last year are expected to exceed £2bn. The unions claim it should be more generous in its bargaining.

They point to the enormous changes that have taken place at Barclays since 1991 with cuts of more than 18,000 staff as productivity has improved through the introduction of new operational methods, wider use of new technology and centralisation of key functions such as securities.

This year Barclays intends to extend opening hours and introduce more flexible working in its branches and this will add to pressures on staff. In its response to Barclay's offer, Bifu has warned the bank about the 'low morale and disillusionment with the bank as an employer' among staff.

Talks are continuing at National Westminster, where in its initial offer management has admitted many branch staff will not be receiving a basic increase at all, and many must expect a rise of less than the inflation rate.

Mr Martin Gray, NatWest's chief executive, has already warned staff that 1995 will be a 'tough year' with intensive pressure on costs.

Next week Lloyds is expected to give its response to pay demands. Its staff want a 5 per cent improvement in salaries with a minimum rise of £500. Profits, to be announced tomorrow, are forecast to show an improvement on last year's £1bn to £1.3bn.

Pay talks at Midland have not yet started but the bank has already indicated that it wants to introduce performance-related pay for all staff grades this year.

Source: the *Financial Times*, 9.2.1995.

1. **What is the role of a trade union? Give examples from the passage to illustrate your answer.**
2. **To what extent were banking trade unions in a strong position in 1995 to negotiate a pay increase? Use demand and supply diagrams to illustrate your answer.**
3. **In what ways are the banks seeking to reduce the power of unions in the workplace?**

unit 52 Labour market failure

Summary

1. In a perfectly competitive labour market, there is no unemployment, no discrimination and market forces allocate workers to their highest paid occupations.
2. In practice, there are many examples of market failure in labour markets.
3. One major cause of labour market failure in the UK is the lack of mobility of labour, in turn caused principally by failure in the housing market and by a lack of skills amongst workers.
4. In segmented labour markets, the formal sector is unlikely to make short term adjustments to unemployment and hence labour markets may be prevented from clearing.
5. Trade unions and monopsonist employers, such as government, may reduce employment in the market. So too might government policy.
6. Governments attempt to correct labour market failure in a variety of ways, including minimum wage legislation and equal pay legislation. These may lead to an increase in wages for some workers but may also lead to unemployment for others.

Efficiency, equity and market failure

An economy where all markets are perfectly competitive is Pareto efficient (☞ unit 34). All labour markets will clear. Everyone who wants a job at the going wage rate is able to obtain one and therefore there is no unemployment. There is perfect factor mobility and therefore there can be no regional or sectoral unemployment. The market mechanism will allocate workers to their highest value occupations, ensuring that total output in the economy is maximised.

In a real modern industrialised economy, few markets are perfectly competitive. There are many instances of market failure and this is true not just in the goods market (☞ unit 35) but also in labour markets. Market failure can be judged against a number of criteria of efficiency including:

- full employment - the extent to which the market mechanism provides jobs for those who wish to work;
- maximum labour productivity - the extent to which the potential, the talents and the skills of workers in jobs are fully utilised in an economy.

Market failure can also be judged against different criteria of equity:

- equal opportunities - the extent to which all groups in society including women, the young, the elderly and those from ethnic minorities are not discriminated against in the labour market;
- wage differentials - the extent to which individual workers receive a 'fair' wage for the work they do.

Causes of labour market failure

There are a considerable number of ways in which labour markets are imperfect.

Mobility of labour In a perfect labour market, there is complete mobility of labour. Workers are free at no cost to themselves, to move jobs between industries and between regions. In practice, there are major obstacles to mobility.

- Many workers have job-specific skills. For instance, a teacher could not easily become a manager. A manager could not easily become a concert pianist. A concert pianist could not easily become a chef. When industries, such as the steel industry or the shipbuilding industry, shrink as they did in the 1970s and 1980s in the UK, redundant skilled workers in these industries find it difficult to find any employment except unskilled, low paid jobs. Industrial training by firms and by government favours young workers. So older workers find it difficult to move from industry to industry, even if they so wish.
- Knowledge is imperfect in the labour market, particularly in occupations where there is a long tradition of labour immobility. There are high SEARCH COSTS for workers and employers in finding out about employment opportunities. These search costs include time spent looking for jobs, or job applicants, and money costs such as travel, postage and advertisements. The higher the search costs, the less likely a search will take place and the less labour mobility there will be.
- Workers are not just workers. They belong to families and local communities. They take a pride in their area or in the skills they have acquired over a long period of time. Many people prefer not to move round the country in pursuit of a job or a career. They prefer to remain unemployed or stay in a job which is not particularly rewarding rather than move.
- The housing market can also be a major barrier to mobility. In the UK, the rented sector declined in importance in the post-war period (☞ unit 4). Today, most rented property is owned by local authorities or housing associations and is available mainly to low income families. Long waiting lists mean that workers in higher unemployment areas such as Scotland cannot move to lower unemployment areas such as the South East and secure family accommodation at a low rent. Young single workers are better catered for because there is a relatively plentiful supply of cheap low quality bed-sit/flat accommodation available nationally. Private good quality family accommodation is available in small quantities but at such high rents that it is only affordable by workers on above average

incomes. Most homes, however, are now owner occupied. In the 1980s, this caused mobility problems because a large price differential opened up between the South and the rest of the country. Home owners in, say, Yorkshire couldn't afford to move to jobs in, say, London because they couldn't afford to buy a house. From late 1988, a new problem arose. House prices started to fall sharply and the number of sales collapsed. Home owners found they couldn't sell their houses to move to a new job elsewhere. Many also found they had **negative equity** in their homes, i.e. because of a fall in house prices, they owed more in mortgage than the current market value of the house. They then couldn't afford to sell their house because they would have had to pay the balance between the mortgage and the sale price to the building society or bank providing the mortgage. This problem was particularly acute in the South of England. Consequently, many workers became reluctant to take new jobs elsewhere in the country.

QUESTION 1 A survey published in 1993 by the CBI and Black Horse Relocation Services suggested that employee resistance to job relocation was growing. Nearly 40 per cent of the 251 companies surveyed said a working spouse 'represented a key inhibitor to relocation'. Ms Sue Shortland, head of the Confederation of British Industry's relocation group, said: 'The issue of the working partner will increase with more women working and more dual-income families.' She pointed out that it was not only the temporary loss of income that caused problems but also the damage to the partner's career, promotion and income potential.

A third mentioned concern was children's education and just more than a quarter of the survey sample quoted family ties and roots as reasons for reluctance to move with the company.

The current property price slump is the most serious barrier to relocation. As many as 44 per cent of the sample said inability to sell their home inhibited them from being moved to another part of the country by their employer. When asked how employees' needs for relocation support would change in the next three years, 10 per cent of companies mentioned the property slump whilst a further 7 per cent discussed negative equity problems.

Source: adapted from the *Financial Times*, 12.1.1995.

(a) What barriers to labour mobility were highlighted by the 1993 survey?
(b) Explain why labour immobility can lead to inefficiency in the economy.

Trade unions and monopsony employers It is argued that trade unions and monopsony employers create unemployment in the market. A full explanation of this was given in units 50 and 51.

Segmented labour markets Some economists have argued that labour markets are segmented so that there is little movement of labour from one market to another. One version of this argument is the DUAL LABOUR MARKET HYPOTHESIS. In the formal, primary or planning sector of the economy, workers, often unionised, are employed by large employers such as oligopolistic or monopoly firms or by government. Workers in the formal sector tend to be better qualified and better paid. In the informal, secondary or market sector, workers, mainly non-unionised, are employed by small firms or are self-employed. These workers tend to be low-skilled or unskilled workers on low pay.

In the formal sector, workers are seen as important assets by their employers. They are trained and are expected to pursue a life-long career in their occupation. They are seen as reliable, dependable and loyal. In return for these qualities, firms are prepared to give a complete remuneration package, including not just pay, but also benefits such as pension schemes, sickness benefit and paid holidays. At times, this package may be far in excess of the equilibrium wage rate (i.e. the firm could employ workers at far lower wages). However, reducing wages to take advantage of short term weaknesses in the labour market would be counter-productive in the long run. It might lead to lower morale, greater uncertainty and lower productivity amongst existing staff. If workers are brought in from outside the company, it may take time for new staff to become familiar with often complex work routines and there may be friction between these outsiders and existing company staff. Reducing wages in the short term may also deter young people, who see that wages can be volatile, from entering the industry.

In the informal sector, workers are expected to be mobile. Job security is low. Training is minimal. Workers are not expected to stay with their employers and hence little is provided in the form of extra benefits, such as sickness benefits or pension schemes.

If the economy is in fact divided into these two sectors, there are important implications for unemployment and discrimination. Market economists argue that unemployment in an industry can only be a short term phenomenon because wages will fall to clear the market. However, employers do not react to unemployment by cutting wages in the formal sector of the economy. On the contrary, workers may continue to receive pay rises in line with their career expectations. In the informal sector, there will be wage cuts which will expand employment. Overall it will take much longer for the economy to return to full employment because only the informal sector behaves in the way economic theory suggests. What is more, the process of adjustment will lead to widening income differentials. Whilst workers in the formal sector will be receiving pay rises, those in the informal sector will receive wage cuts. So the burden of adjustment falls disproportionately hard on those most likely to receive low wages.

For a variety of reasons discussed below, women and those from ethnic minorities tend to form a much larger percentage of the workforce in the informal sector of the economy than in the formal sector. Hence, this dual economy reinforces discrimination against these groups.

QUESTION 2

Table 52.1 *Average earnings, inflation and unemployment, 1990-1993*

	1990	1993
Average earnings 1990 = 100		
Electricity, gas, other energy and water supply	100	122.2
Food, drink and tobacco (manufacture)	100	125.0
Education and health services	100	120.2
Motor vehicles and parts (manufacture)	100	119.5
Whole economy	100	118.5
Hotels and catering	100	118.0
Leather, footwear and clothing (manufacture)	100	117.2
Construction	100	116.5
Distribution and repairs	100	113.3
Retail price index (1990=100)	100	114.3
Unemployment (millions)	1.66	2.92

Source: adapted from Department of Employment, *Employment Gazette.*

Electricity, gas, other energy and water supply, food, drink and tobacco, education and health services and motor vehicles and parts are industries which are characterised by an above average proportion of full time permanent jobs. Hotels and catering, leather, footwear and clothing, construction and distribution and repairs are industries which have above average proportions of part-time workers and casual workers.

How might the theory of segmented labour markets help to explain the difference in the earnings increase between the sectors show in the data?

Government policy Government policies, ranging from taxation on cigarettes to interest rate policy to health and safety legislation, affect the labour market in a variety of ways. Each individual policy lessens market failure or leads to an increase in market failure. Many aspects of the debate on this issue are discussed in units on supply-side economics, but it is important to realise that government policies designed specifically to deal with labour market failure may well themselves create further labour market failure.

Correcting market failure

Governments have adopted a variety of policies in an attempt to improve both efficiency and equity in the labour market. However, some economists believe that the problems created by these policies are worse than the problems they were originally designed to counter.

Minimum wage legislation One way of tackling low pay is for the government to enforce minimum wage rates on employers.

This would seem to be an ideal solution to the problem of poverty amongst workers. However, economic theory predicts that the policy will have undesirable secondary effects. Figure 52.1 shows the demand and supply curves for labour in an industry. The equilibrium wage rate is OE whilst the equilibrium level of employment is OB. The government now imposes a minimum wage of OF, forcing industry wage rates to rise to OF. Firms demand AB less labour whilst BC more workers wish to gain jobs in the industry. The result is AC unemployment.

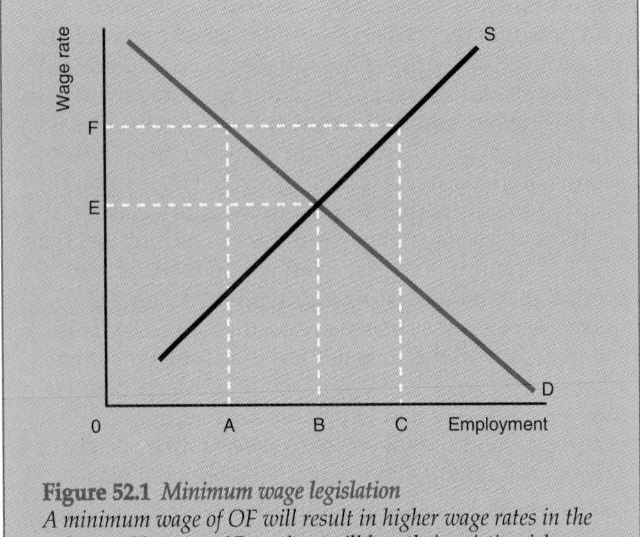

Figure 52.1 *Minimum wage legislation*
A minimum wage of OF will result in higher wage rates in the industry. However, AB workers will lose their existing jobs whilst a total of AC unemployment will be created.

Existing workers have not necessarily benefited. OA workers have gained higher wages. But AB workers have lost their jobs as a result of the legislation. What is more, the workers who have lost their jobs are likely to be the least employable. Firms will have fired their least productive employees.

Minimum wage legislation can also prevent the market from clearing when there is an increase in unemployment. In Figure 52.2, D_1 and S are the original demand and supply curves respectively. Assume that the minimum wage is set at OF. Then the equilibrium market wage rate is equal to the minimum wage rate and there is no unemployment. Now assume that the economy goes into recession. Demand for the industry's product falls and so the demand for labour in the industry falls (remember, labour is a derived demand). The new demand curve is D_2. If the market had been free, wage rates would have fallen to OE and any transitional unemployment in the market would have disappeared. But with a minimum wage of OF, unemployment of AC is created. So it is argued that minimum wage legislation can cause unemployment.

Equal pay legislation Equal pay legislation is designed to raise the wage rates of groups of workers who perform work of equal value to other workers doing the same job who are at present paid higher wages. In the UK, equal pay legislation has been applied particularly to women and to workers from ethnic minorities.

Economic theory suggests that equal pay legislation will

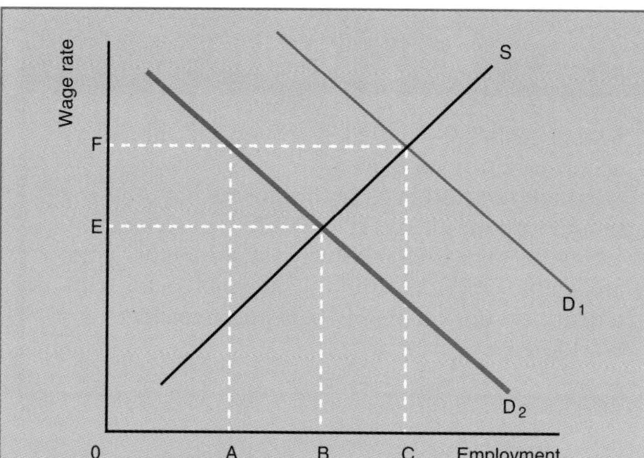

Figure 52.2 *Minimum wages can cause unemployment*
A fall in demand for labour from D_1 to D_2 should lead to a fall in wage rates from OF to OE. However, a minimum wage of OF will prevent this and will cause unemployment of AC to arise.

have the same effect as the imposition of a minimum wage. Equal pay legislation is designed to raise the wages of workers who are discriminated against. In the UK, there is evidence to suggest that it has been partially successful in achieving this (☞ unit 50). However, raising wages will reduce the demand for and increase the supply of labour. If the market was in equilibrium to start with, then the introduction of legislation will cause unemployment amongst those groups whom it is designed to benefit. There is a direct trade-off between higher pay and fewer jobs.

Health and safety legislation and other employment protection measures Government has passed many acts designed to improve the living standards of workers. For instance, health and safety legislation is designed to protect workers against accidents at work. These measures have the effect of raising the cost to firms of employing labour. Not only do firms have to pay workers a wage, but the legislation also forces a rise in labour-related costs. For instance, machines have to be made safe and minimum and maximum work temperatures have to be maintained. This shifts the supply curve upwards and to the left. At any given level of employment, workers will only work for a given wage rate plus the cost of protection measures, in turn leading to a fall in employment. Hence it is argued by free market economists that measures designed to protect the employee usually lead to a fall in employment.

The extent to which government legislation giving workers extra rights leads to a rise in unemployment depends crucially upon three factors.

- The first relates to the difference between the new rights and existing free market rights. For instance, if the market wage rate is £4 per hour and a minimum wage is set at £3 per hour, the minimum wage will have no effect. It won't raise wages in the market or create unemployment. If the minimum wage is set at £3 when market clearing rates are £2.75 per hour, there will be a small increase in average wages but equally it is unlikely that much unemployment will be created. A minimum wage of £6 with market clearing rates of £2 per hour, on the other hand, will give substantial benefits to workers employed but is likely to create substantial unemployment.
- Second, the amount of unemployment created depends on the relative elasticities of demand and supply for labour. Consider Figure 52.3 and compare it to Figure 52.1. Both diagrams relate to the introduction of a minimum wage. The market clearing wage is OE and the minimum wage set is OF. Unemployment of AC is created by the introduction of the minimum wage. In Figure 52.1, the demand and supply curves are relatively elastic between OE and OF. The unemployment created is large. In Figure 52.3, the demand and supply curves are relatively inelastic between OE and OF. The unemployment created is relatively small.
Indeed if the demand for labour is perfectly inelastic, a rise in wages will have no effect on the demand for labour. One conclusion that could be drawn from the argument above is that the demand for labour is relatively less elastic in the formal sector of the economy than in the informal sector. So minimum wage legislation or equal pay legislation will have a much greater impact on jobs in the informal sector than in the formal sector. This would correspond with evidence which suggests that semi-skilled and unskilled workers have suffered disproportionately from unemployment in the 1970s and the 1980s in the UK.
- Third, what might be true for a single industry might not be true for the economy as a whole. For instance, minimum wage legislation in the hairdressing industry might result in unemployment amongst hairdressers. But minimum wage legislation across all industries might have little or no effect on unemployment. In economics, it is not possible to conclude that the economy as a whole will behave in the same way as an individual market.

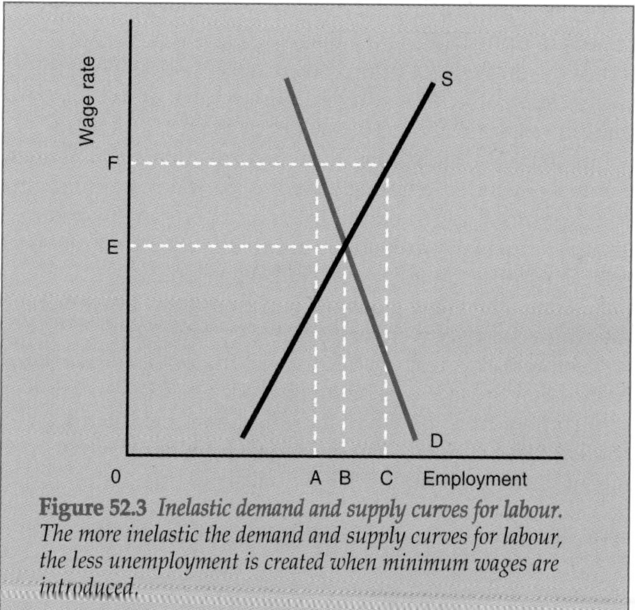

Figure 52.3 *Inelastic demand and supply curves for labour. The more inelastic the demand and supply curves for labour, the less unemployment is created when minimum wages are introduced.*

QUESTION 3 In 1995, the government announced plans to create more rights for disabled people in the workplace. The measures would require employers to make a 'reasonable adjustment' to working conditions to overcome the practical difficulties of a disability. Employers would also have to provide a right of access to goods and services, including the removal of barriers and provision of aids 'where reasonable and readily achievable'. The minister for the disabled estimated that the changes to physical access required by the legislation would impose an overall cost to industry of no more than £1.1bn, with an 'average cost to the average business' of between £500 and £1 500.

Employers' organisations found it hard to oppose the principles behind the measures. However, they were worried that they were too vague. Mr Ian Smedley, the Institute of Directors' small business executive, said: 'The government has in effect issued a blank cheque which business will have to pay.'

Source: adapted from the *Financial Times*, 13.1.1995.

Using diagrams, discuss the possible impact of the government measures described in the data on employment.

Key terms

Search costs - costs, such as money and time, spent searching for a job.

Dual labour market hypothesis - the hypothesis that the labour market is split into two sectors: the formal sector with a relatively skilled, highly paid and stable workforce and the informal sector with a relatively unskilled, low paid and unstable workforce.

Applied economics

A national minimum wage

The Labour Party in the 1990s has argued the case for the introduction of a national minimum wage. National minimum wages are common in many countries as Figure 52.4 shows. The UK, in fact, had a system of statutory minimum wages in certain industries for most of this century. They were set by **Wages Councils**.

Wages Councils were first established in 1909 when the Liberal government of the day set up a number of trade boards in industries with a history of low pay. Before 25 out of the 26 Wages Councils were abolished in 1993, they were responsible for setting minimum rates of pay for 2.5 million workers, about 10 per cent of the workforce, in about 400 000 establishments. Industries covered by Wages Councils included retailing, catering, garment manufacture and hairdressing. Women workers and part-time workers, groups particularly vulnerable to exploitation by employers, were disproportionally present in Wage Council industries. The Wage Councils had 'statutory' powers, i.e. the wages they set were enforceable by law. An inspectorate was responsible for visiting places of work to ensure that the law was being obeyed. The Conservative government from 1979 had indicated that it wanted to abolish these councils, but resistance from employers meant that it took until 1993 to abolish all but one.

Arguments in favour of minimum wages

The main argument in favour of a national minimum wage is one of **horizontal equity** (☞ unit 43). Every worker should receive the same rate of pay for working an hour. In a market economy, this is not possible. The market produces wage differentials in order to create an efficient economy where wages act as signals, creating incentives for workers with high skills to take on jobs with high marginal revenue products. However, the workings of the market can be modified if a floor is placed on wage rates. The abolition of Wages Councils in 1993 according to a 1994 report by the Low Pay Network did result in a substantial fall in wage rates, indicating that inequality had increased. The report stated that a survey covering 1 500 vacancies at 46 Jobcentres found 18.1 per cent of jobs paying below the last reported Wage Council rate for that industry. Underpayment ranged from an average 9.2 per cent in the clothing sector to 22.6 per cent in hairdressing.

Another argument is that minimum wages discourage employers in industrialised countries from utilising resources to produce goods which could be as easily produced in Third World economies. Instead, higher wages encourage First World employers to train their workforce to make them productive enough to justify the higher wages they are now forced to pay. If a country like the UK wants all its workers to share a high living standard, it is vital that firms play their part in increasing the human capital of all workers, including the low paid.

Many employers were in favour of retaining Wages Councils in the UK. They were employers who were

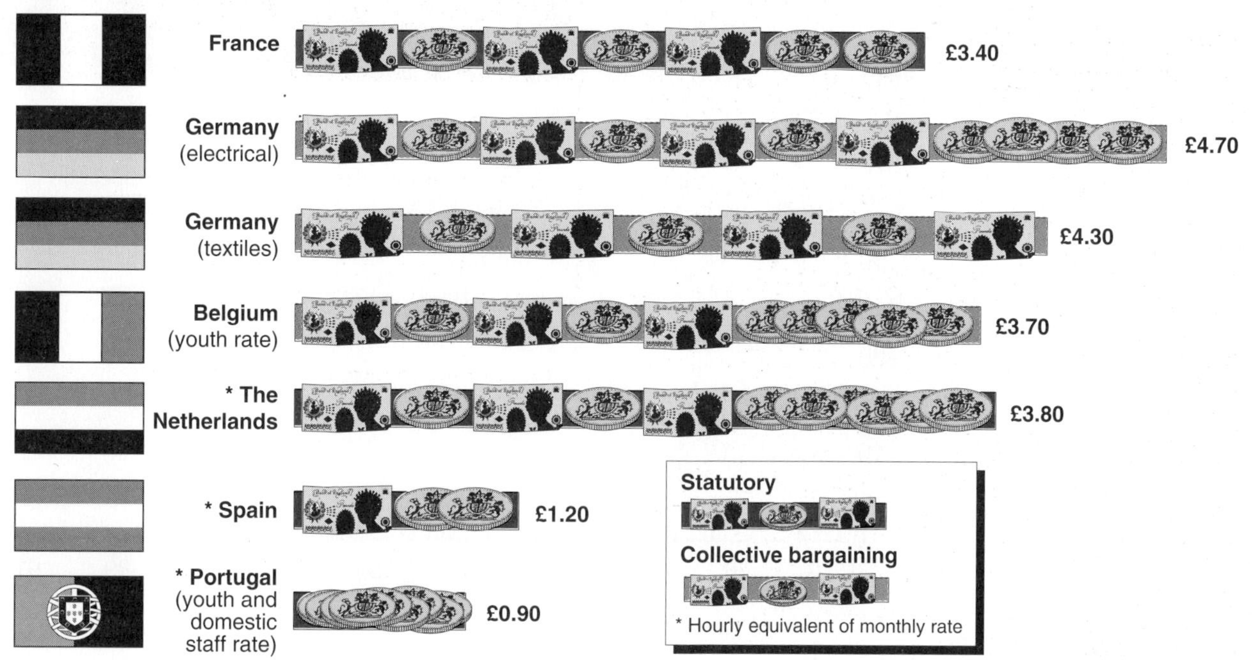

Source: adapted from Income Data Services Ltd.

Figure 52.4 *How minimum wages compared in Europe, 1991*

paying workers above the minimum wage. They were already under competitive pressure from employers who illegally paid wages below the minimum set. They feared that they could lose business or even be driven out of business if they continued to pay existing wage rates.

Arguments against minimum wages

The main argument against minimum wages is that it creates unemployment. Professor Patrick Minford suggested in 1985 that unemployment would fall by 300 000 if Wages Councils were abolished. This assumed that Wages Councils raised pay by about an average of 10 per cent for workers covered by orders. However, other estimates for job gains suggested far lower numbers and H Neuberger (1984) estimated that only 8 000 jobs would be created across the whole economy from abolition.

Evidence from abroad where national minimum wages are relatively common gives contradictory evidence. The United States, for instance, operates a national minimum wage with little seeming effect on unemployment. This is partly because the minimum wage is relatively low. In a 1992 study of 314 fast food restaurants in Texas, L Katz and A Krueger found that, following a 45 per cent rise in the US minimum wage in 1991, employment rose and that the restaurants which had had to raise their wages the most also tended to have the largest increase in employment. A 10 per cent wage increase was predicted to raise relative full-time employment by 25 per cent. In contrast, a study of the extension of the US minimum wage to Puerto Rico in 1974 showed the more expected result, a rise in unemployment. By 1980, the Federal minimum wage was 75 per cent of the average wage in Puerto Rico's manufacturing compared to 43 per cent in mainland USA. Unemployment rose from 11.3 per cent to 23.4 per cent between 1974 and 1983, of which one-third was attributed to the rise in the minimum wage. These results show that the exact economic effects of imposing a minimum wage cannot always be predicted. However, in general, minimum wages imposed on industries where there is little international competition or where it is difficult to recruit substitute cheap labour are unlikely to have much effect on employment.

Another argument is that minimum wages impose compliance costs on individual firms. Wages Councils in the UK were opposed mainly by smaller employers who complained of the administration cost in finding out what they ought to be paying to workers and dealing with the Wages Councils Inspectorate.

A third argument against minimum wages is that they do little to reduce poverty. Partly this is because minimum wages tend to be set at levels little above the market clearing level anyway. More importantly, most poor people are not in work; they are unemployed, married to an unemployed person, at home on their own bringing up children or pensioners. Even low paid workers are not necessarily poor because they tend to be married to a partner who is earning a higher wage. Figure 52.5 illustrates one aspect of this. Women are more likely to be paid less than men. The proportion of married women not in work has fallen over time from 45 per cent in 1973 to 35 per cent in 1991. Nearly all of the married women not in work in 1973 came from households where their husbands worked. But by 1991, nearly a third of non-working married women came from households where their husbands did not work, i.e. of the new jobs created in the 1970s and 1980s, a disproportionate number had gone to women earning a second income for the household. Imposing a minimum wage will not help the 10 per cent of married women in households where neither the husband nor the wife has a job.

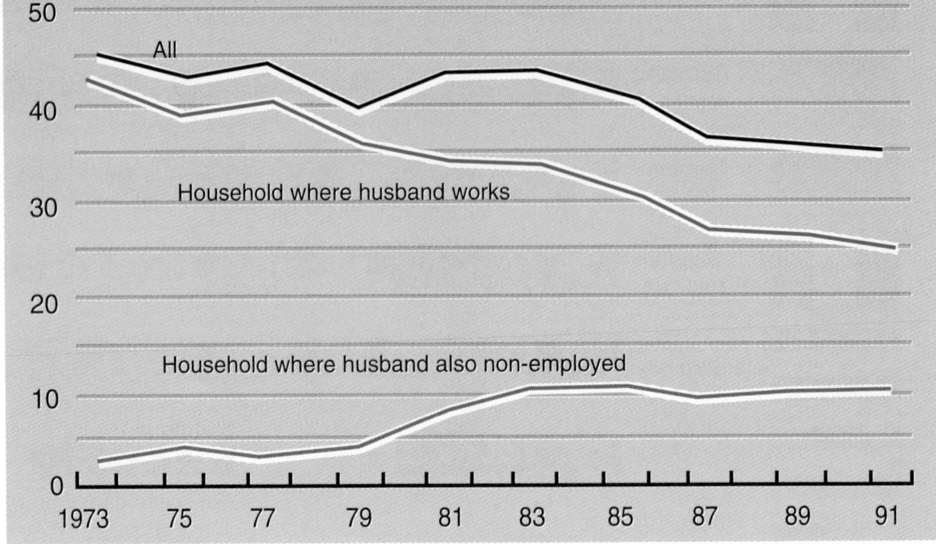

Source: adapted from General household survey.

Figure 52.5 *Distribution of non-employment among working age married women (%)*

DATA QUESTION

The Social Charter

The Maastricht Treaty

In December 1991, European governments gathered together at a Dutch town called Maastricht to hammer out a treaty which would take the European Union through into the next century. A number of key issues were agreed upon including a timetable for European Monetary Union and moves towards greater political union. Possibly the most controversial issue was the Social Charter. The UK secured an opt-out. The other 11 countries would proceed with implementing the Social Charter whilst the UK, it was agreed, would not have to abide by any new rules and regulations.

The Single European Market

The Single European Market came into force on the first of January 1993. European Union States had agreed in 1986 to dismantle all non-tariff barriers to trade between member countries to create a genuine Single Market. The key was harmonisation of policies. So what was legal and possible for a UK firm selling to UK customers would also be legal and possible for a German firm selling into the UK. There was a fear that firms would respond by moving production to the lowest cost country in the EU, enabling them to exploit local workers. Hence, the European Commission was keen to create a harmonisation of policies on labour to complement that on goods.

The Social Charter

The Social Charter, or the European Community Charter of Workers' Fundamental Social Rights, was put forward in the 1980s and approved by the European Commission in 1989. The European Commission is gradually putting forward directives, known as the Social Action Programme. They then have to be approved by the Council of Ministers. Once approved, they must be passed into national law by individual parliaments. Individual directives can be and sometimes are rejected by the Council of Ministers. However, once approved there, they become legally enforceable in all member states (apart from the UK which has secured an opt-out clause) whether or not national parliaments have passed the necessary legislation because individuals can always go to the European Court to have European law upheld. The Social Charter has covered issues such as:

- the granting of the same rights to part-time and casual workers as those of full-time workers in areas such as training and holidays;
- restrictions on the amount of shift and night work that a worker can be asked to do - for instance, workers must have at least 11 consecutive hours of rest in 24 hours and are entitled to a rest day in every seven days, whilst night work is restricted to 8 hours per night averaged over two weeks;
- regulations on maternity leave; women are entitled to at least 14 weeks' maternity leave with a right to job protection, assuming they have worked for an employer for 9 months;

UK a 'paradise for investment'

'Britain will become a paradise for investment', was the verdict of Mr Jacques Delors, president of the European Commission. His angry reaction to Britain's decision to opt out of an extension of the European Community's social and employment policy at December's Maastricht summit is now approvingly echoed by British ministers.

They believe they have preserved the right of British employers and employees to conduct their affairs free from centralised, continental meddling, to the benefit of the UK economy. Britain is poised to become the Hong Kong of Europe, its barely protected labour sucking in foreign capital. This might be an unwelcome development but, to Mr Delors, it is preferable to the alternative, a social dimension that would be limited to a few health and safety directives, with the UK blocking attempts to establish a true set of EU-wide minimum standards at work.

Source: adapted from the *Financial Times*, 28.2.1992

Views on the Social Chapter

Razia Begum's sewing machine clattered through another poppy-dappled curtain tie-back, while Sagar Hussain hoisted more bales of completed linen out to the delivery van bay. There wasn't a lot of time to contemplate the niceties of the Maastricht Social Chapter as Greatmade Textiles of Bradford got on with another fully-occupied day. But at 4.30 pm, gathering around a portable gas stove in their draughty former woollen mill, the company's 17 staff were almost entirely behind John Major's reluctance to sign on the dotted line. 'He's OK by us, so we're OK by him,' said Mr Hussain, nodding at Greatmade's owner, Chadrey Ahmad Miraj. 'We're all right here. We want work. We don't need a lot of rules and regulations.' The others nodded. Several have worked for more than three years at Greatmade, which pays a standard £2.50 an hour, with extra for merit and experience. Their supervisor, Aslam Choudhury, was a bit more circumspect about the complications of Maastricht. 'What a big subject!', he said. 'Difficult to understand, and on something like this, it's important to understand what you are talking about.' The owner, Mr Miraj, said: 'We are up against fierce competition in textiles from other countries - Japan and the Far East especially.'

In another traditionally low-paid industry, David Dickenson of Group 4 Security took the opposite view. His firm, based in Worcester, is well up the pay-and-conditions league for security companies. They dearly want regulation. 'We're at one with the unions on this, perhaps surprisingly,' he said - citing 'cowboy' rivals in Yorkshire paying as little as £1.80 an hour with no frills. 'They're a minority but they lower the customers' expectations generally', he said.

Source: adapted from *The Guardian*, 12.12.1991.

How will European workers be affected by the Social Charter?

You are an economist working for a trade union. You have been asked to prepare a report on the implications of the Social Charter for workers.

1. **Write an introduction outlining the history of the Social Charter and giving examples of provisions in the Charter.**
2. **Outline ways in which workers (a) in Europe and (b) in the UK are likely to benefit from it.**
3. **Using diagrams, analyse how workers in (a) Europe and (b) the UK might lose out from its implementation.**
4. **Evaluate whether the trade union should put pressure on the UK government to sign the Social Charter in the near future.**

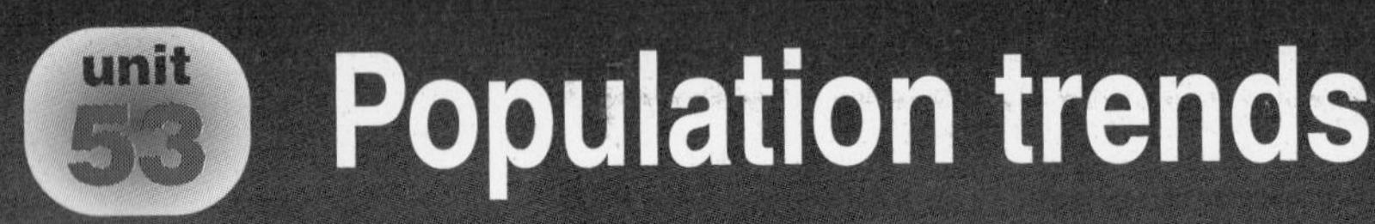

unit 53 Population trends

Applied economics

Population change in the UK

The population of the UK has increased this century from 38 million in 1901 to a current figure of nearly 59 million. There are three ways in which a country's population can increase.

The numbers being born can rise As Figure 53.1 shows, there has been a considerable fluctuation in the number of births this century. The two World Wars saw sharp falls in the number of births. Other periods of economic uncertainty or recession - the 1920s and 1930s, and the late 1960s and early 1970s - were also associated with falls in births. The period of sustained economic growth from 1950 to the mid-1960s saw an increase in births - the so-called post-war baby boom. Subsequently the number of births did not begin to increase again until the late 1970s.

The BIRTH RATE, the numbers of live births as a proportion of the total population, is determined by two factors. First, the larger the number of women of child bearing age, the higher the birth rate is likely to be. For instance, the bulge in births in the 1950s and mid-1960s produced an increase in the numbers of women of child-bearing age from the late 1970s onwards. Hence this provides a partial explanation for the increase in the birth rate from the late 1970s. Second, the birth rate is determined by the FERTILITY RATE, the numbers of live births as a proportion of women of child-bearing age.

What determines the fertility rate is difficult to say. One reason why fertility rates were much higher in the pre-First World War era was the high infant mortality rate. Because so many children died, women needed to have a large number of children if some of these were to survive into adulthood. Today few children die and therefore parents are fairly confident that if they have two children, then those two will survive into adulthood.

Increased use of contraception and abortion too are likely to have affected the fertility rate. However, it should be remembered that contraception and abortion only became widely practised in the 1960s with the introduction of the pill and the legalisation of abortion. So they are unlikely to be major determinants of the changes in the birth rate seen in the first half of this century.

The economics of child rearing is likely to provide a more significant explanation of the trend in all developed countries to lower fertility rates. The opportunity cost of rearing children has steadily increased. In many Third World countries, children are economic assets for the parents. They can be put to work at an early age and custom often demands that children have a duty to look after parents in their old age - having children is the equivalent of investing in a pension scheme. In developed countries, the average leaving age for children from full time education is slowly increasing. More and more children need to be supported through to the age of 21. Children are expensive to keep. There is little tradition in

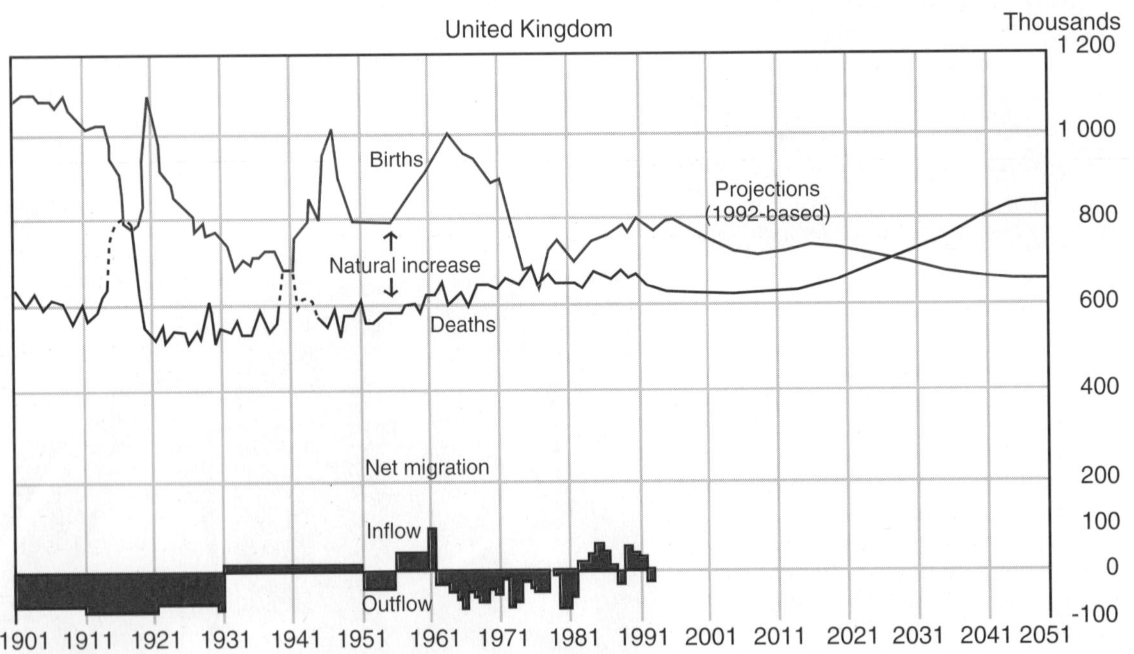

Note: the dots cover the periods 1914-18 and 1938-45 which include deaths of non-civilian and merchant seamen who died outside the country.
Source: adapted from *Social Trends*.

Figure 53.1 *Population changes and projections*

the UK of financial support of parents in old age. What's more, the opportunity cost for women of staying at home to rear children has increased. Women have been able to obtain higher and higher wages and leaving employment for any length of time has a devastating effect on a woman's long term earnings potential (☞ unit 50). In countries such as West Germany, the birth rate today is so low that the population is actually falling.

The number of deaths can fall Figure 53.1 shows that the number of deaths has increased since the Second World War. This is due to increased numbers in the population. However, the DEATH RATE, the proportion of deaths to the total population, has been falling as life expectancy has increased. Better food, improved housing, safer working conditions as well as medical advances have been the cause of this trend towards greater longevity.

Net migration can be positive Net migration is the difference between immigration and emigration. If it is positive, it means that more people enter the country than leave to settle abroad. Figure 53.1 shows that the UK has tended to suffer a loss of population through migration over time. However, the numbers involved are relatively small. In the 1980s, net migration tended to be positive. In 1993, approximately half of all immigrants were British citizens returning home. One-tenth of the total were citizens of other European Union countries. Nearly another tenth were citizens of Australia, New Zealand and Canada. Only approximately three-tenths were from new Commonwealth countries such as Pakistan and Caribbean countries. The change in total population resulting from migration was a mere 0.01 per cent.

Some predict that, with the Single European Market and the Social Charter, migration to and from other European Union countries will increase over the next 10-20 years. They point to the considerable migration flows experienced between states in the USA over time. However, language and cultural barriers are much greater in the EU than in the USA. The main flows are likely to be of three types. One is of managerial workers, transferring from country to country employed by pan-European companies. Another is of young skilled workers wanting to gain language skills before returning home. The third is of migrants from outside the EU who initially settle in one country but then choose to go to live in another European country.

The changing age structure of the population

The death rate has changed only slowly over time, and has tended to fall. However, the birth rate in the UK this century has fluctuated significantly and it is this fluctuation which has caused major changes in the age structure of the population. Table 53.1 summarises the most important changes which have occurred since 1971 and are projected to occur by the year 2025. Four major changes can be singled out.

Children The number of pupils in schools, shown by the population aged 5-15, declined during the 1970s and 1980s. This resulted in widespread closure of schools. However, the increase in the birth rate from 1978 has led to an increased demand for school places in the 1990s although it will fall again in the next century. This means that there has been an increase in demand for goods such as school buildings, children's books and clothing, and teachers in the 1990s.

Young workers The number of school leavers and young workers aged 16-19 grew substantially in the 1970s. This is likely to have been a significant factor in the growth of youth unemployment in that decade. However, in the 1990s, the number of young workers has fallen significantly - the so-called 'demographic timebomb'. It was widely predicted in the late 1980s that employers

Table 53.1 *Selected social and economic needs of population groups by age*

UK — Indices 1991 = 100

	1971	1981	1986	1991	2001	2011	2025	Social and economic needs of different age groups of the population
People aged								
Under 1	110	89	92	100	93	87	93	Maternity services, Health visiting, Preventive medicine.
1-4	118	87	93	100	102	91	97	Day care, Nursery education.
5-15	125	116	103	100	113	107	104	Compulsory education.
16-19	101	125	119	100	95	110	93	Further and higher education, Training,Employment.
15-44 (females)	86	95	100	100	95	91	89	Maternity services.
20-49	86	90	95	100	96	94	90	Employment, Housing,Transport.
50-59/64[1]	111	106	102	100	117	126	133	Pre-retirement training, Early retirement.
60/65[2]-74	99	103	101	100	95	108	123	Retirement, Pensions.
75-84	70	86	95	100	104	101	126	Retirement pension, Health care, Home
85 and over	55	68	81	100	132	150	154	helps, Sheltered housing, Retirement homes.

Notes: 1. 59 for females, 64 for males.
2. 60 for females, 65 for males

Source: adapted from CSO, *Social Trends*.

would be faced with a severe shortage of youngsters on the job market. However, the deep and prolonged recession of 1990-92 led to a sharp fall in demand for young workers which in the first half of the 1990s was probably greater than the fall in supply. The result was increased youth unemployment. A shortage may occur in the second half of the 1990s if there is a significant fall in overall unemployment caused by high economic growth.

The 'baby-boomers' The generation of workers born in the post-war baby boom is now moving through the age structure of the population. In the 1970s and early 1980s as they entered the workforce, they suffered unemployment. In the 1990s and the early part of the next century, they will constitute a growing proportion of the labour force as the number of young people entering the workforce declines. This has important implications for employers. Increasingly they will have to look to older people to fill vacancies. In the Lawson boom 1986-88 employers in the South East, the area of greatest labour shortage, showed greater willingness to promote older workers and to attract mature females back into jobs. The 'baby-boomers' are also likely to be of increasing significance to sellers of goods and services. The 1960s and 1970s were decades when young people represented an important and growing market for firms. However, the numbers of young people are now in decline. Therefore firms have increasingly had to switch their products to appeal to middle-aged people - 'the baby-boomers'.

The elderly A growing proportion of the population is now retired. In 1971, there were 7.4m aged 65 and over, 13.3 per cent of the total population. This grew to 8.5m in 1981 and by 1993 was 9.2m, 15.8 per cent of the total population. The 1990s will see little change in the numbers of over 65s, but in the first decade of the next century the numbers are projected to rise to 10.2m in 2011, 12.0m in 2021 and 14.0m in 2031 as the baby-boomers retire. As Table 53.1 shows, these overall numbers mask significant changes in the composition of the elderly population. In the 1990s, there will be little change in the total figure. But the number of 75 year olds and over (born before or immediately after the First World War) will increase whilst the numbers of 65-74 year olds (the generation born in the 1920s and 1930s) will decrease.

This has major implications for the state. Those aged 75 and over tend to be on very low incomes and therefore need income support. Many are unable to look after themselves and therefore need care in the community or in institutions such as old people's homes. They are particularly expensive for the National Health Service (NHS). Therefore NHS, social security and social services budgets will have to increase in real terms in the 1990s if the standard of living of the elderly is to be maintained at its present levels, or there will have to be much more private provision by individuals. Even in the next century, the number of 75 year olds and over will continue to increase, imposing strains upon government finance. However, the balance of population amongst the elderly will start to change as the baby-boomers begin to retire. In the 2020s and 2030s, the baby-boomer 65-75 year olds, retiring on good pensions and having been brought up accustomed to post-war affluence, are likely to be a powerful force in society and in the market place.

An international comparison

In the developing world, most countries have a relatively young population compared to the UK. Their problems are those of paying for the education of their children and the provision of jobs as these children move into the workforce. In the developed world, the major problem that countries now face is the ageing of the population. Figure 53.2 shows the change in the percentage of the population aged 65 and over in selected OECD countries. Of the countries shown, the UK will be least affected by the 'greying' of its population. Over the period from 1960 to 2020, the percentage of the population over retirement age is projected only to increase by 50 per cent. In Japan, it will nearly quadruple and in West Germany it will double.

As argued above, this has considerable implications for government spending and the economy. For instance, currently health spending is more than four times as high per capita on the over-65s as on the under-65s in OECD countries. For the over-75s, the proportion rises to nearly 6 times.

However, it also has implications for the standard of living of workers in the population. The higher the DEPENDENCY RATIO, the proportion of dependants (i.e. non-workers) to workers in the population, the lower will be the after-tax incomes of workers if dependants are to receive a given income. For instance, workers will see their share of national income fall over the next 70 years in France and West Germany if pensioners are to increase their incomes at the same rate as workers. The worsening ratio of people aged 15-64 to pensioners in OECD countries is shown in Figure 53.3.

One response to this is for the government to cut expenditure on state pensions. In the early 1980s, the UK government, faced with projections that state pensions would take an ever increasing percentage of the total budget in the next century, reduced future benefits to workers in the State Earnings Related Pension Scheme (SERPS). In the late 1980s, the government encouraged workers to opt out of SERPS altogether by offering National Insurance rebates to those who left SERPS and instead took out a personal pension scheme. The

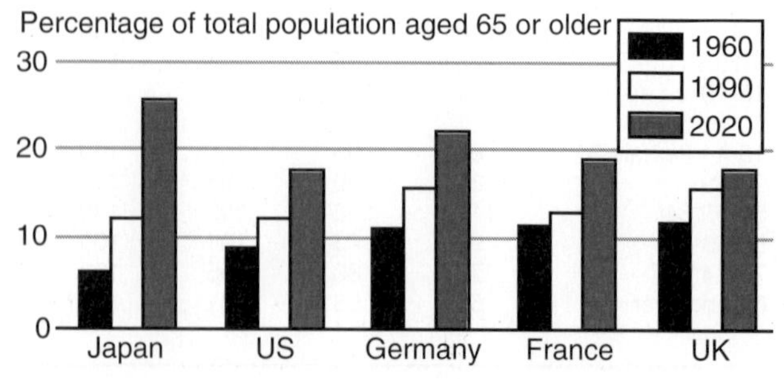

Source: adapted from OECD.

Figure 53.2 *Percentage of total population aged 65 or older*

combined effect of these two changes will mean that total expenditure on state pensions should be lower in future. Future workers who would have had to pay taxes and National Insurance contributions to pay for the pensions of today's workers will now be better off.

The danger with this approach is that those who are contracted into SERPS will be worse off and also that workers who contracted out will not make adequate payments into their private pension scheme. This will tend to increase income inequalities as, already today, pensioners are the largest single group on low incomes.

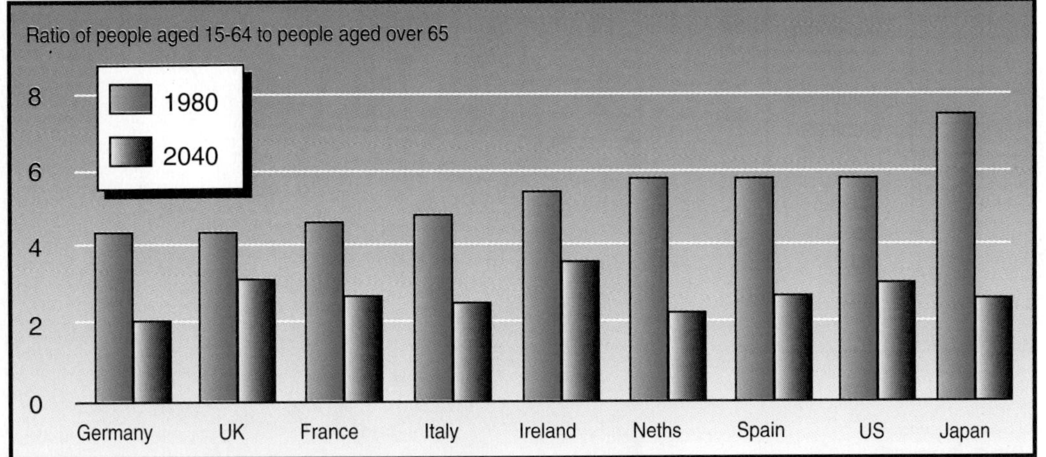

Source: adapted from Hills (1993).

Figure 53.3 *Support ratios*

Key terms

Birth rate - the numbers of live births as a proportion of the total population.

Fertility rate - the numbers of live births as a proportion of women of child-bearing age.

Death rate - the number of deaths as a proportion of the total population.

Dependency ratio - the proportion of dependants (i.e. non-workers) to workers in the population.

Growth of the elderly population

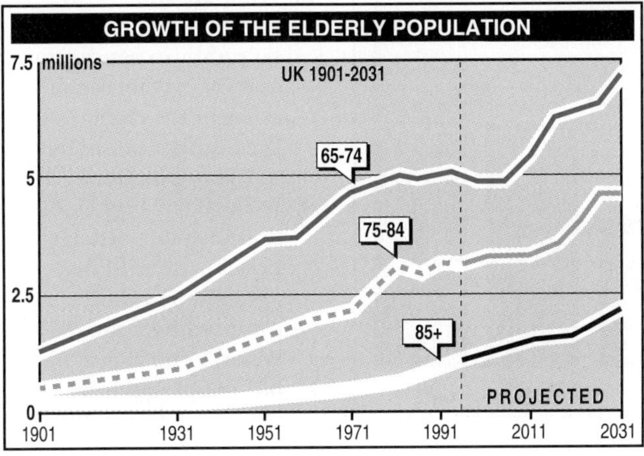

Source: adapted from Laing and Buisson.

Figure 53.4 *Growth of the elderly population*

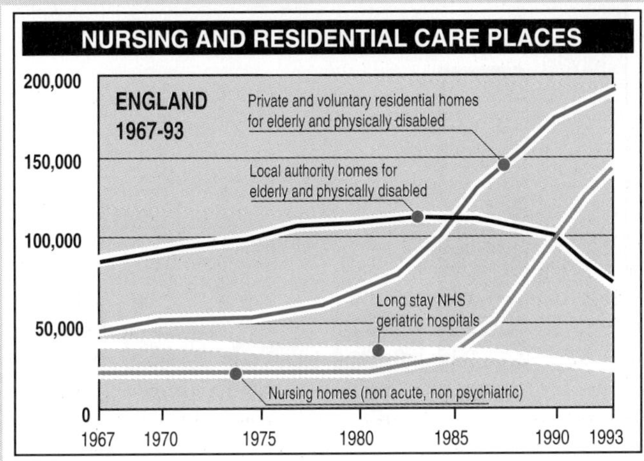

Source: adapted from Laing and Buisson.

Figure 53.5 *Nursing and residential care places*

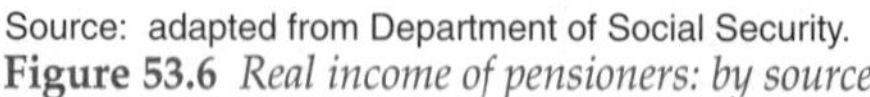

Source: adapted from Department of Social Security.
Figure 53.6 *Real income of pensioners: by source*

Table 53.2 *Benefit expenditure by government on the elderly in real terms*

	1971-72	1981-82	1986-87	1991-92	1993-94	1996-97[1]
Benefit expenditure on the elderly (£bn at 1993-94 prices)	16.7	27.2	32.1	33.6	36.8	38.4
Real GDP at market prices (1990=100)	64.7	75.9	88.6	98.0	99.7	110.0

1. Estimated.

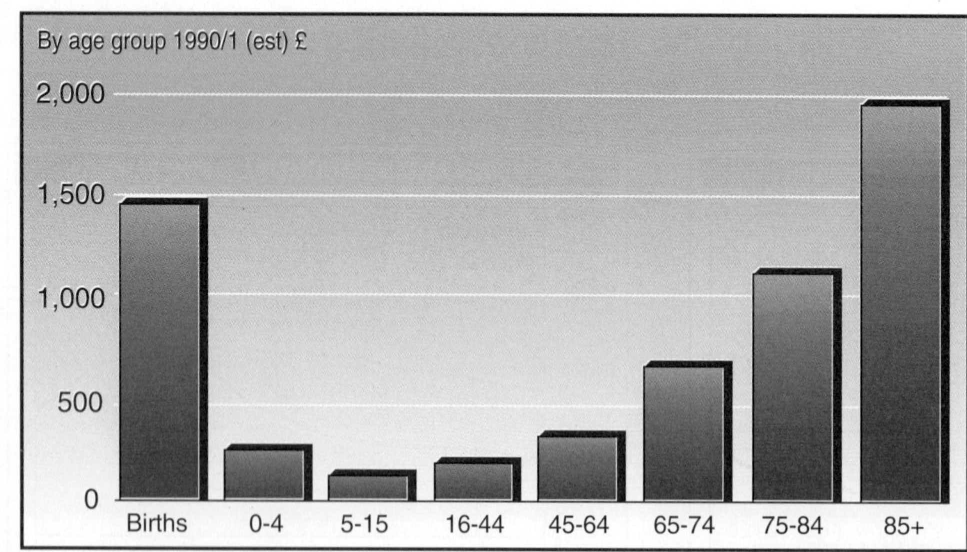

Source: adapted from *Department of Health.*
Figure 53:7 *NHS spending: where the money goes*

1. **How, according to the data, have pensioners' living standards changed in the 1980s and 1990s?**
2. **What are the implications for (a) public expenditure and (b) private sector firms of the changes in the number of old people in the population?**
3. **It has been suggested that the state old age pension should be abolished and be replaced by a means-tested benefit aimed at old people on low income. Discuss the implications of such a change (a) for taxpayers and (b) for old people.**

The functional distribution of income and economic rent

Summary

1. The functional distribution of income is the share of national income received by each factor of production.
2. A factor receives economic rent if its earnings are above its transfer earnings. Quasi rent is rent earned only in the short run.
3. Economic rent will be greater, the more inelastic the supply curve.
4. A change in economic rent will not affect the allocation of resources.

The functional distribution of income

The factors of production are classified into **land**, **labour**, **capital** and **entrepreneurship** (☞ unit 2). The owners of factors of production receive a reward for renting out their factors. Landowners receive rent, labour receives wages, capitalists receive interest and entrepreneurs earn profits.

The FUNCTIONAL DISTRIBUTION OF INCOME shows the share of national income received by each factor of production. This is different from the **personal distribution of income** described in unit 43. An individual or household may receive income from several factors of production. For instance, a pensioner may have a part time job, receive rent from a property which she owns and receive dividends from shares.

The functional distribution of income depends in part upon the price that each factor of production is paid. Neo-classical economic theory suggests that the price of a product is determined by the forces of demand and supply. For instance, the wage rate of labour will be determined by the demand for labour and the supply of labour (☞ unit 50). Rent on land will be determined by the demand for land and the supply of land. The laws of demand and supply are as applicable in factor markets as they are in the goods markets.

The exact shapes of the demand and supply curves for land, labour and capital are discussed at length in the units which precede and follow this unit. However, they are broadly the same shape as in a goods market (i.e. the demand curve is downward sloping whilst the supply curve is upward sloping).

Demand and supply analysis can be used to show the functional distribution of income. In Figure 54.1, the equilibrium wage rate in the labour market is OC. OA workers are employed and therefore the total wage bill is OA x OC (the number of workers employed x the wage rate per worker). The value to the employer of OA workers is given by the area OEBA, the sum of the marginal revenue product of each worker employed up to OA workers (the marginal revenue product of each worker is the vertical distance between the MRP curve and the horizontal axis).

Total revenue received by the employer is OEBA. OCBA is paid in wages. Therefore BCE is the amount left, after wages have been paid, to reward the other factors of production employed by the firm. Out of BCE it has to pay rent, interest and profits to the owners of land and capital and to entrepreneurs.

Figure 54.1 shows the market for labour. The same analysis would apply if the market for land or capital were shown.

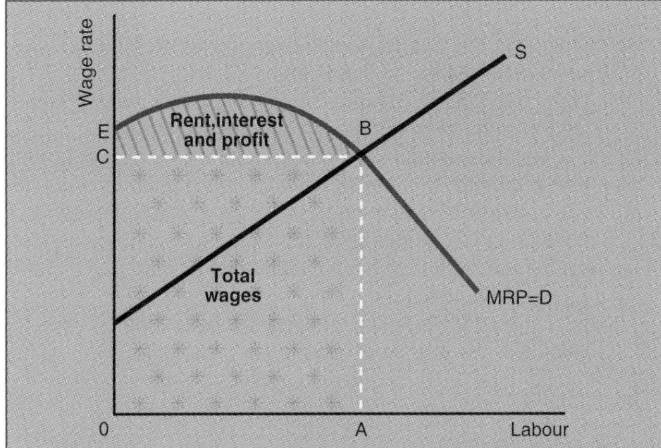

Figure 54.1 *The functional distribution of income*
Total revenue for the firm is the sum of the marginal revenue product of each worker (i.e. OEBA). The total wage bill for the firm is OCBA. Therefore BCE is left to distribute in the form of rent, interest and profit.

Economic rent

David Ricardo, writing in the early part of the 19th century, developed a theory of economic rent which today can be applied to all factors of production. During the Napoleonic Wars, land rents rose steeply at the same time as the price of corn. Many argued that the rise in the price of corn was due to landowners increasing rents on agricultural land. Ricardo, however, argued that it was the rise in the price of corn that resulted in farmers demanding more land for corn production and thus bidding up the price of land. Rent, he argued, was price determined and not price determining.

In Figure 54.2, the supply of land is shown to be perfectly inelastic. There is only a fixed amount of land available for corn production. An increase in the derived demand for land to rent, due to an increase in the price of corn, will push the demand curve for land from D_1 to D_2 and the price or rent of land will increase from OA to OB

QUESTION 1

Table 54.1 *The functional distribution of income in the UK*

at current prices

	1968 £m	1968 % of total	1978 £m	1978 % of total	1988 £m	1988 % of total	1994 £m	1994 % of total
Income from employment and self - employment	29 086	76	112 382	74	302 746	74	428 289	73
Profits	6 640	17	27 991	18	71 519	18	94 083	16
Property rents	2 152	6	10 036	7	29 904	7	60 379	10

Note: Percentages do not add up to 100 because of rounding and because the input charge for consumption of non-trading capital is not shown on the table.

Source: adapted from CSO, *UK National Accounts.*

(a) Describe the changes in the functional distribution of income in the UK between 1968 and 1994.
(b) Using diagrams, explain the following arguments which might account for the data in Table 54.1:
(i) wage rates have risen because the increasing use of capital has made workers more productive;
(ii) the rate of return on capital has not fallen over time because innovation and technical progress have pushed the marginal efficiency of capital schedule to the right;
(iii) property rents have increased over time because the supply of land is very inelastic.

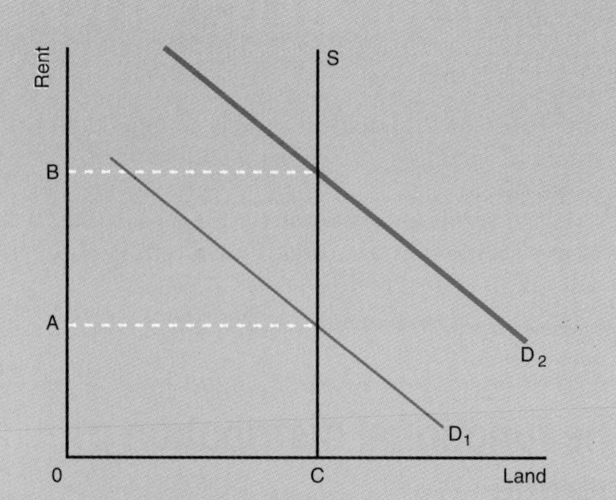

Figure 54.2 *Land in fixed supply*
If the supply of land is perfectly inelastic, any increase in its demand will raise rents but will have no effect on allocation of land as a resource in the economy.

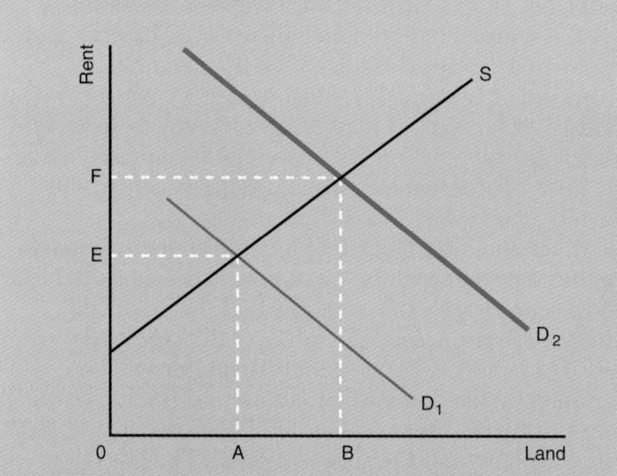

Figure 54.3 *Land in elastic supply*
If the supply of land is not perfectly inelastic, then an increase in its demand will affect not only its price but also the allocation of land within the economy.

A change in the rent on land in Figure 54.2 caused by a change in demand would have no effect on the allocation of resources in the economy. Because the supply is perfectly inelastic, land would be used to grow corn whether the price was almost zero or much higher than OB.

However, supply is not perfectly inelastic for most factors of production. For instance, the land used for growing corn in our example above could have alternative uses, such as growing vegetables or grazing animals. A change in the price of the factor will then have an allocative effect. In Figure 54.3, an increase in demand from D_1 to D_2 will lead to an increase of AB units of the factor being used.

The theory of economic rent distinguishes between two elements in the payment made to a factor of production.

- The TRANSFER EARNINGS of the factor. This is the **minimum** payment needed to keep the factor in its present use. If a worker is paid £200 a week, but could only earn £150 a week in her next best paid occupation, then her transfer earnings would be £150 per week. Transfer earnings are the **opportunity cost** of employing the factor. A change in transfer earnings will affect the allocation of resources. If the worker could now earn £250 a week in her next best paid occupation, economic theory would predict that all other things being equal she would leave her present £200 a week job and take the more highly paid job.
- The ECONOMIC RENT of the factor. Economic rent is the payment over and above the minimum needed to keep the factor in its present use (i.e. it is the difference between its current payment and its transfer earnings). Economic rent will not affect the allocation of resources. If the transfer earnings of a worker were £150, she would remain in her present job whether she earned £200 a week or £250 a week.

The theory of economic rent can be explained using a demand and supply diagram. In Figure 54.4 (a), the equilibrium wage rate of labour is OC. However, only the last worker employed has transfer earnings of OC. The first worker would be prepared to work for a wage rate of OE. We know this because the supply curve shows the

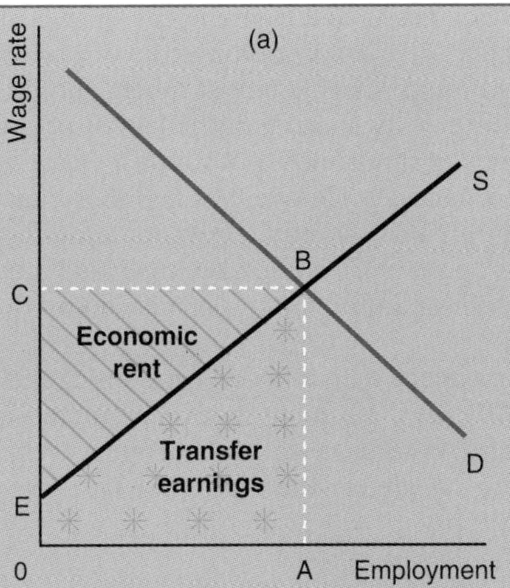

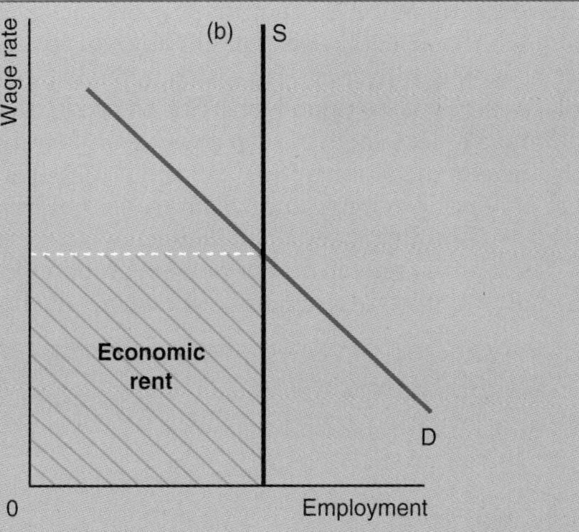

Figure 54.4 *Economic rent*
In Figure 54.4 (a), the total transfer earnings of OA labour is the area OABE. Total wages paid are OABC. So the economic rent paid to the factor is EBC. The less elastic supply of a factor, the greater the element of economic rent. If the supply is perfectly inelastic, as in Figure 54.4 (b), all the payment to the factor is economic rent.

minimum wage rate for which workers would be prepared to work. As successive workers are employed, so the transfer earnings of the marginal worker (the last worker employed) increase. The transfer earnings of the first worker are OE whilst those of the last worker are AB (i.e. it is the vertical distance between the horizontal axis and the supply curve). So the total transfer earnings of all the workers employed, OA, is the area OABE.

The total earnings of OA workers is the area OABC (total number of workers OA times the wage rate per worker OC). The difference between the total payment to a factor and its transfer earnings is its economic rent.

QUESTION 2 Tax changes and falling oil prices have discouraged further oil exploration in the North Sea. A recent study by Arthur Anderson suggests that companies have firm plans to drill only 100 exploration or assessment wells in 1994 compared with 121 in 1993 and more than 200 in 1990. The tax changes have meant that oil companies can offset less of the cost of exploration against the tax they have to pay on profits earned from existing fields, effectively raising the cost of exploration. Falling oil prices have also hit the potential profitability of any newly discovered field. Even in 1992, oil prices were $20 a barrel but by 1994 they had fallen to $14 a barrel.

But at $14 a barrel, existing fields are highly profitable. The average cost of production on existing fields is $5 a barrel. Most of current production comes from fields where production costs are less than $10 a barrel.

Source: adapted from the *Financial Times*, 28.1.1994.

(a) Explain, using a diagram, the amount of economic rent being earned by oil fields in the North Sea in 1994.
(b) What has happened to the amount of economic rent being earned as the price of oil fell in the first half of the 1990s? Explain your answer using a diagram.
(c) Discuss, again with the help of a diagram, why oil exploration in the North Sea fell in 1993 and 1994.

Hence the economic rent of labour in Figure 54.4 (a) is the area EBC.

Economic rent will be greater the more inelastic the supply curve. If, as in Figure 54.4 (b), supply is perfectly inelastic, then all the factor payment is economic rent and the transfer earnings of the factor are zero. Transfer earnings are zero because the factor will be supplied whether the payment received is zero or infinity (as shown by the vertical supply curve). Similarly, if demand is perfectly elastic (i.e. the demand curve is horizontal), all the factor payment is transfer earnings and economic rent is zero. Whatever quantity bought, a higher price would result in demand for the factor falling to zero. The factor cannot earn any more than the minimum needed to keep it in its present use.

Quasi-rent

Sometimes, economic rent can be earned in the short run, but not in the long run. Economic rent which can only be earned in the short run is called QUASI-RENT. For instance, a firm may buy a piece of machinery which is so specialised that it has no alternative uses. Then its transfer earnings are zero and hence all the payments received from the use of the machine are quasi-economic rents. In the long run, the machinery must be replaced completely or not at all, and hence part or all of the earnings of this piece of capital will be transfer earnings. In the long run the machine will need at least to cover its economic cost or it will not be replaced.

Government policy

The amount of economic rent earned by a factor of production will not affect the allocation of resources within the economy. Hence, it is theoretically possible for the government to tax economic rent from a factor without altering economic efficiency in the economy (it was argued in unit 47 that taxes might have an adverse effect on economic efficiency). For instance, the UK government places heavy taxes upon North Sea oil production, but attempts to levy them in such a way as not to discourage the development of marginal fields (i.e. oil fields which are only just profitable and which would not be developed if costs, including taxes, were higher).

Those who argue in favour of taxing economic rents usually want to see a redistribution of income from rich to poor. They argue that it offends against principles of equity that owners of some factors of production should receive high payments whilst others should receive little or nothing. Why should footballers or popstars earn hundreds of thousands of pounds a year when many workers earn a wage which is less than one per cent of that figure? Why should a farmer suddenly acquire a windfall gain of £1 million because his land has been given residential planning permission by the local council?

The problem with a tax on economic rents is that it is very difficult to tax just economic rent and not tax transfer earnings. As soon as transfer earnings are taxed, there will be allocative effects and there may be a loss of efficiency in the economy.

QUESTION 3

(a) Explain why this field in Lancashire might be worth around £1 700 an acre as farming land but £170 000 an acre as building land.
(b) Should farmers be allowed to keep any capital gain on land following the decision by a local authority to grant planning permission for building on the land?

Key terms

Functional distribution of income - shows the share of national income received by each factor of production.
Transfer earnings - the minimum payment needed to keep a factor of production in its present use. It is the opportunity cost of the factor.
Economic rent - the payment made to a factor over and above its transfer earnings in the long run.
Quasi-rent - economic rent earned only in the short run.

Applied economics

Crossing the channel

In 1994, the Channel Tunnel finally opened for business. Twelve months late, and having cost nearly twice as much to build as originally forecast, the project is on the knife edge of financial survival. Nearly all of its costs today are interest payments on its loans and repayment of the loans. The running costs of the Tunnel are relatively small because the operation is highly capital intensive. This poses a problem for competing ferry companies. They know that if Eurotunnel, the company which owns the tunnel, went bankrupt, the Tunnel would simply re-open immediately under new owners but with less debt because some debtors would lose their right to be repaid. In the worst case scenario for debtors, it would still be worth running the business so long as the Tunnel at least covers its day to day operating costs. The ferry companies are in a different position. If their Dover-Calais operations become unprofitable, they can simply transfer their ships to other routes.

The concepts of economic rent and transfer earnings can be used to explain and analyse this situation. In the case of Eurotunnel, the Tunnel has no alternative use. Its transfer earnings are therefore zero and all its earnings are economic rent. In terms of Figure 54.5, the supply curve is perfectly inelastic. The Tunnel will continue in operation whether demand is D_1 or D_2. For the ferry companies, however, their supply curve is very elastic as shown in Figure 54.6. Almost all of their earnings are transfer earnings and very little are economic rent. If the rates of return of their Dover-Calais routes fall to any significant extent, they will stop offering services and transfer the ships to other routes. A fall in demand from D_1 to D_2 would be enough to leave Eurotunnel with a monopoly on the route.

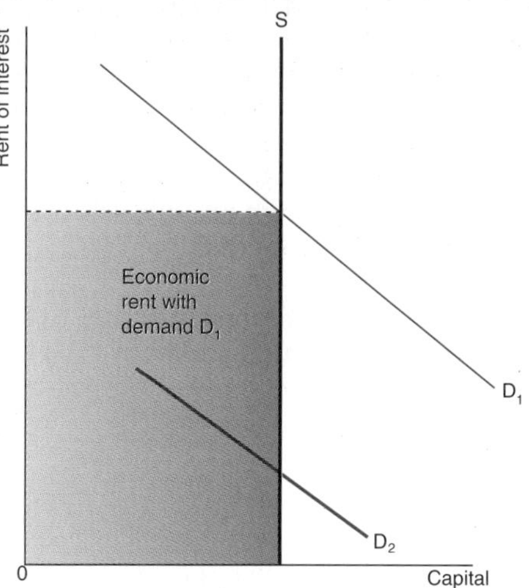

Figure 54.5 *The market faced by Eurotunnel*

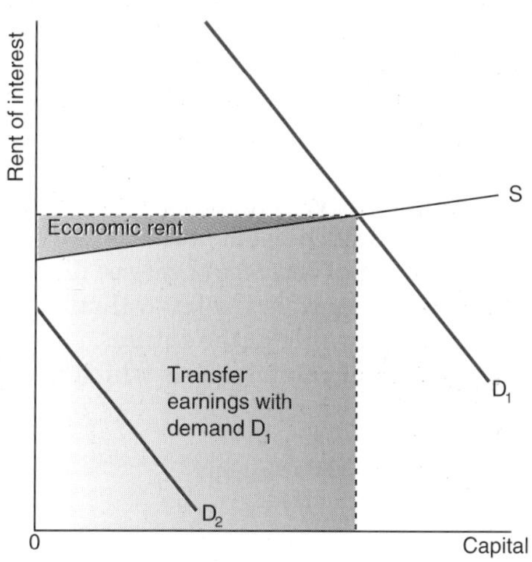

Figure 54.6 *The market faced by the Channel ferry companies*

DATA QUESTION

Economic rents

The July 1995 issue of 'Q' magazine reported that the *Mail on Sunday's* list of the highest paid women in Britain contained a number of music stars. These included Dolores O'Riordan, singer with The Cranberries (£3.2 million during the year), Sade (£2.06 million), Enya (£1.8 million) and Lisa Stansfield (£1.3 million).

The summer of 1995 saw a transfer merry-go-round in the Premier League. Notable transfers for million pound fees included Les Ferdinand (Queens Park Rangers to Newcastle United) and Stan Collymore (Nottingham Forrest to Liverpool) as well as foreign stars such as Denis Bergkamp (Inter Milan to Arsenal). The *Daily Mirror* (8 June 1995) reported the wages of some of the top earning players in the league at that time. These included: Les Ferdinand (£15,000 a week), Eric Cantona (£13,000 a week), Alan Shearer (£13,000 a week) and Andy Cole (£12,000 a week).

The Times, 27.4.1995, reported that the previous day Lord Young (Chair of the privatised company Cable and Wireless and former Cabinet Minister) had defended the pay of executives in privatised utilities. At the Institute of Directors' Conference he argued that 'Enterprise is not greed'. *The Times* reported his salary at the time as £948,000 a year.

1. **Account for the size of the economic rent of the workers/individuals above.**
2. **Should high income earners have a large part of their income taxed away? In your answer, include a discussion of both efficiency and equity considerations.**

Asset prices and the rate of interest

Summary

1. Interest payments increase the value of money over time. Conversely, the value of money available in the future is less than its value today when it is discounted back to its present value.
2. The higher the rate of interest or rate of discount and the longer the time period, the less valuable today is a fixed sum that is payable in the future.
3. The present value of capital goods which yield a stream of benefits in the future can be calculated using the rate of discount.
4. A firm should invest if the present value of the capital is equal to or more than the current cost of the capital.
5. The higher the rate of interest or discount, the lower the present value of capital and hence the less investment there will be.

Present and future values

A saver places £100 in a building society. The advertised rate of interest is 10 per cent per annum. At the end of one year her £100 will have grown to £110 ({£100 + [£100 x 10 per cent]} **or** £100 x 1.1). At the end of two years, it should have grown to £121 (£110 x 1.1 **or** £100 x 1.1 x 1.1). At the end of three years, it should have grown to £133.10 (£121 x 1.1 **or** £100 x 1.1 x 1.1 x 1.1). If the rate of interest had been 20 per cent, £100 would have grown to £120 at the end of the first year, £144 at the end of the second year and £172.80 at the end of the third year.

This illustrates an important point. Money grows over time if it is deposited or lent with interest. Put another way, a fixed sum of money payable in the future is worth less than that fixed sum paid today. £100 placed in the building society grew to be worth more than £100 at the end of three years. Therefore a fixed sum of £100 available in three years' time is worth less than £100 available today. How much less depends upon a number of factors.

The rate of interest or rate of discount The higher the RATE OF INTEREST or RATE OF DISCOUNT, the less valuable is a fixed sum of money available at a future point in time. For instance, at a rate of interest of 10 per cent, £133.10 in three years' time would be worth exactly £100 today. If the rate of interest were 20 per cent, £172.80 in three years' time would be worth £100 today.

The length of time The farther into the future that the money is available, the less valuable it is today. For instance, at a rate of interest of 10 per cent, £133.10 in three years' time is only worth £100 today. If £100 were available in 25 years' time, it would only be worth £9.23 today at 10 per cent per annum (i.e. £9.23 saved today at 10 per cent per annum would grow to be worth £100 in 25 years' time).

QUESTION 1

(a) Using a calculator, work out what £100 saved today at a compound rate of interest of 8 per cent would be worth at the end of each year for the next 10 years.

(b) What would each of the following be worth today if the interest rate were 8 per cent: (i) £108 available in 1 year's time; (ii) £116.64 available in two years' time; (iii) £251.94 available in three years' time; (iv) £25.89 available in 10 years' time; (v) £999.50 available in 9 years' time?

Rental payments and asset prices

Firms use factories, offices, machines and stocks to produce goods and services. If a firm wants to buy a piece of machinery, it has to decide the maximum price that it is prepared to pay for it. The machinery will give a stream of benefits to a company over a long period of time. The firm therefore has to assess what the future benefits are worth today, because it is today that it has to pay the money for the machinery. This is where the discussion above about present and future values can provide some answers to the question: what price should be put on an asset?

A firm can acquire the use of capital in two ways:

- it can buy capital outright;
- it can rent or lease capital.

The purchase price of capital and the RENTAL VALUE or YIELD are two different ways of measuring the price of capital. (Note that labour can also have two prices. If people could be bought and sold under a system of slavery, then it would be possible to buy labour outright. However, in a modern economy this is illegal; the only way to buy labour is to rent it. The rental value of labour is the wage rate. In the case of land, it can either be purchased outright, or rented.)

Economic theory suggests that firms should calculate the price they are prepared to pay for a piece of capital by **discounting** future yields.

Example 1 A firm wishes to buy a machine today. The machine will last for one year, has no scrap value and will give a yield of £110 in one year's time (i.e. after all other costs, including an allowance for normal profit, have been taken away, £110 of revenue is left in one year's time). The amount the firm will pay for the machine will depend upon the rate of interest or rate of discount. Assume that it is 10 per cent. Then the firm will pay a maximum of £100 (the maximum purchase price from the company's viewpoint). This is because £110 in one year's time is the same as £100 today if the rate of interest is 10 per cent.

Example 2 A firm wishes to buy a lorry today for use over a two year period. The lorry will give a yield of £5 500 at the end of the first year, £12 100 at the end of the second year and then can be sold to another company for £24 200. The rate of interest or rate of discount is 10 per cent. So the present value of £5 500 available in one year's time is £5 000. The present value of £12 100 available in two years' time is £10 000, and the value of £24 200 in two years' time is £20 000. So the total present value is £35 000 and the firm would be prepared to pay up to £35 000 for the lorry.

QUESTION 2

Table 55.1

Year	Value of £100, at a compound rate of interest of 10 per cent [1]	Net yield from a machine
0	£100	0
1	£110	£110 000
2	£121	£121 000
3	£133	£133 000
4	£146	£292 000
5	£161	£483 000
6	£177	£885 000
7	£195	£780 000
8	£214	£642 000
9	£236	£472 000
10	£259	£259 000

1. Rounded to the nearest £1.

A firm is considering the purchase of a machine. The machine produces the yield each year shown in Table 55.1. At the end of 10 years, the machine wears out and has no scrap value. What is the maximum price the firm should pay for the machine if the rate of discount is 10 per cent? To calculate this, you will need to work out the present value (in £) of each year's net yield and then add them together.

Discounting

The relationship between the two prices of capital, the rental value of yield and the asset price can be expressed more formally.

It has already been explained how a given money payment in the future is worth less today. How much less is determined by the rules of compound interest. For instance:

- £110 in one year's time is worth only £100 today at 10 per cent - this is calculated by dividing the yield, £110, by (1 + the rate of interest).
- If £121 is available in two years' time, then it is worth £121 ÷ (1 + r) in one year's time and £121 ÷ (1 + r) ÷ (1 + r) today where r is the rate of interest. This is equivalent to £121 ÷ $(1 + r)^2$.

In general if a benefit is available in n years' time, then it needs to be divided by $(1 + r)^n$ to calculate its present value. For instance:

- £100 available in 25 years' time is worth only £100 ÷ $(1 + r)^{25}$ today;
- £1 million available in 50 years' time is worth only £1 million ÷ $(1 + r)^{50}$ today. At a rate of interest of 10 per cent per annum, that is worth just £8 519 today!

The PRESENT VALUE of capital is equal to the discounted sum of future yields (and hence is sometimes also called the DISCOUNTED CASH FLOW). This can be expressed mathematically:

$$\text{Present value (PV)} = \frac{A_1}{(1+r)} + \frac{A_2}{(1+r)^2} + \cdots + \frac{A_n}{(1+r)^n}$$

PV is the present value, A is the amount of rental value or yield received by the firm from owning the capital, r is the rate of interest or rate of discount, and 1, 2, ... n are time periods such as years. The formula is saying that the present value of capital can be calculated by adding the discounted rental values the capital produces in each year. The following examples illustrate this point.

- A company invests in a machine which at the end of the first year gives a yield of £110, at the end of the second year a yield of £121 and at the end of the third year a yield of £133.10. The machine then wears out and has no scrap value. If the rate of discount is 10 per cent, the present value of the machine is the sum of the discounted yields of £110, £121 and £133.10. From the explanation above, each of the three figures discounted back to the present is worth £100. So the present value of the machine is £300.
- A company buys a machine which at the end of the first year yields £12 million, at the end of the second year yields £28.8 million, at the end of the third year yields £17.28 million and at the end of the fourth year yields £20.736 million. It then wears out and has no scrap value. If the rate of discount is 20 per cent, the present value is equal to:

$$\frac{\text{£12m}}{(1+0.2)} + \frac{\text{£28.8m}}{(1+0.2)^2} + \frac{\text{£17.28m}}{(1+0.2)^3} + \frac{\text{£20.736m}}{(1+0.2)^4}$$

$$= \text{£10m} + \text{£20m} + \text{£10m} + \text{£10m} = \text{£50m}$$

So the present value of yields which in the future will be worth £78.816 million is just £50 million discounted back to the present at a discount rate of 20 per cent. The present value of the machine is therefore £50 million.

QUESTION 3 A firm buys a machine which yields £1 000 a year each year for 5 years and then wears out. The machine has no scrap value. What would be the present value of the machine in the year of purchase if the discount rate were:
(a) 2 per cent; (b) 5 per cent; (c) 10 per cent; (d) 20 per cent; (e) [illegible] per cent?

Rate of return

The two ways of expressing the price of capital - the present value of capital and the yield or rental value - are related by the rate of interest or rate of discount. So far, a rate of interest and rental values have been given and the present value calculated. However, it is possible to calculate the RATE OF RETURN or PERCENTAGE YIELD if the present value and the rental values are given. For instance, if a firm buys a machine today for £100 and it gives a yield of £110 in one year's time and has no value thereafter, what is the rate of return? The answer is 10 per cent.

The rate of return or percentage yield is the amount of yield or rental value divided by the asset price of capital. In the equation above, if the present value (PV) and the amount of yield (A) are known, then a rate of return (r) can be calculated.

When should a company buy capital?

A company uses a rate of discount of 10 per cent. It is offered a machine which will provide a yield of £110 in one year's time and be of no value thereafter. From the above discussion, we know that the present value of the machine is £100. So the company is prepared to pay up to £100 for the machine. Therefore:

- if the price of capital is less than or equal to the present value of capital, a firm will buy capital (i.e. it will invest);
- if the price of capital is greater than the present value of capital, the firm will not buy capital.

The present value of capital depends upon the rate of interest or rate of discount used. A firm could use any rate of discount it wished. However, economic theory suggests that firms should link the rate of discount with rates of interest available in financial markets. The opportunity cost of money used to buy capital is the interest foregone from saving it with a bank or other financial institution. For instance, if a firm could gain 10 per cent per annum in a bank, it should not invest in capital if the rate of return on capital is only 5 per cent. Another way of looking at this is to consider that many firms borrow money to finance the purchase of capital. The rate of discount on capital must be at least as high as the rate of interest that has to be paid to borrow money.

In fact, it has to be higher because there is risk attached to buying capital whereas there is little or no risk if the money is saved with a bank. The risk is that the goods or services produced by the capital won't sell, or won't sell at the estimated price, or other factors such as a machine breakdown might affect the profitability of the capital.

The higher the risk, the higher the rate of discount (made up of the rate of discount on a riskless investment plus a **risk premium**). The higher rate of return is compensation to the owners of capital for taking risks.

So another way of deciding whether to invest is to compare the rate of return on a project with current rates of interest.

- If the rate of return on a piece of capital is higher than the current market rate of interest, then a company should buy the capital.
- If the rate of return is less than the current market rate of interest, the company should not buy capital but instead place the money on the financial markets.

QUESTION 4

In 1994, British Aerospace sold the Rover Group to BMW for £800 million.

(a) What was the profit in £ that BMW expected to make from the deal over the next 5 years if it wished to make a rate of return of 20 per cent per annum on the purchase?

(b) Would BMW have paid £800m for Rover if it had wished to make a rate of return of (a) 10 per cent and (ii) 30 per cent per annum? Explain your answer.

Key terms

Rate of interest or rate of discount - the opportunity cost of capital, the rate used to discount future income back to present value.
Rental value or yield - the price paid for the use of a factor of production over a period of time.
Present value or discounted cash flow - the purchase price of capital. It is the maximum price that would be paid for an asset which gave a stream of benefits or rental values over time.
Rate of return or percentage yield - the amount of yield or rental value divided by the value of capital. It is expressed as a percentage.

Applied economics

Brick manufacturing

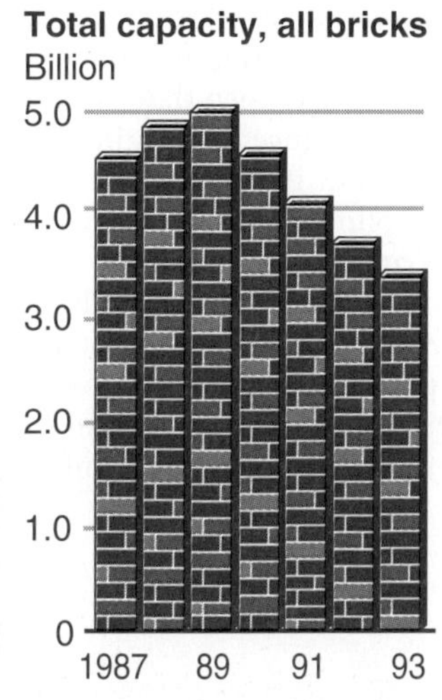

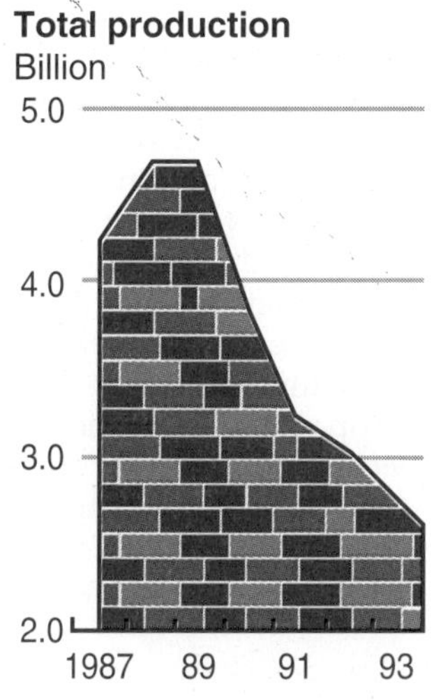

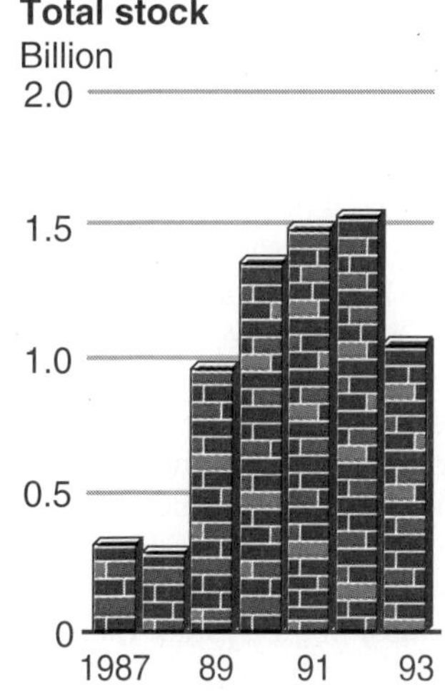

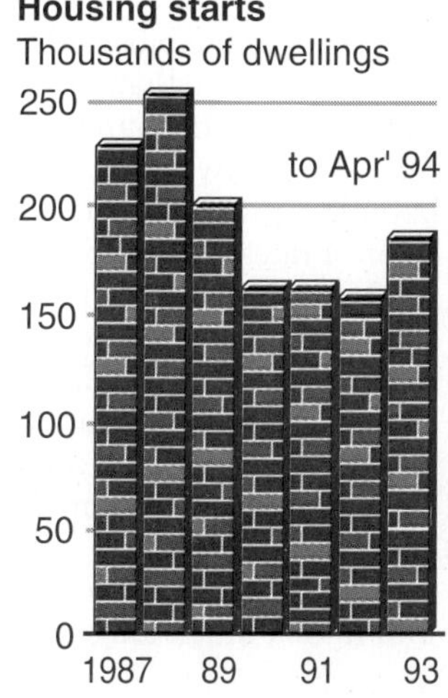

Source: adapted from Brick Development Association.

Figure 55.1 *UK Brick manufacturing, indicators*

In 1994, UK brick manufacturers held 900m bricks in stock, enough to build a Great Wall of China, 6 feet high for 5 300 miles between London and Beijing. The stock is a reflection of the very difficult times that the UK brick industry went through from 1989 onwards. During the late 1980s, new house building and commercial and industrial property development boomed. Sales peaked at 4.7bn bricks in 1987, a little before the peak in production. By 1993, the property market was still in slump and sales had fallen to 3.13bn.

All this can be reflected in the rate of return on capital in the brick industry. In the late 1980s, when brick prices peaked at about £160 per thousand, manufacturers were making an estimated 50 per cent rate of return. What this means is that for every £1 of capital employed in the firm, it was making 50p profit. Not surprisingly, firms considerably increased their capacity during this period, spending £200m to increase potential production from 4.5bn to 5.0bn bricks. In the slump that followed, rates of return crashed. Most brick makers made losses. Much higher interest rates further reduced the present value of any capital. The result was that brick manufacturers closed down capacity. This fell from a peak of 5bn in 1989 to 3.45bn in 1993. Even then, there was still excess capacity in the industry with production of only 2.64bn bricks in 1993 and stocks of over 1bn bricks. Rates of return on existing capital were still below the 20 per cent that the brickmakers would need to justify spending on new capacity. The 20 per cent return reflects what the brickmakers could earn if they simply put the money into relatively risk free financial assets like lending it to a bank plus a large risk premium. Brick making is risky because there have been large swings in the demand for bricks over the past 30 years.

By 1994, it looked as through rates of return were picking up in brick making. Housebuilding starts began to increase and this was reflected in both higher sales and higher prices for bricks. The 20 per cent increase in price between a low of £100 a thousand in autumn 1992 and £120 a thousand in summer 1994 will have directly increased the yield on brick manufacture. Lower stocks too will help increase yields because stocks cost money to keep. Not only are there the costs of storage, but there are also the costs of interest on any money borrowed to keep the stock. Whether the brick industry will expand again during this decade depends very much on what happens in the property market.

The Channel Tunnel

The Channel Tunnel was originally forecast to cost £4.8bn when work began on the project in 1987. By the time most of the bills had been paid in 1994, the cost had climbed to more than £10bn. The cost overruns came from a variety of sources. The Tunnel was started at the time of the Lawson boom when construction was booming, pushing up the cost of materials and labour. Interest rates were very high in the late 1980s and early 1990s, pushing up the interest rate bill. Technical specifications were also changed. For instance, a cooling system had to be installed in the Tunnel after it was realised that temperatures in the Tunnel would rise to 500 degrees centigrade because of friction of the trains on the tracks and the heat from the signalling, communications and other equipment.

What's more, the Channel Tunnel was completed late and it took much longer to commission the system (i.e. check that everything ran smoothly) than anticipated. Many services were at least one year late in starting. Rolling stock was also delivered late, resulting in delays to the build up of services. The result has been that the rate of return on the project has fallen since the original 1987 offering of shares to the public. In 1994, Mr Terry Smith, an investment analyst at Collins Stewart, calculated that, on Eurotunnel's own projections, shareholders will not receive any dividend till 2003. They would then need to receive £300m a year, increasing at a compound rate of interest of 9 per cent for the lifetime of the operating concession which expires in 2052, for the 1994 price of 405p per share to represent the net present value of the investment.

Source: adapted from the *Financial Times*, 3.5.1994 and 20.5.1994.

1. Explain why the estimated rate of return on the Eurotunnel project fell.

2. Discuss what would happen to the rate of return if:

(a) revenues are much larger than forecast;

(b) interest rates rise;

(c) operating costs are much larger than forecast;

(d) the ferry companies pull out of the Dover-Calais market.

unit 56 Capital and land

Summary

1. The demand curve of capital for a firm is the marginal efficiency of capital (MEC) schedule.
2. The MEC schedule will shift if, for instance, there are changes in the cost of production, in the price of output, in risk or in the 'animal spirits' of businesspeople.
3. The supply of capital can be equated with the supply of loanable funds to the market (i.e. the supply of savings).
4. The loanable funds theory states that the rate of interest is determined by the demand for and supply of loanable funds.
5. The price of land is determined by the demand for and supply of land.
6. The supply of land for a particular use, such as agricultural use or residential use, is likely to be inelastic but not perfectly inelastic.

The marginal efficiency of capital

The **law of diminishing returns** states that the marginal product of a factor, such as capital, will eventually decline if increasing quantities of that factor are combined with fixed quantities of other factors. For instance, the marginal physical product of capital for a firm will eventually decline if it uses more and more machines with a fixed quantity of workers and raw materials.

Marginal physical product can be changed into a monetary figure in a number of ways. In labour market theory, it is usual to calculate the marginal revenue product of labour (☞ unit 48). Capital theory usually expresses the marginal productivity of capital in terms of the **percentage yield** or **rate of return** on capital (i.e. the yield or rental value of capital divided by the value of capital). For instance, if a machine gives a return of £200 per year when the value of the machine is £1 000, then the rate of return on the machine is 20 per cent (£200 ÷ £1 000 expressed as a percentage).

This yield or rate of return on the last unit of capital employed is called the MARGINAL EFFICIENCY OF CAPITAL. Because of the law of diminishing returns, the marginal efficiency of capital declines as a firm's stock of capital increases.

QUESTION 1

Table 56.1

Number of machines	Marginal physical product of capital (units of output)	Marginal revenue product of capital (£)	Marginal efficiency of capital (%) £1 000 machine	£2 000 machine
1	30			
2	25			
3	20			
4	15			
5	10			
6	5			

Table 56.1 shows the marginal physical product of capital (i.e. the extra output gained by employing an extra machine using the same amount of land and labour). Complete the table by calculating:

(a) the marginal revenue product of capital if each unit of output could be sold for £10;

(b) the marginal efficiency of capital if each machine could be bought for: (i) £1 000; (ii) £2 000.

(c) Complete a new table assuming that the marginal physical product were twice that shown in Table 56.1 for every machine and each machine could be bought for [illegible].

The demand for capital

The marginal revenue product curve for labour is the demand curve for labour. Similarly, the marginal efficiency of capital curve is the demand curve for capital.

To understand why, remember that a demand curve shows the quantity that will be demanded at any given price over a period of time. Quantity in this case is quantity of capital. The price of capital is measured by the rate of return on capital. Figure 56.1 shows the falling marginal efficiency of capital schedule facing a firm.

A firm will demand capital if it can make a profit by buying or renting capital (i.e. if the rate of return on

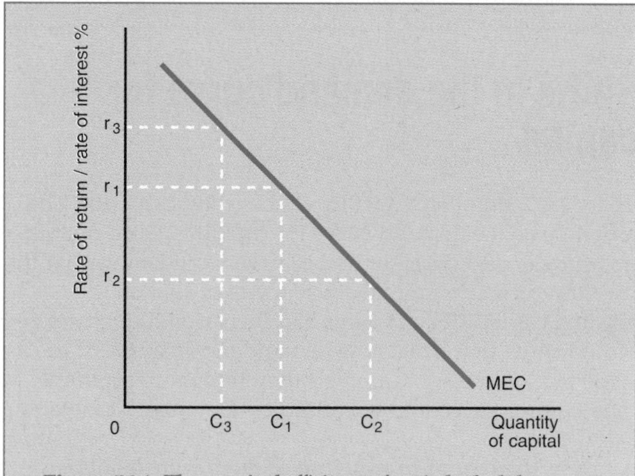

Figure 56.1 *The marginal efficiency of capital schedule*
The MEC schedule is downward sloping because of diminishing returns. It is the demand curve for capital because it is the line which equates the rate of return on capital with the cost of capital, the rate of interest.

capital is equal to or greater than the cost of capital). There are two senses in which the cost of capital can be equated with the rate of interest.

- The firm has the money to buy capital goods. In which case, it could save that money with a financial institution such as a bank and earn interest. The opportunity cost of buying capital is then the interest foregone on the money spent. The firm will only invest (i.e. buy capital goods) if the rate of return on capital, including a risk premium, is greater than the return on money placed with a financial institution.
- The firm has to borrow the money to finance capital expenditure. The cost of borrowing money is the interest that has to be paid on the loan. The firm will only invest if the rate of return on capital (which will include an allowance for normal profit) is equal to or greater than the cost of borrowing the money.

If the rate of interest is r_1 in Figure 56.1, then the firm will demand C_1 of capital. It would not demand C_2, for instance, because the rate of return on C_2 would only be r_2. The rate of return, r_2, would then be less than the rate of interest, r_1, and the firm would lose money relative to the best alternative. Nor would it demand C_3 of capital as the rate of return on C_3 is r_3, which is above the rate of interest r_1. It could therefore profitably expand its capital stock to C_1. This is the equilibrium amount of capital demanded if the rate of interest is r_1 because it is the point where the cost of capital (the rate of interest) is equal to the return from capital (the rate of return).

QUESTION 2

(a) Draw the marginal efficiency of capital schedule from the data in Table 56.1 assuming a cost per machine of £1 000.

(b) How many machines would the firm buy if the rate of interest were: (i) 30 per cent; (ii) 20 per cent; (iii) 10 per cent?

(c) How would your answer to (b) be different if the marginal physical product of each machine were 3 times that shown in Table 56.1?

Shifts in the demand curve for capital

There are a number of factors which could cause the MEC schedule or the demand curve for capital to shift. A shift upwards and to the right in the curve would show that the rate of return or marginal efficiency of capital on the existing capital stock of firms had increased. Equally, it would show that firms now demand more capital at the same rate of interest. Capital is therefore more profitable than before. This could be caused by a number of factors.

A fall in the cost of production If there were a fall in the cost of production, then the yield on capital would rise. For instance, a fall in the cost of building factories or buying new machines will increase the rate of return on marginal capital. Hence, at a given rate of interest, more capital will be bought.

An increase in the price of output If the firm can sell its product for a higher price, then the rate of return on capital will increase.

A reduction in risk All investment is risky. Capital is bought to produce a stream of services in the future and the future is always uncertain. A firm will include an allowance for risk when it calculates the potential rate of return on an investment project. The higher the risk, the higher the rate of return needed to persuade a firm to invest. Hence, if a firm downgrades the risk associated with the purchase of capital, it will be prepared to undertake more investment at the same market rate of interest.

Animal spirits John Maynard Keynes argued that investment was crucially dependent upon the animal spirits of investors. He argued that firms swung from pessimism to optimism about the future and vice versa. The more optimistic firms are about the future, the higher the rate of return they expect from new capital and hence the further to the right will be the MEC schedule.

QUESTION 3 In late 1994, UK machine tool companies were feeling much more confident about their own economic situation than they had twelve months previously. Demand for machine tools was rising after the deepest, longest recession in living memory. 'Things are picking up', said Mr John Wareing, managing director of Leicester-based Jones & Shipman, which makes grinding machines. Its UK orders were up 50 per cent on 1993. The machine tool industry is normally one of the last to recover from a recession, and large machine orders and multi-million pound manufacturing projects tend to trail behind the less costly contracts from smaller, standard machines.

Mr Wareing at J&S said that the upturn in orders reflected confidence among large and small customers. 'Most people are feeling pretty perky now in industry', he said. The one possible obstacle is interest rate increases. Mr Taylor at Leicester-based Bridgeport Machines said: 'As soon as you start playing around with interest rates, it sends shudders through industry, which needs stability for a while.' At Giddings & Lewis, a Merseyside based company, Mr Don McBean, the sales director said: 'The last thing we would want to see is anything that would stop a customer making a decision'.

Source: adapted from the *Financial Times*, 4.10.1994.

(a) Using a diagram, explain why there was an increase in demand for machine tools in 1994.

(b) Discuss what factors could lead to a reversal of this trend.

The supply of capital

The demand for capital can be seen as the demand by firms to borrow money for investment, an increase in their capital stock, at any given rate of interest. Similarly, the supply of capital can be defined as the quantity of money available to firms for investment purposes at any given rate of interest.

Interest is the reward for lending money. Saving takes place for a number of reasons: one is that savers will have more money to spend in the future if they save now (i.e. current consumption has an opportunity cost in terms of future consumption). The higher the rate of interest, the more can be earned in the future and the more attractive saving money becomes today. The more money that is saved, the more there is available for firms to borrow.

Hence, the supply curve of funds available for firms to borrow to invest is upward sloping as in Figure 56.2. An increase in the rate of interest from OA to OB will increase the supply of funds available for investment in capital from OE to OF.

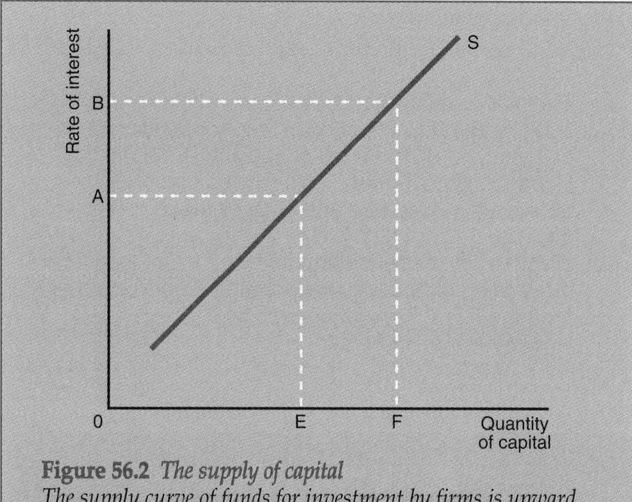

Figure 56.2 *The supply of capital*
The supply curve of funds for investment by firms is upward sloping. An increase in the rate of interest from OA to OB will increase the quantity of loanable funds supplied from OE to OF.

Determination of the rate of interest

Prices are determined by the forces of demand and supply. The price of capital is the rate of interest. Hence the rate of interest must be determined by the demand for and supply of capital. The demand for capital is the demand for investment goods. The higher the rate of interest, the lower will be investment demand and hence the lower will be the demand for borrowed or loanable funds to finance the investment. The supply of capital can be equated with the supply of loanable funds to the market (i.e. the volume of saving). The higher the rate of interest, the more money will be saved, which can then be lent out to firms to borrow for investment.

The LOANABLE FUNDS THEORY of the rate of interest argues that the rate of interest is determined by the demand and supply for loanable funds (i.e. the demand for and supply of capital). The theory is a simplification because consumers and governments borrow money too. A more complete explanation of interest determination is given in unit 75.

QUESTION 4 For each of the following, explain using a diagram:
(a) whether it will affect the demand for or supply of loanable funds;
(b) the effect it will have on the equilibrium rate of interest.
(i) Government gives tax relief on savings; (ii) government cuts tax concessions on pension schemes; (iii) business people become more optimistic about the economy; (iv) wages increase at a faster rate than the price of capital; (v) firms increase the price of their products.

Land

Land as a factor of production is not just land itself but all natural resources (☞ unit 2). The price of land is determined by the demand and supply of land. As with capital, the price of land can be expressed in two ways:
- the purchase price of land;
- the rental value of land.

To illustrate the pricing of land as a factor, take the example of land itself. It might seem that land is in fixed supply and therefore its supply is infinitely price inelastic. There is only a finite amount of land on this planet. The supply of land can be increased through land reclamation, for instance, but the resulting addition to the stock of land can only be very small.

However, there are many markets for land and the land can be switched from one use to another. For instance, industrial land can be used for housing. Housing land can be used for shops. Agricultural land can be used for industrial purposes. Hence the supply of land, although likely to be inelastic, is not perfectly inelastic.

Figure 56.3 shows the demand and supply curves for land used for housing. An increase in the population will increase the demand for housing land from D_1 to D_2. The result will be a rise in the price of housebuilding land and an increase in quantity supplied. In the UK, this extra land is likely to be found by taking agricultural land and using it for house building.

Using agricultural land for housing purposes is controversial in the UK. The government, through Green Belt policies, has limited the supply of agricultural land for housing. This has had the effect of making the supply of land for housing far more inelastic than it would otherwise have been. It has also pushed up the price of building land from what it would have been without the Green Belt policies. This is shown in Figure 56.4. Initially, the market is in equilibrium with price at OE and quantity bought and sold OA. An increase in population, leading to a shift in the demand curve from D_1 to D_2, would lead to an increase in the price of land by EF. However, if the government has imposed limits on the sale of agricultural land for building purposes, the supply curve is not S_1 but S_2. The result is that the increase in the price of land is not EF but EG. Moreover, instead of an extra AC land being released for building purposes, only AB more is sold. Fewer houses are likely to be built, resulting in either homelessness or overcrowding in the existing stock of houses.

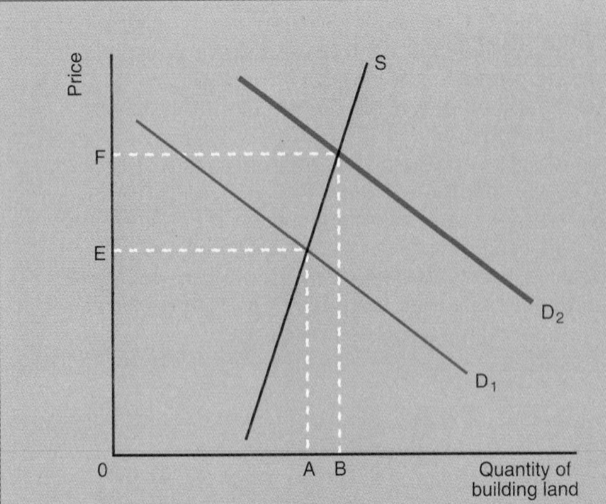

Figure 56.3 *The price of land*
An increase in the demand for building land resulting from an increase in the population will increase land prices from OE to OF.

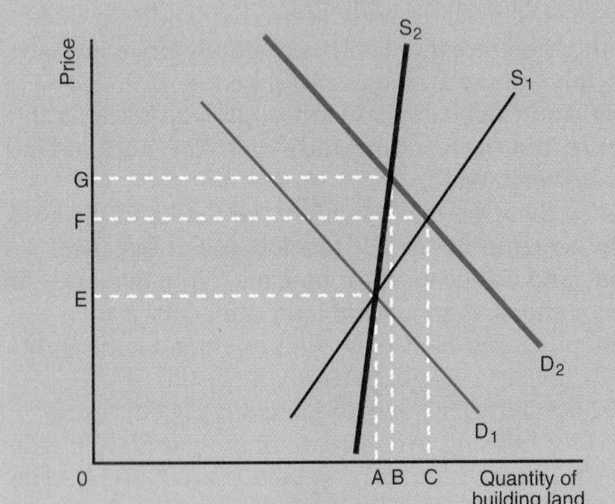

Figure 56.4 *Green belt regulations*
The effect of green belt regulations is to make the free market supply curve S_1 more inelastic. With a 'Green Belt supply curve' for building land, S_2, an increase in the demand for housing will result in a large increase in the price of land of EG and only a small increase, AB, in the quantity of building land.

QUESTION 5 In 1994, John Gummer, the environment secretary, suggested to Berkshire County Council that it should limit the supply of housing land in its forthcoming structure plan to 40 000 homes between 1991 and 2006. This was one-sixth less than the 48 000 homes recommended by Department of the Environment inspectors following a public enquiry the previous year. It was also less than the 52 000 homes which the Housebuilders' Federation had been pressing for. It was slightly more than the 37 000 homes which Berkshire County Council had proposed.

The Housebuilders' Federation warned that a shortage of development sites had already pushed housing land prices up by 50 per cent in the south-east during the past year. The Council for the Protection of Rural England, on the other hand, which supported Berkshire's limit of 37 000 homes, was dissatisfied with the 40 000 figure, which it said did not recognise environmental damage.

Source: adapted from the *Financial Times*, 18.6.1994.

(a) Explain, using diagrams, what the effect would have been on (i) the price of land for residential building and (ii) the price of agricultural land if the Housebuilders' Federation's wishes had been accepted in Berkshire and in other areas of the country.

(b) Discuss who might benefit and who might lose from the limiting of housing land to 40 000 homes rather than the 52 000 recommended by the Housebuilders' Federation.

Key terms

Marginal efficiency of capital - the rate of return on the last unit of capital employed. It is measured by dividing the rental value or yield by the cost of the last unit of capital employed.

Loanable funds theory - the loanable funds theory of interest rate determination argues that the rate of interest is determined by the demand for and supply of loanable funds, in particular for purchase of capital.

Applied economics

Capital

The stock of capital

If an economy grows over time, it is almost certain that this will be reflected in the growth of its capital stock. Table 56.2 shows the composition of the stock of physical capital in the UK in 1993. The largest category of physical capital is 'Other buildings and works'. This comprises buildings such as factories, offices and warehouses. 'Dwellings' are private homes, either owner occupied or rented from landlords such as local councils. Examples of 'plant and machinery' are machine tools, industrial computers and photocopiers as well as large plant such as chemical works.

Table 56.2 *UK physical capital*

	Gross capital stock by type of asset at 1990 replacement cost. £bn at 1990 prices
Road vehicles	81.9
Trains, ships and aircraft	15.9
Plant and machinery	662.4
Other buildings and works	901.9
Dwellings	932.0
Total	2 594.1

Source: adapted from CSO, UK National Accounts.

Marginal efficiency of capital theory

Marginal efficiency of capital theory suggests that the stock of capital will increase if industry becomes more profitable. At any given rate of interest, there will be more investment if the rate of return on that investment has increased. This is shown by a shift to the right in the MEC schedule. On the other hand, a fall in the rate of return on capital will lead to a fall in investment.

Figures 56.5 and 56.6 give some support to this theory. During the late 1960s and early 1970s, the real rate of return on capital fell in the UK. This subsequently led to a fall in the level of investment as a percentage of GDP from 1968 to 1981. The rate of return on capital picked up again in the mid-1970s and, having fallen again in the 1979-81 recession, rose to levels not seen since the 1960s. Rates of return subsequently fell when the economy went into the 1990-92 recession, as did investment.

However, the figures are not conclusive as:

- the correlation between the real rate of return and investment as a percentage of GDP is not particularly close;
- nothing is said about other factors which will have affected investment and which changed over the period, such as the rate of interest;
- whilst increases in demand in the economy, which would affect the MEC schedule, have been taken into account by dividing investment by GDP, it could be argued that a more sophisticated demand variable is needed;
- care must be taken when interpreting investment statistics. Total investment in Figure 56.5 includes investment by government which is not interest sensitive. The private investment figures in Figure 56.5 do not represent a consistent series. This is because the privatisation process of the 1980s and early 1990s transferred large parts of the public sector to the private sector. Part of the increase in private sector investment from the early 1980s therefore simply represents the reclassification of what had been public sector investment before privatisation to private sector investment. Figure 56.5 do not represent a consistent series. This is because the privatisation process of the 1980s and early 1990s transferred large parts of the public sector to the private sector. Part of the increase in private sector investment from the early 1980s therefore simply represents the reclassification of what had been public sector investment before privatisation to private sector investment.

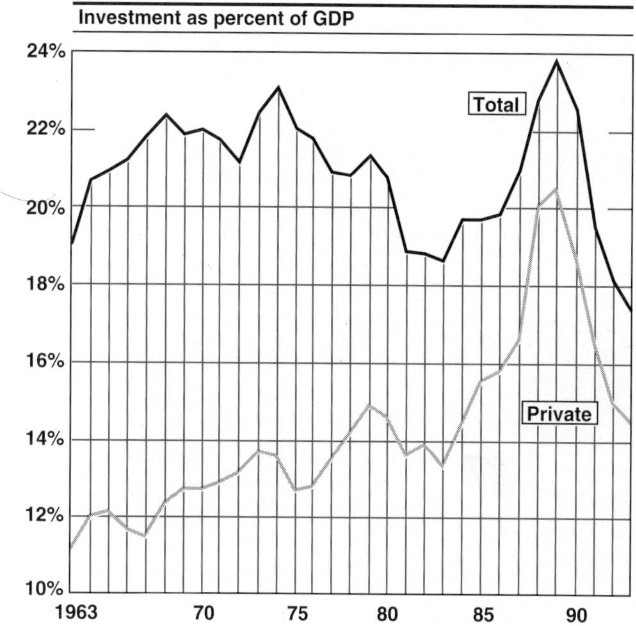

Source: adapted from CSO, *Economic Trends Annual Supplement.*
Figure 56.5 *Investment as a percentage of GDP (at market prices)*

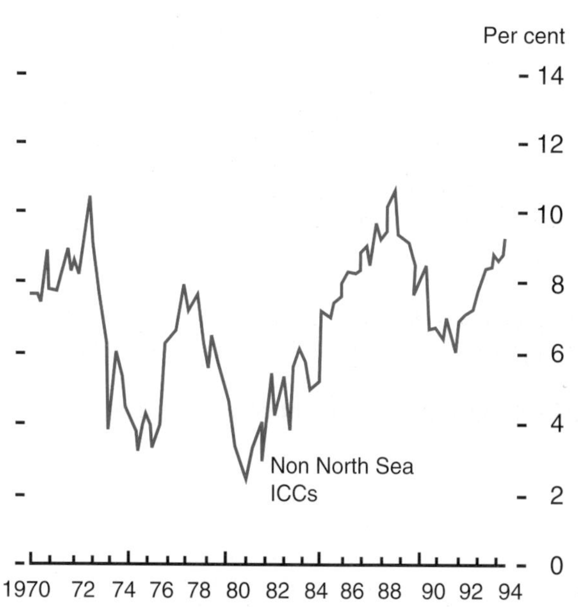

*Pre-tax rate of return on capital stock at replacement cost.
Figure 56.6 *Companies' real rate of return**

Oil reserves

Source: adapted from NatWest Securities.

Figure 56.7 *Levels at which North Sea production is profitable*

Oil reserves in the North Sea are an example of the factor of production land. Recovering oil from oil fields requires a considerable amount of capital, another factor of production. So, what determines the demand for and supply of both of these factors in the context of the North Sea?

The North Sea is split into two halves. Rights to exploit the western half are owned by the British government. Rights to exploit the eastern half are owned by the Norwegian government. Both governments grant licences to explore and then exploit blocks of areas to individual companies or consortia. In the late 1960s and 1970s, blocks which initially looked the most promising in terms of finding oil were auctioned off. The largest oil fields currently in production, such as the Forties and Brent fields, date from this period. In the 1980s and 1990s, less promising areas have been auctioned, but there has continued to be a steady number of new fields. The supply, then, of fields to explore is controlled by the British and Norwegian governments which, on a regular basis, offer companies the chance to bid for new fields. There is also a market in proven oil discoveries. A company may have explored a block and found enough oil to justify production. It may then sell the rights for production to another company. So the supply of proven reserves is controlled by exploration companies. The higher the price a production company is prepared to pay for rights to a field, the more likely it is to find another company willing to sell a field.

The demand for fields depends upon a number of factors. One is the price of oil. Figure 56.7 shows that North Sea oil production would be lower if the price were $10 a barrel than if it were $14 a barrel. Some fields are marginal; that is, at $14 a barrel, they are profitable, but at $10 a barrel, they are unprofitable. Note, however, that the fall in production from a lower price is relatively small. In fact, most UK fields are profitable even at $5 a barrel. Another factor is the rate of interest. The higher the rate of interest, the lower will be the return on a field if the money to finance the field has been borrowed. A third factor is the opportunity cost of exploring and developing a field in the UK. Oil producers have preferred the North Sea to many other locations round the world partly because the infrastructure which has been built up to deal with large oil discoveries, such as the Forties field, leads to lower costs of production than for other fields.

Another important factor is the political stability of the UK. Developing a field in Nigeria or Vietnam, for instance, is a much higher risk because a government could nationalise a field or there could be civil war.

Part of the capital employed in the North Sea has no alternative use. These, for instance, are the pipelines which connect drilling platforms to the coast. Much of the capital has alternative uses. An increasing amount of production now takes place from movable platforms and ships. These can be moved to other areas of the world if production in the North Sea falls. Costs of exploration and production are falling all the time as new advances in technology improve the equipment used and the way it is constructed. Oil recovery rates are also much higher, particular due to the ability now to drill horizontally through rock.

According to estimates by Wood Mackenzie, new technology has halved production costs in the North Sea between 1985 and 1995. Capital is also used more intensively than before. Gas, a by-product of many fields, used to be flared off. Nowadays, it is the norm for it to be collected, making many marginal fields viable.

Source: adapted from the *Financial Times*, 27.10.1993 and, 11.1.1994.

1. **An oil company is considering whether to put in a bid for the rights to explore an off-shore block (a) in the North Sea and (b) in Indonesia. What factors would affect the price it would be prepared to pay for those rights?**
2. **(a) Interest rates worldwide increase. Explain, using a diagram, what effect this would have on the demand for capital in the North Sea. (b) Would your answer be different if interest rates increased in the UK but remained the same in other industrialised countries?**
3. **Suggest what might determine the supply of capital in the North Sea.**

unit 57 Entrepreneurship

Summary

1. Entrepreneurship involves the organisation of production, risk taking and innovation.
2. Owner managers of small firms are likely to combine all these three functions and therefore are most likely to be classified as entrepreneurs.
3. Managers too can be seen as entrepreneurial if they take risks on behalf of their companies and if they are responsible for innovation.
4. Shareholders too risk their capital and therefore could be seen as entrepreneurial.
5. Pure or abnormal profit is the reward for entrepreneurship.
6. An 'enterprise culture' may increase economic welfare if entrepreneurs are responsible for a disproportionate share of innovation, job creation and wealth creation in the economy.
7. An entrepreneurial spirit can be created in large firms if pay and other rewards of managers are linked to their performance.

Entrepreneurs - Anita Roddick (Body Shop) and Richard Branson (Virgin)

The nature of entrepreneurship

There is no standard definition of an **entrepreneur** in economic theory. However, different economists have identified three possible elements of the entrepreneurial function.

The organisation of production The entrepreneur is the factor of production which brings together the other factors in the production process. Land and capital are inert objects. Workers wait for the instructions of their bosses. It is the entrepreneur who buys land and capital, hires labour and then organises all three factors to produce goods and services for sale. The entrepreneur can then be seen as the key to production in the economy. It could be argued that if there were no entrepreneurs, there would be no production.

Risk Production is a risky process. In many industries, land, labour and capital have to be purchased before there is any certainty that the finished product will be sold. For instance, a car manufacturer is likely to make cars without there being any firm orders for their sale. If it makes too many cars, they will have to be stockpiled for sale at a later date. Too big a stockpile and too few orders could result in the bankruptcy of the firm. Hence firms face uncertainties and have to take risks.

The American economist, F H Knight, working in the inter-war period, defined such risk in terms of unquantifiable risk. Some risks are quantifiable and can therefore be insured against. For instance, a firm can insure itself against the risk of fire damage or theft. However, other risks, such as whether a new product will sell, or whether a new production technique will lead to a reduction in costs, are unquantifiable and therefore cannot be insured against.

Entrepreneurs are those who take unquantifiable risks and suffer the consequences if they get it wrong.

Innovation New products are being launched all the time but evidence suggests that only a few will be successful. New production techniques are also being constantly pioneered with varying degrees of success. Joseph Schumpeter, the Austrian economist working in the inter-war years, argued that the entrepreneur is someone who innovates within an organisation.

QUESTION 1 In March 1976, Anita Roddick opened her first shop in Brighton. She had been turned down for a loan by a major bank because her business idea was thought to be a recipe for disaster. After all, who would want to lend money to someone who promises to sell foot lotion made with peppermint and lip balm with apricots? Equally, the idea of promoting 'health rather than glamour and reality rather than the dubious promise of instant rejuvenation' in the cosmetics industry was quite revolutionary. Since that initial opening, the business has never looked back. In 1984, it secured a stock exchange listing and by 1995 had shops in North America and Asia as well as Europe, and a stock market value of over £300m.

Anita Roddick has continued to confound the financial sceptics. She argues that a company can be both commercially successful and ethical. In fact, one of the key reasons why customers shop at Body Shop is because they like the company's attitude to health, animal welfare rights and the environment. She spends her time not just helping to manage the company in a conventional sense but also promoting the ethics of the company through speaking at conferences, visiting the Third World to establish links and gather ideas, and through interaction with her own employees.

In what senses might Anita Roddick be called an entrepreneur?

Entrepreneurs

Most economists would accept that the owner manager of a newly set up company that produced an innovative product could be described as an entrepreneur. This is a person who combines all three of the characteristics described above. She organises production because she is the manager of the company. She takes risks because she has put money into the firm to start it and is producing an innovative product which could well fail. She is an innovator because her product is new to the market.

However, this type of person is only likely to be found in the small firm sector of the economy where an individual is likely to:

- have sufficient capital to be able to finance the setting up of the firm;
- have total control over the organisation of production;
- be exposed to considerable risk if the enterprise fails.

So entrepreneurship has tended to be associated with new, small firms. However, economists have suggested that other workers could be classed as entrepreneurs, or have an entrepreneurial function.

Managers A manager of a company may have no shares in the company for which she works (i.e. she is not an owner or part owner of the company). Hence she does not risk her capital in the business. She could still be regarded as an entrepreneur if she were involved in one of two areas.

- According to Knight's definition above, she would be an entrepreneur if she took decisions which involved an uncertain outcome. For instance, it would be entrepreneurial behaviour if a manager gave the go-ahead for the launch of a new flavour of yoghurt. The flavour might be very successful or it might not. Hence the outcome of the decision is uncertain. Managers of large companies can, in this view, be as entrepreneurial as owner-managers of small companies.
- According to Schumpeter's definition, she would be an entrepreneur if she took decisions which led to innovation. So again, managers of large companies can be seen to be entrepreneurial if they are responsible for pushing their companies into new areas.

Individual managers can be entrepreneurial, but so can groups of managers. If managers work together as a team and innovate or take risks, then the group is entrepreneurial. Hence, large Japanese companies, which often have a tradition of group decision making, can be just as entrepreneurial as the lone businessman who sets up and runs his own business.

Capitalists Millions of individuals in the UK today directly own shares in companies. Does this make them into entrepreneurs? In one sense it does. A few shareholders are 'Aunt Sallys' - friends, relations or business acquaintances of individuals who want to set up their company. These shareholders risk their money to back an individual or an idea which attracts them. They are backing change and may even be in a position to give advice to the person setting up the company. On a wider front, all shareholders in both small and large companies carry the risk of the success or failure of the enterprise. If the company fails, shareholders lose their money. On the other hand, shareholders are unlikely to be involved in organising production. Nor are they involved in innovation in the firm. So some economists argue that capitalists are in some senses entrepreneurs, whilst others disagree.

QUESTION 2 ICI, one of Britain's largest companies, was founded in the 1920s. A solid company, it was rarely called 'entrepreneurial'. The two oil crises of the 1970s wrought havoc with the finances of the company and by 1982 some commentators wondered whether it would survive. In that year, the directors took a gamble. They appointed John Harvey Jones as chairperson, a man famous for loud ties and bad haircuts. He never took work home with him, never answered business calls, never entertained business contacts at home, and did the family shopping at the weekend. But he did turn ICI round. He integrated parts of the business to achieve economies of scale. He closed down or sold off other parts which were unprofitable and expanded those where profit margins were higher and which showed potential future growth. When he retired in 1987, he was seen by many to be the model of an entrepreneur.

(a) In what sense could Harvey Jones be seen as an entrepreneur?
(b) Was the board of directors of ICI entrepreneurial when it appointed Harvey Jones as chairperson?

Profit - the reward for entrepreneurship

In traditional economic theory, profit is seen as the reward for entrepreneurship. Profit is the revenue left over after the other factors of production have been paid. If the entrepreneur is successful, there will be a large residue after wages, interest and rents have been paid. If the entrepreneur is unsuccessful, profits will be negative and the firm could go bankrupt.

Not all profit is the reward for entrepreneurship. **Normal profit** (☞ unit 22) is the opportunity cost of factors such as labour and capital which receive no money payment for their use. Only **abnormal profit** or **pure profit** can be seen as the payment which entrepreneurs receive.

Entrepreneurship and economic welfare

Over the past 15 years, there has been a resurgence of interest amongst policy makers in entrepreneurs and their activities. A number of arguments have been put forward as to why entrepreneurs play such an important role in the economy.

- Innovation. It is claimed that entrepreneurship is essential for innovation. Indeed Schumpeter defined entrepreneurship in terms of this key role in the economy. Without innovation, the economy would stagnate. There would no improvement in living standards. Innovation is therefore vital if economic welfare is to increase.
- Job creation. Successful entrepreneurs create jobs. In particular, there has been much interest in the ability of small firms to create jobs and help ease the unemployment problems of the 1970s and 1980s.
- Wealth creation. Entrepreneurs create wealth by their activities. The small firms of today will become the large successful firms of tomorrow.

QUESTION 3 It was reported in 1990 that small businesses employing fewer than 20 people had contributed the most to job creation in the late 1980s despite employing little more than one fifth of all workers. A study by the Dun and Bradstreet credit rating group found that of companies listed by the group, those employing between 5 and 19 staff generated 295 000 jobs between 1985 and 1987, whilst there was a loss of 106 000 jobs among companies employing more than 1 000 workers. Total net job creation over the period was put at 307 000 - only half the official government estimate of the increase in private sector employment over the same period.

(a) Why might entrepreneurs contribute disproportionately to the growth of welfare in an economy?
(b) Why might the findings of the report not be totally accurate?

On the other hand, it is argued that entrepreneurs, whilst they can play a part in raising economic welfare, are not essential in this process. There is little evidence to suggest that small firms, often seen as more entrepreneurial than large firms, contribute disproportionately to job creation or wealth creation. If any form of innovation is classified as 'entrepreneurial', then entrepreneurs are essential in an economy. But innovation can lead to failure as well as success. It is noticeable that the UK and the USA, economies where the small firm entrepreneur has been seen by many as a folk hero, have had lower economic growth rates than economies such as Japan and Germany where greater stress is placed on team work and co-operation. On the other hand, perhaps the difference between the USA and Japan is that in the USA it is the individual which classically undertakes entrepreneurial activity whilst in Japan it is a team of workers which is entrepreneurial.

Creating an 'enterprise culture'

It is common to equate entrepreneurship with the small business sector of the economy. Many of the claimed advantages of the 'entrepreneurial spirit' are in fact the possible advantages of having an active small business sector in an economy. On this view, the entrepreneur is the owner manager of a small company. Hence government can best support the creation of an enterprise culture by measures which will support the creation and expansion of small firms in the economy. An evaluation of policies taken over the past 15 years by government is contained in the applied economics section below.

Economic theory, however, suggests that the entrepreneurial spirit need have nothing to do with small

QUESTION 4 In November 1994, Mr Cedric Brown, chief executive of British Gas, was awarded a 75 per cent pay rise, taking his basic annual salary to £475 000 at a time when British Gas staff were typically receiving a 3 per cent pay increase. The pay rise was defended on the grounds that Cedric Brown had previously been grossly underpaid for leading such a large company which had recently been so successful. Like many other executives, Cedric Brown also had rights to a number of bonuses linked to performance. The commonest bonus found in the privatised utilities are share options. Executives are given the opportunity to buy shares in their company at some point in the future, such as five years, at today's price. If the company is successful, then this should be reflected in the share price. In 1994, for instance, Richard Young, managing director of Midland's Electricity, left the company with accumulated share options which were estimated to be worth £500 000 in profit to him.

Source: adapted from the *Financial Times*, 16.7.1994 and 21.11.1994

Discuss whether ordinary pay increases or share option schemes are more likely to make executives more entrepreneurial.

firms. Both innovation and risk taking can be as much if not more the concern of large firms as small firms. How then can a more entrepreneurial spirit be created in large firms?

In recent years, there has been a move towards paying managers by results. Some managing directors, for instance, are paid a basic salary but can earn far more if their company achieves a range of objectives. These could include increases in sales, increases in profits, increases in the share price of the company or reductions in the cost of production. Extra payments may come in the form of cash or shares in the company. The idea is to make managers who are employees of the firm accept more risk. If the firm does well, the managers will do well. If the firm does badly, so too do the managers.

Applied economics

The enterprise culture

The growth of self-employment in the UK

The self-employed have traditionally constituted only a small percentage of the total labour force in the UK. Figure 57.1 shows that the number of self-employed workers was approximately 2.2 million or about 8 per cent of the working population throughout the 1970s. However, there was a growth of self-employment during the 1980s so that by 1994 the number of self-employed was nearly 3.3 million, and they formed nearly 13 per cent of the working population.

Superficially, this increase in numbers of self-employed might seem to indicate that more people were becoming entrepreneurs, setting up their own businesses and taking risks with the aim of making profits. However, some economists believe this was not the case. The growth in self-employment took off in 1980-1982 when the economy was in deep recession. Unemployment then remained at very high levels (over three million) till 1986, when it began to fall. This would suggest that unemployment and recession were the key reasons why self-employment rose.

- Some of those made redundant received substantial redundancy payments and therefore had financial capital to set up their own business.
- Some of the unemployed could see no way in which they would get a job in the near future. Self-employment was a way out of this situation, earning money and regaining self-respect.
- Industry itself encouraged the growth of self-employment. In a recession, employers are reluctant to take on new staff because there might be no work for them in six months' or a year's time. Instead, recession and uncertainty provide a powerful incentive to employers to contract work out. For instance, there was a sharp decline in the number of employees of major construction companies in the 1980s. Construction companies increasingly used casual labour or contracted small firms to do jobs.

The substantial shift in employment from manufacturing to service industry during the 1980s is also likely to have been a factor in the growth of self-employment. Figures 57.2 and 57.3 show that most of the the growth in self-employment has come from service industries. Service industry is far more labour intensive than manufacturing. Hence there are far lower financial barriers to entry for a would be entrepreneur in the tertiary sector than in the secondary sector of the economy. Note that the growth in self-employment in manufacturing was particularly concentrated amongst males. This is not surprising given that many manufacturing industries have almost no female self-employed workers. The percentage rise in female self-employment in services, on the other hand, was greater than that for males. The largest proportion of female self-employed workers is found in distribution, hotels, catering and repairs.

The recession of the 1990s led to a fall in the numbers of self-employed, from a peak of 3.5 million in 1990 to a low of 3.2 million in 1993, since when numbers have slowly

Source: adapted from CSO, *Annual Abstract of Statistics*; *Employment Gazette*, February 1995.

Figure 57.1 *Self-employment and the total working population, UK*

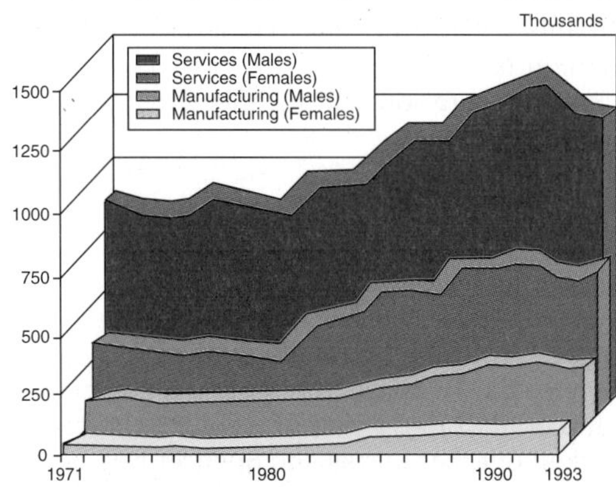

Source: adapted from *Employment Gazette Historical Supplement*, October 1994.

Figure 57.2 *Self-employment by industry and gender, Great Britain (1971-93)*

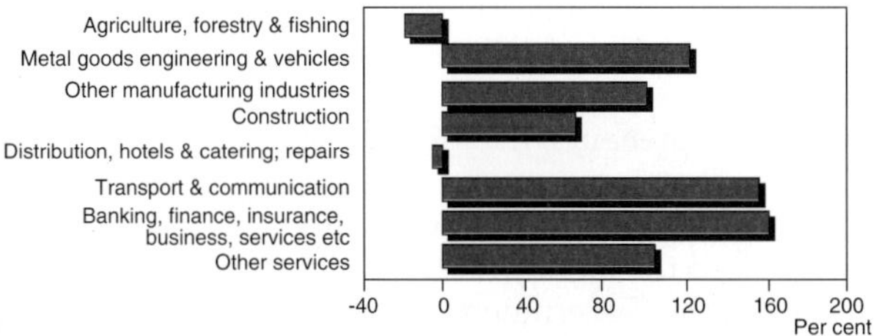

Source: adapted from *Employment Gazette Historical Supplement*, October 1994.

Figure 57.3 *Self-employment by industry, percent changes (1991-93)*

begun to recover. It could be argued that self-employment is unlikely to grow much in the future since self-employment opportunities are unlikely to grow much. Figure 57.4 shows that, by 1992, the UK had a proportion of self-employed workers which was very similar to many other industrialised countries. Indeed, self-employment was greater than in the USA and Germany and on a par with Japan, all countries with which the UK is often compared.

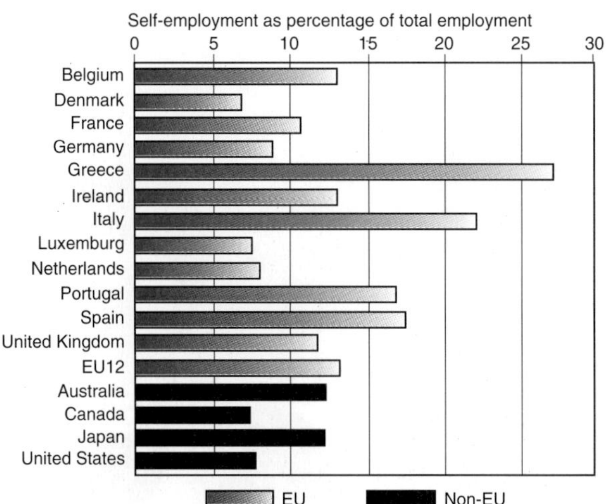

Source: adapted from *Small Firms in Britain (1994).*

Figure 57.4 *International comparisons of self-employment rates (excluding agriculture), 1991*

Government policy

Although high unemployment and structural changes in the UK economy were important factors in the growth of self-employment in the 1980s, it is also true that the decade was one where government economic policy created a climate favourable to entrepreneurial activity.

- Taxes were cut to increase incentives. The highest rate of tax on earned income fell from 83 per cent to 40 per cent between 1979 and 1988. The main rate of corporation tax fell from 52 per cent to 35 per cent and the small companies rate was reduced from 42 per cent to 25 per cent. The burden of administering VAT was lightened, for instance by allowing small companies to make just one VAT return a year.
- The government attempted to reduce the amount of 'red tape' imposed on small businesses. A whole variety of measures was introduced. For instance, some small businesses were exempted from certain requirements relating to industrial tribunals, unfair dismissal procedures and maternity reinstatement. In 1994, the government announced plans to reduce the audit requirements for small firms.
- Small companies found it easier to obtain financial capital to start up and expand. The government encouraged banks to lend more to the small business sector. It also encouraged the growth of the venture capital industry, firms which specialise in putting in share capital to new or expanding businesses. In 1983, it introduced the Business Expansion Scheme which enabled investors to put money into a business and take any profit made tax free. Withdrawn in 1993, the scheme failed to achieve its aim of providing large amounts of share capital for small businesses, but it was an attempt by the government to help small businesses in an area of finance which has often proved difficult for them. The Loan Guarantee Scheme, introduced in 1981, has proved more successful. This is a scheme whereby firms can borrow money from banks and if the firm defaults on its loan, the government will repay the bank any money outstanding. In some ways, the government proved too successful in persuading banks to change their lending attitudes to small businesses. In the recession of 1990-92, when many small businesses went bankrupt, entrepreneurs claimed that banks had lent them too much.
- In 1988, the Department of Trade and Industry (DTI) launched the Enterprise Initiative. This initiative offered free or subsidised training and consultancy for small businesses in areas such as marketing, new technology and production. Local Training and Enterprise Councils (TECs) and Local Enterprise Agencies both carry out the advice and training offered in the Enterprise Initiative.
- The unemployed were encouraged to set up their own enterprises through the Enterprise Allowance Scheme. Participants needed to produce a business plan and they were given help to do this through initial enterprise training provided by the government. They were then given £40 a week for one year to help them establish their own businesses. Between its start in 1983

and April 1991, half a million participated in the scheme. Since 1991, each local TEC has offered a similar scheme tailored to local needs. About 75 per cent of participants survive the first 18 months (including the first 12 months when they are likely to be on a grant) and 65 per cent are still trading after 3 years.

Entrepreneurs

Geoff Brown

Geoff Brown is the son of a Birmingham scaffolder. After travelling extensively as a professional keyboard player in the 1970s, he founded CentreGold in 1983. He realised that there was a market for foreign computer games in the UK. In 1983, he started by buying £200 worth of games from the USA which he began selling in Birmingham. The business has grown into one of the largest publishers and distributors of computer and video games in the UK. He runs the business from a small office on a Birmingham industrial estate.

In 1993, he bought the firm to the stock market where it was valued at £50m. At the time of flotation, he sold part of his stake in the company, realising over £1m. Twelve months later, he sold another 1.38 million shares, realising £1.36m and cutting his share in the company to 29 per cent.

In 1994, the company bought Core, a game developer, for £5.34m. Core employed 34 programmers and designers at the time, and produces games for arcades, personal computers and games machines. Justifying the acquisition, Geoff Brown said: 'They have nine products they are developing, but only for a limited number of formats. We will expand the formats. Also, they licence products into the US; we will publish ourself, which is much more profitable.'

1994, however, proved a difficult year for the company. Fierce competition during the Christmas period saw profit margins cut. There was also growing consumer resistance to buying games on old formats given that new CD technologies were widely predicted to be the formats of the future. The company plunged into loss. Shares which had been sold at flotation at 150p went down to 20p.

Source: adapted from the *Financial Times* 25.9.1994; *The Independent*, 27.10.1994, 29.10.1994; *The Times* 22.2.1995.

The rise and fall of Sock Shop

Sock Shop was founded by Sophie Mirman with her husband Richard. Ms Mirman originally worked for Marks and Spencer and then for the Tie Rack. She spotted a gap in the market when she couldn't find a pair of woolly tights to match a dress. She checked out that Marks and Spencer had only 12 per cent of the hosiery market, and with a belief that women were fed up with fighting their way through crowded department stores every time their tights laddered, she opened her first shop in Knightsbridge Underground station. The design, size and typical locations of the shops were based on the successful Tie Rack formula. They were small, bright, cheerful, and situated wherever there was a large volume of passing customers.

Like so many entrepreneurs, the Mirmans had problems obtaining finance. They were refused venture capital by banks who thought the idea unworkable. Eventually with £1 000 each in capital, they raised the money for the Knightsbridge shop with the backing of the Government Loan Guarantee Scheme.

The shop was an instant success. By 1987 they had 47 shops, the company has been floated on the Unlisted Securities Market with a capital value of over £50 million and the Mirmans were millionaires.

Then came disaster. Sock Shop expanded into the USA but the shops became the targets of hit and run raids by youths. Eventually, the company had to employ a security guard for each shop which made the venture unviable. By 1990, they pulled out, having lost millions of pounds. In the UK, the long hot summer of 1989 resulted in dramatic falls in the sales of tights and socks. Sock Shop moved into loss and in 1990 administrators were appointed under the Insolvency Act. The Mirmans, along with the rest of the shareholders, lost all their money.

Within nine months, the Mirmans had bounced back, opening a children's toy and clothes shop in London. Their entrepreneurial spirit was still very much alive, despite one spectacular failure.

1. **What is meant by 'entrepreneurship'? Illustrate your answer with examples from the data.**
2. **In what ways might the entrepreneurs described above have contributed to the economic welfare of the UK?**
3. **Evaluate ways in which the government could create a more favourable economic climate for entrepreneurs.**

INVESTIGATIONS 4

A. Demographic changes

Aims

- To describe the changes in the numbers of 16-21 year olds in the UK population over the period 1970 to 2020.
- To analyse the possible effects of these changes on employment opportunities, rates of pay and unemployment for 16-21 year olds compared to other workers.
- To evaluate what response, if any, government should make to these changing demographic trends in the future.

Research activity

Start by finding out the age structure or estimated age structure of the population over the period 1970 - 2020. In particular, you need to find the numbers of 16 to 21 year olds in the population over the period. If possible, break down the UK figures by sex and by region. Also establish what proportion of 16-21 year olds are in full time education, what proportion are in work and what proportion are unemployed. Then find out what has happened to the relative pay of young workers aged 16-21 compared to the rest of the population in recent years. Also, find figures for unemployment rates of 16-21 year olds compared to the average for all workers over the period.

Conduct a newspaper and magazine search to find out what predictions have been made recently about young people and their role in the labour market. What impact is this likely to have on older workers and the increased trend towards early retirement? How might government respond to this?

Sources

The CSO *Guide to Official Statistics* gives sources for all government published statistics. General statistics about the population are contained in CSO, *Social Trends*, *Annual Abstract of Statistics* and *Regional Trends*. Large public reference libraries may well also stock OPCS *Monitor Population Projections*, *Population Trends* and *Regional Population Projections*.

CSO, *Social Trends* and CSO, *Annual Abstract of Statistics* also give numbers in full time and part time education. More detailed figures can be obtained from CSO, *Education Statistics for the United Kingdom*. Activity rates are given in CSO, *Social Trends*. A more detailed breakdown can be obtained from occasional articles published in the *Department of Employment Gazette*, a monthly magazine.

Relative earnings can be obtained on a yearly basis from the Department of Employment, *New Earnings Survey*. The *Department of Employment Gazette* also publishes regular articles on earnings which may have relevant material. For your newspaper and magazine search, use one or more indexes. The *Financial Times, The Times, The Guardian* and the *Economist* all publish indexes for past issues. The library may also carry other indexes such as the *Research Index*, published by Business Surveys Ltd., which covers articles of financial interest in 100 newspapers and periodicals on a monthly basis. The newspapers and an index may also be available on CD-Rom.

Structuring your report

Introduction Outline the aim of your investigation. The aim should be put in the form of a hypothesis or question which will allow you to come to some conclusions.
Economic theory Outline the economic theory to be used in this investigation. This is likely to include demographic concepts such as age ratios, and economic concepts such as the demand for and supply of labour, marginal revenue productivity theory, unemployment and market failure.
Techniques used to collect your data Outline how you collected your data.
Changing demographic trends Describe the change in the numbers of 16-21 year olds in the population. Contrast this with other changes in the population. Outline the distribution of young people between work and education. Describe the changes in the ratio of females to males in the 16-21 age range. If possible, present regional as well as national data. Use charts, tables or diagrams to present or illustrate your findings.
Effects on earnings and employment What would economic theory suggest would happen to earnings of 16-21 year olds and to youth unemployment as a result of the demographic changes you have already described? Outline what has happened to these variables since 1970 and what has been suggested will happen in the future. What other effects on industry and employment might result from changing demographic trends, particularly the ratio of females to males and the ratio of 16-21 year olds to total population in regions of the UK? To what extent is the evidence you have gathered consistent with the predictions of economic theory?
Government response Outline what measures the government could take to deal with any problems likely to result from changing numbers of 16-21 year olds in the population in the future. Evaluate the likely effectiveness of such policies.
Sources Outline the sources of information you used. What problems did you encounter in gathering relevant data? What data would you have liked to have obtained but could not? To what extent was the data reliable?
Bibliography Write down a list of your sources in alphabetical order.

Other suggestions

Instead of considering the economic effects of changes in the numbers of 16-21 year olds in the population, it would be possible to investigate the likely economic effects of changes in the numbers of any group in the population. For instance, what are the likely effects of the 'greying' of the population or what is likely to happen to the size of the working population over the next 20 years and what effects will this have?

Alternatively, survey the local job market. What rates of pay can 16-21 year olds gain in different occupations? To what extent can economic theory account for these differences in pay rates? This investigation could involve primary research, for instance a survey of 16-21 year olds in the local area. Local business people could be interviewed on their views about the effects of changing demographic trends on local business. A survey of local newspapers may also provide information about local rates of pay.

B. Entrepreneurship

Aims

- To gather data through the use of interviews and desk research.
- To present the findings of that research in a clear and logical manner.
- To assess the extent to which those interviewed could be considered to be 'entrepreneurs'.
- To evaluate the importance of entrepreneurship in the economy.
- To compare and contrast research findings with the predictions of economic theory.

Research activity

This investigation involves interviewing two entrepreneurs. Your first task is to find a number of people who might be worth approaching. They might own their own companies or be self-employed. Alternatively, they might work for a company in a role which could be seen as an obvious starting point. You may also have a part time job employed by an entrepreneur and therefore have a suitable contact there. National figures, such as Alan Sugar or Richard Branson, are most unlikely to give interviews.

Select two potential entrepreneurs and make an approach either personally or by letter. You need to outline the purpose of your investigation, when and where you propose the interview might take place and give some examples of questions you are likely to ask. You may decide to ask the person to come to your school or college and the whole group can participate in the interview. Alternatively, you may go to the place of work or home of the individual. You could perhaps link this with a work experience placement.

Before the interview, draw up a questionnaire. Think carefully about what information you must have if the investigation is to have substance. What supplementary questions will you need to ask if your original question does not draw forth a sufficiently detailed answer? Equally, think about what information the entrepreneur may well be unwilling to divulge (e.g. sales figures and profit figures).

In the interview, be confident and remain in control of the interview. Do not be afraid to ask the interviewee to explain or elaborate on an answer. It is usually easiest if you tape record the interview and make notes on it afterwards. However, if you use a tape recorder, you **must** obtain consent before the interview.

The second part of your research is to collect material about entrepreneurs and entrepreneurship in general. Read what textbooks and other materials have to say about the characteristics of entrepreneurs and the role of entrepreneurs in the economy. Conduct a newspaper and magazine search on entrepreneurs, the role of small businesses in the economy and on individuals who might be called 'entrepreneurs'. To conduct your search, it is easier if you use an index. The quality newspapers and magazines, such as the *Financial Times*, publish their own indexes. Otherwise, use any index which your local large public library might have available, such as the *Research Index*, published by Business Surveys Ltd., which covers articles of financial interest in 100 newspapers and periodicals on a monthly basis. Newspapers may also be available on CD-Rom.

Structuring your report

Introduction Outline the aim of your investigation. The aim should be put in the form of a hypothesis or question which will allow you to come to some conclusions.

Economic theory Outline the economic theory to be used in this investigation. This is likely to include concepts such as risk, the factors of production, entrepreneurship, and economic efficiency.

Techniques used to collect your data Outline how you collected your data.

A description of the two entrepreneurs interviewed Introduce the two entrepreneurs you interviewed - their names, their occupation, whether or not they owned their own company, etc. Outline the main questions you asked (you may wish to include the whole questionnaire as an appendix) and briefly summarise the responses.

Application and analysis To what extent could the two people interviewed be considered to be entrepreneurs? Compare their role with the role of the entrepreneur in economic theory. Compare too their activities with those of other 'entrepreneurs' whom you have discovered from your newspaper and magazine search.

Evaluation Consider the extent to which entrepreneurs perform a useful role in a market economy like that of the UK. Illustrate your answer from the material gathered during the interviews and your newspaper and magazine search. To what extent is entrepreneurship essential for economic success?

Bibliography Write down a list of your sources in alphabetical order.

Other suggestions

A wide variety of people could be interviewed to illustrate the role of workers in an economy and the rewards to other factors of production.

- One or more trade unionists could be interviewed to consider the role of trade unions in today's Britain. To what extent do they protect their workers' interests? Does a trade union mark-up exist? Do trade unions cause unemployment?
- A manager could be interviewed. What is the role of a manager in an organisation? To what extent are managers entrepreneurial? To what extent could management be seen as part of the inefficiency of production (X-inefficiency ☞ unit 33).
- Workers in two contrasting markets could be interviewed to evaluate the extent of economic rent. What do they consider to be their transfer earnings? What factors might affect their level of economic rent?
- The process of wage determination could be investigated by interviewing a number of employees in different occupations. What factors determine their wage rates/earnings and how does this correlate with the predictions of economic theory?

The circular flow of income

Summary

1. In a simple circular flow model of the economy, households spend all their earnings on goods produced by firms, which in turn pass back all earnings to households. There is no government and no foreign trade.
2. Income, output and expenditure are defined as being equal in the circular flow model.
3. If it is assumed that households save as well as spend, whilst firms produce not only goods for consumption but also investment goods, then saving becomes a leakage from the circular flow whilst investment is an injection.
4. Actual injections must equal actual withdrawals.
5. In the real world, it is the financial system which links investment and savings.
6. In an economy with government, public spending is an injection whilst tax revenues are a withdrawal from the circular flow.
7. In an open economy where there is foreign trade, exports are an injection whilst imports are a withdrawal.

A simple economy

Macro-economics is the study of the workings of the whole economy. An economy is a complicated structure and not surprisingly there is much disagreement amongst economists about exactly how it works. Just as in micro-economics, where the model of demand, supply and the market provides a basic framework for the analysis of many problems, so in macro-economics there is an accepted general model of economic behaviour. This is the CIRCULAR FLOW OF INCOME model.

In a pure **subsistence economy**, there is no trade between individuals. People consume only the goods and services that they themselves produce. In a more sophisticated market economy, producers and consumers become separated.

- **Households** own the wealth of the nation. They own the land, labour and capital used to produce goods and services. They supply these factors to firms in return for rents, wages, interest and profits - the rewards to the factors of production. They then use this money to buy goods and services.
- **Firms** produce goods and services. They hire factors of production from households and use these to produce goods and services for sale back to households.

The flow from households to firms is shown in Figure 58.1. The flow of money round the economy is shown in red. Households receive payments for hiring their land, labour and capital. They spend all that money on the goods and services produced by firms (consumption). An alternative way of putting this is to express these money payments in **real** terms (☞ unit 3 explains the distinction between real and monetary values). The real flow of products and factor services is shown in black. Households supply land, labour and capital and in return receive goods and services.

This model of the economy is a very simple one because it has been assumed that:

- Households spend all of their income on goods and services produced by firms whilst firms spend all of their revenues on factors of production owned by households;

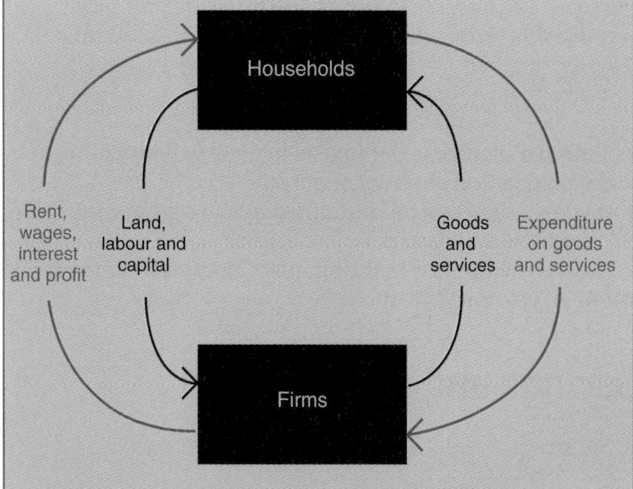

Figure 58.1 *The circular flow of income in a simple economy*
Households supply factors of production to firms in return for rent, wages, interest and profit. Households spend their money on goods and services supplied by firms.

QUESTION 1

Table 58.1

	£bn
Rent	5
Wages	75
Interest and profit	20

The figures in Table 58.1 represent the only income payments received by households. There are no savings, investment, government expenditure and taxes or foreign trade in the economy.

(a) Construct a circular flow of income diagram showing the income and expenditure of households and firms.
(b) How would your answer be different if wages were £100bn?

- there is no government sector and hence there is no government spending or taxes;
- the economy is CLOSED (i.e. there is no foreign sector).

Income, output and expenditure

The amount of money flowing round the system gives a value to the level of economic activity. As can be seen from Figure 58.2, this can be measured in three different ways. Going from right to left, the level of economic activity can be measured as the value of:

- national expenditure (E) - spending by households on the goods and services produced by firms;
- national output (O) - the output of firms (i.e. the value of what they produce);
- national income (Y) - the income paid by firms to households.

In national income accounts, the three are identical because they are defined in such a way as to be identical:

$$O \equiv E \equiv Y$$

- National income is defined as income generated from the production of national output.
- National expenditure is defined as the expenditure needed to purchase national output.

This is true not just in the simplest circular flow model but in all circular flow models.

Savings and investment

In the simple model above, it was assumed that households spent all of their income. In practice not all household income is spent. Some of it is saved.

Saving (☞ unit 62) is called a LEAKAGE or WITHDRAWAL from the circular flow of income and expenditure because the money saved leaves the circular flow. Withdrawals lower the level of economic activity in the system.

Firms too do not spend all of their money on existing factors of production. They spend money on **investment goods**. These are goods such as machines, factories, offices and other capital equipment used to produce other goods and services. As well as this **fixed capital**, there is **circulating capital** (also called stocks, or stocks and work in progress or inventories). These are goods which have been produced by firms but have not been sold to consumers. They could, for instance, be coal at a steel mill, steel at a car plant, or cars in a dealer's showroom. Investment expenditure is an INJECTION to the circular flow. Injections increase the level of economic activity in the system.

Savings and investment are shown in Figure 58.3. Money saved leaks from the circular flow, whilst money spent on goods and services flows round the system. Those firms manufacturing investment goods receive payments for those goods. Real goods and services and the services of real factors of production flow round the system in the opposite direction.

In the real world, savings in the economy are linked to investment through the financial system. For instance, households save money and deposit their savings in a bank. The bank then lends out the money to firms to finance their investment programmes.

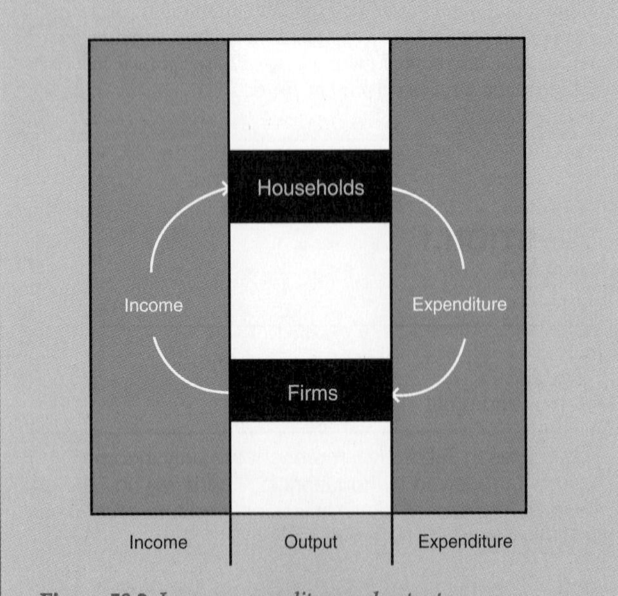

Figure 58.2 *Income , expenditure and output*
The value of the flow of money round the system can be measured at three different points - as income , output or expenditure. These three must be identical because they measure the same flow.

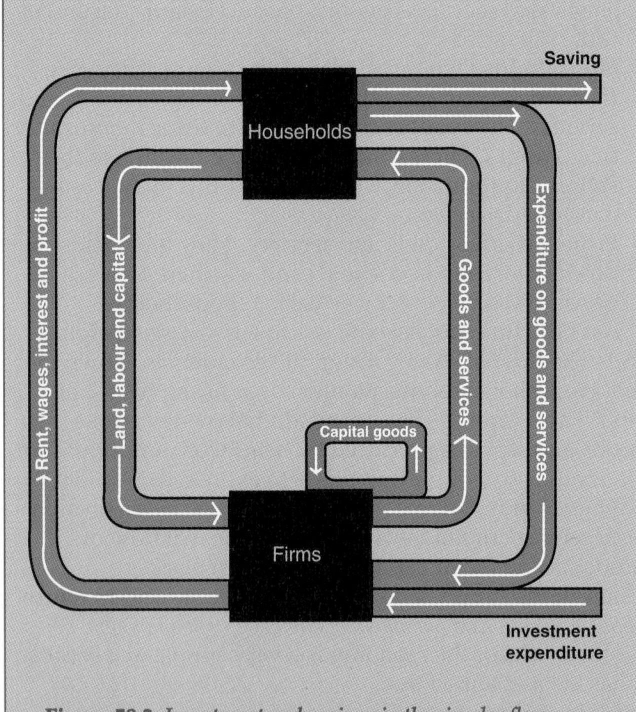

Figure 58.3 *Investment and savings in the circular flow*
Investment is an injection to the circular flow whilst saving is a leakage.

Injections must equal withdrawals

So far nothing has been said about the size of the flows round the economy. In the simplest model, the circle is closed. Hence, the flow of money round the system will be constant and the economy will be in **equilibrium** (i.e. there will be no tendency to change within the system).

But if investment and saving take place, money enters and leaves the system. Common sense suggests that the two will be equal at some point. Consider what would happen if they were not. If investment spending were greater than saving, the amount of money entering the system would be greater than the amount leaving. Every time money went round the circular flow it would increase, leading eventually to an infinite amount of money and a corresponding infinite level of production in the system. If on the other hand, savings were greater than investment, there would be a net drain of money from the system. Eventually there would be no money left in the system and all production would stop.

To understand why injections must equal withdrawals, it is necessary to introduce two **identities**. An identity is something which is true by definition. For instance, a quadruped must always have four legs by definition. Therefore 'quadrupeds are four legged animals' is an identity. Identities are shown by the symbol ≡.

It was assumed above that households either spend their income or save it. Hence by definition, income must equal consumption expenditure plus savings:

$$Y \equiv C + S$$

where Y is income, C is consumption expenditure and S is savings.

It was also assumed that there were only two components of total spending on goods and services in the economy. Households bought goods and services, whilst firms spent money on investment goods. Hence, by definition, total expenditure must equal consumption expenditure plus investment:

$$E \equiv C + I$$

where E is total expenditure and I is investment.

Income and expenditure are two ways of measuring the same flow round the economy. Y and E are therefore always the same value. Hence:

$$C + S \equiv C + I$$

and it must therefore be true that:

$$S \equiv I$$

In the circular flow model, withdrawals (in this case savings) must always be equal to injections (in this case investment). This is true of **actual** savings and **actual** withdrawals. In unit 80, we shall see that economic agents may **plan** to save and invest different amounts but that their plans may be frustrated because **actual** injections and withdrawals must always be equal.

QUESTION 2

Table 58.2

£bn

	Consumption	Saving	Investment	National income
(a)	70	30		
(b)	20			25
(c)	50		10	
(d)		250		800
(e)			8	48

The table shows actual consumption, saving, investment and national income in a simple closed economy with no government. Fill in the missing figures in the table for each line a to e.

The government sector

Governments exist in all national economies. Governments raise money through taxes to finance their expenditure on services such as defence and education.

Taxes represent a withdrawal of money from the circular flow. Government takes money from households and firms in a variety of taxes. Government spending, on the other hand, is an injection to the circular flow. Government spending puts money back into the flow.

In a closed economy, (i.e. one where there is no foreign trade), there are thus two injections and two withdrawals. Investment and government spending are injections and savings and taxes are withdrawals. It was argued above that actual injections must always equal actual withdrawals. Hence, it must be true that:

$$I + G \equiv S + T$$

Note that it need not be true that I ≡ S if there is a government sector. Investment could be greater than savings if taxes were greater than government spending. What must be true, however, is that total injections (I + S) must always equal total withdrawals (S + T).

Foreign trade

Nations trade with each other. Consumers spend money on imported goods. This is money which leaves the domestic circular flow of income to be given to foreigners.

Imports are therefore a withdrawal from the circular flow. On the other hand, foreigners spend money on goods and services produced domestically. This is therefore represented as an injection into the circular flow.

In an OPEN ECONOMY (i.e. a country with foreign dealings) with a government sector, there are now three injections and three withdrawals:

- the injections are investment, government spending and exports;
- the withdrawals are savings, taxes and imports.

Actual injections must equal actual withdrawals.

Hence:

$$I + G + X \equiv S + T + M$$

where X is exports and M is imports.

It is now possible to draw a circular flow diagram for this economy. Figure 58.4 does not attempt to show exactly how the injections and withdrawals fit into the circular flow. Such a diagram would be extremely complicated. For instance, taxes can be paid not only by households and firms but also by foreigners on exports and imports. Computer models of the circular flow for the UK can use hundreds of different equations to describe the interactions within the economy.

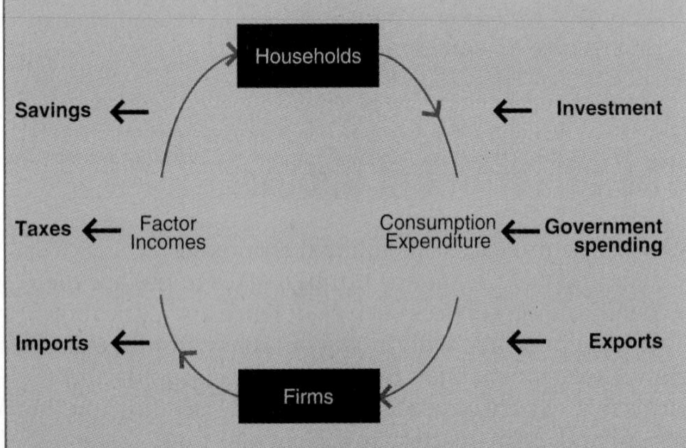

Figure 58.4 *The circular flow for an open economy with government*
Savings, taxes and imports are withdrawals whilst investment, government spending and exports are injections.

QUESTION 3 Draw a circular flow diagram for the UK economy. Where would you place on it: (a) the purchase by a UK firm of new machinery manufactured domestically; (b) the deposit of money by a household into a bank; (c) the payment of wages by a firm; (d) the purchase by a UK household of a car manufactured in Germany; (e) the purchase of theatre tickets by American tourists in London; (f) the purchase by a UK household of a meal in Glasgow; (g) the payment of profits to Japan from a Japanese owned factory in Wales?

Measures of national income

Figure 58.2 shows that there are three ways of measuring national income - by income, by output or by expenditure. All three must be equal because they provide snapshots at different stages of the same money flowing round the economy. National income is then usually expressed as GDP or GNP.

- GROSS DOMESTIC PRODUCT or GDP is the most commonly quoted measure of national income. It measures income generated within the domestic economy.
- GROSS NATIONAL INCOME or GNP adds in income that has been earned abroad minus any income that the UK has had to pay abroad. Examples of this income are interest paid on loans and dividends received on shares. Note that earnings from exports are already included in gross domestic product because the expenditure method of calculating GDP includes this.

There is also a third measure of national income which is called 'national income'. The difference between GNP and national income is that national income includes an allowance for **depreciation** (☞ unit 59). Each year, the capital stock of the country wears out or depreciates, rather like a car as it gets older. National income is the income of the country (GNP) minus depreciation.

GDP and GNP tend to be quoted in articles and publications more often than national income. The reason is because figures for depreciation are usually not given in month by month estimates of current national income. It is also difficult to estimate and tends not to fluctuate very much as a percentage of national income. As Figure 58.5 shows, changes in GDP and GNP are good indicators of changes in national income. GDP is often used in preference to GNP because it is a better indicator of output and employment trends in the domestic economy and because accurate figures for income from abroad take a considerable time to collect. Again, from Figure 58.5, it can be seen that over long periods of time, changes in GDP and GNP tend to be almost the same and hence using the crudest measure of income, GDP, provides a reasonably reliable guide to what is happening to more complete measures of income.

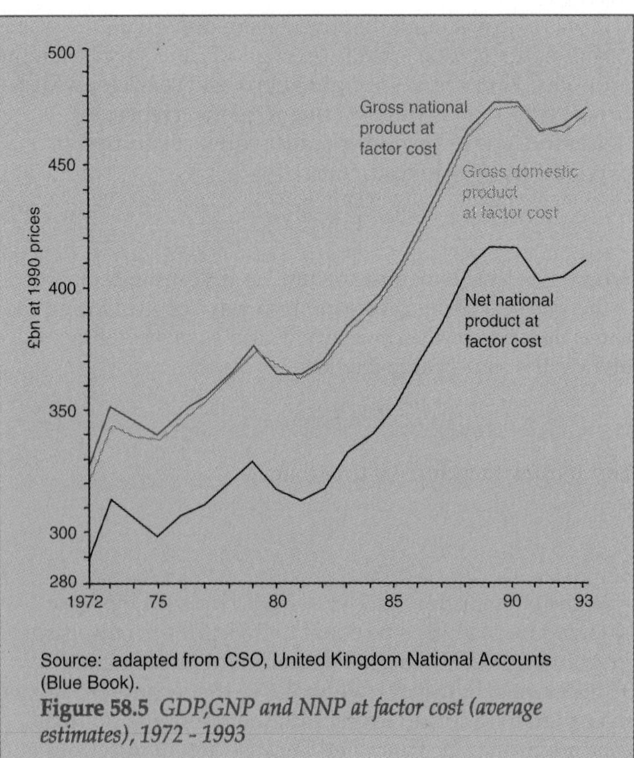

Source: adapted from CSO, United Kingdom National Accounts (Blue Book).

Figure 58.5 *GDP,GNP and NNP at factor cost (average estimates), 1972 - 1993*

Transfer payments

Not all types of income are included in the final calculation of national income. Some incomes are received without there being any corresponding output in the economy. For instance:

- the government pays National Insurance and social security benefits to individuals, but the recipients produce nothing in return;
- students receive student grants from government, but again produce nothing which can be sold;
- children receive pocket money and allowances from their parents;
- an individual selling a second hand car receives money, but no new car is created.

These incomes, called TRANSFER PAYMENTS, are excluded from final calculations of national income. For instance, government spending in national income is **public expenditure** (☞ unit 44) minus spending on benefits and grants.

QUESTION 4 The Gray family: Pete Gray, teacher aged 45; Mary Gray, accountant and mother aged 44; Enid Gray, retired aged 70; John Gray, unemployed, aged 22; Sara Gray, university student aged 20; Emma Gray, sixth former at school aged 18.

(a) Make a list of the likely sources of income for each member of the Gray family.
(b) Explain which of these are transfer earnings and which would be included as part of national income.

Key terms

Circular flow of income - a model of the economy which shows the flow of goods, services and factors and their payments round the economy.
Closed economy - an economy which has no trade with foreign countries. There are therefore no exports or imports.
Leakage or withdrawal - national income which is not spent on current consumption and therefore leaves the circular flow of income. Savings, taxes and imports are usually considered to be leakages.
Injection - national expenditure in addition to consumption expenditure in the circular flow of income. Investment, government spending and exports are usually considered to be injections.
Open economy - an economy with economic trade with foreigners.
Gross domestic product (GDP) - a measure of national income before property income from abroad and depreciation have been accounted for.
Gross national product (GNP) - a measure of national income including net property income from abroad but before depreciation.
Transfer payments - income payments for which there is no corresponding output. They are excluded from national income accounts.

Applied economics

The Channel Tunnel Rail Link

The Channel Rail link, between London and the Channel Tunnel, is forecast to be built at the end of this century or the beginning of next century. It will be a major piece of civil engineering work, the first major new railway line to be built in Britain for over a hundred years.

The projected cost is in excess of £3bn. Its impact on the economy can be traced through the circular flow of income. The link will be an example of investment in the economy. As such, it is an injection (flow 1) into the circular flow, as shown in Figure 58.6. Part of the total cost of the project will be spent directly on labour (4) and materials by the construction company which builds the link. Part will be used to pay other firms employed for subcontracting work (flow 2). Both the construction company and its subcontractors will spend money on imported goods and services, a leakage from the circular flow of the UK economy (3). They will also pay interest, profits and dividends to debtors and shareholders (5). Taxes on earnings, a withdrawal from the circular flow, will be deducted at source and paid to the government (6). Households then receive income net of tax.

In Figure 58.6, the flow of income is traced back from households to firms. Households will save part of the money (7), a leakage from the circular flow. The rest will be used to purchase consumer goods (8). Some consumer goods will be imported (9). Most consumer goods will be subject to VAT or other indirect taxes (10). Money paid in taxation or imports will leak out of the UK circular flow. The rest will flow back to the UK firms supplying the consumer goods. They, in turn, will use the money to pay for materials from other firms, to pay their workers, their shareholders, etc. and so the money will flow back round the left hand side of the circular flow shown in Figure 58.6.

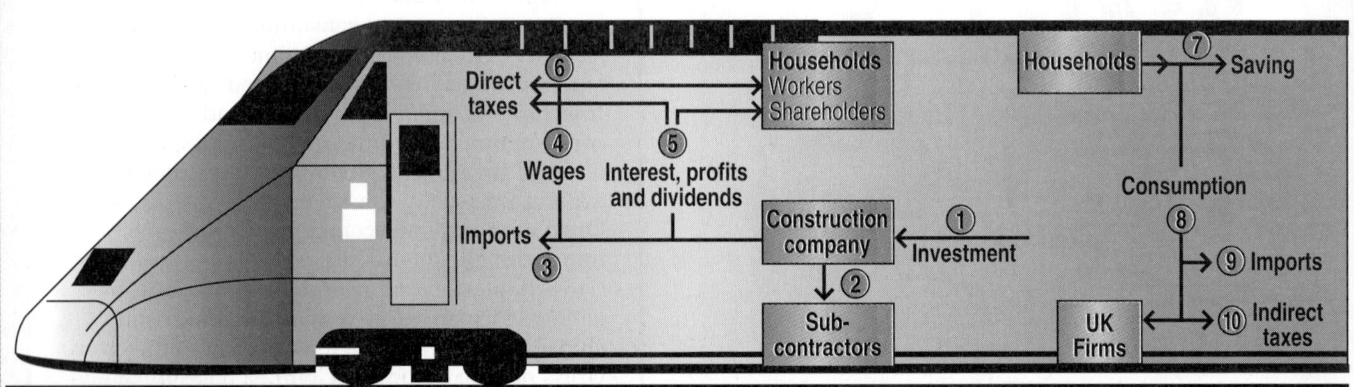

Figure 58.6

NEC

The Scottish Office has asked for a report on the economic implications of the announcement that NEC is to invest in Scotland and a comment on its relative merits. Look at the information on the next page.

1. **Outline briefly the proposed investment.**
2. **Using a circular flow model of the economy, illustrate (i) the extra flows of money round the Scottish economy from the investment and the subsequent operation of the facility and (ii) what would be happening in the Scottish economy if there hadn't been inward investment in Silicon Glen during the 1980s and 1990s.**
3. **Discuss, again using a circular flow model, whether it would not be better for the Scottish economy if it could have seen a £530 million investment by a number of Scottish electronics companies to make components and sub-assemblies to be used in the production of computers and other finished products built in Scotland rather than the NEC semiconductor investment.**

NEC locates in Scotland

In September 1994, NEC, the Japanese electronics company, announced that it was to locate its next-generation semiconductor plant in Scotland at its existing Livingston facility. 'This is an extremely good investment for Scotland', one figure in the Scottish electronics industry said. 'These semi-conductor plants have to invest to survive. If NEC didn't invest here, the Livingston plant would eventually run down. Meanwhile the Japanese would have built their new plant somewhere else.'

Even so, the scale of the investment needs to be kept in proportion. Of the £530m total cost of the investment - Japan's largest in Scotland - three-quarters will be spent on equipment to manufacture the memory chips, and almost all of this will come from Japan. That part which is actually spent in the UK will go mainly on the construction of the high-specification buildings on the 100-acre site. The impact of the investment on local manufacturing may be less great than that of electronics assembly plants which involve smaller capital outlays.

Semiconductor plants have only one principal input, crystalline silicon, which NEC at Livingston obtains mostly from its fellow Japanese company Shin-Etsu, which also has a plant in Livingston. Unlike, for example, the assembly of personal computers, the making of semiconductors does not involve collating inputs from a wide range of suppliers, many of which could in theory be local. Thus the 'upstream linkages' from a chip plant to the local economy are limited, and probably involve mainly suppliers of gases, chemicals, clean-room services and garments.

The new NEC plant will make an important contribution to the Scottish economy by employing 430 staff in addition to the 900 it already employs. 'These are high quality jobs', said Mr Peter Timms, managing director of Flexible Technology, a printed circuit board assembler.

The Japanese company's investment not only confirms Scotland as a prime location for multinational electronics manufacturers, but strengthens the array of companies operating there. Scotland currently produces 11 per cent of Europe's semiconductors, 35 per cent of its personal computers, over 50 per cent of its automated banking machines and 60 per cent of its workstations. Silicon Glen, as the Scottish electronics industry is often called, includes many of the leading US and Japanese electronics companies and employs about 45 000. As Figure 58.7 shows, electronics (classified as electrical and instrument engineering) has been responsible for ensuring an increase in manufacturing output in Scotland over the period 1988 to 1994.

However, critics point out that the plants are largely producing items designed in the US or Japan. And though it is tricky to identify the exact source of material inputs, the most recent survey suggested that only 10 per cent came from Scotland in 1993-94 in spite of a 16 per cent rise in the industry's turnover to £9bn. Only a tiny number of Scottish-based companies is engaged in the large scale supply of components and sub-assemblies to the multinationals.

Source: adapted in part from the *Financial Times*, 22.9.1994 and 7.4.1995.

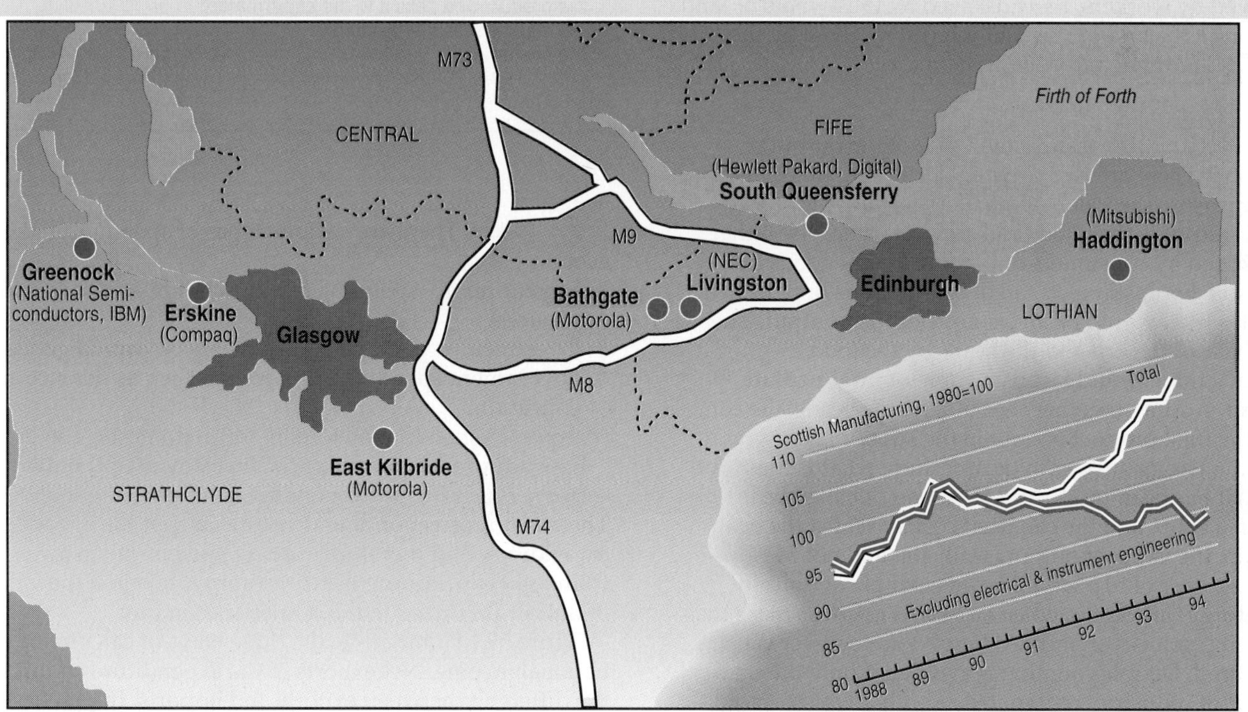

Source: adapted from Scottish Office Industry Department.

Figure 58.7 *Change in manufacturing output in the Scottish economy and recent manufacturing growth in Scotland*

Measuring national income

Summary

1. National income can be measured in three different ways:- national income, output and expenditure.
2. National income is equal to wages, rents, interest and profit.
3. National output is equal to the sum of the output of individual industries. It is important to avoid double counting in the output method.
4. National expenditure is equal to consumption, investment, government spending and exports minus imports.
5. National income is equal to domestic income plus net property income from abroad.
6. Expenditure at factor cost is equal to expenditure at market prices minus indirect taxes plus subsidies.
7. The difference between gross and net national income is capital consumption.
8. Transfer payments such as National Insurance benefits should not be included in national income.
9. The value of the real increase in stocks must be included in national expenditure.

Income, output and expenditure

The circular flow model, discussed in the previous unit, forms the basis for national income accounting. In the model, there are three way of measuring the same flow of money round an economy. Actual income, output and expenditure must always be identical. Income, output and expenditure are **flows** of money which pay for goods, services and factors over a period of time, and are made up a number of different components.

Income Income is payment received for the hire of factors of production. Therefore income is made up of wages received by workers, rents received by the owners of land and property, and profits and interest received by the owners of capital and entrepreneurs.

Output Output measures the value of the output of industry. There are two ways of calculating this. One way is to measure the value of the final output of industry. **Final output** is the goods and services which are either purchased by consumers or used as capital goods by industry. For instance, a can of baked beans bought in a supermarket would be an example of final output. The purchase of the can and the beans by the food manufacturer would be an example of **intermediate output**. Adding together the value of the beans, the can, and the final product bought in the supermarket would give the wrong answer to the question: what is the value of what has been produced? If the can of baked beans cost 40p in a shop, and the can itself cost 4p whilst the beans cost 7p, the value of output is still 40p and not 51p.

An answer of 51p would be an example of **double counting**. This occurs when an item is counted more than once. It produces an inflated figure for whatever is being measured. Double counting is avoided if only the final output of industry is computed. Another way to avoid double counting is to calculate VALUE ADDED. Instead of counting the value of the final output of a product, it is possible to calculate the value added at each stage of production. For instance, if the manufacturer sells a can of baked beans to the supermarket for 35p and the supermarket sells it to the consumer for 40p, then the value added by the supermarket is 5p. As can be seen from Table 59.1, the sum of the value added at each stage of production must equal the value of final output.

Table 59.1

	Value added	Total value of output
Raw materials (beans, can etc.) bought by a baked bean manufacturer	20p	20p
Baked bean manufacturer 'makes' the product and sells it to the supermarket	15p	35p
Supermarket sells the product to the customer	5p	40p
Final output	40p	40p

Expenditure There are various types of spending in the economy:

- consumption - spending by households on goods and services;
- investment - spending by producers on capital goods;
- government spending - on services such as defence and education;
- exports - spending by foreigners on domestic goods.

Expenditure on consumption, investment and public sector services includes spending on imported goods. There is no corresponding domestic output for import expenditure and therefore imports must be taken away from total expenditure if expenditure is to equal the value of output produced in the domestic economy.

Figure 59.1 summarises the three ways of calculating national income. Net exports in the expenditure column is the difference between exports and imports. In practice, calculating national income is extremely complex. We will now discuss some of the most important details of this calculation.

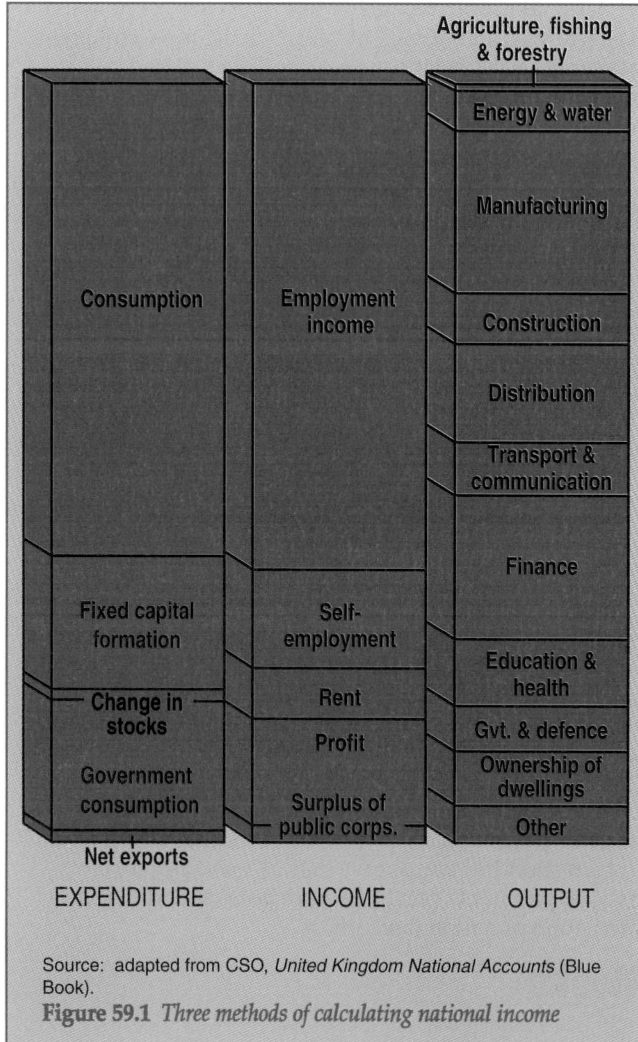

Source: adapted from CSO, *United Kingdom National Accounts* (Blue Book).

Figure 59.1 *Three methods of calculating national income*

QUESTION 1 The following are extracts from the national income accounts of a country.

Table 59.2

	£ million
Wages and salaries	35
Investment	10
Output of manufacturing industry	10
Government expenditure	15
Rents	5
Interest and profits	10
Exports	15
Consumers' expenditure	20

(a) Calculate national income by the income method assuming that all the necessary information on incomes is contained in the data.
(b) What must be the value of national expenditure?
(c) What must be the value of imports?
(d) Why is it not possible to calculate national income by the output method from the data given?

Domestic income to national income

In a real economy, foreigners own some domestic resources. For instance, the Japanese car manufacturer Nissan owns a car plant in Sunderland and Japanese banks have lent money to British firms. On the other hand, UK citizens and companies own assets abroad. These assets give rise to corresponding income. Nissan repatriates profits to Japan, whilst Japanese banks earn interest on their loans. British assets abroad give a flow of income from abroad to the UK.

So DOMESTIC INCOME is distinguished from NATIONAL INCOME in national income accounts. Domestic income is the nation's income before income paid and received from abroad has been included. National income is income which includes not only domestic income but also incomes earned and paid abroad.

In the UK national income statistics, this income is called NET PROPERTY INCOME FROM ABROAD. So:

Domestic income + Net property income from abroad = National income.

QUESTION 2
What was the value of national product or income in the following years?
(a) In 1991, domestic product (i.e. income) was £495 900, property income from abroad was £ 76 958, whilst property income paid was £77 175.
(b) In 1992, domestic product (i.e. income) was £516 027, property income from abroad was £69 167, whilst property income paid was £64 874.
(c) In 1993, domestic product (i.e. income) was £546 589, property income from abroad was £74 040, whilst property income paid was £70 978.

At market prices to factor cost

If you were to buy some eye shadow at £2.35 the price would include 17.5 per cent Value Added Tax (VAT). The actual value of the output is therefore £2. This is the amount that the retailer receives after paying the VAT to the government. The remainder is used to pay factor incomes - wages, rents, etc. So £2 and not £2.35 passes round the circular flow of income.

Some goods are **subsidised**. For instance, in 1975 the government subsidised the price of bread. This meant that the amount paid by consumers for bread was less than the value of the output of bread. The difference between what the consumer paid and what the producer received was the subsidy. The amount flowing round the circular flow in this case is the expenditure on bread plus the subsidy paid by government. This is equal to the value of total output of bread and of total incomes received from bread production.

The value of expenditure including indirect taxes such

as VAT and subsidies is called expenditure AT MARKET PRICES. Expenditure excluding taxes and subsidies is called expenditure AT FACTOR COST. To go from market prices to factor cost, it is necessary to take away indirect taxes and add subsidies. So:

Expenditure at factor cost = Expenditure at market prices - Indirect taxes + Subsidies.

QUESTION 3

Table 59.3

£ million

	Expenditure at market prices	Indirect taxes	Subsidies	Expenditure at factor cost
1989	519 345	79 980	5782	
1990	552 099	78 298		479 867
1991	575 104		5995	495 683
1992		87 506	6412	520 320
1993	633 085	91 361	7458	549 182

Source: adapted from CSO, *United Kingdom National Accounts (Blue Book).*

Copy out and complete the table.

Gross national income to net national income

Gross and net have different precise meanings in different contexts. In national income accounting, the difference between gross income and net income is depreciation. Over a period of time, the capital stock of a country - factories, offices, machines, roads, hospitals etc. - wears out. This is called DEPRECIATION or CAPITAL CONSUMPTION.

Depreciation should be excluded from national income. To see why, consider an individual who spent £12 000 over a year. £2 000 of this was drawn from her savings. Her income therefore must have been £10 000 and not £12 000. The capital stock of a country is like an individual's wealth. If it has been run down to provide money for spending, then the value of that depreciation or capital consumption must be taken away to arrive at a true value of income.

Another way of seeing this is to consider gross and net investment. Gross investment is the total value of investment expenditure over a period of time. Part of that investment simply replaces capital goods which have worn out over the period. This is the value of depreciation. The rest, net investment, is the increase in the capital stock. Net investment rather than gross investment shows how much the productive potential of the country has increased over time. So:

Gross national income - Capital consumption = Net national income

NATIONAL INCOME is, strictly speaking, defined as net national product at factor cost. It is equal to national expenditure and national output. It is the most complete measure of national income currently calculated by government. Note that 'national income' is the term used in economic theory to refer to all three measures of the flow of money around the circular flow.

QUESTION 4

Table 59.4

£ million

	Gross investment at factor cost	Net investment at factor cost	Gross national product	Net national product	Capital consumption
1989	100 559		445 147		56 716
1990	98 252			418 606	61 261
1991	85 063		495 683	432 081	
1992	84 937		520 320		63 998
1993	87 025		549 182		65 023

Source: adapted from CSO, *United Kingdom National Accounts (Blue Book).*

Copy out and complete the table.

Transfer payments

Transfer payments are payments of income which have no corresponding output (☞ unit 58 for examples). Transfer payments must therefore be excluded from any calculation of national income.

Stocks

A company might produce £10 million worth of goods but only sell £9 million to consumers. Output is therefore £10 million, but only £9 million is received in consumer expenditure. The other £1 million of goods will have been added to the firm's STOCKS or INVENTORIES. These are goods which a firm has produced or bought from another firm but is waiting to sell. A company may also buy stocks of raw materials. These stocks are awaiting transformation into new goods and services.

In national income accounts, changes in stocks are treated as expenditure by the firm. In the above example, the company has been forced to buy from itself the £1 million of goods that it had hoped to sell. Equally, if it had bought raw materials and held them in stock, this would have been classified as expenditure.

Note that it is **changes** in stocks and not stocks themselves that are treated as expenditure in national income accounts. Income, expenditure and output are money or real flows over a period of time. The corresponding flow is the change in stocks and not stock levels.

There is a further complication resulting from inflation. Profits of companies include an allowance for stock appreciation. For instance, a company may have held 100 units of raw material in stock throughout the period. Their total value may have increased because of inflation. But this increase in value has no corresponding output - there are still 100 units in stock at the end of the period even if their value has increased. Therefore stock appreciation must be deducted from national income if income is to equal output.

Key terms

Value added - the difference between the price paid for inputs by one producer to another and the value of the output of the producer.
Domestic and national income - domestic income is income which excludes the value of incomes generated by assets owned overseas and of domestic assets owned by foreigners. National income includes these.
Net property income from abroad - the difference between income received from overseas assets and that paid on domestic assets owned by foreigners.
Market prices and factor cost - national income at market prices includes taxes on expenditure and subsidies. Factor cost excludes these.
Depreciation or capital consumption - the cost of replacing the capital stock which has been used up or has depreciated over the time period.
National income - net national product at factor cost.
Stocks or inventories - goods held by a firm either for future production or sale.
Gross domestic fixed capital formation - gross investment (i.e. before depreciation)

QUESTION 5

Table 59.5

					£ million
	1989	1990	1991	1992	1993
National income					
Total domestic income	448 820	485 017		517 859	548 162
Stock appreciation	7 061		2 010		2 359
Gross domestic product at factor cost		478 886	495 900	516 027	
National expenditure					
Total expenditure excluding stock changes	513 253	552 918		598 818	
Value of physical increase in stocks and work in progress		-1 800	-4 631	-1 697	-185
Gross domestic product at market prices	515 957	551 118	575 321		630 023
less indirect taxes *plus* subsidies	74 198	72 232	79 421	81 094	
Gross domestic product at factor cost	441 759				546 120

Source: adapted from CSO, *United Kingdom National Accounts (Blue Book).*

Copy out and complete the table.

Applied economics

The national income accounts of the United Kingdom

Income, expenditure and output

The current UK national income statistics show calculations of gross domestic product at factor cost by each of the income, output and expenditure methods. National income is then derived from the figure obtained.

In practice, estimates of gross domestic product at factor cost calculated by the expenditure method differ from those calculated by the income method and both differ from figures for the output method. This is hardly surprising. National income statistics are calculated from millions of individuals' returns. Inaccuracies are inevitable. Returns can also be falsified or not submitted to evade taxes such as income tax and VAT. So a figure for a **statistical discrepancy or residual error** is included in the calculation of each method of national income. It is the difference between the actual estimate of gross domestic product at factor cost as calculated by one method and the average estimate of GDP calculated by the three methods. For instance, if GDP by the income method were £98, by the output method £99, and by the expenditure method £103, then the average estimate of GDP would be £100 [(£98 + £99 + £103) ÷ 3]. So the statistical discrepancy for income would be +£2, for output +£1 and for expenditure -£3.

Gross domestic product by the expenditure method

Table 59.6 shows how GDP by the expenditure method is calculated. National expenditure is made up of consumption, investment, government spending and net exports.

- The table shows that consumers' expenditure is by far the largest single item.
- Government expenditure is split into two parts.

Investment by government on roads, new hospitals, new schools etc. is included in the figure for investment. General government final consumption measures non-investment expenditure such as wages and salaries, and purchases of consumable items from toilet paper to school textbooks to petrol.

- Investment is called GROSS DOMESTIC FIXED CAPITAL FORMATION in national income accounts. It is investment both by the private and the public sectors.
- The addition to stocks is also classified as part of investment expenditure as explained above.

The total of these components of expenditure is called **total domestic expenditure**. Exports are added to arrive at **total final expenditure**. However, imports must be taken away because there is no corresponding output figure for imports. This then gives a figure for **gross domestic product at market prices**.

The statistical discrepancy in 1993 was negative, indicating that the estimate for domestic expenditure was more than the average of the three methods. To go from market prices to factor cost (see above), it is necessary to take away indirect taxes like VAT and excise duties and add subsidies. The figure now arrived at is **GDP at factor cost**.

Table 59.6 *GDP by the expenditure method, 1993*

	£ millions
Consumers' expenditure	405 639
General government final consumption	138 224
Gross domestic fixed capital formation	94 715
Value of physical increase in stocks and work in progress	-197
Total domestic expenditure	638 381
Exports of goods and services	157 999
Total final expenditure	796 380
less imports of goods and services	166 266
Statistical discrepancy	-91
Gross domestic product at market prices	630 023
less taxes on expenditure	91 361
plus subsidies	7 458
Gross domestic product at factor cost	546 120

Source: adapted from CSO, *United Kingdom National Accounts (Blue Book).*

GDP by the income method

Incomes in the circular flow are factor incomes - wages, profits and rents. Table 59.7 shows the breakdown of domestic income.

- Wages paid to workers are split into two categories. Income from employment is the measure of salaries and wages paid to employed workers. The earnings of the self-employed are classified separately.
- Profits too are split into two categories. Gross trading profits of companies refers to the profits earned by private sector businesses. Gross trading surpluses of public corporations and general government enterprises refers to the profits made by state owned companies, ranging from the Post Office to local authority swimming pools.
- Rent is the payment received by individuals from the lease of property. Government too owns property. The imputed charge for consumption of non-trading capital is an estimate of how much the state would have had to pay in rent if the property had been owned within the private sector.

These added together make up **total domestic income**. The value of the monetary increase in the value of stocks must now be deducted (see above). Adjusting the figures with the statistical discrepancy gives the value of GDP at factor cost.

Table 59.7 *GDP by the income method, 1993*

	£ millions
Income from employment	352 896
Income from self-employment	61 346
Gross trading profits of companies	73 397
Gross trading surpluses of public corporations and general government enterprises	3 709
Rent	52 872
Imputed charge for consumption of non-trading capital	3 942
Total domestic income	548 162
less stock appreciation	-2 359
less statistical discrepancy	317
Gross domestic product at factor cost	546 120

Source: adapted from CSO, *United Kingdom National Accounts (Blue Book).*

GDP by the output method

Table 59.8 shows the breakdown of domestic output. The figures are for the value added by each industry rather than final output. In some industries, such as defence and education, little or nothing is traded in the market place. Therefore there can be no price set upon the products. So the value of the output of these industries is assumed to be equal to the value of the inputs. For instance, the output of the defence industry is assumed to be equal to the salaries paid to personnel, equipment bought over the time period, etc.

Table 59.8 *GDP by the output method, 1993*

	£ millions
Agriculture, hunting, forestry and fishing	10 373
Mining & quarrying including oil & gas extraction	12 147
Manufacturing	118 294
Electricity, gas and water supply	13 994
Construction	29 221
Wholesale & retail trade; repairs; hotels and restaurants	78 348
Transport, storage and communication	46 263
Financial intermediation, real estate, renting & business activities	133 956
Public administration, national defence and compulsory social security	38 199
Education, health, social work	57 457
Other services including sewage and refuse disposal	31 292
Total	569 544
less adjustment for financial services	23 741
Statistical discrepancy	317
Gross domestic product	546 120

Source: adapted from CSO, *United Kingdom National Accounts* (Blue Book).

From GDP to GNP

Gross domestic product measures income, output and expenditure generated from resources in the UK. But the UK owns assets abroad and foreigners own assets in the UK. So property income received from abroad needs to be added to GDP whilst property income paid abroad must be subtracted from GDP, giving a figure for net property income from abroad. Table 59.9 shows the movement from GDP to GNP.

From GNP to national income

Gross national product at factor cost is an estimate of national income before consumption has been deducted. Table 59.9 arrives at net national product at factor cost or national income by deducting capital consumption.

Table 59.9 *From GDP at factor cost to national income, 1993*

	£ millions
Gross domestic product at factor cost	546 120
Net property income from abroad	3 062
Gross national product at factor cost	549 182
less capital consumption	65 023
National income	484 159

Source: adapted from CSO, *United Kingdom National Accounts (Blue Book)*.

GDP statistics aim at a moving target

Financial markets are always eager to hear the latest gross domestic product statistics from the government. But the reaction from economists is often more muted. In spite of the attention paid to GDP, many economists suspect the data are one of the more ambiguous elements of the statistical series.

Part of the problem is that calculating GDP requires a huge pool of data on output, expenditure and income. Since this data arrives at different times, new data can prompt revisions, not least because the three methods the Central Statistical Office (CSO) can use to calculate GDP rarely result in the same figure.

The CSO points out that these revisions have fallen in the past four years. It recently set itself a target to keep revisions in annual GDP data below 0.4 per cent. Some observers believe the data still understate the recovery. Mr Andrew Cates of brokers UBS points out that annual GDP data have been revised upwards on average by 0.5 per cent over the past 25 years.

But the second difficulty dogging the statisticians is the speed of economic change.

As Mr Doug McWilliams, head of the centre for economics and business research, said: 'The CSO is chasing a moving target. The economy is restructuring so fast it is hard to pick up these shifts.'

The issue revolves around 'weightings'. The CSO calculates the relative weight of sectors in the economy every five years. The weighting given to the oil and gas sector, for example, fell from about 60 parts per 1,000 in 1985 to 21 parts in 1990, following the decline in the North Sea sector in the late 1980s.

But since this rebasing occurs only every five years, changes in the performance of sectors within this period are not reflected.

A big question mark hangs over rapidly changing sectors such as financial services and electronics. With the computer sector having increased turnover by 50 per cent in the past year, according to the Engineering Employers Federation, observers such as Mr McWilliams suspect a five-year rebasing is too clumsy to reflect these shifts.

The CSO itself argues that any discrepancies from this are small. Nevertheless, alternative systems of updating are being considered, not least because other approaches are being developed elsewhere. The Danish government has introduced a continual rebasing method into its data.

CSO officials fear that introducing this would be costly, could lead to less accuracy in the actual rebasing used, and provide an additional statistical burden for businesses.

Faced with these problems most observers, such as Ms Kate Barker, chief economist at the Confederation of British Industry, simply take the data with a pinch of salt.

She said: 'I am not sure it is worse now than before. But the general point is that financial markets sometimes get too excited about figures, as if they represented reality - which of course they don't.'

Source: adapted in part from the *Financial Times*, 18.11.1994.

1. **What does GDP measure?**
2. **Why are there problems with the measurement of GDP, according to the article?**
3. **Discuss the problems which firms supplying (a) the North Sea oil industry and (b) the computer industry might have if they used GDP figures to assess likely demand in those industries.**
4. **(a) Suggest ways in which the Central Statistical Office could improve the accuracy of GDP statistics and (b) assess the costs and benefits of your proposals.**

The use of national income statistics

Summary

1. National income statistics are used by academics to formulate and test hypotheses. They are used by policy makers to formulate economic policy both on a micro-economic and macro-economic level. They are often used as a proxy measure for the standards of living and to compare living standards between countries and within a country over time.
2. National income statistics can be inaccurate because of statistical errors, the existence of the black economy, of non-traded sectors, and difficulties with valuing public sector output.
3. Problems occur when comparing national income over time because of inflation, the accuracy and presentation of statistics, changes in population, the quality of goods and services and changes in income distribution.
4. Further problems occur when comparing national income between countries. In particular, an exchange rate has to be constructed which accurately reflects different purchasing power parities.

Why is national income measured?

National income is a measure of the output, expenditure and income of an economy. National income statistics provide not only figures for these totals but also a breakdown of the totals. They are used in a number of different ways.

- Academic economists use them to test hypotheses and build economic models of the economy. This increases our understanding of how an economy works.
- Government, firms and economists use the figures to forecast changes in the economy. These forecasts are then used to plan for the future. Government may attempt to direct the economy (☞ for instance unit 68 on fiscal policy), making changes in its spending or its taxes at budget time. Groups such as trade unions or the CBI will make their own recommendations about what policies they think the government should pursue.
- They are used to make comparisons over time and between countries. For instance, national income statistics can be used to compare the income of the UK in 1950 and 1995. Or they can be used to compare France's income with UK income. Of particular importance when making comparisons over time is the rate of change of national income (i.e. the rate of economic growth).
- They are used to make judgements about economic welfare. Growth in national income, for instance, is usually equated with a rise in living standards.

QUESTION 1

GNP per capita ($)

0 5,000 10,000 15,000 20,000 25,000 30,000 35,000 40,000

Chad
France
Germany 23,030
Indonesia
Ireland 12,210
Italy
Korean Republic
Nigeria
Oman
Peru
Portugal 7,450
Romania
South Africa 1,221
Switzerland
Thailand
United Kingdom 17,790
United States

Source: adapted from the World Bank, *World Development Report.*

Figure 60.1 *Where they rank in the world (GNP per capita)*

(a) What statistics do governments need to collect in order to be able to calculate GNP per capita?

(b) How might (i) an economist and (ii) a government use these statistics?

The accuracy of national income statistics

National income statistics are inaccurate for a number of reasons.

Statistical inaccuracies National income statistics are calculated from millions of different returns to the government. Inevitably mistakes are made - returns are inaccurate or simply not completed. The statistics are constantly being revised in the light of fresh evidence. Although revisions tend to become smaller over time, national income statistics are still being revised ten years after first publication.

The black economy Taxes such as VAT, income tax and National Insurance contributions, and government regulations such as health and safety laws, impose a burden on workers and businesses. Some are tempted to evade taxes and they are then said to work in the **black, hidden** or **informal economy**. In the building industry, for instance, it is common for workers to be self-employed and to under-declare or not declare their income at all to the tax authorities. Transactions in the black economy are in the form of cash. Cheques, credit cards, etc. could all be traced by the tax authorities. Tax evasion is the dominant motive for working in the black economy but a few also claim welfare benefits to which they are not entitled. The size of the hidden economy is difficult to estimate, but in the UK estimates have varied from 7 to 15 per cent of GDP (i.e. national income statistics underestimate the true size of national income by at least 7 per cent).

Home produced services In the poorest developing countries in the world, GNP per person is valued at less than £100 per year. It would be impossible to survive on this amount if this were the true value of output in the economy. However, a large part of the production of the agricultural sector is not traded and therefore does not appear in national income statistics. People are engaged in subsistence agriculture, consuming what they themselves produce. Hence the value of national output is in reality much higher. In the UK, the output of the services of housewives and househusbands is equally not recorded. Nor is the large number of DIY jobs completed each year. The more DIY activity, the greater will be the under-recording of national output by national income statistics.

The public sector Valuing the output of much of the public sector is difficult because it is not bought and sold. This problem is circumvented by valuing non-marketed output at its cost of production. For instance, the value of the output of a state school is the cost of running the school. This method of valuation can yield some surprising results. Assume that through more efficient staffing, the number of nurses on a hospital ward is reduced from 10 to 8 and the service is improved. National income accounts will still show a fall in output (measured by a drop in the two nurses' incomes). In general, increased productivity in the public sector is shown by a fall in the value of output. It looks as though less is being produced when in fact output remains unchanged.

QUESTION 2 The size of the black economy in the UK is disputed. Stephen Smith of the Institute of Fiscal Studies estimated that the black economy is between 3 and 5 per cent of GDP. This is based on research into consumer spending in areas where such activity is prevalent, such as painting, decorating, cleaning and gardening. The Inland Revenue, on the other hand, estimates the size is between 6 and 8 per cent of GDP or up to about £50bn. Employed workers paying PAYE (Pay as you earn, a system where tax is deducted from a worker's pay packet by the employer) have little opportunity to fiddle their taxes. They account for approximately 21 million taxpayers. The rest, about 3.4 million, are self-employed. Many of them are able to conceal earnings whilst at the same time exaggerating their expenses which they can offset against tax. Stephen Smith estimates that between 16 and 20 per cent of income of the self-employed is not declared to the tax authorities.

(a) Explain why the black economy is concentrated particularly amongst the self-employed.
(b) In the 1980s and 1990s, the government aimed to create a more flexible workforce, with more part time, casual and self-employed workers as a proportion of the total workforce. What are the implications of this for the size of the black economy in the UK?

Comparing national income over time

Comparing the national income of the UK today with national income in the past presents problems.

Prices Prices have tended to increase over time. So an increase in national income over the period does not necessarily indicate that there has been an increase in the number of goods and services produced in the economy. Only if the rate of increase of national income measured in money terms (the nominal rate of economic growth) has been greater than the increase in prices (the inflation rate) can there be said to have been an increase in output. So when comparing over time, it is essential to consider **real** and not **nominal** changes in income (☞ unit 3).

The accuracy and presentation of statistics National income statistics are inaccurate and therefore it is impossible to give a precise figure for the change in income over time. Moreover, the change in real income over time will also be affected by the inflation rate. The inevitable errors made in the calculation of the inflation rate compound the problems of inaccuracy. The method of calculating national income and the rate of inflation can also change over time. It is important to attempt to eliminate the effect of changes in definitions.

Changes in population National income statistics are often used to compare living standards over time. If they are to be used in this way, it is essential to compare national income per capita (i.e. per person). For instance, if the population doubles whilst national income quadruples, people are likely to be nearer twice as well off than four times.

Quality of goods and services The quality of goods may improve over time due to advances in technology but they may also fall in price. For instance, cars today are far better than cars 80 years ago and yet are far cheaper. National income would show this fall in price by a fall in national income, wrongly implying that living standards had fallen. On the other hand, pay in the public sector tends to increase at about 2 per cent per annum faster than the increase in inflation. This is because pay across the economy tends to increase in line with the rate of economic growth rather than the rate of inflation. Increased pay would be reflected in both higher nominal and real national income but there may well be no extra goods or services being produced.

Defence and related expenditures The GDP of the UK was higher during the Second World War than in the 1930s, but much of GDP between 1940 and 1945 was devoted to defence expenditure. It would be difficult to argue that people enjoyed a higher standard of living during the war years than in the pre-war years. So the proportion of national income devoted to defence, or for instance to the police, must be taken into account when considering the standard of living of the population.

Consumption and investment It is possible to increase standards of living today by reducing investment and increasing consumption. However, reducing investment is likely to reduce standards of living from what they might otherwise have been in the future. As with defence, the proportion of national income being devoted to investment will affect the standard of living of the population both now and in the future.

Externalities National income statistics take no account of **externalities** (☞ unit 36) produced by the economy. National income statistics may show that national income has doubled roughly every 25 years since 1945. But if the value of externalities has more than doubled over that time period, then the rate of growth of the standard of living has less than doubled.

Income distribution When comparing national income over time, it is important to remember that an increased national income for the economy as a whole may not mean that individuals have seen their income increase. Income distribution is likely to change over time, which may or may not lead to a more desirable state of affairs.

QUESTION 3

Table 60.1

	Nominal GNP £ bn	Index of Retail Prices (1985 = 100)	Population (millions)
1948	10.6	8.3	48.7
1958	20.5	13.0	51.7
1968	38.3	17.5	55.2
1978	150.4	52.8	56.2
1988	405.9	113.0	57.1
1994	589.5	148.7	58.4

Source: adapted from CSO, *Annual Abstract of Statistics*; CSO, *Economic Trends Annual Supplement.*

(a) For each year, calculate the value of real GNP (at 1985 prices) per head of the population.
(b) To what extent is it possible to judge from the data whether living standards increased over the period 1948-1994?

Comparing national income between countries

Comparing national income between economies is fraught with difficulties too. Income distributions may be different. Populations will be different and therefore it is important to compare per capita income figures. National income accounts will have varying degrees of inaccuracy, caused, for instance, by different sizes of the informal economy in each country. National income accounting conventions will differ.

There is also the problem of what rate of exchange to use when comparing one country's national income with another. The day to day market exchange rate can bear little relation to relative prices in different countries. So prices in some countries, like Switzerland or West Germany, can be much higher at official exchange rates than in France or Italy. Therefore if national income statistics are to be used to compare living standards between countries it is important to use an exchange rate which compares the cost of living in each country. These exchange rates are known as **purchasing power parities**. For instance, if a typical basket of goods costs 10 francs in France and £1 in the UK, then national income should be converted at an exchange rate of 10 francs to the £1 - even if the market exchange rate gives a very different figure.

Even this is not accurate enough. In some countries, consumers have to purchase goods which in others are free. For instance, Sweden spends a greater proportion of its national income than Italy on fuel for heating because of its colder climate. But this extra expenditure does not give the Swedes a higher standard of living. Again, countries are different geographically and one country might have higher transport costs per unit of output than another because of congestion or having to transport goods long distances. In practice, it is almost impossible to adjust national income figures for these sorts of differences.

QUESTION 4

Table 60.2 *Output and living standards*

Country	Currency units per £		GDP	Population
	Market exchange rates	Purchasing power parities		
USA	1.77	1.57	$5 920 bn	255.4m
Japan	223.7	283.7	464 000 bn Yen	124.5m
Switzerland	2.47	3.36	336.9bn Swiss francs	6.9m
France	9.32	9.97	FF 6 951bn	57.4m
Italy	2 163	2 265	L1 494 547bn	57.8m
Germany	2.75	3.21	Dm 2 780bn	80.6m
Spain	179.9	178.7	64 272bn pesetas	39.1m
UK	1.00	1.00	£510.2bn	57.8m

Source: adapted from OECD, *Main Economic Indicators*; World Bank, *World Development Report.*

(a) Rank in order the countries in the table according to (i) GDP and (ii) GDP per head. To do this you need to convert GDP and GDP per head into pounds sterling using the purchasing power parity exchange rate.
(b) Would your rank order have been different if you had converted GDP at market exchange rates rather than purchasing power parity exchange rates? If so, explain why.

Applied economics

France and the United Kingdom

France has a higher GDP than the UK. In 1994, French GDP was FF 7 060 bn compared to £625.4 bn for the UK. At an exchange rate of FF8.49 to the £, this meant that the French economy produced 33 per cent more than the UK economy.

Crude national income statistics like these don't say very much when making inter-country comparisons. For a start, populations may be vastly different. In this case, France and the UK have almost identical populations of approximately 58 million, with the UK having a slightly larger population than that of France. So GDP per capita gives little extra information compared to total GDP when making comparisons. Purchasing power parities (PPPs) do, however, differ substantially from market exchange rates. In the 1990s, market exchange rates have over-valued the franc in comparison with PPPs. French GDP, when converted in £ using PPPs in 1994 was £696.0 bn, 11 per cent higher than that of the UK. The conclusion must be that France had a higher GDP and GDP per head than that of the UK.

In making comparisons about living standards, national income is only one among many factors to be taken into account. One such is the distribution of income. Table 60.3 shows that income in the UK in the late 1980s was less evenly distributed than that in France. Not only does France have a higher national income, but there is less inequality in income in the country compared to the UK.

Another group of factors which are important relate to how national income is distributed between different types of expenditure. In 1992, 15 per cent of GDP in France was accounted for by general government consumption on items such as education and environmental services compared to 18 per cent in the UK. Government spending on defence was much higher in the UK at 11.3 per cent of total government spending compared to 6.4 per cent in France. On the other hand, the French government spent more on health services - 16.0 per cent of total government spending compared to 13.2 per cent in the UK.

Investment in the French economy both by the private and public sectors was higher than that in the UK - 20 per cent of GDP compared to 15 per cent. This meant that UK citizens spent more of their national cake than the French:- 64 per cent of GDP compared to 60 per cent. This higher spending from GDP will, to some extent, have helped narrow the gap for consumers between French and UK GDP.

Quality of life is difficult to measure. The French are less urbanised than their UK counterparts. In 1992, 73 per cent of French people lived in towns and cities compared to 89 per cent in the UK. Important too is the fact that France is over twice the size of the UK and hence population density is much lower in France. Certainly, French roads are on average far less congested than in the UK and lower population densities and a more dispersed industry and population mean that air pollution is less in France than in the UK.

Many other factors need to be taken into account before concluding that the French have a higher standard of living than the British. However, on the indicators chosen above, it would seem that the British are lagging behind their French counterparts.

Table 60.3 *Income distribution*
Percentage share of income or consumption

	Lowest 20%	Next 20%	Middle 20%	Next 20%	Highest 20%	Highest 10%
France (1989)	5.6	11.8	17.2	23.5	40.3	24.4
UK (1988)	4.6	10.0	16.8	24.3	44.3	27.8

Source: World Bank, *World Development Report.*

Living standards

Table 60.4 *Health indicators*

	Years	Per thousand of the population		%		
	Life expectancy at birth	Crude birth rate	Crude death rate	Married women of childbearing age using contraception	Prevalence of malnutrition (under 5s)	Pop. per physician
	1992	1992	1992	1988 - 93	1987 - 92	1990
1 Burundi	48	45	17	-	31.0	6 870
2 Indonesia	60	25	10	50	39.9	7 030
3 Peru	65	27	7	55	10.8	960
4 Poland	70	13	10	-	-	490
5 Greece	77	10	10	-	-	580
6 Australia	77	15	8	-	-	-
7 UK	76	14	11	-	-	-
8 Germany*	76	10	11	-	-	370
9 USA	77	16	9	74	-	420
10 Sweden	78	14	11	-	-	370
11 Japan	79	11	7	56	-	610

* Before unification

Table 60.5 *Central government expenditure*

% of total government spending, 1992

	Defence	Education	Health	Housing, social security, welfare
1 Burundi	n.a.	n.a.	n.a.	n.a.
2 Indonesia	6.8	9.8	2.8	2.0
3 Peru	n.a.	n.a.	n.a.	n.a.
4 Poland	n.a.	n.a.	n.a.	n.a.
5 Greece	n.a.	n.a.	n.a.	n.a.
6 Australia	8.6	7.0	12.7	31.2
7 UK	11.3	13.2	13.8	31.8
8 Germany	n.a	n.a.	n.a.	n.a.
9 USA	20.6	1.8	16.0	31.1
10 Sweden	5.5	9.3	0.8	56.2
11 Japan	n.a.	n.a.	n.a.	n.a.

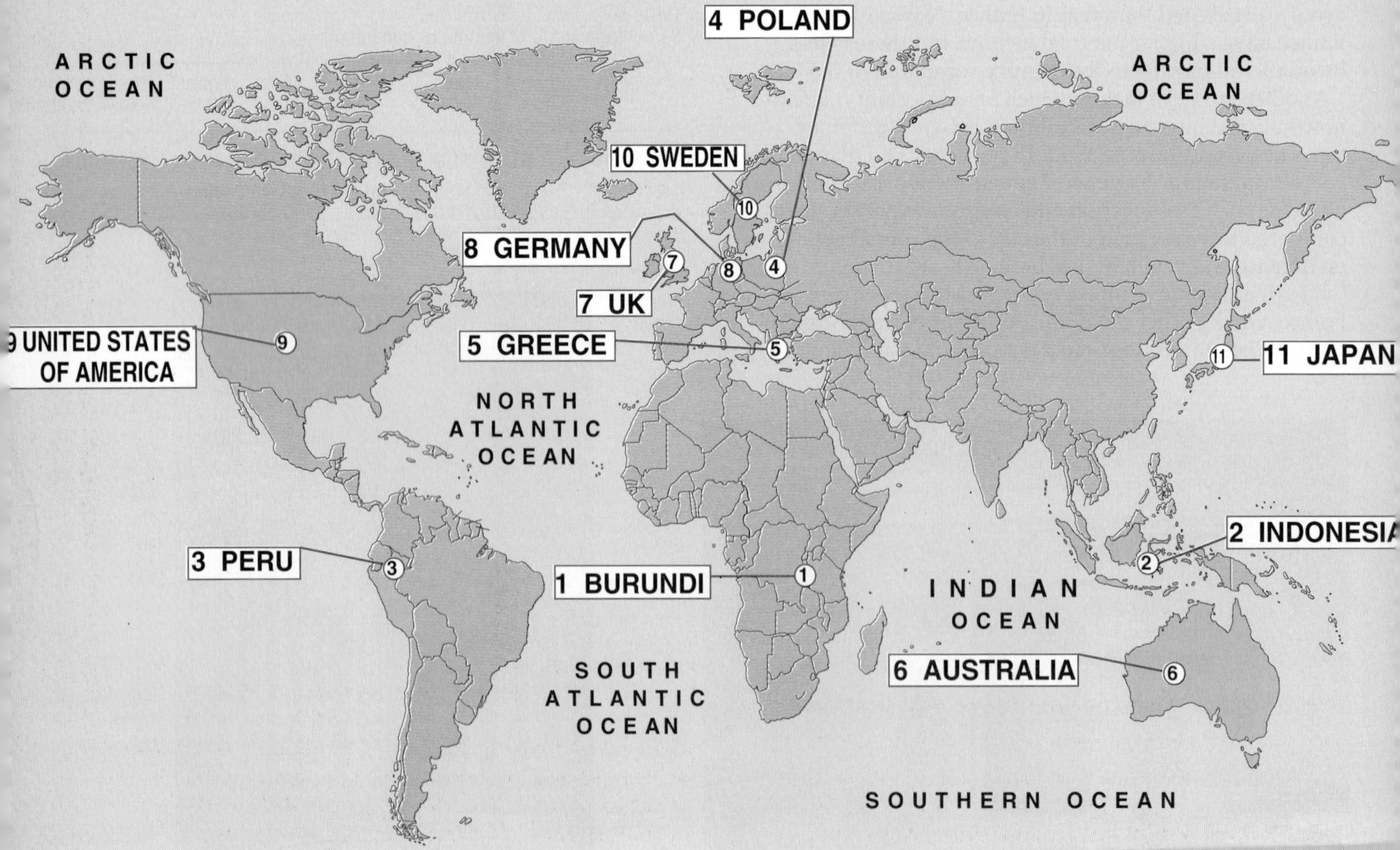

4 POLAND
ARCTIC OCEAN
ARCTIC OCEAN
10 SWEDEN
8 GERMANY
7 UK
9 UNITED STATES OF AMERICA
5 GREECE
11 JAPAN
NORTH ATLANTIC OCEAN
2 INDONESIA
3 PERU
1 BURUNDI
INDIAN OCEAN
6 AUSTRALIA
SOUTH ATLANTIC OCEAN
SOUTHERN OCEAN

Table 60.6 *Education*

	Adult Literacy (%)[1]		Percentage of group enrolled in education	
	Female	Total	Primary	Secondary
	1990		1991	1991
1 Burundi	60	50	37	6
2 Indonesia	32	23	23	45
3 Peru	21	15	-	70
4 Poland	-	-	96	83
5 Greece	11	7	97	98
6 Australia	e	e	97	82
7 UK	e	e	100	86
8 Germany	e	e	100	-
9 USA	e	e	99	90
10 Sweden	e	e	100	91
11 Japan	e	e	100	97

1. % of adults who are illiterate e Illiteracy is less than 5 per cent.

Table 60.7 *Population and infrastructure*

	Pop. (millions)	Area (thousands sq. km)	Urban pop. (as % of total pop.)	Households with electricity (% of total)	Pop. with access to safe water (% of total)	Telephone mainlines (per 1000 persons)
	mid - 1992		1992	1984	1990	1990
1 Burundi	5.8	28	6	1	45	2
2 Indonesia	184.3	1 905	32	14	51	6
3 Peru	22.4	1 285	71	90	53	26
4 Poland	38.4	313	63	96	89	86
5 Greece	10.3	132	64	89	98	391
6 Australia	17.5	7 713	85	98	100	456
7 UK	57.8	245	89	-	100	442
8 Germany	80.6	357	86	100	100	483
9 USA	255.4	9 373	76	100	-	545
10 Sweden	8.7	450	84	96	100	683
11 Japan	124.5	378	77	-	96	441

Table 60.8 *National income indicators*

1992

	GDP ($ million)	GDP per capita ($)	PPP estimates of GNP per capita US = 100	Distribution of GDP (%) Agriculture	Industry	Services	Gvt. consumption	Private consumption	Gross domestic investment
1 Burundi	986	210	3.2	54	20	26	10	92	19
2 Indonesia	126 364	670	12.8	19	40	40	10	53	35
3 Peru	22 100	950	13.3	-	-	-	6	81	16
4 Poland	83 823	1 910	21.1	7	51	42	9	68	23
5 Greece	67 278	7 290	34.6	-	-	-	19	73	18
6 Australia	294 760	17 260	75.0	3	30	67	19	62	20
7 UK	903 126	17 790	72.4	-	-	-	22	64	15
8 Germany	1 789 261	23 030	89.1	2	39	60	18	54	21
9 USA	5 920 199	23 240	100.0	-	-	-	18	67	16
10 Sweden	220 834	27 010	76.2	2	32	66	28	54	17
11 Japan	3 670 979	28 190	87.2	2	42	56	9	57	31

Table 60.9 *Energy and the environment*

	Energy use per capita (kg oil equivalent)	Natural forest area: Total area (thousand sq. km)	Natural forest area: Annual deforestation (% of total area) 1981-90	Nationally protected areas (% of total area) 1993
	1992	1990		
1 Burundi	24	2	0.6	3.2
2 Indonesia	303	1 095	1.0	10.2
3 Peru	330	679	0.4	3.2
4 Poland	2 407	87	-0.1	7.2
5 Greece	2 173	60	-0.0	0.8
6 Australia	5 263	1 456	-0.0	10.6
7 UK	3 743	24	-1.1	18.9
8 Germany	4 358	107	-0.5	24.6
9 United States	7 662	2 960	0.1	10.5
10 Sweden	5 395	280	-	6.6
11 Japan	3 586	247	0.0	12.3

Table 60.10 *Income distribution*

Percentage share of income or consumption

	Quintile groups					
	Lowest 20%	Next 20%	Middle 20%	Next 20%	Highest 20%	Highest 10%
1 Burundi	n.a.	n.a.	n.a.	n.a.	n.a.	n.a.
2 Indonesia (1990)	8.7	12.1	15.9	21.1	42.3	27.9
3 Peru (1985-86)	4.9	9.2	13.7	21.0	51.4	35.4
4 Poland	9.2	13.8	17.9	23.0	36.1	21.6
5 Greece	n.a.	n.a.	n.a.	n.a.	n.a.	n.a.
6 Australia (1985)	4.4	11.1	17.5	24.8	42.4	25.8
7 UK (1988)	4.6	10.0	16.8	24.3	44.3	27.8
8 Germany (1988)	4.7	11.8	17.1	23.9	40.9	24.4
9 USA (1985)	4.7	11.0	17.4	25.0	41.9	25.0
10 Sweden (1981)	8.0	13.2	17.4	24.5	36.9	20.8
11 Japan (1979)	8.7	13.2	17.5	23.1	37.5	22.4

Source for all tables: adapted from World Bank, *World Development Report*.

You have been asked to write an article for an 'A' level General Studies magazine. The editor wants you to compare the standard of living of 11 countries using national income statistics. In your article:

- **make such a comparison;**
- **then discuss the limitations of using national statistics to compare living standards between countries, giving examples of how different economic indicators might provide an additional or perhaps even better basis for making a comparison.**

Output

Applied economics

The structure of the economy

The UK economy is structured into three main sectors. In the PRIMARY SECTOR of the economy, raw materials are extracted and food is grown. In the UK national income accounts, the primary sector corresponds approximately to agriculture, forestry and fishing, and parts of energy and water supply. In the SECONDARY SECTOR of the economy, raw materials are transformed into goods. The secondary sector approximates in the UK national income accounts to manufacturing, construction and the rest of energy and water supply not included in primary industry. The TERTIARY SECTOR produces services, such as transport, distribution services, financial services and education.

Figure 61.1 shows shares of output in 1993. Manufacturing accounted for approximately 22 per cent of output, whilst services were 71 per cent. Agriculture was relatively insignificant at approximately 2 per cent, whilst mining and North Sea oil and gas extraction accounted for little more. Water, gas and electricity supply again was about 2 per cent of output, whilst the construction industry produced 5 per cent of national output. (The figures add up to more than 100 per cent because of rounding and because an allowance needs to be made for double counting of financial services.)

Changes in economic structure

There have been significant changes in the structure of the UK economy over time. Before the industrial revolution of 1750-1850, output was concentrated in the rural sector of the economy. Production was heavily weighted towards the production of food or household services. In the 19th century, manufacturing grew as a percentage of total output. By 1950, as Figure 61.2 shows, the share of manufacturing output in total output was 34 per cent whilst the share of services was 49 per cent. Since then, the share of manufacturing has declined whilst that of services has increased.

Not only has manufacturing declined in relative terms, but it has also declined in absolute terms over certain periods in the past 20 years. Figure 61.3 shows the index of output of manufacturing and services, and of GDP. Whilst GDP and services show a general upward trend, manufactures have seen severe declines of 6 per cent between 1973 and 1976, 14 per cent between 1979 and 1981 and another 6 per cent between 1990 and 1992. It wasn't until 1988 that manufacturing output reached the same levels as those achieved in 1973, and the recession of 1990-92 meant that output was no higher in 1993 than it was in 1988. Whilst manufacturing output was 16 per cent higher in 1994 than in 1970, service output was 70 per cent higher.

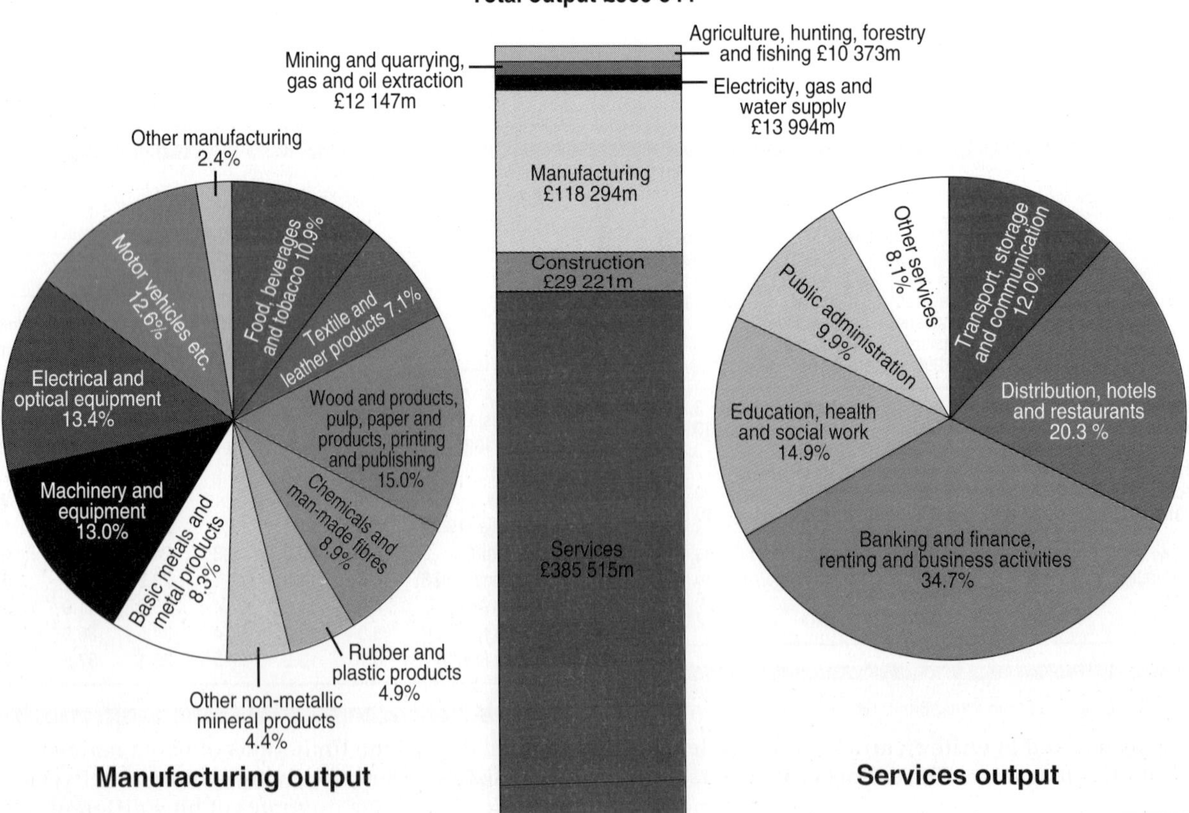

Figure 61.1 *Share of output, 1993*

Source: adapted from CSO, *Annual Abstract of Statistics.*

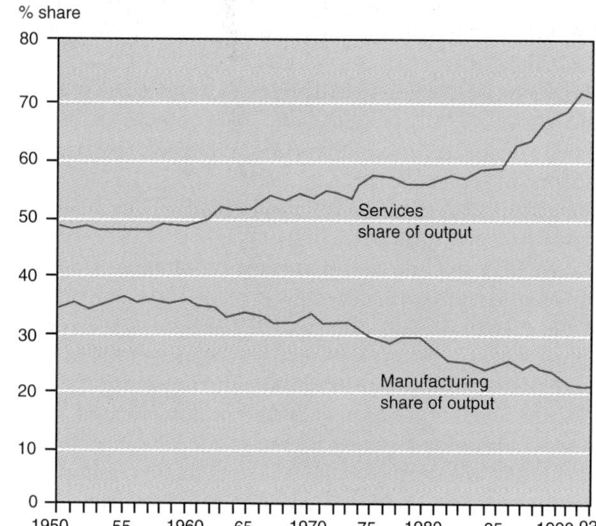

Source: adapted from CSO, *United Kingdom National Accounts.*

Figure 61.2 *Manufacturing and service sector output as a share of GDP*

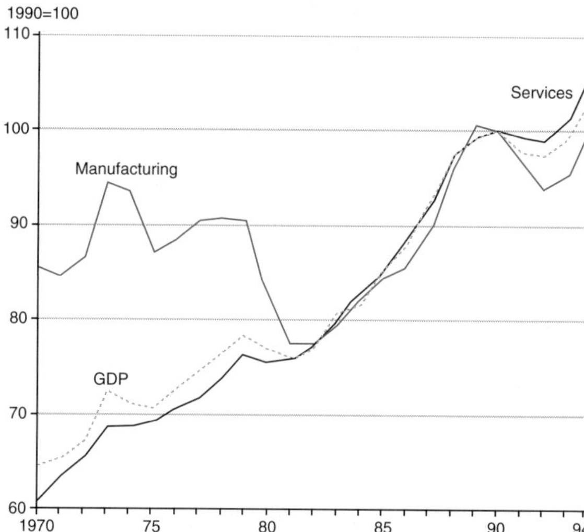

Source: adapted from CSO, *United Kingdom National Accounts.*

Figure 61.3 *GDP, manufacturing and service sector output, 1990=100*

Certain manufacturing industries have done better than others. Table 61.1 shows the 14 groupings of manufacturing in the Standard Industrial Classification. 1990 is the base year, and therefore output for each industry is given an index number of 100 in 1990. In 1982, the economy was just beginning to grow again after a deep recession which particularly hit manufacturing industry. In 1990, most of manufacturing industry was still producing at levels reached in 1988-89 at the height of the Lawson boom. In 1994, the economy, like in 1982, was beginning to grow again after a deep recession. The Table shows that all industries saw growth in output between 1982 and 1990. Some industries, such as textiles and 'other manufacturing', were badly hit by the recession of the early 1990s and were still producing below their 1990 level in 1994. The Table also shows that there have been large differences in the rate of growth of output of different industries between 1982 and 1994. Chemicals and man-made fibres have been success stories, as has rubber and plastic products. The revival of motor manufacturing, led by new Japanese plants in Sunderland and Derby, helped increase transport equipment output after previous declines. The fastest growing industry was electrical and optical equipment, which includes computer equipment.

Table 61.1 *Manufacturing output by industry at constant factor cost*

1985 = 100

	1983	1986	1989	1993
Manufacturing				
Food and drink	91.5	94.1	98.9	101.2
Tobacco products	104.9	87.6	96.3	100.3
Textiles & leather products	96.0	104.4	102.5	89.8
Wood & wood products	77.9	83.9	101.5	87.2
Pulp, paper products, printing & publishing	69.7	77.8	97.8	98.9
Solid & nuclear fuels, oil refining	94.9	105.2	103.0	112.8
Chemicals & man-made fibres	75.2	84.1	100.3	107.4
Rubber & plastic products	64.6	75.7	97.2	100.8
Other non-metallic mineral products	84.4	88.0	105.2	89.7
Basic metals & metal products	82.6	86.4	102.8	86.1
Machinery & equipment	85.2	87.2	97.8	84.0
Electrical & optical equipment	67.1	80.0	99.8	101.5
Transport equipment	76.0	79.5	101.7	88.2
Other manufacturing	75.6	80.6	98.5	80.3
Total manufacturing (revised definition)	79.2	85.6	100.2	95.3

Source: adapted from CSO, *Annual Abstract of Statistics*; CSO, *Monthly Digest of Statistics.*

Employment

Not surprisingly, the change in the share of output of the manufacturing and service sectors of the economy has produced changes in the structure and pattern of employment, as can be seen in Figure 61.4. In 1971, 7.9 million workers were employed in manufacturing out of a

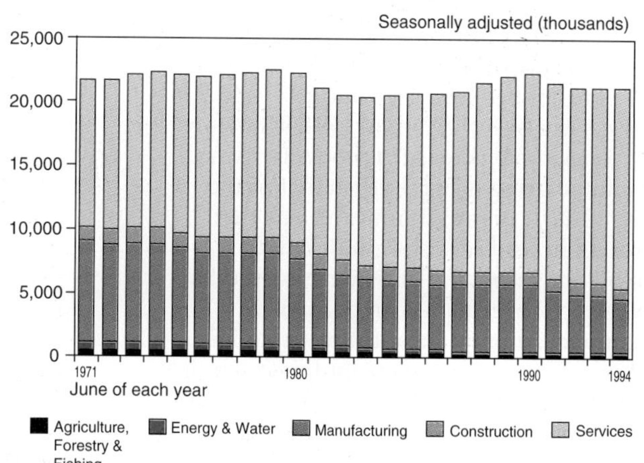

Source: adapted from Department of Employment, *Employment Gazette*, October 1994.

Figure 61.4 *Employees in employment by industrial sector: Great Britain (1971-1994)*

total number of employees in employment of 21.6 million (the self-employed and unemployed are not included here). By 1994, employment in manufacturing had fallen to 4.2 million out of a total 20.9 million employees. A rise in manufacturing output of 18 per cent was accompanied by a 47 per cent fall in employment. Employment in primary industry had fallen too. On the other hand, service sector employment rose considerably, from 11.4 million employees in 1971 to 15.4 million in 1994, a rise of 35 per cent which accompanied a 69 per cent increase in total output. Figure 61.5 shows that in 1971, approximately half of all employees worked in service sector industries. By 1994, this had grown to nearly three-quarters. The share of manufacturing employment, on the other hand, has fallen from nearly two-fifths to one-fifth.

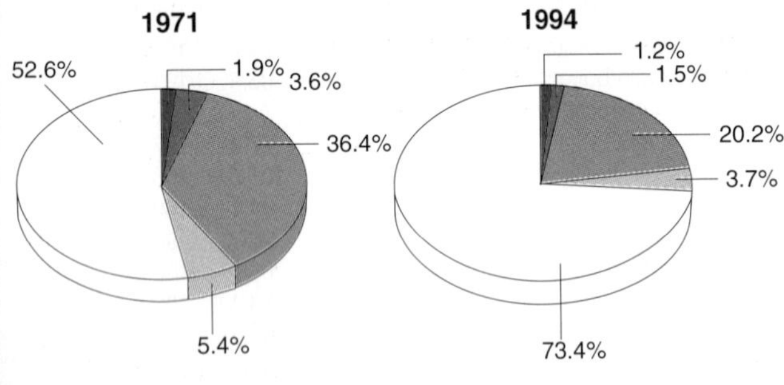

Source: adapted from Department of Employment, *Employment Gazette*, October 1994.

Figure 61.5 *Employment by sector (employees in employment as a percentage of the total), Great Britain, 1971 and 1994*

Labour productivity

Labour productivity (output per worker) has risen substantially in the post-war period. Productivity in manufacturing rose by an average of 3.0 per cent per year in the 1960s, 2.2 per cent between 1970 and 1979 and 3.8 per cent between 1979 and 1994. Productivity growth in the whole economy has been slower - 2.4 per cent in the 1960s, 1.8 per cent between 1970 and 1979 and 2.0 per cent between 1979 and 1994. Therefore, given that the increase in productivity in manufacturing is higher than that of the rest of the economy, it must be true that growth in service sector productivity was below the average. This is what would be expected. Large gains can be made in manufacturing by substituting capital for labour. There is less scope for this in service industries, particularly in personal services and tourism where high labour to customer ratios are equated with quality.

De-industrialisation

The process of decline in manufacturing industry is known as DE-INDUSTRIALISATION. There is no standard definition of the term but it has at times been used to describe:

- the absolute decline in output of manufacturing industry;
- a significant decline in the share of manufacturing output in total output;
- the absolute decline in the numbers of workers employed in manufacturing;
- the relative decline in the proportion of all workers employed in manufacturing.

In the case of the UK, the past 20 years have seen an absolute decline in employment and relative falls in both employment and output of manufacturing industry. De-industrialisation has also been a major cause of changes in employment by region in the UK. Figure 61.6 shows that male employment has declined in regions which have traditionally relied on manufacturing employment - the Midlands, Wales, the North and Scotland. The South East, the largest employment region in the country with 32 per cent of the UK workforce, suffered a loss of 1.2 million manufacturing jobs between 1971 and 1994. Female employment, on the other hand, has grown and this has largely been the result of increased service sector jobs.

The causes of de-industrialisation

It has been argued that de-industrialisation is inevitable in developed economies. Over time, consumers choose to

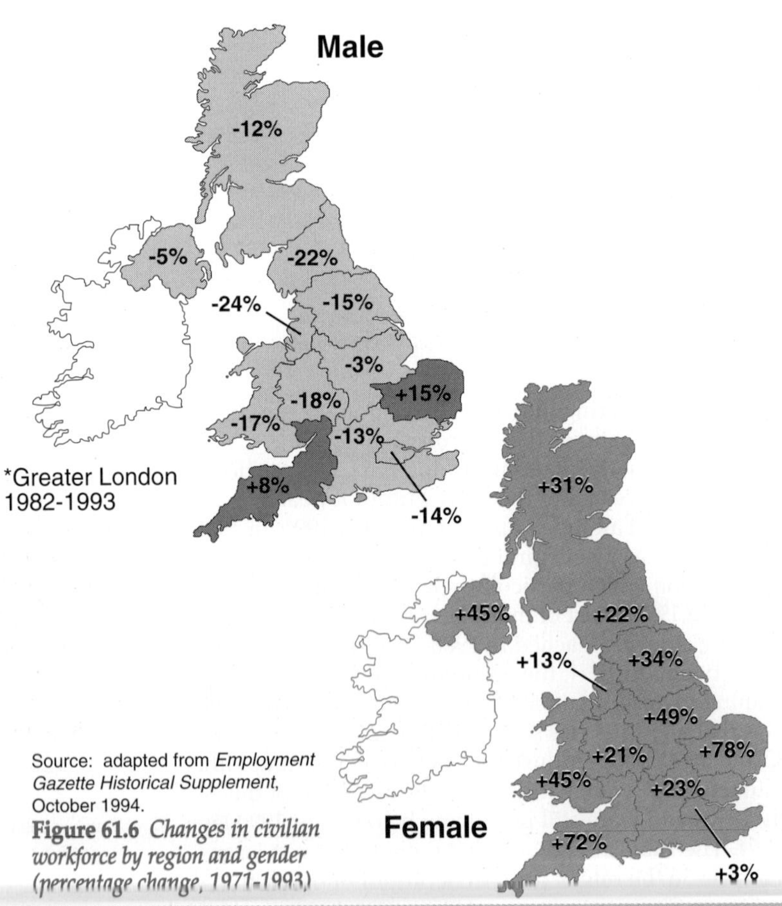

Source: adapted from *Employment Gazette Historical Supplement*, October 1994.

Figure 61.6 *Changes in civilian workforce by region and gender (percentage change, 1971-1993)*

spend an ever greater proportion of their income on services rather than manufactures (i.e. services have an income elasticity of demand greater than 1 whilst manufactures have an income elasticity of demand of less than 1). Table 61.2 would give some support to this hypothesis. It shows that manufacturing output as a share of GDP has fallen in all G7 economies (the 7 largest industrial economies in the world). Equally, whilst employment grew in manufacturing industries of the G7 countries in the 1960s and 1970s, it tended to fall in the 1980s. However, the UK suffered the largest fall in manufacturing output amongst the 7 countries between 1960 and 1990. Also, the UK was the only country to show a consistent fall in employment over the whole period. If all G7 countries are in the process of de-industrialisation, the UK has de-industrialised at a much faster rate than its international competitors.

Table 61.2 *Manufacturing output and employment in the G7 countries, 1960-1990*

	Manufacturing						
	Output as a percentage of GDP			Annual percentage growth in employment			
	1960	1979	1992	1960-67	1968-73	1974-79	1980-90
United States	28	23	18	1.9	1.0	1.5	-0.5
Japan	35	29	26	4.0	2.5	-0.4	1.1
Germany	40	34	26	-0.2	0.9	-1.8	0.8
France	29	26	19	1.1	1.6	-1.1	-1.7
United Kingdom	32	25	17	-0.3	-1.1	-1.2	-3.1
Italy	29	28	20	0.8	0.4	0.3	-1.1
Canada	n.a.	19	17	2.5	2.2	1.9	-0.3

Source: adapted from OECD, *Historical Statistics.*

Moreover, the change in UK consumer expenditure should have favoured UK manufacturers. UK consumer spending on goods rose by 28.7 per cent in real terms between 1979 and 1994, whilst UK manufacturing output rose by only 9.3 per cent. The failure of British manufacturing industry to satisfy domestic demand has led to a significant increase in imports of manufactured goods into the country. Not only that, but this has been paralleled by disappointing export performance in manufactures. (This important shift in the structure of foreign trade is discussed in more detail in unit 84.)

From this, it could be argued that much of the blame for British de-industrialisation must be put on British manufacturing itself. It has failed to compete successfully on world markets and the result has been a declining share of world exports, and declining output. Although productivity in UK manufacturing has increased, it has not increased at a sufficiently high rate. In the second half of the 1980s, it looked as though British manufacturing industry might be regaining some of its lost ground. Productivity increases were matching those of its industrial rivals, whilst the fall in Britain's share of manufactured trade bottomed out. However, the recession of 1990-92 dealt a further blow to British industry. In 1992, manufacturing output fell back again to its 1973 level - little more than its 1979 level. Even so, the prospects for the 1990s look reasonably good. Much of British industry is now internationally competitive. It has had to be to survive into the 1990s. Moreover, the UK has attracted key inward investment from, amongst others, Japanese producers. Often, they want to use the UK as a place to manufacture to sell into the EU. The motor industry in particular, which in the 1970s and 1980s mirrored the decline of UK manufacturing, has been rejuvenated by foreign ownership and investment and looks set to expand substantially in the rest of the decade.

A whole variety of arguments have been put forward to explain why British manufacturing industry proved so uncompetitive in the 1970s and 1980s and why its future is still uncertain in the 1990s. Many of these arguments are equally used to suggest why the UK has such a low growth rate (☞ unit 99). They range from a failure to invest, to 'short-termism' in the City, to over-powerful trade unions, to a failure by government to support industry.

Does de-industrialisation matter?

There are two main reasons which would suggest that Britain's de-industrialisation is of crucial significance. First, the very rapid pace of de-industrialisation meant that the market economy found it impossible to redeploy all the resources released from manufacturing into service industries in the 1970s and 1980s. The result was high structural unemployment, with traditional manufacturing regions suffering higher rates of unemployment than those in the service-based South. In the 1990-92 recession, although the percentage decline in manufacturing output was greater than that of service output, the nearly 4 to 1 ratio of service employment to manufacturing employment meant that the service-based South for the first time was much worse hit than traditional manufacturing regions. Even so, unemployment in the mid-1990s was much higher than it was in 1970, and part of this could be argued to have been the result of a failure by the market mechanism to replace the 4 million jobs lost in manufacturing over the period.

Second, the UK has suffered from balance of payments problems. Unlike in Germany and Japan, both countries with very strong manufacturing industries and persistent balance of payments surpluses, imports have regularly exceeded exports. When the country grows very fast, such as in the Lawson boom of 1986-88, huge deficits on the balance of payments can rapidly build up as imports of manufactures are sucked in to satisfy consumer demand. If this is to be prevented, UK manufacturing industry must be more competitive than before and it must be larger. UK manufacturing industry at the moment is almost certainly too small to cope with a return to low levels of unemployment in the economy.

Key terms

Primary industry - extractive and agricultural industries.
Secondary industry - production of goods, mainly manufactures.
Tertiary industry - production of services.
De-industrialisation - the process of decline of industry, particularly manufacturing industry, measured for instance by declines in absolute levels of employment and output, or declines in relative share of employment or output in the economy of manufacturing industry.

De-industrialisation in the UK

Table 61.3 *Output by industry in selected regions*

£ billion at 1990 prices

	1974		1983		1993	
	Manufac -turing	Services	Manufac -turing	Services	Manufac -turing	Services
South East	27.5	84.2	28.5	95.2	26.4	134.9
East Anglia	7.6	5.6	3.0	7.3	3.8	11.8
West Midlands	13.6	14.9	9.9	18.2	11.5	25.2
Wales	4.5	7.4	3.3	9.0	5.3	12.7
Scotland	8.9	16.6	7.6	19.8	8.3	28.4
Northern Ireland	1.9	3.9	1.4	5.5	2.1	7.8
United Kingdom	102.8	201.3	91.6	233.7	103.0	335.8

Source: adapted from CSO, *Regional Trends.*

Table 61.4 *Employment by industry in selected regions*

Millions

	1974		1983		1993	
	Manufac -turing	Services	Manufac -turing	Services	Manufac -turing	Services
South East	2.03	4.78	1.53	5.05	1.02	5.51
East Anglia	0.21	0.36	0.18	0.43	0.16	0.56
West Midlands	1.09	0.97	0.71	1.06	0.56	1.29
Wales	0.34	0.50	0.21	0.55	0.21	0.67
Scotland	0.68	1.13	0.44	1.21	0.36	1.43
Northern Ireland	0.17	0.26	0.11	0.33	0.10	0.40
United Kingdom	7.72	12.24	5.42	13.17	4.27	15.33

Source: Department of Employment, *Employment Gazette.*

Table 61.5 *Regional indicators*

	GDP per head £ at 1990 prices			Personal disposable Income per head £ at 1990 prices			Unemployment %		
	1974	1983	1993	1974	1983	1993	1974	1983	1993
South East	6 815	7 581	9 345	5 410	6 053	7 583	1.3	7.5	10.2
East Anglia	5 586	6 182	8 195	4 559	5 209	7 017	1.5	8.0	8.1
West Midlands	6 045	5 609	7 498	4 856	4 916	6 639	1.8	12.8	10.8
Wales	5 203	5 334	6 821	4 243	4 756	6 262	3.0	12.9	10.3
Scotland	5 622	6 137	7 930	4 626	5 216	7 025	3.3	12.2	9.7
Northern Ireland	4 495	4 641	6 598	3 824	4 623	6 457	4.2	15.6	13.8
United Kingdom	6 018	6 366	8 056	4 856	5 363	6 918	2.0	10.5	10.3

Source: adapted from CSO, *Regonal Trends.*

1. Compare the distribution of output and employment between the regions shown in the data.
2. (a) What is meant by 'de-industrialisation'?
   (b) To what extent has there been de-industrialisation in these regions?
3. Assess whether there is any link between de-industrialisation and economic prosperity.

Consumption and saving

Summary

1. Consumption can be divided into spending on durable goods and non-durable goods.
2. The consumption function shows the relationship between consumption and its determinants, the main one being income.
3. Increases in wealth will lead to an increase in consumption.
4. Expected inflation tends to lead to a rise in saving and a fall in consumption. The effect of households attempting to restore the real value of their stock of savings more than outweighs the effect of households bringing forward their purchases of goods.
5. The rate of interest and the availability of credit particularly affect the consumption of durable goods.
6. A change in the structure of the population will affect both consumption and saving. The greater the proportion of adults aged 35-60 in the population, the higher is likely to be the level of saving.
7. Keynesians hypothesise that consumption is a stable function of current disposable income in the short run.
8. The life cycle hypothesis and the permanent income hypothesis both emphasise that consumption is a stable function of income only in the very long run. In the short run, other factors such as the rate of interest and wealth can have a significant impact upon consumption and savings.

Defining consumption and saving

CONSUMPTION in economics is spending on consumer goods and services over a period of time. Examples are spending on chocolate, hire of videos or buying a car. Consumption can be broken down into a number of different categories. One way of classifying consumption is to distinguish between spending on **goods** and spending on **services**. Another way is to distinguish between spending on DURABLE GOODS and NON-DURABLE GOODS. Durable goods are goods which, although bought at a point in time, continue to provide a stream of services over a period of time. A car, for instance, should last at least 6 years. A television set might last 10 years. Non-durable goods are goods and services which are used up immediately or over a short period of time, like an ice-cream or a packet of soap powder.

SAVING is what is not spent out of income. For instance, if a worker takes home £1 000 in her wage packet at the end of the month, but only spends £900, then £100 must have been saved. The saving might take the form of increasing the stock of cash, or an increase in money in a bank or building society account, or it might take the form of stocks or shares. Income in this case is DISPOSABLE INCOME, income including state benefits such as child benefit and interest on, say, building society shares, but after deductions of income tax and National Insurance contributions.

Consumption and income

There are a number of factors which determine how much a household consumes. The relationship between consumption and these factors is called the CONSUMPTION FUNCTION. The most important determinant of consumption is disposable income. Other factors, discussed in sections below, are far less important but can bring about small but significant changes in the relationship between consumption and income.

Assume that a household one year has an income of £1 000 per month. The next year, due to salary increases, this rises to £1 200 per month. Economic theory predicts that the consumption of the household will rise.

How much it will rise can be measured by the MARGINAL PROPENSITY TO CONSUME (MPC), the proportion of a change in income that is spent:

$$\text{MPC} = \frac{\text{Change in consumption}}{\text{Change in income}} = \frac{\Delta C}{\Delta Y}$$

where Y is income, C is consumption and Δ is 'change in'. If the £200 rise in income leads to a £150 rise in consumption, then the marginal propensity to consume would be 0.75 (£150 ÷ £200).

For the economy as a whole, the marginal propensity to consume is likely to be positive (i.e.greater than zero) but less than 1. Any rise in income will lead to more spending but also some saving too. For individuals, the marginal propensity to consume could be more than 1 if money was borrowed to finance spending higher than income.

Evidence suggests that the AVERAGE PROPENSITY TO CONSUME (APC) for an economy tends to fall over long periods of time. The average propensity to consume is the proportion of total income that is spent on consumption

$$APC = \frac{\text{Consumption}}{\text{Income}} = \frac{C}{Y}$$

This is because a rise in **real** incomes (incomes after the inflation element has been taken out) will leave consumers better off. They are therefore more likely to be able to afford to save more of their income.

QUESTION 1

Table 62.1

£bn (at 1990 prices)

	Consumption	Disposable income
1953	126.4	132.0
1954	131.6	136.3
1963	170.9	185.4
1964	176.0	193.2
1973	228.6	254.3
1974	225.3	252.4
1983	261.2	289.2
1984	266.5	295.5
1993	349.3	395.5
1994	358.4	400.1

Source: adapted from CSO, *Economic Trends Annual Supplement.*

(a) Calculate (i) the APC for each year and (ii) the MPC for 1954, 1964, 1974, 1984 and 1994.

(b) (i) What has broadly happened to the average propensity to consume over time?
(ii) Suggest why this has occurred.

QUESTION 2

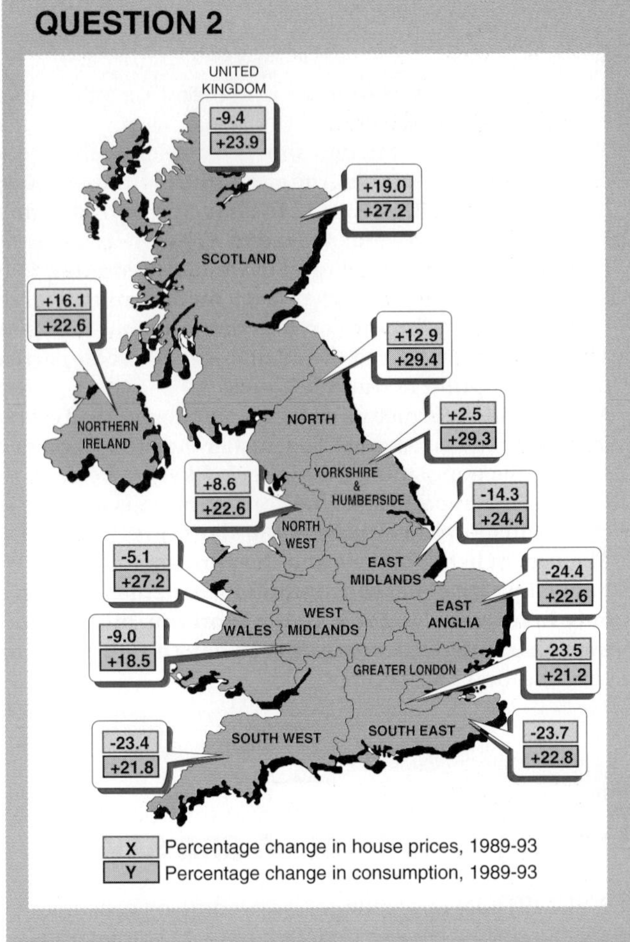

Source: adapted from CSO, *Regional Trends.*

Figure 62.1 *Percentage change in house prices and consumption, 1989-93*

(a) What happened to house prices between 1989 and 1992?

(b) To what extent do the data support the hypothesis that wealth is a determinant of consumption?

Wealth

The wealth of a household is made up of two parts. **Physical wealth** is made up of items such as houses, cars and furniture. **Monetary wealth** comprises items such as cash, money in the bank and building societies, stocks and shares, assurance policies and pension rights.

If the wealth of a household increases, consumption will increase. This is known as the WEALTH EFFECT. There are two important ways in which the wealth of households can change over a short time period.

- A change in the price of houses. If the real price of houses increases considerably over a short period of time, as happened in the UK from 1985 to 1988, then households feel able to increase their spending. They do this mainly by borrowing more money secured against the value of their house.
- A change in the value of stocks and shares. Households react to an increase in the real value of a household's portfolio of securities by selling part of the portfolio and spending the proceeds. The value of stocks and shares is determined by many factors. One of these is the rate of interest. If the rate of interest falls, then the value of stocks will rise (☞ unit 72). So consumption should be stimulated through the wealth effect by a fall in the rate of interest.

Inflation

Inflation, a rise in the general level of prices, has two effects on consumption. First, if households expect prices to be higher in the future they will be tempted to bring forward their purchases. For instance, if households know that the price of cars will go up by 10 per cent the next month, they will attempt to buy their cars now. So expectations of inflation increase consumption and reduce saving.

However, this seems to be more than outweighed by the effect of inflation on wealth. Rising inflation tends to erode the real value of money wealth. Households react to this by attempting to restore the real value of their wealth (i.e. they save more). This reduces consumption.

Overall, rising inflation tends to reduce consumption.

The negative effect on consumption caused by the erosion of real wealth more than offsets the positive effect on consumption caused by the bringing forward of purchases.

The rate of interest

Households rarely finance expenditure on **non-durables** such as food or entertainment by borrowing money. However, much of the money to buy **durables** such as cars, furniture, kitchen equipment and hi-fi equipment comes from credit finance. An increase in the rate of interest increases the monthly repayments on these goods. This means that, effectively, the price of the goods has increased. Households react to this by reducing their demand for durables and thus cutting their consumption.

Many households also have borrowed money to buy their houses. Increased interest rates lead to increased mortgage repayments. Again, this will directly cut spending on other items and perhaps, more importantly, discourage households from borrowing more money to finance purchases of consumer durables.

It has already been explained above that a rise in the rate of interest reduces the value of stocks on stock markets and thus reduces the value of household wealth. This in turn leads to a fall in consumption.

QUESTION 3

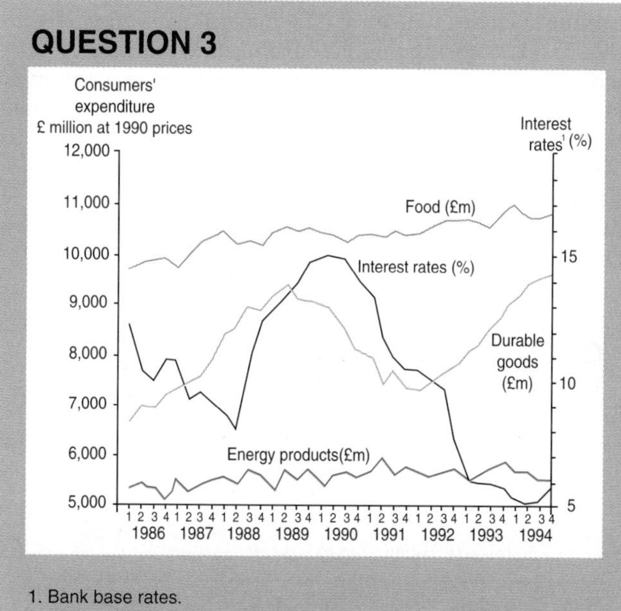

1. Bank base rates.
Source: adapted from CSO, *Economic Trends Annual Supplement.*

Figure 62.2

(a) Describe the trends shown in Figure 62.2.
(b) Explain, using examples from the data, the extent to which interest rates affect consumption.

The availability of credit

The rate of interest determines the price of credit. However, the price of credit is not the only determinant of how much households borrow. Governments in the past have often imposed restrictions on the availability of credit. For instance, they have imposed maximum repayment periods and minimum deposits. Before the deregulation of the mortgage market in the early 1980s in the UK, building societies rationed mortgages. They often operated queueing systems and imposed restrictive limits on the sums that could be borrowed. When these restrictions are abolished, households increase their level of debt and spend the proceeds. Making credit more widely available will increase consumption.

Expectations

Expectations of increases in prices tend to make households bring forward their purchases and thus increase consumption. Expectations of large increases in real incomes will also tend to encourage households to increase spending now by borrowing more. So when the economy is booming, autonomous consumption tends to increase. On the other hand, if households expect economic conditions to become harsher, they will reduce their consumption now. For instance, they might expect an increase in unemployment rates, a rise in taxes or a fall in real wages.

The composition of households

Young people and old people tend to have higher APCs than those in middle age. Young people tend to spend all their income and move into debt to finance the setting up of their homes and the bringing up of children. In middle age, the cost of homemaking declines as a proportion of income. With more income available, households often choose to build up their stock of savings in preparation for retirement. When they retire, they will run down their stock of savings to supplement their pensions. So if there is a change in the age composition of households in the economy, there could well be a change in consumption and savings. The more young and old the households, the greater will tend to be the level of consumption.

The determinants of saving

Factors which affect consumption also by definition must affect saving (remember, saving is defined as that part of disposable income which is not consumed). The SAVINGS FUNCTION therefore links income, wealth, inflation, the rate of interest, expectations and the age profile of the population with the level of saving. However, because a typical AVERAGE PROPENSITY TO SAVE (the APS - the ratio of total saving to total income calculated by Saving ÷ Income) is 0.1 to 0.2 in Western European countries, income is far less important in determining saving than it is in determining consumption. Factors other than income are therefore relatively more important. This explains why, in the UK, for instance, the APS has varied from 0.03 to 0.15 in the 1980s and 1990s. The MARGINAL PROPENSITY TO SAVE (the proportion that is saved out of a change in income calculated by Change in saving ÷ Change in income) is equally unstable for these reasons.

QUESTION 4 Consumers proved impervious to the effects of high interest rates, according to City interpretations of the trend in 1989 of high borrowing costs and buoyant spending.

This was a marked shift in behaviour from the mid-1970s, when high rates of inflation were associated with negative real interest rates and subdued consumer spending.

Credit control and inflation forced home owners to save in order to meet interest payments. Those with funds on deposit had to save more to offset the erosion of the real value of their money.

In the 1980s the absence of credit controls allowed consumers to accumulate debt, not savings, said economists from the London Business School and Shearson Lehman Hutton, the securities house.

A January 1990 Gallup survey indicated that the 1980s trend was set to continue. The 1990s had begun with a 'worrying bounce' in consumer confidence. It also showed that people were more willing to buy consumer durables.

Other City analysts were less certain. Flemings Research said that the engine of the consumer boom - vehicles, durables, luxury goods and services - had had its fuel supply cut off by high interest rates.

With the aid of a diagram, explain the different influences upon consumption and saving during the 1970s and 1980s.

The Keynesian consumption function

John Maynard Keynes was one of the greatest economists working in the first half of the twentieth century. He was the founder of modern macro-economics, the subject of much of the rest of this book. It was he who first popularised the idea that consumption was linked to income. 'Keynesian' means that an idea is linked to an idea first put forward by Keynes. Keynesian economists are economists who work within the framework first established by Keynes.

The Keynesian consumption function lays stress upon the relationship between planned current consumption and current disposable income. Other factors, particularly the availability of credit, can have an important impact upon expenditure on consumer durables. However, in the short term at least, income is the most significant factor determining the level of consumption. Changes in wealth and changes in the rate of interest (the two can be interrelated as argued above) have little impact upon short term consumption. This means that the consumption function is relatively stable. It is not subject to frequent large scale shifts.

Keynes himself was worried that increasing prosperity would lead to a stagnant economy. As households became better off, they would spend less and less of their increases in income. Eventually their demand for consumer goods would be completely satiated and without increases in spending, there could be no more increases in income.

The evidence of the past 40 years has proved Keynes wrong. There does not seem to be any indication that households are reducing their MPCs as income increases. However, this view has also led Keynesians to argue that higher income earners have a lower MPC (and therefore save a higher proportion of their income) than low income earners. Therefore, redistributing income from the poor to the rich will lower total consumption. The reverse, taking from the rich to give to the poor, will increase total consumption. But as we shall now see, this too seems to be contradicted not only by the evidence but also by alternative theories of the consumption function.

The life cycle hypothesis

Franco Modigliani and Albert Ando suggested that current consumption is not based upon current income. Rather, households form a view about their likely income over the whole of their lifetimes and base their current spending decisions upon that. For instance, professional workers at the start of their careers in their early 20s may earn as much as manual workers of the same age. But the APC of professional workers is likely to be higher. This is because professional workers expect to earn more in the future and are prepared to borrow more now to finance consumption. A professional worker will expect, for instance, to buy rather than rent a house. The mortgage she takes out is likely to be at the top end of what banks or building societies will lend. The manual worker, on the other hand, knowing that his earnings are unlikely to increase substantially in the future, will be more cautious. He may be deterred from buying his own home and, if he does, will take out a small rather than large mortgage.

During middle age, households tend to be net savers. They are paying off loans accumulated when they were younger and saving for retirement. During retirement they spend more than they earn, running down their savings.

QUESTION 5

Table 62.2 *Population by age (mid year estimates and projections)*

United Kingdom						Percentages and millions	
	%					%	Millions
	Under16	16-39	40-64	65-79	80 and over	All ages	
1993	20.6	34.9	28.8	11.9	3.9	100.0	58.2
Projections							
2001	20.7	32.9	30.6	11.4	4.3	100.0	59.8
2011	19.2	30.0	34.1	11.9	4.7	100.0	61.3
2021	18.3	29.7	32.7	14.3	5.1	100.0	62.1
2031	18.2	28.4	30.5	16.3	6.6	100.0	62.2
2041	17.6	27.8	30.1	16.8	7.8	100.0	61.2
2051	17.6	28.0	30.3	14.9	9.2	100.0	59.6

Source: adapted from Office of Population Censuses and Surveys; Government Actuarys Department; General Register Office (Scotland); General Register Office (Northern Ireland).

What effects do you think the changing structure of the population over the next 50 years is likely to have on consumption and saving?

The permanent income hypothesis

Developed by Milton Friedman, this in many ways develops the insights of the life cycle hypothesis. Friedman argued that households base their spending decisions not on current income but on their PERMANENT INCOME. Broadly speaking, permanent income is average income over a lifetime.

Average income over a lifetime can be influenced by a number of factors.

- An increase in wealth will increase the ability of households to spend money (i.e. it will increase their permanent income). Hence a rise in wealth will increase actual consumption over a lifetime.
- An increase in interest rates tends to lower both stock and share prices. This leads to a fall in wealth, a fall in permanent income and a fall in current consumption.
- An increase in interest rates also leads to future incomes being less valuable. One way of explaining this is to remember that a sum of money available in the future is worth less than the same sum available today (☞ unit 55 for a full explanation). Another way is to consider borrowing. If interest rates rise, households will need either to earn more money or cut back on their spending in the future to pay back their loans . Therefore, the real value of their future income (i.e. their permanent income) falls if interest rates rise.
- Unexpected rises in wages will lead to an increase in permanent income.

Friedman argued that the long run APC from permanent income was 1. Households spend all their income over their lifetimes (indeed, Friedman defined permanent income as the income a household could spend without changing its wealth over a lifetime). Hence, the long run APC and the MPC are stable.

In the short run, however, wealth and interest rates change. Measured income also changes and much of this change is unexpected. Income which households receive but did not expect to earn is called **transitory income**. Initially, transitory income will be saved, as households decide what to do with the money. Then it is incorporated into permanent income. The MPC of the household will depend upon the nature of the extra income. If the extra income is for instance a permanent pay rise, the household is likely to spend most of the money. If, however, it is a temporary rise in income, like a £10 000 win on the pools, most of it will be saved and then gradually spent over a much longer period of time. Because the proportion of transitory income to current income changes from month to month, the propensity to consume from current income will vary too. So in the short run, the APC and the MPC are not constant. This contradicts the Keynesian hypothesis that current consumption is a stable function of current income.

Important notes

Saving and savings Saving is that part of income which is not spent. It is a **flow** concept because saving takes place over a period of time. Saving is added to a **stock** of savings. A household's stock of savings is the accumulation of past savings. For instance, you might have £100 in the bank. This is your stock of savings. You might then get a job over Christmas and save £20 from that. Your saving over Christmas is £20. Your stock of savings before Christmas was £100 but afterwards it was £120. The savings function explains the relationship between the flow of savings and its determinants. It attempts to explain why you saved £20 over Christmas. It does not explain why you have £100 in the bank already.

Aggregate flows Utility theory (☞ units 14 and 15) is used to explain individual consumer behaviour. The theory of the consumption function is a **macro-economic theory** explaining the behaviour of **all individuals** in an economy. Some individuals may reduce spending when income increases but the theory of the consumption function predicts all households taken together will increase their spending.

Key terms

Consumption - total expenditure by households on goods and services over a period of time.
Saving (personal) - the portion of households' disposable income which is not spent over a period of time.
Durable goods - goods which are consumed over a long period of time, such as a television set or a car.
Non-durable goods - goods which are consumed almost immediately like an ice-cream or a packet of washing powder.
Disposable income - household income over a period of time including state benefits, less direct taxes.
Consumption function - the relationship between the consumption of households and the factors which determine it.
Marginal propensity to consume - the proportion of a change in income which is spent. It is calculated by $\Delta C \div \Delta Y$.
Average propensity to consume - the proportion of total income spent. It is calculated by $C \div Y$.
Wealth effect - the change in consumption following a change in wealth.
Savings function - the relationship between the saving of households and the factors which determine it.
Average propensity to save - the proportion of a total income which is saved. It is calculated by $S \div Y$.
Marginal propensity to save - the proportion of a change in income which is saved. It is calculated by $\Delta S \div \Delta Y$.
Permanent income - the income a household could spend over its lifetime without reducing the value of its assets. This approximates to the average income of a household over its lifetime.

Applied economics

Consumption in the UK

The composition of consumption expenditure

Total real consumption since 1950 has more than trebled. However, as Figure 62.3 shows, there were significant differences in the rate of growth of the components of expenditure. Spending on food, for instance, only increased by a third whilst spending on durables, such as cars, furniture and carpets, increased more than 10 times. In general, expenditure on necessities such as food and energy products increased at a lower rate than expenditure on luxuries such as durable goods and services. It is interesting to note that expenditure on alcoholic drink and tobacco fell between 1979 and 1994. Within this total, spending on drink rose slightly but spending on tobacco fell sharply, almost certainly the result of increased awareness of the health risks associated with its consumption.

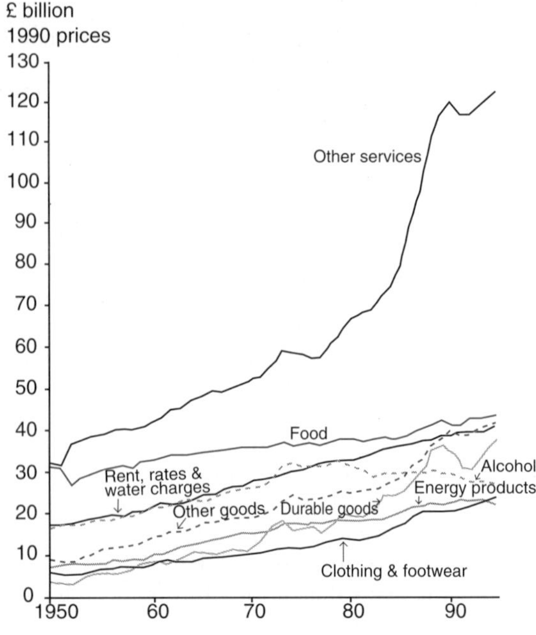

Source: adapted from CSO, *Economic Trends Annual Supplement.*
Figure 62.3 *Composition of consumer expenditure, 1950-1994*

Consumption and income

Keynesian theory suggests that income is the major determinant of consumption. The evidence in Figure 62.4 would tend to support this theory. Over the period 1948 to 1994, real personal disposable income rose 235 per cent whilst real consumers' expenditure increased 205 per cent. Keynesian theory would also suggest that the average propensity to consume declines as incomes rise over time. Figure 62.5 lends some support to this. The APC between 1950 and 1959 averaged 0.96, in the 1960s was 0.92, in the 1970s was 0.90 and remained the same at 0.90 in the 1980s. The first half of the 1990s saw it fall further to 0.89. There is some fluctuation, however, around these long term averages. In particular, whilst the APC was under 0.90 in all years but one between 1973 and 1985, there was a sharp rise in the APC between 1986 and 1988 to a peak of 0.94 before falling away to its longer term average in the 1990s. This would suggest that other factors can be important in determining consumption apart from income.

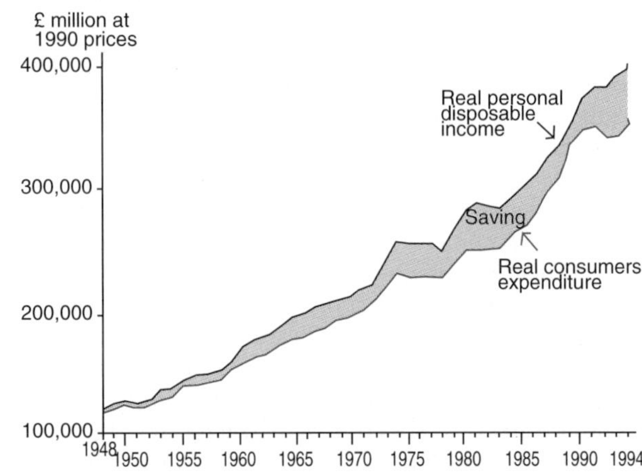

Source: adapted from CSO, *Economic Trends Annual Supplement.*
Figure 62.4 *Consumption, saving and personal disposable income*

Other determinants of consumption

Economists in the 1960s and early 1970s were fairly confident that the relationship between consumption and income was highly stable. However, from the mid-1970s to the early 1990s, a number of key variables which can affect consumption were themselves subject to large changes and this had a small but significant effect on the average propensity to consume. The period of the Lawson boom from 1986 to 1988, when the APC rose from 0.89 in 1985 to 0.94 in 1988, is particularly interesting.

Wealth A sharp appreciation in household wealth was a key feature of most of the 1980s. Figure 62.6 shows that share prices rose considerably between 1980 and 1987, increasing over $2^1/_2$ times until Black Monday in October 1987 when world stock markets crashed and 25 per cent of the value of shares on the London Stock Exchange was wiped out. This considerable increase in stock market values was one key element in persuading households to increase their spending in 1986 and 1987.

Another factor was the sharp rise in house prices. As Table 62.3 shows, house prices more than trebled between 1971 and 1981 which may have been a factor in preventing a further fall in the APC in the 1970s compared to the 1960s. Between 1981 and 1989, house prices more than doubled again. House prices in the South of England rose by far more than this. Individuals made large paper gains when they moved house. Homeowners generally felt wealthy. This fuelled the consumer boom of 1986-88. Equally, the sharp fall in house prices from 1989 onwards led to a fall in household wealth. Homeowners caught with negative equity (i.e. negative wealth tied up in their house because the value of their mortgage was greater than the present market value of their house) were in no mood to carry on spending at high levels.

Source: adapted from CSO, *Economic Trends Annual Supplement.*

Figure 62.5 *The average propensity to consume (APC), UK*

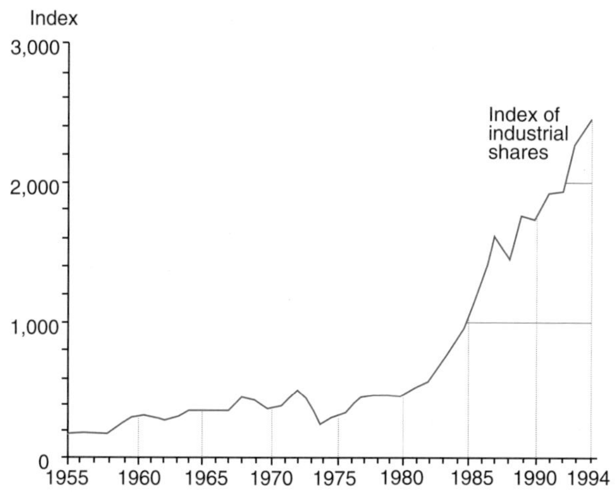

Source: adapted from CSO, *Economic Trends Annual Supplement.*

Figure 62.6 *London stock market prices (FT Ordinary share index, 1st July 1935 = 100)*

Inflation Periods of high inflation tend to be marked by a falling APC and vice versa. During the Lawson boom, inflation at around 4 per cent per annum was very low in comparison with the 1970s and early 1980s as Figure 62.7 shows. This helped increase the real return on saving and allowed consumers to save less in order to accumulate their desired stock of savings. A reduced need to save released household resources for spending.

The rate of interest and the availability of credit As Figure 62.8 shows, rates of interest during the Lawson boom were relatively low. This encouraged households to borrow money to spend. In particular, large amounts of

Table 62.3 *Average price of new dwellings (£)*

	Average price of new dwellings: mortgages approved (£)
1956	2 280
1957	2 330
1958	2 390
1959	2 410
1960	2 530
1961	2 770
1962	2 950
1963	3 160
1964	3 460
1965	3 820
1966	4 100
1967	4 340
1968	4 640
1969	4 880
1970	5 180
1971	5 970
1972	7 850
1973	10 690
1974	11 340
1975	12 406
1976	13 442
1977	14 768
1978	17 685
1979	22 728
1980	27 244
1981	28 028
1982	28 508
1983	31 678
1984	34 160
1985	37 304
1986	43 647
1987	51 290
1988	64 615
1989	74 976
1990	78 917
1991	76 443
1992	73 093
1993	74 854
1994	75 769

Source: adapted from CSO, *Social Trends.*

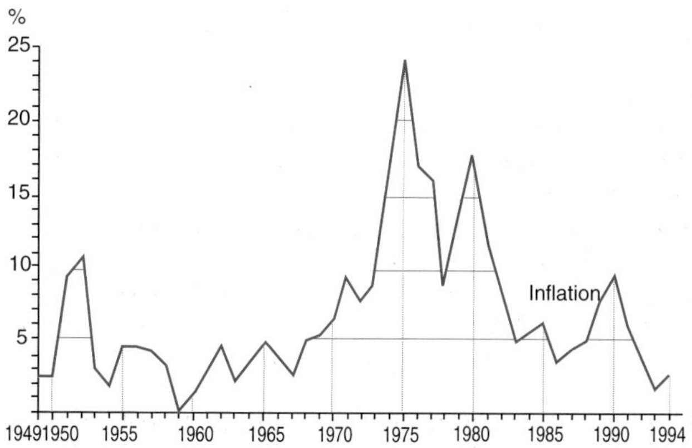

Source: adapted from CSO, *Economic Trends Annual Supplement.*

Figure 62.7 *Inflation (percentage change year on year)*

money were borrowed to purchase houses, fuelling the house price rises. The 1980s also saw **financial deregulation**. Government restrictions on the ability of banks and building societies to lend money to consumers, which had been slowly loosened since the end of the Second World War, were abolished. The result was that there was fierce competition between financial institutions to lend money. The amount of credit increased by 15 per cent a year during most of the 1980s. Low interests and easy availability of credit were major factors in increasing spending in the Lawson boom.

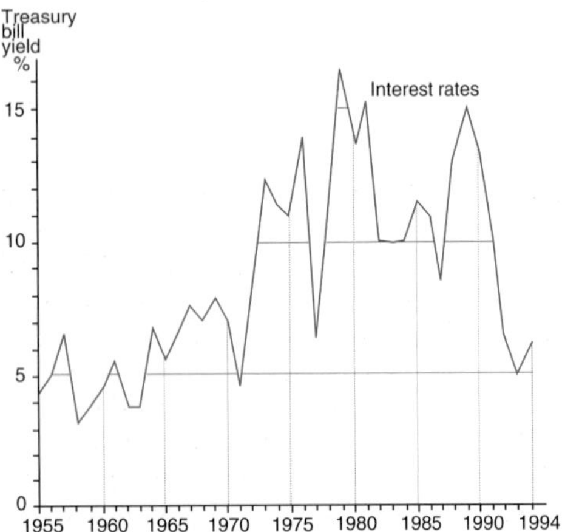

Source: adapted from CSO, *Economic Trends Annual Supplement.*
Figure 62.8 *Interest rates (Treasury bill yield %)*

Expectations During the Lawson boom, consumer confidence was very high. This is hardly surprising given the economic indicators of booming incomes, increasing house prices and low inflation. One key indicator not so far mentioned was the fall in unemployment, shown in Figure 62.9. This had risen from 1.3 million in 1979 to over 3 million by 1982, where it stayed till 1986. Then it began to fall sharply and by 1990 had reached a low of 1.5 million. Between 1986 and 1988, the fear of unemployment, which might have constrained spending and borrowing, lessened considerably.

The composition of households The life cycle hypothesis suggest that consumption patterns change over an individual's lifetime. For instance, 45-64 year olds will be the significant savers in the economy as they put aside money for their retirement. The 1980s saw a fall in numbers in this age group, from 12.3 million in 1981 to 12.2 million in 1989, at a time when the total population increased from 55.1 million to 57.2 million. This might have played a small part in increasing the APC.

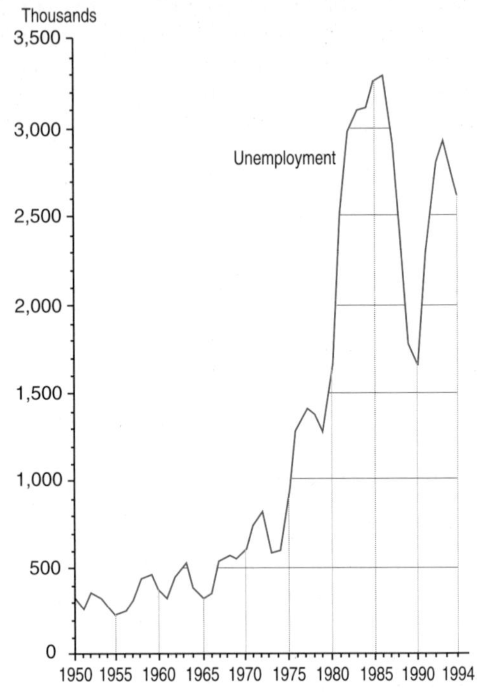

Source: adapted from CSO, *Economic Trends Annual Supplement.*
Figure 62.9 *Unemployment*

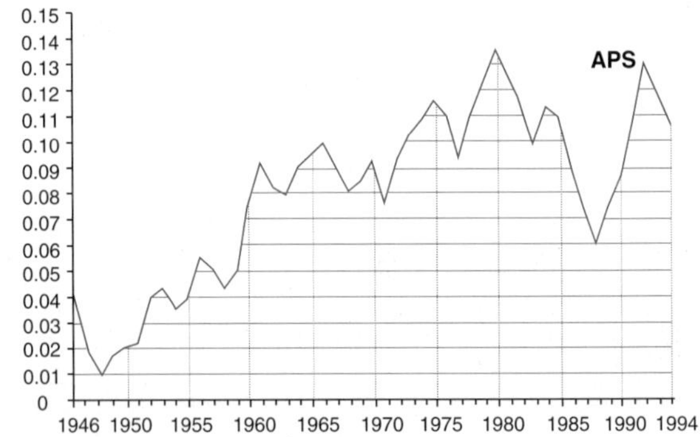

Source: adapted from CSO, *Economic Trends Annual Supplement.*
Figure 62.10 *The average propensity to save (APS), UK*

The determinants of saving

You have been asked to write a report for a bank on the determinants of saving in the economy. Use the data in the Applied Economics section to construct your report.

- **Briefly outline trends in saving and the APS since 1950.**
- **Briefly outline the main factors which affect saving in the economy.**
- **Produce two small case studies to illustrate how these factors affect saving; the first case study should be of the period 1975 to 1977; the second case study should be of the period 1989 to 1994.**

unit 63 Investment

Summary

1. Investment is the purchase of capital goods which are then used to create other goods and services. This differs from saving, which is the creation of financial obligations.
2. The marginal efficiency of capital theory suggests that investment is inversely related to the price of capital - the rate of interest.
3. Factors which shift the MEC or investment demand schedule include changes in the cost of capital goods, technological change, and changes in expectations or animal spirits.
4. The accelerator theory suggests that investment varies with the rate of change in income.
5. The past and current profitability of industry too may be more important than future rates of return on capital in determining current investment.

A definition of investment

Economists use the word INVESTMENT in a very precise way. Investment is the addition to the **capital stock** of the economy - factories, machines, offices and stocks of materials, used to produce other goods and services.

In everyday language, 'investment' and 'saving' are often used to mean the same thing. For instance, we talk about 'investing in the building society' or 'investing in shares'. For an economist, these two would be examples of saving. For an economist, investment only takes place if real products are created. To give two more examples:

- putting money into a bank account would be saving; the bank buying a computer to handle your account would be investment;
- buying shares in a new company would be saving; buying new machinery to set up a company would be investment.

A distinction can be made between **gross** and **net** investment. The value of the capital stock depreciates over time as it wears out and is used up. This is called **depreciation** or **capital consumption**. Gross investment measures investment before depreciation, whilst net investment is gross investment less the value of depreciation. Depreciation in recent years in the UK has accounted for about three-quarters of gross investment. So only about one-quarter of gross investment represents an addition to the capital stock of the economy.

Another distinction made is between investment in **physical capital** and in **human capital**. Investment in human capital is investment in the education and training of workers. Investment in physical capital is investment in factories etc.

Investment is made both by the public sector and the private sector. Public sector investment is constrained by complex political considerations. In the rest of this unit, we will consider the determinants of private sector investment in physical capital.

QUESTION 1

From the photograph, give examples of: (a) past investment in physical capital; (b) past investment in human capital; (c) saving; (d) capital consumption.

Marginal efficiency of capital theory

Firms invest in order to make a profit. The profitability of investment projects varies. Some will make a high **rate of return** (☞ unit 54), some will yield a low rate of return and others will result in losses for the company. The rate of return on an investment project is also known as the **marginal efficiency of capital** (☞ unit 55).

At any point in time in the economy as whole, there exists a large number of possible individual investment projects. Table 63.1 shows an economy where there are £4bn of investment projects with an MEC of 20 per cent and above, £8bn with an MEC of 15 per cent and above and so on

How much of this investment takes place will depend upon the rate of interest in the economy. If the rate of interest is 20 per cent, then firms having to borrow money

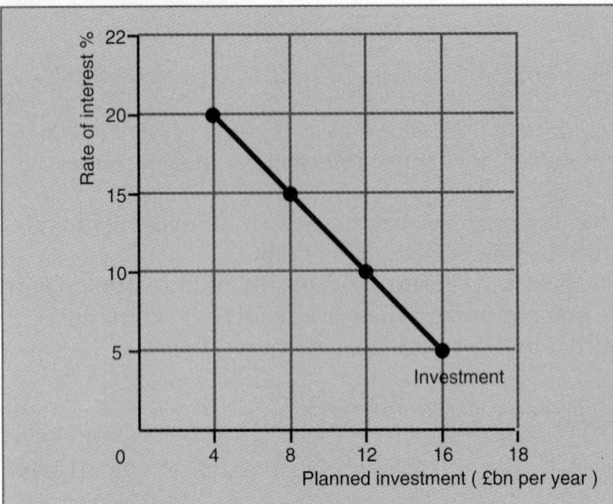

Figure 63.1 *The planned investment schedule*
A fall in the rate of interest will make more investment projects profitable. Planned investment will rise if the rate of interest falls.

QUESTION 2

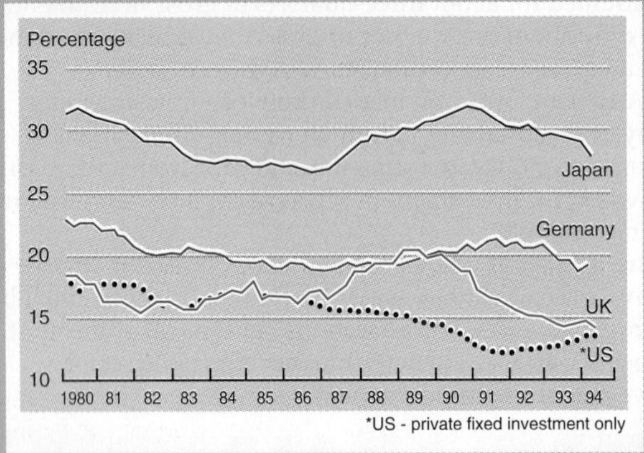

Figure 63.2 *Gross fixed capital formation (as a percentage of GDP/GNP)*

In 1994, the governor of the Bank of England, Eddie George, criticised British industry for underinvestment. A recent CBI survey found that most UK companies were insisting on a return on capital of at least 20 per cent. Whilst interest rates and inflation were high, this might have been appropriate. However, the true overall cost of capital internationally was then in the region of 11-12 per cent. British industry's insistance on returns which are much higher than those of her international competitors may explain why the UK has one of the lowest rates of investment amongst industrialised countries.

Source: adapted from the *Financial Times*, 2.3.1994 and 29.8.1994.

(a) Explain, using a diagram, the effect of high expected rates of return by UK industry on its investment.

(b) Why might high expected returns explain why the UK's relative investment record compared to other countries is so low?

Table 63.1 *Planned investment and the marginal efficiency of capital*

Marginal efficiency of capital (% per year)	Planned investment (£bn per year)
20	4
15	8
10	12
5	16

will make a loss if they undertake any project with an MEC of less than 20 per cent. Hence, planned investment will be £4bn. If, on the other hand, the rate of interest is 5 per cent, then all investment projects with an MEC of 5 per cent or more will be profitable. Hence, planned investment will be £16bn. So the conclusion of marginal efficiency of capital theory is that planned investment in the economy will rise if the rate of interest falls. This relationship, using the figures from Table 63.1, is shown in Figure 63.1.

In our explanation above, the rate of interest was assumed to be the rate of interest at which firms have to borrow money. However, most investment by firms in the UK is financed from **retained profit** (☞ unit 22). This does not alter the relationship between the rate of interest and investment. Firms which keep back profits have a choice about what to do with the money. They can either invest it or save it. The higher the rate of interest on savings, such as placing the money on loan with banks or other financial institutions, the more attractive saving the money becomes and the less attractive becomes investment. Put another way, the higher the rate of interest, the higher the **opportunity cost** of investment and hence the lower will be the amount of planned investment in the economy.

Factors which shift the planned investment schedule

Cost of capital goods If the price of capital goods rises, then the expected rate of return on investment projects will fall if firms cannot pass on the increase in higher prices. So increases in the price of capital goods, all other things being equal, will reduce planned investment. This is shown by a shift to the left in the planned investment schedule in Figure 63.3.

Technological change Technological change will make new capital equipment more productive than previous equipment. This will raise the rate of return on investment projects, all other things being equal. Hence, technological change such as the introduction of computer aided machinery will raise the level of planned investment at any given rate of interest. This is shown by a shift to the right in the planned investment schedule.

Expectations Businesses have to form views about the future. When calculating the possible rate of return on future investment, they have to make assumptions about

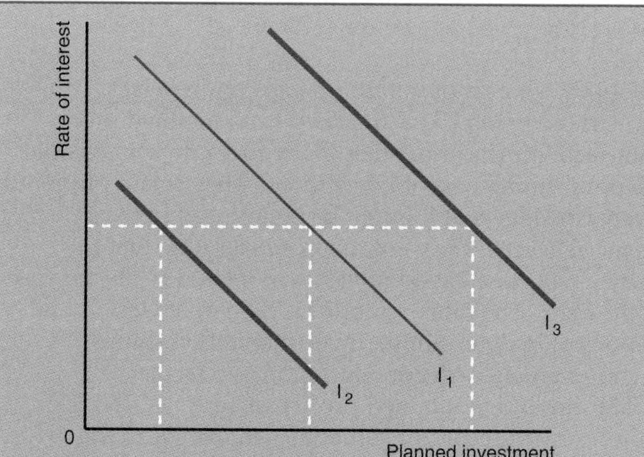

Figure 63.3 *Shifts in planned investment*
An increase in the cost of planned capital will reduce the rate of return on investment projects. Therefore at any given rate of interest, planned investment will fall. This is shown by a shift to the left in the planned investment schedule. Changes in technology which make capital more productive raise the level of planned investment, shown by a shift to the right of the schedule.

future costs and future revenues. If managers become more pessimistic about the future, they will expect the rate of return on investment projects to fall and hence planned investment will be reduced. If, on the other hand, they become more optimistic their expectations of the rates of return on investment projects will tend to rise. Hence planned investment will rise and this will be shown by a shift to the right in the investment schedule. Keynes called the expectations of businessmen their 'animal spirits'. He believed that expectations were crucial in determining changes in investment, and that these expectations could change suddenly.

Government policy Government can play a crucial role in stimulating private sector investment. This will be discussed in more detail in units 68 and 69.

QUESTION 3 Assume that I_1 in Figure 63.3 shows the planned investment schedule for the UK. Is it more likely to shift to I_2 or I_3 if: (a) there is a rise in the real prices of commercial property; (b) the government announces a billion pound programme to encourage the use of micro-computers in industry; (c) the economy grew much faster than expected last year and forecasts show this set to continue; (d) the price of computers and computer aided tools falls; (e) the New York Stock Exchange crashes?

The accelerator theory

The ACCELERATOR THEORY of investment suggests that the level of planned investment varies with the rate of change of income or output rather than with the rate of interest.

To see why this might be the case, consider Table 63.2.

Table 63.2

Year	Annual output £m	Number of machines required	Investment in machines
1	10	10	0
2	10	10	0
3	12	12	2
4	15	15	3
5	15	15	0
6	14	14	0

A firm producing toys needs one machine to produce £1m of output per year. The machines last 20 years and for the purpose of this example we will assume that none of the firm's machines need replacing over the time period being considered (so we are considering net and not gross investment). Initially in year 1 the firm has £10m worth of orders. It already has 10 machines and therefore no investment takes place. In year 2, orders remain unchanged and so again the firm has no need to invest. However, in year 3 orders increase to £12m. The firm now needs to invest in another two machines if it is to fulfil orders. Orders increase to £15m in year 4. The firm needs to purchase another 3 machines to increase its capital stock to 15 machines. In year 5, orders remain unchanged at £15m and so investment returns to zero. In year 6, orders decline to £14m. The firm has too much capital stock and therefore does not invest.

In this example investment takes place when there is a change in spending in the economy. If there is no change in spending, then there is no investment. What is more, the changes in spending lead to much bigger changes in investment. For instance, the increase in spending of 25 per cent in year 4 (from £12m to £15m) resulted in an increase in investment of 50 per cent (from 2 machines to 3 machines). In reality, it should be remembered that about 75 per cent of gross investment is replacement investment which is far less likely than net investment to be affected by changes in income. Even so, the accelerator theory predicts that investment spending in the economy is likely to be more volatile than spending as a whole.

The simplest form of the accelerator theory can be expressed as:

$$I_t = a\,(Y_t - Y_{t-1})$$

where I_t is investment in time period t, $Y_t - Y_{t-1}$ is the change in income during year t and a is the accelerator coefficient or CAPITAL-OUTPUT RATIO. The capital-output ratio is the amount of capital needed in the economy to produce a given quantity of goods. So if £10 of capital is needed to produce £2 of goods, then the capital-output ratio is 5. The theory therefore predicts that changes in the level of investment are related to past changes in income.

This accelerator model is very simplistic. There are a number of factors which limit the predictive power of the model.

- The model assumes that the capital-output ratio is constant over time. However, it can change. In the long term, new technology can make capital more productive. In the shorter term, the capital-output ratio is likely to be higher in a recession when there is excess capacity than in a boom.

- Expectations may vary. Businesses may choose not to satisfy extra demand if they believe that the demand will be short lived. There is little point in undertaking new investment if the extra orders will have disappeared within six months. On the other hand, businesses may anticipate higher output. Despite constant income, they may believe that a boom is imminent and invest to be ahead of their rivals.
- Time lags involved are likely to be extremely complicated. Changes in investment are likely to respond to changes in income over several time periods and not just one.
- Firms may have excess capacity (i.e. they can produce more with current levels of capital than they are at present doing). If there is an increase in income, firms will respond not by investing but by bringing back into use capital which has been mothballed or by utilising fully equipment which had been underutilised.
- The capital goods industry will be unable to satisfy a surge in demand. Some investment will therefore either be cancelled or delayed.

Despite these qualifications, evidence suggests that net investment is to some extent linked to past changes in income. However, the link is relatively weak and therefore other influences must be at work to determine investment.

QUESTION 4

$$I_t = 2\,(Y_t - Y_{t-1})$$

(a) In year 0 income was £100m. In subsequent years, it grew by 5 per cent per annum. Calculate the level of investment in years 1 to 5.
(b) Compare what would happen to investment in each year if income grew instead by (i) 10 per cent and (ii) 2½ per cent.

Profits

About 70 per cent of industrial and commercial investment in the UK is financed from retained profit. Some economists argue that many firms do not consider the opportunity cost of investment. They retain profit but rarely consider that it might be better used saved in financial assets. They automatically assume that the money will be spent on investment related to the activities of the firm. The rate of interest is then much less important in determining investment. Investment becomes crucially dependent upon two factors.

- The amount of retained profit available. So the poor investment record of companies in the UK in the 1970s, for instance, was a direct reflection of their inability to generate profits needed to plough back into their operations.
- The availability of suitable investment projects. If firms do not have suitable investment projects to hand, they will bank the cash or pay it out to shareholders in dividends. New technology or new products can act as a spur to investment on this view.

Key terms

Investment - the addition to the capital stock of the economy.
Accelerator theory - the theory that the level of planned investment is related to past changes in income.
Capital-output ratio - the ratio between the amount of capital needed to produce a given quantity of goods and the level of output.

Applied economics

Investment in the UK

The composition of investment

Gross investment is called **gross domestic fixed capital formation** (GDFCF) in UK official statistics. Figure 63.4 shows the composition of investment in 1979 and 1994. Significant changes in this composition are apparent from the data. Whilst investment in private sector housing has grown, public sector housing investment, mainly council housing, has fallen. This reflects government policy during the period of promoting home ownership. Expenditure on vehicles, ships and aircraft has fallen. On the other hand, investment expenditure on plant and machinery and other new buildings and works has increased.

Table 63.3 shows how the composition of investment has changed by industry. Between 1982 and 1993, gross investment grew faster than GDP, raising the percentage of GDP allocated to investment from 18.5 per cent to 20.3 per cent. However, within this total, there are striking differences. Manufacturing investment has grown by only one-third of the average growth of investment. On the other hand, electricity, gas and water supply investment, of which water supply is the most significant part, has grown by nearly double the average rate. But it is service industries, such as financial services, which have seen the greatest increase. The difference in investment rates between manufacturing and services is a major factor in explaining the process of **de-industrialisation** (☞ unit 61) in the UK in the 1980s.

Table 63.3 *GDP and gross domestic fixed capital formation by industry*

	£ million, at 1990 prices			% change
	1982	1989	1993	1982 - 93
GDP at factor cost	370 493	476 228	476 423	28.6
Total GDFCF	68 404	111 470	96 611	41.2
of which				
Agriculture, hunting, forestry and fishing	1 772	1 537	1 142	-35.5
Mining & quarrying including oil gas extraction	5 674	4 252	5 693	0.3
Manufacturing	9 518	14 984	10 989	15.5
Electricity, gas & water supply	3 640	4 094	6 211	70.6
Construction	865	1 180	745	-12.8
Wholesale & retail trade; repairs; hotels & restaurants	5 611	9 923	7 800	39.0
Transport, storage & communication	4 932	10 100	9 608	94.8
Financial intermediation, real estate, renting & business activities	6 411	21 387	13 455	109.9
Other services	8 828	14 505	17 946	103.3
Dwellings	16 433	24 789	19 238	17.0

Source: adapted from CSO, *United Kingdom National Accounts (Blue Book).*

Table 63.4 *Determinants of investment*

	£ million, at 1990 prices			Per cent
	Private sector investment	Annual change in GDP	Company profits	Interest rate[1]
1979	54 795	10 054	63 221	13.68
1980	52 438	-7 758	51 027	16.32
1981	49 075	-4 161	45 493	13.27
1982	52 963	6 438	48 485	11.93
1983	53 194	13 858	58 129	9.83
1984	59 953	7 716	61 246	9.68
1985	65 820	15 777	67 743	12.25
1986	67 877	16 370	61 161	10.9
1987	78 099	19 603	72 654	9.74
1988	92 481	21 929	74 242	10.9
1989	95 745	10 482	71 621	13.85
1990	89 963	2 658	64 748	14.77
1991	80 896	-9 973	55 595	11.70
1992	77 970	-2 349	54 376	9.56
1993	78 190	9 859	64 542	6.01
1994	79 429	18 643	76 572	5.46

1. Bank base rate.
Source: adapted from CSO, *Economic Trends Annual Supplement*; CSO, *Monthly Digest of Statistics.*

The determinants of investment

Economic theory suggests that there may be several determinants of private sector investment. The accelerator theory suggests that investment is a function of past changes in income. Neo-classical theory argues that the rate of interest is the important determinant, whilst other theories point to the current level of profits as significant.

The evidence tends to support the idea that the level of investment is determined by a number of variables. In Table 63.4, there is some superficial correlation between investment and changes in income, profits and the rate of interest. However, it should be remembered that these variables may move together through the business cycle (☞ unit 67) and that changes in investment may in themselves affect the three variables in the data.

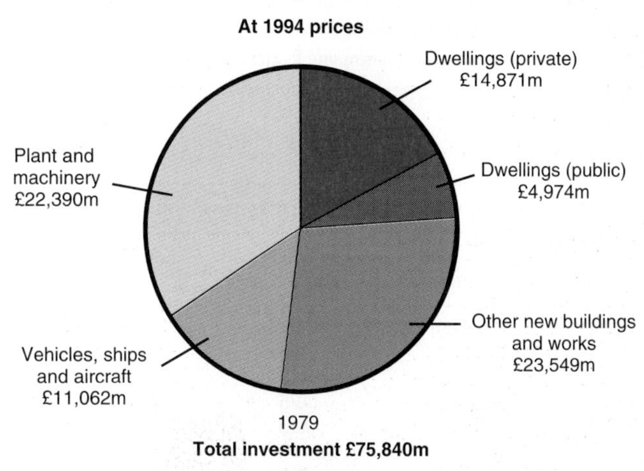

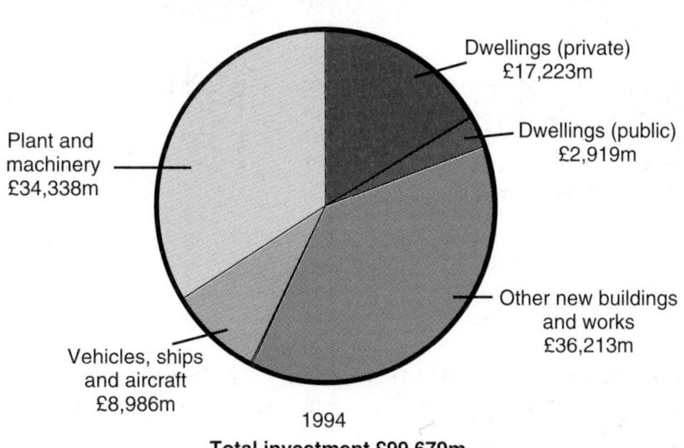

Source: adapted from CSO, *Economic Trends Annual Supplement*; CSO *Monthly Digest of Statistics.*

Figure 63.4 *Gross domestic capital formation by type of asset, 1979 and 1994*

Investment

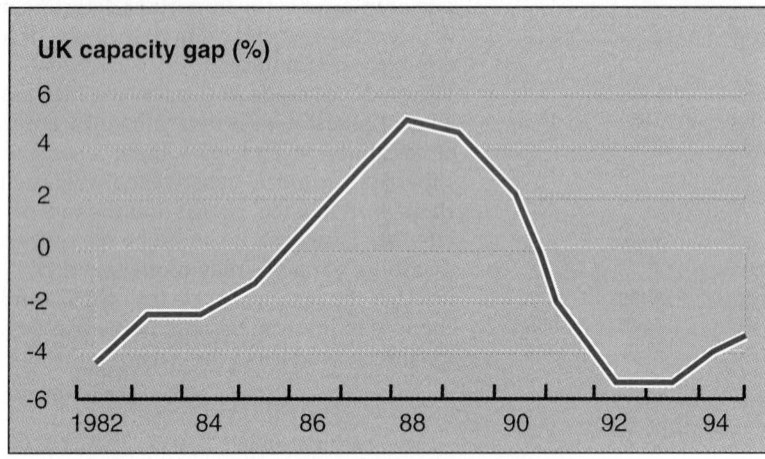

Source: adapted from Datastream. **Figure 63.5** *UK capacity gap*

The capacity gap measures the difference between the capital needed to produce the current level of GDP (the zero line on the graph) and the actual amount of capital in the economy. If the gap is positive, the economy is working above its capacity. This implies that there are large amounts of overtime, shift work and weekend work taking place, which increases the average cost of production. If the gap is negative, then there is too much capital in the economy for the current level of output. Firms therefore can increase production without increasing their need for capital.

Table 63.5 *Investment and some possible determinants*

	£ million at 1990 prices					%
	Gross fixed investment in manufacturing industry			GDP	Company profits[1]	Interest rate[2]
	Plant and machinery	New buildings and works	Total			
1987Q1	2 409	334	2 975	108 559	17 293	10.80
Q2	2 527	380	3 135	110 101	17 171	9.35
Q3	2 605	413	3 217	112 021	18 388	9.58
Q4	2 717	425	3 314	113 136	19 792	9.20
1988Q1	2 666	440	3 318	114 908	18 311	8.75
Q2	2 869	466	3 542	115 522	17 514	8.17
Q3	2 879	480	3 577	117 213	18 165	11.09
Q4	2 755	451	3 409	118 103	20 201	12.38
1989Q1	2 950	490	3 663	118 668	17 998	13.00
Q2	3 021	546	3 834	118 898	17 978	13.43
Q3	3 019	524	3 775	119 131	17 223	14.00
Q4	3 008	484	3 712	119 531	18 527	14.95
1990Q1	3 042	527	3 791	120 154	16 330	15.00
Q2	2 920	620	3 741	120 581	16 485	15.00
Q3	2 851	327	3 359	119 514	15 821	15.00
Q4	2 718	433	3 336	118 637	16 127	14.08
1991Q1	2 688	463	3 323	117 785	13 697	13.52
Q2	2 650	492	3 258	117 300	13 546	11.86
Q3	2 523	506	3 174	116 893	12 664	10.92
Q4	2 472	439	3 048	116 935	15 678	10.50
1992Q1	2 312	423	2 875	116 189	13 324	10.50
Q2	2 345	444	2 953	116 206	12 822	10.17
Q3	2 330	408	2 889	116 827	12 193	9.83
Q4	2 348	378	2 873	117 342	16 024	7.64
1993Q1	2 247	387	2 801	117 821	14 754	6.25
Q2	2 202	368	2 733	118 314	15 157	6.00
Q3	2 184	360	2 728	119 350	15 393	6.00
Q4	2 164	403	2 727	120 404	18 595	5.79
1994Q1	2 137	404	2 695	121 726	17 397	5.35
Q2	2 174	431	2 774	123 388	17 652	5.25
Q3	2 229	441	2 823	124 501	18 364	5.37
Q4	2 383	429	2 947	125 451	22 698	5.88

1. Gross trading profits of companies. 2. Bank base rates.
Source: adapted from *Economic Trends Annual Supplement*.

A large manufacturer of machine tools, a key component of manufacturing industry investment, has asked you to prepare a report on manufacturing investment and its determinants.

1. **Briefly outline trends in manufacturing investment over the period 1987-94.**
2. **Taking each possible determinant of investment, explain why economic theory suggests there is a link between the two variables and suggest whether the evidence from 1987-1994 supports the theory.**
3. **Write a conclusion, discussing which economic indicators are most likely to forecast future changes in manufacturing investment.**

Aggregate demand

Summary

1. The aggregate demand curve is downward sloping. It shows the relationship between the price level and equilibrium output in the economy.
2. A movement along the aggregate demand curve shows how equilibrium income will change if there is a change in the price level.
3. A shift in the aggregate demand curve is caused by a change in variables such as consumption and exports at any given price level.
4. Keynesian economists argue tha demand curve is steep (i.e. chang have little effect on equilibrium i economists argue that the aggrega curve is much shallower (i.e. increases in the prices will significantly depress the equilibrium level of income).

Aggregate demand

In unit 4, there was a discussion of what determined the demand for an individual product. Demand was defined as the quantity that would be bought at any given price. In this unit, we will consider what determines AGGREGATE demand. 'Aggregate' in economics means a 'total' or 'added up' amount. AGGREGATE DEMAND is the total of all demands or expenditures in the economy at any given price.

National expenditure was defined in units 58 and 59 as consumption expenditure (C), investment expenditure (I), government expenditure (G), expenditure on exports by foreigners (X), **minus** all the import expenditure which is included in C, I, G and X. Import expenditure must be taken away because national expenditure only measures expenditure on goods and services produced in whole or in part in the DOMESTIC ECONOMY. The domestic economy is the economy of a single country, like the UK or Germany. Within a domestic economy, there are likely to be a number of **regional economies**, like the Midlands or the South East in the UK. Domestic economies form part of the **world economy**.

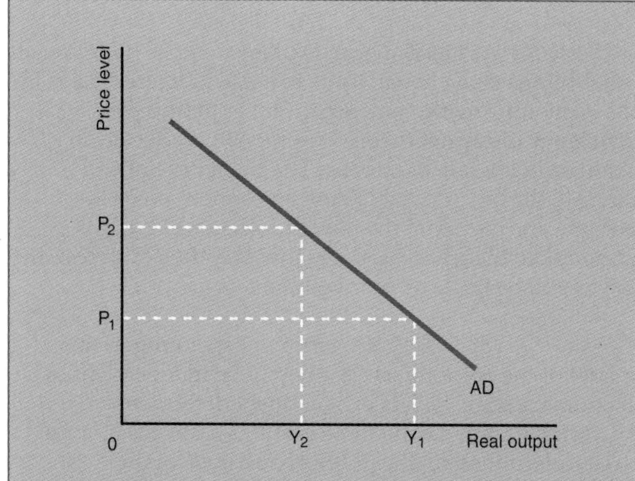

Figure 64.1 *The aggregate demand curve*
A rise in the price level will lead, via a rise in interest rates, to a fall in the equilibrium level of national income and therefore of national output. Hence the aggregate demand curve is downward sloping.

The aggregate demand curve

The AGGREGATE DEMAND CURVE shows the relationship between the price level and the level of real expenditure in the economy. Figure 64.1 shows an aggregate demand (AD) curve. The price level is put on the vertical axis whilst real output is put on the horizontal axis.

The **price level** is the average level of prices in the economy. Governments calculate a number of different measures of the price level. In the UK, for instance, the most widely quoted measure is the **Retail Price Index**, figures for which are published every month and are widely reported in the news. A change in the price level is **inflation** (☞ unit 93).

Real output on the horizontal axis must equal real expenditure and real income. This is because, in the circular flow model of the economy, these three are different ways of measuring the same flow (☞ unit 59). The aggregate demand curve plots the level of expenditure where the economy would be in an equilibrium position at each price level, all other things being equal.

Demand curves are nearly always downward sloping. Why is the aggregate demand curve the same shape? One simple answer is to consider what happens to a household budget if prices rise. If a household is on a fixed income, then a rise in average prices will mean that they can buy fewer goods and services than before. The higher the price level in the economy, the less they can afford to buy. So it is with the national economy. The higher the price, the less goods and services will be demanded in the whole economy.

A more sophisticated explanation considers what happens to the different components of expenditure when prices rise.

Consumption Consumption expenditure is influenced by the rate of interest in the economy (☞ unit 62). When prices increase, consumers (and firms) need more money to buy the same number of goods and services as before. So the **demand for money** increases (☞ units 70 and 74).

...ase in demand will raise the price of money ...se consumers are competing amongst themselves to ...rrow from a fixed pool of money available from banks, building societies and other financial institutions. The price of money is the **rate of interest** (☞ unit 75). A rise in interest rates leads to a fall in consumption, particularly of durable goods such as cars which are commonly bought on credit.

Another way a rise in the price level affects consumption is through the **wealth effect** (☞ unit 62). A rise in the price level leads to the real value of an individual consumer's wealth being lower. For instance, £100 000 at today's prices will be worth less in real terms in a year's time if average prices have increased 20 per cent over the 12 months. A fall in real wealth will result in a fall in consumer spending.

Investment As has just been explained, a rise in prices, all other things being equal, leads to a rise in interest rates in the economy. Investment, according to **marginal efficiency of capital** theory (☞ unit 63), is affected by changes in the rate of interest. The higher the rate of interest, the less profitable new investment projects become and therefore the fewer projects will be undertaken by firms. So, the higher the rate of interest, the lower will be the level of investment.

Government spending Government spending in this model of the economy is assumed to be independent of economic variables. It is **exogenously** determined, fixed by variables outside the model. In this case, it is assumed to be determined by the political decisions of the government of the day. Note that government spending (G) here does **not** include **transfer payments**. These are payments by the government for which there is no corresponding output in the economy, like welfare benefits or student grants (☞ units 59 and 60).

Exports and imports A higher price level in the UK means that foreign firms will be able to compete more successfully in the UK economy. For instance, if British shoe manufacturers put up their prices by 20 per cent, whilst foreign shoe manufacturers keep their prices the same, then British shoe manufacturers will become less competitive and more foreign shoes will be imported. Equally, British shoe manufacturers will find it more difficult to export charging higher prices. So a higher UK price level, with price levels in other economies staying the same, will lead to a fall in UK exports.

Hence, aggregate demand falls as prices rise, first, because increases in interest rates reduce consumption and investment and, second, because a loss of international comptitiveness at the new higher prices will reduce exports and increase imports.

QUESTION 1 In 1975, inflation rose to a peak of 24.1 per cent. Real GDP fell in both 1974 and 1975. In 1980, inflation rose to a peak of 18.0 per cent and real GDP fell in 1980 and 1981. In 1990, inflation rose to a peak of 9.5 per cent. GDP fell in 1991 and 1992.

How might economic theory account for this?

Shifts in the AD curve

The aggregate demand (AD) curve shows the relationship between the price level and the equilibrium level of real income and output. A change in the price level results in a **movement along** the AD curve. High prices lead to falls in aggregate demand.

Shifts in the aggregate demand curve will occur if there is a change in any other relevant variable apart from the price level. When the AD curve shifts, it shows that there is a change in real output at any given price level. In Figure 64.2, the shift in the AD curve from AD_1 to AD_2 shows that at a price level of P, real output increases from Y_1 to Y_2.

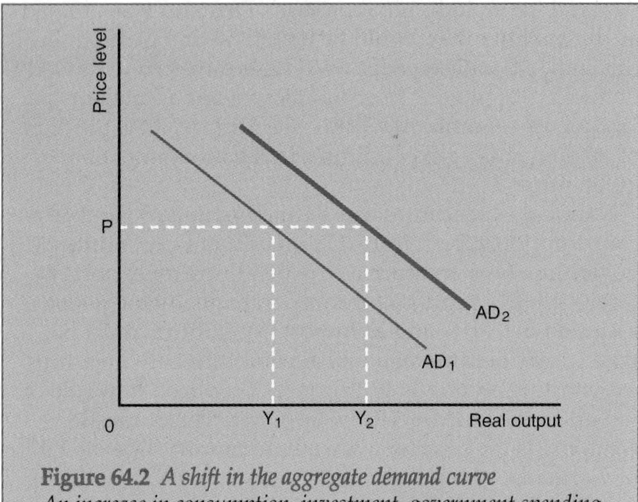

Figure 64.2 *A shift in the aggregate demand curve*
An increase in consumption, investment, government spending or net exports, given a constant price level, will lead to a shift in the aggregate demand curve from AD_1 to AD_2.

There are a number of variables which can lead to a shift of the AD curve. Some of these variables are **real** variables, such as changes in the willingness of consumers to spend. Others are changes in **monetary** variables such as the rate of interest.

Consumption A number of factors might increase consumption spending at any given level of prices, shifting the AD curve from AD_1 to AD_2 in Figure 64.2. For instance, unemployment may fall, making consumers less afraid that they will lose their jobs and more willing to borrow money to spend on consumer durables. The government might reduce interest rates, again encouraging borrowing for durables. A substantial rise in stock market prices will increase consumer wealth which in turn may lead to an increase in spending. A reduction in the relative numbers of high saving 45-60 year olds in the population will increase the **average propensity to consume** (☞ unit 62) of the whole economy. New technology which creates new consumer products can lead to an increase in consumer spending as households want to buy the these new products. A fall in income tax would increase consumers' disposable income, leading to a rise in consumption (☞ unit 62).

Investment One factor which would increase investment spending at any given level of prices, pushing the AD curve from AD_1 to AD_2 in Figure 64.2, would be an increase in business confidence - an increase in 'animal spirits' as John Maynard Keynes once put it. This increase in business confidence could have come about, for instance, because the economy was going into boom. A fall in interest rates ordered by the government would lead to a rise in investment. An increase in company profitability would give firms more retained profit to use for investment. A fall in taxes on profits (corporation tax in the UK) would lead to the rate of return on investment projects rising, leading to a rise in investment.

Government spending A change of government policy might lead to a rise in government spending at any given level of prices, pushing the AD curve to right from AD_1 to AD_2 in Figure 64.2.

Exports and imports A fall in the exchange rate of the currency will make exports more competitive and imports less competitive. So exports should rise and imports fall, pushing the AD curve to the right in Figure 64.2. An improvement in the quality of domestically-made goods would again increase domestic competitiveness and increase exports and reduce imports.

QUESTION 2 Explain, using a diagram, the likely effect of the following on the aggregate demand curve for the UK.

(a) The increase in real investment expenditure between 1988 and 1990.
(b) The cuts in planned government expenditure by the Labour government between 1976 and 1978.
(c) The large cuts in taxes in the Lawson Budget of 1987.
(d) The fall in the savings ratio during the 1980s from its peak of 13.4 per cent in 1980 to a low of 5.7 per cent in 1988.
(e) The 10 per cent fall in the exchange rate following the UK leaving the Exchange Rate Mechanism in September 1992.
(f) The high inflation experienced by the UK in the mid-1970s.
(g) The pushing up of interest rates by the Thatcher government from 12 per cent in June 1979 to 17 per cent in November 1979.
(h) The 25 per cent fall in London stock market prices in October 1987.

The multiplier

If there is an increase in, say, investment of £1, what will be the final increase in national income? John Maynard Keynes argued in his most famous book, *The General Theory of Employment, Interest and Money*, published in 1936, that national income would increase by more than £1 because of the MULTIPLIER EFFECT.

To understand why there might be a multiplier effect, consider what would happen if firms increased spending on new factories by £100m. Firms would pay contractors to build the factories. This £100m would be an increase in aggregate demand. The contractor would use the money in part to pay its workers on the project. The workers would spend the money, on everything from food to holidays. This spending would be an addition to national income. Assume that £10m is spent on food. Food

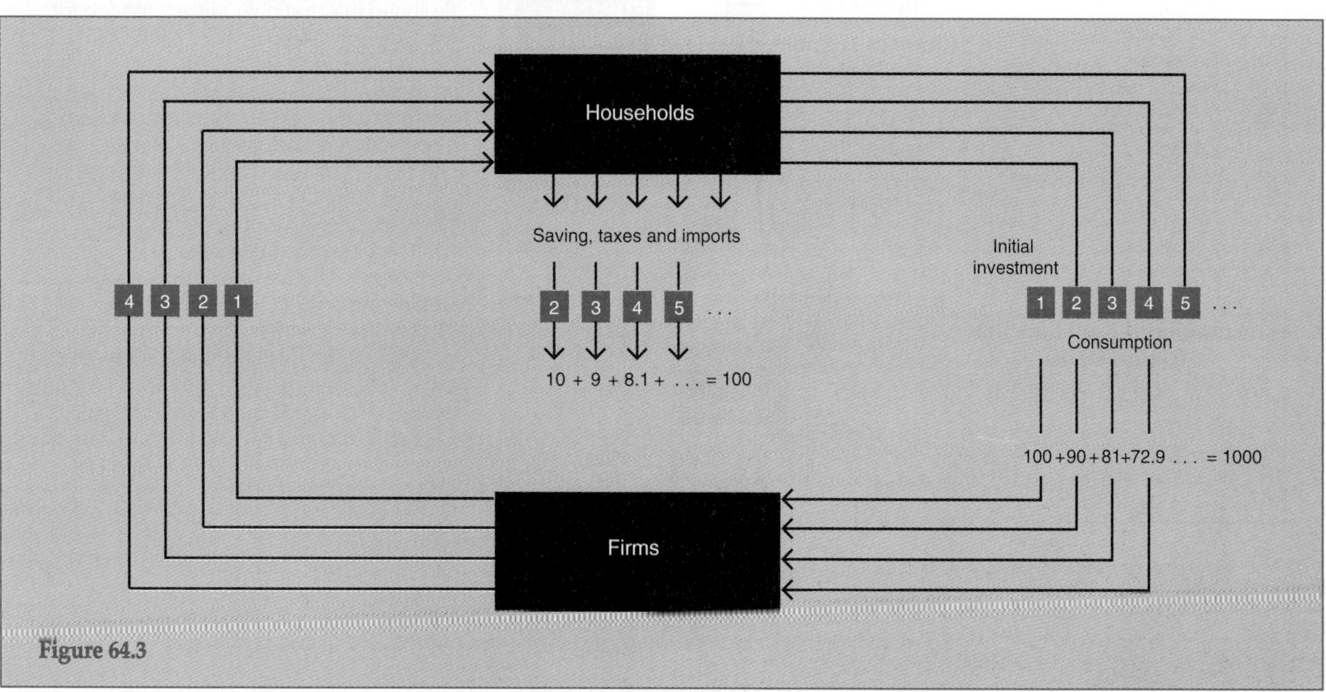

Figure 64.3

manufacturers would in turn pay their workers who would spend their incomes on a variety of products, increasing national income further. John Maynard Keynes argued that this multiplier effect would increase jobs in the economy. Every job directly created by firms through extra spending would indirectly create other jobs in the economy.

This process can be shown using the **circular flow of income model** (☞ unit 58). Assume that households spend 9/10ths of their gross income. The other 2/10ths are either saved or paid to the government in the form of taxes. Firms increase their spending by £100m, money which is used to build new factories. In Figure 64.3, this initial £100m is is shown in stage 1 flowing into firms. The money then flows out again as it is distributed in the form of wages and profits back to households. Households spend the money but remember that there are **withdrawals** of 0.1 of income because of savings and taxes. So only £90m flows back round the economy in stage 2 to firms. Then firms pay £90m back to households in wages and profits. In the third stage, £81m is spent by households with £19 million leaking out of the circular flow. This process carries on with smaller and smaller amounts being added to national income as the money flows round the economy. Eventually, the initial £100m extra government spending leads to a final increase in national income of £1 000m. In this case, the value of the MULTIPLIER is 10.0.

If leakages from the circular flow in Figure 64.3 had been larger, less of the increase in investment would have continued to flow round the economy. For instance, if leakages had been 0.8 of income, then only £20m (0.2 x £100m) would have flowed round the economy in the second stage. In the third stage, it would have been £4m (0.2 x £20m). The final increase in national income following the initial £100m increase in investment spending would have been £125m.

The multiplier model states that the higher the leakages from the circular flow, the smaller will be the increase in income which continues to flow round the economy at each stage following an initial increase in spending. Hence, the higher the leakages, the smaller the value of the multiplier.

The multiplier effect and increases in government spending and exports

Extra investment spending is only one possible reason why there might be a multiplier effect on aggregate demand. Any increase of the **injections** into the circular flow will lead to a multiple increase in income in the economy. So, an increase in government spending would lead to a multiple increase in income. So too would an increase in export spending.

The shape of the aggregate demand curve

Economists disagree about the shape of the AD curve. **Keynesian economists** argue that the curve is relatively

QUESTION 3

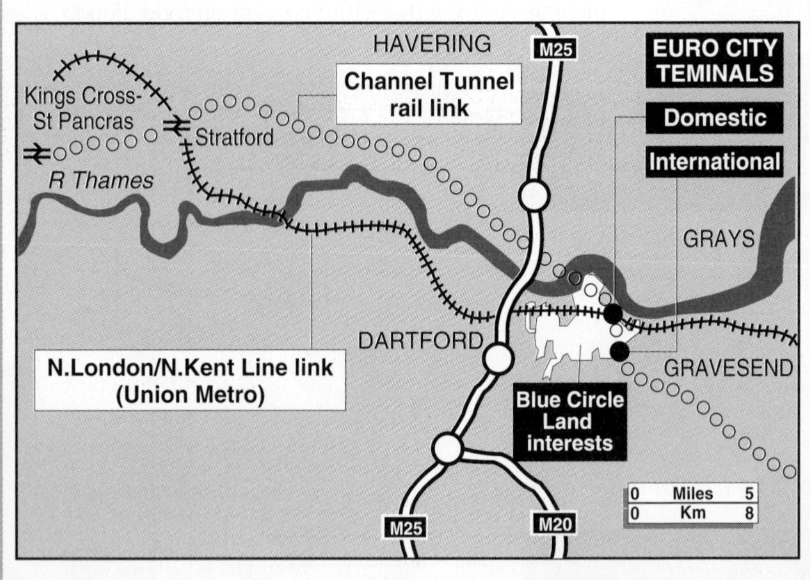

In 1993, Blue Circle Industries announced proposals to build a privately financed international railway station for the planned Channel Tunnel link near Dartford in north-west Kent. The station, which would cost up to £500m, would occupy about 250 acres of chalk quarries and waste ground, part of a 2 500-acre site owned by Blue Circle, Britain's biggest cement producer. The land is on the route of the £2.5bn rail link. Blue Circle's plans include hotels, a conference centre, offices and shops as well as international and domestic passenger terminals. The company hopes that the development could act as a catalyst for a much bigger development of the entire 2 500 acres owned by Blue Circle. This could include construction of a new town with up to 12 500 homes, offices, shops, a conference centre, business and industrial parks, and recreational and social amenities, creating some 34 000 jobs.

Source: adapted from the *Financial Times*, 27.3.1993.

Explain how there might be a multiplier effect on income if the proposed investment near Dartford went ahead.

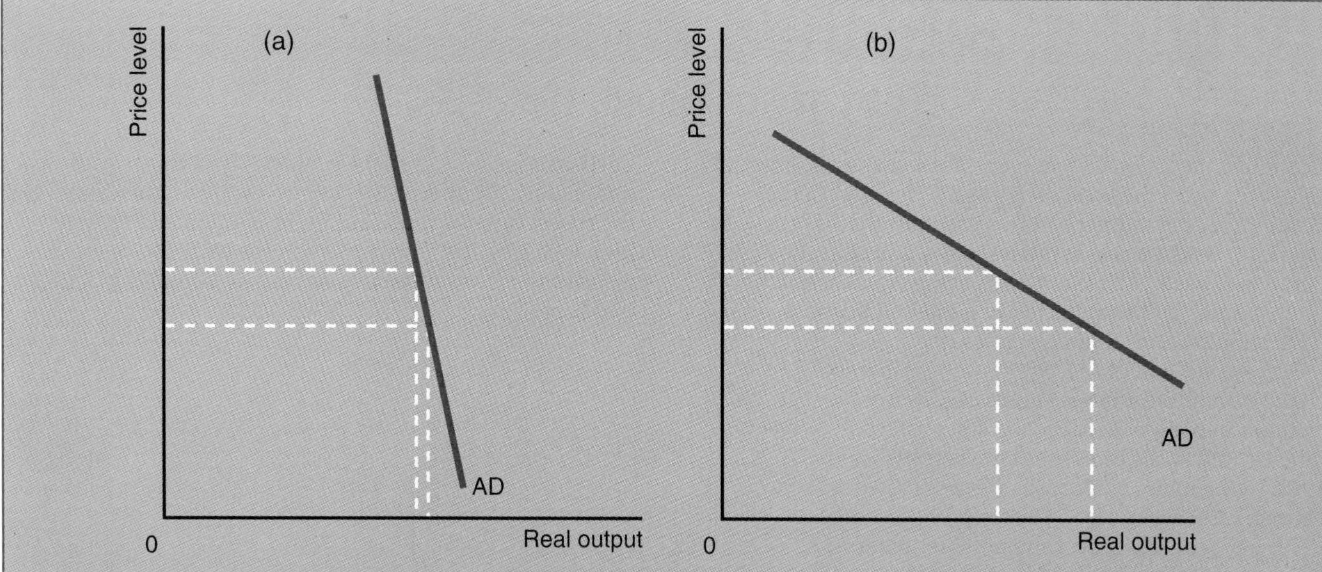

Figure 64.4 *The responsiveness of equilibrium real output to changes in the price level*
Keynesians argue that the AD curve is relatively steep because real output changes little when the price level changes. Classical economists argue that the AD curve is relatively shallow because price changes have a significant effect on real output.

steep, i.e. that changes in the price level have little impact on aggregate demand, as shown in Figure 64.4 (a) . They argue that increases in the price level have little impact on interest rates. In turn, changes in interest rates have little impact on consumption and investment expenditures. Keynesians argue that the main determinant of consumption is disposable income (☞ unit 62) whilst the main determinants of investment are past changes in income (☞ unit 63). So the link between changes in the price level and aggregate demand is very weak.

Classical economists argue that the link between the price level and aggregate demand is a strong one as shown in Figure 64.4(b). Classical economists are economists who are strongly influenced by the economic theories developed before Keynes. They look back to the nineteenth century when the basics of micro-economics were developed. In particular, they tend to argue that markets usually work efficiently and that labour market failure is relatively unimportant. In this case, they argue that increases in the price level have a strong impact on interest rates (☞ unit 75). In turn, changes in interest rates have a considerable impact on consumption and investment. Interest rates are much more important, they argue, in determining expenditure on consumer durables than Keynesian economists would suggest. Also, investment is strongly influenced by interest rates - the **marginal efficiency of capital theory** (☞ unit 63).

Important note

Aggregate demand analysis and aggregate supply analysis outlined in unit 66 is more complex than demand and supply analysis in an individual market. You may already have noticed, for instance, that a change in interest rates could lead to a movement along the aggregate demand curve or lead to a shift in the curve. Similarly, an increase in consumption could lead to a movement along or a shift in the curve. To distinguish between movements along and shifts in the curve it is important to consider what has caused the change in aggregate demand.

If the change has come about because the price level has changed, then there is a movement **along** the AD curve. For instance, a rise in the price level causes a rise in interest rates. This leads to a fall in consumption. This is shown by a movement up the curve.

If, however, interest rates or consumer spending have changed for a different reason than because prices have changed, then there will be a **shift** in the AD curve. A government putting up interest rates at a given price level would lead to a shift in the curve.

Key terms

Aggregate - the sum or total.

Aggregate demand - is the total of all demands or expenditures in the economy at any given price.

Domestic economy - the economy of a single country.

Aggregate demand curve - shows the relationship between the price level and equilibrium national income. As the price level rises the equilibrium level of national income falls.

Multiplier effect - an increase in investment or any other autonomous expenditure will lead to an even greater increase in income.

Multiplier - the figure used to multiply a change in autonomous expenditure, such as investment, to find the final change in income. It is the ratio of the final change in income to the initial change in autonomous expenditure.

Applied economics

The Lawson boom, 1986-1989

Economic theory would suggest that a change in interest rates will affect the level of aggregate demand in the economy. A fall in interest rates will shift the AD curve to the right, whilst a rise in interest rates will shift the AD curve to the left. All other things being equal, a fall in interest rates will be reflected in higher GDP and a fall in GDP should result if interest rates rise.

The second half of the 1980s saw considerable changes in interest rates. Figure 64.5 shows changes in bank base rates, the key short term interest rate in the economy, between 1985 and 1992. In the main, bank base rates fell between February 1985 and May 1988 from 14 per cent to 7.5 per cent. The government then tightened its interest rate policy. Within six months, base rates had risen to 13 per cent before climbing even further to 15 per cent by October 1989. They then stayed at this very high level for 12 months before falling again.

Figure 64.5 also shows the percentage year on year changes in GDP between 1985 and 1992. 1985-1988 were years of high growth, averaging approximately 4.0 per cent per annum, well above the $2^1/_2$ per cent trend rate of growth in the post-war period. The annual growth rate peaked in the first quarter of 1988 at 5.6 per cent. Then it began to decline markedly. In the third quarter of 1990, GDP fell, and continued to decline for 7 quarters, the longest recession since the 1930s.

It can be argued that the growth of GDP in the mid-1980s was directly related to the reduction in interest rates. Furthermore, although the economy had begun to slow a little before the sharp rises in interest rates from May 1988, the rise in interest rates and their maintenance at very high levels by the government in the early 1990s was a significant factor in causing aggregate demand to fall at that time.

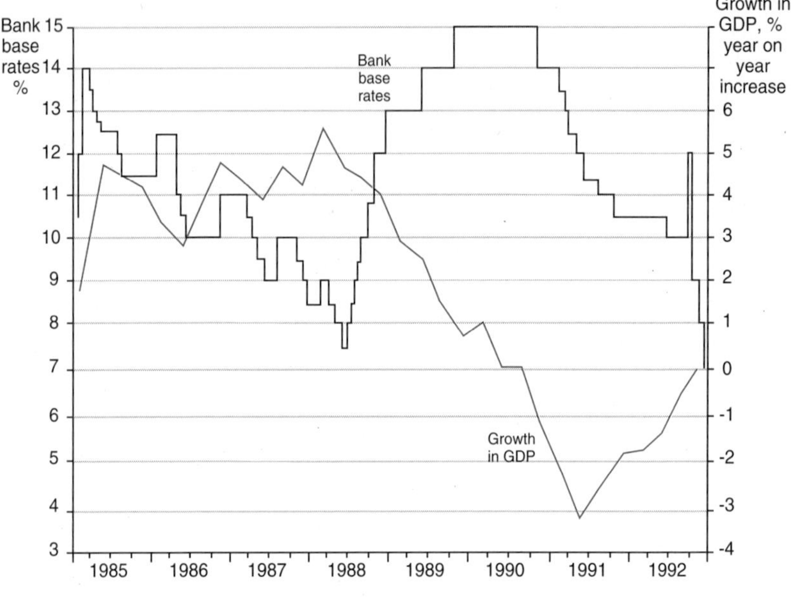

Source: adapted from CSO, *Economic Trends Annual Supplement.*

Figure 64.5 *Bank base rates and economic growth, 1985-1989*

Aggregate demand, 1992-95

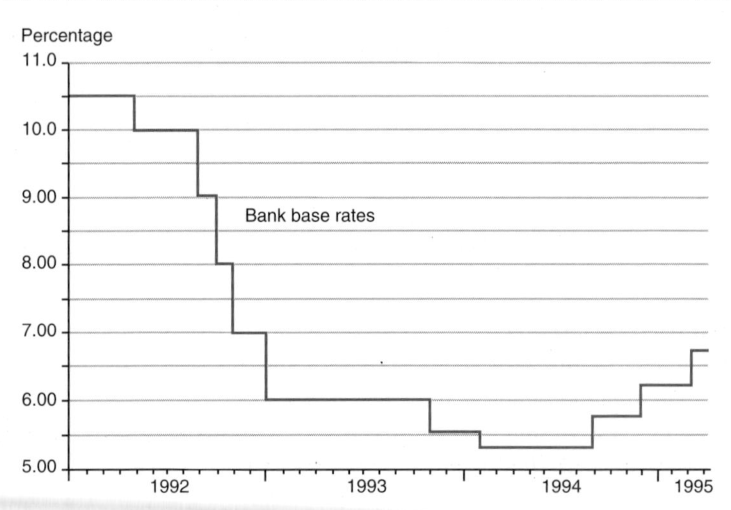

Figure 64.6 *Bank base rates*

From the data, discuss what is likely to have happened to aggregate demand and its components between 1992 and 1994/5. Use diagrams to illustrate your answer.

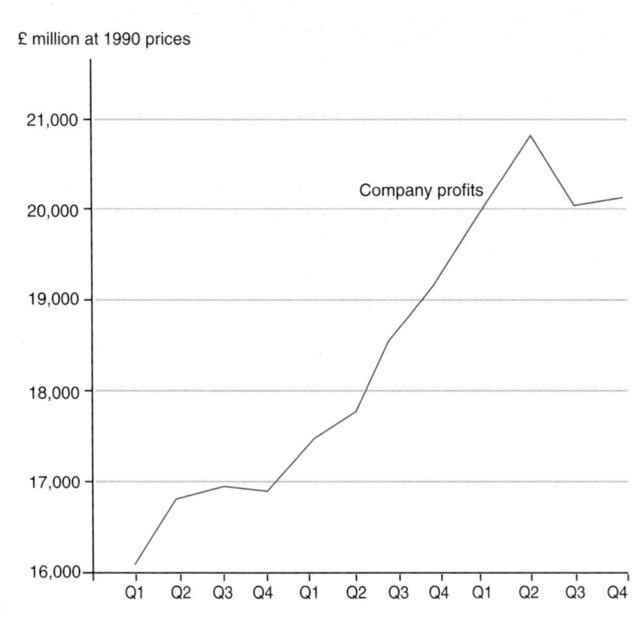

1. Gross trading profits of industrial and commercial companies net of stock appreciation adjusted by the GDP deflator.

Figure 64.7 *Company profits[1] (at 1990 prices)*

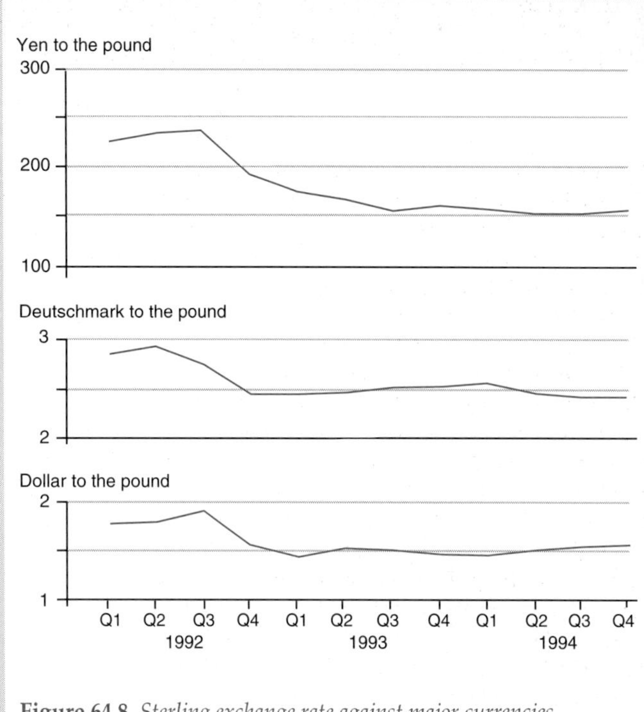

Figure 64.8 *Sterling exchange rate against major currencies*

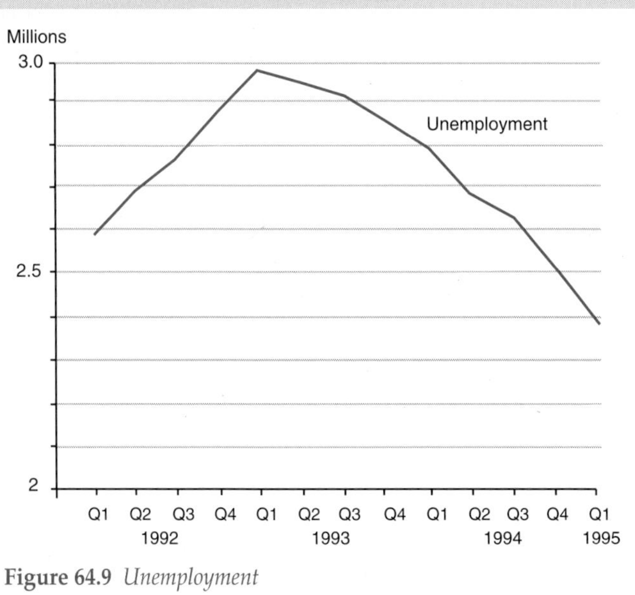

Figure 64.9 *Unemployment*

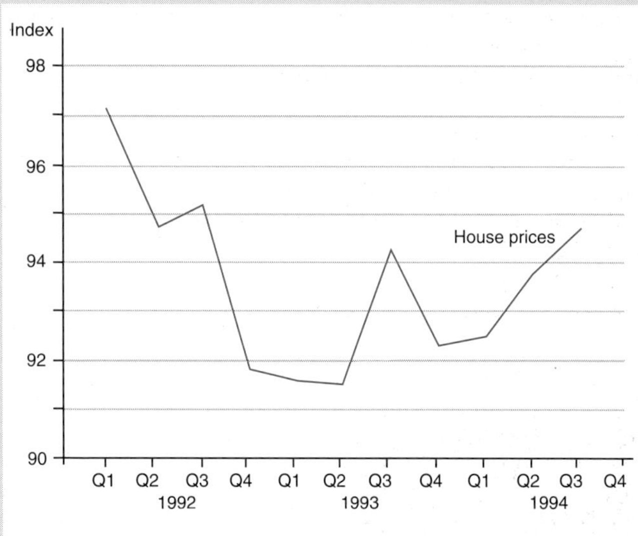

Figure 64.10 *Average house prices (DoE Index 1990=100)*

Figure 64.11 *Price level - Index of Retail Prices, January 13, 1987=100*

Source: adapted from Department of Employment.

Aggregate supply

Summary

1. The aggregate supply curve shows the level of output in the whole economy at any given level of average prices.
2. In the short run, it is assumed that money wage rates are constant. Firms will supply extra output if the prices they receive increase. Hence, in the short run, the aggregate supply curve is upward sloping.
3. An increase in firms' costs of production will shift the short run aggregate supply curve upward, whilst a fall in costs will shift it downwards.
4. In the long run, wage rates may go up or down. Classical economists argue that if wages are perfectly flexible, unemployment will be eliminated by a fall in real wage rates. With full employment in the economy, the long run aggregate supply curve must be vertical at an output level equal to the full employment level of income.
5. Keynesian economists argue that real wages may not fall far enough to eliminate unemployment even in the long run. The long run aggregate supply curve is then horizontal or upward sloping at levels of output below full employment income but becomes vertical at full employment.
6. Shifts in the long run aggregate supply curve are caused by changes in the quantity or quality of factors of production or the efficiency of their use.

The short run aggregate supply curve

In unit 9, it was argued that the supply curve for an industry was upward sloping. If the price of a product increases, firms in the industry are likely to increase their profits by producing and selling more. So the higher the price, the higher the level of output. The supply curve being talked about here is a **micro-economic** supply curve. Is the **macro-economic** supply curve (i.e. the supply curve for the whole economy) the same?

The macro-economic supply curve is called the AGGREGATE SUPPLY CURVE, because it is the sum of all the industry supply curves in the economy. It shows how much output firms wish to supply at each level of prices.

In the short run, the aggregate supply curve is upward sloping. The short run is defined here as the period when money wage rates and the prices of all other factor inputs in the economy are fixed. Assume that firms wish to increase their level of output. In the short run, they are unlikely to take on extra workers. Taking on extra staff is an expensive process. Sacking them if they are no longer needed is likely to be even more costly, not just in direct monetary terms but also in terms of industrial relations within the company. So firms tend to respond to increases in demand in the short run by working their existing labour force more intensively, for instance through overtime.

Firms will need to provide incentives for workers to work harder or longer hours. Overtime, for instance, may be paid at one and a half times the basic rate of pay. Whilst basic pay rates remain constant, earnings will rise and this will tend to put up both the average and marginal costs per unit of output. In many sectors of the economy, where competition is imperfect and where firms have the power to increase their prices, the rise in labour costs will lead to a rise in prices. It only needs prices to rise in some sectors of the economy for the average price level in the economy to rise. So in the short term, an increase in output by firms is likely to lead to an increase in their costs which in turn will result in some firms raising prices. But the increase in prices is likely to be small because, given constant prices (e.g. wage **rates**) for factor inputs, the increases in costs (e.g. wage **earnings**) are likely to be fairly small too. Therefore the short run aggregate supply curve is relatively price elastic. This is shown in Figure 65.1. An increase in output from Q_1 to Q_2 leads to a moderate rise in the average price level of $P_1 P_2$.

If demand falls in the short run, some firms in the economy will react by cutting their prices to try and stimulate extra orders. But the opportunities to cut prices will be limited. Firms will be reluctant to sack workers and their overheads will remain the same, so their average cost and marginal cost will barely be altered. Again, the aggregate supply curve is relatively price elastic.

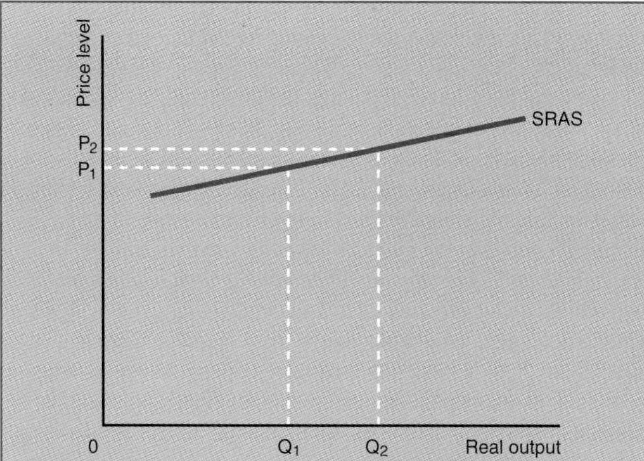

Figure 65.1 *The short run aggregate supply curve*
The slope of the SRAS line is very shallow because, whilst it is assumed that in the short run wage rates are constant, firms will face some increased costs such as overtime payments when they increase output.

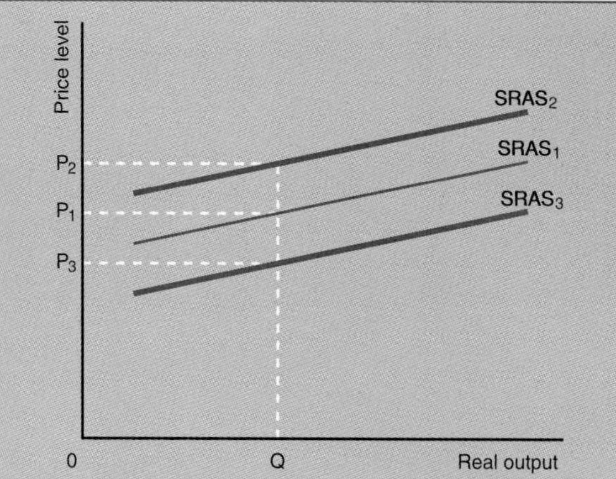

Figure 65.2 *Shifts in the short run aggregate supply curve*
The short run aggregate supply curve is drawn on the assumption that costs, in particular the wage rate, remain constant. A change in costs is shown by a shift in the curve. For instance, an increase in wage rates would push $SRAS_1$ up to $SRAS_2$ whilst a fall in wages rates would push the curve down to $SRAS_3$.

QUESTION 1 During 1963, output in the UK economy boomed. GDP rose by 5.5 per cent. Using an aggregate supply curve, show the likely effect of this on prices assuming that money wage rates did not rise during the period.

Shifts in the short run aggregate supply curve

The SHORT RUN AGGREGATE SUPPLY CURVE shows the relationship between aggregate output and the average price level, assuming that money wage rates in the economy are constant. But what if wage rates do change, or some other variable which affects aggregate supply changes? Then, just as in the micro-economic theory of the supply curve, the aggregate supply curve will shift. The following are three of the factors which might cause SUPPLY SIDE SHOCKS, factors which cause the short run aggregate supply curve to shift.

Wage rates An increase in wage rates will result in firms facing increased costs of production. Some firms will respond by increasing prices. So at any given level of output, a rise in wage rates will lead to a rise in the average price level. This is shown in Figure 65.2 by a shift in the short run aggregate supply curve from $SRAS_1$ to $SRAS_2$.

Raw material prices The prices of many commodities, such as copper and rubber, fell in the the early 1980s. A general fall in the prices of raw materials will lower industrial costs and will lead to some firms reducing the prices of their products. Hence there will be a shift in the short run aggregate supply curve downwards. This is shown in Figure 65.2 by the shift from $SRAS_1$ to $SRAS_3$.

Taxation An increase in the tax burden on industry will increase costs. Hence the short run aggregate supply schedule will be pushed upwards, for instance from $SRAS_1$ to $SRAS_2$ in Figure 65.2.

QUESTION 2 Using diagrams, show the the likely effect of the following on the short run aggregate supply curve.

(a) Output in 1959 was 4.1 per cent higher than in 1958 but the price level was the same.
(b) Output in 1982 was the same as in 1978, yet wage rates had increased by approximately 50 per cent over the period.
(c) In 1973-4, the price of crude oil approximately quadrupled.

The long run AS curve and the labour market

In the short run, it was assumed that wage rates were fixed. Most groups of workers today in the UK economy renegotiate their wage rates annually. The short run could be seen as a period of months rather than years. What happens in the labour market in the long run?.

Assume that the economy goes into recession. The demand for labour will fall because the demand for goods in the economy is falling. In Figure 65.3, this is shown by the shift to the left in the demand curve for labour (☞ unit 50 for a full discussion of labour market equilibrium). The old equilibrium real wage rate was OE. For equilibrium now to be restored, the real wage rate needs to fall to OF. If wages get stuck at OE, there will be unemployment in the economy of AC. Economists differ about how workers will respond to changed demand for labour and the consequent change in unemployment.

The classical view At one extreme are some classical, monetarist or supply side economists. They argue that the market for labour is like the market for bananas. Excess

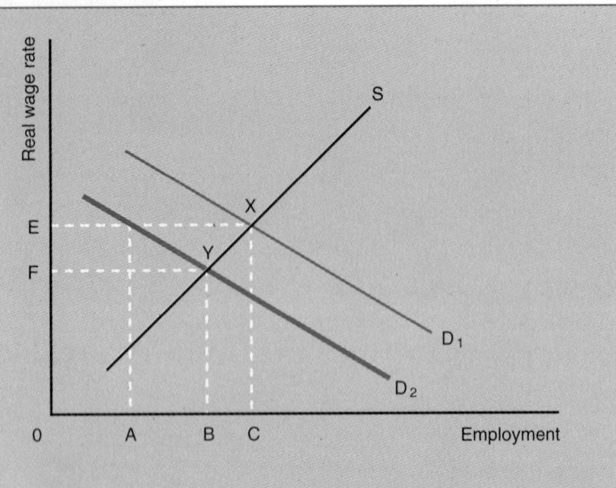

Figure 65.3 *A fall in the demand for labour*
A fall in the demand for labour from D_1 to D_2 will result in short term unemployment of AC. However, the equilibrium level of unemployment will fall from OC to OB in the longer term as a result of a fall of EF in real wage rates. This will restore the economy to full employment.

supply of bananas will bring about a rapid fall in price to clear the market. So too in the labour market. Unemployed workers will realise that they will have to accept cuts in pay if they are to get another job. Those in work will know that there is a pool of unemployed workers waiting to take their jobs if they do not show at least restraint in their wage claims. Firms know that they can pick up workers at low rates of pay. Hence in an effort to maximise profitability by minimising costs they will not be prepared to pay their existing workforce such high real wages.

Classical economists differ as to how quickly the labour market clears. Some argue that the labour market takes time to bring about a fall in wages and unemployment. This was the view taken by many during the Great Depression of the 1930s. Their view is based on a theory of ADAPTIVE EXPECTATIONS. This means that expectations of what will happen is based on what has happened in the past. In the short term, workers who are unemployed will hope that the economy will pick up and they will be able to get a job.

Firms will be reluctant to damage relations with existing workers by cutting their wages when, in fact, they could hire new workers at a lower wage rate than that being paid to existing workers. Hence, in the short term, disequilibrium can exist in the labour market. In the longer term, however, unemployed workers will realise that they will never get a job if they stick out for too high a wage. Firms will realise that the new lower level of wages is here to stay and will adopt pay cutting policies. Wages will then fall, bringing the market back to equilibrium.

New Classical economists, in contrast, believe that markets will clear instantaneously. The idea of RATIONAL EXPECTATIONS was developed in the 1970s in America by two economists, Robert Lucas and Thomas Sergeant. They argued that economic agents, such as workers and firms, base their decisions on all the information they have, including current information and predictions of future events. Because they are using all the information they have, they are making their decisions about what to do in a rational way. In the labour market, workers know that long term unemployment can only be solved by accepting wage cuts. Equally, firms know that they can enforce wage cuts when unemployment rises. Therefore, the labour market will clear immediately. In Figure 65.3, a fall in demand for labour will lead to an immediate move from X to Y. In comparison, the adaptive expectations school would argue that it takes time to move from X to Y because workers and firms are basing their decisions on past events, without thinking clearly about where the future equilibrium will be in the market.

A traditional Keynesian view At the other extreme are some Keynesian economists who argue that unemployment will persist until there is an opposing expansion of demand for labour. They argue that real wages will never fall sufficiently to clear the labour market completely if the market goes into disequilibrium. To understand why real wage rates are unlikely to fall, it is necessary to think clearly about the nature of the labour market in a modern industrialised economy like the UK. In Victorian England, it might have been true that firms hired and fired at will, taking on unemployed workers who were prepared to work for lower wages whilst sacking those who refused to take pay cuts. It might also be true that workers were forced to submit to the iron law of the market place, taking real wage cuts when the demand for labour fell. But conditions are very different in a modern industrialised economy (☞ unit 52 for a fuller explanation of the following points).

- Medium to large employers have little to gain by forcing down wages in the short term. Such action is likely to demotivate the existing workforce and lead to a loss of employee loyalty and goodwill. Employees represent valuable assets of the firm. They have received training and are familiar with working practices. Hiring new labour is a costly process if workers leave because of dissatisfaction with the firm. So such employers are likely to take a long term view of the labour market.
- Trade unions act to protect the interests of their members. Trade union members are almost all in jobs. Therefore they are not particularly concerned with the plight of the unemployed (just as firms are not in business to help alleviate unemployment). Trade unions will naturally not only resist real wage cuts but will press for higher real wages. Can a trade union be said to have achieved its objectives if the workforce of a firm shrinks through natural wastage by a few per cent and those who keep their jobs gain real wage increases?
- If there is minimum wage legislation, then employers of low paid workers will find it difficult if not legally impossible to cut wage rates.
- Benefits for the unemployed discourage workers from taking low paid jobs, preventing employers from offering very low pay when unemployment rises.
- The economy comprises a large number of different

labour markets. Labour is immobile geographically in the UK, particularly low paid unskilled workers because of problems with renting low cost housing (☞ unit 52). Labour is immobile occupationally because of the ever increasing division of labour within the economy and the failure of both firms and government to provide the level of training which would make workers mobile.

According to this view, a modern labour market is inevitably imperfect. Real wage rates may conceivably fall sufficiently in the long run to bring the economy back to full employment but then, as Keynes said, 'in the long run we are all dead'. It is little comfort to a 45 year old made redundant today to know that in 15 years' time the economy will have returned to full employment and he may then have a chance of getting a low paid job.

A moderate Keynesian view New classical economists argue that the labour market adjusts instantaneously. Moderate classical economists argue that it might take a few years. Traditional Keynesians argue that it might take decades. Moderate Keynesians argue that the process might take 5-10 years. According to this view, labour market rigidities are strong. However, in the medium term, employers in the formal sector of the economy will push down real wage rates from what they would otherwise have been. Even if this is only one per cent per year, it amounts to over 5 per cent over a five year period.

QUESTION 3 Money wage rates in an economy increase by 50 per cent in the long run but full employment output remains unchanged. Show the effect of this on the long run aggregate supply curve for the economy.

Moreover, there is a significant small business economy where wages are more flexible. Some of those made unemployed will become self-employed, accepting a lower wage in the process.

The long run aggregate supply curve

What happens in the labour market determines the shape of the LONG RUN AGGREGATE SUPPLY CURVE. Classical or supply side economists see the labour market as functioning perfectly. Unemployment represents a disequilibrium position in the market. Real wages, the price of labour, will therefore fall until demand exactly equals supply. At this equilibrium point there will be no unemployment. The classical viewpoint therefore argues that in the long run firms will always employ all workers who wish to work at the equilibrium wage. Similarly, the markets for the other factors of production, land and capital, will be in equilibrium at their full employment level. Hence in the long run firms will supply the maximum potential output of the economy. This is true whatever the level of prices. Therefore the long run aggregate supply curve is vertical and is at the full employment level of output. This is shown in Figure 65.4.

Keynesian economists argue that, even if unemployment exists, workers who have got jobs will carry on negotiating and receiving higher pay rises as the economy grows. There will be little tendency for real wages to fall, allowing the labour market to clear (they are **sticky downwards**). Traditional Keynesian economists argue that, even in the long run, the labour market may not clear. Unemployment could be a long run feature of an economy. Three possibilities then present themselves.

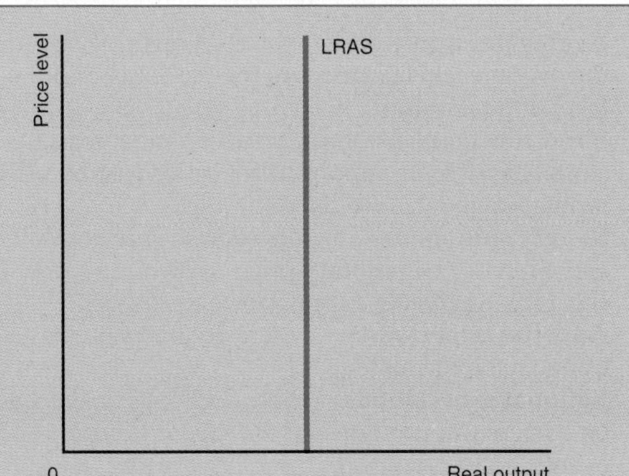

Figure 65.4 *The classical long run aggregate supply curve*
Classical economics assumes that in the long run wages and prices are flexible and therefore the LRAS curve is vertical. In the long run, there cannot be any unemployment because the wage rate will be in equilibrium where all workers who want a job (the supply of labour) will be offered a job (the demand for labour). So, whatever the level of prices, output will always be constant at the full employment level of income.

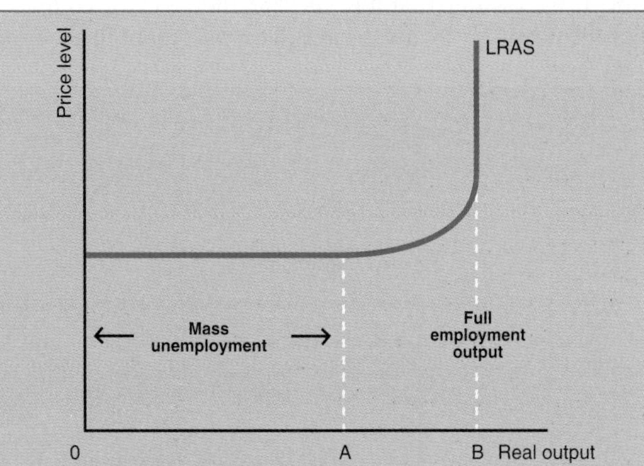

Figure 65.5 *The Keynesian long run aggregate supply curve*
Traditional Keynesian economists argue that, even in the long run, unemployment may persist because wages don't necessarily fall when unemployment occurs. When there is mass unemployment, output can be increased without any increases in costs and therefore prices. As the economy nears full employment, higher output leads to higher prices. At full employment, the economy cannot produce any more whatever prices firms receive.

- If the economy is in massive recession, an increase in output is unlikely to increase prices. Workers will be too frightened of losing their jobs to negotiate pay rises even if an individual firm is expanding. Here the aggregate supply curve would be horizontal because firms could expand production without experiencing a rise in costs.
- If unemployment is relatively low, workers will be in a position to bid up wages in response to increased demand. Here the aggregate supply curve is upward sloping. The nearer full employment, the more workers will be able to obtain wages increases.
- If the economy is at full employment, firms by definition won't be able to take on any more labour, however much they offer. The economy cannot produce more than its full employment output. Hence at full employment the aggregate supply curve will be vertical.

These three possibilities are shown in Figure 65.5. At levels of output between O and A, mass unemployment exists. The aggregate supply curve is therefore horizontal. Between output levels A and B, the economy is experiencing some unemployment, so the aggregate supply curve is upward sloping. At the full employment level of output, B, the supply curve becomes vertical.

Note that both classical and Keynesian economists agree that at full employment, the long run aggregate supply curve is vertical. Whatever prices are charged, industry cannot increase its output. But Keynesian economists argue that, in the long run, the economy may operate at less than full employment, in which case the aggregate supply curve is horizontal or upward sloping.

Shifts in the long run aggregate supply curve

The long run aggregate supply curve is likely to shift over time. If we assume that it is vertical, then we are saying that the economy is always at full employment in the long run. This means that the position of the aggregate supply curve is determined by the potential output of the economy. Economic growth occurs because the quantity or quality of the factors of production available to an economy increase or because existing resources are used more efficiently.

Figure 65.6 shows how a growth in potential output is drawn on an aggregate supply diagram. Assume that the education and skills of the workforce increase. This should lead to labour becoming more productive, in turn leading to an increase in the productive potential of the economy at full employment. The long run aggregate supply curve will then shift from $LRAS_1$ to $LRAS_2$, showing that at a given level of prices, the economy can produce more output. A fall in potential output, caused for instance by a fall in the size of the labour force, would be shown by a leftward shift in the curve, from $LRAS_1$ to $LRAS_3$.

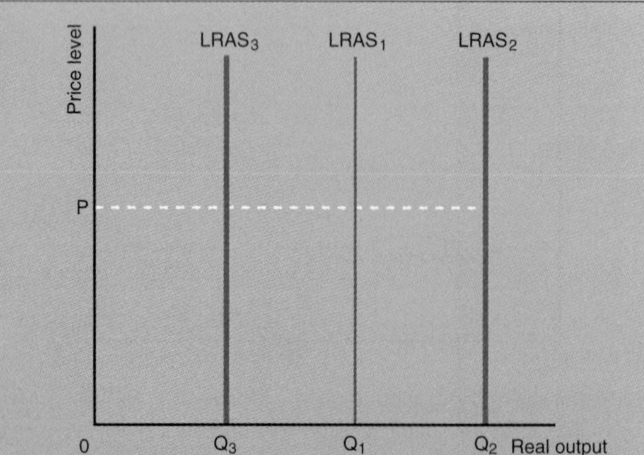

Figure 65.6 *A shift in the long run aggregate supply curve*
An increase in the productive potential in the economy pushes the long run aggregate supply curve to the right, for instance from $LRAS_1$ to $LRAS_2$. A fall in productive potential, on the other hand, is shown by a shift to the left of the curve, from $LRAS_1$ to $LRAS_3$ for instance.

QUESTION 4

(a) The economy was arguably at full employment in both 1964 and 1973. Show the effect on the long run aggregate supply curve of the increase in real GDP over that period from £263 billion in 1964 to £346 billion in 1973 (at 1990 prices).

(b) GDP (at 1990 prices) fell from £376 billion in 1979 to £364 billion in 1981. The fall in output was particularly concentrated amongst manufacturing industry. At the time, the closure and break up of factories and the sale of equipment, sometimes sold second hand to overseas buyers, was widely reported. Employment in manufacturing fell 16 per cent during the period. Show the likely effect on the long run aggregate supply curve of this.

Key terms

Aggregate supply curve - the relationship between the average level of prices in the economy and the level of total output.
Short run aggregate supply curve - the upward sloping aggregate supply curve which assumes that money wage rates are fixed.
Supply side shocks - factors such as changes in wage rates or commodity prices which cause the short run aggregate supply curve to shift.
Adaptive expectations - where decisions are based upon past information.
Rational expectations - where decisions are based on current information and anticipated future events.
Long run aggregate supply curve- the aggregate supply curve which assumes that wage rates are variable, both upward and downwards. Classical or supply side economists assume that wage rates are flexible. Keynesian economists assume that wage rates may be 'sticky downwards' and hence the economy may operate at less than full employment even in the long run

Applied economics

The case of oil

As Figure 65.7 shows, in 1973 a barrel of oil cost $2.83. A year later the price had risen to $10.41. This price rise was possibly the most important world economic event of the 1970s. The trigger for the rise came from a war - the Yom Kippur war - when Egypt attacked Israel and was subsequently defeated. The Arab nations, to show support for Egypt, decreed that they would cut off oil supplies from any country which openly supported Israel. Because the demand for oil in the short run is highly price inelastic, any small fall in the supply of oil is enough to bring large increases in prices. After the war finished, the oil producing nations through their organisation OPEC (the Organisation of Petroleum Exporting Countries) realised that it was possible to maintain a high price for oil by limiting its supply (i.e. by operating a cartel). Since then OPEC has operated a policy of restricting the supply of oil to the market.

Oil prices rose rather more slowly between 1974 and 1978. But between 1978 and 1982 the average price of a barrel of oil rose from $13.03 to $31.80. Again, a political event was a major factor in triggering the price rise. The Shah of Iran, ruler of an important oil producing country,

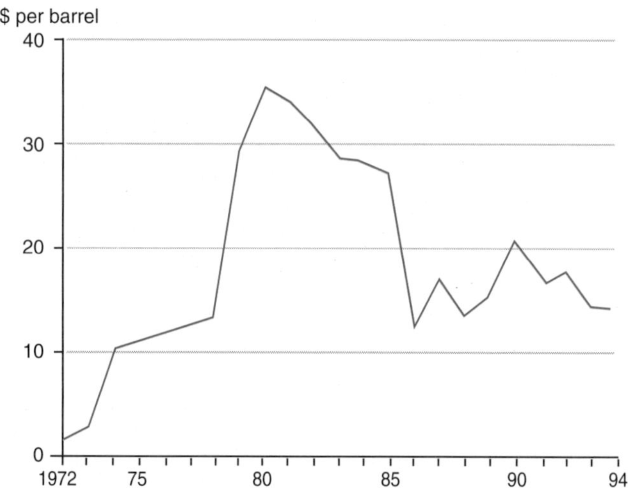

Source: adapted from *BP Statistical Review of World Energy.*

Figure 65.7 *Price of oil, Arabian Light/Dubai, $ per barrel*

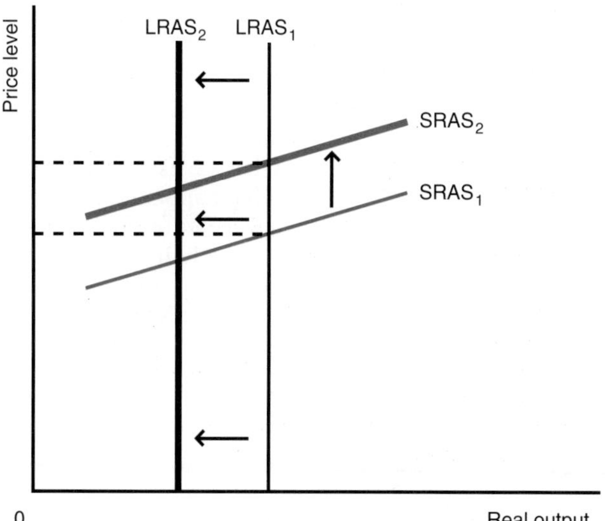

Figure 65.8

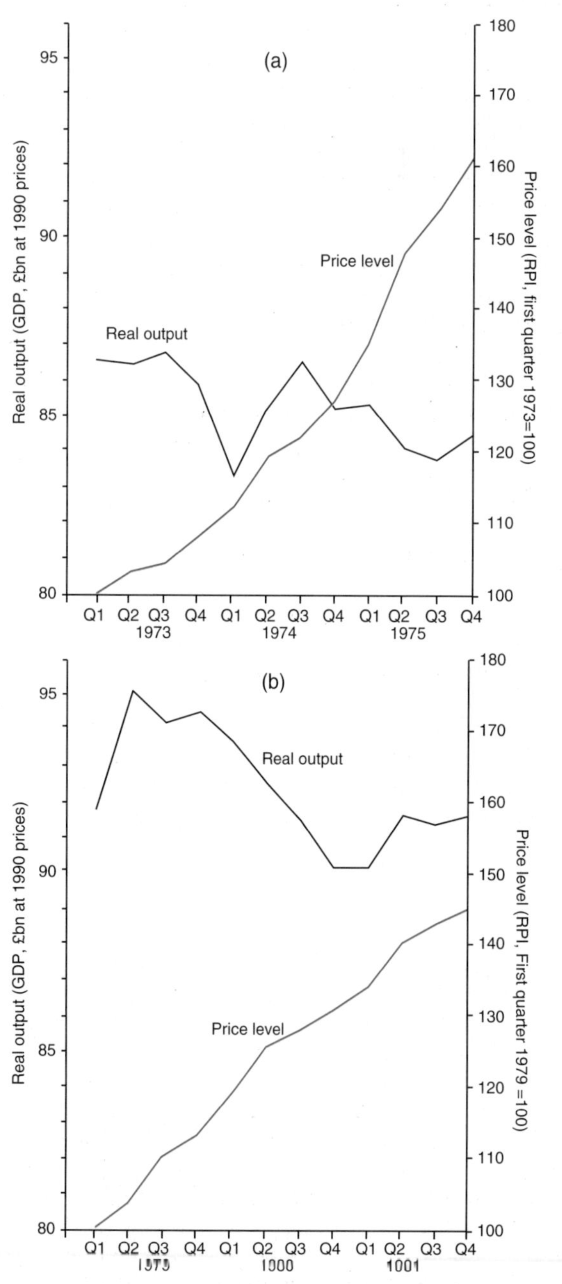

Source: adapted from CSO, *Economic Trends Annual Supplement.*

Figure 65.9 *Real output and prices in two periods of oil price shocks*

was deposed by Muslim fundamentalists led by the Ayatollah Khomeini. The revolution plunged Iran into economic chaos and the new rulers, fiercely anti-Western, showed little interest in resuming large scale exports of oil. A small disruption in oil supplies, a situation exploited by OPEC, was again enough to send oil prices spiralling.

The rise in oil prices had an important effect on the aggregate supply curve of the UK economy. It increased the costs of firms. So at any given level of output, firms needed to charge higher prices to cover their costs. This means that the short run aggregate supply curve shifted upwards as shown in Figure 65.8. This is supported by evidence from the UK economy. There is little doubt that the rise in oil prices helped push up UK prices by 16 per cent in 1974, 25 per cent in 1975, 17 per cent in 1979 and 15 per cent in 1980, as shown in Figure 65.9.

It could also be argued that the long run aggregate curve was pushed back to the left by the oil price rises (from $LRAS_1$ to $LRAS_2$ in Figure 65.8). The rise in oil prices meant that some capital equipment which was oil intensive became uneconomic to run. This equipment was mothballed and then scrapped, leading to a once-and-for-all loss in the productive potential of the economy.

Higher prices and lost output arguably led the UK to experience the most difficult economic circumstances since the Second World War.

Aggregate supply, 1974-79

Between February 1974 and May 1979, there was a Labour government in the UK. It is often considered to have been a disastrous period for the economy. In 1975, inflation rose to a post-war peak of 24.2 per cent. Unemployment rose from half a million in 1974 to one and half million in 1977. Share prices halved in 1974. The pound fell to an all time low against the dollar in October 1976. The UK government was forced to borrow from the IMF (the International Monetary Fund in late 1976 to shore up the value of the pound. In 1978-79, during the 'winter of discontent', the economy seemed racked by strikes as workers pressed for double digit pay rises.

However, the second half of the 1970s were difficult times for all industrialised economies. Growth rates worldwide fell as economies accommodated the supply-side shock of the first oil crisis in 1973-4. Table 65.1 shows that the growth in real GDP in the UK economy was above its long run trend rate of growth of 2.4 per cent per annum in four of the six years during the period; and although the average yearly growth rate over the six years was only 1.4 per cent, if 1973, a boom year for the economy were included, the average rate of growth would be 2.3 per cent. Investment spending in the economy remained static, with investment as a percentage of GDP slightly declining. This perhaps reflected a lack of confidence in the future of the economy. Even so, this should be contrasted with the experience of the early 1980s. Investment fell in 1980 and 1981 and did not reach its 1979 levels till 1984.

The 1970s were inflationary times throughout the world. Inflation in the UK accelerated from 7.5 per cent in 1972 to 15.9 per cent in 1974 and 24.1 per cent in 1975. However, the government adopted firm anti-inflationary policies in 1975 and inflation subsequently fell to 8.3 per cent in 1978, before rising again to 13.4 per cent in 1979 as pressure from wages and import prices, including the second round of oil price rises, worsened.

Table 65.1 *Selected economic indicators, UK 1974-79*

	Real growth in GDP	Gross investment		Price level	Import prices	Wage levels
	%	£bn at 1990 prices	% of GDP	1974=100	1974=100	1974=100
1974	- 1.5	73.2	18.8	100.0	100.0	100.0
1975	- 0.7	71.7	18.5	124.1	114.1	126.5
1976	2.7	72.9	18.3	144.7	139.9	146.2
1977	2.6	71.6	17.6	167.7	161.6	161.0
1978	2.8	73.8	17.5	181.4	167.9	184.3
1979	2.7	75.8	17.5	205.8	178.7	213.1

Source: adapted from CSO, *The Blue Book; Economic Trends Annual Supplement.*

Consider both the passage and the table carefully. Discuss, using diagrams, what happened to aggregate supply in the second half of the 1970s:
(a) in the short run and
(b) in the long run.

unit 66 Equilibrium output

Summary

1. The economy is in equilibrium when aggregate demand equals aggregate supply.
2. In the classical model, where wages are completely flexible, the economy will be in long run equilibrium at full employment. In the Keynesian model, where wages are sticky downwards, the economy can be in long run equilibrium at less than full employment.
3. In the classical model, a rise in aggregate demand will in the short run lead to an increase in both output and prices, but in the long run the rise will generate only an increase in prices. In the Keynesian model, a rise in aggregate demand will be purely inflationary if the economy is at full employment, but will lead to an increase in output if the economy is below full employment.
4. A rise in long run aggregate supply in the classical model will both increase output and reduce prices. Keynesians would agree with this in general, but would argue that an increase in aggregate supply will have no effect on output or prices if the economy is in a slump.
5. Factors which affect aggregate demand may well affect aggregate supply and vice versa, although this may occur over different time periods. For instance, an increase in investment is likely to increase both aggregate demand and aggregate supply.

Equilibrium output in the short run

Units 64 and 65 outlined theories of aggregate demand and aggregate supply. Both Keynesian and classical economists agree that in the short run the aggregate demand curve is downward sloping whilst the aggregate supply curve is upward sloping. The equilibrium level of output in the short run occurs at the intersection of the aggregate demand and aggregate supply curves. In Figure 66.1, the equilibrium level of income and output is OQ. The equilibrium price level is OP.

Equilibrium output in the long run

The main disagreement amongst economists is about long run equilibrium in the economy. Classical economists argue that in the long run the aggregate supply curve is vertical, as shown in Figure 66.2. Long run equilibrium occurs where the long run aggregate supply curve (LRAS) intersects with the aggregate demand curve. Hence equilibrium output is OQ and the equilibrium price level is OP. Associated with the long run equilibrium price level is a short run aggregate supply curve (SRAS) which passes through the point where LRAS = AD. The long run aggregate supply curve shows the supply curve for the economy at full employment (☞ unit 65). Hence there can be no unemployment in the long run according to classical economists.

Keynesian economists argue that the long run aggregate supply curve is as shown in Figure 66.3. The economy is at full employment where the LRAS curve is vertical at output OR - a point of agreement with classical economists. However, the economy can be in equilibrium at less than full employment. In Figure 66.3 the

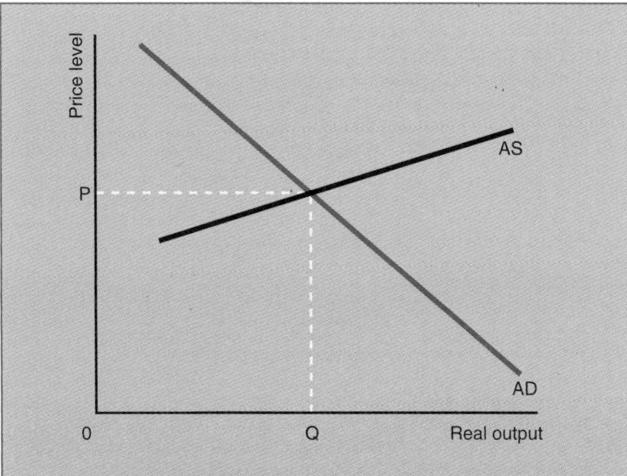

Figure 66.1 *Equilibrium output*
The equilibrium level of national output is set at the intersection of the aggregate demand and supply curves at OQ. The equilibrium price level is OP.

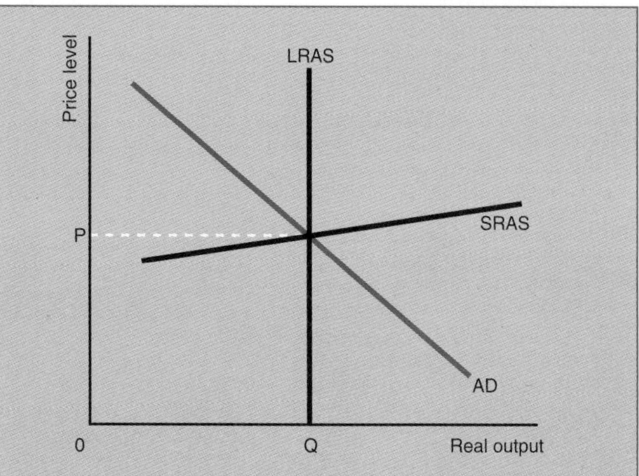

Figure 66.2 *Long run equilibrium in the classical model*
Long run equilibrium output is OQ, the full employment level of output, since wages are flexible both downwards as well as upwards.

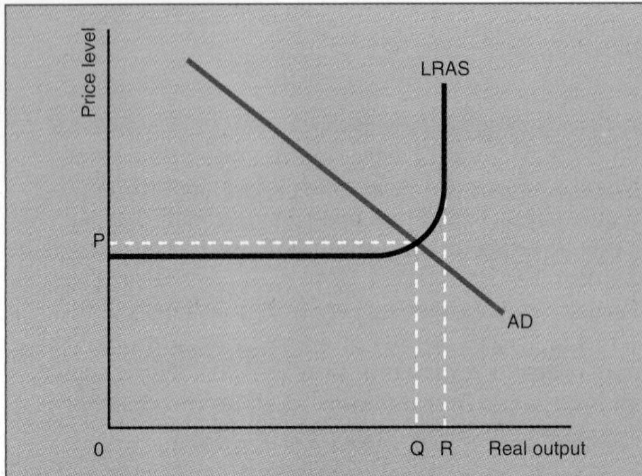

Figure 66.3 *Long run equilibrium in the Keynesian model*
Long run equilibrium output OQ may be below the full employment level of output OR because it is argued that wages are sticky downwards.

equilibrium level of output is OQ where the AD curve cuts the LRAS curve. The key point of disagreement between classical and Keynesian economists is the extent to which workers react to unemployment by accepting real wage cuts.

Classical economists argue that a rise in unemployment will lead rapidly to cuts in real wages. These cuts will increase the demand for labour and reduce its supply, returning the economy to full employment quickly and automatically. Economists like Patrick Minford, of the rational expectations school of thought, argue that this short term disequilibrium is corrected so quickly that the short run can be disregarded. Keynesian economists, on the other hand, argue that money wages are sticky downwards. Workers will refuse to take money wage cuts and will fiercely resist cuts in their real wage. The labour market will therefore not clear except perhaps over a very long period of time, so long that it is possibly even not worth considering.

QUESTION 1

What would be the effect on equilibrium income in the long run if the workers in the photograph were (a) successful and (b) unsuccessful with their demands?

Having outlined a theory of equilibrium output, it is now possible to see what happens if either aggregate demand or aggregate supply change.

A rise in aggregate demand

Assume that there is a rise in aggregate demand in the economy with long run aggregate supply initially remaining unchanged. For instance, there may be an increase in the wages of public sector employees paid for by an increase in the money supply, or there may be a fall in the marginal propensity to save and a rise in the marginal propensity to consume. A rise in aggregate demand will push the AD curve to the right. The classical and Keynesian models give different conclusions about the effect of this.

The classical model A rise in aggregate demand, which shifts the aggregate demand curve from AD_1 to AD_2 in Figure 66.4, will move the economy from A to B. There will be a movement along the short run aggregate supply curve. Output will rise from OL to OM and this will be accompanied by a small rise in the price level from ON to OP.

But the economy is now in long run disequilibrium. The full employment level of output is OL, shown by the position of the long run aggregate supply curve. The economy is therefore operating at over-full employment. Firms will find it difficult to recruit labour, buy raw materials and find new offices or factory space. They will respond by bidding up wages and other costs. The short run aggregate supply curve is drawn on the assumption that wage rates and other costs remain constant. So a rise in wage rates will shift the short run aggregate supply curve upwards. Short run equilibrium output will now

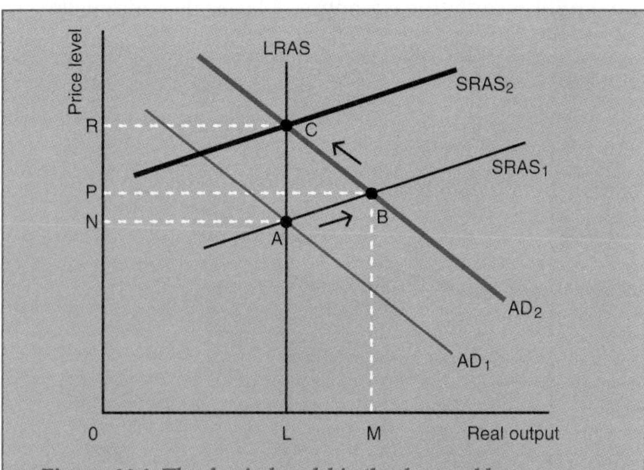

Figure 66.4 *The classical model in the short and long run*
A rise in aggregate demand shown by a shift to the right in the AD curve will result in a movement along the SRAS curve. Both output and prices will increase. In the long run, the SRAS curve will shift upwards with long run equilibrium being re-established at C. The rise in demand has led only to a rise in the price level.

fall and prices will keep rising. The economy will only return to long run equilibrium when the short run aggregate supply curve has shifted upwards from $SRAS_1$ to $SRAS_2$ so that aggregate demand once again equals long run aggregate supply at C.

The conclusion of the classical model is that increases in aggregate demand will initially increase both prices and output (the movement from A to B in Figure 66.4). Over time prices will continue to rise but output will fall as the economy moves back towards long run equilibrium (the movement from B to C). In the long term an increase in aggregate demand will only lead to an increase in the price level (from A to C). There will be no effect on equilibrium output. So increases in aggregate demand without any change in long run aggregate supply are purely inflationary.

The Keynesian model In the Keynesian model, the long run aggregate supply curve is shaped as in Figure 66.5. Keynesians would agree with classical economists that an increase in aggregate demand from, say, AD_4 to AD_5 will be purely inflationary if the economy is already at full employment at OD.

But if the economy is in deep depression, as was the case in the UK during the early 1930s, an increase in aggregate demand will lead to a rise in output without an increase in prices. The shift in aggregate demand from AD_1 to AD_2 will increase equilibrium output from OA to OB without raising the price level from OP as there are unused resources available.

The third possibility is that the economy is a little below full employment, for instance at OC in Figure 66.5. Then a rise in aggregate demand from AD_3 to AD_4 will increase both equilibrium output and equilibrium prices.

In the Keynesian model, increases in aggregate demand may or may not be effective in raising equilibrium output.

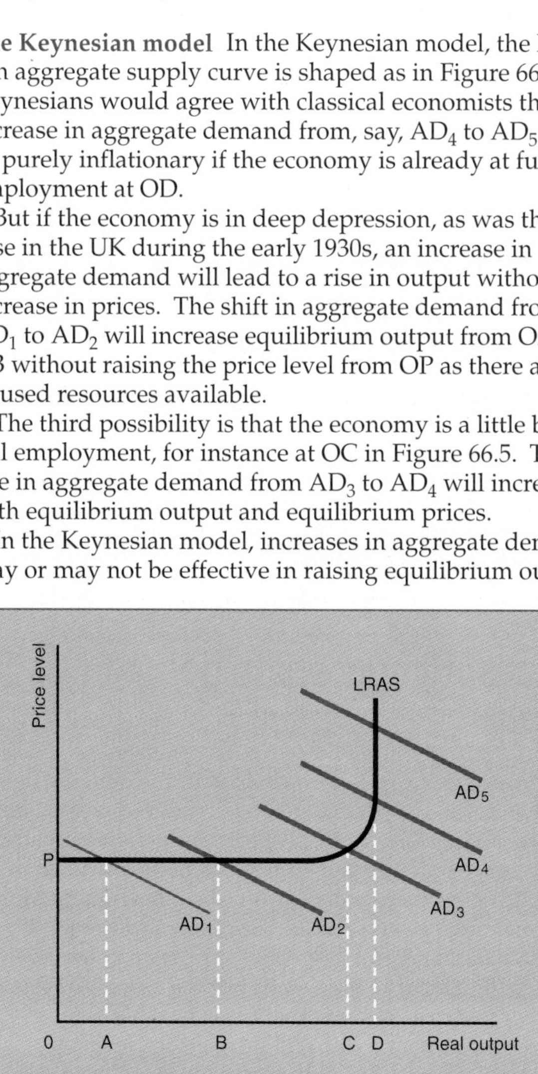

Figure 66.5 *The Keynesian model*
If the economy is already at full employment, an increase in aggregate demand in the Keynesian model creates an inflationary gap without increasing output. In a depression, an increase in aggregate demand will increase output but not prices. If the economy is slightly below full employment, an increase in aggregate demand will increase both output and prices.

It depends upon whether the economy is below full employment or at full employment.

QUESTION 2 In his Budget of 1981, with unemployment at 3 million and still rising, the Chancellor of the Exchequer Geoffrey Howe raised the level of taxes and significantly reduced the budget deficit in order to squeeze inflationary pressures. In a letter to *The Times*, 364 economists protested at what they saw as the perversity of this decision.

(a) Geoffrey Howe was influenced by classical economic thinking. Using a diagram, explain why he believed that his policy (i) would help reduce inflation and (ii) not lead to any increase in unemployment.
(b) The economists who wrote the letter to *The Times* could broadly be described as Keynesian. Using a diagram, explain why they believed that it was folly to increase taxes at a time when the economy was in the grip of the worst recession since the 1930s.

A rise in long run aggregate supply

A rise in long run aggregate supply means that the potential output of the economy has increased (i.e. there has been genuine economic growth). Rises in long run aggregate supply which are unlikely to shift the aggregate demand curve might occur if, for instance, incentives to work increased or there was a change in technology.

The classical model In the classical model, an increase in long run aggregate supply will lead to both higher output and lower prices. In Figure 66.6 a shift in the aggregate supply curve from $LRAS_1$ to $LRAS_2$ will increase equilibrium output from OL to OM. Equilibrium prices will also fall from ON to OP. Contrast this conclusion with what happens when aggregate demand is increased in the classical model - a rise in prices with no increase in

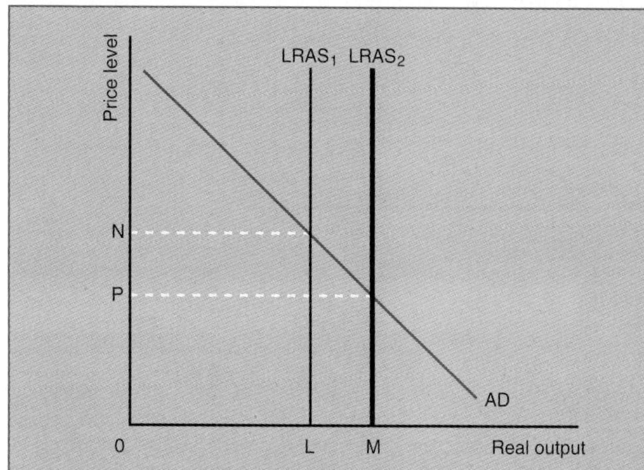

Figure 66.6 *An increase in aggregate supply in the classical model*
A shift to the right of the LRAS curve will both increase equilibrium output and reduce the price level.

output. It is not surprising that classical economists are so strongly in favour of **supply side** policies (☞ unit 69 - this is why they are often referred to as 'supply side' economists).

The Keynesian model In the Keynesian model, shown in Figure 66.7, an increase in aggregate supply will both increase output and reduce prices if the economy is at full employment. With aggregate demand at AD_1, a shift in the aggregate supply curve from $LRAS_1$ to $LRAS_2$ increases full employment equilibrium output from Y_E to Y_F. If the economy is at slightly less than full employment, with an aggregate demand curve of AD_2, then the shift to the right in the LRAS curve will still be beneficial to the economy, increasing output and reducing prices. But Keynesians disagree with classical economists that supply side measures can be effective in a depression. If the aggregate demand curve is AD_3, an increase in aggregate supply has no effect on equilibrium output. It remains obstinately stuck at Y_D. Only an increase in aggregate demand will move the economy out of depression.

It is now possible to understand one of the most important controversies in the history of economics. During the 1930s, classical economists argued that the only way to put the millions of unemployed during the Great Depression back to work was to adopt supply side measures - such as cutting unemployment benefits, reducing trade union power and cutting marginal tax rates and government spending. John Maynard Keynes attacked this orthodoxy by suggesting that the depression was caused by a lack of demand and suggesting that it was the government's responsibility to increase the level of aggregate demand. The same debate was replayed in the UK in the early 1980s. This time it was Keynesians who represented orthodoxy. They suggested that the only quick way to get the millions officially unemployed back to work was to expand aggregate demand. In the Budget of 1981, the government did precisely the opposite - it cut its projected budget deficit, reducing aggregate demand and argued that the only way to cure unemployment was to improve the supply side of the economy.

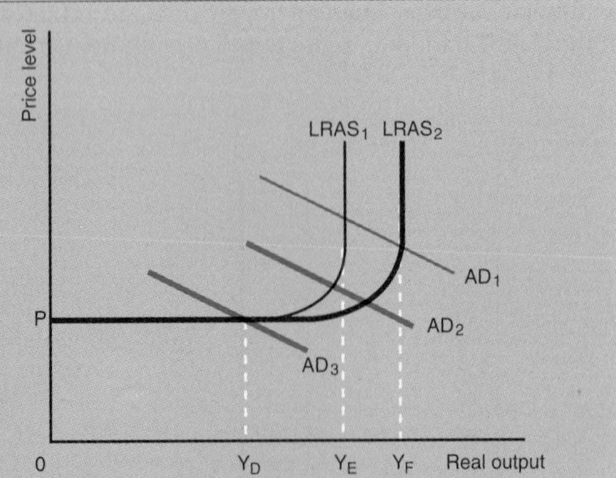

Figure 66.7 *An increase in aggregate supply in the Keynesian model*
The effect of an increase in long run aggregate supply depends upon the position of the aggregate demand curve. If the economy is at or near full employment, an increase will raise output and lower prices. However, if the economy is in depression at Y_D*, an increase in LRAS will have no impact on the economy.*

QUESTION 3 In June 1995, a new French government unveiled a stiff budget designed to reduce high unemployment levels by 700 000 and bring down a high budget deficit from 5.7 per cent of GDP to 5.1 per cent of GDP within the fiscal year. The measures included:

- a substantial FF19bn cut in government spending affecting all ministries apart from justice and culture, with defence bearing nearly 50 per cent of the cuts;
- a rise in corporation tax from 33.3 per cent to 36.6 per cent;
- a rise in the standard rate of VAT from 18.6 per cent to 20.6 per cent;
- a 10 per cent rise in wealth tax;
- a 40 per cent cut in employment taxes paid by firms on employment of workers at or near the minimum wage level;
- new programmes targeted particularly at youth in difficulties, offering training, apprenticeship and other policies to bring people into the workforce;
- a rise in the minimum wage by 4 per cent;
- a rise in state pensions by 0.5 per cent;
- measures to stimulate the housing market, particularly focused on lodgings for people on lower incomes.

Using diagrams, explain what effect these measures would have on aggregate supply according to
(a) classical or supply side economists and
(b) Keynesian economists.

Increasing aggregate demand and supply

In micro-economics, factors which shift the demand curve do **not** shift the supply curve as well and vice versa. For instance, an increase in the costs of production shifts the supply curve but does **not** shift the demand curve for a good (although there will of course be a **movement along** the demand curve as a result). But in macro-economic aggregate demand and aggregate supply analysis, factors which shift one curve may well shift the other curve as well. For instance, assume that firms increase their planned investment. This will increase the level of aggregate demand. But in the long run it will also increase the level of aggregate supply. An increase in investment will increase the capital stock of the economy. The productive potential of the economy will therefore rise. We can use aggregate demand and supply analysis to show the effects of an increase in investment.

An increase in investment in the classical model will initially shift the aggregate demand curve in Figure 66.8 to the right from AD_1 to AD_2. There will then be a movement along the short run aggregate supply curve from A to B. There is now long run disequilibrium. How this will be resolved depends upon the speed with which the investment is brought on stream and starts to produce goods and services. Assume that this happens fairly quickly. The long run aggregate supply curve will then shift to the right, say, from $LRAS_1$ to $LRAS_2$. Long run equilibrium will be restored at C. Output has increased and the price level fallen slightly. There will also be a new short run aggregate supply curve, $SRAS_2$. It is below the original short run aggregate supply curve because it is assumed that investment has reduced costs of production.

Not all investment results in increased production. For instance, fitting out a new shop which goes into receivership within a few months will increase aggregate demand but not long run aggregate supply. The long run aggregate supply curve will therefore not shift and the increased investment will only be inflationary. Equally, investment might be poorly directed. The increase in aggregate demand might be greater than the increase in long run aggregate supply. Here there will be an increase in equilibrium output but there will also be an increase in prices. The extent to which investment increases output and contributes to a lessening of inflationary pressure depends upon the extent to which it gives a high rate of return in the long run.

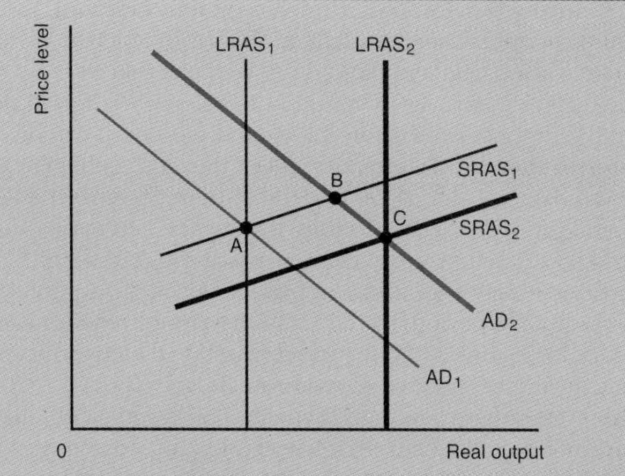

Figure 66.8 *An increase in investment expenditure*
An increase in investment will increase aggregate demand from AD_1 to AD_2, and is likely to shift the long run aggregate supply curve from $LRAS_1$ to $LRAS_2$. The result is an increase in output and a small fall in prices.

QUESTION 4 Using a classical model of the economy, explain the effect of the following on (i) aggregate demand; (ii) short run aggregate supply; (iii) output and prices in the long run.

(a) A 10 per cent rise in earnings.
(b) An increase in real spending by government on education and training.
(c) An increase in the average long term real rate of interest from 3 per cent to 5 per cent.

Applied economics

Stagflation, 1974-76 and 1979-1981

In a simple Keynesian model, rising inflation is associated with falling unemployment and vice versa. The experience of the 1950s and 1960s tended to support the hypothesis that there was this trade off between the two variables. However, in 1974-75 and 1979-1981 there was both rising inflation **and** rising unemployment: this combination of stagnation and inflation came to be called **stagflation**.

The stagflation of both these periods can be explained using an aggregate demand and supply model of the economy. The rise in oil prices in each period was an external supply side shock to the UK economy. It had the effect of raising the short run aggregate supply curve (☞ unit 65) from $SRAS_1$ to $SRAS_2$ in Figure 66.9. The economy shifted from A to B. As can be seen from the diagram, prices rose and output fell.

In the first oil crisis, inflation rose from 9.1 per cent in 1973, to 15.9 per cent in 1974, and 24.1 per cent in 1975, before falling back to 16.5 per cent in 1976. Real GDP on the other hand fell by 1.5 per cent in 1974 and 0.8 per cent in 1975, before resuming an upward path in 1976.

In the second oil crisis, inflation rose from 8.3 per cent in 1978, to 13.4 per cent in 1979, and 18.0 per cent in 1980, before falling back again in 1981. Real GDP fell by 2 per cent in 1980 and 1.2 per cent in 1981.

The classical model would suggest that, all other things being equal, the economy would fall back to A from B. Full employment would be restored at the old price level. The above figures indicate that this did not happen. This was because the aggregate demand curve shifted to the right at the same time as the short run aggregate supply curve was shifting to the left. This led to continued inflation as output rose from 1976 and again from 1982. The rise in aggregate demand in the first period was partly due to the then Labour government increasing the budget deficit, as well as increases in the money supply (the inflation was **accommodated** ☞ unit 94). In the second period, taxation rose and government spending fell during the downturn in the economy, although the money supply increased again. This difference in fiscal stance is a partial explanation of why the rise in unemployment was lower and the rise in inflation higher in the first period than in the second period. It can be argued that the shift to the right in the aggregate demand curve was greater in the mid-1970s than the early 1980s.

In Figure 66.9, the economy is now at C. In reality, the AD and AS curves are constantly shifting to the right, producing new equilibrium price levels and output levels in each time period, so the economy would not remain at C for long. But could the economy stay at C in theory? According to classical economists, the answer is no. At C, given that there is unemployment, real wages will fall, shifting the SRAS curve down and leading to a new equilibrium with lower prices and higher output. Keynesians would argue that C could well be an equilibrium position for a number of years because the labour market is not a perfect market. Extreme Keynesians would argue that the labour market does not clear in the face of unemployment and therefore the economy could remain at C even in the long run. Did the economy in practice move back to a full employment level? The second oil price shock followed quickly after the first and therefore it is difficult to answer this from the experience of the 1970s. However, unemployment did fall between 1976 and 1979, indicating perhaps a movement towards full employment. Following the second oil price shock, unemployment continued to increase until the third quarter of 1986. Then it fell rapidly, halving by late 1989. Whether the economy had moved back onto its long run aggregate supply curve is debatable. If it had, then the natural rate of unemployment must have been considerably higher in 1989 than it was, say, in the early 1970s, a somewhat surprising conclusion given the array of labour market measures implemented in the 1980s.

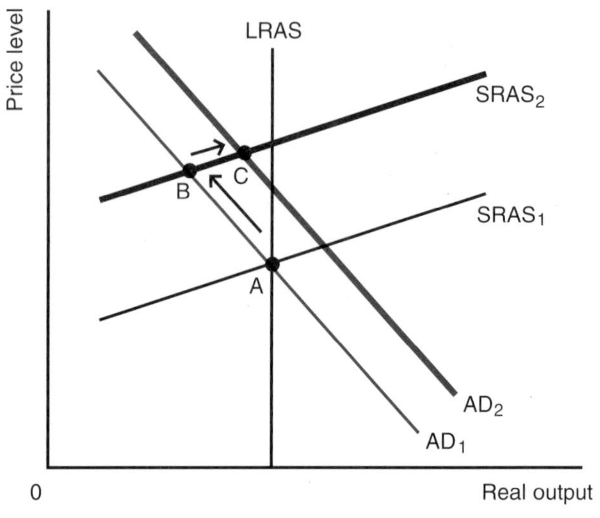

Figure 66.9

The 1990-92 recession

Table 66.1 *Change in GDP and its components*

Percentage change on previous year at constant prices, seasonally adjusted

		Consumers' expenditure	General government final consumption	Gross domestic fixed capital formation	Exports	Imports	GDP
1988	Q1	8.1	1.9	19.4	0.0	13.2	5.6
	Q2	7.3	0.9	19.5	3.1	12.4	4.7
	Q3	7.7	-0.9	11.0	0.1	10.3	4.4
	Q4	7.0	1.0	7.0	-1.3	14.5	4.1
1989	Q1	4.9	-0.2	11.4	5.4	14.7	3.0
	Q2	4.6	0.2	5.7	1.4	8.0	2.6
	Q3	2.0	3.9	5.0	3.4	7.6	1.4
	Q4	1.6	1.8	2.2	8.5	0.2	0.9
1990	Q1	1.2	2.2	-2.1	5.3	1.3	1.0
	Q2	1.1	3.5	-2.5	7.2	3.0	0.0
	Q3	0.7	1.2	-4.3	4.3	-1.1	0.0
	Q4	-0.6	3.3	-5.1	3.2	-1.3	- 1.1
1991	Q1	1.3	3.2	-10.1	-3.5	-7.2	- 2.3
	Q2	-3.0	3.0	-10.3	0.2	-7.3	- 3.1
	Q3	-2.4	2.9	-9.4	1.5	-4.9	- 2.6
	Q4	-2.0	1.2	-7.1	-1.1	-1.7	- 1.8
1992	Q1	1.8	1.6	-2.6	5.0	3.8	- 1.7
	Q2	-0.0	0.6	-1.5	2.8	7.8	- 1.3
	Q3	0.6	-1.6	-0.5	0.8	6.8	- 0.4
	Q4	1.3	-0.6	0.0	3.9	6.5	0.0

Source: adapted from CSO, *Economic Trends; Economic Trends Annual Supplement.*

Table 66.2 *GDP and its components*

£ million at 1990 prices, seasonally adjusted

	Consumers' expenditure	General government final consumption	Gross domestic fixed capital formation	Stocks	Exports	Imports	GDP at market prices	GDP at factor cost
1988 Q1	81 906	27 346	25 480	237	29 930	32 410	132 489	114 908
1992 Q4	85 750	28 837	24 180	-497	34 551	37 919	134 902	117 342

Table 66.3 *Money supply growth and the rate of interest*

		Money supply M4, percentage change on previous year	Banks' base rate %
1988	Q1	3.8	8.75
	Q2	3.6	8.17
	Q3	4.9	11.09
	Q4	4.5	12.38
1989	Q1	3.9	13.00
	Q2	4.0	13.43
	Q3	4.1	14.00
	Q4	4.2	14.95
1990	Q1	4.4	15.00
	Q2	3.9	15.00
	Q3	2.6	15.00
	Q4	2.2	14.08
1991	Q1	1.7	13.52
	Q2	1.7	11.86
	Q3	1.3	10.92
	Q4	1.4	10.50
1992	Q1	1.2	10.50
	Q2	1.2	10.17
	Q3	1.0	9.83
	Q4	0.4	7.64

Source: adapted from CSO, *Financial Statistics.*

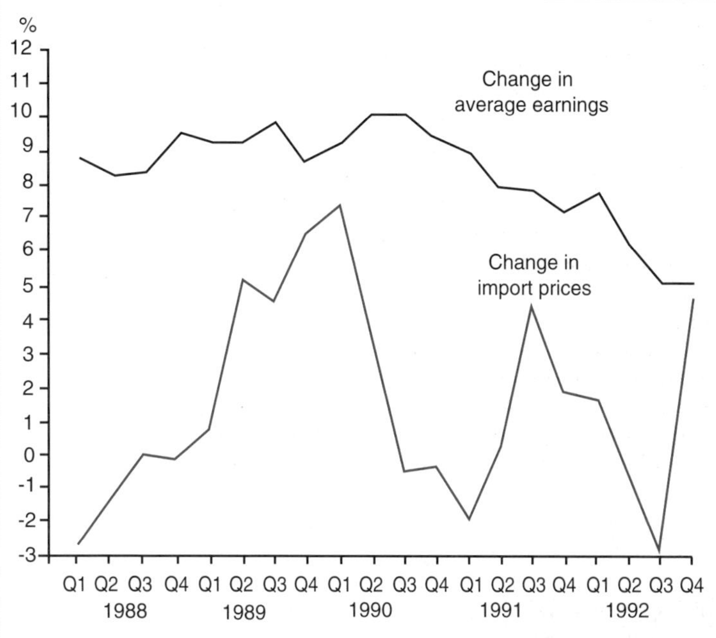

Figure 66.10 *Changes in costs*

Table 66.4 *Inflation, house prices, unemployment and the PSBR*

		Inflation, % change over previous 12 months	House prices, % change on previous year	Unemployment, millions	PSBR (-) or PSDR (+) £ millions at 1990 prices
1988	Q1	3.3	20.9	2.7	+3 375
	Q2	4.3	22.6	2.5	+2 002
	Q3	5.5	32.6	2.3	+2 420
	Q4	6.5	32.9	2.1	+5 916
1989	Q1	7.8	30.3	2.1	+6 188
	Q2	8.2	27.3	1.9	+64
	Q3	7.7	16.2	1.8	+475
	Q4	7.6	7.4	1.6	+3 327
1990	Q1	7.7	2.9	1.6	+4 410
	Q2	9.6	-1.6	1.6	-5 928
	Q3	10.4	-3.2	1.7	+464
	Q4	10.0	-2.7	1.8	+3 169
1991	Q1	8.6	-2.0	1.9	+2 466
	Q2	6.0	-1.5	2.2	-6 717
	Q3	4.8	-1.4	2.4	-3 477
	Q4	4.2	-0.8	2.5	+441
1992	Q1	4.1	-1.0	2.6	-3 313
	Q2	4.1	-3.0	2.7	-9 515
	Q3	3.6	-4.4	2.8	-6 831
	Q4	3.0	-7.0	2.9	-6 196

Source: adapted from CSO, *Economic Trends; Economic Trends Annual Supplement.*

1. **Describe the changes in output between 1988 and 1992.**
2. **What factors might have affected (a) aggregate demand between 1988 and 1992 and (b) aggregate supply over the same period?**
3. **Discuss, using diagrams, why the economy went into a period of stagflation in 1990 followed by a period of falling inflation and falling output.**

The business cycle

Summary

1. Business cycles have been a feature of capitalist economies in the 19th and 20th centuries.
2. The business cycle has four phases - boom, recession, slump and recovery.
3. The business cycle can be explained using the AD/AS model of the economy.
4. The multiplier-accelerator theory states that cycles are caused by the interaction of the Keynesian multiplier and the accelerator theory of investment.
5. The inventory cycle theory argues that cycles are caused by regular fluctuations in the levels of stocks in the economy.
6. Long wave cycles have been explained by changes in construction levels and by changes in technology.
7. Monetarists believe that trade cycles are caused by changes in the money supply.

Characteristics of cycles

It has long been observed in economics that income and employment tend to fluctuate regularly over time. These regular fluctuations are known as BUSINESS CYCLES or TRADE CYCLES.

Figure 67.1 shows the various stages of a traditional cycle, such as occurred during the 19th century, during the 1930s or during the 1970s and 1980s in the UK.

- **Peak or boom**. When the economy is at a peak or is in a boom, national income is high. It is likely that the economy will be working at beyond full employment. **Overheating** is therefore present (although the economy could be at less than full employment, according to Keynesians, if there are bottlenecks in certain industries in the economy). Consumption and investment expenditure will be high. Tax revenues will be high. Wages will be rising and profits increasing. The country will be sucking in imports demanded by consumers with high incomes and businesses with full order books. There will also be inflationary pressures in the economy.
- **Recession**. When the economy moves into recession, output and income fall, leading to a fall in consumption and investment. Tax revenues begin to fall and government expenditure on benefits begin to rise. Wage demands moderate as unemployment rises. Imports decline and inflationary pressures ease.
- **Trough or slump**. At the bottom of the cycle, the economy is said to be in a trough or slump. Economic activity is at a low in comparison with surrounding years. Mass unemployment exists, so consumption, investment and imports will be low. There will be few inflationary pressures in the economy and prices may be falling (there will be **deflation** in the strict sense of the term).
- **Recovery or expansion**. As the economy moves into a recovery or expansion phase, national income and output begin to increase. Unemployment falls. Consumption, investment and imports begin to rise. Workers feel more confident about demanding wage increases and inflationary pressures begin to mount.

During the 1950s and 1960s, the UK saw much milder trade cycles, as shown in Figure 67.2. National income did not fall but there were regular fluctuations in the rate of economic growth. A recession occurred when the rate of economic growth fell. Recovery or expansion was present when the growth rate picked up again. The economy was

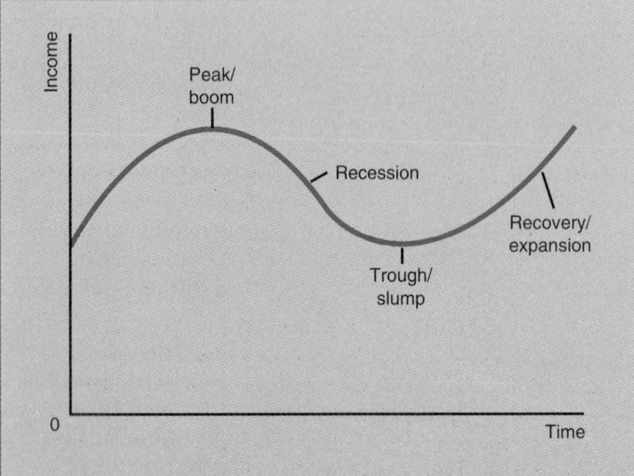

Figure 67.1 *The traditional business cycle*
The economy moves regularly from boom through recession to slump before recovering again.

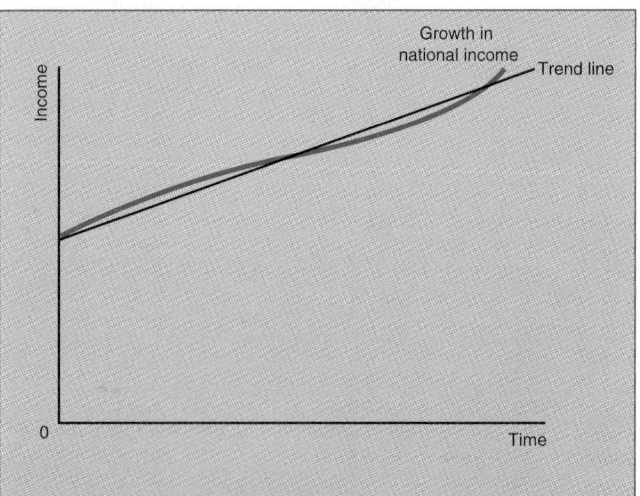

Figure 67.2 *The UK trade cycle of the 1950s and 1960s*
Peaks and troughs occurred when economic growth is high or low respectively.

in a boom when economic growth was at its highest compared to surrounding years. There were troughs too when growth was particularly low but they were not really 'slumps' in the traditional sense. In the post-war period in the UK, the business cycle has tended to last four or five years from peak to peak. This contrasts with longer seven to nine year cycles in the 19th century. Some economists have claimed that there are longer 50 year KONDRATIEV CYCLES, so named after the Russian economist who first put forward the idea.

QUESTION 1

Table 67.1

	Growth of GDP	Investment	Balance of payments current balance	Unemployment
	%	(£ billion at 1985 prices)		(millions)
1978	2.9	54.9	1.7	1.4
1979	2.8	56.5	- 0.9	1.3
1980	- 2.0	53.4	3.9	1.6
1981	- 1.2	48.3	8.4	2.5
1982	1.7	50.9	5.4	2.9

Identify the four phases of the business cycle from the data.

Business cycle models

Business cycle models can be divided into two types. **Exogenous models** argue that business cycles are started by a shock to the economic system, such as wars, revolutions, gold discoveries or large movements of population. It could be argued that the four-fold increase in the price of oil in 1973-74 gave a significant supply side shock to world economies. These effects rippled through time until economies returned to equilibrium.
Endogenous theories argue that trade cycles are caused by factors which lie within the economic system. Even if there were no supply side shocks, the economy would fluctuate regularly over time, although the fluctuations might be quite mild.

QUESTION 2 Explain how a major world recession, an exogenous shock to the UK economy, could trigger a business cycle.

Aggregate demand and aggregate supply analysis

The business cycle can be explained using aggregate demand and aggregate supply analysis. Consider Figure 67.3. The economy is in both short run and long run equilibrium at A.

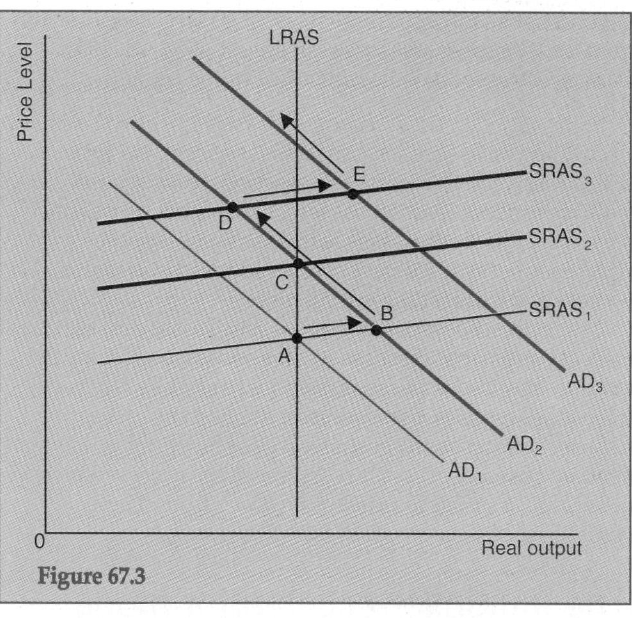

Figure 67.3

Boom An exogenous shock to the economy now shifts the aggregate demand curve from AD_1 to AD_2. For instance, the government might reduce income tax in the run up to a general election, or the stock market might suddenly boom, increasing the real wealth of households and encouraging them to spend more. The economy now moves from A to B. This is a long run disequilibrium point. The economy has overheated, with aggregate demand being greater than long run aggregate supply. The result will be over-full employment. Wage rates and other factor prices will rise. This rise in factor prices shifts the short run aggregate supply curve upwards, eventually reaching $SRAS_2$, with the economy at C. This ought to be the new long run equilibrium point.

Recession However, why should the SRAS curve stop rising at $SRAS_2$? It is possible that it will overshoot, eventually stopping at, say, $SRAS_3$ with the economy in recession. It will be the recession which eventually brings wage inflation to a halt, not a possible long run equilibrium position. With the economy in recession, equilibrium output will have fallen, shown on the diagram by D being left of C.

Recovery Eventually, though, there will be an increase in aggregate demand at the given price level. In the move from B to D, consumers and producers have cut their real spending. Consumers will have particularly cut spending on consumer durables whilst firms will have cut investment spending. There comes a point when expenditure on these items has to start rising. Consumers, for instance, having delayed buying new cars, eventually have to replace their old cars. Firms, having deferred new investment spending, have to replace worn out machinery or stop producing. So the AD curve shifts again to the right, producing the upturn in the cycle.

Boom As consumer and business confidence returns, spending further increases to AD_3. But this produces a new short run equilibrium point where the economy is again at over-full employment, a long run disequilibrium position. Wages start to rise, pushing the SRAS curve upwards to produce the downturn in the economy.

Figure 67.3 shows an economy where the initial demand shock produces smaller and smaller cycles over time. Eventually, the economy will converge to a long run equilibrium position on the long run aggregate supply curve. It is likely that, before this happens, another exogenous shock will have occurred which yet again increases the amplitude of the cycle.

Different schools of economists emphasise different aspects of this basic explanation. Keynesian economists tend to emphasise the change in real variables, such as investment, which then produce fluctuations in output which characterise the business cycle. Monetarist economists tend to emphasise the role of money in the process which lead to fluctuations in prices as well as output. These individual explanations will now be discussed.

The multiplier-accelerator model

One Keynesian explanation of the business cycle is the MULTIPLIER-ACCELERATOR MODEL. The **accelerator theory** of investment says that investment is a function of past changes in income (☞ unit 63). If national income is growing, so too will investment. This increase in investment will lead to a multiple increase in national income via the **multiplier effect** (☞ unit 64). This leads to a further increase in investment. Hence the economy keeps on growing. On the other hand, if income falls, so too will investment, feeding through via the multiplier process to a further fall in income. Investment then falls again. The economy is on a downward path.

So far we have a possible explanation of why an economy might grow or contract over time but there is as yet no explanation of the trade cycle in it. There are two ways of using the multiplier-accelerator model to construct a business cycle model. The first is to construct a far more complicated accelerator model than, for instance, the $I_t = k\ (Y_t - Y_{t-1})$ theory developed in unit 63. Some formulations of the accelerator model will produce regular cycles. Whether these formulations are realistic can only be gauged when they are tested against real data.

The other way is to postulate the existence of **ceilings** and **floors** in the cycle. An annual growth rate of 5 to 6 per cent has proved unsustainable for the post-war UK economy. The economy moves to full employment and then beyond full employment. There simply isn't any more labour to be hired to sustain the boom. This puts a brake on the economy. As the rate of increase in output slows down, so the rate of growth of investment falls, producing the downturn in the economy. Similarly, national income will not keep falling to zero. At some point firms have to increase investment to replace worn-out machinery. Consumers will increasingly resist falls in their consumption and will be prepared to call on savings or borrow money to prevent their living standards falling even further. This is the turning point for the economy. Output will begin to rise, pulling up consumption expenditure and encouraging investment expenditure.

QUESTION 3 In an economy, $I_t = 2\ (Y_t - Y_{t-1})$. It is also assumed that an increase in investment, I, in time period t will lead to an increase in income, Y, in the **next** time period, t+1, via the multiplier process. The value of the Keynesian multiplier is 2.

There are ceilings and floors in the economy. The maximum increase in investment in any one time period is 150. Investment can never be negative. If investment falls to zero in one time period, it is assumed that it will rise to 10 in the next time period. Table 67.2 shows a cycle in the economy.

Table 67.2

Time period	Y	I
1	100	10
2	120	40
3	180	120
4	340	150 (max.)
5	400	120
6	340	0 (min.)
7	100	10 (min.)
8		
...		
16		

In time period 1, Y is assumed to be 100 and I is assumed to be 10. In time period 2, Y is assumed to increase to 120 because of an increase in demand for exports. The change in income in period 2 is therefore 20 and investment will increase to 40 (because 2 x [120 - 100] equals 40). An increase in investment of 30 (40 - 10) in time period 2 leads to a multiple increase in income in time period 3 of 60 (2 x 30). So income in time period 3 is 180 (120 + 60) and investment is 120 (2 x 60). With an increase in investment of 80 (120 - 40) and a multiplier of 2, the increase in income in time period 4 is 160. This should generate an increase in investment of 340. However there is a ceiling on investment of 150.

(a) Explain in words how income and investment change in periods 5 to 7.

(b) Complete the table by calculating the levels of income and investment in years 8 to 16.

The inventory cycle

Another Keynesian explanation of the business cycle is the INVENTORY CYCLE hypothesis. **Inventories** is another name for stocks of raw materials and finished products held by producers. For instance, a car manufacturer will hold stocks of steel, car components and finished cars.

Some economists argue that there is an inventory cycle of business activity in the economy. Changes in inventories cause regular fluctuations in the level of national income. For instance, assume that the government increases its expenditure in real terms. Firms will initially meet part of the extra demand by supplying goods from existing stocks. So they will need to increase their production levels, firstly to replace those stocks and secondly to meet the continued extra demand from government. This leads to an increase in national income via the multiplier process. Eventually firms will have replenished their stocks to their desired levels. They will then reduce their orders from other firms to the level needed to satisfy long term demand. But this reduction in orders will produce a downturn in the economy via the multiplier process. The economy will only pick up once firms have so run down their stocks that they are forced to increase their orders again.

QUESTION 4

Table 67.3 *Change in stocks and GDP, 1979-1983*

	£ billions at 1985 prices	
	Increase in stocks and work in progress[1]	GDP[2]
1979	3.3	283.4
1980	- 3.4	277.4
1981	- 3.2	274.3
1982	- 1.3	279.2
1983	1.4	289.2

1. At market prices.
2. At factor cost.
Source: adapted from CSO, *Economic Trends Annual Supplement.*

Explain how the changes in stocks and work in progress might have contributed to the change in GDP over the period 1979-1983.

Long wave cycles

A number of economists have argued that long wave cycles exist. Like the multiplier-accelerator theory and the inventory cycle theory, these theories emphasise that cycles are caused by changes in real variables.

In the inter-war period, Kuznets claimed that there was a 15-20 year building cycle. Economic fluctuations were caused by regular long cycles in building and construction.

Again in the inter-war period, a Russian economist named Kondratiev suggested that 50 year cycles existed. These were caused by lumpiness in the pace of technological change. The idea was further developed by the Austrian economist, Schumpeter, who identified waves of technological progress. For instance, in the mid-nineteenth century the development of the railways was a major boost to world demand. In the early part of this century, it was the motor car and electricity that provided the stimulus to technological advance. In the post-war period up to 1970, it was the development of chemicals, plastics, nuclear power and a wide range of electrical consumer goods. Today, the world economy is making a start on exploiting the micro-chip and biotechnology.

These waves of innovation produce characteristic cycles. Take the micro-chip revolution; in the 1970s and early 1980s, microchips began to make an impact on products and output. Initially, some new products came onto the market (like calculators). But the biggest impact was on existing products. Costs were cut by incorporating micro-chips into existing machines. This led to a shake out of employment because the new machines could produce more output with less labour.

The world economy moved to slump both in the mid-1970s following an oil price shock, and again in the early 1980s. On both occasions, unemployment rose substantially and remained at very high levels historically. The 1980s and the 1990s have been decades of high unemployment. The long wave cycle hypothesis would suggest that the new products appearing on the market - ranging from virtual reality machines to integrated personal computer/television/video/games/CD rom machines to satellite communication - will lead to an upturn in the world economy in the 1990s and the first decade of the next century. By the year 2010, the micro-chip revolution will reach maturity and the economy will be at the top of its 50 year boom. Exciting new products will begin to be more difficult to invent. So economic growth rates will begin to fall. The economy will then be in its recession phase. By 2020-30, the economy will be again approaching a slump which should occur in the 2030s. Once again new technologies will emerge, but they will only help lift the world economy from recession by the 2040s.

A monetarist explanation

Milton Friedman has suggested that trade cycles are essentially monetary phenomena, caused by changes in the **money supply** (☞ unit 94). In their important book *A Monetary History of the United States, 1867-1960*, Milton Friedman and Anna Schwartz argued that US business cycles were preceded by changes in the money supply.

The argument put forward is that changes in the money supply lead to changes in real variables, such as unemployment and national income, before finally leading to an increase in prices. The path to an increased price level is not a smooth one but is cyclical. The oscillations in the cycle become more and more damped as time goes on. Of course they can become more amplified again if there is another excessive increase in the money supply.

The link between changes in the money supply and changes in income is known as the **transmission mechanism**. Assume that there is a once and for all increase in the money supply when the economy is in long run equilibrium. The money supply is now greater than the **demand for money** (☞ unit 70). Economic agents, such as banks, firms and consumers, will adjust their portfolio of assets. Some of the excess supply will be used to buy physical assets - goods and services. The rest will be saved, reducing interest rates and thus encouraging the borrowing of money again to buy physical assets. The increase in consumption and investment will result in an increase in income. The economy is now in boom. Prices will begin to rise. This, together with increased real spending, will increase the demand for money. It is most unlikely that the economy will return to equilibrium with the demand and supply for money being equal. What will happen is that the demand for money will carry on increasing so that the demand for money exceeds the supply of money. Once this happens, economic agents will start to adjust their portfolios in the opposite direction. They will cut back on purchases of physical and financial assets. Interest rates will rise. Investment and consumption will begin to fall. The economy is now in recession with falling income. This reduces the demand for money, bringing it back past the equilibrium point to the bottom of the cycle where once again supply is greater than demand for money. There will be a further bout of portfolio adjustment and aggregate demand will start to rise, bringing the economy into the recovery phase of the cycle. This will carry on, although Friedman argues that without further shocks the oscillations will become smaller and smaller over time.

QUESTION 5 Monetarists argue that the business cycle can be explained by changes in the money supply. For instance, Friedman and Schwartz (1963) argue that the Great Depression of the 1930s in the USA was caused by a drastic fall in the supply of money. They write: 'An initial mild decline in the money stock from 1929 to 1930, accompanying a decline in Federal Reserve credit outstanding, was converted into a sharp decline by a wave of bank failures beginning in late 1930.' Those failures produced (a) widespread attempts by the public to convert deposits into currency and hence a decline in the deposit-currency ratio, and (b) a scramble for liquidity by the banks and hence a decline in the deposit-reserve ratio.

(a) How and why, according to Friedman and Schwartz, did the US money supply contract from 1929?
(b) Suggest how this contraction in the money supply then led to depression.

Key terms

Business or trade cycle - regular fluctuations in the level of economic activity.
Kondratiev cycles - long 50 year trade cycles caused by the 'lumpiness' of technological change.
Multiplier-accelerator model - a model which describes how the workings of the multiplier theory and the accelerator theory lead to changes in national income.
Inventory cycle - fluctuations in national income caused by changes in the level of inventories or stocks in the economy.

Applied economics

The UK business cycle in the post-war period

The duration of the business cycle in the UK in the post-war era has averaged 4 to 5 years from peak to peak. As Figure 67.4 shows, during the 1950s and 1960s, booms and recessions were very mild. Recessions meant declines in the rate of growth of output rather than falls in output. However, the 1970s and 1980s saw much greater swings, and the recession of 1980-82 was the severest since the Great Depression of the 1930s, whilst the recession of 1990-92 was the longest.

In the 1950s, 1960s and early 1970s, booms in the economy (1954-5s, 1959-60, 1964, 1968 and 1973) were associated with low unemployment, high inflation and a current account deficit on the balance of payments. It is noticeable from Figure 67.4 that unemployment shifted upwards in the late 1960s. The fall in unemployment that could have been expected in the boom of 1968 did not take place. This represented an upward shift in the **natural rate** of unemployment in the economy (☞ unit 90). It is an example of **hysteresis**, where an economic variable changes but does not bounce back to its original position when economic circumstances change.

The recession of 1974-75 was unusual in that it coincided with a severe supply side shock to the economy. The quadrupling of oil prices pushed the current account on the balance of payments into record deficit, whilst it led to an increase in the inflation rate. This produced the phenomenon of **stagflation** in 1974. There was rising inflation, a worsening balance of payments, rising unemployment and a fall in output. Within a couple of years, however, more traditional patterns reasserted themselves. The boom of 1978-79 saw faster growth, falling unemployment coupled with rising inflation and a deteriorating current account.

The recession of 1979-81 was even more severe than that of 1974-75 and again there was stagflation. Unemployment more than doubled and output fell by 4.2 per cent. Manufacturing industry was very badly affected, experiencing a 14.6 per cent fall in output from peak to trough. At the same time, inflation increased from 13.4 per cent in 1979 to 18.0 per cent in 1980 before falling back to 11.9 per cent in 1981. The balance of payments current account moved strongly into surplus. The recession of 1979-81 was untypical when compared to recessions of the 1950s and 1960s in many ways. The second oil crisis of 1978-79 fuelled inflation and created a downturn in the international economy which fed through to lower demand for UK exports. At the same time, North Sea oil was beginning to have a major impact on the balance of payments and led to a rise in the exchange rate, again dampening demand for UK non-oil exports. The government also, for the first time in the post-war era, reduced aggregate demand as the economy went into recession, firstly by increasing domestic interest rates and secondly by cutting public spending and raising taxes.

Perhaps not surprisingly, the economy took some time to recover. There was a faltering in the economy in 1984, but no major recession as the experience of the previous 30 years would have suggested. However, there was a boom in the economy in 1987-89, approximately ten years after the last major boom of 1977-79. The boom had many of the characteristics of two previous booms, in 1963-64 and 1972-74. All, in different ways, were fuelled by government policy changes. The Barber boom of 1972-74 was fuelled by a disastrous loosening of monetary policy combined with a large fiscal expansion driven by tax cuts and increases in government spending. The Lawson boom of 1987-89 too saw a failure to control growth in the money supply at an early enough point in the boom. Whilst overall fiscal policy remained broadly neutral, major income tax cuts in 1987 further boosted already strong consumer confidence which fed through into higher consumption, spending and borrowing.

Increasing house prices at the time were both a symptom of inflation and a cause of rising demand and rising prices. Fast increases in house prices increase the wealth of households and encourage them to borrow and spend more. Over the three year period 1963-65, house prices rose by 20 per cent, higher than the average for the 1950s and 1960s. Over the three year period 1972-74, house prices rose 90 per cent, whilst over the four years of 1986-89 they increased 72 per cent. Certainly, the house price boom of the mid-late 1980s was encouraged by the government through generous tax concessions on mortgages and a political climate which equated home ownership with success.

In all three booms, the current account on the balance of payments went into substantial deficit; 1.2 per cent of GDP in 1964, 4.2 per cent of GDP in 1974 (although this was partly caused by the oil supply side shock) and a record 5.1 per cent of GDP in 1989. This was because these booms sucked in imports as British industry failed to meet domestic demand.

The Lawson boom was followed by a prolonged recession. It was caused by a considerable tightening of monetary policy. Interest rates were doubled in 1988-89 from $7\frac{1}{2}$ per cent to 15 per cent in a bid by the government to stem a small rise in inflation. In 1990, the UK joined the ERM at too high a rate of the pound against other European currencies. The result was that the government was forced to maintain high interest rates to defend a weak pound throughout 1991 and 1992, long after the inflationary threat had passed. As a consequence, the recession was the longest since the 1930s. It was only when the UK was forced to leave the ERM and the government quickly cut interest rates down to $5\frac{1}{2}$ per cent by 1994 that the economy came out of recession.

By 1995, the UK found itself in a very unusual situation. In previous recoveries, the current account has tended to worsen whilst inflation has risen. However, partly due to the sizeable devaluation of the pound from 1992, the current account improved as the economy came out of recession whilst inflationary pressures remained subdued. It would be difficult to believe, however, that the UK could break with its history and achieve a 'golden scenario' of fast growth with low inflation and a current account surplus.

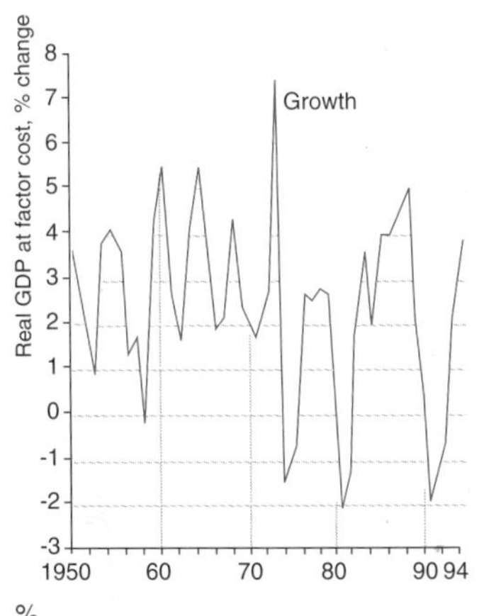

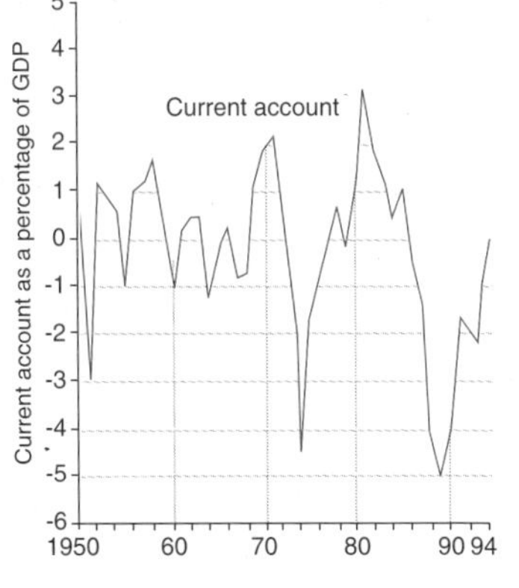

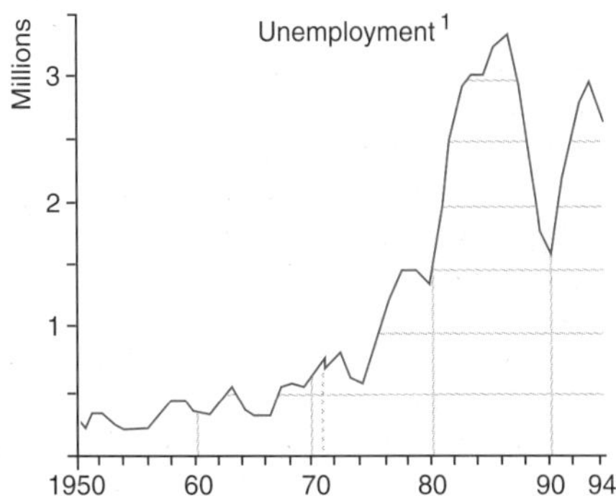

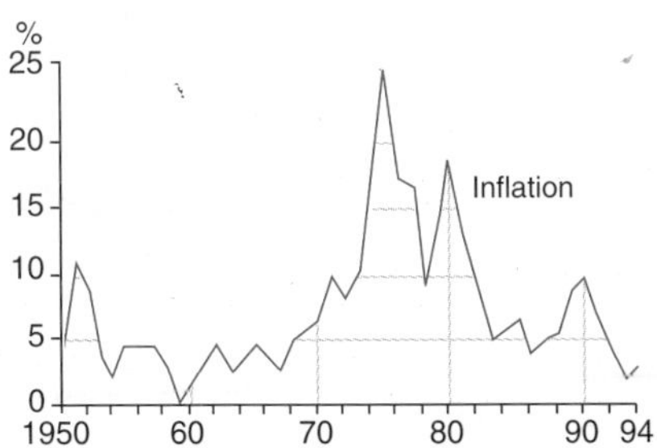

1. There were over 20 revisions to the way in which unemployment was measured in the 1980s. The figures here from 1971 are calculated on the basis of the 1982 definition of unemployment when the count was changed from those registered at Jobcentres for work to those registered as in receipt of benefits for being unemployed. Despite this, there are further discontinuities in the series in 1982, 1983 and 1985.

Source: adapted from CSO, *Economic Trends Annual Supplement;* CSO, *Monthly Digest of Statistics.*

Figure 67.4 *The business cycle: growth, unemployment, inflation and the current account*

'Output gap' leads to inflation alert

The strong growth in the US has now eroded all of the spare capacity in the US economy, suggesting that inflationary pressures may soon intensify, the OECD outlook said yesterday.

Germany also has a relatively low level of spare capacity in its economy, even though recovery has started only recently there. However, the UK has more spare capacity than any other of the six largest industrialised economies, closely followed by France.

These findings are likely to fuel the debate about the timing of interest rate rises in OECD countries and the significance of the so-called 'output gap', not least because the OECD yesterday announced reforms in its calculations of this gap.

In recent years, western governments have attached growing significance to the concept of an output gap, since it has been assumed that an erosion of the spare capacity will lead to higher inflation. The output gap is usually defined as the difference between the actual growth rate in an economy and its theoretical potential growth rate if all capacity were used.

However, economists and governments have remained sharply divided over the correct way to measure the output gap. Although the Bank of England, for example, uses its own calculations of the UK output gap to help determine the timing of interest rate rises, it refuses to publish figures on this.

In the past, the OECD's own calculations of the output gap have relied on a mixture of historical statistical analysis, and judgements about broader trends in the economy, such as changes in labour market flexibility.

However, the OECD is now relying on a more complicated modelling technique that seeks to estimate the total productive capacity in an economy, compared with its actual growth.

The OECD admits that the concept remains extremely slippery. Nevertheless, its finding that the US economy has now eroded all of its spare capacity may add to pressure for a further rise in US interest rates.

'There is widespread agreement that full employment has been reached (in the US),' the OECD said. It forecasts that inflation in the US will rise to more than 3 per cent in the next 18 months. Conversely, the surprising conclusion that the UK now has more spare capacity than most other European countries not only highlights the depth of the recent UK recession - but may also fuel complaints from some economists that further rises in the UK interest rates are unnecessary.

France is also estimated to have a relatively large output gap, which again may indicate the depth of its recent recession.

Meanwhile the output gap in Japan, which is only now emerging from recession, is predicted to remain little changed over the next two years, highlighting the fact that inflationary pressures are likely to remain subdued, creating little need for interest rate rises.

The OECD warned that Italy, in particular, was one country that needed to address the problem of the budget deficit, although the Italian government had introduced some reforms.

Source: the *Financial Times*, 21.12.1994.

Table 67.4 *Output gaps*

Deviations of actual GDP from potential GDP as percentage of potential GDP

	US	Japan	Germany	France	Italy	UK	Canada
1986	-0.4	-3.8	-1.3	-2.2	0.1	0.5	1.0
1987	0.2	-3.8	-1.8	-2.3	1.5	2.8	2.6
1988	1.7	-1.2	-0.5	-0.5	2.9	5.0	4.6
1989	2.2	0.1	0.2	1.1	4.0	4.6	4.0
1990	1.4	1.8	2.3	1.2	3.7	2.2	0.8
1991	-1.4	3.1	3.8	-0.2	2.6	-2.5	-3.5
1992	-1.3	2.0	2.5	-1.0	0.8	-5.1	-4.8
1993	-0.4	-0.2	-1.2	-3.7	-2.1	-5.2	-4.4
1994	1.0	-2.3	-1.2	-3.5	-2.0	-3.9	-2.9
1995	1.5	-2.8	-1.1	-2.6	-1.4	-2.9	-1.7
1996	1.0	-2.5	-0.5	-1.6	-0.7	-2.3	-0.8

Source: OECD, [illegible]

1. **What does it mean when the article states that 'Japan ... is ... now emerging from a recession'?**
2. **Explain the link between a recession in the economy and an 'output gap'.**
3. **Using Table 67.4, discuss in which years different countries were**
   (a) in a recession and
   (b) in a boom.
4. **Discuss, using diagrams, why governments might have wanted to raise interest rates in 1995.**

Aggregate demand and government policy

Summary

1. The main economic goals of government policy are usually seen as maintaining low unemployment and inflation with a high growth rate, given a current account balance of the balance of payments.
2. Government attempts to manipulate its budget deficit or surplus (its PSBR or PSDR) to achieve economic goals are called fiscal policy.
3. Changes in tax and government spending levels will have an effect on aggregate demand. An increase in government spending, for instance, will have a multiplier effect on national income.
4. Government expenditure and tax revenues which change automatically as income changes are called automatic stabilisers. They break the fall of national income when the economy moves towards a depression and limit the rise of income when the economy is in boom.
5. Active fiscal policy is the term used to describe the deliberate manipulation of government expenditure and taxes to influence the economy.
6. Demand management through the use of fiscal policy has its limitations. There are time lags involved in the implementation of policy, economic data on which to base decisions are inadequate, economic theory itself is not sufficiently well developed for governments to be able to fine tune the economy to meet precise targets and continued deficits lead to national debt problems.
7. Monetary policy can also be used to influence aggregate demand.

The goals of government policy

Governments are generally argued to have four main macro-economic goals:
- to maintain full employment;
- to ensure price stability;
- to achieve a high level of economic growth;
- to keep exports and imports in balance.

Sometimes it is argued that governments have a major responsibility to ensure an equitable distribution of income and wealth. It is also arguable that governments today have a major responsibility for ensuring that the workings of the economy are consistent with a sustainable environment. These issues are explored in many other units of this book.

Fiscal policy

The UK government has been responsible for between 40 and 50 per cent of national expenditure over the past 20 years. The main areas of public spending are the National Health Service, defence, education and roads (☞ unit 44). In addition, the government is responsible for transferring large sums of money round the economy through its spending on social security and National Insurance benefits. All of this is financed mainly through taxes, such as income tax and VAT (☞ unit 47).

In the post-war era, governments have rarely balanced their budgets (i.e. they have rarely planned to match their expenditure with their receipts). In most years, they have run BUDGET DEFICITS, spending more than they receive. As a result, in most years governments have had to borrow money. In the UK, the borrowing of the public sector (central government, local government and other state bodies such as nationalised industries) over a period of time is called the PUBLIC SECTOR BORROWING REQUIREMENT (PSBR). In two periods, between 1969-70 and 1988-90, the UK government received more revenue than it spent. The normal budget deficit was turned into a BUDGET SURPLUS. The UK budget surplus is called the PUBLIC SECTOR DEBT REPAYMENT (PSDR). As the name implies, a budget surplus allows the government to pay off part of its accumulated debt. This debt, called the NATIONAL DEBT, dates back to the founding of the Bank of England in 1694.

The government has to make decisions about how much to spend, tax and borrow. It also has to decide on the composition of its spending and taxation. Should it spend more on education and less on defence? Should it cut income tax by raising excise duties? These decisions about spending, taxes and borrowing are called the FISCAL POLICY of the government.

The key date in the year for fiscal policy is the day of the BUDGET. Since 1993, Budget day in the UK has been in late November or early December. The Budget gives a forecast of government spending and taxation in the coming year, and it fixes spending totals and tax rates, usually mainly covering the next financial year. In the UK, the financial year starts on 6 April and runs till 5 April in the following year.

QUESTION 1

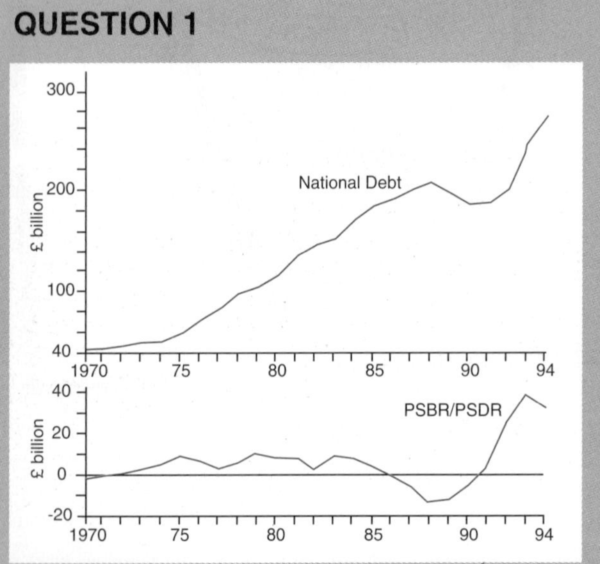

Source: adapted from CSO, Financial Statistics; Economic Trends Annual Supplement.

Figure 68.1 *The PSBR, the PSDR and the national debt*

(a) (i) Distinguish between a PSBR and a PSDR.
(ii) In which years did the UK have a PSDR?
(b) Using examples from the data, explain the link between the PSBR or PSDR and the national debt.
(c) If a government wanted to pay off its national debt over a number of years, how could it achieve this?

Aggregate demand

Government spending and taxation changes have an effect on aggregate demand. A rise in government spending, with the price level constant, will increase aggregate demand, pushing the AD curve to the right as in Figure 68.2.

Equally, a cut in taxes will affect aggregate demand. A cut in taxes on income, such as income tax and National Insurance contributions, will lead to a rise in the disposable income of households. This in turn will lead to a rise in consumption expenditure and hence to a rise in aggregate demand. This rise, because the price level is assumed to remain constant, will shift the AD curve to the right, as in Figure 68.2.

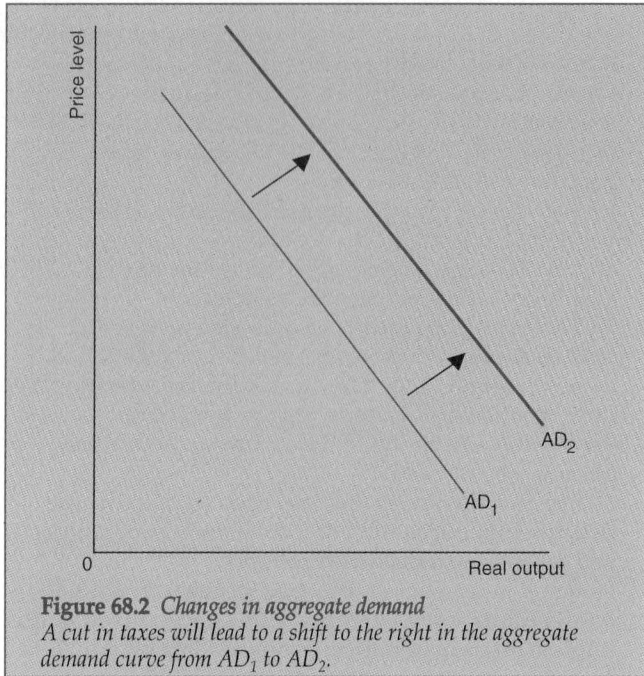

Figure 68.2 *Changes in aggregate demand*
A cut in taxes will lead to a shift to the right in the aggregate demand curve from AD_1 to AD_2.

QUESTION 2 Explain the probable effect the following would have on aggregate demand, all other things being equal:
(a) a rise in income tax rates;
(b) a cut in council tax rates;
(c) a cut in spending on education;
(d) a rise in VAT rates combined with an increase in spending on the NHS.

The multiplier

In unit 64, it was explained that a rise in government spending (G) will not just increase aggregate demand by the value of the increase in G. There will be a multiple increase in aggregate demand. This **multiplier effect** will be larger the smaller the leakages from the circular flow (☞ unit 81).

In a modern economy, where leakages from savings, taxes and imports are a relatively high proportion of national income, multiplier values tend to be small. However, Keynesian economists argue that they can still have a significant effect on output in the economy if the economy is below full employment.

Automatic stabilisers

In the 1930s, large falls in export earnings and investment spending led to the Great Depression. Today, any reduction in export earnings or investment would have

QUESTION 3 The Labour government which took office in February 1974 barely had a majority in Parliament and therefore was unwilling to increase taxes and cut public expenditure to tackle soaring inflation and a large balance of payments deficit. In November 1974, another general election took place and this time the Labour government secured a workable majority. In the 1975 Budget, it cut planned public expenditure and increased taxes, both by over £1 000 million. Further cuts in public expenditure were announced in 1976. The PSBR fell from £10 161 million in 1975 to £8 899 million in 1976 and to £5 419 million in 1977. However, the government relaxed its fiscal stance in 1978, and the PSBR increased to £8 340 million.

(a) What is meant by 'the multiplier'?
(b) Explain, using the concept of the multiplier, the likely effect that the change in fiscal policy between 1974 and 1976 had on national income.
(c) Using a diagram, discuss the impact that the change in the government's fiscal stance in 1978 is likely to have had on prices and output.

less impact on the economy because AUTOMATIC or BUILT-IN STABILISERS are greater. Automatic stabilisers are expenditures which automatically increase when the economy is going into a recession. Conversely, they automatically fall when national income begins to rise.

Government spending and taxation are both automatic stabilisers. When the economy goes into recession and unemployment rises, the government automatically increases its social security spending, paying out more in unemployment benefits and other related benefits. The fall in aggregate demand is therefore less than it would otherwise have been. Tax revenues fall too at a faster rate than the fall in income. This is because tax rates tend to be higher on marginal income than on average income. For instance, a worker paid on commission may sell less in a recession. Her tax rate might then fall from the higher rate of 40 per cent to the basic rate of 25 per cent. If household spending has to be cut, then it is likely that consumption items such as consumer durables taxed at 17½ per cent VAT will see falls rather than zero rated food. With the government collecting less tax, disposable incomes are higher than they would otherwise be and therefore consumption can be at a higher level than would be the case without this automatic stabiliser.

When the economy goes into boom, government spending falls as the benefit budget falls automatically. Tax revenue increases at a faster rate than the increase in income. An unemployed person will pay very little tax. Once the unemployed get jobs, they start to pay substantial amounts of direct and indirect tax. So aggregate demand is lower than it would otherwise be with these automatic stabilisers.

Discretionary fiscal policy

ACTIVE or DISCRETIONARY FISCAL POLICY does not rely on the economy automatically changing the amount the government spends or collects in taxes. It is the deliberate manipulation of government expenditure and taxes to influence the economy. The deliberate decision by government to cut tax rates, leading to a fall in tax revenues, would be an example of active fiscal policy. Another would be a decision to increase spending on education.

There are a large number of reasons why governments use discretionary fiscal policy. They might be influenced by non-economic arguments. For instance, the Conservative government between 1979 and 1983 deliberately increased spending on defence in the belief that the UK spent too little on defence in the 1970s. The government may also alter government spending and taxation to win votes (☞ unit 44). They may wish to influence the **supply side** of the economy (☞ unit 69). It may wish to influence aggregate demand. This is known as **demand management**.

QUESTION 4 Explain whether the following are likely to be examples of automatic stabilisers or active fiscal policy:
(a) the rise in VAT rates from 8 to 15 per cent in 1979;
(b) the cut in the highest rate of income tax on earned income from 83 per cent to 60 per cent in 1979;
(c) the rise in payments of unemployment benefit from £680 million in 1979-80 to £1 328 million in 1980-81;
(d) the one per cent fall in the real value of taxes on income during 1980;
(e) the abolition of earnings related unemployment benefit in January 1982.

Demand management

Keynes developed his ideas about changing demand in the 1930s against the backdrop of the Great Depression. During the depression of the 1930s, millions of workers all over the world lost their jobs. In both the USA and Germany, unemployment levels reached 25 per cent. The economic orthodoxy of the time advocated **balanced budgets**, where government spending equalled taxation, and argued that the government could do little directly to influence the level of income and employment. Keynes argued that an increase in demand would cut unemployment. If firms wouldn't increase demand by increasing investment, and consumers wouldn't increase their demand by increasing their average propensities to consume, then the government would have to step in and, through creating a budget deficit, increase demand in the economy.

This view became the economic orthodoxy of the 1950s and 1960s. After the terrible unemployment of the 1930s, the goal became to create FULL EMPLOYMENT. In the 1944 White Paper *Employment Policy* (Cmnd 6527), it was stated that: 'The government accepts as one of their primary aims and responsibilities the maintenance of a high and stable level of employment after the war.' Full employment is the level of output at which all the factors of production in the economy are fully utilised at given factor prices. For instance, it is where every worker who wants a job at the current wage rate is in employment.

So, when the economy was suffering from a rise in unemployment, government would increase the budget deficit. When the economy was at full employment, aggregate demand was threatening to rise even further and inflation was increasing (a situation known as OVER-HEATING), government would reduce the budget deficit to reduce aggregate demand.

In fact, unemployment levels in the 1950s and 1960s tended to fluctuate between 1 and 2 per cent. As time went on, economists and politicians felt more and more that the economy could be FINE-TUNED to a very precise level of unemployment through the use of fiscal levers. This was called DEMAND MANAGEMENT of the economy - the use of government policy to manage the level of aggregate demand in the economy. But even in the 1950s and 1960s, it was recognised that there were limitations to fine tuning.

The limitations of demand management policies

Conflicting policy objectives Governments in the 1950s and 1960s found it impossible to maintain a **stable** level of low unemployment. The economy tended to move from boom to mild recession - what came to be known as the STOP-GO CYCLE. When unemployment was low, economic growth tended to be high. However, inflation tended to rise and the balance of payments slipped into deficit. It was particularly the balance of payments which worried governments at the time. So when the balance of payments moved into deficit, the government would reduce the budget deficit and the economy would move into mild recession. Then the balance of payments would move into surplus, the government would apply the fiscal levers again, expanding the economy and the cycle would start all over again.

Time lags Assume that the government announces a £500 million increase in civil servant salaries and a £500 million increase in road building. If the multiplier were 2, this would lead to a £2 000 million increase in equilibrium income in the Keynesian model. However, it may take some years for the full increase to work through the economy. The increase in civil servant salaries will work through relatively quickly. Civil servants will increase their spending within a few months of receiving the pay increase. The road building programme may take years even to start. So a government needs to be careful to take account of lags in spending when using fiscal policy to fill or remove deflationary or inflationary gaps. If a government wishes to reflate or deflate the economy quickly, it needs to change those taxes and those items of expenditure which will have an immediate impact on aggregate demand. Changing income tax rates, social security payments and public sector wages will all act quickly to change demand. Long term capital projects, such as road building or hospital building, are inappropriate for short term changes although they may be ideal in a serious longer term depression such as that which occurred during the 1930s and early 1980s.

In the past, governments have been accused of even destabilising the economy through the use of active fiscal policy. Government would reflate the economy just at a time when the economy was moving into boom of its own accord, just as it arguably was in 1972 when the Chancellor reflated the economy. The combination of extra private sector spending and extra public sector spending would then create an inflationary gap. The more inherently stable the economy, the more potential damage there would be from wrong timing in active fiscal policy. Hence some economists argue that the inability to predict time lags accurately makes it impossible to use fiscal policy to fine tune the economy.

Inadequacy of economic data Active fiscal policy assumes that the Chancellor knows the current state of the British economy. But statistics are notoriously unreliable. Unemployment statistics and inflation statistics are not revised after publication, but national income statistics and the balance of payments statistics are frequently revised. Moreover, the 'black holes' in these statistics (the 'residual errors', 'balancing items' or 'statistical discrepancies' ☞ unit 59) have become increasingly large over time. If the balance of payments is in deficit, the Chancellor will not know how much of this is due to a genuine deficit and how much is due to inaccurate recording of statistics. Fine-tuning then becomes very difficult. The Chancellor could well reflate the economy even though it was at full employment because he had been misled by statistics showing a recession.

Inadequate economic knowledge Active fiscal policy assumes that we know how the economy behaves. However, there is scepticism that economics will ever be able to predict changes in variables to the last few per cent. This is important because so many of the variables which governments wish to control have very small values. For instance, the government may wish to reduce economic growth from 3 per cent to 1½ per cent. But active fiscal policy is unlikely ever to be sufficiently sensitive to achieve exactly that 1½ per cent fall.

The inadequacy of the model An increased budget deficit will fill a deflationary gap. A reduced budget deficit will close an inflationary gap. These are the conclusions of the simple Keynesian model of income determination. But it should be remembered that the model makes a large number of assumptions. In the 1950s and 1960s, it seemed to many that these were reasonable assumptions to make. In the 1970s and 1980s, these assumptions seemed far less reasonable. Much of the rest of this book will be devoted to exploring why the simple Keynesian model needs to be modified if it is to be used to explain the very unusual economic events of the past two decades, or whether other models are more applicable.

The national debt Since the Second World War, many governments have abandoned attempts to balance their budgets. They find it politically easier to spend more than they tax and borrow the difference. Demand management policies then become a question of increasing budget deficits when the economy has high unemployment and reducing them when the economy is at full employment. In the long term, this can present a major problem for governments.

Governments are no different from individuals. If they continually borrow money, then eventually a national debt is built up which is increasingly difficult to **service** (i.e. pay interest on the debt). For instance, assume that a government is taking 40 per cent of national income in taxes. It has a national debt equivalent to 100 per cent of national income. Interest on the debt averages 10 per cent per annum. Then, the government has to pay 10 per cent of national income in interest, which amounts to one-quarter of its tax revenues (10%÷ 40%). If it is continuing to run a budget deficit, then the proportion of taxation going on servicing the debt will increase further over time.

Eventually, lenders will begin to be scared that the government will default on its debt (i.e. it will not pay the interest and will not pay back loans as they mature). Governments in this position have to offer higher rates of interest on new loans in order to persuade lenders to take the risk of lending to them. This makes the situation worse, because the government is how having to pay even more interest on its debt. In the worst case, lenders will refuse to lend or the government will become overwhelmed by its debt and begin to default on its loans. Either way, the government will have gone bankrupt.

There is a way around this in the short term. The government, unlike an individual, can pay its debt by simply printing money. More money in the economy is likely to lead to inflation (☞ unit 94). Inflation reduces the real value of the debt. For instance, in the example above, if the government creates a doubling of prices, then the real value of the national debt will fall from 100 per cent to 50 per cent because national income at current prices will double but the national debt at current prices will stay the same. However, this is not a long term solution. Lenders will demand much higher rates of interest if there is high inflation in a country. Budget deficits will continue to increase the size of the national debt. The government will have to be creating large amounts of inflation simply to stand still in terms of national debt.

QUESTION 5 In 1988 and 1989, the government sharply increased interest rates to curb rising inflation and a growing balance of payments deficit. In 1989, the current account deficit was nearly £20 000 million. However, the balancing item, the net amount of transactions which went unrecorded, stood at + £15 024 million.

Suggest why the large balancing item may have hindered the government in its attempt to formulate economic policy.

Keynes never advocated running budget deficits over long periods. He thought that a short term budget deficit would be a useful shock to help bring the economy back towards full employment. Today, the size of the national debt in relation to national income is one of the key indicators in the European Union for the decision as to whether countries could adopt a single currency. The larger the debt, the more potentially unstable is the economy of a country and the less likely it is that that country could survive successfully in a monetary union (☞ unit 98).

Monetary policy

Monetary policy (discussed at length in units 77 and 78) is the attempt by government or the central bank of an economy to manipulate the money supply, the supply of credit, interest rates or any other monetary variables to achieve the fulfilment of policy goals. In this unit, we will concentrate on the effects of changes in interest rates on aggregate demand. Governments lowering interest rates at a given level of prices will lead to a rise in aggregate demand, from AD_1 to AD_2 in Figure 68.2. This is because a fall in interest rates leads to a rise in spending on consumer durables and an increase in investment spending (☞ units 62 and 63). Conversely, a rise in interest rates will lead to a fall in aggregate demand, shown by a shift to the left in the aggregate demand curve.

Monetary policy can therefore be used as part of the demand management policies of a government, either on its own or with fiscal policy. Keynesian economists have traditionally emphasised the importance of fiscal policy. This is because they argue that consumption and investment are only weakly linked to interest rates. Therefore, monetary policy is relatively ineffective. Classical or monetarist economists, on the other hand, argue that fiscal policy is weak (☞ unit 103).

Key terms

Budget deficit or Public Sector Borrowing Requirement (PSBR) - a deficit which arises because government spending is greater than its receipts. Government therefore has to borrow money to finance the difference.
Budget surplus or Public Sector Debt Repayment (PSDR) - a government surplus arising from government spending being less than its receipts. Government can use the difference to repay part of National Debt.
The National Debt - the accumulated borrowings of government.
Fiscal policy - decisions about spending, taxes and borrowing of the government.
Budget - a statement of the spending and income plans of an individual, firm or government. The Budget is the yearly statement on government spending and taxation plans in the UK.
Automatic or built-in stabilisers - mechanisms which reduce the impact of changes in the economy on national income.
Active or discretionary fiscal policy - the deliberate manipulation of government expenditure and taxes to influence the economy.
Full employment - the level of output in an economy where all factors of production are fully utilised at given factor prices.
Over-heating - the economy over-heats when planned expenditure is greater than full employment income (i.e. when there are strong inflationary tendencies at full employment income).
Fine-tuning - the attempt by government to move the economy to a very precise level of unemployment, inflation, etc. It is usually associated with fiscal policy and demand management.
Demand management - government use of fiscal and other policies to manipulate the level of aggregate demand in the economy.
Stop/go cycle - the movement from boom to recession in the trade cycle.

Applied economics

A history of fiscal policy

1950-1975

During the period 1950-75, fiscal policy was probably the most important way in which governments manipulated aggregate demand. During the 1950s, governments learnt to use the 'fiscal levers' with more and more confidence. In a recession, such as in 1958, the government would cut taxes to stimulate spending in the economy. This might also be accompanied by public spending increases, although it was recognised that these would take longer to multiply through the economy than tax cuts. In a boom, when the economy was over-heating, as in 1960, the government would increase taxes and possibly cut public spending.

Borrowing in the economy was mainly controlled through direct controls on banks and building societies, specifying who was allowed to borrow money, or through controls on hire purchase, the most common way of financing the purchase of consumer durables.

In the 1960s, governments began to recognise some of the limitations of fiscal policy. The Labour government of 1964-66 experimented briefly with a National Plan, an attempt to model the economy in terms of the inputs and outputs of each industry. This plan was then to be used to help the government identify where particular industries were failing or creating 'bottlenecks' and might need further investment. This supply side experiment was abandoned as the economy faced yet another sterling crisis, which ultimately ended in the pound being devalued in 1967. Another policy used from 1966 was an incomes policy - government limits on the pay rises that could be given to workers. This supply side measure was designed to lower inflation whilst allowing the economy to grow and enjoy low rates of unemployment.

The last bout of traditional Keynesian demand management came in 1972-73 when the government cut taxes and increased public spending to put the economy into boom. This boom, called the Barber boom (after Anthony Barker, the then Chancellor of the Exchequer), ended disastrously as inflation spun out of control, fuelled by the oil price increases of 1973-74.

1975-1995

The mid-1970s saw a wholesale disillusionment with traditional Keynesian demand management techniques. A classical model of the economy became increasingly accepted as the model for governments to work with. In 1976, the Labour Prime Minister of the day, Jim Callaghan, in addressing his party conference, stated that: 'We used to think that you could just spend your way out of a recession, and increase employment by cutting taxes and boosting government spending. I tell you in all candour that that option no longer exists, and that in so far as it ever did exist, it worked by injecting inflation into the economy.'

The view was taken that cutting taxes produced only a temporary increase in aggregate demand. Unemployment would fall and growth would rise. However, as in the Barber boom, the medium term consequences would be a rise in the inflation rate. To reduce inflation, the government would have to tighten its fiscal stance by raising taxes. Aggregate demand would fall and the economy would return to its equilibrium position but at a higher level of prices and of inflation.

From 1979, when Margaret Thatcher won her first general election, fiscal policy was used for two separate purposes. First, it was used for micro-economic objectives as part of supply side policy for the government (☞ unit 69). For instance, income tax was cut to increase incentives to work. Second, it was used to ensure that monetary targets were met. In particular, it was felt that changes in the PSBR, such as might come about if taxes were cut, would have no effect on aggregate demand if the money for the tax cuts was genuinely borrowed from the non-bank sector. For instance, if the government cut taxes by £1 and financed this by borrowing from the non-bank sector, then there could be no increase in aggregate demand. The taxpayer would have £1 extra to spend but the lender to the government would have £1 less to spend. On this view, increases in the PSBR completely **crowd-out** other expenditure in the economy resulting in no increase in aggregate demand. They could only work in a Keynesian manner if the increase in the PSBR was financed through printing the money (the government has the unique power in the economy to print money) and thus increasing the money supply.

During the period of the Lawson boom (1986-89, named after Nigel Lawson the then Chancellor) and the following recession (1990-92), the government allowed public spending and taxes to act as automatic stabilisers. So in the boom, the government allowed a large PSDR to emerge. In the recession, the PSBR was allowed to grow and by 1993 had reached over 5 per cent of GDP. In 1994-95, the government used active fiscal policy to cut this large deficit, increasing taxes whilst keeping a tight rein on public spending. On Keynesian assumptions, this put a brake on aggregate demand as it increased during the recovery. On classical assumptions, the tax increases have had no effect on aggregate demand because the accompanying cuts in government borrowing released resources for the private sector to borrow and spend. One of the main reasons why the government felt it was so important to reduce the PSBR was because of concerns that otherwise the national debt would grow out of control.

Preparing a Budget

March 1993 Budget

The Chancellor, Norman Lamont, announced a package which included steep increases in taxes, but which would take effect mainly from April 1994. In particular, he announced that from April 1993 these would be:

- a freeze on personal allowances on income tax;
- a small widening in the 20 per cent of income tax;
- a 5 per cent rise in excise duties on beer and wine;
- a $6^1/2$ per cent increase in tobacco duty;
- a 10 per cent rise in tax on petrol.

From April 1994:

- employees National Insurance contributions would rise by 1 per cent;
- VAT would be extended to domestic fuel and power;
- tax relief on mortgages would be cut by allowing interest to be only offset against a 20 per cent income tax rate.

Overall, the tax package was broadly neutral in 1993-94 because the small increases in tax revenues were offset by falls in tax revenues because of the weak growth in the economy in 1992-93. However, tax revenues were predicted to grow strongly in 1994-95 and subsequent years as the effects of the April 1994 Budget and growth in the economy began to take effect.

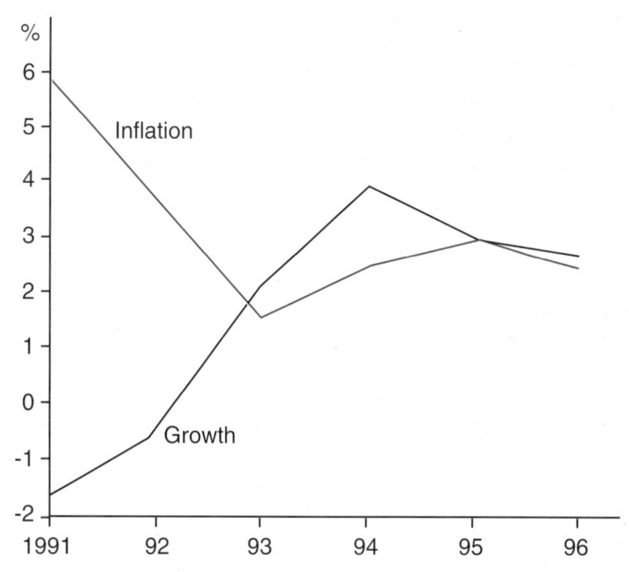

Figure 68.3 *Real growth in GDP and inflation*

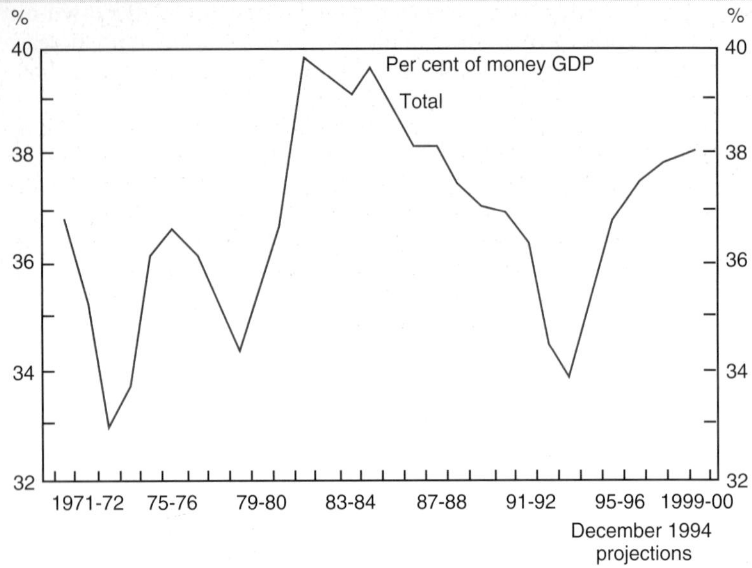

1. Includes local authority taxes.

Figure 68.4 *Taxes and social security[1] contributions as a percentage of GDP*

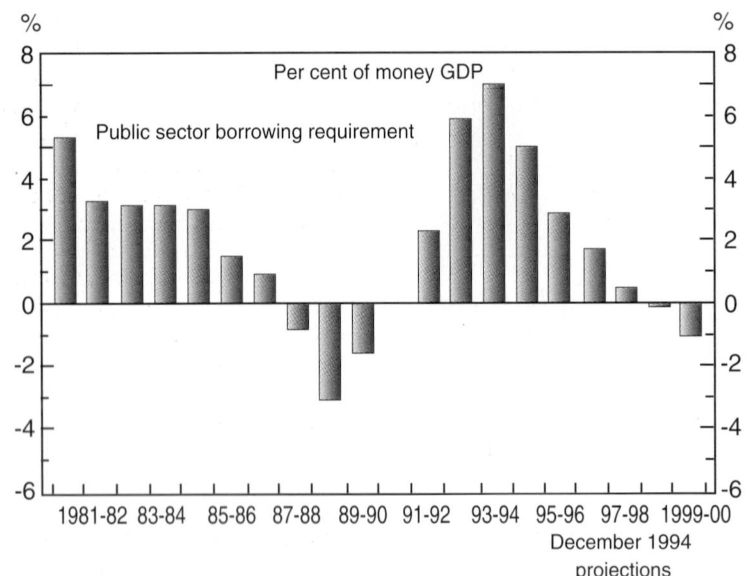

1. Negative values indicate a public sector debt repayment.

Figure 68.5 *PSBR[1]*

December 1994 Budget

The Chancellor, Kenneth Clarke, restated the plans for tax increases in 1995-96 announced in his December 1993 budget. He was defeated in his bid to further raise VAT on domestic fuel to 17.5 per cent, but made up the short-fall in revenue by further increasing taxes on petrol, drink and tobacco. Government spending remained broadly neutral.

December 1993 Budget

This was the first 'unified Budget' bringing together tax and government spending plans for the first time. The Budget confirmed the April 1993 tax increases as well as adding extra tax increases. In particular:

- income tax allowances were frozen;
- the married couple's income tax allowance was limited to a 20 per cent tax rate and this was to be cut to 15 per cent in April 1995;
- the 20 per cent tax band was further widened by £500 to £3 000;
- mortgage interest tax relief was restricted to 20 per cent and a further cut to 15 per cent was announced for April 1995;
- new indirect taxes were to be imposed from October 1995 on general insurance and airline flights out of the UK;
- increased excise duties were imposed on tobacco, wine and petrol;
- VAT at 8 per cent was imposed domestic fuel in line with the announcement in the April 1993 Budget.

Overall, taxes were predicted to rise by £8½bn in 1994-95, rising to £16.4bn in 1996-97. Taxes as a percentage of GDP were to increase from 36½ per cent in 1993-94 to 40¾ per cent in 1998-99. Real government spending was set to fall by a very small amount in 1994-95.

The Chancellor of the Exchequer is preparing for his December 1995 Budget. He wishes to maintain above average growth of around 3 per cent with low inflation of 3 per cent or less. Write a report for the Chancellor:

(a) outlining the main tax and government spending changes made in his 1993 and 1994 Budgets;

(b) explaining why it was sensible not to increase tax revenues in 1993-94 given that the main priority was to get the economy out of the recession and grow by above its trend rate of 2½ per cent;

(c) analysing the effect of the 1994-95 tax changes on aggregate demand, output and prices from what they otherwise might have been in the second half of the 1990s;

(d) advising the Chancellor whether there is room for tax cuts in his December 1995 or 1996 Budgets if 3 per cent growth is to be maintained with low inflation.

unit 69

Government and aggregate supply

Summary

1. Some economists, called supply side economists, believe that governments should not intervene in the workings of the free market. The government's role, they argue, is to remove restrictions to the operations of individual markets. Keynesian economists believe that governments need to intervene on the supply side to correct market failure.
2. Aggregate supply in the economy can be increased if government intervenes to ensure that labour markets operate more efficiently and if there is an increase in human capital over time.
3. Governments need to encourage firms to invest and take risks if aggregate supply is to increase.
4. Privatisation, deregulation and increased competition can increase aggregate supply.
5. Regional policy and inner city policy can also increase aggregate supply.

Different approaches

Economists agree that government can affect the supply side of the economy. However, they disagree about how this should be done.

Supply side economists Supply side economists come from the same broad school of thought as neo-classical, new classical and monetarist economists. They believe that free markets promote economic efficiency and that government intervention in the economy is likely to impair economic efficiency. Government still has a vital role to play in the economy, according to these economists. Government is responsible for creating the environment in which free markets can work. This means eliminating the barriers which exist to the perfect working of markets. SUPPLY SIDE ECONOMICS therefore tends to be the study of how government can intervene using **market orientated** policies.

Keynesian and neo-Keynesian economists Keynesian and neo-Keynesian economists believe that free markets often fail to maximise economic efficiency in the economy. Governments therefore have to correct **market failure** (☞ unit 36). This means intervening in free markets to change the outcome from that which it would otherwise have been.

In the rest of this unit, we will consider these two types of supply side policy - market orientated policies and interventionist policies.

Labour market policies

The level of aggregate supply is determined in part by the quantity of labour supplied to the market and the productivity of that labour. For instance, all other things being equal, an economy with 10 million workers will produce less than an economy with 20 million workers. Equally, an economy where workers have little **human capital** (☞ unit 2) will have a lower output than one where there are high levels of human capital. Classical economists argue that there are a number of ways in which the quantity and quality of labour are restricted because markets are not allowed to work freely.

Trade unions The purpose of a trade union is to organise workers into one bargaining unit. The trade union then becomes a monopsonist, a sole seller of labour, and prevents workers from competing amongst themselves in the job market. Economic theory predicts that if trade unions raise wage rates for their members, then employment and output will be lower in otherwise competitive markets (☞ unit 51). So classical economists argue that government must intervene to curb the power of trade unions, for instance, by reducing their ability to strike.

State welfare benefits Workers are unlikely to take low paid jobs if state benefits are a little below or equal to the pay being offered. Hence, state benefits reduce the level of aggregate supply because more workers remain unemployed. Classical economists argue that the solution is to cut state unemployment benefits to encourage workers to take on low paid jobs.

Minimum wages If there is a minimum wage which is set above the market clearing wage, then unemployment will be created (☞ unit 52). Minimum wages prevent some workers who would be prepared to work for lower pay from getting jobs. Hence aggregate supply is lowered. Classical economists argue that minimum wages should be abolished.

Marginal tax rates High marginal rates of tax on incomes discourage economic activity. A tax on cigarettes leads to fewer cigarettes being bought. A tax on work (income tax) leads to people working less. A tax on profits (corporation tax) is a disincentive to firms to make profits. Lowering certain taxes will therefore raise the level of economic activity and increase aggregate supply.

Supply side economists believe that the supply of labour is relatively elastic. A reduction in marginal tax rates on income will lead to a significant increase in 'work'. This could mean individuals working longer hours, being more willing to accept promotion, being more geographically mobile, or simply being prepared to join the workforce.

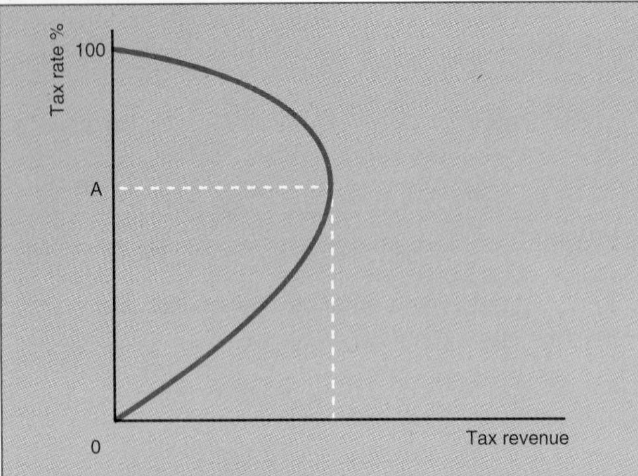

Figure 69.1 *The Laffer curve*
As tax rates increase, economic activity is discouraged and hence the rate of growth of tax revenues falls. Above OA, an increase in tax rates so discourages economic activity that tax revenues fall.

Work is, arguably, an inferior good, whilst leisure, its alternative, is a normal good. The higher an individual's income, the less willing he or she is to work. So a cut in marginal tax rates will have a negative income effect at the margin (i.e. the worker will be less willing to work). However, a cut in marginal tax rates will have a positive substitution effect because the relative price of work to leisure has changed in favour of work (i.e. the worker will be more willing to work ☞ unit 49 for a fuller explanation). Supply side economists believe that the substitution effect of a tax cut is more important than the income effect and hence tax cuts increase incentives to work. If cutting marginal income tax rates encourages people to work harder and earn more, then in theory it could be that tax revenues will increase following a tax cut. For instance, if 10 workers, each earning £10 000 a year, pay an average 25 per cent tax, then total tax revenue is £25 000 (10 x £10 000 x 0.25). If a cut in the tax rate to 20 per cent were to make each worker work harder and increase earnings to, say, £15 000, tax revenues would increase to £30 000 (10 x £3 000). This is an example of the LAFFER CURVE effect, after Professor Arthur Laffer who popularised the idea in the late 1970s. Figure 69.1 shows a Laffer curve, which plots tax revenues against tax rates. As tax rates increase, the rate of growth of tax revenue falls because of the disincentive effects of the tax. OA shows the maximum revenue position of the tax. At tax rates above OA, an increase in the tax rate so discourages economic activity that tax revenues fall.

QUESTION 1 A number of studies have been completed discussing the link between income tax cuts and incentives to work. For instance, Brown and Dawson (1969) surveyed all the studies published between 1947 and 1968 making links between tax rates and hours worked. They found that high taxation acted as a disincentive to working longer hours for between 5 and 15 per cent of the population. These workers were mainly people who could choose to vary their hours of work relatively easily - the wealthy, rural workers, the middle aged and those without families. On the other hand, a smaller group of people tended to increase their hours of work when taxes were higher. These were typically part of large families, young, less well-off urban dwellers.

In a 1988 study by C V Brown, it was found that the substantial increase in tax allowances in the 1988 Budget only increased the number of hours worked in the economy by 0.5 per cent. The cut in the basic rate of tax had no effect at all on hours worked whilst the massive cut in the top rate of tax from 60 per cent to 40 per cent only had a small effect in stimulating extra hours of work by the rich.

(a) Explain why tax rates might have an effect on incentives to work.
(b) To what extent have tax cuts increased the number of hours worked?
(c) What are the implications of the two studies described in the passage for the shape of the Laffer curve?

Taxes on labour Firms will not take on workers if their total wage cost is too high. Part of the total cost is the wages of workers. However, many countries tax firms for employing labour, often by imposing employer contributions to state social security funds. In the UK, for instance, employers have to pay National Insurance employers' contributions. The higher the tax, the fewer workers will be employed and hence the lower will be the level of aggregate supply.

Reducing the cost of changing jobs In a modern fast-changing economy, workers are likely to be changing jobs on a relatively frequent basis. Some workers will even become **portfolio workers**, having a mix of part-time jobs at any one time rather than a single full time job. If the labour market is such that workers find it difficult to get new jobs when they are made redundant, then unemployment will rise and aggregate supply will fall. So the government must ensure that **barriers to mobility** between jobs are as low as possible. One important barrier to mobility can be pensions. If pension rights are typically provided by individual employers, then a worker who is frequently moving from employer to employer will lose out. Hence, governments should give workers the opportunity to provide for their own pension which they can take with them them from job to job. Another problem in the UK has been a lack of geographical mobility due to rigidities in the housing market. If house prices in the South of England are much higher than in the North, then workers will be discouraged from moving from North to South. Equally, if workers are unable to rent houses at an affordable rent in an area, then low paid workers will not be able to move into that area to take up jobs.

Education and training Increasing the level of human capital of workers is vital if economies are to develop. Increased levels of education and training will raise the marginal revenue product of workers (i.e. will raise the value of output of workers). This in turn will shift the aggregate supply curve to the right. The value of human capital in the economy is one of the most important determinants of the level of aggregate supply.

QUESTION 2 A shortage of skilled labour is now seen as a major constraint in the expansion of the Welsh economy. In one initiative, the Welsh Office announced in June 1994 that it would fund a £3.6m scheme to support 550 engineering apprenticeships, provide engineering equipment for colleges and instruct workplace trainers.

Better school results are also needed. Welsh boys have lagged behind their English and, in particular, Northern Irish and Scottish counterparts in gaining A levels (or their equivalent). However, there has been a big rise in the numbers of those in Wales who go on to further education, from 36 per cent in 1988-89 to 53 per cent in 1993-94. Female students, who achieve better school results than males, also outnumber them in further education by 20 per cent.

If women are better educated, they also form a smaller part of the workforce and are in less responsible positions. 57 per cent of employees in 1993 were male, whilst only 43 per cent were female. And in a report, '*People and Prosperity, a challenge to Wales*', published by the Welsh Office in November 1993, women were 'much more likely than men to be in unskilled and semi-skilled jobs, and in those jobs without long-term career prospects. They are in turn under-represented at the senior levels of industry, public service and the professions as compared with UK averages. Employers in Wales are losing by this waste of resources.'

One organisation attempting to reduce this waste is Chwarae Teg, the women's fair pay body launched in 1992. It received Welsh Office funding of £50 000 and aims to encourage good practice in training, flexible working and better child care to enable women to return to work or training. It has become a role model for similar initiatives in England.

Source: adapted from the *Financial Times*, 7.9.1994.

(a) Using an aggregate supply diagram, explain why a 'shortage of skilled labour' could be a major constraint on the Welsh economy.
(b) How is the government tackling this problem? In your answer, discuss the part being played by public sector organisations and by organisations in the private sector supported by the public sector.

The capital market

Increasing the capital stock of the country - its factories, offices, roads etc.- will push the aggregate supply curve to the right. According to classical economists, the government has a key role to play in this.

Profitability Firms invest in order to make a profit. The higher the rate of profit, the more investment will take place. Hence, government must create an environment in which firms can make profits for their owners. One way of doing this is by reducing taxes on company profits. Another is to reduce inheritance tax which might be paid by a small business owner when passing on his or her business to a family relative. Another is to reduce taxes on employing workers. Reducing the amount of government red tape, like planning permissions, can also help reduce costs and increase profitability.

Allocating scarce capital resources The government is in a poor position to decide how to allocate resources. It should leave this as much as possible to the private sector. Hence, state owned companies should be **privatised** wherever possible. Government should offer only limited taxpayers' money to subsidise industry. The government should stay well clear of trying to 'back winning companies'.

QUESTION 3 The government is taking a tougher line on applications for regional aid from foreign investors who are considering England as a location and from UK companies wanting to relocate within the UK. The Department of Trade confirmed that it was scrutinising applications for Regional Selective Assistance (RSA) in England more stringently as part of government promises to cut public spending. However, it pointed out that its spending in 1994-95 was set to be £101m compared to £89.2m in 1993-94.

Some economic development bodies are afraid that the government's belief that the UK is now a highly attractive location for inward investment - thanks to de-regulation, labour market flexibility and low inflation - is lessening ministers' commitment to a grant regime about which it may be ideologically lukewarm.

Their worries have been highlighted by the government's decision last month to lay greater stress in granting RSA on the quality of jobs created. This may make it more difficult to win grants for projects offering the kind of less skilled work attractive to the jobless in high unemployment areas. For instance, Mr Bryn Sidaway, leader of Sunderland Council, is known to have written to the Prime Minister complaining that the level of RSA offered to Lucus SEI Wiring Systems, automotive components manufacturer, for a proposed Wearside plant, was lower than expected. However, the company recently announced that the project, which will create 650 jobs in its £10m first phase, will go ahead.

In the 40 years to 1991, the UK secured 36 per cent of US direct investment into the European Union, and between 1951 and March 1992, 40.9 per cent of Japanese EU direct investment.

Source: adapted from the *Financial Times*, 23.6.1994.

(a) How can offering RSA grants increase aggregate supply (a) in a region of the UK and (b) in the UK itself?
(b) (i) Why might a government committed to freeing up markets be 'ideologically lukewarm' to RSA?
(ii) Why might the decision of Lucus to site itself in Wearside support this view?
(c) Discuss whether aggregate supply would increase more if the government offered RSA on the criteria of the 'quality of jobs created' rather than the number of jobs created.

Increasing the range of sources of capital available to firms Firms can be constrained in their growth if they are unable to gain access to financial capital like bank loans or share capital. Government should therefore encourage the private sector to provide financial capital particularly to small businesses. They may, for instance, offer tax incentives to individuals putting up share capital for a business.

The goods market

Inefficient production will lead to a lower level of aggregate supply. For instance, if UK car workers produce 50 per cent fewer cars per worker with the same equipment as German workers, then the level of aggregate supply in the UK can obviously be increased if UK labour productivity is raised. The government has a key role to play in increasing efficiency.

Classical economists argue that the most important way of securing increased efficiency is through encouraging **competition**. If firms know that they will go out of business if they do not become efficient, then they have a powerful incentive to become efficient producers. The government can increase competition in the market in a number of ways.

Encouraging free trade (☞ unit 85) Fierce foreign competition results in a domestic industry which has to be efficient in order to survive. The government should therefore liberalise trade, removing tariffs (taxes) and other barriers to imports.

Encouraging small businesses (☞ units 40 and 57) Small businesses can operate in markets where there are no large businesses. Competition here is intense. However, small businesses can operate in markets where there are very large firms. Small businesses then force larger firms to remain cost competitive. Otherwise the larger firms will lose market share.

Privatisation (☞ unit 45) Privatising firms, and in the process creating competition between newly created firms, eliminates the distortions created by the operation of public sector monopolies.

Deregulation (☞ unit 46) Removing rules about who can compete in markets will encourage competition.

Interventionist approaches

Keynesian economists would tend to take a different approach to government policy and aggregate supply. They would tend to focus on issues of where free markets fail. For instance, they would agree with classical economists that a key aspect of government policy must be to increase education and training. However, whereas classical economists would argue that training should be left to individual companies or groups of companies in a local area, Keynesians would argue that training is best organised by government. The state should, for instance, impose levies on firms to finance state organised training placements and schemes.

With regard to investment in physical capital, classical economists would argue that profit should direct the level and pattern of investment. Keynesian economists would argue that if investment is insufficient in the economy, then the government should intervene and, for instance, use taxes to set up state owned companies or subsidise investment by private industry.

In the 1950s and 1960s in the UK, the main supply side problem was that of regional inequality with the North of England, Scotland and Northern Ireland experiencing higher unemployment rates than the South and the Midlands. The Keynesian policy response was a mixture of offering incentives to firms investing in high unemployment regions and making it difficult for firms to expand in low unemployment regions.

QUESTION 4 In 1993, Merseyside received the first instalment of a £1.6bn European investment programme for the economic regeneration of the area. The initial £176 million package of funds was made up of £75 million of European grant topped up with funds from the government, plus private sector money. The money has come because the region's gross domestic product per head had fallen to 75 per cent of the European average, a trigger point that gave Merseyside access to structural funds.

Projects are envisaged in construction, investment promotion, small business development, training, technology and leisure. The 1993 awards were intended to create 3 900 jobs, 20 000 training places and 341 000 sq ft of industrial space. Bruce Millan, European Commissioner for Regional Policy, said the five year objective was 49 000 jobs.

Source: adapted from *The Times*, 1.11.1994.

(a) How might the EU regional grant increase aggregate supply in the local Merseyside economy?

(b) (i) What is the estimated cost to the EU per job created over the five years?
(ii) To what extent does this represent good value for money for the EU taxpayer?

Key terms

Supply side economics - the study of how changes in aggregate supply will affect variables such as national income; in particular, how government micro-economic policy might change aggregate supply through individual markets.

Laffer curve - a curve which shows that at low levels of taxation, tax revenues will increase if tax rates are increased; however, if tax rates are high, then a further rise in rates will reduce total tax revenues because of the disincentive effects of the increase in tax.

Applied economics

Supply side policies in the UK

Since 1979, the government has been committed to implementing supply side policies aimed at improving the workings of free markets. A wide range of measures have been introduced which are described below.

The labour market

Reducing trade union power Industrial relations had long been recognised as a problem for the UK. Some have argued that the solution was to increase the power of trade unions over their members and legalise their rights in the workplace in order to make trade unions more responsible decision making bodies. Others argued that trade union power needed to be drastically curtailed. In 1969, the Labour government of the time published *In Place of Strife*, a White Paper on trade union reform which floundered on trade union opposition within the government. In 1971, the Conservative government under Edward Heath passed the Industrial Relations Act which attempted to curtail trade union powers. However, the legislation was flawed and trade unions circumvented the provisions of the Act. The Labour government of 1974-79, if anything, increased the power of trade unions by repealing the Industrial Relations Act and giving unions further rights. The election of a Conservative government in 1979, however, completely transformed the industrial relations scene. A number of Acts were passed (☞ unit 51) which effectively made secondary picketing illegal as firms gained the power to sue trade unions involved for damages. Industrial action called by a union now had to be approved by a secret ballot of its membership. Secret ballots were also made compulsory for elections of trade union leaders. Closed shops became more difficult to maintain and enforce. The government also took an extremely hard line with strikes in the public sector, refusing to give in to union demands. The breaking of strikes, such as the miners' strike of 1983-95, increased the confidence of private employers to resist trade union demands. By the mid-1990s, with the loss of over one-quarter of their members since 1979, trade unions had become marginalised in many places of work and considerably weakened in others.

Wage bargaining Employers will only take action against employees if it is profitable for them to do so. Supply side economists view collective bargaining as an inflexible way of rewarding workers. They advocate individual pay bargaining with payment systems based on bonuses and performance related pay. By reducing the power of trade unions, the government has gone some way to breaking collective bargaining. It has encouraged employers to move away from national pay bargaining to local pay bargaining and has itself, in the public sector, attempted to move away from national pay agreements to local ones.

Reducing state welfare benefits Reducing benefits to those out of work increases incentives for people to take jobs. Within three years of coming to office in 1979, the government abolished earnings-related unemployment benefit and also abolished the index linking of benefits to the rise in average earnings. Benefits since that time have only been indexed to the RPI, the inflation rate.

Unemployment benefit was made subject to income tax in 1982. In 1988, in a major overhaul of the social security system, the problems of both the **poverty trap** (where an increase in wages leads to a fall in income for a worker after tax has been paid and benefits withdrawn) and the **unemployment trap** (where unemployed workers find that they can receive a higher income from remaining unemployed than by taking low paid jobs) were addressed by increasing benefits paid to those in low paid work and cutting benefit rates to those not in a job. Even so, low income families continued to face effective marginal tax rates of around 80 per cent. In another move, the government initiated the Restart programme in 1986 which forced any worker claiming benefits for being out of work to attend an interview at a Jobcentre at least once a year to review his or her position. Between 1986 and 1990, there was a dramatic fall in unemployment from 3.0 million to 1.6 million. Partly this was due to the Lawson boom in the economy. But the Restart programme was instrumental in getting many of the long term unemployed to cease claiming benefits for being unemployed, getting them onto training schemes or getting them reclassified so that they could receive invalidity benefits. From the viewpoint of increasing aggregate supply, only training leading to a subsequent job would have led to a shift to the right in the aggregate supply curve.

Repealing social legislation Legislation was passed during the 19th and early 20th centuries which protected the rights of women and children in the workplace in the UK. For instance, workers under the age of 18 were not allowed to work more than 48 hours a week or for more than 9 hours a day. Much of this legislation was still in force in 1979, although working conditions had changed considerably. The legislation was said to restrict the ability of employers to use young workers or women flexibly in the workplace and therefore discouraged their employment. The 1989 Employment Act repealed much of this legislation, effectively removing the special protection given in law to female and young workers. The UK has also resisted agreeing to European social legislation. In 1992, at Maastricht, it secured an opt-out clause for the Social Charter. Measures, such as giving women new maternity rights, which will be implemented in the other member countries, will not necessarily be passed into law in the UK.

Training and education Education and training are now recognised by the government as keystones of their supply side policies. In education, the government announced in 1988 that it would implement a National Curriculum in schools, one of the aims being to raise national standards in education. The establishment of city technology colleges and grant maintained schools was also designed to increase educational attainment levels. In higher education there was a large expansion of numbers taking degree courses in the late 1980s and early 1990s.

Vocational training has undergone change with the establishment of a national system of awards - NVQs (National Vocational Qualifications) and GNVQs (General National Vocational Qualifications) - which are replacing a large variety of different, often little known, awards. NVQs are work based qualifications whilst GNVQs are taught within schools and colleges. The government has set ambitious targets for the numbers of workers to have achieved different levels of these qualifications by the year 2000.

In the late 1980s, training provision was completly reorganised on a local basis. Each area had a local TEC (Training and Enterprise Council). Unlike previous training programmes, which were a partnership between trade unions, employers and government at a national level, TECs are dominated by employers at a local level. Much of their finance comes from national government but they also sell training packages to local businesses. The change from national to local provision was implemented because it was felt that local employers were best placed to decide on training needs in their local area.

Many of the schemes offered by TECs were offered before by government. For instance, training schemes offered to unemployed young workers were first introduced in the second half of the 1970s. The Youth Training Scheme was introduced in 1983 as a six month scheme for unemployed 16-17 year olds. In 1986, this was expanded to a possible 2 years for 16 year olds and 1 year for 17 year olds. Subsequently, 16-17 year olds lost the right to claim any form of benefit for being unemployed on the grounds that they ought to be in work, in full time education or on a guaranteed training scheme. The Employment Training Scheme began in 1988 and offered a year's training to unemployed adults. It replaced 34 different schemes which the government had previously been offering. The third major scheme was the Enterprise Allowance Scheme started in 1983 which offered financial assistance and training to those wanting to set up their own businesses. All these schemes were ended when the TECs became operational and TECs are now responsible for delivering training schemes for the unemployed and for providing support for those wanting to set up in business.

Reducing marginal tax rates Cutting direct taxes was high on the list of government priorities after 1979. The basic rate of tax was cut from 33 per cent in 1979 to 25 per cent by 1988, whilst the highest rate of tax on earned income fell from 83 per cent to 40 per cent. In 1992, a new lower rate of income tax was established at 20 per cent on the first few thousand pounds of taxable income. Income tax cuts were designed in part to increase incentives to work. Incentives to accumulate wealth were given by cuts in both inheritance tax and capital gains tax rates. Employers too have gained with the National Insurance Surcharge, a tax of $3\frac{1}{2}$ per cent on company wages paid by employers, being abolished in 1984. The UK has continued to have almost the lowest social security taxes on employers in Europe.

Pensions With fewer workers having life time work with a single employer, it has become important to ensure that mobile workers are not penalised in their pensions by shifting jobs. Personal pensions, pension rights which could be taken from job to job, became available from the mid-1980s. Whilst personal pensions are satisfactory for some, the evidence suggests that they have not been as successful as at first thought. First, workers have been unwilling to make the pension contributions needed to provide a satisfactory pension. It should be remembered that in ordinary pension schemes provided by employers, a typical 15 per cent of an employee's salary is put aside for pension contributions. Second, there was a gross mis-selling of personal pensions with many workers being persuaded to leave good employers' schemes to take out personal pensions which provided inferior benefits.

Housing Housing can be a major barrier to mobility. Housing policy since 1979 has, if anything, tended to discourage mobility and hence increase unemployment and reduce aggregate supply. Between 1981 and 1989, large differentials in house prices between regions in the UK opened up, making it difficult for workers to move from higher unemployment, low house price areas outside the south of England to lower unemployment, high house price areas in the south. The house price collapse since 1989, whilst reducing house price differentials between regions, has led to a stagnant housing market and negative equity. Many have been unable to sell their homes or have not been able to afford to sell. In the rented housing market, the policy of selling council houses to tenants from 1980 reduced the stock of affordable rented council housing. On the other hand, changes in rent controls in the late 1980s meant that landlords could, under certain circumstances, charge much higher rents. This, together with an increase in demand for rented accommodation resulting from the collapse of property prices, has led to some increase in renting at the top end of the market in the 1990s.

Small businesses are important because they provide jobs and can become the big businesses of tomorrow.

Help to businesses

If aggregate supply is to increase, the private sector needs to expand. Hence, according to supply side economists, the government needs to create an environment in which business can flourish.

Deregulation of the capital and money markets For instance, Big Bang in 1986 swept away the restrictive practices found in the City of London and particularly the Stock Exchange, making money and capital markets more competitive. The Building Societies Act 1986 gave Building Societies the power to compete with banks in offering a wide range of financial services. The abolition of exchange controls in 1979 allowed free movement of financial capital in and out of the UK.

Tax privileges for saving The tax system in the UK has traditionally favoured group savings schemes, such as pensions and assurance policies. It has therefore discouraged individuals from lending money directly to industrial companies, or buying shares in businesses. The government after 1979 wished to see a far more 'level playing field', where tax privileges are evened out between different types of saving. In particular, it has sought to establish a **share owning democracy**. Wider share ownership has been encouraged particularly through the privatisation programme and through Personal Equity Plans (PEPS), a scheme whereby investors in shares gain tax relief. At the same time, assurance companies have lost some of their tax privileges.

Reduction of public sector borrowing If government spends more than it receives, it will need to borrow the money. But if the government borrows the money, and the supply of money is fixed, that means there will less money for firms to borrow (i.e. there will be financial **crowding-out**). The government reduced its borrowing during the 1980s and in the late 1980s there was even a period of time when debt was repaid. However, the 1990s have seen a sharp deterioration again in the government's finances. The government has also seemed less concerned that financial crowding-out is an important factor in determining low investment in the economy.

Help to small businesses Small businesses are important in the economy (☞ unit 57) because they provide new jobs and can become the big businesses of tomorrow. The government, since 1979, has placed particular importance on the development of an 'enterprise culture'. For instance, the small companies' rate of corporation tax was reduced from 42 per cent in 1979 to 25 per cent by the early 1990s. Income tax for the self-employed was cut too, as described above. Reductions in the power of trade unions and the repeal of restrictive employment legislation has helped create a freer labour market for small businesses. The government encouraged the banks in the 1980s to increase their lending to small businesses. In 1981, it set up the Loan Guarantee Scheme, whereby the government guaranteed payment of 70 per cent of specified loans to small businesses. These loans were ones which banks would not normally make under their lending criteria (i.e. they were loans which carried above average risk for the banks). In the 1980s and early 1990s, the government gave tax breaks through the Business Expansion Scheme to investors willing to put money into small businesses. The Enterprise Allowance Scheme, where unemployed workers were given an allowance for setting up in business on their own, also encouraged the growth of small businesses. The government has also been very conscious of the amount of 'red tape' with which small businesses have to comply. It has attempted to reduce this. For instance, the burden of VAT administration has been reduced by various means.

Goods markets

It is argued that competition increases both productive and allocative efficiency. Markets should therefore be made as competitive as possible. Encouraging competition was central to government policy after 1979.

Deregulation and privatisation The government has concentrated on measures to make the public sector more competitive. A significant number of public corporations, like British Telecom and British Gas, have been privatised. Central government departments and local authorities have been encouraged to put such services as waste collection or cleaning to tender rather than employing staff directly to provide the service. Many controls have been abolished, one of which was the ending of some of the legal restrictions on pub opening hours. In 1994, the government finally succeeded in introducing new Sunday Trading regulations which have allowed shops to open legally on Sundays.

Elimination of state subsidies to inefficient producers If industries are making losses, this is a clear signal from the market place that the products of those industries are no longer wanted in such large quantities. Government propping up loss-making industries just to prevent unemployment results in a misallocation of resources. That money could be better used in growing industries in the economy. Hence, after 1979 government attempted to make all nationalised industries profitable (in the sense of private profit). In the case of industries like coal or shipbuilding, this has necessitated radical cuts both in plant and manpower. The government has refused to come to the help of declining industries in the private sector, despite calls for subsidies.

Encouragement of international free trade Fierce foreign competition results in a domestic industry which has to be efficient in order to survive. The government has had little sympathy for industrialists who have called for protectionist measures to save them from the effects of what they might call 'unfair' competition. In contrast to most other EC countries, the government has also welcomed inward investment, for instance from Japanese companies. The government argued that not only did these companies create wealth and jobs in the UK, but they also set competitive standards for existing UK firms to reach.

Regional and industrial policy

Before 1979, the main focus of supply side policies was regional and industrial policy. Since the time when manufacturing industry began to decline, arguably from the 1920s onwards, the UK government provided a variety of incentives to encourage firms to locate themselves in high unemployment areas. A variety of incentives have been used at different times:

- grants for new investment;
- tax relief on new investment;
- subsidies on employment;
- expenditure on infrastructure, such as motorways or factory buildings then available for subsidised rent;
- a requirement for firms to obtain permission from government to set up or expand in a low unemployment area of the UK (permissions called Industrial Development Certificates).

In the 1970s and early 1980s, the main incentive used was grants for new investment. It was felt that this was not only costly to the Exchequer, but also encouraged the siting of capital intensive manufacture rather than labour intensive manufacture or service industries in high unemployment areas. It was calculated, for instance, that the average cost between 1972 and 1983 to the government of creating an extra job in the assisted regions was £35 000 (at 1982 prices), whilst a total of 500 000 jobs had been created over the period (K Hartley and N Hooper, 1990).

In 1984, government implemented a new system of more selective regional assistance. The areas eligible for assistance were substantially reduced, and were graded into two levels: development areas and intermediate areas. Firms creating new jobs in development areas were automatically eligible for a regional development grant (RDG) of 15 per cent of investment expenditure up to a ceiling of £3 000 per new job created. Regional selective assistance (RSA) was made available to firms creating jobs or safeguarding jobs in both development and intermediate areas, but was discretionary. The Department of Industry attempted to provide the minimum financial support needed to secure the creation of new jobs.

The recession of 1990-92, which particularly affected the South of England but had far less impact on the rest of the country, led to a levelling out of disparities between regions. This led to a major review by government of the areas which could claim assistance. In future, only small areas, rather than whole regions, will be able to get regional development assistance. The South, for the first time, will have a number of areas which fall into this category. In addition, the EU provided regional grants, but these were not necessarily tied to specific job creation. They were provided for new road building or land reclamation, as well as the building of factories.

There have also been a large number of measures aimed at revitalising inner cities. The creation of Enterprise Zones, where companies setting up were offered tax incentives, reduced government 'red tape' and possibly subsidised premises, is one example of how government has attempted to regenerate old industrial areas.

Part-time workers win new rights

The UK's 6 million part-time workers are to have most of the statutory employment rights of those in full-time jobs, the government announced today. It will bring Britain in line with European Union equality laws. An estimated 750 000 employees, mainly women, working less than 16 hours a week and in continuous service with their employer for over two years, will now have rights covering unfair dismissal and redundancy payments, extended maternity leave, a written statement of employment, time off for union activities and notice of dismissal. Under current legislation passed in 1975 they have had to wait five years to qualify for equal treatment with full-time employees.

The decision follows a judgement against the government in the House of Lords earlier this year over the different legal rights of part-time and full-time workers.

The Lords' case was brought by the Equal Opportunities Commission, which claimed the law discriminated against women workers; 87 per cent of part-time workers are women. Ms Kamlesh Bahl, OEC chair, said last night she was 'delighted' at a 'major victory' for women workers. Mr John Monks, TUC general secretary, said trade unions would continue campaigning for complete equality between part-time and full-time workers.

Dr Ann Robinson, head of the Institute of Directors' policy unit, described the government's decision as 'another submission to a piece of nonsense legislation from Europe.' It was the 'thin end of the wedge' that would lead on to equal rights for part-timers in holiday entitlement and pension provision. The Federation of Small Businesses said it was gravely concerned about the effect of the decision on its members. Mr Robbie Gilbert, the Confederation of British Industry's employment affairs director, said the decision brought a 'welcome clarification to the law' though it would hit small employers.

The decision to grant new rights to part-time workers represents a humiliating climb down for the government. Only two weeks ago, it had vetoed a draft European Union directive on part-time workers. Mr Michael Portillo, then employment secretary, had said it would impose intolerable constraints on job creation. In announcing the decision to accept the House of Lords' ruling, he said the government was still convinced the removal from UK employment protection legislation of all existing distinctions based on the number of hours worked each week would make employers reluctant to create new part-time jobs for women and threaten the security of existing employees. The effects of the changes would be 'carefully monitored to assess their impact on business and on employment opportunities', he said. 'The government will reconsider the position in due course if objective evidence of adverse effects emerges.'

Source: adapted from the *Financial Times*, 21.12.1994.

The government has asked you to write a report on the possible effects of its decision to grant new rights to part-time workers in 1994. In your report:

1. **summarise the main changes and state who is likely to be affected by them;**
2. **using diagrams showing labour demand and supply curves, analyse the potential effect of the changes on employment and wages; in your answer contrast the predictions of industry with those who might argue that there will be little effect;**
3. **discuss the possible implications of the change for the aggregate supply curve of the UK economy;**
4. **assess whether equal rights should be given to part-timers for holiday entitlement and pension provision.**

INVESTIGATIONS 5

A. Consumer expenditure

Aims

- To gather appropriate data to investigate the relationship between consumer expenditure, the components of consumer expenditure and their determinants.
- To put forward hypotheses about the relationships between these economic variables.
- To correlate the data collected to establish whether there are any statistical relationships.
- To use these findings to make recommendations concerning business strategies.

The task

You are to assume that you are a private consultancy company. You have been approached by several companies which are seeking to expand their businesses.

- Company X is a company which has a cyclical demand for its product. It wishes to diversify and buy a company which has a relatively stable demand for its product when the economy goes into recession and incomes either grow more slowly or actually fall.
- Company Y is seeking to diversify and is interested in buying a furniture manufacturing company with the use of borrowed funds. It is worried about the extent to which an increase in interest rates, which would push up the costs of its borrowing, would affect the furniture business.
- Company Z is a conglomerate, producing a range of goods and services. It is thinking of increasing its investment expenditure in the next couple of years and wants to know whether you think it ought to proceed given the outlook for the economy in the medium term.

Your task is to give advice to each of these companies and make recommendations about their courses of action.

Research

Obtain figures for consumer expenditure (total and component categories), personal disposable income and the rate of interest (such as base rate and deposit account rate for selected retail banks) on a quarterly and yearly basis from *Economic Trends Annual Supplement* (data goes back to 1948). Update the figures from the latest edition of *Economic Trends*. A more detailed breakdown of consumer expenditure can be obtained from CSO, *Annual Abstract of Statistics*, but only annual figures are given over the past 10 years. CSO, *Monthly Digest of Statistics* gives quarterly figures but only for the previous 12 quarters.

Establish from textbooks what relationship you would expect to see between consumption expenditure and these other variables. What other variables might also influence total consumption or individual components of consumption?

You may have access to a computer data base such as SECOS. A powerful computer package will enable you to correlate data over time much more easily than if you have to do it by hand.

You could use newspaper and magazine articles to support your recommendations. Use articles which deal with the factors affecting consumption or the effect of changes in consumption on the economy.

Structuring your report

Introduction Outline the aim of your investigation. The aim should be put in the form of a hypothesis or question which will allow you to come to some conclusion.
Economic theory Outline the economic theory to be used in this investigation. This is likely to include concepts such as consumption, personal disposable income, wealth and interest rates.
Techniques used to collect your data Outline how you collected your data.
Presentation of evidence Using tables, graphs and any other appropriate diagrams, outline your findings. For instance, what are the trends in consumer expenditure? To what extent is total consumption determined by disposable income? What other factors, if any, determine consumption? To what extent is expenditure on food determined by interest rates?
Recommendations What recommendations would you make to each of the three companies? Your comments must be supported by evidence.
Sources Outline the sources of information you used. What problems did you encounter in gathering relevant data? What data would you have liked to have obtained but could not? To what extent was the data reliable?
Bibliography Write down a list of your sources in alphabetical order.

Other suggestions

It is possible to investigate a number of macro-economic relationships using data from *Economic Trends Annual Supplement* and the *Annual Abstract of Statistics*, together with *Economic Trends* and the *Monthly Digest of Statistics* (all published by CSO).

- The relationship between saving and its determinants such as income and the rate of interest.
- The relationship between investment and determinants such as past changes in income and the rate of interest.
- The relationship between imports and income.

B. The business cycle

Aims

- To outline a model of the business cycle.
- To investigate the characteristics and causes of the business cycle in post-war Britain.
- To use evidence to suggest which stage of the business cycle the UK economy is currently passing through.
- To analyse the contribution of government to stabilising the cycle or to creating fluctuations in the level of economic activity.

Research

Start by reviewing how economic theory characterises the business cycle and what it suggests might be the causes of the cycle. Make a list of those variables which change through the various stages of the cycle. Make another list of those variables, changes in which are argued to cause regular economic fluctuations.

Then, using CSO, *Economic Trends Annual Supplement*, chart the business cycle for the UK economy since 1948. Using recent newspaper articles, or publications such as the *Monthly Digest of Statistics* or *Economic Trends*, find figures for recent changes in output, prices, stocks, etc. in order to assess whether the UK economy is currently in the boom, slump, recession or recovery phase of the cycle.

In particular, consider recent figures for government spending and taxation. According to economic theory, these should act as automatic stabilisers over the cycle. If the economy is currently in recession, for instance, is there any evidence to suggest that tax receipts are slowing down or even falling; are social security payments related to unemployment rising? Investigate too, particularly by listening to the news on radio or television, or by reading the quality press, whether the government is using government spending and taxation to create a favourable economic climate for when it next has to call a general election. What evidence is there that this has been the case in the past?

Structuring your report

Introduction Outline the aim of your investigation. The aim should be put in the form of a hypothesis or question which will allow you to come to some conclusion.
The business cycle Using economic theory, describe the various phases of the typical business cycle. Explain how variables such as prices, investment, consumption and taxes change over the cycle. Use charts and diagrams wherever appropriate.
Techniques used to collect your data Outline how you collected your data.
The UK business cycle Using the data you have gathered, describe the UK business cycle in the post-war period. Identify peaks and troughs in the economy. Show how different variables have changed in the cycle. Suggest whether changes in any one variable have been particularly important in creating a boom or recession in the economy at any point in time. Again, use charts and diagrams wherever appropriate.
The current phase of the business cycle In what phase of the business cycle is the economy at the time of your investigation? Explain your reasoning carefully, backing up your arguments with evidence that you have gathered.
Causes of the business cycle Identify possible causes of the business cycle in the UK economy. You may be able to identify causes which are common throughout post-war British economic history. Alternatively, you may choose to concentrate on the possible causes of one or two booms or recessions in particular trade cycles.
The business cycle and the government To what extent are government spending and taxation acting as automatic stabilisers in the current phase of the cycle? To what extent is government overriding these automatic stabilisers for its own political gains and therefore creating a political stop-go cycle? What are likely to be the consequences of such manipulation for the economy after a general election?
Sources Outline the sources of information you used. What problems did you encounter in gathering relevant data? What data would you have liked to have obtained but could not? To what extent were the data reliable?
Bibliography Write down a list of your sources in alphabetical order

Other suggestions

Instead of considering the whole post-war period, you could choose to focus in on a particular fluctuation in the business cycle. For instance, you could investigate the nature and causes of the 1972-1976 phase of the business cycle.

Alternatively, you could concentrate your investigation on how one variable changes over the cycle.

- How has investment changed in the post-war period?
- Are the changes cyclical in nature?
- How has the money supply changed over the cycle?
- How has the current account on the balance of payments changed?

You could investigate the Kondratiev long wave cycle. Outline what he suggested was the cause of long wave cycles. Does the economic evidence from the UK support or refute his hypothesis?

Money, its supply and demand

Summary

1. Money has four functions: as a medium of exchange; a unit of account; a store of value; and a standard for deferred payment.
2. Characteristics of good money include acceptability, portability, durability, divisibility and limited supply.
3. In a modern economy, cash and sight deposits are the assets which best fulfil the function of a medium of exchange. These are known as narrow monies.
4. Near monies, assets which are good units of account and stores of value and can easily be converted into assets which are a medium of exchange, include time deposits in banks and building societies. Broad money is narrow money plus near money.
5. Money substitutes, such as credit cards, are items which act as a medium of exchange but are not stores of value.
6. The money supply is the total amount of money circulating in the economy.
7. Households and firms hold their wealth in money, in non-money financial assets or in physical assets. The opportunity cost of holding money is the benefits foregone from holding other financial or physical assets.
8. The demand for money varies with income and with the rate of interest.

Is this the only form of money?

The functions of money

Most people today in Britain, if asked 'what is money?', would reply 'notes and coins'. What is it about notes and coins that make them money, and is there anything else which possesses these same properties? If something is to be money, it must fulfil four FUNCTIONS (i.e. it must do four things).

A medium of exchange This is the most important function of money. Money is used to buy and sell goods and services. A worker accepts payment in money because she knows that she will be able to use that money to buy products in the shops.

There is no money in a BARTER economy. Exchange is conducted directly by swopping one good with another. For instance, a farmer might pay a dozen eggs to have his horse shod or a woman might trade a carpet for a cow. This requires a **double coincidence of wants**. If the blacksmith didn't want eggs, then he might refuse to shoe the farmer's horse. If the woman with a carpet was offered a horse instead of a cow, again she might refuse to trade. Barter requires that each party to the transaction wants what the other has to trade. This is costly and difficult, if not impossible, and therefore trade is discouraged. Without trade there can be no specialisation. Without specialisation, there can be little or no increase in living standards. So barter is associated with types of economy where individuals or small groups are self-reliant, and so the need for trade is small.

Money separates the two sides of a barter transaction. The farmer can sell his eggs for money. The blacksmith will accept money for shoeing the farmer's horse because he knows that he will be able buy the goods that he wants with the money.

Unit of account Money acts as a measure of value. If a dress costs £30 and a skirt costs £15, we know that the value of one dress equals the value of two skirts. At times of very high inflation, such as in Germany in 1923, money ceases to act as a unit of account. Prices may change by the hour. A dress costing £30 in the morning might only buy one skirt in the evening. High inflation therefore destroys the ability of money to perform this function. It is very difficult under a barter sytem to establish an agreed unit of account as people's opinions of the value of certain items differ greatly.

A store of value A worker who receives wages is unlikely to spend the money immediately. She may defer spending because it is more convenient to spend the money later. She will do this only if what she can buy in the future is approximately equal to what she can buy today. So money links the present and the future. It acts as a store of value. High inflation destroys this link because money in the future is worth far less than money today. In the German hyperinflation of 1923, people started to refuse payment in German money because it would lose so much value by the time they had spent it.

A standard for deferred payment If a person lends money today, she will only do so if she thinks that she will be able to buy roughly the same amount of goods when it is paid back. In trade, a company which accepts an order at a fixed price today for delivery and payment in a year's time will only do so if it is confident that the money it receives will have a value which can be assessed today. So again money must link different time periods when it comes to borrowed as well as saved money.

When money ceases to have this function, credit and borrowing collapse and this is very damaging to investment and economic growth in an economy.

QUESTION 1

Explain which of these items might be considered 'money' and which would not.

The characteristics of money

Pigs, silver, gold, teeth, and even wives have been used as money in the past. Some cultures today still use animals as currency. However most, if not all, of these have been unsatisfactory because of their characteristics. Ideally, money should be:

- acceptable to all - it is inconvenient if a type of money is only accepted in some shops but not others for instance;
- portable - pigs, for instance, are not easy to carry around and this limits the trade which is conducted using pigs as a medium of exchange;
- durable - pigs die and teeth deteriorate; ideally money should be durable over time;
- divisible - whole live pigs can't be used to buy the small things in life because they are too valuable; money must be capable of being split into small denominations;
- limited - if ordinary stones are used as money, prices of goods are likely to be very high in terms of stones because they are so easy to obtain;
- difficult to forge - forgeries make money worth less and can lead to its becoming unacceptable in exchange.

QUESTION 2 To what extent do each of the items in the previous question possess the characteristics of a good money?

Forms of money in a modern economy

In a modern economy there are a number of assets which can be classified as money.

Cash Cash means notes and coins. Cash is a **token money**. It has little or no intrinsic value (unlike gold which would be classified along with items such as pigs and cigarettes as **commodity money**). It is issued either by government or with the permission of government. Government reinforces the acceptability of cash by making it **legal tender**. This means that it must be accepted by law as a means of payment.

During much of the 19th century, bank notes were **convertible**. This meant that it was possible to go into a bank and convert the notes into something of real value: in this case, gold. However, more notes were issued than their value in gold. The value of notes and coins printed over and above the value of gold in bank vaults was called the **fiduciary issue**. Today UK bank notes are not convertible into gold and therefore all notes are **fiat** money, money made legal tender by government decree.

Cash is not perfect money. In the UK it is an almost perfect medium of exchange. But inflation affects three of the functions of money - those of a unit of account, a store of value and a standard of deferred payment. In 1975 for instance, UK inflation was nearly 25 per cent. Anyone holding £1 at the beginning of the year could only buy 75 pence worth of goods with it at the end of the year. The higher the rate of inflation, the less it can be said that cash is a 'good' money.

Money in current accounts Banks and building societies in the UK offer customers current account facilities.

Current accounts (called SIGHT DEPOSIT ACCOUNTS in economic theory) have two distinguishing features. First, cash can be withdrawn on demand from the account if it is in credit. So deposits can be immediately converted into money if the account holder so wishes. Second, account holders are provided with a cheque book. Cheques can be used to purchase goods and services. Cheque book money therefore is a medium of exchange. It is not perfect because people and firms can refuse to accept cheques in a transaction. Moreover, little or no interest is offered on accounts and so current account deposits lose value over time with inflation, damaging their store of value function. But deposits in current accounts are nearly as good a form of money as cash.

Near monies NEAR MONIES are assets which fulfil some but not all of the functions of money. In particular, they act as units of account and stores of value but cannot be used as mediums of exchange. However, they are convertible into a medium of exchange quickly and at little cost. (The ease with which an asset can be converted into money without loss of value is termed LIQUIDITY. The more liquid an asset, the more easily it is convertible into money.) In the UK, the most obvious type of near monies is TIME DEPOSITS with banks and building societies. They pay higher rates of interest than current accounts. They are therefore used more for saving and less for making transactions than current accounts. Depositors need to give notice if they wish to withdraw from the account (hence the term 'time' deposit). Alternatively, many accounts offer instant access if an interest rate penalty is paid (i.e. the saver loses money for the privilege of instant withdrawal).

Non-money financial assets All financial assets can be converted into money. However, for most assets the potential penalties for doing this are great. There can be a long waiting time for withdrawal and there can be considerable loss of money from conversion. This impairs their functions as units of account and stores of value. Economists do not classify these assets as money. Shares, for instance, are easily sold, but it can take up to a month to receive the money from the sale. Shares can also change value rapidly and are therefore not a good store of value (when share prices fall) or a standard for deferred payment (when share prices rise).

Money substitutes

Money is not the only means of payment for goods and services. Charge cards and credit cards have become increasingly important over the past 20 years as a medium of exchange. But they are not stores of value. This is because possession of a card does not show that the cardholder has money in the credit card account. The card only represents an ability to borrow money instantly. So credit cards are not money but they are MONEY SUBSTITUTES (i.e. they are used instead of money).

QUESTION 3 Emma Higgins has £250 in a building society share account. She owns a £100 000 house but owes £50 000 in the form of a mortgage loan. Her current account at her bank is in credit by £200 and she has an overdraft facility of £300. In her purse she has £20 in cash. She has recently purchased £50 worth of goods using her credit card. Her credit card limit is £1 000.

Explain how much money Emma Higgins possesses.

The money supply

The MONEY SUPPLY is the total amount of money circulating in the economy. It has been argued above that there is no financial asset which perfectly possesses all the functions of money. So financial assets can be placed on a spectrum as in Figure 70.1. At the left of the spectrum is the asset which comes closest to fulfilling most of the functions of money today - cash. At the other end are assets which are extremely illiquid, such as shares in companies not traded on a stock exchange. In between there is a range of assets. As we move right assets possess

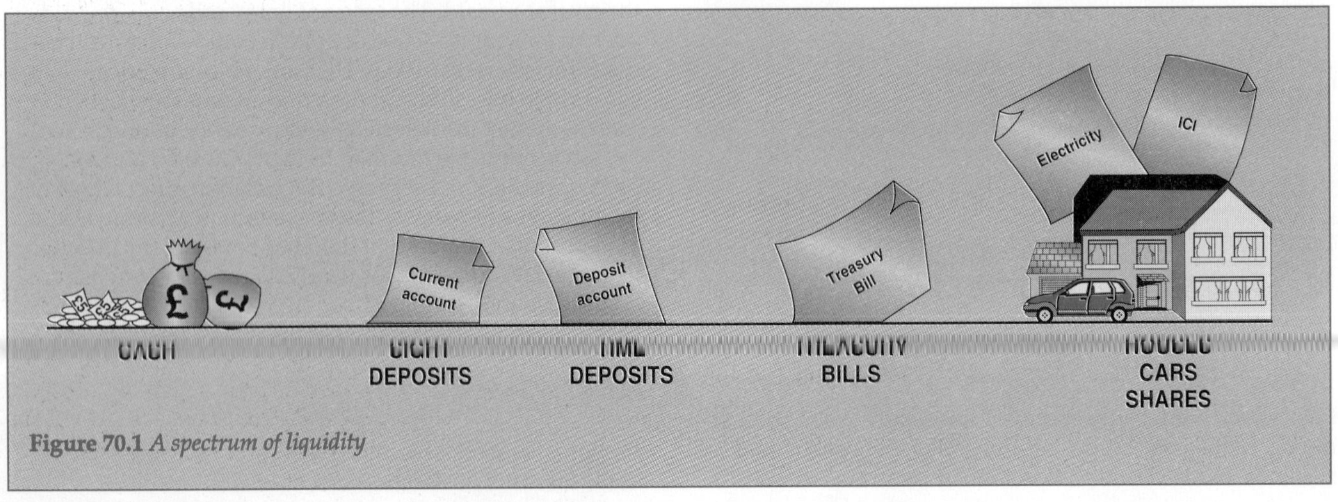

Figure 70.1 *A spectrum of liquidity*

fewer and fewer of the functions of money.

It is now clear that the cut off point between those assets which are money and those which are not is to some extent arbitrary. In the UK, there is a number of official definitions of the money supply. There are two broad types of money supply definition.

- NARROW MONEY - money which can be used as a medium of exchange.
- BROAD MONEY - narrow money plus near monies.

Current money supply definitions used in the UK are described below in the applied economics section.

The demand for money

Households and firms hold their wealth in a variety of different assets. Two main types of assets can be distinguished:

- **financial assets**, either monetary assets, such as cash and deposits in current accounts at banks, or non-money assets such as stocks and shares;
- **physical assets**, such as houses, buildings, cars, furniture, machinery, computers and inventories.

When economists talk about the DEMAND FOR MONEY, they do not refer to how much money people would like to have in a world where they were infinitely rich. What they mean is how much households and firms choose to hold in the form of money as opposed to holding either non-money financial assets or physical assets.

There is therefore an **opportunity cost** to a household if it holds £300 in cash. It could instead buy shares, and receive dividends and possibly capital gains. It could put money into a pension plan and increase the value of pension payments at some time in the future, or it could buy a new television and enjoy the services which it provides. Hence the price of holding money is the benefits foregone from holding another type of asset.

The demand for money is determined by two main factors.

Income The higher the level of income in the economy, the greater the demand for money. This is because the higher the level of income, the greater will be spending in the economy. The more households spend, the more money they need to use to complete transactions.

The rate of interest One of the alternative uses for money is to buy financial assets which yield interest. A household could, for instance, hold bonds which are issued by the government and on which interest is payable. The higher the rate of interest, the greater the opportunity cost of holding money. If interest rates on government bonds are 5 per cent, then the opportunity cost of holding £100 for one year in money is £5 in lost interest. If the rate of interest is 20 per cent, the opportunity cost is £20.

Figure 70.2 shows this relationship between the demand for money and interest rates and income. The higher the rate of interest, the lower will be the demand for money. A rise in income would shift the demand for money curve to the right, from MD_1 to MD_2. This is because a rise in income raises the demand for money at any given rate of interest. Conversely, a fall in income would lead to a shift in the demand for money curve to the left.

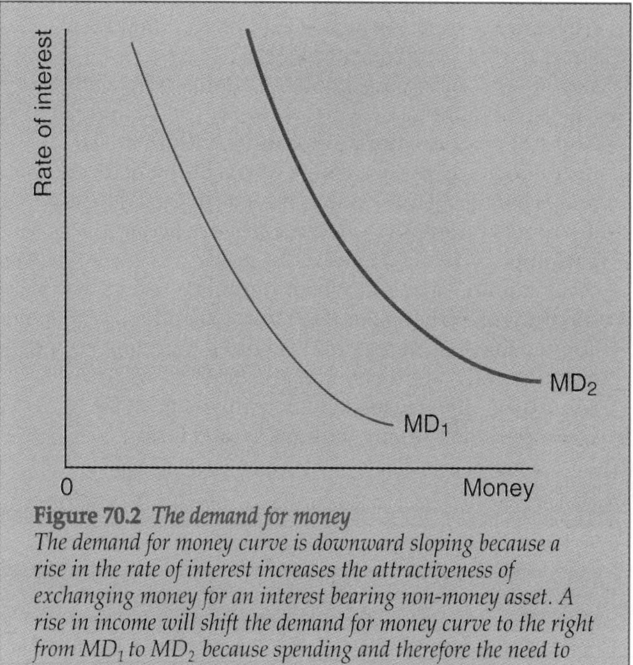

Figure 70.2 *The demand for money*

The demand for money curve is downward sloping because a rise in the rate of interest increases the attractiveness of exchanging money for an interest bearing non-money asset. A rise in income will shift the demand for money curve to the right from MD_1 to MD_2 because spending and therefore the need to have money to spend will rise.

QUESTION 4 Kim Yip has £250 in cash, £500 in a building society account earning 5 per cent per annum interest, £400 worth of government bonds with a market rate of interest of 7 per cent, £900 worth of British Telecom shares earning a 3 per cent dividend, a house valued at £70 000 on which there is a mortgage of £40 000, furniture and personal possessions insured for £30 000, and a car worth £2 500 secondhand.

(a) What might be the opportunity cost for Kim of holding: (i) the £250 in cash; (ii) the £900 in British Telecom shares; (iii) the £70 000 house?

(b) Long term interest rates on government bonds rise by 3 per cent, all other things being equal. How might this affect Kim's holding of money?

Key terms

Functions of money - money must be a medium of exchange, a store of value, a unit of account and a standard for deferred payment.
Barter - swopping one good for another without the use of money.
Sight deposit accounts - Accounts with financial institutions where deposits are repayable on demand and where a cheque book is issued. In the UK, they are more commonly called current or cheque accounts.
Near money - an asset which cannot be used as medium of exchange in itself but is readily convertible into money and is both a unit of account and a store of value.
Liquidity - the degree to which an asset can be converted into money without capital loss.
Time deposit accounts - accounts where interest is paid but savers are not able to withdraw without either giving notice or paying an interest rate penalty.
Money substitutes - those which can be used as a medium of exchange but which are not stores of value. Examples are charge cards or credit cards.
Money supply - the total amount of money in circulation in the economy.
Narrow money - money which is primarily used as a medium of exchange.
Broad money - narrow money plus near monies.
The demand for money - the total amount of money which households and firms wish to hold at a point in time.
The demand for money - the total amount of money which households and firms wish to hold at a point in time.

Applied economics

The money supply in the UK

There is no single definition of money because no financial asset possesses all the characteristics or fulfils all the functions of money perfectly. A variety of different financial assets possess some of the functions to some degree, and hence it is possible to provide a number of definitions of the money supply. In the United States, over 40 definitions are used, but for the UK there are only 2 main measures (M0 and M4) calculated by the Bank of England together with another 3 (M2, M3H and M4c) which are rarely commented on. Figure 70.3 shows the relationship between the different measures of the money supply.

- M0 is the narrowest definition of the money supply. It is equal to the notes and coins in circulation together with cash in the tills of banks and the balances held by banks with Bank of England for operational reasons (☞ unit 71).
- M2 is notes and coins in circulation plus retail account deposits with banks, building societies and the National Savings Bank. These retail deposits with banks are both cheque book accounts, which offer little or no interest, and savings accounts. Deposit accounts at building societies are special accounts which tend to be used by charities, social clubs etc. rather than ordinary customers who tend to put their money into share accounts. The National Savings Bank account is a low interest ordinary account.
- M4 is approximately equal to M2 plus money in building society share accounts and private sector holdings of certificates of deposit (☞ unit 71 for an explanation of certificates of deposit).

M0 and M2 are **narrow monies**. This means that notes and coins in circulation together with money in bank accounts are used mainly as a medium of exchange. Households and firms hold this money to use to buy goods with. M4 is a definition of **broad money**, money which is used for both spending and for saving. These definitions are not perfect. For instance, money in high-interest accounts at banks, included in M2, are mostly held as savings. Equally, much of what is held in building society share accounts, included in M4, is held for spending purposes rather than as longer term savings. The problem for the Bank of England, which compiles the statistics, is that it is impossible to know exactly which monies are being held for transactions purposes and which for savings.

The other two definitions of the money supply currently calculated are M4c and M3H. M4c is approximately M2 plus all foreign currency deposits held with UK banks and building societies. This is a measure which might be useful when considering the impact of foreign currency flows on the money supply and therefore on the economy in the UK. M3H is a slightly broader measure of M4c. It is approximately M4c plus sterling and foreign currency deposits held by UK public corporations with banks and building societies. It has been published to provide a money supply figure which is similar to money supply figures calculated by other EU countries, and therefore allows comparisons between countries of changes in broad money in individual economies.

The difficulty of defining what is money in the UK can

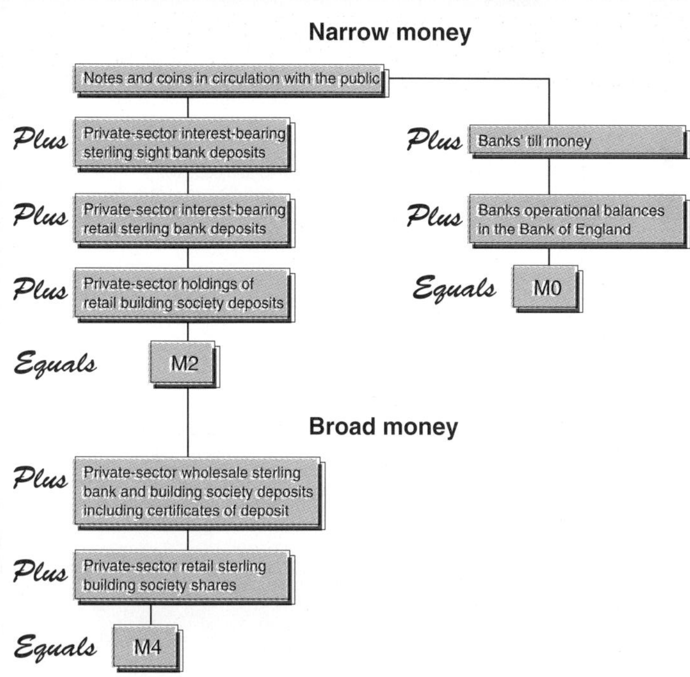

Figure 70.3 *Relationships between measures of the money supply*

also be illustrated by looking at the changing nature of building societies. 30 years ago, money in building society accounts was quite clearly savings, and not typically used for transactions purposes. In the 1970s and the1980s, however, building societies began to compete more aggressively with banks. A growing proportion of building society customers used their accounts as they would a bank cheque account to store money briefly before spending it. Building societies encouraged this by expanding their branch networks, making it easier for customers to pay in and withdraw money. They also began to offer cheque book accounts. So building society share account money has increasingly become part of narrow money.

The Abbey National provides another example of how building societies have affected the money supply. In 1989 the Abbey National changed its legal status from that of a building society to a bank. Before this date, the Bank of England had published figures for M1 and M3, which were two measures of notes and coins in circulation plus money in bank accounts. The change meant that suddenly these measures jumped by the value of deposits with the Abbey National. The Bank of England decided to abandon calculation of M1 and M3 because there would now be no continuity between the pre-1989 and post 1989 figures. They were also afraid that a number of other building societies would follow the Abbey National in becoming banks, which would distort even further the statistics.

Figure 70.4 shows the relative size of each of the 3 main measures of the money supply currently calculated. Note that M0 is a fraction of the size of M4. Most money today is bank and building society deposit and share money.

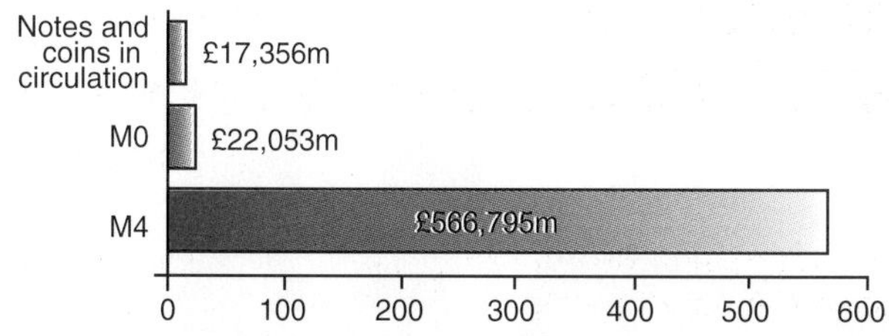

Source: adapted from CSO, *Monthly Digest Of Statistics.*

Figure 70.4 *The relative sizes of different measures of the money supply, 1994*

DATA QUESTION

Money in the UK

A manufacturer of bank notes and plastic cards has commissioned a report on prospects in the UK market for money. Write the report:

(a) distinguishing between money and money substitutes;

(b) explaining how the market for (i) money and (ii) money substitutes has changed over the period;

(c) discussing how means of payment are likely to change in the future and the implications this will have for the money supply in the UK.

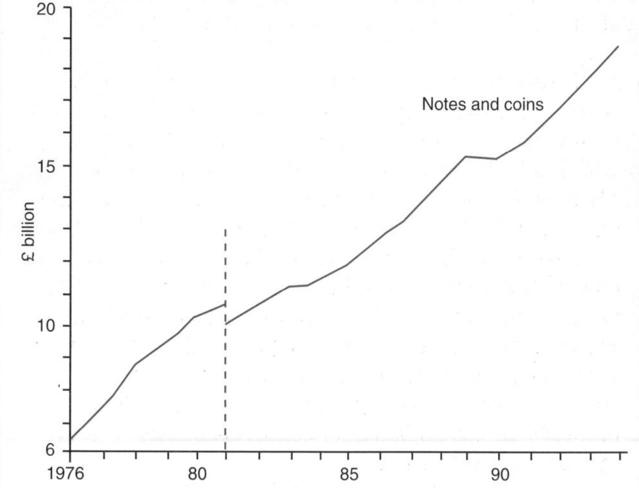

Note. Discontinuity in 1981.
Source: adapted from CSO, *Financial Statistics.*

Figure 70.5 *Notes and coins in circulation (with the M4 private sector)*

Great Britain				Percentages			
	1976	1981	1984	1989	1990	1991	1992
All payments							
Cash[1]	93	88	86	80	78	78	76
Non-Cash	7	12	14	20	22	22	24
Non-cash payments							
Cheque	68	68	64	55	52	50	46
Standing order/ direct debit	21	20	22	23	23	24	25
All plastic payment cards	7	9	13	18	20	23	25
of which -							
Credits/charge card	6	8	12	15	15	14	14
Retailer card	-	1	-	1	1	1	1
Debit card	0	0	0	2	4	8	11
Other[2]	2	2	1	4	4	3	4

1 Cash payments under fifty pence in 1976, and £1 from 1981 onwards, are excluded.

2 Includes deductions made directly from wages and salaries, and payments made by Postal Order.

Source: CSO, *Social Trends*, 1994.

Table 70.1 *Consumer payment: by method (GB, percentages)*

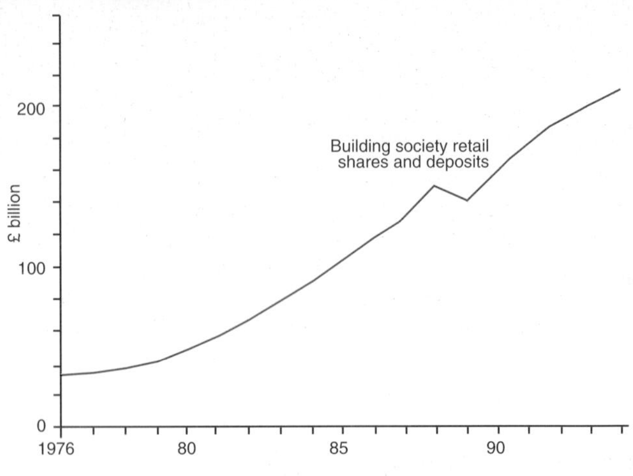

Source: adapted from CSO, *Financial Statistics.*

Figure 70.6 *Building society retail shares and deposits*

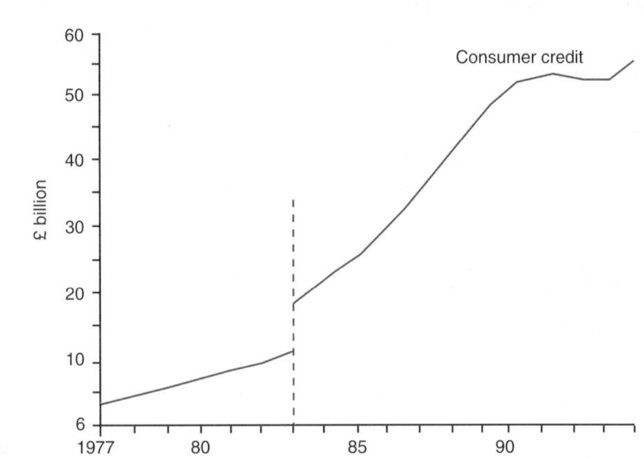

Note. Discontinuity in 1983.
Source: adapted from CSO, *Financial Statistics.*

Figure 70.7 *Consumer credit*

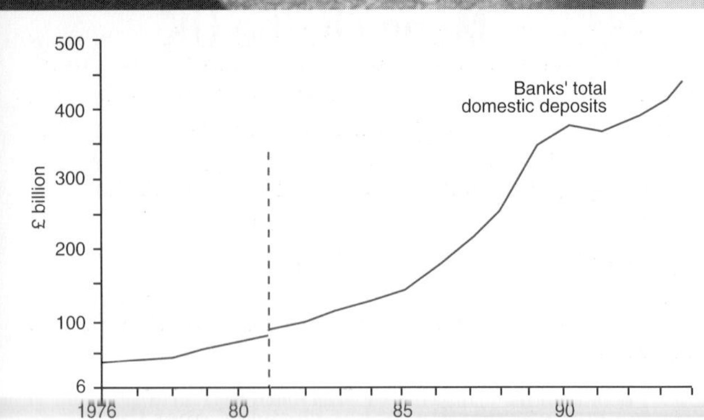

Note. Discontinuity in 1981.
Source: adapted from CSO, *Financial Statistics.*

Figure 70.8 *Bank domestic deposits*

The creation of money

Summary

1. Commercial banks are financial intermediaries that borrow and lend money.
2. Banks have the power to create money because they need only retain a fraction of the cash which is deposited with them. The rest can be loaned out, leading to an increase in the money supply.
3. A new £1 deposited in the banking system will lead to an increase of up to £1 times the credit multiplier in the volume of bank credit and therefore the money supply.
4. The credit multiplier is 1 divided by the reserve ratio.
5. The monetary base of the economy is the name given to the stock of money which banks or other financial intermediaries need to have in order to be able to create credit.

The commercial banks

Commercial banks, such as the Midland Bank or Barclays Bank, are **financial intermediaries**. They link customers together, just as supermarkets link shoppers with food manufacturers. They provide a wide range of financial services including money transmission services. But their main activity is the borrowing and lending of money. They borrow from customers who place money in a variety of different accounts. They then lend money to individuals, businesses and governments. They make a profit by charging a higher rate of interest on loans than they pay on the money they have borrowed.

Credit creation in a single bank system

In the process of borrowing and lending money, banks have the ability to create money. To explain why, some simplifying assumptions need to be made.

- There is only one bank in the economy.
- The public already holds enough money to satisfy its needs and any new money it receives will be deposited with the bank.
- The bank, by law, has to hold 10 per cent of its deposits in cash.

When a customer deposits cash with the bank, the bank will not keep that money in its vaults. It knows that customers, on average, do not demand all of their money back all at once. On any one day, the bank might have to pay back say 10 per cent of deposits made by the public.

The public will also be depositing money with the bank on that day, so it only needs to keep less than 10 per cent of its customers' total deposits in cash on a day to day basis. The more its customers use cheques and money substitutes like credit cards, the less it will need to keep in cash. In the UK today, the major banks only keep between 1 and 2 per cent of total deposits in the form of cash. The ratio between the amount of cash a bank has to keep and its **total liabilities** (the money the bank owes to its customers) is called the **cash ratio**. The cash ratio is an example of a RESERVE RATIO. With a cash ratio, cash is the reserves in the banking system (other assets such as gold could equally be used as reserves). We have assumed above that the reserve ratio is 10 per cent. Today's banking system is called a FRACTIONAL RESERVE BANKING SYSTEM because banks only keep a fraction of total deposits as reserves.

Table 71.1 shows the balance sheet of the one bank in the economy. Liabilities (what the bank owes) are placed on the left hand side whilst assets (what the bank owns) are put on the right. A 'balance sheet' is so called because the liabilities must equal the assets. Customers have deposited £100m with the bank. Thus the bank has liabilities of £100m to its customers. The bank will not keep this in its vaults. It knows that it only needs to keep £10m in cash to satisfy the day to day requirements of its customers. It can lend out the other £90m. This will earn interest and make profit for the bank.

Now assume that the government prints an extra £10m in notes. It gives these to the general public in the form of a tax rebate. It was assumed above that the public was already satisfied with its holdings of cash. So it will deposit all of the £10m with the bank. The new balance sheet will look as in Table 71.2. The bank assets are now £20m in cash and £90m in loans. But it does not need to hold £20m in cash. With a cash ratio of 10 per cent, it only needs to hold £11m in cash (£110m x 10 per cent). It could

Table 71.1 *Balance sheet of a single bank*

£ million

Liabilities		Assets	
Deposits	100	Cash	10
		Loans	90
Total	100		100

Table 71.2 *Balance sheet following the deposit of £10m cash*

£ million

Liabilities		Assets	
Deposits	110	Cash	20
		Loans	90
Total	110		110

Table 71.3 *Balance sheet following the loan and redeposit of £9m*

£ million

Liabilities		Assets	
Deposits	119	Cash	20
		Loans	99
Total	119		119

Table 71.4 *Final balance sheet following an additional £10m cash in the economy*

£ million

Liabilities		Assets	
Deposits	200	Cash	20
		Loans	180
Total	200		200

lend out the extra £9m. When it lends out the £9m, the money will probably be spent and returned as a new deposit to the bank (remember the public already holds all the cash it wants to hold). The new balance sheet will look as in Table 71.3. Loans have increased to £99m. The bank still has £20m in cash because, although it lent out £9m in cash, the cash was redeposited with the bank. Liabilities have increased by £9m to £119m.

The bank now holds £20m in cash but only has liabilities of £119m. Its cash ratio is well above 10 per cent. It only needs to hold £11.9m in cash. So it will lend out a further £8.1m (£20m - £11.9m). This will be spent and redeposited with the bank, allowing it to further increase its loans. This process will carry on until the bank achieves a cash ratio of 10 per cent. This is shown in Table 71.4. Total assets and liabilities are £200m. Therefore with cash of £20m, its cash ratio is 10 per cent. £180m have been lent out to customers. This represents an equilibrium position for a bank seeking to maximise profits.

It cannot lend out any more because, although the amount of cash it would have would remain the same (customers keep on returning cash lent out to the bank), its assets and liabilities would be too great in relation to its holdings of cash. For instance, with £20m cash and £400m in liabilities, its cash ratio would fall to 5 per cent, below the legal minimum. The cash ratio therefore sets a limit on a bank's ability to borrow and lend money.

Note that an extra £10m in cash has led to a growth of £100m in deposits at the bank. Deposits in the bank are part of the money supply (☞ unit 70). So the bank has created an extra £90m (£100m - £10m) of money in the system. This money does not belong to the bank. It belongs to customers. But the bank is happy to help create this money for its customers because it can make a profit by lending it out at higher rates of interest than it borrows it for.

QUESTION 1

Table 71.5 *Balance sheet of a single bank*

£ million

Liabilities		Assets	
Deposits	400	Cash	40
		Loans	360
Total	400		400

There is one bank in an economy which has to keep a cash ratio of 10 per cent. Its initial balance sheet is shown in Table 71.5. All money lent out by the bank is redeposited in the bank. The bank always aims to maximise its loan book subject to the 10 per cent cash ratio. The government gives customers a tax rebate of £60 million cash which they deposit in the bank. Draw up balance sheets showing the assets and liabilities of the bank:

(a) stage 1 immediately following the deposit of the money;
(b) stage 2 after the bank has initially lent out part of the £60 million;
(c) stage 3 after the bank has received new deposits from the money lent out;
(d) the final stage when the bank is in equilibrium.

The credit multiplier

In the above example, an injection of £10m in cash to the banking system led to a final increase of £100m in the money supply. So the initial £10m was multiplied ten fold. The value of this multiplier is given a variety of names. It is called the CREDIT MULTIPLIER, or MONEY MULTIPLIER, or BANK MULTIPLIER or BANK DEPOSIT MULTIPLIER. The increase in the money supply is given by the formula:

$$(C) + (C \times 0.9) + (C \times 0.9 \times 0.9) + \ldots$$

where C is the initial cash injection to the bank and 0.9 is the fraction of any new cash which can be lent out by the bank. This is shown in diagrammatic form in Figure 71.1 where it is assumed that £10 cash is injected into the banking system and there is a 10 per cent reserve ratio.

The above is a geometric progression and the value of the final increase can be calculated more easily by multiplying the initial cash injection by the credit multiplier, the formula for which is:

$$\text{Credit multiplier} = \frac{1}{\text{reserve ratio}}$$

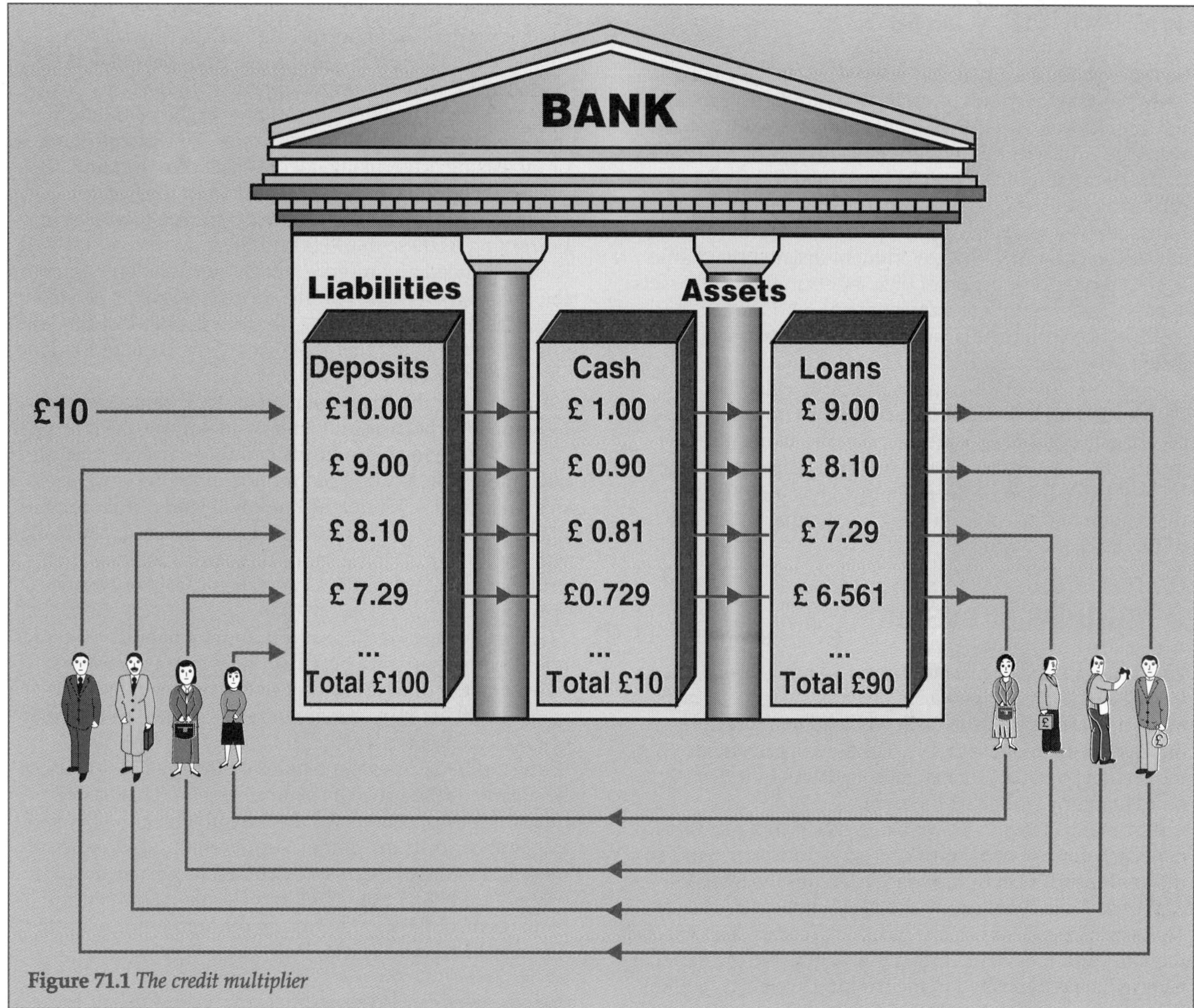

Figure 71.1 *The credit multiplier*

For instance, if banks have to keep 10 per cent of their deposits in the form of cash, then the reserve ratio is 10 per cent or 0.1. The credit multiplier is then 1÷ 0.1 or 10. A £10 increase in cash in the system increases the money supply by £10 x 10 or £100.

The larger the reserve ratio, the smaller will be the value of the credit multiplier. For instance, if the banks have to keep 20 per cent of the assets in cash, then the reserve ratio is $^1/_5$. The credit multiplier is therefore 1÷ $^1/_5$ or 5. If banks have to keep only 1 per cent in cash, then the credit multiplier is 1÷ $^1/_{100}$ or 100.

In practice, the credit multiplier is smaller than the above formula would suggest. This is because the public do not redeposit all the cash that they receive when banks lend out money. They keep back some of it mainly to use in day to day transactions. The larger the proportion of cash lent out by banks that the public keeps rather than redepositing, the smaller will be the value of the money multiplier. Note that the reserve ratio is a minimum ratio. If banks by law have to maintain a 10 per cent cash ratio, then it would be illegal for them to have a 6 per cent cash ratio, but legally they could have a 12 per cent or 20 per cent cash ratio if they so wished. However, in practice, banks are likely to wish to maintain the lowest reserve ratio possible because reserve assets, such as cash, yield little or no financial return.

QUESTION 2 There is only one bank in an economy. All money loaned out by the bank is redeposited with the bank. Cash is the only reserve asset required to be held by banks. By how much will the money supply increase if the reserve ratio and the initial sum of new cash deposited in the bank are:

(a) 10 per cent and £500m;
(b) 20 per cent and £100m;
(c) 25 per cent and £200m;
(d) 50 per cent and £1000m;
(e) 5 per cent and £1bn;
(f) 1 per cent and £120m?

The monetary base

So far we have assumed that reserve assets have been cash. But they need not be cash. Two hundred years ago when gold was the equivalent of cash, and bank notes were the equivalent of modern day cheques, it was gold that was the reserve asset. The banks had to keep back a certain amount of gold to satisfy the day to day transactions demands of their customers. During the 1960s and 1970s in the UK, the government insisted that banks keep a certain proportion of their assets in financial assets such as Treasury Bills, commercial bills and money at short notice with the discount houses. These assets were called 'reserve assets'.

RESERVE ASSETS are sometimes also called HIGH POWERED MONEY. The money is 'high powered' because its possession enables the banks to create extra money. Equally, reserve assets are sometimes called the MONETARY BASE of the economy. They are the base of the system because it is on this base that banks are able to build the credit pyramid.

A multi-bank system

We can now drop the last of our simplifying assumptions. It has been shown that in a single bank system, an increase in reserve assets, such as cash, will lead to a multiple increase in the money supply. The bank has created money. The overall conclusion is no different if there is more than one bank in the system.

Assume that there are two banks. One bank receives a new cash deposit of £10m. The reserve ratio is 0.1 and so the bank keeps £1m in cash and lends out the £9m. We cannot say into which bank the £9m will be redeposited. That will depend on which customers receive the £9m and the market shares of the respective banks. We can say that £9m will be redeposited in the banking system as a whole. We can also predict that the two banks between them will keep £0.9m and lend out £8.1m. By the time the process has finished, the banking system as a whole will have created £90m of bank money to add to the £10m cash. But depending upon competition in the banking industry, different banks will have created different amounts within that total.

Asset and liability management

So far, we have outlined a banking system where the amount of reserves that a bank holds determines its total assets and loans. For instance, with a 10 per cent cash ratio system, a bank holding £10 cash can create a total of £90 in loans, with total assets and liabilities being £100. This type of **asset management** system can be found in the United States, Germany, Australia, New Zealand, South Africa, Mexico and Venezuela.

However, in the UK, banks use a **liability management** system. In this sort of system, banks decide whether they wish to increase their loans. If they do, then they go out and borrow the money to finance the loans. The attraction of lending out more money is that banks can earn interest on the loans. On the other hand, the more they lend out, the higher the cost of borrowing the funds to achieve those loans. The funds could come from personal customers increasing their deposits with the bank. To persuade them to lend more money to the bank might involve offering higher interest rates, lower bank charges or increasing advertising, all of which cost the bank money. The funds could also come from the London wholesale money markets. However, large increases in borrowing in these markets will push up interest rates. If the banks need any reserve assets, they will 'buy' them in the financial markets. For instance, if UK banks needed extra cash, they could buy cash from the Bank of England and pay for it using their balances at the Bank of England (☞ applied section).

Under a liability management system, banks decide how much to borrow and lend by looking at the marginal cost of borrowing extra funds and the marginal revenue to be gained from lending out more. If marginal cost is less than marginal revenue, the bank will lend out more. If marginal cost is greater than marginal revenue, the bank will cut its borrowings. Banks therefore maximise their profits where MC = MR (as neo-classical theory argues ☞ unit 26).

The process of credit creation under a liability system is no different than under an asset management system. However, the limit to the amount of money that banks create is not set by a scarcity of reserve assets (a **quantity** of financial assets). Instead, it is set by the cost of acquiring those assets in relation to the revenues that can be obtained (the **price** of financial assets). This has very important implications for the way in which the Bank of England controls the money supply through the price of money, the rate of interest (discussed in greater detail in units 77 and 78). In the USA and Germany, the central banks control the money supply through manipulating the quantity of reserve assets.

Key terms

Reserve ratio or reserve asset ratio - the ratio between the assets which the bank has to keep to meet either customer or legal requirements and the total amount deposited with the bank.
Fractional reserve banking system - a system in which banks only keep a fraction or proportion of total customer deposits in reserves and lend out the rest.
Credit multiplier, or money multiplier or bank multiplier or bank deposit multiplier - the number of times a change in reserve assets will change the money supply.
Reserve assets, high powered money or the monetary base - those assets which banks have to keep either because they are needed to satisfy customers' requirements (like cash) or because the government insists upon them during times of regulation.

Applied economics

UK banks and the creation of money

The UK clearing banks

The four largest clearing banks in the UK are Lloyds, Barclays, Midland and National Westminster. Traditionally, one of their main functions has been to borrow money from customers who make deposits in **current accounts** or **deposit accounts**. The banks lend out that money in the form of overdrafts or loans. Sometimes the clearing banks are called **high street banks** or **retail banks**. Both of these names refer to the fact that the clearing banks get a large proportion of their total funds from millions of customers through a network of branches in the UK.

'Clearing banks' are so-called because these banks clear cheques. For instance, a customer of Barclays bank may write out a cheque to a customer of Lloyds. The Lloyds customer will accept the cheque because she knows that Barclays bank is prepared to transfer money to Lloyds upon receipt of the cheque. On any one day, millions of cheques need to be cleared. This is done through a number of regional clearing houses including the principal **clearing houses** in London. Banks send cheques to clearing houses to be sorted. Then balances are transferred between banks. For instance, if Lloyds has £500 million worth of cheques drawn on Barclays bank and Barclays Bank has £750 million worth of cheques drawn on Lloyds Bank then Lloyds will transfer £250 million to Barclays.

Balance sheets

The major UK clearing banks today are financial conglomerates, offering a complete range of financial services to their customers, but their traditional business has been the borrowing and lending of money. The ways in which banks borrow and lend money can be seen from their **balance sheets**. Table 71.6 shows the combined balance sheet of UK clearing banks in March 1995. The balance sheet can be divided into two: the assets of banks in pounds sterling and in foreign currencies, and their liabilities.

Almost all liabilities (i.e. money that the banks owe to their customers or clients) are deposits of one type or another. 'Notes outstanding' are notes issued by the Scottish and Northern Ireland banks. Like the Bank of England, they have the legal power to issue £5, £10, £20 and £50 pound notes. They are a liability to these banks because holders of these notes can return them to the issuing bank and demand payment in another form such as English bank notes. Certificates of deposit are long term bonds issued by the banks mainly to raise finance for long term loans to companies or governments. Items in suspense and transmission etc. are items such as monies received but unaccounted for and monies being transferred between accounts.

The assets of the banks (i.e. what the bank owns) range in liquidity and profitability. In general the less liquid the asset the more profitable it is (☞ unit 75). So banks try to keep as much of their assets as is prudent in the form of advances. The rest of their balance sheet is made up of more liquid assets which provide a buffer in case of a run on the bank.

- Cash. Less than 1 per cent of assets is kept in the form of cash. Banks know that that is all they need to satisfy the everyday transaction needs of their customers.
- Balances with the Bank of England. The banks have to keep 1/2 per cent of their **eligible liabilities** (broadly the sterling resources of the banks) in a non-interest bearing account with the Bank of England. These could be used to control the money supply through monetary base control (☞ unit 77). In practice they are used as a cheap source of finance by the Bank of England and to settle the day to day clearing needs of the banks.
- Market loans. Banks lend money **at call and short notice**. This means that the money can be recalled very quickly should the need arise. Call money is money which can be recalled immediately. Banks lend money to other banks in the **inter-bank market**. They also lend money to **discount houses** in the discount market (☞ unit 73).
- Certificates of deposit (CDs). Banks borrow money by issuing **certificates of deposit** but they also hold them for liquidity reasons. An equivalent would be homeowners who owe a building society £30 000 on a mortgage and have £1 000 with the same building society in a share account. They don't use the £1 000 to pay off the mortgage today because they may need to withdraw £500 next week.
- Local authority loans. Banks lend money to local authorities who use the money to finance capital projects such as the building of sports centres or road building.
- Bills. These are short term loans (normally maturing within 91 days of issue). Bills offered for sale by the government are called **Treasury Bills**. When issued by firms they are known as **commercial bills**. Local authorities also issue bills to finance their day to day activities.
- Bonds. Banks buy bonds issued not only by the government (called gilt-edged stock) but also by individual firms.
- Advances. Advances are the single most important asset of banks. Advances earn banks the highest rate of interest and therefore they try to maximise the level of advances subject to constraints of liquidity and prudence.

Table 71.6 *Retail banks: balance sheet, March 1995*

	£ million
Liabilities	
Sterling liabilities	
Notes outstanding	2 104
Deposits: UK private sector	454 634
Certificates of deposit and other short term paper	66 258
Other	80 017
Foreign currency deposits	938 475
Sterling and other currency liabilities: items in suspense and transmission, capital and other funds	87 832
Total liabilities	1 629 220
Assets	
Sterling assets	
Notes and coins	3 695
Balances with Bank of England	1 539
Market loans: Discount houses	6 806
Other UK banks	93 216
UK bank CDs	24 739
Building society CDs & time deposits	5 036
UK local authorities	1 656
Overseas	39 741
Bills: Treasury Bills	6 914
Eligible bank bills	13 342
Other	655
Advances: UK public sector	3 358
UK private sector	386 942
Overseas	12 814
Banking department lending to central government (net)	753
Investments: British government stocks	15 377
Other	43 017
Miscellaneous assets	31 417
Other currency assets	
Market loans and advances	749 921
Investments	148 375
Other	28 800
Total assets	1 629 220

Source: adapted from *The Bank of England Quarterly Bulletin.*

The credit multiplier

To what extent can UK banks create money (i.e. what is the value of the credit multiplier for the clearing banks)? They must keep at least 1/2 per cent of their eligible liabilities (eligible liabilities in March 1995 were only £1 489m) with the Bank of England. In addition, they need to keep a proportion of their liabilities in the form of cash to satisfy day to day withdrawals by their customers. The cash ratio has fallen over time as greater use has been made of cheques, credit cards and debit cards for transactions purposes. As can be seen from the balance sheet in Table 71.6, the banks kept approximately 0.2 per cent (£5 184m ÷ £1 629 220m) of their assets as cash plus deposits at the Bank of England. So it might seem that the current credit multiplier for banks is approximately 500 (1 ÷ 0.002). (Note that this is the credit multiplier for money in the UK and for overseas money dealt with by the banks. It is possible but more complicated to calculate a credit multiplier for sterling assets alone.)

However, because UK banks run under a liability management system, this sort of calculation is irrelevant when considering how much banks are willing to lend. After all, the banks can always buy notes and coins from the Bank of England and the Bank of England is always prepared to accept new deposits from the Banks. There are, in fact, three important considerations taken into account by banks when deciding how much to lend.

First, they need to keep a proportion of their assets in forms which are more liquid than advances. If there were ever a run on a bank (i.e. suddenly a large number of customers wanted their money back because they were afraid that the bank would go bankrupt), the bank would want to liquidate some of its assets very quickly to obtain cash to reassure customers. (Of course, if all customers wanted all their money back from a bank immediately, it would necessarily go bankrupt however sound its balance sheet.) So the clearing banks keep a proportion of their assets in liquid financial assets such as Treasury Bills.

Second, banks will not lend if the risk is greater than the return on a loan. For instance, it would be foolish to lend money to someone who on average had a 50 per cent chance of complete default on a loan if the bank could only charge 5 per cent interest a year on it. In general, the riskier the loans that a bank is prepared to make, the higher the rate of interest. Hence, the higher the interest rate, the greater will be the desire of banks to lend to the limit set by the credit multiplier.

Third, it could be that banks are unable to lend all the money they would like to lend because customers are unwilling to borrow. Between the first quarter of 1987 and the first quarter of 1990, bank lending in the UK doubled. This included the period of the Lawson boom in the economy in 1987 and 1988. However, in the recession which followed, banks found it very difficult to expand their loan books because consumers and businesses had become very reluctant to increase their debt. So, between the first quarter of 1991 and the first quarter of 1993, total loans increased by a mere 1.5 per cent. Increasing their stock of high powered money during this period would have given banks the capability to lend more but would not have altered an economic climate in which customers refused to borrow more.

DATA QUESTION

Bank lending

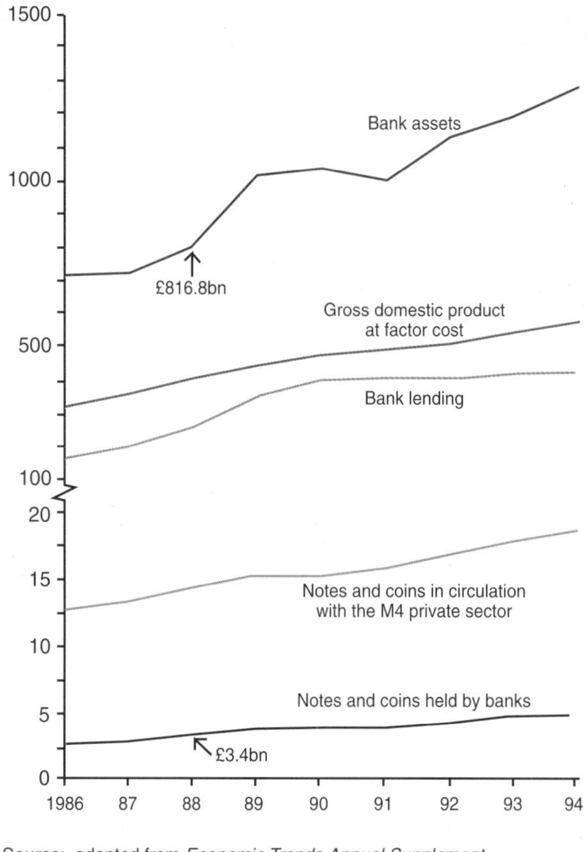

Source: adapted from *Economic Trends Annual Supplement*.

Figure 71.2

Great Britain							Percentages
	1976	**1981**	**1984**	**1989**	**1990**	**1991**	**1992**
All payments							
Cash[1]	93	88	86	80	78	78	76
Non-Cash	7	12	14	20	22	22	24
Non-cash payments							
Cheque	68	68	64	55	52	50	46
Standing order/ direct debit	21	20	22	23	23	24	25
All plastic payment cards	7	9	13	18	20	23	25
of which -							
Credits/charge card	6	8	12	15	15	14	14
Retailer card	-	1	-	1	1	1	1
Debit card	0	0	0	2	4	8	11
Other[2]	2	2	1	4	4	3	4

1 Cash payments under fifty pence in 1976, and £1 from 1981 onwards, are excluded.

2 Includes deductions made directly from wages and salaries, and payments made by Postal Order.

Source: CSO, *Social Trends*, 1994.

Table 71.7 *Changing methods of payment*

1. (a) What has happened to notes and coins held by banks as total bank assets have changed over time?
(b) Explain why banks should change their holdings of notes and coins.
2. Assume that the Bank of England was concerned about the growth of bank lending in 1988 and imposed a cash ratio of 0.5 per cent on the banks.
(a) What would have been the immediate effect of this on bank assets and bank lending?
(b) How might the banks have attempted to get round this restriction?
3. Assume that in 1991 the Bank of England removed the obligation on banks to keep a cash ratio of 0.5 per cent. What effect do you think this would have had on the banks' ability to lend money?

Bonds, bills and shares

Summary

1. Bonds are loans which can be bought and sold second hand on world bond markets.
2. The price of (second hand) bonds rises when interest rates fall and falls when interest rates rise.
3. A bill is a loan which pays no interest. Lenders make a return by buying the bill at a discount (i.e. for less than its maturity value).
4. Owners of shares are part owners of companies who are entitled to receive a share of the profits of the company in dividends.

Bonds

BONDS are a form of loan. If a company decides to borrow money through an issue of bonds, it will sell the issue on the market. The purchaser will usually receive a piece of paper - the bond itself. On the bond, there should be three pieces of information.

- The nominal price of the bond - usually the price at which the bond was originally sold.
- The nominal rate of interest payable - this is the rate of interest on the nominal price of the bond, fixed for the term of the bond. The bond will also state the frequency of payment of interest.
- The date on which the nominal value or price of the bond will be repaid.

If the nominal price were £100 and the nominal rate of interest 5 per cent per annum, then £5 interest would be paid each year for the lifetime of the bond. £100 would be repaid when the bond **matured**.

There are a variety of types of bonds and of borrowers. Government borrows money through the issue of bonds. UK government bonds are called GILT EDGED STOCK. Particular bond issues are referred to by their nominal interest rate and date of maturity. For instance, Treasury 10 per cent 2004 is stock which will be repaid in the year 2004 and in the meantime pays 10 per cent interest on the nominal price of the stock (usually £100 per bond). CONSOLS (or consolidated stock) are IRREDEEMABLE BONDS. This means that there is no date for repayment on the bond certificate (and it is most unlikely that the UK government will ever pay back the loan given that the nominal rate of interest on the bonds is a mere 2½ per cent). However, consols have value because the government promises to pay the holders interest each year. Consols were issued in the past when interest rates were much lower. A 2½ per cent consol, for instance,

QUESTION 1

0010000 GB0005902332 00 000000

U.S.$10,000

Midland Bank plc

(Incorporated with limited liability in England)

U.S.$750,000,000
Undated Floating Rate Primary Capital Notes

This Note is one of a duly authorised issue of U.S.$750,000,000 Undated Floating Rate Primary Capital Notes (the "Notes") in the aggregate principal amount of U.S.$750,000,000 in bearer form in the denomination of U.S.$10,000 each with coupons attached. The Notes are issued pursuant to Resolutions of meetings of duly authorised committees of the Directors of Midland Bank plc (the "Bank") passed on 6th and 23rd May, and 14th June, 1985 and constituted by a Trust Deed dated 17th June, 1985 made between the Bank and The Law Debenture Trust Corporation p.l.c. as Trustee and are subject to and have the benefit of such Trust Deed.

THIS IS TO CERTIFY that the Bank will pay to the bearer on such date as the principal sum hereinafter mentioned may become repayable in accordance with the Terms and Conditions endorsed hereon (the "Conditions"), upon presentation and surrender of this Note, the principal sum of

U.S.$10,000 (Ten thousand United States dollars)

except in the event of the winding up in England of the Bank, in which event the bearer's entitlement shall be as set out in Condition 9(b) endorsed hereon.

Interest will be payable (subject in respect of Interest Periods prior to June 1995 to a minimum rate of 5 per cent. per annum) at rates determined in accordance with the Conditions on the Compulsory Interest Payment Dates and otherwise as specified in the Conditions, subject to and in accordance with the Conditions.

AS WITNESS whereof the Bank has caused this Note to be sealed and the Coupons appertaining thereto to be signed manually or in facsimile on its behalf.

Issued as of 19th June, 1985.

Securities Seal

SPECIMEN

(a) What is the name of the borrower?
(b) What is the nominal value of the bond?
(c) What is the minimum nominal rate of interest on the bond?
(d) When will the bond mature?

with a nominal value of £100, would give a yearly income of £2.50.

Companies issue bonds, usually called STOCKS or DEBENTURES, to finance investment. In the UK, these are relatively unimportant as a source of finance today, mainly because firms are unwilling to borrow at current high fixed interest rates over long periods of time.

Eurobonds are bonds issued by companies and governments which are **denominated** in a currency other than that of the borrower. For instance, ICI might borrow money to finance expansion in Germany by issuing eurobonds denominated in deutschmarks. These Eurobonds could be bought by, say, a French bank, a British company or an American individual.

A key feature of a bond is that it is is negotiable. Buyers of bonds need not wait until the loan matures to get their money back. Bonds can be bought and sold second hand, but the market price of a bond will not necessarily be the same as the nominal value of the bond.

QUESTION 2

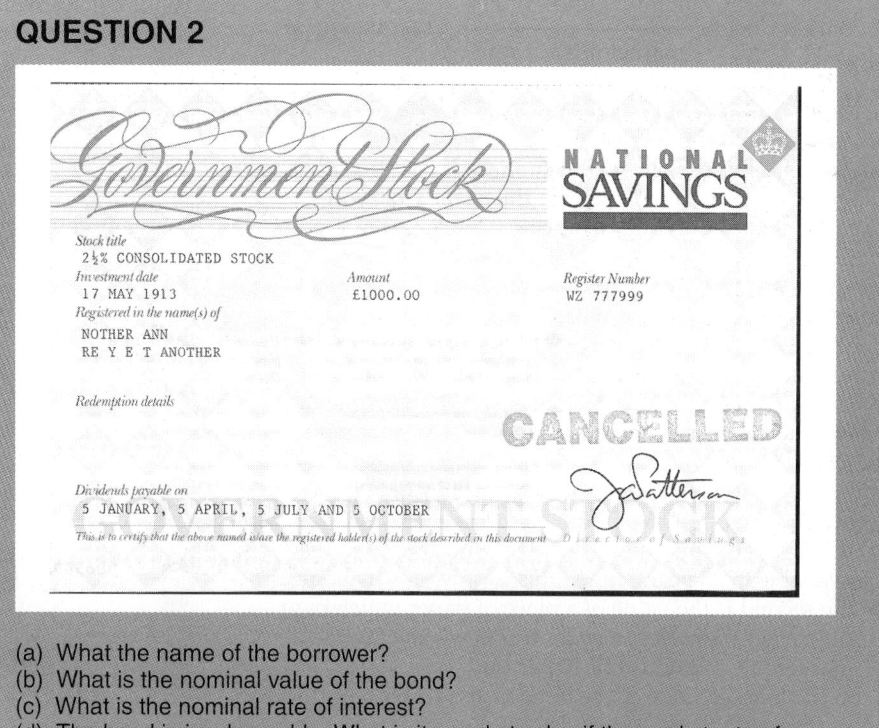

(a) What the name of the borrower?
(b) What is the nominal value of the bond?
(c) What is the nominal rate of interest?
(d) The bond is irredeemable. What is its market value if the market rate of interest on similar assets is: (i) 5 per cent (ii) 7½ per cent (iii) 10 per cent (iv) 12½ per cent (v) 20 per cent?

The price of bonds

Economic theory suggests that the higher the rate of interest, the lower will be the price of existing bonds. For consols, for example, a doubling of the rate of interest will halve the market value of the bond.

To understand why this is the case, consider irredeemable stock which has been issued at £100 nominal price and with a nominal interest rate of 2½ per cent per annum. This bond therefore yields £2.50 interest each year. Assume the market rate of interest on comparable assets now rises to 5 per cent. On £100 saved, £5 interest would be paid. So savers would not pay £100 for a bond which yielded only £2.50 interest. In fact, they would be prepared to pay a maximum £50 for this bond [{£2.50÷ £50} x 100 = 5 per cent]. If the market rate of interest rose again, this time to 10 per cent, a saver would only pay £25 for a £100 bond which gave only £2.50 interest per year (because £2.50 is 10 per cent of £25). Put as a formula:

QUESTION 3

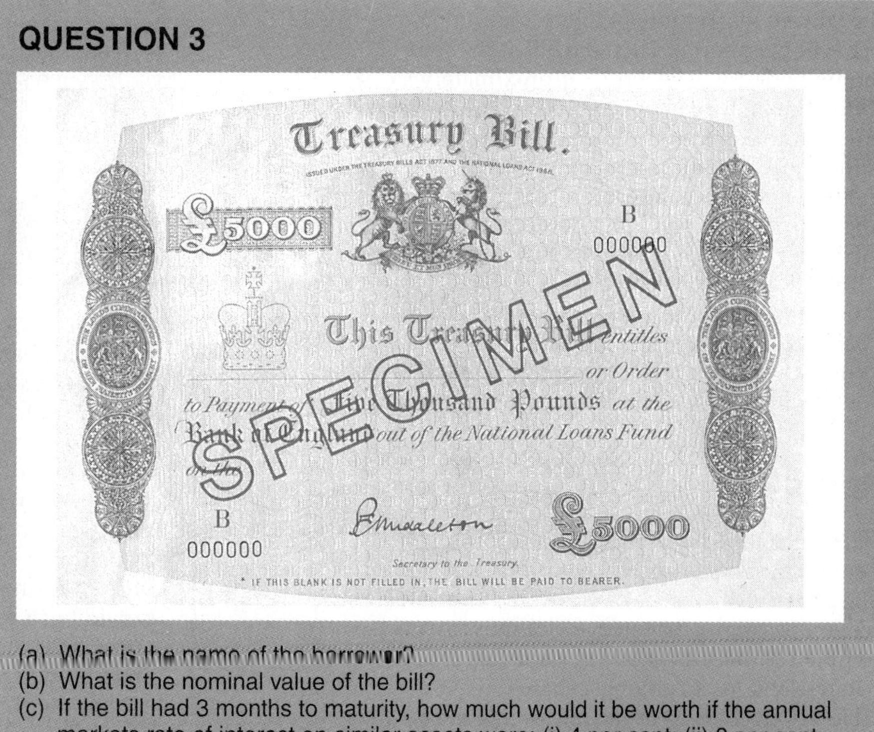

(a) What is the name of the borrower?
(b) What is the nominal value of the bill?
(c) If the bill had 3 months to maturity, how much would it be worth if the annual markets rate of interest on similar assets were: (i) 4 per cent; (ii) 8 per cent; (iii) 12 per cent; (iv) 16 per cent?

$$\text{Market price} = \frac{\text{nominal interest rate}}{\text{market interest rate}} \times \text{nominal price}$$

Most bonds are not irredeemable. However, the same inverse relationship between market price and the rate of interest applies to redeemable bonds.

The economic principle is that the farther away in time the payment of the loan, the greater will be the influence of the rate of interest on price. For instance, a £100 government stock repayable tomorrow with a nominal interest rate of 5 per cent when the market rate is 10 per cent will be worth almost £100 (plus any interest due). The same stock repayable in 25 years' time would be worth only about £60. In the first case, whatever the rate of interest on the bond, the government has guaranteed to pay £100 tomorrow and therefore the stock is worth almost £100 today. In the second case, the value of the bond is made up of two parts:

- the first is the discounted value (☞ unit 55) of £100 available in 25 years' time - this is only worth about £10;
- the second is the value of a piece of paper which pays the owner £5 interest a year - this is worth £50 at a market rate of interest of 10 per cent.

So the market value of the bond is about £60.

Bills

A BILL is a loan on which no interest is paid. For instance, the government might issue a Treasury Bill of £100 for repayment in 3 months' time. No one will lend the government £100 free for three months. So the government has to sell the bill at a **discount**. Assume that the current market rate of interest on similar assets is 12 per cent per annum. Then the bill at the start of the three month period will be worth **approximately** £97. The £3 difference in price between £100 and £97 represents the interest or return on the bill. (£3 interest for three months is the equivalent approximately of £12 interest for 12 months, and hence the rate of 12 per cent per annum.) The nearer to the point of redemption, the nearer will be the market value of the bill to its redemption value.

The UK government issues bills, called **Treasury Bills**. Companies too issue a large volume of bills in the UK. These are called **commercial bills.** Bills are used for short term borrowing, typically over 3 or 6 months, unlike bonds which are used for long term borrowing.

Shares

SHARES entitle the owner to a proportion of the profits of a company. This proportion of profit is called a **dividend**. The prices of shares move erratically over time. Some economists argue that share price movements are completely random and hence it is impossible to pick winners and losers amongst shares.

However, changes in the rate of interest are likely to change share prices. There are two ways of explaining this. Firstly a rise in interest rates will make interest bearing assets relatively more attractive. At the margin, shareholders will sell their shares and buy bonds or put their money in the bank or building society. Secondly, shares will give a stream of dividend payments into the future. When interest rates rise, the present value of those future dividends falls (☞ unit 55). Hence buyers are only prepared to pay a lower price for the shares.

QUESTION 4

THORNTONS PLC

Offer
by
S. G. Warburg & Co. Ltd.
and
Granville & Co. Limited
of
16,973,980 Ordinary Shares of 10p each
at 125p per share payable in full on application

(a) What is the name of the company selling new equity in itself?
(b) Name the two merchant banks which are organising the sale of the new equity.
(c) How many shares are being issued?
(d) What is the nominal price of each share?
(e) How much money will the issuing company receive from the sale (before payments of fees relating to the sale)?

Key terms

Bond or stock - a type of long term borrowing where the loan can be traded during its lifetime.
Gilt-edged stock - bonds issued by the UK government.
Consols - Irredeemable gilt-edged stock.
Irredeemable stock - bonds which have no time limit on repayment of the loan. They are held because they give a guaranteed interest payment.
Debentures - stocks issued by companies.
Bills - a form of short term loan where no interest is paid but a return is made by buying the bill at a lower price than its final redemption value.
Share - ownership of part of a company which entitles the shareholder to dividends, a share of the profits of the company.

Applied economics

Government stock and Treasury Bills

Yields on government stock and Treasury Bills have fluctuated considerably since 1955 as Figures 72.1 and 72.2 show. The 1950s and 1960s were decades of relatively low yields and high prices. The 1970s and 1980s were decades of relatively high yields and low prices. An individual holding 2½ per cent Consols in 1955 saw their value fall considerably by 1974 as the market rate of interest (the yield) rose considerably. On the other hand, an individual buying 2½ per cent Consols in 1974 would have seen a considerable capital gain if he or she had held them until 1994.

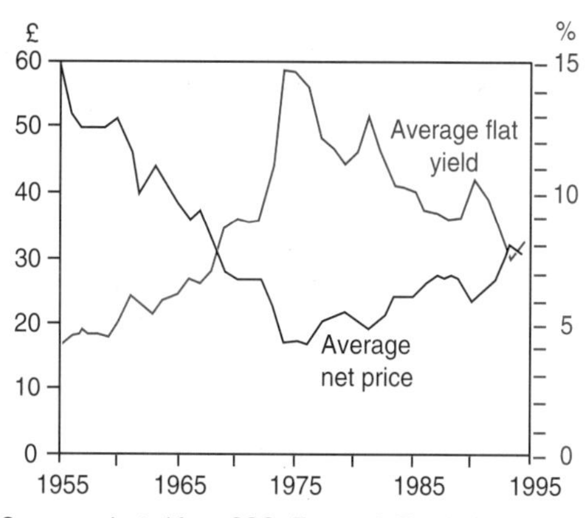

Source: adapted from CSO, *Economic Trends Annual Supplement.*

Figure 72.1 *2½ per cent Consols; average net price and average flat yield*

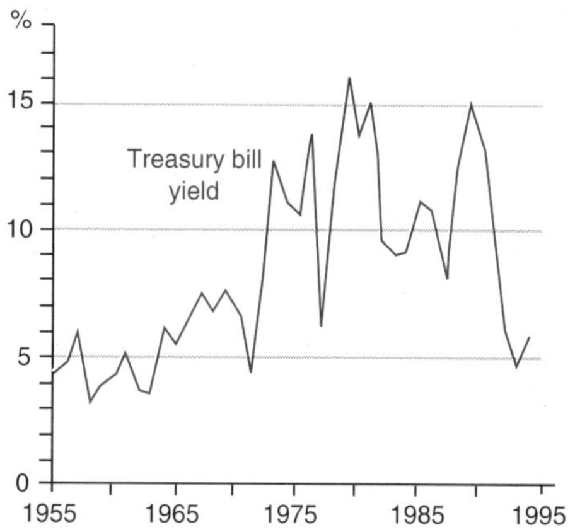

Source: adapted from CSO, *Economic Trends Annual Supplement.*

Figure 72.2 *Treasury Bill yield (percentages)*

As will be discussed in unit 75, the main factor determining the rate of interest in the long run is the rate of inflation in the economy. The 1950s and 1960s were periods of relatively low inflation. Hence, interest rates were relatively low. The 1970s and 1980s were periods of relatively high inflation. Hence, interest rates were relatively high.

Share prices, in contrast to government stock and Treasury Bill prices, have risen consistently over the period. This is because they reflect the growth in value in companies, which in turn reflects underlying growth in national income in the economy. The dividend yield (equivalent to the rate of interest on bonds or bills) has averaged approximately 5 per cent over the 40 year period. Periods when the dividend yield increased above this tended to be periods of economic uncertainty, when investors were reluctant to buy for fear that company profits would collapse. 1974, for instance, when dividend yields rose to 8.23 per cent, was the year of the first oil crisis, when oil prices quadrupled and the British economy began to enter a deep recession.

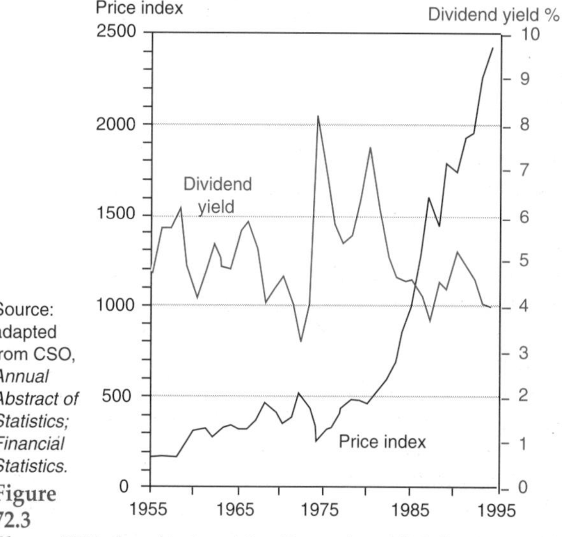

Source: adapted from CSO, *Annual Abstract of Statistics; Financial Statistics.*

Figure 72.3 *Shares, FT index of industrial ordinary shares (1 July 1935=100) and dividend yield (percentages)*

Pension fund investment

Consider the data in Figures 72.1-72.3. In the 1970s and 1980s, UK pension funds gradually increased their holdings of shares and reduced their holdings of government stock as a percentage of their total funds. Write an article for a quality newspaper:

(a) describing trends in prices and yields on government stocks and shares;

(b) explaining why these trends have led pensions funds to change their investment strategy over time;

(c) discuss whether, in the low inflation of the late 1990s, pension funds should change their strategy again.

Money and capital markets

Applied economics

Financial intermediaries and markets

Banks, building societies and other financial institutions are financial intermediaries. They are like supermarkets, acting as middlemen between buyers and sellers. They charge for the services they provide in order to make a profit.

Most of the work of financial institutions involves borrowing and lending money. For instance, banks borrow money from some individuals and firms and then lend it back to others. Building societies borrow money from some individuals and lend it back again to the same or other individuals mainly to finance house purchases. Pension funds collect money from individuals and companies and use that money to buy stocks, shares, property and other assets. Financial institutions also provide services such as accounting services, advice on tax, and organisation of mergers and takeovers.

The markets where financial institutions borrow and lend money amongst themselves and their clients are known as money markets and capital markets.

Banks

Banks can be divided into two types. **Retail banks** collect deposits from and lend money to a large number of customers. Retail banks in the UK are the clearing banks such as Lloyds and the Midland Bank. **Wholesale banks** survive by trading only in very large sums of money with a relatively small number of clients. Retail banks have branches throughout the UK whilst a wholesale bank, like the US bank, Chase Manhattan, may only have one branch, almost certainly in London.

The activities and balance sheets of the UK retailing banks were described in unit 71. **Foreign** or **overseas banks** have long had branches in the City of London, but there was an explosion in their number in the 1960s. Foreign banks set up in the City of London for two reasons. Firstly they wanted to be able to offer a service to their clients with interests in the UK. For instance, a Japanese company with a factory in the UK may prefer to deal with a Japanese bank in London rather than with a UK bank. Secondly, foreign banks need to be physically located in London, one of the most important financial centres of the world, if they are to do business concerned with the London markets efficiently and effectively for their international clients.

Many foreign banks with a branch in London are concerned only with satisfying the needs of the customers in their own countries. A few, however, have established themselves as a major force in the City of London, fighting for custom in financial markets against established UK banks and other financial institutions.

Finance houses

Finance houses, or secondary banks as they are sometimes known, are banks which traditionally have specialised in leasing and hire purchase contracts. By offering higher rates of interest than the banks, they have been able to attract larger single savings deposits from individual customers. They also borrow a significant proportion of their funds from the money markets in London.

Today these banks are tending to offer a wider range of financial services to customers by opening branches in high streets. For instance, today they now offer life assurance and pension fund contracts.

Merchant banks

Traditionally, merchant banks such as Rothschild and Morgan Grenfell were banks which specialised in the finance of trade and commerce (hence the name 'merchant'). One important service they offer is the accepting of commercial bills (or bills of exchange). A company might issue a bill payable in three months' time to another company from which it has bought materials. The receiving company then sells the bill in the London discount market to obtain the money now, but it will have to sell it at a discount (☞ unit 72). It would, however, get a better price for the bill if it was accepted by an accepting house (a merchant bank which belongs to the Accepting Houses Committee). Accepting a bill means that the accepting house will guarantee payment of the bill even if the issuing company goes bankrupt. It is essentially a form of insurance for which the accepting houses charge a fee.

Today merchant banks offer a broad range of services. One of their main activities is the organisation of share issues for companies wishing to sell new shares (hence they are sometimes called issuing houses). They are also prominent in takeover battles. Companies will often hire a merchant bank to assist in a takeover or in defence against another predator company. Merchant banks act as financial advisers, managing the portfolios of wealthy individuals, trusts and pension funds. Many are unit trust managers. They borrow and lend money internationally too, but this is not a major part of their business.

The Bank of England

The Bank of England is the **central bank** of the UK. Owned by the government, it is responsible for carrying out government monetary policy. It has a number of major functions.

- It is responsible for the issue of notes and coins. These are issued on demand to the banking system.
- It supervises the financial system of the UK. For instance, it attempts to prevent fraud and dishonest trading by financial institutions.
- It advises the government on and implements monetary policy (☞ units 77 and 78).
- It manages the Exchange Equalisation Account, the account used to buy and sell foreign currency in order to maintain a given level of sterling in the foreign exchange markets (☞ unit 97).
- It acts as banker to the government, managing the National Debt, and arranging for the issue of new loans to cover any financial shortfall by the government.
- It acts as banker to the banking system. All banks have to keep ½ per cent of their liabilities with the Bank of England and these balances are used to settle accounts between individual banks after all cheques have been cleared (☞ unit 71). The Bank of England also provides liquidity to the banking system if banks are short of cash and other liquid assets. They do this through discount houses.

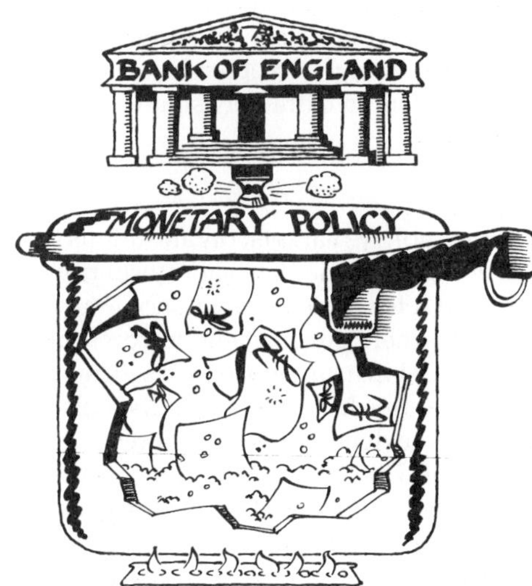

Discount houses

Discount houses are a peculiarly British institution. In 1995, there were only nine members of the London Discount Market Association and even the largest discount house is very small compared to a clearing bank or merchant bank. But they play a role in the London money markets which is far more important than their size would suggest.

Traditionally the discount houses have borrowed money at very short notice. Banks, for instance, lend money overnight (known as **money at call**). These funds represent very short term operating surpluses of the banks. The discount houses have then used this money to buy bills, such as Treasury Bills. Discount houses **have** to lend short term because they borrow short term.

On some days banks lend surplus funds to the discount houses. On other days, they need to withdraw their funds to maintain the liquidity needed to pay customers who withdraw money from their bank accounts. What would happen if, for instance, Barclays Bank needed money to pay customers who demanded payment, but it didn't have enough? This means that Barclays has too little cash and too few operating balances at the Bank of England, and too many of its assets tied up in advances, government stock, bills or loans to the discount houses. Barclays would react by withdrawing money from the discount houses, or recalling money at call with other banks. They might also be forced to sell other liquid assets such as Treasury Bills. There would be no problem if other banks had surplus funds. They would buy the bills and make deposits with the discount houses. But if all the banks faced the same liquidity crisis, they would all be trying to withdraw money from the discount houses and sell assets without there being enough buyers. In particular, the discount houses would not be able to sell the Treasury Bills and commercial bills they hold to repay the money Barclays had deposited with them. The whole of the banking system could go into bankruptcy. In the past, in the 19th century for instance, there were spasmodic bouts of bankruptcies amongst banks. Most went bankrupt because of mismanagement but some fell victim to crises of confidence. Everybody wanted their money back and the bank could not pay them immediately.

The Bank of England has a responsibility for ensuring the smooth working of the UK financial system. It does not want to have financially sound banks going bankrupt because of a minor liquidity crisis. So it has created a safety valve within the system. The discount houses have the unique privilege of being able to go to the Bank of England and either sell bills or borrow money, giving bills as security. This allows them to obtain short term money to give to the banks, thus preventing a crisis. However, the Bank of England reserves the right to charge a penal rate of interest, called Bank Rate before 1971 and Minimum Lending Rate between 1971 and 1981. This penal rate is higher than the market rate of interest which means that the discount houses lose money if they are **forced into the Bank**.

The Bank of England in turn uses the discount market for **monetary policy** (☞ units 78 and 79). If there were no Bank of England intervention, a shortage of money in the market would drive up its price (i.e. interest rates would rise). Banks would have to offer higher rates of interest in order to be able to get the cash they needed to prevent themselves going bankrupt. If there is a surplus of funds in the money markets, borrowers of money will be able to reduce the interest rates they offer to pay. On any one day there will almost certainly be either a surplus or a shortage of funds in the money markets, implying that there should be sharp changes in interest rates on a day to day basis. The Bank of England for a long time has seen interest rate fluctuations as undesirable. It therefore intervenes on a day to day basis, supplying money when there is a shortage of funds in the market and selling bills when there is a surplus, so that money market interest rates remain constant over time.

When the Bank of England wants to change short term interest rates, it lets the market know its wishes. The market cannot ignore the Bank because the Bank can charge a penal rate on its transactions with the market, which would then stand to lose a great deal of money.

Building societies

Building societies have traditionally borrowed money from small savers and lent money out to finance house purchases. During the 1980s, there was a revolution in the way in which building societies operated. The Building Societies Act 1986 freed the building societies from previous regulations which limited their ability to offer a wide range of financial services. Today, many of the larger building societies are transforming themselves into financial institutions which look increasingly like banks. They have begun to offer services ranging from current accounts to credit cards to pensions. The 1990s has seen fierce competition in the market for retail financial services. Some building societies, such as the Abbey National and the Halifax and Leeds have or intend to convert themselves legally into banks. The Cheltenham and Gloucester Building Society was taken over by Lloyds Bank in 1995. These trends are likely to continue in the second half of the 1990s.

Assurance and pension companies

Assurance companies and pension funds provide long term saving plans. They take money from a large number of small savers who usually pay regular premiums into life assurance or pension plans. Today the money that is paid in is used principally to buy shares. Assurance companies and pension funds - so-called **institutional investors** - now dominate shareholdings in the UK. Whether this is desirable or not is debateable (☞ unit 22).

Money markets

There are a large number of different money markets in the UK. They are all interlinked because funds from one market will flow into others if the interest rate differential changes (e.g. if interest rates stay the same in the first market but rise in the others). The main borrowers and lenders in each market are the financial institutions described above.

The discount market Until the early 1960s, the discount market was the main money market in London. As described above, the clearing banks lent money to discount houses overnight or very short term. The money could be withdrawn rapidly if the banks needed extra liquidity because it was deposited at call or at very short notice. The Bank of England guaranteed liquidity in the market by acting as a **lender of last resort**.

Parallel or secondary markets There are five other important sterling markets in London. The largest of these is the **inter-bank market**. In the late 1960s, the newly-arrived foreign banks in London began to lend money at call or short notice amongst themselves instead of to established discount houses. They did this because they were able to get higher rates of interest on money lent. Very quickly, UK banks also began to borrow and lend on the inter-bank market. The oldest parallel money market, started in 1955, is the **local authority market** where local authorities borrow money directly from City institutions. In the **inter-company market**, dating back to 1969, large companies cut out the middleman (the banks and other financial institutions) and borrow and lend between themselves. Finance houses borrow money from other financial institutions through the **finance house market**. Lastly, there is significant trade on the **sterling certificate of deposit market** in certificates of deposit (☞ unit 71) issued in sterling by banks.

Eurocurrency markets The London sterling money markets are completely dwarfed in size by the eurocurrency markets operated from London. Eurocurrency transactions are transactions in any currency apart from the currency of the country where the transaction takes place. In London, this means any transaction in any currency apart from sterling. A complete range of money market instruments or assets is found on eurocurrency markets. For instance, it is possible to borrow and lend money through loans, overdrafts and bonds (called Eurobonds). Governments, industrial companies and financial institutions use the markets for borrowing and lending. Transactions start in millions of dollars. This is very different from the retailing operations of the UK high street banks, where money can be borrowed and lent in extremely small quantities.

Capital markets

On the London money markets, organisations borrow and lend money for their immediate short term use. **Capital markets** are markets where firms finance long term development or where government borrows money long term. The financial instruments used by firms and government to do this have been described elsewhere.

- Companies issue debentures and shares (☞ units 22 and 72).
- The UK government issues government stock (☞ unit 72).

Traditionally, the major capital market in the UK has been the London Stock Exchange. The Stock Exchange is primarily a secondary market where existing (i.e. second hand) securities such as shares and gilts have been traded. It has functioned as a primary market to the extent that the UK government has sold new stock on the market, but it is not a primary market for shares. New shares are usually offered for sale to financial institutions or to the public directly by the company issuing the shares. Traditionally these sales have been organised with the help of merchant banks or stockbrokers. To guarantee that all the shares will be sold, the issue can be underwritten. This means that one or a number of financial institutions will buy any shares left unsold at a fixed price. In return for this guarantee, the company has to pay an underwriting fee, payable whether or not the underwriters have to buy any shares.

Embarrassment of riches

After five years of grappling with huge bad debts, inadequate profits and dissatisfied customers, British high-street banks face an unfamiliar concern. They may be about to start making too much money. 'It makes me more worried about the industry than I've been for a long time,' says one director whose bank is moving from bad times into good ones.

The broker Barclays de Zoete Wedd estimates that the nine biggest UK banks will add £3.7bn to their capital this year, 10 times their retained (after tax and dividends) profits of £369m in 1992. As bad debts fall, a big rise in banks' income will show through. 'Banks have been huge consumers of capital, but are becoming cash cows,' says Mr Peter Toeman, an analyst at Hoare Govett, the stockbroker.

Some improvement appeared inevitable. Banks' profits usually rise when economies recover because bad debts fall, and they can earn more from lending. But the scale on which UK banks are now starting to generate cash is greater than in the past for a number of reasons.

- Management tried to offset the unprecedented bad debts of the downturn by raising income. They widened interest rate margins on loans, and charged higher fees to businesses and personal customers for services such as cheque clearing. Mr Toeman estimates that returns on assets such as loans have risen about 25 per cent since 1989 as a result.
- They have also boosted profits by shedding staff and cutting branch networks. Barclays and National Westminster this week announced that they plan 7 700 job losses between them on top of previous cuts. While cost-cutting and the introduction of new technology raise short-term profits, income may be curtailed in the long term because there are fewer branches through which to sell products.
- Banks traditionally absorb excess capital by taking on fresh loans. But there has been weak demand for loans so far as the economy picks up. Some companies have repaid bank loans and replaced them with equity and debt securities. Many private customers are wary of taking on debt. So banks may find they are holding capital without the conventional means of employing it.
- Banks are inherently more profitable as a result of shedding businesses which made inadequate returns. National Westminster decided last year to abandon retail banking in France after it reviewed its operations to see what return they were likely to achieve, on average, during complete economic cycles. Such judgements have made banks smaller and more profitable despite short-term costs.

For all these reasons, banks are likely not only to make but to retain more money than in recent recoveries. As bank executives point out, this might not be a problem in other sectors. 'When industrial companies have cash, people view it as a war chest, a sign of strength,' says Sir Nicholas Goodison, chairman of TSB Group. But banks face distinct pressures, both because of public perception, and the constraints of the industry.

First, customers, may be offended by large profits because they have become disenchanted at standards of service. 'There is a hard core of dissatisfaction with banks,' says Mr Jean Eaglesham, head of money policy at the Consumers' Association.

Second, banks with capital to spend are at risk of losing more money than other types of company if their investments turn sour. Banks are allowed to lend about 20 times their capital, using money from their depositors and money markets. This means that if a banking venture goes wrong, they stand to lose not just their own investment, but up to 20 times that amount. Thus, shareholders tend to be worried if their banks acquire excess capital.

Third, well-capitalised banks may try to lend more despite weak demand. This will lead to competition that could push down margins on lending, and erode fees. There is already evidence of falling margins on loans to large companies, and some banks have frozen small business charges this year.

Finally, the more capital a bank has, the harder it is to achieve good returns on it. Banks have adopted returns on equity as their main measure of profit. Barclays is aiming for a 15 per cent after-tax return, and NatWest for a return of 17.5 per cent. The targets are testing in an era of low interest rates.

These factors will militate against banks holding excess capital. The problem is defining the right amount. Banks must have at least a 4 per cent ratio of core capital - mostly equity and reserves - to risk-weighted assets. But ratios of 7 per cent are common in the US. 'Four per cent has become old hat,' says Mr Brian Pearse, Midland's chief executive.

Most banks are rebuilding capital lost as a result of bad debt problems, and are yet to reach the core capital-to-assets ratio of 6 per cent which most industry experts now regard as reasonable. Even after reaching that point, the size of losses from bad debts in the last recession - four times that of previous cycles - could make them anxious to retain capital.

'We face a lot of uncertainty. The view that the world is now a smooth and easy place is not the only one,' says Mr Derek Wanless, NatWest's chief executive. Yet banks cannot simply sit indefinitely on their cash. 'Banks with too much capital may be able to tough it out for a couple of years, but they will have to do something eventually,' says Mr Ian Harley, Abbey National's finance director.

Source: the *Financial Times*, 14.1.1994.

1. (a) What is a bank and (b) how can it 'lose money'?

2. (a) Explain how a bank can increase its profitability. (b) What are the potential disadvantages of a bank earning high profits?

3. 'Capital' of a bank is money and other financial assets which are owned by the bank (and therefore its shareholders). It is NOT money which is owed to customers who lend to the bank. The Basle convention, which UK banks conform to, states that banks must have at least £4 of their own capital for every £100 they accept from customers as deposits or lend out.
(a) Why did the capital of UK banks rise in the first half of the 1990s? (b) Discuss what the banks could have done with the increased capital they were accumulating.

The demand for money

Summary

1. Households and firms hold their wealth in money, in other financial assets or in physical assets.
2. The opportunity cost of holding money is the benefits foregone from holding other financial or physical assets.
3. The traditional Keynesian approach distinguishes three motives for holding money: a transactions demand, a precautionary demand and a speculative demand. The total demand for money is a function of both income and the rate of interest.
4. A more modern Keynesian approach sees money being held in a portfolio of financial assets. The demand for money is dependent upon the opportunity cost of holding that money.
5. A monetarist approach sees money being held in a portfolio of both financial and physical assets.
6. The major difference between Keynesian and monetarist approaches is that in the former the demand for money is far more interest elastic than in the latter.

A portfolio of assets

It was explained in unit 70 that holding or **demanding** money has an opportunity cost. Other **financial assets**, such as bonds or shares, could be held and interest and dividends could be received from those holdings. Alternatively, **physical assets** could be held, such as cars or stocks. Hence, the price of holding money is the benefits foregone from holding another type of asset.

A traditional Keynesian theory of the demand for money

Traditional Keynesian theory identifies three reasons or motives why households and firms hold money rather than other types of assets.

The transactions demand Money is needed to buy goods and services. Cash or cheques are used to pay for everything from a newspaper to a meal or a supermarket bill. This is known as the TRANSACTIONS DEMAND FOR MONEY. The amount of money needed depends upon the level of real expenditure in the economy. The most important determinant of this is the level of real income. The higher the level of real income, the more households and firms will have to spend and hence the higher the level of expenditure.

The transactions demand for money is also dependent upon the level of inflation. Shoppers will need twice the amount of money to buy the same trolley load of goods if the price of supermarket goods doubles over a period of time.

The precautionary demand We live in a world of uncertainty. Tomorrow the car might break down or an important creditor go bankrupt. So households and firms tend, if possible, to hold more money than is needed just for transactions purposes. The higher the level of income, the greater the bill is likely to be from something going wrong. For instance, the cost of repairing an expensive car is likely to be greater than that of a cheap car. So the PRECAUTIONARY DEMAND FOR MONEY is a function of (i.e. varies with) income.

The speculative demand for money One reason why people change the amount of money they choose to hold is because they wish to speculate on the stock market. This component of the total demand for money is called the SPECULATIVE DEMAND FOR MONEY. Assume that the only alternative to holding money is to hold bonds. Remember that the price of bonds is inversely related to the rate of interest. The higher the price of bonds, the lower the rate of interest and vice versa (☞ unit 72).

Now assume that the markets think that interest rates are high. If they are considered 'high', the market is likely to think there is more chance of them falling than going even higher. Hence the market will expect bond prices to rise rather than fall in the future.

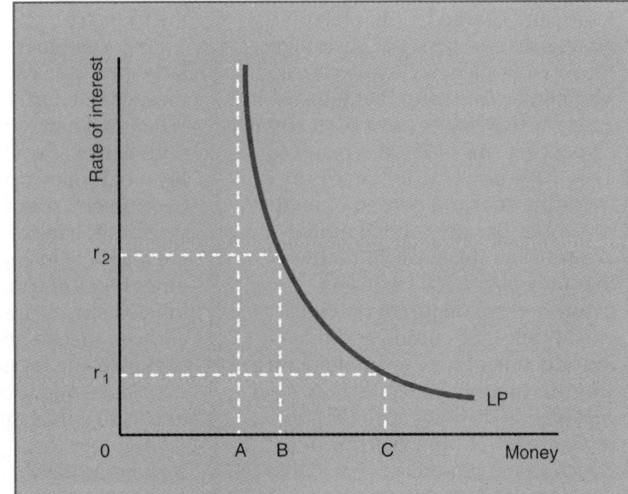

Figure 74.1 *The Keynesian liquidity preference schedule*
OA is the transactions and precautionary demand for money. Both are determined by real income and the price level, independently of the rate of interest. The demand for money above OA is the speculative demand, which is inversely related to the rate of interest.

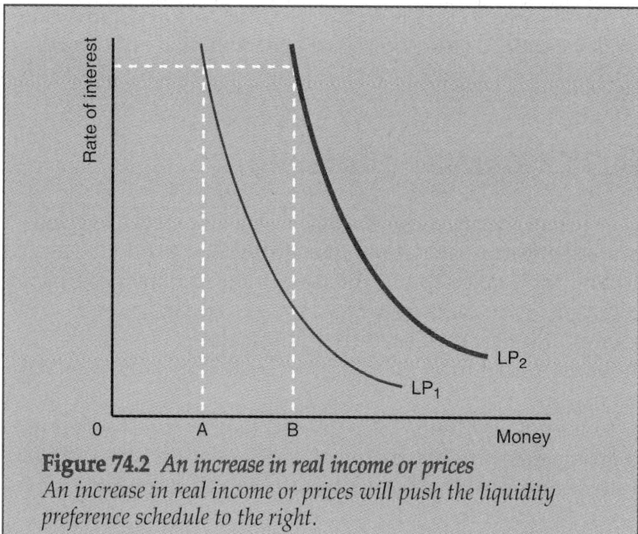

Figure 74.2 *An increase in real income or prices*
An increase in real income or prices will push the liquidity preference schedule to the right.

How will market speculators react to this? It is possible to make a capital gain by buying bonds when their prices are low and selling them when they are higher. Hence speculators will buy bonds when interest rates are high hoping that interest rates will fall and therefore bond prices will rise. Bonds will be bought with money. So a high demand for bonds means a low speculative demand for money.

QUESTION 1

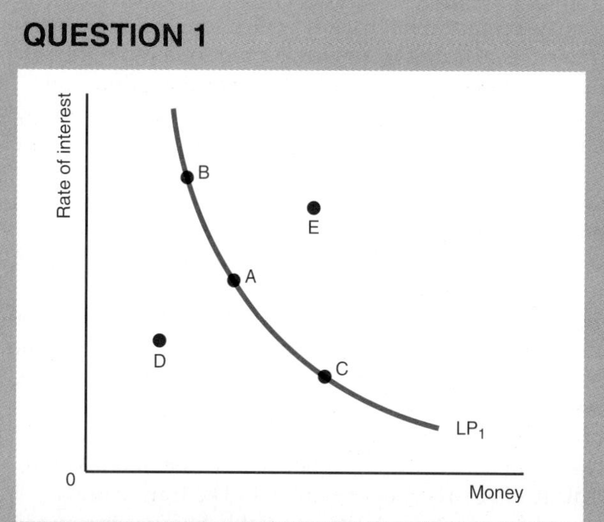

Figure 74.3

Figure 74.3 shows a liquidity preference schedule LP_1 for an economy. The economy is in equilibrium at the point A. Which point would the economy be most likely to move to if there were:
(a) an increase in real national income;
(b) a fall in interest rates;
(c) a rise in the price level;
(d) a fall in bond prices;
(e) a fall in money wages with prices constant;
(f) an increased perception of economic risk amongst the population?

When interest rates are very low, they are likely to rise in the future. Hence, speculators are likely to sell bonds for money. Thus the demand for money is likely to be high when interest rates are low.

This theory predicts that the speculative demand for money will be low when interest rates are high (people preferring to buy bonds), but high when interest rates are low.

Figure 74.1 combines the three motives for holding money. The demand for money curve is called the LIQUIDITY PREFERENCE SCHEDULE. It shows the relationship between the demand for money and the rate of interest. OA of money is demanded whatever the rate of interest. This is the amount demanded for transactions and precautionary purposes. At an interest rate of r_1, OC of money is demanded. OA is demanded for transactions and precautionary purposes. AC is demanded for speculative purposes. When interest rates rise to r_2, the demand for money falls. The transactions and precautionary demands remain the same at OA. But the speculative demand falls to AB.

The transactions and precautionary demands for money will increase if real income in the economy rises or if there is inflation. This, shown in Figure 74.2, has the effect of pushing the liquidity preference schedule to the right. If the transactions and precautionary demands increase from OA to OB, then the liquidity preference schedule will shift from LP_1 to LP_2.

A modern Keynesian approach

The theory of a speculative demand for money is now widely rejected by economists. The idea that bonds are the only alternative to holding money is simplistic in a world where there are so many different money market instruments. Moreover, the theory assumes that there is some 'normal' rate of interest against which speculators can judge whether interest rates are high or low. The experience of the past 20 years suggests that no such normal interest rate exists.

The modern Keynesian approach is based upon ideas first published in 1958 by the American economist Professor James Tobin. Asset holders can hold their wealth in a wide range of financial assets, from cash to bonds to shares. Each type of asset provides a different mix of benefits. In particular:

- money can be used immediately for making transactions;
- non-money assets should yield a return in the form of interest, dividends or capital gain.

The opportunity cost of holding money is then the yield foregone on holding non-money assets. The opportunity cost of holding non-money assets is the advantage of liquidity - being able to spend the money when you like.

It is now possible to explain what happens to the demand for money as different variables change.

A rise in nominal income This is likely to lead to an increase in the number of transactions in the economy. Hence the demand for money will increase.

An increase in prices Households and firms now need more money to complete each transaction. Hence the demand for money will rise.

An increase in interest rates An increase in interest rates increases the opportunity cost of holding money. Therefore, the demand for money will fall and the demand for interest bearing assets will rise. For instance, if the rate of interest on building society money is 2 per cent, there is no great incentive to put money into interest bearing accounts. But when the interest rate is 10 per cent, people are much more aware of the advantages of getting interest on their assets. They are prepared to spend time moving savings around from current accounts (some of which don't pay interest) to interest bearing accounts and back again to maximise interest payments.

An increase in risk Many assets are risky. The rate of return can be positive but it can also be negative. For instance, the prices of shares over long periods of time have tended to increase. In October 1987, world stock markets saw a 25 per cent fall in share price. If the annual rate of return (including capital gains) on shares averaged 5 per cent, many would decide that they didn't want to invest in shares because it was too risky. But if the rate of return on shares increased to 30 per cent per year, then more people would be prepared to buy shares because the rewards would be much greater. Tobin argued that households and firms would trade off higher interest for less risk. But the higher the rate of interest, the greater would be the opportunity cost of holding assets in the form of riskless money. So the higher the rate of interest, the less the demand for money. The higher the risk on non-money assets, the lower will be their demand and the higher the demand for money.

The portfolio balance approach of Tobin yields the same overall conclusions as the traditional Keynesian approach - the demand for money varies directly with nominal income and inflation but inversely with the rate of interest.

It is also possible within the approach to analyse why narrow definitions of the money supply (notes and coins and money in bank current accounts) have grown more slowly over time than broader measures of the money supply (which also include interest bearing deposit accounts with banks and building societies). During the 1970s and 1980s there has been a large expansion in the use of credit cards, a **money substitute**. The convenience of use of credit cards and the availability of free credit has proved so attractive that the use of narrow money for transactions purposes has fallen as a ratio of the total volume of transactions made. On the other hand, interest rates have increased considerably. Customers have found it worthwhile to lose a certain amount of liquidity to gain high interest. Hence there has been a switch out of cash and current account money into interest bearing accounts.

QUESTION 2 Following the October 1987 stock market crash, the net sales of UK unit trusts fell sharply. At the same time, net inflows of money into building society accounts increased sharply. Explain why this happened.

A monetarist approach

Keynesian theory assumes that financial assets are good **substitutes** for each other. For instance, a good alternative to holding cash is to put the money into a bank account; alternatives to bank account deposits are stocks and shares. But it is assumed that physical assets, such as houses or furniture, are not good substitutes for financial assets.

In monetarist theory it is argued that physical assets are a good substitute for financial assets. For instance, if the rate of interest falls, both Keynesians and monetarists would predict that asset holders will sell some of their interest bearing assets. These are now no longer so attractive as before. Keynesian theory would suggest that the assets will be converted into money (i.e. the demand for money will rise). Monetarist theory suggests that part will be converted into money but part will be spent. Asset holders will use the opportunity of the sale of interest bearing financial assets to buy physical assets such as furniture, cars or houses.

This debate about whether physical assets are a good substitute for financial assets is important when considering the shape of the liquidity preference schedule. In Figure 74.4, the initial rate of interest is r_1 and the quantity demanded of money is OA. Interest rates now fall to r_2. According to Keynesian theory, asset holders will reduce their holdings of interest bearing financial assets and increase their holdings of money as shown by the curve LP_k. But according to monetarist theory, part of the fall in demand for interest bearing financial assets will be used to buy physical assets and consumption goods. Hence the liquidity preference schedule is LP_m and the increase in the demand for money is only AB and not AC as under Keynesian assumptions.

Monetarists argue that the liquidity preference schedule is far more interest inelastic than Keynesians believe, and that large falls in interest rates are needed to increase the demand for money to any extent. According to monetarists, the dominant demand for money is the transactions demand. The speculative demand is small.

This leads to another conclusion. The transactions demand for money is relatively stable because income is relatively stable. But the speculative demand is dependent upon perceptions of risk. If, as after the stock market crash of October 1987, there is an increased perception of risk, then the liquidity preference schedule will shift to the right. If the demand for money is essentially a transactions demand, then the demand for money schedule will be relatively stable. If on the other hand risk and speculation play an important part in determining the demand for money, then the liquidity preference schedule will shift frequently as perceptions of risk change.

Keynesians, then, argue that the demand for money is interest elastic and unstable. Monetarists argue the converse - that the demand for money is interest inelastic and stable.

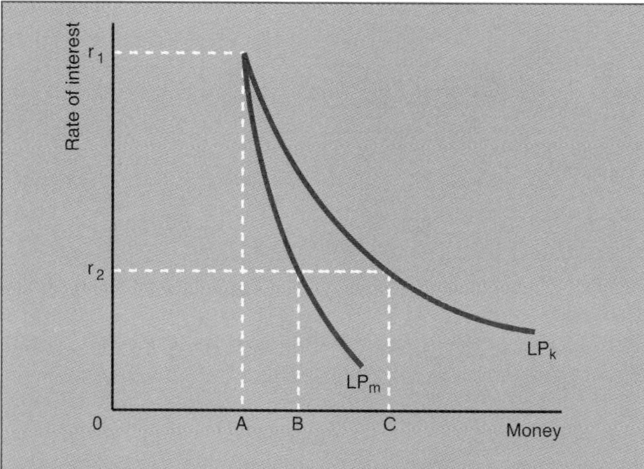

Figure 74.4 *The shape of the liquidity preference schedule*
Monetarists argue that physical assets are a good substitute for financial assets. Hence they argue that the demand for money curve is far more interest inelastic than Keynesians argue.

Key terms

The transactions demand for money - the demand for money to make purchases of goods and services.
The precautionary demand for money - the demand for money to safeguard against unforeseen events.
The speculative demand for money - the demand for money arising from speculation in financial assets such as bonds.
Liquidity preference schedule - the demand for money curve, showing the relationship between the quantity of money demanded and the rate of interest.

Applied economics

The demand for money in the UK

Economic theory suggests that the demand for money is a function of several variables, including income and the rate of interest. Statistics for different measures of income and the rate of interest are readily available but how can the demand for money be measured?

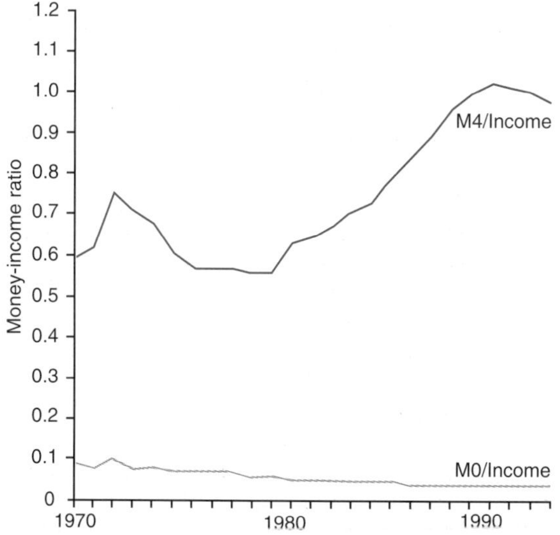

1. M0 and M4 outstanding at end year ÷ GDP current market prices for the year.
Source: adapted from CSO, *Economic Trends Annual Supplement; Economic Trends.*

Figure 74.5 *The ratio of money to income*[1]

At any point in time, the demand for money must equal the supply of money, so it is possible to measure the demand for money by measuring the money supply. There are a number of definitions of the money supply and hence a number of different demands for money can be measured too.

The transactions demand for money is perhaps best measured using M0 (notes and coins in circulation). Figure 74.5 shows the ratio of M0 to GDP (income) since 1970. If incomes were the sole determinant of the transactions demand for money, then the ratio of M0 to income would be constant over time. However, the ratio has consistently fallen over time. The main reason why the M0-income ratio has fallen over time is that there has been an increase in the use of other means of payment apart from cash. With cheques, debit cards and credit cards, consumers have been reducing their holdings of cash in relation to their rising incomes.

As economic theory would suggest, there is far less correlation between broad money, M4, and income than, for instance, between M0 and income because income is only one of several variables which affect the demand for broad money. The M4-income ratio varies from 0.57 to 1.02 in Figure 74.5. One variable influencing the demand for broad money is the rate of interest. Figure 74.6 is a scatter diagram showing the relationship between the rate of interest and the M4-income ratio. Whilst the correlation is not particularly good, it would suggest that the higher the rate of interest, the lower the M4-income ratio - the relationship predicted by economic theory.

Income and the rate of interest are not the only variables which affect the demand for money according to economic theory. However, factors such as wealth and risk are more difficult to measure than income and the rate of interest and, overall, economists have found it difficult to establish a demand for money function which works well over long periods of time.

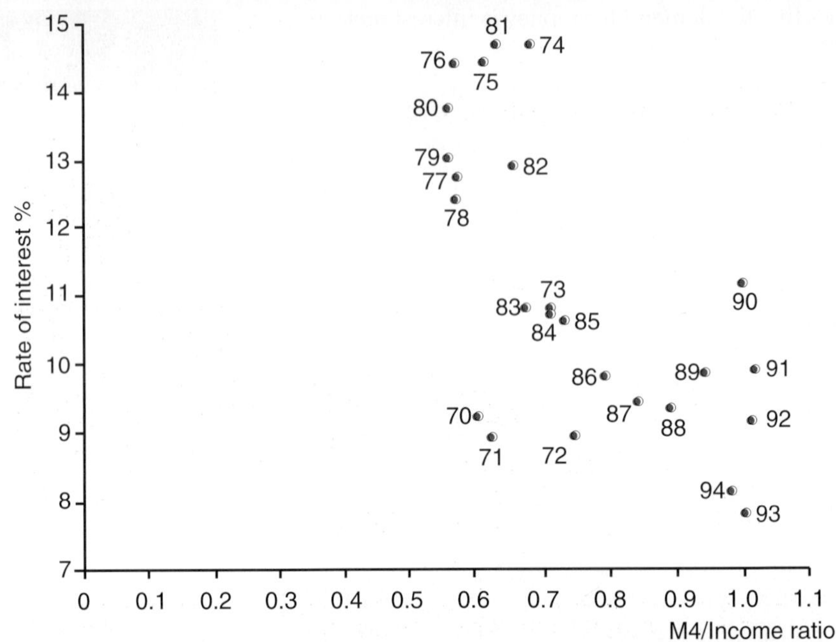

1. British government securities, long dated 20 years.
Source: adapted from CSO, *Economic Trends Annual Supplement; Economic Trends.*

Figure 74.6 *The demand for money and the rate of interest*[1]

Holding cash

When Mr Brian Pitman, chief executive of Lloyds Bank, argues that something is one of 'the biggest destroyers of shareholder value' in his bank, one might expect him to be taking steps to get rid of it. The trouble is that the culprit is something that most people regard as retail banks' most staple product - cash.

Mr Pitman's remarks at a conference - held this month by De La Rue, the banknote printers, to discuss the costs of cash - indicate the size of the problem for banks. The associated Boston Consulting Group study estimated that cash distribution now costs the equivalent of 25 per cent of banks' branch network costs.

The study is the first time for 20 years that the workings of the British cash-handling system have been exposed. The costs break down into two forms: the physical expense of moving notes and coins around; and the interest forgone by people, businesses and banks in holding rather than investing cash.

Individuals' £800m cost is calculated as forgone interest on the £10.1bn cash they hold at any one time. This £10.1bn - £460 per household - is higher than the stocks held by other participants; businesses hold £5.1bn, while bank branches hold only £3.1bn and building society branches a mere [illegible] in total.

The only way individuals could gain such interest would be not to use cash, a distant prospect despite the growth in credit and debit cards. Those with most steps at their disposal are the banks, which incur only £300m in lost interest on their cash holdings but pay a further £1.9bn a year to move cash around.

A comparison with a 1973 study by the banks' Association for Payment and Clearing Services shows that banks have made matters worse for themselves by increasing access to cash. Banking cash transactions per year have fallen in value from £180bn to £120bn, yet the number has risen from 650m to 1.6bn.

The costs are even higher in France and Germany, in the latter case probably because there has been less expansion of the use of credit and debit cards which have staunched some of the growth in cash in the UK. This suggests that banks can devise ways of altering the UK system, and so reduce their own costs.

The Boston Consulting Group study argues that banks can reduce costs by cutting the number of cash withdrawals through branches, and by managing their stocks of cash more efficiently to avoid lost interest on excess stocks. One Spanish bank is estimated to have saved 35 per cent on cash costs by improved management.

However, the study suggests that banks also have motives to try to develop new means of taking cash out of the banking system. One alternative to cash now being considered is the use of 'smart cards' that can hold a nominal cash amount. These could be used at retailers with the appropriate counter technology.

Source: the *Financial Times*, 19.10.1993.

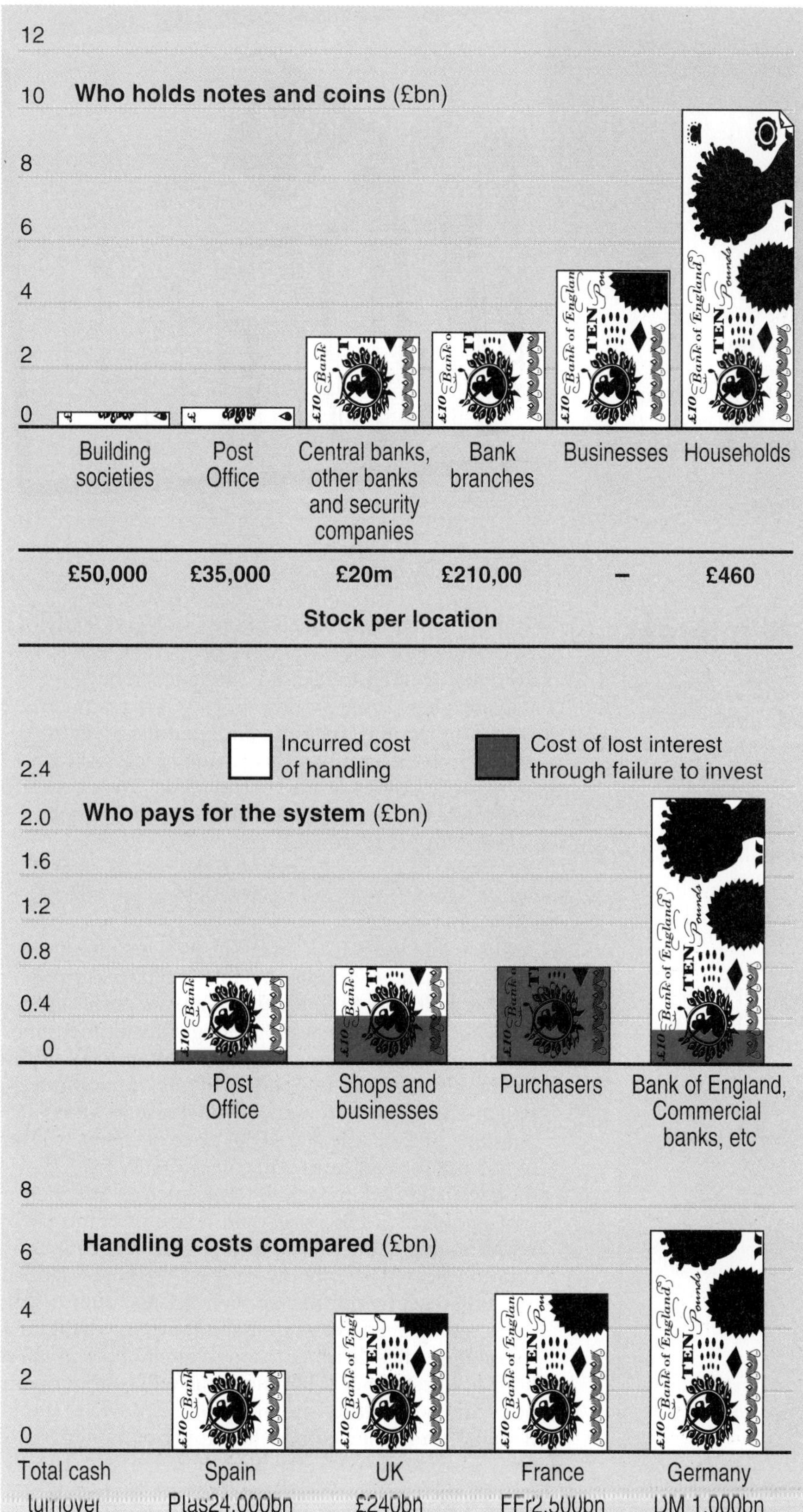

Source: adapted from Boston Consulting Group.

Figure 74.7

1. Why is cash held by individuals, businesses and financial institutions?
2. Explain what the article argues is the opportunity cost of having cash in an economic system like that of the UK.
3. (a) Discuss how households and businesses might adjust their portfolio of assets if there was a halving of cash in the economic system because of increased use of debit and credit cards.
   (b) What implications does this have for the interest rate elasticity of demand for money?

unit 75 The rate of interest

Summary

1. The price of money is the rate of interest.
2. The rate of interest is determined by the demand for and supply of money.
3. An increase in the demand for money or a fall in the supply of money will increase the rate of interest. A fall in the demand for money or an increase in the supply of money will lead to a fall in the rate of interest.
4. Different interest rates exist in different money markets. Interest rates tend to move together in the same direction over long periods of time.
5. Factors which cause interest rates to differ in the same market include time, risk and administrative cost.
6. The real rate of interest is the nominal rate adjusted for inflation.

Determination of the rate of interest

Economic theory suggests that, just as the price of a good is determined by the forces of demand and supply (☞ unit 6), so too is the price of money. So what is the price of money? It is how much needs to be paid if money is borrowed - it is the **rate of interest**.

Figure 75.1 shows the demand and supply curves of money. The demand curve for money is usually called the **liquidity preference schedule** (☞ unit 74). It is downward sloping because the higher the rate of interest, the more households and firms will wish to hold non-money assets such as bonds or shares. The money supply is drawn as a vertical line, showing that the supply of money remains constant whatever the rate of interest. This assumes that the central bank can and does control the supply of money in the economy independently of its price (☞ unit 78). The money supply is then said to be **exogenous**. It would make no difference to our conclusions here if the money supply were assumed to be upward sloping and therefore **endogenous**, with the money supply determined by the rate of interest rather than by the decisions of the central bank. The equilibrium rate of interest r_e occurs where the demand for money equals the supply of money.

Figure 75.1 *The equilibrium rate of interest*
r_e is the equilibrium rate of interest - the rate of interest where the demand for and supply of money are equal.

Economic theory suggests that if the rate of interest is above or below this level then it will tend towards its equilibrium value.

- Assume that the rate of interest is r_1 (i.e. there is an excess demand for money). Households and firms want to hold more money than they are currently holding. They will react by selling some of their non-money assets and converting them into money. If they sell bonds, the price of bonds will fall. If bond prices fall, interest rates automatically increase (☞ unit 72). Similarly, if they sell shares the price of shares will tend to fall and interest rates will consequently rise. If money is defined in narrow terms such as M0, then households could increase their holdings of money by withdrawing some from building society accounts. Building societies will now have a shortfall of deposits and will react by putting up their interest rates to attract more savings. So excess demand for money will push up interest rates, leading to a movement back along the liquidity preference schedule. This will continue until households and firms are in equilibrium where the demand for money equals the supply of money.
- Now assume the converse: that there is excess supply of money such as would exist at a rate of interest of r_2. Households and firms hold more money than they wish, so they will attempt to put it into the building society, or buy bonds, shares or other types of assets. This will lead to a fall in interest rates back towards the equilibrium interest rate r_e.

Shifts in the money demand and supply curves

What happens if the demand or supply of money changes (i.e. there is a **shift** in either the money demand or supply curves)?

Assume that the liquidity preference schedule shifts to the right as in Figure 75.2. This means that more money is demanded at any given rate of interest. This could be caused by an increase in income, an increase in the price level (we are assuming that the LP curve shows the demand for nominal balances) or an increase in the perceived risk of holding non-monetary assets such as bonds or shares (☞ unit 72). The rate of interest will consequently increase from r_1 to r_2. So an increase in liquidity preference shown by a shift to the right in the LP curve will increase interest rates, but not change the supply of money which is fixed by the authorities.

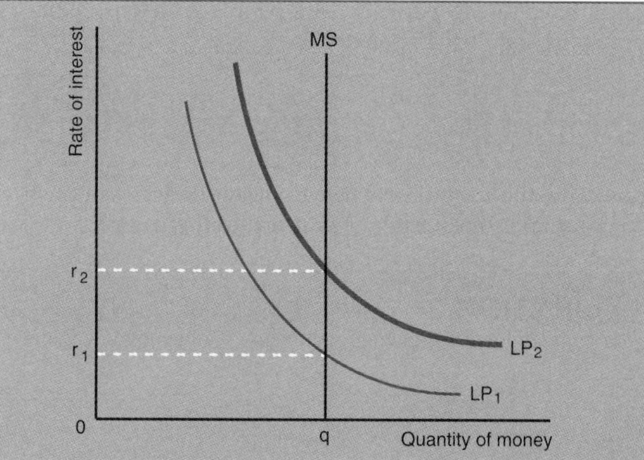

Figure 75.2 *An increase in the demand for money*
An increase in the demand for money, shown by a shift in the liquidity preference schedule to the right, will increase the rate of interest from r_1 to r_2.

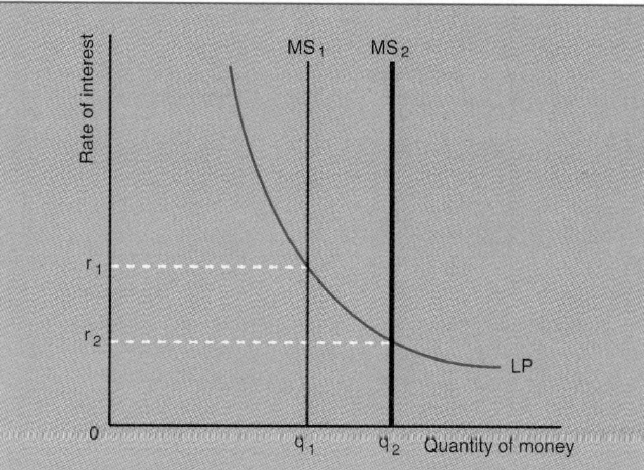

Figure 75.3 *An increase in the money supply*
An increase in the money supply, shown by a shift in the money supply curve to the right, will lead to a fall in the rate of interest from r_1 to r_2.

Conversely, a fall in the demand for money will lead to a fall in interest rates.

Now assume that the government increases the supply of money. This is shown by a shift to the right in the supply curve in Figure 75.3. The result will be a fall in the rate of interest from r_1 to r_2. Conversely a fall in the money supply will lead to an increase in interest rates.

QUESTION 1 Draw a diagram showing the liquidity preference schedule and the money supply curve. Show the likely effect on the equilibrium rate of interest if there is:
(a) a fall in the money supply;
(b) an increase in the price level;
(c) increased use of credit cards in payment for goods and services;
(d) a fall in national income at current prices;
(e) an increase in notes and coins in circulation in the economy;
(f) a fall in speculative activity in the bond market at any given rate of interest.

Different markets, different rates of interest

So far, it has been implicitly assumed that there is one market for money and one equilibrium rate of interest in the economy. This is a very useful simplification in macro-economic theory. However, in reality there are many markets for money and many rates of interest in an economy. For instance, in the discount market (☞ unit 73) banks and discount houses borrow and lend money from each other. In the local authority bill market, local authorities borrow and lend money from banks and other financial institutions. In the mortgage market, building societies and banks lend money to households purchasing property. If all these markets were perfect, and all loans and borrowing were identical, then the rate of interest in all markets would be the same. But there are many barriers between markets and loans are not identical. Hence interest rates differ. One major barrier between different money markets is imperfect knowledge. For instance, when banks offer higher rates of interest on their accounts than building societies, the building societies will not suffer major drains of funds. This is partly because customers find it inconvenient to change money from one account to another. But also many customers are unaware of differences in interest rates. Equally, in some markets borrowers and lenders are locked into fixed term contracts. These are likely to be short - anything up to, say, 6 months. This means that money cannot flow into another market to take advantage of higher interest rates.

Barriers to the flow of money between markets exist but on the whole they are not high enough to insulate markets completely. When interest rates increase in the City of London, the major banks will almost certainly increase their interest rates too. The effect will ripple out into the rest of the economy. Building societies may not respond initially but they will suffer a drain of funds in the medium term if they do not increase their interest rates. So interest rates tend to move in the same direction over a period of time.

There are a number of factors which can cause interest rates to differ in the same market.

- Time. The longer the period of the loan, the higher tends to be the rate of interest. If money is lent out for just 24 hours, the lender has complete flexibility either to stop lending the money or to switch money to another market. If it is lent out for 25 years, there is no such flexibility. So higher interest is necessary to compensate lenders as the length of the term of a loan increases.
- If the market expects interest rates to fall in the near future, then longer term loans could attract a lower rate of interest than shorter term loans. For instance, if current interest rates are 12 per cent for overnight loans, but you expect them to fall to 10 per cent in a month's time, then you might be prepared to lend money for three months at somewhere between 10 and 12 per cent.
- Risk. Lending money to an unemployed worker is likely to be far more risky than lending it to the Midland Bank. So the greater the risk of default on the loan, the higher will be the rate of interest.
- Administrative cost. Lending out £100 million in lots of £100 at a time is likely to be far more administratively costly than lending out £100 million to one customer. So the higher the administration cost, the higher will tend to be the rate of interest.

QUESTION 2

Table 75.1 *Selected interest rates and yields, 28 April 1995*

Source	Period of loan	%
Interbank money markets	overnight	4
	seven days	$5\frac{1}{2}$
	one month	$6\frac{7}{16}$
	three months	$6\frac{7}{8}$
	one year	$7\frac{5}{8}$
Treasury Bills	one month	$6\frac{3}{8}$
	three months	$6\frac{3}{8}$
Gilt edged stock (high yield)	five years	8.52
	fifteen years	8.64
Mortgage rate		8.0
Personal loan, unsecured, Midland Bank		15.4
Overdraft, unauthorised Abbey National		29.5
Royal Bank of Scotland MasterCard		14.5
Marks & Spencer store card		26.8

Source: adapted from the *Financial Times*, 29.4.1995.

Suggest reasons why the interest rates in Table 75.1 differ from each other.

Nominal and real interest rates

When a building society offers a rate of interest of 10 per cent, it is offering a NOMINAL RATE OF INTEREST. The interest is unadjusted for inflation. But each year, prices in the economy are likely to rise. £100 placed in the building society today will, excluding any interest payments, buy fewer goods and services in a year's time.

The REAL RATE OF INTEREST is the rate of interest adjusted for inflation. For instance, the real rate of interest would be 5 per cent if the nominal rate of interest were 10 per cent and the rate of inflation were 5 per cent. With a nominal rate of interest of 12 per cent and a rate of inflation of 8 per cent, the real rate of interest would be 4 per cent.

Real interest rates can be negative as well as positive. In 1975, with the UK inflation rate at 25 per cent and nominal interest rates about 7 per cent, the real rate of interest was **minus** 18 per cent. Anyone saving at 7 per cent would have lost 18 per cent of the purchasing power of their money during 1975. Why do people save when real interest rates are negative? One reason is that much saving is highly illiquid. People can't liquidate assurance or pension fund contracts easily or without cost for instance. Another reason is that people need to save if only because they do not wish to spend all their income when they receive it on pay day. What's more, savers might have lost 18 per cent. But people who kept their money in cash lost 25 per cent!

Nominal interest rates and inflation

Economic theory predicts that higher inflation will push up nominal interest rates. Assume that there is zero

QUESTION 3

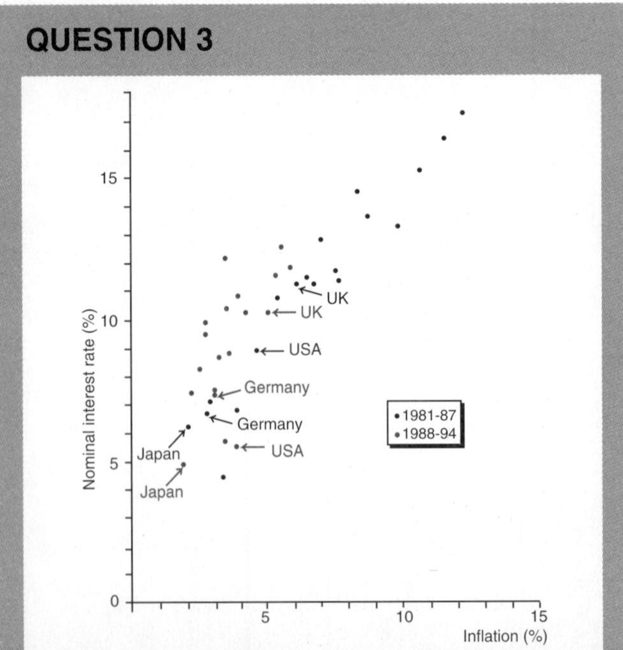

1. Short term rates, annual average.
2. Average annual percentage change in consumer prices.

Figure 75.4 *Nominal interest rates[1] and inflation[2] in 19 OECD countries*

(a) Explain the possible link between nominal interest rates and inflation rates.
(b) To what extent does the data in Figure 75.4 support economic theory?

inflation and the nominal rate of interest is 3 per cent (i.e. the real rate of interest is 3 per cent). Then, £100 today would grow into £103 in a year's time. That £100, if saved rather than spent today, would enable the saver to buy 3 per cent more goods and services in 12 months time. Now assume that inflation rises to 5 per cent. If nominal interest rates are still 3 per cent, then £100 today would only buy £98 worth of goods in a year's time because the real rate of interest is - 2 per cent. Savers would therefore save less. Borrowers, on the other hand, would borrow more because they are effectively being paid to borrow money. The market for loanable funds would therefore fall into disequilibrium. It can only return to equilibrium when nominal rates of interest have risen sufficiently to approximately the original real rate of interest of 3 per cent.

Irving Fisher, an American economist in the early part of this century, argued that a 1 per cent increase in inflation would be associated with a 1 per cent increase in nominal interest rates. So, if the real rate of interest is 3 per cent, then nominal interest rates would be 13 per cent if the inflation rate were 10 per cent, 23 per cent if the inflation rate were 20 per cent and so on.

This can be seen in Figure 75.2. The demand for money is a demand for real balances. So when prices rise, the demand for money increases, shown by the shift to the right in the liquidity preference curve in Figure 75.2. But this rise in demand raises interest rates. The analysis is more complex than this, though. As will be seen in the next unit, large increases in prices will be associated with large increases in the money supply. So high inflation will be associated with shifts to the right in the money supply curve too. What the Fisher hypothesis implies is that the shift to the right in the demand for money curve would be greater than the shift to the right in the money supply curve, and this would produce rising nominal interest rates.

Key terms

Nominal interest rates - interest rates unadjusted for inflation.

Real interest rates - nominal interest rates adjusted for inflation.

Applied economics

The rate of interest in four money markets

The rate of interest in each money market in the UK is determined by the demand for and supply of money in that market. It is possible to identify the main borrowers and lenders in most money markets. For instance, in the UK domestic mortgage market, banks and building societies are the two most important suppliers of money. People wanting to borrow money to buy a house demand money. The rate of interest on a mortgage loan is low compared to, say, an ordinary overdraft or bank loan. This is mainly because a mortgage loan is secured on a property. If a borrower defaults on the loan, the bank or building society can force the borrower to sell the property and pay back the loan with the money raised. So a mortgage loan is regarded as being relatively free of risk by lenders.

Banks have traditionally been the main source of loans and overdrafts, although secondary banks and building societies have recently entered the market too. The demand for money comes from individuals and companies who want to borrow to finance everything from repairs to a car, to a new kitchen or a new factory. Interest rates tend to be set according to risk of default. Large companies can usually get lower rates of interest on loans than small companies, whilst individuals are charged much higher rates than on a mortgage loan. It could be argued that loans through credit cards form part of this market too. Interest rates on credit cards tend to be above overdraft and personal loan rates for individuals. Not only is the risk of default higher on a credit card than on a personal loan but there are much greater administrative costs in handling credit card loans than in handling personal loans and overdrafts.

In a City money market, such as the discount market or local authority market, individual transactions tend to be for far greater sums of money. In the discount market, the government demands money by issuing Treasury Bills (☞ unit 72) and money is supplied for their purchase mainly by discount houses and banks. In the local authority market, local authorities demand money whilst banks and other financial institutions supply funds. Table 75.3 shows interest rates in these two markets at a point in time. Treasury Bills carried a lower rate of interest than local authority deposits because central government was considered a marginally better risk than local authorities.

Table 75.2 *Selected interest rates, 28.4.1995*

Per cent

	Overnight	7 days notice	1 month	3 months
Treasury Bills	-	-	$6^{1}/_{2}$	$6^{5}/_{8}$
Local authority deposits	$6^{5}/_{16}$	$6^{1}/_{16}$	$6^{9}/_{16}$	$6^{15}/_{16}$

Source: adapted from the *Financial Times*, 29.4.1995

The rate of interest on Treasury Bills with three months to maturity was slightly higher than with one month to maturity. This is what economic theory would predict. In the local authority market, again, interest rates tended to rise, the longer to maturity the deposit. Interestingly, the 7 day notice deposit carried a lower rate of interest than the overnight rate. This probably reflects an excess supply of 7 day deposit money rather than a response to interest rate fundaments such as risk or time.

DATA QUESTION

Interest rates and inflation

Table 75.3 *Inflation and selected interest rates*

	Inflation rate	Banks base rate	Average rate of interest paid on building society share accounts	British government securities, long dated 20 years.
1980	18.0	16.32	10.3	13.78
1981	11.9	13.27	9.2	14.74
1982	8.6	11.93	8.8	12.88
1983	4.6	9.83	7.3	10.80
1984	5.0	9.68	7.7	10.69
1985	6.1	12.25	8.7	10.62
1986	3.4	10.9	7.8	9.87
1987	4.2	9.74	7.5	9.47
1988	4.9	10.90	7.0	9.36
1989	7.8	13.85	n.a	9.58
1990	9.5	14.77	n.a	11.08
1991	5.9	11.70	n.a	9.92
1992	3.7	0.56	n.a	9.13
1993	1.6	6.01	n.a	7.07
1994	2.5	5.46	n.a	8.05

1. (a) What is meant by a 'real rate of interest'?

(b) During which years shown in the data were real interest rates positive in the UK?

2. Why are some interest rates higher than others? Illustrate your answer from the data.

3. Discuss whether changes in interest rates reflect changes in the rate of inflation.

The quantity theory of money

Summary

1. Money is neutral if changes in the supply of money only affect the price level of the economy.
2. The Fisher equation of exchange states that MV≡PT.
3. The quantity theory of money states that changes in M, the money supply, are the sole determinants of changes in P, the price level.
4. Monetarists argue that V is constant in the short term and changes only slowly in the long run.
5. They also argue that the money supply must grow over time to match any increase in T, the level of real income; if the growth in T were greater than the growth in M, there would be a fall in prices.
6. Keynesian economists dispute whether V is constant in the short run. They also suggest that increases in prices may well lead to increases in the money supply.

The neutrality of money

In 1960, the President of France, General Charles de Gaulle, cut the value of all French money by a factor of 100. He passed a law which decreed that on the 1 January 1960, 100 Francs would be called 1 Franc. So a 1 000 Franc note was reduced in value to 10 Francs. 10 000 Francs in a French bank account was only worth 100 Francs. A company which had borrowed 100 million Francs would only have to repay 1 million Francs. This change in the value of the Franc had little or no effect on the **real economy**. Because all monetary values were changed on the same day, relative values remained unchanged. Prices were only 1 per cent of their former level, but so too were wages. The company which had its loan cut by a factor of 100 still had to earn 100 times more in Francs to pay off the loan. The owner of a 1 000 Franc note saw its value reduced 100 fold, but then prices were reduced by the same factor. The note bought exactly the same quantity of goods and services as before.

This is an example of the neutrality of money. Money is said to be NEUTRAL if changes in the money supply only affect the level of prices in the economy. But economists disagree about the extent to which money is neutral. Some economists argue that changes in the money supply can have important effects on the real economy, in particular on variables such as national income and unemployment, whilst others argue that it is neutral.

The equation of exchange

The EQUATION OF EXCHANGE distinguishes between the real and the money side of the economy. The most famous formulation of the equation was made by Irving Fisher, an American economist who worked during the first half of this century. The FISHER EQUATION is:

$$MV \equiv PT$$

M is the total amount of money in the economy (i.e. the money supply). V is the VELOCITY OF CIRCULATION of money (sometimes also called the INCOME VELOCITY). V is the number of times the money supply changes hands over a period of time, such as a year. P is the average price of each transaction made in the economy. T is the total number of transactions made over a period of time.

The equation of exchange is an identity (i.e. it is true by definition ☞ unit 59). Assume that there is £100 of money (M) in circulation in the economy. On average, each £1 changed hands 4 times (V) during the year. So we know that £400 must have been spent during the year (M x V). If the average price of each transaction was £2 (P), there must have been 200 separate transactions (T) over the period. Similarly, if 100 transactions (T) take place over a year and each transaction was for an average of £5 (P), then the total amount spent was £500. If there was only £50 of money in circulation (M), that money **must** have changed hands on average 10 times during the year. So the velocity of circulation of money (V) must have been 10.

Different formulations

There are a number of other ways of expressing the equation of exchange.

- T, the number of transactions in the economy over a period of time, can be equated with real national income, the physical volume of output in the economy. Hence:

  $$MV \equiv PY$$

  where Y is real national income.
- P times Y, the average price of each transaction times the level of real national income, is equal to y, the level of nominal national income, or national income at current prices. So:

  $$MV \equiv y$$

- If $MV \equiv PY$ and we divide both sides of the identity by V, then:

$$M \equiv \frac{PY}{V}$$

- If $1 \div V$ is called k, we then have:

$$M \equiv kPY$$

- Alternatively, if $Y \div V$ is called a, we have:

$$M = aP$$

We will now use these different formulations to explain the quantity theory of money.

QUESTION 1 The money supply M is £200, V is 10 and T is 100.
(a) What is the value of P?
(b) The money supply now doubles. If V and T remain constant, what is the new value of P?
(c) At the new money supply level, T now increases from 100 to 150. What will happen to the price level if there is no change in the money supply and V remains constant?
(d) At the new money supply level, what is the level of (i) national income at constant prices and (ii) national income at current prices?
(e) If $M = aP$, what is the value of a at the new money supply level?

The quantity theory of money

The QUANTITY THEORY OF MONEY is one of the oldest economic theories, dating back at least 500 years if not more. The theory states that increases in prices are caused solely by increases in the money supply. As Milton Friedman put it in his 1968 book *Dollars and Deficits*, 'inflation is always and everywhere a monetary phenomenon'.

It is necessary to make a number of key assumptions if we are to make the transition from the equation of exchange, which is an identity and therefore always true, to the quantity theory of money. The simplest way of doing this is to assume that k, the inverse of the velocity of circulation of money, and Y, the real level of national income, are both constant. Then:

$$M = aP$$

where a is the constant kY (or $Y \div V$). If M increases, then so must P. In the crudest form of monetarism, M and P will change by the same percentage. So a 10 per cent increase in the money supply will increase prices by 10 per cent. Money is therefore neutral.

Advocates of the quantity theory of money are called MONETARISTS and the belief that inflation is caused solely by increases in the money supply is called MONETARISM. Why do monetarists argue that V and Y can be assumed to be constant?

The velocity of circulation The velocity of circulation of money is the average number of times a unit of money changes hands over a period of time. For instance, a £10 note may change hands 50 times a year.

One factor which determines the velocity of circulation is the way in which households receive money and make purchases.

- The velocity of circulation of broad money will tend to fall if there is a change from paying workers once a week to once a month. Households will now hold money for longer periods of time to cover expenditure later in the month.
- The increased use of **money substitutes**, such as credit cards, will also reduce the velocity of circulation of money itself. Instead of making many separate money transactions, the card holder will make one transaction at the end of the month to the credit card company.

On the other hand, increased use of cheques and debit and credit cards will tend to lead to an increase in the velocity of circulation of notes and coins (M0). Households and firms increasingly do not keep cash as savings at home, but use it for transactions purposes. Cash card machines mean that households keep less and less cash as a proportion of income and spend it very quickly.

Another factor which is important in determining the value of V is the extent to which money is used for speculation. If there is a large **speculative demand for money** (☞ unit 74), then V can vary as asset portfolios are switched in and out of money. Keynesians argue that when the rate of interest rises, households and firms desire to hold less money because the opportunity cost of holding money will have risen. The opportunity cost is the interest or return they could have obtained if they had placed their money in, say, a building society account or in stocks or shares. When the rate of interest rises, less money will be held to make the same number of transactions. Households and firms will make their smaller stock of money work harder (i.e. the velocity of circulation will rise).

So the debate about the value of the velocity of circulation of money is the same debate as the one about the determinants of the demand for money. Monetarists argue that the speculative demand for money is relatively unimportant because money is held mainly for transactions purposes. In the long run V can change as institutional factors change, but the change will be slow. In the short run, V is broadly constant because the demand for money is a stable function of income. Keynesians on the other hand argue that changes in the rate of interest lead to significant changes in **liquidity preference** (i.e. the demand for money) and therefore the velocity of circulation is volatile in the short run.

National income Real national income tends to rise slowly over time. The annual growth rate of the UK economy over the past 40 years has averaged about $2\frac{1}{2}$ per cent. If $M = kPY$, and k is constant, then the money supply can grow by the rate of growth of real income without generating a rise in prices. Monetarists indeed argue that the money supply should be expanded in line with real growth, otherwise prices will fall. Falling prices can be just as undesirable as inflation. But any expansion of the money supply over and above the rate of growth of real income will be inflationary, according to monetarists.

QUESTION 2

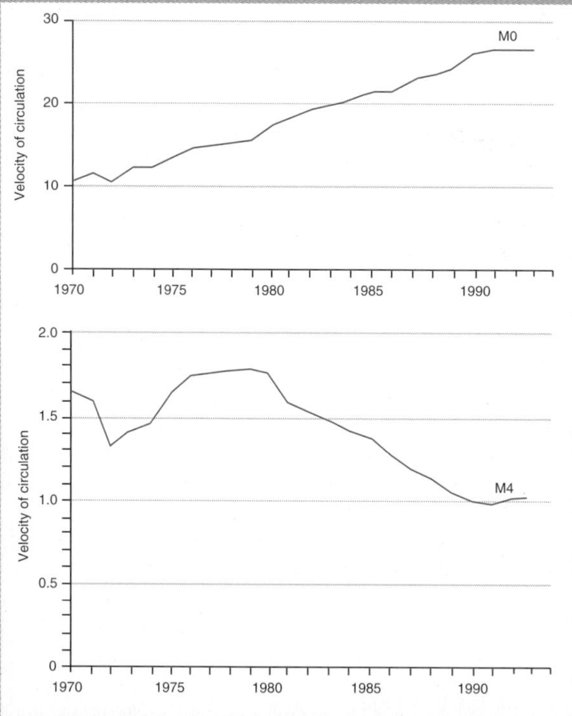

Figure 76.1 *Velocity of circulation*

Figure 76.1 shows two different measures of the velocity of circulation of money: that of M0, narrow money and of M4, broad money.

(a) To what extent is the velocity of circulation of money constant over time?

(b) Suggest reasons why the velocity of circulation may have changed over the period shown.

The money supply and inflation

The quantity theory of money, according to monetarists, shows that price increases are the result of increases in the money supply. This conclusion is dependent upon the assumptions that the velocity of circulation of money is constant and that income (and therefore transactions and output) changes only slowly over time. Keynesians, on the other hand, argue that the demand for money is unstable and therefore the velocity of circulation of money is unstable too. A rise in M could be offset by an decrease in V rather than leading to a change in the price level. Keynesians also point out that monetarists assume that causality runs from M to P. But logically it could equally be true that price increases could lead to an increase in the money supply. There are two ways in which this might occur.

- Assume that the money supply is **endogenous** (i.e. it cannot be controlled by the central bank but instead is created by the banking system). A rise in wages will lead to increased demand for money from the banks. Firms will need more money to pay their workers, whilst workers will increase their demand for money because their incomes have gone up. An increased demand for money will push up interest rates and banks will find it more profitable to create money. Therefore the money supply will expand.
- If the money supply is **exogenous**, (i.e. its size is controlled by the central bank), it is not necessarily true that the central bank will choose to restrict the growth of the money supply. It may well allow the money supply to expand rather than accept the consequences of restricting its growth. This policy is known as **accommodating** the factors, causing the increase in demand and therefore supply of money.

The quantity theory of money equation also suggests that an increase in the money supply **could** lead to an increase in real income. If M = kPY, and k and P are assumed to be constant, then an increase in M will lead to an increase in Y. Some monetarists (such as Patrick Minford and others from the Rational Expectations school of thought) argue that an increase in M will feed through so quickly to an increase in P that Y will not be affected at all (i.e. there will no time lag between an increase in M and an increase in P). Other monetarists, such as Milton Friedman, argue that, in the short term, much of the increase in the money supply will indeed initially lead to an increase in real income. This link between increases in M and increases in Y is known as the monetary **transmission mechanism** (☞ unit 94). But, they argue, in the longer term, real income will revert to its previous level whilst all of the increase in the money supply will have fed through to an increase in prices (i.e. there is a time lag between increases in the money supply and increases in the price level).

Economists are agreed that very large increases in the money supply will inevitably lead to high inflation. If the

Key terms

Neutrality of money - the theory that a change in the quantity of money in the economy will affect only the level of prices and not real variables such as unemployment.

The equation of exchange (the Fisher equation) - the identity $MV \equiv PT$ where M is the money supply, V is the velocity of circulation of money over time, P is the price level and T is the number of transactions over time.

The velocity of circulation of money/income velocity - the number of times the stock of money in the economy changes hands over a period of time.

The quantity theory of money - the theory, based on the equation of exchange, that increase in the money supply, M, will lead to increases in the price level P.

Monetarists - economists who believe that the quantity theory of money shows that inflation is always and everywhere caused by excessive increases in the money supply.

money supply increases by 200 per cent over a year, it would be impossible for either V or Y to change sufficiently for P to be unaffected. The monetarist-Keynesian debate centres round the effects of relatively small increases in the money supply. Are money supply increases of 5 or 10 or even 20 per cent necessarily inflationary?

QUESTION 3 The time was when the publication of figures for broad money growth would be one of the economic highlights of the month. Not any more. The Conservative government of 1979-83 believed devotedly in a link between money supply and inflation, as did many distinguished City economists. However, Thursday's publication of M4 figures caused hardly a stir. Growth in M4 in the year to September was just 4.8 per cent, at the bottom of the government's target rate of between 3 and 9 per cent. It would seem that there is no need to worry about inflation. However, a month ago, base rates were increased from 5.25 per cent to 5.75 per cent with both the Chancellor and the Governor of the Bank of England saying that they were worried that inflation might be beginning to rise again.

There are still some economists who believe that money supply growth is the key determinant of inflation. Tim Congdon, of Lombard Street Research, argues that it was the slow growth of broad money in late 1990 and early 1991 which has led to the lowest inflation rates since the late 1950s and 1960s. He also believes that the subdued growth rate of M4 means that inflation will stay low.

There is general agreement on the reasons for slow growth in M4. Consumers and businesses borrowed heavily in the 1980s and became highly indebted. When interest rates rose in the late 1980s and the economy went into recession, many went bankrupt. They are now reducing their indebtedness and are wary of repeating their mistakes by borrowing again. However, enough confidence has returned for consumer credit figures, covering items such as credit cards, to begin to rise again.

Tim Congdon argues that this is not significant. Mortgage lending, which is about 7 times the size of consumer credit lending, is very subdued and is likely to remain so with the ratio of mortgage debt to housing stock being over 30 per cent when the average between 1960 and 1990 was only 20 per cent. Other economists disagree. Kevin Gardiner, UK economist at Morgan Stanley, argues that the recent rise in consumer credit is significant because it shows that consumers, while not yet sufficiently relaxed to borrow for mortgage purposes, have rediscovered some of their 1980s borrowing habits. Rather than M4 being a forward indicator of the economy, Mr Gardiner believes that the economy's strength will eventually lead to M4 growth. The debate may seem arcane but it is important. If believers in the significance of M4 are right, the Bank of England may seriously damage the recovery if it pushes for higher interest rates when credit growth is so weak.

Source: adapted from the *Financial Times*, 24.10.1994.

(a) Tim Congdon is a monetarist. How can you tell this from the passage?

(b) Why might (i) the mortgage market and (ii) the 'economy's strength' have an effect on the growth of M4?

(c) (i) Using a diagram, analyse what impact a rise in the rate of interest will have on the money supply.
(ii) Discuss whether a rise in interest rates of a few per cent could 'seriously damage the recovery'.

Applied economics

Inflation and the money supply

The quantity theory of money suggests that inflation is caused by increases in the money supply over and above the rate of real growth in the economy. If this were true, it would be possible to see a strong correlation between money supply growth and the rate of change of prices across a number of countries.

Figure 76.2 is a scatter diagram, giving data for OECD countries. On the horizontal axis is the average annual percentage growth of broad money. On the vertical axis is the average annual percentage change in prices. As can be seen, if a line of 'best fit' is drawn, there does seem to be some correlation between the two variables: the higher the percentage increase in the money supply, the higher the rate of inflation. Figure 76.3 shows the relationship between the four variables in the Fisher equation for the UK from 1970. The 1970s and the 1990s would tend to support the view that changes in the money supply lead to a change in the rate of inflation.

- The growth in M4 between 1970 and 1972 led first to a fall in the velocity of circulation of money and then to an increase in growth in GDP. This was shortly followed by a rise in the inflation rate in 1974 and 1975. It was this experience which was particularly influential in converting many economists and politicians to monetarism.
- The fall in the rate of growth of M4 in 1973-7 led to initial rises in the velocity of circulation of money and falls in the growth of GDP, followed by falling inflation rates between 1975 and 1978.
- The fall in the rate of growth of M4 from 1989 led to falls in the rate of inflation from 1991 onwards.

However, there is little correlation between growth of M4 and inflation in the late 1970s and most of the 1980s. During this time, there was an increasing disillusionment amongst economists and politicians with what was sometimes called 'crude' monetarism

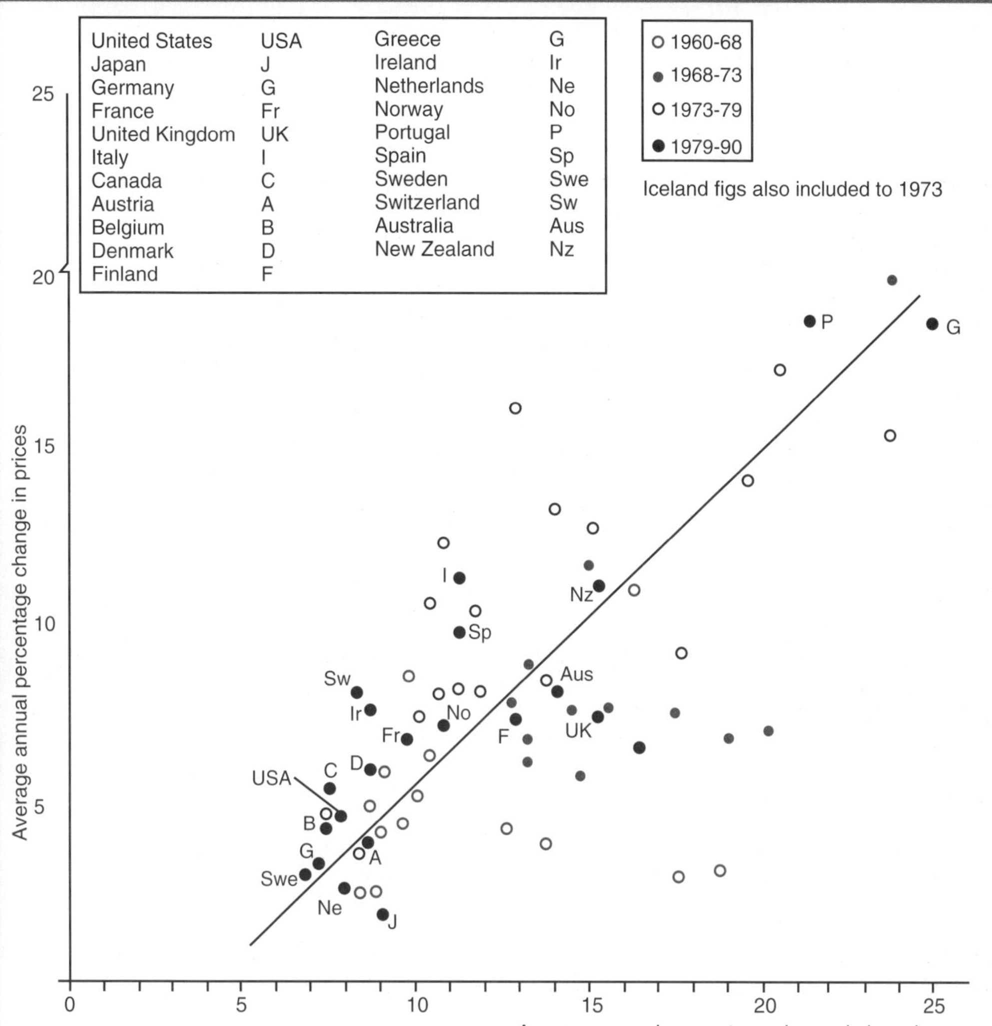

1. GDP deflator. 2. Broad money.
Source: adapted from OECD, *Historical Statistics*, 1960-90.

Figure 76.2 *Inflation[1] and the percentage change in the money supply[2] for OECD countries*

(Denis Healey, Chancellor of the Exchequer from 1976 to 1979 called it 'punk' monetarism!). The targeted measures of the money supply (M1 and M3, now no longer calculated) grew at a much faster rate than inflation. In the middle 1980s, for instance, with inflation at around 5 per cent, M4 was growing in the 12-16 per cent range.

Monetarists today would argue that this arose mainly because of financial deregulation. For instance:

- exchange controls were abolished in 1979;
- controls on bank lending were removed in 1980;
- competition in the banking sector was increased, by allowing building societies to offer banking services under the Building Society Act 1986;
- the London Stock Market was deregulated in 1986.

This led to individuals and companies increasing their demand for money (i.e. controls had rationed the amount of money available to them). Increases in money holdings relative to all other variables led to falls in the velocity of circulation of money, previously thought by monetarists to be broadly constant over time.

However, the increase in money holdings was a one-off effect and by the early 1990s, a more normal relationship between changes in the money supply and inflation became re-established.

For monetarists, the evidence of the 1970s and the 1990s shows clearly that inflation is a monetary phenomenon. They also have an explanation for the unusual relationship between the money supply and prices in the 1980s. For Keynesians, the whole period shows that there is no predictable relationship between the money supply and prices and changes in V often absorb changes in M. Moreover, it may be that the causality is running from increases in prices to increases in the money supply, rather than the other way around as monetarists would suggest. In short, the evidence could be used to support a wide variety of conflicting opinions about the causes of inflation.

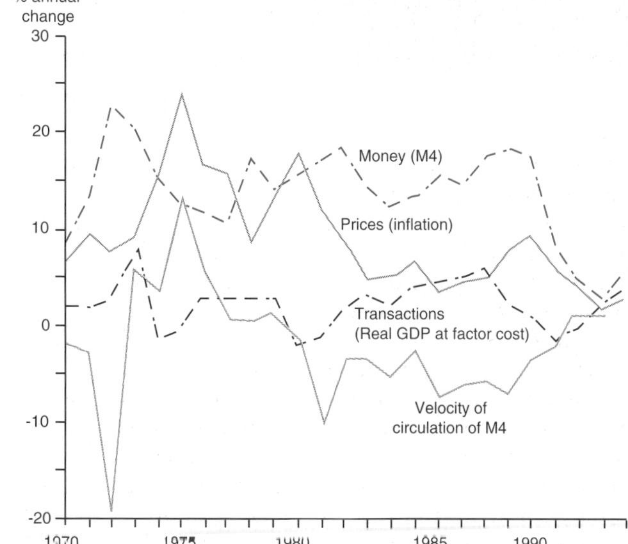

Source: adapted from CSO, *Economic Trends Annual Supplement*.

Figure 76.3 *Annual percentage change in prices, real GDP, the money supply (M4) and the velocity of circulation of M4*

Black economy blurs M0 message

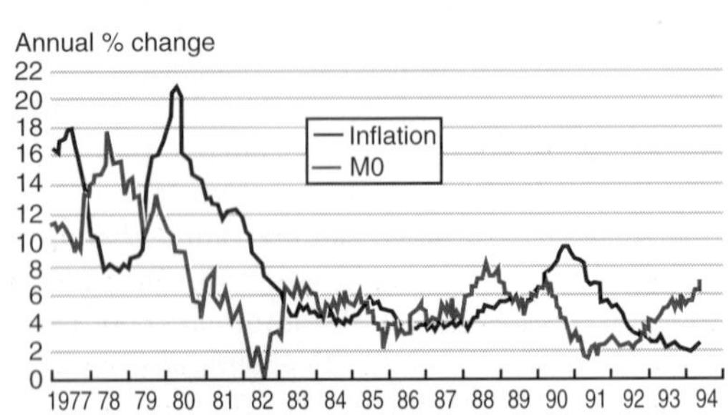

Source: adapted from the Bank of England; CSO.
Figure 76.4 *Money supply, M0 and inflation*

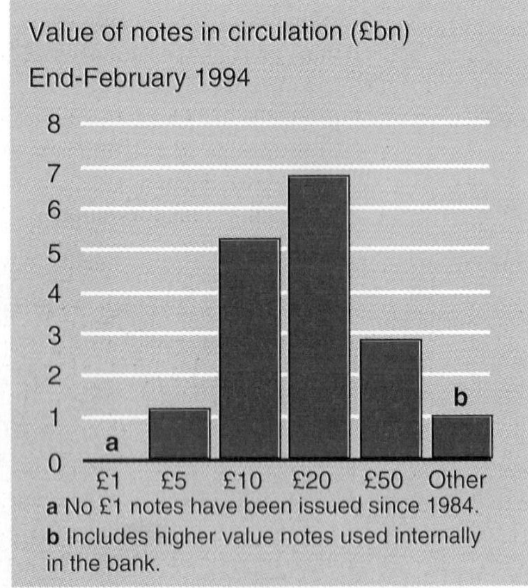

Source: adapted from the Bank of England; CSO.
Figure 76.5 *Value of notes in circulation (£bn)*

If an economist from Mars had picked up a copy of yesterday's money supply figures he or she might have had cause to blink.The annual rate of growth in June of M0, the narrowest measure of money supply, was 6.8 per cent. For more than a year the government and the Bank of England have been solemnly proclaiming that M0's 'monitoring' range should be zero to 4 per cent.

So, the question that an onlooker might ask, as M0 has been soaring out of its target range for several months, is why the rise had not prompted more outcry from the City or the Bank itself?

The main reason, economists say, is a new scepticism about the reliability of M0 as an indicator of high street activity. Many analysts suspect the data are being skewed by low interest rates, changes in banking technology and even the growth of new black-economy activities such as car-boot sales.

M0, which chiefly comprises notes and coins in circulation, has traditionally been of interest to economists for two reasons. First, the figures have been a useful guide to future inflation. Second, they have often provided an early guide to retail sales because more spending creates a greater demand for cash.

In the past six months this relationship has broken down as M0 has surged at a much faster rate than high street spending. The Bank blames the rise primarily on low interest rates. If consumers are not receiving much interest on their bank accounts, the argument goes, they will tend to hold more cash, and so the 'velocity' at which money circulates will slow.

This analysis has been accepted by many City economists, who point out that a similar pattern has occurred in the US. Some analysts are resorting to recalculating the target band to take account of the low velocity. Mr John Marsland of the UBS bank believes that if interest rates are considered the 'real' target limit should be 6.5 per cent. But as a recent Bank of England research report on the subject admitted: 'Gauging the extent to which this fall [in velocity] arises from recent changes in interest rates is difficult.' The guesswork is made harder because interest rates are only one of the factors that influence how consumers use cash. Mr Don Smith of Midland Global Markets believes another influence on M0's growth may be the recent shift towards part-time work, where employees are more likely to be paid in cash.

Meanwhile, the growing use of large-denomination bank notes may indicate that consumers are spending more in the cash-based, black-market economy. Mr Bernard Tennant, retail sales director at the British Chambers of Commerce, says its research shows there has been an 'explosion' in the number of car-boot sales, with at least 1,500 taking place every week.

But calculating whether this kind of factor affects M0 is extremely difficult because of the lack of information about the black economy. Meanwhile, changes in banking technology may be affecting the use of cash. The fact that the number of £20 notes has risen by almost 30 per cent in the past three years and overtaken the £10 note as the most common denomination, for example, is presumed to reflect their popularity in bank cash-dispensers.

In spite of this uncertainty the Bank shows no sign of abandoning its emphasis on M0 yet. As the Bank's report pointed out, comparisons between retail price inflation and M0 in the past 25 years show that M0 has been an accurate predictor of inflation up to six months ahead.

Nevertheless, the same report admitted that it could 'find no convincing explanation' why M0 should have these predictive powers. Indeed, with the government committed to maintaining inflation well below the current M0 data, the Bank has every reason to hope that the current mis-match between M0 and retail sales will produce another statistical discrepancy in six months - this time between M0 and retail price inflation.

Source: the *Financial Times*, 5.7.1994.

1. **(a) What is M0 and (b) why is it considered to be an important economic indicator?**
2. **Explain why, according to the article, the velocity of circulation of M0 might have slowed.**
3. **Why, according to economic theory, should a slowing of the velocity of circulation of M0 affect the predictive power of M0?**
4. **To what extent do you think the changes discussed in the article are likely to continue to distort the long term trend growth in M0?**

unit 77 Monetary policy

Summary

1. Policy goals are established by government. Policy instruments are used to achieve these goals. Intermediate targets are used to monitor the success of government intervention in the economy.
2. One policy instrument is monetary base control, the control of high powered money in the economy.
3. Open market operations can affect the money supply through the purchase and sale of government stock.
4. Manipulating interest rates can affect the demand for money.
5. Other policy instruments include credit controls and controls on the growth of bank lending.

Goals, targets and instruments

Governments today set general **policy goals** such as full employment, price stability, a balance of payments equilibrium and high economic growth. All too often the economy is in crisis. Perhaps there is unemployment, inflation or the balance of payments is in deficit. The government may then choose to act to steer the economy back to a more desirable position. It will use a variety of **policy instruments** to achieve this aim, such as changes in interest rates.

How can the government judge whether it is succeeding in achieving its policy goals? The number of vacancies notified to Jobcentres could be used to judge whether the economy is at full employment - the fewer the number notified, the nearer the economy is to full employment. Notified vacancies would then be called an **intermediate target** - a target to aim for in attempting to reach the policy goal of full employment.

The money supply and the rate of interest are examples of intermediate targets too. It is widely believed, for instance, that excessive increases in the money supply lead to inflation (☞ unit 76). Hence it is important to target the rate of growth of the money supply. MONETARY POLICY is defined as the attempt by government or a central bank to manipulate the money supply, the supply of credit, interest rates or any other monetary variables to achieve the fulfilment of policy goals.

In this unit we shall consider what policy instruments government might use to control monetary variables. In the next unit, we will consider how effective such control might be. Before we proceed, it is important to note two points.

- Some monetary variables such as the rate of interest may be used by government as a policy instrument as well as being an intermediate target. This is one of the problems of policy which can make it difficult for government to control the economy effectively.
- There are various definitions of the money supply ranging from M0 (notes and coins plus bank deposits at the Bank of England) to M4 (the main constituents of which are M0, bank current account deposits, bank deposit account deposits, building society deposits and National Savings deposits). The Bank of England has total control over the issue of notes and coins in the UK. However, less than 1 per cent of M4 is made up of notes and coins. So if it wishes to control anything other than M0, it has to control the amount of money in the banking system and in the wider financial system too.

Monetary base control

Banks have the power to create money (☞ unit 71). But there is a limit to the amount of money that can be created. This is set by the amount of **high powered money** within the system and by the **reserve ratio**. For instance, banks might need to keep 1 per cent (i.e. 0.01) of their total deposits in the form of cash because customers withdraw some cash on a day to day basis from bank branches. Cash is then the high powered money within the system. The money multiplier is 1 ÷ 0.01 or 100. So if the banks held £1 billion in cash, they could create a maximum of £100 billion in deposits. The money supply would then consist of any cash in circulation with the public plus £100 billion of bank deposit money.

One possible way in which a central bank can influence the size of the money supply is if it alters the size of the reserve ratio. Suppose in our example that the central bank issued a directive ordering banks in future to keep 2

QUESTION 1 The money supply is £110 billion. Of this, £10 billion is cash held by the general public and £100 billion is bank deposits. The central bank has decreed that banks must keep 10 per cent of their total liabilities in the form of cash. So the banking system has £10 billion worth of cash in bank vaults and £90 billion worth of loans on its books.

(a) Which asset is high powered money?
(b) What is the reserve ratio?
(c) What is the value of the credit multiplier?
(d) The central bank increases the reserve ratio to 25 per cent. Assuming that there is no change in the amount of cash held by the general public, what will be (i) the new level of bank assets and liabilities and (ii) the new level of the money supply?
(e) What would the answers be in (d) if the reserve ratio were 5 per cent?
(f) Assume that the reserve ratio stays at 10 per cent. The central bank orders all other banks to deposit 1 per cent in cash of their total assets in a special account at the central bank.
   (i) If the general public maintain their cash holdings of £10 billion, what will be the effect on the money supply of this directive?
   (ii) If the banking system could persuade the general public to deposit an extra £1 billion in cash in bank accounts, what would be the effect on the money supply?

per cent of their deposits in the form of cash. With only £1 billion in cash, banks could then only hold £50 billion in deposits. The money supply would have fallen by £50 billion (£100 billion - £50 billion). So increases in the reserve ratio will reduce the money supply, whilst falls in the reserve ratio will increase it.

The central bank can also restrict the supply of reserve assets to the banks. Suppose the central bank forced banks to deposit £ ½ billion of notes with it. They are then not allowed to include these deposits as part of their reserve assets. The banks will therefore see their holdings of reserve assets fall from £1 billion to £ ½ billion. They will be forced to cut the amount of deposits held by the public from £100 billion to £50 billion (1 per cent of £50 billion equalling the £ ½ billion in cash the banks now hold). So restricting the availability of reserve assets to the banks will lead to a fall in the money supply.

Open market operations

The central bank has the unique power to create bank notes or destroy them at almost no cost to itself (the cost being that of printing and distributing the notes). Assume that the central bank prints £1 million in notes and uses the money to buy financial securities such as government bonds (☞ unit 72) from the general public. The public now hold fewer bonds but they hold £1 million more in bank notes. They are likely to deposit most of these in banks. Assume for simplicity that they deposit all the cash in the banking system. If the reserve ratio is 1 per cent and cash is the reserve asset, then £1 million of extra cash deposited in the banks will enable them to create £100 million of extra money through the credit multiplier process.

The reverse is also true. If the central bank sells £1 million of financial securities, the public are likely to pay for these by withdrawing £1 million from the banking system by issuing cheques to the central bank. The central bank will then present the cheques to the banks for payment in cash. The banking system will now lose £1 million of cash and therefore of reserve assets. With a reserve ratio of 1 per cent (i.e. a credit multiplier of 100), the banking system has to reduce assets and liabilities by £100 million.

QUESTION 2 Cash is defined as the reserve asset. The central bank imposes a 5 per cent reserve ratio on the banking system.

(a) What is the credit multiplier?
(b) By how much will the money supply change if the central bank sells the following amounts of government bonds to the general public:
(i) £1 billion; (ii) £250 million; (iii) £500 million?
(c) By how much will the money supply change if the central bank buys the following amounts of government bonds from the general public:
(i) £2 billion; (ii) £200 million; (iii) £600 million?

This process of buying and selling financial securities in exchange for high powered money (cash in our example) is known as OPEN MARKET OPERATIONS. In practice credit multipliers are nowhere near as large as in our examples, but open market operations are still likely to produce a multiple increase or contraction of the money supply.

The discount rate

Banks can go bankrupt whilst still being perfectly sound financially. They only keep enough cash or other liquid assets to meet their day to day needs. They lend out the rest for a longer term. If all the customers of a bank wanted their money back today, the bank would be unable to pay and therefore it would be technically bankrupt. To prevent this from happening, central banks act as lenders of last resort. When there is a shortage of cash in the financial system, the central bank will buy securities for cash. In the UK, discount houses are the channel through which the Bank of England acts as lender of last resort (☞ unit 73).

Banks will suffer no financial penalties for running short of liquid assets such as cash if the central bank is prepared to buy financial assets at their current market value. The current market value of assets such as Treasury Bills, commercial bills, and government stock is determined by the rate of interest (☞ unit 72). The higher the rate of interest, the lower the market value of outstanding bills and bonds. So if the **discount rate** (the interest rate which the central bank uses to calculate the price it will pay for bills and bonds) is equal to the current market rate of interest, the banks will not lose money if they are forced to sell assets to the central bank.

But the higher the central bank sets the discount rate above market rates of interest, the greater will be the loss that banks face if they are forced to sell assets to the central bank when short of cash. So the higher the discount rate above market rates, the greater will be the banks' desired ratio of cash to total assets (i.e. their reserve ratio). With cash holdings constant, they can only increase this ratio by reducing their total assets and thus reducing the money supply.

Increases in the discount rate are also likely to increase bank **base rates** as well as other interest rates in the economy. An increase in interest rates will reduce the demand for money (☞ unit 74). In equilibrium, the demand for money is equal to the supply of money. So in theory an increase in interest rates, with the demand curve for money (the liquidity preference schedule ☞ unit 74) unchanged, can only be sustained if the money supply has fallen too. To achieve higher interest rates, the central bank must be prepared to buy and sell financial assets such as bills and bonds on a day to day basis at the constant higher rate of interest. What the central bank cannot do is choose both an interest rate level and a money supply level. Either it fixes the money supply and allows the rate of interest to find its equilibrium level or it fixes the rate of interest and allows the money supply to adjust.

Funding

In the traditional sense of the term, FUNDING refers to the replacement of short term debt by long term debt. Funding was used in the 19th and early 20th centuries in the UK to manage the National Debt (☞ unit 68), the money which governments had borrowed in the past normally to finance wars. In modern monetary policy, changing the structure of the Debt can affect intermediate targets.

- Reducing the amount of short term debt, such as Treasury Bills, and increasing the amount of long term debt by a corresponding amount will lower short term interest rates (because there is less demand now for loanable funds) and increase long term interest rates (because there is now a greater demand for long term funds). In the early 1980s, the Bank of England adopted a policy similar to this where it issued more long term debt than it needed and used the money from the sales of that debt to buy mainly commercial bills. This policy was called **over-funding** and was designed to increase long term interest rates and reduce the rate of growth of broad money.
- Replacing short term debt with long term debt can also be an instrument of monetary base control. If short term debt is counted by the Bank of England as part of the reserve assets of the banking system (i.e. part of high powered money in the economy), then a reduction in short term debt will lead to a contraction in the money supply.

Since the mid-1980s, the Bank of England has broadly adopted a policy of full funding. This simply means that if the government borrows money, it does so through the issue of long term term stock and it does not 'print' the money. If, as was true in the later 1980s, the government is paying back the National Debt because tax receipts and other revenues are higher than government spending, then the government buys back an equivalent amount of government stock from the market with money (i.e. public borrowing or debt repayment has a neutral effect on the money supply).

Rules and regulations

Central banks have used a variety of other techniques in an attempt to control the money supply. For instance, in the 1970s UK banks were subject to limits on growth of their deposits. Called the **supplementary special deposit** scheme (and nick-named the 'corset'), the Bank of England imposed interest rate penalties on excessive deposit growth. Throughout the post-war period up to 1981, governments used hire purchase controls to limit the amount of hire purchase credit in the economy. During the late 1960s, banks were told to give special priority to firms wishing to borrow money for exports. This was an example of how monetary policy was used to favour certain sectors of the economy at the expense of others.

QUESTION 3 For most of the quarter, the Bank of England adopted a broadly neutral stance in its money market operations. There were brief periods of speculation about an interest rate cut in January, most notably on 19 January, when the three-month rate implied by the futures contract for March fell from 5.31 per cent to 5.17 per cent. The next day, the Bank declined to offer an early round of assistance, despite a money market shortage of £1.2bn. The market's reaction allowed the Bank to resume a broadly neutral stance.

In late January, technical money market conditions tightened and for a period of several days bills were not readily forthcoming in the regular operations. On 27 January, the combination of the settlement of the January gilt auction, speculation that the Bundesbank might reduce its official rates and that this would facilitate lower UK rates, and reluctance on the part of several market participants to sell bills before the end of the month led borrowing from the Bank at 2.45 p.m. to be unusually high, at £915 million.

Source: adapted from Bank of England, *Bank of England Quarterly Bulletin*, May 1994.

(a) On January 19, the money markets thought that short term interest rates were going to be cut by the Bank of England. Using the concepts of demand for and supply of money, explain how the next day, the Bank of England showed the markets that interest rates were not going to be cut.
(b) Why, in late January, were holders of bills reluctant to sell them?
(c) On 27 January, there was a 'settlement of the January gilt auction', when those who had purchased new issue gilts at the gilts auction earlier in the month had to pay for them. (i) Who paid money to whom in this settlement? (ii) There was now a shortage of money in the markets. Why? (iii) If the Bank of England had not intervened, what would have happened to interest rates as a consequence? Use a demand and supply diagram to illustrate your answer. (iv) How did the Bank of England prevent interest rates from changing?

Key terms

Monetary policy - the attempt by government or a central bank to manipulate the money supply, the supply of credit, interest rates or any other monetary variables, to achieve the fulfilment of policy goals such as price stability.
Open market operations - the buying and selling of financial securities in exchange for high powered money in order to increase or decrease the size of the money supply.
Funding - the replacement of short term debt by long term debt.

Applied economics

UK monetary policy, 1950 - 1979

1950 - 1971

Before 1971, the two main intermediate targets of UK monetary policy were the rate of interest and the growth in credit. The rate of interest was considered significant because it could affect the level of investment in the economy and, more importantly, influence the value of the pound on foreign exchange markets. The amount of credit offered by banks and finance houses affected the total demand for goods and services in the UK, including the demand for imports.

The Bank of England exercised control over interest rates through operations in the discount market, setting a bank rate (the discount rate explained above) which then influenced all other money market interest rates.

The volume of credit was in part controlled through the imposition of **lending ceilings**. These were an example of **quantitative** controls. The Bank of England set limits on the growth of bank lending. There was a **qualitative** element in that restrictions on lending were made far tighter for personal customers than for businesses. A company wanting to borrow money for a factory to produce exports, for instance, would be far more likely to be granted a loan than an individual wanting to borrow to buy a car. There were also controls on **hire purchase**. Credit cards were only introduced in the late 1960s, and hire purchase was a very important way in which ordinary people borrowed money. The Bank of England set maximum repayment periods and minimum deposits in an attempt to regulate the demand for hire purchase.

In theory, the Bank of England had the power to use monetary base control. Banks had to keep 8 per cent of their liabilities in cash and 28 per cent in other liquid assets such as Treasury Bills and commercial bills. By limiting the amount of cash held by the banks or by reducing the supply of liquid assets, the Bank of England could have induced a multiple contraction in the money supply. Indeed, in 1960, the Bank moved one step towards this when it introduced the **special deposits** scheme. This allowed the Bank of England to force the banks to deposit with it a proportion of their assets. Special deposits were, therefore, forced loans by the banks to the Bank of England and in theory reduced their ability to make loans to consumers and industries. However, except possibly in 1969, the banks were not, in practice, constrained in their lending by the scheme.

1971-1976

In the 1960s, as the number of banks and other financial institutions in the UK grew, it became increasingly apparent that a significant number of borrowers were avoiding the lending ceilings imposed on the main clearing banks by borrowing money from financial institutions not subject to Bank of England controls (this is known as **disintermediation** ☞ unit 78). The Bank responded by changing its approach to monetary policy. In 1971, in a document entitled *Competition and Credit Control*, it declared that it would control credit in future not through lending ceilings (a form of rationing) but via the price mechanism. The rate of interest would be used to restrict credit and control the growth of the money supply. Lending ceilings and hire purchase restrictions were abolished, although the special deposits scheme was retained. The 8 per cent cash ratio and 28 per cent liquid assets ratio were replaced by a $12\frac{1}{2}$ per cent reserve asset ratio (reserve assets were a variety of liquid assets such as Treasury Bills, but not cash) with banks agreeing to keep $1\frac{1}{2}$ per cent of their assets as balances with the Bank of England. Bank rate was renamed minimum lending rate (MLR), although its function remained the same as before.

Competition and Credit Control proved to be a failure. Its introduction was followed by an explosive increase in the money supply. M4 increased by 70 per cent between 1971 and the end of 1973. Part of the failure was due to the fact that borrowers who had been limited in their borrowing before 1971 increased their borrowings. Perhaps more importantly, it was introduced at a time when the Conservative government of Edward Heath and his Chancellor Anthony Barber was preparing to spend its way out of a recession. Interest rates needed to be kept low if investment and consumer spending were to be encouraged. But low interest rates encouraged record borrowing. In December 1973, the Bank of England was forced to reintroduce hire purchase controls. It also introduced the **supplementary special deposits scheme**, the 'corset', which penalised banks exceeding lending limits by forcing them to deposit money with the Bank of England at a zero rate of interest.

Essentially, *Competition and Credit Control* failed because the government was unwilling to impose sufficiently high interest rates to curb the credit boom. Instead it reverted to the quantitative controls of the 1950s and 1960s.

1976-1979

Before 1976, the intermediate targets of monetary policy had been the rate of interest and the volume of credit. In 1976, the Labour Chancellor of the Exchequer, Denis Healey, introduced a new intermediate target, growth of the money supply M3 (notes and coins plus bank deposits, a definition of the money supply now no longer calculated). In the first half of the 1970s, many economists had become convinced that changes in the money supply caused changes in inflation (the belief known as **monetarism** ☞ unit 76). Therefore, control of the money supply was essential if governments were to reduce inflation.

It was not intended that monetary policy should actively be used to achieve the target set. Rather, the target was to be used as an indicator when planning the level of government borrowing or setting interest rates. In practice, since 1976 the money supply has always tended to grow at a faster rate than the target set by the government.

The Labour government of 1974-9 used a range of monetary policy instruments to constrain credit and the growth of the money supply. Quantitative controls in the form of the corset were in use, as were restrictions on hire purchase. There was also much greater awareness that the way in which the Public Sector Borrowing Requirement (PSBR) was financed and its size could have an important impact on the growth of the money supply and on interest rates. The Bank of England was no longer allowed to print the money needed by government to cover the PSBR (printing money would otherwise have led to an increase in the money supply). This was achieved by ensuring that new government debt was sold only to the non-bank sector. It was also recognised that the size of the PSBR would have an impact on interest rates. The lower the PSBR, the lower could be the rate of interest.

Tradition in the balance

The role of discount houses has been questioned for the post 30-40 years. The following, written in 1992, gives one view of the debate.

Some people regard them as the most noble institutions in the City of London. Others think that they should die.

The City's discount houses are in the thick of a revolution. For as long as anyone can remember, these money market dealers have played a crucial role in the Bank of England's sterling operations, acting as the valves through which liquidity passes from the Bank to the commercial banks. But now, nearly three centuries after they were founded, voices in the City are saying these dealers have outlived their usefulness. 'They are ancient history, a complete anachronism,' says Mr Neil MacKinnon, chief economist of Yamaichi International in London.

Critics argue that London is looking increasingly out of step as the only European financial centre to use such intermediaries as discount houses in its money market operations.

'Given the expansion of the money markets globally, they now have a place only in the history books,' Mr MacKinnon says.

Their relationship with the central bank is jealously guarded. If the commercial banks are short of cash, one way they can balance their books is by borrowing money from a discount house. The commercial banks obtain cash by selling an eligible bill, essentially a post-dated cheque, to a discount house which, in turn, sells it to the Bank. The rates at which the Bank lends to the discount houses influence the level of lending rates throughout the banking system. This intermediary role is now under attack from several fronts.

- **British clearing banks**. In the past year, the balance of power in the money market has shifted towards the clearers, as the Bank of England has allowed the protection given to the discount market to be eroded.In the 1970s, the Bank ruled that the commercial banks had to place a proportion of assets in the form of secured callable deposits with the discount market. This cash, which averaged around 5 per cent of a bank's eligible liabilities, was known as 'club money' and gave the discount houses an assured source of funding at lower rates than those in the market.In the past year, the 'club money' practice has faded. Commercial banks no longer have to place a minimum level of funds with the discount houses. Instead, they have begun keeping larger stocks of bills on their books. This gives the bigger clearing banks greater leverage over the market. A common practice among clearers is to push short-term rates in the money markets downwards when it suits their books, by passing many bills on to the discount houses at once. They can deploy bills in the quantities they need to, rather than relaying on the liquidity services of the discount houses.
- **Monetary convergence**. Another challenge comes from the plans for monetary convergence envisaged in the Maastricht Treaty on European Monetary Union (EMU). The Bank of England's operations are unlike those in the other 11 EC countries. In Germany, for example, the Bundesbank deals directly with the nation's banks rather than through intermediaries. It keeps a tight rein over day-to-day money market developments by obliging banks to place minimum reserves in non-interest-bearing accounts at the central bank and, by way of compensation, operates a limited discount window for the banks at favourable interest rates.The Bundesbank operates only once a week in the open market, rather than every day as the Bank of England does. 'It is a lot simpler on the continent,' says one money market trader in London. 'If there is monetary union, Britain will have to resort to the European way.'Last month, Mr Eddie George, deputy governor of the Bank of England, also hinted that the Bank was less committed to the discount market principle. He said some of the subtlety of national money market techniques, 'tailored to national market circumstances', could be lost in the move to EMU.
- **Government policy**. The discount houses' profits are being eroded by the British government's cautious policy on base rates. When base rates move sharply downward, the discount houses make larger profits because the capital value of the bills they hold rises. But in the past year, the Bank has pursued a policy of infrequent rate cuts. Sterling's membership of the Exchange Rate Mechanism has tended to reduce volatilities in the cash market, and in the short sterling futures market where the discount houses are also big players.

It is unlikely that the Bank of England will desert the discount houses in the immediate future, having had such a close relationship with them over the centuries.But the market is unsure how the Bank will react in the long term, both to the pressures from Britain's clearing banks and the need to conform to continental-style monetary operations in the run-up to EMU.

Source: adapted from the *Financial Times*, 22.6.1992.

1. (a) What is a discount house?
(b) How can discount houses make a loss?
2. Describe the role of discount houses in the London money markets.
3. Explain the difference between the way in which the Bundesbank and the Bank of England operate monetary policy.
4. Discuss whether the Bank of England could continue to operate monetary policy successfully without using discount houses.

The limitations of monetary policy

Summary

1. There is much controversy about the ability of central banks to control the money supply.
2. Attempts to control the growth of bank lending have resulted in disintermediation.
3. Monetary base control could well result in highly volatile short term interest rates. The central bank would also need to have a firm control on the assets which form the monetary base of the economy. Even then monetary policy may be rendered ineffective because of disintermediation.
4. Controlling the money supply through the control of interest rates assumes that the demand for money is stable. Keynesian economists would question this assumption.
5. It is not possible to control simultaneously the money supply, the rate of interest, the level of government borrowing and the exchange rate because all are interlinked.
6. Economists differ as to whether the money supply is exogenous or endogenous.

Monetary policy

The economic theory outlined in unit 77 would suggest that the central bank has a battery of policy instruments with which to control either the money supply or the rate of interest. In practice, monetary policy is extremely complex and it is far from clear whether the central bank has any real control over monetary variables. Why is this?

Disintermediation

A student wishing to buy a magazine has two alternatives if the one she wants is not available at the local shop. Either the student could give up the search altogether, or she could try another shop. Bank loans can be seen to be like the magazine. Assume the central bank is attempting to control the money supply by restricting the growth of bank lending. Potential borrowers then have two choices. Either they don't borrow, in which case the central bank has achieved its policy objective, or they find another way of borrowing the money.

In practice, both are likely to occur. For instance, the operation of the supplementary special deposits scheme (the 'corset' ☞ unit 77) probably led to some reduction in bank lending. But it also encouraged banks and their customers to find new ways of borrowing and lending money which would not appear on the officially controlled balance sheets of the banks. At the time, banks got firms to lend directly to each other. The bank put the two sides in contact with each other and provided insurance cover to the lender in case of default by the borrower. The bank charged a fee for its work - equivalent to the profit it would have earned if it had received a deposit and then lent out the money in the normal way.

This process is an example of DISINTERMEDIATION and it results in the measured money supply being lower than the actual supply of money. When the corset was abolished in 1980, there was a significant jump in broad money figures as money which had been driven underground by monetary control measures returned to the official system.

Disintermediation becomes easier the more alternative forms of borrowing and lending are available. The abolition of **exchange controls** (☞ unit 87) in 1979 meant that there was nothing to prevent a firm which had been refused a loan in London from borrowing the money in New York or Frankfurt. Equally, the abolition of many of the legal restrictions in the financial markets in the 1980s (known as **deregulation**), including 'Big Bang' and the freeing of building societies to provide many banking services, has made it even more difficult for the Bank of England to prevent disintermediation taking place.

Disintermediation is an example of GOODHART'S LAW. Professor Charles Goodhart argued that if the

QUESTION 1 In 1989, in the Mansion House Speech, given each year by the Chancellor of the Exchequer, Nigel Lawson said: 'I am urged by some to consider a return to some form of direct credit controls ... Any attempt to impose restrictions on UK lending institutions would very soon be as full of holes as a colander, not least because of offshore flows.'

What did he mean?

authorities attempted to manipulate one variable which had a stable relationship with another variable, then that relationship would change or break down as behaviour adapts to manipulation. Controlling bank lending won't reduce the money supply - but it will lead to a breakdown in the former stable relationship between bank lending and monetary growth as borrowers borrow outside the banking system.

Monetary base control

Many monetarists have argued that the only effective way of controlling the money supply is through monetary base control. But there are a number of problems with this. First, the central bank is likely to define the monetary base in very narrow terms. High powered money is likely to be defined as cash, or bank balances with the central bank. On any one day, banks are likely to find themselves with too much high powered money or too little. Because the stock of high powered money is relatively small, these surpluses or deficits are likely to lead to large day to day fluctuations in short term interest rates. If the banks are short of high powered money, they will need to borrow the money and this will push up interest rates, and vice versa. Sharp fluctuations in short term money market interest rates will be unsettling for the financial markets as a whole. The Bank of England in the post-war era has always placed a great emphasis upon the stability of day to day short term interest rates. So monetary base control would conflict with this objective.

Second, there is doubt about the ability of the central bank to control the stock of high powered money. Assume that the central bank declares that banks must keep 1 per cent of their assets in cash. The central bank then reduces the amount of cash in circulation, hoping to reduce the money supply by bringing about a multiple contraction in bank assets and liabilities. The banks may respond by tempting their customers to place more of the cash in circulation with the banks. For instance, they could increase interest rates, hoping to make deposits of cash more attractive, or they could make it easier or less costly to use money substitutes such as credit cards. There is only one type of high powered money which cannot be manipulated in this way - balances by the banks with the central bank. If the central bank were to use this as a policy weapon, banks would have every incentive to devise deals which did not show up on their balance sheets (i.e. engage in disintermediation).

QUESTION 2 In the same 1989 Mansion House speech quoted above, the Chancellor of the Exchequer, Nigel Lawson, said: 'It has ... been alleged recently that Germany does indeed use credit controls, operated through their use of reserve ratios for the banking system. This is a complete misunderstanding. The reserve ratio, which in practice is rarely changed, is the mechanism by which the German authorities generate the money market shortages necessary to give them control over interest rates. We achieve precisely the same effect by different technical means. To suppose that the German reserve ratio requirement somehow separately doubles as a direct credit control, let alone a consumer credit control, is moonshine.'

(a) Explain, using a diagram, how the German authorities use reserve ratios to 'give them control over interest rates'.
(b) How, in theory, could reserve ratios be used as a 'direct credit control'?

The demand for money

The main thrust of UK monetary policy in the post-war era has been the control of interest rates rather than the money supply. Even after 1976 when the Bank of England first announced money supply targets, interest rates were used to shift the money supply curve. This is shown in Figure 78.1. Assume that the central bank wishes to reduce the money supply from MS_1 to MS_2. To achieve this it would raise interest rates from r_1 to r_2 on the assumption that there could be a movement back up the liquidity preference schedule (i.e. there would be a reduction in the quantity of money demanded) and therefore the money supply would have to fall to achieve equilibrium. But this assumes that the central bank knows the shape of the liquidity preference schedule. If it is more interest inelastic than it thinks, then an increase in interest rates will not reduce the money supply by as much as the central bank hoped. Moreover, if the liquidity preference schedule is unstable, there will be frequent shifts of the schedule, making interest rate policy unpredictable in its effects. This is often argued by Keynesian economists.

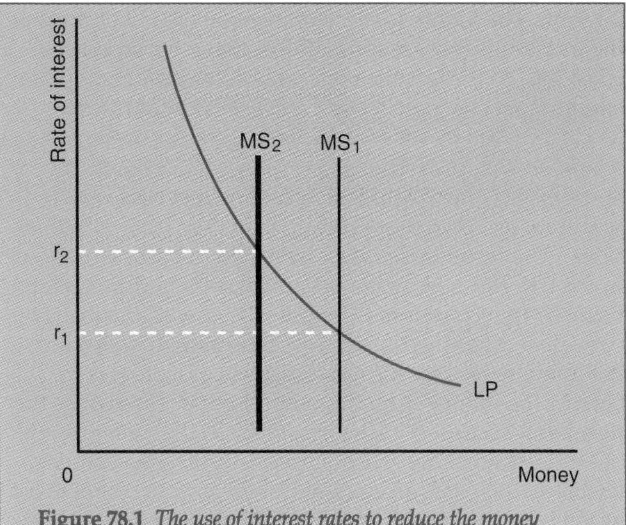

Figure 78.1 *The use of interest rates to reduce the money supply*
An increase in the rate of interest from r_1 to r_2 will be accompanied by a fall in the supply of money if the liquidity preference schedule is stable.

Policy constraints

Even if the central bank could control the money supply, it

QUESTION 3

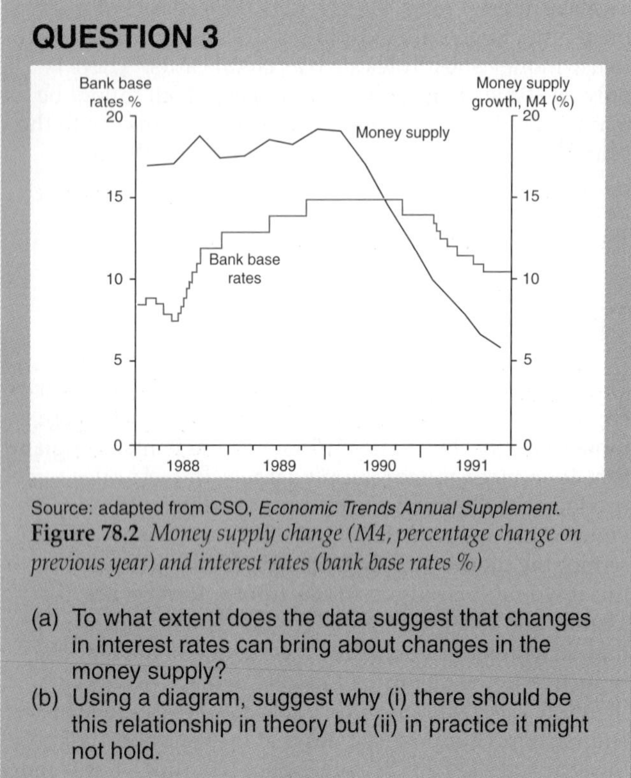

Source: adapted from CSO, *Economic Trends Annual Supplement.*

Figure 78.2 *Money supply change (M4, percentage change on previous year) and interest rates (bank base rates %)*

(a) To what extent does the data suggest that changes in interest rates can bring about changes in the money supply?

(b) Using a diagram, suggest why (i) there should be this relationship in theory but (ii) in practice it might not hold.

might not choose to do so because of other policy constraints.

The money supply and the rate of interest The central bank cannot fix both the money supply and the rate of interest. The higher the rate of interest, the lower must be the money supply assuming the demand for money is constant. So the government cannot, for instance, operate a tight monetary policy and have low interest rates.

The money supply, the rate of interest and the PSBR Since the Second World War, governments have traditionally spent more money than they have raised in taxes. The result is that they have had to borrow money. In the UK, this borrowing is known as the **public sector borrowing requirement** (☞ unit 68). Governments have two ways of raising this money, assuming that they are not going to borrow it from foreigners. The first is to borrow the money from the general public (known as the **non-bank sector**). This has no effect on the money supply but it does affect the rate of interest. If the government wishes to increase the amount, it will have to compete for funds with consumers and firms. This extra demand for borrowed funds will increase their price (i.e. the rate of interest will rise). Conversely, a fall in the PSBR will reduce total demand for borrowed funds and thus the rate of interest will fall. So the government cannot choose both the level of the PSBR and the rate of interest if genuine borrowing takes place.

The government has a second option when financing the PSBR. It could choose to print the money. In a modern economy, it does this by selling government debt to the **banking sector**. Tables 78.1 and 78.2 show how this is achieved. Before, in a one bank economy, the bank has £100 of deposits from customers and, with a 10 per cent cash ratio, keeps £10 in cash and lends the rest out in loans (☞ unit 71). The government now sells the bank £10 of stock which the bank pays for with cash. The government spends the cash and it reappears in the banking system in

Table 78.1

			£
Deposits	100	Cash	10
		Loans	90
		Government stock	0
Total	100		100

Table 78.2

			£
Deposits	110	Cash	11
		Loans	89
		Government stock	10
Total	110		110

the form of new deposits. Deposits therefore increase to £110. As assets, the bank has £10 of government stock. If it is to maintain a 10 per cent cash ratio, it has to reduce its loans to £89 and keep an extra £1 in cash to increase its cash holdings to £11. The important figure is the one for total deposits because these appear in the money supply. They have increased from £100 to £110. Hence, the central bank has effectively 'printed' the money it needed through the banking system. Note that if it had sold government stock to the non- bank sector, bank customers who bought the stock would initially have withdrawn cash from the bank to pay for it. There would then have been an equal and opposite movement as other customers who had received extra cash from the government deposited this in the bank. Overall, the balance sheet of the bank would have remained the same.

There is a long history of governments resorting to the printing presses to finance spending. This method has the advantage that the government does not need to raise taxes. It also means that interest rates do not need to rise. Indeed, they are likely to fall because the money supply will rise. So the government cannot choose both the level of the PSBR and the money supply if it resorts to the printing presses to finance borrowing.

The money supply, the rate of interest and the exchange rate The **exchange rate** is the rate at which one currency can be exchanged for another (☞ unit 87). It is a market price, and therefore the exchange rate is determined by the forces of demand and supply. Governments can intervene to try and fix the exchange rate at a particular level by either buying or selling currency. For instance, if the Bank of England wanted to make the value of the pound fall against other currencies, then it could sell pounds for currencies such as dollars and deutschmarks. But the pounds it sells must come from somewhere. If the Bank prints the money, it will raise the money supply. If it borrows the money from the public, it will raise the demand for loans and hence raise the rate of interest.

Alternatively the value of the pound can be changed by changing interest rates. A rise in interest rates in the UK will attract an inflow of funds to the country increasing the demand for the currency and hence raising its price. The rise in interest rates can only be engineered through a fall in the money supply. So the Bank of England again faces a trade-off in its policy objectives.

The money supply, the rate of interest, the PSBR and the exchange rate are all interlinked. If the government fixes a value for one, it cannot fix a value for others. Hence a government may choose not to control the money supply in order to control other variables such as the rate of interest.

QUESTION 4 In 1987 and early 1988, the value of the pound against other currencies rose. The Chancellor of the Exchequer, Nigel Lawson, believed that this would prove damaging to the economy and he attempted to limit this rise by cutting interest rates. Bank base rates fell from 11 per cent at the start of 1987 to a low of $7^{1}/_{2}$ per cent in mid-1988. However, there were worrying signs that inflation was beginning to increase. The government sharply increased interest rates to 15 per cent by the end of 1988 to brake the rise in the money supply. At the same time, the foreign exchange markets lost confidence in the pound, the value of the pound fell and the Chancellor had to raise interest rates again in 1989 to prevent the pound from falling further.

Using illustrations from the passage, explain the policy conflict between control of the money supply, control of interest rates and exchange rate control.

The flow of funds equation

Many of the points already made can be seen from using a FLOW OF FUNDS EQUATION. This breaks down any increase in the money supply into individual components. The flow of funds equation differs for different measures of the money supply. However, for M4, any increase in the money supply equals:

- the PSBR - Public Sector Borrowing Requirement (or *minus* the Public Sector Debt Repayment);
- *minus* the sales of government stock and any other public sector debt to the non-bank private sector (or *plus* purchases of public sector debt from the non-bank sector);
- *plus* banks and building societies' sterling lending to the UK private sector;
- *plus* the external effect.

The increase in the money supply (ΔMS) =

+ PSBR

- non-bank private sector lending to the government

+ bank lending to the non-bank private sector

+ external effect

To understand why this is the case, it is important to consider how money is being injected into or withdrawn from the economy. The government injects money into the economy when it spends more than it raises in taxes and other revenues. So the larger the PSBR the greater the increase in the money supply. On the other hand, money is withdrawn from the economy when the government sells stocks and other securities to private individuals and non-bank firms (i.e. the government is engaged in **open market operations**). If the government fully funds the PSBR (i.e. sells £1 of government stock to private individuals and non-bank firms to pay for every £1 of the PSBR), then there is no effect on the money supply. If, on the other hand, the PSBR is greater than sales of government stock to the non-bank private sector, then there will be an increase in the money supply.

The money supply can also increase if there is a growth in banks' and building societies lending to individuals and firms. A very small proportion of the money lent will end up as an increase in notes and coins in circulation, part of M4. The rest will end up as new deposits in banks and building societies, which again will form part of the measured increase in M4.

Finally, the money supply can increase if there is a net inflow of funds from abroad. This external effect is made up of three components. If the government sells government stock to foreigners, then this has a minus effect on the flow of funds and the money supply. This is because foreigners have to buy pounds or use the pounds they own to buy the government stock. The pounds are given to the government and therefore removed from the money supply. The second component is bank lending by UK banks to foreigners. If UK banks lend pounds to foreigners, then the money supply of pounds will increase. The third component is changes in the Bank of England's currency reserves. The Bank of England keeps reserves of gold and foreign currencies (☞ unit 97). It uses these to intervene in the foreign currency markets to change the price of the pound. When the Bank of England buys foreign currency by issuing pounds, this increases the UK money supply. If, on the other hand, the Bank of England sells foreign currency for pounds, the money supply is reduced because there will be fewer pounds in circulation.

The dilemmas facing the Bank of England now become very clear.

- If the government increases the PSBR but doesn't finance that by borrowing from the non-bank private sector or from overseas, then the money supply will

QUESTION 5

Table 78.3 *Flow of funds, M4*

£ million

	PSBR 1	Purchases by non-bank private sector of government debt 2	Bank and building society lending to the private sector 3	External effect 4	Change in M4 5
1987	-143	- 4 124	45 291	2 038	41 817
1988	-11 868	3 840	69 435	-8 737	52 670
1989	-9 276	12 821	78 811	-18 113	64 229
1990	-2 125	-651	63 221	-8 968	51 413
1991	7 693	- 5 543	28 142	-2 526	27 682
1992	28 650	- 20 092	13 422	-3 702	18 112
1993	42 503	- 30 009	8 553	3 170	24 219
1994	37 195	-23 056	16 586	-6 675	24 052

Note: columns 1 + 2 + 3 + 4 = 5. For statistical reasons the numbers may not always add up.
Source: adapted from CSO, *Financial Statistics.*

(a) Describe the change in M4 over the period 1987-1994.
(b) (i) To what extent did the change in bank and building society lending to the private sector mirror the changes in M4?
(ii) Interest rates fell in 1987-88 but then rose sharply before beginning to fall again in 1991. How might this account for the changes in bank and building society lending?

increase - it will have effectively 'printed' the money.

- If the Bank of England finances the PSBR by borrowing from the non-bank private sector, then interest rates will tend to rise because there will be an increased demand for loanable funds in the UK.
- If the PSBR is financed by borrowing the money from abroad, this will tend to raise the exchange rate of the pound because it is increasing the demand for pounds on foreign exchange markets.
- If the Bank of England wishes to change the exchange rate using its foreign currency reserves, then there will inevitably be an effect on the money supply.
- Even if the PSBR and the foreign currency reserves are having no impact on the money supply, it can still increase if bank and building society lending is increasing. But the many attempts to control lending in the past through rules, regulations, funding, etc. have not been very successful. So the UK government today has come to rely on manipulating interest rates to achieve changes in growth in lending. However, the government then can't control both the rate of increase of the money supply and the rate of interest.

Money supply: exogenous or endogenous?

Keynesians tend to argue that central banks can, at best, only loosely control the money supply, and then only in the short term. In the long term it is the financial system which determines the money supply. The money supply is then said to be **endogenous** (i.e. determined within the system). The money supply curve is then drawn upward sloping as in Figure 78.3. The higher the rate of interest, the higher the price the banks will receive for the creation of money. Therefore the higher the rate of interest, the higher will be the amount of money supplied to the market.

Monetarists tend to argue that central banks can control the money supply. They often cite the US Federal Reserve Bank and the German Bundesbank as examples of strong central banks which have achieved monetary stability.

They argue that the failure of a central bank to control its money supply is a failure of will often caused by political interference from government more interested in controlling other variables such as the exchange rate than in controlling the money supply. The Bank of England is often cited as an example of such a central bank. If the central bank does control the money supply then the money supply curve is vertical as in Figure 78.1. It shows that whatever the rate of interest, the central bank fixes the amount of money in circulation.

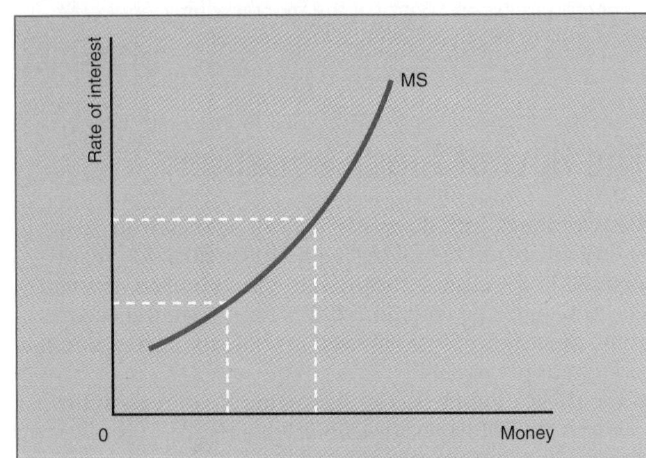

Figure 78.3 *An endogenous supply of money curve*
The banking system increases the supply of money as the rate of interest increases.

Key terms

Disintermediation - in the financial system, the process of bypassing established financial intermediaries to achieve the same result as would have occurred if a financial intermediary had been used.

Goodhart's law - if the authorities attempt to manipulate one variable which had a stable relationship with another variable before, then the relationship will change or break down.

Flow of funds equation - shows how money is injected and withdrawn from the economy to produce a change in the money supply.

Applied economics

UK monetary policy, 1979 - 1995

The Conservative administration that came into office in June 1979 was, to start with at least, monetarist in its views. Its most important policy goal was the reduction of inflation and it believed that inflation was caused by excessive increases in the money supply. It therefore attached far more importance to money supply targets than the previous Labour administration. Money supply targets (the **intermediate target** of monetary policy, along with the PSBR) were written by the Chancellor of the Exchequer Geoffrey Howe into the **Medium Term Financial Strategy**, first published with the 1980 Budget. A reduction in the money supply was to be achieved by:

- setting interest rates high enough to lower the demand for money;
- financing the PSBR without printing money by selling government debt to the non-bank sector;
- allowing the exchange rate to float, to prevent the buying and selling of foreign currencies from affecting the money supply.

Interest rates, the PSBR and the exchange rate therefore became the **monetary instruments** of government policy.

High interest rates were achieved through increasing Minimum Lending Rate in the discount market. Within five months of coming into office, the government increased MLR from 12 per cent to 17 per cent.

The government attempted to cut the PSBR by reducing government expenditure and raising taxes. Cuts in the PSBR were seen as essential, partly because it was feared that the PSBR would in practice be financed through printing money (despite the sale of new debt to the non-bank sector), and partly because cuts in the PSBR were essential if interest rates were to be reduced from their record levels.

The absence of government intervention in the foreign exchange market resulted in an increase in the value of the pound. The effective exchange rate index increased from 107 in the second quarter of 1979 to 127 in the first quarter of 1981, an appreciation of 19 per cent in less than two years.

Unfortunately for the government, its policy instruments proved neither adequate nor suitable to the task of constraining the money supply within pre-set targets. In the early 1980s, the money supply grew at approximately twice the rate set by the government. In part, this can be explained by the government's desire to deregulate financial markets. In 1979, the government abolished **exchange controls**, controls on the amount of sterling that could be taken abroad for investment purposes. The corset was abolished in June 1980, leading to a sudden jump in the money supply as hidden money returned to the official banking system. There were therefore no quantitative controls on bank lending left. This led to an increase in bank borrowing, and therefore the money supply, as individuals and companies increased their borrowings to their 'free market' level. Increases in debt as a proportion of income rose throughout most of the 1980s fuelled by further measures such as the deregulation of building societies in 1985.

In part, however, it came to be realised that there was no simple connection between the rate of interest, increases in the money supply (however measured) and the rate of inflation. One explanation of this is that controlling the money supply through interest rates assumes that the demand for money is a stable function of income - which it cannot have been in the early to mid-1980s. Indeed, the demand for money must have considerably increased, indicating that the controls of the 1960s and 1970s had artificially depressed the demand for money.

By the mid-1980s, the government had effectively abandoned attempts to control the growth of the money supply, and in November 1985 abandoned M3 as an intermediate target.

The government was divided about whether or not the exchange rate should be used as a new intermediate target (☞ unit 98 for a further discussion about what follows). The Chancellor of the Exchequer, Nigel Lawson, believed that fixing the value of the pound against the deutschmark would prevent increases in inflation resulting from devaluations of the pound. He also believed that a fixed value of the pound would impose a discipline on government and industry. To prevent devaluation, the UK inflation rate would have to fall to the level of the German inflation rate. Governments therefore would be forced to set sufficiently high interest rates to reduce growth of the money supply and therefore the level of inflation. Industry could not expect government to finance inflationary pay awards by increasing the money supply and then devaluing the pound to restore UK industrial competitiveness on world markets. Others, led by the Prime Minister Margaret Thatcher, believed that the UK should use interest rates as the main policy weapon to reduce the money supply and bring down inflation, and allow the exchange rate to find its own level.

In 1987, the Chancellor indicated that the pound would 'shadow' the deutschmark. For a variety of reasons, the pound almost immediately began to rise against the deutschmark, and the Chancellor reacted by bringing down interest rates. By mid-1988, it became clear that inflationary pressures were building up again in the UK economy. The government decided to combat inflation by raising interest rates. But raising interest rates would also lead to a rise in the value of the pound against the deutschmark. The Chancellor lost the argument about pegging the exchange rate and bank base rates were increased from 7.5 per cent in May 1988 to 15 per cent by October 1989 whilst the value of the pound increased from 3.00 deutschmarks in the second half of 1987 to nearly 3.25 deutschmarks in the first quarter of 1989. But by October 1990, the government, due to pressure from its EU partners, reversed its policy of allowing the pound to float and joined the European Exchange Rate Mechanism, thus putting stability of the exchange rate as an intermediate target once again.

Britain's entry to the ERM was, in retrospect, a disastrous move. For those economists against Britain's membership, it was a disaster because it forced the Bank of England to keep interest rates at too high a level. Bank base rates were cut in October 1990 to 14 per cent and then slowly came down to 10 per cent by May 1992. However, real interest rates increased over the period, from 3.6 per cent in the third quarter of 1990 to 5.8 per cent in the second quarter of 1992. The result was that the economy remained stuck in a what became the longest recession since the 1930s. Critics of ERM membership said that inflation had been defeated in 1990-91 and there should have been a substantial relaxation in monetary policy then aimed at getting the economy moving again. Many proponents of Britain's membership of the ERM felt that the UK had entered at too high an exchange rate. The decision to go in at a very high exchange rate was based on previous thinking which had led to the shadowing of the deutschmark in 1987. A high pound would force firms to cut costs and keep them low. If they didn't, they would lose business and could go bankrupt because they were in direct competition with low inflation German and French firms.

On 16th September 1992, 'Black Wednesday', the government's economic policies were shattered when the foreign exchange markets forced the pound out of the ERM (☞ unit 97). This, arguably, proved a turning point for the success of government policy. It enabled the government to bring down interest rates rapidly, from their 10 per cent level before Black Wednesday to 6 per cent in January 1993 and to a low of 5.25 per cent in February 1994. The economy quickly got moving again with much lower interest rates and a pound which had been devalued by approximately 13 per cent. The government was even prepared in 1993-4 to underfund the PSBR by £5bn by selling government stock to the bank sector, thus directly increasing the money supply.

Money supply growth during 1992-5 remained very subdued. This was despite a pick up in the economy and a huge £46bn PSBR in 1993-4. In fact, the government and the Bank of England increasingly discounted the evidence from money supply figures about what was going on in the economy at the time and what the future rate of inflation might be. M0 growth was erratic, with speculation that a growth in the **black economy** (☞ unit 60) at a time of high unemployment was fuelling demand for high denomination notes. M4 growth was dampened because of subdued bank and building society lending. Investment till 1995 was low, and hence firms were not borrowing to expand. Consumers only began to increase their net consumer debt in 1995. High real interest rates, previous indebtedness, high unemployment and a lack of confidence all made consumers cautious about borrowing. More importantly, mortgage lending was stagnant with the housing market stuck in a deep rut. On the other hand, by 1994 the economy was growing at above long term average growth rates and there were signs that bottlenecks were already appearing in a few industries. International commodity prices were increasing along with many raw material prices. Consequently, the government began to put interest rates up again in September 1994, reaching 6.75 per cent in March 1995.

Since Black Wednesday, the short term rate of interest has been the key instrument of monetary policy, alongside a continuing commitment broadly to full fund the PSBR and allow the exchange rate to float without much Bank of England intervention.

The Bank of England has continued to control short term interest rates though open market operations in the discount market. It then allows other interest rates in the economy to be determined by market forces around that rate. On the whole, money and capital markets are so inter-linked that increases in discount market rates will lead to increases in other interest rates in the economy and vice versa.

Note that monetary base control has never been used in the UK. Quantitative controls (rules and regulations) were abandoned in the early 1980s. Open market operations are confined solely to the discount market and are used not directly to control the supply of money, but to control short term interest rates.

DATA QUESTION

Monetary policy, 1971-73

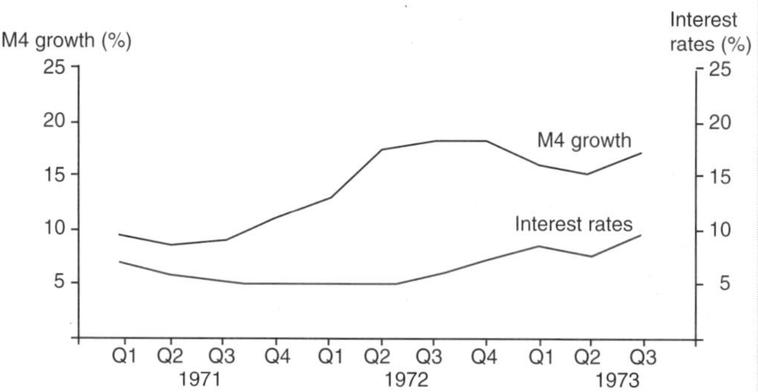

Source: adapted from CSO, *Economics Trends Annual Supplement.*

Figure 78.4 *M4 growth (% change on previous year) and interest rates (%, bank base rate)*

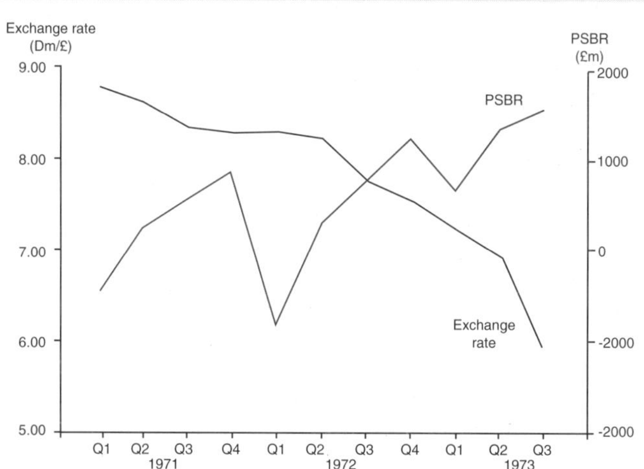

Source: adapted from CSO, *Economics Trends Annual Supplement.*

Figure 78.6 *Exchange rate (value of £ against German deutschmark) and PSBR (£millions)*

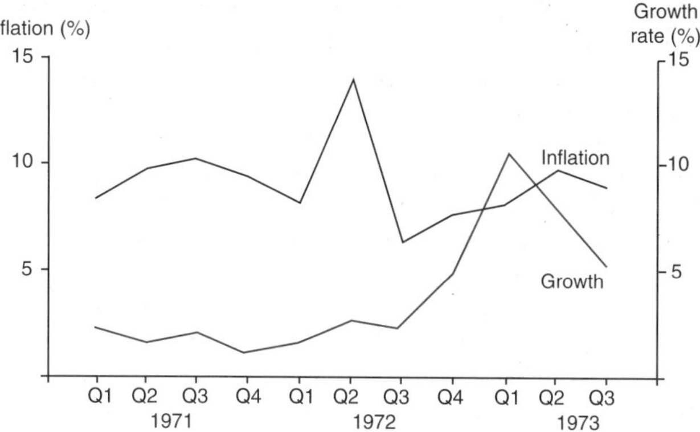

Source: adapted from CSO, *Economics Trends Annual Supplement.*

Figure 78.5 *Inflation and real economic growth (% change on previous year)*

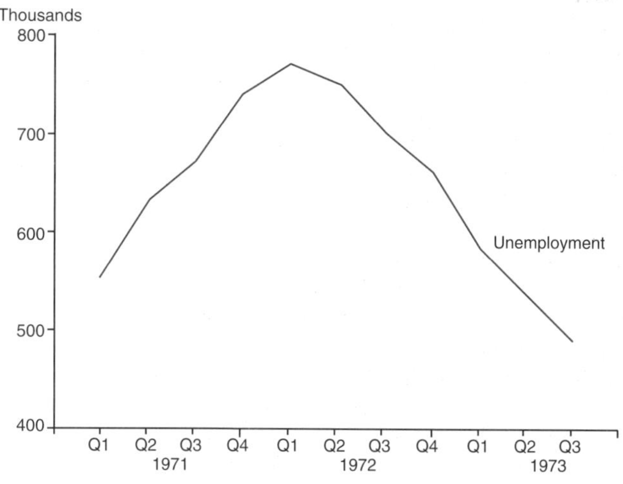

Source: adapted from CSO, *Economics Trends Annual Supplement.*

Figure 78.7 *Unemployment*

1971 was a difficult year for the economy. Economic growth was below the long term trend figure of 2.4 per cent whilst unemployment was rising to record post-war levels. In 1972, the government decided to reflate the economy. In his two Budgets of 1972 and 1973, the Chancellor, Anthony Barber, cut taxes and increased government spending. By 1973, the economy was booming but inflation was rising from its 1972 level. Then, at the end of 1973, British miners went on strike for large pay rises at a time when the price of oil on international markets was rocketing.

In 1971, the Bank of England announced a major change in the way in which it operated monetary policy. In a document entitled *Competition and Credit Control*, it declared that it would control credit in future not through lending ceilings (a form of rationing) but via the price mechanism. The rate of interest would be used to restrict credit and control the growth of the money supply. Lending ceilings and hire purchase restrictions were abolished although the Special Deposits scheme was retained. Banks would have to keep 12½ per cent of their assets as 'reserve assets', a variety of liquid assets which included Treasury Bills. The 12½ per cent reserve asset ratio would not, however, be used for monetary base control purposes. It was there to ensure that banks had enough liquid assets to meet the needs of their customers.

(a) Outline the trends in the economy between 1971-73.

(b) Suggest alternative ways in which the Bank of England could have operated its monetary policy, giving advantages and disadvantages of each.

(c) It is January 1974. Discuss how the Bank of England should have reacted to economic events over the period.

INVESTIGATIONS 6

A. Interest rates

Aims

- To gather data about the structure of interest rates in the UK over a period of time.
- To investigate the characteristics of the money markets in which those interest rates are set.
- To analyse what determines the structure of UK interest rates.
- To analyse why interest rates change over time.

Research

You need to find out about the current structure of interest rates and how and why it can change. Either research a past period (e.g. the past three months or the past five years) or follow the money markets now for a period of time (such as a month or three months). Interest rates are the price of money in a particular money market. For each interest rate you follow, find out who are the buyers and sellers (i.e. the borrowers and lenders) in each market. You may be able to obtain information from local branches of banks, building societies and other financial institutions.

A wide variety of interest rates are quoted on a daily or weekly basis in the *Financial Times*. Other quality newspapers and periodicals, such as *The Times* and *The Independent*, carry a more limited range of interest rates. If you attempt to explain how and why interest rates have changed over a period of years rather than a few months, then statistical publications such as *Economic Trends*, *Economic Trends Annual Supplement*, *Financial Statistics* and the *Annual Abstract of Statistics*, all published by CSO, will be easier to use than daily newspapers.

Quality newspapers and magazines, such as the *Financial Times* and the *Economist*, are the best source of material which might explain why interest rates have changed in the short term. If you are looking back over a period of time rather than attempting to explain why interest rates are changing at the moment, then use an index to help you conduct a newspaper and magazine search. Newspapers such as the *Financial Times* and *The Times* publish their own indexes. The public library you use may construct its own index, or it may carry an index such as the *Research Index* (Business Surveys Ltd.) which covers articles of financial interest from 100 newspapers and periodicals on a monthly basis. Newspapers may also be available on CD-Rom.

Structuring your report

Introduction Outline the aim of your investigation. The aim should be put in the form of a hypothesis or question which will allow you to come to some conclusions.
Economic theory Outline the economic theory you will use in your analysis. This will include concepts such as financial markets, the demand and supply of money and loanable funds, risk and time.
Techniques used to collect your data Outline how you collected your data.
Presentation of research findings Using tables, graphs, charts or whatever might be appropriate, describe the structure of interest rates in the UK and how they have changed over the period of time you have chosen to research. Describe the borrowers and lenders in each money market about which you have gathered data and the characteristics of the market.
Analysis Suggest reasons why interest rates are structured as they are. For instance, why are bank deposit rates below bank base rates? Why are interest rates on credit card loans higher than inter-bank rates? What barriers are there between money markets which prevent all interest rates from being identical?

Then analyse why interest rates have changed over the period you have chosen. What has caused these changes in interest rates? To what extent have all interest rates changed in the same direction or at the same speed or the same magnitude? For instance, a change in bank base rates may only have been followed by a change in building society mortgage rates two weeks later. Credit card interest rates may have remained the same, however. Suggest reasons to account for these different types of change.
Sources Outline the sources of information you used. What problems did you encounter in gathering relevant data? What data would you have liked to have obtained but could not? To what extent was the data reliable?
Bibliography Write down a list of your sources in alphabetical order.

Other suggestions

- Instead of investigating interest rates, describe and analyse changes in the prices of bills and bonds in the money markets. Daily information about bill and bond prices is given in the *Financial Times* together with an excellent summary describing and explaining price movements. Investigate the factors which may have affected bond and bill prices. To what extent is there a relationship between the rate of interest and the price of bills and bonds?
- Investigate changes in the velocity of circulation of money. Monthly figures for nominal GDP and the money supply are issued by CSO and the Bank of England. Why have changes taken place? To what extent are movements in the different measures of the velocity of circulation similar and why? To what extent can velocity of circulation be said to be stable?

B. Monetary policy

Aims

- To chart changes in the money supply over a period of time.
- To analyse why those changes have taken place and in particular to consider the influence of monetary policy on changes in the money supply.
- To analyse the effects of monetary policy on the wider economy.

Research activity

Your research needs to be concentrated on three areas.

- How has the money supply changed over the past few months?
- How has the government attempted to influence the growth of the money supply if at all (i.e. how has it conducted its monetary policy)?
- What are the possible current effects of monetary policy on variables such as inflation, expenditure and the balance of payments?

Before you start, review material about definitions of the money supply, the types of monetary policy available and the implementation and effectiveness of monetary policy from any books or other materials available to you.

Money supply figures (for the range of measures from M0 to M5) are announced monthly and are widely reported in the quality financial press.

Alternatively, they are published in *Economic Trends*, the *Monthly Digest of Statistics* and *Financial Statistics* all published by CSO. The quality financial press will also suggest reasons to account for the magnitude of the announced money supply figures. Use an index such as the *Financial Times* index, or the *Research Index* (published by Business Surveys Ltd) which covers articles in 100 newspapers and periodicals on a monthly basis, to help you find such articles.

The *Financial Times* publishes daily reports about Bank of England intervention in the discount market to steady interest rates. It also publishes major articles, along with other quality newspapers and periodicals, on the effects of interest rate changes after a major change in interest rates by the Bank of England. Again, use indexes to find these articles.

Structuring your report

Introduction Outline the aim of your investigation. The aim should be put in the form of a hypothesis or question which will allow you to come to some conclusions.
Economic theory Outline the economic theory you will use in your analysis.
Techniques used to collect your data Outline how you collected your data.
Changes in the money supply Describe, using charts, graphs or any other appropriate form of diagram, how the money supply has changed in recent months. Explain the different definitions of the money supply and indicate any observed relationship between them.
Analysis of money supply changes Suggest why the money supply has changed. To what extent has this been due to government monetary policy? How did you evaluate this? How has the Bank of England intervened to influence the rate of growth of the money supply? What measures of the money supply changed the greatest? Which measures show greatest correlation between the money supply and monetary policy? Explain why you think this is the case.
Analysis of the effects of monetary policy How is current monetary policy influencing the economy? Consider its possible effects on inflation, expenditure, unemployment, growth and the balance of payments.
Sources Outline the sources of information you used. What problems did you encounter in gathering relevant data? What data would you have liked to have obtained but could not? To what extent was the data reliable and unbiased?
Bibliography Write down a list of your sources in alphabetical order

Other suggestions

- Instead of considering the past few months, it would be possible either to take a longer time period (e.g. the past 5 years) or to follow changes in the money supply as they happen over say a three month period, or to investigate a period in the past.
- You could concentrate your investigation upon the effects of monetary policy upon the economy. This would involve monitoring the effects of changes in the money supply on other economic variables such as unemployment, inflation, consumption, saving, investment, exchange rates and the balance of payments.

unit 79 The Keynesian consumption function

Summary

1. **In the Keynesian model, a distinction is made between planned consumption and actual consumption.**
2. **The Keynesian consumption function shows the relationship between planned consumption and actual disposable income.**
3. **Planned consumption plus planned saving are equal to disposable income.**
4. **A movement along the consumption function line shows the effect on consumption of a change in income. A shift in the line is caused by a change in variables other than income which determines the autonomous level of consumption.**

Planned consumption

In unit 62, it was explained that Keynesian economists believe that the main determinant of consumption is disposable income. In the Keynesian model which follows, a distinction is made between PLANNED (or DESIRED or EX ANTE) CONSUMPTION and ACTUAL (or REALISED or EX POST) CONSUMPTION. Planned consumption, as the term implies, is what households plan to spend. Actual spending is what they end up spending. Actual spending is what is recorded in national income statistics. Planned spending may equal actual spending, but often households' plans are frustrated because of changes in the economy. A sudden rise in unemployment, for instance, would frustrate many households' spending plans.

The consumption function

In the Keynesian model, planned consumption varies with actual income. Columns 1 and 2 in Table 79.1 show a hypothetical consumption function. As income increases, so does the level of planned consumption. This is plotted in Figure 79.1. The consumption function, the line showing the relationship between income and planned consumption, is upward sloping. Note that at low levels of income, households spend more than they earn. It is assumed that they prefer to borrow money or draw on their stock of savings rather than allow their spending to fall below a certain level (i.e. they **dissave**).

What households do not spend out of their disposable income, they must save. So:

$$Y \equiv C + S$$

where the ≡ sign shows that this must be true by definition. C is planned consumption and S is planned saving. It is now possible to calculate planned saving in Table 79.1. If income is £400 and planned consumption is £360, then planned saving must be £40. If income is £300 and planned consumption £280, then planned saving must be £20. At an income level of £100, planned dissaving of £20 takes place. This is summarised in columns 1-3 and illustrated in Figure 79.2.

If households either spend or save all of their income, it must be true that the average proportion spent out of income and the average proportion saved must be equal to 1. The average proportion spent is the **average propensity to consume** (APC ☞ unit 62) whilst the average proportion saved is the **average propensity to save** (APS). For instance, if an individual spent 0.8 of her income, she must have saved 0.2. So:

$$APC + APS = 1$$

Table 79.1 *Consumption, saving and income*

(1) Income Y	(2) Planned consumption C	(3) Planned saving S	(4) Average propensity to consume C ÷ Y	(5) Change in income ΔY	(6) Change in planned consumption ΔC	(7) Marginal propensity to consume ΔC ÷ ΔY
0	40	-40	-			
				100	80	0.8
100	120	-20	1.2			
				100	80	0.8
200	200	0	1.0			
				100	80	0.8
300	200	20	0.93			
				100	80	0.8
400	360	40	0.9			

Similarly, if an individual spent 0.6 of her annual pay rise, she must have saved 0.4 of it. So:

$$MPC + MPS = 1$$

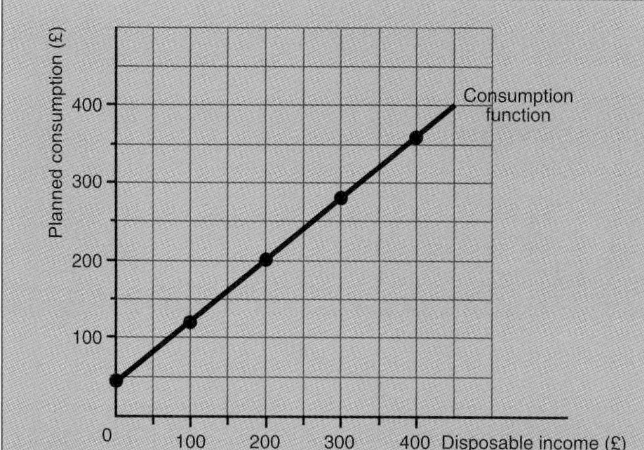

Figure 79.1 *A consumption function*
As income rises, so too does the level of planned consumption.

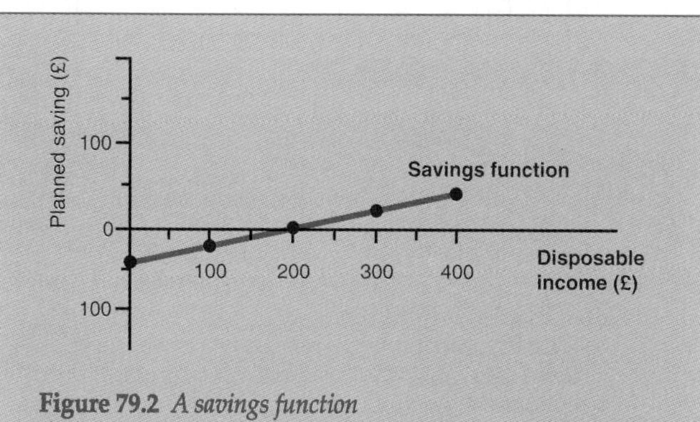

Figure 79.2 *A savings function*
As income rises, so too does the level of planned saving.

QUESTION 1

Consumption is equal to £100 plus ¾ of income.

(a) Calculate the level of consumption at income levels of: (i) £200; (ii) £400; (iii) £600; (iv) £800; (v) £1 000.

(b) What is the level of saving at each of these levels of income?

(c) Plot both the consumption and savings functions on the same graph.

(d) On a different graph, plot the consumption and savings functions for income levels between 0 and £1 000 assuming that consumption was; (i) £200 plus ¾ of income; (ii) £400 plus ¾ of income; (iii) £100 plus ½ of income.

A graphical presentation

It is possible to illustrate many of the points made above using graphs. Figure 79.3 shows the consumption and saving functions from Table 79.1.

A 45° line is drawn on the graph. This line shows all points where planned consumption is equal to income. If the consumption function lay along this line, the average propensity to consume would be exactly 1 (i.e. all income would be spent).

The consumption function starts where income is zero and consumption is £40. This is called the level of AUTONOMOUS CONSUMPTION. It is consumption unrelated to the level of income. Whatever the level of income, consumption will always be at least £40. It is the irreducible minimum which will be consumed. Since income must equal consumption plus savings by definition, then a consumption level of £40 when income is zero must mean that saving is - £40. Hence - £40 is where the savings function starts on the vertical axis. Consumption then increases as income increases. This consumption is known as INDUCED CONSUMPTION because it is induced or caused by changes in income.

At an income level of £200, the consumption function passes through the 45° line. The 45° line shows all points where consumption and income are equal. So at an income of £200, consumption is £200 and saving must be zero. Therefore this is the level of income where the savings function cuts the horizontal axis.

At levels of income up to £200, consumption is greater than income and dissaving takes place. At income levels over £200, consumption is less than income and saving is positive. The vertical distance between the consumption function and the 45° line is the level of saving. For instance, at an income level of £300, consumption is £280. So saving must be £20 and this is shown by the savings function. The shaded area on the diagram, then, is either saving (to the right of the point where the consumption

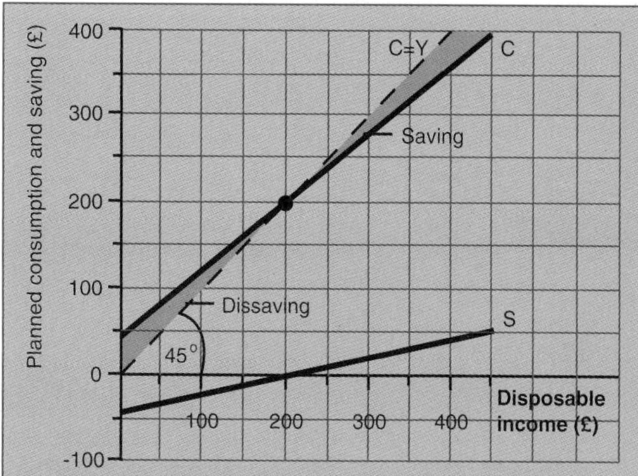

Figure 79.3 *Consumption and savings functions*
The point where the consumption function crosses the 45° line is the break even point. Savings are zero and income equals consumption. The level of autonomous consumption is £40. The slope of the line gives the value of the MPC and the MPS.

function cuts the line) or dissaving (to the left).

The average propensity to consume is found by dividing total planned consumption by total income. For instance, at an income level of £100, consumption is £120 and so the APC is 1.2. At an income level of £200, consumption is £200 and so the APC is 1.0. At an income level of £400 it is 0.9 (360÷400). For a straight line consumption function which does not pass through the origin, the APC therefore falls as income increases.

The marginal propensity to consume is found by dividing the change in planned consumption by the change in income. For instance, the MPC between an income level of £300 and £400 is 0.8. The change in planned consumption is measured by the vertical distance between two points on the consumption function (for instance from £280 to £360) and the change in income by the horizontal distance (for instance from £300 to £400). Mathematically this is also the slope or gradient of the line. So the marginal propensity to consume between two points is the slope of the consumption function between those two points. In Figure 79.3, the MPC is in fact the same at all points along the line (0.8). You can see this at a glance if you know that the slope of a straight line graph is constant.

The same applies to the average and marginal propensities to save. The average propensity to save increases as income increases (if the APC is falling, the APS must be rising). The MPS is constant, shown by the straight line of the savings function. It is equal to 0.2.

The gradient of the 45° line is 1. Any change in income is exactly matched by a change in consumption. The slope of the consumption and savings functions is shallower than the 45° line, showing that they must be less than 1. So if we draw a consumption function which, starting from the consumption axis, passes through the 45° line, we are stating that the MPC is less than 1.

Figure 79.4 shows a number of different consumption functions. Consumption function 1 is a straight line graph passing through the origin. Because it passes through the origin, it means that there is no autonomous consumption. Total planned consumption divided by total income (the APC) measures the slope of the line. So the APC is equal to the MPC at all levels of income.

Consumption function 2 is not a straight line and so the gradient of the curve or the MPC is constantly changing. In this case, the slope is getting progressively shallower and therefore the MPC is falling as income increases. Consumption function 3, on the other hand, shows a function where the MPC is increasing as income increases.

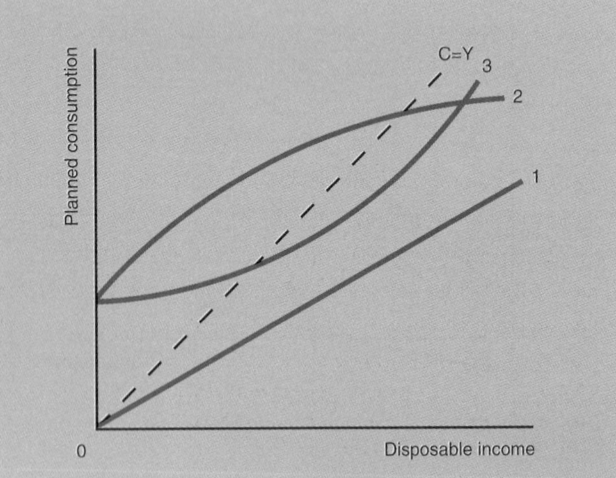

Figure 79.4 Different consumption functions
Line 1 shows a function where the MPC = APC. Line 2 shows a function where the MPC is falling as income increases whilst line 3 shows a function where the MPC rises as income rises.

QUESTION 2

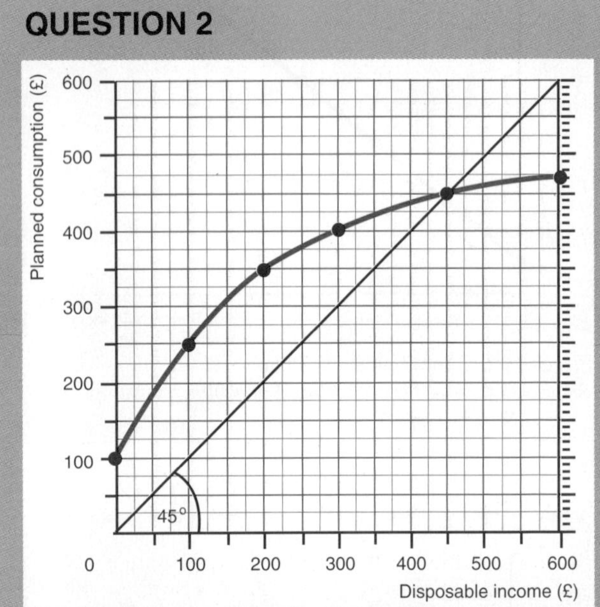

Figure 79.5

(a) Calculate the APC at an income level of: (i) £100; (ii) £200; (iii) £300; (iv) £450; (v) £600.
(b) Calculate the MPC between income levels of: (i) £0 and £100; (ii) £100 and £200; (iii) £200 and £300; (iv) £450 and £600.
(c) Assume that autonomous consumption was not £100 but £200, and that therefore consumption was £100 higher at each level of income in Figure 79.5. What then would be (i) the APC and (b) the MPC at each of the income levels in (b) and (c) respectively?

The value of the APC and the MPC

The straight line consumption function drawn in Figure 79.3 shows a function where:

- the average propensity to consume is greater than 1 at low levels of income but less than 1 at higher levels of income;
- the marginal propensity to consume is constant and less than 1.

This is broadly the Keynesian view of the consumption function. Other views were explained in unit 62.

The formula for the consumption function

The straight line simple Keynesian consumption function can be expressed using an equation:

$$C = a + bY$$

- a is the **autonomous element** which does not vary with income;
- bY is the **induced element** which varies directly with disposable income;
- b is the marginal propensity to consume;
- C is planned consumption;
- Y is income.

Other factors affecting consumption

In unit 62, it was explained that other factors apart from income have some influence on consumption. These factors include changes in interest rates, wealth and consumer confidence. Changes in these other factors can be shown on a diagram.

In Figure 79.6, a change in income in shown by a **movement along** the consumption function, for instance from point A to point B. A change in other factors affecting planned consumption, such as changes in interest rates, will lead to a change in the autonomous element of consumption (i.e. that part of consumption which is not determined by income). This would be shown by a **shift** in the function. In Figure 79.6, a fall in interest rates leads to a rise in autonomous consumption from a_1 to a_2. The consumption function then shifts upwards from C_1 to C_2.

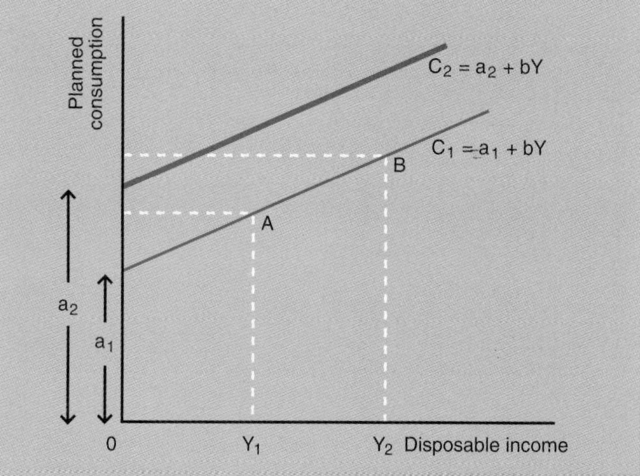

Figure 79.6 *Shift in the consumption function*
A rise in the autonomous level of consumption from a_1 to a_2 will shift the consumption function upwards from C_1 to C_2.

QUESTION 3 Explain, using a diagram, the effect that each of the following would have had on (i) autonomous consumption and (ii) the consumption function.

(a) The rise in interest rates from $7^1/_2$ per cent in 1987 to 15 per cent in 1989.
(b) The fall in house prices between 1989 and 1993.
(c) The increase in inflation from 9.1 per cent in 1973 to 24.1 per cent in 1975.
(d) The rise in expectations that unemployment would remain high in the early 1980s.
(e) The increase in the proportion of 40-64 year olds in the population in the 1990s and the first decade of the next century.
(f) The sharp rise in disposable income during the Lawson boom of 1986-1988.

Important notes

Income and disposable income It was explained early on in this unit that the consumption function linked planned consumption with disposable income. However, later in the unit, we talked simply about 'income' rather than disposable income. National income and disposable income are the same in a simple economy where there is no government and no foreign trade. However, they are not the same if there is government because disposable income is income adjusted for taxes and benefits. This is important to remember in more advanced theory.

Real and not nominal values The theory of the consumption and savings function links real consumption and real saving with real income. Changes in the price level, as will be explained in the next unit, can shift the consumption and saving functions.

Key terms

Planned, desired or ex ante consumption - the amount households intend to spend.
Actual, realised or ex post consumption - the amounts households succeed in spending.
Autonomous consumption - consumption which is not determined by changes in income.
Induced consumption - consumption expenditure which is related to income.

Applied economics

The consumption function

Keynesian theory would suggest that current disposable income is the major determinant of consumption. Figure 79.7 plots actual real consumption against real disposable income for the UK since 1948. As can be seen, the correlation is very high indicating that consumption is indeed largely determined by income over a long period of time.

In the short term, the correlation is lower. Figure 79.8 shows quarterly data for consumption and disposable income at current prices since 1987. The period of the Lawson Boom, was one where the long term relationship between consumption and income became more unstable. Even so, the correlation is still clear - rising income is linked with rising consumption.

Figure 79.9 gives a third example of correlation between consumption and income. Income here is not disposable income but GDP because GDP figures are available across countries. The fact that GDP figures rather than disposable income figures have been used should mean that there is less correlation between consumption and income because the income measure chosen is only an approximation to disposable income. Income and consumption per head have been used to distinguish between countries at different levels of development. However, there is a clear correlation present across countries. As countries develop and enjoy higher incomes per head, their average propensity to consume falls.

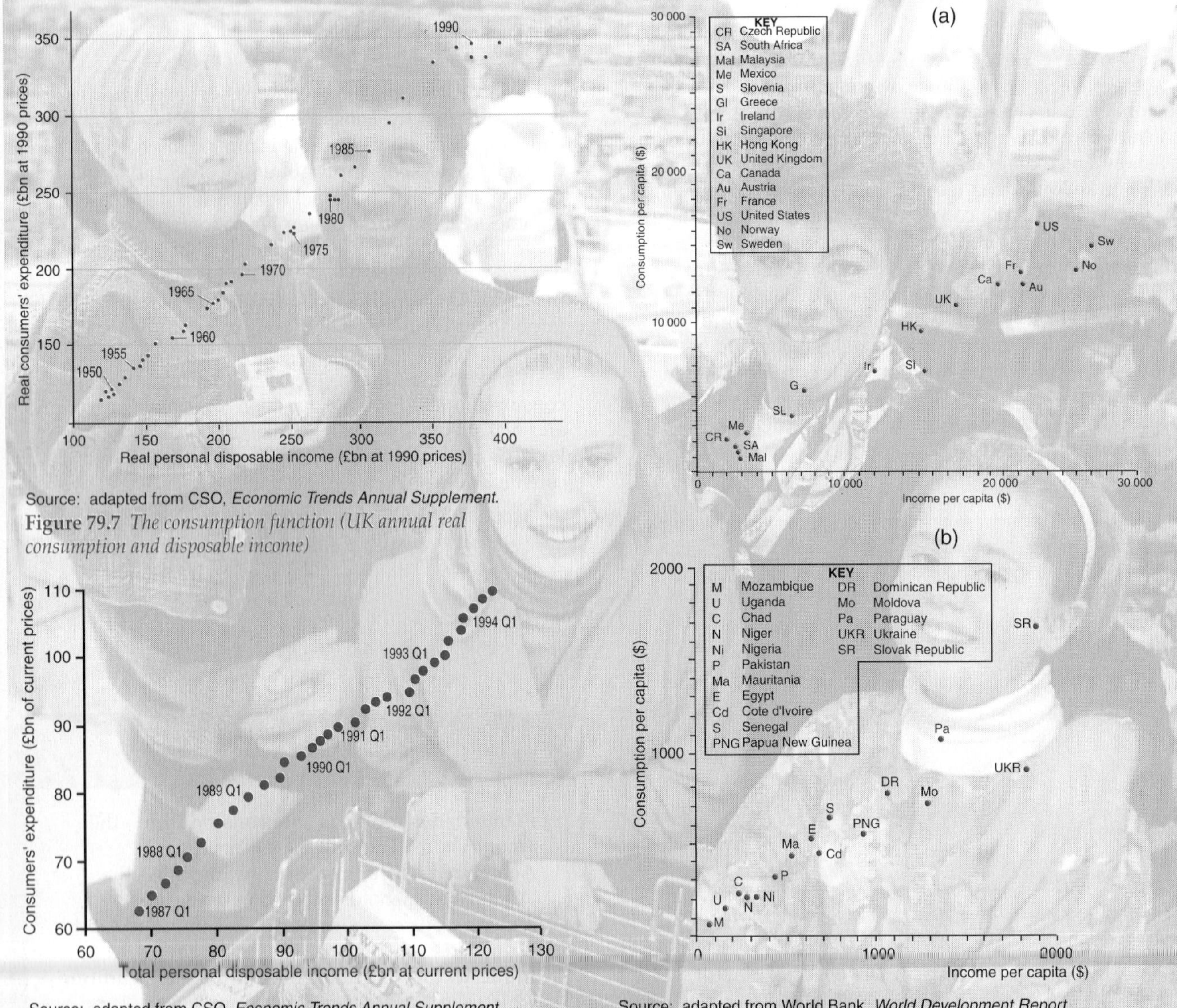

Source: adapted from CSO, *Economic Trends Annual Supplement.*

Figure 79.7 *The consumption function (UK annual real consumption and disposable income)*

Source: adapted from CSO, *Economic Trends Annual Supplement.*

Figure 79.8 *The consumption function (UK quarterly consumption and disposable income at current prices)*

Source: adapted from World Bank, *World Development Report.*

Figure 79.9 *The consumption function (international comparison of consumption and GDP per head in $, 1992)*

Estimating consumption

Table 79.2 *Key indicators in the economy, 1978-1982*

		Personal disposable income £bn at current prices	Interest rate[1] %	Inflation rate[2] %	Unemployment millions
1978	Q1	26.0	6.5	9.4	1.4
	Q2	27.8	8.5	7.6	1.3
	Q3	29.0	10.0	7.9	1.5
	Q4	30.0	11.5	8.2	1.3
1979	Q1	30.5	13.5	9.6	1.4
	Q2	32.5	13.0	10.7	1.2
	Q3	34.6	14.0	15.9	1.3
	Q4	37.9	15.5	17.1	1.3
1980	Q1	37.5	17.0	19.1	1.4
	Q2	39.5	17.0	21.6	1.5
	Q3	41.0	16.0	16.3	1.8
	Q4	41.9	15.0	15.4	2.0
1981	Q1	42.8	14.0	12.6	2.3
	Q2	43.8	12.0	11.8	2.4
	Q3	44.4	12.0	11.4	2.6
	Q4	45.6	15.0	11.9	2.8
1982	Q1	46.2	14.0	11.2	2.9
	Q2	47.5	13.0	9.4	2.8
	Q3	48.2	11.0	7.9	2.9
	Q4	49.0	9.5	6.2	3.1

1. Bank base rates, quarterly average. 2. Year on year increases. Source: adapted from CSO, *Economic Trends Annual Supplement.*

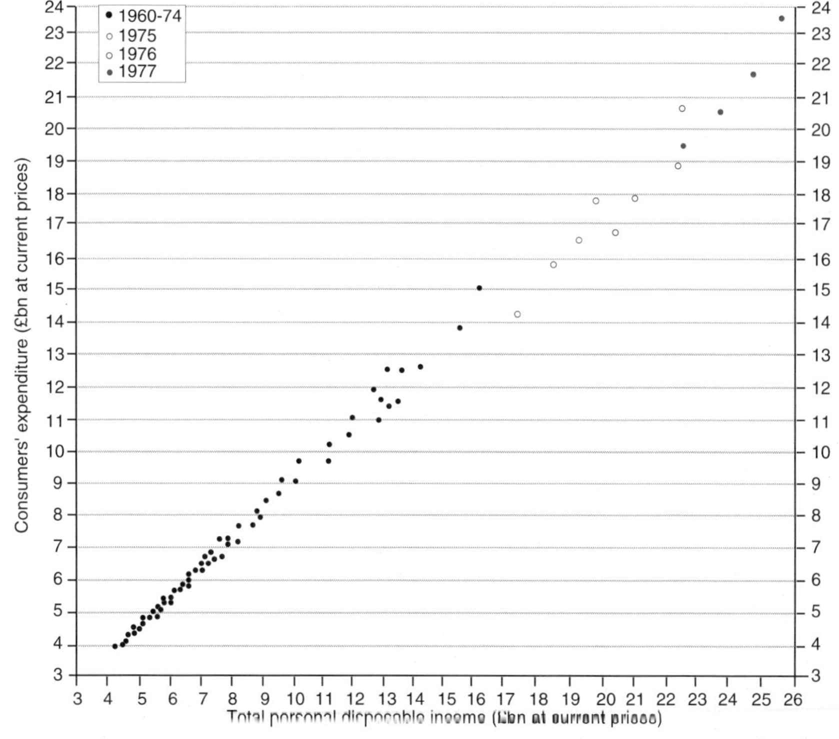

Source: adapted from *Economic Trends Annual Supplement.*

Figure 79.10 *Consumption and personal disposable income, 1960-1977, quarterly at current prices*

You have been asked to estimate the value of quarterly consumption during the period 1978-1982. Write a report:

(a) detailing the economic theory behind your estimates, using diagrams where appropriate;
(b) giving the quarterly estimates;
(c) explaining, using the theory outlined in (a), why you have chosen those particular figures.

Planned expenditure in a simple economy

Summary

1. In the simplest Keynesian model of national income determination, there is no government or foreign trade, wage rates are constant and money is neutral.
2. Aggregate demand (or planned expenditure) is then equal to planned consumption plus planned investment.
3. The equilibrium level of national income occurs where planned expenditure is equal to actual income.
4. The equilibrium level of national income is unlikely to be equal to the full employment level of income.
5. Equilibrium national income also occurs where planned investment equals planned saving.
6. Equilibrium income can be shown either on a 45° line diagram (the income-expenditure approach) or on a Keynesian cross diagram (the injections - leakages approach).

The Keynesian model

In units 64-66, a model of aggregate demand and aggregate supply was developed, which led to the determination of equilibrium output in the economy. In unit 79, this unit, and units 80-82, we go behind the aggregate demand curve and see how it is derived. The derivation comes from two sources. First, there is a Keynesian model of income determination, developed simply in this unit. Second, there is a model of the demand and supply for money, developed in units 74 and 75. In unit 83, we will put these models together to see why the aggregate demand curve is downward sloping.

Simplifying assumptions

In order to keep the analysis as simple as possible, a number of assumptions need to be made.

- The economy has no government sector. This means that total personal disposable income, the determinant of consumption, is equal to national income.
- The economy is closed (i.e. there is no foreign trade). Hence GNP and GDP are equal because there is no net property income from abroad (☞ unit 59).
- There is no depreciation of the capital stock and hence national income and GNP are equal.
- Wages and prices in the economy will remain constant as demand changes at all levels of income below full employment. Full employment ☞ unit 65 is the level of output at which all the factors of production in the economy are fully utilised at given factor prices. For instance, every worker who wants a job at the current wage rate is in employment.
- Money is neutral so that changes in real variables which affect monetary variables such as the money supply don't feed through to further changes in real variables.

Much of the rest of this book will be spent looking at what happens when we relax these assumptions but to start with we will build a simple model of income determination.

Aggregate demand

AGGREGATE DEMAND in the Keynesian model (often called AGGREGATE EXPENDITURE or PLANNED EXPENDITURE) is defined as the amount of desired expenditure in the economy at any level of income. Total spending in the economy is made up of consumption expenditure, investment, government expenditure and net exports (☞ unit 64). In our simple model of the economy, there is no government and no foreign trade. So aggregate demand or planned expenditure (E) is equal to planned consumption (C) plus planned investment (I):

$$E = C + I$$

Table 80.1 shows an example of how aggregate demand would change as income (Y) increases. Planned consumption is assumed to be a function of income (☞ unit 79). As income increases, so does the level of consumption. The formula for the consumption function in the table is $C = 100 + 0.5Y$. Planned investment is assumed to be determined solely by changes in the rate of interest. So investment remains the same as income increases (i.e. investment is **autonomous** or **exogenous**). Aggregate demand or planned expenditure is calculated by simply adding planned consumption to planned investment.

Table 80.1 *Aggregate demand*

£

Actual income Y	Planned consumption C	Planned investment I	Planned expenditure E (i.e. C + I)
0	100	100	200
100	150	100	250
200	200	100	300
000	250	100	350
400	300	100	400
500	350	100	450
600	400	100	500

QUESTION 1

(a) C = 200 + 0.75Y and I is a constant £600. Calculate the value of planned expenditure if income is: (i) 0; (ii) £800; (iii) £1 600; (iv) £2 400; (v) £3 200; (vi) £4 000.
(b) Consumption changes such that C = 300 + 0.8Y whilst I is now a constant 800. Calculate the value of planned expenditure at the income levels in (a).

Equilibrium income

Figure 80.1 shows the data from Table 80.1 plotted on a graph. The consumption function is drawn first. When income is zero, consumption is 100. This is the level of autonomous consumption (i.e. that part of planned consumption expenditure which does not vary with income). Consumption then rises as income rises. The rise in consumption is less than the rise in income because the **marginal propensity to consume** is less than 1 (in this case it is 0.5).

Planned investment is then added to the planned consumption line. The C + I line is parallel to the C line because planned investment remains constant as income changes. The level of planned investment is the vertical distance between the two lines. The 45° line on the diagram shows all points where planned expenditure equals actual income.

It is now possible to find the equilibrium level of income. The EQUILIBRIUM LEVEL OF NATIONAL INCOME is the level of income where there is no tendency for it to change. It occurs when the plans of neither households nor firms are frustrated. This is true only when planned expenditure equals actual income (i.e. at an income level of £400 where the planned expenditure line or aggregate demand schedule crosses the 45° line). To understand why this is true, consider what would happen if planned expenditure were not equal to actual income.

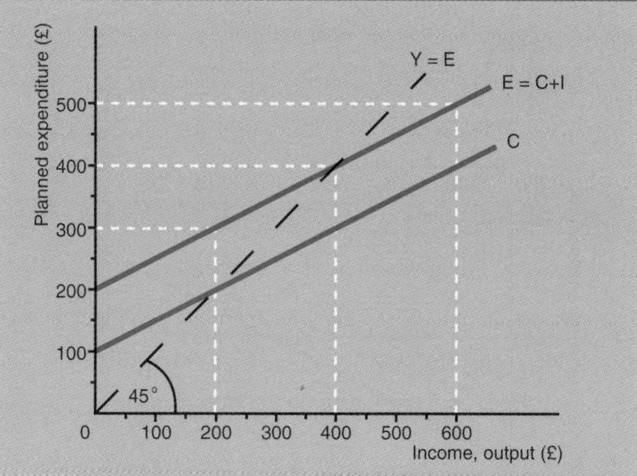

Figure 80.1 *The 45° line diagram*
Equilibrium income is established where the aggregate demand schedule crosses the 45° line (i.e. where planned expenditure equals actual income).

Planned expenditure more than actual income Assume that the level of income and therefore the level of output is £200 (actual or realised national income must equal national output and national expenditure according to national income definitions). Reading from the graph or table, the level of planned expenditure is therefore £300. A combination of two things is now likely to occur. First, households and firms will attempt to buy consumption and investment goods and find that firms will turn away their orders. The output of firms is not great enough to satisfy the level of demand in the economy. Second, firms will destock. They will have goods in stock which they were not planning to sell at that point in time. They will sell these stocks in an attempt to satisfy demand. But these sales are unplanned or undesired. They will then increase output to increase their stocks back to their planned or desired level. So destocking and unfulfilled orders will act as a signal to firms to increase production. Firms will have an incentive to increase output so long as planned expenditure is greater than actual income or output.

Planned expenditure less than actual income Assume that the level of income and therefore output is £600. Reading from the graph or table, we can see that the level of planned expenditure is then £500. If output is greater than expenditure, firms will not be able to sell all their production. They will have to make unplanned increases to their stock levels. They will react by cutting production, using up their existing stocks. They will only stop this when their stock levels are back to their desired level and when planned expenditure equals actual output.

QUESTION 2

(a) Plot on a graph the two planned expenditure lines derived from your answers to Question 1(a) and 1(b).
(b) What is the equilibrium level of income in each case?

Equilibrium employment and full employment

One of the key predictions of the simple Keynesian model of income determination is that the economy may well settle down to an equilibrium level of output which is not the full employment level of output. On Figure 80.1, it is not possible to determine which is the full employment level of output. The economy will tend towards an equilibrium level of income of £400. But what if the full employment level of income were £600? There is no mechanism within the system to increase the equilibrium level of income to the full employment level. Hence the economy can be stable and there can be large scale unemployment.

Keynes argued that the depression of the 1930s showed that mass unemployment could persist over long periods of time. It was argued earlier (☞ unit 65) that some economists believe the contrary; that unemployment cannot persist in the long run because wages will fall to clear the labour market. However, in the simple Keynesian model, we have assumed that wage rates are constant and therefore the wage rate mechanism cannot lead to a fall in unemployment.

Another approach

Another way of determining the equilibrium level of national income is to use the concepts of injections and leakages from the circular flow of income. In our simple model there is only one injection - investment. There is also only one leakage - savings (savings are that part of income which is not consumed because Y = C + S). Actual investment and actual savings must always be equal (for a proof of this ☞ unit 58). Keynes pointed out that savers and investors are two different sets of economic agents. Investors are firms whilst savers are households (although firms too save). So there is no reason why the planned saving should equal planned investment.

National income is in equilibrium when planned investment is equal to planned savings. To understand why, consider what would happen if they were different.

Planned investment greater than planned savings Income is equal to consumption (or that part of income which is not saved) plus investment. In Table 80.2, it can be seen that if income is £100 and consumption £150, then there must be dissaving of £50. On the other hand if income is £600 and consumption £400, then saving must be £200. If planned investment is greater than planned savings, firms must be planning to spend more than that which households want to save. So planned consumption plus planned investment must be greater than actual income. For instance, in Table 80.2, at an income level of £200, households plan to save nothing and spend £200, whilst firms plan to invest £100. So total planned expenditure is £300. With planned expenditure greater than actual income either firms will be forced to turn away orders or they will make unplanned reductions in their stock levels. Either way, firms will now want to increase output and therefore national income will rise.

Planned investment less than planned savings If this is the case, then planned spending will be less than actual output. For instance, in Table 80.2 at an income level of £600 households plan to save £200 but firms plan to invest only £100. Total planned expenditure will be £500 (£400 by households and £100 by firms) but income or output will be £600. Firms will therefore be producing more than they can sell. Unplanned stocks will start to build up. Firms will respond by cutting back production. Output and therefore income will fall.

So if planned investment is greater than planned savings, income will tend to rise. If I is less than S, income will tend to fall. Only when planned investment and planned savings are equal will there be no tendency for income to change.

Table 80.2 *Aggregate demand*

£

Actual income Y	Planned consumption C	Planned saving S	Planned investment I	Planned expenditure E (i.e. C + I)
0	100	-100	100	200
100	150	-50	100	250
200	200	0	100	300
300	250	50	100	350
400	300	100	100	400
500	350	150	100	450
600	400	200	100	500

The Keynesian cross diagram

The bottom graph in Figure 80.2 illustrates the points that have just been discussed. Actual income and output are put on the horizontal axis. Planned investment and saving are put on the vertical axis. The saving function is upward sloping, showing that saving increases as income increases. The investment line is horizontal, showing that planned investment remains constant whatever the level of income. The equilibrium level of output is £400 where planned investment equals planned saving. If planned savings is greater than planned investment to the right of the equilibrium point, there will be a tendency for output and income to fall. If planned investment is greater than planned savings to the left of the equilibrium point, there

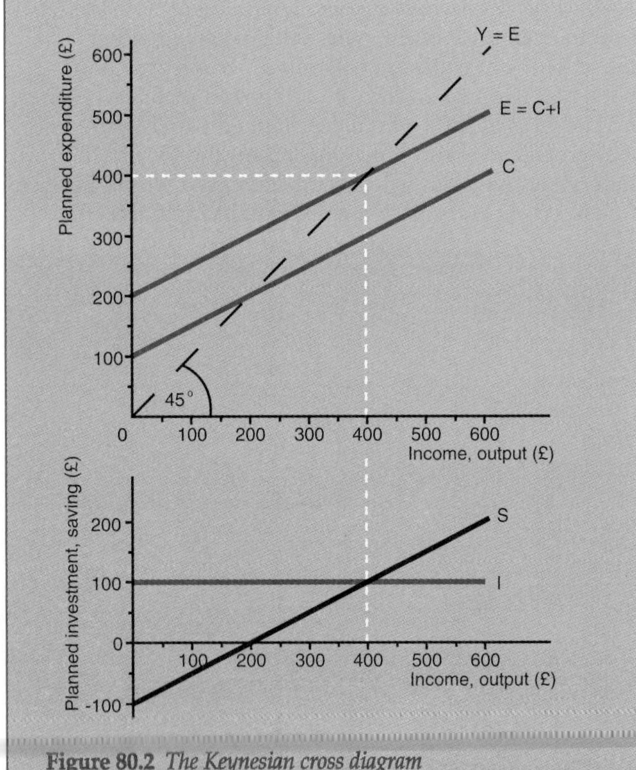

Figure 80.2 *The Keynesian cross diagram*
Income and output will be in equilibrium when the level of planned investment equals the level of planned savings.

will be a tendency for output and income to rise.

The top graph in Figure 80.2 is a copy of Figure 80.1. Placing the two together shows that the two ways of establishing equilibrium income are equivalent. Both the income-expenditure approach and the injections-leakages approach give exactly the same result.

QUESTION 3

S = -200 + 0.25Y and I is a constant £600.

(a) Calculate the level of planned savings at income levels of: (i) 0; (ii) £1 200; (iii) £2 000; (iv) £3 200; (v) £4 000.
(b) Plot the values of planned saving and planned investment on a Keynesian cross diagram.
(c) What is the equilibrium level of national income?
(d) How would your answers to the above be different if S = -300 + 0.25Y and I = 700?

Key terms

Aggregate demand or expenditure in the Keynesian model - the desired expenditure in the economy at any level of income.
Equilibrium level of national income - that level of income or output where there is no tendency to change. This only occurs where planned expenditure equals actual income (i.e. where the aggregate demand schedule crosses the 45° line).

Applied economics

Stocks and income, 1979-1982

In the Keynesian model of income determination, national income will be in equilibrium if planned expenditure equals actual income. The national income accounts of the UK do not give figures for planned expenditure - they only record actual expenditure. However, the accounts do give some clues as to how changes in planned expenditure lead to changes in actual income.

Table 80.3 shows the value of the physical increase in stocks and work in progress and GDP, both at constant market prices, between 1979 and the first quarter of 1983. Increases in stocks are classified as part of total investment in the Keynesian model. So a fall in stock levels, fixed investment remaining equal, would lead to a fall in investment expenditure.

In June 1979, a new Conservative government came into office, committed to reducing inflation. To achieve this, it sharply increased interest rates and allowed the level of the pound to rise to record levels. Both of these factors contributed to a fall in the level of stocks which firms wished to hold (i.e. there was a fall in planned expenditure on new stock). Economic theory would suggest that this fall in planned investment would cause a fall in planned expenditure. The economy would then be in disequilibrium. With planned expenditure less than actual income, firms could not sell all their output. They would respond by cutting their output and stocks even further until once again planned expenditure equalled actual income.

The data in Table 80.3 can be explained in terms of this model. In 1977 and 1978, the quarterly increase in stocks averaged approximately £800m. The first two quarters of 1979 saw similar expenditure. However, in the third quarter, there was an exceptional increase in stocks of £1.6bn, an indication perhaps that planned expenditure was now greater than actual income. There then followed two years of destocking. This fall in planned expenditure resulted in a fall in actual income and output, from £85bn in the fourth quarter of 1979 to a low of £78bn in the second quarter of 1981. By 1983, the process of destocking had run its course and for the rest of the 1980s, stockbuilding was on the whole positive, as was the change in GDP.

Table 80.3 *Quarterly GDP and change in stocks, 1977-1983*

£ million at 1985 prices

		At market prices	
		Value of physical increase in stocks and work in progress	Gross domestic product
1977	Quarterly	854	77 849
1978	average	717	80 645
1979	Q1	1 067	78 672
	Q2	764	82 721
	Q3	1 627	83 228
	Q4	-130	85 485
1980	Q1	-643	80 492
	Q2	139	78 569
	Q3	-524	81 904
	Q4	-2 343	82 756
1981	Q1	-1 223	79 181
	Q2	-1 112	77 850
	Q3	188	80 478
	Q4	-1 053	82 738
1982	Q1	919	79 990
	Q2	560	78 644
	Q3	-482	81 285
	Q4	-2 278	84 552
1983	Q1	445	84 415

Source: adapted from CSO, *Economic Trends Annual Supplement.*

Consumption, investment and GDP

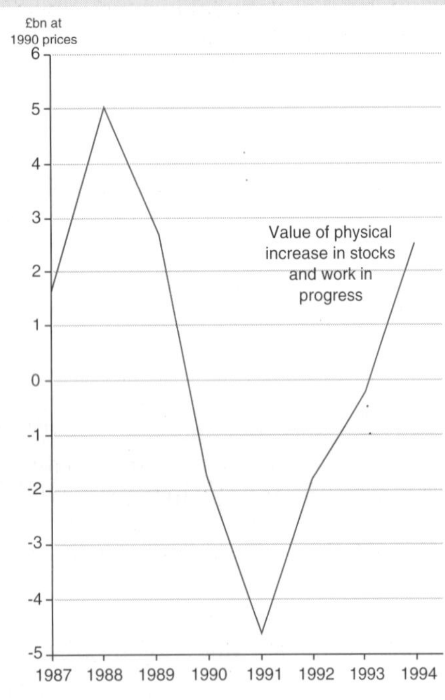

Source: adapted from CSO, *Economic Trends Annual Supplement.*

Figure 80.3 *Value of physical increase in stocks and work in progress, 1987-1994 (£bn at 1990 prices)*

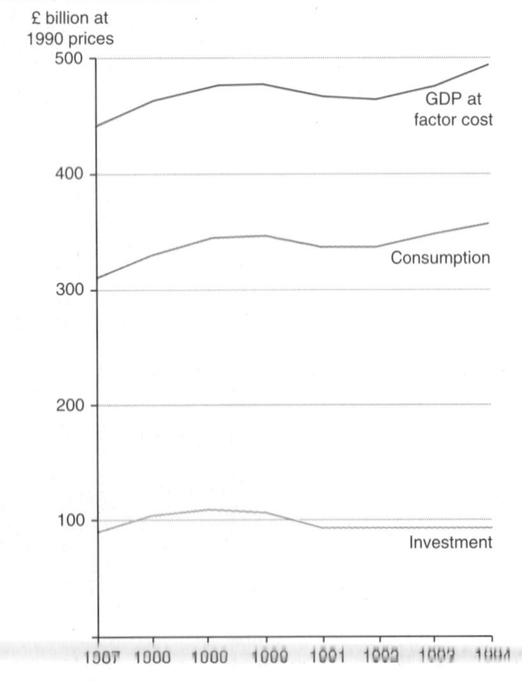

Source: adapted from CSO, *Economic Trends Annual Supplement.*

Figure 80.4 *Consumption, gross investment and gross domestic product, 1987-1994 (£bn at 1990 prices)*

1. What are 'stocks and work in progress' for firms?
2. Explain why changes in stocks can be an important indication of disequilibrium in the economy. Illustrate your answer with examples from the data.
3. (a) Using a diagram, explain why changes in consumption and investment led to changes in national income between 1987 and 1994. (b) Suggest why consumption and investment changed over the period.

The multiplier and the paradox of thrift

Summary

1. An increase in planned investment or the autonomous level of consumption will lead to an increase in planned expenditure.
2. An increase in planned expenditure will lead to a multiple increase in national income.
3. The value of the multiplier is given by the formula 1 ÷ MPS.
4. The paradox of thrift states that an increase in planned saving will lead not to an increase in actual saving but to a fall in income.

Assumptions

In unit 80, it was shown that national income would be in equilibrium when planned expenditure equalled actual income. A number of important simplifying assumptions were made: the economy was closed and without a government sector; wages and prices were stable; the economy was at less than full employment so that national income could increase or decrease as aggregate demand changed; money was neutral.

In this unit, we will continue to make these assumptions. The purpose of this unit is to show how aggregate expenditure might change in our simple model and what happens to national income if it does so.

Changes in aggregate expenditure

What happens if consumers spend more money at any given level of income, or businesses increase their investment expenditure? We know that aggregate demand (AD, also called aggregate expenditure or planned expenditure E) is equal to planned consumption (C) plus planned investment (I). So a change in either C or I will lead to a change in E. Common sense suggests that if consumers and businesses plan to spend more money, then the income of the economy will rise. This is indeed what the Keynesian model predicts.

Traditional Keynesian economics assumes that consumption is relatively stable but investment can be volatile, fluctuating with the **animal spirits** (or confidence in the future) of businessmen. Assume that firms plan to spend more on investment goods at every level of income. Then aggregate expenditure will rise. This is shown by the shift in the aggregate expenditure line in the 45° line diagram in Figure 81.1 from E_1 to E_2. The two lines are parallel because it has been assumed that planned investment rises by the same amount whatever the level of income. It can be seen that the equilibrium level of national income rises from Y_1 to Y_2. Hence an increase in planned investment will lead to an increase in the equilibrium level of income.

Exactly the same conclusion can be arrived at using the Keynesian cross diagram in Figure 81.1. An increase in planned investment pushes up the planned investment line from I_1 to I_2. The result is that equilibrium income rises from Y_1 to Y_2.

A fall in planned investment will have the opposite effect. A fall will lead to a shift downwards in the aggregate expenditure line and hence a fall in equilibrium income.

A change in the **autonomous** component of consumption (☞ unit 79) will lead to similar changes in national income. If households plan to spend a constant amount more at every level of income, the aggregate expenditure line will shift upwards, raising the equilibrium level of national income. Figure 81.2 shows the same point using the Keynesian cross diagram. An increase in the autonomous element of planned consumption will lead to a fall in the autonomous element in planned savings. The shift downwards in the savings function from S_1 to S_2 shows that, at any given level of

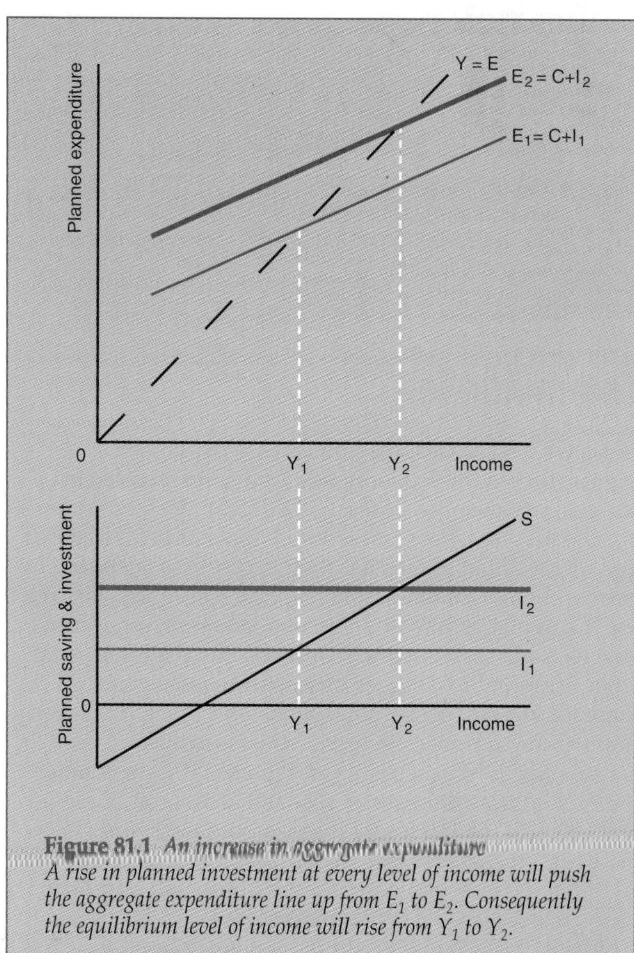

Figure 81.1 *An increase in aggregate expenditure*
A rise in planned investment at every level of income will push the aggregate expenditure line up from E_1 to E_2. Consequently the equilibrium level of income will rise from Y_1 to Y_2.

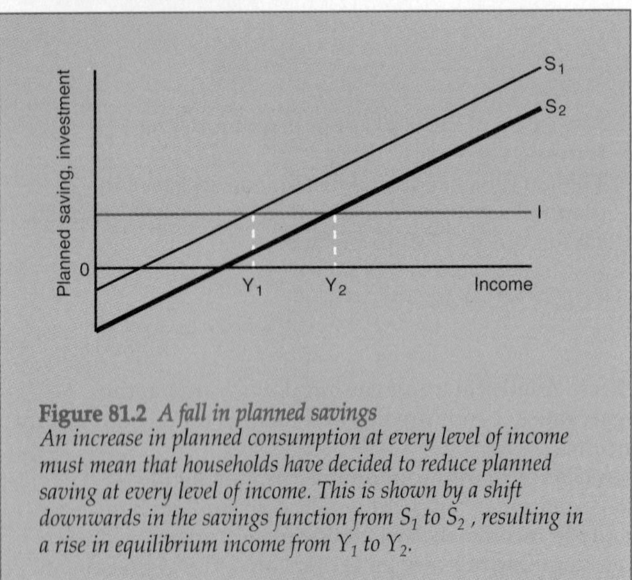

Figure 81.2 *A fall in planned savings*
An increase in planned consumption at every level of income must mean that households have decided to reduce planned saving at every level of income. This is shown by a shift downwards in the savings function from S_1 to S_2, resulting in a rise in equilibrium income from Y_1 to Y_2.

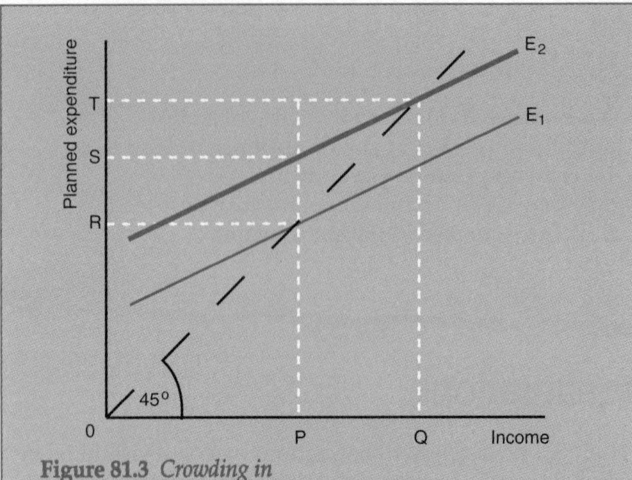

Figure 81.3 *Crowding in*
An increase in planned investment expenditure of RS crowds in extra consumption expenditure of ST leading to a final increase in planned expenditure of RT and in income of PQ.

income, households now plan to save less. Equilibrium income consequently rises from Y_1 to Y_2. A fall in planned consumption will have the opposite effect, decreasing the level of equilibrium income in the economy.

QUESTION 1 C = 50 + 0.8Y, S = -50 + 0.2Y and I is a constant £50.
(a) Plot the planned expenditure line on a 45° line diagram for income levels up to £1 000 and find the equilibrium level of income.
(b) I now rises to £100. Draw the new planned expenditure line on your diagram and find the new equilibrium level of income.
(c) What would the equilibrium level of income be if investment fell to £10?

The multiplier

So far we have shown that an increase in planned expenditure in the economy will lead to an increase in national income. But how large will that increase in income be? Imagine what would happen if firms decided that they wanted to increase their investment spending by borrowing more money from banks, for instance. Firms use the money to buy investment goods from other firms, which would then pay their workers, buy materials from other firms and pay bigger dividends to company shareholders etc. These households then spend the money again and so it returns to firms, who in turn pay it back to households in wages, profits and interest (this of course is the circular flow of income). The initial amount of money will keep circulating round the economy, each time increasing the level of national income. This suggests that an initial increase in planned expenditure will lead to an even greater increase in national income.

Indeed, this is what the simple Keynesian model predicts. A rise in aggregate demand will lead to a multiple increase in the equilibrium level of expenditure. Look at Figure 81.3. Aggregate expenditure rises from E_1 to E_2. Assume that the rise comes entirely from an increase in planned investment. The increase in investment is RS, the vertical distance between E_1 and E_2. But the increase in aggregate demand and national income is RT and PQ respectively. (RT and PQ are the same because this is shown by the 45° line.) An increase in investment has led to an even greater increase in income. This is the **multiplier effect** discussed in unit 64.

QUESTION 2 Draw a circular flow diagram showing the effect of an increase in planned investment expenditure of £1 000 assuming that the marginal propensity to save is 0.5.

The value of the multiplier

The value of the multiplier can be calculated using a formula:

$$\text{Multiplier (k)} = \frac{1}{\text{MPS}}$$

where MPS is the marginal propensity to save. In our simple economy, households can only save or spend any increase in their income. Therefore the marginal propensity to save plus the marginal propensity to consume must be equal to 1.

$$\text{MPS} + \text{MPC} = 1$$

Hence the MPS is equal to 1 minus the MPC. This gives an alternative formula for the multiplier:

$$\text{Multiplier (k)} = \frac{1}{1 - \text{MPC}}$$

Assume the MPS is 0.1 and there is an increase in investment expenditure of £100. The value of the multiplier is 1 ÷ 0.1 or 10. An increase in planned investment expenditure of £100 therefore leads to a £1 000 increase (£100 x 10) in national income. Exactly the same answer could be obtained if we use the alternative formula. The MPC is 0.9. Therefore the value of the multiplier is:

$$\frac{1}{1 - 0.9} \quad \text{or } 10.$$

Sometimes the multiplier is called the INVESTMENT MULTIPLIER, although we have already seen that there would be a multiplier effect if there were a change in autonomous consumption. The multiplier is also sometimes called the KEYNESIAN MULTIPLIER after John Maynard Keynes who first made the concept popular. It is also called the REAL MULTIPLIER to distinguish it from the **credit multiplier**, used to calculate the increase in the money supply following an increase in high powered money held by the banking system (☞ unit 71), and the **money multiplier** which shows the relationship between increases in the money supply and increases in income.

QUESTION 3 Calculate the change in income if there is:
(a) an increase in planned investment of £100 and the MPS is 0.5;
(b) a fall in planned investment of £1 000 and the MPS is 1/2;
(c) a fall in planned autonomous consumption of £600 and the MPS is 0.4;
(d) a fall in planned investment of £500 and the MPC is 0.5;
(e) a rise in planned investment of £250 and the MPC is 0.8;
(f) an increase in planned autonomous consumption of £200 and the MPC is 0.75;
(g) a fall in planned investment of £800 and C = 100 + 0.5Y;
(h) a rise in planned investment of £700 and S = -50 + 0.25Y.

The Keynesian cross diagram

The Keynesian cross diagram can also be used to show the effect of different multipliers. In Figure 81.4, national income is initially Y_1. If the savings function is S_1, then an increase in planned investment from I_1 to I_2 will lead to a final increase in equilibrium income of Y_1Y_2. There are two ways of calculating the multiplier from the diagram.

- The ratio of the increase in income to the increase in investment is $Y_1Y_2 \div I_1I_2$ (i.e $\Delta Y \div \Delta I$). So this is the value of the multiplier.
- The marginal propensity to save is given by the slope of the savings function (☞ unit 79). So the MPS is BD ÷ AB. The value of the multiplier is 1 ÷ MPS and hence it is equal to AB ÷ BD. Since AB = Y_1Y_2 and BD = I_1I_2, this is equivalent to the first way of calculating the multiplier.

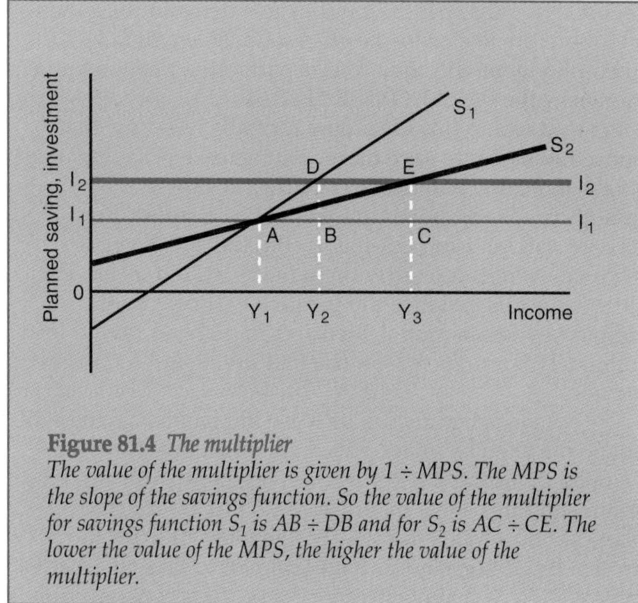

Figure 81.4 *The multiplier*
The value of the multiplier is given by 1 ÷ MPS. The MPS is the slope of the savings function. So the value of the multiplier for savings function S_1 is AB ÷ DB and for S_2 is AC ÷ CE. The lower the value of the MPS, the higher the value of the multiplier.

If the savings function, however, is S_2 and not S_1, the final increase in equilibrium income Y_1Y_3 is even larger. The slope of the savings function S_2 is shallower than S_1, and therefore the MPS is lower. This indicates that the lower the value of the MPS, the higher the value of the multiplier.

The paradox of thrift

If people plan to save more, is this good or bad for the economy? Savings are usually considered to be good. But the simple Keynesian model suggests that this might not be so. If people plan to save more, they must plan to

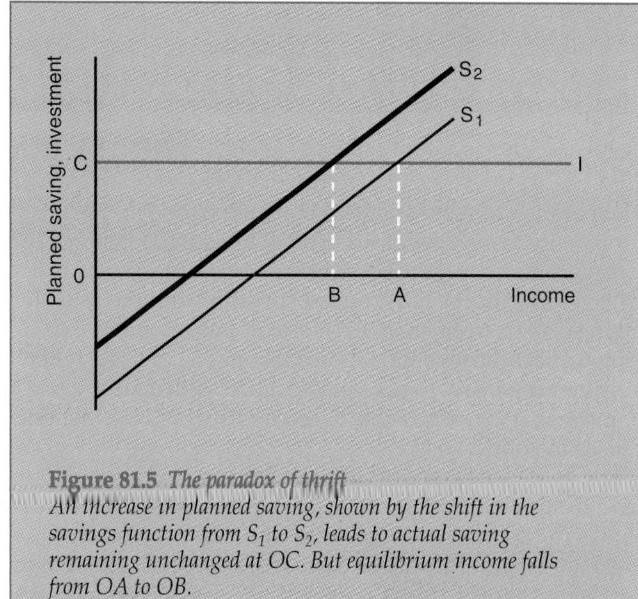

Figure 81.5 *The paradox of thrift*
An increase in planned saving, shown by the shift in the savings function from S_1 to S_2, leads to actual saving remaining unchanged at OC. But equilibrium income falls from OA to OB.

spend less. Less spending means less demand for goods and therefore lost orders for firms. Income will fall and unemployment will rise. This is part of the phenomenon known as the PARADOX OF THRIFT.

Let us develop this idea more formally. Assume that households plan to save more. An increase in saving at all levels of income will lead to an upward shift in the savings function, shown in Figure 81.5. Equilibrium income will fall from OA to OB. But the new level of planned savings is exactly the same as the old level. This surprising conclusion is the paradox of thrift. In our simple Keynesian model, increases in planned saving lead ultimately not to increases in actual saving but to falls in income.

The reason is because an increase in planned saving will not be matched by an increase in planned investment. Planned investment remains unchanged because we have assumed at this stage that there is no link between the plans of households to save and the plans of firms to invest. But if households have planned to save more, they must also have planned to spend less. Less consumption means lower orders for firms. Firms will cut back production and lay off workers. So the income of households will fall. This will carry on until once again consumption, savings and investment are in equilibrium.

Another way of understanding this is to see that an increase in planned saving must mean that households now plan to save a greater proportion of their income than before. For instance, they might plan to increase savings from 0.1 of their income to 0.2 of their income. The level of savings in the Keynesian model cannot change if there is no change in the level of investment. Hence, the only way that households can succeed in doubling their savings ratio is if their income is halved.

It is important to remember that we have assumed so far that the economy is at less than full employment. The paradox of thrift tells us that if there is unemployment in the economy, extra saving and less consumption can only make matters worse. The cure for unemployment is not less spending but more spending.

However, if the economy were to be at full employment, the story might be very different. If we relax another of our assumptions - that there is no direct link between investment and savings because savers and investors are two distinct groups in the economy - then a rise in saving (and therefore a fall in consumption) might allow investment to rise. This is likely to lead to increases in national income in the future (i.e. lead to economic growth). Indeed, the discussion of the causes of economic growth in unit 99 suggests that one of the reasons for the UK's low growth rate has been her low savings ratio.

QUESTION 4 S = -200 + 0.25Y and I = 1 000.

(a) On a Keynesian cross diagram, plot the values of S and I between income levels of 0 and 6 000.
(b) What is the equilibrium level of income?
Households now change their saving habits and decide to plan to save half of any increase in their income.
(c) What is the new savings function?
(d) Plot the new savings function on your graph.
(e) What is the new level of equilibrium income?
(f) By how much has equilibrium income changed?

Key terms

Investment multiplier, Keynesian multiplier or real multiplier - the multiplier defined in unit 64.
The paradox of thrift - increases in planned saving lead to a fall in national income with actual saving remaining unchanged.

Applied economics

The paradox of the thrift

The paradox of thrift suggests that an increase in the propensity to save will lead to a fall in national income. In a real economy there are a number of variables, such as changes in exports, government spending and the rate of interest, apart from changes in the propensity to save which affect the level of national income. Therefore, when a rising propensity to save is associated with a falling level of income, it is not possible to conclude decisively that one causes the other.

The evidence from the UK economy, however, would tend to support the hypothesis. Consider Table 81.1, which shows the personal savings ratio (the APS expressed as a percentage) and the rate of change of real GDP. The major recession years of 1974-75, 1980-81 and 1990-92 are all associated with high savings ratios. The Lawson boom of 1986-88 was associated with very low savings ratios.

Figure 81.6, a scatter diagram, presents the same data as in Table 81.1. It shows that there is some correlation between the savings ratio and real growth. The higher the savings ratio, the lower the rate of growth in the economy.

It could be that the causality runs the other way, from changes in growth of GDP to changes in the savings ratio. Economic theory would tend to support that there is this reverse link. For instance, in a recession, unemployment rises. Unemployment causes uncertainty and a fall in consumer confidence. The result is a fall in the propensity to consume and a rise in the propensity to save.

It is likely, then, that a whole number of different

variables are affecting both the propensity to save and the rate of growth of GDP. However, the evidence in Table 81.1 and Figure 81.6 would support the hypothesis that there is some link between changes in the propensity to save and changes in the equilibrium level of income.

Table 81.1 *The APS and growth in GDP*

Percentage

Year	Personal saving ratio (APS)	Annual growth in real GDP at factor cost
1970	9.1	2.0
1971	7.4	1.7
1972	9.2	2.8
1973	10.1	7.5
1974	10.7	-1.5
1975	11.5	-0.7
1976	10.8	2.7
1977	9.2	2.6
1978	10.9	2.8
1979	12.1	2.7
1980	13.4	-2.1
1981	12.6	-1.1
1982	11.3	1.8
1983	9.7	3.7
1984	11.1	2.0
1985	10.7	4.0
1986	8.7	4.0
1987	7.1	4.6
1988	5.7	5.0
1989	7.2	2.2
1990	8.4	0.4
1991	10.5	-1.7
1992	12.8	-0.5
1993	11.7	2.1
1994	10.4	3.9

Source: adapted from *Economic Trends Annual Supplement.*

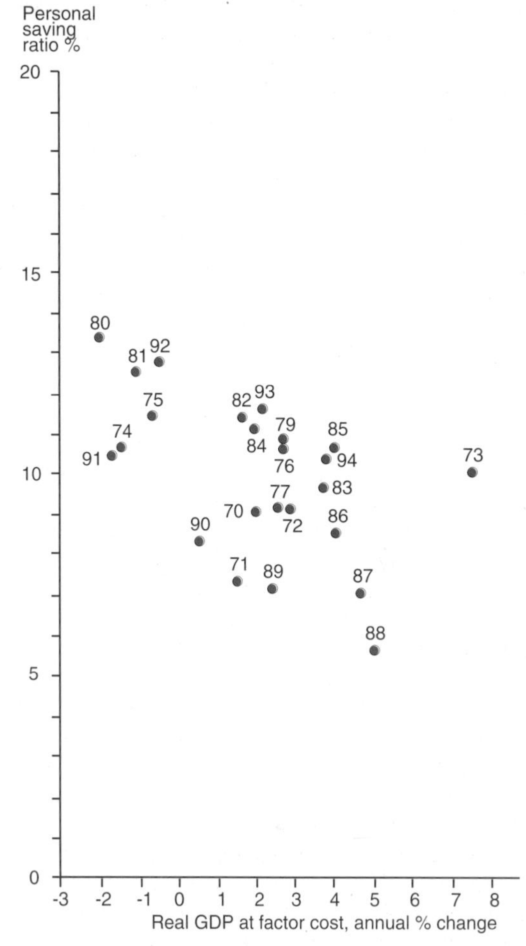

Source: adapted from Economic Trends, *Annual Supplement.*

Figure 81.6 *The relationship between the APS and real growth*

The Northern Ireland economy

In a report on exports in Northern Ireland published in 1995, it was stated that exports of manufactured goods and services from the province were increasing more quickly than those of the UK as a whole. In the three years to March 1994, exports by companies operating in Northern Ireland companies increased by 25 per cent compared with a UK growth rate of 18 per cent. Total external sales, including shipments to the mainland UK, grew slightly slower, at 16 per cent, reflecting the UK recession. The main export growth areas were chemicals, electrical and instrument engineering and transport equipment. Clothing and textile sales, which also increased sharply, continued to be dependent on the UK market.

The figures, compiled before the ceasefires at the end of 1994, underscore the fact that Northern Ireland output has outstripped that of the UK as a whole since the third quarter of 1991. Industrial output is growing at 4 per cent per year. The performance of the Northern Ireland economy in part reflects the increase in inward investment, which reached record levels in 1993-94. Exports have been helped by the withdrawal of sterling from the European exchange rate mechanism in September 1992 and its consequent 15 per cent devaluation. Northern Ireland companies have also benefited from buoyant domestic demand, helped by sustained levels of public spending.

Source: adapted from the *Financial Times*, 26.4.1995.

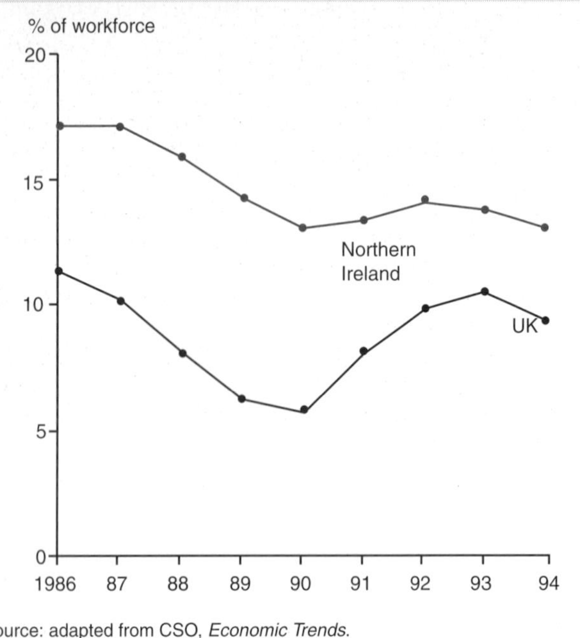

Source: adapted from CSO, *Economic Trends.*

Figure 81.7 *Unemployment, % of workforce*

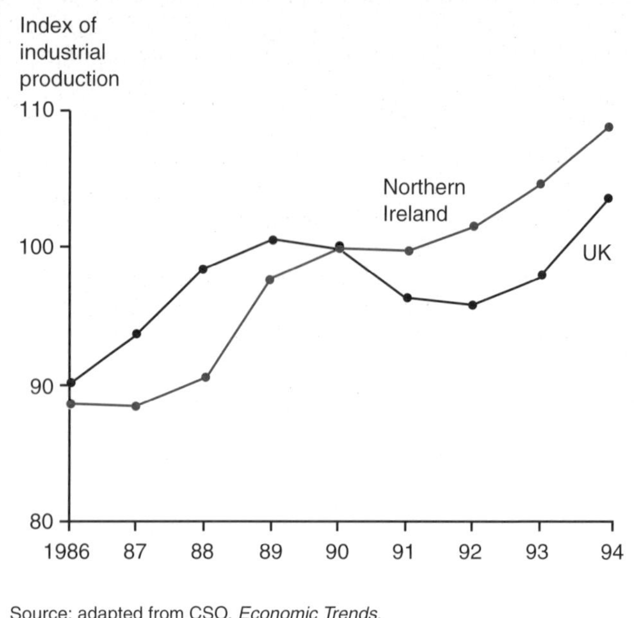

Source: adapted from CSO, *Economic Trends.*

Figure 81.8 *Index of industrial production, 1990=100*

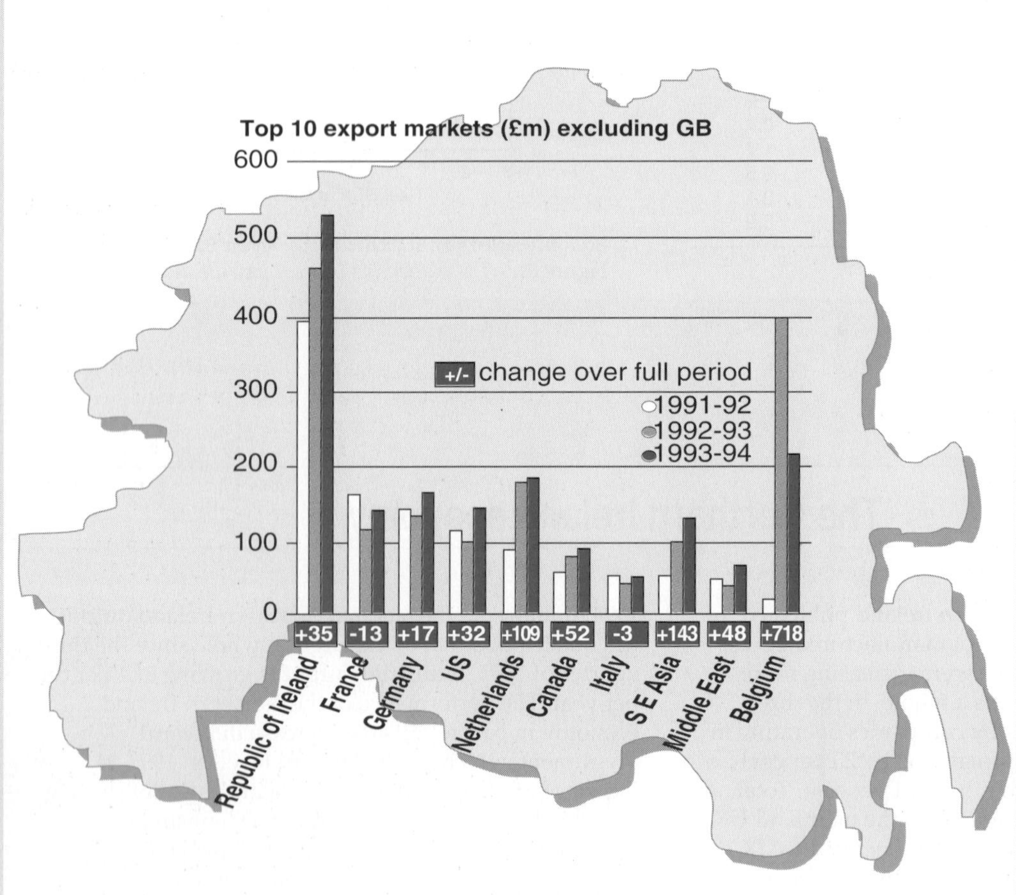

Source: adapted from Northern Ireland Economic Research Centre.

Figure 81.9 *Growth in Northern Ireland exports*

1. **Compare the performance of the Northern Ireland economy with that of the UK in the early 1990s.**
2. **Explain how 'the multiplier' might help explain Northern Ireland's relatively strong economic performance. (Note that changes in exports and government spending as well as investment can lead to a multiple increase in national income as will be discussed in units 82 and 83.)**
3. **Discuss what effect the IRA and unionist ceasefires in late 1994 are likely to have had on the national income of Northern Ireland.**

Government and national income

Summary

1. Aggregate demand in an economy with government is equal to C + I + G.
2. The economy is in equilibrium when planned C + I + G is equal to actual income. Alternatively, it is in equilibrium when planned injections I + G equal planned withdrawals S + T.
3. An increase in planned government expenditure will lead, via the multiplier process, to an increase in income. The value of the multiplier is equal to 1 ÷ (MPS + MPT).
4. An increase in tax rates will lead to a fall in national income.
5. If the economy is below full employment, a deflationary gap is said to exist. The government can fill this by an increase in spending or a reduction in taxes.
6. If the economy is at full employment, increased government spending or lower taxes cannot, by the definition of full employment, increase output. Instead it will raise prices, and an inflationary gap is then said to exist.
7. Keynesian theory suggests that there is a balanced budget multiplier. Increasing government spending and taxes by the same amount will lead to a rise in national income.

Assumptions

In the simple Keynesian model of income determination developed in units 80 and 81, a number of assumptions were made:

- the economy was closed and there was no government activity;
- the economy was below full employment;
- wages and prices were stable;
- money was neutral.

In this unit, the simplifying assumption that there is no government economic activity will first be dropped, and in the next unit we will consider what happens if there is foreign trade.

Aggregate expenditure in an economy with government

In the simplest model of the economy, aggregate expenditure or aggregate demand is equal to planned consumption plus planned investment. With a public sector, there is a further component of expenditure: planned government expenditure (G). So the new aggregate expenditure equation is:

$$E = C + I + G$$

It is important to understand what constitutes and what determines C, I and G when the activities of government are added to the model.

Consumption Planned consumption is a function of **disposable income** (☞ unit 79):

$$C = f(Y_d)$$

Disposable income is income after tax but includes transfer payments. In our model, we need to express planned consumption as a function of national income. In the simplest model, with no government, disposable income and national income are the same, so no adjustment needs to be made. In a model with government, disposable income (Y_d) is equal to national income (Y) minus net taxes (T). 'Net taxes' in turn is defined as the difference between taxes paid and transfer payments (such as child benefit or unemployment benefit) received. So:

$$Y_d = Y - T$$

Since consumption is a function of disposable income it must be a function of national income minus net taxes:

$$C = f(Y - T)$$

Investment Planned investment, as in the simple model, is assumed to be autonomous. It is determined by firms independently of the level of income.

Government spending Planned government spending in this model is not equal to public expenditure. Public expenditure includes **transfer payments** (☞ unit 59). These are transfers of income from taxpayers to the recipients of benefits such as the unemployed, students and pensioners. In the circular flow model, expenditure must not only create income but there must also be a corresponding output. Expenditure on, say, unemployment benefits produces no corresponding flow of output of real goods and services. So any spending on transfer payments by government is excluded from the definition of G, government spending, used in our model. What is included, however, is spending on goods and services such as hospitals, schools, the police and the army. An assumption is made within the model that G is autonomous (i.e. it is not determined by the level of income). It is assumed that G is determined by political rather than economic considerations. So when national income rises, the government may or may not choose to change the level of government spending.

QUESTION 1 A government spends money in just two ways. £5 000 million is spent on its army. £2 000 million is spent on welfare payments to citizens of the country. It raises £6 000 million in taxes and national income is £34 000 million.
(a) In the circular flow of income model, what would be the value of (i) G and (ii) T where G is government spending and T is net taxes?
(b) What is the value of disposable income?
(c) What is the value of consumption expenditure if $C = £1\,000m + 0.6Y_d$?
(d) What would the answers be to (b) and (c) if taxes were not £6 000 million but: (i) £4 000 million; (ii) £8 000 million?

Equilibrium income

In equilibrium, planned expenditure equals actual income (☞ unit 80). So in an economy with government, there is equilibrium when planned consumption plus planned investment plus planned government spending equals income:

$$Y = C + I + G$$

Figure 82.1 shows this using the 45° line diagram and the Keynesian cross diagram. In the 45° line diagram, the consumption line is drawn upward sloping. This shows that consumption increases as income increases. Investment is autonomous. Whatever the level of income, planned investment expenditure is PQ. Hence the C + I line is parallel to the C line. Planned government expenditure too is autonomous, remaining constant at a level of QR whatever the level of income. Hence the C + I + G line is parallel to the other two lines. Planned expenditure is equal to actual income where the C + I + G line crosses the 45° line. Hence the equilibrium level of national income is OS.

The Keynesian cross diagram shows injections and leakages in the economy. Income is in equilibrium when planned injections equal planned withdrawals. The two injections are investment and government spending. Both are autonomous and therefore the I + G line is horizontal, showing that neither changes as income changes. Both S and T are assumed to increase with income. At higher levels of income, households plan to save more and they have to pay more in taxes such as income tax and VAT which in practice are linked to income. Equilibrium income is OS where planned injections equal planned leakages.

QUESTION 2 C = 1 000 + 0.75Y, planned investment is a constant 9 000 and planned government expenditure is a constant 10 000.
(a) Plot the aggregate expenditure line on a 45° line diagram between income levels of 0 and 100 000.
(b) What is the equilibrium level of income?
(c) (i) Draw the aggregate expenditure line if government spending were not 10 000 but only 5 000. (ii) What would be the new level of equilibrium income?

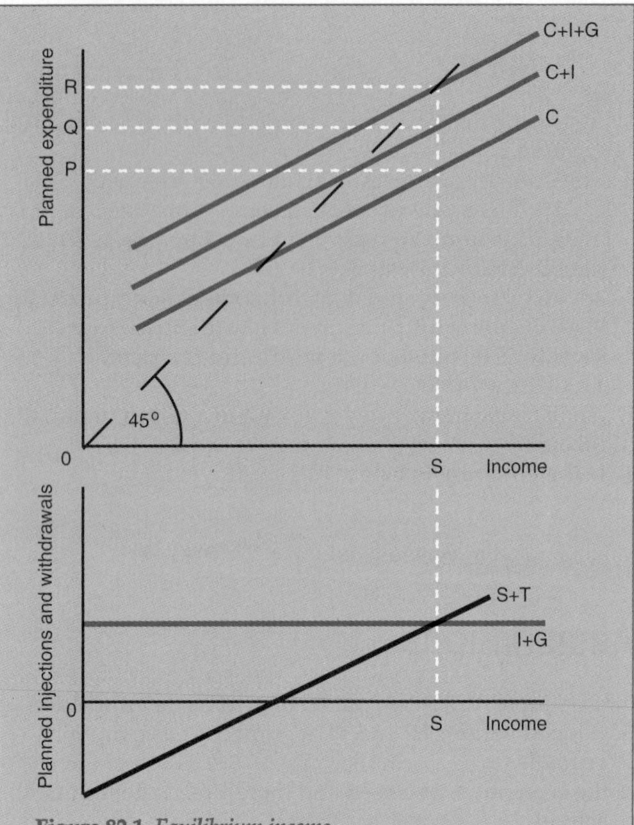

Figure 82.1 *Equilibrium income*
Equilibrium income in an economy with a government sector will occur where planned expenditure, C+ I + G, equals actual income at OS. The same result can be obtained by equating planned injections I + G with planned leakages S + T.

Changes in government spending

An increase in government spending will raise the level of aggregate expenditure. More spending in the economy will in turn raise the level of equilibrium income (☞ units 64 and 81 for an explanation of how exactly this occurs). This is shown in Figure 82.2. A rise in planned government spending from G_1 to G_2 will lead to an upward shift in the aggregate expenditure schedule, from $C + I + G_1$ to $C + I + G_2$. Equilibrium national income will now rise from OS to OT.

The increase in government spending in Figure 82.2 was PQ. However, the final increase in planned expenditure was PR. QR consumption expenditure has been crowded in through the multiplier effect. Remember that the multiplier is the ratio of the final change in income to the initial change in planned expenditure:

$$\text{Multiplier} = \frac{\Delta Y}{\Delta J}$$

where ΔY is the change in income and ΔJ is the change in the two injections I and G. We can also express the multiplier in another way as:

$$\text{Multiplier} = \frac{1}{MPS + MPT}$$

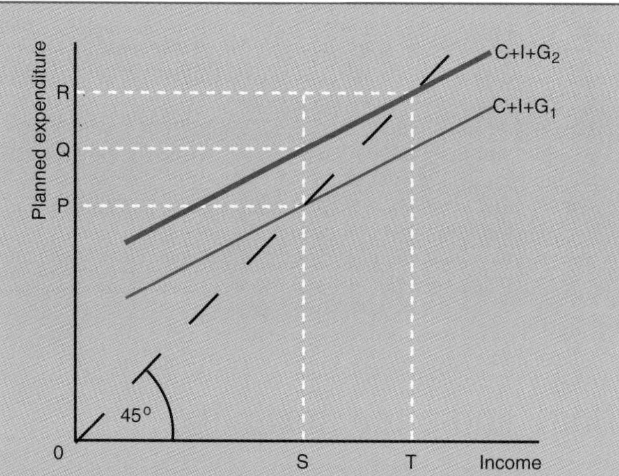

Figure 82.2 *An increase in government spending*
An increase in government spending will shift the aggregate expenditure line up from $C + I + G_1$ to $C + I + G_2$. The result is an increase in the equilibrium level of income from OS to OT.

where the MPS is the marginal propensity to save and the MPT is the marginal propensity to tax. The MPS can be defined as the proportion of a change in income that is saved. The MARGINAL PROPENSITY TO TAX is defined as the proportion of a change in income that is taken in taxes by government. For instance, if the government collects an extra £20 in tax when national income increases by £100, then the MPT is 0.2.

The multiplier can again be expressed in terms of the marginal propensity to consume.

$$\text{Multiplier} = \frac{1}{1 - \text{MPC}}$$

The MPC in this formula is the marginal propensity to consume out of **national income**. This is not the same as the marginal propensity to consume out of disposable income which is found in the consumption function. In the next section we will see how the two MPCs are related mathematically.

The multiplier is used to calculate the change in equilibrium income resulting from a change in either planned investment or planned government spending.

QUESTION 3 What is the change in equilibrium national income if:

(a) MPS = 0.15, MPT = 0.1 and there is an increase in investment of £100m;
(b) MPS = 0.1, MPT = 0.2 and government spending increases by £6 000m;
(c) G increases by £1 000m at the same time as I increases by £2 000m, MPS = 0.3, MPT = 0.2;
(d) G increases by £5 000m at the same time as I increases by £2 000m, MPS = 0.05, MPT = 0.05;
(e) S = -200m + 0.35Y, T = 0.15Y, I increases by £3 000m at the same time as G increases by £5 000m;
(f) S = - 400m + 0.2Y, T = 0.05Y, I increases by £2 000m at the same time as G increases by £4 000m?

For instance, if the multiplier is 2 and planned government spending increases by £500 million, then equilibrium national income will rise by £1 000 million. If the multiplier were 3, a fall in G of £1 000 million would lead to a fall in equilibrium income of £3 000 million.

Equally, if we know that the marginal propensity to save is 0.3 and the marginal propensity to tax is 0.2, then the value of the multiplier is 1 ÷ (0.3 + 0.2) or 2. So a change in G of £300 million will lead to a change in equilibrium income of £600 million.

Changes in taxation

A change in tax rates is a little more difficult to analyse than a change in government spending. Assume that taxes change in proportion to income. So we are assuming that taxes are like income tax where an increase in national income will lead to an increase in tax revenue for the government.

We know that consumption is a function of disposable income. Assume the formula for the consumption function is:

$$C = a + b\,Y_d$$

where a is autonomous consumption and b is the marginal propensity to consume. It has been explained above that Yd, disposable income, is equal to Y - T. So:

$$C = a + b\,(Y - T)$$

Taxes are proportional to income. If there is no autonomous element in taxation and taxes are assumed to be net of benefits, then taxes are equal to the marginal propensity to tax (t) times income:

$$T = tY$$

Substituting this in the previous equation we get:

$$C = a + b\,(Y - tY)$$

or

$$C = a + b\,(1 - t)\,Y$$

For instance, if the marginal propensity to consume out of disposable income (b) is 0.9 and the marginal propensity to tax (t) is 0.2, then the marginal propensity to consume out of national income is 0.9 x (1 - 0.2) or 0.72.

This example shows that the marginal propensity to consume out of disposable income is higher than the marginal propensity to consume out of national income. This is what should be expected. Disposable income is smaller than national income because of taxes. So the proportion spent out of disposable income is bound to be higher than the proportion spent of national income.

Figure 82.3 shows the relationship between the two consumption functions. C_1 shows the relationship between consumption and disposable income. C_2 shows the relationship between consumption and national income. The marginal propensity to consume is the gradient of the line. So C_1 is steeper than C_2 because the marginal propensity to consume out of disposable income is higher than the marginal propensity to consume out of

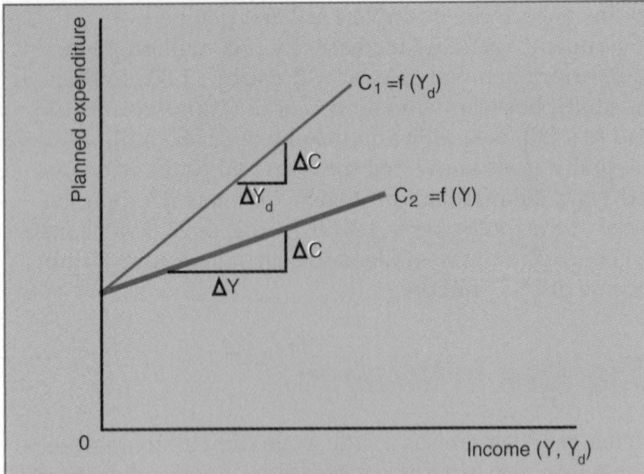

Figure 82.3 *Disposable income and national income*
The MPC out of disposable income is higher than the MPC out of national income. Hence C_1 is steeper than C_2.

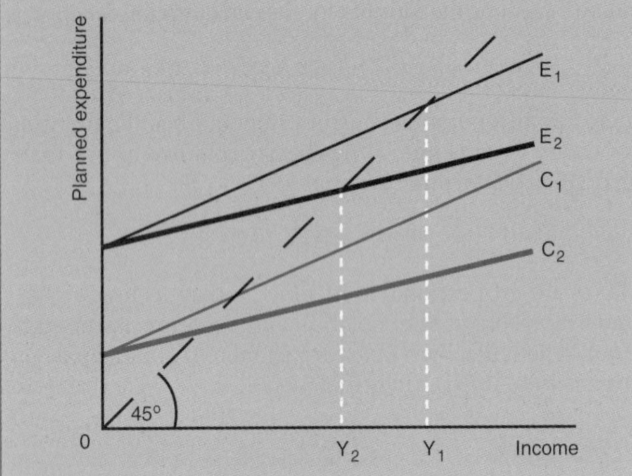

Figure 82.4 A rise in tax rates
A rise in tax rates and revenues will lead to a fall in the consumption line from C_1 to C_2 and hence a fall in aggregate expenditure from E_1 to E_2 due to a fall in planned consumption. As a result, equilibrium income will fall from Y_1 to Y_2.

national income.

It is now possible to see what happens if the government increases rates of tax so that more tax is paid at every level of income. An increase in the marginal propensity to tax will lower the marginal propensity to consume out of taxed income. This can be shown by a swing downwards in the consumption function from C_1 to C_2. If we now add planned investment and government spending, we arrive at the aggregate expenditure lines in Figure 82.4. A rise in tax rates has led to a fall in aggregate expenditure from E_1 to E_2. The result is that equilibrium national income falls from Y_1 to Y_2.

This is the result that would be expected. A rise in tax rates will lead to an increase in tax revenues for the government. Consumers are therefore spending less money. Hence national income will fall. On the other hand, a fall in tax rates will put money into consumers' pockets. They will increase their consumption expenditure, raising the level of national income.

QUESTION 4 Using diagrams, explain how the following might have affected equilibrium income according to the Keynesian model.

(a) In 1994 and 1995, the Chancellor of the Exchequer substantially raised taxes in the economy in order to reduce the PSBR.
(b) In 1963, the Chancellor substantially cut taxes to combat unemployment and low growth.
(c) In 1979, the Chancellor raised VAT from 8 per cent to 15 per cent but cut income tax rates resulting in no overall change in tax revenues.

Wage and price flexibility

In the simple Keynesian model of the economy first outlined in unit 80, a number of important simplifying assumptions were made. One was that wages and prices were stable. Another was that the economy operated at below **full employment**. Hence, when aggregate demand or expenditure rose, prices remained constant whilst output and income expanded.

These two assumptions will now be modified. We will still assume that income can change without causing a change in prices so long as the economy operates below full employment. But any increase in aggregate demand when the economy reaches full employment will result not in a rise in output but in a rise in prices. For instance, in the early 1930s when there was mass unemployment in the UK, an increase in spending in the economy would have raised output and put people back to work. But ten years later, with Britain at war, with no unemployment and factories working at full stretch, an increase in spending would not have led to extra output. The economy could not produce any more because it was at full employment. What would have happened, but for a system of rationing, would have been severe inflation, as indeed happened during the First World War under

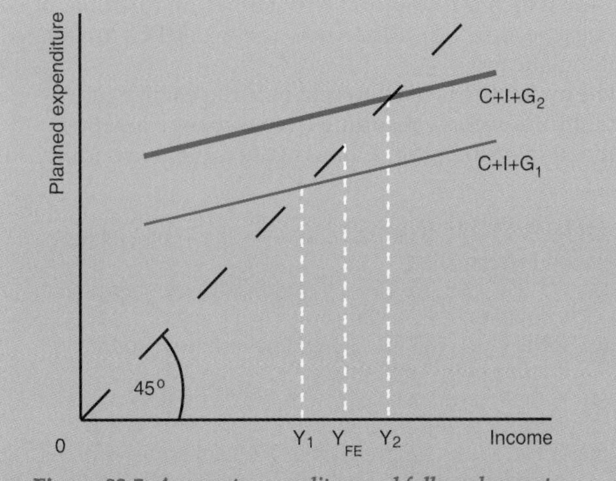

Figure 82.5 *Aggregate expenditure and full employment*
If Y_{FE} is the full employment level of income, then a rise in government spending from G_1 to G_2 will lead to a rise in real output and income of Y_1Y_{FE} and a rise in prices to bring Y_{FE} up to Y_2.

similar circumstances.

This can be shown in Figure 82.5. The economy is initially in equilibrium at income Y_1. The full employment level of income is Y_{FE}. Government now increases its spending from G_1 to G_2, raising the level of planned expenditure from $C + I + G_1$ to $C + I + G_2$. The new equilibrium level of income is Y_2. There will be a rise in real output and income from Y_1 to Y_{FE}. But Y_{FE} by the definition of full employment is the maximum level of output for the economy. Therefore the rise in output and income from Y_{FE} to Y_2 cannot be a rise in real output. It must be a rise in nominal output (i.e. output at current prices) caused solely by an increase in prices.

Inflationary and deflationary gaps

An INFLATIONARY GAP is said to exist when planned expenditure is greater than the full employment level of i income (i.e. when there are inflationary pressures in the economy). In Figure 82.6, the equilibrium level of income, Y_E, is greater than the full employment level of income, Y_{FE}. If inflation is to be avoided, income needs to fall by Y_EY_{FE}. This will be achieved if planned expenditure falls from E_1 to E_2. This fall could, for instance, come from a fall in government expenditure. The size of the fall needed is AB. Note that this is less than the fall in national income. This is because a fall in autonomous expenditure, such as G or I, will lead to a multiple fall in income through the multiplier effect. AB is then the size of the inflationary gap.

A DEFLATIONARY GAP exists when planned expenditure is less than the full employment level of income (i.e. when there is unemployment in the economy). There must be an increase in autonomous expenditure such as investment or government spending if planned expenditure is to rise to equal full employment income. In Figure 82.7, the rise needed is AB. Again, AB is less than Y_EY_{FE} because of the multiplier effect. A rise in government spending of AB will crowd-in extra consumption

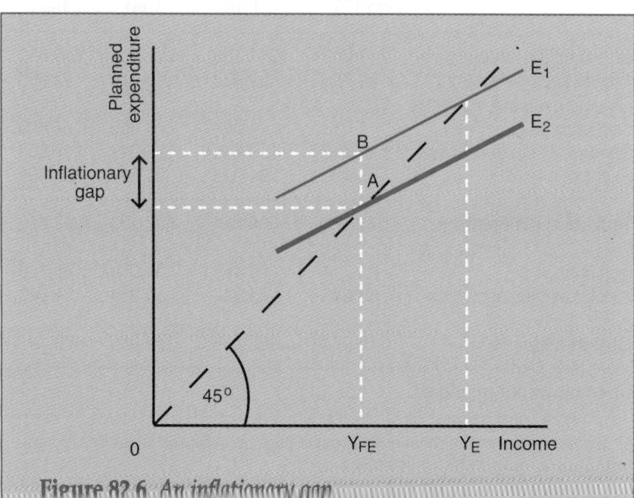

Figure 82.6 An inflationary gap
An inflationary gap exists when full employment income is below equilibrium income. Without a fall in planned autonomous expenditure of AB, the economy will suffer inflation.

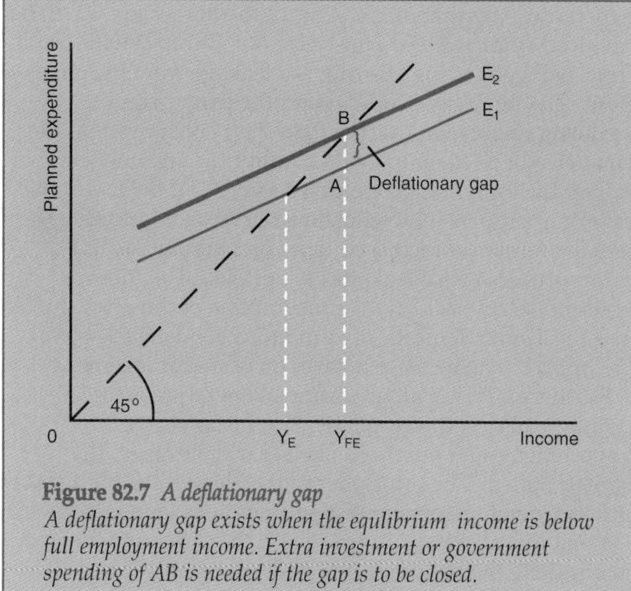

Figure 82.7 A deflationary gap
A deflationary gap exists when the equlibrium income is below full employment income. Extra investment or government spending of AB is needed if the gap is to be closed.

expenditure to give the final rise of Y_EY_{FE} in income.

In the simple Keynesian model, it is possible then for government to intervene to stabilise the economy at its full employment level. If the economy is at below full employment, it should increase its budget deficit to fill the deflationary gap. If the economy is threatening to go beyond full employment, it should reduce its budget deficit or run a surplus to remove the inflationary gap.

QUESTION 5 C = 1 000 + 0.6Y, where C is consumption and Y is national income. Government spending is a constant 10 000 and investment is 5 000.
(a) On a 45° line diagram, plot the aggregate expenditure line from income levels of 0 to 70 000.
(b) What is the equilibrium level of income?
(c) What is the size of the inflationary gap if the full employment level of income is (i) 20 000 and (ii) 30 000?
(d) What is the size of the deflationary gap if the full employment level of income is (i) 50 000 and (ii) 60 000?

The balanced budget multiplier

So far we have shown that increases in government spending or reductions in tax will raise the level of national income whilst falls in G or rises in T will lead to a fall in Y. But what if the Chancellor in his budget raised both G and T by the same amount? Keynesian theory predicts that this would be likely to increase aggregate demand.

Assume that the Chancellor raises government spending by £1 000m and the value of the multiplier is 2. This will lead to an increase in the equilibrium level of income of £2 000 million. On the other hand, an increase in taxes of £1 000 million will reduce the equilibrium level of income. However, income will fall by less than £2 000 million. This is because households will not reduce their expenditure by that much. Part of the higher taxes will be financed from reduced consumption. But part will come from reduced saving. Saving is a leakage from the circular flow. The more households fund the extra taxes by reducing their saving rather than their consumption, the smaller will be the impact on equilibrium income (i.e. the higher the marginal propensity to save and the lower the marginal propensity to consume out of taxed income, the less the impact of increased taxes on national income).

Imports are also a leakage (☞ unit 58). The more households cut back on the consumption of imported goods and the less on domestically produced goods, the less will the impact of an increase in taxes on domestic income.

Furthermore, not all government spending is on domestically produced goods. For instance, the government may purchase nuclear missiles from the United States. The multiplier will be lower, the higher the proportion of government spending on foreign goods.

What this all means in practice is that governments can manipulate their expenditure and taxation to change the size of the balanced budget multiplier. For instance, spending extra money on house building which has a very high domestically produced component and financing it by taxing the better off, who have above average propensities to save and import, according to Keynesians, will raise national income. Spending extra money on defence equipment, which has a higher import content, and taxing the poor who have a low propensity to save, will increase national income far less.

Key terms

The marginal propensity to tax - the proportion of a change in income that is taken in taxes by government.
Inflationary gap - exists when planned expenditure is greater than the full employment level of income. It is the fall in autonomous expenditure needed to reduce income to its full employment level.
Deflationary gap - exists when planned expenditure is less than the full employment level of income. It is the rise in autonomous expenditure needed to increase income to its full employment level.

Applied economics

A deflationary gap, 1979-1982

The Barber boom of 1972-4 was caused by government increasing public spending and reducing taxes to fill a deflationary gap which emerged in the UK economy during 1971. It was the last time that a UK government was to use the insights of the simple Keynesian model to direct policy. By the mid-1970s, it was generally recognised that increasing the PSBR would have important consequences for inflation even if the economy was below full employment. The Conservative administration which came into office in 1979 saw the control of inflation as their main priority. They believed that increasing government expenditure would lead only to inflation and no long term fall in unemployment. In pursuit of their policies, they cut public expenditure, raised tax revenues, raised the rate of interest and allowed the exchange rate to rise substantially.

Table 82.1 shows the effect of this on national income and employment, between 1979 and 1981.

- Increases in interest rates led to sharp falls in stock levels held by companies. They also contributed to a sharp decline in private sector investment.
- Exports fell slightly as exporters found it difficult to sell abroad due to the high value of the pound.
- Government expenditure fell. This change was entirely made up of falls in public sector investment since public sector current consumption in fact rose slightly.

Overall, actual I + G + X at constant market prices fell by £10 418 million in 1980 and £6 697 million in 1981 before increasing again by £7 730 million in 1982.

In the simple Keynesian model, falls in injections to the circular flow, I + G + X, lead to falls in national income

Table 82.1 *Expenditure, income and unemployment, 1979-82*

£ millions at 1990 prices

	1979	1980	1981	1982
Consumption expenditure	247 212	247 185	247 402	249 852
Private sector investment	54 795	52 438	49 075	52 963
Change in stocks and work in progress	4 013	- 4 064	- 3 859	- 1 545
Government expenditure[1]	119 416	119 644	116 812	117 555
Exports	95 130	94 918	94 211	94 996
Total final expenditure[2]	521 191	509 274	502 130	512 372
less imports	89 714	86 469	84 050	88 146
less taxes plus subsidies	56 943	55 347	54 054	54 846
GDP at factor cost[3]	375 974	368 216	364 055	370 493
Unemployment (millions)	1.3	1.7	2.5	2.9

1. General government final consumption plus public corporation investment plus general government investment.
2. Totals slightly differ from the sum of components because not all investment expenditure has been allocated between sectors by CSO.
3. Totals different from sum of components because of the method used to re-base on 1990 prices.
Source: adapted from CSO, *Economic Trends Annual Supplement*, CSO *United Kingdom National Accounts*.

and rises in unemployment. As can be seen from Table 82.1, this is indeed what happened. GDP at factor cost fell by £7 758 million in 1980 and £4 161 million in 1981 before increasing in 1982 by £6 438 million. Unemployment more than doubled between 1979 and 1982.

Keynesian economists at the time bitterly opposed government policies. They argued that the government needed to close the widening deflationary gap by increasing government spending and reducing taxes. In 1981, to their dismay, the Chancellor Geoffrey Howe sharply increased taxes in his March Budget. A letter to *The Times* shortly afterwards, signed by 364 UK economists, protested vigorously at what they saw as the folly of government policy. In fact, by 1982 exports and investment had begun to rise, and there was a slight increase in government expenditure too. This pushed up the aggregate demand line and increased GDP, but not sufficiently to prevent a further large increase in unemployment. For the rest of the 1980s, the government refused to use demand management techniques of a fiscal nature to influence either unemployment or inflation. However, the experience of the early 1980s suggests that changes in government spending and taxation may influence the level of income in the economy, at least in the short term.

The UK economy, 1960-62

1. **How, according to the data, was the economy changing in the period 1960-1962?**
2. **Discuss, using diagrams, what were the main variables affecting the change in**
   (a) consumption and
   (b) national income over the period.
3. **The Conservative government of the time managed the economy on Keynesian lines. What do you think the Chancellor should have done in his 1963 Budget? Use diagrams to help explain your answer.**

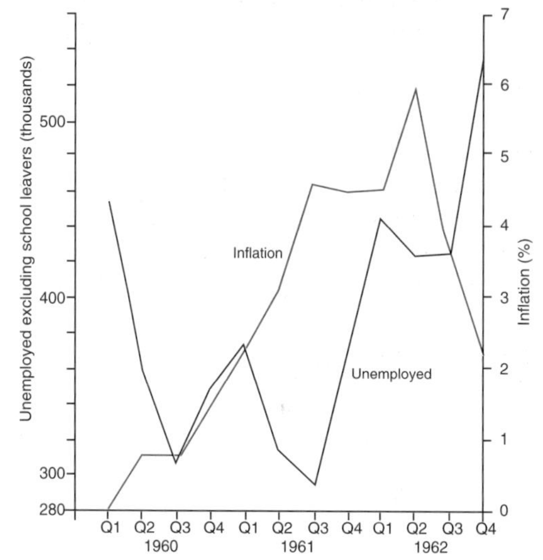

Source: adapted from CSO, *Economic Trends Annual Supplement.*

Figure 82.8 *Unemployment and inflation, 1960-62*

Table 82.2 *Income and expenditure, 1960-62*

		Consumption [1,6]		Investment [1,2,6]		Government spending [3,6]		Disposable income [4]		GDP[5]	
		£bn at 1990 prices	% change on previous year	£bn at 1990 prices	% change on previous year	£bn at 1990 prices	% change on previous year	£bn at 1990 prices	% change on previous year	£bn at year prices	% change on previous year
1960	Q1	39 159	6.3	5 939	14.2	19 934	4.7	41 282	7.2	57 232	7.8
	Q2	39 059	3.9	5 979	8.0	20 058	3.2	42 059	5.7	56 889	5.9
	Q3	39 262	3.9	6 042	8.7	20 077	2.6	42 710	6.6	57 874	5.3
	Q4	39 255	1.5	6 256	5.6	20 513	2.9	43 148	6.9	57 009	3.5
1961	Q1	39 958	2.0	6 502	9.5	20 863	4.7	43 589	5.6	58 757	2.7
	Q2	39 961	2.3	6 665	11.5	21 021	4.8	44 297	5.3	59 200	4.1
	Q3	40 151	2.3	6 791	12.4	21 325	6.2	44 324	3.8	59 224	2.3
	Q4	40 129	2.3	6 623	5.9	21 311	3.9	44 046	2.1	59 023	1.7
1962	Q1	40 447	1.2	6 683	2.8	21 645	3.7	44 029	1.0	59 151	0.7
	Q2	41 173	3.0	6 890	3.4	21 548	2.5	44 048	0.0	59 989	1.3
	Q3	40 931	1.9	7 021	3.4	21 356	0.1	44 750	0.1	60 507	2.2
	Q4	41 374	3.1	6 878	3.9	21 394	0.4	45 459	3.2	60 072	1.8

1. Private sector.
2. Figures for 1960-61 are estimated.
3. General government final consumption and investment. Figures for 1960-61 are estimated.
4. Real personal disposable income.
5. Gross domestic product at factor cost.
6. At market prices.

Source: adapted from CSO, *Economic Trends Annual Supplement.*

Foreign trade and the derivation of the aggregate demand curve

Summary

1. Exports are exogenously determined in a simple Keynesian model of the economy but imports are assumed to be a function of income.
2. Aggregate demand in an open economy is equal to C + I + G + X - M.
3. The economy is in equilibrium when planned expenditure C + I + G + X - M is equal to actual income.
4. An increase in planned exports will lead to a multiple increase in income.
5. The value of the multiplier is given by the formula 1÷ (MPS + MPT + MPM).
6. An increase in imports caused by an increase in the marginal propensity to import will lead to a fall in national income.
7. The downward sloping aggregate demand curve can be derived from combining what happens in the money market with a Keynesian model of income determination.

Exports and imports

Countries trade with each other because they need the goods and services other countries produce. Goods and services purchased from abroad are called **imports**, whilst domestically produced goods and services sold abroad are called **exports**. A TRADE DEFICIT occurs if the value of imports is greater than exports. If the value of exports is greater than imports, then there is said to be a TRADE SURPLUS.

The value of exports is determined by a large variety of factors. In the simple Keynesian model of the economy, with fixed exchange rates, it is assumed to be determined by the level of income of foreigners. The higher their income, the more goods and services they will buy, including imported goods. This means that exports are **autonomous** or **exogenous**. They are not determined by factors within the domestic economy.

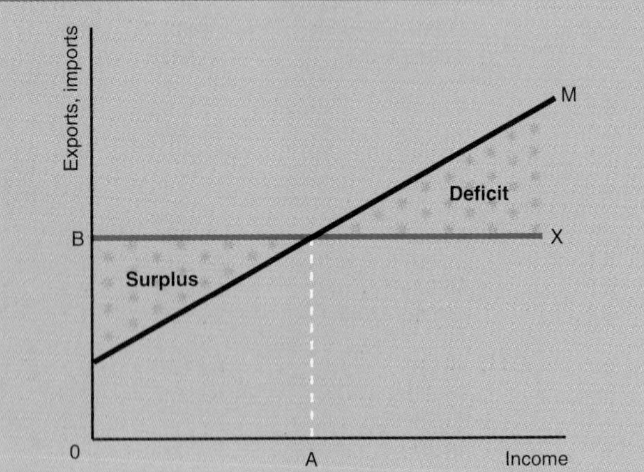

Figure 83.1 *The trade balance*
As income increases, the trade balance moves from being in surplus at income levels below OA to being in deficit.

Imports, however, are assumed to be **endogenous**. If domestic income rises, households and firms will buy more goods, including imported goods. If you were to receive an increase in income of £20 a week, you might increase your spending by £15 on domestically produced products and £5 on imported products. Hence imports are assumed to be a function of income.

Just as it is possible to calculate the marginal propensity to save and the marginal propensity to tax, so it is possible to calculate the MARGINAL PROPENSITY TO IMPORT (MPM). This is defined as the proportion of a change in income which is spent on imported goods. It is calculated

QUESTION 1

Table 83.1 *UK exports, imports and GDP, 1990-1994*

£ billion

	1990	1991	1992	1993	1994
Exports	217	218	214	237	258
Imports	235	226	224	249	258
Income (GDP at factor cost)	479	496	516	547	578

Source: adapted from CSO, *Economic Trends.*

(a) Calculate the trade deficit or surplus for each year from 1990 to 1994.
(b) What was the marginal propensity to import, all other things being equal, in: (i) 1991; (ii) 1992; (iii) 1993; (iv) 1994?
(c) Explain why the values for the marginal propensity to import for 1991 and 1992 are not what you would expect.

by dividing the change in imports (ΔM) by the change in income (ΔY):

$$\text{Marginal propensity to import (MPM)} = \frac{\Delta M}{\Delta Y}$$

So in our example above, the MPM of an increase in your income of £20 is 0.25 (5 ÷ 20).

Figure 83.1 illustrates the points made above. Exports are autonomous and therefore remain constant at a level of OB whatever the level of income. Imports increase as income increases. At income levels below OA, there is a trade surplus. At income OA the trade balance is zero. At income levels above OA, there is a trade deficit.

Aggregate demand in an open economy

In an economy with no government and no foreign trade, aggregate demand or aggregate expenditure is equal to planned consumption plus planned investment. In unit 82, a government sector was introduced and aggregate demand was redefined as C + I + G. Planned consumption was said to be consumption out of taxed income.

In an economy with government and foreign trade, aggregate demand is commonly defined as:

$$E = C + I + G + X - M$$

Planned exports, X, are an addition to aggregate expenditure. C, I and G are planned spending on goods and services produced both at home and abroad. The goods produced abroad, although they raise domestic spending, have no corresponding impact on either domestic output or domestic income. Hence to find the level of demand within the economy which is equal to national income and national output it is necessary to take away imports. We could do this by redefining C, I and G as expenditures solely on domestically produced goods. For instance, C would be total consumption minus the consumption on imported goods. Aggregate expenditure would then be equal to C + I + G + X. However, it is more usual to leave our definitions of C, I and G unchanged, place imports M into a separate category and then take M away from C + I + G + X.

Equilibrium income

The economy is in equilibrium when planned expenditure equals actual income or when planned injections equal planned withdrawals (☞ unit 74). So in an open economy (i.e. where there is foreign trade) with government, national income is in equilibrium when either:

$$Y = C + I + G + X - M$$

or when:

$$I + G + X = S + T + M$$

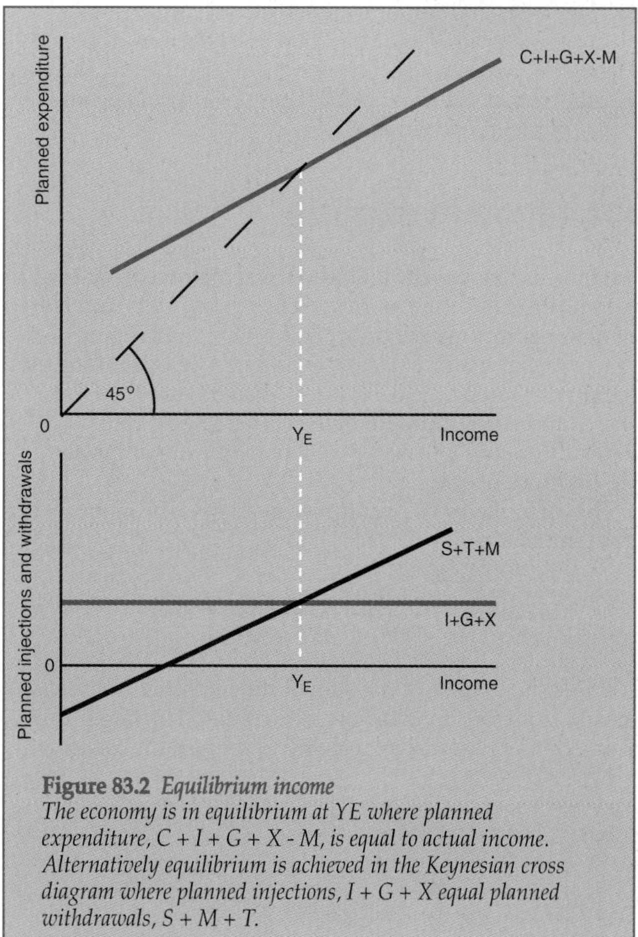

Figure 83.2 *Equilibrium income*
The economy is in equilibrium at YE where planned expenditure, C + I + G + X - M, is equal to actual income. Alternatively equilibrium is achieved in the Keynesian cross diagram where planned injections, I + G + X equal planned withdrawals, S + M + T.

Figure 83.2 shows these conditions diagrammatically. In the 45° line diagram, equilibrium is achieved where the aggregate demand or expenditure line crosses the 45° line (☞ unit 80 for an explanation of why this should be so). In the Keynesian cross diagram, there are three injections (planned investment, government spending and exports) and three withdrawals (planned saving, imports and taxes). Each of the three injections is assumed to be autonomous. Investment is determined by the decisions of businesses, government spending by government and exports by foreigners. None of these is assumed to change as income changes. Hence the I + G + X line is horizontal.

QUESTION 2 C = 20 + 0.5Y and M = 0.25Y where C is consumption, M is imports and Y is national income. G is 80, I is 30 and X is 50.

(a) On a 45° line diagram, plot aggregate demand between income levels of 0 and 300.
(b) What is the equilibrium level of income?
(c) What is the trade surplus or deficit at the equilibrium level of income?
(d) (i) At what level of income would there be an exact trade balance?
(ii) What would be the inflationary or deflationary gap at this level of income if the full employment level of income were equal to the equilibrium level of income in (a) above?

Saving, taxes and imports, on the other hand, are endogenous variables. They increase as income increases. Hence the withdrawals line, S + T + M, is upward sloping. Equilibrium is achieved at Y_E where planned injections equal planned withdrawals.

A change in exports

An increase in exports will lead to an increase in aggregate expenditure in the economy. Hence the equilibrium level of national income will rise. This is shown in Figure 83.3. A rise in exports of PQ leads to an increase in equilibrium national income of ST. PQ is less than ST and therefore there has been a multiplier effect. Increased export expenditure of PQ has crowded in extra consumption expenditure of QR.

The formula for the multiplier in an open economy with government is:

$$\text{Multiplier} = \frac{1}{\text{MPS} + \text{MPT} + \text{MPM}}$$

(i.e. it is the inverse of the sum of the marginal proportion leaked from the circular flow of income). The larger the value of the marginal propensity to import, the lower will be the value of the multiplier. For instance, if the MPS were 0.1, the MPT 0.2 and the MPM 0.1, the value of the multiplier would be 2.5 [1 ÷ (0.1 + 0.2 + 0.1)]. If the MPM rose to 0.2, the multiplier would fall to 2 [1÷ (0.1 + 0.2 + 0.2)].

So if the multiplier were 2.5 and exports rose by £1 000 million, equilibrium income would rise by £2 500 million crowding in an extra £1 500 million of spending. If the multiplier were 2 and exports fell by £500 million, equilibrium income would fall by £1 000 million.

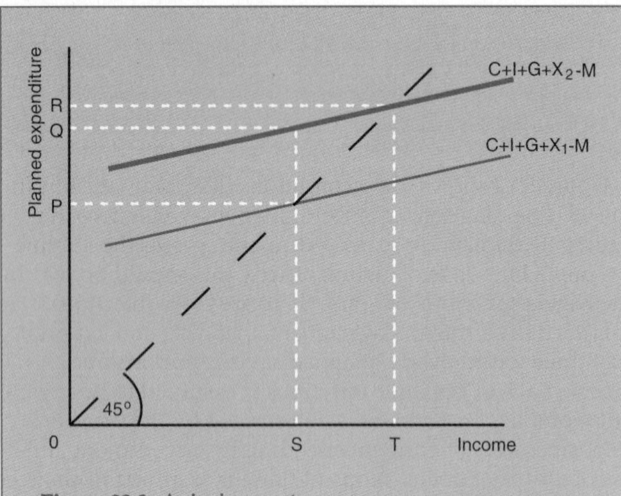

Figure 83.3 *A rise in exports*
A rise in planned export expenditure of PQ will shift the aggregate expenditure line upwards from $C + I + G + X_1 - M$ *to* $C + I + G + X_2 - M$.

QUESTION 3 Calculate the change in income if:
(a) MPS = 0.1, MPT = 0.2 and MPM = 0.2 with an increase of £500 million in government spending;
(b) MPS = 0.2, MPT = 0.1 and MPM = 0.1 with a decrease of £600 million in investment;
(c) MPS = 0.1, MPT = 0.05 and MPM = 0.1 with an increase of £1 000 million in exports;
(d) MPS = 0.05, MPT = 0.1 and MPM = 0.05 with an increase of £200 million in government spending;
(e) MPS = 0.1, MPT = 0.2 and MPM = 0.1 with an increase of £400 million in exports.

A change in imports

Imports are a function of income. So the level of imports and therefore the level of planned expenditure will change as income changes. This change in planned expenditure is shown by a movement along the planned expenditure line in the 45° line diagram. However, if there is a rise in the level of planned imports at any given level of income because the marginal propensity to import has risen, the planned expenditure line will shift downwards from E_1 to E_2 as shown in Figure 83.4. The line will pivot round rather than make a parallel shift because the size of the change in planned imports increases as income increases. It can be seen that the equilibrium level of national income falls. This is what would be expected. If households and firms plan to increase their spending on imports, they must also be planning to spend less on domestic goods. A fall in demand for domestic goods will lead to lower output and lower incomes within the domestic economy.

Note that there could be a rise in the **average** propensity to import without a rise in the **marginal** propensity to import. If, for instance, a country revalued its currency, then imports would become cheaper and at every level of income, planned imports would then be greater. A change in the average propensity to import (APM) would be shown by a parallel shift in the planned expenditure line, shifting it upwards if the APM were to fall, and downwards if it were to rise.

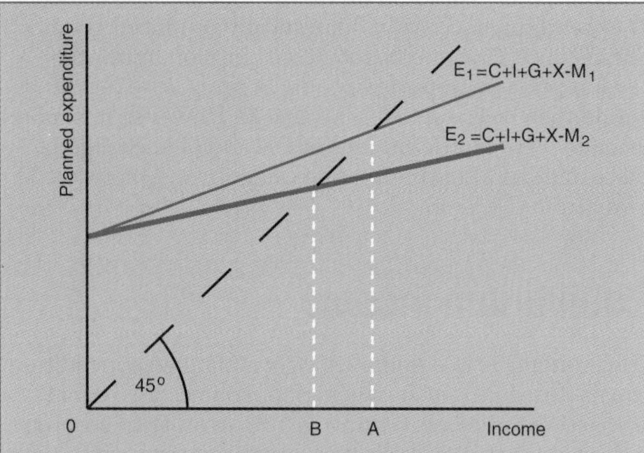

Figure 83.4 *A rise in the propensity to import*
An increase in the propensity to import will lead to a fall in the aggregate expenditure line from $C + I + G + X - M_1$ *to* $C + I + G + X - M_2$. *This will reduce the level of equilibrium income from OA to OB.*

QUESTION 4 In 1980, the value of the pound rose strongly so that by the end of the year the trade weighted index (an average value of the pound against other currencies) was 30 per cent above its value at the beginning of 1979. As a consequence, UK goods became much less competitive against foreign produced goods and therefore there was a rise in the average propensity to import. National income fell by approximately 2 per cent.

Explain, using a 45° line diagram and assuming all other things are equal, why the change in the average propensity to import in 1980 should have affected the level of national income.

Deriving the aggregate demand curve

The **aggregate demand curve** shows the relationship between output in the economy and the price level. It was explained in unit 64 that the aggregate demand curve was downward sloping. We can now formally derive the aggregate demand curve from the Keynesian model of income determination and from the theory of money markets.

Assume that there is an increase in the price level (i.e. there is inflation). What will happen?

The money market An increase in the price level will increase the transactions demand for money (☞ unit 74). If prices have risen, consumers and firms will need more money to buy the same number of goods. Therefore they will hold (i.e. demand) more money and reduce their holdings of non-monetary assets. In Figure 83.5, this is shown by a shift to the right in the liquidity preference schedule from LP_1 to LP_2. As a result, the equilibrium rate of interest will rise from r_1 to r_2. So an increase in the price level, ceteris paribus, results in an increase in interest rates.

Figure 83.5 *The money market*
A rise in the price level will increase the transactions demand for money, pushing the liquidity preference schedule from LP_1 to LP_2. As a consequence the rate of interest will rise from r_1 to r_2.

Consumption and investment An increase in interest rates will affect both consumption and investment. A rise in the cost of borrowing will reduce spending on consumer durables such as cars and furniture. A rise in interest rates will also tend to reduce the wealth of individuals because the prices of stocks and shares are inversely related to the rate of interest (☞ unit 72). A reduction in wealth will reduce consumption (the **wealth effect** (☞ unit 62). Investment will fall because there will be a movement back up the marginal efficiency of capital schedule (☞ unit 63). Hence there is an inverse relationship between the rate of interest and the level of

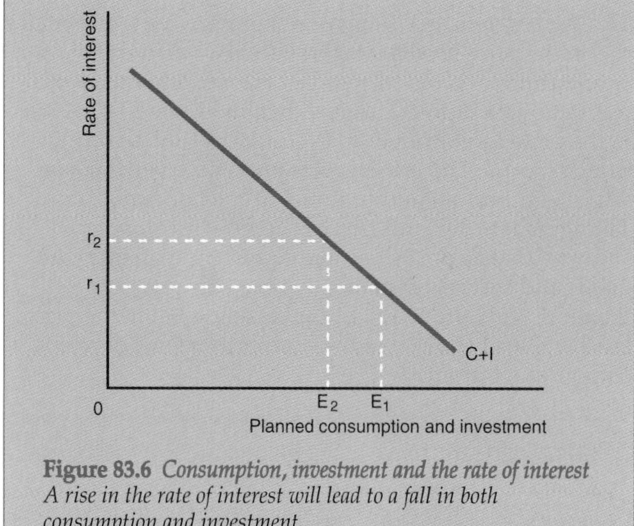

Figure 83.6 *Consumption, investment and the rate of interest*
A rise in the rate of interest will lead to a fall in both consumption and investment.

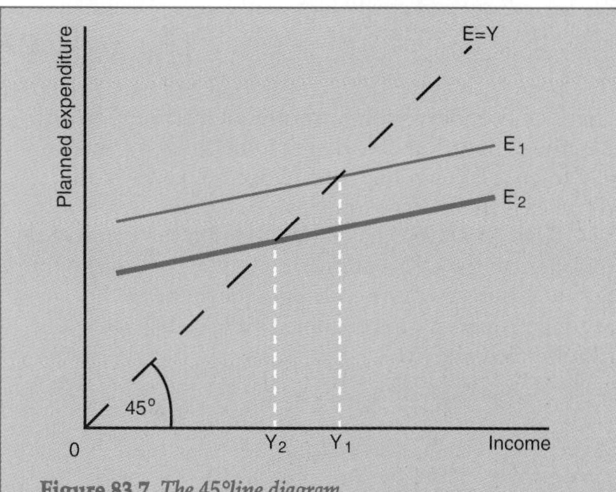

Figure 83.7 *The 45°line diagram*
A fall in the level of planned consumption and investment will lead to a fall in the planned aggregate expenditure line from E_1 to E_2. This in turn leads to a fall in the equilibrium level of national income and output from Y_1 to Y_2.

consumption and investment as shown in Figure 83.6.

The 45° line diagram A rise in interest rates will cause a fall in planned autonomous consumption (i.e. consumption not related to income) and in planned investment. So a rise in interest rates will lead to a fall in the planned aggregate expenditure line on the 45° line diagram (☞ units 80 and 81). This is shown in Figure 83.7. The fall in planned expenditure will result in a fall in the equilibrium level of income from Y_1 to Y_2.

The aggregate demand curve What we have seen is that a rise in the price level feeds through to a fall in the equilibrium level of real national income and therefore of real national output. This is shown in Figure 83.8. A rise in the price level from P_1 to P_2 results in a fall in output from Y_1 to Y_2. The price level is put on the vertical axis whilst equilibrium output is put on the horizontal axis. The aggregate demand curve is downward sloping showing that as prices rise, the equilibrium quantity of goods and services demanded in the economy, and therefore real output, falls. Conversely, a fall in the price level will lead to a rise in the equilibrium level of real income and output.

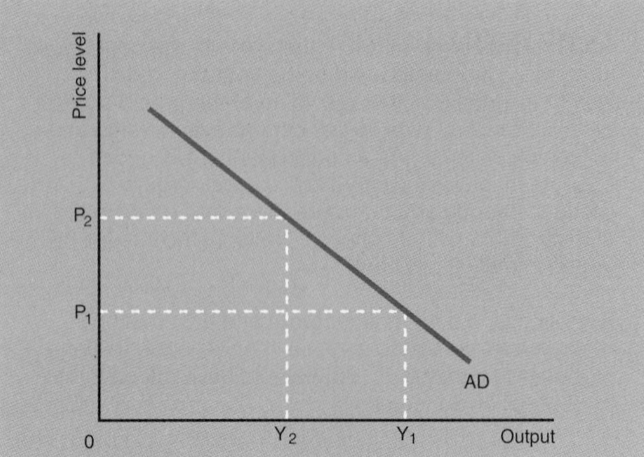

Figure 83.8 *The aggregate demand curve*
A rise in the price level will lead, via a rise in interest rates, to a fall in the equilibrium level of national income and therefore national output. Hence the aggregate demand curve is downward sloping.

QUESTION 5 Between 1987 and 1990, there was a jump in the rate of inflation from around 5 per cent to over 9 per cent. Show how (a) an inflation rate of 5 per cent per annum affects different markets in the economy and the aggregate demand curve and (b) what the effect would be on the aggregate demand curve of a 9 per cent inflation rate compared to a 5 per cent inflation rate.

Key terms

Trade surplus and deficit - there is a surplus if the value of exports is greater than imports, and a deficit if exports are less than imports.
Marginal propensity to import (MPM) - the proportion of any change in income which is spent on imported goods.

Applied economics

The value of the multiplier

In an open economy with government intervention and trade, the proportion of leakages to national income is likely to be relatively high and hence the value of the multiplier is likely to be low.

M C Kennedy (1992) has estimated that the value of the multiplier for the UK is approximately 1⅓. To make this estimate it is necessary to calculate the value of the marginal propensity to consume (MPC), since the multiplier is equal to:

$$\frac{1}{1 - \text{MPC}}$$

where MPC is the change in consumption of domestically produced goods (net of taxes) as a proportion of a change in national income. Kennedy assumed that national income is measured by GDP.

We start by calculating personal income from GDP. Assume that GDP increases by £100m. GDP calculated by the income method can be divided into employment income, approximately 80 per cent of the total, and profit, approximately 20 per cent of the total. Of the £100m increase in GDP, £80m is therefore employment income and £20m can be assumed to be profit. Of the £20m profit, £7m will be undistributed profits and £7m will be paid in corporate taxes, leaving £6m to be distributed to shareholders to form part of their income. The increase in income will increase employment and thus reduce unemployment benefits. Kennedy estimated this fall in transfer payments to households to be £4m. Thus, a £100m rise in GDP will lead to a £82m (£80m + £6m - £4m) rise in personal income.

This £82m rise is an increase in personal income. To calculate personal disposable income it is necessary to take away direct taxes on income. The standard rate of income tax is 25 per cent, whilst National Insurance contributions for the average income earner are approximately 10 per cent. Marginal tax rates are therefore 35 per cent, leaving 65 per cent of an increase in personal income in the hands of consumers. Hence, personal disposable income from the above £82m is approximately £55.3m (£82m x 0.65).

Of the £55.3m, approximately 0.9 will be spent on the basis of recent national income figures, according to Kennedy. So consumer spending is £48m (£55.3 x 0.9). Not all of that represents factor income from spending on goods because indirect taxes are levied on purchases. The average rate of tax on goods (VAT plus excise duties) is 0.2. Factor income from expenditure on goods is therefore £38.4m (£48m x 0.8).

Factor income generated by expenditure on goods is split between domestically produced goods and imported goods. Kennedy estimated the marginal propensity to import to be 0.39. Of the £38.4m spent, only £23.4m [£38.4 x (1 - 0.39)] will represent purchases of domestically produced goods net of tax.

The marginal propensity to consume out of GDP is therefore 0.234. The value of the multiplier is then 1.31 [1÷ (1- 0.234)]. This means that if exports, for instance, increase by £100m, the final increase in GDP is £13m. £100m represents the extra expenditure on exports. The £31m is an increase in consumer spending on domestically produced goods net of all taxes.

Kennedy points out that this estimate assumes the economy is at less than full employment. Increases in I, G or X can lead to an increase in national income because there are unutilised resources of labour and capital. He also assumes that interest rates remain constant and there is a policy of monetary accommodation (☞ unit 94). Lastly he assumes that the exchange rate does not change.

The propensity to import and national income

Table 83.2 *Imports as a percentage of total final expenditure*

	%
1950 - 1954	14.0
1955 - 1959	14.7
1960 - 1964	15.6
1965 - 1969	16.6
1970 - 1974	19.0
1975 - 1979	19.4
1980 - 1984	20.6
1985 - 1989	21.4
1990 - 1994	20.6

Source: adapted from CSO, *Economic Trends Annual Supplement*; CSO, *Monthly Digest of Statistics.*

Table 83.2 shows imports as a percentage of national income (measured by total final expenditure), averaged over five year periods from 1950.

1. **What has happened to the average propensity to import for the UK between 1950 and 1994?**
2. **Explain the effect this has had on the value of the multiplier for the UK economy.**
3. **A government wishes to expand demand by increasing government spending. What would be the difference in (a) the amount of government spending needed to raise aggregate expenditure and (b) the impact on the trade balance in 1990-94 compared to 1950-54?**
4. **Discuss why a local council in the UK would find it almost impossible to raise income substantially in the local area by increasing its own spending.**

unit 84

The theory of comparative advantage

Summary

1. If one country has lower costs of production for a good than another country, then it is said to have an absolute advantage in the production of that good.
2. International trade will take place even if a country has no absolute advantage in the production of any good. So long as it has a comparative advantage in the production of one good, international trade will be advantageous.
3. Transport costs will limit any welfare gain from international trade. However, economies of scale in production will increase the gains from trade.
4. The terms of trade (the ratio of export prices to import prices) will determine whether trade is advantageous for a country.
5. David Ricardo thought that comparative advantage existed because of differences in labour costs between countries. In the Heckscher-Ohlin model, comparative advantage is explained by differences in factor endowments.
6. The theory of comparative advantage argues that international trade takes place because of differences in the price of products. However, much world trade is the result of non-price competition between countries. Design, reliability, availability and image are some of the factors which determine purchases of foreign goods.
7. In the theory of preference similarity, it is argued that trade takes place because consumers demand more choice than can be provided by domestic producers.

Absolute advantage

Adam Smith, in his famous example of a pin making factory, explained how specialisation enabled an industry to increase the production of pins from a given quantity of resources (☞ unit 2). In an economy, specialisation exists at every level, from the division of labour in households to production at international level.

Consider Table 84.1. Assume that there are only two countries in the world, England and Portugal. They produce only two commodities, wheat and wine. Labour is the only cost, measured in terms of man hours to produce 1 unit of output. Table 84.1 shows that it costs more in man hours to produce a unit of wine in England than in Portugal. Portugal is said to have an ABSOLUTE ADVANTAGE in the production of wine. It can produce both goods but is more efficient in the production of wine. On the other hand, it costs more in man hours to produce wheat in Portugal than in England. So England has an absolute advantage in the production of wheat. It is clear that it will be mutually beneficial for England to specialise in the production of wheat and for Portugal to specialise in the production of wine and for the two countries to trade.

Table 84.1

	Cost per unit in man hours	
	Wheat	Wine
England	10	15
Portugal	20	10

The same conclusion can be reached if we express relative costs in terms of absolute output. If Portugal could produce either 5 units of wheat or 10 units of wine, or some combination of the two, the relative cost of wheat to wine would be 2:1 as in Table 84.1. If England could produce either 9 units of wheat or 6 units of wine, the relative cost would be 3:2 as in Table 84.1. Hence, Portugal could produce wine more cheaply and England wheat more cheaply.

QUESTION 1

Table 84.2

	UK			France		
	Cars		Computers	Cars		Computers
(a)	10	OR	100	9	OR	108
(b)	5	OR	10	4	OR	12
(c)	20	OR	80	25	OR	75
(d)	5	OR	25	4	OR	30
(e)	6	OR	18	8	OR	16

Two countries with identical resources, UK and France, using all these resources, can produce either cars or computers or some combination of the two as shown above. Assuming constant returns to scale, state which country has an absolute advantage in the production of (i) cars and (ii) computers in each of (a) to (e) above.

Comparative advantage

David Ricardo, working in the early part of the 19th century, realised that absolute advantage was a limited case of a more general theory. Consider Table 84.3. It can be seen that Portugal can produce both wheat and wine more cheaply than England (i.e. it has an absolute advantage in both commodities). What David Ricardo saw was that it could still be mutually beneficial for both countries to specialise and trade.

Table 84.3

	Cost per unit in man hours	
	Wheat	Wine
England	15	30
Portugal	10	15

In Table 84.3, a unit of wine in England costs the same amount to produce as 2 units of wheat. Production of an extra unit of wine means foregoing production of 2 units of wheat (i.e. the opportunity cost of a unit of wine is 2 units of wheat). In Portugal, a unit of wine costs 1 ½ units of wheat to produce (i.e. the **opportunity cost** of a unit of wine is 1½ units of wheat in Portugal). Because relative or comparative costs differ, it will still be mutually advantageous for both countries to trade even though Portugal has an absolute advantage in both commodities. Portugal is relatively better at producing wine than wheat: so Portugal is said to have a COMPARATIVE ADVANTAGE in the production of wine. England is relatively better at producing wheat than wine: so England is said to have a comparative advantage in the production of wheat.

Table 84.4

	Production before trade		Production after trade	
	Wheat	Wine	Wheat	Wine
England (270 man hours)	8	5	18	0
Portugal (180 man hours)	9	6	0	12
Total	17	11	18	12

Table 84.4 shows how trade might be advantageous. Costs of production are as set out in Table 84.3. England is assumed to have 270 man hours available for production. Before trade takes place it produces and consumes 8 units of wheat and 5 units of wine. Portugal has fewer labour resources with 180 man hours of labour available for production. Before trade takes place it produces and consumes 9 units of wheat and 6 units of wine. Total production between the two economies is 17 units of wheat and 11 units of wine.

If both countries now specialise, Portugal producing only wine and England producing only wheat, total production is 18 units of wheat and 12 units of wine. Specialisation has enabled the world economy to increase production by 1 unit of wheat and 1 unit of wine. The theory of comparative advantage does not say how these gains will be distributed between the two countries. This depends upon the wheat/wine exchange rate, a point discussed below.

Table 84.5

	Output		
	Good X		Good Y
Country A	20	OR	40
Country B	50	OR	100

The THEORY OF COMPARATIVE ADVANTAGE states that countries will find it mutually advantageous to trade if comparative costs of production differ. If, however, comparative costs are identical, there can be no gains from trade. Table 84.5 shows the maximum output of two countries, A and B of two products, X and Y. The Table shows that country A, for instance, can either produce 20 units of good X or 40 units of good Y or some combination of both. The comparative costs or the opportunity cost of production is identical in both countries: one unit of X costs two units of Y. Hence there can be no gains from trade.

QUESTION 2

Table 84.6

	Cost per unit in man hours	
	Meat	Bread
UK	5	10
France	3	4

(a) Which country has comparative advantage in the production of (i) meat and (ii) bread?

(b) The UK has a total of 300 man hours available for production whilst France has a total of 200. Before any trade took place, the UK produced and consumed 38 units of meat and 11 units of bread. France produced and consumed 20 units of meat and 35 units of bread. How much more could the two countries produce between them if each specialised and then traded?

(c) How would the answer to (a) be different, if at all, if the cost of meat and bread in France were: (i) 4 and 4; (ii) 3 and 7; (iii) 3 and 6; (iv) 6 and 12; (v) 6 and 15; (vi) 1 and 3?

The assumptions of the theory of comparative advantage

The simple theory of comparative advantage outlined above makes a number of important assumptions.

- There are no transport costs. In reality, transport costs always exist and they will reduce and sometimes eliminate any comparative cost advantages. In general, the higher the proportion of transport costs in the final price to the consumer, the less likely it is that the good will be traded internationally.
- Costs are constant and there are no economies of scale. This assumption helps make our examples easy to understand. However, the existence of economies of scale will tend to reinforce the benefits of international specialisation. In Table 84.4 the gains from trade will be more than 1 unit of wheat and 1 unit of wine if England can lower the cost of production of wheat by producing

more and similarly for Portugal.

- There are only two economies producing two goods. Again this assumption was made to simplify the explanation. But the theory of comparative advantage applies equally to a world with many economies producing a large number of traded goods. Table 84.7 shows that Chile has no absolute advantage in any product. However, it has a comparative advantage in the production of copper. Portugal has a clear comparative advantage in the production of wine whilst England has a comparative advantage in the production of apples. Exactly what and how much will be traded depends upon consumption patterns in all three countries. For instance, if neither Portugal or Chile consume apples, England will not be able to export apples to these countries.

Table 84.7

	Cost per unit in man hours			
	Apples	Wine	Wheat	Copper
England	10	15	20	50
Portugal	15	10	30	60
Chile	20	20	50	70

- The theory assumes that traded goods are homogeneous (i.e. identical). Commodities such as steel, copper or wheat are bought on price. But a Toyota car is different from a Rover car and so it is far more difficult to conclude that, for instance, the Japanese have a comparative advantage in the production of cars.
- Factors of production are assumed to be perfectly mobile. If they were not, trade might lead to a lowering of living standards in a country. For instance, assume the UK manufactured steel but then lost its comparative advantage in steel making to Korea. UK steel making plants are closed down. If the factors of production employed in UK steel making are not redeployed, then the UK will be at less than full employment. It might have been to the UK's advantage to have kept the steel industry operating (for instance by introducing quotas) and producing something rather than producing nothing with the resources.
- There are no tariffs or other trade barriers (☞ unit 85).
- There is perfect knowledge, so that all buyers and sellers know where the cheapest goods can be found internationally.

The terms of trade

In Table 84.4 it was shown that England and Portugal could benefit from trade. Whether trade takes place will depend upon the TERMS OF TRADE between the two countries. From the cost data in Table 84.3, England could produce 2 units of wheat for every 1 unit of wine. It will only trade if it receives more than a unit of wine for every 2 units of wheat. Portugal on the other hand can produce 2 units of wheat for every 1⅓ units of wine. It will only trade if it can give England less than 1⅓ units of wine for 2 units of wheat. Hence trade will only take place if the terms of trade are between 2 units of wheat for 1 unit of wine and 2 units of wheat and 1⅓ units of wine (i.e. between 2:1 and 2:1⅓).

This is shown in Figure 84.1. The cost ratios of wine for two units of wheat are drawn. England will only gain from trade if the international price of wine for wheat is to the right of its existing domestic cost line. Portugal on the other hand will only gain if the international price is to the left of its domestic cost line. Hence trade will only be mutually advantageous if the terms of trade are somewhere between the two lines, the area shaded on the graph.

The terms of trade is defined as the ratio between export prices and import prices:

$$\text{Index of terms of trade} = \frac{\text{Index of export prices}}{\text{Index of import prices}} \times 100$$

QUESTION 3

Table 84.8

	Cost per unit in man hours			
	Tapes	Sweaters	Beefburgers	Chocolate
England	20	10	8	20
Portugal	30	8	12	30
Chile	40	8	4	25

(a) Which country has an absolute advantage in the production of (i) tapes; (ii) sweaters; (iii) beefburgers; (iv) chocolates?
(b) Which country has a comparative advantage in the production of (i) tapes; (ii) sweaters; (iii) beefburgers; (iv) chocolates?

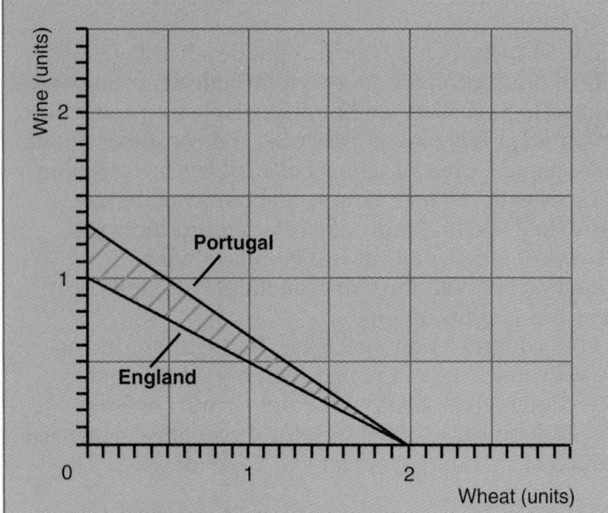

Figure 84.1 *The terms of trade*
England will find it advantageous to trade only if its terms of trade are at least 1 unit of wine for every two units of wheat exported. Portugal will only trade if it can receive at least 2 units of wheat for every 1⅓ units of wine exported. Therefore the terms of trade between the two countries will lie somewhere in the shaded area on the graph.

It is an **index** (☞ unit 3) because it is calculated from the weighted average of thousands of different export and import prices.

QUESTION 4 Look again at the data in Table 84.6.
(a) Show on a graph the price ratios of meat for bread in the two countries before trade.
(b) Would both countries find it mutually advantageous to trade if the international trade price ratio were 1 unit of meat for: (i) 4 units of bread; (ii) 3 units of bread; (iii) $1\frac{1}{2}$ units of bread; (iv) 1 unit of bread; (v) $\frac{1}{2}$ unit of bread; (vi) 2 units of bread; (vii) $1\frac{1}{3}$ units of bread?

Why comparative advantage exists

David Ricardo believed that all costs ultimately could be reduced to labour costs. This belief is known as the **labour theory of value**. Hence the price of a good could accurately be measured in terms of man-hours of production. Following on from this, he argued that differences in comparative costs reflected differences in the productivity of labour.

There is an element of truth in this idea. The theory suggests that high labour productivity countries would have a comparative advantage in the production of sophisticated high technology goods whilst low labour productivity countries would have a comparative advantage in the production of low technology goods. Looking at the pattern of world trade, it is true for instance that developing countries export low technology textiles whilst developed countries export high technology computer equipment.

However, neo-classical price theory suggests that labour is not the only source of differing opportunity costs of production. For instance, the price of a piece of agricultural land can increase several times overnight if planning permission is given for residential building. This increase in value has little to do with man-hours of production. Prices and costs are, of course, linked to quantities of labour inputs, but they are also linked to forces of scarcity which can drive prices up or down.

Heckscher and Ohlin, two Swedish economists working in the inter-war period, suggested that different costs were the result not just of different labour endowments between countries but also of different capital and land endowments. If an economy, such as India, has a large quantity of unskilled labour but little capital, then the price of capital relative to labour will be high. If, on the other hand, an economy like the USA has a large stock of capital relative to labour, then capital will be relatively cheap. Hence India will have a comparative advantage in the production of goods which can be made using unskilled labour. The USA will have a comparative advantage in the production of goods which require a relatively high capital input. Saudi Arabia is much more richly endowed with oil than France. France, on the other hand, has a rich abundance of skilled labour and capital equipment in the defence industry. Hence the theory would suggest that Saudi Arabia will specialise in producing oil, France in producing defence equipment and that the two countries will trade one product for the other.

Non-price theories of trade

The theory of comparative advantage provides a good explanation of world trade in commodities such as oil, wheat or copper. Countries with relatively rich endowments of raw materials or agricultural land specialise in the production of those commodities. It also provides a good explanation of the pattern of trade between First and Third World countries. Third World countries tend to export commodities and simple manufactured goods whilst importing more technologically sophisticated manufactures and services from the First World. However, the theory does not account for much of that half of world trade which occurs between the rich developed economies of the world.

QUESTION 5 Brazil, a middle-income country, is a major export of shoes, particularly to the US market. In 1993, production was 562m pairs, with exports of 183m pairs, 80 per cent of which went to the USA. In 1994, the Brazilian shoe industry found itself in deep trouble. The Brazilian currency, the Real, rose in value by 15 per cent, meaning that manufacturers either had to increase prices by 15 per cent or cut their costs and profit margins to keep the dollar price the same. At the same time, China significantly increased its exports of shoes to the US market.

China, a low-income country, produces low cost shoes in the \$5 to \$8 range, and it is in this bottom end of the market that Brazil is most vulnerable. In the middle range market, where export prices are around \$10, Brazil still has a competitive edge. The Chinese can't compete on quality with the Brazilians whilst the European and US manufacturers can't compete on price. At the top end of the market, European and US manufacturers retain a competitive edge on quality and design.

Some believe that the Brazilian industry must find ways of cutting cost to regain market share at the bottom end of the market lost to the Chinese. If they don't, they will also become vulnerable in the middle range market where the Chinese are likely to improve quality and where the Italians and Spanish could well push down their costs to become price competitive. Others believe that the Brazilian industry must accept that it will lose the bottom end of the market and concentrate on going up market by improving quality and design.

Source: adapted from the *Financial Times*, 13.12.1994.

(a) Suggest why Brazil might be losing its comparative advantage in the production of bottom of the range shoes.
(b) How might Brazil retain a comparative advantage in shoe production even though it ceases to be a low cost producer?

Commodities are **homogeneous** products. There is nothing to choose between one grade of copper from Chile and the same grade from Zambia. Therefore the main determinant of demand is price. Manufactured goods and services tend to be **non-homogeneous**. Each product is slightly different. So when a consumer buys a car, price is only one amongst many factors that are considered. Reliability, availability, image, colour, shape and driving performance are just as important, if not more so. There is a wide variety of cars to choose from on the market, some produced domestically but many produced abroad. **Preference similarity theory** suggests that many manufactured goods are imported not because they are relatively cheaper than domestic goods but because some consumers want greater choice than that provided by domestic manufacturers alone. Domestic manufacturers, however, should have a competitive edge because they should be more aware of the needs of their domestic customers. This limits the extent to which foreign manufacturers can penetrate the home market.

Key terms

Absolute advantage - exists when a country is able to produce a good more cheaply in absolute terms than another country.
Theory of comparative advantage - countries will find it mutually advantageous to trade if the opportunity cost of production of goods differs.
Comparative advantage - exists when a country is able to produce a good more cheaply relative to other goods produced domestically than another country.
Terms of trade - the ratio of export prices to import prices.

Applied economics

UK trade flows

Table 84.9 *UK exports and imports.*

£ million

	Exports		Imports	
	Goods	Services	Goods	Services
1955	3 073	1 748	3 386	1 590
1965	4 913	2 858	5 173	2 675
1975	19 185	15 001	22 441	13 270
1980	47 149	41 041	45 792	39 555
1985	77 991	79 953	81 336	74 010
1990	101 718	114 504	120 527	114 730
1994	135 200	122 793	145 727	112 434

Source: adapted from CSO, *Economic Trends Annual Supplement;* CSO, *Monthly Digest of Statistics.*

The UK trades in both goods and services. During the 1950s and 1960s, exports and imports of goods considerably exceeded those of services as can been seen from Table 84.9. However, during the 1970s and 1980s, services became relatively more important and indeed between 1981 and 1991, service exports exceeded exports of goods. This might seem to indicate that the UK has increased its comparative advantage in services and experienced a fall in comparative advantage in goods. But the situation is more complicated than this.

Table 84.10 gives a breakdown of visible trade (trade in goods) by commodity. There are very striking trends shown here.

- Exports of fuels, approximately 95 per cent of which are oil, have increased. This is due to North Sea oil which first came on stream in 1976. By 1985, due to record production and high oil prices, fuel exports accounted for 21.5 per cent of visible exports. By 1994, this had fallen to only 6.2 per cent as North Sea oil production and the price of oil fell. Imports of oil, on the other hand, have declined as a percentage of total imports.
- Imports of food and raw materials have declined from 76.5 per cent of total imports to 17.9 per cent in 1994. In the Victorian age, Britain was known as the 'workshop of the world', importing raw materials and exporting manufactured goods. A fall in percentage imports of raw materials would suggest that the UK has lost comparative advantage in the production of manufactured goods.
- This loss of comparative advantage in manufactured goods is clear from import figures for manufactures. In 1955, manufactures accounted for only 23.2 per cent of imports. By 1994, this had risen to 74.0 per cent.

The possible reasons for the decline in UK manufacturing have already been discussed in unit 61. Some manufacturing industries have suffered more than others. Industries such as the UK motorcycle industry have been wiped out by foreign competition. Others, such as the motor vehicle industry, have moved from surplus to deficit in the 1980s, part of a more general trend for UK engineering. Textiles and metals have suffered more than most, whilst the picture has been more promising for a few industries such as chemicals and pharmaceuticals.

The theory of comparative advantage is often expressed in terms of relative costs of production. Whilst it is clear that our loss of competitiveness in industries such as textiles has been due to higher relative costs, this is less obvious in industries such as car manufacture. Here, poor quality, unreliability, poor design and long delivery dates have been possibly more important in losing markets than

Table 84.10 *Exports and imports by commodity (% of total value)*

		1955	1965	1975	1985	1994
Food, beverages and tobacco	Exports	6.0	6.6	7.1	6.3	7.5
	Imports	36.9	29.7	18.0	10.6	9.6
Basic materials	Exports	3.9	4.0	2.7	2.7	1.7
	Imports	29.0	19.3	8.4	6.0	3.5
Fuels	Exports	4.9	2.7	4.2	21.5	6.2
	Imports	10.6	10.6	17.5	12.8	4.8
Total food and raw materials	Exports	14.8	13.3	14.0	30.5	15.4
	Imports	76.5	59.6	43.9	29.4	17.9
Semi-manufactured	Exports	36.9	34.6	31.2	25.6	26.2
	Imports	17.9	23.8	23.9	24.8	23.7
Finished manufactured	Exports	43.5	49.0	51.0	41.2	47.6
	Imports	5.3	15.4	29.9	44.0	50.3
Total manufactures	Exports	80.4	83.6	82.2	66.8	73.8
	Imports	23.2	39.2	53.8	68.8	74.0
Unclassified	Exports	4.8	3.1	3.8	2.7	10.8
	Imports	0.3	1.2	2.7	1.8	8.1

Source: adapted from CSO, *Annual Abstract of Statistics; CSO, Monthly Digest of Statistics.*

Table 84.11 *Invisible trade, UK*

£ million

		1975	1985	1990	1994
Total	Exports	15 001	79 593	114 504	122 793
	Imports	13 270	74 010	114 730	112 434
of which					
Sea transport	Exports	2 651	2 986	3 444	3 351
	Imports	2 561	3 515	3 756	4 482
Civil aviation	Exports	780	3 078	4 474	5 406
	Imports	675	2 877	4 769	5 678
Travel	Exports	1 218	5 442	7 785	9 517
	Imports	917	4 871	9 916	13 633
Financial and other services	Exports	2 889	12 061	15 744	20 383
	Imports	1 501	4 608	9 317	10 105
Interest, profit and dividends of the private sector	Exports	6 298	51 270	77 213	77 295
	Imports	5 182	48 222	75 543	63 515

Source: adapted from CSO, *Annual Abstract of Statistics; CSO, Monthly Digest of Statistics.*

high relative prices.

The loss of UK competitiveness in manufactured goods could be argued to be unimportant if manufactures can be replaced by services. However, service exports (or service **credits**) and imports (or service **debits**) are not all traded services. As Table 84.11 shows, the single most important 'service export' today is interest, profits and dividends. These are the earnings from money invested or lent abroad and brought back to the UK. They are the equivalent of interest on a building society account. During the 1970s and 1980s, the UK built up large stocks of foreign investments, but equally foreigners have built up stocks of investments in the UK, from which they take interest, profits and dividends, which become imports or debits for the UK. Interest, profit and dividend credits in 1994 accounted for approximately 30 per cent of total exports (visibles plus invisibles) whilst debits accounted for 25 per cent of total imports. It is as if a household paid 25 per cent of its income in mortgage repayments whilst receiving 30 per cent of its income from interest on money saved.

Traded services - sea transport, civil aviation, travel (tourism) and financial and other services - are only approximately 30 per cent of the value of traded goods. So, despite the fact that the UK has a significant comparative advantage in the provision of financial services, there is no way in which the UK could in the foreseeable future compensate for significant losses in comparative advantage in manufactures by gaining further comparative advantage in traded services. Manufacturing matters!

So far, the composition of UK trade has been discussed. But Table 84.12 shows how the direction of trade in goods has changed over time. In 1955, the UK was still to a great extent following trading patterns established during the Victorian era, buying raw materials from developing countries and selling them manufactured goods. By 1994, UK trade had shifted dramatically. Over half of exports and imports were now with EU countries. Markets in the Third World were relatively unimportant. Note too that trade with Japan, classified under 'other developed countries', is very small in relation to the total - but has grown significantly over time. Over the next ten years, with further economic integration planned by the EU, the percentage total of trade with the EU is likely to continue rising.

Table 84.12 *Visible trade by area*

Percentage of total

		1955	1975	1994
EU[1]	Exports	26.8	41.1	57.2
	Imports	25.9	45.1	55.8
Other Western Europe	Exports	3.8	6.8	4.2
	Imports	2.4	6.0	6.3
North America	Exports	11.3	12.1	14.4
	Imports	19.8	13.5	13.3
Other developed countries	Exports	15.3	9.6	4.0
	Imports	12.4	8.0	7.1
of which Japan	Exports	0.5	1.6	2.2
	Imports	0.6	2.8	5.9
Rest of the world	Exports	42.7	30.4	20.2
	Imports	39.5	27.4	17.4
of which Eastern Europe	Exports	1.3	3.4	2.1
	Imports	2.7	2.4	1.9
oil exporting countries	Exports	5.1	11.6	4.2
	Imports	9.2	13.6	2.1

1 Includes all 1994 EU countries in 1955 and 1975 percentages.

UK car productivity

Wage costs (D-marks per hour)*			
	1980	1990	1993
Germany**	26.84	41.91	52.06
France	19.66	26.09	28.64
Italy	17.73	28.63	27.25
Netherlands	23.33	29.35	31.78
Belgium	28.14	33.58	37.22
UK	14.95	25.05	25.90
Sweden	28.60	42.78	38.96
Spain	12.63	27.01	27.77
US	24.83	33.13	38.55
Japan	13.26	26.83	41.57

*calculated on basis of average exchange rate of each currency against the D-mark during the year concerned **West Germany only Source: VDA

Figure 84.2 *Wage costs*

Wage costs in the British motor industry are now lower than those in America, Japan and all mainland European countries - but UK productivity is so poor that unit labour costs in Britain are higher than anywhere else.

These startling international comparisons are made in the latest annual report of VDA, Germany's equivalent of the Society of Motor Manufacturers and Traders.

According to VDA's findings, which are likely to prove controversial, relative productivity in the British vehicle-assembly and components industry has declined since 1980. VDA says British productivity is now less than a quarter of Japan's - the world leader - and only a third as high as America's or Belgium's.

British productivity is so poor, says VDA, that in terms of total competitiveness it more than wipes out the country's wage-cost advantage. Last year, British wage costs - helped by the pound's decline against the D-mark - were less than half those in Germany, which has by far the highest wage costs of motor-manufacturing countries.

In terms of unit labour costs (which combine wage costs and productivity to give a statistic for total efficiency), Germany's astrónomical wage costs make it the worst-performing of all the countries - except for Britain. The UK is about 18% less efficient than Germany, according to VDA, and half as efficient as Japan, France and America, whose unit costs are all about 40% less than Germany's.

Some British experts say the VDA findings must be put in perspective. Kumar Bhattacharyya, professor of manufacturing systems at Warwick University, said yesterday: 'The figures don't tell the whole story. They may be accurate in strictly mathematical terms, but they don't take full account of the different volumes in each country's motor industry,' As volumes rise in Britain with the increase in Japanese transplant production,the country's unit costs should become more competitive, he said.

'If you take into account Britain's low social costs and high returns on investment, based on the sort of volumes we have, we are not that bad,' Bhattacharyya said. 'Although we are not as good as some people here have suggested, there has been a vast improvement in sales per employee in recent years, and in other areas, such as inventory levels.'

One big exception to VDA's findings is Ford, which revealed earlier this year that unit labour costs in its British plants were lower than in its German factories, although still higher than in Belgium and Spain. In addition, some British component suppliers, such as GKN and T&N, have attained high productivity and low unit labour cost levels.

However, VDA points out that only 29% of value added in vehicle production results from final manufacturing - demonstrating the importance of the supply industry.

In February, Michael Heseltine, president of the Board of Trade, launched a report that savaged the British components industry. Sponsored by the Department of Trade and Industry, it said 'fundamental and profound' barriers existed in the industry, which was characterised by 'acrimony, bad faith, cheating and lying'.

The situation, it continued, 'is clearly not leading to an efficient or developing UK components industry. Nor is it likely to do so in the short term'.

Source: Andrew Lorenz, The *Sunday Times*, 30.10.1994, © Times Newspapers Limited, 1994.

Figure 84.3 *Wage costs and productivity*

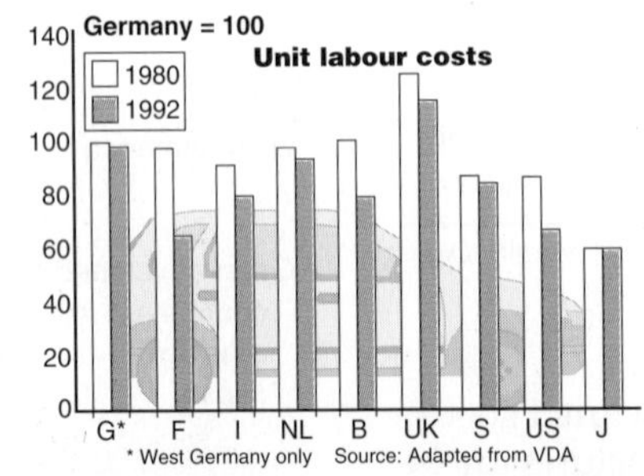

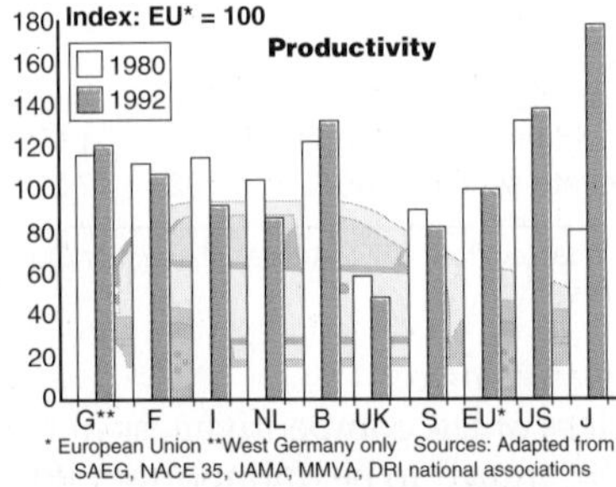

Japanese motor manufacturers have been establishing car plants in the UK. Partly this is because the European Union (EU) restricts imports of cars manufactured outside the EU. Partly this is because of high costs of production in Japan. The UK has received a disproportionate share of Japanese inward car investment over the past ten years in the EU. Japanese car manufacturers have replicated Japanese production methods in their UK plants. They have also worked very hard with suppliers on costs, quality and delivery times. In some cases, Japanese component manufacturers have established UK plants next to the new Japanese car plants.

The Department of Trade and Industry has asked you to prepare a report on the possible implications of this in the light of the article above. In your report:

1. **discuss whether the data shows the UK has an absolute advantage in the production of cars;**
2. **suggest why the Japanese have decided to set up factories in the UK rather than, say, Germany given UK unit labour costs;**
3. **analyse the possible impact of increased Japanese car production on the relative competitiveness of the UK as a car manufacturing economy.**

Free trade and protectionism

Summary

1. Although the gains from trade can be large, all countries choose to adopt protectionist policies to some extent.
2. Tariffs, quotas, voluntary export agreements and safety standards are some of the many ways in which countries limit free trade in goods and services.
3. The infant industry argument is one argument used to justify protectionism. It is claimed that young industries need protection if they are to survive the competition of larger more established industries in other countries. When the industry has grown sufficiently, barriers can be removed.
4. It is claimed that protectionism can save jobs. However, there is a great danger that the erection of barriers for this purpose will lead to retaliation by other trading nations, resulting in an overall welfare loss.
5. Protection against dumping will only lead to a gain in long run welfare for a nation if the dumping is predatory.
6. One valid argument in favour of protectionist policies is if the importing country is a monopsonist. The imposition of tariffs will lead to a fall in the price of imports, leading to a gain in welfare for the nation at the expense of foreign suppliers and an improvement in the terms of trade.

Free trade

The theory of comparative advantage (☞ unit 84) shows that trade between countries will be mutually beneficial if relative costs of production differ. Evidence suggests that the gains from trade can be large. They are often most significant in product areas where **economies of scale** are sizeable and transport costs are relatively low.

Specialisation enables total world production to be very much higher than if there were no international trade. But it is important to realise that not everyone benefits from free trade. Some countries or some individuals may gain at the expense of others. Free trade over time will inevitably involve changes in world income distribution. In the rest of this unit we consider how governments can restrict trade and why they might wish to do so.

Methods of protection

There are a large number of ways in which a country may choose to erect TRADE BARRIERS.

Tariffs A TARIFF is a tax on imported goods. It is sometimes called an IMPORT DUTY or a CUSTOMS DUTY. Tariffs can be used by governments to raise revenue to finance expenditure. However, they are most often used in a deliberate attempt to restrict imports. A tariff, by imposing a tax on a good, is likely to raise its final price to the consumer (although occasionally a foreign supplier will absorb all the tariff to prevent this from happening). A rise in the price of the good will lead

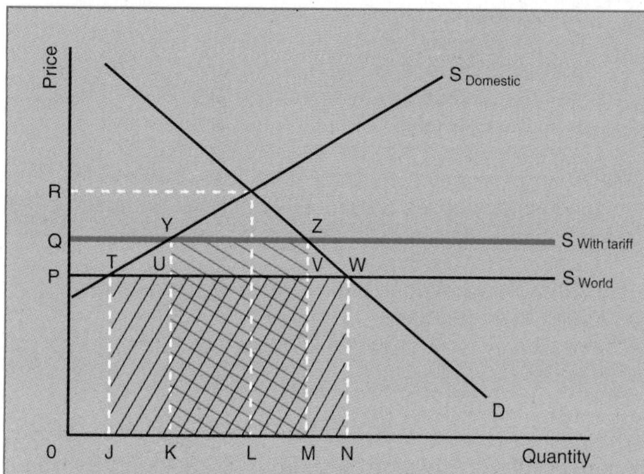

Figure 85.1 *Tariffs*
If the world price of a good is OP, a tariff of PQ will shift the supply curve upwards from S_{World} *to* $S_{With\ tariff}$*. Domestic consumption will fall by MN whilst domestic production will rise by JK. Imports will fall from JN to KM.*

to a fall in demand and the volume of imports will fall. A tariff should also help domestic producers. Some consumers will switch consumption from imported goods to domestically produced substitutes following the imposition of a tariff. For instance, if the UK imposed a tariff on sugar cane imports, British produced sugar beet would become more competitive and demand for it would rise.

This is shown in Figure 85.1. D is the domestic demand for a good. $S_{Domestic}$ is the domestic supply curve of the product. With no foreign trade, equilibrium output would occur where domestic demand and supply were equal at OL. However, with foreign trade, world producers are assumed to be prepared to supply any amount of the product at a price of OP. Consumers will now buy imported goods because the world price OP is below the domestic price of OR. Domestic supply will fall back along the supply curve to OJ. Demand for the good will rise to ON. Imports must be JN if demand is ON and domestic supply is OJ.

Now assume that the government of the country imposes a tariff of PQ per unit. The price to domestic consumers will rise to OQ. Domestic producers will not pay the tariff. Therefore they find it profitable to expand production to OK. Higher prices cause demand to fall to OM. Hence imports will only be KM. Expenditure on imports will fall from JTWN (price JT times quantity bought JN) to KYZM. Of that area KYZM, KUVM will be the revenue gained by foreign firms. The rest, UYZV, is the tax collected on the imports and will therefore go to the government.

QUESTION 1 $Q_D = 100 - \frac{1}{2}P$, $Q_S = 50 + \frac{1}{2}P$ where Q_D is quantity demanded domestically, Q_S is quantity supplied domestically and P is the price of the product.

(a) On graph paper draw the domestic demand and supply curves defined by the two equations between quantities of 0 to 100.

(b) What is the equilibrium price and quantity demanded and supplied domestically?

(c) The country starts to trade internationally. The international price for the product shown is 20. The country can import any amount at this price. What is: (i) the new level of demand; (ii) the new level of domestic supply; (iii) the quantity imported?

(d) The government, alarmed at the loss of jobs in the industry, imposes a tariff of 20 per unit. By how much will: (i) domestic demand fall; (ii) domestic supply rise; (iii) imports fall?

(e) What would happen if the government imposed a tariff of 40 per unit?

Quotas A QUOTA is a physical limit on the quantity of a good imported. It is an example of a **physical control**. Imposing a limit on the quantity of goods imported into a country will increase the share of the market available for domestic producers. However, it will also raise the price of the protected product.

This is shown in Figure 85.2. The world supply price of a product is £8. Domestic demand shown by the demand curve D is 10 million units. Of that, 2 million is produced domestically. The remaining 8 million is imported. Now assume that a quota of 3 million units is imposed on imports. Because output is now 4 million units less than it would otherwise have been, price will rise to £10. Domestic production will rise to 3 million units. Domestic consumption is 6 million units. The rise in price has led to a reduction in demand of 4 million units. It should be noted that quotas, unlike tariffs, can lead to gains by importers. It is true in Figure 85.2 that foreign firms have lost orders for 4 million units. But those firms which have managed to retain orders have gained. They used to sell their units for £8. They can now get £10. This is a windfall gain for them, shown on the diagram by the rectangle EFGH.

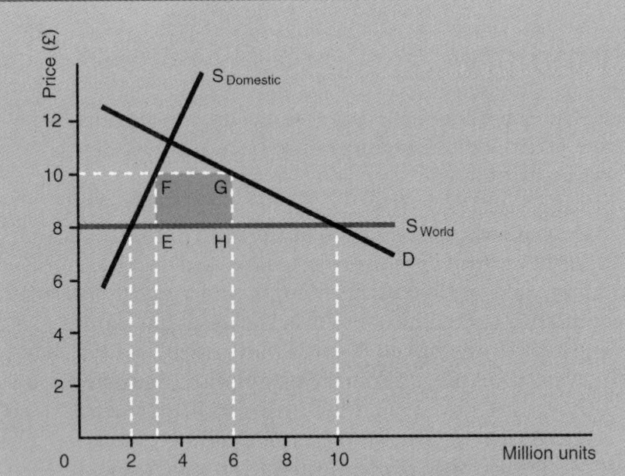

Figure 85.2 *Quotas*
If the world price of a good is £8, the introduction of a quota of 3 million units will reduce supply and raise the domestic price to £10. Domestic consumption will fall from 10 million units to 6 million units whilst domestic production will rise from 2 million units to 3 million units. Importers of the 3 million units subject to quota will make a windfall gain. Before the imposition of the quota they could only get a price of £8 per unit. After the imposition of the quota they can charge £10 per unit.

Other restrictions There are a considerable number of other trade barriers which countries can erect against foreign imports. In the 1970s and 1980s, there was widespread use of **Voluntary Export Agreements**. These are a type of quota which is enforced by importers. For instance, the UK had an agreement with Japanese car manufacturers that they should not take more than 10 per cent of the UK car market. Another widespread barrier is non-competitive purchasing by governments. They are major buyers of goods and services and most governments round the world have a policy of buying only from domestic producers even if this means paying higher prices. Meeting different safety standards can lead to higher costs of production for importers. Simple tactics like lengthy delays at customs posts can also deter imports.

QUESTION 2

Lamp posts The European Commission has brightened the outlook for Europe's lamp post manufacturers by forcing the Spanish government to lift a key trade restriction. The action follows a complaint from a French company, which pointed out that when it attempted to tender for the supply of lamp posts for a Spanish motorway it was rebuffed. It was informed that its product did not conform to local technical requirements.

The Commission stepped in to the dispute by invoking Article 30 of the Treaty of Rome - which guarantees the free circulation of goods - and asked the Madrid government to amend its regulations. This has since been done.

Rum Exports of rum to the EU from Caribbean countries are currently subject to quotas. Most Caribbean countries want the EU to increase the size of the quota, allowing them to increase their exports to the EU. In the long term they would like the EU to abolish the quota altogether. Both last year and this, demand for rum in Europe has increased faster than supply. As a result Caribbean rum producers exhausted their quotas before the end of the year in both years. Not all Caribbean countries are in agreement though. Martinique and Guadeloupe, still French departments, fear that they would be unable to compete if their quotas were taken away and there was a free-for-all in the rum market.

Source: adapted from the *Financial Times*, 1.9.1989, 18.11.1993.

(a) What types of protection are illustrated in the two examples?
(b) What arguments might be used by domestic producers to justify the protectionist measures?
(c) What arguments might be used in favour of greater free trade in the two cases?

Arguments used to justify protection

The theory of comparative advantage states that there are major welfare gains to be made from free trade in international markets. However, protectionism has always been widespread. What arguments can be put forward to justify protectionist policies?

The infant industry argument This is one of the oldest arguments in favour of protection. Industries just starting up may well face much higher costs than foreign competitors. Partly this is because there may be large economies of scale in the industry. A new low volume producer will find it impossible to compete on price against an established foreign high volume producer. Once it is sufficiently large, tariff barriers can be removed and the industry exposed to the full heat of foreign competition. There may also be a learning curve. It takes some time for managers and workers in a new industry to establish efficient operational and working practices. Only by protecting the new industry can it compete until the 'learning' benefits come through.

Some countries, such as Japan, have successfully developed infant industries behind high trade barriers. It is also true that many countries such as the UK have financial systems which tend to take a short view of investment. It is difficult, if not impossible, to find backers for projects which might only become profitable in 10 or even 5 years' time.

However, infant industries in general have not grown successfully behind trade barriers. One problem is that government needs to be able to identify those infant industries which will grow successfully. Governments have a poor record of picking such 'winners'. Second, industries protected by trade barriers lack the competitive pressure to become efficient. Infant industries all too often grow up to be lame duck industries. They only carry on operating because they have become skilled at lobbying government to maintain high trade barriers. Third, it is usually more efficient to use other policy weapons if a government genuinely wishes to encourage the development of a new industry. Specific subsidies, training grants, tax concessions, or even the creation of state enterprises, are likely to be better ways of creating new industries.

QUESTION 3 South Korea is aiming to become one of the world's top 10 producers of cars. Hyundai, Kia and Daewoo are expanding their car production facilities at a rate that recalls the startling growth of the Japanese industry in earlier decades. In 1989, South Korean car production was two-thirds that of the UK and one-tenth that of Japan. It is forecast by 1999 that South Korea will be producing 20 per cent more cars than the UK and 30 per cent that of the Japanese.

The industry has expanded on the back of three main factors. First, the South Korean domestic market is heavily protected such that only 1 per cent of car sales are accounted for by imports. Second, the South Korean government has given large amounts of soft loans - loans at little or no interest - to the three Korean car producers to finance their expansion as part of a state plan to become an industrialised nation. Third, the South Koreans have been helped in the 1970s and 1980s by the Japanese, who shared technology with with them. The South Koreans today have shown that they learnt their lesson well.

Source: adapted from the *Financial Times*, 28.4.1994.

(a) What arguments could be used by the South Koreans to justify high protectionist barriers on car imports?
(b) Discuss whether the European Union and the USA should impose retaliatory barriers to South Korean car imports.

Job protection Another argument with a very long history is the idea that protectionism can create or at least preserve jobs. During the 1970s, the share of the UK car market taken by domestic car manufacturers shrank drastically. It would have been possible to erect trade barriers against foreign imported cars to preserve jobs in the motor car industry. However, there are two major problems with this policy. Firstly, although the policy may benefit manufacturers and their workers, consumers are likely to have less choice and pay higher prices. Much of the gain for producers is an internal transfer of resources from domestic consumers. Moreover, foreign countries could retaliate by imposing trade restrictions on exports, leading to a loss of jobs in the domestic economy. If they do, then all countries participating in the trade war will suffer. Production will be switched from lower cost to higher cost producers, resulting in a loss of welfare for consumers. The gains from trade resulting from comparative advantage will be lost.

Dumping DUMPING can be defined in a number of ways. Broadly speaking it is the sale of goods below their cost of production, whether marginal cost, average total cost, or average variable cost. Foreign firms may sell products 'at a loss' for a variety of reasons.

- They may have produced the goods and failed to find a market for them, so they are dumped on one country in a distress sale. Knickers from China and shoes from Brazil were two examples of this during the 1980s.
- In the short run, a firm may have excess capacity. It will then sell at a price below average total cost so long as that price at least covers its variable cost (☞ unit 27).

QUESTION 4 Three US bicycle manufacturers are seeking protection against Chinese imports which they say severely hit their operating profits last year. The companies filed a complaint yesterday with the Federal government alleging that China is dumping bicycles in the US at 'less than fair market value'. In 1994, the US imported 7.1 million bicycles out of a market of 16.7 million. While import levels have remained steady, China's share of the overall market has risen sharply from 14.6 per cent in 1993 to 23.7 per cent last year.

'This is not a case of volume losses' said a spokesman for the US industry. 'But pricing has been a problem. The domestic industry has been forced to cut prices on every bike sold.' In 1994, China produced 40m bicycles against demand of 34m. In 1992 - the latest figures available for ownership - there were 451m bicycles in Chine, or 38.5 per 100 people. The US action follows the imposition of anti-dumping duties on Chinese bicycles by Canada, Mexico and the European Union. Leading Chinese manufacturers, such as Forever and Phoenix, have been looking to exports - mostly to Asia and Africa - to provide an outlet for excess production. Forever exports about 300 000 bicycles and Phoenix 1m. Less than 5 per cent of these 'low end' products goes to the USA.

Source: adapted from the *Financial Times*, 7.4.1995.

(a) What is meant by 'dumping'?
(b) Discuss how US bicycle manufacturers might argue that Chinese bicycles are being sold in the US at 'less than fair market value'.
(c) What arguments could the Chinese use to defend themselves against accusations of dumping?

Steel and chemical manufacturers tended to sell below total cost during the second half of the 1970s and first half of the 1980s because there was so much excess capacity in those industries as a result of the two oil crises.

- Low prices could represent a more serious long term threat to domestic industry. A foreign producer may deliberately price at a loss to drive domestic producers out of business. Once it has achieved this, it can increase prices and enjoy monopoly profits. Japanese companies have been accused of doing this in, for instance, the European semi-conductor market or in the European video recorder market.

Goals of long term domination by a foreign producer might justify trade barriers, although it might be more efficient to subsidise domestic industries. It is more difficult to say whether short term distress dumping leads to a loss of domestic welfare. On the one hand, domestic producers and their workers may suffer a loss of profits and wages. The impact on employment should be limited if dumping is only a short term phenomenon. On the other hand, consumers gain by being able to buy cheap goods, even if only for a limited period.

Cheap labour Countries which have plentiful sources of cheap labour are often accused of 'unfair competition'. High labour cost countries find it difficult if not impossible to compete against products from these countries and there is pressure from threatened industries to raise trade barriers. However, cheap labour is a source of comparative advantage for an economy. There is a misallocation of resources if domestic consumers are forced to buy from high wage domestic industries rather than low wage foreign industries. Resources which are used in high cost protected industries could be used elsewhere in the economy to produce products for which the country does have a comparative advantage in production.

The terms of trade One argument in favour of tariffs for which an economic case can be made is the optimal tariff argument. In Figure 85.1 it was assumed that a country could import any amount at a given price because it was a relatively small buyer on the world market. However, if a country imports a significant proportion of world production, then it is likely to face an upward sloping supply curve. The more it buys, the higher the price per unit it will have to pay. At the extreme, the country may be a **monopsonist** (i.e. the sole buyer of a product).

If the country faces an upward sloping supply curve, the marginal cost of buying an extra unit will not only be the cost of the extra unit but also the extra cost of buying all other units. For instance, a country buys 10 units at £1. If it buys an eleventh unit, the price rises to £11. The cost of the eleventh unit is therefore £11 plus 10 x £1 - a total of £21. The decision to buy the eleventh unit will be made by individual producers and consumers. The cost to them of the eleventh unit is just £11 - the other £10 extra is borne by the producers and consumers who bought the other 10 units.

Therefore the marginal cost to the economy as a whole

of buying an extra unit of imports is greater than the marginal cost to the individual. But it is the individual which makes the decision about whether to buy or not. If the marginal cost of purchase is lower for the individual than for the economy as a whole, more imports will be bought than if the individual had to pay the whole cost of purchase (i.e. the cost including the increased price of previously purchased units). This would suggest that a tariff which increased prices to the point where the cost to the individual purchaser was equal to the cost borne by society as a whole of that decision would increase economic welfare.

Imposition of a tariff will reduce demand for imported goods, and this in turn will lead to a fall in the price of imported goods (☞ unit 13 - a tariff is a tax which shifts the supply curve for imported goods to the left, resulting in a fall in equilibrium price received by suppliers). Hence the **terms of trade** (the ratio between export prices and import prices ☞ unit 84) will rise in favour of the importing country. The importing country will be able to buy goods more cheaply. But it is important to remember that this gain will be at the expense of the exporting country. If, for instance, the UK imposed a tariff on tea, the price of tea might fall. The UK will gain but only at the expense of India and Sri Lanka. Also, if the exporting country retaliates by imposing its own tariffs, both countries could be worse off than before.

Other arguments A number of other arguments are put forward in favour of trade barriers. It is sometimes argued that a country needs a particular domestic industry for defence purposes. A country may wish to preserve a particular way of life, such as preventing depopulation of remote rural areas heavily dependent upon a particular agricultural product. It may be felt that some imports are too dangerous to be sold domestically. 'Danger' could range from unsafe electrical products, to toxic waste to drugs. Alternatively, a country may decide that it is too dependent upon one industry. Some small Third World countries depend crucially upon one cash crop such as cocoa, bananas or sugar cane for their economic well being. These commodities are subject to large fluctuations in price on world markets. Falls in price can give rise to large falls in living standards in these economies. Diversifying, even if the newly established industries are uneconomic by world standards, could provide a valuable insurance policy against commodity price fluctuations. Trade barriers are one means of sheltering these industries from foreign competition.

In all of this, however, it is important to question whether trade barriers are the best means of achieving the desired objective. Economists tend to argue that other policies, such as subsidising industries, are likely to be more efficient than trade protection.

Key terms

Trade barriers - any measure which artificially restricts international trade.

Tariff, import duty or customs duty - a tax on imported goods which has the effect of raising the domestic price of imports and thus restricting demand for them.

Quota - a physical limit on the quantity of an imported group.

Dumping - the sale of goods at less than cost price by foreign producers in the domestic market.

Applied economics

GATT and protectionism

The Great Depression of the 1930s led countries to adopt policies which 'exported' unemployment. In order to save and create jobs in their domestic markets, they devalued their currencies and erected trade barriers. But because all countries were engaging in the same practices, all that happened was that total trade fell and countries suffered lower standards of living.

After the Second World War, there was a general recognition that these protectionist policies had been self-defeating. The Bretton Woods system of exchange rates (☞ unit 97) banned competitive devaluations, whilst 23 countries in 1947 signed the General Agreement on Tariffs and Trade (GATT). Under GATT rules, member countries were not allowed to increase the degree of protection given to their domestic producers. Also, under the **most-favoured nation** clause of the agreement, a country which offered a cut in tariffs to one country had to offer the same terms to all member countries.

GATT rules prevented protection increasing, but did nothing to reduce protectionism. For this reason, GATT has, over the years, organised a series of negotiations (called 'rounds') aimed at reducing tariffs and quotas. By the end of the last Tokyo round of negotiations in 1979, the average tariff on industrial goods had fallen to 4.7 per cent. Between 1986 and 1994 an eighth round of negotiations, the Uruguay Round, was successfully completed.

The Uruguay Round

The Uruguay Round, so called because the first meeting took place in Uruguay in 1986, differed from previous rounds in that it did not concentrate mainly on trade in manufactured goods. The final treaty in fact covered three main areas, agriculture, textiles and services. The main estimated gains are shown in Figure 85.3.

Agriculture tends to be highly protected throughout the world. The European Union, Japan and the United States in particular have strong protectionist regimes designed to assist their farmers. However, the cost to consumers is very high (☞ unit 34), averaging somewhere between £500 and £1 000 per household per year in the EU according to differing estimates. The Uruguay deal made a start in dismantling protectionist barriers but, even so, they remain very high. An important part of the deal was that non-tariff barriers, such as quotas, have to be converted into tariff barriers. This will make the cost of protectionism much more transparent and could make it more difficult in future for the farming lobby to argue the case for greater protection.

Textiles have traditionally been highly protected too. This is because the major industrialised countries once had important textile industries of their own which have increasingly come under competitive pressure from Third World countries. The response by many First World countries was to allow contraction of the industry but raise barriers to prevent too great a fall in employment. In 1974, this protectionism was formalised in the Multi-Fibre Agreement (MFA), an accord between Third World countries and First World countries, which allowed greater access over time for Third World textile exports to First World markets but within the framework of a highly protectionist First World regime. A World Bank study in 1995 estimated that the abolition of the MFA and the introduction of the Uruguay negotiated tariff reductions would give gains of almost $60bn per year to EU and the USA consumers alone by 2005. This is because they will be able to switch from buying high price domestic textiles to low price Third World imports.

The third part of the Uruguay deal covered services. The USA was particularly concerned that Third World countries were using 'intellectual property' - everything from pirated video games and CDs to drug formulations and manufacturing processes to trade names like Coca Cola and Microsoft- without paying copyright and royalty fees. The Uruguay Round put this firmly on the agenda even if some countries like China continue to flout international conventions. The Uruguay deal also began the process of opening up competition in highly protected national service industries such as finance and telecommunications.

Trading blocs

Since the mid-1970s, the work of GATT (now the WTO, the World Trade Organisation, following a decision made in the Uruguay Round to create a successor to GATT with greater powers) has been made increasingly difficult by the emergence of trading blocs. A few countries have been drawing closer together and offering tariff reductions to some countries but not others in contradiction to the most-favoured national clause. The EU, for instance, has embarked on an ambitious programme under the 1992 Single Market banner, to remove a large number of obstacles to free trade without offering the same trading opportunities to non-EU countries. The USA and Canada

Gatt: who wins what

Total gains in Agriculture $73 billion; Textiles $85 billion; Services $29 billion; Other $23 billion; Total $209.4 billion

Total gain by regions $ bn

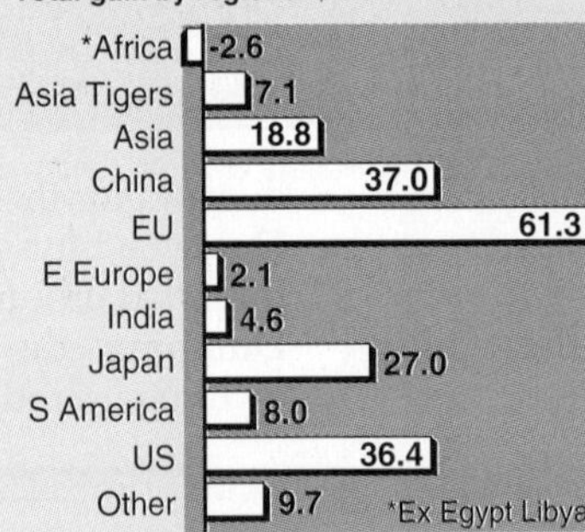

Sources: OECD, GATT

1 US

Largest number of world's 500 biggest global companies, and biggest services exporter ($2 billion benefit). Aerospace, computer software, agriculture ($9.3 billion) and textile ($21.6 billion) sectors will also benefit. Total gain: $36 billion a year by 2002.

2 Japan

Set to gain from liberalisation in high tech goods. Agriculture ($22 billion), manufacturing. Loses $0.5 billion through textile liberalisation. Total gain: $27 billion a year by 2002.

3 Asian Tigers

Gain $3.3 through farm liberalisation, $1.8 billion in textiles, $1.1 billion in services. $7.1 billion overall gain.

4 EU

World's biggest exporting block. Agriculture to see income increase of $30 billion, textiles ($17.2 billion), services ($7 billion), manufacturing ($7.6 billion) all set to gain - but prospects differ in each country. Total gain: $61.3 billion a year by 2002.

5 Eastern Europe

Textile, service sectors likely to benefit. Former Soviet Union set to gain by some $13 billion from liberalisation of services. Total gain: $37 billion a year by 2002.

6 Australia/New Zealand

Large gains from liberalisation of agriculture ($1.0 billion), textile ($1.1 billion). Total gain: $2 billion a year by 2002.

7 China

Set to gain $37 billion a year by 2002.

8 India

Set to gain $4.6 billion a year by 2002.

9 Africa
(excluding Egypt and Libya)

The continent as a whole is set to lose $2.6 billion, with Nigeria alone down $1.0 billion. Morocco, Algeria and Tunisia together lose $0.6 billion, and South Africa loses $0.4 billion.

10 South America

Set to gain $8.0 billion, with Brazil on its own up $3.4 billion. *The estimates also take no account of social costs arising from the structural adjustment of economies in the wake of trade liberalisation.*

Source: adapted from *The Guardian*, 15.12.1993 ©

Figure 85.3 *Gatt: who wins what*

also signed an agreement in 1988 which effectively removed most trade barriers between the two countries. In 1994, this was extended to include Mexico under the North American Free Trade Association (NAFTA) agreement. If this were to carry on, it would be possible to see a world comprised of several large trading blocs, each with common external tariffs and free trade within the bloc. This would contradict the vision of GATT and the WTO which is to remove trade barriers between **all** countries.

Trade imbalances and dumping

In the 1980s and 1990s, there have been growing trade imbalances. Japan and Germany have consistently exported more than they have imported, resulting in trade deficits for other countries. The USA, in particular, has experienced large current account deficits on its balance of payments since the early 1980s, importing far more than it has exported. A number of traditional US industries, such as textiles, car manufacturing and steel, have been badly affected by foreign competition and there have been growing calls for measures to be taken against 'unfair' foreign competition.

It is very difficult to define 'unfair' competition. The whole basis for trade is that it is relatively cheaper to produce goods in some countries than others. It would be foolish for the UK to complain that textiles made by cheap labour in Far Eastern countries represent 'unfair' competition for domestic manufactures given that the source of Far Eastern comparative advantage in textiles lies in its cheap labour. On the other hand, it can be true that countries or companies disrupt markets through **dumping**, which GATT (now the WTO) defines as the sale of a product in an export market at a cheaper price than is charged in the domestic market.

Both the USA and EU have increasingly taken action against what they see as dumping. In the EU, up to 100 anti-dumping suits are investigated each year, and suits have been brought against Japanese manufacturers of photocopiers, printers and video tape recorders. But under GATT and now WTO rules, the USA and EU should take the issue to the WTO and allow the WTO to judge it. Countries don't do this, partly because GATT judgements often take years, by which time the damage has been done, and partly because they are uncertain of winning the case. In many instances, anti-dumping suits have more to do with protecting inefficient domestic producers which have lobbied their governments hard, than with unfair trading practices of, say, Japanese companies which may simply be offering the best products at the cheapest prices.

Protectionism in South Africa

Table 85.1 *Current and proposed tariffs in clothing and textile industries (South Africa)*

TEXTILES	CURRENT DUTY LEVELS	GATT FINAL DUTY LEVELS	SWART FINAL DUTY LEVELS	GATT PHASE-DOWN PERIOD	SWART PHASE-DOWN PERIOD	NATIONAL CLOTHING FEDERATION PROPOSAL
Fibres	25%	10%	7.5%	12 years	10 years	0% in 2 years
Yarn	32%	17.5%	15%	12 years	10 years	0% in 4 years
Fabrics	45%	25%	22%	12 years	10 years	15% in 5 years
Clothing	90%	45%	40%	12 years	10 years	40% in 10 years

Source: adapted from Textile Federation of South Africa.

The GATT Accord

In 1993, countries finally hammered out a deal on a reduction in protectionist barriers - the Uruguay Round deal. South Africa, amongst many other measures, agreed to large cuts in tariffs on clothing and textiles to be completed over a 12 year period.

The Swart plan 1993

In response to the GATT deal, the clothing and textile industry, together with the South African Clothing and Textile Workers Union (SACTWU) pressed the government to help them meet the increased competition from abroad that would result from the GATT deal. In negotiations, the government and the industry agreed on the Swart plan, stating that the 12 year period for implementation of the GATT proposals would be reduced to 10 and that there would be slightly lower import duties than agreed. However, the government was to provide R4.5bn in government aid to help with training and new investment.

New government policy March 1995

In March 1995, the government announced that it was discarding the Swart plan. The R4.5bn aid package was not to be implemented. Moreover, tariffs were to be brought down in a shorter time and by more than that required to conform to the GATT agreement.

The South African clothing and textile industry

The South African clothing and textile industry has been protected by very high tariff barriers since before the Second World War. The R7.7bn textile industry (fibres, yarn and fabrics production) is capital intensive and enjoys considerable economies of scale. As a consequence, the industry is relatively concentrated, dominated by a few large companies mostly based in KwaZulu-Natal province and around Johannesburg. Historically, output has been of relatively poor quality. However, more recently, there has been a push to replace outdated technology which has helped to improve output and establish some export markets. Raw material costs are high and the workforce is poorly trained.

The R5.5bn clothing industry faces different economic circumstances. It is relatively labour intensive. Production is scattered amongst thousands of small companies and the few larger companies have a relatively small market share. Like the textile industry, it has recently begun to find export markets but productivity is low by global standards.

Conflicting views

The government is keen to reduce its own expenditure in order to be able to balance its budget. It also believes that steeper cuts in tariffs will bring about faster productivity gains in the clothing and textile industries.

The National Clothing Federation, representing clothing manufacturers, wants all tariffs on textiles to be abolished over a two year period. It believes that South African textiles are too expensive and wants to be able to buy at world prices from countries such as Pakistan and India. It predicts that another 65 000 jobs could be created in the South African clothing industry for very little capital expenditure if its raw material costs were cut. 'We are very competitive internationally already in terms of quality', said Mr Arnold Werberlof, deputy director of the NCF. 'We're still weak on productivity and training, but a reduction in costs would boost us tremendously.'

The Textile Federation, representing textile manufacturers, argues that too rapid cuts in tariffs would decimate the industry. This would put all the jobs of the 80 000 workers who work directly in the industry and 260 000 workers who work in ancillary industries at risk.

SACTWU, the textile and clothing trade union, faces a difficult decision about what to recommend. Abolishing tariff barriers could mean large job losses amongst its textile members but also the creation of more jobs in the clothing industry. It is demanding that government and employers fund retraining schemes for redundant workers.

Source: adapted from the *Financial Times*, 1.3.1995.

An international agency has asked you to prepare a report on the proposed changes in tariffs on clothing and textiles by South Africa. In the report, you need to evaluate the economic consequences of the changes and make a recommendation about whether the international agency should encourage the South African government to press ahead with its latest plans. In your report:

1. **outline the different policy options on tariffs and aid to industry;**
2. **analyse different economic arguments for and against protection of the clothing and textile industry in South Africa;**
3. **suggest who would be the winners and losers (i) in South Africa and (ii) in the rest of the world of the different policy options facing the South African government;**
4. **make a recommendation about which policy option the South African government should pursue given that the goal of the international agency you are working for is to maximise world welfare.**

The balance of payments account

Summary

1. The balance of payments accounts are split into two parts. The current account records payments for the exports and imports of goods and services. The capital account records saving, investment and speculative flows of money.
2. The current account is split into two parts: trade in visibles and trade in invisibles.
3. The balance of payments accounts must always balance. However, component parts of the accounts may be positive or negative. If there is a surplus on the current account, then outflows on the capital account must be greater than inflows.
4. In practice, the balance of payments does not balance and for this reason a balancing item is included in the accounts.
5. A current account surplus is often seen as a sign of a healthy economy, whilst a current account deficit is seen as a cause for worry. But current account deficits are not necessarily bad as they may be a sign of borrowing which could finance expansion.
6. A current account deficit is most unlikely to be financed by government. The balance of payments deficit and the government deficit, the PSBR, are two completely different entities.

The balance of payments

The BALANCE OF PAYMENTS ACCOUNT is a record of all financial dealings over a period of time between economic agents of one country and all other countries. Balance of payments accounts can be split into two components:

- the CURRENT ACCOUNT where payments for the purchase and sale of goods and services are recorded;
- the CAPITAL ACCOUNT where flows of money associated with saving, investment, speculation and currency stabilisation are recorded.

Flows of money into the country are given a positive (+) sign on the accounts. Flows of money out of the country are given a negative (-) sign.

The current account

The current account on the balance of payments is itself split into two components.

Visible trade VISIBLE TRADE is trade in goods, from raw materials to semi-manufactured products to manufactured goods. Visible EXPORTS are goods which are sold to foreigners. Goods leave the country, whilst payment for these goods goes in the opposite direction. Hence visible exports of, say, cars result in an **inward** flow of money and are recorded with a positive sign on the balance of payments account. Visible IMPORTS are goods which are bought by domestic residents from foreigners. Goods come into the country whilst money **flows out**. Hence visible imports of, say, wheat are given a minus sign on the balance of payments. The difference between visible exports and visible imports is known as the BALANCE OF TRADE.

Invisible trade INVISIBLE TRADE is trade in services. A wide variety of services is traded internationally, including financial services such as banking and insurance, transport services such as shipping and air travel, and tourism. Also included are transfers of money resulting from the loan of factors of production abroad. For instance, a British teacher working in Saudi Arabia and sending back money to his family in England would create an invisible import for Saudi Arabia and an invisible export for Britain. Similarly, a Japanese company repatriating profits made from a factory based in Britain back to Japan would create an invisible import for the UK and an invisible export for Japan. The easiest way to distinguish between invisible exports and imports (or **invisible credits** and **invisible debits** as they are known in the official UK balance of payments account) is to consider flows of money rather than flows of services. The British teacher in Saudi Arabia is sending money back to the UK. An inflow of money means that this is classified as an export. The Japanese company repatriating profits is sending money out of the UK. An outflow of money means that this is classified as an import. The difference between invisible exports and invisible imports is known as the BALANCE ON INVISIBLE TRADE or NET INVISIBLES.

The CURRENT BALANCE is the difference between

QUESTION 1 A country has the following international transactions on current account: exports of manufactured goods £20bn; imports of food £10bn; earnings from foreign tourists £5bn; interest, profits and dividends paid to foreigners £4bn; purchase of oil from abroad £8bn; earnings of nationals working overseas which are repatriated £7bn; sale of coal to foreign countries £2bn; payments by foreigners to domestic financial institutions for services rendered £1bn.

(a) Which of these items are: (i) visible exports; (ii) visible imports; (iii) invisible exports; (iv) invisible imports?
(b) Calculate: (i) the balance of trade; (ii) the balance on invisible trade; (iii) the current balance.
(c) How would your answers to (b) be different if it cost the country £3bn to transport its exports (i) in its own ships and (ii) in the ships of other countries?

total exports (visible and invisible) and total imports. It can also be calculated by adding the balance of trade to the balance on invisible trade.

The capital account

Almost all transactions on the capital account of the balance of payments are private sector transactions. They can crudely be split into two types.

- Short term money flows, sometimes called flows of HOT MONEY, are mainly speculative. Financial institutions, companies and speculators seek to make a profit by buying and selling currencies. A speculator may decide that the value of the dollar will rise over the next week. He buys dollars today, places it perhaps on loan with instant access in New York to earn interest, and then sells dollars in a week's time to take advantage of the next speculative bet. Short term money flows are crucially dependent upon expectations of currency movements and upon interest rates in competing financial centres. If the financial markets expect the pound to fall tomorrow, then they sell today. If interest rates in New York rise, there will be an inflow of hot money into New York to take advantage of the higher interest rates.
- Long term money flows are mainly associated with long term investment and saving. For instance, a Japanese company may set up a car plant in the UK. To finance its building and operation, it sends money from Japan to the UK. Alternatively, a Japanese pension fund may decide that it needs to broaden its international portfolio. So it buys shares on the Paris Stock Exchange, thus creating an outflow of money from Japan and an inflow of money into France.

Just as on the current account, flows of money into the country on the capital account are given a plus sign whilst outflows of money are given a minus sign. For instance, Japanese investment in the UK would be given a positive sign on the balance of payments whilst a UK company lending money to a foreign company would be given a minus sign.

QUESTION 2 Would the following be given a plus or a minus sign on the balance of payments account of the United Kingdom?
(a) Investment overseas by UK residents.
(b) Foreign currency lending abroad by UK banks.
(c) Borrowing from banks abroad by general government.
(d) Portfolio investment in the UK by overseas residents.
(e) Deposits with and lending to banks abroad by the UK non-bank private sector.

The balance of payments must always balance

The balance of payments account must always balance. To understand why, consider a situation where a country experiences a CURRENT ACCOUNT DEFICIT (i.e. imports are greater than exports and outflows of money are greater than inflows). The money to finance the net outflow of money must come from somewhere. Foreigners could lend the money or invest in the country; or the country could run down its savings abroad by selling its assets and bringing the money back home. Either way, in this instance the deficit on the current account will be matched by a surplus (a net inflow of money) on the capital account, reducing the balance on the whole of the balance of payments to zero.

There is a third way in which a current account deficit could be financed. The central bank of the country could sell some of its GOLD AND FOREIGN CURRENCY RESERVES. Central banks hold gold and reserves of other currencies in order to be able to intervene on the foreign exchange markets to alter the value of their own country's currency. The sale of some of its reserves for domestic currency will produce an inflow of domestic money which will be recorded on the balance of payments account.

The balancing item

In theory, it must be true that the addition of the current and capital accounts with the change in gold and foreign currency reserves must be equal to zero; the balance of payments account must balance. In practice this never happens because there is significant under-recording of transactions on the current and capital accounts. Part of the problem is that the accounts are calculated from millions of different returns from firms engaged in exporting and importing or foreign exchange transactions. Completing a form takes time and therefore costs money to the firm. Costs can be cut by not sending in the legally required information to the government. It is also true that some transactions are not recorded to avoid tax or avoid police detection. The balance of payments must always balance. Hence, a **balancing item** is included in the balance of payments to make the accounts balance. As more information about transactions in any one time period becomes available, the balance of payments accounts are changed, including the value of the balancing item. In theory, the size of the balancing item on each revision should go down as more 'missing' items are found.

Balance of payments disequilibria

Whilst it is true that the balance of payments as a whole must balance, individual components of the account are most unlikely to balance. Often the phrase 'a balance of payments deficit' is used in the news. This usually refers to a deficit on the current account, although sometimes it is a deficit on the balance of trade only which is being talked about.

Deficits on current account and therefore surpluses on the capital account are generally considered to be undesirable, whilst surpluses on current account and

QUESTION 3

Table 86.1 *UK Balance of payments*

£ million

	1980	1984	1988	1990	1992	1994
CURRENT ACCOUNT						
Visible trade						
Exports	47 149	70 265	80 346	101 718	107 343	135 200
Imports	45 792	75 601	101 826	120 527	120 447	145 727
Balance of trade						
Invisible trade'						
Credits	41 041	77 031	87 307	114 504	107 164	122 793
Debits	39 555	70 213	82 444	114 730	103 891	112 434
Invisible balance						
Current balance						
CAPITAL ACCOUNT						
Net transactions excluding official reserves	-4 231	- 7 626	-13 736	18 117	4 776	-6 789
Official reserves						
BALANCING ITEM	917	1 033	5 642	842	6462	5 913

Source: adapted from CSO, *Economic Trends Annual Supplement.*

The table shows all the transactions on the UK balance of payments apart from changes in the gold and foreign currency reserves.

(a) Copy out the table and calculate the balance of trade, the invisible balance and current balance for each year.

(b) For each year, calculate the addition to (which would be shown by a minus figure) or drawings on (shown by a plus figure) the official reserves held by the Bank of England.

(c) (i) What has happened to the balancing item as a proportion of visible exports over time?
(ii) Calculate the current balance if half the balancing item were allocated to the current account balance.
(iii) In the late 1980s, the current account position deteriorated sharply, according to official figures. Would this still be true if half the balancing item were missing current account transactions?
(iv) In the early 1980s, the government cut the amount of money spent on the collection of official statistics. Why might this have affected the size of the balancing item?

associated deficits on capital account are considered a sign of economic strength. The main reason for this is that a deficit on current account indicates the country is importing more than it is exporting. Expenditure is therefore higher than income. The deficit is financed either by borrowing from abroad or by running down savings. In any one year, it matters little whether a country is a net borrower internationally. However, if the current account deficit is large and persists over a long period of time, the country will get deeper and deeper into debt. Eventually other countries will refuse to lend any more. The debtor country will have to move back to a current account balance. Not only that but lenders are likely to insist upon repayment of debt. The current account will have to move into surplus to allow this. The 1970s and 1980s saw a large number of Second and Third World countries such as Poland and Brazil first borrowing large sums and then becoming effectively bankrupt because they have been unable to pay back their debts. What has happened is analogous to a household consistently spending more than it is earning and therefore getting into deeper and deeper debt problems.

Current account surpluses are seen as desirable for two reasons. First, it is assumed that exports create jobs whilst imports destroy jobs. Therefore the more exports and the fewer imports for an economy, the healthier the economy will be. This crude argument is a fallacy. An economy can just as well be at full employment with a current account deficit as with a surplus. What is true, however, is that two very successful post-war economies - Japan and West Germany - have tended to run persistent current account surpluses. But these surpluses are the result of economic strength rather than their cause.

Second, current account surpluses are seen as desirable because they are associated with capital account deficits. A capital account deficit means that the country is a net saver internationally. A persistent deficit on capital account is likely to result in growing international wealth. This wealth should generate interest, profits and dividends which can be repatriated to provide an income for the country.

However, current account deficits which necessitate net borrowing from abroad are not necessarily undesirable. The USA ran large, persistent current account deficits in the 1980s. But this was not particularly worrying to many because the deficit was only a small fraction of US national income. Moreover, there is little point in producing without consuming. There is no point in building up a stock of savings unless at some point it is used for spending.

There is also a long tradition of countries borrowing money to finance investment. To take the analogy of a firm, few firms would consider it good business practice never to borrow money. There are times when it is essential to borrow if good investment opportunities are not to be lost. Similarly, the United States in the 1830s and 1840s was a net borrower of international capital and therefore ran a current account deficit. It used the money to finance its economic development. One reason why Third World countries borrow so much money is because the money is, in theory at least, to be used for development purposes. Once factories and offices and farms have been established, they then export a share of the increased output to pay back the foreign debt.

Economic theory and economic history therefore suggest that current account deficits are not always undesirable. Some of today's most affluent economies have run current account deficits for a lengthy period of time in the past. However, there is risk associated with this - the risk that the country will not be able to repay and be forced into the hands of its creditors as are so many Third World countries today.

Government deficits and balance of payments deficits

One very common fallacy is to equate current account deficits with government deficits (the PSBR ☞ unit 68). Most transactions on the balance of payments are made by private individuals and firms. If the country is a net borrower, it is more than likely that this is because private individuals and firms have borrowed more from foreigners than they have lent to foreigners. There is a relationship between government borrowing and the current account deficit but the relationship is complicated, and it could well be the case that the public sector might be in surplus domestically when the current account was in deficit. So the current account deficit is **not** a government deficit in any sense.

Key terms

The balance of payments account - a record of all financial dealings over a period of time between economic agents of one country and all other countries.
Current account - that part of the balance of payments account where payments for the purchase and sale of goods and services are recorded.
Capital account - that part of the balance of payments account where flows of savings, investment and currency are recorded.
Visible trade - trade in goods.
Exports - goods and services produced domestically and sold to foreigners. Payments for exports come into the country.
Imports - goods and services purchased from foreign producers. Payments for imports leave the country.
Balance of trade - visible exports minus visible imports.
Invisible trade - trade in services.
Balance on invisible trade or net invisibles - invisible exports minus invisible imports.
Current balance - the difference between total exports (visible and invisible) and total imports. It can also be calculated by adding the balance of trade to the balance on invisible trade.
Hot money - short term flows of money across the foreign exchanges.
Current account deficit or surplus - a deficit exists when imports are greater than exports; a surplus exists when exports are greater than imports.
Gold and foreign currency reserves - gold and foreign currency owned by the central bank of a country and used mainly to change the foreign exchange value of the domestic currency by buying and selling currency on the foreign exchanges.

Applied economics

The UK balance of payments

The balance of payments account of the UK can be split into two broad categories.

- Transactions on current account include visible and invisible trade.
- Transactions on capital account include flows of money for borrowing, saving and investment. Currently, inflows of money on capital account are called **transactions in liabilities**. They are a liability for the UK because they represent increased borrowing by UK citizens or companies, purchase by foreigners of UK assets or dissaving by the UK when money is brought home following the sale of UK owned assets abroad. Outflows of money on capital account are called **transactions in assets** since money leaving the UK which is recorded on the capital account creates assets (or reduces liabilities) abroad for the UK.

Flows of money into the country must equal outflows of money (i.e. the balance of payments must always balance). So in Figure 86.1, inflows of money to the UK in 1994 (exports plus transactions in liabilities) must equal outflows of money from the UK (imports and transactions in assets). In 1994, the balancing item was positive, indicating that recorded inflows of money were less than recorded outflows.

Another way of expressing this is to consider the balances on the two parts of the account. As shown in Figure 86.2, the current balance (exports minus imports - equal to the balance of trade plus the balance on invisible trade) plus net transactions on the capital account plus the balancing item must equal zero. Not included in Figure 86.2 are transactions with the IMF (allocation of SDRs and subscriptions to the IMF), because in 1994 there were none.

Since the end of the Second World War, there have been a number of consistent trends on the UK balance of payments.

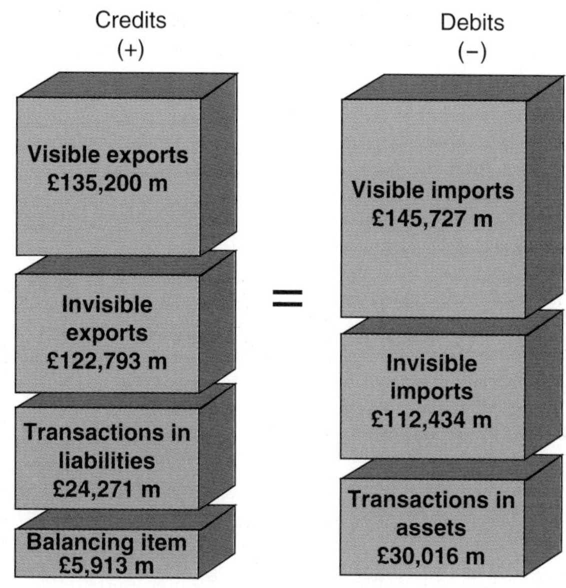

Source: adapted from CSO, *Monthly Digest of Statistics.*
Figure 86.1 *Inflows and outflows on the balance of payments, 1994*

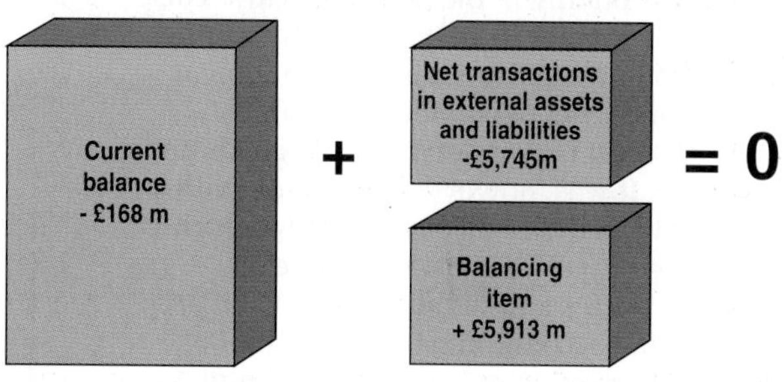

Source: adapted from CSO, *Monthly Digest of Statistics.*
Figure 86.2 *The balance of payments, 1994*

- The balance of trade has been negative, as can be seen from Figure 86.3. Visible exports have tended to be less than visible imports.
- The balance on invisible trade has been positive. Invisible credits (exports) have been greater than invisible debits (imports).
- The current balance has tended to move from surplus to deficit in a cyclical manner. Figure 86.4 shows that, during the 1950s and 1960s, the current account moved into deficit about every 5 years, coinciding with booms in the economy (☞ unit 67). The two oil crises of the 1970s and the revenue from North Sea oil disturbed this simple relationship in the decade following 1974, but the boom of 1987-89 produced the expected current account deficit. Unlike previous deficits, the current account failed to return to surplus in the recession of 1990-92. This is perhaps a reflection of the degree of de-industrialisation experienced in the UK economy in the 1980s where manufacturing industry shrunk so much that, even in a deep recession, the country was still buying large quantities of imported finished manufactured goods. It is also perhaps a reflection of the sheer size of the deficit during the Lawson boom. The current account deficit in 1989, as a percentage of GDP, was nearly a fifth higher than in 1974 when the economy experienced a severe supply side shock in the form of a quadrupling of oil prices. The oil price shock of 1974 severely destabilised all western economies. It is not perhaps surprising, then, that the consumer spending spree of the Lawson years severely disrupted

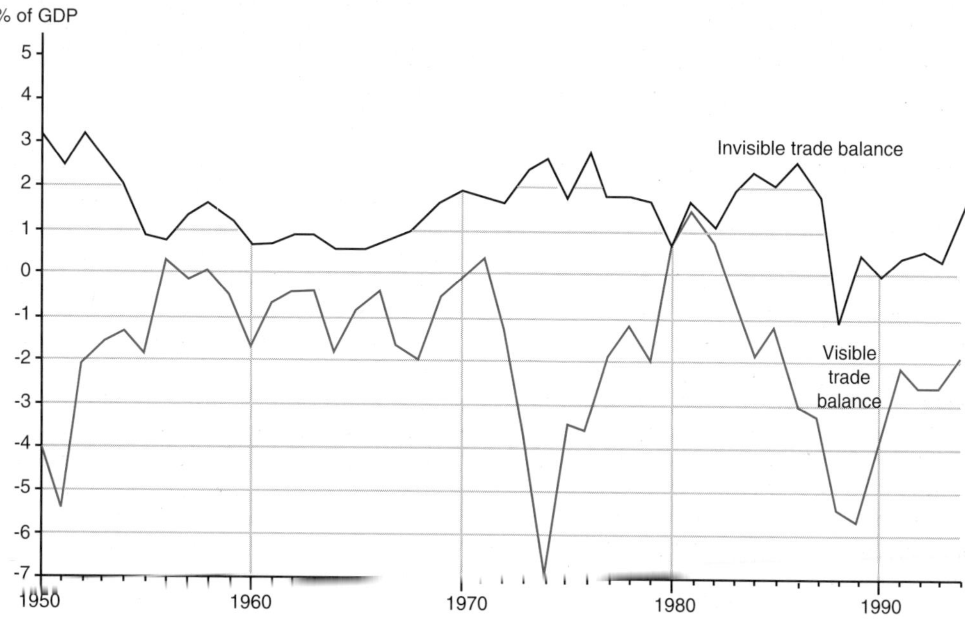

Source: adapted from CSO, *Economic Trends Annual Supplement* ; CSO, *Monthly Digest of Statistics.*
Figure 86.3 *The balance of trade and the invisibles balance as a percentage of GDP, UK*

the UK economy in the next five years. The return to balance in 1994 was partly a reflection of the 15 per cent devaluation of the pound from September 1992 which helped boost exports of tradeable goods and services. It was, however, more to do with a surge in North Sea oil exports and a much improved investment performance on interest profits and dividends from abroad.

- The capital account must move in the contrary direction to the current account, assuming no balancing item, because the balance of payments always balances. A current account surplus necessitates a capital account deficit. Given that there is a balancing item, Figure 86.5 shows that in most years there is indeed this inverse relationship between the current account and capital account. Note that the early 1980s were characterised by large net outflows of capital caused by substantial North Sea oil earnings flowing overseas. In contrast, during the Lawson boom, individuals and firms borrowed large amounts from abroad to finance their consumption and investment. 1989 saw post-war record net borrowing from abroad as a percentage of GDP. These trends in part help explain the very large increase in interest, profits and dividend earnings in the first half of the 1980s, and the collapse of any surplus on these earnings in the early 1990s.

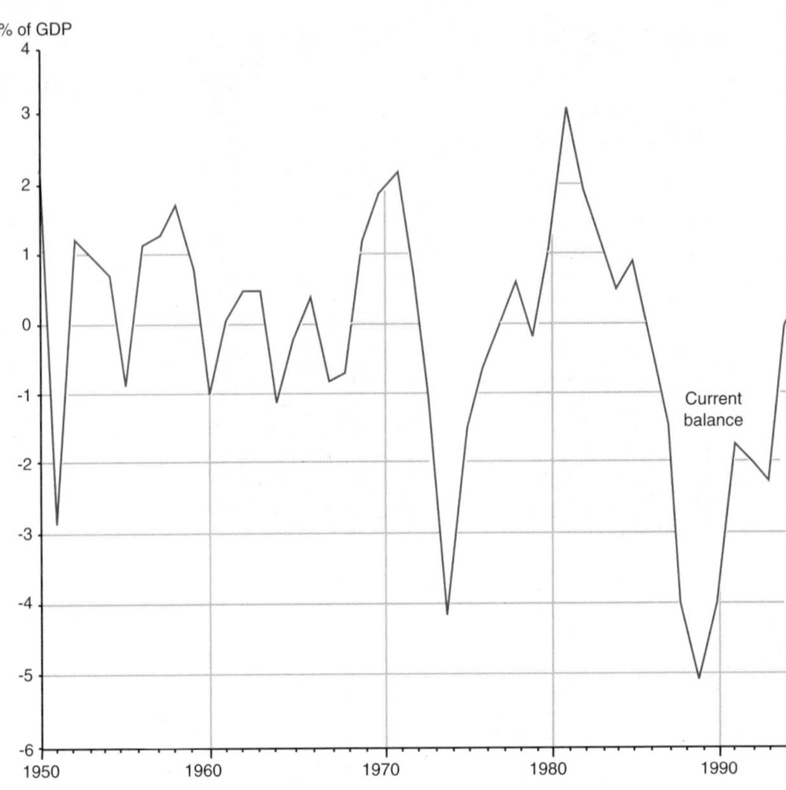

Source: adapted from CSO, *Economic Trends Annual Supplement*; CSO, *Monthly Digest of Statistics*.

Figure 86.4 *Current balance as a percentage of GDP, UK*

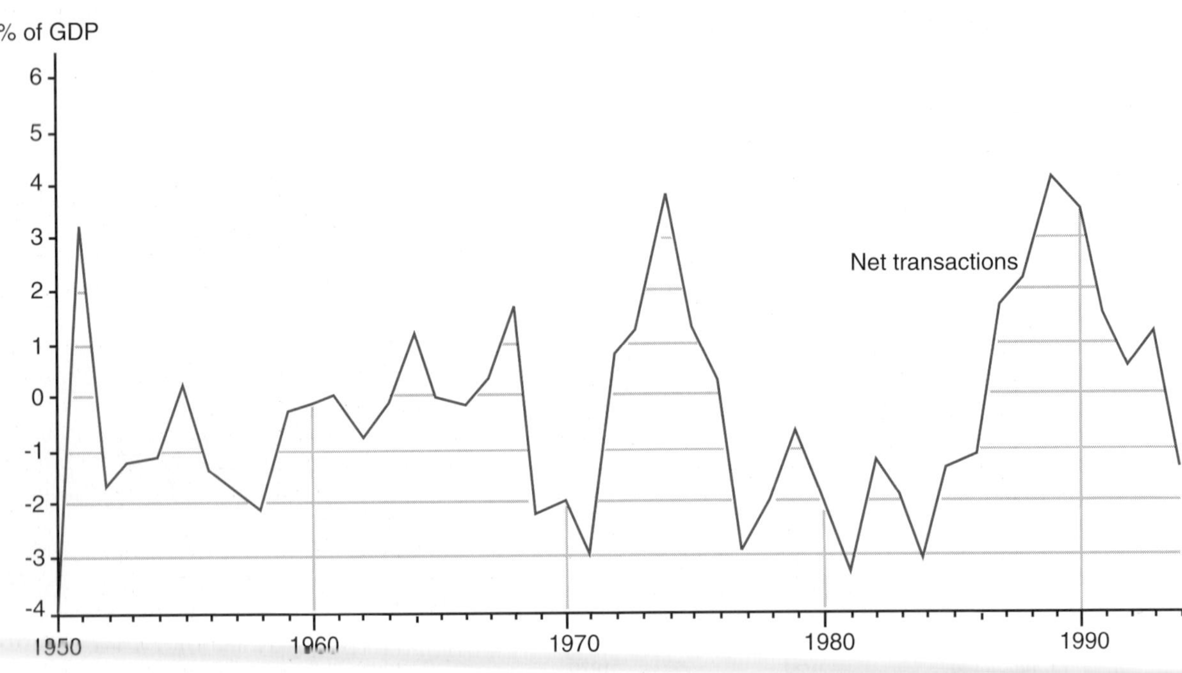

Source: adapted from CSO, *Economic Trends Annual Supplement*; CSO, *Monthly Digest of Statistics*.

Figure 86.5 *Net transactions in external assets and liabilities as a percentage of GDP, UK*

DATA QUESTION

The UK music industry

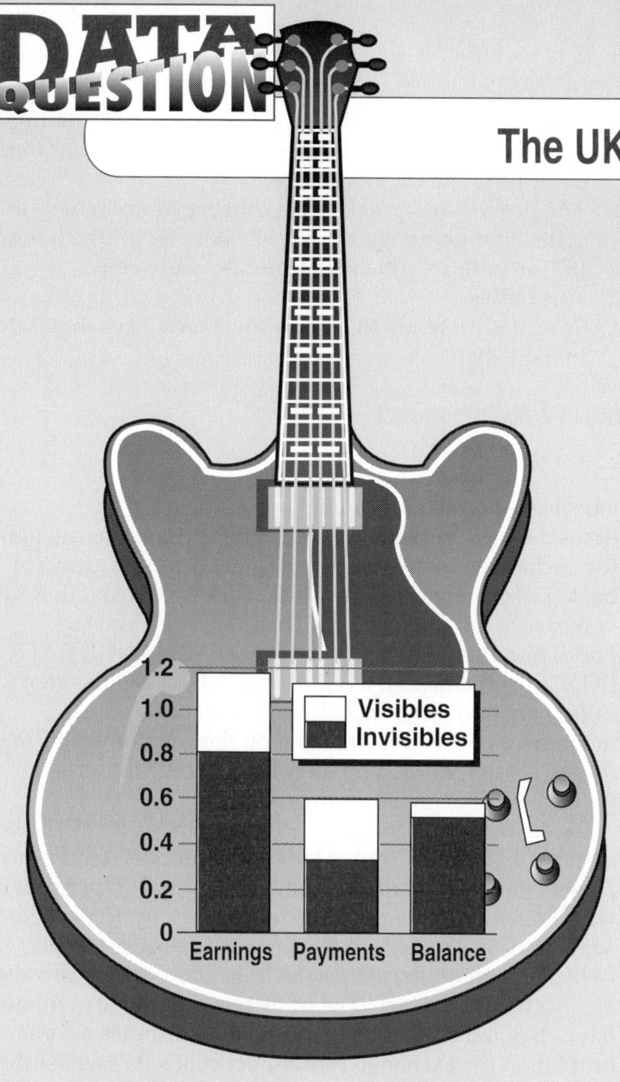

Source: adapted from British Invisibles.

Figure 86.6 *Music industry overseas earnings, 1993 (£bn)*

The music industry - a success story

Britain's music industry is a major exporting success story. Whilst there is a small surplus on trade in visibles such as records, compact discs and instruments, there is a large surplus on trade in invisibles, like royalties for recordings and live performance fees. In 1993, overall exports were almost double that of imports, making a £571m net contribution to the current balance. The music industry is as important today as an exporter as the steel industry. The ratio of exports to imports is exceptionally high, comparable only to a few niche industries such as tobacco, caravans and wallcoverings.

'We are fortunate that British music sells well in 70 or 80 countries around the world. French and German bands do not translate so well.'

Richard Branson, founder of the Virgin music label.

'No one disputes the importance of music in everyone's lives, but what may not be so obvious is the financial benefit the UK economy derives from music.'

Ian Taylor, Trade and Technology Minister.

Future problems

The recording industry's earnings come largely from back catalogues of established artists like the Beatles, Eric Clapton, Elton John and Phil Collins. In the 1990s, however, the UK music industry has found it difficult to find new British talent which sells into international markets. In early 1995, for instance, the only UK artist in the US top 30 singles chart was Des'ree, the female soul singer. Some claim that British recording companies are not spending enough on bringing on new talent. They find it easier to put their resources into selling old material. Others argue that the 1990s has seen a fragmentation of the music world in response to a fragmentation of the music listening public. Today's youngsters, 'Generation X', are not a single mass market in the way that teenagers were in, say, the 1960s. The result is that there is still plenty of good music being produced, but sales volumes are much lower than before because each record is selling into a niche market.

Source: adapted from the *Financial Times*, 10.2.1995.

Produce a report for the Department of Trade and Industry discussing the impact of the music industry on the balance of payments at the moment and in the future. In your report:

1. **explain the contribution made by the music industry to the UK export and import of goods and services;**
2. **discuss possible future trends in the contribution made by the music industry to the current balance on the balance of payments;**
3. **evaluate the impact that a possible takeover of a major UK music recording company, such as Thorn EMI, by a Japanese electronics manufacturer like Sony might have on the current and capital accounts of the UK balance of payments (i) in the short term and (ii) in the longer term.**

Exchange rate determination

Summary

1. The exchange rate is the price at which one currency is convertible into another.
2. The equilibrium exchange rate is established where demand for a currency is equal to its supply.
3. The equilibrium exchange rate will change if there is a change in the value of exports or imports, the value of net long term foreign investment, or the volume or direction of speculative flows.
4. On a day to day basis in a free exchange market, speculation tends to be the dominant influence upon the price of a currency.
5. In the longer term, economic fundamentals relating to exports, imports and long term capital flows tend to determine the exchange rate.
6. The purchasing power parity theory of exchange rates states that exchange rates will in the long run change in line with relative inflation rates between economies.
7. Speculation tends to lead to short term exchange rate instability.

The exchange rate

Different countries use different types of **money** or **currency**. In the UK, goods and services are bought and sold with pounds sterling, in France with the French franc, and in Germany with the German deutschmark.

The rate at which one currency can be converted (i.e. bought or sold) into another currency is known as the EXCHANGE RATE. For instance, a French company may wish to purchase pounds sterling. If it pays 10 million francs to purchase £1 million, then the exchange rate is 10 francs to the pound. A UK household may wish to buy US dollars to take on holiday to Florida. If they receive $2 000 in exchange for £1 000, then the exchange rate is $2 to the pound, or 50p to the dollar.

Exchange rates are normally expressed in terms of the value of one single currency against another single currency - pounds for dollars for instance, or deutschmarks for yen. However, it is possible to calculate the exchange rate of one currency in terms of a group or **basket** of currencies. The EFFECTIVE EXCHANGE RATE (a measure calculated by the International Monetary Fund) and the TRADE WEIGHTED EXCHANGE RATE INDEX (or the EXCHANGE RATE INDEX as it is often called) are two different calculations of the average movement of the exchange rate on the basis of weightings (☞ unit 3) determined by the value of trade undertaken with a country's main trading partners.

To illustrate how the trade weighted index is calculated, assume that the UK trades only with the USA and France. 70 per cent of UK trade is with the USA and 30 per cent is with France. The value of the pound falls by 10 per cent against the dollar and by 20 per cent against the franc (which, incidentally, means the franc has gone up in value against the US dollar). The trade weighted index will now have changed. The fall in the dollar contributes a 7 per cent fall in the exchange rate (10 per cent x 0.7) whilst the fall in the franc contributes a 6 per cent fall (20 per cent x 0.3). The average fall is the sum of these two components (i.e. 13 per cent). If the trade weighted index started off at 100, its new value will be 87.

QUESTION 1

Table 87.1

Original value of the trade weighted index	Change in exchange rate %		New value of the trade weighted index
	Country X	Country Y	
100	+10	+20	
100	+20	+10	
100	-10	+10	
100	+10	-10	
100	- 6	- 6	

Country A trades only with two countries. 60 per cent of its trade is with country X and 40 per cent with country Y.

(a) Complete the table by calculating the new value of the trade weighted index for country A following changes in its exchange rate with countries X and Y.

(b) What would be the values of the trade weighted index if country A had 90 per cent of its trade with country X and 10 per cent with country Y?

(c) Calculate the new values of the trade weighted index in (a) if the original value of the trade weighted index were not 100 but 80.

Equilibrium exchange rates

Foreign exchange is bought and sold on the FOREIGN EXCHANGE MARKETS. Governments may buy and sell currencies in order to influence the price of a currency. Here we will assume that governments do not intervene and that currencies are allowed to find their own price levels through the forces of **demand** and **supply**. There are then three main reasons why foreign exchange is bought and sold.

- International trade in goods and services needs to be financed. Exports create a demand for currency whilst imports create a supply of currency.
- Long term capital movements occur. Inward investment to an economy creates a demand for its currency. Outward investment from an economy creates a supply.
- There is an enormous amount of speculation in the

foreign exchange markets.

The equilibrium exchange rate is established where the demand for the currency is equal to its supply. Figure 87.1 shows the demand and supply of pounds priced in dollars. The market is in equilibrium at an exchange rate of \$2 = £1. £1 000 million are bought and sold each day.

The demand curve is assumed to be downward sloping. If the price of the pound falls against the dollar, then the price of British goods will fall in dollar terms. For instance, if the exchange rate falls from \$2 = £1 to \$1 = £1, then a British good costing £1 000 will fall in price for Americans from \$2 000 to \$1 000. Americans should therefore buy more British goods and demand more pounds to pay for them. So a fall in the price of the pound should lead to an increase in quantity demanded of pounds, giving rise to thedownward sloping demand curve. Similarly the supply curve is upward sloping because a fall in the value of the pound will increase the price of foreign imports for the British, leading them to reduce their purchases of foreign goods and therefore of foreign exchange.

All other things being equal, a fall in the value of the pound from, say, \$2 to \$1 is likely to make the pound look cheap and this may attract speculative buying of the pound and discourage speculative selling. This would then produce downward sloping demand curves and upward sloping supply curves for the pound sterling. However, in general on the capital side, it is unclear how buyers and sellers will react to rises and falls in the price of a currency. Given this, the justification for downward sloping demand curves and upward sloping supply curves for foreign exchange tends to rest on arguments about the buying and selling of currency for export and import payments.

Figure 87.2 shows that the exchange rate will change if either the demand or supply curve shifts. Equilibrium is at price OB and output OQ.

- If British exports to the USA increase, American firms will need to buy more pounds than before to pay for them. Hence an increase in the value of UK exports will increase the demand for pounds, shifting the demand curve from D_1 to D_2. The exchange rate will therefore rise from OB to OC.
- If imports from the USA increase, British firms will need to buy more dollars than before to pay for them. They will buy these dollars with pounds. Hence an increase in the value of UK imports will increase the supply of pounds. The supply curve will shift to the right from S_1 to S_2. The equilibrium value of the pound will fall from OB to OA.
- If the rate of interest in the London money markets increases, US savers will switch funds into the UK. This is likely to be short term money or **hot money** which flows from financial centre to financial centre attracted by the highest rate of return. An increase in inflows on the capital account of the balance of payments will increase the demand for pounds, shifting the demand curve from D_1 to D_2, and increasing the value of the pound from OB to OC.
- If there is an inflow of funds for long term investment in the UK, again the demand for pounds will rise. For instance, Japanese investment in car plants in the UK will raise the demand for pounds (and increase the supply of yen) shown by the shift in the demand curve from D_1 to D_2, raising the value of the pound from OB to OC.
- Speculation is the single most important determinant today of the minute by minute price of the pound. If speculators believe that the value of the pound is going to fall against the dollar, they will sell pounds and buy

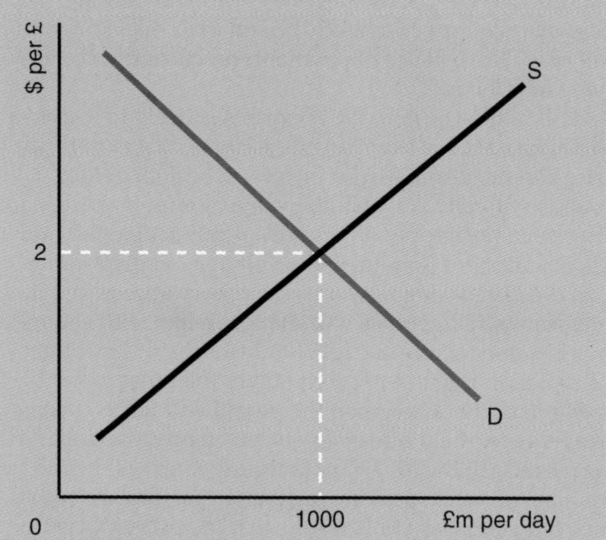

Figure 87.1 *Floating exchange rate systems*
In a free exchange rate market, the price of a currency is determined by demand and supply. Equilibrium price is \$2 to the pound whilst equilibrium quantity demanded and supplied is £1 000 million per day.

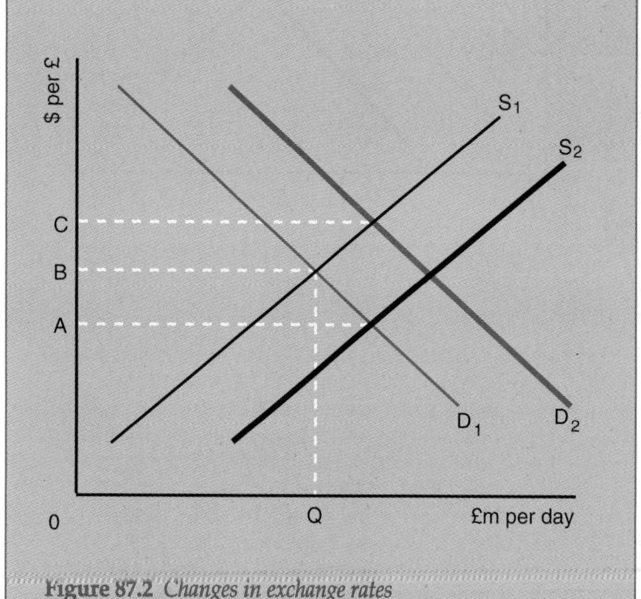

Figure 87.2 *Changes in exchange rates*
The equilibrium value of the pound will change if there is a change in either the demand for or supply of pounds (or both).

dollars. An increase in the supply of pounds on the market, shown by the shift in the supply curve from S_1 to S_2, will lead to a fall in the price of the pound from OB to OA.

It is difficult to assess the level of speculative activity on the foreign exchange markets. Less than 5 per cent of daily foreign exchange transactions in London is a result of a direct buying or selling order for exports and imports or long term capital flows. However, each order tends to result in more than one transaction as foreign exchange dealers cover their exposure to the deal by buying and selling other currencies. Even if every order were to result in an extra three transactions, this would still only account for at most 20 per cent of transactions, which would suggest that speculative deals form the majority of trading on a daily basis.

Thus, in the short term, the value of a currency is dominated by speculative activity in the currency. However, there is evidence to suggest that in the longer term, the value of a currency is determined by economic **fundamentals** - by exports, imports and long term capital movements.

QUESTION 2 Figure 87.3 shows the demand and supply of pounds. D and S are the original demand and supply curves respectively.

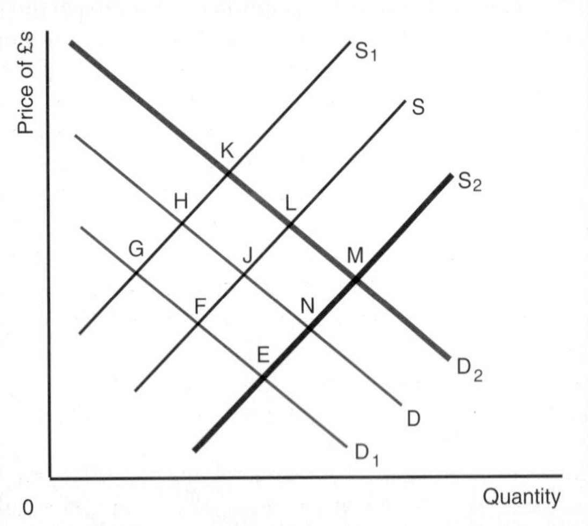

Figure 87.3

(a) At which point (E to N) is the market in equilibrium?

(b) To which point will the market be most likely to move in the short term if there is: (i) an increase in exports; (ii) an increase in imports; (iii) a fall in interest rates in the London money markets; (iv) a rise in takeovers of US companies by British companies; (v) a belief that the value of the deutschmark will rise in the near future; (vi) the discovery of a huge new oil field in the North Sea; (vii) bad summer weather in the UK which sharply increases the number of foreign holidays taken; (viii) a series of prolonged strikes in the UK engineering sector of the economy?

The purchasing power parity theory of exchange rates

If purchasing power parity exists, then a given amount of currency in one country, converted into another currency at the current market exchange rate, will buy the same bundle of goods in both countries. For instance, if £1 = $2, and consumers only buy jeans, then purchasing power parity will exist if a £20 pair of jeans costs $40 in the USA. It won't exist if a pair of jeans priced at £20 in the UK is priced at $50 or $30 in the USA. If there are only two goods in the economy, food and clothing, then purchasing power parity will exist if an identical bundle of food and clothes costs £100 when it costs $200 in the USA, or £500 when it costs $1 000 in the USA.

The PURCHASING POWER PARITY (PPP) THEORY states that exchange rates in the long term change in line with different inflation rates between economies. To understand why exchange rates might change in line with inflation rates, assume that the balance of payments of the UK is in equilibrium with exports equal to imports and capital outflows equal to capital inflows, but it is suffering from a 5 per cent inflation rate (i.e. the prices of goods are rising on average by 5 per cent per year). Assume also that there is no inflation in the rest of world. At the end of one year, the average price of UK exports will be 5 per cent higher than at the beginning. On the other hand, imports will be 5 per cent cheaper than domestically produced goods. At the end of the second year, the gap will be even wider.

Starting from a PPP rate of $2 = £1, this change in relative prices between the UK and the rest of the world will affect the volume of UK exports and imports. UK exports will become steadily less price competitive on world markets. Hence sales of UK exports will fall. Imports into the UK on the other hand will become steadily more price competitive and their sales in the UK will rise. The balance of payments on current account will move into the red.

A fall in the volume of UK exports is likely to lead to a fall in the value of exports (this assumes that exports are **price elastic** ☞ unit 8) and therefore the demand for pounds will fall. A rise in the value of imports will result in a rise in the supply of pounds. A fall in demand and a rise in supply of pounds will result in a fall in its value.

So the purchasing power parity theory argues that in the long run exchange rates will change in line with changes in prices between countries. For instance, if the annual UK inflation rate is 4 per cent higher than that of the USA over a period of time, then the pound will fall in value at an average annual rate of 4 per cent against the dollar over the period. In the long run, exchange rates will be in equilibrium when **purchasing power parities** are equal between countries. This means that the prices of typical bundles of traded goods and services are equal.

The causes of inflation are complex. However, one fundamental reason why economies can become less price competitive over time is **labour productivity** (i.e. output per worker). If output per worker, for instance, increases at a rate of 2 per cent per annum in the UK and 5 per cent per annum in Japan, then it is likely that the UK will become less competitive internationally than Japan over time. Wage costs are the single most important element on average in the final value of a product. In the UK, approximately 70 per cent of national income is made up of wages and salaries. Hence changes in labour productivity are an important component in changes in final costs.

QUESTION 3 Figure 87.4 shows the real exchange rate of sterling between 1975 and 1991. 1975 is taken as the base year (i.e. 1975 = 100). If purchasing power parities were the sole determinant of the exchange rate, the real exchange rate would remain constant at 100 over time (assuming that the exchange rate was in long run equilibrium in 1975).

Note: The real exchange rate has been calculated by dividing the effective exchange rate by the average (weighted) price index of the UK's trading partners relative to the UK Retail Price Index.
Source: adapted from Prest and Coppock's *The UK Economy*, edited by M J Artis, Weidenfeld and Nicolson.

Figure 87.4 *Sterling's real exchange rate*

(a) To what extent has the real exchange rate deviated from its purchasing power parity value?
(b) The mid-1970s saw a collapse in confidence in the British economy as record levels of inflation gripped the country. By 1977, inflation was abating and it was becoming increasingly clear that the North Sea would provide the UK with substantial exports of oil over at least the next decade. How might these two factors explain the deviation of the real exchange rate from its PPP level in the years between 1975 and 1982?

Other factors affecting competitiveness

Price is an important factor in determining purchasing decisions, but it is not the only consideration. Other factors include design, quality, reliability or availability for instance. Over long periods of time, countries can become increasingly uncompetitive internationally in one or more of these factors. Indeed it is often argued that the UK has suffered this fate over the past century. What then happens is that the economy finds it more and more difficult to export whilst the **marginal propensity to import** (☞ unit 83) increases. There is therefore a continual downward pressure on the exchange rate. The debate about what makes a country internationally uncompetitive is the same as the debate about why a country grows at a slower rate than other countries (☞ unit 99).

Long term capital movements

During much of the 19th century, the USA was a net capital importer. It financed its development in part by borrowing money from Europe. Countries which are in a position to borrow money will have a higher long term exchange rate than they would otherwise have done. For instance, during the 19th century, Europeans demanded dollars to invest in the USA. This rise in demand led to a rise in the value of the dollar. Similarly, net long term lending by a country will tend to depress the exchange rate.

Speculation

Day to day exchange rate movements today are affected by speculation or short term flows of capital. Thirty years ago this was different, as nearly all countries imposed a variety of EXCHANGE CONTROLS upon their currency movements. At the most extreme, currency could only be bought and sold through the central bank. In more liberal regimes, purchases could be made on the open market, but individuals and firms often had to seek permission from the central bank to trade in currency. Exchange controls have now largely been swept away in the major industrialised trading nations of the world. Vast sums of money are committed internationally and flows of just a fraction of these across exchanges can lead to large currency fluctuations.

Classical or monetarist economists in the 1960s and 1970s predicted that speculation would dampen exchange rate fluctuations and help stabilise currencies. They argued that the exchange rate in the long term was fixed by economic fundamentals such as the balance between exports and imports. Economic fundamentals only change slowly over time and therefore market expectations of future exchange rates will only change slowly over time too. If the market believes that in two year's time the value of the pound against the dollar will be $2 = £1, and today the value of the pound is $3 = £1, then speculators will sell pounds, driving down the value of the pound towards its longer term value.

The evidence of the 1970s and 1980s suggests that this is not true. In the above example, it is just as likely that the value of the pound will go up as down even if speculators agree that in the long term the pound is overvalued at today's prices. The reason is that speculation by its very nature is short term. Speculators are not very interested in the price of sterling in 2 years' time. They are far more interested in the price of sterling in the next 30 minutes. Large sums of money can be made by buying and selling in the very short term.

It is impossible to pin-point exactly what drives short term exchange rate markets. Certainly markets tend to react in a predictable way to news about changes in economic fundamentals. A bad set of trade figures, for instance, which points to a future fall in the exchange rate, tends to lead to selling pressure today. A rise in domestic interest rates will tend to increase today's exchange rate as speculators anticipate future capital inflows to take advantage of the higher rates of interest. But many exchange rates are inexplicable. Speculators 'lose confidence' or 'gain confidence'. They are very influenced by the opinions of other speculators. Some individuals in the market may be extremely influential. A word spoken in a television interview or written in an article may spark off feverish buying or selling.

Some economists argue that there is no pattern at all to exchange rate movements: that they are on a random walk and the market is totally chaotic.

Even though speculation can be highly destabilising in the short term, economists tend to believe that economic fundamentals prevail in the long term.

QUESTION 4

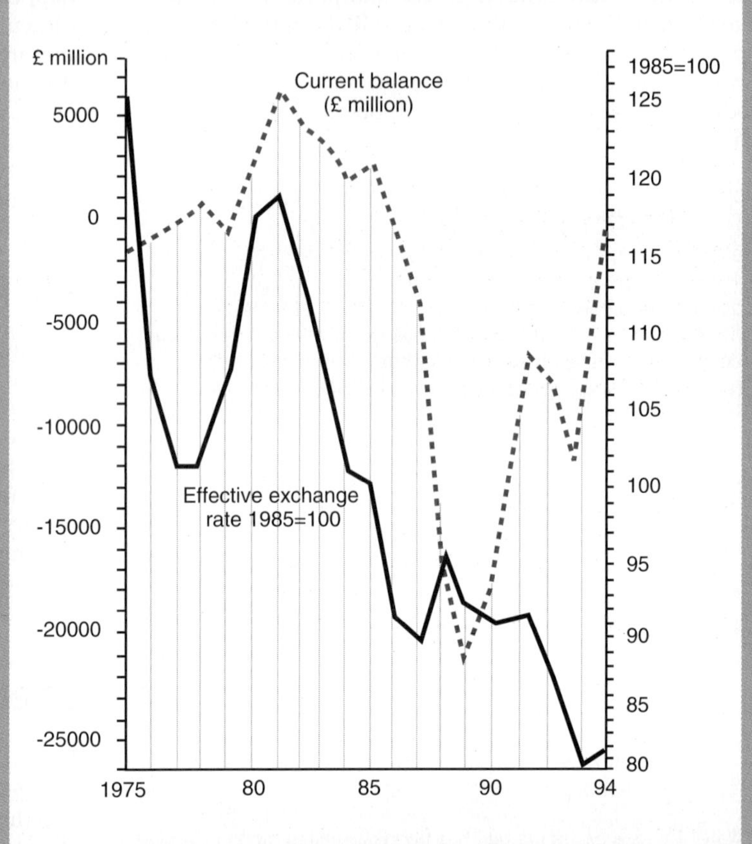

Source: adapted from CSO, *Economic Trends Annual Supplement*; CSO, *Monthly Digest of Statistics*.

Figure 87.5 *Effective exchange rate (1985 = 100) and the current balance*

(a) Explain what economic theory predicts is likely to happen to the exchange rate if the current account position deteriorates.

(b) Speculative activity should anticipate changes in economic fundamentals such as changes in the current account position. Do the data provide any evidence for suggesting that currency speculators have correctly anticipated changes in the UK current account position?

Key terms

Exchange rate - the price at which one currency is exchanged for another.

Effective exchange rate and trade weighted exchange rate index - measures of the exchange rate of a country's currency against a basket of currencies of a country's major trading partners.

Foreign exchange markets - the markets, organised in major financial centres such as London and New York, where currencies are bought and sold.

Purchasing power parity theory - the hypothesis that long run changes in exchange rates are caused by differences in inflation rates between countries.

Exchange controls - controls on the purchase and sale of foreign currency by a country, usually through its central bank.

Applied economics

The exchange rate, 1978-1981

Between 1978 and 1981, the effective exchange rate (EER) of the pound rose by over twenty five per cent before falling back a little, as can be seen in Table 87.2. There are a number of possible reasons why there should have been such a significant change in the EER.

One important factor was the change in the oil balance on the balance of payments. 1976 had seen the first production of North Sea oil and by the early 1980s production had reached its highest level. The effect was to transform a traditional deficit on trade in oil (with the UK importing all her oil requirements) to a substantial surplus. As Table 87.2 shows, there was a £5 000 million turnaround in the oil balance. The effect of increased production was magnified by the second oil crisis of 1978-9 which increased the price of oil from approximately $15 a barrel in 1978 to $36 a barrel in 1981. Increased exports result in greater demand for pounds and hence a higher value of the pound. So the positive change in the oil balance helped increase the EER.

Table 87.2 *Factors affecting the exchange rate, 1979-1981*

		Effective exchange rate 1985 = 100	Interest rate[1] %	Change in official reserves[2] £million	Current account balance £million	Oil balance £million	Net external assets £billion
1978	Q1	105.0	6½	-46	-146		
	Q2	99.2	9	-2 026	509	-2 129.1	12.0
	Q3	100.1	10	54	151		
	Q4	99.6	12½	-311	422		
1979	Q1	101.6	13½	955	-658		
	Q2	106.9	12	68	4	-1 070.7	11.0
	Q3	111.9	14	152	310		
	Q4	107.7	14	-166	-205		
1980	Q1	113.1	17	457	-96		
	Q2	115.5	17	140	-125	60.5	16.8
	Q3	118.3	16	-223	1143		
	Q4	123.6	16	-83	1 873		
1981	Q1	127.1	14	319	2 888		
	Q2	122.7	12	-1 448	1 932	2 871.9	31.1
	Q3	114.1	12	-1 167	510		
	Q4	112.2	15	-123	1 309		

1. Bank base rate at 15 February, 15 May, 15 August, 15 November.
2. Additions to reserves (+), falls in reserves (-).

Source: adapted from CSO, *Economic Trends Annual Supplement*; CSO, *Annual Abstract of Statistics*; CSO, *United Kingdom National Accounts (Blue Book)*.

Despite the positive change in the oil balance, the current balance (total exports minus imports) deteriorated in 1978-9. This was because the economy was enjoying a boom, and imports were being sucked into the country to satisfy domestic demand. However, by the early part of 1980, the economy was spiralling downwards into deep recession, which was to see a fall of 5 per cent in GDP and nearly 20 per cent in manufacturing output before the bottom in mid-1981. That led to a sharp fall in imports which, together with the effect of North Sea oil, led to a record current account surplus in 1981. This move from deficit in 1979 to record surplus in 1981, a turnaround of approximately £7 000 million on an annual basis, must have contributed to the rise in sterling between 1979 and 1981.

A further factor which is likely to have put upward pressure on the pound was the rise in interest rates. Between 1978 and 1980, bank base rates rose from 6½ per cent to 17 per cent. This increased the interest rate differential between London and other financial centres round the world, attracting speculative flows of money into sterling. Falls in interest rates in 1980 and 1981 were followed by falls in the exchange rate in 1981.

Speculation too must have played a part in sending the EER to record levels. In 1978, there was still grave international concern about the competitiveness of the UK economy and the pound. By 1979, the pound was being seen as a petro currency. It didn't take much to look at what was happening to the oil balance to realise that the UK was likely to be in substantial surplus on current account in the early 1980s. Substantial surpluses would be likely to increase the EER, and therefore speculators bought pounds, which had the effect of further raising the EER.

There were two factors which helped prevent the rise in the pound between 1979 and 1981 being even greater than it was. First, in November 1979, the government abolished exchange controls. These had limited the outflow of money on the capital account, reducing outflows from their free market levels. Following abolition, there was a substantial outflow of capital from the UK, reflected in the increase in net external assets of the UK shown in Table 87.2.

Second, the Bank of England intervened in the foreign exchange markets, on the whole buying foreign currency in exchange for pounds (i.e. the supply of pounds increased). The fact that the Bank of England was intervening like this can be seen from the increase in the official foreign currency reserves of the UK during this period. When the exchange rate began to fall in 1981, the Bank of England reversed its policy. It began to buy pounds with foreign currency. This helped break the fall in the pound, but official foreign currency reserves fell.

Sterling against the deutschmark

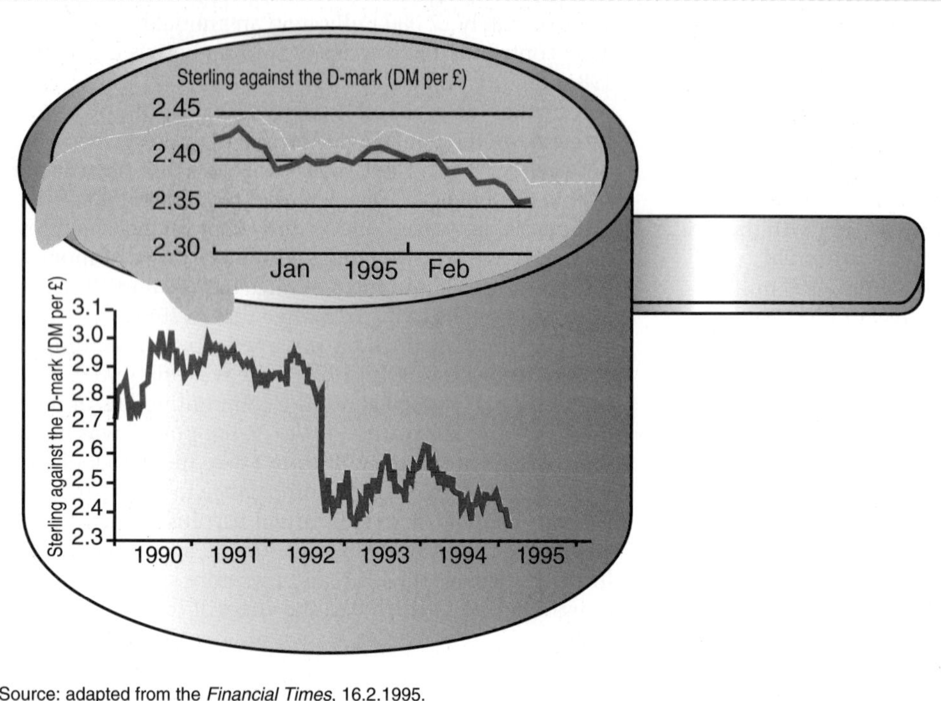

Source: adapted from the *Financial Times*, 16.2.1995.

Figure 87.6 Sterling in hot water against the deutschmark

In the second half of 1993, the value of sterling rose on the foreign exchanges. Economic fundamentals of strong growth, low inflation and a healthy current account made sterling attractive to investors. On purchasing power parity levels, the UK was, for the first time in the 1990s, 'not particularly overvalued versus the deutschmark' according to the Swiss Bank Corporation. The stable political background was also very attractive. Research by Merrill Lynch, the stockbrokers, showed clients holding 'fairly significant' overweight positions in sterling.

In the first half of 1994, the value of sterling fell sharply. Investors who had been overweight in sterling in late 1994 became sellers of sterling. They were worried about the political climate in the UK. Back bench Conservative opposition to the proposed peace plan for Northern Ireland raised the spectre of a general election which the Conservatives could lose to Labour. So too did Conservative Party feuding on the European issue. A Labour government, it is feared by foreign investors, might go for policies which would raise taxes, raise inflation and lead to a deterioration in the current account position. Current UK inflation was also a cause for concern. In January 1995, producer price inflation figures were much worse than market predictions. There were also indications that economic growth was slowing, perhaps caused by a slowdown in export orders.

The Mexican crisis was another factor in causing sterling's weakness. In late 1994, the Mexican government had been forced to devalue the Mexican Peso. This was largely unpredicted by the markets and led to a 'flight towards quality'. Having lost money over the Mexican devaluation, some investors wanted to reduce their risk and hence invest in currencies which were seen as very safe. The German deutschmark was the main beneficiary of this. The pound sterling, because it was seen as a risky currency, was a loser.

Even the low turnover on the foreign exchanges was a factor. A spokesperson for Merrill Lynch said: 'When there is less activity in the markets in general, they tend to gang up on whatever is hot at the moment. The result is that movements of currencies, and the news that generates these moves, are not necessarily in sync.'

Source: adapted from the *Financial Times*, 16.2.1995.

1. A number of different factors are mentioned in the data which affected the value of the pound in 1994 and 1995. Take each factor and explain, using diagrams, why it influenced the value of the pound at the time.

2. To what extent were the movements in the pound described in the data caused by changes in 'fundamentals' rather than by speculation?

3. In 1954, the pound was valued at 11.7 deutschmarks. By 1964, it had fallen to 11.1 deutschmarks, in 1974 to 6.0 deutschmarks and in 1984 to 3.8 deutschmarks. What factors will influence the future value of the pound against the deutschmark and what do you predict will be a possible value of the pound against the deutschmark in 2004?

unit 88 Common markets

Summary

1. In a common market, there is free movement of goods and services, and factors of production. Goods and services imported from outside the common market face a common external tariff.
2. Free trade involves harmonisation in a wide range of areas, including product standards and taxation.
3. The formation of a common market will lead to trade creation and trade diversion. The greater the trade creation and the less the trade diversion, the greater will be the welfare benefits to member countries.
4. Dynamic gains from membership include economies of scale in production. Competition is likely to increase in the short run but mergers and takeovers are likely to lessen competition amongst firms in the long run.
5. Common market spending and taxation will lead to a redistribution of resources between member countries. Inevitably some countries will gain and others will lose from the common market budget.
6. Common markets may be the first step towards complete monetary and political union between member countries.

A common market

A COMMON MARKET or CUSTOMS UNION is a group of countries between which there is free trade and which impose a COMMON EXTERNAL TARIFF on imported goods from outside the market. In theory, free trade between member countries involves goods and services as well as the factors of production.

- Land. There should be free trade in natural resources. In Europe, for instance, a British company should be free to buy land in Paris, whilst a French company should be free to own a licence to exploit North Sea oil.
- Labour. Workers should be free to work in any member country. For instance, an Italian should be able to work in London on exactly the same terms as a worker born in Birmingham.
- Capital. Capital should flow freely between countries. Of particular importance is **financial capital**. A Scottish firm should be free to borrow money in Paris to set up a factory in Italy, just as a London based firm could borrow money from a Scottish bank to invest in Wales.

Imports from outside the common market present a problem. For instance, assume that the UK imposes a tariff of 10 per cent on imports of foreign cars whilst France imposes a tariff of 20 per cent. With free trade between France and the UK, foreign importers would ship cars intended for sale in France to the UK, pay the 10 per cent tariff, and then re-export them 'tariff-free' into France. There are two ways to get round this problem.

- One way is to impose a common external tariff. All member countries agree to change their tariff structures so as to impose the same tariff on imported items. In our example, France and the UK would have to change or HARMONIZE their tariffs on cars to an agreed European Union (EU) figure.
- The other way is for member countries to impose tariffs on re-exports. In our example France could impose a 10 per cent tariff on the original price of cars imported from non-member countries.

This second solution is a feature of FREE TRADE AREAS. A free trade area differs from a common market partly because of its different approach to dealing with non-member imports. It also differs because member countries are not committed to working towards closer economic integration. In a free trade area, the sole objective is free trade between member countries.

In a common market, the goal is to establish a single market in the same way that there is a single market within an individual economy. Ultimately this involves a large number of changes including:

- no customs posts between countries; just as goods and people are free to travel between Manchester and London, so they should be free to travel between London and Milan;
- identical product standards between countries; the existence of individual national safety standards on cars, for instance, is a barrier to trade just as it would be if cars sold in London had to meet different safety

QUESTION 1

- In 1986 the European Commission proposed the introduction of a standardised two pin plug throughout the EU. The proposal was eventually dropped, but was revived again in 1994.
- In 1994, insurance companies were, for the first time, allowed to sell their insurance policies in any country in the EU so long as they conformed to the rules and regulations of their own country. Previously, an insurance company had to comply with the different rules and regulations of each country in which it wished to sell.
- In 1993, UK companies spent over £5bn acquiring companies in other EU countries
- In 1994, a group of countries, including France, Germany, Holland and Belgium, dismantled all frontier posts between their countries.
- The Maastricht Treaty laid down a timetable for the creation of a single currency in Europe.

Explain why each of these illustrates how a common market works.

requirements from cars sold in Bristol;

- harmonisation of taxes; if the tax on the same car is £2 000 more in the UK than in France, then UK residents will buy their cars in France and take them back to England, distorting the pattern of trade; equally if direct taxes on income are an average 15 per cent in France and 30 per cent in the UK, some UK workers may be tempted to go and work in France;
- a common currency; having to buy foreign exchange is a barrier to trade, especially if there are exchange rate movements; hence there should a single common market currency just as there is a single currency in the UK.

Trade creation and trade diversion

The **theory of comparative advantage** (☞ unit 84) shows that free trade between countries is likely to increase total world production. When a small number of countries form a common market, there will be gainers and losers.

TRADE CREATION is said to take place when a country moves from buying goods from a high cost country to buying them from a lower cost country. For instance, country A might have imposed a 50 per cent tariff on imported cars. As a result, all cars sold in country A were produced domestically. It now joins a customs union. The common external tariff is 50 per cent but cars from member countries can be imported free of the tariff. Country A now buys some cars from common market countries because they are lower priced than those previously produced domestically. Consumers in country A have benefited because they are able to buy cars from a cheaper source.

TRADE DIVERSION takes place when a country moves from buying goods from a low cost producer to buying them from a higher cost producer. For instance, before entry to the European Union, the UK had low or zero tariffs on imported foodstuffs. It bought from the lowest cost producers round the world such as New Zealand and the USA. After entry, the UK had to impose the much higher EU common external tariff. As a result it became cheaper to buy food from other EU countries such as France and Italy. France and Italy are higher cost producers than the USA and New Zealand for many food items.

In general the higher the tariffs imposed by a country before entry to a common market, the more likely it is that trade creation rather than trade diversion will take place. It is also true that the net gains will tend to be larger, the greater the volume of trade between the countries in the common market.

QUESTION 2

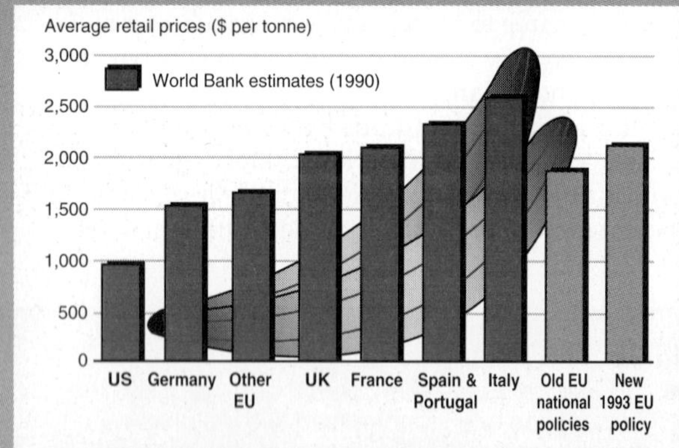

Source: adapted from IMF.

Figure 88.1 *Average retail prices of bananas*

The Single European Market came into existence on 1 January 1993. Its purpose was to abolish the remaining barriers to trade between EU countries. One of its effects was to prevent individual countries from imposing their own trade restrictions on individual products. An example of this was bananas.

Before 1993, some EU countries, notably Germany, had bought their bananas from the cheapest world source. This, in practice, was Latin American countries such as Guatemala. Other countries, notably France and the UK, had imposed tariff barriers on these bananas to allow the import of dearer bananas from ACP (African, Caribbean and Pacific) countries. These are countries which are former colonies of the UK and France. The banana growers are mainly Caribbean countries.

From 1993, the EU imposed a common tariff and quota policy on all bananas coming into the Union. The result was a rise in prices of bananas in Germany and other countries, with little reduction in price in the UK and France.

A World Bank study published in 1995 estimated that EU consumers were paying $2.3bn a year more for their bananas than if they were bought at lowest world prices. Before 1993, the extra cost of buying higher priced bananas had been only $1.6bn. Average prices in the Union had increased by 12 per cent as a result of the new regime. The World Bank report also pointed out that only $300m of the extra $2.3bn paid for bananas reached the ACP producers. The rest benefits mainly the European companies which market bananas. ACP countries would be better off if the EU abolished its banana policy and gave them direct aid instead. Alternatively, the EU should limit the distortions caused by the scheme by making quotas transferable.

Source: adapted from the *Financial Times*, 20.1.1995.

(a) Using examples from the data, distinguish between trade creation and trade diversion.

(b) (i) Using the theory of comparative advantage, explain why the ACP countries might be better off in the long run if they accepted abolition of the banana import policy in return for a guaranteed payment of $300m a year for the next 20 years. (ii) What would be the economic implications if instead of the current policy of giving banana quotas to ACP countries (which allow them to import a fixed amount of bananas into the EU tariff free), the quotas became transferable and tradeable? This would mean that any producer, whether in Africa, the Caribbean or Latin America, could buy banana quotas from ACP producers allowing them to import bananas tariff-free into the EU.

Economies of scale

Gains from trade creation are **static** gains. They occur once and for all following the creation of, or entry to, a common market. Membership of a common market may also result in **dynamic** gains or losses - gains or losses which occur over a period of time. One important such gain comes from **economies of scale** (☞ unit 20). In a common market, the potential size of the customer market is inevitably larger than in a national market. For instance, the European Union has 300 million inhabitants compared to 57 million for the UK. This means that important economies of scale can be achieved by national companies if they carve out a market for themselves throughout the common market. This is no easy task given that each country is likely to have different consumer preferences. However, there are some products, such as basic chemicals, which are demanded by all countries. Other products, such as cars, are relatively easily sold across national boundaries. Yet other products, such as cosmetics, may need different packaging for different countries, but the basic product is the same.

Economies of scale will be achieved over a period of time as companies expand internally or merge with other foreign companies. The size of the potential gains will be greater, the more homogeneous the tastes of consumers within the market. For instance, the gains are likely to be higher for a market comprising France and the UK than for the UK and Iran. Economies of scale bring benefits to consumers because average costs of production fall, and therefore prices are likely to fall too.

QUESTION 3 The Cecchini Report, published in 1988, argued that there would be a 5.3 per cent increase in national income of the European Union following the creation of the Single Market from the beginning of 1993. One major gain would arise from economies of scale. For instance, there were 50 tractor manufacturers in the EU fighting over a market similar in size to that served in the US by just 4 manufacturers. Similarly in the US there were 4 producers of domestic appliances compared to 300 in the EU.

(a) Why is there scope for increased economies of scale in the EU following 1992?
(b) (i) What benefits might consumers receive from increased economies of scale?
(ii) What might be the costs to workers?
(iii) What are the implications for merger and monopoly policy in the EU?

Competition

Another possible dynamic gain arises from increased competition between firms. A common market should eliminate restrictions on trade between member countries. Domestic industries will therefore face greater competition than before from firms in other member countries. Competition will encourage innovation, reduce costs of production and reduce prices. There will therefore be gains in productive and allocative efficiency (☞ unit 34).

Although there is likely to be greater competition in the short run, evidence suggests that this competition will be reduced in the long run. Competition will drive the least efficient firms out of the market, as the theory of perfect competition predicts. Other firms will seek to maintain monopoly profits by re-establishing control over their markets. They will do this by merging with or taking over foreign firms within the common market. Over time, the oligopolistic nature of competition in domestic markets will be recreated on a common market level. This may benefit the consumer through economies of scale but it certainly will not bring the benefits that free market economists suggest.

The Austrian school of Economics argues that competition is not necessarily beneficial to the consumer. Large international monopolies, earning considerable abnormal profit, will have the resources to devote to research, development and investment. If they fail to develop products that satisfy consumer wants, their monopoly will be lost through the process of creative destruction. Competitors will break their monopoly by creating new products. This constant development of new products is far more beneficial to consumer welfare than a few per cent off the price of existing products which might result from a perfectly competitive environment.

QUESTION 4 A study by Richard Baldwin of the Centre for Economic Policy Research, published in 1989, suggested that the gains from the 1992 programme could produce an increase of between 3.5 and 19.5 per cent in Europe's real standard of living. The central argument of the study was that, as well as increasing the efficiency of the existing capital stock, 1992 would encourage both European and other companies to make fresh investments in Europe, further boosting output and growth.

Although the boost would wear off in time, some economists argued that increased returns on capital lead to accelerated technological innovation, increasing economic growth still further.

(a) What dynamic gains were suggested by the Baldwin study?
(b) Why might 'increased returns on capital' have led to 'accelerated technological innovation'?

Transfers of resources

Common markets may differ in the size and power of their institutions. The European Union has a sizeable bureaucracy, a parliament and a large budget. Money is paid into a Union budget by member countries. The money is used to pay for administration and the implementation of Union-wide policies. In the case of the

European Union, about 70 per cent of the budget has traditionally been allocated to one area of policy - the **Common Agricultural Policy** (☞ unit 12 and 34). Any budget of any size opens up the possibility that some member countries may pay more into the budget than they receive. There may therefore be a net transfer of resources from one country to another within a common market. These represent static losses and gains (i.e. once and for all losses and gains).

Perhaps more importantly, there can also be transfers of real resources from country to country. Countries in the common market which are particularly dynamic and successful are likely to attract inflows of labour and capital. Countries which have lower growth rates are likely to suffer net capital outflows and lose some of their best workers to other economies. This could heighten regional disparities, making the richer nations relatively even richer.

The process may be magnified if the successful countries are at the geographical centre of the common market whilst the less successful countries are on the fringe. Transport and communication costs tend to be lower for companies sited at the centre and higher for those at the periphery. Hence central countries tend to have a competitive advantage over fringe countries.

Neo-classical economic theory suggests that free market forces would equalise the differences between regions. An unsuccessful region will have cheap labour and cheap land. Firms will be attracted into the region to take advantage of these. In practice, this effect seems to be very weak. Cheap labour economies can easily become branch economies. Firms set up branches in these regions, employing cheap labour to perform low productivity tasks. Tasks which have high value added are completed at headquarters in higher cost areas. The result is growing economic divergence, with poorer regions losing the most skilled of their labour force to the richer regions and being left with less dynamic and less skilled workers to do less well paid jobs.

Monetary and political union

An internal common market where there are different currencies in each country imposes costs upon producers. Therefore a common market implies a move to a common currency. A common currency implies common monetary and fiscal policies. The economic implications of monetary union are discussed further in unit 98.

A common market may eventually lead to political union. Political union inevitably involves a loss of national sovereignty. Decisions which previously were made at national level will now be made at community level. This may have economic implications in that a member country will lose the ability to direct its economic affairs to its own advantage. On the other hand, it can be argued that any country which is very **open** (i.e. exports a high proportion of its national product) has already lost most of its ability to direct its own economic affairs because so much of its economy depends upon the spending and saving decisions of foreigners.

Key terms

Common market - a group of countries between which there is free trade in products and factors of production, and which imposes a common external tariff on imported goods from outside the market.
Common external tariff - a common tariff set by a group of countries imposed on imported goods from non-member countries.
Harmonization - establishing common standards, rules and levels on everything from safety standards to tariffs, taxes and currencies.
Free trade area - a group of countries between which there is free trade in goods and services but which allows member countries to set their own level of tariffs against non-member countries.
Trade creation - the switch from purchasing products from a high cost producer to a lower cost producer.
Trade diversion - the switch from purchasing products from a low cost producer to a higher cost producer.

Applied economics

The European Union

The historical background

At the end of the Second World War, Europe's economies were shattered. It was realised by many western politicians that this was the direct outcome of unwise political decisions made at the end of the First World War when Germany was economically penalised for having lost the war. Huge war reparations and the isolation of Germany politically had given German fascists the chance to gain support and power, which in turn led to the

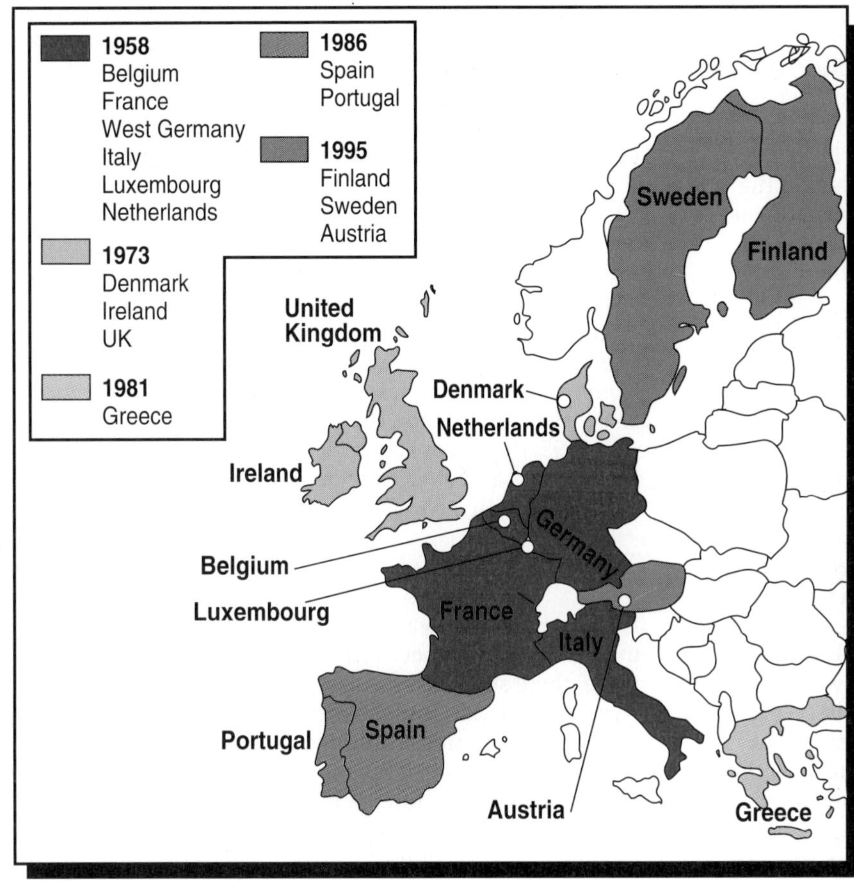

Figure 88.2 *EU countries, 1958-1995*

Second World War. Some had a vision of co-operation and a united peaceful Europe. This vision led to the creation of today's European Union (EU).

The first step on the road to today's EU was the formation in 1952 of the European Coal and Steel Community (ECSC) by France, Germany, Italy, Luxembourg, Belgium and the Netherlands. This created a free trade area for coal and steel, at the time crucial industries in those countries. It enabled the six countries to protect their industries more from US competition. Greater output then enabled ECSC producers to reduce costs through greater economies of scale and thus become more competitive.

In 1957, the European Atomic Energy Community was formed by the same six countries to encourage the growth of the peaceful use of nuclear power. By the time the treaty had been signed, negotiations were well under way for the creation of the far more ambitious European Economic Community (EEC) or Common Market. This came into existence on 1 January 1958 after the signing of the Treaty of Rome in 1957.

The Treaty of Rome established a customs union, with provisions for the phased withdrawal of all tariffs between the six member countries and the imposition of a common external tariff on goods coming into the Community. This was finally completed in 1986. The Treaty also contained provisions which would in future allow the free flow not just of goods but also of capital and of labour between countries. Another aspect was the creation of a European policy on competition and restrictive trade practices.

The Treaty of Rome created a number of important institutions.

- The **European Commission**, based in Brussels, is the equivalent of the civil service in the UK. At the top are 17 Commissioners, each with a particular responsibility for an area of community policy. The Commission is responsible for implementing agreed policies and for proposing new policies. It can be a very powerful body, partly because it is responsible for the day to day running of Community policies, but also because it is the main agent of change and progress in policy.
- The **European Council of Ministers** is a powerful body too. It is made up of a ministerial representative from each member state. When agriculture is being discussed, then countries are represented by their agriculture ministers. When broad economic issues are discussed, it will be finance ministers who are present. New policies put forward by the European Commission are either approved or rejected by the Council of Ministers. Hence, the Council of Ministers is the most important decision-making body. In most areas, there has to be a unanimous vote for a policy to be approved. However, in some areas, only a majority vote is needed.
- The **European Parliament**, based in Strasbourg, is made up of elected representatives (MEPs) from the member states. The European Parliament is a relatively weak body. Until recently, it had almost no decision-making powers at all and even since the Treaty of Maastricht (1992), when its powers were increased, it has been able to do little more than rubber stamp decisions made elsewhere. The intention is that the European Parliament will, over time, increase its powers to become more like a national parliament.
- The **European Court of Justice**, which meets in Luxembourg, is another powerful body. It is the ultimate court of law and is responsible for making judgements on EU law. It regularly passes judgements which have a significant impact on individual countries or the entire community. For instance, its judgement on equal pension rights in 1992 forced the UK government to move towards equalising the state retiring age for men and women in the UK at 65.

The Treaty of Rome envisaged the creation of a number of common policies. The first of these to be implemented under Article 39 of the Treaty was the **Common Agricultural Policy** (CAP). This was established in 1962 and is discussed in much greater detail in units 12 and 34. Article 85 of the Treaty covers **competition policy**, aspects of which are discussed in unit 40. **Regional policy** has been used to reduce income and wealth differentials between member countries. This is discussed in unit 69. **Transport policy**, covered in Articles 3 and 74-84 of the Treaty, has been difficult to implement because national governments have been reluctant to cede powers to the Community over transport issues. However, both competition policy and the Single Market have had a considerable impact on national transport policies. **Social Policy**, covered in Articles 117-128 of the Treaty, envisages the creation of a single market for labour where all workers in the community are covered by common laws. Social policy was given a major boost by the signing of the Treaty of Maastricht in 1991 which contained the Social Charter, discussed in unit 52.

The UK had decided not to join the EEC (now the EU) in 1958, feeling that it would turn out to be largely irrelevant in European terms and preferring to maintain strong links with the USA and its colonies and ex-colonies in the Commonwealth. Instead, it helped create the **European Free Trade Association** (EFTA) in 1960 along with Austria, Denmark, Norway, Portugal, Sweden and Switzerland. Finland joined a little later. EFTA was a free trade area rather than a customs union. There was no intention that EFTA would develop into anything more than an association which dealt with trade, unlike the EEC where there was a vision from the start that a united European state could be formed. The UK quickly recognised that it had probably made the wrong decision and in 1962 applied to the join the EEC. The French blocked the proposal, fearing that Britain's entry would destroy the dominance of France and Germany. Ten years later, the UK was again negotiating for entry and this time, along with Denmark and Eire, was successful in its application. The three countries joined in 1973, enlarging the community to nine members.

An attempt was made in the 1970s to move the EEC in the direction of a single currency. The turbulent economic conditions at the time meant that little was achieved. However, in 1979, the **European Monetary System** was established which became the framework for the move towards a single currency in the 1980s and 1990s. This is discussed further in unit 98.

The 1980s saw the further enlargement of the Community. Greece joined in 1981 whilst Spain and Portugal joined in 1986. This helped shift the political balance in the Community and increased the relative importance of agriculture. The 1980s also saw the signing of possibly the most important act since the Treaty of Rome. The Single European Act (SEA) of 1985, which came into force in 1987, committed member states to take the second step towards the creation of a genuine common market by 1 January 1993. The 1950s and 1960s had seen the removal of tariff and quota barriers on trade in most goods between member countries. The SEA committed governments to removing the many other barriers to trade which still existed. This is discussed in further detail below. The SEA saw a change in the name of the community. To show that the Community was now not just about economic issues, the 'economic' was dropped from EEC and the Community was now officially called the European Community (EC).

In 1989, the European Commission put forward proposals for a Social Charter which would guarantee workers' rights. This Social Charter became the Social Chapter in the Maastricht Treaty in 1992. This Treaty was another important stepping stone in the move towards a united Europe. It laid down a timetable for the creation of a single currency. It also established a framework for co-operation in foreign policy between member countries. To signify the move forward by the Treaty, the name of the Community was changed from the European Community to the European Union (EU).

In 1995, three more countries joined the Union, Austria, Finland and Sweden. The opportunities and problems associated with enlargement are discussed below.

The Single Market

Although the removal of tariff and quota barriers between member countries between 1958 and 1968 promoted free trade, there still existed substantial barriers to trade. First, barriers existed in trade in services. For instance, UK insurance companies could not sell most types of insurance in France or Spain. There were legal restrictions on road haulage by foreign transport in domestic markets. Different regulations prevented UK companies borrowing in France, in spite of the fact that French companies might be able to borrow in London. Second, different standards presented a major obstacle to trade in goods. For instance, a tractor manufacturer had to produce a different tractor for sale in each member country because each imposed different safety regulations. Third, governments tended to buy only from domestic companies (government purchases are known as 'public procurement'). The French government would only buy computers from a French manufacturer, whilst the UK tended to buy military equipment only from UK companies. Lastly, everything from customs posts, import and export forms to different VAT rates and corporation taxes imposed heavy administrative costs on companies trading across country boundaries.

In 1985, member countries signed the Single European Act. This committed members to removing all trade obstacles by 31 December 1992. To get round the problems of trying to harmonise 3 000 European product standards, the EU adopted the principle of mutual recognition. This meant that so long as a manufacturer made its products conform to the rules and regulations of one country in the EU, it could be sold throughout the EU even if it did not conform to the rules and regulations of other countries. So a UK tractor manufacturer can sell a British made tractor in Italy even if it does not conform to Italian safety regulations, so long as it conforms to UK safety regulations.

The benefits of a single European market were put forward in the Cecchini report published by the European Commission in 1988 and are summarised in Table 88.1.

Table 88.1 *EU gains from the internal market*

	% of GDP
Removal of barriers affecting trade	0.2 - 0.3
Removal of barriers affecting overall production	2.0 - 2.4
Total gains from removing barriers	2.2 - 2.7
Exploiting economies of scale more fully	2.1
Gains from intensified competition reducing business ineffectiveness and monopoly profits	1.6
Total gains from market integration	2.1 - 3.7
Total gains	4.3 - 6.4

Source: European Commission.

Removal of border controls, technical regulations and other adminstrative hurdles could increase Union GDP by up to 2.7 per cent. Exploitation of greater economies of scale because producers will now be able to sell across the whole European market rather than in just their domestic markets will add up to 2.1 per cent of GDP. The resulting increase in competition, particularly in the area of public procurement, would increase GDP by up to 1.6 per cent.

These one-off gains would amount to between 4.2 and 6.4 per cent of GDP. However, the dynamic gains might be even greater. In a study by Richard Baldwin (1989), it was estimated that the gains could be up to four times as great as the Cecchini report estimated. This was because the static boost in GDP would lead to an investment boom as more capital was needed to produce the extra output created by the 1992 process. This once and for all increase in investment could add another 15 per cent to GDP on top of the extra 5 per cent (a middle estimate of the 4.2 and 6.4 per cent gain) which might be expected from the static gains.

In all this process, there will be gainers and losers. Inefficient national companies which had been protected from international competition by relying upon public procurement contracts would either have to become more efficient or go bankrupt. Either of these would be likely to lead to a loss of jobs. However, overall the Cecchini report estimated that a total of between 1.75 and 5 million extra jobs would be created in the Union in the medium term.

Enlargement of the union

Perhaps the most important reason why the UK joined the Union was a belief that membership would increase the growth rate of the country. In Britain's case, increased prosperity was to come from the benefits of greater trade. However, other applicants have also been aware that there are transfers of resources within the Union and that they might be significant beneficiaries of such transfers. Transfers can come from the EU budget, such as regional grants or subsidies paid to farmers under CAP. There can also be significant transfers of private sector capital as firms set up in a country to take advantage of selling into its markets or to exploit cheap labour or land. It is difficult to establish whether the UK did benefit from joining. However, it is clearer in the case of Spain and Portugal whose growth rates went up in the second half of the 1980s.

These transfers can pose a threat to existing members and in part explain the opposition of some members to the enlargement of the Union. By the mid-1990s, there was a considerable queue of countries wanting to join the EU, including Eastern European countries such as Poland and Hungary, southern European countries such as Albania and Slovenia, and an Asian country, Turkey. The threats to existing members are mirror images of the opportunities to applicant countries.

- Existing members are afraid that their markets will be swamped by cheap imports from these countries. The markets which are most at risk are politically sensitive markets, such as agriculture and textiles, where the EU has traditionally imposed high tariff barriers to protect domestic industries.
- There is a fear that the contributions of rich countries to the EU budget would rise considerably following enlargement. If much poorer countries join the community, and regional and CAP payments are maintained, it is inevitable that there will be large budget transfers to the new members, paid for by existing members.
- Some countries fear that enlargement will delay plans to move towards even greater economic and political union. It would be difficult, for instance, to implement a single currency in 1999 if in that year 3 countries joined the Union.
- Movements of labour and capital can also pose problems. There is a fear that capital would move to newly joined cheap labour countries whilst workers would move in large numbers from these countries to existing member countries, attracted by much higher wages.

So what might develop is a range of membership or association options. In 1992, the EU signed an agreement with EFTA, the European Free Trade Association (which at the time comprised Switzerland, Iceland, Norway, Liechtenstein, Finland, Sweden and Austria), extending to them EU freedom of movement of goods, services, people and capital. This created a European Economic Area (EEA). Industrial tariffs between EFTA and the EU were already zero but the new agreement further reduced barriers to trade in agricultural goods. So EFTA countries get the benefit of free trade with Europe but without the complications of the next step, a common market. It could be that countries like Estonia and Latvia will chose to join EFTA initially before applying to join the EU. It could also come about that the EU will offer second tier membership to countries. They could join the free trade area without necessarily being given access to agricultural markets, regional funds or a common currency. In the longer term, Eastern European countries and Mediterranean countries such as Malta, Cyprus and Turkey are likely to become members. In the even longer term, North African countries such as Tunisia and Morocco may well want to join too, creating greater opportunities but also greater problems for the enlarged Union.

Enlarging the EU

'The Visegrad-4 countries are two and a half times more agricultural and less than one-third as rich as the EU-15. Adding just the Visegrad-4 countries to the EU would double the budgetary cost of CAP and increase the total budget cost of the EU by 70 per cent because the 4 countries would also be entitled to large amounts of structural aid.'

Table 88.2 *European countries: selected indicators 1992*

	EU members				Visegrad-4[1]				Other Eastern European	
	UK	France	Germany	Italy	Poland	Hungary	Czech Republic	Slovak Republic	Bulgaria	Romania
GDP per head ($)	17 790	22 260	23 030	20 460	1 910	2 970	2 450	1 930	1 339	1 130
PPP estimate of GNP per capita, United States = 100	72.4	83.0	89.1	76.7	21.1	24.8	31.0	24.3	22.2	11.9
Population (millions)	57.8	57.4	80.6	57.8	38.4	10.3	10.3	5.3	8.5	22.7
Agriculture, % of total GDP	2	3	2	3	7	7	6	6	14	19
Exports, average annual growth rate 1980-92 (%)	3.5	5.2	4.6	4.1	3.0	1.6	na	na	na	- 10.4
Telephone mainlines per thousand persons	442	495	483	388	86	96	na	na	na	102

Source: adapted from World Bank, *World Development Indicators.*

[1]The Visegrad-4, Hungary, Poland, the Czech Republic and Slovakia, are the four most developed countries in Eastern Europe.

Figure 88.3 *EU countries in 1995 and future potential members*

Prepare a report for the European Commission on the potential benefits and problems of enlarging the European Union to include Eastern European countries. In the report:

1. give a brief outline of the history of the EU to date;
2. summarise the main advantages of EU membership for existing members;
3. discuss the likely impact enlargement would have on existing members and the Eastern European countries which joined concerning
   (i) agriculture and the CAP budget;
   (ii) non-agricultural industries and trade in goods;
   (iii) services and their trade;
   (iv) contributions to and receipts from the EU budget;
   (v) migration between countries.

INVESTIGATIONS 7

A. The Common Agricultural Policy

Aims

- To describe the operation of the Common Agricultural Policy.
- To assess its impact on an individual farmer in the UK, and on an individual family.
- To evaluate proposed reforms of CAP, with particular reference to an individual farmer and an individual family.
- To argue the case for a particular set of reforms, considering them both from the viewpoint of economic efficiency and equity.

Research activity

This is likely to be best done as a group task. A group could undertake the research and then individuals could write reports based upon the group's findings.

Your first task is to find a farmer who is willing to be interviewed. One of your teaching group may have a parent, or other relation or friend who is a farmer. Alternatively, write off to the local branch of the NFU (National Farmers' Union).

Prepare a questionnaire. You want to find out what effect the Common Agriculture Policy has on the farmer, what could be the effect of proposed reforms and what reforms the farmer thinks are necessary. For instance, what crops does the farmer grow which are covered by price regulation under CAP? What livestock is reared which is subject to intervention pricing or quotas? What is the effect of set-aside on the farmer's activities? What does the farmer think about proposals to cut farm subsidies? Does the farmer think that he or she should be paid an allowance for 'keeping the country tidy'?

Agree with the farmer upon a place and a time for the interview. This could be in school or college, or it could be at the farm. Before the interview, outline the sort of questions that you will be asking at the interview. State that the more facts and figures that he or she can give, the better you will be able to understand the effect of CAP on farming. You may wish to record the interview rather than taking notes at the time. Permission to do so **must** be asked in advance.

Before the interview, familiarise yourself as much as possible about the operations of CAP and proposed reforms. For instance, go to your local public library and undertake a newspaper and magazine search for any articles about CAP published over the last 6 months. Use an index to help you with your search. The librarian will be able to tell you what indexes are available in the library. Follow the news on radio and television. Listen in particular to the daily radio broadcast on Radio 4, Farming Today, at 6.10 a.m.

At the same time as you are working through the process of interviewing a farmer, consider the impact of CAP on your own family and other consumers throughout the EU. How much does it cost taxpayers to fund CAP? How much extra does the average family have to pay in higher food prices because it has to buy expensive EU food rather than food from outside the EU available at lower world prices?

Structuring your report

Introduction Outline the aim of your investigation. The aim should be put in the form of a hypothesis or question which will allow you to come to some conclusions.
Economic theory Outline the economic theory you will use in your analysis. This will include concepts such as demand, supply, price, intervention in markets economic efficiency.
Techniques used to collect your data Outline how you collected your data.
The Common Agricultural Policy Explain briefly how the Common Agricultural Policy works. Outline, also briefly, any proposed reforms of CAP currently being discussed.
Effects of CAP on an individual farmer Explain your research findings. Assess the impact of CAP on the prices received for produce by the farmer, the influence CAP has on levels of output, and the effect of CAP on costs, revenues and profits of the farm.
CAP and the consumer What is the impact of CAP on the taxpayers and consumer in the EC? How much lower could the annual food bill of your family be if CAP were abolished and food were available at world prices?
Analysis of proposed reforms What effect would proposed reforms have on the individual farm surveyed? For instance, what would be the effect on prices, output, revenues and profits? What would be the effect on the taxpayer and the consumer?
Evaluation of reforms Outline what you think would be an equitable and efficient reform of CAP. When coming to a conclusion, consider the impact of your proposals on the farmer you have interviewed, as well as on the average family.
Sources Outline the sources of information you used. Evaluate critically the reliability of the information given by the interviewee. What data would you have liked to have obtained but could not?
Bibliography Write down a list of your sources in alphabetical order.

Other suggestions

Instead of considering the impact of the CAP on farmers and on individuals, it would be possible to consider the impact of the 1992 process on a firm and on individual families. Find out as much as possible from books, newspapers and magazines about the Single European Market before interviewing a local business person. Evaluate the costs and benefits to the firm, to a household as a consumption unit, and to a household as a provider of factors of production, particularly labour.

Alternatively, consider the impact of the moves towards a single European currency. What was the UK's experience of membership of the ERM between 1990 and 1992? What effect did it have on a particular business or a particular family? Should the UK rejoin the ERM? Who, in the UK, would benefit and who would lose from the completion of a single currency with the UK included in the currency union?

B. Comparative advantage

Aims

- To undertake a household survey.
- To present the findings of the survey.
- To apply economic theory in order to analyse and account for patterns of world trade.
- To evaluate reasons for the lack of international competitiveness of UK industry.
- To assess how British industry and the UK government could improve the competitiveness of industry.

Research activity

Your first task is to survey the contents of your house. Select 50 items at random and for each write down its country of origin. Then choose 10 goods from your list. These should represent a variety of different goods, rather than be a bundle of similar goods. No more than 25 per cent of the goods should be of British origin. Include if possible the family car.

You now need to find reasons why the goods you have selected from your survey are produced in a particular country. Use the theories of trade that you have learned (such as the theory of comparative advantage) to formulate a hypothesis for each good about the reasons for its origin. Then attempt to find evidence to support or refute the hypothesis. For instance, does the country of origin enjoy the benefit of cheap labour, or abundant reserves of a particular raw material? Has the country a reputation for high quality design or manufacture of the good? Do trade statistics show that the country is a particularly strong exporter of the good?

A wide variety of statistics about world trade and world economies are available in publications from the UN (United Nations), the World Trade Organisation (WTO, formerly GATT, the General Agreement on Tariffs and Trade), UNCTAD (United Nations Conference on Trade and Development), the IMF (International Monetary Fund), OECD (Organisation for Economic Co-operation and Development) and the World Bank (IBRD, the International Bank for Reconstruction and Development). Large public reference libraries tend to take a variety of these publications but exactly what is available varies from library to library. Ask the librarian for help in locating what they carry in stock.

CSO publish several publications detailing UK trade. The standard reference source is *UK Balance of Payments (Pink Book)*. Some statistics are published in the *Annual Abstract of Statistics* (updated monthly in the Monthly Digest of Statistics) whilst detailed figures are given in *Overseas Trade Statistics of the UK*.

In addition, quality newspapers and magazines publish occasional articles about world trade in particular commodities. It should be relatively easy to find articles about world trade in cars, clothes or shoes for instance. Use whatever indexes are available in your local large public reference library. For instance, the *Financial Times* and the *Economist* produce indexes to their publications, whilst the *Research Index*, published by Business Surveys Ltd., covers 100 newspapers and magazines on a monthly basis. Your library may have some of these publications on CD-Rom.

Structuring your report

Introduction Outline the aim of your investigation. The aim should be put in the form of a hypothesis or question which will allow you to come to some conclusions.
Trade theory Describe briefly one or more theories of trade. Identify the main factors which are likely to explain why world trade takes place. In the light of these factors, state the hypotheses you formulated about the reasons for the origin of each good.
Techniques used to collect your data Outline how you collected your data.
Analysis of survey results To what extent does evidence support or refute your original hypotheses? In some cases, you will have found it more difficult to gather evidence than in others. Don't be afraid of stating this. Equally, don't be afraid of saying that the evidence refutes your original hypothesis. In some cases, it may be unclear as to why a particular country should have produced a particular product.
Evaluation On the basis of your analysis, state what you think British firms need to do if they are to regain market share in the domestic market and gain increased market share abroad? What policies should governments pursue to help them achieve this?
Sources Outline the sources of information you used. What problems did you encounter in gathering relevant data? What data would you have liked to have obtained but could not? To what extent were the data reliable?
Bibliography Write down a list of your sources in alphabetical order.

Other suggestions

Instead of looking at a number of different goods for a number of different countries, it would be possible to concentrate on the reasons for trade for a particular economy, such as Hong Kong, Singapore, Japan or France. Describe the trade flows from the country and then assess the extent to which theories of trade can account for these particular patterns.

Alternatively, it would be possible to consider changing patterns of trade for a particular good or commodity. For instance, how has world trade in cars changed over the past 30 years? Can economic theory account for this changing pattern of trade?

You could also choose a particular good and consider how its UK production and trade have changed over time. What factors might account for the changes you have found?

Unit 89 Unemployment

Summary

1. Unemployment is a stock concept, measuring the number of people out of work at a point in time.
2. Unemployment will increase if the number of workers losing jobs is greater than the number of people gaining jobs.
3. The costs of unemployment include financial costs to the unemployed, to taxpayers, and to local and national economies. They also include non-financial costs such as possible increased vandalism or increased suicides.

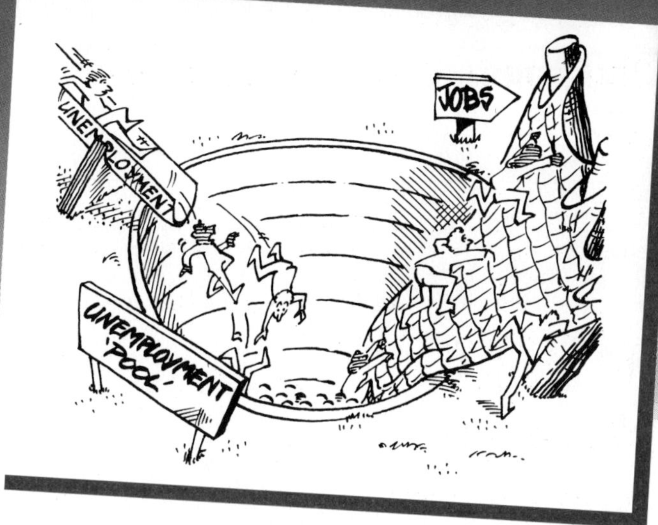

The measurement of unemployment

Unemployment, the number of people out of work, is measured at a point in time. It is a **stock concept** (☞ unit 115). However, the level of unemployment will change over time. Millions of people seek jobs each year in the UK. Young people leave school, college or university seeking work. Former workers who have taken time out of the workforce, for instance to bring up children, seek to return to work. Workers who have lost their jobs, either because they have resigned or because they have been made redundant, search for new jobs. Equally, millions of workers lose their jobs. They may retire, or leave work to look after children or they may resign or be made redundant from existing jobs.

Unemployment in an economy with a given labour force will fall if the number of workers gaining jobs is greater than the number of people losing jobs. In 1994, for instance, between 290 000 and 400 000 workers a month lost their jobs. However, the numbers gaining jobs were slightly higher per month than the numbers losing jobs. The result was a net fall in unemployment over the year. This flow of workers into or out of the stock of unemployed workers is summarised in Figure 89.1.

Unemployment will also increase if there is a rise in the number of people seeking work but the number of jobs in the economy remains static. During most years in the 1970s and 1980s, there was a rise in the number of school leavers entering the job market as well as more women wanting a job in the UK. It can be argued that at least some of the increase in unemployment in these two decades was a reflection of the inability of the UK economy to provided sufficient new jobs for these extra workers in the labour force.

The costs of unemployment

Long term unemployment is generally considered to be a great social evil. This is perhaps not surprising in view of the following costs of unemployment.

Costs to the unemployed and their dependants The people who are likely to lose the most from unemployment are the unemployed themselves. One obvious cost is the loss of income that could have been earned had the person been in a job. Offset against this is the value of any benefits that the worker might receive

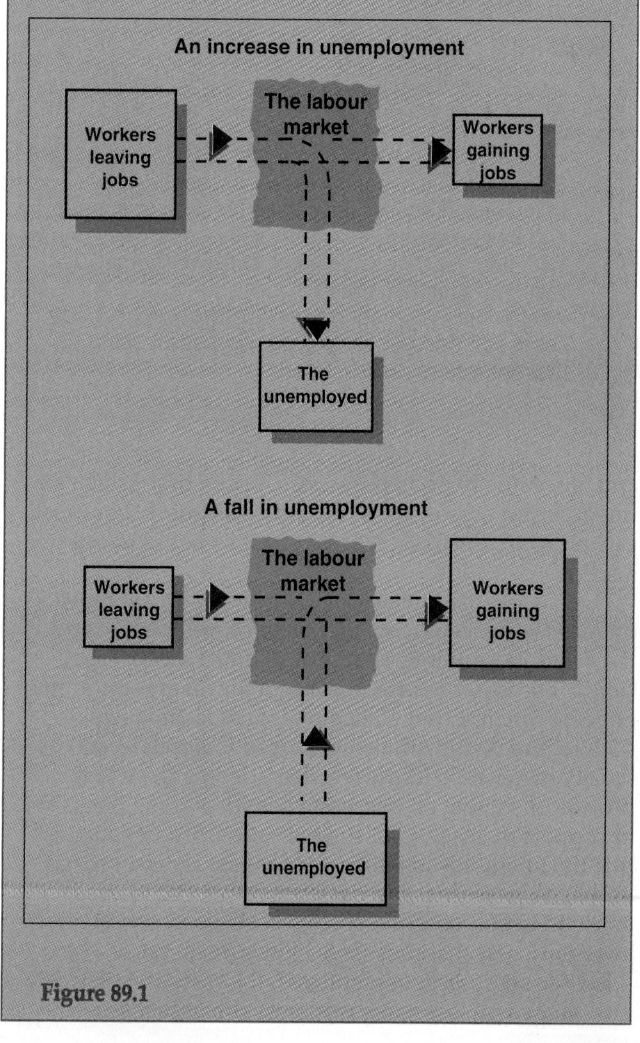

Figure 89.1

QUESTION 1

Table 89.1 *Unemployment flows, 1994*

Thousands

		August	Sept	October	Nov	Dec
Under 25						
Male	Inflow	83.7	79.4	71.8	72.0	68.9
	Outflow	76.5	82.0	108.4	77.3	63.8
Female	Inflow	52.6	48.4	47.6	39.5	32.9
	Outflow	44.9	53.8	66.5	45.5	38.1
25-44						
Male	Inflow	99.2	95.7	102.9	104.2	102.5
	Outflow	111.3	113.9	130.6	112.1	96.9
Female	Inflow	43.6	37.8	37.2	37.9	31.6
	Outflow	37.8	49.6	49.8	41.4	34.5
Over 45						
Male	Inflow	41.7	41.1	45.0	47.2	43.7
	Outflow	51.7	50.4	54.9	51.5	46.3
Female	Inflow	19.9	16.0	15.9	18.0	14.2
	Outflow	16.8	23.3	21.0	19.7	16.0
All ages						
Male	Inflow	224.6	216.6	229.7	223.6	215.2
	Outflow	239.7	246.5	293.8	240.8	206.9
Female	Inflow	116.3	102.2	100.6	95.4	78.7
	Outflow	99.4	126.6	137.5	106.7	88.6

Source: adapted from Department of Employment, *Employment Gazette.*

(a) Explain in which months unemployment (i) increased and (ii) decreased for each age group and by gender.
(b) Was unemployment higher or lower in August 1994 than in December 1994?
(c) When unemployment overall is falling, suggest why some age and gender groups might have rising unemployment.

and any value placed on the extra leisure time which an unemployed person has at his or her disposal. For most unemployed it is likely that they will be net financial losers.

The costs to the unemployed, however, do not finish there. Evidence suggests that unemployed people and their families suffer in a number of other ways. One simple but very important problem for them is the stigma of being unemployed. Unemployment is often equated with failure both by the unemployed themselves and by society in general. Many feel degraded by the whole process of signing on, receiving benefit and not being able to support themselves or their families. Studies suggest that the unemployed suffer from a wide range of social problems including above average incidence of stress, marital breakdown, suicide, physical illness and mental instability, and that they have higher death rates.

For the short term unemployed, the costs are relatively low. Many will lose some earnings, although a few who receive large redundancy payments may benefit financially from having lost their job. The social and psychological costs are likely to be limited too.

However, the long term unemployed are likely to be major losers on all counts. The long term unemployed suffer one more cost. Evidence suggests that the longer the period out of work, the less likely it is that the unemployed person will find a job. There are two reasons for this. First, being out of work reduces the human capital of workers. They lose work skills and are not being trained in the latest developments in their occupation. Second, employers use length of time out of work as a crude way of sifting through applicants for a job. For an employer, unemployment is likely to mean that the applicant is, to some extent, deskilled. There is a fear that the unemployed worker will not be capable of doing the job after a spell of unemployment. It could show that the worker has personality problems and might be a disruptive employee. It could also be an indication that other employers have turned down the applicant for previous jobs and hence it would be rational to save time and not consider the applicant for this job. The long term unemployed are then in a catch-22 situation. They can't get a job unless they have recent employment experience. But they can't get recent employment experience until they get a job.

Costs to local communities Costs to local communities are more difficult to establish. Some have suggested that unemployment, particularly amongst the young, leads to increased crime, violence on the streets and vandalism. Areas of high unemployment tend to become run down. Shops go out of business. Households have no spare money to look after their properties and their gardens. Increased vandalism further destroys the environment.

Costs to taxpayers The cost to the taxpayer is a heavy one. On the one hand, government has to pay out increased benefits. On the other hand, government loses revenue because these workers would have paid taxes if they had been employed. For instance, they would have paid income tax and National Insurance contributions on their earnings. They would also have paid more in VAT and excise duties because they would have been able to spend more. So taxpayers not only pay more taxes to cover for increased government spending but they also have to pay more because they have to make up the taxes that the unemployed would have paid if they had been in work.

Costs to the economy as a whole Taxpayers paying money to the unemployed is not a loss for the economy as a whole. It is a **transfer payment** (☞ unit 58) which redistributes existing resources within the economy. The actual loss to the whole economy is two-fold. Firstly there is the loss of output which those workers now unemployed could have produced had they been in work. The economy could have produced more goods and services which would then have been available for consumption. Secondly there are the social costs such as increased violence and depression which are borne by the unemployed and the communities in which they live.

QUESTION 2 In a study of 6 000 employed and unemployed workers, a team of academics found that the unemployed had poor psychological health. They were more likely to be depressed, less likely to mix with people in work and had little access to social support networks or to information about jobs. One of the team, Richard Lampard of Warwick University, concluded that unemployment directly increases the risk of marriage break-up, finding that the chances of the marriage of an unemployed person ending in the following year are 70 per cent higher than those of a person who has never been out of work.

The study also found that men in low-paid insecure jobs suffered almost the same level of psychological distress as those who were out of work altogether. It was found that there was a close correlation between perceived job security and psychological well-being. Women were found to be just as distressed by lack of paid work, but less affected by the prospect of an insecure low-paid job. .

Source: adapted from *The Guardian*, 10.3.1994.

(a) What problems face the unemployed, according to the article?
(b) Why might these problems give rise to costs not just for the unemployed but also for society as a whole?

Applied economics

Unemployment

Measures of unemployment

In economic theory, the unemployed are defined as those without a job but who are seeking work at current wage rates. Measuring the number of unemployed in an economy, however, is more difficult than economic theory might suggest. There are two basic ways in which unemployment can be calculated.

- Government can undertake a survey of the population to identify the employed and the unemployed. This is the approach taken in countries such as the USA, Japan and Sweden. The UK government does a quarterly survey of the workforce, called the Labour Force Survey, but this does not provide the main unemployment statistic for the UK economy.
- The government can count all those who register as unemployed. In some countries, a register of the unemployed is kept by trade unions because unemployment benefit is linked with union membership. In the UK, before 1982, the official monthly unemployment count was based on the numbers who had signed on at Jobcentres. The count was then changed to those who were claiming benefit for being unemployed from the Department of Health and Social Security (now the Department of Social Security, DSS).

How many unemployed?

Underestimation The way in which unemployment is calculated is very important because the method used to some extent determines the number of people officially counted as unemployed. For instance, during the 1980s, the UK government made a number of important changes in the method of calculating the numbers unemployed. Critics would argue that these changes mean that the unemployment figures in the UK now underestimate the number of unemployed.

- In November 1981, males over 60 were offered higher supplementary benefit rates to induce them to declare themselves as retired rather than claim unemployment benefit which would have put them on the register of the unemployed. This cut the numbers unemployed by an estimated 37 000.
- Before October 1982, anyone registered with a Jobcentre as seeking work and not in paid employment was counted as unemployed. Registration at a Jobcentre was a condition for receiving any form of unemployment benefits.
- In October 1982, the count was transferred from Jobcentres to the DHSS. There was a 190 000 fall in the number of unemployed. Most of these were women who had registered at Jobcentres because they were seeking work but were unable to claim benefits because their husbands were earning too much and because they were unable to claim National Insurance benefits in their own right.
- In March 1983, another 162 000 non-working males over 60 left the count when they no longer had to register as unemployed in order to be given free contributions to the National Insurance Fund.
- In March 1986, 50 000 disappeared from the register when a two week time lag in counting the unemployed was introduced.
- In July 1986, the government changed the method of calculating the percentage unemployment rate. Before 1986, the total number unemployed was divided by the numbers of employed and unemployed. After May 1986, the percentage unemployment rate was calculated by dividing the unemployed by the total of employed, unemployed, self-employed and HM Forces. By making the denominator larger, the government cut the percentage unemployment rate by 1.5 per cent.
- A further 50 000 disappeared in September 1988 when no youngster under the age of 18 was allowed to register as unemployed. It was argued that any unemployed 16 or 17 year old could not be genuinely unemployed because all were guaranteed a place on the

Youth Training Scheme.

- It can also be argued that the government has put greater pressure on the long term unemployed either to join a training scheme or to go on the Enterprise Allowance Scheme (☞ unit 57) through its Restart Programme introduced in 1986. It did this by threatening to withdraw unemployment benefits from those who refused. Exactly how many joined government schemes unwillingly is impossible to estimate.

The official UK count also does not capture a large number of hidden unemployed workers. These are mostly women who never signed on at Jobcentres or who now are not eligible for benefit but who would accept employment if offered. The size of this hidden unemployment can be gauged from the fact that 220 000 workers disappeared from the workforce between 1980 and 1983 at a time when unemployment rose from 1.6 million to 3.1 million. Yet between 1983 and 1986 the workforce rose by 1.2 million and the number of females in employment rose by 700 000 at a time when unemployment hovered at just above the 3 million level. Equally, in the 1990-92 recession the workforce fell from 28.5 million in the second quarter of 1990 to 27.8 million in the first quarter of 1993, a disappearance of 700 000 workers. The fall in unemployment in the recovery from 3.0 million in the first quarter of 1993 to 2.5 million in the last quarter of 1994 was half accounted for by a growth in jobs in the economy, but the other half was caused by workers no longer signing on as unemployed.

Overestimation Some economists argue that the official UK count vastly overestimates the numbers unemployed. They argue that more accurate figures could be obtained if the following were removed from the official count.

- They argue that there are a large number of officially unemployed workers not actively seeking work and who therefore cannot be called 'unemployed'.
- The severely disabled and the mentally or physically handicapped are unemployable and therefore again should be stripped out of any calculation of unemployment.
- Some workers have jobs in the black economy but continue to claim benefits.
- Workers who are between jobs, for instance those workers out of work for four weeks or less, should not be included as part of the unemployment total as they may not actually be 'unemployed'.

Labour Force Survey and claimant counts

There are two main ways in which unemployment is measured in the UK. The first, which has been in place since 1982, is based on a complete count of all who sign on for benefits and pass eligibility tests for unemployment. Unemployment figures based on this count are published monthly.

The second, which was first started on a biannual basis in 1973, increased to yearly in 1984 and has been quarterly since 1993, is the ILO (International Labour Organisation) based survey of the unemployed. The ILO count is taken from a wider survey of employment called the Labour Force Survey (LFS). 60 000 households, with over 100 000 adults, are surveyed every three months. The questionnaire used covers household size and structure, accommodation details, basic demographic characteristics such as age, sex, marital status and ethnic origin, and economic activity. To be counted as unemployed, an individual has to be without a paid job, be available to start a job within a fortnight and has either looked for work at some time in the previous four weeks or be waiting to start a job already obtained.

Figure 89.2 shows how the two different measures of unemployment have compared over time. The ILO measure shows less change than the claimant count measure. When unemployment was falling at a faster rate on the claimant count than on the ILO count from 1986, it could be argued that this was due to the Restart programme which pushed the unemployed off the claimant count when they were still in fact looking for work. When unemployment rose faster on the claimant

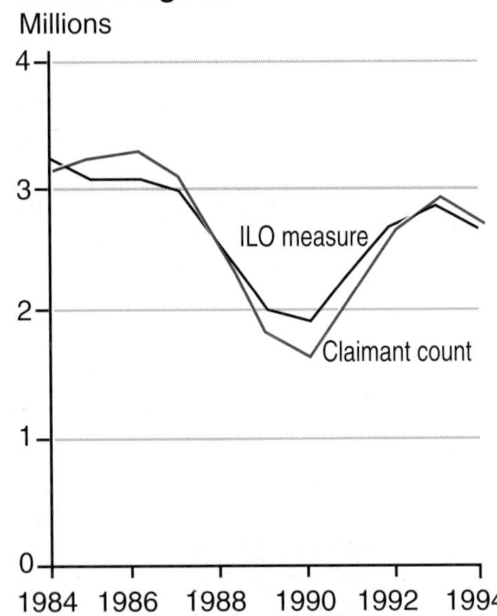

Source: adapted from Employment Department.

Figure 89.2 *ILO and claimant count measures of unemployment*

Table 89.3 *International unemployment rates*

Percentages

	1976	1981	1986	1991	1994
Spain	4.6	13.9	21.0	16.0	23.8
France	4.4	7.4	10.4	9.4	12.6
Canada	7.1	7.5	9.5	10.2	10.4
Australia	4.7	5.7	8.0	9.5	9.7
United Kingdom	5.6	9.8	11.2	8.8	9.6
Italy	6.6	7.8	10.5	9.9	11.8
Belgium	6.4	10.8	11.2	7.2	9.7
Sweden	1.6	2.5	2.7	2.7	8.0
United States	7.6	7.5	6.9	6.6	6.0
Germany	3.7	4.4	6.4	4.2	6.8
Portugal	-	-	8.4	4.1	6.8
Japan	2.0	2.2	2.8	2.1	2.9

Source: adapted from OECD

count from 1990, it could be argued that this was because some of those claiming benefits for being unemployed became discouraged from looking for work and therefore didn't show up on the ILO count.

One of the great advantages of the ILO count is that it is the internationally recognised way of measuring unemployment. Unemployment rates can therefore be compared between countries. It is also only a small part of the outcome of the Labour Force Survey which covers all employment. Hence, it is possible to provide detailed pictures of employment and unemployment by characteristics such as age, sex, marital status and ethnic origin. On the other hand, it is more costly to collect than the claimant count and figures are currently only available three monthly, with a greater time period needed to calculate the statistics from collection to publication. Like any survey, it is subject to sampling and response errors and because of this is not always suitable for studying small geographical areas or very small groups of workers.

The claimant count, on the other hand, is not an internationally recognised way of measuring unemployment. It is based on administrative benefit rules which do not necessarily accurately reflect unemployment. It also provides only limited analysis of the characteristics of the unemployed. Its three main advantages are that it is cheap to collect, it is available quickly and frequently, and, because it is a complete count and not a survey, it gives accurate figures for unemployment in small geographical areas.

Table 89.3 shows international unemployment rates from the 1970s. The UK was fairly typical in Europe in seeing a large increase in unemployment in the 1980s. Nevertheless, some countries such as Japan and the USA have tended to enjoy lower unemployment rates than the UK.

Unemployment costs

It is 20 years since the European economies suffered the first oil shock and with it the great upward shift in unemployment. In Europe, 21 million people, more than 11 per cent of the labour force, are now without work.

The unemployment problem is even more chronic than the orthodox claimant count figures suggest. Include the economically inactive and discouraged who are not claiming benefit and one in four men aged between 16 and 64 are out of work.

Government priority has been to lower inflation, arguing that jobs growth follows. This, however, has only been possible because of the derided social democratic institution of the Welfare State. Immediately after the oil shock there were fears of social unrest when unemployment was half today's levels, but the safety net stilled dissent.

As a result, governments have arguably taken risks with civil society that those who knew the conditions of the late 19th century and first half of this would never have dared. Unalloyed sound money and free trade before 1914 depended upon mass migration, and when that imploded there was mass unemployment that gave birth to fascism and communism. Now the same policy mix is again giving rise to ugly political currents. Who is to say that Britain will remain untouched?

Endemic unemployment blights everyone, with and without work. Those with work may think themselves virtuous and unaffected, but ultimately they, too, are brought down by the slowing growth rate caused by the sheer waste of people - their incomes, spending and skills. And the longer the unemployed are idle, the harder it is to become employable again. The economy starts to lock in the underperformance with a whole set of self-reinforcing low expectations of growth, investment and employment. There is a drift towards a high unemployment equilibrium.

This is compounded by the reaction of those in work. They begin to find promotion and pay increases ever harder to secure, and as everyone starts to know somebody made unemployed through no fault of their own, the fear spreads. The employed begin to spend more carefully too; the low-growth trap is springing shut.

As millions find themselves turning to the state for support so there is a structural deterioration in public finances. Welfare states were designed to accommodate people in transition from job to job - not vast pools of the permanently jobless. The growth in welfare spending seems to warrant the call for scaling back the competence of government generally - and that adds to the vicious circle.

Yet there is another and perhaps more insidious effect. Unemployment degrades the spirit. It is not just the jobless trying to get through each bleak day. It is that the employed are party to what is happening. In the same way those who hate become degraded by their venom, so living in a society that can carry the wound of unemployment uncomplainingly for a generation demeans us all. It denies our humanity.

Source: adapted in part from *The Guardian*, 21.2.1994.

1. What is meant by 'endemic unemployment'?

2. Outline the costs of unemployment discussed in the article: (a) to the unemployed; (b) to those in work; (c) to the government; (d) to the economy as a whole.

3. To what extent would a substantial increase in the number of unemployed workers on government training schemes reduce the costs of unemployment?

Types of unemployment

Summary

1. There is equilibrium in the labour market when the demand for and supply of labour are equal.
2. If supply exceeds demand in the labour market and it is therefore in disequilibrium, then unemployment is either cyclical or classical.
3. Unemployment can still exist even if the labour market is in equilibrium. Unemployment would then be frictional, seasonal or structural.
4. Voluntary unemployment occurs when workers choose not to take jobs offered at existing wage rates. Frictional, seasonal, structural and classical unemployment are all examples of voluntary unemployment.
5. The rate of unemployment in the economy given voluntary unemployment is called the natural rate of unemployment.
6. Involuntary unemployment occurs when workers are willing to work for existing wage rates but jobs are not offered to them. Cyclical unemployment is an example of involuntary unemployment.

Labour market equilibrium

Equilibrium in the labour market is achieved when the demand for labour is equal to the supply of labour (☞ unit 50). The demand for labour in an economy is determined by the **marginal revenue product** of labour. As more and more workers are combined with a fixed stock of land and capital, the marginal revenue product of labour (the addition to output of the extra worker) declines (an example of the **law of diminishing returns**). Hence the demand curve for labour is downward sloping.

The supply curve for labour in an economy is likely to be upward sloping. As real wage rates increase, more adults, particularly women, are attracted into the workforce. In the very short term, employers can also persuade existing workers to work overtime if they offer higher rates of pay.

Figure 90.1 shows the equilibrium level of employment in the economy. Employment is OE whilst the equilibrium wage rate is OW. Unemployment in the economy then occurs for two reasons. Either the labour market moves away from its equilibrium position, with actual wages being above OW, or there is still some measured unemployment even when the labour market is in equilibrium. These two possibilities are explored in this unit.

Real wage rate
Supply
W
Demand
0
E
Employment

Figure 90.1 *Labour market equilibrium*
The labour market is in equilibrium when the demand for labour is equal to the supply of labour.

Unemployment when the labour market is in disequilibrium

Sometimes the labour market moves away from its equilibrium position. Figure 90.2 shows such a situation. The actual wage rate, OV, is above the market clearing wage rate of OW. Compared to the equilibrium position:

Figure 90.2 *Equilibrium and disequilibrium in the labour market*
At a wage rate of OW, there will be equilibrium in the labour market. At a wage rate of OV, however, there will be disequilibrium with unemployment of FG.

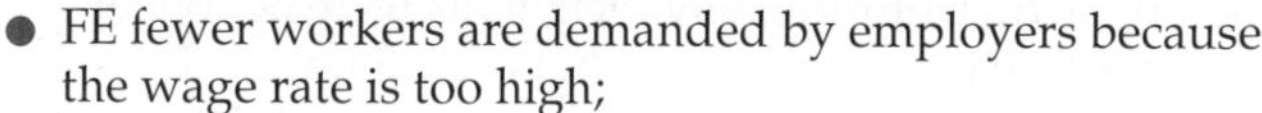

- FE fewer workers are demanded by employers because the wage rate is too high;
- EG more workers want a job because the wage rate is so high.

The result is that there is FG unemployment in the economy.

If wage rates were to fall to OW, unemployment would fall as firms demanded more workers and some workers dropped out of the labour market, not willing to work at the lower wage rates. There are a number of reasons why the labour market can be in disequilibrium and each gives rise to a particular type of unemployment.

Cyclical or demand-deficient unemployment When an economy goes into recession, unemployment rises because there is insufficient demand within the economy. It is not just labour which becomes unemployed, factories, machines, mines, offices and farms (i.e. land and capital) become unemployed too. Figure 90.3 shows what happens in the labour market in a recession. The demand for labour falls, shown by a shift to the left in the demand curve. Employment used to be at OE. Now it is at OG with the old wage rate of OW. This is because OE workers want a job but only OG workers are demanded by firms.

This unemployment of GE is CYCLICAL or DEMAND-DEFICIENT UNEMPLOYMENT. It is also sometimes called KEYNESIAN UNEMPLOYMENT because it was Keynes who argued in the 1930s that the Great Depression was caused by a lack of demand within the economy. In a recession, the economy is in disequilibrium. Macro-economic forces will work to restore the economy to its long run equilibrium position. The extra demand for goods will then generate extra demand for labour. Therefore, in the long run the demand curve for labour will shift back to the right in Figure 90.3. In the short run, however, there is unemployment.

Classical unemployment CLASSICAL UNEMPLOYMENT or REAL WAGE UNEMPLOYMENT

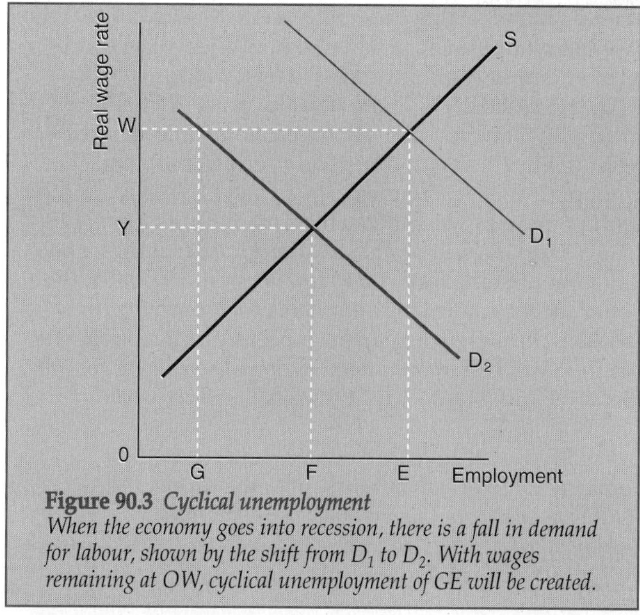

Figure 90.3 *Cyclical unemployment*
When the economy goes into recession, there is a fall in demand for labour, shown by the shift from D_1 to D_2. With wages remaining at OW, cyclical unemployment of GE will be created.

exists when the real wage rate is above that needed to clear the labour market even when the economy is booming. Jobs exist but workers choose not take them because they are not prepared to accept the wages being offered, or they are unable to take them because of trade union power or government legislation. In Figure 90.2, the actual wage rate of OV is too high to clear the market. What's more, wages are 'sticky downwards'. This means that there are factors preventing wages from falling to clear the market.

One reason why unemployed people refuse to take jobs is because unemployment benefit levels are too near the level of pay being offered. If benefit levels are above OW in Figure 90.2, there is no point in workers accepting a job at a wage rate of OW. The ratio between the benefit actually received and the wage a worker could receive is known as the **replacement ratio**. If the ratio were 1.0, then the unemployed would receive exactly the same from working as from being unemployed. If the ratio were 2.0, the unemployed would be half as well off working as on the dole. One way of reducing the replacement ratio and giving the unemployed a greater incentive to take a job is to cut unemployment benefits.

Another reason why the labour market may fail to clear is because of minimum wage legislation. If the minimum wage is OV in Figure 90.2, then there will inevitably be unemployment (☞ unit 52).

Another factor could be trade unions forcing up wages above their equilibrium level. Trade unions serve the interests of their members, nearly all of whom are in employment. Pushing up wage levels, even if this means long term job losses, is likely to be seen as advantageous by the trade union (☞ unit 51).

Unemployment when the labour market is in equilibrium

Even when the labour market is in equilibrium, there might be still be unemployment for a variety of reasons.

Frictional and search unemployment Most workers who lose their jobs move quickly into new ones. This short-term unemployment is called FRICTIONAL UNEMPLOYMENT. There will always be frictional unemployment in a free market economy and it is not regarded by most economists as a serious problem. The amount of time spent unemployed varies. The higher the level of unemployment benefits or redundancy pay, the longer workers will be able to afford to search for a good job without being forced into total poverty. Equally, the better the job information available to unemployed workers through newspapers, Jobcentres, etc. the shorter the time workers should need to spend searching for jobs. Hence SEARCH UNEMPLOYMENT will be lower.

Seasonal unemployment Some workers, such as construction workers or workers in the tourist industry, tend to work on a seasonal basis. SEASONAL UNEMPLOYMENT tends to rise in winter when some of these workers will be laid off, whilst unemployment falls in summer when they are taken on again. There is little that can be done to prevent this pattern occurring in a market economy where the demand for labour varies through the year.

QUESTION 1 April 1990 marked a turning point in unemployment. The numbers of those out of work had been falling since late 1986, from 3.1 million to 1.6 million. Unemployment was now set to rise again, reaching 3 million by early1993. London and the South East were particularly badly affected by this rise, as was the construction industry. Explain how you would classify each of the following London workers, interviewed in April 1990, by type of unemployment.

(a) Mr Robert Quinn, 24, has been unemployed for two months after being laid off from his labouring job. 'I think the firm was short of money', he said. He could not find any jobs and his marriage had broken up.
(b) Mr David Kimber, 26, originally from Liverpool, became unemployed three weeks ago when his contract as a tower crane driver expired. 'I have been promised contracts but jobs are being put back.'
(c) Mr Kirpal Singh, 24 and single, quit two months ago after two years as a computer operator for Harrods, the department store, 10 miles away. 'It was just too far to travel every day', he said. He was optimistic about getting another job and said he was being called for second interviews.
(d) Ms Susan Morrison, 19, was pessimistic about getting another job in word processing. She left one job in January after a month when she was told she 'not the right person' for the job. She previously resigned from British Telecom because she believed she was the lowest paid person in her office.
(e) Ms Patricia Jones, 24, a former deputy catering officer at a large London further education establishment, said: 'There was no career development being offered. I have got all the qualifications to progress in catering so I want a good job with a salary in five figures.'
(f) Mr Peter Vass, 24, a former merchandiser with Maples, the furniture group, resigned because: 'I was paid about £8 000 a year and it just was not enough.' Unemployed for 10 weeks, he was optimistic about getting a new job.

Source: adapted from the *Financial Times*, 18.4.1990.

Structural unemployment Far more serious is the problem of STRUCTURAL UNEMPLOYMENT. This occurs when the demand for labour is less than its supply in an individual labour market in the economy. One example of structural unemployment is **regional unemployment**. Throughout the post-war period, the South of England has tended to be at full employment while regions such as Northern Ireland have consistently suffered unemployment. This has occurred because of a lack of mobility of factors of production between the regions (☞ unit 52). Another example is **sectoral unemployment**. The steel and shipbuilding industries in the UK declined sharply in the late 1970s and early 1980s leaving a considerable number of skilled workers unemployed. Unfortunately their skills were no longer needed in the economy and without retraining and possible relocation, they were unable to adapt to the changing demand. **Technological unemployment** is another example of structural unemployment. Groups of workers across industries may be put out of work by new technology. Again, without retraining and geographical mobility these workers may remain unemployed.

The natural rate of unemployment

In a boom period, there is no cyclical unemployment. When the economy goes into recession, workers lose their jobs and they have difficulty getting another job because there are too few jobs in the economy at existing wage rates. Cyclical unemployment is therefore INVOLUNTARY UNEMPLOYMENT. It is involuntary because unemployed workers can't choose to go back to work, because there are no jobs available.

However, all other types of unemployment are examples of VOLUNTARY UNEMPLOYMENT. This occurs when workers refuse opportunities of work at existing wage rates. For instance, a worker who is frictionally unemployed could choose to spend less time searching for work and take a job which is less well paid than he or she might have wanted. Seasonal workers could find odd jobs, such as working in pubs or cleaning, to fill in the months when they are out of work from their main occupation. Those suffering from structural unemployment could get a job if they were prepared to accept a lower rate of pay or worse conditions of work. For instance, unemployed workers in Northern Ireland could come to the South of England to find jobs. Redundant steel workers could become bar attendants or security guards. Classical unemployment is voluntary because individual workers, trade unions or governments choose to allow unemployment to exist by maintaining too high wages. The NATURAL RATE OF UNEMPLOYMENT is the percentage of workers who are voluntarily unemployed. The economy is said to be at **full**

employment when there is no involuntary unemployment in the economy. The distinction between voluntary and involuntary unemployment can be shown on diagrams. In Figure 90.4, the long run aggregate supply curve for the economy is drawn with an equilibrium output level of OE. At this output level, the economy, including the labour market, is in long run equilibrium. However, some workers choose not to work at the equilibrium wage level in the economy. In Figure 90.4, the equilibrium wage rate is OW. Two supply curves for labour are drawn. $S_{workers}$ shows the number of workers who are prepared to accept a job at any given wage rate. $S_{Labour\ force}$ is $S_{workers}$ plus those who claim they wish to work, but are not prepared to work at the given wage rate. Official statistics therefore show that there is EF unemployment in the economy. This unemployment is voluntary and OE is the **natural level of**

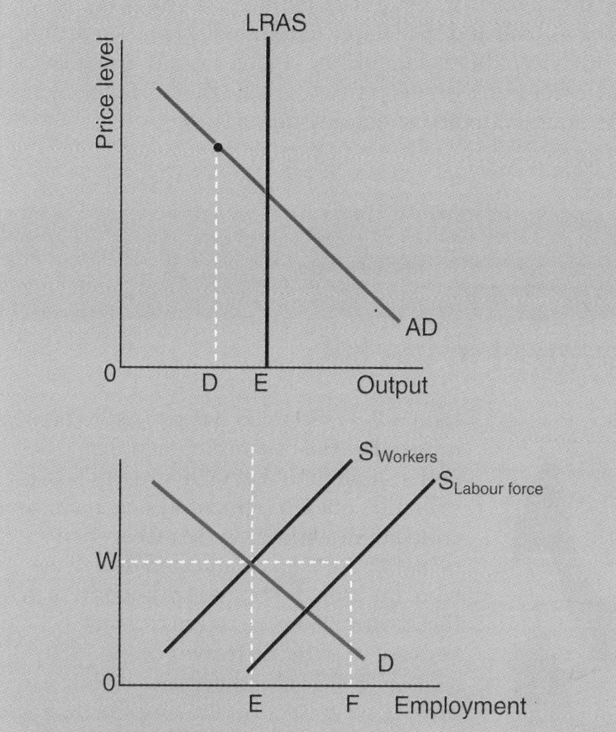

Figure 90.4 *Voluntary employment*
Voluntary unemployment exists when a part of the labour force refuses to work at the going wage rate. Equilibrium full employment exists at OE. At OW the equilibrium wage rate, EF workers choose not to work. The natural rate of unemployment is therefore EF÷OF. Cyclical unemployment occurs if the economy is below equilibrium output and employment of OE, such as OD.

QUESTION 2 In a study of 6 000 employed and unemployed workers, a team of academics found that, contrary to popular opinion, the jobless were more committed to employment than those already in work. 77 per cent were willing to take a job even if there were no financial necessity, compared with 66 per cent of those with jobs who said they would continue to work. There was no evidence that the unemployed were difficult to please in the job market. Only 12 per cent of the unemployed said they expected pay above that of the average of their employed counterparts. 45 per cent of all those out of work said they had seriously considered re-training in order to find work, with 40 per cent prepared to move area.

The study also considered whether the unemployed were intrinsically less 'employable'. Two methods were used to compare the unemployed and those in work. First, an examination of the work histories of the unemployed showed that people out of work had previously held almost exactly the same number of jobs as the employed - by far the biggest factors determining work experience were age, sex and industry. Second, the fact that the average duration of the longest jobs of the unemployed was 74 months, and for the employed 76 months which, the study says, 'suggests employability rather than behavioural instability.'

Source: adapted from *The Guardian*, 10.3.1994.

To what extent does the study outlined in the article suggest that unemployment is mainly voluntary?

Key terms

Cyclical, demand-deficient or Keynesian unemployment - when there is insufficient demand in the economy for all workers who wish to work at current wage rates to obtain a job.
Classical or real-wage unemployment - when real wages are kept at such a high level that the demand for labour is greater than the supply of labour.
Frictional unemployment - when workers are unemployed for short lengths of time between jobs.
Search unemployment - when workers spend time searching for the best job available.
Seasonal unemployment - when workers are unemployed at certain times of the year, such as building workers or agricultural workers in winter.
Structural unemployment - when the pattern of demand and production changes leaving workers unemployed in labour markets where demand has shrunk. Examples of structural unemployment are regional unemployment, sectoral unemployment or technological unemployment.
Involuntary unemployment - unemployment which exists when workers are unable to find jobs despite being prepared to accept work at the existing wage rate.
Voluntary unemployment - workers who choose not to accept employment at the existing wage rate.
The natural rate of unemployment - the proportion of the workforce which chooses voluntarily to remain unemployed when the labour market is in equilibrium.

employment in the economy. EF is the **natural level of unemployment**. The natural rate of unemployment is the natural level of unemployment divided by the labour force, EF ÷ OF.

What if the economy is at output level OD in Figure 90.4? Here, the economy is in a recession with output below the full employment level of OE. There will therefore be cyclical unemployment, which is involuntary unemployment. The market will return to equilibrium at OE and in the process will reduce the level of cyclical unemployment to zero.

The extent to which unemployment is voluntary or involuntary has been a major controversy in economics. Keynesian economists have argued that most of the unemployment in the Great Depression of the 1930s and the major recessions of 1980-82 and 1990-92 was demand-deficient in nature. At the other extreme, classical economists of the rational expectations school of thought have argued that labour markets will adjust almost instantaneously to large rises in unemployment. Wage rates will fall and the labour market will clear. According to this view, there were plenty of jobs around in the 1930s and 1980s but workers refused to take them. Hence there was no involuntary unemployment.

Applied economics

The causes of unemployment in the UK

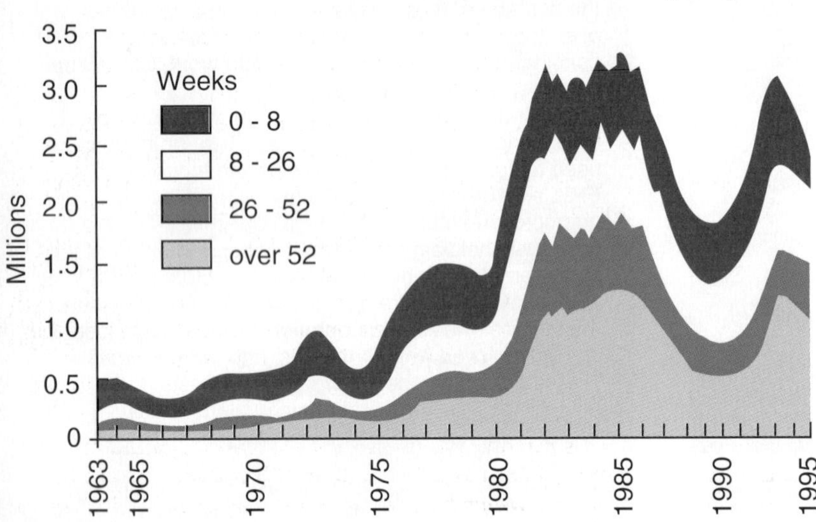

Figure 90.5 *Unemployment by duration*

Figure 90.5 shows that unemployment in the 1980s and 1990s was much higher than in the 1960s. This is not just a UK phenomenon. Unemployment rates throughout Europe have increased in contrast to the the US and Japanese experience. Why is this the case?

Involuntary unemployment

Unemployment patterns correspond closely to movements in the **trade cycle**. In the past, unemployment has tended to lag behind the other main indicators such as changes in GDP. This is because firms have tried to avoid making workers redundant in a recession in the hope that it will not be too prolonged. In a boom, firms have been reluctant to take on new staff because they fear that the boom may not last. The major recessions of the 1970s, 1980s and 1990s (1971-72, 1974-76, 1980-82 and 1990-92) can be seen in Figure 90.5 with this lagged response. The recovery from the 1990-92 recession has proved to be unusual in that unemployment has fallen at the same time that GDP growth has risen (i.e. unemployment has been almost co-incident with the cycle rather than being lagged). It is suggested that firms were far more willing to sack workers in the downturn in the recession, first because of bitter memories of the 1980-82 recession and second because labour is now easier to sack and re-employ than before as a consequence of changes in the law in the 1980s. When the upturn came in 1993, firms had little slack labour and therefore were forced to go out and hire workers in order to cope with the improved economic climate. Whilst it is clear that the trade cycle has been the most important determinant of short term changes in unemployment, it can't explain why the underlying rate of unemployment rose in every cycle from the late 1960s.

Keynesian economists argue that at least part of the growth in unemployment in the 1980s has been caused by a lack of demand in the economy. Between 1979 and 1986, it can be argued that the government kept aggregate demand too low through a combination of high interest rates (restrictive monetary policy) and tight control of government borrowing (restrictive fiscal policy). When it allowed aggregate demand to rise during the Lawson boom, unemployment fell rapidly. However, there was a severe tightening of monetary policy and a deflationary exchange rate policy between 1988 and 1992, when unemployment rose back to its early 1980 levels. Then, a loosening of monetary policy and the 15 per cent devaluation of the pound in September 1992 once again led to a rise in aggregate demand and a rapid fall in unemployment in 1993 and 1994. On this argument, aggregate demand was only great enough to return the economy to something near full employment in 1987 and

1988, and then the rise in demand was so rapid that, not surprisingly, other key variables such as inflation and the current account on the balance of payments deteriorated sharply.

It is interesting to note that in each of the major downturns in the economy from 1971 to 1982, unemployment rose in the recession but did not fall to its previous level in the following boom. In 1979, for instance, unemployment fell to 1.3 million. In the aftermath of the Lawson boom, unemployment only fell to 1.7 million in 1990. Some economists have argued that cyclical unemployment in itself can create long term unemployment. If someone is made unemployed during a recession, and then stays unemployed for over a year, then they are likely to become to some extent de-skilled, making it more difficult for them to get a job in an upturn. The pace of technological change today makes this more of a problem than, say, 50 years ago. Some workers will become discouraged from looking for work, and as a result miss opportunities for employment when vacancies begin to increase again. The major recessions of 1974-76 and 1980-82 were also particularly damaging to manufacturing industry, with a substantial proportion of the capital stock of manufacturing being dismantled. With it went forever the jobs of the people who were employed in those factories. Cyclical unemployment causing structural unemployment is an example of **hysteresis** - the current value of a variable (in this case unemployment) being directly affected by its previous value (in this case, previous levels of unemployment).

Voluntary unemployment

Classical economists tend to argue that the rise in unemployment was mainly due to rises in voluntary unemployment. A number of key variables are singled out in Layard, Nickell and Jackson's estimate of the causes of unemployment shown in Table 90.1.

Frictional and search unemployment rose in the 1960s and 1970s because of a significant rise in the late 1960s of the replacement ratio, the ratio of unemployment benefits relative to wages. Workers could now afford to remain unemployed longer, searching for the right job. This rise can in part be seen by the change in short term unemployment of 0-8 weeks duration, shown in Figure 90.5. In the 1960s, approximately 250 000, half of the total, were unemployed for less than 8 weeks. By the early 1980s, this had risen to half a million, but this represented only approximately 15 per cent of the total.

Table 90.1 *The causes of UK unemployment*

	1956-59	1960-68	1969-73	1974-80	1981-87
Actual rate of unemployment (%)	2.2	2.6	3.4	5.2	11.1
Estimated natural rate of unemployment (%)	2.2	2.7	3.8	6.1	6.6
Change in natural rate (%)		+0.5	+1.1	+2.3	+0.5
of which:					
North Sea Oil		0	0	-0.3	-2.6
Terms of trade		-0.4	-0.1	1.5	1.3
Skill mismatch		0.1	0.3	0.6	1.5
Unemployment benefits		0.3	0.6	-0.3	0.3
Trade union power		0.4	0.3	0.8	0.1
Tax wedge		0.1	0	0	-0.3

Sources: P.R.G. Layard, S.J.Nickell, and R. Jackman, *Unemployment*, 1991, by permission of Oxford University Press.

Structural unemployment has risen for a number of reasons. First, there has been a devastating run down of some primary industries, such as coal mining, and most manufacturing industries. This process of de-industrialisation (☞ unit 61) has left many unemployed workers with the wrong skills. Layard *et al* in Table 90.1 see this skills mismatch as an important contributor to raising the natural rate of unemployment. North Sea oil has made matters worse by raising the exchange rate of the pound, particularly between 1978 and 1981, which made imports cheaper to British consumers but UK exports more expensive to foreigners. Labour has also been left in the wrong regions. The primary and secondary jobs that disappeared were spread fairly evenly over the country as a proportion of the labour force. However, the South experienced much faster growth in service industries than the rest of the country over the period. This enabled the South to transfer workers from manufacturing into service jobs relatively easily. But it took much longer elsewhere. Inappropriate housing policies, which encouraged expensive home ownership and discouraged affordable renting (☞ unit 69), then prevented lower paid workers from moving out of high unemployment regions to the South. Only by the mid-1990s had regional unemployment rates converged, much of this due to the contraction of service sector jobs in the South in the recession of 1990-92. This might be an indicator that the economy has now broadly adjusted to the shift in patterns of production of the last 40 years.

This run down in primary and secondary industry employment has to be set against broader trends in the economy which have made matters worse. The 1970s and early 1980s saw a substantial increase in the numbers of 16 year olds in the population who needed to find jobs. This trend has now been reversed, which should help reduce long term unemployment in the 1990s. There has also been a substantial decrease in the number of well paid semi-skilled and unskilled jobs traditionally taken by males. These were jobs in primary and manufacturing industry, such as coal mining or working on a production line in a car factory. There are still plenty of unskilled jobs available, but they now tend to be low paid, in service industries and have traditionally been performed by women. The result has been a large expansion in female employment in the economy. Unskilled male workers have been reluctant to take these 'women's jobs'.

Moreover, these males are now caught in the **poverty trap,** where they can receive almost as much in benefit as working in these low paid occupations. Even if they are tempted to take work, they know that very high marginal rates of tax on low pay will severely limit any increase in take-home pay they might receive through working longer hours or getting promotion. This 'tax wedge' in Table 90.1 became less of a disincentive to work in the 1980s because of falls in tax rates on the low paid, but marginal rates of tax in the mid-1990s still remain high.

There are several possible causes of **classical unemployment**. Layard *et al* in Table 90.1 place some importance on trade unions as causing unemployment. Trade unions were arguably most powerful in the 1970s. In the 1980s, trade unions came under severe pressure from government, which enacted a large number of laws restricting trade union freedoms. The severe recession of 1980-82 also led to a substantial and continuing erosion of the membership base of British trade unions (☞ unit 51). By the 1990s, it could be argued that trade unions were relatively weak and therefore could not be a major contributor to voluntary unemployment. 1994 saw the abolition of **wages councils** (☞ unit 52) in the UK, which some economists argued were a major cause of classical unemployment. The major barrier which currently remains to the downward mobility of wages is the benefit system. Hence, some economists argue that unemployment and other benefits should be cut even further to increase incentives for the unemployed to take low paid work. Other economists question the extent to which the replacement ratio is a cause of unemployment and point out that further cuts in benefits would lead to even greater **inequalities** in society (☞ units 43 and 102).

The causes of unemployment

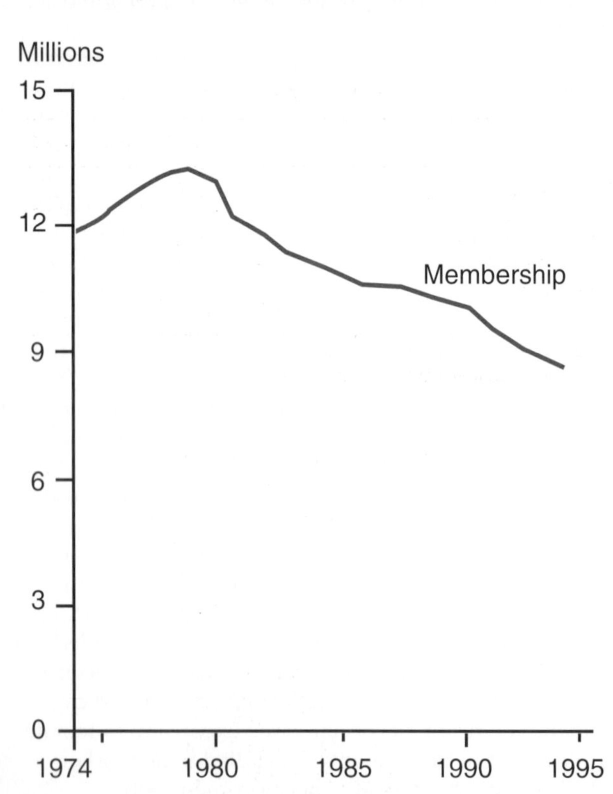

Source: adapted from Department of Employment, *Employment Gazette*, June 1994.

Figure 90.6 *Trade union membership*

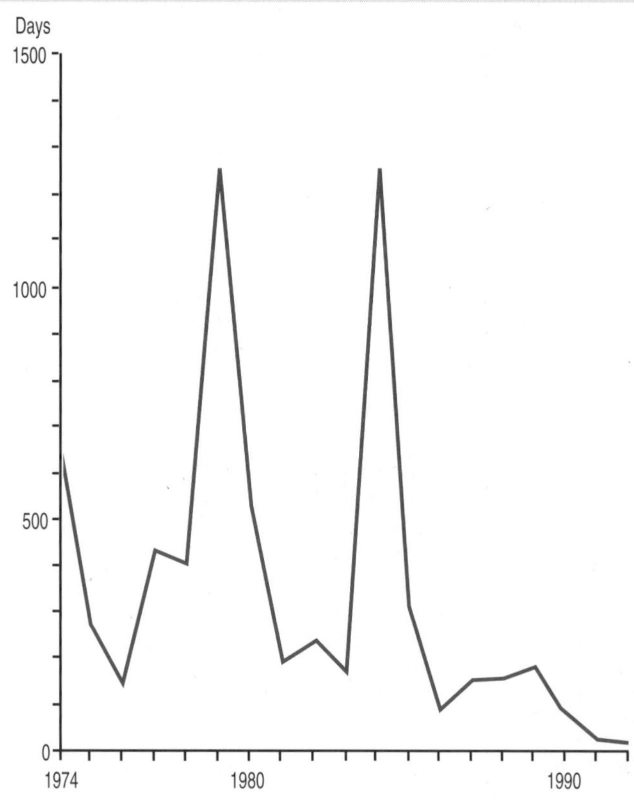

Source: adapted from Department of Employment, *Employment Gazette*, June 1994.

Figure 90.7 *Strikes - working days lost per thousand employees*

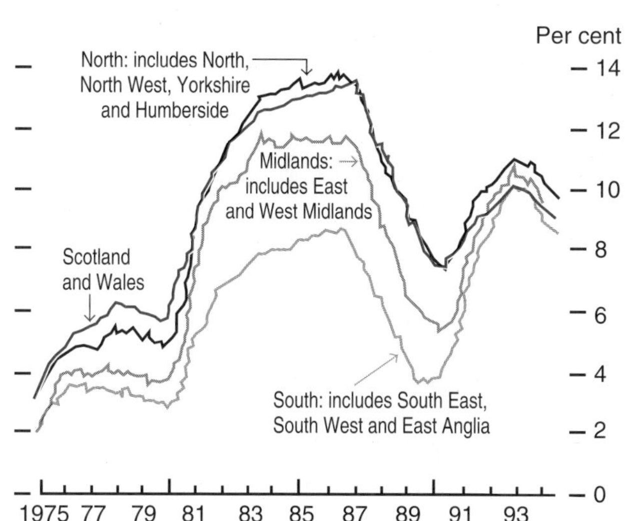

Source: adapted from Bank of England, *Bank of England Quarterly Bulletin,* November 1994.

Figure 90.8 *Regional unemployment rates*

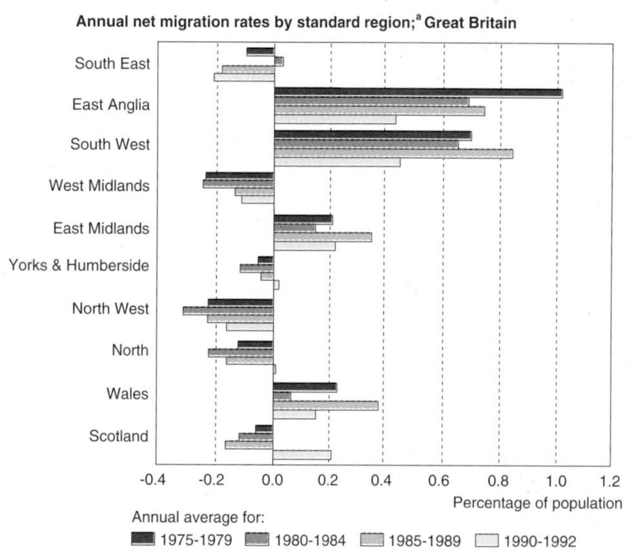

Source: adapted from Department of Employment, *Employment Gazette,* February1995.

Figure 90.9 *Average net migration rates by standard region: Great Britain*

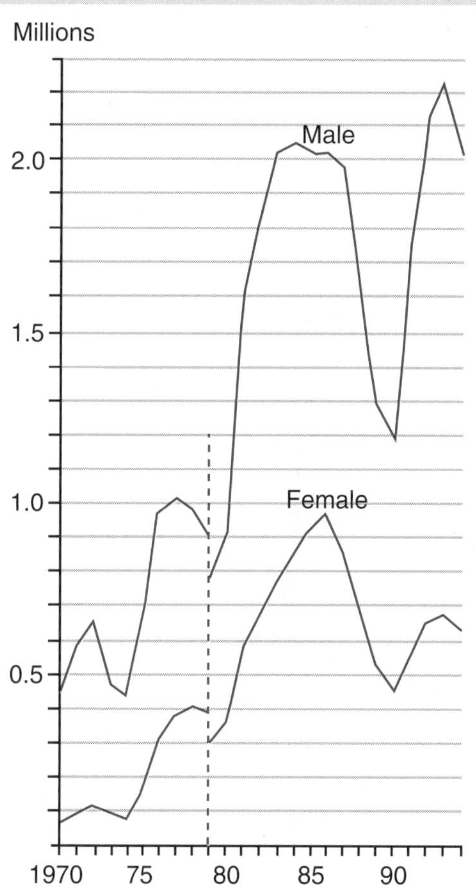

1. Discontinuity in 1979.
2. Note that male employment fell from 14.0 million in 1970 to 10.9 million in 1994, whilst female employment rose from 8.5 million to 10.7 million over the same period.

Source: adapted from CSO, *Annual Abstract of Statistics.*

Figure 90.10 *Male and female unemployment*

Table 90.2 *Unemployment rates by occupation**

	1979	1984	1989	1992
Professional		2.2	1.4	3.1
Intermediate	3.1	3.8	2.5	4.3
Skilled non-manual		6.4	3.8	6.4
Skilled manual	1.9	8.7	5.1	11.4
Semi-skilled	10.4	11.2	7.3	13.5
Unskilled		13.6	9.7	14.6

* Excludes people unemployed for more than 3 years.
Source: adapted from Labour Force Survey.

Income support claimants
% of population directly claiming income support

12
8
4
0
1973 80 85 90 93

Figure 90.11 *Income support claimants - % of population claiming income support*

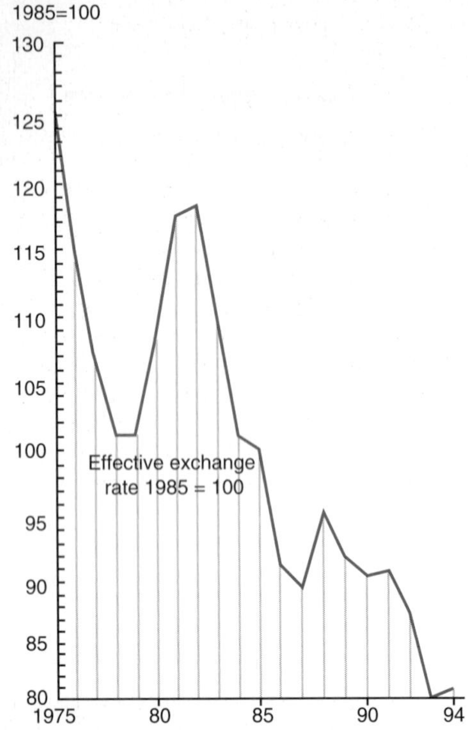

1985=100

Effective exchange rate 1985 = 100

Figure 90.12 *Effective exchange rate of the pound*

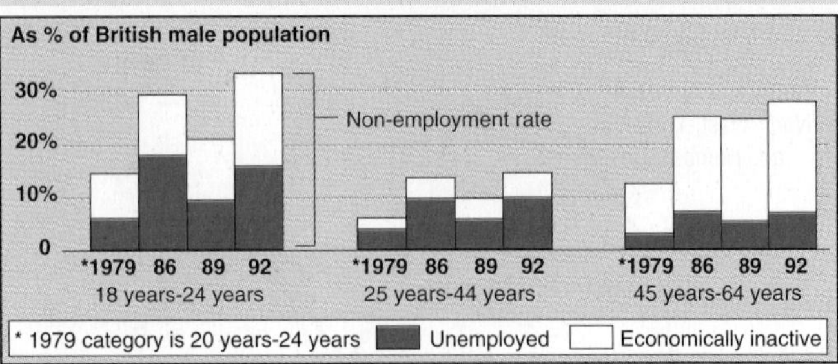

Source: adapted from Labour Force Survey.

Figure 90.14 *Male unemployment and non-employment rates, by age*

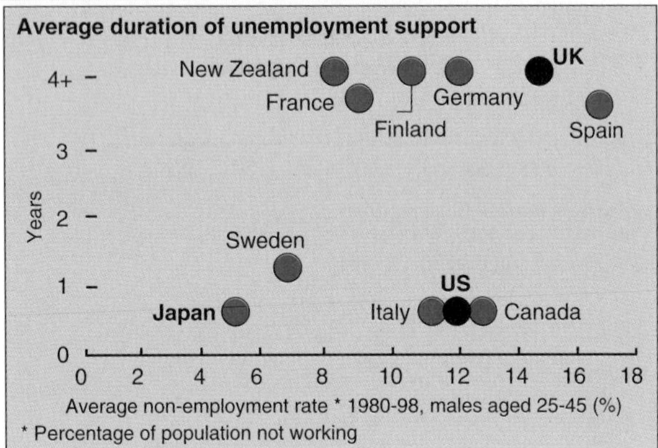

1. The vertical axis shows the average length of time an unemployed worker can expect to receive unemployment benefits from the state. The horizontal axis shows the percentage of the male workforce aged 25-54 who are not in a job. This includes both the officially unemployed and 'discouraged workers' - workers who would like a job but have become discouraged from looking and therefore no longer appear on the unemployment statistics.
Source: adapted from Layard and Jackman; OECD.

Figure 90.15 *Period of time during which unemployment benefits are given compared to the non-employment rate of males[1]*

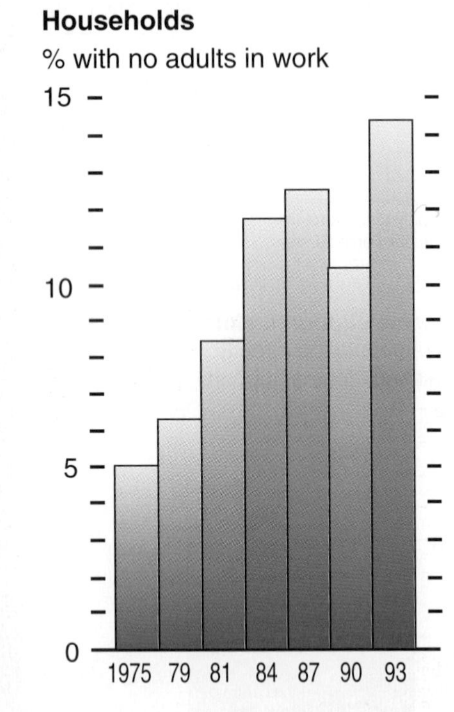

Figure 90.13 *Households - % with no adults in work*

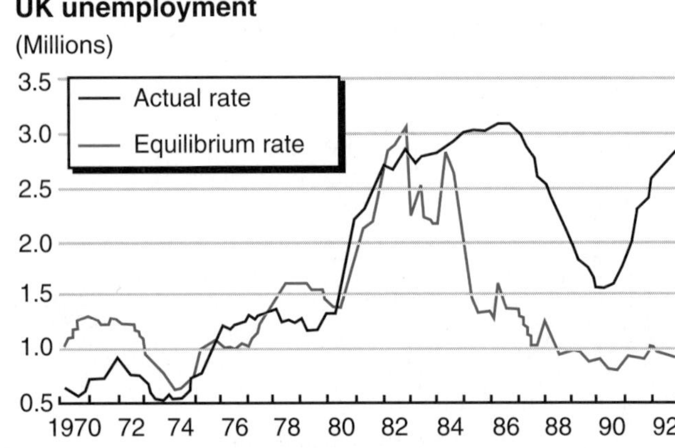

1. This estimate of the 'equilibrium' rate - the natural rate of unemployment - was produced by Patrick Minford, a classical economist who firmly believes that trade unions, wages councils, high tax rates and too high benefit rates have been major causes of unemployment in the past.

Source: adapted from Minford, NIESR.

Figure 90.16 *UK unemployment[1]*

A magazine has asked you to write an article on the causes of UK unemployment in the 1990s. In your article:

(a) outline the main trends in unemployment during the period shown in the data;

(b) discuss the possible causes of unemployment, distinguishing between the main types of unemployment identified by economists;

(c) evaluate which factors have been most important in determining unemployment levels.

Unit 91 The Phillips curve

Summary

1. The Phillips curve shows the relationship between the rate of change of money wages and unemployment. High unemployment is associated with a low rate of change of money wages, whilst low unemployment is associated with a high rate of change of money wages.
2. Following publication of Phillips's findings in 1958, a view developed that there was a trade-off between unemployment and inflation.
3. From the mid-1960s, the Phillips curve relationship broke down in the UK. The most widely accepted explanation of this is that the original Phillips curve shows the short run adjustment process of the economy, assuming money illusion on the part of workers. From the mid-1960s onwards, workers ceased to have money illusion.
4. Classical economists argue that the long run Phillips curve is vertical. Unemployment will always return to its natural rate. The Phillips curve trade off exists only in the short run.
5. A government which increases demand in the economy will succeed in reducing unemployment at the cost of high inflation in the short run, but in the long term unemployment will return to its natural rate at a higher rate of inflation.
6. Policies which succeed in reducing inflation will create unemployment in the short run. Keynesians tend to argue that the unemployment cost will be severe and prolonged. At the other extreme, new classical economists argue that the unemployment cost will be negligible and that the short run adjustment process is rapid.

The original Phillips curve

In 1958, Professor A W Phillips at the London School of Economics published *The Relation between Unemployment and the Rate of Change of Money Wage Rates, 1861-1957*. He showed that there was a remarkably stable relationship between the rate of change of money wages and the level of unemployment. As can be seen from Figure 91.1, high rates of unemployment were associated with low (and even negative) rates of change of money wage rates whilst low rates of unemployment were associated with high rates of change of money wage rates. The line of best fit came to be called the PHILLIPS CURVE.

This relationship provides a useful insight into the causes of inflation. Changes in money wage rates are a key component in changes in prices. Assume money

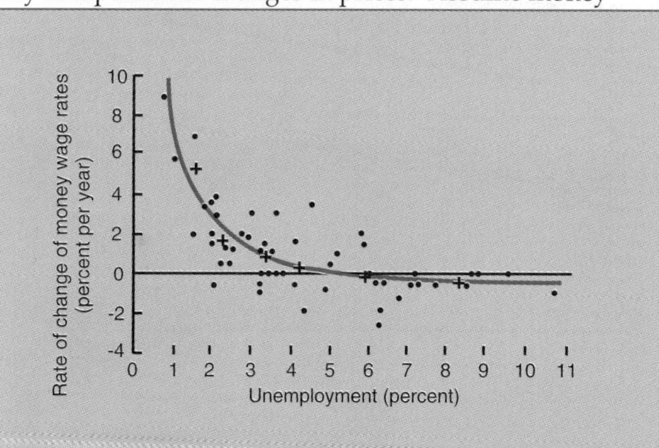

Figure 91.1 *The Phillips curve*
The original Phillips curve was derived from data from the period 1861 to 1913. Phillips then showed that the curve predicted the relationship between the rate of change of money wage rates and unemployment in the period 1913 to 1957.

QUESTION 1

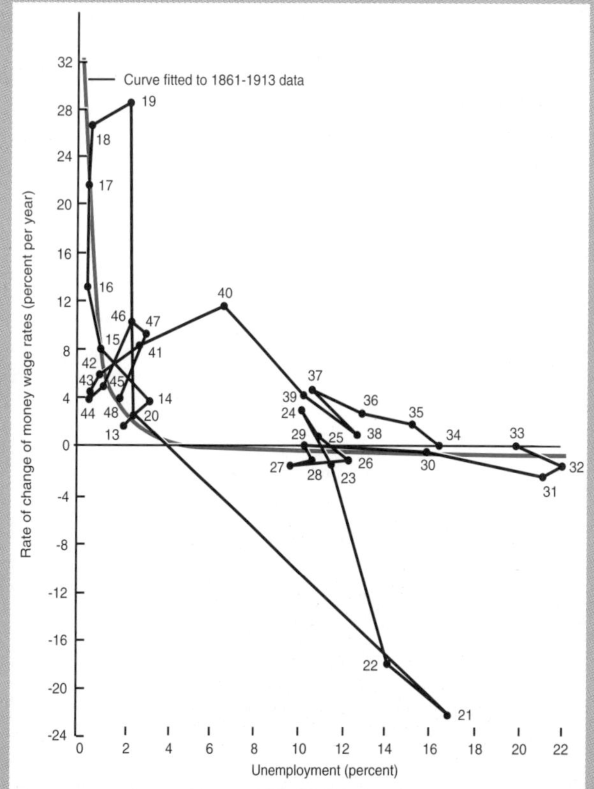

Figure 91.2 *Phillips curve data, 1913-1948*

To what extent do the data shown in Figure 91.2 support the view that there is a stable relationship between unemployment and the rate of change of money wage rates?

wage rates rise by 10 per cent whilst all other factors remain constant. If 70 per cent of a firm's costs are wages, then its costs will rise by 7 per cent. It is likely to pass these costs on in the form of higher prices. These higher prices will feed through to higher costs for other firms or directly into the inflation rate (for instance, the Retail Price Index in the UK). The higher the rate of change of money wages, the higher the likely rate of inflation. Hence the Phillips curve hypothesis can be altered slightly to state that there is an inverse relationship between inflation and unemployment. When unemployment is low, inflation will be high. When unemployment is high, inflation will be low or even negative (i.e. prices will be falling).

The initial importance of the Phillips curve

The article was important initially for two reasons. First, it helped Keynesians to develop a more sophisticated theory of inflation. In the simplest Keynesian model, the aggregate supply curve is shaped as in Figure 91.3.

Up to the full employment level of income, the supply curve is horizontal. Any increase in aggregate demand will increase output without causing inflation. At full employment, the supply curve is vertical. Any increase in aggregate demand will increase prices without increasing output. But the evidence of the 1950s suggested that the aggregate supply curve was upward sloping near the full employment level of output. Changes in aggregate demand affected both output and inflation.

Second, policy makers (and particularly governments) changed their views about how the economy might be managed. Many became convinced that there was a trade-off between unemployment and inflation. Zero inflation (i.e. price stability) could be achieved but only by keeping unemployment at what for the time seemed a relatively high level. On the other hand lower unemployment could be achieved by accepting higher levels of inflation. But it was impossible to set both the rate of unemployment and the rate of inflation.

The breakdown of the simple Phillips curve relationship

Following publication of Phillips' article, a great deal of work was done in the UK and abroad to test the relationship between unemployment and inflation. In general, the relationship seemed to be true in other countries too. In the early 1960s the relationship continued to hold true in the UK. Then from 1966 onwards, it broke down completely. Year after year, points to the right of the original Phillips curve were recorded as shown in Figure 91.7. Even more serious was the fact that no new pattern seemed to emerge. Some economists argued that the original Phillips curve never existed anyway. The accepted theory today is that the Phillips curve as originally plotted was a special case and can be understood only in the wider context of aggregate demand and aggregate supply analysis.

The short run Phillips curve

Assume that prices are stable and that there is an increase in aggregate demand. Perhaps planned investment has increased, or the government wishes to increase its expenditure. This will shift the aggregate demand curve to the right in Figure 91.4. The economy moves along its short run aggregate supply curve from A to B. Note that

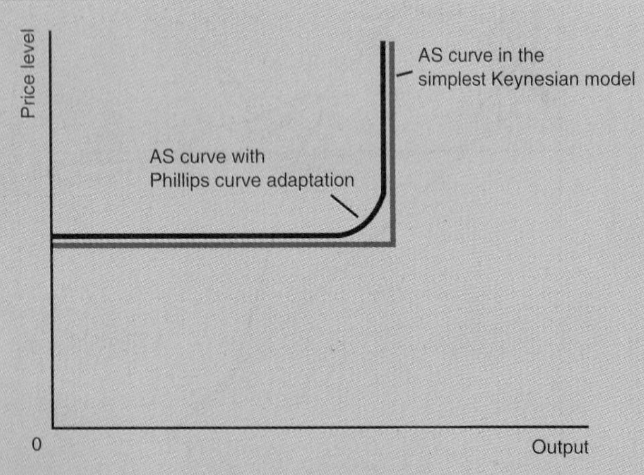

Figure 91.3 *The Keynesian aggregate supply curve*
The simplest Keynesian model assumes that the aggregate supply curve is horizontal at less than full employment levels of output and then vertical at full employment. With a Phillips curve relationship introduced into the model, the aggregate supply curve becomes upward sloping before reaching full employment output.

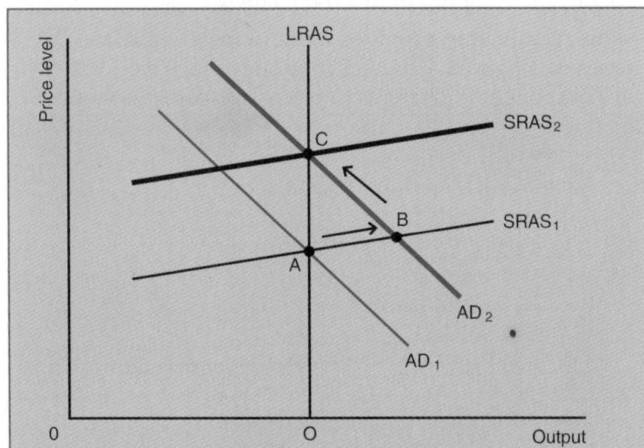

Figure 91.4 *Aggregate demand and aggregate supply*
An increase in aggregate demand from AD_1 to AD_2 will increase prices. It will also increase output and therefore reduce unemployment. This movement from A to B shows the short run Phillips curve relationship. In the long run the economy moves back to C. There is no trade off in the long run between unemployment and inflation.

the movement involves an increase in output and an increase in the price level. An increase in output is usually associated with a fall in unemployment. The increase in the price level is of course inflation. Hence the move from A to B shows the Phillips curve trade-off - higher inflation for lower unemployment. The relationship would be no different if aggregate demand fell, shifting the aggregate demand curve to the left except that lower inflation would be traded off for higher unemployment. So the Phillips curve as originally plotted by Phillips shows what happens when the economy adjusts in the short run to a **demand-side shock**.

The long run Phillips curve with zero inflation

On classical assumptions, point B in Figure 91.4 is not a long run equilibrium point (☞ unit 90). Given that the economy is at full employment at the point A, the economy has moved to a position of over-full employment at B. In the labour market, workers will be able to bid up wage rates, shifting the short run aggregate supply curve upwards. The economy will only return to equilibrium at the point C where aggregate demand once again equals long run aggregate supply. The movement from B to C involves a rise in measured unemployment whilst inflation falls back to zero again when the economy reaches the point C (remember we assumed that the economy had no inflation at A and once the economy reaches C there are no forces which will increase prices any more). In the long run, therefore, there is no trade-off between inflation and unemployment.

The vertical long run Phillips curve

Over the past 40 years, the UK has suffered from persistent inflation. Up to the mid-1960s, inflation rates were very low, typically in the range 0 to 2 per cent per annum. Since then inflation rates have been very much higher, the peak being nearly 25 per cent in 1975. Households, workers and firms are likely to react very differently to the low creeping inflation seen up to the mid-1960s and the much higher rates experienced since then. Up to the mid-1960s, it is likely that economic agents in the UK suffered from MONEY ILLUSION. This is the belief that prices are stable when in fact they are not. For instance, if a worker received a money wage increase of 2 per cent, she may believe that she is 2 per cent better off. However, if inflation is also running at 2 per cent then she is in fact no better off. She is said to be suffering from money illusion. Her real wage has not changed.

From the mid-1960s, inflation has never been very far away from the main news in the UK. Workers became aware that rises in prices eroded their real standard of living. So they started to negotiate in real terms. Instead of negotiating for a pay increase of 2 per cent, they would negotiate for 2 per cent plus the expected rate of inflation. This affected the position of the short run Phillips curve.

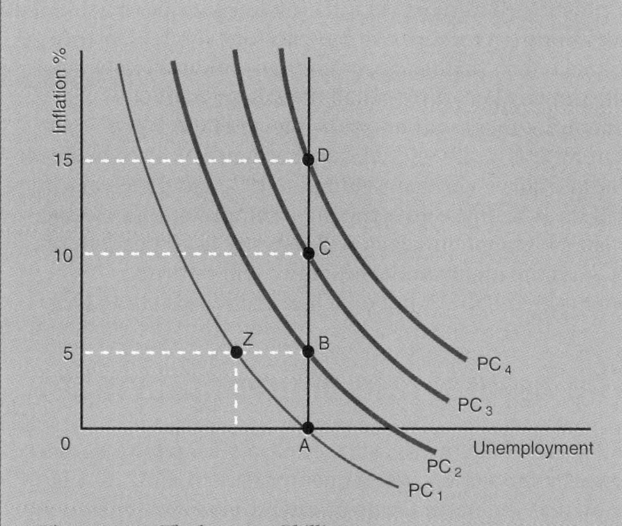

Figure 91.5 *The long run Phillips curve*
In the long run, the Phillips curve is vertical. Attempts by government to reduce unemployment below the natural rate of unemployment OA will be successful in the short run, for instance moving the economy from A to Z. But in the long run the only result will be higher inflation.

In Figure 91.5, the original Phillips curve is PC_1. Workers and firms assume that there will be no price changes and the economy is in equilibrium at the point A. The government now increases aggregate demand, pushing the economy to the point Z on the short run Phillips curve PC_1, reducing unemployment and increasing inflation to 5 per cent. If workers suffer from money illusion, the economy will eventually return to the point A as explained above. But assume that they are more

QUESTION 2 In September 1994, the year on year inflation rate was 2.2 per cent. A number of pay deals were concluded in September and October 1994 including:

- a 3.5 per cent increase plus a £325 lump sum from October 1 for manual workers at British Aerospace's plant at Woodford in Cheshire after a 24 hour stoppage by operators;
- Anglesey Aluminium increased pay by 4.7 per cent at its Holyhead plant after an earlier offer was turned down by the workforce;
- Honeywell Controls Systems in Motherwell reached a two year deal with a 4 per cent rise from October plus a 1.5 per cent rise next March and the next deal to be from March 1 1996;
- employees at Westland received a 3.25 per cent pay increase after a number of groups staged one or two day strikes;
- Britannia Airways improved its pay offer for 1 400 cabin staff after a strike ballot vote with a guarantee that no rises would be less than 3 per cent.

Source: adapted from the *Financial Times*, 22.10.1994.

Explain whether these workers' decisions to accept their pay offers would have been different if inflation had been running at: (a) 0 per cent and (b) 15 per cent.

sophisticated and expect inflation to continue at 5 per cent per annum. Workers will bargain for even higher money wages which further push up prices. Hence real wages fall and workers drop out of the labour market. Unemployment will return to a level of OA but a 5 per cent inflation rate will become permanent. The short run Phillips curve will have shifted to PC_2 and the economy will be at B. If the government attempts again to reduce unemployment, inflation will rise, say to 10 per cent on PC_2. In the long run the economy will return to unemployment OA but on a higher Phillips curve PC_3.

The natural rate of unemployment

In Figure 91.5, why does the economy keep tending back towards the same level of unemployment, OA? OA is known as the **natural rate of unemployment** (☞ unit 90). It is the rate of unemployment which exists when the economy is in long run equilibrium (i.e. where aggregate demand equals long run aggregate supply). It was explained in unit 65 that the economy, based on classical assumptions, tends towards its long run equilibrium level through changes in wages and prices. If the economy is below the natural rate of unemployment, then aggregate demand is above long run aggregate supply, as at the point B in Figure 91.4. Workers will be able to bid up wage rates, and the short run aggregate supply curve will shift upwards till long run equilibrium is once again re-established. If unemployment is above its natural rate, aggregate demand is less than long run aggregate supply. Unemployment will force workers to accept wage cuts. Firms will then take on more labour, expanding output and lowering unemployment to its natural level.

If the economy is in long run equilibrium, the labour market will also be in equilibrium. So another definition of the natural rate of unemployment is that it is the rate of unemployment which occurs when the demand for labour equals the supply of labour.

In the long run, the economy will always tend towards its natural rate of unemployment. Hence the long run Phillips curve is vertical. It is the line ABCD in Figure 91.5. There is no long run trade-off between unemployment and inflation. A government can reduce unemployment below its natural rate in the short run but, in the long run, unemployment will climb back up again and inflation will be higher.

Reducing inflation

Yet another way of defining the natural rate of unemployment is that it is the rate of unemployment which can be sustained without a change in the inflation rate. Sometimes it is called the NAIRU - THE NON-ACCELERATING INFLATION RATE OF UNEMPLOYMENT. To understand why, consider what happens if the government attempts to reduce inflation. In Figure 91.6, the government wishes to reduce the inflation rate from 10 per cent to 5 per cent. It can only do this by travelling down the short run Phillips curve from the point A to the point B, increasing unemployment in the short term from 1½ million to 3 million. The economy will now slowly return to its natural rate of unemployment of 1½ million at the point C. So to reduce inflation, the government must accept higher unemployment in the short run. If it is not prepared to pay this price, inflation will remain constant at 10 per cent with 1½ million unemployed.

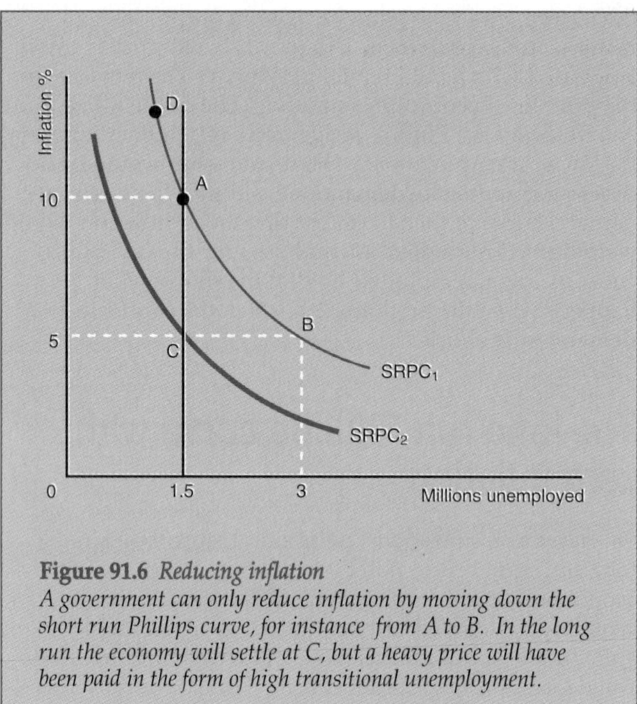

Figure 91.6 *Reducing inflation*
A government can only reduce inflation by moving down the short run Phillips curve, for instance from A to B. In the long run the economy will settle at C, but a heavy price will have been paid in the form of high transitional unemployment.

An increase in the inflation rate above 10 per cent can only come about through an increase in aggregate demand over and above what it would otherwise have been. This increase will again move the economy off the point A, this time up the short run Phillips curve to D.

So the labour market can be in equilibrium at the natural rate of unemployment (at the NAIRU) with any inflation rate. Hence, once again the long run Phillips curve is vertical.

The only way to reduce the NAIRU (i.e. push the vertical long run Phillips curve to the left), according to classical economists, is to adopt supply side policies (☞ unit 69).

Keynesians, monetarists and classical economists

The theory that the Phillips curve was vertical in the long run was put forward by the founder of modern monetarism, Milton Friedman. It was he too who suggested that workers might not suffer from money illusion. Hence his theory is sometimes called the **expectations-augmented Phillips curve hypothesis** or **adaptive-expectations hypothesis**.

Many Keynesians doubt the existence of a natural rate

of unemployment. This is because they believe that it takes a very long time for labour markets to clear if there is mass unemployment. In Figure 91.6, a government which creates unemployment of CB in order to reduce inflation may well find that the economy gets stuck with an unemployment level of 3 million. Unless it is prepared to wait perhaps a decade or more, it can only reduce unemployment by expanding demand again and accepting higher inflation.

On the other hand, New Classical economists, led in the UK by Professor Patrick Minford of Liverpool University, have suggested that the short run Phillips curve does not exist. In their theory of **rational expectations** they argue that economic agents, such as workers, trade unions and employers, are able to see whether inflation and unemployment are likely to rise or fall in the future. If the government states that it is prepared to accept a rise in unemployment in order to reduce inflation, workers will immediately moderate their wage demands in order to avoid unemployment. Inflation therefore falls immediately. So the conclusion is that the economy will always be on the vertical long run curve because economic agents perfectly adapt their expectations in the light of economic news.

Key terms

The Phillips curve - the line which shows that higher rates of unemployment are associated with lower rates of change of money wage rates and therefore inflation and vice versa.
Money illusion - when economic agents such as workers believe that changes in money values are the same as changes in real values despite inflation (or deflation) occurring at the time.
NAIRU, the non-accelerating inflation rate of unemployment - the natural rate of unemployment, the level of unemployment which can be sustained with a change in the inflation rate.

QUESTION 3

Table 91.1 *Unemployment and inflation*

Per cent

	Unemployment	Inflation
1979	4.1	13
1980	5.1	18
1981	8.1	12
1982	9.6	9
1983	10.5	5
1984	10.7	5
1985	10.9	6
1986	11.1	3
1987	10.0	4
1988	8.1	5
1989	6.5	8
1990	5.8	10
1991	8.0	6
1992	9.7	4
1993	10.3	2
1994	9.4	3

Source: adapted from CSO, *Economic Trends Annual Supplement.*

In 1979, a Conservative government was elected with a promise to bring down the rate of inflation.

(a) Using a diagram, explain why reducing the rate of inflation might increase the rate of unemployment.
(b) Do the data suggest that counter-inflation policies in the 1980s and 1990s had an unemployment cost?

Applied economics

The Phillips Curve, 1963-1994

Between 1957, the date of publication of Phillips' original article, and 1965 the UK economy behaved in a way that the original Phillips curve would have predicted. In Figure 91.7, the points for 1963, 1964 and 1965 lie on the original Phillips curve. However, from 1967 combinations of unemployment and inflation rates moved to the right of the original curve. Indeed, rising inflation became associated with rising unemployment, contrary to the predictions of the Phillips curve which suggests a negative correlation between the two variables.

The expectations-augmented Phillips curve hypothesis would suggest that the downward sloping short run Phillips curve had shifted to the right because workers had increased their expectations of future inflation rates. They no longer suffered from money illusion and hence they took into account future price rises when bargaining for wage increases. Is there any evidence to suggest that workers ceased to suffer from money illusion from the mid-1960s onwards?

One factor must be that inflation from 1964 onwards was much higher than it had been over the previous 40 years. Apart from a brief period during the Korean War in the early 1950s, inflation had at worst been 1 or 2 per cent per annum. Therefore it was a reasonable assumption on the part of workers that money wage increases would roughly equal real wage increases. However, from 1964 onwards, inflation increased substantially, and by 1975 had peaked at 24.1 per cent. It would be surprising if workers had not lost their money illusion after 1964 given these trends.

Another factor must be that 1965 saw the implementation of the first statutory prices and incomes

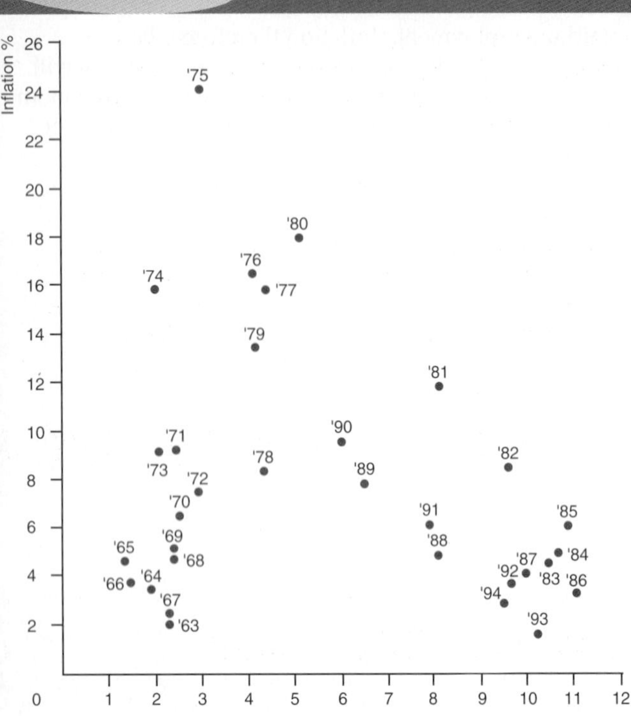

Source: adapted from CSO, *Economic Trends Annual Supplement.*

Figure 91.7 *Phillips curve data, 1963-1994*

policy (☞ unit 95). The Labour government of Harold Wilson announced that no wage increases could be awarded for a period of six months in order to curb rising inflation. This ensured that inflation and its control became a central issue in British politics. Workers could not help but become aware that inflation was important for the purchasing power of their wage packets.

The Edward Heath government of 1970-1974 positively encouraged trade unions in 1972-3 to settle for index-linked pay deals with employers as part of its prices and incomes policy. It believed that inflation would fall in the short term and that therefore such deals would produce lower pay rises than if unions had bargained on the basis of the current rate of inflation. In fact, rising world commodity prices, particularly of oil, made these deals inflationary.

During the 1970s and 1980s, it could be argued that trade unions bargained on the basis of 'RPI+' (the RPI, the Retail Price Index, is the most commonly used measure of inflation in the UK ☞ unit 93). If inflation was running at 10 per cent, then trade unions negotiated on the basis of

To what extent is there a link between rising prices and unemployment in the UK?

securing 10 per cent plus a real pay increase.

This pattern of bargaining could lead to perverse effects. Assume the government attempted to reduce inflation by increasing interest rates (monetary policy) or increasing indirect taxes (to reduce aggregate demand through fiscal policy). Both of these in the short term have the effect of increasing the inflation rate because both the mortgage interest rate and indirect tax rates are included in the RPI measure of inflation. Unions would then negotiate higher wage rises based on the higher RPI, which had in part been caused by government policy attempting to reduce inflation.

Since 1979, the government has attempted to break the link running from increases in inflation to wage increases. It has done this through a variety of **supply side measures**, including reducing trade union power and encouraging individual rather than collective bargaining. In the first half of the 1990s, certain employers have managed to push through pay increases which have been below the rate of inflation. Some economists argue that lower unemployment in the second half of the 1990s will lead to a return to inflation based bargaining. Other economists believe that a new economic climate has been created in which inflation and wage rises have become decoupled. If this is the case, then it might be possible even in the short run to have stable inflation at the natural rate of unemployment.

Unemployment and inflation in OECD countries

Table 91.2 *Inflation (percentage change on previous year)*

	United Kingdom	Germany	France	Italy	EU	United States	Japan	Canada	Major 7 OECD countries[1]	All OECD countries[2]
1985	6.1	2.2	5.9	8.6	6.2	3.5	2.1	4.0	4.0	4.9
1986	3.4	-0.1	2.7	6.2	3.7	1.9	0.4	4.1	2.0	3.0
1987	4.2	0.2	3.1	4.6	3.3	3.7	-0.2	4.4	2.9	3.6
1988	4.9	1.3	2.8	5.0	3.6	4.0	0.5	4.0	3.4	4.3
1989	7.8	2.8	3.5	6.6	5.3	4.9	2.2	5.1	4.5	5.4
1990	9.5	2.7	3.4	6.0	5.6	5.4	3.1	4.7	5.0	5.8
1991	5.9	3.5	3.2	6.5	5.1	4.2	3.3	5.6	4.3	5.2
1992	3.7	4.0	2.4	5.3	4.2	3.1	1.6	1.5	3.1	4.0
1993	1.6	4.2	2.1	4.2	3.4	3.0	1.1	1.9	2.6	3.6

Table 91.3 *Unemployment rates (percentage of total labour force)*

	United Kingdom	Germany	France	Italy	EU	United States	Japan	Canada	Major 7 OECD countries[1]	All OECD countries[2]
1985	11.2	7.1	10.2	9.6	10.8	7.1	2.6	10.4	7.2	7.8
1986	11.2	6.4	10.4	10.5	10.8	6.9	2.8	9.5	7.1	7.7
1987	10.3	6.2	10.5	10.9	10.6	6.1	2.8	8.8	6.7	7.3
1988	8.6	6.2	10.0	11.0	9.9	5.4	2.5	7.7	6.1	6.7
1989	7.2	5.6	9.4	10.9	9.0	5.2	2.3	7.5	5.7	6.2
1990	6.8	4.8	8.9	10.3	8.4	5.4	2.1	8.1	5.6	6.1
1991	8.8	4.2	9.4	9.9	8.7	6.6	2.1	10.2	6.3	6.8
1992	9.9	4.6	10.4	10.5	9.5	7.3	2.2	11.2	6.9	7.5
1993	10.3	5.8	11.7	10.2	10.7	6.7	2.5	11.1	6.9	7.8

1. UK, Germany, France, Italy, USA, Japan and Canada.
2. 25 countries.

Source: adapted from CSO, *Economic Trends*.

1. **Distinguish between short run and long run Phillips curves.**
2. **Do the data suggest that Phillips curves exist in OECD countries?**
3. **To what extent can governments use demand management policies to reduce unemployment without affecting inflation?**

Unemployment and government policy

Summary

1. Demand management techniques can be used to reduce cyclical unemployment in the economy.
2. Voluntary unemployment is best tackled by a variety of supply side policies. Supply side economists would advocate measures such as improving job search information, reducing the benefit to wage ratio, training, abolishing minimum wages and increasing the mobility of workers.
3. The natural rate of unemployment can be reduced if long run aggregate supply in the economy grows.

Demand management

Unemployment can be classified into five types (☞ unit 90). If unemployment is Keynesian, or demand-deficient in nature (i.e. caused by too little spending in the economy), then it may be appropriate for government to use policies which lead to an increase in aggregate demand.

During the 1950s and 1960s, successive British governments used **demand management** techniques (☞ unit 68) to keep unemployment at extremely low levels by historical standards. If the economy was below full employment, the government intervened to fill the existing **deflationary gap**. A deflationary gap is the increase in autonomous spending needed to bring the economy back to full employment. Because the government could most easily control its own spending, or change consumption spending by changes in tax, it could affect total spending in the economy by spending more or reducing taxes (i.e. increasing the PSBR). It would also loosen monetary policy, mainly by relaxing controls on the availability of credit in the economy (☞ unit 77). Similarly, if there were excess demand in the economy and inflationary pressures built up, the government would eliminate the **inflationary gap** - the fall in autonomous spending needed to eliminate inflation in the economy - by reducing the PSBR and tightening credit controls.

The change in the budget deficit or surplus did not need to be of the same magnitude as the deflationary gap. This was because of the **multiplier** effect. For instance, if the deflationary gap were £10 000 million and the multiplier were 2, then the government would only need to increase its spending by £5 000 million to fill the deflationary gap.

The deflationary gap could even be filled if the government's budget deficit remained unchanged. If the government increased both government spending and taxation by the same amount, then aggregate demand would rise because of the **balanced budget multiplier effect** (☞ unit 82).

The effects of demand management policies can be seen in Figure 92.1. A Keynesian aggregate supply curve is assumed (☞ unit 65). The economy is initially at A, below the full employment level of output of OR. An increase in aggregate demand from AD_1 to AD_2 will restore the economy to full employment, albeit at some cost in terms of higher prices. However, a further increase in aggregate demand, from AD_2 to AD_3, will be purely inflationary, since the economy is already at full employment.

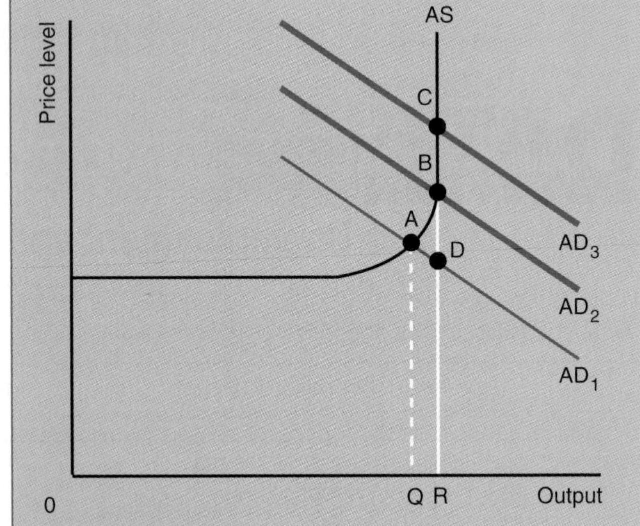

Figure 92.1 *Demand management*
According to Keynesians, expansionary fiscal or monetary policy can shift the AD curve to the right. If the economy is at A, at less than full employment, then an increased budget deficit could move the economy to B. If the economy is already at B, fiscal expansion will be purely inflationary.

Keynesians today recognise that the demand management policies undertaken in the 1950s and 1960s were too simplistic and failed to take account of both inflation and the natural rate of unemployment. Despite this, modern Keynesians argue that **cyclical unemployment** can be tackled by fiscal policy. For instance, in a recession, it would be wrong for a government deliberately to set out to keep its budget balanced as happened in the 1930s. It should allow the **automatic stabilisers** (☞ unit 68) of reduced tax revenues and increased spending on unemployment benefit to break the fall in output. It could also use **active fiscal policy**, deliberately increasing public spending and cutting taxes, to speed up the recovery. Governments, though, need to be very careful not to overstimulate the economy given the inflation and balance of payments constraints (☞ unit 103). With high natural rates of unemployment as well, demand management policies can only be part of the solution to reducing unemployment rates.

Classical economists argue that the long run aggregate supply curve is vertical (☞ unit 65). The economy will always revert to its full employment level. Demand management policies are therefore at best unnecessary and at worst seriously damaging to the economy. If nothing else, expansionary policy will always lead to higher inflation than would otherwise be the case. In Figure 92.1, with an aggregate demand curve of AD_1 and the economy initially at A, there would be a movement back to full employment at D if there were no government intervention. Active demand management, which shifts the aggregate demand curve to AD_2, results in the same output level but higher prices at B.

QUESTION 1 In his 1959 Budget, the Chancellor of the Exchequer, Heathcoat Amory, substantially reduced taxes. He justified this in the following words: 'The prospect for home production as I have set it out does not represent a full enough use of the capital resources which have been created in recent years. Nor can we be content with the possibility that unemployment might continue at around the present levels ... (However) we must at all costs make it our business not to return to an overload on the economy, which would make a resumption of inflation inevitable. At the present time, however, this is clearly not an immediate danger.'

(a) Using an aggregate demand and supply diagram, explain why the Chancellor cut taxes.
(b) Would his policy have been any different if inflation had been rising at the time?
(c) The economy grew very strongly in the second half of 1959 and in 1960. Over the next three years the government was to restrict the growth of demand both through fiscal and monetary policies. Using a diagram, suggest why the government adopted deflationary policies.

Supply side policies

Economists are divided about the best way to tackle cyclical unemployment. However, they agree that demand management policies cannot be used to tackle other types of unemployment. These need to be reduced by **supply side policies**.

Frictional unemployment If unemployment is short term, then there is a variety of measures which the government could employ to reduce this type of unemployment. One is to increase the flow of information to unemployed workers by providing better employment services. In the UK, for instance, this would mean more spending on Jobcentres. If unemployed workers can be matched to vacancies more quickly, they will spend less time on the dole and frictional unemployment will fall.

Another measure would be reduce or withdraw benefits to the short term unemployed. For instance, if all benefits were cut after three months, rather than, say, six months or a year, there would be a greater incentive for unemployed workers to find work quickly. Increased benefit rights and increased redundancy payments can only act as incentives for the short term unemployed to spend longer searching for jobs.

Measures to combat structural unemployment, such as increasing the mobility of labour between regions or industries might also help reduce frictional unemployment.

QUESTION 2 In 1995, the government passed legislation which would replace unemployment benefit, a non-means tested benefit, by a new Jobseeker's allowance. Unemployment benefit was payable for up to 12 months to workers. Those receiving the benefit could continue receiving it even if they turned down jobs which they considered were unsuitable for them.

The Jobseeker's allowance, in contrast, would last only 6 months before being means tested. Jobseekers must take any job offered, regardless of the level of pay. If they don't, then they will lose their entitlement to the allowance. Anyone failing to look for work under a jobseeker's agreement, a contract which the unemployed person must sign, or refusing to be directed into a job on offer, could have benefit entitlement withdrawn for up to 26 weeks, with only discretionary payments available where a claimant can prove hardship. Any person judged to be 'voluntarily' unemployed will have their entitlement to the allowance withdrawn. They will then be forced to rely on hardship payments for a possible 26 weeks.

It is estimated that the government will save £400 million a year through the change as fewer workers become entitled to receive the Jobseeker's allowance compared to the old unemployment benefit.

Source: adapted from the *Financial Times*, 23.5.1995.

(a) How might the introduction of the Jobseeker's allowance help reduce frictional unemployment?
(b) Discuss whether it would have an impact on any other type of unemployment.

Structural unemployment Longer term structural unemployment is difficult to deal with. If the unemployment is regional, with some regions having much higher unemployment rates than other regions, then Keynesian economists would argue that the government should give financial incentives for firms to move to those areas. All countries in the EU, for instance, have regional funds which they use to lure large companies to set up in high unemployment regions. Spending on infrastructure, such as motorways, or on human capital such as retraining, can also lure firms into a region. Classical economists would tend to rely more on free market forces. They argue that high unemployment regions are likely to be characterised by low land and labour costs. This, in itself, should attract inward investment. They also argue that regional funds tend to pay out money to firms which would have moved into the region anyway . They are therefore largely a waste of taxpayers' money.

If the unemployment is industrial, caused for instance by the decline of a traditional industry, then Keynesian economists would argue that governments should spend money on retraining workers from those industries. Declining industries also tend to create local unemployment blackspots and therefore an injection of regional funds can be helpful too. Classical economists would again tend to rely more on free market forces. In particular, they would suggest that large redundancy benefits and high unemployment benefits will prolong any search for work. They would therefore suggest lower benefits and cutting benefits to workers who refuse to take lower paid jobs.

Some unemployed workers remain unemployed because of their length of time out of work. The longer the time spent out of the workforce, the lower will be a worker's human capital. On the other hand, employment creates human capital if only because of the addition made through experience of work. There is also considerable evidencethat employers sift through applications on the basis of length of unemployment. The long term unemployed are unlikely even to be invited for interview. In one sense, this discrimination represents rational behaviour on the part of employers because unemployment destroys human capital. Some economists have argued that employers who take on the long term unemployed should receive a subsidy, such as a proportion of the benefits that the unemployed worker would have received if he or she had remained unemployed.

QUESTION 3 Darren Chow, 25, unemployed, father of one baby with another due in March, is a scheme veteran. He has been on five training schemes since leaving school with almost no qualifications, but has never had a proper job. 'At the end of the training, I just get thrown back on the dole. They don't get you into work.' Chow lives in the Benwell area of Newcastle-on-Tyne. The men locally used to work at the Vickers engineering complex and other heavy industrial works along the River Tyne. Vickers is still there, but like most of the new workplaces along the river, it now employs not masses of labourers but a highly trained, skilled elite.

Chow has picked up Youth Training qualifications as a painter and decorator and a City and Guilds in catering from a year at college. This month, he starts at a Job Club, a government sponsored initiative to help the unemployed find work. If it proves fruitless, he plans to return to college for more catering training.

Disillusion with training schemes is widespread. However, one scheme in Newcastle, the West End scheme, offers some real prospects for unskilled men. The government-funded Newcastle City Challenge urban regeneration initiative has employed Larry Watt, an experienced construction project manager, to persuade companies to which it awards building contracts to recruit local people to work on site. His job is not easy. Many contractors believe trainees lack skills. However, Watt is persistent. The West End trainees he offers do have skills, having attended a Tyneside scheme run by Jarvis, the construction company, which offers 39 weeks of concentrated training, including site experience, in brick laying or joinery, and a National Vocational Qualification. So far, 50 West End men have taken up this scheme. Half are now employed and the rest are still in training with Jarvis. As Robert Oxley, someone who has got a job from the scheme, says: 'It's up to employers to give people a chance. There needs to be better quality of training and better prospects. It's no good having a lot of training if there are no prospects at the end of it.'

Source: adapted from the *Financial Times*, 18.1.1994.

To what extent can training schemes reduce structural unemployment? Use evidence from the passage in your answer.

Real wage unemployment As has already been mentioned, cutting real wage unemployment can be accomplished by cutting unemployment benefits. This gives a greater incentive for workers to take on low paid work. Paying employers to take on unemployed workers would also cut real wage unemployment. This is because at given wage rates, the demand for the long term unemployed is less than its supply. Equally, the government giving benefits to low paid workers cuts real wage unemployment because those employed workers might otherwise not be willing to take on that low paid work.

Classical economists would also argue that reducing trade union power and abolishing minimum wages are solutions to real wage unemployment. Trade unions act to increase the real wages of workers. Without unions, wages would be lower and therefore employers would be willing to take on more workers. Equally, minimum wage legislation prevents employers from creating jobs below the minimum wage and hence unemployment is increased.

The natural rate of unemployment

The supply side measures outlined so far are only some of the measures which can be taken to reduce the **natural rate of unemployment** (☞ unit 90). They tend to be measures which make existing labour markets function more efficiently. However, another way of reducing the natural rate of unemployment is to increase the growth rate of the whole economy. This assumes that increased economic activity will increase the number of jobs in the economy and therefore reduce the rate of unemployment.

Classical economists believe that tax rates are crucial to economic decision making. Hence, cuts in the marginal rate of income, social security or profit taxes will lead to significant increases in incentives to work, take risks and increase wealth (☞ unit 69). Policies such as **privatisation, increased competition** and **deregulation** will also increase the productive potential of the economy according to classical economists. Keynesian economists tend to emphasise more the role of investment in both physical and human capital and policies which governments can adopt to increase investment in the economy.

Applied economics

Unemployment policy in the UK, 1950-1995

The experience of the 1930s and 1940s

During the period of the Great Depression in the 1930s, unemployment in the UK rose to 13 per cent of the labour force. Some regions were worse affected than others, and many industrial towns had unemployment rates exceeding 25 per cent. The poverty that unemployment caused scarred this generation of workers. Therefore, when the ideas of John Maynard Keynes, put forward throughout the 1930s, most famously in his *General Theory of Employment, Interest and Money*, held out the promise that the problem of unemployment could be solved by increasing government spending, they were eagerly taken up in the post-war period. In 1944, a White Paper stated that it would become a government policy objective to secure a 'high and stable level of employment' after the war was over. The experience of the war itself, when unemployment fell to almost zero, was confirmation for many that government could achieve this aim of low unemployment.

1950-65, the era of demand management

The 1950s and early 1960s saw governments using Keynesian demand management policies with increasing confidence. Unemployment throughout the period remained low by historical standards, averaging only 1.7 per cent. When unemployment rose in a recession, the government would increase its spending, reduce taxes and loosen credit controls. When the economy overheated, with low unemployment but rising inflation and a worsening current account balance, the government would reduce aggregate demand by raising taxes, reducing government spending and tightening credit controls.

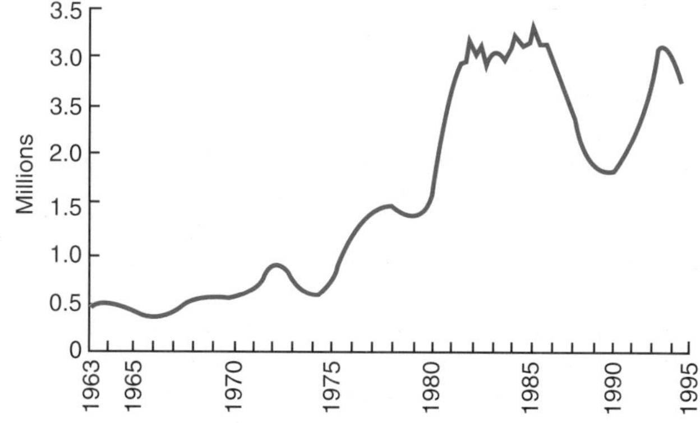

Figure 92.2 *Unemployment, 1963-94*

For instance, in 1963, with unemployment rising to nearly half a million, a post-war peak, and growth faltering, the Conservative government of the day put forward a highly reflationary Budget. Unemployment fell sharply to 300 000 by 1965 but the current account went into deficit, giving rise to exchange rate crises for the pound.

Structural unemployment was a problem throughout the period. It was caused mainly by the decline of traditional primary industries such as coal mining, heavy manufacturing such as shipbuilding, and certain other manufacturing industries such as textiles. These industries were concentrated in the North of England, Scotland, Wales and Northern Ireland. Hence, structural unemployment manifested itself primarily as regional unemployment. The government tackled this through a range of regional incentives to firms setting up in high unemployment regions (☞ unit 69).

1966-1979, the growing disenchantment with demand management

By the mid-1960s, governments were finding it increasingly frustrating that they could not achieve both low unemployment and low inflation combined with a current account surplus. It was recognised that demand management techniques had their limitations. In 1966, the Labour government under Harold Wilson imposed a **prices and incomes policy** (☞ unit 95). The aim of the policy was to reduce inflation without having to deflate the economy through higher taxes or reduced government spending. Nevertheless, deflationary fiscal unemployment designed to combat the current account deficit, and a rising **natural rate of unemployment**, led to a near doubling of unemployment between 1966 and 1967 and it remained at a post-war high of half a million till 1970.

The incoming Conservative government under Edward Heath was quickly faced by a recession in the economy. In the winter of 1971-72, unemployment gradually increased to nearly 1 million. The government felt forced to do a U-turn in its free market policies and in 1972, the Chancellor, Anthony Barber, gave a large fiscal boost to the economy in his March Budget - his 'dash for growth' as it was called at the time. This was to be the last time that any government put the control of unemployment as its main economic priority. In the resulting boom, growth accelerated to near record levels, unemployment fell back towards the half a million level, but inflation went out of control and the current account went into a large deficit. A vicious twist to the Barber boom was then given by the quadrupling of oil prices in 1973-74 (☞ unit 8). The government lost an election in February 1974 and the incoming Labour government, still committed to the 1944 objective of low unemployment, failed to provide any coherent policy response to the huge problems imposed by the **stagflation** of the time.

The following year, however, the government made the

control of inflation its main economic priority, with the recognition that the current account had to be returned to balance in the medium term.

Deflationary fiscal and monetary policies were combined with a prices and incomes policy to deflate the economy. The commitment to full employment was abandoned, at least in the short term, although the Labour Party continued to see this as a long term objective. This enormous change in thinking, which was led by a revival of interest in monetarist ideas, is perhaps best summarised in a speech given by the Labour Prime Minister of the day, Jim Callaghan, to his Party Conference in 1976. He said: 'We used to think that you could just spend your way out of a recession, and increase employment, by cutting taxes and boosting government spending. I tell you in all candour that that option no longer exists, and that in so far as it ever did exist, it worked by injecting inflation into the economy.'

Unemployment rose quickly from 600 000 in 1974 to nearly 1.5 million in 1978. The government had little coherent response to this rise in unemployment. Youth unemployment was tackled by introducing what is now Youth Training. A variety of make-work schemes were offered to adult unemployed workers, which eventually became the adult training schemes of today. However, the rise in unemployment was considered a necessary price to pay for the fall in inflation, which fell from 24 per cent in 1975 to 8 per cent in 1978. Nevertheless, the government was unwilling to see unemployment rise further. In 1978-79, against a backdrop of a reflationary fiscal and monetary policy, it attempted to bring inflation down further by tightening the pay ceiling in its incomes policy. Workers rejected this, and in the 'winter of discontent' of 1978-79 a series of major damaging strikes which secured large pay rises for the workers concerned ripped the incomes policy apart. The government was left with no credible anti-inflationary policy.

1979-1995, the abandonment of the objective of full employment

Labour lost the election of June 1979 and the Conservative Party came into power under Margaret Thatcher committed to a complete abandonment of many of the policies which had characterised the post-war period. The government believed that its main objective should be to control inflation through the pursuit of sound monetary policy. It should also reduce state involvement in the economy in order to allow private sector markets to work more efficiently. Sound money and less government intervention would provide higher economic growth and greater prosperity. In the short term, a price that might have to be paid to achieve this was a further rise in unemployment. The government abandoned any commitment to keeping unemployment low or stable. Unemployment would settle down at the NAIRU, the non-accelerating inflation rate of unemployment (☞ unit 91). This was the natural rate of unemployment at which stable prices could be maintained.

The government abandoned any attempt to manipulate aggregate demand through fiscal or monetary policy. Demand management was seen to be counter-productive given that the long run aggregate supply curve in the economy was vertical. Short run falls in unemployment could be secured by moving down the Phillips curve and up the short run aggregate supply curve. However, the consequent boom could only lead to a following recession in which all the gains in unemployment would be lost again. The only way to reduce unemployment was through supply side policies designed to reduce the natural rate of unemployment.

The incoming government in 1979 immediately began to tackle rising inflation by sharply increasing interest rates. With a rising pound as well, caused by high interest rates and North Sea oil, the economy quickly went into a recession. The recession of 1980-82 was the worst recession since the Great Depression. Unemployment rose to over 3 million, almost matching the unemployment rate of the 1930s. A traditional Keynesian response would have been to reduce taxes and increase public spending in 1981 to get the economy out of recession. The Chancellor at the time, Geoffrey Howe, actually increased taxes in his 1981 budget in order to reduce the PSBR, thus putting less pressure on interest rates which are affected by the size of government borrowing.

Unemployment remained stubbornly high between 1982 and 1986, hardly changing at all from the 3 million figure. The government then made a fundamental policy mistake, pursuing too lax a fiscal and monetary policy in the mistaken belief that their supply side reforms could now enable the economy to grow above its trend rate for the post-war period. In the ensuing Lawson boom, unemployment fell rapidly, from 3.3 million in 1986 to 1.6 million in 1990. However, the expansion of aggregate demand which caused this fall in unemployment also led to a small build up of inflationary pressures. In 1988, the government reacted savagely to this by doubling interest rates. The economy slowly went into recession. However, when the recession came in 1990-92, it proved to be the longest recession since the 1930s and led to unemployment climbing back up again to 3 million. From 1993, unemployment began to fall again fairly rapidly to 2.5 million in 1995.

Throughout the period 1979-95, the government made no attempt to use demand management policies to change the level of unemployment, leaving it to find its own 'natural' level. However, the government did vigorously pursue **supply side policies** (☞ unit 69) designed mainly to increase efficiency in the economy, but with the hoped-for outcome that employment would rise. Many supply side policies led directly to job losses in the economy. For instance, privatisation has led to a shake-out of jobs in the privatised industries, the result of increased **productive efficiency**. To reduce unemployment, these needed to be more than matched by new jobs created in the economy. The government attempted to create an 'enterprise culture' (☞ unit 69), particularly encouraging the growth of small firms in the economy. It had a positive attitude to inward investment, for instance from Japanese companies. This was in marked contrast to the attitude of some European governments which saw inward investment as being harmful to their domestic industries. From the late

1980s, there was considerable emphasis put on education and training in order to increase levels of human capital in the economy.

Creating a climate where businesses could set up, expand and earn high profits was seen as essential for higher economic growth and therefore lower unemployment. But equally, the government believed that high unemployment could only be tackled through reform of the labour market. Trade unions were seen as driving up wages and creating uncertainty through constant industrial action, thus destroying jobs. So the government introducing sweeping trade union reforms which broke the power of the union movement. Government legislation which gave protection to women and children in the workplace was repealed in order to 'free' markets. Wages councils, which set minimum wages in low pay industries, and which were claimed to create unemployment, were finally abolished in 1994. Encouragement was also given to employers to reduce employment costs by making it easier to cut staff when necessary. There was a marked increase in the numbers of workers working part-time or on fixed term contracts. These moves to create a 'flexible' labour market were driven by a belief that jobs could be created and prosperity increased if the UK could become a lower wage, less regulated economy than her main trading partners, particularly in Europe. The rapid fall in unemployment in 1993 and 1994 as the economy came out of recession is claimed by some economists to be the direct result of this new flexibility in the labour market. Firms which fired labour as the economy went into recession were confident enough to hire again as the economy came out of recession.

No political party in the second half of the 1990s has committed itself to securing full employment in the future. The high unemployment experienced by the UK is little different from the experiences of other European countries since the mid 1970s. In an integrated Europe, it is almost impossible to conceive of the UK being able rapidly to reduce unemployment to levels which would be, say, half the value of her Continental partners. Nevertheless, some economists believe that demand management techniques should be used when the economy is below full employment and remain sceptical that supply side policies are the only effective unemployment policies in the long term.

60 point strategy for putting people back to work

- **To enhance the creation and diffusion of technological know-how:**

Invest in the creation of new knowledge through basic scientific research and help companies gain access to such knowledge.

Promote and strengthen mechanisms for international co-operation to gain economies of scale and avoid duplication of R&D.

Reduce uncertainties that impair the creation and diffusion of new technologies. Measures could include promoting multilateral agreements on intellectual property rights and standards, introducing transparent rules on government support for strategic technologies and ensuring a sound legal framework for spreading know-how.

Ease the absorption of new technologies in companies through, for example, making better use of public procurement and removing regulatory barriers to new information infrastructures.

- **To increase working time flexibility:**

Remove obstacles in labour legislation that impede flexible working time arrangements.

Extend part-time work to the public sector.

Move from the household to the individual as the base for income tax.

Reduce or remove non-neutral fiscal incentives to early retirement of workers.

Realign policies to give older workers more opportunities to stay in work.

- **To nurture an entrepreneurial climate:**

Lower start up costs and simplify compliance rules to boost new company start-ups.

Help small businesses to grow by improving information and advice on such matters as business planning, equipment and access to training and R&D.

Identify and cut out unwarranted regulatory impediments to small businesses gaining access to credit.

- **To increase wage and labour cost flexibility:**

Reassess the role of statutory minimum wages as a method of redistributing incomes. If countries decide to keep a legal minimum wage to combat poverty, they should index it to prices rather than average earnings and ensure sufficient differentiation of wage rates by area and region to prevent minimum wages hitting youth employment or jobs in low productivity areas.

Reduce non-wage labour costs, especially in Europe, by cutting taxes on labour.

Reduce or remove provisions in

the structure of tax and social security contributions that discourage hiring or part-time employment.

Reduce direct taxes on the low-paid where this would boost demand for workers, while protecting their incomes.

Refocus, as a medium-term measure, collective bargaining to cover framework agreements that would leave employers free to respond flexibly to market trends.

Introduce 'opening clauses' that would allow collective agreements covering many workers to be renegotiated a lower level.

Increase competition in product markets through such means as deregulation and privatisation.

- **To reform employment security provisions:**

Prevent dismissals on unfair grounds but allow firings if needed on economic grounds.

Loosen mandatory restrictions on dismissals in countries (such as Spain) where they hinder new hiring.

Allow fixed-term contracts but keep the mandatory protection for such contracts relatively light.

- **To expand and enhance active labour market policies:**

Improve public employment services by integrating placement and counselling, unemployment benefit payments and management of labour market programmes.

Ensure benefit claimants stay in regular contact with employment service monopolies.

Maintain training for the jobless in economic downturns, but target training programmes in line with labour market needs.

Allow the labour market authorities to buy and sell training places for the unemployed and involve employers in design and execution of training programmes.

Target job creation measures at groups where unemployment could do great harm, such as long-term unemployed youths. Measures could include special employment subsidies for high unemployment groups. But pay on job-creation programmes should be low and training linked to temporary employment programmes in the public sector.

- **To improve labour force skills:**

Improve initial education. Measures could include provisions of pre-school training for those from disadvantaged backgrounds, measures to reduce early school-leaving, greater involvement of parents in schools and better incentives to motivate teachers.

Improve school-to-work transitions. Measures could include greater partnership between industry and schools, new forms of apprenticeship, new national skill standards, effective career guidance at school, a better balance between academic and technical and vocational studies and a "training wage" low enough to encourage companies to offer many training places.

Improve incentives for companies and workers to invest in continued learning. Measures could include training credits for adult workers or accountancy changes that would make the value of skills clear to companies and workers.

- **To reform unemployment and related benefit systems:**

Restrict unemployment insurance benefit entitlements in countries where these last a long time, to the period of intense job search.

Reduce the amount of dole where it is high relative to a claimant's previous post-tax income.

Restrict benefits of indefinite duration for employable people.

Limit support for collective short-time working to companies in temporary difficulty.

Adjust benefits to ensure low-paid workers are better off when in work, that spouses of the unemployed have an incentive to take part-time work and that long-term unemployed only receive benefit if they take part in 'active labour market programmes'.

Improve information about claimants available to the employment services.

Make employers pay some of the cost of lay offs.

Attack benefit fraud.

Keep a local financing element in assistance benefits to discourage the view that benefits are costless to the local economy.

Source: the *Financial Times* ,8.6.1994.

In June 1994, the OECD published a report, *The OECD Jobs Study*, on how to reduce unemployment in member countries, particularly in Europe where job growth had been poor by international standards and where unemployment in the 1980s and 1990s had consequently risen. Their main recommendations were given in the data above.

1. **Using economic theory, briefly distinguish between different types of unemployment.**
2. **Using the data above, analyse what policies could be used to reduce each different type of unemployment you have described in question 1.**
3. **Assess what policies would be most successful in reducing youth unemployment.**

unit 93 Inflation

Summary

1. Inflation is a general sustained rise in the price level.
2. Inflation is measured by calculating the change in a weighted price index over time. In the UK this index is called the Retail Price Index.
3. A price index only measures inflation for average households. It also cannot take into account changes in the quality and distribution of goods over time.
4. Inflation is generally considered to give rise to economic costs to society. These include shoe-leather and menu costs, psychological and political costs, and costs which arise from the redistribution of income in society. Some economists believe that inflation also results in higher unemployment and lower growth in the long term.
5. Unanticipated inflation tends to give rise to higher economic costs than anticipated inflation.

The meaning of inflation

INFLATION is defined as a sustained general rise in prices. The opposite of inflation - DEFLATION - is a term which can have two meanings. Strictly speaking it is defined as a fall in the PRICE LEVEL. However it can also be used to describe a slowdown in the rate of growth of output of the economy. This slowdown or **recession** is often associated with a fall in the **rate of inflation**. Before the Second World War, recessions were also associated with falls in prices and this is the reason why deflation has come to have these two meanings.

A general rise in prices may be quite moderate. CREEPING INFLATION would describe a situation where prices rose a few per cent on average each year. HYPER-INFLATION, on the other hand, describes a situation where inflation levels are very high. There is no exact figure at which inflation becomes hyper-inflation, but inflation of 100 or 200 per cent per annum would be deemed to be hyper-inflation by most economists.

Measuring inflation

The inflation rate is the change in average prices in an economy over a given period of time. The price level is measured in the form of an **index** (☞ unit 3). So if the price index were 100 today and 110 in one year's time, then the rate of inflation would be 10 per cent.

Calculating a price index is a complicated process. Prices of a representative range of goods and services (a **basket** of goods) need to be recorded on a regular basis. In the UK, the most widely used measure of the price level is the Retail Price Index. In theory, each month, on the same day of the month, surveyors are sent out to record 150 000 prices for 600 items. Prices are recorded in different areas of the country as well as in different types of retail outlets, such as corner shops and supermarkets. These results are averaged out to find the average price of goods and this figure is converted into **index number form**.

Changes in the price of food are more important than changes in the price of tobacco. This is because a larger proportion of total household income is spent on food than on tobacco. Therefore the figures have to be **weighted** before the final index can be calculated. For

QUESTION 1

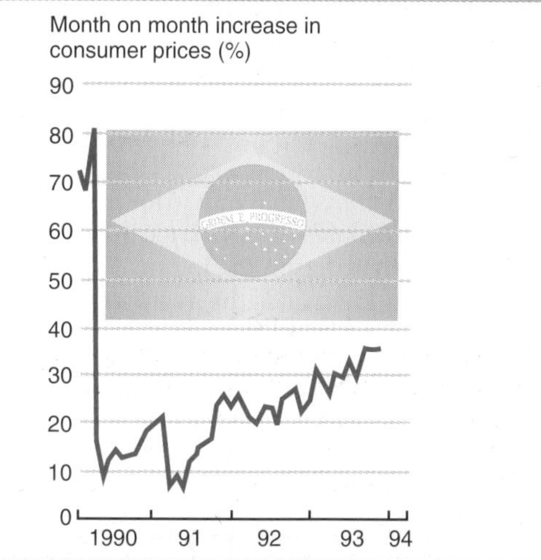

Source: adapted from Datastream.

Figure 93.1 *Inflation in Brazil, 1990-1994*

(a) By how much were prices rising over the period shown in the graph?
(b) To what extent could Brazil be said to have experienced hyper-inflation between 1990 and 1994?

instance, assume that there are only two goods in the economy, food and cars, as shown in Table 93.1. Households spend 75 per cent of their income on food and 25 per cent on cars. There is an increase in the price of food of 8 per cent and of cars of 4 per cent over one year. In a normal average calculation, the 8 per cent and the 4 per cent would be added together and the total divided by 2 to arrive at an average price increase of 6 per cent. But this provides an inaccurate figure because spending on food is more important in the household budget than spending on cars. The figures have to be weighted. Food is given a weight of 3/4 (or 0.75 or 750 out of 1 000) and cars a weight of 1/4 (or 0.25 or 250 out of 1 000). The average increase in prices is 8 per cent multiplied by 3/4 added to 4 per cent multiplied by 1/4 (i.e. 6 per cent + 1 per cent). The weighted average is therefore 7 per cent. If the RPI were 100 at the start of the year, it would be 107 at the end of the year. In order to calculate a weighting, it is necessary to find out how money is spent. In the case of the Retail Price Index, the weighting is calculated from the results of the Family Expenditure Survey. Each year, a few thousand households are asked to record their expenditure for one month. From these figures it is possible to calculate how the average household spends its money. (This average household, of course, does not exist except as a statistical entity.)

Table 93.1

Commodity	Proportion of total spending	Weight	Increase in price	Contribution to increase in RPI
Food	75%	750	8%	6%
Cars	25%	250	4%	1%
Total	100%	1 000		7%

QUESTION 2

Table 93.2

Year	Weights: Food	Weights: All other items	Weights: Total	% annual increase in prices: Food	% annual increase in prices: All other items
1	300	700	1000	10	10
2	250	750	1000	5	10
3	200	800	1000	4	6
4	150	850	1000	3	2
5	125	875	1000	4	4
6	120	880	1000	6	4
7	120	880	1000	5	7
8	110	890	1000	8	10

Table 93.2 shows the price index weights given to food and to all other items in each of eight years. It also shows the percentage annual increase in prices of those items.

(a) Calculate the rate of inflation (i.e. the percentage increase in prices) in each year 1 to 8.

(b) What would the price index in years 2-8 be if the price index were 100 in year 1?

The accuracy of price indices

It is important to realise that any price index is a weighted average. Different rates of inflation can be calculated by changing the weightings in the index. For instance, the Retail Price Index calculates the average price level for the average household in the UK. But it is possible, again using data from the Family Expenditure Survey, to calculate price indices for pensioner households or one parent households. One major difference between these households and the average household is that they spend a larger proportion of their income on food. So a 10 per cent rise in the price of food compared to a 5 per cent rise in the price of all other items will result in a higher rate of inflation for pensioners and one parent households than for the average household. In fact each individual household will have a different rate of inflation. The Retail Price Index only measures an average rate of inflation for all households across the UK.

The household spending patterns upon which the index is based also change over time. For instance, food was a far more important component of the Retail Price Index 30 years ago than it is today because spending on food was then a higher proportion of total spending. The index cannot indicate changes in the quality of goods. Cars might increase in price because their specification improve rather than because there has been an inflationary price rise. The weights for the Retail Price Index are changed annually to take account of changes in spending patterns. But this does not get round the fact that the average 'basket' or 'bundle' of goods purchased in 1950 and upon which the RPI for 1950 was calculated was very different from the average bundle of goods purchased in 1990.

QUESTION 3

Table 93.3 *Index of Retail Prices*

	Average annual percentage change: 1977-81	1982-86	1987-91	1992	1993	1994
General index	13.4	5.5	6.5	3.7	1.6	2.5
Pensioner index, two person household	12.8	5.3	5.3	3.9	2.9	2.1

Source: adapted from CSO, *Economic Trends Annual Supplement.*

(a) Explain why the change in the General Index of Retail Prices may differ from the change in the Pensioner Index.

(b) A two person pensioner household where the pensioners retired in 1976 receives pensions linked to the General Index of Retail Prices. In which years would it, on average, have seen (i) an increase and (ii) a decrease in its real purchasing power? Explain why this occurs.

The costs of inflation

Inflation is generally considered to be a problem. The higher the rate of inflation the greater the economic cost. There are a number of reasons why this is the case.

Shoe-leather costs If prices are stable, consumers and firms come to have some knowledge of what is a fair price for a product and which suppliers are likely to charge less than others. At times of rising prices, consumers and firms will be less clear about what is a reasonable price. This will lead to more 'shopping around', which in itself is a cost.

High rates of inflation are also likely to lead to households and firms holding less cash and more interest bearing deposits. Inflation erodes the value of cash, but since nominal interest rates tend to be higher than with stable prices, the opportunity cost of holding cash tends to be larger, the higher the rate of inflation. Households and firms are then forced to spend more time transferring money from one type of account to another or putting cash into an account to maximise the interest paid. This time is a cost.

Menu costs If there is inflation, restaurants have to change their menus to show increased prices. Similarly, shops have to change their price labels and firms have to calculate and issue new price lists. Even more costly are changes to fixed capital, such as vending machines and parking meters, to take account of price increases.

Psychological and political costs Price increases are deeply unpopular. People feel that they are worse off, even if their incomes rise by more than the rate of inflation. High rates of inflation, particularly if they are unexpected, disturb the distribution of income and wealth as we shall discuss below, and therefore profoundly affect the existing social order. Change and revolution in the past have often accompanied periods of high inflation.

Redistributional costs Inflation can redistribute income and wealth between households, firms and the state. This redistribution can occur in a variety of ways. For instance, anybody on a fixed income will suffer. In the UK, many pensioners have received fixed pensions from private company pension schemes which are not adjusted for inflation. If prices double over a five year period, their real income will halve. Any group of workers which fails to be able to negotiate pay increases at least in line with inflation will suffer falls in their real incomes too.

If **real** interest rates (☞ unit 75) fall as a result of inflation, there will be a transfer of resources from borrowers to lenders. With interest rates at 10 per cent and inflation rates at 20 per cent, a saver will lose 10 per cent of the real value of saving each year whilst a borrower will see a 10 per cent real reduction in the value of debt per annum.

Taxes and government spending may not change in line with inflation. For instance, if the Chancellor fails to increase excise duties on alcohol and tobacco each year in line with inflation, real government revenue will fall whilst drinkers and smokers will be better off in real terms assuming their incomes have risen at least by as much as inflation. Similarly, if the Chancellor fails to increase personal income tax **allowances** (the amount which a worker can earn 'tax free') in line with inflation, then the burden of tax will increase, transferring resources from the taxpayer to the government.

Unemployment and growth Some economists, mainly monetarists, have claimed that inflation creates unemployment and lowers growth. Inflation increases costs of production and creates uncertainty. This lowers the profitability of investment and makes businessmen less willing to take the risk associated with any investment project. Lower investment results in less long term employment and long term growth.

There is also a balance of payments effect. If the exchange rate does not fully adjust to **purchasing power parity** levels (☞ unit 87), exports will become less competitive and imports more competitive. The result will be a loss of jobs in the domestic economy and lower growth.

QUESTION 4 In 1993, the Index of Retail Prices rose by 1.6 per cent and in 1994 by 2.5 per cent. How might the following have been affected by the change?
(a) A pensioner on a fixed pension.
(b) A bank deposit saver, given that the rate of interest on a bank deposit account was 3.00 per cent in 1993 and 3.75 per cent in 1994.
(c) A worker whose personal income tax allowance was £3 445 between April 1992 and March 1993, was the same in 1993-94 and was £3 525 in 1994-95.
(d) A mother with one child who received £9.65 in child benefit between April 1992 and March 1993, £10.00 in 1993-94 and £10.20 in 1994-95.

Anticipated and unanticipated inflation

Much inflation is **unanticipated**; households, firms and government are uncertain what the rate of inflation will be in the future. When planning, they therefore have to estimate as best they can the expected rate of inflation. It is unlikely that they will guess correctly and hence their plans will be to some extent frustrated. On the other hand, inflation may be **anticipated**. Inflation may be a constant 5 per cent per year and therefore households, firms and government are able to build in this figure to their plans.

Unanticipated inflation imposes far greater costs than anticipated inflation. If inflation is anticipated, economic agents can take steps to mitigate the effects of inflation. One way of doing this is through INDEXATION. This is where economic variables like wages or taxes are increased in line with inflation. For instance, a union might negotiate a wage agreement with an employer for staged increases over a year of 2 per cent plus the change in the Retail Price Index. The annual changes in social security benefits in the UK are linked to the Retail Price Index.

Economists are divided about whether indexation provides a solution to the problem of inflation. On the one hand, it reduces many of the costs of inflation although some costs such as shoe leather costs and menu costs remain. On the other hand, it reduces pressure on government to tackle the problem of inflation directly. Indexation eases the pain of inflation but is not a cure for it.

Moreover, indexation may hinder government attempts to reduce inflation because indexation builds in cost structures, such as wage increases, which reflect past changes in prices. If a government wants to get inflation down to 2 per cent a year, and inflation has just been 10 per cent, it will not be helped in achieving its target if workers are all awarded at least 10 per cent wage increases because of indexation agreements.

Key terms

Inflation - a general rise in prices.
Deflation - a fall in the price level.
Price level - the average price of goods and services in the economy.
Creeping inflation - small rises in the price level over a long period of time.
Hyper-inflation - large increases in the price level.
Indexation - adjusting the value of economic variables such as wages or the rate of interest in line with inflation.

Applied economics

The Retail Price Index

Calculating the index

The Retail Price Index is a complex index compiled from a large amount of data. Each month, 150 000 prices are collected from shops in 180 locations round the country. The 150 000 prices are gathered on 600 items, ranging from microwave ovens to grapefruit to ferry charges. The prices are then averaged out using weights. The weights are calculated from the yearly Family Expenditure Survey. This survey asks 7 000 households a year to keep diaries of what they spend over a fortnight. A spending pattern for the average family can then be worked out.

The weights are revised each year to take account of changing patterns of expenditure. Figure 93.2 shows how weights have changed between 1962 and 1995. The proportion spent on food in the average budget has been declining over time as incomes have risen (food has a very low positive income elasticity of demand). Travel and leisure and housing and household expenditure, on the other hand, have been rising. In 1995, for instance, cabbage greens, calculators and frozen Victoria sponges were removed from the weights. Included for the first time were smoke alarms, chewing gum and replica football strips.

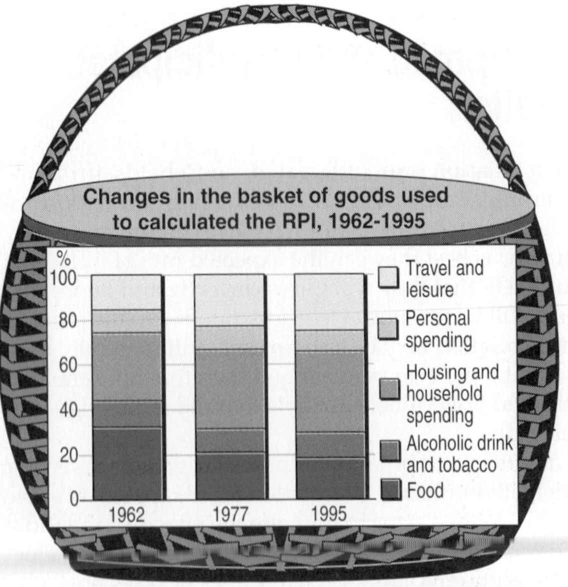

Source: adapted from CSO.

Figure 93.2 *Changes in the basket of goods used to calculate the RPI, 1962-1995*

Is the RPI reliable?

The RPI, as a statistical measure of inflation, has many problems. One problem, highlighted by the House of Commons Public Accounts Committee in 1990 following publication of a report earlier in the year by the National Audit Office (NAO), was that, in practice, prices were not necessarily collected each month. Of the 175 000 prices nationally collected at that time, only about 95 000 prices were recorded. Of nine offices surveyed in detail by the NAO, eight of them collected between 42 and 84 per cent of the theoretical maximum. The ninth, Camden, was on strike and therefore provided no data. There were a number of reasons why prices were not collected. In Camden, for instance, only one-third of prices were collected regularly because of lack of staff. For the remaining two-thirds, price data was copied forward from price collection forms for the previous month. In general, almost 30 per cent of specific items for which prices were collected at the beginning of the year became unavailable in the course of the year. There was a high turnover of staff collecting the statistics, and staff had no formal training in their task. Obviously, all this brings into question the reliability of the Retail Price Index.

A second, similar problem relates to the Family Expenditure Survey (FES). The Survey is nationally based on 10 000 households but 30 per cent of those asked refuse to take part. A disproportionate number of those refusing are households from ethnic minorities, manual workers and the very rich. The result is that these households are under-represented in the FES, eventually distorting the RPI. The 'average household' which emerges from the FES does not, of course, exist in reality. Hence, no inflation rate based on this 'average household' is the same as the inflation rate for a given household. The government does publish inflation rates for a few different household groups, including pensioner households. Even then, no pensioner household will be exactly the same as the average pensioner household constructed from the FES. As a result, the rate of inflation for a given household can differ significantly from that implied by the RPI.

Mortgage payments and indirect taxes

There has been considerable debate in recent years about whether mortgage interest rates and indirect taxes should be included in the compilation of the RPI. The argument in favour of inclusion is a simple one. Increases in mortgage payments and prices due to indirect tax changes are genuine price changes faced by households. Therefore they should be included in a measure of changes in average prices.

The arguments against are more complex. The main argument is that changes in mortgage interest rates, the main determinant of changes in mortgage payments, and changes in indirect taxes are political decisions by government. They do not reflect underlying trends in prices in the economy. Since the 1980s, changing interest rates has been the main way in which government has attempted to influence the level of aggregate demand in the economy. When aggregate demand is rising too fast and causing inflation to rise, as in 1988, the government has responded by increasing interest rates. However, these interest rates then feed through to higher mortgage repayments and a higher RPI. A policy designed to curb inflation in the long run has the perverse effect of increasing it in the short run. Increasing short run inflation can then influence wage bargaining (☞ unit 91), with unions demanding higher wage increases to compensate for higher inflation. This magnifies the short term increase in inflation.

As for changes in indirect taxes, again a rise in indirect tax which is designed to increase overall tax revenues and therefore reduce the PSBR is likely to be taking place at a time when there are inflationary pressures in the economy. But these increases lead to higher inflation rates measured by the RPI. Even if the indirect tax increase is not designed primarily to help combat inflationary pressures - as was the case in 1979 when VAT was increased from 8 per cent to 15 per cent to finance large cuts in income tax, or in 1990 when the poll tax was introduced in England and Wales - it can give the RPI an unwanted upward twist which is then used as a bargaining tool by unions in pay negotiations.

What is more, there are methodological arguments against including mortgage interest payments in the RPI. Only one-quarter of households have a mortgage, and yet mortgage payments were, until 1995, the only measure of changes in the cost of owning or renting a home in the RPI. In France and Italy, mortgage costs of owner-occupation are deliberately excluded from their indices. Instead, changes in rents are measured and from that a change in the cost of owning a home is imputed (i.e. estimated). On the other hand, the proportion of houses that are rented in France and Italy is nearly twice as high as in the UK and hence rents are a more reliable statistic to include in the index than in the UK.

Since 1995, the importance of mortgage payments has been lessened by the inclusion of a measure of the cost to homeowners of keeping their houses in good condition. This has been assumed to be in proportion to the price of a house. Hence, house price changes now feed directly into the rate of inflation.

Indexation

An opposition political party has asked for a discussion paper on a proposal to index link various types of income (wages, benefits, interest rates, etc.). In your paper:

1. **outline what is meant by 'indexation' in the context of inflation, illustrating your answer with reference to Brazil;**
2. **(a) explain the main costs of inflation and**
   (b) analyse which costs might be lessened by the introduction of indexation;
3. **discuss the extent to which indexation would protect individuals from inflation;**
4. **evaluate the disadvantages of introducing indexation.**

Use the data over as a basis for your answers.

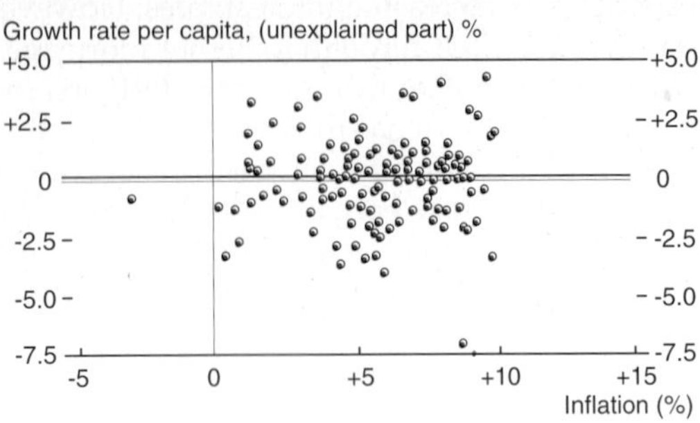

1. Average over the period 1960-1990 for countries with less than 10 per cent inflation on average out of a sample of 100 countries.
Source: adapted from Bank of England, *Bank of England Quarterly Bulletin*, May 1995.

Figure 93.3 *Growth and inflation: countries with less than 10% average inflation*[1]

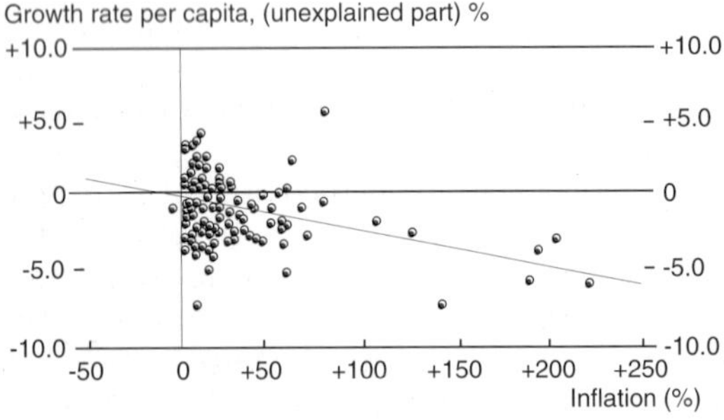

1. Average over the period 1960-1990, 100 countries.
Source: adapted from Bank of England, Bank of England Quarterly Bulletin, May 1995.

Figure 93.4 *Growth and inflation: all countries*[1]

Inflation hits rich harder than poor

Poorer households have been less affected by the officially defined measures of inflation during the recent period of Conservative party rule than richer ones, a new study claims. The research, carried out by the Institute of Fiscal Studies, shows that the rate of inflation experienced by households has varied significantly from the official inflation data shown in the Retail Prices Index. Between 1979 and 1992, for example, the rate of inflation experienced by the poorest 10 per cent of the population was about a 1 percentage point lower than the officially published data, the report notes.

Rich households spend a large proportion of their budgets on luxury items, with two-thirds of their income spent on items that have been subject to value added tax. Poor households, by contrast, spend more on basic necessities such as food, fuel and clothing, with only a third of their income spent on items subject to VAT. Because the cost of luxuries has risen faster than overall inflation, not least because of the rise in VAT on luxury items, this has meant that richer households have been disproportionately affected. Poorer households, by contrast, have benefited from the fact that the relative cost of food and clothing and fuel has fallen during this period.

Source: adapted from the *Financial Times*, 23.9.1994.

No 'feelgood' factor for the middle classes

In a report published by the Reward research group in April 1995, it was argued that the amount of money needed by an average family to maintain its standard of living rose by 6.4 per cent in the year to February, at a time when the official RPI increase was only 2.8 per cent. The increase in average earnings at the time was running at 3.5 per cent across the economy as a whole. The Reward research group, which specialises in providing information for companies trying to relocate employees, calculates the cost of living index by tracking 250 prices in almost 100 locations. The Reward index is skewed towards reflecting the 'real' lifestyles of typical employees by creating a series of 'benchmark' lifestyles, from council accommodation to big family houses.

The report shows that, broken down on a lifestyle basis, the cost of living rose faster for lower income families than for richer ones. A typical family of four living in a three-bedroomed terraced house and eating 46 meals out a year saw the cost of their lifestyle rise 7 per cent last year. A family living in a six-bedroom house with a cleaner, golf club membership, private school fees and 250 meals out a year saw their lifestyle costs rise only 5.1 per cent. These differences partly reflect sharp sectoral variations between goods and services.

Source: adapted from the *Financial Times*, 12.4.1995.

Brazilian inflation

Inflation in Brazil is expected to remain higher than hoped until the end of the year, and is adding to pressure for the government to outlaw the use of indices which keep salaries and taxes rising in line with prices. The government's official inflation figure for the period, due to be published later this week, is likely to show the monthly inflation rate rising from 1.98 per cent in October to about 3 per cent. Unexpectedly high inflation in the government index is worrying because, according to law, salaries have to be increased in line with the index. Congress passed this law because it feared that inflation would otherwise eat away at workers' spending power. The government also at the time got Congress to pass a law which said that overdue tax payments would be increased in line with inflation.

However, advisers to the new president, Mr Fernando Henrique Cardoso, are now starting to study how to remove or modify these links, which most economists agree fan inflation. One idea is to allow companies to negotiate wages directly with their workers, which then would mean in law that workers did not have inflation protection, instead of relying on the current system of industry-wide union agreements. Many congressmen and some ministers oppose this because they believe that Brazilian workers do not have sufficient bargaining power against their employers.

Source: adapted from the *Financial Times*, 22.9.94.

The causes of inflation

Summary

1. Monetarists argue that inflation is caused by excessive increases in the money supply.
2. Some Keynesians believe that excess demand in the economy is the principal cause of inflation - the demand-pull theory of inflation.
3. Other Keynesians argue that inflation is primarily cost-push in nature.
4. If inflation is caused by shifts in the aggregate demand or aggregate supply curves, it can only persist if it is either validated or accommodated by an increase in the money supply.

The monetarist explanation

Monetarists argue that the sole cause of inflation is a rise in the money supply. As Milton Friedman put it, 'inflation is always and everywhere a monetary phenomenon'.

This view can be explained using the Fisher formulation of the **quantity theory of money**:

$$MV \equiv PT$$

where M is the money supply, V is the velocity of circulation of money, P is the price level and T the number of transactions over a period of time. In the short run, increases in M will feed through to higher levels of transactions (i.e. national income will rise and unemployment is likely to fall), and a fall in V. This is known as the **monetary transmission mechanism**. But in the long run, with V constant, increases in M over and above the rate of real growth in the economy (the change in T) will feed through to changes in P (☞ unit 76).

The effects of an increase in the money supply can be explained using aggregate demand and aggregate supply analysis (☞ units 64-66). An increase in the money supply will lead to an increase in aggregate demand through the transmission mechanism. Consider Figure 94.1. Monetarist or classical economists would argue that the long run aggregate supply curve is vertical. The equilibrium level of output is the full employment level Y_F and the initial price level is P_1. An increase in the money supply shifts the aggregate demand curve to the right from AD_1 to AD_2. Initially the economy moves up the short run aggregate supply curve $SRAS_1$ from K to L. But in the longer run, with increased prices and over-full employment, workers will demand and gain wage rate increases which will push the short run aggregate supply curve up to $SRAS_2$ and then to $SRAS_3$. N is the new long run equilibrium point where aggregate demand is once again equal to long run aggregate supply. Output, having initially risen, has returned to its long run full employment level. But prices have risen from P_1 to P_2.

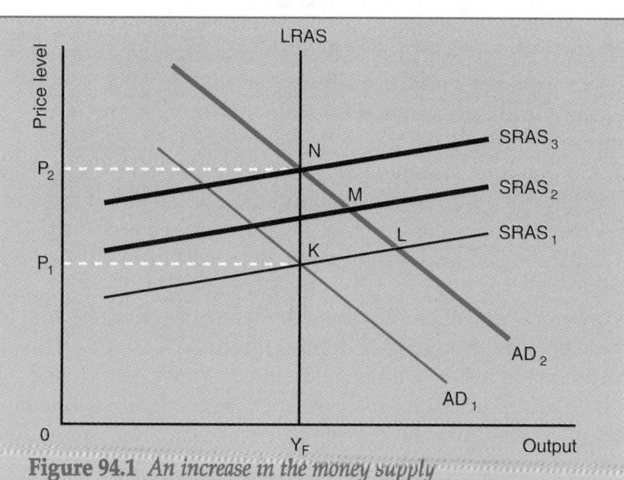

Figure 94.1 *An increase in the money supply*
An increase in the money supply will shift the aggregate demand curve from AD_1 to AD_2. After an initial rise in output, shown by the movement from K to L, the economy will return to long run equilibrium at N. Prices have risen but output remains unchanged.

Keynesian analysis suggests that the monetary transmission mechanism is weak. Rises in the money supply tend to reduce V, the velocity of circulation, rather than increase T, real aggregate demand. Hence rises in the money supply have little impact on the price level. This is not to say that extremely large increases in the money supply will not cause serious inflation. But it makes little difference to inflation whether the money supply grows by, say, 10 per cent a year or 12 per cent a year.

QUESTION 1

Table 94.1 *The money supply and inflation*

	Percentage change		
	Money supply (M4)	Real GDP	Prices
1970	8.6	2.3	6.5
1971	13.8	1.4	9.2
1972	22.8	3.5	7.5
1973	20.6	5.9	9.1
1974	15.7	- 0.6	15.9
1975	12.8	- 2.1	24.1
1976	11.8	4.0	16.5
1977	10.9	2.2	15.8
1978	17.2	3.5	8.3

Source: adapted from CSO, *Economic Trends Annual Supplement.*

(a) How do monetarists account for the causes of inflation?
(b) To what extent do the data support this view?

The monetary transmission mechanism

The MONETARY TRANSMISSION MECHANISM, the short run link between the money supply and output, can be analysed in more depth using the concepts of the demand for and supply of money. Assume that the money market starts off in equilibrium with the demand for money (☞ unit 74) equal to the supply of money (☞ unit 70). Then assume that, for some reason such as the government wanting to reduce interest rates in order to reduce unemployment, there is an increase in the money supply. Disequilibrium in the money market will now be present. The money supply will be greater than the demand for money (i.e. households and firms, including financial institutions such as banks, will be holding more money than they desire). Two things will happen according to the theory of the demand for money.

- Money will be exchanged for physical assets. Households and firms will change their portfolio of assets to hold less money and more goods. In simple language, this means that households and firms will spend more money.
- Money will be exchanged for non-monetary financial assets. Households and firms will buy more stocks and shares etc. Greater demand will increase the price of financial assets but it will therefore reduce the rate of interest (remember the price of bonds for instance is inversely related to the rate of interest ☞ unit 72). A fall in the rate of interest will increase the level of consumption and investment in the economy (i.e. households and firms will spend more money).

So an increase in the money supply will result both directly and indirectly in a rise in the level of aggregate demand in the economy. This is known as the monetary transmission mechanism:- the mechanism through which a change in the money supply affects the real economy. Some monetarist economists even calculate **money multipliers** (not to be confused with credit multipliers used in creation of credit theory). The money multiplier is the number of times an increase in the money supply is multiplied to give the final increase in national income. Many monetarists argue that the money multiplier is large. Hence, small changes in the money supply produce large shifts in the aggregate demand curve. Keynesians on the other hand argue that the money multiplier is very small. They argue that physical assets are a poor substitute for financial assets such as money. Therefore an increase in the money supply will mainly affect holdings of financial assets such as stocks and shares and have little effect on holdings of physical assets. Secondly, they argue that consumption and investment are relatively insensitive to the rate of interest (☞ units 62 and 63). Hence quite large changes in the rate of interest will have little impact upon planned aggregate expenditure.

Economists agree that an increase in the money supply, through the transmission mechanism, will shift the aggregate demand curve to the right whilst a decrease will push it to the left. They disagree about the size of the shift that will occur (i.e. they disagree about the size of the money multiplier). In the long run, monetarists argue that output will fall back to its long run position. Any short term increase in output will only be temporary. The only long term effect of excessive increases in the money supply will be a rise in prices.

QUESTION 2

Table 94.2 *Inflation, money and economic growth, 1983-1992*

Per cent

	Change in M4	Inflation	Economic growth
1983	14.0	4.6	3.7
1984	12.5	5.0	2.0
1985	13.1	6.1	4.0
1986	15.9	3.4	4.0
1987	14.7	4.2	4.6
1988	17.2	4.9	5.0
1989	18.2	7.8	2.2
1990	17.6	9.5	0.4
1991	8.0	5.9	-1.7
1992	4.4	3.7	-0.5

Source: adapted from CSO, *Economic Trends Annual Supplement.*

Between 1983 and 1987, broad monetary growth averaged 14.0 per cent whilst inflation averaged 4.7 per cent. Broad money growth then jumped to an average of 17.7 per cent between 1988 and 1990 whilst inflation rose to a peak of 9.5 per cent in 1990 from 4.9 per cent in 1988.

(a) How would monetarists account for this?

The average real growth rate of GDP over the period 1983-1987 was 3.7 per cent. At the time, there was a substantial deregulation of financial markets which led to an explosion of borrowing both by households and companies.

(b) How would a monetarist explain why, despite 14 per cent per annum increases in the money supply, there was only 4.7 per cent per annum average increases in inflation over the period?

The annual rate of growth of the money supply fell from 18.2 per cent in 1989 to 2.6 per cent in 1993. At the same time, the rate of growth of the economy collapsed from a peak of 5.0 per cent in 1988 to - 1.7 per cent in 1991.

(c) Why might this be an example of how the monetary transmission mechanism operates?

Demand-pull inflation

Monetarists stress that inflation is a **monetary phenomenon**. Keynesians have traditionally argued that inflation occurs because of changes in **real** variables in the economy. One important Keynesian theory is that inflation is caused by excess demand in the economy. The DEMAND-PULL THEORY of inflation says that inflation will result if there is too much money chasing too few goods in the economy.

Figure 94.2 shows an aggregate demand curve with a Keynesian aggregate supply curve (☞ unit 65). The economy is at full employment at income Y_F. Assume that there is a rise in aggregate demand from AD_1 to AD_2. This could be the result of an increase in consumer confidence which raises autonomous consumer spending. Investment might rise because the rate of return on capital increases. The government might increase its spending. Alternatively, there might be a rise in exports because of strong economic growth in other countries. The result of these increases in real expenditure is a rise in both output and inflation. Output rises from OA to OB whilst the price level rises from OE to OF. Rising output will lead to a fall in unemployment.

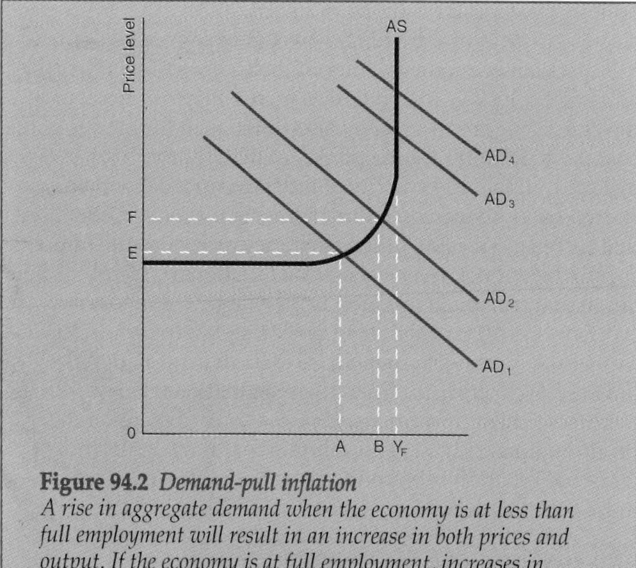

Figure 94.2 *Demand-pull inflation*
A rise in aggregate demand when the economy is at less than full employment will result in an increase in both prices and output. If the economy is at full employment, increases in aggregate demand simply lead to increases in inflation.

Falling unemployment accompanied by rising inflation is the **Phillips curve** relationship (☞ unit 91).

If the economy is already at full employment, with the aggregate demand curve at AD_3, then a rise in real expenditure which shifts the aggregate demand curve to AD_4 will lead only to a rise in inflation with no rise in output or decrease in unemployment. The Phillips curve then becomes vertical.

The demand-pull theory of inflation therefore says that inflation is caused by an increase in spending in the economy (i.e. an increase in demand). This increase in demand pulls up prices.

QUESTION 3

Table 94.3 *Excess demand and inflation*

	Real GDP % change	Unemployment %	Inflation %
1970	2.3	2.6	6.5
1971	1.4	2.6	9.2
1972	3.5	2.9	7.5
1973	5.9	2.0	9.1
1974	-0.6	2.1	15.9
1975	-2.1	3.1	24.1
1976	4.0	4.2	16.5
1977	2.2	4.4	15.8
1978	3.5	4.4	8.3

Source: adapted from CSO, *Economic Trends Annual Supplement.*

(a) Outline a demand-pull theory of inflation.
(b) To what extent do the data support a demand-pull theory of inflation?

Cost-push inflation

A second Keynesian theory of inflation is the COST-PUSH theory of inflation. This states that inflation is caused by increases in costs of production. There are four major sources of increased costs.

- Wages and salaries. They account for about 70 per cent of national income and hence increases in wages are normally the single most important cause of increases in costs of production.
- Imported goods. An increase in the price of finished manufactured imports, such as television sets or cars, will lead directly to an increase in the price level. An increase in the price of imported semi-manufactured goods and raw materials, used as component parts of domestically produced manufactured goods, will feed through indirectly via an increase in the price of domestically produced goods.
- Profits. Firms can raise their prices to increase their profit margins. The more price inelastic the demand for their goods, the less will such behaviour result in a fall in demand for their products.
- Taxes. Government can raise indirect tax rates or reduce subsidies, thus increasing prices. It can also order nationalised industries to raise their prices more than they might have wished to otherwise. This represents a 'hidden' tax.

There are a number of occasions in the past when there has been a significant rise in prices due to an increase in one of these costs. For instance, all Western economies suffered sharp rises in prices after the four-fold increase in the price of oil in 1973-4.

However, Keynesian economists have argued that a cost-push spiral can develop which leads to a long term cycle of inflation. Consider a developed economy with zero inflation and few natural resources. International commodity prices of products such as oil, gas and coal increase by 50 per cent in one year. Domestic prices rise by 10 per cent as a result. Workers will now be 10 per cent worse off in real terms. So they will press for higher wages. If in the past they have become accustomed to receive a 2 per cent increase in real wages per year, they will be prepared to settle for 12 per cent. Firms pay the 12 per cent and pass on the increase in their costs in the form of higher prices. This fuels inflation. The following year, trade unions will once again fight for pay increases of 2 per cent plus the rate of inflation. In the meantime, the profits of firms will have been declining in real terms. So firms are likely to attempt to increase their

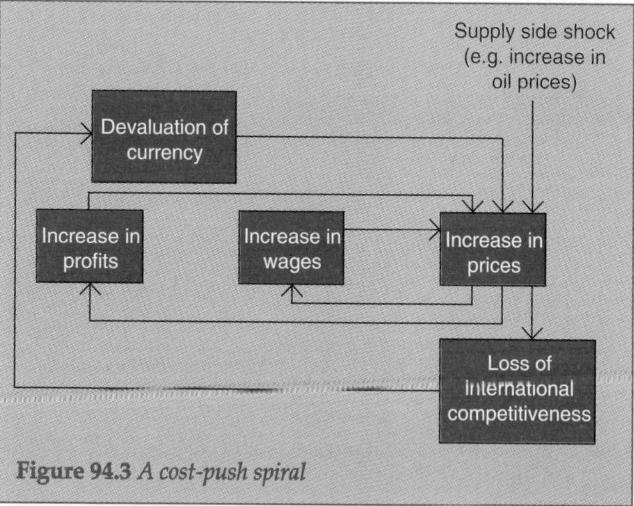

Figure 94.3 *A cost-push spiral*

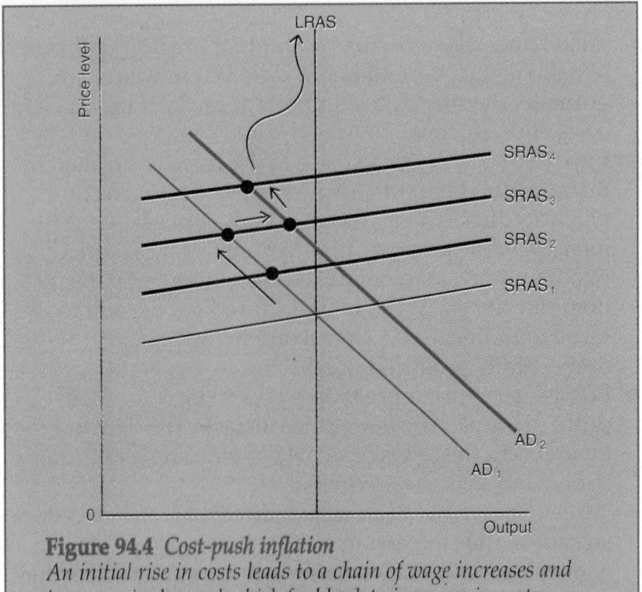

Figure 94.4 *Cost-push inflation*
An initial rise in costs leads to a chain of wage increases and increases in demand which feed back to increases in costs. Hence, the short run equilibrium level of prices in the economy is constantly moving upwards.

profit margins in money terms, again fuelling inflation. This process, shown in Figure 94.3, is called a WAGE-PRICE SPIRAL or sometimes a COST-PUSH SPIRAL.

This wage-price spiral can also be seen in Figure 94.4. An initial price shock, say from a large increase in oil prices, shifts the short run aggregate supply curve up from $SRAS_1$ to $SRAS_2$. With higher prices, workers demand higher wages which employers concede. This pushes the short run aggregate supply curve up even further to $SRAS_3$. The increase in wages leads to an increase in aggregate demand which shifts the aggregate demand curve to the right from AD_1 to AD_2. This further raises the price level. So workers again demand higher wage increases which employers concede. So the short run aggregate supply curve shifts up again to $SRAS_4$. And so it goes on, with wage rises fuelling

QUESTION 4

Table 94.4 *Costs and prices*

	Percentage change		
	Average weekly earnings	Import prices	Retail Price Index
1970	12	4	6.5
1971	11	5	9.2
1972	13	5	7.5
1973	14	28	9.1
1974	18	46	15.9
1975	27	14	24.1
1976	16	22	16.5
1977	9	16	15.8
1978	13	4	8.3

Source: adapted from CSO, *Economic Trends Annual Supplement.*

(a) Outline a theory of cost-push inflation.
(b) To what extent do the data support the view that inflation is mainly cost-push in origin?

both increases in costs to firms, hence shifting the SRAS curve upwards, and fuelling increases in aggregate demand.

Keynesian economists differ in their views of whether the spiral is explosive, with inflation increasing over time, as is the case in Figure 94.4. They also differ as to the causes of the cost-push inflation. Some point out that, for the UK for instance, all the major bouts of inflation since 1918 have been started by large increases in the price of imports. Others say that increases in trade union militancy can cause the initial supply side shock which starts the inflationary spiral. Others argue that cost-push inflation is inevitable in a modern economy because of the struggle between workers and capitalists. Both wish to increase their share of national income. Workers force firms to give inflationary pay increases whilst firms increase prices so as to increase their profit margins. There is no solution to this struggle and therefore inflation is bound to be endemic in a modern industrialised society.

Monetary accommodation

Keynesians tend to argue that whilst hyper-inflations are caused by excessive increases in the money supply, the creeping inflation experienced in recent decades in the industrialised world has been caused mainly by changes in real variables. Either there has been excessive spending (demand-pull inflation) or there have been supply side shocks which have increased costs of production. Monetarists would not deny that a supply side shock like the four-fold increase in oil prices in 1973-4 increased prices. But they would argue that this was a once-and-for-all increase, rather like a seasonal increase in the price of tomatoes. It was an increase in prices but it was not inflationary (i.e. it did not in itself cause a general and sustained increase in prices).

Consider Figure 94.5. An increase in oil prices has shifted the short run aggregate supply curve from $SRAS_1$ to $SRAS_2$. The economy has moved from full employment at A to below full employment at B and prices have risen. The economy is now in a position of STAGFLATION or SLUMPFLATION with both price increases and unemployment. Keynesian theory would suggest that workers will now demand higher wage increases to compensate them for increases in prices. But monetarists would question where the money to pay these inflationary wage increases is going to come from. If the money supply is fixed, the aggregate demand curve cannot shift. Wage increases for some workers must be compensated for by wage losses for others. Some workers will 'price themselves out of jobs' as the short run aggregate supply curve rises to $SRAS_3$.

Unemployment therefore increases. Eventually workers will start to accept cuts in their wages and this will start to shift the short run aggregate supply curve downwards. Eventually the economy will return to full employment at A at the original price level. So a supply side shock will only be inflationary in the long run if the government allows the money supply to rise to ACCOMMODATE the inflationary pressures within the economy.

Accommodation is a very attractive political solution in the short run. Faced with unemployment and inflation, a government can at least reduce unemployment by increasing the money supply and thus increasing aggregate demand. But in the long run such a policy is simply inflationary. What is more, monetarist economists argue that the economy would have returned to full employment anyway through the process of real wage cuts.

The same argument applies to increases in aggregate demand. Assume that government increases its spending when the economy is already at full employment, thus increasing aggregate demand. Prices rise slightly. The increase in spending will almost certainly result in an increase in the demand for borrowed funds. This will increase interest rates. Consumption will fall, whilst on the foreign exchanges there will be an inflow of money from abroad which will finance an increase in imports. Hence domestic aggregate demand will fall to its original level. The expansion in demand is said not to have been VALIDATED if the money supply is not increased. If the money supply had been expanded, firms would have reacted by bidding up the price of labour, shifting the short run aggregate supply curve upwards, producing a potential inflationary spiral.

So monetarists argue that demand and supply side shocks cannot cause inflation. It is only if the money supply is allowed to increase that inflation will ensue.

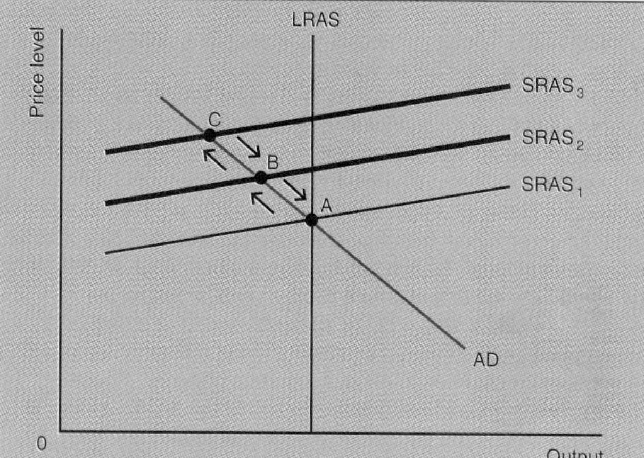

Figure 94.5 *Monetary accommodation*
A supply side shock which shifts the short run aggregate supply curve from SRAS$_1$ to SRAS$_2$ may lead workers to demand inflation-compensating wage increases, shifting the short run aggregate supply curve even farther upward and to the left. But the economy will return to the original point A so long as the government does not accommodate the price rise (i.e. does not increase the money supply which would have the effect of shifting the aggregate demand schedule to the right).

Key terms

Monetary transmission mechanism - the mechanism through which a change in the money supply leads to a change in national income and other real variables such as unemployment.
Demand-pull inflation - inflation which is caused by excess demand in the economy.
Cost-push inflation - inflation caused by increases in the costs of production in the economy.
Wage-price or cost-push spiral - the process whereby increases in costs, such as wages, lead to increases in prices and this in turn leads to increases in costs to firms.
Stagflation or slumpflation - a situation where an economy faces both rising inflation and rising unemployment.
Monetary policy accommodation - a change in the nominal money supply which the government permits following a supply side shock in order to keep the real money supply constant.
Monetary policy validation - a change in the nominal money supply which the government permits following a change in aggregate demand in order to keep the real money supply constant.

QUESTION 5

(a) Distinguish between monetary accommodation and monetary validation.
(b) Consider the data in Tables 94.1, 94.2 and 94.3. Is there any evidence to suggest that monetary accommodation or validation occurred in the period 1970 to 1978?

Applied economics

Inflation in the Lawson boom, 1986-1989

In the first half of the 1980s, the inflation rate fell from 18.0 per cent in 1980 to 4.6 per cent in 1983. Inflation then hovered in the 5 per cent range for the next five years but in mid-1988 it began to increase again. By the end of 1990, the annual growth of the Retail Price Index was over 10 per cent. Why was there this doubling of the inflation rate?

From a monetarist view, the increase in inflation in 1988 can be linked to the jump in the rate of growth of the money supply from 1986. In the early part of the 1980s, the money supply, whether measured as M1, M2, M3 or M4, had grown considerably faster than the level of nominal GDP (i.e. faster than PT in the Fisher equation). As Table 94.5 shows, the annual rate of growth of M4 increased from below 15 per cent per annum to over 15 per cent in 1986 and by 1988 was averaging over 17 per cent. This increase was sufficient to produce the increase in inflation from the middle of 1988. It would suggest that there was a one to two year time lag between initial increases in the rate of growth of the money supply and subsequent increases in the inflation rate at the time.

Keynesians too can provide an explanation of the increase in inflation. As can be seen from Table 94.5, the rate of growth of real GDP increased from a rate of about 3 per cent per annum between 1983 and 1986 to over 4 per cent from the last quarter of 1986. By the first quarter of 1988, annual growth was an unsustainable 5.6 per cent. This very fast growth quickly reduced unemployment from over 3 million in the first half of the 1980s to 1.6 million by the last quarter of 1989, with areas such as the South East of England suffering severe shortages of many types of labour. In Keynesian terms, it could be argued that an inflationary gap had opened, leading to demand-pull inflation.

Table 94.5 also shows figures for the rate of increase in earnings. Wages are the most significant cost for employers on average. From 1984, there was a gradual increase in the rate of growth of earnings. In the first quarter of 1984, it was 6.1 per cent per annum, but by 1989 it was nearly 10 per cent. This could provide evidence for a cost-push explanation of the rise in inflation.

In fact, it is likely that the increased inflation from 1988 onwards was due to a combination of the above factors. Most economists would accept that aggregate demand increased from 1986 relative to aggregate supply. The increase in the money supply came about, partly because of lower interest rates, but also because of deregulation in the financial markets. In particular, the second half of the 1980s saw the aggressive selling of mortgages as building societies, freed from many of their previous constraints, encouraged customers to borrow money. Banks too entered the mortgage market in an aggressive manner. People moving houses tended to borrow more than they needed to cover the cost of the house purchase and used the cash to buy everything from carpets and curtains to new cars. Increased lending also led to rapid increases in house prices. This encouraged home owners to borrow money secured against the increase in value of their houses.

The consequent increase in consumption then led to increased investment by industry at a time when export sales were growing fast too. Extra spending which led to increased output meant that unemployment fell. With increased tightness in the labour market, workers were able to secure higher wage increases, which led to pressures on costs and prices.

Between 1986 and the middle of 1988, the government **accommodated** the increase in demand by allowing the money supply to rise. However, between 1988 and 1989, in a bid to curb inflation, it doubled interest rates. It takes time for policy to work. The economy began to slow down in 1989 and by 1991 was in recession. Paradoxically, the increases in interest rates, designed to curb inflation, led in the short term to increases in the Retail Price Index, which may well have led to increased wage demands by workers attempting to prevent the erosion of their real wage levels. However, by 1991, inflation was beginning to fall.

Table 94.5 *Inflation and its possible determinants*

		Percentage change over previous 12 months				Millions
		Inflation	Money supply	Real GDP	Average earnings	Unemployment
1983	Q1	4.9	14.7	3.2	8.8	3.2
1984	Q1	5.2	11.7	3.4	6.1	3.2
1985	Q1	5.4	14.0	2.3	7.5	3.3
1986	Q1	5.0	13.7	3.3	8.4	3.4
	Q2	2.8	15.3	2.9	8.1	3.3
	Q3	2.7	15.6	4.0	7.4	3.3
	Q4	3.5	15.9	4.8	8.0	3.2
1987	Q1	3.9	14.6	4.3	7.2	3.2
	Q2	4.2	14.1	4.0	7.5	3.1
	Q3	4.3	15.4	4.7	7.9	2.9
	Q4	4.1	16.2	4.2	8.4	2.8
1988	Q1	3.3	16.8	5.6	8.8	2.7
	Q2	4.3	16.9	4.7	8.3	2.5
	Q3	5.5	18.6	4.4	8.4	2.3
	Q4	6.5	17.6	4.1	9.6	2.1
1989	Q1	7.8	18.0	3.0	9.3	2.1
	Q2	8.2	18.6	2.6	9.3	1.9
	Q3	7.7	17.6	1.4	9.9	1.8
	Q4	7.6	18.3	0.9	8.7	1.6

Source: adapted from CSO, *Economic Trends Annual Supplement;* CSO, *Monthly Digest of Statistics.*

Inflation, 1990-94

The Bank of England has asked you, as one of their economists, to prepare a report on the main causes of inflation during the period 1990-1994.

1. **Briefly describe the main trends in the economy during the period.**
2. **Outline each main theory of inflation which you know, and discuss the extent to which the evidence from the period supports the explanation.**
3. **Write a conclusion in which you evaluate which theory best explains the pattern of inflation during the period.**

Table 94.6 *Inflation and its possible determinants*

		Percentage change over previous 12 months					
		GDP at 1990 prices	Inflation	Money supply (M4)	Average earnings	Import prices	Profits[1]
					at current prices		
1990	Q1	1.0	5.2	4.4	9.3	7.4	-4.0
	Q2	0.0	6.2	3.9	10.1	3.2	7.8
	Q3	0.0	5.9	2.6	10.1	-4.1	2.3
	Q4	-1.1	5.8	2.2	8.6	-0.3	-4.6
1991	Q1	-2.3	8.6	1.7	9.0	-1.8	5.3
	Q2	-3.1	6.0	1.7	8.0	0.3	-3.5
	Q3	-2.6	4.8	1.3	7.9	4.5	-4.5
	Q4	-1.8	4.2	1.4	7.3	1.9	8.3
1992	Q1	-1.7	4.1	1.2	7.8	1.8	-4.0
	Q2	-1.3	4.1	1.2	6.3	-0.3	0.1
	Q3	-0.4	3.6	1.0	5.2	-2.8	4.9
	Q4	0.0	3.0	0.4	5.2	4.8	-1.6
1993	Q1	1.5	1.8	0.7	4.1	8.5	13.6
	Q2	2.0	1.3	0.9	3.7	10.0	8.1
	Q3	2.4	1.7	1.3	3.2	11.2	11.6
	Q4	2.6	1.6	1.8	1.8	3.7	18.3
1994	Q1	3.3	2.4	1.6	3.7	1.3	19.0
	Q2	4.1	2.6	0.7	4.0	3.7	15.9
	Q3	4.1	2.3	5.2	3.9	4.2	19.5
	Q4	4.2	2.6	4.1	3.9	4.9	11.0

1. Gross trading profits net of stock appreciation of industrial and commercial companies, but not including North Sea oil companies.

Source: adapted from CSO, *Economic Trends Annual Supplement*

Counter-inflation policy

Summary

1. Economists disagree over the causes of inflation. Monetarists argue that inflation is caused solely by increases in the money supply. Keynesians tend to emphasise that inflation is caused by changes in real variables, in particular excess demand or supply side shocks.
2. If inflation is caused by excessive increases in the money supply, then it can only be curbed by reducing the rate of growth of the money supply through monetary policy. However, a reduction in inflation will necessitate transitional costs of higher unemployment and lower growth.
3. The operation of monetary policy will tend to be more effective if government borrowing is low and if the central bank is independent of government control.
4. Keynesian economists argue that the money supply is endogenous and therefore difficult if not impossible to control. They argue that inflation can only be controlled through control of real variables in the economy. Aggregate demand can be manipulated via fiscal policy. Micro-economic fiscal policies can also be used to break wage-price spirals.
5. Maintaining a stable exchange rate is likely to help in the fight against inflation.
6. Keynesians advocate prices and incomes policies as a possible way of reducing the inflationary impact of supply side shocks. However, it is inappropriate to use them to control inflation caused by excess demand in the economy.

The causes of inflation

A rise in prices is caused either by a rise in aggregate demand or a fall in aggregate supply or some combination of both (☞ unit 66). Any single rise in prices is not necessarily 'inflationary' because inflation is defined as a sustained rise in prices. For inflation to occur, therefore, there must be a sustained rise in aggregate demand or fall in supply.

Economists disagree about the fundamental causes of such a sustained rise in prices. Monetarists argue that a rise can only be sustained if there is a sustained rise in the money supply over and above the rise in the level of output. Hence inflation is a monetary phenomenon. Keynesians would not disagree with part of this analysis. For inflation to occur, rises in aggregate demand must be **validated** by a rise in the money supply. The same is true of aggregate supply. A fall in aggregate supply is only inflationary if supply side shocks are **accommodated** by increases in the money supply (☞ unit 94). However Keynesians stress that the inflation seen in the post-war era in Western industrialised economies has been caused by changes in real variables.

The emphasis placed on a particular cause of inflation will influence the choice of policy used to control it. Monetarists would argue that the control of the money supply is the only effective means of regulating inflation. This is because the price level is determined by the amount of money in the economy. Keynesians argue that the control of real variables, such as aggregate demand and aggregate supply, would be more effective in controlling inflation. Put another way, monetarists argue that inflation can only be controlled through **monetary policy** (☞ units 77 and 78). Keynesians argue that monetary policy is ineffective. Inflation is best controlled through policies such as fiscal policy (☞ unit 68) and **incomes policy** (☞ below).

Monetary policy

The monetarist view According to monetarists, monetary policy is the only effective tool available to control inflation. Assume that a government wishes to eliminate inflation from the economy. To do this, it must restrict the growth of the money supply. The link between a fall in the money supply (or a moderation in its rate of growth) and inflation is known as the monetary **transmission mechanism** (summarised in Figure 95.1). A restrictive monetary policy will result in a fall in the supply of money relative to the demand for money (i.e. households and firms now hold less money than they desire). They will react by attempting to increase their holdings of money. They will sell some of their non-money financial assets, such as stocks and shares, or they will borrow money. They may also reduce their expenditure on goods and services thus enabling them to hold more money in their pockets or accounts. Sales of financial assets, or increasing demand for borrowed funds, will force up the rate of interest (☞ unit 75) which in turn will lead to a reduction in both consumption and investment. So both directly and via the interest rate mechanism, restrictive monetary policy will moderate the growth of aggregate demand or even reduce it. This leads to a fall in inflation.

Note that the government may choose to attempt to restrict the money supply by raising interest rates. This is what the UK government did in the late 1980s to reduce inflation. High interest rates, as just described, lead to a fall in consumption and investment and therefore aggregate demand, which in turn leads to a fall in inflation.

Political considerations If it is so easy to reduce inflation, why then is inflation such a persistent problem in many economies such as the UK? Monetarists would argue that it is because governments lack the political will to control inflation. In the short run, a reduction in the rate of

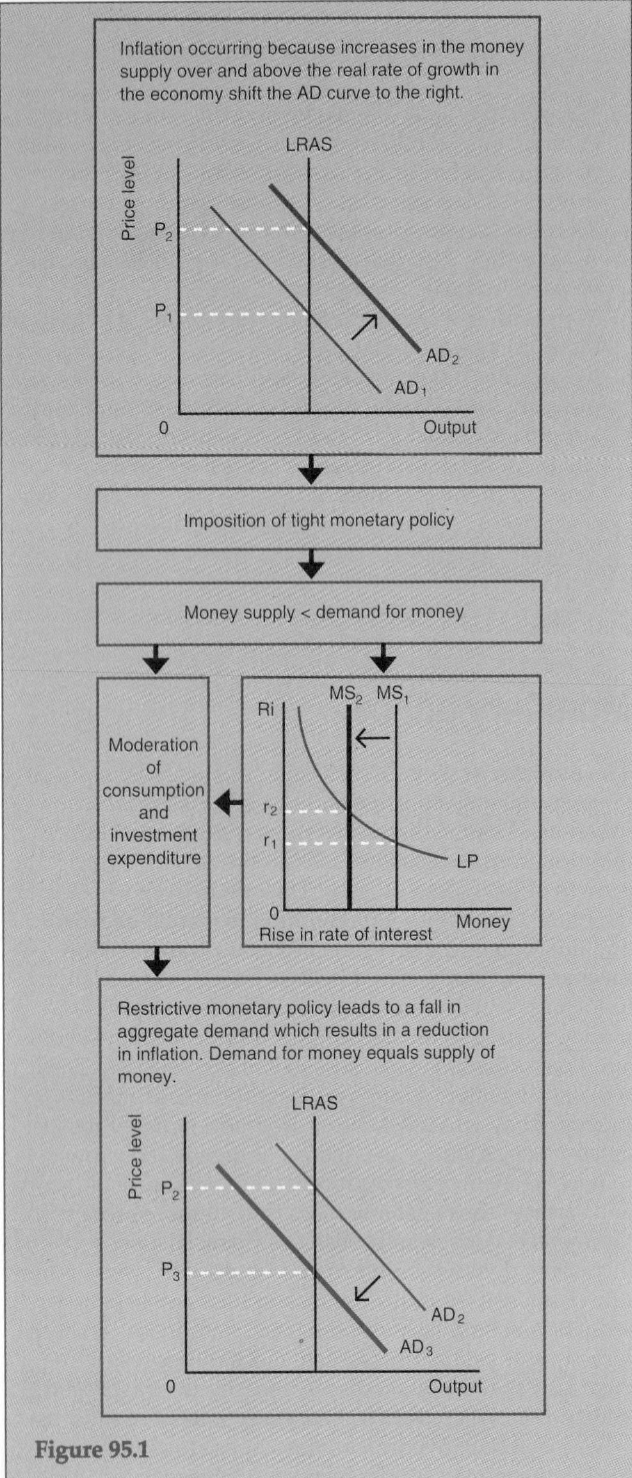

Figure 95.1

growth of the money supply, which in turn leads to a fall in aggregate demand, will lead to a fall in output and a rise in unemployment. This is the short run Phillips curve relationship (☞ unit 91). Unemployment and low growth is politically unpopular and governments are often swayed not by what is best for the economy in the long run but by short term electoral considerations.

Moreover, governments can gain short term political popularity by **increasing** the rate of growth of the money supply. Votes can be won by cutting taxes and raising public spending. If this is financed not by genuine borrowing but by printing the money (achieved by borrowing from the banking sector), then interest rates will fall. This will stimulate consumer and investment spending and reduce unemployment. The government has created an artificial boom. In the long run the economy must return to its **natural rate of unemployment**, but the price level will have risen in the process of adjustment.

The greatest danger, according to monetarists, is that governments will become more and more afraid of tackling inflation because of the consequences for unemployment and output in the short term. To avoid short term political unpopularity, government will continually validate (i.e. print the money to finance) ever increasing rates of inflation. The higher the rate of inflation, the more severe is likely to be the slump needed to return the economy to a low inflation point.

Regulations and rules Monetarists tend to be deeply suspicious of government intervention. They argue that there are ways of ensuring that governments are restricted in their power to print money. One way is to limit the amount that the government can borrow in any one year. Government borrowing in the UK is known as the PSBR (Public Sector Borrowing Requirement). The larger the PSBR, the higher will need to be the rate of interest in the economy (☞ unit 78) if the PSBR is financed by genuine borrowing. High interest rates are politically unpopular. Therefore the higher the PSBR, the more tempted governments will be to finance their borrowing by resorting to printing the money.

Secondly, monetarists tend to support the creation of independent central banks whose duty is to maintain price stability. In an economy like the UK, the central bank is effectively controlled by the government. Therefore there is no institution which can resist inflationary policies. In Germany and the USA, central banks are independent and are free to pursue counter-inflationary monetary policy without the need to worry about short term political pressures.

The Keynesian view Keynesians do not deny that controlling the money supply will lead to a reduction in inflation. But they are sceptical of the efficacy of monetary policy. The problem according to Keynesians is that governments cannot control the growth of the money supply directly. The money supply is determined not by the central bank but by the banking system. The money supply is not **exogenous** but **endogenous** (☞ unit 78).

Moreover, there is no precise relationship between the money supply and inflation. Keynesians would not dispute that an annual growth rate of the money supply of 1 000 per cent will increase prices by roughly 1 000 per cent. But as recent evidence from the UK economy shows, the money supply can grow by anything up to 20 per cent a year and inflation can still be very low. Raising interest rates might be effective in reducing aggregate demand, but it is an inefficient policy. It disproportionately affects demand for durable goods traditionally bought on credit, and those with large mortgages. High interest rates also reduce investment. Raising income tax spreads the burden across far more individuals and far more sectors of industry and works far quicker.

Keynesians would also question the priority given to the control of inflation. It is not obvious that creating millions of unemployed people in the short term is worth a long term reduction in inflation. Moreover, the labour market is highly inflexible. The 'short term' could be five, ten, fifteen or even twenty years (☞ unit 65). Validating or accommodating inflation by increasing the money supply could lead to less loss of economic welfare, for instance, than the slump that occurred for instance in the early 1980s in the UK.

One final point is that a tight monetary policy causes increased inflation in the short term. Higher interest rates mean higher mortgage repayments which in the UK are a component part of the Retail Price Index. This is likely to lead to higher wage claims which make the process of adjustment to a lower inflation rate a more difficult and longer process.

QUESTION 1 In the UK it has long been taken for granted that the government has the right to use public resources to purchase election victories ... Since the Second World War, growth in the UK has tended to peak at around the time of an election, with inflation duly following a year or two thereafter ... A government that wishes to increase public expenditure or lower taxes will find it politically more effective to do so by increasing its borrowing than by raising taxes or cutting spending. In time, a larger deficit will usually result in monetary expansion and so inflation ... The solution is to tie the government's hands ... The Prime Minister should sacrifice political control and choose an independent Bank of England that would be as good as the German Bundesbank.

Source: adapted from an article by Martin Wolf in the *Financial Times*, 19.10.1989.

(a) Explain why there might be a link between elections and inflation.
(b) Why might giving independence to the Bank of England help break this link?

Fiscal policy

Demand-pull inflation If inflation is demand-pull in nature, then reducing the level of aggregate demand in the economy will reduce inflationary pressures. Assume in Figure 95.2 that the aggregate demand curve over the next 12 months will shift from AD_1 to AD_3. Prices would therefore rise from OA to OC. By cutting the rise in aggregate demand to AD_2, the government can reduce the rate of inflation with prices rising only to OB.

Keynesians tend to argue that fiscal policy can play a crucial role in cutting aggregate demand. The key variable which the government can manipulate is the PSBR, government borrowing. If it reduces the level of borrowing it will cut aggregate demand. It can cut borrowing either by reducing the level of government spending or by increasing taxes. If it reduces government spending, there will be a **multiplier effect** on national income with aggregate demand falling by more than the initial cut in government spending (☞ units 64 and 68).

Cost-push inflation Governments can also influence wage-push spirals by artificially manipulating indirect tax rates. In a wage-push spiral, workers press for wage increases which are equal to a real increase plus the rate of inflation. For instance, if workers want a 2 per cent real increase and the expected inflation rate is 8 per cent, then they will press for a 10 per cent pay rise. But if the inflation rate is 18 per cent they will press for a wage rise of 20 per cent. Governments can reduce the expected rate of inflation by not raising indirect taxes in money terms. For instance, in the UK excise duties tend to be raised each Budget in order to maintain the real value of the tax. Fully indexing all excise duties tends to add about 1 per cent to the Retail Price Index each year. If the Chancellor chooses not to raise duties, the expected rate of inflation will fall, thus moderating pay claims.

If the government owns key industries, like the railways or the Post Office, it can again reduce expected inflation by not raising prices in line with inflation. The result is that these industries make lower profits or even losses, but this may be a small price to pay for lower inflation.

Lower taxes paid by industry will reduce industry's costs. Reducing corporation tax or employers' National Insurance contributions may therefore help break a cost-push spiral. It would be foolish for a government to lower taxes and leave government spending unchanged if the aim were to reduce inflation. It would replace an element of cost-push inflation with more demand-pull inflation. So real public expenditure must be reduced too. One way of reducing real public expenditure is to keep public sector

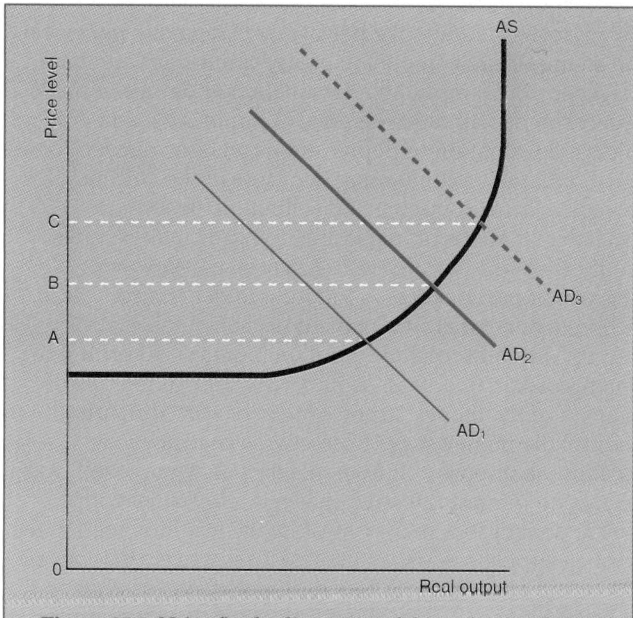

Figure 95.2 *Using fiscal policy to control demand-pull inflation*
Reducing the PSBR so that an increase in aggregate demand is moderated from AD_3 to AD_2 will reduce the rate of inflation.

pay below the rate of inflation. This has the added counter-inflationary bonus that government can set an example to private sector workers of what might be the 'going-rate' of pay increase. If the government sets a ceiling of 4 per cent instead of 8 per cent on public sector pay increases when the rate of inflation is 8 per cent, then private sector workers may be prepared to accept 9 per cent wage increases instead of 10 per cent.

The monetarist view Monetarists see all such measures as futile. Tinkering around with indirect taxes to achieve an artificially low rate of inflation can only be a short term measure. It fails to tackle the underlying cause of inflation which is too high a rate of growth of the money supply. As for demand side measures, they only work because the government is simultaneously reducing the rate of growth of the money supply. If the government raised taxes and reduced public spending but allowed the money supply to continue to grow, inflation would still continue. Fiscal austerity only works if its implementation involves monetary austerity.

QUESTION 2 Each year, the Chancellor in his Budget is faced with choices about whether or not to change tax rates. Explain, using diagrams, why the following might lead to a fall in the inflation rate:
(a) raising income tax rates;
(b) on cost-push grounds, reducing duties on alcohol, tobacco and petrol;
(c) increasing a PSDR;
(d) increasing public sector pay by less than the rate of inflation.

Exchange rate policy

In an open economy like the UK, exchange rate policy can be an important component of any counter-inflationary package. Put simply, any devaluation or depreciation of the currency will raise the price of imports (☞ unit 96). Hence devaluation or depreciation can be a source of cost-push inflation. Maintaining the value of the currency, for instance through buying and selling on the foreign exchange markets or increasing domestic interest rates, could therefore, according to Keynesians, play an important part in keeping inflation under control.

Some monetarists, too, favour exchange rate stability but for different reasons. A fall in inflation, according to monetarists, can only arise if there is a fall in the rate of growth of the money supply. It can be very difficult to control the money supply directly, so central banks wishing to impose a tight monetary policy may well resort to raising interest rates. (A rise in interest rates with a stable demand for money must be the result of a fall in the money supply.) A rise in interest rates will curb domestic spending and reduce inflationary pressures. Higher interest rates will also attract inflows of financial capital from abroad. The result will be a rise in the exchange rate. This will help reduce inflation because the price of imports will fall. It will also make domestically produced goods less competitive against imported goods, forcing domestic producers to cut costs if they wish to stay in the market.

However, the price of a fall in inflation will be unemployment and loss of output, as implied by the short run Phillips curve. To avoid part of this cost, some monetarists argue that it would be far better for a currency to be pegged to a low inflation currency. An example would be the pegging of the pound to the deutschmark via the EMS (the European Monetary System ☞ unit 98). The free market mechanism would then set to work to reduce inflation. If inflation in the UK continued to be higher than in Germany, UK goods would become less competitive in relation to German goods. UK imports would rise and UK exports would fall. This would impose a deflationary effect on the UK economy. Unemployment would rise and firms would be unable to offer inflationary pay rises to their workers without going out of business. Pay settlements would moderate, the growth in the demand for money would slow and hence inflation would fall. But the unemployment costs would be lower than if the exchange rate were allowed to rise.

So some monetarists believe that pegging the currency is an effective alternative **intermediate target** (☞ unit 77) to control of the money supply. Other monetarists argue that the only way to control the money supply effectively is to control the money supply itself. But it should be remembered that economists disagree about whether or not this is possible.

QUESTION 3
'The exchange rate is the link between one country's price level and another's. If sterling is linked to a non-inflationary currency such as the D-Mark, there is no way in which the movement of prices in traded goods and services in Britain can diverge from that of Germany's in the long run; and a link with the D-Mark becomes a partial substitute for the Gold Standard anchor.'

Source: Samuel Brittan, *Financial Times*, 22.6.1989.

Explain why Samuel Brittan argues that UK inflation can be reduced if it is linked to the deutschmark.

Prices and incomes policies

PRICES AND INCOMES POLICY is a policy designed to limit the growth of prices and incomes directly. For instance, a government could impose a price freeze and/or an incomes freeze. This means that prices and incomes are not allowed to rise. The government, however, could just control incomes, limiting their growth to 2 per cent for instance, or allowing them to rise only in line with inflation.

Incomes policies became fashionable in the 1960s when it was hoped that their introduction could push the short run Phillips curve to the left. This would enable a government to run the economy with a given level of unemployment at a lower rate of inflation than would otherwise be the case. Unfortunately this displayed a lack of understanding of the economics behind the Phillips curve.

Incomes policies can help reduce inflation caused by supply side factors. Assume that there is a sharp rise in the price of imports which in turn leads to a sharp rise in the Retail Price Index. Workers increase their wage demands, threatening to set off a wage-price spiral. The government could react by tightening monetary policy, allowing the economy to fall into recession and purging the economy of inflation through increased unemployment. An incomes policy offers a less harsh solution. By imposing maximum pay increases, the government breaks inflationary expectations and hence the cost-push spiral and helps the economy return to price stability at much lower cost in terms of unemployment.

However, prices and incomes policies cannot be used to repress inflation caused by demand side factors indefinitely. If government continues to allow aggregate demand to exceed aggregate supply, for instance through its own excessive spending or through excessive money supply expansion, then prices will rise sharply following the ending of an incomes policy compared to what they would have been without the policy. Indeed the excess demand will tend to contribute to the breakdown of the incomes policy. This is because firms and workers will expect prices to rise given demand conditions in the economy. Firms will know that they could charge higher prices for their products because there is excess demand. Therefore they will be more prepared to award higher wage rises to workers than if there were no excess demand. Workers will realise that firms are prepared to pay higher wages and will be prepared to fight, for instance by taking industrial action. The incomes policy collapses leading to a surge of inflationary wage increases.

An incomes policy may help curb inflation in the short run if inflation is caused by supply side factors by breaking inflationary expectations. But there is considerable debate about whether an incomes policy has any place in the long run management of an economy. Any guidelines or maximum levels of pay imposed by a policy tend to become norms - every worker receives the government set pay increase. Pay differentials between workers therefore do not change. But pay differentials would change over time if all markets were free. This creates grave problems. In expanding industries, for instance, employers would probably like to pay their workers more in order to recruit labour, whilst in declining industries employers might want to pay their workers less, unworried that they might then lose workers. Firms and workers therefore become increasingly resentful of the operation of the incomes policy and have an ever increasing incentive to break it.

QUESTION 4

Table 95.1

	1974	1975	1976	1977	1978
Change in money supply[1] %	11	6	8	9	15
Change in prices %	16	24	17	16	8

1. £M3.
Source: adapted from CSO, *Economic Trends Annual Supplement.*

In 1973-74, the UK economy suffered a severe supply side shock arising from large increases in the price of imported commodities, particularly oil. Import prices rose 46 per cent in 1974. In 1975, the Labour government negotiated an incomes policy with the trade unions which was to last till 1979. However, by 1978, workers were becoming increasingly frustrated with low pay increases. In the winter of 1978-79, the 'winter of discontent', key groups of workers succeeded in breaking the pay guidelines.

(a) Why might the incomes policy described in the passage have helped reduce inflationary pressures?
(b) Why might the changes in the money supply shown in Table 95.1 help explain why workers found it possible to break the incomes policy in 1978-79?

Key terms

Prices and incomes policy - a policy designed to limit the growth of prices and incomes directly.

Applied economics

The control of inflation in the UK

The 1950s and 1960s

In the 1950s and first half of the 1960s, governments used a mixture of fiscal and monetary policies to control rising prices. Apart from the period of the Korean war in the early 1950s, inflation at the time was invariably associated with booms in the economy. Hence, measures to reduce the growth rate of the economy also helped reduce this demand-pull inflation. Favoured weapons were increases in taxes, tighter controls on bank lending and hire purchase lending. It was felt that these, compared to, say, decreases in government spending, would have a rapid impact on aggregate demand.

In 1966, a new policy was implemented to control

inflation. Inflation had risen from 2.1 per cent in 1963 to 4.7 per cent in 1965 as the economy expanded. The new Labour government, under Harold Wilson, decided that a prices and incomes policy might enable the economy to enjoy both a cut in inflation and maintain the relatively low unemployment at the time (i.e. it hoped to shift the short run Phillips curve back to the left). In August 1966 a **statutory** (i.e. legally enforceable) policy was imposed. It became illegal for firms to raise prices or award pay increases. Inflation during the rest of the year and in 1967 moderated. However, as the policy was relaxed inflation began to creep up again, despite a highly deflationary Budget in 1968 which was designed to tackle the balance of payments problem at the time. By 1969, annual inflation had risen to 5.1 per cent, higher than when the prices and incomes policy was first imposed.

The 1970s

In the 1970 election, whether an incomes policy should be continued was a key issue. The opposition Conservatives promised to scrap the policy whilst the Labour government remained committed to its use, despite rising inflation. The Conservatives won the election and duly scrapped the policy. However, for the following two years they failed to have any coherent policy response to the ever rising inflation rate. Indeed, in his 1972 Budget, the Chancellor, Anthony Barber, gave a fiscal boost to the economy by making a sizeable cut in taxes which in Keynesian terms could only have fuelled inflation. The boost given to the money supply by the printing of money to pay for the increased budget deficit was compounded by the 1971 reform of the way in which monetary policy was operated. **Competition and Credit Control** (☞ unit 77), led to an unplanned explosion in the money supply which, on monetarist grounds, could only have led to higher inflation. Another factor adding to inflationary pressures was the abandonment of the UK's fixed exchange rate in 1972 and the consequent fall in the value of the pound which pushed up import prices. Finally, there was an explosion of commodity prices in 1972-73 which culminated in a quadrupling of the price of oil in 1973-74. This led to severe cost-push inflation.

To tackle the growing problem, the government announced in November 1972 the reintroduction of a statutory prices and incomes policy. Like the previous policy, it started with a wage and price freeze, and was followed by a gradual relaxation of policy. For a short time, inflation fell, but the inflationary pressures on the economy were so strong that price increases soon resumed their upward march. Interest rates were slowly raised from 6 per cent in July 1972 to 13 per cent by November 1973. Competition and Credit Control was abandoned in December 1973 and replaced by tighter controls on bank lending. However, the government lost a snap election held in February 1974 on the issue of whether miners could receive a pay increase above the limit allowed in the incomes policy.

The incoming Labour government, without a majority in Parliament, did little to curb inflation. It held a second election later in 1974 when it won a majority but continued to seem to have little policy response to the enormous economic problems - growing inflation, growing unemployment, a recession and a large balance of payments deficit - facing the economy. It had hoped that its 'Social Contract', negotiated with the unions during 1974, which promised to increase pensions, repeal anti-union laws and take other measures which would favour trade union members in return for moderation in pay bargaining, would reduce cost-push inflation. However, the unions only paid lip-service to the contract. In 1975, the government then negotiated another more binding, but still voluntary, Contract with the unions. The trade unions agreed to accept a maximum £6 a week pay increase, with nothing for those earning over £8 500 a year, for one year from August 1975. This, together with falls in worldwide commodity prices, led, according to cost-push proponents, to the rapid fall in inflation from 24.1 per cent in 1975 to 16.5 per cent in 1976 and to a low of 8.3 per cent in 1978.

However, there were also demand side factors at work in the fall in inflation between 1975 and 1978. There were considerable cuts in planned government spending in 1975 and 1976, as well as tax rises. As a consequence, the PSBR fell from £10.2bn in 1975 to £5.4bn in 1977. This deflationary fiscal policy was accompanied by a tightening of monetary policy. On the money side, the first official money supply targets were announced in July 1975 and a tight rein was kept on money supply growth. M4, which had grown by 56 per cent in 1972 alone following the introduction of Competition and Credit Control, grew by only 10 per cent in 1975. Bank base rates were kept very high, in the 10-14 per cent range, for nearly all of 1975 and 1976.

Success in reducing inflation led the government to relax its fiscal and monetary policy from 1977 onwards. The economy began to grow strongly again, with aggregate demand increasing because of increases in spending from the private sector. Inflation, even at 8 per cent, was still higher than our major industrial competitors and still high in historical terms. So the government attempted to enforce a tightening of its incomes policy from August 1978. It demanded a reduction in the target rate of wage increases from the 10 per cent of 1977-78 to 5 per cent in 1978-79. The unions refused to endorse this and in the autumn and winter of 1978-79 (the **winter of discontent**) there was a series of crippling strikes. The government had no legal power to force private sector employers to keep to the 5 per cent guideline because the incomes policy was voluntary. Strikes in the public sector were eventually ended by a promise to set up a commission to consider pay comparability. These pay awards came to be called 'Clegg awards' after the Chairman of the Commission set up to judge the claims. However, the incomes policy had effectively been pushed aside by the unions and the winter of discontent was an important factor in causing the Labour Party to lose the June 1979 election to the Conservatives.

The 1980s and 1990s

The incoming Conservative government of Margaret Thatcher was firmly monetarist. It argued that incomes policies were completely irrelevant to the control of inflation. An incomes policy could paper over the cracks for a short time, but if the economy was continually being fuelled by increases in the money supply, then the inevitable longer term consequence was inflation.

The incoming government faced a difficult challenge. Commodity prices, particularly oil, had once again risen sharply in the world boom of 1978-79, causing a considerable jump in import prices. Wage increases were into double figures with large salary increases promised to public sector workers through the Clegg Commission. On the demand side, 1978-79 were boom years for the economy. The government made matters worse by increasing VAT from 8 per cent to 15 per cent in their first Budget in July 1979. This move paid for a substantial cut in income tax rates. The overall tax impact was neutral, but the 7 per cent increase in VAT fed immediately through to an estimated 5 per cent increase in the RPI, the inflation index. Workers then attempted to regain that 5 per cent by pressing for higher wage increases in 1979-80.

As a monetarist government would, it chose to tighten monetary policy. Interest rates were raised from 12 per cent before the election to 17 per cent in November 1979. In its 1980 Budget, it announced a Medium Term Financial Strategy (MTFS). Money supply growth was to be curbed. This would be achieved by high interest rates and by a commitment to fully fund the PSBR (i.e. not to allow any printing of money to fund government borrowing). The PSBR itself was to be reduced in order to allow interest rates to come down, since the government believed that higher government borrowing increased interest rates in the economy (because higher borrowing led to a higher demand for funds in the loans markets). The publication of the MTFS was also meant to lead to a lowering of inflationary expectations in the economy (based on a **rational expectations model** ☞ unit 65). The argument was that workers based their wage demands on inflation. If workers could be made to believe that future inflation would very low, then wage demands would be low and this would help reduce inflationary pressures in the economy in itself.

Between 1980 and 1981, the economy went into a deep recession. High interest rates caused massive destocking by British industry, which in turn led to lay offs and rapidly rising unemployment. At the same time, the exchange rate of the pound rose considerably due to increased exports of North Sea oil. This helped reduce import prices and hence inflation, but it led to a large contraction of manufacturing industry which found itself unable to compete against cheap foreign imports. So a tight monetary policy, combined with an exchange rate policy which allowed the pound to go up in value, helped reduce inflation from 18.0 per cent in 1980 to 11.9 per cent in 1981. In his 1981 Budget, the Chancellor, Sir Geoffrey Howe, further tightened the squeeze by substantially increasing taxes, producing a fiscal deflationary impact. By 1982, inflation had fallen to 8.6 per cent and in 1983 it was 4.6 per cent.

Throughout the 1980s and early 1990s, fiscal policy was used only to achieve micro-economic objectives, such as cutting income tax rates to increase incentives to work, or as a means of achieving monetary or exchange rate targets. Monetary policy became the chief weapon in the fight against inflation, helped by exchange rate policy.

The government rapidly became disillusioned with targeting the money supply directly. The first half of the 1980s saw double digit annual growth of the money supply despite rapidly falling inflation. It became clear that a simple link between money supply growth and inflation did not exist. In consequence, in 1982, the government stopped targeting just one money supply measure, sterling M3, and set targets for another two money supply measures and, by 1985, the government had downgraded sterling M3 from a targeted variable to one of many variables which it monitored.

By the mid-1980s, the focus of anti-inflationary policy had moved to the exchange rate. Falls in the value of the pound would feed through to higher import prices and therefore higher inflation. If the pound could be pegged against a low inflation currency, in practice the deutschmark, then UK inflation rates would have to remain at the levels of that country. From 1987, the government operated an exchange rate policy where the pound shadowed the deutschmark. Interest rates were raised or lowered according to whether the pound was falling or rising against the deutschmark. This policy proved misguided.

The problem was that economic growth moved from an annual average of 2.5 per cent in 1982-84 to 4.0 per cent in 1985-86 to 4.8 per cent in 1987-88. This growth in demand was unsustainable and began to show through in a deteriorating balance of payments situation and eventually in 1987-88 in rising inflation. The government in the meantime had decided that it had transformed the economy through its supply-side measures and that non-inflationary growth of 4 to 5 per cent was now feasible. It was only in Summer 1988 that the government became convinced that the economy was over-heating and that action would have to be taken to control inflation. It broke the link with the deutschmark and raised interest rates, from 7.5 per cent in May 1988 at the height of the Lawson boom, to 13 per cent by November 1988 and 15 per cent by October 1989. The government hoped for a rapid fall in inflation and a 'soft-landing' for the economy where growth might fall back a little without the economy going into recession. Inflation, however, continued to climb. The government's interest rate policy contributed to its short-term problems. The unprecedented 7.5 per cent increase in interest rates fed through to rises in mortgage interest rates and then into the retail price index. The result was that the headline RPI figure increased at a faster rate than most other measures of inflation in the economy and workers pressed for wage increases based on the higher RPI rates.

However, throughout this period, the then Chancellor of the Exchequer, Nigel Lawson, remained convinced that that pegging the pound to the deutschmark was the only credible anti-inflationary policy. The Prime Minister, Margaret Thatcher, a fierce anti-European, believed that monitoring the domestic money supply was still the key to inflation policy, and that the problems of rising inflation in 1988 were directly linked to the lax monetary policy which the government had been forced to maintain with low interest rates as a result of the shadowing of the deutschmark in 1987 and early 1988. That disagreement was one of the key factors in the political events that led to the ousting of Margaret Thatcher as Prime Minister and her replacement by John Major. It was under his leadership that a decision was finally made in 1990 to join the ERM (☞ unit 98), pegging the pound against the deutschmark at the very high central level of £1 = DM2.95. The level was deliberately chosen to provide a further counter-inflationary twist to the higher interest rate policy of the time. Firms competing against foreign companies found it almost impossible to pass on any price increases to customers at this rate of exchange and consequently were forced to give very low wage increases, if any, to their workers. The high exchange rate was also deflationary because exporters found it hard to increase exports at that rate whilst importers found it easier to compete against UK firms in the UK.

The headline rate of inflation reached a peak of 9.5 per cent in 1990 before falling eventually to a low of 1.6 per cent in 1993. Very high interest rates and then a high exchange rate proved successful in reducing inflation. Fiscal policy remained neutral, with the government allowing its budget to move from substantial surplus in 1988 to a very large deficit by 1993. However, between 1993 and 1996, the government increased taxes to reduce the PSBR and this in itself led to a fiscal squeeze on the economy, which contributed to continuing low rates of inflation. Monetary policy began to ease from 1990 with interest rate cuts. The exchange rate policy of the government collapsed in September 1992 when it was forced to leave the ERM. The subsequent 15 per cent fall in the value of the pound undoubtedly helped raise inflation from 1.6 per cent in 1993 to 2.5 per cent in 1994. However, the long recession of 1990-92, with unemployment nearly doubling from 1.6 million in 1990 to 2.9 million in 1993, kept a tight lid on inflationary pressures in the economy.

By 1995, the government had a target rate of growth for inflation of 1-4 per cent, as shown in Figure 95.3. It was using a wide range of indicators, from house prices to money supply growth to the exchange rate, to judge whether inflationary pressures were increasing or decreasing in the economy. The pound was being allowed to float relatively freely and any attempt to use the exchange rate to anchor the UK economy to a low inflation country like Germany had been abandoned. Interest rates were the main obvious weapon the government was using to control inflation, having raised interest rates in 1994 as the economy began to grow strongly again. Fiscal policy was not officially being used to control inflation. However, the tightening fiscal stance of the government in 1994-95 cannot but have helped reduce inflationary pressures.

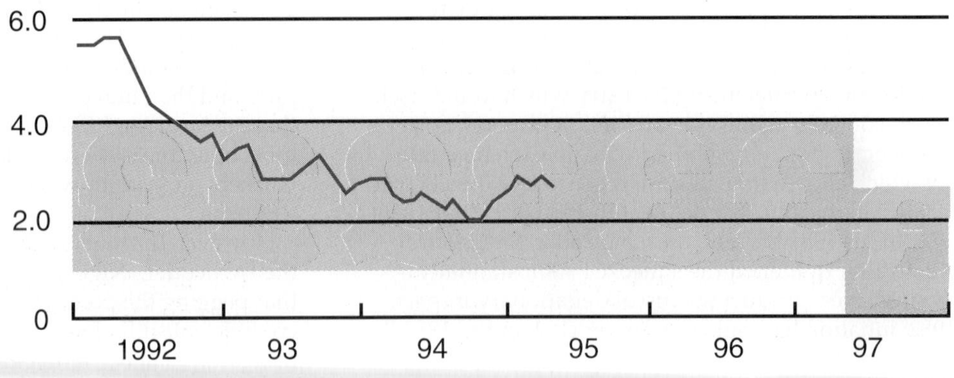

Source: adapted from Datastream.
Figure 95.3 *Inflation targets, 1995*

An evaluation of policy

In retrospect, it can be argued that anti-inflation policy in the UK has often been misguided. Prices and incomes policies (a policy aimed at the supply-side of the economy) failed to work when the government was allowing the economy to grow rapidly (i.e. there were demand pressures building up). Governments have reacted too late in the inflationary cycle to stem inflationary pressures (e.g. in 1973) and have sometimes then over-reacted, producing too deep a recession (e.g. in 1989 and 1990). Warning signs have been ignored (e.g. the excessive monetary growth in 1972) whilst some measures designed to reduce inflation have, at least in the short term, increased inflation (e.g. the increases in interest rates in 1988-89). The reaction to inflation has often been ambivalent because of conflicting policy objectives (e.g. in 1994 when the government relaxed policy to encourage recovery in the economy). However, the commitment to full employment, which many economists now believe was a major contributor to rising inflation in the 1960s and 1970s, was abandoned in the late 1970s. It is difficult to see any future government abandoning a commitment to low inflation in order to pursue a policy of reducing unemployment.

Inflation, 1986-88

Table 95.2 *Changes in GDP and its components at 1990 prices, seasonally adjusted*

	Percentage change over previous 12 months					% of GDP[1]
	GDP	Consumers' expenditure Consumption	Investment	Exports	Imports	PSBR(-)/PSDR(+)
1986						
Q1	3.3	6.1	-4.7	4.4	1.2	+2.4
Q2	2.9	7.8	1.4	1.7	7.6	-3.1
Q3	4.0	6.9	6.5	4.8	10.4	-4.3
Q4	4.8	6.4	7.6	7.0	8.5	+2.0
1987						
Q1	4.3	4.7	4.2	6.8	4.4	+0.9
Q2	4.0	4.1	10.4	4.4	5.9	-1.6
Q3	4.7	5.4	11.5	7.4	10.0	-0.5
Q4	4.2	6.8	14.9	4.1	10.6	+2.6
1988						
Q1	5.6	8.1	19.4	0.0	13.2	+2.9
Q2	4.7	7.3	19.5	3.1	12.4	+1.7

1. Not seasonally adjusted.

Table 95.3 *Prices and earnings*

	Percentage change over previous 12 months				
	RPI	House prices[1]	Import prices	Output of manu-factured goods[2]	Average earnings
1986					
Q1	5.0	13.5	- 8.5	- 16.1	8.1
Q2	2.8	18.8	- 8.2	- 16.5	7.4
Q3	2.7	19.8	- 3.7	- 16.6	8.0
Q4	3.5	15.9	+ 2.6	- 16.7	7.2
1987					
Q1	3.9	17.3	+ 4.4	+ 3.7	7.5
Q2	4.2	14.2	+ 4.1	+ 3.8	7.9
Q3	4.3	16.3	+ 4.3	+ 3.6	8.4
Q4	4.1	21.3	- 0.5	+ 3.8	8.8
1988					
Q1	3.3	27.3	- 2.7	+ 3.9	8.3
Q2	4.3	27.8	- 1.3	+ 4.1	8.4

1 Average price of new dwellings purchased with a mortgage.
2 Producer price index. Output of all manufactured products, home sales.

Table 95.4 *Unemployment, the exchange rate and interest rates*

	Unemployment (millions)	Exchange rate (sterling against the deutschmark)	Bank base rate
1986			
Q1	3.4	3.38	12.30
Q2	3.3	3.39	10.45
Q3	3.3	3.10	10.00
Q4	3.2	2.87	10.85
1987			
Q1	3.2	2.84	10.80
Q2	3.1	2.96	9.35
Q3	2.9	2.97	9.58
Q4	2.8	2.99	9.20
1988			
Q1	2.7	3.01	8.75
Q2	2.5	3.14	8.17

Source: adapted from CSO, *Economic Trends*; *Economic Trends Annual Supplement*.

An economics magazine has asked you to write an article about the Lawson boom and what might have been an alternative policy response to the one chosen at the time by the government to combat rising inflation.

1. Outline the economic conditions prevailing between the first quarter of 1986 and the second quarter of 1988.
2. Explain, using diagrams, how the chosen policy of the government - to raise interest rates from 7.5 per cent in May 1988 to a peak of 15 per cent in November 1989 - should, in theory, reduce inflation.
3. Evaluate, using diagrams, what alternative policies the government could have pursued at the time.
4. The chosen policy response - to raise interest rates in 1989 and 1990 and then to join the ERM in 1990 - led to the longest recession since the 1930s. Discuss whether it might not have been better simply to have done nothing in 1988, 1989 and 1990.

Government policy, the balance of payments and exchange rates

Summary

1. The balance of payments is likely to be in disequilibrium if the value of exports and imports differs over a long period of time.
2. One policy weapon available to governments to tackle a current account deficit is to devalue the currency or allow it to depreciate. The Marshall-Lerner condition states that devaluation will be successful if the combined elasticities of demand for exports and imports exceed unity.
3. In the short term, devaluation is likely to lead to a deterioration in the current account position because of the J curve effect. In the longer term, the competitive benefits of devaluation may be eroded by cost-push inflation.
4. Deflationary policies will act to reduce imports because of the fall in total demand in the economy. Raising interest rates is one way of implementing a deflationary policy.
5. Raising interest rates is also likely to lead to a rise in the value of the currency in the short term as speculative funds are attracted into the country.
6. Protectionist measures can reduce imports but the ability of governments to implement such policies today is severely limited by international agreements.
7. Supply side policies should lead to an increase in international competitiveness over long periods of time.
8. In the short term, a country may choose to impose currency controls, restricting the supply of its currency for use in international transactions.

Balance of payments equilibrium

The balance of payments can be said to be in **equilibrium** when there is no tendency for it to change. This is most likely to occur in the short to medium term if exports are equal to imports and hence both the current and the capital account are in balance. However, equilibrium could also exist if:

- imports are greater than exports and the country is using borrowed foreign money to develop its economy as the USA did in the early part of the 19th century;
- exports are greater than imports and the country is investing the money abroad in order to finance increased imports in the future. It can be argued that Japan is in this position today given that it faces a sharp decline in its workforce and a sharp rise in the number of pensioners in the next 30 years.

In the long term, countries are unlikely to be able to continue as substantial net borrowers because other countries will refuse to lend to countries which get deeper and deeper into debt (as has happened with many Third World countries during the 1980s). In the long term, therefore, equilibrium will occur when exports equal imports.

If the balance of payments is in equilibrium there will be no tendency for the exchange rate to change. If, on the other hand, a country tends to export more than it imports over long periods, its exchange rate will tend to rise. The demand for the country's currency to pay for its exports will continually exceed the supply of currency offered for sale to pay for imports. Speculation may cause the exchange rate to fluctuate randomly in the short term if exchange rates are floating but the exchange rate trend is likely to be upward in the long term. If the country runs a persistent current account deficit, its exchange rate will tend to fall.

If the current account is in persistent deficit (or surplus), what measures can government take to rectify this situation? How can governments keep exchange rates up when there is persistent selling pressure from the markets?

Devaluation and revaluation

One possible way of curing a current account deficit is for the government to DEVALUE the currency. This means that it lowers the value of the currency against other currencies. Devaluation affects exports and imports because it changes their relative prices and thus their international competitiveness. The opposite of devaluation is REVALUATION, an increase in the value of the currency.

Devaluation assumes that the government pegs the value of its currency against other currencies. (This is done by European countries within the Exchange Rate Mechanism or ERM, for instance.) However, exchange rates may **float**, which means that governments allow free market forces to determine the value of the currency. A fall in the value of the currency is then called a DEPRECIATION of the currency. The opposite of depreciation is APPRECIATION of the currency. In what follows, it will be assumed that the government does control the value of the currency and therefore the term 'devaluation' rather than 'depreciation' will be used. However, devaluation and depreciation have the same effects, as do revaluation and appreciation.

The effects of devaluation

Assume that the pound falls in value against other currencies by 20 per cent. The price of imports will therefore rise in pounds sterling. With an exchange rate of

10F = £1, a French car sold to UK importers for 100 000 francs would have cost £10 000 in pounds sterling. With a 20 per cent devaluation of the pound, the new exchange rate will be 8F = £1. So the cost of a 100 000 franc car will be £12 500. At the new price, demand is likely to fall. The effect on the total value of imports will depend upon the elasticity of demand for French cars. If demand is elastic, the percentage rise in the price of French cars will be more than offset by a percentage fall in the demand for cars. Hence the total sterling value of imported French cars will fall. (This is an application of the relationship between elasticity and revenue ☞ unit 9). If demand is price inelastic, a rise in price will lead to a rise in expenditure on French cars and hence a rise in the sterling value of French car imports.

In summary, a devaluation of the pound will:

- leave the French franc **price** unchanged but increase the sterling price of imported goods;
- result in a fall in **import volumes**;
- lead to a fall in the **total sterling value** of imports assuming that domestic demand for imports is elastic; if demand is inelastic, there will be a rise in the sterling value of imports.

Devaluation of the pound should have no effect on the sterling price of exports. A £10 000 car exported to France will still be £10 000 after devaluation. But the price will have fallen in French francs. If the value of the pound falls from 10F = £1 to 8F = £1, the £10 000 car will fall in price in France from 100 000 francs to 80 000 francs. This should lead to a rise in demand for UK cars.

A devaluation will therefore:

- leave the **sterling price** of exports unchanged but reduce the price in foreign currency terms;
- lead to a rise in **export volumes**;
- increase the **total sterling value** of exports.

QUESTION 1 In October 1993, it was reported that exports of steelwork for construction had risen by up to a fifth since sterling left the ERM in September 1992 and the pound had fallen in value by over 10 per cent. Invitations to tender for international contracts had risen even faster, according to a survey of orders received by the 12 largest UK constructional steel producers.
The survey, by British Constructional Steelwork Association, showed that the companies had received international invitations to tender and requests for price quotations involving more than 400 000 tonnes of steel since September 1992, compared to just 20 000 tonnes in the preceding 12 months. Mr Rollo Reid, director of John Reid & Sons in Dorset, said: 'We have been quoting prices up to 25 per cent lower than local German fabricators. We have even been asked, for the first time, to price jobs in Japan.' Mr Joe Lock, managing director of Watson Steel, part of the Amec construction group, said: 'Opportunities to bid for international work have increased considerably following sterling's devaluation.'

Source: adapted from the *Financial Times*, 1.10.1993.

Explain, using examples from the passage, what is likely to happen to (a) price, (b) volumes and (c) revenues of exports following a devaluation of a currency.

Devaluation and elasticity

Overall, devaluation of the pound will increase the sterling value of exports, but may or may not lead to a fall in the value of imports depending upon the elasticity of demand for imports. It is likely that, even if import values increase, export values will increase even more. Hence devaluation will result in an improved current account position. The MARSHALL LERNER condition states that, given very stringent conditions, devaluation will result in an improvement on current account if the combined elasticities of demand for exports and imports are greater than 1. If the combined elasticities for exports and imports are less than 1, then the correct policy response to a current account deficit should be a currency **revaluation**.

Devaluation and pricing strategies

So far it has been assumed that UK exporters will choose to keep the sterling price of the products constant and change the foreign currency price, whilst importers will choose to keep the foreign currency price of their goods the same and change the sterling price. However, exporters and importers may choose a different strategy. Jaguar, for instance, may price a model at $40 000 in the USA. If the value of the pound is $2 = £1, it will receive £20 000 per car. If the pound is now devalued to $1 = £1, Jaguar has a choice of strategies. It could keep the sterling price constant at £20 000 and reduce the dollar price to $20 000. However, a fall in price of a luxury car may give the wrong signals to US car buyers. They may assume that Jaguar cars are no longer luxury cars. They may think that Jaguar is not doing well in the US and is having to reduce prices in order to maintain sales. The fall in the dollar price may generate few extra sales. So Jaguar is likely to hold constant the dollar price of $40 000 and consequently increase its profit margins. When the value of the pound rises against the dollar, Jaguar may again choose to hold constant the dollar price. A rise in the dollar price may lead to large falls in sales if Jaguar is in a competitive market with other luxury car manufacturers.

If both exporters and importers adopt the strategy of leaving the prices they charge to their customers unchanged, devaluation will still improve the current account position. Assume the pound is devalued.

- The sterling value of exports will rise because exporters have chosen to increase the sterling price of exported goods rather than reduce their foreign currency price. Export volumes will remain unchanged because the foreign currency price has remained unchanged. Therefore sterling export values will increase because of the sterling price increase.
- The sterling value of imports will stay the same. Foreign firms have chosen to keep the sterling price of their goods constant. Hence volumes will not change. Neither, therefore, will the sterling value of imports.

With export values increased and import values unchanged, there will be an improvement in the current account position.

QUESTION 2 In the first quarter of 1995, the value of the pound fell sharply against its main trading partners. Mr Malcolm Taylor, managing director of Bridgport Machines, the Leicester-based machine tool maker, said his company intended to use the competitive bonus offered by a lower pound to increase market share in Europe. 'Our strategy will be to let the distributors take the advantage of the currency movement to win more market share', he said. The ambition was to raise exports overall by up to one quarter this year. But some companies were not going to take the same view, according to Mr Richard Brown, deputy director-general of the British Chamber of Commerce: 'They are unlikely to use a temporary change in sterling's value to increase market share and are much more likely to take windfall profits'. China manufacturer, Royal Worcester, which had not yet seen any additional boost to overseas sales because of the fall in the pound, may choose this option. Mr Tim Westbrook, managing director at Royal Worcester, said: 'We will have to see where sterling settles before considering whether to readjust prices. If the weakness is only short-term, we may just see a blip in profit margins.'

Source: adapted from the *Financial Times*, 22.3.1995.

(a) Compare the impact on the current account of the balance of payments of the two different reactions to a fall in the value of the pound described in the article.
(b) Why might a machine tool company be more willing to change its prices than a manufacturer of fine china like Royal Worcester?

Problems associated with devaluation

There are two major problems with using devaluation as a policy weapon.

The J curve The current account following devaluation is likely to get worse before it gets better. This is known as the J CURVE EFFECT and it is shown in Figure 96.1.

Assume the UK has a current account deficit and attempts to devalue its currency. In the short run the demand for exports and imports will tend to be inelastic. Although the foreign currency price of UK exports will fall, it takes time before other countries react to the change. Hence, the volume of exports will remain the same in the short term, before increasing in the longer term. This means that in the short term, there will be no increase in sterling export values.

Similarly, although the sterling price of imports rises, in the short term UK buyers may be stuck with import contracts they signed before devaluation. Alternatively, there may be no alternative domestic suppliers and hence firms may have to continue to buy imports. Hence, in the short term, sterling import values will rise. In the longer term, contracts can be revised and domestic producers can increase supply, thus leading to a reduction in import volumes.

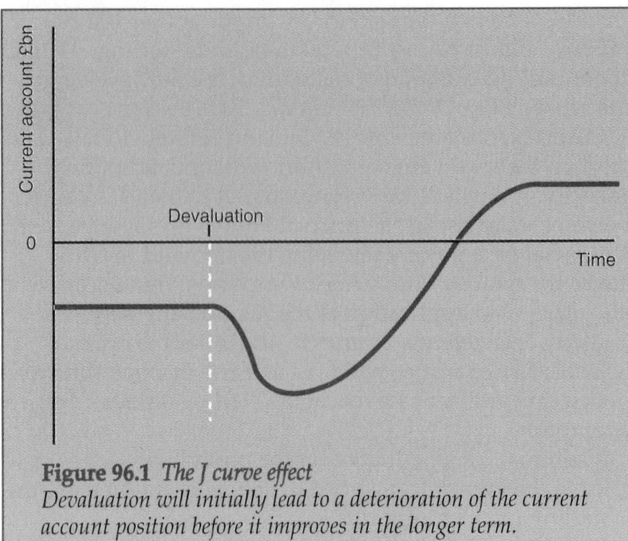

Figure 96.1 *The J curve effect*
Devaluation will initially lead to a deterioration of the current account position before it improves in the longer term.

Overall, in the short term, import values will rise but export values will remain constant, thus producing a deterioration in the current account. In the longer term, export values will rise whilst import values might fall, producing an improvement in the current account position.

Cost-push inflation Devaluation generates imported inflation. This is not serious if there is a once and for all increase in prices. But if it starts up or fuels a cost-push **inflationary spiral**, then the increased competitiveness achieved by the devaluation will be quickly eroded. Keynesian economists have become increasingly sceptical of the value of devaluation as a policy weapon to cure a balance of payments deficit unless it is part of a much wider package of measures designed to increase the competitiveness and performance of a deficit economy.

QUESTION 3 In the first quarter of 1995, the value of the pound fell sharply against its main trading partners. David Walton, UK economist at Goldman Sachs, compared this situation to the one in late 1992 when the pound equally fell in value. He pointed out that: 'The difference between now and 1992 is that inflation was heading down but now it is already rising'. He believed that if sterling's weakness were to be maintained, then it would take inflation outside the government's target range in 1996.

Some companies were already passing on increased costs and others were preparing to do so. Mr Bob Bischoff, chair of Boss Group, the Bedfordshire-based fork lift truck maker which exports 65 per cent of its vehicles, said Boss now had an added competitive edge against its German, Japanese and Scandinavian rivals, but he also bought components from Germany and import costs were already rising. 'If these continue, we will increase our prices,' he warned.

Source: adapted from the *Financial Times*, 22.3.1995.

What problems might be associated with a falling value of the pound? Illustrate your answer with examples from the passage.

Deflation

Devaluation results in **expenditure switching**. Foreigners buy more of our exports and less of their own and other countries' production, whilst domestic consumers buy fewer imports and more domestically produced goods. An alternative approach to curing a current account deficit is **deflation**. This is an **expenditure reducing** policy. If the government reduces aggregate demand in the economy, for instance by raising interest rates or increasing taxes, people have less money to spend so they reduce their consumption of domestically produced goods and imported goods. Imports therefore decline. Exports may also rise if domestic firms switch sales from the depressed domestic market to foreign markets.

For the UK, deflation has proved very successful in reducing imports, particularly because the UK has a very high **marginal propensity to import** in manufactured goods. The effect on exports has been less noticeable. Firms may well choose to reduce output in response to a recession in the economy rather than seek export orders.

One important policy advantage of deflation is that it is likely to reduce inflationary pressures in the economy, assuming those pressures come from the demand side of the economy. On the other hand, it also reduces growth and increases unemployment, both undesirable in themselves. In the long term, the economy must increase its international competitiveness unless the economy is to remain permanently below full employment.

Interest rates

Increased interest rates will initially bolster the value of the currency. They attract speculative inflows into the country, raising the demand for the currency. In the longer term, a rise in interest rates which must have been generated by a fall in the supply of money (☞ unit 78) will lead to a fall in aggregate demand through the transmission mechanism. Higher interest rates deflate the economy, leading to a fall in imports and hence an improvement in the current account.

QUESTION 4 In 1988, with a worsening balance of payments situation and rising inflation, the UK government raised interest rates. Bank base rates between 1988 and 1990 rose from $7\frac{1}{2}$ per cent to 15 per cent.

Explain how a rise in domestic interest rates might lead to an improvement in the balance of payments current account position.

Protectionism

Increasing tariffs or quotas or other protectionist measures will reduce imports thus improving the current account position. Tariffs and quotas can both have a significant impact in the short term. However, protectionism is not much favoured by economists. First, the country is likely to find itself becoming even more internationally uncompetitive in the long run as its domestic industries have no incentive to improve their efficiency. Second, protectionism in one country invites retaliation from its trading partners. The country could find that the gains on current account from reduced imports are more than matched by losses of exports as a result of retaliation (☞ unit 85).

Increased protectionist measures are also forbidden except under certain specific circumstances by the WTO (the World Trade Organisation). Membership of a trading bloc like the European Union severely limits the ability of individual countries to limit imports through protectionist policies.

Currency controls

A government may choose to impose or tighten currency controls. These are controls on the purchase of foreign currency by domestic citizens and firms. In the late 1960s, for instance, the UK government limited the amount of currency that could be taken abroad on holiday to £50 per person. Governments could equally restrict finance for investment abroad or even for imports. The government abolished exchange controls in 1979, and today, the UK government is unable to impose currency controls because of its membership of the European Union.

Supply side policies

One way of making domestically produced goods more competitive is through devaluation: altering the relative price of exports and imports. However, there are many other ways in which domestic industry can become more competitive internationally. **Supply side policies** (☞ unit 69) aimed at reducing unit labour costs, increasing investment, increasing the skills of the labour force and improving the quality and design of products should lead to increased exports and reduced imports. Supply side policies tend to be long term policies. They cannot cure a current account deficit within, for instance, 12-24 months.

QUESTION 5 In February 1990, the government of Bangladesh, faced with a swelling of the country's current account deficit, tightened its currency controls. Importers were required to provide a 50 per cent cash deposit when opening new letters of credit.

A letter of credit is a type of loan common in the export/import trade. Explain why the government measure outlined in the passage could lead to (a) an improvement in the current account position and (b) a rise in the value of the Bangladesh currency, the Taka.

Key terms

Devaluation and revaluation - a fall or rise in the value of the currency when the currency is pegged against other currencies.
Depreciation or appreciation - a fall or rise in the value of the currency when the currency is floating and market forces determine its value.
Marshall Lerner condition - devaluation will lead to an improvement in the current account so long as the combined price elasticities of exports and imports are greater than 1.
J curve effect - in the short term a devaluation is likely to lead to a deterioration in the current account position before it starts to improve.

Applied economics

Government policy

The 1950s and 1960s

For much of the 1950s and 1960s, the balance of payments and the exchange rate posed major problems for the UK government. Whenever the economy went into boom, the current account slipped into deficit. This would tend to be associated with exchange rate crises. Speculators would sell sterling, forcing its price down. At the time the UK was a member of the **Bretton Woods system** (☞ unit 97) of exchange rates, where the pound was fixed in value against other currencies. To keep the pound fixed the government tended to deflate the economy, putting it into recession. This led to falling imports and an improved balance of payments situation. However, by the mid-1960s, it was argued by many that the UK had a structural deficit on its balance of payments (i.e. in the long term deficits would outweigh surpluses and thus there would be a long term deficit on the current account). In 1964, an incoming Labour government under Harold Wilson rejected the policy option of devaluing the pound. His government then spent the next three years dealing with intermittent exchange rate crises and finally, in June 1967, devalued the pound by 15 per cent.

The next nine months saw a sharp deterioration in the current account position - probably the working out of the J curve effect. The government therefore decided that its March 1968 Budget needed to be severely deflationary. The current account rapidly improved and by 1969 was back in surplus. Which was the most important factor in this - the 15 per cent devaluation or the most deflationary Budget since the Second World War - is difficult to judge.

The 1970s

The current account continued in surplus in 1970 and 1971 as the economy went into a recession. The March 1972 Budget was highly reflationary, designed to reduce unemployment. The government recognised that this might have implications for the current account and announced that it was not committed to maintaining the existing exchange rate. In June 1972, following heavy selling of the pound, the UK left the Bretton Woods system and the pound depreciated in value.

The pound fell rapidly. Against the deutschmark, for instance, it fell from DM8.26 in the second quarter of 1972 to DM6.05 in the last quarter of 1973, a 27 per cent depreciation. This should have allowed the current account to remain in balance. However, government policy was so reflationary that the current account moved deeper and deeper into the red. The final twist was the oil crisis of 1973-74, which quadrupled the price of imported oil.

The government's policy response was to continue to allow the pound to float downwards. By the end of 1975, the pound was only worth DM5.30 and by the last quarter of 1976 it was worth only DM3.98, a 52 per cent depreciation against its second quarter 1972 value. Budgets in 1975 and 1976 were deflationary. This did not prevent a major sterling crisis in late 1976 when the government was forced to borrow money from the IMF to prop up its reserves. However, the current account position was already improving by 1975-76 and in 1977 it moved into surplus. Again, it is difficult to judge the extent to which this improvement was due either to depreciation of the currency or to deflationary budgets.

The current account position was then transformed by exports of North Sea oil. The first oil was produced in 1976 and by 1980 oil exports were greater than oil imports. The government produced mildly reflationary Budgets in 1977 and 1978 to stimulate growth and reduce unemployment. Inevitably, the current account position worsened and by 1979 the current account was back in deficit. However, the exchange rate remained broadly stable and, indeed, the pound began to go up in value in 1979 as the foreign currency markets anticipated the effect the North Sea oil bonanza would have on the current account.

The 1980s and 1990s

In the 1950s, 1960s and 1970s, current account deficits were seen as a problem which demanded a policy response from government. Since 1979, the government has believed that the current account is self correcting and therefore does not demand a policy response. Between 1980 and 1982, the current account benefited from a growing oil surplus and a deep recession in the economy. In contrast, the value of the pound soared. Against the deutschmark, for instance, it rose from DM3.81 in the last quarter of 1979 to DM4.81 in the first quarter of 1981, an appreciation of 26 per cent. But for this appreciation, the current surpluses in 1980-82 would have been even larger.

The appreciation did, however, have the disastrous effect of destroying a sizeable part of UK manufacturing industry. Unable to compete internationally, firms went out of business. Manufacturing output fell 18 per cent between the second quarter of 1979 and the last quarter of 1982. The trade balance on finished manufactures, which had fluctuated between +£2bn to £3bn per annum in the 1970s, plunged to a deficit of £4bn by 1984 and then, after a short period of stabilisation, plunged to a £13bn deficit by 1989. From 1982, the pound began to fall again as it became apparent that much of the increased oil revenues on the current account had been offset by large falls in the trade balance on manufactured goods. In the second half of the 1980s, the government began to consider, and then in 1987 finally implemented, a policy of shadowing the deutschmark. This culminated in the UK joining the ERM in 1990. However, this exchange rate policy was designed to combat inflation (☞ unit 92) and was not aimed at correcting the growing current account deficit of the time.

The current account remained broadly in balance till 1986. Then, as the economy went into the Lawson boom, it deteriorated sharply and deficits, measured as a percentage of GDP, began to be recorded which were as large as those during the oil crisis of the mid-1970s. The government refused to accept there was any problem. It argued that the deficits showed a desire on the part of consumers and firms to borrow abroad to finance spending. If that is what they wanted, then the government should not intervene to prevent them from doing so. As the economy went into recession following the Lawson boom, the current account deficit fell, but even at the height of the recession in 1991-92, it remained obstinately in deficit. Then the government was forced to take the pound out of the ERM in September 1992. The pound went down in value by 15 per cent. With deflationary Budgets in 1994 and 1995, the current account began to move towards balance despite the recovery in the economy from 1993. Government policy remained in the mid-1990s, not to intervene actively to tackle balance of payments problems.

Depreciation of the pound, 1992-94

Table 96.1 *Current balance 1990-1994*

	£m
1990	- 19 035
1991	- 8 176
1992	- 9 831
1993	- 11 800
1994	- 168

Table 96.2 *Components of the current balance*

£ million

	Visible trade		Invisible trade	
	Oil balance	Non-oil balance	Traded services balance	Other services balance
1990	1 529	- 20 338	3 689	- 3 915
1991	1 208	- 11 492	3 708	- 1 600
1992	1 548	- 14 652	4 089	- 816
1993	2 457	- 15 851	5 213	- 3 619
1994	4 158	- 14 685	4 759	+ 5 600

Table 96.3 *Non-oil visible balance*

	£m		£m		£m
1992		1993		1994	
Q1	- 3 100	Q1	- 3 893	Q1	- 4 295
Q2	- 3 336	Q2	- 3 972	Q2	- 3 596
Q3	[illegible]	Q3	- 3 945	Q3	- 2 781
Q4	- 4 553	Q4	- 4 041	Q4	- 4 031

Table 96.4 *Volume indices[1] for exports and imports*

1990 = 100

	All goods		Non-oil goods		Services[2]	
	Exports	Imports	Exports	Imports	Exports	Imports
1992						
Q1	101.9	97.0	102.1	97.3	98.6	101.4
Q2	103.9	101.4	104.0	101.4	99.1	100.1
Q3	103.0	101.8	102.5	101.7	97.9	97.6
Q4	105.9	103.5	105.6	103.8	96.9	97.2
1993						
Q1	106.3	104.4	105.7	104.5	100.8	94.4
Q2	104.7	102.3	103.8	102.0	98.5	99.0
Q3	107.2	104.4	105.8	104.4	103.6	97.6
Q4	109.3	107.5	107.4	107.4	105.4	101.9
1994						
Q1	112.1	110.0	110.0	111.0	104.3	105.4
Q2	116.6	108.0	113.8	108.8	102.4	102.9
Q3	120.9	108.9	119.5	109.8	104.9	102.2
Q4	124.0	115.5	122.4	116.8	107.8	108.9

1. Quantity sold, expressed in index number form.
2. Traded services. This does not include 'other services' (i.e. investment income and public sector and private sector transfers).

Table 96.5 *Average prices of exports and imports*

1990 = 100

	All goods		Non-oil goods		Services[1]	
	Exports	Imports	Exports	Imports	Exports	Imports
1992						
Q1	102.4	101.3	104.2	102.4	105.4	103.6
Q2	103.2	100.6	104.7	101.4	106.1	103.0
Q3	102.8	99.8	104.4	100.5	106.3	104.8
Q4	105.4	106.7	106.6	107.2	112.0	111.6
1993						
Q1	114.2	110.1	116.0	110.9	115.4	118.8
Q2	114.2	110.8	115.9	110.8	114.1	115.9
Q3	115.5	111.0	117.7	112.4	116.0	115.7
Q4	115.1	110.7	117.9	112.4	115.8	117.1
1994						
Q1	115.9	111.0	119.2	112.8	116.0	116.5
Q2	117.3	114.8	120.0	116.6	115.5	115.8
Q3	117.7	116.3	120.3	117.7	118.3	116.2
Q4	117.0	115.9	119.7	117.5	118.8	117.6

1. Traded services. This does not include 'other services' (i.e. investment income and public sector and private sector transfers).

Table 96.6 *Exchange rates*

	Sterling exchange rate against deutschmark	Sterling exchange rate index (1985 = 100)
1992		
Q1	2.866	90.5
Q2	2.916	92.3
Q3	2.786	90.9
Q4	2.445	79.8
1993		
Q1	2.414	78.5
Q2	2.484	80.2
Q3	2.522	81.0
Q4	2.510	81.0
1994		
Q1	2.563	81.3
Q2	2.497	80.0
Q3	2.421	79.2
Q4	2.446	80.2

Table 96.7 *Economic growth*

	% change in real GDP on previous 12 months
1990	
Q1	1.0
Q2	0.0
Q3	0.0
Q4	- 1.1
1991	
Q1	- 2.3
Q2	- 3.1
Q3	- 2.6
Q4	- 1.8
1992	
Q1	- 1.7
Q2	- 1.3
Q3	- 0.4
Q4	0.0
1993	
Q1	1.5
Q2	2.0
Q3	2.4
Q4	2.6
1994	
Q1	3.3
Q2	4.1
Q3	4.1
Q4	4.2

Source: tables adapted from CSO, *Economic Trends*.

On 16 September 1992, the government suspended the pound from the ERM. The result was an immediate double digit fall in the value of the pound. The suspension came at a time when the economy was only slowly coming out of a prolonged recession in the economy. In the period following the suspension, the government rapidly cut interest rates in the economy, from 10 per cent to 5½ per cent in early 1994.

1. **Explain, using a diagram, what the J curve model suggests will happen to the current account on the balance of payments (a) in the short term and (b) in the longer term.**
2. **What would you expect to happen to the current account when an economy comes out of recession?**
3. **To what extent do your answers to questions 1 and 2 help you understand what happened to the current account on the balance of payments between 1992 and 1994?**

Exchange rate systems

Summary

1. There are a number of different types of exchange rate system - mechanisms for determining the conditions of exchange between one currency and another.
2. The Bretton Woods system was an example of an adjustable peg system. In the short term, currencies were fixed in value against each other. In the longer term, currencies could be devalued or revalued. Currencies were fixed in the short term by central bank intervention - the buying and selling of currency using foreign currency reserves.
3. In a floating exchange rate system, the value of a currency is determined, without central bank intervention, by the forces of demand and supply in foreign currency markets.
4. With a managed or dirty float, the price of a currency is determined by free market forces, but occasionally central banks will intervene using their reserves to steady the price of the currency.
5. The Gold Standard was an example of a fixed exchange rate system. Currencies were pegged in value against gold and therefore they could not change in value against each other.
6. The European Monetary System is an example of a currency bloc. A group of currencies maintain fixed exchange rates against each other, but float against other currencies.

Exchange rate systems

An EXCHANGE RATE SYSTEM is any system which determines the conditions under which one currency can be exchanged for another. In unit 87, it was assumed that exchange rates were determined purely by the free market forces of demand and supply. This type of system is known as a free or floating exchange rate system. In contrast fixed exchange rate systems have existed in the past, where currencies have not been allowed to change in value against each other from year to year. In between, there is a variety of adjustable peg systems which combine elements of exchange rate stability in the short term with the possibility of exchange rate movements in the long term.

The Bretton Woods system

An ADJUSTABLE PEG SYSTEM is an exchange rate system where, in the short term, currencies are fixed or pegged against each other and do not change in value, whilst in the longer term the value of a currency can be changed if economic circumstances so dictate. Between the end of the Second World War and the early 1970s, exchange rates were determined by an adjustable peg system. It was known as the BRETTON WOODS SYSTEM after the town in the USA where Allied powers met in 1944 to discuss new international trade arrangements for the post-war era.

How it worked Under the system, each country fixed its exchange rate against other currencies. For instance, between 1949 and 1967, the pound was valued at US $2.80. This was known as the par value for the currency. The Bank of England guaranteed to maintain prices within a narrow 1 per cent boundary. So the price of the pound could fluctuate on a day to day basis between $2.78 and $2.82. Prices were maintained because central banks bought and sold currency. When the price of pounds threatened to go below $2.78, the Bank of England would intervene in the market and buy pounds. When the price threatened to go over $2.82, the Bank of England would sell pounds.

This is illustrated in Figure 97.1. The free market demand curve for pounds is $D_1 D_1$. In contrast, the demand curve under an adjustable peg system, $D_2 D_2$, is kinked. Above a price of $2.78, the demand curve is the same as the free market demand curve. But at $2.78, the Bank of England is prepared to buy any amount of foreign currency to maintain the value of the pound at this minimum level. Therefore the demand curve for pounds becomes horizontal (i.e. perfectly elastic) at this price.

Assume that the supply curve is initially S_1, resulting in an equilibrium price of $2.80. OA is bought and sold and the Bank of England does not intervene in the market.

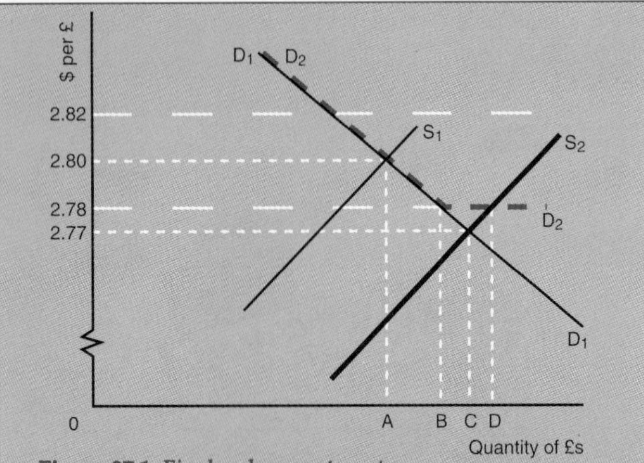

Figure 97.1 *Fixed exchange rate systems*
The pound is pegged at $2.80 but is allowed to fluctuate within a very narrow band from $2.78 to $2.82. If market forces shift the supply curve from S_1 to S_2, the Bank of England will need to buy BD pounds to maintain the minimum price of $2.78.

Now assume that imports into the UK increase, shifting the supply curve for pounds to the right to, say, S_2. The new free market equilibrium price would be $2.77, below the minimum **intervention price** within the system, with OC currency bought and sold. The Bank of England would react to this by buying pounds with gold or foreign exchange held in its **reserves** (☞ unit 86). To restore the exchange rate to the minimum $2.78, it has to buy BD pounds, the difference between the OB pounds demanded by the rest of the market at $2.78 and OD, the quantity supplied for sale.

If the value of the pound threatened to rise above the maximum price of $2.82, the Bank of England would sell pounds on the market, increasing the supply of pounds and thus forcing their price down. Note that on Figure 97.1, the supply curve of sterling under an adjustable peg system would be kinked like the demand curve, becoming horizontal (i.e. perfectly elastic) at a sterling price of $2.82. The Bank of England would be prepared to supply any amount of sterling in exchange for foreign currencies at a price of $2.82.

QUESTION 1

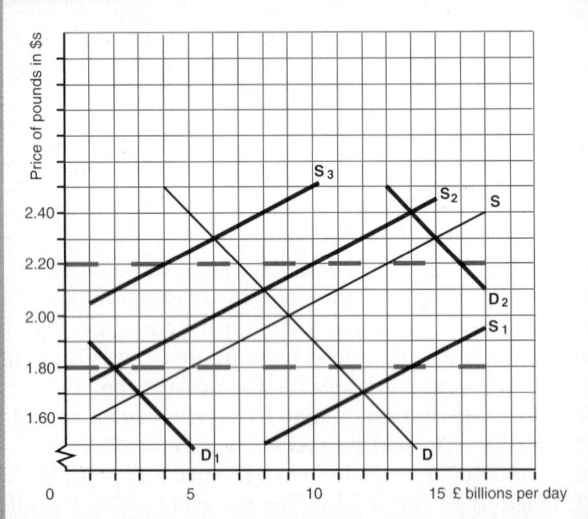

Figure 97.2
D and S are the free market demand and supply curves for pounds in $s. The Bank of England is committed to keeping the dollar price of sterling between $2.20 and $1.80.

(a) What is the free market price of the pound?
(b) With a demand curve D, how much currency (in £) will the Bank of England have to buy or sell per day if the supply curve shifts from S to: (i) S_1; (ii) S_2; (iii) S_3?
(c) With a supply curve S, how much currency (in £) will the Bank of England have to buy or sell per day if the demand curve shifts from D to: (i) D_1; (ii) D_2?

Adjustment mechanisms Under the Bretton Woods system, countries were committed to two major policy objectives:
- in the short term, to maintaining stable exchange rates;
- in the long term, to maintaining a balance of payments equilibrium (which they would be forced to do anyway by free market forces).

In the short term, exchange rate stability was maintained by buying and selling currencies as explained above. The system was therefore crucially dependent upon the existence of gold and foreign currency reserves held by central banks. In theory, the price of the currency was set at its long term equilibrium level. A run down in reserves caused by the need to buy the domestic currency when the currency was weak would be offset by increases in the reserves at other times when the currency was strong.

However, free market speculation could lead to very rapid depletions of a country's gold and foreign currency reserves. The UK suffered a series of **sterling crises** in the 1950s, 1960s and 1970s as speculators sold pounds believing that the UK government might devalue sterling. Governments had a limited number of options open to them if they wanted to maintain the value of their exchange rate.
- The most likely response to heavy selling pressure on the currency was to raise interest rates. This attracted speculative money from abroad, raising the demand for and therefore the price of the currency. In the medium term, a rise in interest rates would have a deflationary impact via the **transmission mechanism**.
- The government could also attempt to prevent a fall in the value of the currency by introducing **currency controls** (☞ unit 96).
- As a last resort, the central bank would turn to the **International Monetary Fund** (IMF). The founders of the system realised that there would be times when an individual country would run out of reserves. So it set up an international fund, the IMF, which would lend money to central banks when needed. Central banks would deposit part of their gold and foreign currency reserves with the IMF and in return would be able to borrow a limited amount of money when in a crisis.

Short term measures were unlikely to satisfy the market for long if speculators were selling a currency because they judged that there was a FUNDAMENTAL DISEQUILIBRIUM on the country's balance of payments. If imports were greater than exports over a long period of time, the central bank of the country would continually be buying its currency and thus running down its reserves. Eventually the reserves, including any money borrowed from the IMF, would be exhausted and the currency would have to fall in value. Governments could adopt a number of long term policies to prevent this happening (☞ unit 96 for more detail).

- It was intended that governments would officially devalue their currency before markets forced this anyway.
- In practice, governments tended to deflate their economies, reducing imports and thus restoring a current account balance.
- Protectionist measures, such as raising tariffs and quotas, were a possibility but were illegal under GATT (now the WTO) rules (☞ unit 85). This severely limited their use by major industrialised countries.
- Supply side policies designed to improve long term competitiveness were also a possibility.

QUESTION 2 In 1952, the ratio of world central bank gold and foreign currency reserves to total world imports stood at 70 per cent. By 1966, this had fallen to 38 per cent.

Suggest reasons why this fall is likely to have contributed to the collapse of the Bretton Woods system in the early 1970s.

Floating exchange rate systems

In a pure FLOATING or FREE EXCHANGE RATE SYSTEM, the value of a currency is determined on a minute by minute basis by free market forces. This is the exchange rate system described in detail in unit 97. Governments, through their central banks, are assumed not to intervene in the foreign exchange markets.

In theory there is no need for intervention because the balance of payments must always balance (☞ unit 87). The balance of payments will look after itself. In practice, governments find it impossible not to intervene because changes in exchange rates can lead to significant changes in domestic output, unemployment and inflation. Moreover, sharp falls in a currency are usually damaging politically and hence governments are tempted at these times to shore up the currency by buying in the market.

A system where the exchange rate is determined by free market forces but governments intervene from time to time to alter the free market price of a currency is known as a MANAGED or DIRTY FLOAT. Governments intervene by buying and selling currency as under the Bretton Woods system explained above. It is 'managed' by governments. It is 'dirty' because it is a deliberate interference with 'pure' forces of demand and supply.

Adjustment mechanisms Since the collapse of the Bretton Woods system in the early 1970s, world trade has been regulated not under a pure free exchange system but under a system of managed or dirty floats. Governments have used interest rates and their gold and foreign currency reserves to manipulate the value of their currencies. Depreciation, appreciation and deflation have all been used in an attempt to alter current deficits or surpluses. Governments have found it more difficult to pursue openly protectionist policies because of international pressure for greater free trade. Currency controls too have fallen into disfavour as supply side economics has stressed the value of free markets and deregulation in promoting the international competitiveness of economies.

QUESTION 3 Currency speculators were left licking their wounds yesterday as an unexpected round of central bank support for the dollar caught the market napping. The Federal Reserve was joined by the Bundesbank, Bank of Japan, Bank of Canada and nine European central banks. The dollar finished in London at DM1.4130 and Y84.565, nearly three pfennigs and two yen up from the levels where the central banks first started buying dollars. With most European central banks selling D-Marks to support the dollar, the German currency lost ground across the board.

The timing of the intervention would appear to have been more significant than the amount. Estimates from banks involved in executing Fed orders suggest that the total support effort may have amounted to around $1bn, split equally between the Fed and the other banks. Notable about the timing was that it came early in New York trading, when the market is likely to be most impressionable. It was also deft in the sense that the Fed intervened just when the market was looking ready to test key technical levels at DM1.38 and Y82. Had the dollar fallen below these levels, analysts believe that any remaining positive sentiment in favour of the US currency would have been irretrievably shattered.

Scepticism about the dollar's recovery prospects remains too deep-seated for yesterday's intervention to have prompted any fundamental assessment about the currency's outlook. The markets believe that the dollar will continue to fall. In recent weeks, weak economic statistics have led to selling of the dollar. If tomorrow's publication of the US employment report shows that economic fundamentals are continuing to deteriorate, there is likely to be a fresh bout of selling from the market.

Source: adapted from the *Financial Times*, 1.6.1995.

(a) At the time the article was written, the dollar was floating freely against other currencies. What does this mean?
(b) The dollar had been falling in value since the beginning of 1995. What must have been occurring in the foreign exchange markets for this to happen?
(c) The float of the dollar was a 'dirty float'. How do you know this from the passage?
(d) Explain, using a diagram, how the value of the dollar was forced upwards on 31 May 1995.
(e) What could cause the value of the dollar to fall further in June 1995?

The Gold Standard

How it worked During much of the 19th century and the start of the 20th century exchange rates were determined by the GOLD STANDARD, an example of a FIXED EXCHANGE RATE SYSTEM. The major trading nations made their domestic currencies **convertible** into gold at a fixed rate. For instance, in 1914 a holder of a £1 note could go to the Bank of England and exchange the note for 0.257 ounces of gold. Because French citizens could exchange French francs for a fixed amount of gold, and German citizens the same, and so on, it meant that there was a **fixed exchange rate** between the major trading currencies of the world. The domestic money supply was directly related to the amount of gold held by the central bank. For every extra 0.257 ounces of gold held by the Bank of England, it could issue £1 in paper currency (the currency was backed by gold). On the other hand, a fall in the gold reserves at the Bank of England meant an equivalent fall in the paper money in circulation.

Adjustment mechanisms A deficit on the current account of the balance of payments could not be corrected by devaluation of the currency. By the rules of the Gold standard mechanism, the currency was fixed in value. Imbalances on the current account were corrected instead through deflation and reflation or changes in interest rates.

Assume that the UK is on the Gold Standard and that the current account is in deficit. There is therefore a net outflow of pounds to foreigners. Foreigners have no use for pounds so they will exchange those pounds for gold at the Bank of England. With less gold, the Bank of England will be forced to reduce its issue of notes (the notes handed in by foreigners for gold will effectively be destroyed). The money supply will fall and interest rates will rise. This will produce a deflation in the economy through the **transmission mechanism**. Not only will demand fall, reducing imports, but there will also be a fall in prices (predicted by the **quantity theory of money** ☞ unit 76). Exports will thus become more competitive and imports less competitive. The current account will return to equilibrium. The initial rise in unemployment caused by the fall in demand will be reversed as exports increase, returning the economy to full employment.

Currency blocs

A country may choose to peg its currency against one other currency but allow the currency to fluctuate against all others. This would be a minimal example of a CURRENCY BLOC, a group of currencies fixed in value against each other but floating against all others.

Possibly the most important currency bloc today is the EUROPEAN MONETARY SYSTEM (EMS). Most member countries of the European Community have agreed to keep their currencies within a 15 per cent band of each other. If a currency threatens to break out of the band, central banks of EMS countries will intervene in the market, buying or selling currency to keep the currency within the band. The bloc of currencies floats freely against all other world currencies, including the dollar and the yen.

Like the Bretton Woods system, this is an example of a hybrid system, combining elements of fixed and floating exchange rate systems.

QUESTION 4 The Italian lira remained very firm, at the top of the European Monetary System. In Milan the Bank of Italy bought D-Marks at the fixing and also intervened to support the French franc, as the lira threatened to move above its cross rate limit against the franc. At the finish of trading in London the D-mark had rallied against the lira, advancing to L737.95 from L737.70.

Source: the *Financial Times*, 9.3.1990.

Using diagrams, explain how intervention by the Bank of Italy affected the value of (a) the D-mark against the lira and (b) the French franc against the lira.

Key terms

Exchange rate system - a system which determines the conditions under which one currency can be exchanged for another.
Adjustable peg system - an exchange rate system where currencies are fixed in value in the short term but can be devalued or revalued in the longer term.
Bretton Woods system - an adjustable peg exchange rate system which was used in the post-Second World War period until its collapse in the early 1970s.
Fundamental disequilibrium on the balance of payments - where imports are greater than exports over a long period of time resulting in unsustainable levels of international borrowing.
Free or floating exchange rate system - where the value of a currency is determined by free market forces.
Managed or dirty float - where the exchange rate is determined by free market forces but governments intervene from time to time to alter the free market price of a currency.
The Gold Standard - an exchange rate system under which currencies could be converted into gold at a fixed rate, hence providing a relative price between each currency.
Fixed exchange rate - a rate of exchange between at least two currencies which is constant over a period of time.
Currency bloc - a group of currencies which are fixed in value against each other but which may float freely against other world currencies.
European Monetary System - a currency bloc where the participating currencies are fixed against each other within a 15 per cent band and where the bloc as a whole fluctuates freely against other currencies.

Applied economics

The Bretton Woods system

The Bretton Woods system first devised in 1944 provided exchange rate stability. Hence, it can be argued that it encouraged the growth of world trade during the 1950s and 1960s.

It was intended that governments could choose how to resolve a current account deficit. They could deflate the economy, creating unemployment, reducing imports and reducing domestic inflation. This was the same adjustment mechanism as present under the Gold Standard. They could also devalue the currency. By changing the relative price of exports and imports, the economy could be made more internationally competitive without creating unemployment. However, there would be some cost in terms of imported inflation.

In practice, countries tended not to devalue except in a crisis. This was because devaluation, wrongly in the view of many economists, came to be associated with economic failure. Deficit countries tended to use deflation as the main policy weapon to deal with balance of payments problems, negating the flexibility of adjusting relative prices built into the system. The burden of adjustment also fell solely on deficit countries. There was little pressure within the system for surplus countries to reduce their surpluses, for instance by revaluing their currencies. The result was that the system became increasingly brittle. Deficit countries like the UK tended to lurch from one foreign exchange crisis to the next whilst surplus countries like West Germany resisted pressures to take any action to reduce their surpluses.

Problems were compounded by the fall in the value of gold and currency reserves as a ratio of world trade over the 1950s and 1960s. To maintain exchange rate stability, central banks bought and sold currency. So long as the central banks were the main buyers and sellers in the market, they could dictate the price of foreign exchange. However, during the 1950s and 1960s world trade expanded at a much faster rate than gold and foreign currency reserves.

In an attempt to inject greater liquidity into the international financial system, the IMF issued **Special Drawing Rights** (SDRs) to member countries in 1969. SDRs are a form of international currency which can only be used by central banks to settle debts between themselves or with the IMF. When a country needs foreign currency to defend its own currency, it can buy it with the SDRs it holds. Whilst SDRs, effectively a handout of 'free' money, increased liquidity in the system at the time, the IMF failed to allocate further SDRs to member countries. The countries which control the IMF, the industrialised nations of the world, particularly the USA, are afraid that further creation of SDRs would encourage countries, particularly in the Third World, to put off dealing with fundamental balance of payments problems by using newly distributed SDRs to finance their large current account deficits. Today, SDRs account for only about 5 per cent of world reserves.

The Vietnam war from 1965 onwards made matters worse. To finance the war the USA ran a large current account deficit and therefore was a net borrower of money on its capital account. Individuals and firms were quite happy to lend their pounds, francs, deutschmarks and other currencies to the US and in exchange receive dollars because exchange rates were fixed to the dollar and dollars were seen to be as safe as gold itself.

By the late 1960s there was a large amount of money, particularly dollars, being held outside its country of origin. Americans were holding pounds, Japanese were holding deutschmarks, Germans were holding dollars, etc. This provided the base for large speculative activity on the foreign exchanges. It had become obvious that the United States would need to devalue the dollar if it were to return to a balance of payments equilibrium. On the other hand, it was obvious that Germany and Japan, two large surplus countries, would have to revalue their currencies. There was persistent selling pressure on the dollar and buying pressure on the D-mark and yen. Central banks found it more and more difficult to match the speculative waves of buying and selling. In the early 1970s, after some traumatic devaluations and revaluations, one country after another announced that it would float its currency.

The Bretton Woods system provided a long period of exchange rate stability during which there was a significant expansion of world trade. The cost of adjustment to current account deficits was probably less than under the Gold Standard. Although deflation was widely used in response to this problem, countries also devalued their currency, trading off slightly higher imported inflation for less unemployment. However, the system was not sufficiently robust to prevent its collapse in the early 1970s.

The CFA franc zone

History

The CFA franc zone has a long history dating back to before the Second World War when most of its current members were African French colonies. Local currencies were pegged to the French franc and colonies kept their foreign exchange reserves in France at the Bank of France, the French Central Bank. When the colonies became independent, many decided to retain their link with the French franc because the majority of their trade was with France or other European countries and not, for instance, with other African countries. This reflected the nature of trade - the exports of commodities and the import of manufactured goods.

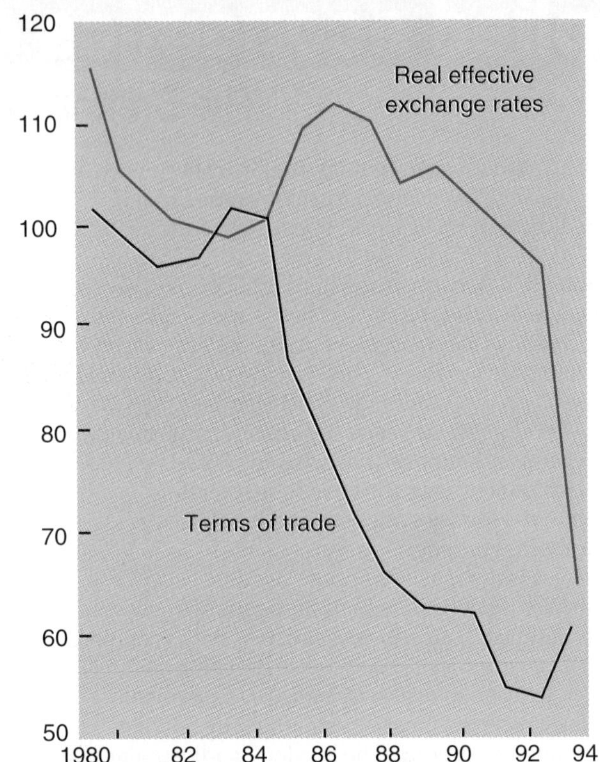

Source: adapted from IMF, Information Notice System; and *World Economic Outlook.*

Figure 97.3 *CFA countries, real effective exchange rates and terms of trade, 1980-94 (weighted by 1994 GDP, 1985=100)*

Table 97.1 *Macro-economic indicators of CFA and selected non-CFA countries*

	GDP per capita (US$ at PPP rates) 1992	GNP per capita (Annual growth, %) 1980-92	Inflation rate (Average annual rate, %) 1980-92	Primary commodity exports (% of total) 1992	Export growth (Average annual rate, %) 1980-92	Current balance	
						$ million 1992	% of GDP 1992
West African Economic and Monetary Union							
Benin	1 500	- 0.7	1.7	70	10.5	- 162	- 7.4
Burkino Faso	730	1.0	3.5	88	7.7	- 468	- 16.8
Cote d'Ivoire	1 640	- 4.7	1.9	90	7.6	- 1 468	- 16.8
Mali	500	- 2.7	3.7	92	6.5	- 414	- 14.6
Niger	740	- 4.3	1.7	98	- 4.3	- 156	- 6.7
Senegal	1 750	0.1	5.2	78	2.5	- 547	- 8.7
Togo	1 100	- 1.8	4.2	89	2.9	- 190	-11.8
Central African Economic and Monetary Community							
Cameroon	2 300	- 1.5	3.5	83	10.4	- 834	- 8.0
Central African Republic	1 040	- 1.5	4.6	56	5.1	- 183	- 14.6
Chad	710	3.4	0.9	95	9.5	- 325	- 26.1
Congo	2 450	- 0.8	0.5	97	7.8	- 402	- 14.3
Equatorial Guinea	-	-	-	-	-	-396	-12.2
Comoros	-	-	-	-	-	-	-
Other countries							
Tanzania	630	- 1.9	25.3	85	- 1.2	- 866	- 36.9
Malawi	730	- 0.1	15.1	96	5.8	- 432	- 25.8
Sierra Leone	770	0.0	60.8	67	0.7	-	-
Uganda	1 070	-	-	99	1.9	- 346	- 11.5
Kenya	1 360	0.2	9.3	71	4.1	- 312	- 4.5
Ghana	1 890	- 0.1	38.7	99	8.0	- 592	- 8.6
Zimbabwe	1 970	- 0.9	14.4	68	- 0.8	- 859	- 17.1
Nigeria	2 160	- 0.4	19.4	92	1.7	+ 1 537	+ 5.2
France	19 200	1.7	5.4	22	5.2	+ 9 164	+ 0.7

Source: adapted from World Bank, *World Development Report.*

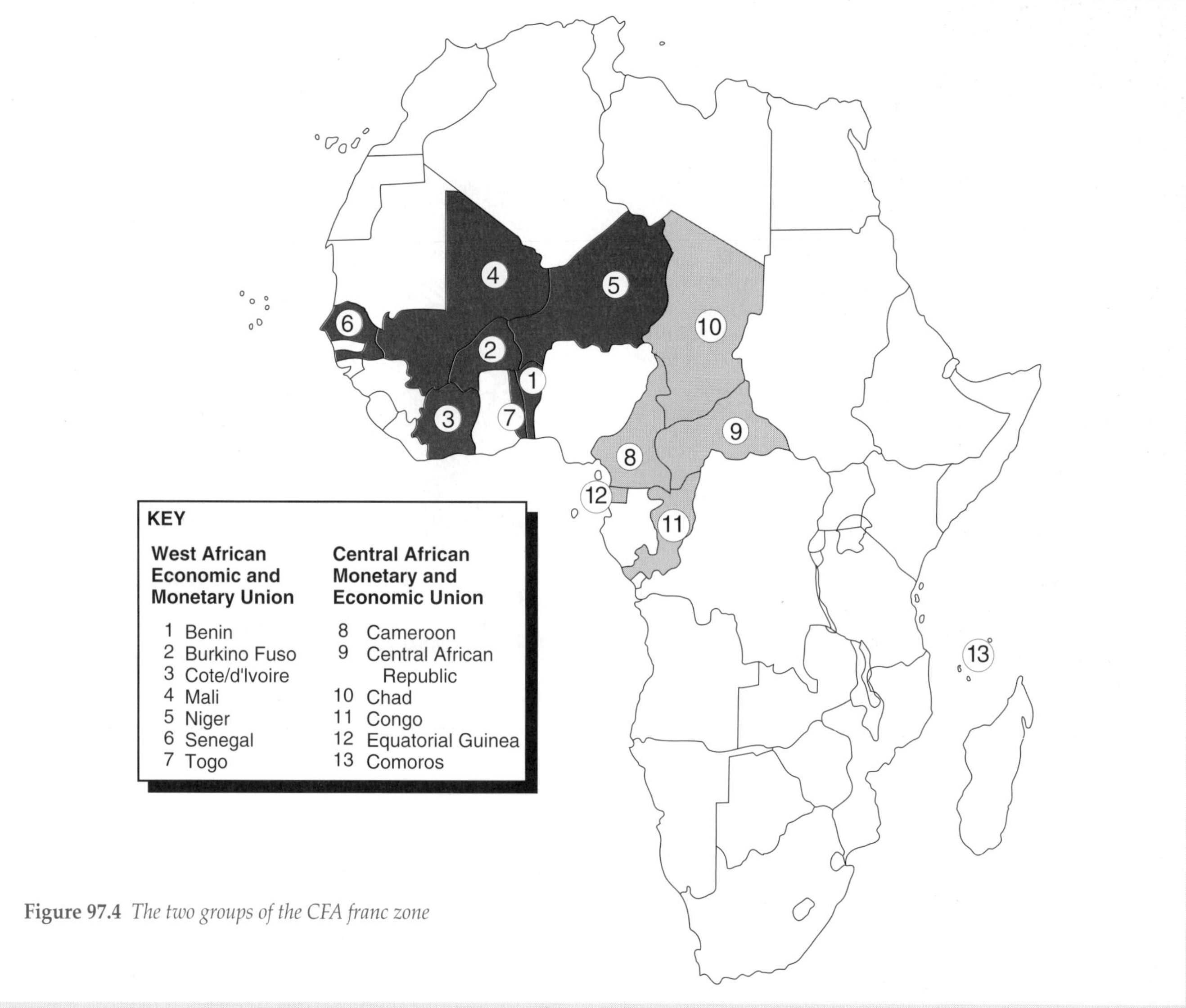

Figure 97.4 *The two groups of the CFA franc zone*

Maintaining the CFA franc zone

Since 1985, there have been 13 member countries in the zone, split into two groups, the West African Economic and Monetary Union, and the Central African Economic and Monetary Community. Each group has a single central bank which operates monetary and exchange rate policy. There is a complex formula for controlling monetary growth in each group. The formula effectively prevents the governments of member countries from printing money to finance excessive government spending. It also raises interest rates when monetary growth becomes excessive.

In 1993, the CFA franc was pegged at 50 CFA francs to 1 French franc. This exchange rate has been maintained since the early 1950s.

In 1993, the CFA franc zone was facing a crisis. Its competitiveness had deteriorated sharply during the 1980s due to large falls in commodity prices compared to the prices of the manufactured goods it imported from abroad. This had led to a number of other economic problems which needed addressing urgently. Write a report for the International Monetary Fund (IMF) detailing:

- **the problems that countries in the CFA franc zone faced in the early 1990s;**
- **the potential advantages and problems for individual countries of a large devaluation of the CFA franc but a maintenance of a pegged exchange rate system;**
- **the potential advantages of a break up of the system with individual currencies being free to float against other currencies.**

In your report, compare the economic experience of non-CFA franc zone countries with floating exchange rates against that of the CFA countries.

The advantages and disadvantages of exchange rate systems

Summary

1. An exchange rate system should encourage world trade, particularly through exchange rate stability. Floating exchange rate systems have proved very poor at providing exchange rate stability.
2. Economic costs of adjustment when the balance of payments of a country is in fundamental disequilibrium should be low. Adjustment mechanisms within fixed exchange rate systems, such as the Gold Standard, and to a lesser extent adjustable peg systems, such as the Bretton Woods system and the EMS, tend to create unemployment because they rely upon deflation of the economy. In contrast, floating exchange rate systems tend to give rise to inflation when currencies depreciate following current account deficits.
3. Fixed exchange rate systems, and to a lesser extent adjustable peg systems, force governments to maintain inflation rates comparable to their industrial competitors.
4. Exchange rate systems should be robust. Free exchange rate systems are the most robust because they require the least government intervention.

Judging between systems

Over the past 200 years, a variety of exchange rate systems have been in operation. This would suggest that no system is without its problems. A number of criteria can be used to judge the relative merits of different exchange rate systems.

Encouragement of world trade

World trade enables countries to specialise in the production of those goods and services in which they have a **comparative advantage** (☞ unit 84). This specialisation increases the total amount of goods available for world consumption. Hence exchange rate systems could be judged upon the extent to which they encourage or discourage world trade.

It has long been argued that exchange rate volatility, such as occurs under free floats or managed floats, discourages trade. If exchange rates fluctuate by large amounts on a day to day basis, exporters and importers will find it impossible to know what price they will receive or have to pay for deliveries in the future. For instance, a UK exporter may agree to sell goods to the US for payment in US dollars in 3 months' time. Built into the $1 million price is a 10 per cent profit margin. Over the 3 months, the pound falls in value against the dollar by 15 per cent. Not only will the exporter lose its planned profit, but it will also make a loss on the contract of about 5 per cent.

There are ways around this problem in a free or managed float regime. **Futures markets** exist, where foreign exchange can be bought at a fixed price for delivery at some point in the future. So the exporter could have bought pounds **forward**. At the time it signs the export agreement, it would have taken out a contract in the foreign exchange markets to buy $1 million worth of pounds in three months' time (which it will pay for using the $1 million gained from the export contract). It now has a guaranteed price in pounds for its contract. Of course the forward price of pounds may be less than the price of pounds today (the spot price). But this is not important in the sense that the UK exporter will have based the export agreement price on the forward rate of the pound, and not on the current spot price. This process of buying currency forward to prevent losses is known as **hedging**.

Unfortunately, futures markets are limited in their scope. It is not possible, for instance, to buy a currency for delivery in 5 years' time. So long term contracts need other forms of insurance. This is often provided by government agencies which guarantee prices in the domestic currency for large long term export contracts. Hedging and insurance cost money and they therefore either discourage trade or raise its cost. Companies that are unable or unwilling to hedge or to insure have to decide whether or not to take the risk of proceeding with the export or import contract.

So, in general, the less volatile the currency movement, the less likely that international trade will be discouraged.

Fixed exchange rate systems, such as the Gold Standard, and adjustable peg systems, such as the Bretton Woods system, are on these criteria considered to be 'better' systems than free or managed float systems.

QUESTION 1 Moves towards European monetary union would lift a heavy burden from the backs of Europe's smaller businesses, most of which lack the expertise to deal with the complexities of foreign exchange markets. Smaller businesses pay a high cost for converting small amounts of foreign currencies, says Ms Jane Waters, a foreign exchange consultant. Banks typically charge 1 per cent on small deals of up to $10 000, but only 0.1 per cent on larger amounts.

Van Halteren, a Dutch meat processor with annual sales of £23m, pays about £25 000 each year to hedge the riskier currencies, such as sterling.

Many small businesses are frightened off from using the textbook exchange hedges - forward transactions or currency option arrangements - because of their perceived complexity and cost. They take evasive action. They invoice customers in their own currency; some delay making transfers of funds until currency rates are favourable; others boost prices to cover the currency risk.

All these manoeuvres carry risks. Better by far, smaller owners argue, to establish a foreign exchange framework which allows companies to get on with their business rather than having to watch currency movements.

Source: adapted from the *Financial Times*, 28.7.1989.

Explain, using examples from the passage, why exchange rate stability might encourage world trade.

Economic costs of adjustment

A country's balance of payments on current account can move into disequilibrium. Different exchange rate systems have different mechanisms for returning the balance of payments to equilibrium. The movement back to equilibrium may involve economic costs, such as increased unemployment or lower economic growth. The larger these transitional costs, the less attractive the exchange rate system.

The main cost of adjustment within a fixed exchange rate system or an adjustable peg system is likely to be increased unemployment. Under the Gold Standard, a current account deficit was automatically eliminated in the long term through a fall in domestic prices. However, economists disagree about the extent to which money wage rates fall quickly in response to unemployment. Keynesian economists tend to argue that wage rate adjustment is slow. Classical or monetarist economists argue that it is a relatively quick process. The slower the adjustment, the higher the cost in terms of unemployment and lost output. Countries abandoned the Gold Standard in the early 1930s because they felt that floating exchange rates would enable their economies to reduce unemployment at a faster rate than if the exchange rate was linked to gold.

Under the Bretton Woods system, countries tended to avoid devaluing their currencies (☞ unit 97). When current accounts moved into deficit, governments tended to deflate their economies, imposing higher taxes or reducing government expenditure. Unemployment therefore rose as the rate of economic growth fell.

One of the main criticisms of floating and managed exchange rate systems is that they encourage inflationary behaviour on the part of governments. Assume that an economy has a higher inflation rate than its major trading partners and that, consequently, the current account is in deficit. Under the Bretton Woods system, governments would have been likely to tackle these two problems through deflating the economy. Under the Gold Standard, deflation would have occurred automatically. Rising unemployment and lost output are politically unpopular as well as costly economically. Under a floating exchange rate system, the exchange rate should fall automatically with a current account deficit. This leads to **imported inflation**. A government can avoid tackling domestic inflation and the current account deficit simply by allowing the exchange rate to fall continually. Hence there is no anti-inflation discipline built into the floating exchange rate system.

Moreover, tackling inflation under a floating exchange rate system can be more costly than under fixed exchange rate systems. Assume that the government reduces the money supply and raises interest rates as part of an anti-inflation package. The rise in domestic interest rates will encourage an inflow of speculative funds on the capital account. This will increase the price of the currency. An increase in the exchange rate will make the economy less internationally competitive. Exports will fall and imports will rise, leading to a worsening of the already bad current account deficit. But falling exports and rising imports also lead to a fall in aggregate demand, pushing the economy into recession. This recession is part of the process by which inflation falls and the economy becomes more internationally competitive. The current account will only return to equilibrium when the market exchange rate is approximately equal to the **purchasing power parity rate** (☞ unit 87). It will only stay in equilibrium when the country's inflation rate is equal to that of its trading partners. Lowering inflation is a painful process and will certainly not be politically popular.

Financial disciplines

Today, there are some who argue that inflation is the most important economic problem facing economies and governments. Monetarists argue that inflation is caused by excessive increases in the money supply. Under the Gold Standard, governments are unable to expand the money supply unless stocks of gold in the central bank rise first (although countries did issue a fixed amount of notes which were not backed by gold - the **fiduciary issue** - this did not affect the principle that central banks could not increase notes in circulation without corresponding increases in their stocks of gold). Changes in stocks of gold are unlikely to be very large in the short term. Hence the Gold Standard provides an important check on the ability of governments to generate inflation through the creation of money.

Equally, under an adjustable peg system, such as the Bretton Woods system, governments could not allow their inflation rates to differ greatly from those of their industrial competitors because otherwise they would lose international competitiveness, their current account would go into deficit and they would then be likely to deflate to solve this problem.

However, under a floating exchange rate system, as argued above, governments can always solve problems of international competitiveness, caused by domestic inflation, by allowing their currencies to fall in value. There is no financial discipline imposed by the system.

QUESTION 2 Throughout the 1980s the UK exchange rate was determined under a floating exchange rate system, whilst the exchange rate of her main EU trading partners was determined under an adjustable peg system - the ERM. Inflation rates in all EU countries tended to fall in the first half of the 1980s and then remained low till the end of the decade. UK inflation rates tended to be 2-3 per cent higher than those of France and Germany during the period, whilst the value of pound tended to fall. By 1987 the value of the pound was 15 per cent lower against the ECU (the basket or average of European currencies) than in 1980. However, between 1982 and 1988, average annual economic growth in the UK exceeded that of most European countries. In 1988, inflation in the UK began to accelerate again with the UK government responding by doubling interest rates to 15 per cent. The economy began to slow down. Then, in 1990, the UK joined the ERM at the very high central exchange rate of DM2.95, the same rate of exchange as prevailed on average in 1986. To maintain the value of the pound, the UK government was forced to keep interest rates at much higher levels than it probably would have wanted. The UK economy was in a very long prolonged recession between 1990 and 1992, with inflation falling rapidly to levels not seen since the 1960s. In September 1992, speculative pressure forced the pound to be suspended from the ERM. The value of the pound immediately fell over 10 per cent and the government cut interest rates from 10 per cent to 5½ per cent over the next 12 months. Growth in the economy rapidly picked up and the economy came out of recession.

(a) (i) What was true about the UK's inflation rate and rate of economic growth during the period 1982-88 compared to those of her main EU partners?
(ii) With these trends, explain what you would have expected to happen to the UK current account on the balance of payments if the value of the pound had remained constant.
(iii) Some economists and politicians argued at the time that allowing the pound to float downwards was inflationary. Explain this view.

(b) (i) Why might the fact that the UK joined the ERM in 1990 have prolonged the recession of 1990-1992?
(ii) Explain the likely impact of Britain's membership of the ERM on domestic inflation.

Robustness of the system

Some exchange rate systems are extremely robust; that is, they are unlikely to break up when economic conditions are unfavourable. The more likely it is that an exchange rate system will break up under strain, the less attractive the exchange rate system.

Fixed exchange rate systems, or adjustable peg systems, are less robust than free or managed float exchange rate systems. Countries abandoned the Gold Standard in the early 1930s during the Great Depression because they wanted to be able to devalue their currencies in order to gain competitive advantage. By devaluing, they hoped to be able to reduce imports, boost exports and thus reduce domestic unemployment. However, the rest of the 1930s, with a managed float system of exchange rates, saw a series of competitive devaluations with countries trying to export their unemployment. Competitive devaluations are ultimately self-defeating because devaluation by one country, matched by a devaluation by another country simply left exchange rates unchanged.

The unsatisfactory experience of the 1930s led to the creation of the Bretton Woods system. It broke up in the early 1970s, partly because countries failed to devalue and revalue when there was a fundamental disequilibrium on their current accounts and partly because central banks lacked reserves to counter the growing mountain of speculative money which moved so quickly from country to country.

The managed float system of the 1970s, 1980s and 1990s has had to cope with three oil crises, and in the early 1980s, the worst world slump since the 1930s. Free and managed float systems are extremely robust because governments can allow free market forces to determine the value of the exchange rate without intervening in the market. However, the extreme volatility of exchange rates over the period has led many to advocate a return to some sort of fixed or adjustable peg system. The robustness of the system is less attractive than the exchange rate stability that can be found, for instance, within the European Monetary System (☞ applied).

QUESTION 3 In the early 1970s, the Bretton Woods system of exchange rates broke up. Explain why the system proved insufficiently robust.

Applied economics

European Monetary Union

History

The debate about European Monetary Union (EMU) has a long history in the the European Union (EU). Different currencies within Europe can be argued to be a major obstacle to trade, in the same way as tariffs or quotas. In 1970, the Werner Report proposed the creation of a European Monetary Union and for a short period in the early 1970s, the 6 member countries of the EU pegged their currencies against each other. However, the inflationary pressures of the time, culminating in the oil crisis of 1973-74, broke the system as one country after another either devalued or revalued.

The late 1970s saw more stable economic conditions and a fresh start was made in 1979 with the creation of the European Monetary System (EMS), the most important component of which was the Exchange Rate Mechanism (ERM). Member countries agreed to peg their currencies within a 2¼ per cent band of a weighted average of European currencies. This weighted average is called the ECU (the European Currency Unit). Between 1979 and 1987, there were 11 **realignments** within the EMS as countries devalued or revalued. In general, the low inflation, current account surplus countries, such as West Germany and Holland, revalued their currencies, whilst higher inflation, current account deficit countries, such as France and Italy, devalued their currencies.

The Maastricht Treaty

In 1989, Jacques Delors, President of the European Commission, presented a radical report suggesting that member countries should move to full European Monetary Union. His proposals formed the basis for the part of the Maastricht Treaty, signed in 1992, which dealt with EMU. A timetable was laid down for the progression to full EMU.

Stage 1 An EU 'Monetary Committee' was to be set up which would advise governments and the European Commission about the steps needed to move onto the next two stages.

Stage 2 During this stage, which in theory started on 1 January 1994, a new 'European Monetary Institute' was to be established which would help countries work towards stage 3. In particular, during stage 2, countries would have to adjust their own domestic policies to achieve 4 **convergence criteria**. These convergence criteria were considered vital to the success of a single currency.

- Inflation. Inflation rates must be within 1.5 per cent of the average rate in the three lowest inflation countries in the EU. This is because a country with considerably higher inflation than other countries would, in a floating exchange rate mechanism, normally see its currency sink lower against its trading partners as it becomes less and less competitive. It can only maintain purchasing power parity through a falling exchange rate. To maintain a stable exchange rate, it must therefore align its inflation rate approximately to those its trading partners.

- Interest rates. Long term interest rates must be no more than two per cent above the average rate in the three lowest interest rates countries in the EU. If long term interest rates were much higher than this in one country, then there would be short term flows of money into that country to take advantage of the higher interest rates. This would then destabilise currency flows putting pressure on the currency of that country to move upwards. Stable exchange rates can only be maintained if there is little or no incentive to move large sums of short term money from country to country within the EMS.

- Fiscal stance. Governments must have budget deficits of no more than 3 per cent of GDP (at market prices) and a national debt of less than 60 per cent of GDP (at market prices). Governments which are heavily indebted, or need to borrow large sums of money in a year will tend to have to offer high rates of interest on the debt being issued. High interest rates on government bonds will tend to attract flows of money from overseas which could destabilise the currency. Equally, there is a danger that governments will find it difficult to finance their debt and as a result foreigners will refuse to lend to the country. This too will tend to destabilise the currency. Hence, for currency stability, there must be fiscal stability too.

- Durability of convergence. A country's currency must have been in the narrow band of the ERM for at least two years with no realignments or 'severe tensions'. This is to ensure that there has been at least some history of stability of the currency.

Stage 3 In this stage, there would be a move towards fixed currencies. A new body, the European System of Central Banks (ESCB) would hold and manage the official reserves of all the member countries. The ECU would become an official currency. Whether countries would retain their national currencies for use domestically, or whether a single currency would operate throughout all the Union, would have to be negotiated. In theory, there would be no problem in allowing national currencies to be retained in exactly the same way as Scotland and Northern Ireland have kept the right to issue their own pound notes within the UK. The Maastricht Treaty states that countries and the European Commission must decide whether to launch Stage 3 in 1996 to start on 1 January 1997. If monetary union is not launched on that date, then a review must take place by mid-1998. If no date is set for future starting, the Treaty lays down that Stage 3 will start on 1 January 1999.

The possible future of EMU

At the time the Maastricht Treaty was signed, in February 1992, there seemed a reasonable chance that EMU would be accomplished by the turn of the century. However, events since then make it unlikely that a single currency will be established in the short term. The problem has been that, unlike the period 1987-1992 when most member countries were moving closer towards the convergence criteria as shown in Figure 98.1, there was between 1992 and 1995 a move away from the criteria.

For a start, the UK was forced out of the ERM in September 1992 by speculative selling of the pound. In the same crisis, the Spanish peseta, the Portuguese escudo and the Italian lira were devalued. In February 1993, the Irish punt was devalued, followed in May 1993 by yet another devaluation of the peseta and escudo. In August 1993, the franc was effectively devalued when it broadened its bands from $2^1/_4$ per cent to 15 per cent. In March 1995, the peseta and the escudo were devalued yet again. The size of these fluctuations is shown in Figure 98.2. The convergence criteria concerning 2 years of currency stability for the UK, Italy, Spain and Portugal are unlikely to be met in the near future.

A number of countries are moving away from the other convergence criteria. Nearly all countries have increased their debt/GDP ratios, with three countries, Belgium, Greece and Italy, having debt/GDP ratios in 1995 of over 110 per cent, nearly twice the ratio laid down in the Maastricht Treaty. These three countries have little or no hope of reducing their debt ratios to 60 per cent or less within the next ten years. In 1994, only three countries - Germany, Ireland and Luxembourg - had budget deficits of less than 3 per cent. Inflation rates remained out of line for many countries.

If the Maastricht Treaty deadlines are to be adhered to, it now seems almost certain that EMU would only happen in 1999. Most commentators, however, now believe that there is little chance of the convergence criteria being met even in 1999. Three possibilities then emerge. One is that the whole timetable is put back, new target dates set and EMU occurs sometime early next century. The second possibility is that a 'two-speed' Europe emerges. Germany, France, the Netherlands, Belgium and Luxembourg, which as Figure 98.2 shows have had reasonable currency

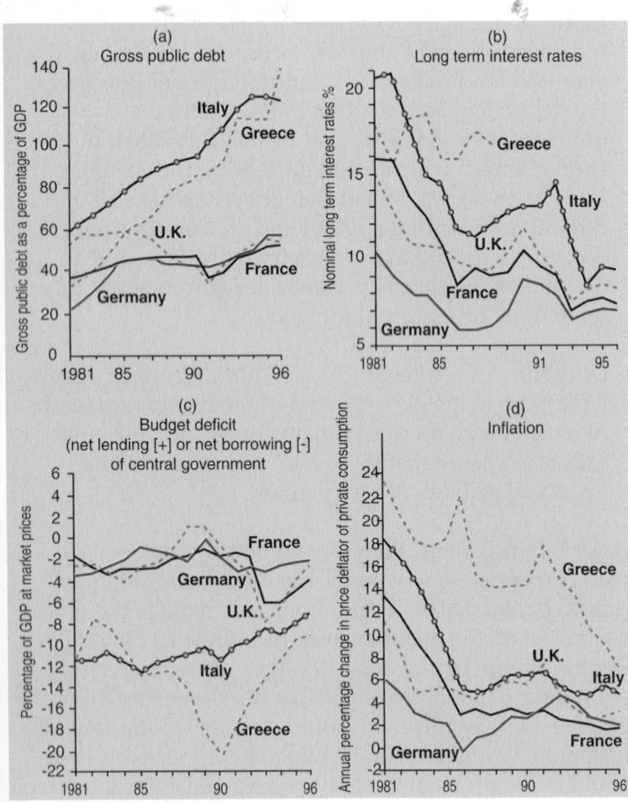

* 1995-96 projections
Source: adapted from Datastream, IMF.
Figure 98.1 *Convergence criteria in the EU*

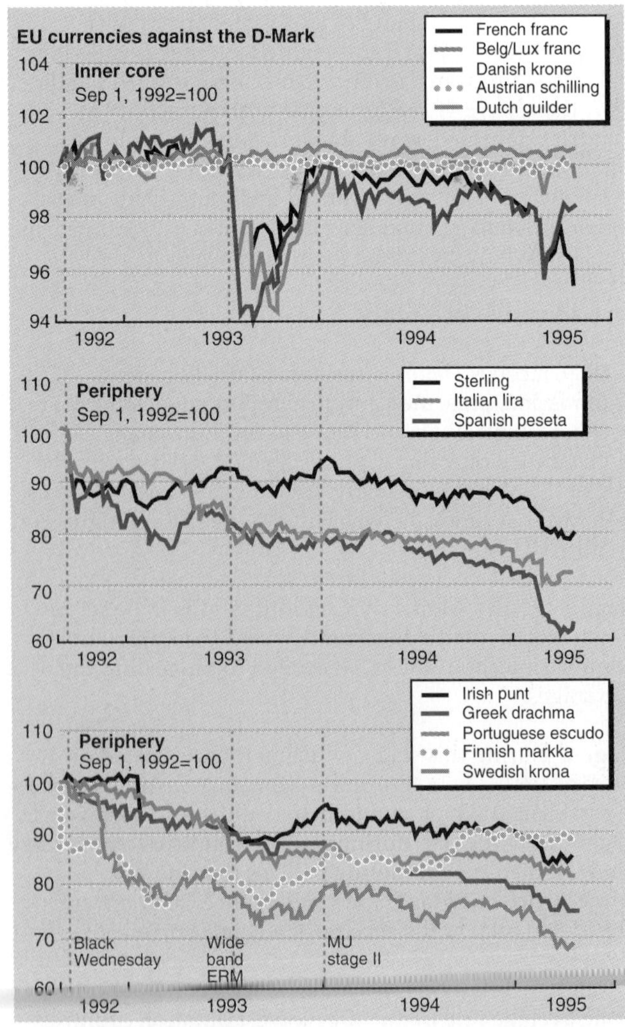

Source: adapted from Datastream.
Figure 98.2 *Exchange rates within and outside the ERM*

stability, would proceed to monetary union in 1999. Other countries, such as Italy and the UK, would stay out. A third possibility is that EMU never comes into being simply because the advantages of moving to a single currency never outweigh the disadvantages when governments have to make a decision about whether to move forward. To understand why this might be the case, it is necessary to understand the possible advantages and disadvantages of EMU.

The advantages of EMU

Increased trade and reduced costs to firms Proponents of the move argue that it brings considerable economic benefit to member countries because it not only increases trade through the elimination of exchange rate fluctuations, but it also lowers costs to industry because firms will not have to buy foreign exchange for use within the EU. For them, EMU represents the completion of the **Single European Market**. It is vital if Europe is to compete with the other large trading blocs of North America and the Far East.

The political agenda There is also a political agenda to EMU. It can only be achieved by the creation of a central European bank (the European System of Central Banks - ESCB), the complete removal of national control over monetary policy and the partial removal of control over fiscal policy. Individual nation states will lose sovereignty (i.e. the ability to control their own affairs). It will be a considerable step down the road towards political union. There are many in the EU who favour economic and political union and they are very much in favour of EMU. There are also many who wish to retain national sovereignty and are fighting hard to prevent EMU, whatever its other merits might be, from going ahead.

Inflation From the mid-1980s onwards, there was a number of economists and politicians who argued that, for the UK at least, EMU provided the best way forward to achieve low inflation rates throughout the EU. During the first half of the 1980s, high inflation countries, such as France and Italy, were forced to adopt policies which reduced their inflation rates to something approximating the German inflation rate. If they had not done this, the franc and the lira would have had to be periodically devalued, negating the fixed exchange rate advantages of the system. Effectively, the German central bank, the Bundesbank, set inflation targets and therefore monetary targets for the rest of the EU.

At the time, there was much discussion of why Germany had a better inflation record than many other European countries. A consensus emerged that it was because the Bundesbank, the German central bank, was independent of the German government. In countries such as the UK and France, central banks were controlled by governments. If the UK government decided to loosen monetary policy, for instance, by reducing interest rates, it had the power to order the Bank of England to carry out this policy on its behalf. There have always been especially strong pressures before an election for UK governments to loosen the monetary reins and create a boom in the economy, with a subsequent increase in inflation following the election. The Bundesbank, in contrast, was independent of government. By law it has a duty to maintain stable prices. It can resist pressures from the German government to pursue reflationary policies if it believes that these will increase inflation within the economy.

Events of the early 1990s have shaken a naive faith that linkage to the independent ESBC, the central bank of Europe, would solve all inflationary problems. This is because German inflation rates in the early 1990s rose to over 4 per cent as Germany struggled with the consequences of unification. In 1993, inflation was nearly three times as high in Germany as in the UK and twice as high as that in France. Some countries, such as France, have made their central banks independent on the German model and therefore arguably don't need the EMU link to Germany to maintain low inflation. The UK has gone a little way towards giving more power to the central bank by publishing reports of monthly meetings between the Chancellor of the Exchequer and the Governor of the Bank of England. This forces the government to justify its monetary policy publicly and makes it more difficult for it to use interest rates for short term political ends.

The disadvantages of EMU

The instability of the system Throughout most of the 1980s, the UK refused to join the ERM. It argued that it would be impossible to maintain exchange rate stability within the ERM, especially in the early 1980s when the pound was a petro-currency, and when the UK inflation rate was consistently above that of Germany. When the UK joined the ERM in 1990, there had been three years of relative currency stability in Europe and it looked as though the system had become relatively **robust**. The events of September 1992, when the UK and Italy were forced to leave the system, showed that the system was much less robust than had been thought. Critics of EMU argue that the system will never be robust enough to get beyond Stage 2 of the timetable laid out at Maastricht.

Over-estimation of trade benefits Some economists argue that the trade and cost advantages of EMU have been grossly over-estimated. There is little to be gained from moving from the present system, which has some stability built into it, to the rigidities which EMU would bring.

Loss of sovereignty On the political side, it is argued that an independent central bank is undemocratic. Governments must be able to control the actions of the central banks because governments have been democratically elected by the people, whereas an independent central bank would be controlled by a non-elected body. Moreover, there would be a considerable loss of sovereignty. Power would be transferred from London to Brussels. This would be highly undesirable because national governments would lose the ability to control policy. It would be one more step down the road towards a Europe where Brussels was akin to Westminster and Westminster akin to a local authority.

Deflationary tendencies Perhaps the most important economic argument relates to the deflationary tendencies within the system. In the 1980s and 1990s, France succeeded in reducing her inflation rates to German levels, but at the cost of higher unemployment. For the UK, it can be argued that membership of the ERM between 1990 and 1992 prolonged unnecessarily the recession of the period. This is because the adjustment mechanism in the ERM acts rather like that of the Gold Standard. Higher inflation in one ERM country means that it is likely to generate current account deficits and put downward pressure on its currency (the **purchasing power parity theory** ☞ unit 87). To reduce the deficit and and reduce inflation, the country has to deflate its economy.

In the UK, it could be argued that the battle to bring down inflation had been won by the time the UK joined the ERM in 1990. However, the UK joined at too high an exchange rate. It was too high because the UK was still running a large current account deficit at an exchange rate of around 3 deutschmarks to the pound. The UK government then spent the next two years defending the value of the pound in the ERM with interest rates which were too high to allow the economy to recover. Many forecasts predicted that, had the UK not left the ERM in September 1992, inflation in the UK in 1993 would have been negative (i.e. there would have been falling prices). The economic cost of this would have been continued unemployment at 3 million and a stagnant economy. When the UK did leave the ERM, and it rapidly cut interest rates from 10 per cent to 5½ per cent, there was strong economic growth and the current account position improved, but there was an inflation cost.

Another problem that the early 1990s highlighted was that the needs of one part of Europe can have a negative impact on the rest of Europe. In the early 1990s, the Germans struggled with the economic consequences of German reunification. There was a large increase in spending in Germany with a consequent rise in inflation. The Bundesbank responded by raising German interest rates. As a result, there was an upward pressure on the deutschmark as speculative money was attracted into Germany. Germany's ERM partners were then forced to raise their interest rates too to defend their currencies. However, higher interest rates forced most of Europe into recession in 1992-93. Countries such as France couldn't then get out of recession by cutting interest rates because this would have put damaging strains on the ERM. The overall result was that Europe suffered a recession because of local reunification problems in Germany. Critics of the ERM and EMU argue that this could be repeated frequently if EMU were ever to be achieved. Local economies would suffer economic shocks because of policies, foisted on them, designed to meet the problems of other parts of Europe.

One way around this would be to have large transfers of money from region to region when a local area experienced a recession. For instance, Northern Ireland, which suffered structural unemployment for most of the post-war period, has had its economy propped up by large transfers of resources from richer areas of the UK with lower unemployment. However, regional transfers are very small at the moment. Moreover, to approximate the regional transfers which occur at the moment in, say, Britain, there would have to be a huge transfer of expenditures from national governments to Brussels - just what anti-Europeans are most opposed to.

DATA QUESTION

In praise of the international monetary non-system

The floating exchange rate non-system comes of age this month. It was 21 years ago, in March 1973, that the attempt to sustain the post-war system of fixed but adjustable exchange rates was abandoned. But that is not the only anniversary. It was also 50 years ago, in July 1944, that the conference at Bretton Woods, New Hampshire, designed the system that expired in 1973.

It is timely, therefore, to ask whether the global system of dirty floating either will, or should, endure for the next 21 years, or more. The answer is that it both will and should.

Floating exchange rates have had relatively few friends and many enemies. Yet nothing successful has been put in their place. Small countries are able to make credible commitments to fixed exchange rates, be it through currency boards (in the case of Hong Kong), the ERM (in the case of the Netherlands) or just a unilateral target (in the case of Austria). Large countries find it far more difficult. Even France, most devoted to the cause of fixed exchange rates of the members of the group of seven leading industrial countries, had to concede 15 per cent fluctuation bands within the ERM last summer.

It looks as though the world must learn to stop worrying and love floating exchange rates. Would that be so bad?

The chart shows what has happened to exchange rates of the three major currencies - the dollar, the yen and the D-Mark - since 1971, the year when President Nixon's administration devalued the dollar, a decision that led ultimately to generalised floating. Five points emerge:

- there is a considerable amount of

short term 'noise' in the movement of nominal exchange rates;

- there was one huge swing in nominal exchange rates which began in 1980 and ending in 1987;
- that swing went into reverse in early 1985, well before the celebrated meeting of the G7 finance ministers at the Plaza Hotel in New York;
- there has been a fairly close correlation between swings in nominal and real exchange rates, although this has been less true for the D-Mark than for the other two, because Germany is shielded by the ERM;
- there have now been some seven years of reasonable exchange rate stability.

This last fact explains why schemes to reform the international monetary system - common in the mid-1980s - have ceased to attract much attention today. But it also helps put the earlier dollar 'bubble' in proper perspective.

Neither credible exchange rate commitments nor intervention explain the long period of relative stability, at least after 1987. This underlines the point made by Professor Max Corden of the Johns Hopkins University School of Advanced International Studies in Washington DC, in a book to be published later this year, that 'managed floating is not incompatible with considerable exchange rate stability'.

The conditions for this are low and stable inflation in all participants and the absence of major shocks. Destabilising shocks do have to be major ones. Even the fall of the Berlin Wall resulted in only a modest appreciation of the D-Mark against the dollar, though it did lead to a melt-down in the more rigid ERM.

In the mid-1980s, the non-system looked far more erratic. Now it is possible to recognise that the ultimate cause of the rise of the dollar was an exceptionally large shock in the world's biggest economy: the tightening of monetary policy under Paul Volcker, chairman of the Federal Reserve, combined with the loosening of fiscal policy, under President Ronald Reagan.

It is also unlikely that any other exchange rate system could have coped better with such a shock. Professor Corden's book, which shows just how economic analysis ought to be used to clarify important questions for an educated general public, indicates why.

Suppose that it is accepted that the dollar had begun to overshoot seriously by 1983 and 1984, what would have been the consequences of using monetary policy to stop the trend? The likely answer, as we know from British experience with a similar bubble in 1987 and 1988, is that US inflation would have risen instead. It is possible that the total real exchange rate appreciation would then have been smaller. What is much more important is that the loss of competitiveness would have been more difficult to reverse under greater exchange rate stability. It would have required falling prices or at the least rapidly falling inflation, rather than the depreciation of the nominal exchange rate that occurred.

Not only has the present non-system been functioning quite well for some years, it is also difficult to conceive of any workable alternatives. The fate of the ERM has demonstrated the vulnerability of any fixed exchange rate system with imperfect credibility and free capital movement. One alternative would be a credibly fixed exchange rate system, such as a currency board or, for large countries, a currency union. The only other would be a float, but the more explicitly the exchange rate is managed within the float, the greater its vulnerability to speculation.

As Professor Corden puts it, 'the current laissez faire international monetary system is simply a market system, which co-ordinates the decentralised decisions reached by private and public actors and is likely to be as efficient at this as the market system within the domestic economy.' In other words, floating exchange rates among major currencies offer the worst possible system, except for all the others.

Source: the *Financial Times*, 28.3.1994.

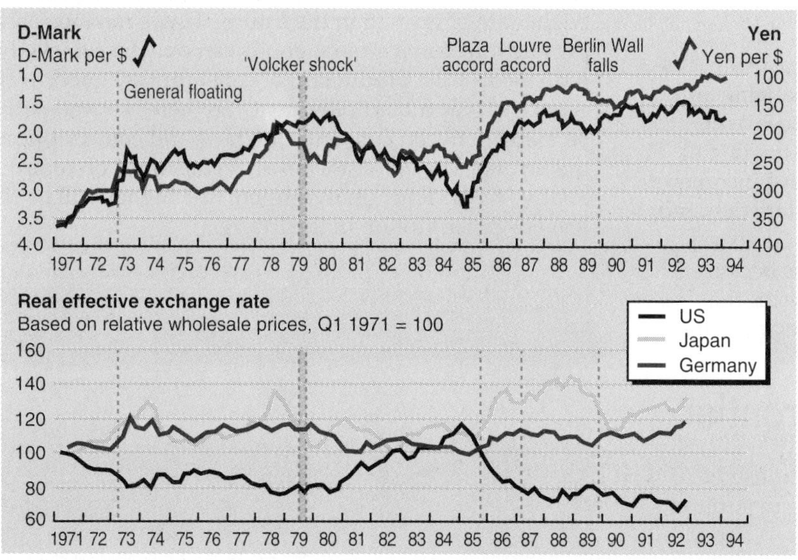

Source: adapted from Datastream; IMF

Figure 98.3 *Exchange rates, 1971-94*

1. **To what extent has there been exchange rate stability since 1973?**
2. **Explain why the floating exchange rate system is 'simply a market system' and why it is often associated with currency instability.**
3. **Between 1982, when Ronald Reagan became president of the United States, and 1985, the value of the dollar rose. At the time, Ronald Reagan pursued an economic policy which led to a large increase in the government's budget deficit. Meanwhile, the Federal Reserve Bank, the central bank of the United States, raised interest rates and thus tightened monetary policy in order to counter what it saw as inflationary trends in the US economy. (a) Explain why the value of the dollar rose between 1982 and 1985. (b) (i) How could monetary policy have been used to stop the rise in the dollar and (ii) what would have been the consequences of using monetary policy to stop the trend?**
4. **Discuss why floating exchange rates are likely to remain as the main exchange rate system over the next decade.**

Economic growth

Summary

1. Economic growth is the change in potential output of the economy shown by a shift to the right of the production possibility frontier. Economic growth is usually measured by the change in real national income.
2. Economic growth is caused by increases in the quantity or quality of land, labour and capital and by technological progress.
3. It is sometimes argued that growth is unsustainable because of the law of diminishing returns. Because land in particular is fixed in supply, diminishing returns will set in. However, most natural resources are not in fixed supply and historical evidence suggests that all factors are variable over time.
4. If all factors of production are variable over time, economies of scale could well be present. Advances in technology in particular may allow economies to grow at even faster rates in the future.

Definition

Economies change over time. One way of measuring this is the rate of change of national income. National income is a measure of how much an economy produces over time. Economists define economic growth as the rate of growth of national income. In practice, national income can be measured in many ways, but growth statistics tend to be presented in terms of either a change in GDP or GNP. Growth must be measured in **real** terms because it is the change in the volume of goods and services that we are attempting to measure and not their monetary value.

The production possibility frontier

Production possibility frontiers (PPFs) can be used to discuss economic growth. The PPF shows the maximum or **potential** output of an economy (☞ unit 1). When the economy grows, the PPF will move outward as in Figure 99.1. A movement from A to C would be classified as economic growth. However, there may be unemployment in the economy. With a PPF passing through C, a movement from B (where there is unemployment) to C (full employment) would be classified as **economic recovery** rather than economic growth. Hence, an increase in national income does not necessarily mean that there has been economic growth. In practice it is difficult to know exactly the location of an economy's PPF and therefore economists tend to treat all increases in GNP as economic growth.

Figure 99.1 can also be used to show the conflict between investment and consumption. One major source of economic growth is investment. All other things being equal, the greater the level of investment the higher will be the rate of growth in the future. However, increased production of investment goods can only be achieved by a reduction in the production of consumption goods if the economy is at full employment. So there is a trade off to be made between consumption now and consumption in the future. The lower the level of consumption today relative to the level of investment, the higher will be the level of consumption in the future.

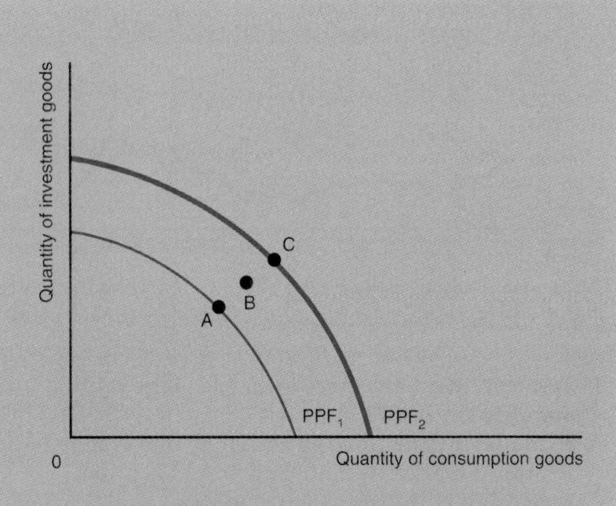

Figure 99.1 *Production possibility frontiers*
A movement from A to C would represent economic growth if there were a shift in the production possibility frontier from PPF_1 to PPF_2. A movement from B to C would represent economic recovery if the production possibility frontier were PPF_2.

The long run aggregate supply curve

Another way of showing economic recovery and economic growth is to use the concept of the **long run aggregate supply curve** (☞ unit 65). The long run aggregate supply curve shows the maximum output of the economy. Hence, economic growth could be shown by an increase in long run aggregate supply. In Figure 99.2, this would be the shift from $LRAS_1$ to $LRAS_2$, with the economy moving from A to C.

Economic recovery would imply that the economy was operating at below its maximum level of output to begin with. With a long run aggregate supply curve of $LRAS_2$, a movement from B to C would be an example of economic recovery.

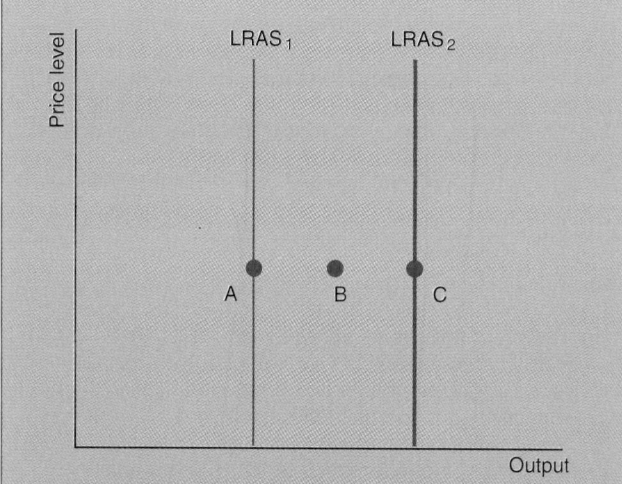

Figure 99.2 *Long run aggregate supply curves*
A movement from A to C would represent economic growth if there were a shift in the long run aggregate supply curve from $LRAS_1$ to $LRAS_2$. A movement from B to C would represent economic recovery if the long run aggregate supply curve were $LRAS_2$.

QUESTION 1

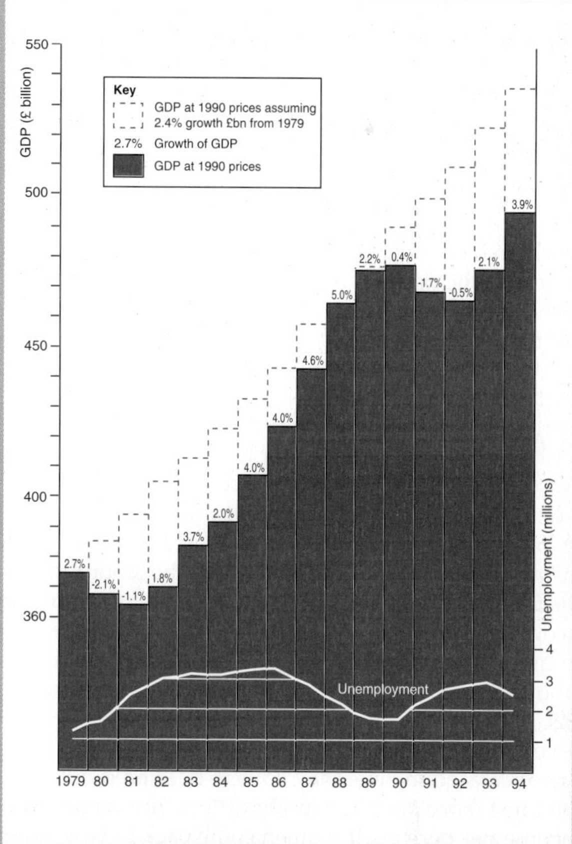

Source: adapted from CSO, *Economic Trends Annual Supplement;* CSO, *Economic Trends.*

Figure 99.3 *GDP and unemployment*

Figure 99.3 shows GDP at 1990 prices, the level of unemployment, and what GDP would have been if the economy had grown from its 1979 base at 2.4 per cent per annum (the average rate of growth between 1960 and 1994).

To what extent might the change in GDP since 1979 be classified as economic recovery rather than economic growth?

The causes of economic growth

National output can be increased if there is an increase in the quantity or quality of the inputs to the production process. Output can also be increased if existing inputs are used more efficiently. This can be expressed in terms of a **production function** (☞ unit 17):

Output = f (land, labour, capital, technical progress, efficiency)

The remainder of this unit will concentrate on the ways in which the quantity and quality of the factors of production can be increased and on what determines technical progress.

Land

Different countries possess different endowments of land. Land in economics is defined as all natural resources, not just land itself. Some countries, such as Saudi Arabia, have experienced large growth rates almost solely because they are so richly endowed. Without oil, Saudi Arabia today would almost certainly be a poor Third World country. Other countries have received windfalls. The UK, for instance, only started to exploit its oil resources in the mid 1970s. Today oil contributes about 3 per cent of GNP. However, most economists argue that the exploitation of raw materials is unlikely to be a significant source of growth in developed economies, although it can be vital in developing economies.

Labour

Increasing the number of workers in an economy should lead to economic growth. Increases in the labour force can result from three factors.

- Changes in demography. If more young people enter the workforce than leave it, then the size of the workforce will increase. In most western developed countries the population is relatively stable. Indeed, many countries will experience falls in the number of young people entering the workforce over the next ten or twenty years because of falls in the birth rate during the late 1960s and the 1970s.
- Increases in participation rates. Nearly all men who wish to work are in the labour force. However, in most Western countries there exists a considerable pool of women who could be brought into the labour force if employment opportunities were present. In the UK, for instance, almost all of the increase in the labour force in the foreseeable future will result from women returning to or starting work.
- Immigration. A relatively easy way of increasing the labour force is to employ migrant labour. Increasing the size of the labour force may increase output but will not necessarily increase economic welfare. One reason is that increased income may have to be shared out amongst more people, causing little or no change in income per person. If women come back to work, they have to give up leisure time to do so. This lessens the increase in economic welfare which they experience.

Increasing the quality of labour input is likely to be far more important in the long run. Labour is not **homogeneous** (i.e. it is not all the same). Workers can be made more productive by education and training. Increases in **human capital** (☞ unit 2) are essential for a number of reasons.

- Workers need to be sufficiently educated to cope with the demands of the existing stock of capital. For instance, it is important for lorry drivers to be able to read, typists to spell and shop assistants to operate tills. These might seem very low grade skills but it requires a considerable educational input to get most of the population up to these elementary levels.
- Workers need to be flexible. On average in the UK, workers are likely to have to change job three times during their lifetime. Increasingly workers are being asked to change roles within existing jobs. Flexibility requires broad general education as well as in-depth knowledge of a particular task.
- Workers need to be able to contribute to change. It is easy to see that scientists and technologists are essential if inventions and new products are to be brought to the market. What is less obvious, but as important, is that every worker can contribute ideas to the improvement of techniques of production. An ability of all workers to take responsibility and solve problems will be increasingly important in the future.

QUESTION 2 According to a report by the National Institute of Economic and Social Research, published in May 1994, British chemical and engineering companies are poorer at training technicians and using postgraduate engineers and scientists than similar German companies. The British engineering plants in the survey had improved productivity substantially over 15 years, but were still behind the German plants. They were also 'followers' in technical innovation. 'British price competitiveness still depends heavily on favourable movements in exchange rates,' says the report.

In the chemicals industry, 'Most British plants were at least equal to and sometimes ahead of their German counterparts in the use of new, sophisticated capital equipment.' The German plants had more skilled workers: in chemicals, 45 per cent of Germans had a craft apprenticeship compared with 23 per cent in Britain. In engineering, the gap was wider: 57 per cent to 20 per cent. These differences were even sharper at the intermediate-technician level, with virtually all German supervisors trained to meister level and only 5 per cent of British supervisors with any specific training for their role. The proportion of technical and higher-degree graduates was similar in the chemicals industry, but the German plants had more than double the British level in engineering. Germany is taking more postgraduate level students who are regarded by UK employers as 'over-qualified' and lacking commercial aptitude.

Source: adapted from the *Financial Times*, 26.5.1995.

(a) Output of the chemicals and man-made fibres industry increased by 11 per cent between 1986 and 1994. Over the same period, output of engineering industries decreased by 3 per cent. What factors might have accounted for this?
(b) Why might the differences outlined in the article account for the UK's slower rate of growth compared to Germany?

Capital

The stock of capital in the economy needs to increase over time if economic growth is to be sustained. This means that there must be sustained investment in the economy.

However, there is not necessarily a correlation between high investment and high growth. Some investment is not growth-related. For instance, investment in new housing or new hospitals is unlikely to create much wealth in the future. Investment can also be wasted if it takes place in industries which fail to sell products. For instance, investment in shipbuilding plants during the late 1970s and early 1980s provided a poor rate of return because the shipbuilding industry was in decline. Investment must therefore be targeted at growth industries.

Technological progress

Technological progress increases economic growth in two

QUESTION 3

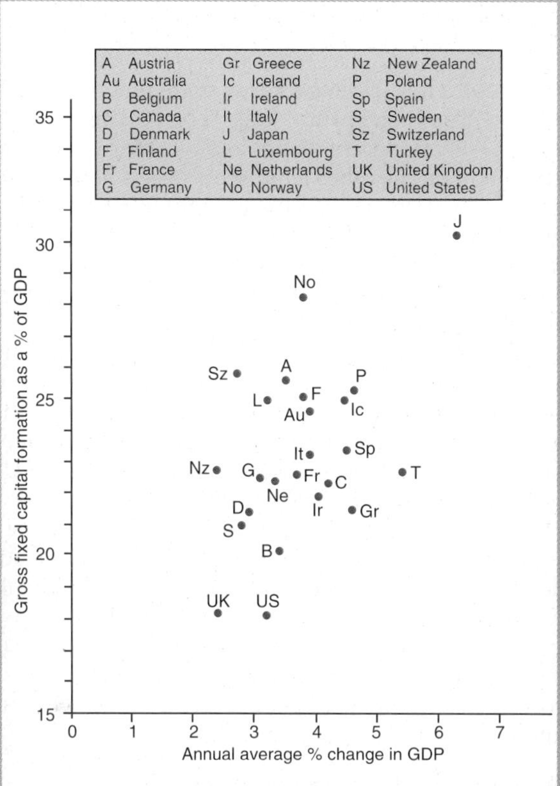

Source: OECD, *Historical Statistics.*

Figure 99.4 *Investment and economic growth in the 24 OECD countries (1960-90)*

(a) What relationship would economic theory suggest exists between investment and economic growth?
(b) To what extent is this relationship shown by the data?

ways.

- It cuts the average cost of production of a product. For instance, a machine which performed the tasks of a simple scientific calculator was unavailable 100 years ago. 50 years ago, it needed a large room full of expensive equipment to do this. Today calculators are portable and available for a few pounds.
- It creates new products for the market. Without new products, consumers would be less likely to spend increases in their income. Without extra spending, there would be less or no economic growth.

Diminishing returns and economies of scale

Some economists have argued that growth is unsustainable because of diminishing returns. The **law of diminishing returns** states that if increasing amounts of factors of production are combined with at least one fixed factor, eventually marginal product and then average product will decline. For instance, if more and more painters are put into a room with the same amount of paint and paintbrushes, then very quickly the productivity of each painter added will be less than that of the last one. Land and labour can be seen as fixed factors. Adding more and more capital will lead to diminishing returns.

Another way of looking at this is to use the concept of the **marginal efficiency of capital** (☞ units 56 and 63). Figure 99.5 shows an economy with a fixed number of investment projects. The more investment projects undertaken, the lower will be the rate of return earned on each project. Eventually the stock of investment projects which yield any positive rate of return will be exhausted. The economy cannot grow any further.

However, it is most unlikely that any factor is fixed. Although the quantity of labour, for instance, might remain unchanged, the quality of labour should increase over time. Equally, land is not fixed. The agricultural industry has had no problems over the past 200 years in steadily increasing the yield per acre in the UK. It has done this partly by increasing the quality of the land input through the use of crop rotation techniques and fertilisers. Evidence suggests that all factors are variable over time.

If this is true, then there may well be economies of scale present. For instance, growth during the inter-war period was higher on average than in Victorian England. Growth since the Second World War has been even higher. Economies of scale could arise, for instance, from the more widespread application of technology across markets. Equally, there is an exponential growth in scientific and technical knowledge. This suggests that the pace of change in production and development of new products will increase at an ever faster rate, allowing countries to enjoy ever faster growth rates. If this is true, then countries which devote a larger proportion of their national income to Research and Development are likely to grow faster than those which lag behind.

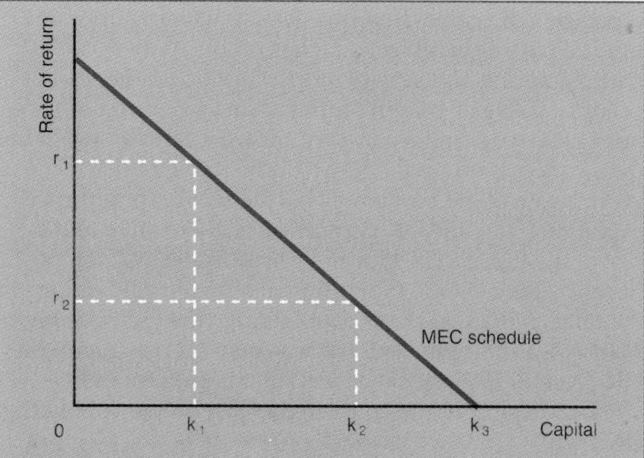

Figure 99.5 ***Limits to growth***

If the marginal efficiency of capital schedule does not shift, then investment over time will slowly reduce the stock of available investment projects. Eventually at k_3 there will be no investment projects left with a positive rate of return and economic growth will stop.

Applied economics

Britain's growth rate

Worries about Britain's growth rate date back over a century. In Edwardian times, for instance, it was not difficult to see the economic advance of Germany and France and compare it with the poor economic performance of the UK economy. Britain's poor growth performance has persisted in the post-war era. As Table 99.1 shows, the UK had the lowest average annual rate of growth between 1960 and 1994 of the seven largest industrial economies of the world (the **Group of Seven** or G7). It doesn't matter which period is taken, the UK has always been bottom of the growth league.

Economists disagree about the causes of the UK's relatively low growth rate and space here only allows some of the arguments to be considered. Economists do agree that the causes of growth are complex and that there are no easy 'quick fixes' in raising a country's growth rate.

Table 99.1 *Average annual growth in GDP, G7 countries, 1960-1994*

	1960-67	1968-73	1974-79	1980-94	1960-94
United States	4.5	3.2	2.4	2.3	3.0
Japan	10.2	8.7	3.6	3.4	6.5
Germany	4.1	4.9	2.3	2.2	3.1
France	5.4	5.5	2.8	1.9	3.5
United Kingdom	3.0	3.4	1.5	1.9	2.4
Italy	5.7	4.5	3.7	2.1	3.6
Canada	5.5	5.4	2.7	2.4	3.7
Average G7	5.0	4.4	2.7	2.3	3.6

Source: adapted from OECD, *Historical Statistics.*

Labour

Catching up Why can China grow by 10 per cent per annum whilst the UK barely manages a quarter of that? One suggestion is that the high economic growth rate represents the gains from transferring workers from low productivity agriculture to higher productivity manufacturing and service industries. If a worker can produce £500 per year in output as an agricultural worker but £1 000 working in a factory, then the act of transferring that worker from agriculture to industry will raise the growth rate of the economy. This theory was popular in explaining why the UK performed badly relative to the rest of the EU in the 1950s and 1960s. In 1960-67, for instance, the average proportion of agricultural workers in the total civilian working population in the then Common Market was 18.1 per cent, but was only 4.2 per cent in the UK. Even in 1980-88, there was still 8.7 per cent of EU workers in agriculture compared to just 2.5 per cent in the UK.

Class and conflict Another argument put forward is that class structures in the UK have been much more firmly entrenched than in other countries. This has led to a 'them' and 'us' attitude. Workers on the one hand see businesses and management as both exploitive and incompetent. They join together in trade unions to seek protection from their natural 'class' enemies and have to struggle to secure decent wages and working conditions. Management on the other hand see workers as lazy and greedy, unable to work effectively without proper supervision.

Whilst this may have been true for much of this century, the 1980s saw a revolution in attitudes. The power of trade unions, organisations which tended to perpetuate the rhetoric of class struggle and division, was considerably reduced by the anti-union legislation/trade union reform of the Conservative government. On the other hand, the era of the incompetent public school boss could arguably be said to have finally disappeared. The shake out in UK manufacturing industry in the early 1980s left only relatively efficient firms in business. The 1980s was the decade when MBAs (degrees in management) and reading the latest management book became fashionable. Finally, Japanese work practices, which emphasised lack of co-operation, hierarchy and had a considerable influence on how firms were structured. If class and conflict were important determinants of poor growth, then the 1990s should be a decade of higher growth.

Education and training There is widespread agreement amongst economists that education and training is one of the key factors - if not, in fact, the most important factor - in determining economic growth rates. The UK has an enviable record in educating the top 20 per cent of its population to the age of 21. However, there are widespread criticisms of its relative success in educating the other 80 per cent of the population and for what happens after 21. There is a considerable body of evidence which suggests that some of the UK's industrial competitors, such as Germany and Japan, educate their bottom 80 per cent of the school population to higher standards than in the UK. In the USA, where standards for all children to the age of 18 tend to be fairly low, there is a widespread acceptance that the majority of post-18 year olds will stay on and do some form of college course. The USA has the highest proportion of 18-24 year olds in full time education of any country in the world. In the workplace, countries like Germany have the reputation of spending more on training existing workers than in the UK.

In the 1980s, the UK government attempted to put in place mechanisms for improving education and training. The National Curriculum was intended to raise education achievement by setting national standards. The implementation of national vocational qualifications (NVQs) and their school or college based equivalent GNVQs) is an attempt to raise educational standards of the bulk of the post-16 population, both in schools and colleges or in work. It is still far too early to assess whether these reforms address the fundamental problem that the UK faces.

Capital

Table 99.2 shows that the UK has consistently devoted less of its GDP to investment than other countries. Economic theory would suggest that investment - the addition to the physical capital stock of the country - is essential for economic growth. How can an economy increase its growth rate if it does not increase the amount it is setting aside to increase the production potential of the country? There are a number of possible explanations for why the UK has such a relatively low growth rate and also one which challenges the assumption that higher investment is needed to increase growth rates.

Table 99.2 *Gross fixed capital formation as a percentage of GDP*

Per cent

	1960-67	1968-73	1974-79	1980-90	1960-90
United States	18.1	18.4	18.8	17.6	18.1
Japan	31.0	34.6	31.8	29.4	31.3
Germany	25.2	24.4	20.8	20.4	22.5
France	23.2	24.6	23.6	20.6	22.6
United Kingdom	17.7	19.1	19.4	17.6	18.2
Italy	24.9	24.0	24.0	21.2	23.3
Canada	22.6	22.1	23.5	21.5	22.3

Source: adapted from OECD, *Historical Statistics.*

Quality, not quantity Some economists have argued that it is not the quantity of investment that is important but its direction. The two classic examples used for the UK are Concorde (the supersonic plane) and the nuclear power programme. Large sums of public money were poured into the development of Concorde and the nuclear power programme in the 1960s. Both proved uncommercial. Switzerland devotes one-third more of its GDP to investment than the UK and yet has a similar growth rate. In this view, increasing investment rates without there being the investment opportunities present in the economy would have little or no effect on growth rates. The money would simply be wasted. Moreover, how could investment be increased in an economy? The simplest way would be for government to spend more on investment, either through its own programmes, by investing directly in industry, or through subsidies. Free market economists would then argue that the government is a very poor judge of industries and projects which need further investment. The money would probably be squandered on 1990s equivalents of Concorde. Only if firms increase investment of their own accord in free markets can growth increase.

Short-termism In this view, the USA and the UK have relatively low growth rates because of the structure of their financial institutions. In the USA and the UK, banks do not invest in companies. They lend to companies over fairly short time periods, typically up to five years, but many loans (e.g. overdrafts) are repayable on demand. Shares in companies are owned by shareholders, and these shares are traded on stock markets. Stock markets are driven by speculators who are not interested in where a company might be in five or ten years time. They are only interested in the size of the next dividend payment or the price of the share today. In contrast, in Germany and Japan banks own large proportions of industry through shareholdings. The banks are interested in the long term development of companies. Losses this year are less important if the long term future of a company is bright and secure. It is therefore argued that US and UK stock markets lead to short-termism. Firms will only invest if they can make a quick profit to satisfy shareholders who are only interested in the financial performance of the company over, say, 12 months. In Germany and Japan, firms can afford to make long term investment decisions even if these involve poorer short term performance, secure in the knowledge that their shareholders are interested in the long term future of the business.

Lack of savings The USA and the UK have relatively low savings ratios. Given that over the long term exports roughly equal imports for a country, and the government budget deficit tends to fluctuate around a fixed proportion of GDP, then using the circular flow of income model (where injections equal withdrawals), savings must roughly equal a constant proportion of investment. Higher savings will thus allow higher investment. In the UK, firms have large tax incentives to save through not distributing all their profits to shareholders. This retained profit could be increased through even lower taxation. Or the government could increase its savings by moving to a budget surplus. Individuals could be persuaded to save more again through tax incentives.

Innovation The UK spends a relatively low proportion of its GDP on research and development (R&D). For most of the post-war period, an above average share of that R&D has been devoted to defence research. Hence, some economists argue that R&D spending in total needs to be increased for higher growth, and a larger proportion needs to be spent on civilian projects. Others argue that it is not so much the quantity that is important as the use to which R&D is put. It is often pointed out that the UK has a good international record in making discoveries and in inventions. However, too many of those have not been taken up by UK businesses. Instead, the ideas have gone overseas and been used by foreign firms as the bases for world-beating products. In this argument, UK firms have been very poor in the past at making a commercial success of R&D.

Taxes Another argument put forward is that the UK has had a tax regime which has discouraged enterprise, work and investment. Before 1979, for instance, the highest marginal rate of tax on earned income was 83 per cent. Since 1979, the government has implemented a large number of reforms, including large reductions in key marginal tax rates on income and profits. The UK now has almost the lowest average rate of tax in the EU.

Possible causes of economic growth

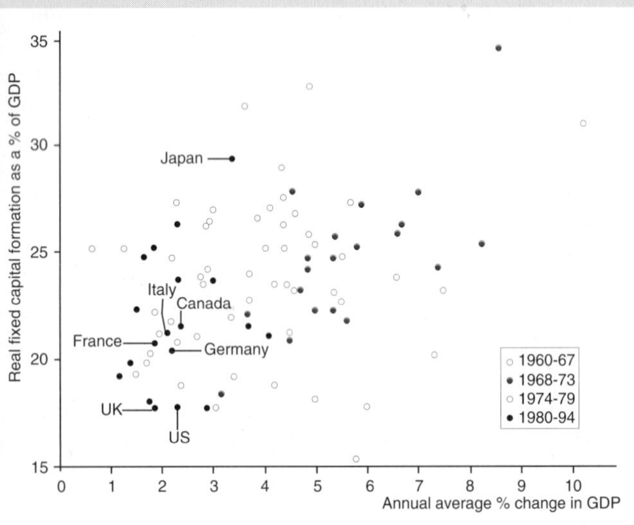

Figure 99.5 *Real growth in gross investment and real growth in GDP*

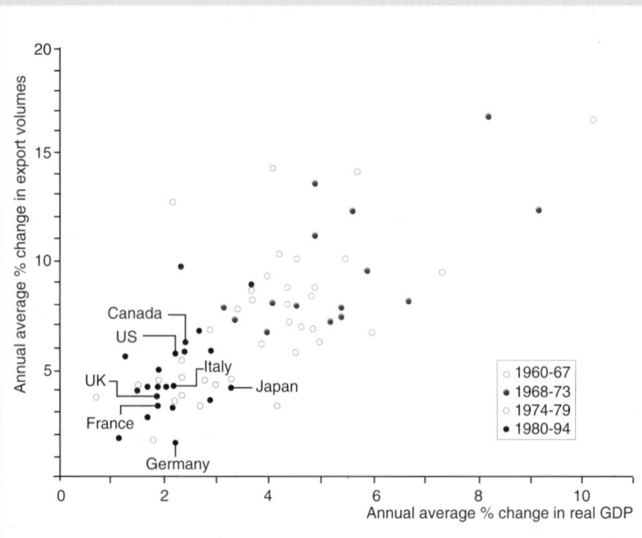

Figure 99.6 *Real growth in exports and real growth in GDP*

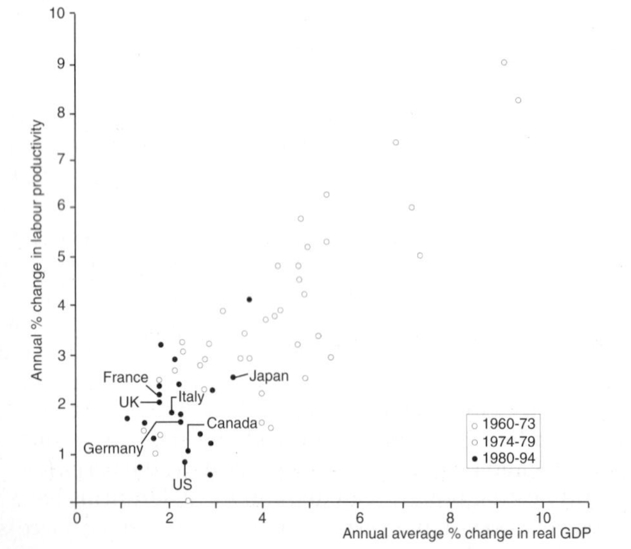

Figure 99.7 *Growth in labour productivity and real growth in GDP*

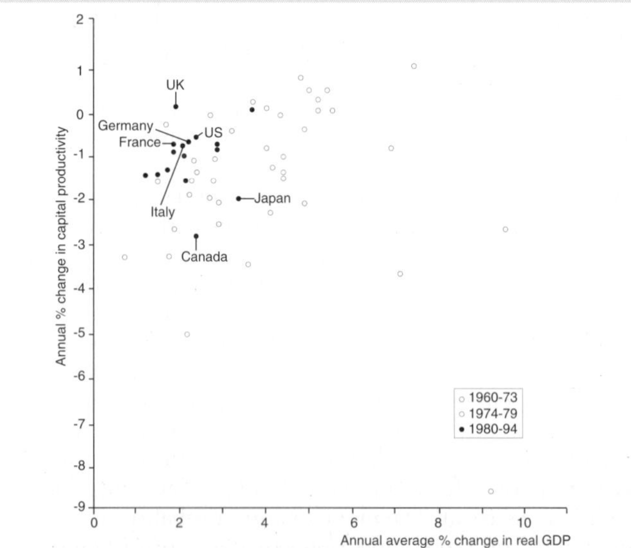

Figure 99.8 *Growth in capital productivity and real growth in GDP*

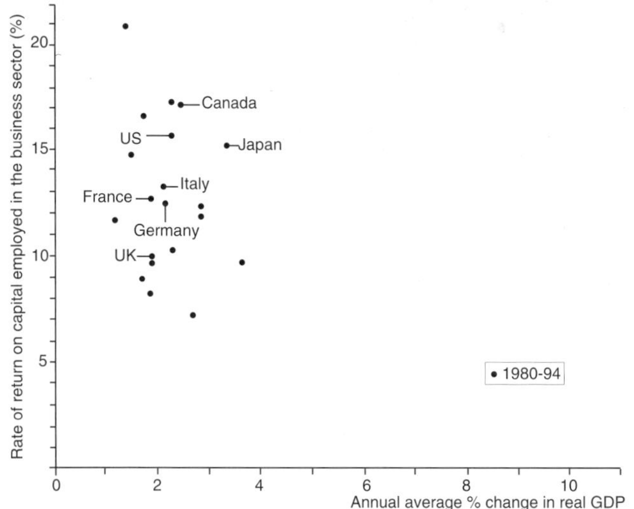

Figure 99.9 *Rates of return on capital in the business sector and real growth in GDP*

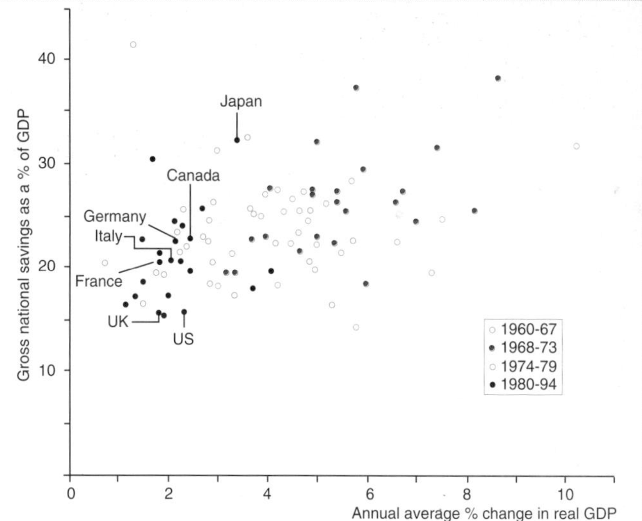

Figure 99.10 *Gross national savings as a percentage of GDP and real growth in GDP*

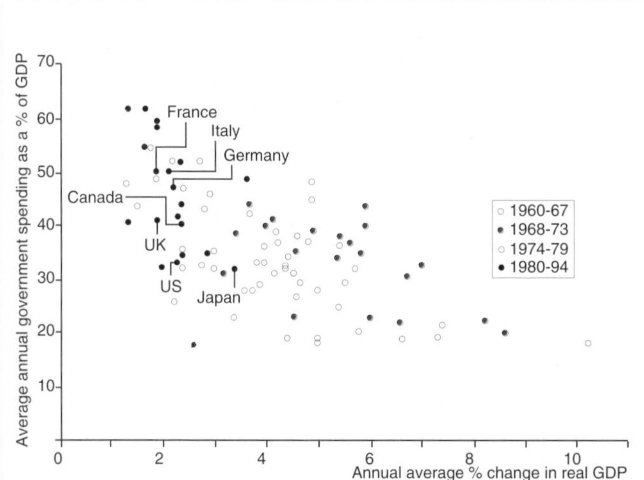

Figure 99.11 *Government spending as a percentage of GDP and real growth in GDP*

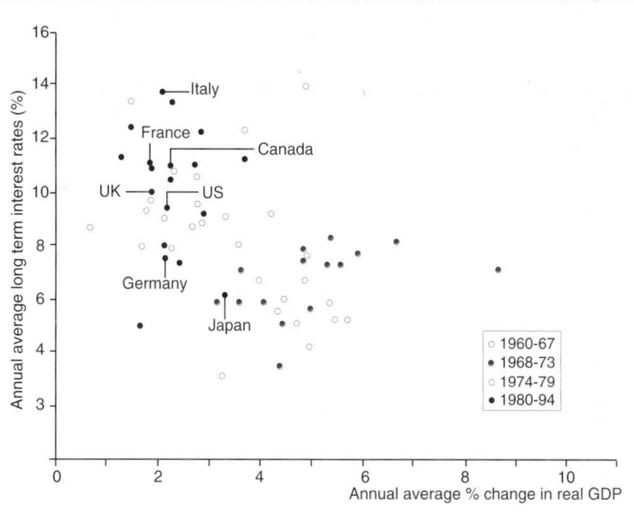

Figure 99.12 *Long term interest rates and real growth in GDP*

Figures 99.5 to 99.12 refer to published data by the OECD for OECD countries (US, UK, Canada, Italy, France, Germany, Japan, Austria, Belgium, Denmark, Finland, Greece, Iceland, Ireland, Luxembourg, Netherlands, Norway, Portugal, Spain, Switzerland, Turkey, Australia and New Zealand). Data is not included for all countries in every period indicated as the OECD did not publish these figures. The 7 major OECD countries' figures for the period 1980-94 are labelled.

An International bank, interested in assessing the long term growth prospects for loan business in different countries, has asked you to prepare a background paper on what key variables might be used to assess the future growth of economies. In your report:

1. **define what is meant by economic growth and how it is commonly measured;**
2. **outline the possible causes of growth;**
3. **use Figures 99.5 to 99.12, and any other data you might find, to assess whether there is any statistical evidence to support these hypotheses about the causes of growth;**
4. **decide which of the 7 major OECD countries (labelled) in the data have the best long term growth prospects after 1994, justifying your decision.**

National income, economic growth and welfare

Summary

1. National income is often used as the main indicator of the standard of living in an economy. A rise in GDP per head is used as an indication of economic growth and a rise in living standards.
2. However, there are many other important components of the standard of living, including political freedom, the social and cultural environment, freedom from fear of war and persecution, and the quality of the environment.
3. Economic growth over the past 100 years has transformed the living standards of people in the western world, enabling almost all to escape from absolute poverty.
4. Economic growth is likely to be the only way of removing people in the Third World from absolute poverty.
5. Economic growth has its costs in terms of unwelcome changes in the structure of society.
6. Some believe that future economic growth is unsustainable, partly because of growing pollution and partly because of the exploitation of non-renewable resources.

National income and economic welfare

National income is a measure of the income, output and expenditure of an economy. It is also often used as a measure of the **standard of living**. However, equating national income with living standards is very simplistic because there are many other factors which contribute to the economic welfare of individuals.

Political freedoms We tend to take civil liberties for granted in the UK. But other governments in the world today are totalitarian regimes which rule through fear. In some countries, membership of an opposition party or membership of a trade union can mean death or imprisonment. The freedom to visit friends, to travel and to voice an opinion are likely to be more valuable than owning an extra television or being able to buy another dress.

The social and cultural environment In the UK, we take things such as education for granted. We have some of the world's finest museums and art galleries. We possess a cultural heritage which includes Shakespeare and Constable. The BBC is seen as one of the best broadcasting organisations throughout the world. But we could all too easily live in a cultural desert where the main purpose of television programming might be to sell soap powders and make a profit. Alternatively, the arts could be used as political propaganda rather than exist in their own right.

Freedom from fear of violence If a person doesn't feel safe walking the streets or even at home, then no number of microwave ovens or videos will compensate for this loss. Equally, fears of war, arbitrary arrest, imprisonment or torture make material possessions seem relatively

QUESTION 1 Economists have long recognised that GDP is only a proxy measurement of living standards. In a book entitled *Alternative Economic Indicators* published in 1995, Victor Anderson, a British economist, argues that other measures apart from GDP should be used as measures of economic well-being. His thesis is that, in pursuing the maximisation of the monetary value of physical production, 20th century economists have neglected the intrinsic value of human beings and their interaction, and the need to protect the natural world. 'Narrowly financial criteria have ruled economic policy-making for too long. It is time to bring human and environmental realities back into economics.'

In the book he details 14 indicators which, he argues, could be considered alongside economic growth in evaluating economic outcomes. The alternative economic indicators include primary school enrolment, literacy, calorie intake, telephones per person, carbon dioxide emissions and operable nuclear reactors.

Source: adapted from the *Financial Times*, 1994.

(a) What does the author mean by 'narrowly financial criteria' when discussing living standards?

(b) Why should indicators such as primary school enrolment have any impact on living standards?

unimportant.

The working environment How long and hard people have to work is vital in evaluating standards of living. One reason why the average worker is far better off today than 100 years ago is because his or her working year is likely to be about half the number of hours of his or her Victorian counterpart's. Equally, the workplace is far safer today than 100 years ago. Industrial accidents were then commonplace and workers received little or no compensation for serious injuries or even death.

The environment Environmental issues are currently at the forefront of people's consciousness. There is an understanding that production activities can damage the environment and that in future we may well have to stop consuming certain products if we are to safeguard the environment.

The growth debate

The rate of economic growth has accelerated historically. Even five hundred years ago, most people would have seen little change in incomes over their lifetimes. In Victorian England, the economy grew at about one per cent per annum. Over the past thirty years, the UK economy has grown at an average of just over 2 per cent. But the recent growth performance of the UK, whilst excellent by historical standards, has been low compared to the growth rates of other countries. Japan, after growing at up to 10 per cent per annum in many years after 1945, averaged 3.4 per cent growth between 1980 and 1994.

Table 100.1 *Economic growth rate of £1 over time*

Year	Growth rates				
	1%	2%	3%	5%	10%
0	100	100	100	100	100
5	105	110	116	128	161
10	110	122	130	163	259
25	128	164	203	339	1 084
50	164	269	426	1 147	11 739
75	211	442	891	3 883	127 189
100	271	724	1 870	13 150	1 378 059

Growth at these rates over the past 50 years has led to undreamt of prosperity for the citizens of the industrialised world. Consider Table 100.1. It shows by how much £1 will grow over time at different rates. At one per cent growth, income will roughly double over the lifetime of an individual. At 2 per cent, it will quadruple over a lifetime. At 3 per cent, it is doubling every twenty five years. At 5 per cent, it only takes about 14 years to double income. At 10 per cent, it only takes about 7 years to double income.

If recent growth rates are a guide to the future, average British workers in 30 years' time will earn in real terms twice what they are earning today. When they are in their seventies, they can expect workers to earn four times as much as their parents did when they were born.

These increases in income have led to the elimination of **absolute poverty** (☞ unit 43) for most citizens in industrialised countries.

- Life expectancy has doubled over the past 300 years and infant mortality rates have plummeted.
- People have enough to eat and drink. What we eat and drink is nearly always fit for human consumption.
- Housing standards have improved immeasurably.
- Nearly everyone can read and write.

Future increases in income are generally desirable. Very few people would prefer to have less income rather than more income in the future (remember economics assumes that people have **infinite wants**). So economic growth has generally been considered to be highly desirable. Moreover, two-thirds of the world's population do not live in the affluent West. Many who live in the Third World suffer absolute poverty. The only way to eliminate malnutrition, disease, bad housing and illiteracy in these countries is for there to be real economic growth.

QUESTION 2

The photographs show a modern kitchen and a kitchen at the turn of the century. To what extent do they show that economic growth has been desirable?

Arguments against growth

Despite the apparent benefits, the goal of economic growth has become increasingly questioned in recent years.

One argument is that the increase in national income has been largely fictitious. Three hundred years ago much of the output of the economy was not traded. Women were not on the whole engaged in paid work. Much of the supposed increase in income has come from placing monetary values on what existed already. Much of the increase in income generated by the public sector of the economy comes not from increased production but from increased wages paid to public sector workers who produce the same amount of services. Whilst there is some truth in this, it cannot be denied that material living standards have increased immeasurably over the past three hundred years. People not only consume more goods and services, they have on average far more leisure time.

Another argument is that modern industrialised societies have created large negative **externalities**. For instance, growth has created a large pool of migrant workers, wandering from job to job in different parts of the country. They become cut off from their roots, separated from their families. The result is alienation and loneliness, particularly of the old, and the collapse of traditional family values. Crime rates soar, divorce rates increase, stress related illnesses become commonplace and more and more has to be spent on picking up the pieces of a society which is no longer content with what it has.

Supporters of this view tend to look back to some past 'golden age', often agricultural, when people lived mainly in villages as parts of large extended families. However, historical evidence suggests that such a rural paradise never existed. Life for many was short and brutish. Drunkenness was always a problem. Family life was claustrophobic and did not allow for individuality. Most people were dead by the age when people today tend to divorce and remarry.

Perhaps the most serious anti-growth argument is that growth is unsustainable. Consider again Table 100.1. If Western European countries continue to grow at an average 3 per cent per annum then in 25 years' time national income will be twice as large as it is today; in fifty years' time, when an 18 year old student will be retired, it will be over 4 times as large; in 75 years' time, when on current life expectancy figures that student would be dead, it will be nearly 9 times as large; and in 100 years' time it will be nearly 19 times as large. If the average wage in the UK today is £12 000 per annum, then in 100 years' time it will have risen to £355 300 per annum in real terms.

Each extra percent increase in national income uses up **non-renewable resources** such as oil, coal and copper. In the late 1970s, the Club of Rome, a forecasting institute, produced a report called 'The Limits to Growth'. The report claimed that industrialised economies as we know them would collapse. They would be caught between a growth in pollution and a decline in the availability of scarce resources such as oil, coal and timber. Oil was projected to run out in the next century and coal by the year 2 400. In the 1980s, the world was gripped by reports that people were destroying the ozone layer and raising the world's temperature through the greenhouse effect. The planet cannot support growth rates of even 1 or 2 per cent per year. Growth must stop and the sooner the better.

Economic theory suggests that the future may not be as bleak as this picture makes out. In a market economy, growing scarcity of a resource, such as oil, results in a rise in price. Three things then happen. First, demand and therefore consumption falls - the price mechanism results in conservation. Second, it becomes profitable to explore for new supplies of the resource. Known world oil reserves today are higher than they were in 1973 at the time of the first oil crisis! Third, consumers switch to substitute products whilst producers are encouraged to find new replacement products. After the massive rise in oil prices in 1973-4, the world car makers roughly halved the fuel consumption per mile of the average car over a period of ten years through more efficient engines. Brazil developed cars which ran on fuel made from sugar.

Governments too respond to pressures from scientists and the public. The activities of industry are far more regulated today in the western world than they were 30 years ago.

What is worrying, however, is that the market mechanism and governments are frequently slow to act. Governments and markets are not good at responding to pressures which might take decades to build up but only manifest themselves suddenly at the end of that time period. Some scientists have predicted that global warming is now already irreversible. If this is true, the problem that we now face is how to change society to cope with this. There is no clear consensus as to how we could reverse economic growth, consume less, and cope with the coming catastrophe, without creating an economic nightmare with mass starvation.

One point to note is that supporters of the anti-growth lobby tend to be people who are relatively well off. Cutting their consumption by 25 per cent, or producing products through expensive environmentally friendly alternative technologies might not create too much hardship for them. However, leaving the mass of people in the Third World today at their present living standards would mean that they would continue to live in absolute poverty with starvation and death an ever present threat. In the Third World, the struggle for survival is far more important than any environmental concern. Green politics tends to be the preserve of the affluent western middle classes.

Applied economics

The standard of living in the UK since 1900

GDP is often used as the major economic indicator of welfare. Table 100.2 shows that, on this basis, living standards in the UK have risen considerably this century. Between 1900 and 1931, GDP rose 23 per cent and between 1900 and 1994 rose 423 per cent. Population has increased too, but even when this has been taken into account, the rise in income per person is impressive.

Table 100.2

	GDP (£bn at 1990 prices)	Population (millions)	GDP per head (£ at 1990 prices)
1901	94.6	38.2	2 476
1911	109.0	42.1	2 589
1921	96.4	44.0	2 190
1931	116.6	46.0	2 426
1951	180.0	50.2	3 586
1961	236.2	52.7	4 482
1971	312.9	55.5	5 638
1981	364.1	55.8	6 525
1991	468.9	57.8	8 112
1994	495.1	58.3	8 492

Source: adapted from CH Feinstein, *National Income, Expenditure and Output in the United Kingdom*, 1855-1965 (Cambridge University Press); CSO, *United Kingdom National Accounts (Blue Book).*

It is possible to chart a multitude of other ways in which it can be shown that the standard of living of the British family has improved. For instance, 14.2 per cent of children in 1900 died before the age of 1. In 1995, the comparable figure is less than 0.7 per cent. In 1900, the vast majority of children left school at 12. Today all children stay on till the age of 16, whilst nearly 40 per cent of 16-19 year olds are in full time education or training. In 1900, few people were able to afford proper medical treatment when they fell ill. Today, everyone in the UK has access to the National Health Service.

Table 100.3 illustrates another way in which we are far better off today than a family at the turn of the century. It shows the weekly budget of a manual worker's family in a North Yorkshire iron town, estimated by Lady Bell in her book *At The Works*. The family lived off 7½ home-made loaves of 4lb each thinly scraped with butter, 4lb of meat and bacon, weak tea, a quart of milk and no vegetables worth mentioning. In 1992, whilst average consumption for five people of bread was only 8.2lb a week, tea 0.4lb and sugar 2.3lb, on the other hand meat consumption was 10.5lb, potato consumption was 9.9lb, and butter, margarine, lard and other oils consumption was 2.7lb. Moreover, today's diet is far more varied and ample with fruit and vegetables apart from potatoes playing a major part. Malnutrition, not uncommon in 1900, is virtually unknown in the UK today.

The budget in Table 100.3 also says a great deal about the very restricted lifestyle of the average family in 1908. Then, a family would consider itself lucky if it could take a day trip to the seaside. In comparison, 60 per cent of all adults took a holiday of 4 days or more in 1993, and 16 per cent took two or more holidays a year. 23.5 million holidays were taken abroad.

Table 100.3

Family budget in 1908
Income 18s 6d, family of five

	s.	d.
Rent	5	6
Coals	2	4
Insurance	0	7
Clothing	1	0
Meat	1	6
14lb of flour	1	5
3½ lb of bread meal	0	4½
1lb butter	1	1
Half lb lard	0	2½
1lb bacon	0	9
4 lb sugar	0	8
Half lb tea	0	9
Yeast	0	1
Milk	0	3
1 box Globe polish	0	1
1lb soap	0	3
1 packet Gold Dust	0	1
3 oz tobacco	0	9
7lb potatoes	0	3
Onions	0	1
Matches	0	1
Lamp oil	0	2
Debt	0	3
Total	18	6

In 1908, houses were sparsely furnished. The main form of heating was open coal fires; central heating was virtually unknown. Very few houses were wired for electricity. Table 100.3 shows that the typical house was lighted by oil. All the electrical household gadgets we take for granted, from washing machines to vacuum cleaners to televisions, had not been invented. The 1lb of soap in the 1908 budget would have been used to clean clothes, sinks and floors. Soap powders, liquid detergents and floor cleaners were not available. 'Gold Dust' was the popular name for an exceptionally caustic form of shredded yellow soap notorious for its ability to flay the user's hands. Compare that with the numerous brands of mild soaps available today.

Workers worked long hours, six days a week with few holidays, whilst at home the housewife faced a life of drudgery with few labour-saving devices. Accidents were frequent and old age, unemployment and sickness were dreaded and even more so the workhouse, the final destination for those with no means to support themselves.

Ecologically, the smoke-stack industries of industrial areas such as London, the Black Country and Manchester created large scale pollution. The smogs which are found in many cities such as Mexico City and Los Angeles today were common occurrences in turn-of-the-century Britain. The urban environment was certainly not clean 90 years ago.

Socially and politically, women, who formed over half the population, were not emancipated. In 1900, they did not have the vote, their place was in the home, they were often regarded as biologically inferior to men, and they were debarred from almost all public positions of influence and authority. In many ways, the standard of living of women has improved more than that of men this century because of the repressive attitude held towards women 90 years ago.

Overall, it would be very difficult to look back on 1900 and see it as some golden age. For the vast majority of those in Britain today, the 1990s are a paradise in comparison. However, whilst there might be little absolute poverty today, it could be argued that there is considerable relative poverty. It could also be argued that the poorest today are probably still worse off than the top 5 per cent of income earners in 1900.

Comparative living standards in the UK

Table 100.4 *Income, prices and population*

	1971	1994
GDP (£bn at current prices)	50.0	578.3
Retail price index (1985 = 100)	21.4	152.3
Population (millions)	55.5	58.3

Table 100.5 *Purchasing power*

	1971	1994
Time necessary to work to pay for		
1lb pork sausages	19 minutes	10 minutes
1lb cod fillets	25 minutes	23 minutes
Ford Escort	2 194 hours	1 788 hours
Colour television licence	19 hours	12 hours
Return 2nd class ticket London to Edinburgh	21 hours	8 hours

Table 100.6 *Government spending on welfare benefits*

	£bn at 1993-94 prices	
	1971-72	1993-94
Elderly	16.7	36.8
Long term sick and disabled	2.9	17.2
Short term sick	2.4	1.2
Family	2.8	14.4
Unemployed	2.8	9.7
Widows and others	2.5	1.7
Total benefit expenditure	30.1	[illegible]

Table 100.7 *Population*

	1971	1993
Percentage of the population		
under 16	14.3	12.0
16-39	17.5	20.3
40-64	16.7	12.0
65-79	6.1	6.9
80 and over	1.3	2.3

Table 100.8 *Male death rates*

	1971	1993
Death rates per 1000 males in each group		
Under 1	20.0	7.8
1-15	0.5	0.2
16.39	1.1	1.0
40-64	11.4	7.0
65-79	59.9	47.5
80 and over	174.0	149.8

Table 100.9 *Number of abortions*

	1971-72	1993
Abortions	63 400	119 600

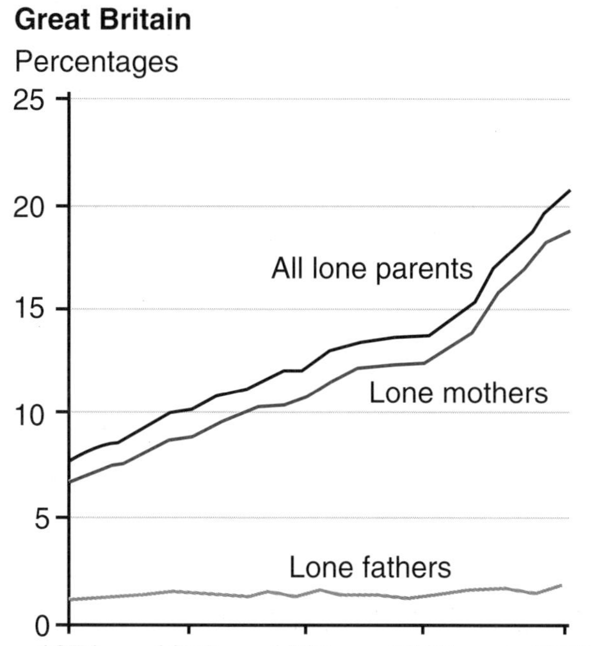

Source: adapted from OPCS.

Figure 100.1 Families headed by lone parents as a percentage of all families

Table 100.10 *Housing*

	1971	1991
% of households with no:		
bath or shower	9.1	0.3
inside toilet	11.5	0.5
Number of mortgages	4.5m	10.4m
Properties taken into repossession	2 800	58 500

Table 100.11 *Percentage of households owning selected consumer durables*

	1972	1993
Television	93	99
Telephone	42	90
Washing machine	66	88
Video recorder	0	73
Microwave	0	62
CD player	0	39

Table 100.12 *Education*

	1970-71	1992-93
Ratio of pupils to teachers in state schools	22.6	18.6
Numbers in higher education	621 000	1 444 000
Government spending on education as % of GDP	5.2	5.2

Table 100.13 *Health*

	1971	1993
Average number of patients per:		
doctor	2 400	1 900
dentist	4 500	3 100

Table 100.14 *Employment*

	1971	1993
Males employees in employment		
full time	13.1m	9.8m
part time	0.6m	1.1m
Female employees in employment		
full time	5.6m	5.8m
part time	2.8m	4.8m
Unemployed	0.75m	2.92m

Table 100.15 *Real gross weekly earnings of selected workers, £ at April 1994 prices*

	1971	1994
Waiter/waitress	105	157
Caretaker	159	220
Bricklayer/mason	198	252
Carpenter/joiner	203	261
Nurse	142	316
Primary teacher	235	394
Solicitor	347	569
Medical practitioner	499	746

Table 100.16 *Leisure*

	1971	1993-94
Average attendance at Football League (1971) - Premier League (1993-94) games	31 352	23 040*
Membership of:		
Cub scouts	265 000	349 000*
Brownies/Guides	376 000	385 000*
Scouts	215 000	192 000*
Girl guides	316 000	225 000*
Youth clubs, boys	179 000	397 000*
girls	140 000	318 000*
Army cadet force	39 000	39 000*
Number of holidays taken abroad	4.2m	23.2m+

* 1992 + 1993

Table 100.17 *Number of enquiries dealt with/client interviews by selected advisory and counselling services*

	1971	1993
Citizens Advice Bureau	1.5m	8.25m
Samaritans	87 000	2.4m
Relate	22 000	76 000
Law Centres Federation	1 000	525 000

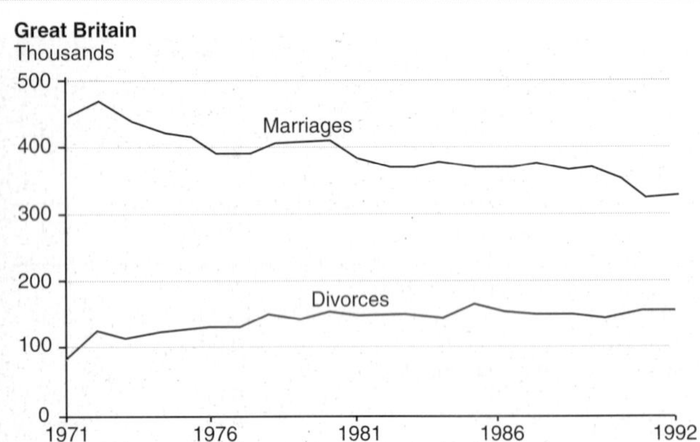

Source: adapted from OPCS; General Register Office (Scotland).
Figure 100.2 *Marriages and divorces*

Table 100.18 *Average daily flow of motor vehicles on motorways*

Thousands

	1971	1993
Vehicles on motorways	20.52	55.2

Crime - the number of notifiable offences recorded per 100 population

The rate tripled in England and Wales between 1971 and 1992, although it fell by nearly 2 per cent in 1993 when there was one offence recorded for every ten people. The rates for Northern Ireland and Scotland have also increased since 1971, but also fell between 1992 and 1993, by 4 per cent and 8 per cent respectively.

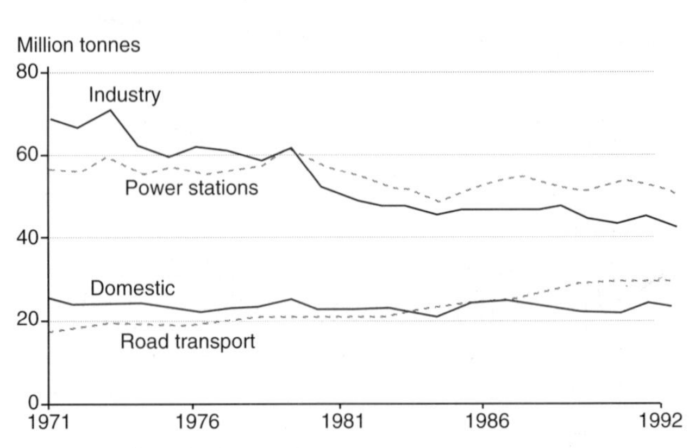

Source: adapted from National Environmental Technology Centre.
Figure 100.3 *Carbon dioxide emissions by source*

Sources for all tables: adapted from CSO, *Social Trends*; *Annual Abstract of Statistics.*

You have been asked to write a magazine article from an economic perspective comparing the early 1970s and the mid-1990s. The focus of the article is a discussion of whether living standards have improved in the UK over the period. Construct the article as follows.

1. **In your introduction, pick out a small number of key statistics which you feel point out the differences between the two periods.**
2. **In the main part of the article, compare and contrast the two periods, pointing out how living standards have improved and also where it could be argued that the UK is worse off in the mid-1990s than in the early 1970s.**
3. **In a conclusion, discuss whether rising GDP over the next twenty years will be sufficient to ensure that the UK is better off in 2015 than in the mid-1990s.**

unit 101

Economic growth and government policy

Summary

1. Government policy to increase economic growth over the long term should be directed towards increasing labour productivity, either by raising the skills of the labour force or by increasing the quantity or quality of the capital stock.
2. Some economists argue that governments should intervene in the market place if high economic growth is to be achieved. They advocate such policies as increased expenditure on education and training, subsidies for investment, direct government investment in the economy and grants or subsidies for Research and Development.
3. Other economists argue that government is poorly placed to judge how resources should be allocated within an economy. They argue that it is the role of government to liberate markets of restrictions. They advocate the use of supply side policies to increase the rate of economic growth.

The causes of economic growth

Economic growth occurs when there is an increase in the quantity or quality of the factors of production or when they are used more efficiently. A government wishing to increase growth in the economy fundamentally must pursue policies which will increase **labour productivity** (i.e. output per worker). There are three main ways to achieve this:

- the quality of the labour force can increase, meaning that each worker on average can produce more output with an existing stock of capital and an existing state of technology;
- the quantity of the capital stock can increase, meaning that workers are able to use more capital, thus raising average output;
- the state of technology can change, meaning that a given capital stock can be more productive with a given labour force.

Government policies to promote growth therefore need to be directed at both the labour and capital markets.

An interventionist approach

Some economists believe that the market mechanism is unlikely to lead to optimal rates of economic growth. There are so many forms of **market failure** (☞ unit 35), that the government must intervene in the market place. For instance, it can be argued that the economic prosperity of countries such as France, Germany and Japan are based upon **interventionist** policies of their governments. There are many ways in which government can act to increase the growth rate of the economy.

Increased public expenditure on education and training The quality of the workforce can be increased if educational standards are raised. This could be achieved if, for instance, more children stay on at school or college after the age of 16, or more people go to university or polytechnic. But a significant increase in the numbers in full time education is likely to require significant increases in the education budgets of government.

Alternatively, employers could provide more training for their staff. But in a free market, firms are under strong cost pressures to spend as little as possible on training. Many firms may find it far cheaper, rather than to train staff directly, to 'poach' trained staff from other firms. The result is market failure - the inability of the free market to provide sufficient training for the country's workforce. Here again there is a crucial role to be played by government. The government could force the private sector to undertake more training, for instance by passing laws which state that firms must pay for at least one day's training a week for all 16 to 18 year olds employed. Or it could encourage training at work by providing generous subsidies to employers with strong training programmes.

Subsidising investment Economic theory suggests that firms will invest more if the cost of capital declines

QUESTION 1 The abolition of industry training bodies in the early 1980s was a grave mistake according to some economists. Firms in industries with a training council paid a levy per employee to the council. They were then able to send workers on courses provided by the council. Firms which chose not to train workers, but instead hired trained workers from other firms when needed, still had to make a financial contribution to training. Today's situation encourages free riding. Firms which train workers may get some financial support from their local TEC (Training and Enterprise Council). However, the bulk of the training cost has to be paid for by the firm. Not surprisingly, small firms spend little or nothing on training and rely on being able to recruit staff trained by other firms when vacancies occur. The result is that the UK's workforce is poorly trained in comparison with those of industrialised competitors such as Germany and Japan.

(a) (i) What is meant by 'free riding'? (ii) Why might the present UK training system encourage free riding whilst the previous system might not?
(b) Explain why firms have an incentive to over-consume training and thus waste training resources if they are provided free or at little cost by government.
(c) What is the possible link between training and economic growth?

(☞ unit 56). So the government could subsidise investment if it wished to increase investment spending in the economy. It has a variety of ways to do this. It could, for instance, provide direct subsidies for new investment, giving a grant for a proportion of any new investment undertaken by a firm, or it could offer tax incentives. Investment could be offset against corporation tax liability. Governments could offer selective assistance to particular industries which it believed would be important in the future. This is known as a policy of 'picking winners'.

Alternatively, the government could reduce the cost of capital by lowering interest rates, leading to a move along the **marginal efficiency of capital schedule**. One way of possibly reducing interest rates is to increase the personal savings ratio. The argument here is that actual injections, I + G + X must equal actual withdrawals, S + T + M (☞ unit 55). If G, X, T and M remain constant, an increase in S, total savings, will lead to an increase in I, the level of investment. This occurs through the interest rate mechanism. Hence measures which encourage saving, such as tax allowances, may increase the level of investment.

Direct government investment Free market forces, even when working in their most efficient way, may still result in a less than socially desirable level of investment in the economy. The government may then be forced to intervene directly, rather than attempting to influence the private sector indirectly. For instance, the government may choose to nationalise firms or industries (i.e. take them into public ownership). It may do this following disappointing performance in the private sector. In some cases, the industry or firm may otherwise go out of business and the government has to step in to rescue it for the nation.

The government may also choose to co-operate with the private sector in developing an industry. The government could set up in partnership with an existing private sector company to develop a new product. In the small business sphere, the government may fund a government owned company to take equity stakes in growing businesses.

QUESTION 2

Sir, It is perplexing that in the UK economic debate there is so little focus on the personal sector savings ratio. To raise the underlying rate of growth there must be, in addition to greater risk-taking activity (via lower corporate and income taxes), a higher average rate of investment.

The principal way this can occur is if the personal sector consistently saves a higher proportion of its income, thereby indirectly increasing the amount of borrowing that the corporate sector can undertake whilst maintaining balance of payments equilibrium.

Reasons for a low savings/investment ratio lie not in cultural characteristics but in fiscal incentives. In particular, the combination of mortgage interest tax relief, no capital gains tax on profits from property sales, and taxation on savings/investment income, engenders a low savings ratio.

The UK economy will only be transformed when deferred consumption (savings) becomes the most attractive means of boosting one's asset-based wealth, a la Japan. This could be achieved by imposing a capital gains tax on property profits while making savings income tax free - ensuring that the bulk of funds saved were indeed redirected to the corporate sector.

Jack Brown

Source: letter in the *Financial Times*, 29.11.1989.

(a) Explain what, in the author's opinion, was the cause of low economic growth in the UK at the time.
(b) How might the measures he advocated increase the growth rate?

Encouraging Research and Development Government can encourage technological progress in a variety of ways. For instance, it can fund universities and polytechnics to engage in fundamental research. It can establish research institutions. It can give grants or tax subsidies to private firms undertaking research and development. It can encourage the widespread dissemination of new inventions and new technologies by subsidising their price, or offering free assistance to firms wanting to know how new technologies might be of benefit to them.

Another way is to encourage the growth of large monopolies and to discourage the existence of small and medium size companies in the market. In the Austrian view(☞ unit 39), large monopolies are the firms which are the most likely to have the money and the incentive to engage in Research and Development. They have the money because they are able to earn abnormal profit. They have the incentive because their monopoly power depends upon their hold over the market with existing technology. In the process of **creative destruction**, monopolies can be destroyed by new competitor firms offering new products to satisfy the same wants. For instance, the monopoly power of the railways of the 19th century was destroyed by the coming of the motor car. On the other hand, firms in perfect competition have no incentive to undertake Research and Development because there is perfect knowledge in the market. Any invention will quickly become common knowledge and will be copied by all firms in the industry.

Protectionism The government may feel that domestic industry is failing to invest because of foreign competition. For instance, the **infant industry argument** (☞ unit 85) says that industries which are just starting up may need initial protection because they do not have the economies of scale available to established large foreign competitors. It could be that the whole economy of a country is inefficient compared to international rivals and that a period behind high protectionist barriers, where domestic industries can earn high profits and afford to make large investments, is needed to prevent a complete collapse of industry.

The limits to interventionism

Countries are finding it more difficult to adopt interventionist policies as time goes on. This is because international agreements are limiting the scope for interventionism. For instance, the UK government is severely limited in its domestic policies by its membership of the EU. It cannot increase subsidies to individual industries without running the risk of being forced to stop by the European Commission. Monopolies are subject to EU law too. The UK obviously cannot put up tariff barriers against goods coming from other Common Market countries. It is also limited in its ability to protect domestic industries against foreign competition by being a signatory to international treaties which limit protectionism, which are now policed by the World Trade Organisation (WTO).

Not only the legal and institutional constraints on interventionism have increased over the past 30 years. The intellectual climate in favour of interventionism has waned, whilst that of the free market alternative has strengthened. Nationalisation, monopolisation and protectionism are policies which many governments around the world have abandoned. The move towards privatisation was, for instance, first started by the UK government in 1980. At the same time, countries like South Korea and Singapore, both of which have had very high growth rates in recent decades, are interventionist in the sense that government has promoted education and training and deliberately worked with the private sector in choosing which sectors of industry should be promoted.

A free market approach

The alternative approach has a long tradition in economics. Free market economists argue that the market is the most efficient way of allocating resources. Government intervention is at best ineffectual and at worst seriously damaging to the long run economic growth of the economy.

For instance, governments are not best placed to judge what type of training is needed by companies. If companies don't train their workers, it is because the economic rate of return on such training is too small. Companies must be using their scarce resources in more profitable ways (i.e. ways which increase national income more than expenditure on training). Subsidising investment too is economically damaging. It alters the balance between present and future consumption, making future consumption seem more valuable than it is. It encourages capital intensive industry and discriminates against labour intensive industry (because capital intensive industry will receive a large subsidy) without there being any economic justification for this distortion.

As for 'picking winners', government has a long history of throwing money at loss making ventures. Concorde, the shipbuilding industry, and nuclear power, are examples of 'winners' that successive UK governments have picked. Nor has the quality of research in British universities given us a competitive advantage over the Japanese and the Germans.

Education and training Whilst recognising that the state has an important role to play in providing or organising education and training, free market economists would emphasise the importance of choice and private sector involvement in provision. Free market economists would stress that individuals and businesses are often better at determining their own needs than governments. Hence, governments should allow choice, for instance by providing individuals with education vouchers which they can use to buy the education of their choice. When it comes to higher education, governments should be mindful of the need to avoid high levels of taxation. Higher education is very expensive and the main beneficiaries of higher education are those receiving education themselves. This is reflected in the higher wages of graduates.

Therefore, the best way to maximise the numbers of those going into higher education is to avoid government funding which can only be limited, but to embrace schemes where students themselves pay for their own education. Students will also work harder at university and be keen to use the skills they have learnt if they have to pay for that education.

In training, businesses are better placed than government to decide the training needs of their workers. Hence schemes such as the system of TECs in the UK, which place training under the control of businesses and encourage joint funding of training between the public sectors and private sectors, are more likely to yield a high rate of return than government directed schemes.

Investment Investment is best left to private industry. Profit maximising firms have the incentive to direct investment towards the highest yielding projects. If government intervenes, it often has other goals such as reducing unemployment or increasing prosperity in a particular area of the country. Yet for high growth, investment should be directed towards investment projects with high yields.

The size of the state The size of the state should be as small as possible, according to free market economists. The state needs to exist to provide a legal and monetary framework in which the free market can operate. It also needs to provide **public goods** (☞ unit 44). However, state spending crowds out free market spending. £1 spent on a council house is £1 that could have been spent in the private sector. In a free market consumers can choose what they want to buy. Their spending patterns are dictated by their aim to maximise their own utilities. But in the public sector the government forces consumers to accept the bundle of goods and services that the state has decided consumers ought to have. This bundle may be very different from the bundle that consumers would buy if they had a choice in a free market. So the conclusion is that welfare will be greater, the more resources are allocated in private free markets. Moreover, the private sector creates wealth through ongoing investment. Although the state does invest, a much greater proportion of its spending goes on consumption goods and services.

Free trade Free trade and competition are vital for growth. Free trade and competition mean that only those firms which are most efficient will survive. Protectionism and monopoly allows firms to remain in business which are likely to be far from efficient, exploiting the consumer through high prices and selling poor quality products.

Free market economists point to the economic success of countries such as Hong Kong and South Korea which have been exported orientated, succeeding in selling products at the right price and the right quality throughout the world.

Free market ideas are at the heart of **supply side economics** (☞ unit 69). They are also at the heart of free trade and the gains to be made from the exploitation of **comparative advantage** (☞ unit 84-85).

QUESTION 3 This week's report by the Organisation for Economic Co-operation and Development on unemployment in Europe seems to come out strongly in favour of the UK government's economic policy, in particular with regard to its Maastricht opt-out of the social chapter. The basic message from both runs like this: Europe's labour and social costs have become too expensive and its labour laws are too inflexible. In particular, they give employees too many rights and too much job protection.

Consider also the following, however. Germany and Switzerland have some 80 per cent higher labour costs per hour than Britain and Spain, about 40 per cent higher than Italy and France, and four times the labour costs of Portugal. This should make Germany very uncompetitive. But no, Germany still has a very healthy trade surplus with Britain, which has been rising again lately at an alarming rate.

Competitiveness depends on capital investment, R&D, processes, management qualities and workforce attitude and skills, rather than on wage rates - in other words, on overall productivity. UK companies believe they can compensate for their lack of investment by focusing on labour costs. A link between low wage cost, international competitiveness and long-term success seems to me at best unproven and at worst to be more likely the reverse. Germany perhaps needs less regulation to produce a more flexible labour force. However, Britain, coming from the opposite side, needs in many areas more, not less, protection and regulation. It should try to learn from its European neighbours. Being so often in a minority of one in Europe does not happen by coincidence. It is invariable a sign of being wrong.

Source: adapted from an article by Robert Bischof, chairman of Boss Group, now part of Jungheinrich, the German fork lift truck maker, in the *Financial Times*, 10.6.1994.

(a) Explain why over-regulation of the labour market could lead to lower economic growth according to free market economists.
(b) Robert Bischof argues that low wage costs are relatively unimportant in determining competitiveness and growth. Explain his view.
(c) Discuss whether measures to free markets of government regulation are the best way to promote higher economic growth.

Applied economics

Industrial policy

In the 1980s and 1990s, various governments, notably in the UK and the USA, have pursued vigorous free market supply side policies in the belief that economic growth can best be stimulated by reducing government intervention in the market and liberating the energy and dynamism of market forces. This non-interventionist approach has already been discussed at length in unit 69. Here we will consider the alternative strategy of interventionist industrial policy.

It has been argued by some economists that countries such as Japan, Germany and France have experienced higher growth rates than the UK as a direct result of interventionist policies pursued by the governments of these countries. In Japan, for instance, the Ministry of International Trade and Industry (MITI) has used a wide range of policies in the post-war period aimed at transforming Japan into a world industrial super-power. Following Japan's defeat after the Second World War, US economists advised Japan to rebuild industries in which it had a comparative advantage, such as textiles and agriculture. This advice was rejected because it was felt that such a development strategy would create a Japan which would always lag behind the USA and Europe in economic development. Instead, through MITI, a number of key industries were identified which would be the industries of the future. Initially these included ships and steel, and later cars, electrical and electronic goods and computers. MITI then used a battery of policies to stimulate growth in these industries. These included:

- indicative plans for the whole economy, showing how output was set to grow industry by industry in the future;
- tax incentives, precisely targeted and withdrawn once a particular goal had been achieved;
- the creation of state owned companies to undertake research and production in high-risk areas of investment;
- large scale public funding of research and development programmes;
- encouraging co-operation between producers where this would enable Japanese companies to compete more successfully in international markets, even if this discouraged domestic competition;
- encouraging the free exchange of views and ideas between companies, particularly with regard to the fulfilling of state plans for the economy;
- subsidising investment in key industries;
- selective use of import controls, particularly to protect emerging industries.

The relationship between MITI and private industry was an informal one. Firms did not need to follow MITI plans. However, the deference to authority within Japanese society meant that Japanese companies on the whole conformed to the plans laid down by the ministry. MITI seems to have been successful at 'spotting winners' - selecting those industries which are likely to have high growth rates in the future.

In France, there have been a succession of state economic plans in the post-war era. Like the Japanese plans, they are indicative plans, showing how the French government expects output to rise over the next five year period. Again, like the Japanese, the French government has been openly interventionist, supporting key industries, particularly high technology industries, through tax incentives, subsidies, tariffs and quotas and the giving of many other forms of support.

The UK has a long history of free trade, dating back to its dominance in trade in manufactures in the 19th century. Industrial policy has been pursued in a much less coherent manner and with far less conviction than in many other industrial countries. One important aspect of UK industrial policy has been **regional policy** (☞ unit 69), but this has been implemented far more to redirect industry to particular locations in the UK than to stimulate industrial growth overall. The Labour government of 1964-1970 has possibly been the government most committed to interventionism in the post-war period. In 1965, it produced a National Plan which was made irrelevant within months of its issue because the government decided to deflate the economy in order to resolve an exchange rate crisis. It also created the Industrial Reorganisation Corporation (IRC), which encouraged key companies to merge in order to be able to exploit economies of scale more fully and be better equipped to compete in international markets. The IRC was abolished by the incoming Conservative administration in the early 1970s. The Labour administration of 1974-1979 created the National Enterprise Board, a holding company for the various relatively small state owned and partially state owned companies in public hands. Lack of funds prevented it from pursuing an aggressive strategy in, for instance, new technologies and it never had a significant impact on the structure of output before it was dissolved by the Conservative administration after 1979. From this evidence, it would be difficult to argue that UK industrial policy has been a key factor in promoting high growth. Advocates of interventionist industrial policy suggest that industrial policy has never really been given a chance to operate in the post-war period in the UK, and this explains its ineffectiveness. Free market economists suggest that it operated but has been ineffective and therefore government intervention in the market should be radically reduced.

South Korea

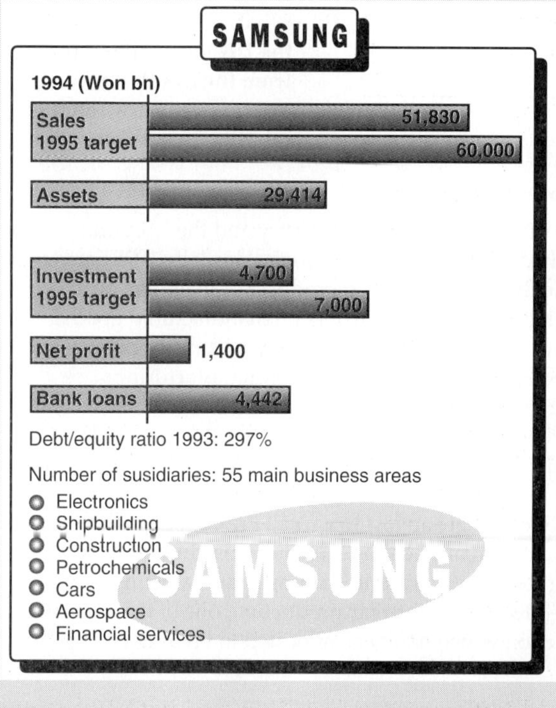

Note: companies in the UK which have a debt to equity ratio of 100 per cent or more are considered to be high risk with the possibility that they might go into bankruptcy.

Source: adapted from *Financial Times*, 2.5.1995.

Figure 101.1 *Performance of the two leading South Korean chaebols*

Table 101.1 *Annual growth in output and expenditure*

% annual growth

	South Korea		Hong Kong		UK	
	1970-80	1980-92	1970-80	1980-92	1970-80	1980-92
GDP	9.6	9.4	9.2	6.7	2.0	2.7
Agriculture	2.7	1.9	-	-	2.4	3.1
Industry	15.2	11.6	-	-	1.1	0.8
of which manufacturing	17.0	11.9	-	-	-0.3	3.5
Services	9.6	9.3	-	-	2.2	2.9
GDP per capita	-	8.5	-	5.5	-	2.4
General government consumption	7.4	6.9	8.3	5.6	2.4	1.2
Private consumption	7.4	8.3	9.0	7.0	1.8	3.6
Gross domestic investment	14.2	12.7	12.1	4.8	0.2	4.5
Exports	23.5	11.9	9.7	5.0	4.4	3.5

Table 101.2 *Distribution of GDP by output and expenditure*

Percentage

	South Korea		Hong Kong		UK	
	1970	1992	1970	1992	1970	1992
By expenditure[1]						
Government consumption	10	63 }	7	9	18	22
Private consumption	75		9	61	62	64
Gross domestic investment	25	37	21	29	20	15
Exports of goods and nonfactor services	14	32	92	144	21	14
Imports of goods and nonfactor services	24	33	88	142	20	16
Gross domestic savings	15	37	25	30	21	14
By output						
Agriculture	26	8	2	0	3	2
Industry	29	45	36	23	44	31
of which manufacturing	21	26	29	16	33	21
Services	45	47	62	77	53	67
Distribution of manufacturing output						
Food, beverages and tobacco	26	11	4	9	13	14
Textiles and clothing	17	11	41	36	9	5
Machinery, transport equipment	11	33	16	21	31	31
Chemicals	11	9	2	2	10	12
Other	36	36	36	33	37	37

1 GDP = General government consumption plus private consumption plus gross domestic investment plus exports minus imports.

Table 101.3 *Percentage of age group enrolled in education*

	South Korea		Hong Kong		UK	
	1970	1991	1970	1991	1970	1991
Primary	99	100	92	-	97	100
Secondary	42	88	36	73	73	86
Tertiary	16	40	11	18	20	28

Source: adapted from World Bank, *World Development Report*.

1979 was a watershed in British economic history. Between the end of the Second World War and 1979, UK governments had been moderately interventionist in their running of the UK economy. After 1979, with the Conservative government of Margaret Thatcher, the government adopted a radical free market approach to running the economy.

Hong Kong is one of the most free market industrialised economies to be found in the world today. It is one of the 'Tiger economies' of East Asia which has enjoyed spectacular growth over the past 30 years.

1. Compare the growth and structure of the South Korean economy with that of the UK and Hong Kong.
2. Contrast the interventionist approach of the South Korean government to the economy with that of Hong Kong and the UK since 1979.
3. What, if anything, could the UK government learn from the South Korean experience if it wanted to raise its growth rate?

The management of the South Korean economy

The South Korean economy has been run on interventionist lines for the past 30 years. Key features of the system are:

- a division of the economy into market segments with companies being allocated marget segments in which they can compete by government;
- the fostering of conglomerate companies called *chaebols*; the two largest of these are Samsung and Hyundai;
- state intervention in industry, with the government giving large loans at low rates of interest to chaebols for investment to meet targets for production and exports set by the government;
- a willingness by the state to get South Korean companies to move into areas of manufacturing which are growing; for instance, in the mid-1980s, Samsung entered the semiconducter chip market despite the fact that it had no record of production in the industry and the USA and Japan had established a technological lead; by 1995 Samsung was the the world's leading producer of memory chips;
- very high protectionist barriers on manufactured goods, whilst at the same time being happy to run current account deficits to import raw materials for manufacturing;
- a willingness by government to penalise *chaebols* which fail to work with the government; between 1992 and 1995, Hyundai lost access to offshore borrowing rights and access to low interest industrial loans from state banks because the founder of the group lost to a rival, President Kim, in the 1992 presidential elections; Hyundai also lost because during the same period its leading rival, Samsung, was allowed to expand into car production, one of the areas of production which had been allocated to Hyundai.

The redistribution of income and wealth

Summary

1. Governments redistribute income and wealth because they believe that this will increase economic welfare.
2. They can do this through fiscal means, raising taxes from the relatively well off to spend on services and benefits for the relatively less well off.
3. Governments can also legislate to promote greater equality, for instance through passing equal pay legislation or imposing minimum wages.
4. Some economists argue that redistribution gives rise to large welfare losses. These include lower economic growth and higher unemployment. They conclude that the poor would be better off in the long term without any redistribution of income and wealth by government.
5. Other economists argue that there is little or no evidence to suggest that economies where government redistributes a considerable proportion of income and wealth perform any differently from more free market economies.
6. Critics of the market approach reply that many groups in society, such as the handicapped and the elderly, can only enjoy rising living standards if government deliberately intervenes in their favour.

The distribution of income and wealth

Free market forces give rise to a particular distribution of income and wealth in society. This distribution is unlikely to be either **efficient** or **equitable**. In units 34 to 47, the causes of inefficiency in a market economy were outlined as were the government policies which might correct this **market failure**. This unit outlines how government might intervene to make the distribution of income and wealth in society more equitable.

The current distribution of income and wealth can be seen by government as undesirable for various reasons.

- **Absolute poverty** (☞ unit 43 for a definition of this and other terms used in this section). Absolute poverty may exist in society. At the extreme, people may be dying on the streets for want of food, shelter or simple medicines.
- **Relative poverty** may be considered too great. The government may consider the gap between rich and poor in society to be too wide.
- **Horizontal equity may not exist**. For instance, men may be paid more for doing the same jobs as women. Workers from ethnic minority groups may be discriminated against in employment and housing.
- The current distribution may be seen to conflict with considerations of **economic efficiency**. For instance, it might be argued that income and wealth differentials need to be increased in order to provide incentives for people to work harder.

The first three of the above arguments suggest that income and wealth differentials should be narrowed. In recent years, however, **supply side economists** (☞ unit 69) have argued strongly that income differentials need to be widened if economic growth is to be increased.

How can governments change the distribution of income and wealth in society?

Government expenditure

Government expenditure can be used to alter the distribution of income. One obvious way is for government to provide monetary benefits to those requiring financial support. Social security and National Insurance benefits now account for over 30 per cent of UK government expenditure.

However, governments may wish to target help more precisely. For instance, an increase in the old age pension will not necessarily relieve absolute poverty amongst

QUESTION 1 The government is proposing to move towards a system of road pricing in the UK in an attempt to solve problems of congestion on British roads. There are a variety of possible technologies available which might be used, one of which is a meter installed in a car which would read signals from road side beacons or gantries across the road. There are also a variety of possible metering tariffs. One possibility is that road users will be charged for the use of roads only when roads are congested or likely to be congested. For instance, motorists might be charged to use main roads into town and city centres at peak rush hour times. Some cities might charge motorists to use roads in the centre at any time of the day. Congested motorways, such as the M25, might be tolled for much of the day.

(a) To what extent is access to a road system which is free at the point of use road system an issue of equality of opportunity?

(b) How would the distribution of income change if the government imposed congestion metering whilst at the same time: (i) cutting the basic rate of income tax by the amount raised in the new road taxes; (ii) using the money raised from the new road taxes to subsidise public transport?

some old people. They may live in houses which are damp and cold and be unable or unwilling to pay considerable sums of money to remedy the situation. So the government may choose to spend money on housing for the elderly, for instance providing low rent housing or offering renovation grants for owner-occupied property. Similarly, governments may choose to help children in need not by increasing child benefit but by offering free clothes or food coupons.

Another important area of government activity is the provision of goods and services which give citizens equality of opportunity in society. The Beveridge Report of 1942 argued that citizens should have access to a minimum standard of health care, housing and education as well as minimum incomes and employment. Some argue that education, housing and health care are no different from cars or holidays. If people have a high income, they should be able to buy better education for their children and better health care for themselves, just as they can buy better cars or more expensive holidays. Others argue that all people should have equal access to the **same** education and health care because these are basic to any standard of living in a modern industrialised economy. Private education and private health care should not be available to those who are capable of affording them.

Taxation

The taxation system plays a crucial role in determining the distribution of income in society. Taxes can be **progressive, regressive or proportional**.

QUESTION 2 Between 1979 and 1994, the government introduced a number of tax changes. These included:

- in 1979, a reduction in the highest rate of income tax from 83 per cent to 60 per cent and a 2p cut in the standard rate of income tax, accompanied by an increase in the standard rate of VAT from 8 to 15 per cent;
- in 1987, a reduction in the highest rate of income tax from 60 per cent to 40 per cent and a further 2p cut in the standard rate of income tax;
- between 1990 and 1993, the replacement of the domestic rating system, a tax on property, by the council tax, another tax on property but which effectively reduced the tax on high priced properties and increased it for low priced properties. At the same time, VAT was raised by $2^1/_2$ per cent to reduce average tax bills;
- in 1994, the imposition of 8 per cent VAT on domestic fuel such as gas and electricity;
- from 1994, the imposition of a yearly 3 per cent real increase in tax on petrol;
- from 1994, the reduction in value of tax relief on the interest on mortgages.

Explain the likely effect of these tax changes on the distribution of income in the UK.

- Income tax, capital gains tax and inheritance tax are broadly progressive (i.e. the higher the level of earnings of the taxpayer, the higher the proportion of income paid in that tax).
- VAT is broadly proportional.
- Excise duties and the council tax are regressive.

If there is to be a significant redistribution of income from the rich to the poor, the tax system has to be progressive in nature. The government needs to tax away a higher proportion of income from the well off than from the poor. On the other hand, if the government wishes to widen income and wealth differentials, it should make the tax system less progressive or more regressive.

Legislation

The government may alter the distribution of income directly through its spending and taxation decisions. However, it can also influence the behaviour of private economic agents through legislation. For instance, governments may choose to introduce minimum wage legislation (☞ unit 52), forcing employers to increase rates of pay for the lowest paid workers. They may also choose to make discrimination illegal through measures such as equal pay legislation, or they may force employers to provide benefits such as sickness benefit, pensions and medical care for their employees, or redundancy payments. They may attempt to raise the incomes of the low paid and the unemployed through effective retraining or helping workers to be more mobile geographically.

The costs of redistribution

Intervention in the economy may well lead to higher economic welfare for some, but it may also lead to lower economic welfare for others.

There is an obvious cost to those in society who lose directly from increased taxation. Some economists argue that any taxation results in a loss of freedom. The taxpayer loses the ability to choose how to allocate those scarce resources which are now being expropriated by the state. Therefore in a free society taxation should be kept to an absolute minimum. On the other hand, **the law of diminishing marginal utility** (☞ unit 14) would suggest that taking resources away from an affluent individual to give to a poor person will lead to an increase in the combined utility of the two individuals. The loss of utility by the rich person will be less than the gain in utility by the poor person. It is difficult to show this conclusively because it is not possible to make direct utility comparisons between individuals.

Classical or supply side economists would suggest that redistribution involves heavy costs in terms of economic growth and employment. Raising income tax rates lowers the incentives of those in employment to work (☞ unit 69) thus reducing the rate at which the aggregate supply curve shifts to the right. Classical economists would also argue that redistribution reduces the incentive of those out of work to find jobs. High unemployment benefits can make it more worthwhile to remain unemployed than to gain employment. This raises the natural rate of unemployment and depresses the level of output in the economy. Minimum wage legislation and equal pay legislation may lead to a loss of employment. Economic theory suggests that if firms are forced to pay higher wages, they will employ fewer staff. High tax rates can lead to a flight of capital and labour from an economy. Individual entrepreneurs may choose to leave the country, taking their money and skills with them. Firms may choose to locate abroad to take advantage of lower tax rates, leading to a loss of domestic jobs and income.

There is also a host of other distortions which become endemic in the system. For instance, some have argued that subsidies to home owners through mortgage income tax relief have led to too great an investment in the housing stock of the country at the expense of investment in wealth-creating industry. Provision of free children's school clothing can lead to some parents selling the clothing immediately and using the money for other purposes. High taxes lead to the growth of tax avoidance and evasion where a considerable amount of resources are devoted to circumventing tax legislation.

QUESTION 3

Table 102.1 *Shares of total income tax liability*

United Kingdom — Percentages

	1976-77	1981-82	1986-87	1992-93
Top 1 per cent	11	11	14	15
Top 5 per cent	25	25	29	32
Top 10 per cent	35	35	39	43
Next 40 per cent	45	46	43	43
Lowest 50 per cent	20	19	16	14

Source: adapted from CSO, *Social Trends.*

During the 1980s, rates of income tax were lowered. The highest rate of tax was reduced from 83 per cent to 40 per cent, whilst the basic rate of tax came down from 33 per cent to 25 per cent.

(a) Explain why these reductions in tax rates may have produced the change in the share of tax paid by different income groups as shown in Table 102.1.
(b) How might a lowering of income tax rates benefit (a) the better off and (b) the less well off?

The role of government

Free market economists argue that the costs of government intervention are extremely large. They are so large in fact that any possible welfare benefits resulting from the redistribution of income from the rich to the poor are far outweighed by the welfare losses which result. They argue that economic growth will increase if taxation is low, if government regulation of the economic activities of the private sector is minimal and if state production of goods and services is kept to the barest minimum. The poor may lose out because there will be little in the way of state benefits. But they will be more than compensated for this through increased economic growth. The wealth generated by the better off in society will trickle down to the less fortunate. For instance, the poor would be better off receiving 10 per cent of a 'national cake' of £20 bn than 15 per cent of a cake of only £10 bn.

The argument that the poor would be better off if income differentials were wider rather than narrower is dependent upon a number of propositions:

- that being better off is a matter of absolute quantities rather than relative quantities;
- it must be true that high marginal income tax rates are a disincentive to work and to enterprise;
- a generous benefit system must act as a disincentive to work;
- there must be a mechanism through which increased wealth in society will benefit not just the rich but also the poor, particularly those who for whatever reason are unable to work.

This could be the case for many employed people but there is no mechanism apart from charity in a free market economy for groups such as the handicapped, the sick and the elderly to benefit from increased prosperity enjoyed by the rest of society.

QUESTION 4 In 1989, the Methodist Conference, the governing body of the Methodist church, attacked the government's 'divisive' social and economic policies which victimised the poor. In reply, the then Prime Minister, Margaret Thatcher, stated: 'Over the past decade living standards have increased at all points of the income distribution - that includes the poorest.'

'After allowing for inflation, a married man with two children who is in the lowest tenth of earnings has seen his take-home pay go up by 12.5 per cent'.

'Of course some have, through their own endeavours and initiative, raised their living standards further. They are also paying more in taxes, and those who earn most are contributing a higher proportion of the total that government receives from income tax'.

'You equate wealth with selfishness. But it is only through the creation of wealth that poverty can be assisted.'

'Our task is to enlarge opportunity so that more and more people may prosper.'

Over the 1980s, the distribution of income became more unequal. Explain how Margaret Thatcher defended this in her reply to the Methodist Conference.

Applied economics

Redistributive policies in the UK

The Welfare State, whose foundations were laid down by Clement Attlee's Labour administration of 1945-51, should ensure that every citizen of the UK enjoys a minimum standard of living. To achieve this, higher income earners are taxed more than lower income earners and the money is used to provide a variety of benefits in kind and in cash.

Table 102.2 is a CSO (Central Statistical Office) estimate of how this redistribution affects incomes. It is based on figures from the Family Expenditure Survey, a yearly sample of approximately 7 000 households in the UK. The households have been split into quintile groups (i.e. fifths) according to original incomes of households. For instance, the 1 435 households which form the bottom fifth of households ranked on original income had an original income of just £1 920 per year. The top fifth of households, the 1 436 households with an original income of £39 370, earned on average 21 times as much.

These sharp inequalities are reduced through the effects of the tax and benefit system. Benefits in cash, contributory (i.e. National Insurance benefits) and non-contributory

Table 102.2 *Redistribution of income through taxes and benefits, 1993*

£ per year and percentages

	Quintile groups of households[1]					
	Bottom fifth	Next fifth	Middle fifth	Next fifth	Top fifth	All households
Average per household						
Wages and salaries	950	3 210	9 640	16 210	29 140	11 830
Imputed income from benefits in kind	10	10	80	300	920	270
Self-employment income	400	580	1 140	1 630	4 160	1 580
Occupational pensions, annuities	240	680	1 220	1 570	1 980	1 140
Investment income	190	360	570	880	2 620	930
Other income	140	180	210	260	550	270
Total original income	1 920	5 020	12 860	20 850	39 370	16 000
plus Benefits in cash						
Contributory	1 780	2 300	1 640	1 100	670	1 500
Non-contributory	2 670	2 050	1 430	830	390	1 470
Gross income	6 380	9 370	15 930	22 780	40 420	18 980
less Income tax[2] and NIC[3]	230	650	2 080	3 870	8 590	3 080
less Local taxes[4] (gross)	560	550	620	660	730	620
Disposable income	5 590	8 170	13 240	18 250	31 100	15 270
less Indirect taxes	1 710	1 950	3 100	3 790	4 900	3 090
Post-tax income	3 870	6 220	10 140	14 460	26 200	12 180
plus Benefits in kind						
Education	1 630	1 080	1 370	1 030	780	1 180
National Health Service	1 750	1 750	1 570	1 360	1 190	1 520
Housing subsidy	80	90	40	20	10	50
Travel subsidies	50	50	50	60	90	60
School meals and welfare milk	100	30	10	10	10	30
Final income	7 480	9 220	13 190	16 940	28 270	15 020
Percentage of households in group which are:						
Retired	39	47	24	15	7	26
Non-retired with 1-2 adults and no children	19	18	30	39	57	32
Non-retired with 1-2 adults plus children	36	26	31	29	24	35
Non-retired, 3 or more adults, with or without children	6	9	16	16	12	12

1. Equivalised disposable income has been used for ranking the households into quintile groups.
2. After tax relief at source on mortgage interest and life assurance premiums.
3. Employees' National Insurance contributions.
4. Gross council tax, community charge, rates and water charges. Rates in Northern Ireland.

Source: adapted from *Central Statistical Office, Social Trends.*

Table 102.3 *Taxes as a proportion of income, 1993*

	Bottom fifth	Next fifth	Middle fifth	Next fifth	Top fifth	All households
Tax rate as percentage of original income						
Income tax, NIC and local taxes	41	24	21	22	25	23
Income tax, NIC and local taxes and indirect taxes	130	63	45	40	36	42
Tax rate as a percentage of gross income						
Income tax, NIC and local taxes	12	13	17	20	23	19
Income tax, NIC and local taxes and indirect taxes	39	34	36	37	35	36

Source: adapted from CSO, *Social Trends*.

benefits increase the incomes of the bottom quintile of income earners from £1 920 to £6 380 a year. Whilst many benefits are targeted on low income households, some benefits are universal benefits, available to all whatever their income. The most important universal benefit is child benefit.

Benefits have to be paid for by taxes and National Insurance contributions (NICs). The tax system is often considered to be **progressive** (☞ unit 47). However, as Table 102.2 and 102.3 show, it is in practice arguably regressive. The indirect tax system is clearly regressive. For instance, the bottom fifth of households paid 27 per cent of their gross income in regressive taxes whilst the top fifth paid only 12 per cent. Direct taxes, including the council tax, are progressive for the bottom 60 per cent of households if income is measured as original income, but regressive over the rest of the income range. Direct taxes are regressive throughout the income range if income is measured as gross income. Overall, the tax system is progressive if income is taken as original income.

However, the system is roughly proportional if income is measured as gross income. Households receive a variety of benefits in kind. The amount received depends on the composition of the household. For instance, the bottom fifth of households, receiving an average £3 610 in benefits, comprise mainly retired people or families with children. Hence, they receive large benefits in the form of free education and health care. Nearly 3 in 5 of the top fifth of households are non-retired adults with no children. Hence, the benefit they get from the NHS and from the education system is less. Their average benefits only total £2 080.

Overall, whilst the top fifth of households received 21 times the amount of original income compared to the bottom fifth of households, in terms of final income the ratio was only 3.8 times. So it would seem that the Welfare State is successful to some extent in reducing inequalities in society. What the statistics fail to show is the growing inequality in society since 1979 which has left the bottom 20 per cent of households little better off in real terms over the period, but has allowed the top 20 per cent to increase their real incomes by over 50 per cent.

Poverty in the UK

Members of a private think tank have come up with a number of different ways to reduce poverty in the UK.

- Impose a minimum wage of £4.00 per hour.
- Raise the state old age pension and the limits below which pensioners can claim other benefits such as housing benefit, by £30 per week per pensioner on average.
- Raise child benefit by an average of £10 per week per recipient.
- Raise the Job Seekers' Allowance by an average of £30 per week per worker.
- Cut the standard rate of income tax by 2p in the pound.
- Cut the higher rate of income tax from 40p in the pound to 30p in the pound.
- Create half a million places on government work schemes for the long term unemployed.
- Provide free nursery care and creche facilities between 8 in the morning and 6 in the evening.
- Abolish National Insurance contributions (both employer and employee) for part-time workers working less than 15 hours per week.
- Cut all benefits to workers able to work but not in work.

Table 102.4 *Households moving between different income groupings, 1991 to 1992*
Great Britain — Percentages

	Income fell 4 or more deciles	Income fell 2-3 deciles	Income stable	Income rose 2-3 deciles	Income rose 4 or more deciles
1991 income grouping					
Lowest decile	0.0	0.0	71.1	21.2	7.7
2nd decile	0.0	0.0	82.2	13.5	4.3
3rd decile	0.0	11.5	69.0	13.9	5.6
4th decile	0.0	14.9	68.3	13.3	3.6
5th decile	6.0	10.6	65.9	16.2	1.3
6th decile	8.1	10.6	68.0	10.9	2.3
7th decile	8.8	11.8	69.3	10.0	0.0
8th decile	7.1	11.2	75.4	6.3	0.0
9th decile	10.0	9.6	80.3	0.0	0.0
Highest decile	7.3	6.3	86.4	0.0	0.0
All households	4.7	8.6	73.6	10.6	2.5

Note: The table shows the percentage of households which moved from one decile group (tenth of the population) ranked by income to another decide group. For instance, 7.3 per cent of households which were in the top 10 per cent of income in 1991 has fallen to 6th decile or lower in 1992. In contrast, 7.7 per cent of households in the poorest bottom decile in 1991 saw their income rise by at least 4 deciles to the fifth decile or higher in 1992. Approximately 75 per cent of households saw no change in their decile group between 1991 and 1992. So 25 per cent moved up or down at least one decile.

Table 102.5 *Percentage of each group whose income is below 50 per cent of average UK income, 1979-1991/92 (net of housing costs).*

	1979	1991-92
Self-employed	15	24
Single or couple, both in full-time work	1	2
Couple, one in full-time work, one in part time	2	5
Couple, one in full-time work, one not working	6	17
One or more in part-time work	15	32
Head or spouse aged 60 or more	20	36
Head or spouse unemployed	58	76
Others	35	62
All economic types (%)	9	25
All economic types (millions)	5.0	13.9

Source: Department of Social Security, Households Below Average Income: a Statistical Analysis 1979-1991-92.

Table 102.6 *The scale of social protection in UK and EU countries*

	UK	EU average per country
As percentage of average earnings in the country		
Sickness and invalidity benefit	28	69
Unemployment benefits, first 12 months, typical worker	23	61
Unemployment benefits for 18 year old	18	25
State pensions	44	75
Social expenditure per head in ECU converted at purchasing power rates	3 700	4 000

Source: Commission of the Communities, (1991) *Final Report on the Second European Poverty Programme*, 1985-89, COM (91) 29 Final.

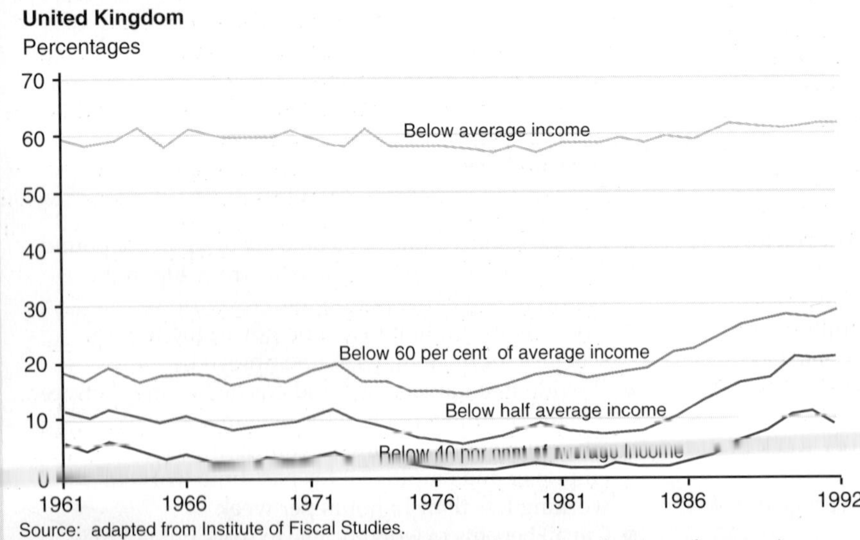

Source: adapted from Institute of Fiscal Studies.
Figure 102.1 *Percentage of people whose income is below various fractions of average income*

You have been asked to evaluate the various proposals for reducing poverty put forward by the private think tank. In your report:

1. **outline the characteristics of poverty in the UK;**
2. **take each proposal, explain why it might have an impact on poverty and assess its advantages and disadvantages;**
3. **put forward a proposal of your own for the relief of poverty and assess its costs and benefits;**
4. **assess which of the proposals, or combination of proposals, is most likely to reduce poverty without imposing too great a cost on the economy.**

The limits of government policy

Summary

1. Government policy is aimed at achieving high growth, low unemployment, price stability and a balance of payments equilibrium.
2. In the Keynesian model, trade-offs exist between high growth and low unemployment, and price stability and a balance of payments equilibrium.
3. Keynesian economists favour the use of fiscal policy to influence the level of aggregate demand in the economy. It can also be used to stimulate investment, training and other supply side variables.
4. Devaluation and prices and incomes policies are also sometimes advocated by Keynesian economists although there are doubts about the long run effectiveness of these policies.
5. Monetarist economists argue that inflation is a monetary phenomenon and can be reduced through control of the money supply.
6. Classical and supply side economists argue that there are no long run trade-offs between macro-economic policy variables. A high economic growth rate can be achieved with price stability and a current account equilibrium if markets are able to adjust to their free market equilibrium levels.

Goals and instruments

It is generally argued that governments have four main macro-economic policy goals:

- to maintain full employment;
- to ensure price stability;
- to achieve a high level of economic growth;
- to keep the balance of payments in equilibrium.

Sometimes it is also argued that governments have a major responsibility to ensure an equitable distribution of income and wealth, whilst, in the 1990s, it is possible that environmental objectives may come to rank in equal importance to these other goals.

Government can achieve these goals by using a wide range of policy instruments, which have been discussed extensively in previous units. These include:

- fiscal policy - e.g. changing tax rates, the size and distribution of government spending and public borrowing;
- monetary policy - e.g. controlling the growth of the money supply, changing interest rates, altering terms of credit;
- exchange rate policy - revaluing or devaluing the currency;
- supply side policies - some of these, such as lowering marginal tax rates on income, could be classified under fiscal policy, but others include trade union reform, competition policy, privatisation and deregulation, and reform of financial markets.

Demand management policies (☞ unit 68) aim to influence the level of aggregate demand in the economy, whilst supply side policies (☞ unit 69) aim to influence the level of aggregate supply.

Competing economic models of the economy produce radically different policy prescriptions to the problems which beset economies. In this unit, the limitations of government policy will be examined within the framework of the different models outlined in previous units.

The Keynesian model

The Keynesian model of the economy suggests that, in the UK at least, governments face difficult trade-offs between inflation and growth on the one hand and unemployment and balance of payments equilibrium on the other. Figure 103.1 illustrates this. The economy starts off at less than full employment at output level OA. The government decides to reflate the economy by expanding aggregate demand. Traditional demand management techniques would see cuts in taxes and increases in public spending, resulting in an increase in the budget deficit or a reduction in the budget surplus. Cuts in interest rates or relaxations in credit or hire purchase controls might be used to reinforce this. Via the multiplier process, there will be an expansion in aggregate demand, pushing the aggregate demand curve in Figure 103.1 to AD_2.

This shift in the AD curve has returned the economy to full employment at OB. The growth rate in the economy will have increased, simply because GDP will have gone up faster than it would have done if aggregate demand had remained at AD_1 (note that, strictly speaking, this is not economic growth but rather economic recovery - economic growth can only result from increases in aggregate supply, the productive potential of the economy ☞ unit 99). However, the price level will have risen from OE to OF and the current account on the balance of payments will have moved from a surplus of JK to a deficit of KL.

Note that the expansion in demand was greater than the minimum needed to secure full employment. Government only needed to increase aggregate demand to AD_3 to secure its objective of returning the economy to full employment. Keynesian economists have long recognised that it is difficult for governments to 'fine-tune' the economy to an exact position.

On Figure 103.1, it is impossible for the government to achieve simultaneously full employment and a current account equilibrium with price stability. The full employment level of income, OB, coincides with a current account deficit and a rise in prices from OE. Keynesian economists have suggested a variety of ways around this possible problem.

Devaluation This would increase exports and reduce

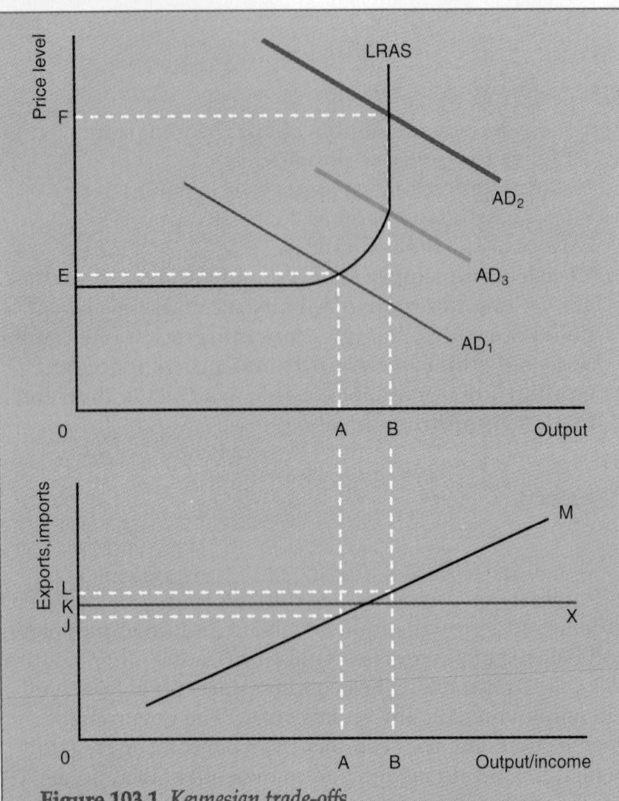

Figure 103.1 *Keynesian trade-offs*
If the economy is at output level OA, it will be below full employment but the current account will be in surplus. If the government expands aggregate demand from AD_1, it will reduce unemployment but increase inflation and lead to a current account deficit.

imports, returning the economy to equilibrium on the current account. However, as many Keynesian economists would recognise, this in itself produces trade-offs. Devaluation will lead to higher import prices and increased aggregate demand because of increased demand for exports and import substitutes. This in turn will lead to cost-push and demand-pull inflation, eroding the competitive gain from devaluation. Some Keynesians would accept that devaluation is likely to lead to current account gains only in the short to medium term. In the longer term, say after 5 years, the increased inflation induced by devaluation will have wiped out any competitive gain.

Supply side measures Measures which simultaneously increase output and stimulate exports could be used. For instance, exporters could receive subsidies in the form of cheap loans, foreign exchange insurance, and reduced tax rates. Alternatively, if unemployment was mainly structural rather than cyclical, government could use regional policies or training policies to reduce unemployment, and this could well result in more exports and fewer imports than if the government adopted expansionary demand side policies.

Prices and incomes policies The inflationary impact of an increase in demand could be reduced by the use of prices and incomes policies. Whilst Keynesian economists would accept that the three periods of prices and incomes policy in the 1960s and 1970s in the UK failed in their objective to reduce long term inflation, there are still many Keynesians who believe that a more sophisticated form of incomes policy (for instance, taxing wage increases above a pay norm) would work.

Keynesians are generally sceptical of the ability of the labour market, by itself, to restore full employment. Doing nothing, when output is below full employment, at OA in Figure 103.1, might lead eventually to more jobs as workers accept real wage cuts, pricing themselves back into work, but the process is long and difficult. Doing nothing is not an appropriate policy response according to Keynesians.

Equally, whilst they agree that long term growth can only be achieved through supply side growth, they would argue that measures such as cutting marginal tax rates on income or reducing unemployment benefit will have little impact on incentives to work. The key to supply side growth is stimulating greater investment, both in physical and human capital. So using a high interest rate policy to curb inflation is more likely to be damaging to growth because high interest rates discourage investment more than, say, increasing income tax.

QUESTION 1 **A business plan for Britain**

Labour will move Britain into the new industrial era of high technology and high skills. A Labour government will:

- manage the economy sensibly in order to avoid the wasteful boom-bust pattern of the Conservative government and lay the foundations for sustainable growth;
- liberate the energies of our people by putting education and training at the heart of our programme;
- encourage finance to increase long-term investment in industry;
- develop the new technologies which will modernise our economy and provide new opportunities for all;
- support small business and promote the growth of medium sized enterprises;
- empower the regions to promote economic growth;
- develop new partnerships between the private and public sector which enable the speedy development of our nation's infrastructure.

Source: The Labour Party, *Rebuilding the Economy*, 1994.

(a) To what extent could Labour Party policy outlined in the 'Business Plan for Britain' be described as 'Keynesian'?
(b) Evaluate whether the Labour Party, in its Plan, might be putting too great an emphasis on securing future growth and not enough on maintaining low inflation.

Monetarist, classical and supply side models

Just as there are as many Keynesian beliefs as there are Keynesian economists, so too there are many differences in thinking between economists who would classify themselves as 'monetarist', or 'classical' or 'supply siders'. These last three terms refer to three different strands of beliefs amongst non-Keynesian economists.

- Monetarism refers to the belief that inflation is caused by increases in the money supply over and above the real rate of growth in the economy (☞ units 76 and 94).
- Classical economists tend to believe that free markets are highly efficient, whereas government intervention in the market tends to lead to economic inefficiency.
- Supply side economists are economists who believe that increased growth in the economy can only be secured through the freeing of markets from government intervention. This can be achieved through micro-economic policy and not through the traditional macro-economic demand management policies popularised by Keynesian economists.

Classical economics and monetarism have a long history. The belief that the duty of government was to protect property rights, maintain a stable currency and provide public goods whilst leaving the production of all other goods and services to free markets was known as **laissez-faire** in the 19th century.

Unemployment Classical economists, faced with the unemployment depicted in Figure 103.1, would argue that the government should not directly intervene. They believe that the long run aggregate supply curve is vertical, as in Figure 103.2. If the economy is below full employment at A, then free market forces will return the economy to equilibrium at B. In the labour market, unemployment will force workers to accept real wage cuts, and thus workers will be priced back into jobs. The cuts in wage rates will mean that the short run aggregate supply (drawn on the assumption of constant wage rates) will shift downwards from $SRAS_1$ to $SRAS_2$. Therefore, there is no long run trade-off between unemployment and inflation as Keynesians would suggest.

Inflation If there is inflation in the economy, this can be reduced through restricting the growth of the money supply. This will have a short run cost. Reducing the rate of growth of the money supply will be initially deflationary. Cuts in money supply growth will, via the transmission mechanism, initially affect output and therefore increase unemployment. But in the longer term, the economy will return to equilibrium with unemployment unaffected at its natural rate. Fiscal policy must be subordinated to monetary policy if the government is to achieve money supply control.

Growth Long term growth can only be raised through increased growth in aggregate supply. If unemployment is considered too high, then again this is a supply side problem. A fall in the natural rate of unemployment and an increase in growth can only be achieved through the successful implementation of supply side policies. Fiscal policy should therefore be used to influence not macro-economic demand, as Keynesians suggest, but micro-economic decisions by workers, firms and consumers.

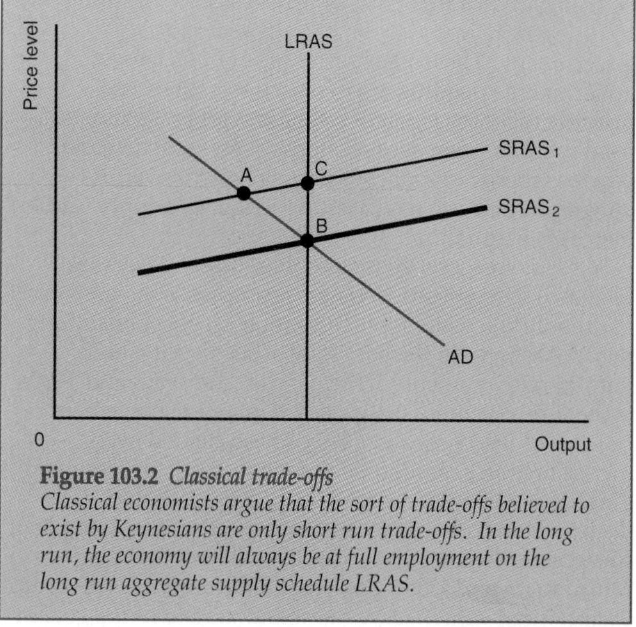

Figure 103.2 *Classical trade-offs*
Classical economists argue that the sort of trade-offs believed to exist by Keynesians are only short run trade-offs. In the long run, the economy will always be at full employment on the long run aggregate supply schedule LRAS.

The balance of payments Classical economists argue that the current account can largely be left to itself if, first, foreign exchange markets are free and, second, a current account deficit is not being caused by excess government spending. If foreign exchange markets are free, the currency will find its own level and markets will ensure that undesirable current account deficits are rectified through depreciations. Excess government spending, however, can hamper this. We know that injections must equal withdrawals, so $I + G + X = S + M + T$. If I and S are roughly equal, then M - X, the current account balance, must equal G - T, the government budget balance. If the government budget is in deficit, this must cause a current account deficit. So the elimination of government budget deficits is important if trade deficits are to be eliminated too.

Trade-offs According to classical economists, the trade-offs which Keynesian economists believe to exist are, if anything, only short term trade-offs. If the economy were at A in Figure 103.2, an increase in aggregate demand would restore the economy to full employment but at the unnecessary cost of higher inflation. Demand management techniques have other limitations.

If the economy is already at B, increased aggregate demand, whilst initially leading to increased output and lower unemployment, will in the longer term be purely inflationary. The economy will return to the natural rate of unemployment at C shown by the vertical long run aggregate supply curve. In the process, government may have increased its share of spending in GDP. This increase in government spending will have resulted from a fall in private sector spending - the process known as **crowding out**.

Demand management will only have its desired effect if the monetary stance of the government changes. For instance, increased government spending which is financed by genuine borrowing will have no effect on aggregate demand. Increased public sector spending will be matched by a reduction in private sector spending resulting from loans by the private sector to the government. The expansionary effect of increased government spending arises only if it is financed by printing the money needed. So fiscal policy cannot be used to influence macro-economic aggregate demand, whereas monetary policy is dangerously powerful - dangerous because increases in the money supply lead to increases in inflation.

Some monetarists go further than this and say that increases in aggregate demand as a result of expansionary fiscal policy actually have the long term effect of shifting the LRAS curve to the left. They argue that the high natural rate of unemployment of the late 1980s and 1990s is the direct result of misguided demand management policies of the 1960s and 1970s. These created ever increasing rates of inflation to maintain full employment. Periods of deflation designed to combat inflation destroyed industry and jobs permanently (the principle of **hysteresis**, the idea that a variable will not necessarily return to its previous value when other variables revert to their normal value). Only the abandonment of the goal of full employment by the Conservative government from 1979 prevented yet more damaging cycles of boom and boost, with the natural rate of unemployment spiralling ever upwards.

QUESTION 2 The Conservative Party won four successive general elections in 1979, 1983, 1987 and 1992. In its election manifestoes, the Party put forward a consistent set of economic policies for the 1980s and 1990s. It argued that the foremost economic priority was the control of inflation. This could be achieved through the use of monetary policy, either by controlling the growth of the money supply directly or through interest rate policy.

It argued that the rejuvenation of the economy could be achieved through supply side policies which would liberate markets. Specific policies to achieve this included privatisation, reform of trade union and other labour laws, a lowering of income tax rates and reform of the benefits system.

It rejected the idea that unemployment could be reduced permanently through increased government spending or increased government borrowing. Permanent jobs in the economy would only be created through investment and the creation of companies.

(a) To what extent could Conservative Party policy outlined in the passage be described as 'classical' or 'monetarist' in its approach?
(b) Explain why, on economic grounds, the Conservative Party rejected using demand management techniques to reduce unemployment.

Applied economics

The Lawson Boom, 1987-1991

The severe recession of 1979-1981 was followed by a period of relative tranquillity. Although unemployment remained stubbornly high at over 3 million, the current account was in surplus, inflation was low at around 5 per cent and growth averaged 3 per cent per annum during 1982-1986.

However, in 1987, as Table 103.1 shows, the rate of growth of the economy began to increase, and by the fourth quarter, the year on year increase was 4.2 per cent. There then followed a boom in the economy, now called the 'Lawson Boom' after Nigel Lawson, the then Chancellor of the Exchequer. Did the Lawson boom show the traditional short term trade-offs predicted by economic theory?

Table 103.1 shows that:
- inflation increased from 3.9 per cent in the first quarter of 1987 to 10.4 per cent in the third quarter of 1990;
- unemployment fell, from 3.2 million in the first quarter of 1987 to £1.6 million by 1990;
- the current account on the balance of payments slumped seriously into deficit, from being broadly in balance in 1986 to an annual deficit of around £22.5bn in 1989.

By the end of 1990, the economy was going into recession. Growth in output had stagnated, unemployment was rising, but inflation was falling and the current account deficit was falling.

The Lawson boom was unlikely to have been caused by government fiscal policy. The PSBR (Public Sector Borrowing Requirement) was turned into a PSDR (Public Sector Debt Repayment) in 1987. The Budget of 1988 did see cuts in income tax rates from 60 per cent to 40 per cent for higher rate taxpayers, and from 27 per cent to 25 per cent for standard rate taxpayers. However, in Keynesian terms, the budget was still broadly neutral. What it did do perhaps was to encourage people to believe that their incomes would continue to rise at a high level for the foreseeable future, and companies to believe that the boom in spending would continue. This then increased the willingness of both consumers and industry to borrow money to finance consumption and investment.

The most likely cause of the Lawson boom was loose monetary policy in the mid-1980s. This fuelled a consumer spending boom, based on increased borrowing by the personal sector. The most visible effect of this was to send house prices rocketing throughout the country. But everything from car sales to expenditure on carpets and curtains and toys saw record increases as well. By mid-1988, it was apparent that the economy was over-heating and that inflation was on the increase whilst the current account deficit was becoming unsustainable. The Chancellor, Nigel Lawson, responded by doubling interest rates within the next 12 months. Keynesian economists doubted whether raising interest rates would be effective in reducing inflationary pressures. They argued for tax increases. It took some time for high interest rates to work their way through the economy. The immediate effect was to bring the house price spiral to a complete stop. In some areas of the country, such as London and East Anglia, house prices soon began to fall. This brought about a slump in sales of low cost furniture and carpets as fewer people changed houses. By the beginning of 1990, it was clear that the high interest rate policy was reducing growth. Indeed, growth completely faltered mid-year and then from the last quarter GDP began to fall. It carried on falling for 8 quarters, the longest recession since the 1930s. Not surprisingly, unemployment rose rapidly and inflation fell to its lowest rate since the 1960s.

The economy was then in a traditional short term recession, with unemployment high and growth low or negative, but with inflation low too. The only difference was that the current account on the balance of payments had not gone into surplus, but had improved considerably since the height of the boom. In the subsequent recovery of 1993-95, unemployment fell, growth picked up, but so too did inflation. The current balance improved too, contrary to what might be expected in a recovery, but this was probably due to the more than 10 per cent devaluation of the pound following Britain's exit from the ERM in September 1992.

Table 103.1 *Inflation, unemployment, growth and the current account balance, 1986-1990*

		Percentage change over previous 12 months		Millions	£ millions
		Inflation	Real GDP	Unemployment	Current account balance
1986	Q1	5.0	3.3	3.4	+ 455
	Q2	2.8	2.9	3.3	- 422
	Q3	2.7	4.0	3.3	- 1 034
	Q4	3.5	4.8	3.2	+ 130
1987	Q1	3.9	4.3	3.2	- 152
	Q2	4.2	4.0	3.1	- 1 347
	Q3	4.3	4.7	2.9	- 1 805
	Q4	4.1	4.2	2.8	- 1 679
1988	Q1	3.3	5.6	2.7	- 3 741
	Q2	4.3	4.7	2.5	- 3 709
	Q3	5.5	4.4	2.3	- 4 042
	Q4	6.5	4.1	2.1	- 5 125
1989	Q1	7.8	3.0	2.1	- 5 220
	Q2	8.2	2.6	1.9	- 6 089
	Q3	7.7	1.4	1.8	- 7 276
	Q4	7.6	0.9	1.6	- 3 927
1990	Q1	7.7	1.0	1.6	- 6 383
	Q2	9.6	0.0	1.6	- 6 279
	Q3	10.4	0.0	1.7	- 4 138
	Q4	10.0	-1.1	1.8	- 1 468
1991	Q1	8.6	-2.3	1.9	- 3 848
	Q2	6.0	-3.1	2.2	- 1 548
	Q3	4.8	-2.6	2.4	- 3 014
	Q4	4.2	-1.8	2.5	+ 234
1992	Q1	4.1	-1.7	2.6	- 3 156
	Q2	4.1	-1.3	2.7	- 3 484

Source: adapted from CSO, *Economic Trends Annual Supplement*; CSO, *Monthly Digest of Statistics.*

Government policy, 1992

The date is 17 September 1992. The day before, sterling had been suspended from the ERM after having joined in October 1990. The value of the pound has fallen over 10 per cent. Your task is to write a report for the Chancellor, Norman Lamont, advising him how government policy should now change given that the pound is free to float. Use the data in Table 103.1 in the Applied Economics section of this unit as well as Tables 103.2 and 103.3. In your report:

(a) describe the current state of the economy - use the second quarter 1992 figures as your most up to date data;

(b) discuss what your policy objectives should be - (for instance, is the most important policy objective to reduce inflation, or is it to increase economic growth?);

(c) decide upon what fiscal, monetary, trade or other policies you think will most effectively achieve your chosen objectives;

(d) evaluate any trade-offs you might be faced with in the use of your chosen policies;

(e) assess what might be the long term equilibrium growth, unemployment and inflation rates for the economy;

(f) discuss whether your chosen policy package could be described as broadly Keynesian or monetarist.

Table 103.2 *Money supply growth, interest rates and the exchange rate*

Per cent

		Change in M4 seasonally adjusted %	Bank base rates %	Exchange rate of the £ against the deutschmark
1986	Q1	4.1	12.30	3.382
	Q2	3.9	10.45	3.387
	Q3	2.9	10.00	3.109
	Q4	3.5	10.85	2.868
1987	Q1	3.3	10.80	2.837
	Q2	3.5	9.35	2.964
	Q3	3.7	9.58	2.974
	Q4	4.5	9.20	2.989
1988	Q1	3.8	8.75	3.013
	Q2	3.6	8.17	3.142
	Q3	4.9	11.09	3.165
	Q4	4.5	12.38	3.175
1989	Q1	3.9	13.00	3.233
	Q2	4.0	13.45	3.140
	Q3	4.1	14.00	3.071
	Q4	4.2	14.95	2.876
1990	Q1	4.4	15.00	2.800
	Q2	3.9	15.00	2.812
	Q3	2.6	15.00	2.965
	Q4	2.2	14.08	2.923
1991	Q1	1.7	13.52	2.920
	Q2	1.7	11.86	2.961
	Q3	1.3	10.92	2.937
	Q4	1.4	10.52	2.885
1992	Q1	1.2	10.50	2.866
	Q2	1.2	10.17	2.916

Source: adapted from CSO, *Economic Trends Annual Supplement*; CSO, *Financial Statistics*.

Table 103.3 *Consumption and investment, 1986-1992*

At 1990 prices

		Consumption			Investment	PSDR (+) / PSBR (-)
		Durables	Non-durables	Total		
1986	Q1	6 729	65 621	73 350	20 471	+ 2 444
	Q2	7 014	66 913	73 927	20 001	- 3 268
	Q3	6 931	67 534	74 465	21 395	- 4 600
	Q4	7 253	67 627	74 880	21 818	+ 2 210
1987	Q1	7 290	68 493	75 783	21 334	+1 025
	Q2	7 479	69 495	76 974	22 091	- 1 762
	Q3	7 647	70 888	78 535	23 850	- 465
	Q4	7 981	71 961	79 942	25 064	+ 2 993
1988	Q1	8 441	73 465	81 906	25 480	+3 375
	Q2	8 605	73 978	82 583	26 396	+ 2 002
	Q3	9 064	75 531	84 595	26 464	+ 2 420
	Q4	8 943	76 564	85 507	26 824	+ 5 916
1989	Q1	9 211	76 666	85 877	28 387	+ 6 188
	Q2	9 404	76 989	86 393	27 892	+ 64
	Q3	9 157	77 131	86 288	27 788	+ 475
	Q4	9 097	77 751	86 848	27 403	+ 3 327
1990	Q1	9 006	77 913	86 919	27 781	+ 4 410
	Q2	8 913	78 430	87 343	27 198	- 5 928
	Q3	8 579	78 317	86 896	26 583	+ 464
	Q4	8 178	78 191	86 369	26 015	+ 3 169
1991	Q1	8 082	77 742	85 824	24 751	+ 2 466
	Q2	7 496	77 190	84 686	24 410	- 6 717
	Q3	7 786	76 997	84 783	24 074	- 3 477
	Q4	7 476	77 146	84 622	24 168	+ 441
1992	Q1	7 384	76 857	84 241	24 119	- 3 313
	Q2	7 564	77 126	84 690	24 038	- 9 515

Source: adapted from CSO, *Economic Trends Annual Supplement*.

INVESTIGATIONS 8

A. The costs of unemployment

Aims

- To gather data through the use of interviews and desk research on the costs of unemployment to the individual and to the economy as a whole.
- To present the findings of that research in a clear and logical manner.
- To assess the extent to which the information gathered through interviews is typical of the national picture.
- To evaluate policy alternatives to reduce the costs of unemployment.

Research

Your first task is to find one or more unemployed people to interview. This is probably best done as a group task. Someone in the group may have an unemployed relative or acquaintance who would be prepared to be interviewed. Given the sensitive nature of the issue of unemployment, however, it might be better to try and interview someone who is not known to anybody in your group. One possible contact would be the local job club. Alternatively, there may be a number of different voluntary organisations who have people working with them under Youth Training (YT) or Employment Training (ET) placements and which could be approached to see if there would be anybody who would be prepared to talk to you. It would be better from the viewpoint of your research and probably for the unemployed people themselves if you could arrange to interview two or three people at the same time in a group interview. Seek permission before the interview to record it on audio tape.

Before the interview, draw up a list of questions. You need to find out what are the costs of unemployment to the individuals being interviewed. Start out by getting them to tell you something about themselves, their education and training and any previous jobs they may have had. Then ask them how unemployment has affected them. Do not be afraid to ask further questions if the information they give you is insufficient for your needs. However, remember to be sensitive at all times - unemployment is never regarded as a success and is usually considered to be a sign of failure on the part of the persons concerned even if they have been made unemployed through no fault of their own. Finally, ask them how they are searching for a new job. You are particularly interested in the costs of that search to the individual. For instance, what monetary costs are there in the process of search? How much time is being spent on the search? To what extent does the search demoralise the individual or give him or her hope and a sense of value?

The second part of your research is to put the cases of the people you have interviewed into a national context. Attempt to make some estimate of the cost of unemployment to the whole economy (☞ unit 89 for an explanation of what costs you need to take into consideration). Average wages, the total numbers unemployed, the numbers receiving different types of benefit for being unemployed (unemployment benefit and income support) and average payments can be found in the *Annual Abstract of Statistics* and the *Monthly Digest of Statistics*, both published by CSO. More detailed figures can be obtained from CSO, *Social Security Statistics.*

Structuring your report

Introduction Outline the aim of your investigation. The aim should be put in the form of a hypothesis or question which will allow you to come to some conclusions.
Economic theory Outline the economic theory you will use in your analysis. These will include concepts such as voluntary and involuntary unemployment, menu costs, shoe leather costs and uncertainty.
Techniques used to collect your data Outline how you collected your data.
National unemployment costs Explain how you attempted to calculate the costs of unemployment nationally. What monetary costs can be placed on current national unemployment? What are the costs on which no monetary value can be placed? Build a picture of the costs for the typical unemployed person.
Case study Present the findings of your interview. Assess the costs of unemployment to the individuals concerned, both financial and non-financial. To what extent were the interviewees typical of the average person unemployed?
Policy alternatives Suggest a variety of ways in which the costs of unemployment could be reduced. Obviously one way would be for the government to reduce unemployment through reflating the economy (i.e. increasing aggregate demand in the economy). However, concentrate here on how unemployment could be reduced through supply side measures, or how the costs of unemployment could be reduced in other ways. Evaluate each policy alternative and suggest a package of measures which you feel would be most suitable and effective.
Sources Outline the sources of information you used. What problems did you encounter in gathering relevant data? What data would you have liked to have obtained but could not? To what extent were the data, particularly the data gathered at the interview, reliable?
Bibliography Write down a list of your sources in alphabetical order.

Other suggestions

If you are unable to find a suitable interviewee for your investigation on the costs of unemployment, it would be possible to consider the costs of inflation. Consider the costs from the viewpoint of a number of different individuals, such as savers, those with mortgages, workers and pensioners. Then consider the costs from a national viewpoint. For instance, is there any evidence to suggest that inflation leads to lower growth in the economy? The research method, sources and presentation of this investigation are very similar to those outlined above.

B. Current economic problems and government policy

Aims

- To describe the current economic problems facing the economy.
- To discuss the relative importance of these problems using primary research as evidence.
- To outline present government policy and the alternatives to those policies.
- To evaluate the effectiveness of government policy.

Research activity

Your first task is to find out what are the main economic problems currently faced by government. You should be aware, simply through following the news and having studied some economics, what are the main preoccupations of government policy. Use this knowledge to devise a simple questionnaire which asks respondents to state the extent to which they think a problem is important at the moment and to rank in order current economic problems in order of importance. Interview at least 10 adults - parents, relations and other adults you are acquainted with.

Your next task is to survey the current state of the economy. Using *Economic Trends* or the *Monthly Digest of Statistics* (both published by CSO), find out current trends in inflation, the balance of payments, unemployment and economic growth, and any other variables which you consider to be important. Alternatively, use recent newspaper articles which you have collected.

Conduct a newspaper and magazine search for comment about the current economic situation and information and analysis about present government policy. Search through the previous month's issues of the *Financial Times*, other quality newspapers such as the *Independent* and magazines such as the *Economist*. If you wish to pursue your search over a longer time period, use whatever indexes are available in your local large public reference library, such as those produced by individual newspapers and magazines, or a more general index such as the *Research Index*, published by Business Surveys Ltd., which covers articles of financial interest in over 100 newspapers and magazines. These publications may also be available on CD-Rom.

Listen to current affairs programmes on the television and the radio.

Structuring your report

Introduction Outline the aim of your investigation. The aim should be put in the form of a hypothesis or question which will allow you to come to some conclusions.
Economic theory Outline the economic theory you will use in your analysis. This will include concepts and theories of unemployment, inflation, growth and the balance of payments.
Techniques used to collect your data Outline how you collected your data.
Current economic problems Describe the current economic problems facing the economy. Use graphs and tables to illustrate your answer. Assess their relative importance with the help of the results from your questionnaire.
Policy alternatives What policies are the government currently using to solve these problems? For instance, what is the government's monetary policy? How is government using fiscal measures to tackle Britain's problems? What is its exchange rate policy? What other policies could be used instead? Evaluate the range of alternative policies and discuss their relative advantages and disadvantages. What economic policies do you think the government should be pursuing today?
Sources Outline the sources of information you used. What problems did you encounter in gathering relevant data? What data would you have liked to have obtained but could not? To what extent were the data, particularly your questionnaire, reliable?
Bibliography Write down a list of your sources in alphabetical order.

Other suggestions

The investigation outlined above is very wide ranging. Instead of looking at all the problems facing the UK economy, it would be possible to concentrate on just one. For instance, why is the balance of payments a problem? What is current government policy on the balance of payments? What are the possible policy alternatives and would these, in your opinion, be more effective at resolving the current difficulties?

Alternatively, consider a particular policy weapon, such as interest rates, exchange rates, the PSBR or privatisation. How is government using it to solve Britain's current economic problems? Is it using it effectively? Would other policy weapons be more suitable for resolving the problem?

First World and Third World

Applied economics

Classification

The world can be divided into groups of countries.

First world countries FIRST WORLD countries are a small group of rich industrialised countries: the United States, Canada, France, Italy, Germany, the UK and Japan (known as the 'G7 countries'), other countries in Western Europe and Australia and New Zealand. Sometimes they are called Western countries, because for the most part they lie in the western hemisphere, as can be seen from Figure 104.1. Sometimes they are called 'North' countries (from the phase 'North-South divide') because, for the most part they lie in the northern hemisphere, as Figure 104.1 shows. They are also known as DEVELOPED COUNTRIES, indicating that they have reached an advanced stage of economic development.

Second world countries The phrase 'SECOND WORLD' countries is rarely used today. However, these are the former communist countries of Eastern Europe and the USSR. They too are included in the 'North', and are usually classified as 'developed', although their GDP is far lower than that of the average First World country.

Third world countries THIRD WORLD countries are a large group of poor countries in Asia, Africa and Latin America. Most are situated in the southern hemisphere, and hence are known as the 'South' (as in the phrase 'North-South divide'). Sometimes they are called DEVELOPING COUNTRIES (DCs), indicating that their economies are still developing, in contrast with the 'developed' economies of the First World. They are also called LESS DEVELOPED COUNTRIES (LDCs), again contrasted with the 'developed' countries of the North.

Third world countries differ greatly amongst themselves and hence they are often sub-divided into further groups. For instance, sometimes the poorest are called **Fourth World** countries or **low income countries**, whilst the richer Third World countries are known as middle income countries. Fast growing **middle income countries,** such as South Korea, Singapore and Mexico, are sometimes called emerging economies, emerging to take their place amongst the developed countries of the world. South Korea, Singapore, Taiwan and others are called **newly industrialised countries (NICs)**, indicating that their economies now have a strong, Western-style, industrial base. Third World countries are also grouped by region, such as sub-Saharan African countries, or South East Asian countries.

Third World countries are all very different from each other, and therefore in some ways it is dangerous to lump them together and talk about 'the characteristics of Third World countries'. However, there are a number of basic problems which are shared by this group of countries, to a greater or lesser extent. These will now be discussed in turn.

Per capita income

As Table 104.1 shows, 85 per cent of the world's population lived in the Third World in 1992. Yet, the total GDP of the Third World is only 20 per cent of the world's total. The First World, with 15 per cent of the world's population, enjoys 80 per cent of its GDP. Low income Third World countries, with 59 per cent of the world's population, enjoy just 5 per cent of world GDP. The figures in Table 104.1 need, however, to be treated with

Table 104.1 *Population and national income, 1992*

	Population millions	GDP US$bn	GNP[3] per capita US$
World	5 438	23 060.6	4 280
Developed world			
High income economies[1]	821.8	18 312.2	22 160
Developing world[2]	4 610	4 695.6	1 040
Low income economies	3 191.3	1 147.8	390
excluding China and India	1 156.6	427.6	370
Middle income economies	1 418.7	3 549.0	2 490
Lower middle income	941.0	1 595.1	1 695
Upper middle income	477.7	1 960.8	4 020
South Asia	1 177.9	297.3	310
Sub-Saharan Africa	543.0	270.0	530
East Asia and Pacific	1 688.8	1 266.8	760
Middle East and North Africa	252.6	454.5	1 950
Europe and Central Asia	494.5	1 124.4	2 080
Latin America and Caribbean	453.2	1 219.1	2 690

Source: adapted from the World Bank, *World Development Report.*

1. Includes Israel, Hong Kong, Singapore and the United Arab Emirates which are classified by the United Nations as developing countries.
2. Includes all Second World countries, Greece, Portugal and Saudi Arabia. These countries are classified as middle income economies. Greece and Portugal, however, are classified by the United Nations as developed countries.
3. The value of GNP in $US is nearly identical to the value of GDP for nearly all countries.

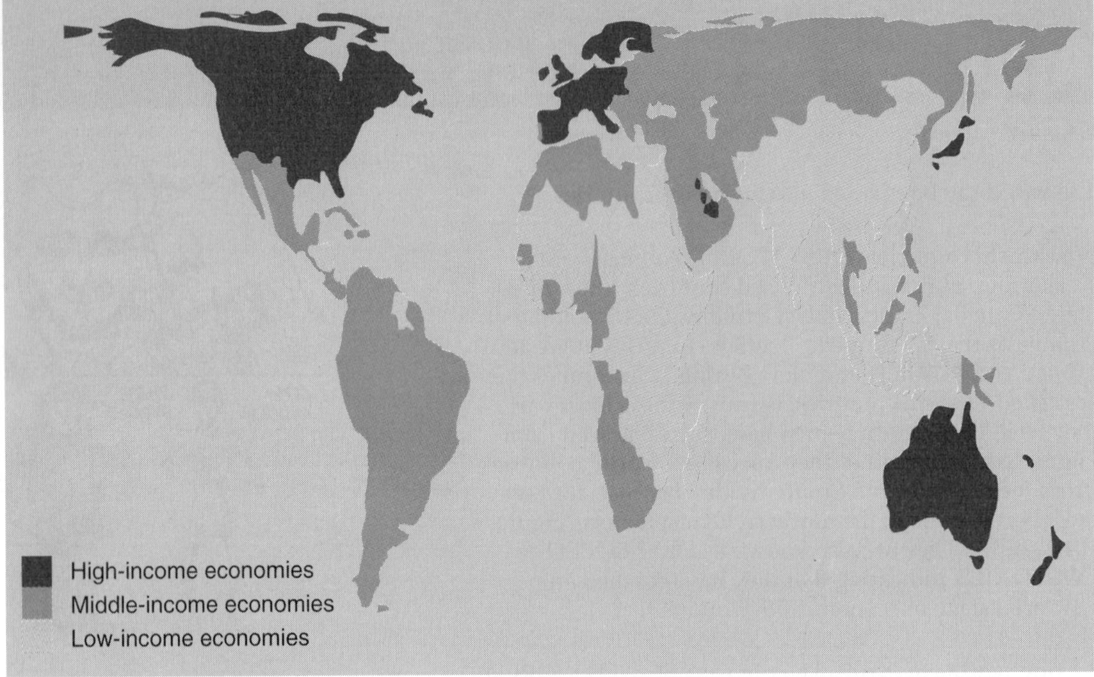

Figure 104.1 *High, middle and low income economies of the world, illustrated on a Peters Projection; a Peters Projection shows the countries of the world with their correct relative areas*

caution for two reasons (☞ unit 60). First, the poorer the country, the greater will be the proportion of output which is not traded in the market economy. For instance, produce from subsistence farming, building houses and providing entertainment is likely to be either underestimated or not included at all in GDP figures for low income economies.

Second, the figures are in US dollars converted at market exchange rates. A more realistic measure of differences in living standards would be to consider GDP converted at **purchasing power parity** rates (☞ unit 87). These compare different GDPs using exchange rates which take account of differences in the cost of living. For instance, in 1992, it was 9.5 times more costly to buy the same bundle of goods in the USA than in Mozambique, according to World Bank estimates. In this case, Mozambique's GDP needs to be multiplied 9.5 times if a fair standard of living comparison is to be made between the USA and Mozambique. Table 104.2 shows GDP per capita figures in US dollars both at market exchange rates and at purchasing power parity rates. The table shows that there can be significant differences between the two figures.

Adjusting GDP at purchasing power parity rates can significantly alter a country's ranking in world GDP league tables. It also considerably reduces the world inequalities in income shown in Table 104.1. Even so, there are still 17 countries which, according to World Bank estimates, have a GDP per capita at purchasing power parities of less than 5 per cent of the US total. Another 20 have a GDP per capita of less than 10 per cent. No middle income country has a GDP per capita of more than 50 per cent of that of the USA, whilst the majority have incomes of between 10 and 30 per cent of the US total.

It should be remembered that the figures in Tables 104.1 and 104.2 relate to average incomes for these countries. Rich elites in poor Third World countries can enjoy incomes which are comparable to First World countries.

Table 104.2 *Purchasing power parity estimates of national income per capita for selected countries, 1992*

		At market exchange rates		At purchasing power parity rates	
				GNP per capita	
	Population millions	GDP US$ millions	GNP[1] per capita US$	US$	%of GNP of USA
Ethiopia	54.8	6 257	110	340	1.5
Mozambique	16.5	965	60	570	2.5
Tanzania	25.9	2 345	110	630	2.7
Malawi	9.1	1 671	210	730	3.2
Uganda	17.5	2 998	170	1 070	4.6
India	883.6	214 598	310	1 210	5.2
China	1 162.2	596 075	470	1 910	9.1
Pakistan	119.3	41 904	420	2 130	9.2
Georgia	5.5	4 660	850	2 470	10.7
Romania	22.7	24 438	1 130	2 750	11.9
Peru	22.4	22 100	950	3 080	13.3
Egypt	54.7	33 553	640	3 670	15.9
Jamaica	2.4	3 294	1 340	3 770	16.3
Poland	38.4	83 823	1 910	4 880	21.1
Brazil	153.9	360 405	2 770	5 250	22.7
Thailand	58.0	110 337	1 840	5 890	24.8
Mexico	85.0	329 011	3 470	7 490	32.4
Chile	13.6	41 203	2 730	8 090	35.0
South Korea	43.7	296 136	6 790	8 950	38.7
Portugal	9.8	79 547	7 450	10 120	43.8
Saudi Arabia	16.8	111 343	7 510	11 170	48.3
South Africa	39.8	103 651	2 670	11 390	49.3
Spain	39.1	574 844	13 970	13 170	57.0
New Zealand	3.4	41 304	12 300	14 400	62.3
Singapore	2.8	46 025	15 730	16 720	72.3
Hong Kong	5.8	77 828	15 360	20 050	86.7
Switzerland	6.9	241 406	36 080	22 100	95.6
United States	255.4	5 920 199	23 240	23 120	100.0

1. The value of GNP in $US is nearly identical to the value of GDP for nearly all countries.
Source: adapted from the World Bank, *World Development Report*.

Equally, the poorest 10 per cent of the population of New York have incomes which are comparable to the average of middle income countries. Problems of inequality within countries are discussed further in unit 105.

Physical capital

Third world countries have far less physical capital per capita than First World countries. This includes not just factories, offices and machines, but also infrastructure capital such as roads and railways, as well as schools and hospitals.

Table 104.3 shows a variety of infrastructure statistics for different countries. In general, a country is less developed:

- the fewer the households with access to electricity;
- the larger the percentage loss of electricity from the electricity system, for instance because of poor maintenance;
- the fewer the number of telephone lines per inhabitant;
- the less well kept is the road system;
- the fewer the people with access to safe water.

Table 104.3 *Infrastructure in selected countries*

	Electricity		Telephone	Roads in	Population with
	Households with electricity (% of total) 1984	System losses (% of total output) 1990	mainlines per 1000 persons 1990	good condition (% of paved roads)1988	access to safe water (% of total) 1990
Mozambique	4	26	3	12	22
Tanzania	6	20	3	25	52
Malawi	16	19	3	56	51
Uganda	-	40	2	10	33
India	54	19	6	32	49
Pakistan	31	24	8	18	55
Romania	49	9	102	30	95
Peru	90	18	26	34	33
Egypt	46	14	33	39	90
Jamaica	49	19	45	10	72
Poland	96	15	86	69	89
Brazil	79	14	63	30	86
Thailand	43	11	24	50	77
Mexico	75	13	66	85	81
Chile	85	19	65	42	87
South Korea	100	6	310	70	93
Portugal	78	11	241	50	92
Singapore	98	3	385	85-100	100
Hong Kong	-	11	434	85-100	100
United States	100	9	545	85-100	100

Source: adapted from the World Bank, *World Development Report.*

The table is rank ordered according to GDP per capita at purchasing power parity rates. It can be seen that, in general, the lower the level of GDP per capita, the poorer the infrastructure level of the country. However, there are large differences between countries which have little correlation with GDP levels. For instance, Malawi, India and Chile all have relatively low system losses from their electicity industries, a sign of greater efficiency in their economies. Poland has 69 per cent of its roads in good condition compared to only 30 per cent in Brazil despite the fact that both have roughly comparable GDP per capita levels. South Korea and Singapore have First World levels of infrastructure although they are classified as Third World countries.

Physical capital is important because the more physical capital, the greater the productive potential of the economy. If a country is to grow, it must increase its stock of physical capital in order to push out its **production possibility frontier** (☞ unit 1).

Human capital

Developing countries have lower levels of human capital than developed countries. It is difficult to measure levels of human capital. However, one indicator is to consider educational statistics. Table 104.4 gives two measures. The first is of the percentage enrolment in different stages of education. Least developed countries would expect to have the lowest proportions of the total age group enrolled in education. For instance, less than ten per cent of children are enrolled in secondary education in Mozambique, Tanzania and Malawi. Fewer than half the children in the 6-11 age group are enrolled in primary education in Pakistan. These enrolments then have an impact on adult literacy. Low enrolments in the past have led to high illiteracy rates in Mozambique, Uganda and Pakistan. On the other hand, relatively high enrolments have led to low illiteracy rates in countries such as China, Peru and Jamaica.

Table 104.4 *Education*

	Percentage of age group enrolled in education[1], 1991			Adult illiteracy, 1990 %
	Primary	Secondary	Tertiary	
Mozambique	63	8	0	67
Tanzania	69	5	0	-
Malawi	66	4	1	-
Uganda	71	13	1	52
India	98	44	-	52
China	123	51	2	27
Pakistan	46	21	3	65
Romania	90	80	9	-
Peru	126	70	36	15
Egypt	101	80	19	52
Jamaica	106	62	6	2
Poland	98	83	22	-
Brazil	106	39	12	19
Thailand	113	33	16	7
Mexico	114	55	15	13
Chile	98	72	23	7
South Korea	107	88	40	4
Portugal	122	68	23	15
Saudi Arabia	77	46	13	38
Spain	109	108	36	5
New Zealand	104	84	45	less than 5
Singapore	108	70	-	-
Hong Kong	108	-	18	-
Switzerland	103	91	29	less than 5
United States	104	90	76	less than 5

Source: adapted from the World Bank, *World Development Report.*

1 Figures may total more than 100 per cent. This is because some children are in primary (usually defined as 6-11 year olds) or secondary (usually defined as 11-17 year olds) education who are older or younger than the defined age group. For instance, 108 per cent of Spaniards are enrolled in secondary education because some 18 and 19 year olds are still in secondary education which is defined as being for 11-17 year olds.

Education levels are vital to the ability of countries to grow in the future. Countries which invest today in education, particularly in primary education where research shows that **rates of return** on the investment are highest, are likely to grow faster in the future. South Korea, for instance, one of the Tiger economies of South East Asia, has invested heavily in its education system, with 40 per cent of the age group in higher education in 1991, a figure larger than most developed countries. The United States, with arguably the highest levels of human capital in the world, has three-quarters of its age group in tertiary education. China, a relatively poor country, has, since the 1949 Revolution, placed a strong emphasis on education. This has been one of the prime reasons why the country has been able to grow at 10 per cent per annum in the 1980s and 1990s.

High population growth

Third World countries have had relatively high rates of population growth compared to First World countries (☞ unit 106 for a fuller discussion). This poses two major problems. Firstly, it means that Third World countries need to invest large amounts in both physical and human capital in order to create the goods and services and jobs needed for their growing populations. However, Third World countries also need to increase their consumption in order to provide a basic standard of living for their populations now. Higher investment to create future prosperity can only be achieved by forgoing consumption now, lowering current prosperity. Some successful Third World countries have avoided this problem by securing large amounts of investment capital from abroad. However, other high growth Third World countries have financed heavy investment by large domestic savings (☞ unit 107).

The second problem that high population growth brings is high dependency ratios. In First World countries, low population growth is causing a crisis because the ratio of retired workers to those in work will increase substantially over the next 30 years in most countries. In the Third World, it is children who are causing the crisis. In some African countries, half the population is under the age of 15. Not only do these children need education, but they also need to be provided with jobs in the future, both points which reinforce the need for high growth in investment.

Health and mortality

People in the Third World on average enjoy poorer health and are likely to die younger than in First World countries. Poor health and high mortality shown in Table 104.5 are caused by a number of factors. One is the standard of nutrition of individuals. Table 104.5 shows that the average daily calorie supply of the poorest countries of the world is only a half to two thirds that of the developed countries of the world. Within this, there are large disparities, with the poor in most Third World countries having a deficient diet. Poor nutrition is a major contributor to ill health and higher mortality rates. Poor nutrition also affects both the physical and mental development of individuals. One of the reasons why individuals are on average taller in First World countries compared to, say, fifty years ago is a better diet. Equally, educational performance is affected by diet.

Another factor is the physical infrastructure of the country. Access to clean water is vital for health. So are proper sanitation facilities, particularly in urban areas. The environment must be healthy too.

Large numbers of people die from diseases such as dysentery or malaria, which are water-born or carried by animals. In First World countries, these diseases have been almost eliminated through proper infrastructure or control of the natural environment.

A third factor is the working environment. People often are forced to work in poor conditions which severely damage their health. If they are agricultural workers, there are many animal carried diseases to which they can be exposed. If they work in industry, poor light, noise, heat and dust can shorten life. Moreover, many start work at a much younger age than in First World countries.

Finally, health care provision is poorer. Table 104.5 shows the number of doctors and nurses per thousand of the population in selected countries. The poorer the country, the fewer doctors and nurses there tend to be. Health provision can be highly effective even on quite low budgets, as the example of, say, Sri Lanka or China has shown. However, this requires a sound infrastructure

Table 104.5 *Health, nutrition and mortality, selected countries*

	Under 5 mortality rate, males (per 1 000 live births) 1992	Babies with low birth weights (%) 1990	Life expectancy at birth (years) 1992	Daily calorie supply (per capita) 1989	Prevalence of malnutrition (under 5) (%) 1987-1992	Population per Physician 1990	Population per Nurse 1990
Ethiopia	216	16	49	1 667	-	32 500	-
Mozambique	283	20	44	1 680	-	-	-
Tanzania	158	14	51	2 206	25.2	24 970	3 310
Malawi	238	20	44	2 139	-	45 740	1 800
Uganda	216	-	43	2 153	23.3	-	-
India	104	33	61	2 229	63.0	2 460	-
China	43	9	69	2 639	21.3	-	-
Pakistan	142	25	59	2 219	40.4	2 940	5 040
Georgia	27	19	72	-	-	170	-
Romania	32	49	70	3 155	-	560	430
Peru	75	52	65	2 186	10.8	960	-
Egypt	93	57	62	3 336	10.4	1 320	490
Jamaica	19	43	74	2 609	7.2	-	-
Poland	20	-	70	3 505	-	490	-
Brazil	76	11	66	2 751	7.1	-	-
Thailand	36	13	69	2 316	13.0	4 360	1 170
Mexico	49	12	70	3 052	13.9	-	-
Chile	24	7	72	2 581	-	2 150	340
South Korea	18	9	71	2 852	-	1 070	1 190
Portugal	13	5	74	3 495	-	490	-
Saudi Arabia	38	7	69	2 874	-	700	450
South Africa	77	-	63	3 122	-	1 750	-
Spain	11	4	77	3 572	-	280	260[1]
New Zealand	11	6	76	3 362	-	-	80[1]
Singapore	7	7	75	3 198	-	820	-
Hong Kong	9	8	78	2 853	-	-	240[1]
Switzerland	9	5	78	3 562	-	630	-
United States	12	7	77	3 671	-	370	70[1]

1. 1984 figures.
Source: adapted from the World Bank, *World Development Report*.

of nurses with some basic training, rudimentary clinics and basic medicines along with effective health education.

Table 104.6 *Structure of production*

	Distribution of gross domestic product (%), 1992		
	Agriculture	Industry	Services
Ethiopia	48	13	39
Mozambique	64	15	21
Tanzania	61	12	26
Malawi	28	22	50
Uganda	57	11	32
India	32	27	40
China	27	34	38
Pakistan	27	27	46
Georgia	27	37	37
Romania	19	49	32
Egypt	18	39	52
Jamaica	5	44	51
Poland	7	51	42
Brazil	11	37	52
Thailand	12	39	49
Mexico	8	28	63
South Korea	8	45	47
Saudi Arabia	7	52	41
South Africa	4	42	54
Singapore	0	38	62
Hong Kong	0	23	77
France	3	29	68
Japan	2	32	66
Germany	2	39	60

Source: adapted from the World Bank, *World Development Report*.

Unemployment and underemployment

Third World countries tend to have much higher unemployment and underemployment rates than First World countries. This arises from a number of factors. The most important is a lack of physical capital. Without the machines, factories and offices, workers are **structurally** unemployed (☞ unit 90). However, factors such as poor government economic policies and protectionism in other countries can also play a part. In countries heavily reliant on agriculture, unemployment is highly **seasonal**.

Structure of the economy

Growth and development alters the structure of output in the economy (☞ unit 61). Developed countries have gradually shifted from primary to secondary and then tertiary production over time. An indicator of the level of development of an economy today is therefore the extent to which its output is dependent upon agricultural production and industrial production. Table 104.6, for instance, shows that the poorest countries, Ethiopia, Mozambique and Tanzania have between 48 and 61 per cent of output accounted for by agriculture. In contrast, France, Germany and Japan have 3 per cent or less. The proportion devoted to industry at first increases, from, say, Ethiopia's 13 per cent to Poland's 51 per cent. It is then likely to decline as demand for services grows within the country. Amongst developed countries, industry accounted in 1992 for between 15 per cent (Australia) and 32 per cent (Japan) of output. Services accounted for between 66 per cent (Japan) and 80 per cent (Ireland).

Structure of foreign trade

The structure of the economy tends to mirror the structure of trade. Third World countries are likely to be more reliant on exports of primary commodities, such as rice or copper, than First World countries. Rapid industrialisation in the Third World over the past 20 years has meant that manufactures now account for a much greater proportion of Third World exports. However, many of these manufactures tend to be low technology products such as textiles or footwear. The problems associated with an over-reliance on commodity exports will be discussed in unit 108.

Key terms

Developed and developing or less developed countries - developed countries are the rich industrialised nations of Europe, Japan and North America, whilst developing or less developed countries are the other, poorer, less economically developed nations of the world.

First World countries - the rich, developed, nations of Western Europe, Japan and North America.
Second World countries - the communist and formerly communist nations of Eastern Europe and the Soviet Union.
Third World countries - the developing nations of the world in Africa, South America and Asia.

The Third World

Consider the data in the tables in this unit.

1. **Explain why Tanzania would be considered a poor Third World country.**
2. **Compare Egypt and South Korea as developing countries.**
3. **Hong Kong is classified as a developing country by the United Nations. To what extent was this classification appropriate in 1992?**
4. **Discuss which Third World countries were (a) most likely and (b) least likely to achieve high growth rates in the future on the basis of the data presented.**

Economic development

Applied economics

Economic growth

In economics, development has traditionally been associated with economic growth. Economic growth measures changes in national income, the sum of all traded output in the economy. Countries which produce a great deal are also able to consume at high levels. Hence, a country like the United States, which has the highest GDP in the world, as well as the highest GDP per capita (measured at purchasing power parity rates), is able to give its citizens a high standard of living. On the other hand, a country like Ethiopia, the poorest country in the world measured in terms of GDP per capita, sees its citizens enjoying a very low standard of living.

It might seem, then, that economic success can be measured in terms of economic growth rates. Countries with high growth rates, such as the Tiger economies of East Asia, are ones which are developing very fast. Countries which have negative growth rates, such as many African countries in the 1980s, are regressing, not developing. Levels of national income were discussed in unit 104. On a GDP measure, Pakistan is 'more developed' than Ethiopia, South Korea more developed than China and the USA more developed than Singapore. In terms of growth, the relative position of countries is changing very fast. Table 105.1 shows real annual growth rates for different areas and countries between 1966 and 1993. The world rate of growth has slowed down considerably over the period, from an average of 5.1 per cent in 1966-73 to 3.0 per cent in 1974-1990. The 1.2 per cent growth in 1991-93 should not be taken as an indication of future growth rates because during this period the major developed economies of the world went into recession. Since most of the world's GDP is accounted for by these economies, a recession in a few countries can seem to indicate a major downturn in growth throughout the world.

However, some areas of the world are growing at a much faster rate than others. East Asia and the Pacific, with countries like China (with one-quarter of the world's population), South Korea and Hong Kong, have grown at over 7 per cent per annum throughout the period. Other areas have performed poorly. African countries in particular have grown very slowly in the 1980s. Latin American countries have only kept pace with growth rates in the developed world. In the former Soviet Union, the early 1990s were disastrous, with half of GDP being wiped out in the first three years of the decade (☞ unit 113).

Table 105.1 shows annual changes in GDP. However, population growth must be taken into account if GDP is to be a reliable indicator of development. Table 105.2 shows annual changes in GDP per capita for the same countries as in Table 105.1. The scale of the African disaster can now be seen. In Sub-Saharan Africa, real GDP per capita fell at an average rate of 0.7 per cent between 1974 and 1990. On average, Africans were 10 per cent poorer in GDP terms

Table 105.1 *Growth of real GDP, 1966-1993*

	1966-73	1974-90	1991-93
World	**5.1**	**3.0**	**1.2**
High-income	**4.8**	**2.9**	**1.3**
Low and middle-income	**6.9**	**3.5**	**0.8**
Excluding Eastern Europe and FSU	6.2	3.5	4.6
Asia	5.9	6.3	7.0
East Asia and Pacific	7.9	7.1	8.7
China	8.5	8.2	12.3
Korea, Rep.	11.2	8.5	6.4
Indonesia	6.6	6.1	6.5
South Asia	3.7	4.9	3.2
India	3.7	4.8	2.9
Latin America and the Caribbean	6.4	2.7	3.2
Brazil	9.8	3.6	1.2
Mexico	6.8	3.4	2.4
Argentina	4.3	0.5	7.9
Europe and Central Asia	7.0	3.6	-9.4
Russian Federation[a]	7.1	3.7	-15.5
Turkey	6.1	4.3	4.9
Poland	7.7	1.9	-0.6
Middle East and North Africa	8.5	0.7	3.4
Iran, Islamic Rep.	10.6	-0.4	6.4
Algeria	6.3	4.4	-0.1
Egypt, Arab Rep.	3.8	7.3	0.9
Sub-Saharan Africa	4.7	2.2	0.6
South Africa	4.7	2.2	-0.9
Nigeria	6.5	1.0	4.1

a. Data for years before 1993 refer to the former Soviet Union (FSU).
Source: adapted from World Bank, *Global Economic Prospects and the Developing Countries.*

Table 105.2 *Growth of real GDP per capita, 1966-1993*

	1966-73	1974-90	1991-93
World	**3.1**	**1.2**	**-0.4**
High-income	**3.8**	**2.2**	**0.7**
Low and middle-income	**4.5**	**1.5**	**-0.9**
Excluding Eastern Europe and FSU	3.6	1.4	2.6
Asia	3.4	4.3	5.2
East Asia and Pacific	5.2	5.4	7.2
China	5.8	6.6	11.0
Korea, Rep.	8.8	7.0	5.4
Indonesia	4.1	3.9	4.7
South Asia	1.3	2.6	1.1
India	1.4	2.6	0.9
Latin America and the Caribbean	3.7	0.5	1.3
Brazil	7.1	1.4	-0.5
Mexico	3.5	0.9	0.3
Argentina	2.7	-1.0	6.6
Europe and Central Asia	6.0	2.6	-9.8
Russian Federation[a]	6.5	3.1	-15.5
Turkey	3.5	1.9	2.8
Poland	7.0	1.2	-0.7
Middle East and North Africa	5.8	-2.4	0.7
Iran, Islamic Rep.	7.6	-4.2	3.5
Algeria	3.3	1.3	-2.4
Egypt, Arab Rep.	1.7	4.7	-1.3
Sub-Saharan Africa	2.0	-0.7	-2.3
South Africa	2.1	-0.3	-3.1
Nigeria	3.8	-1.8	0.3

a. Data for years before 1993 refer to the former Soviet Union (FSU).
Source: adapted from World Bank, *Global Economic Prospects and the Developing Countries.*

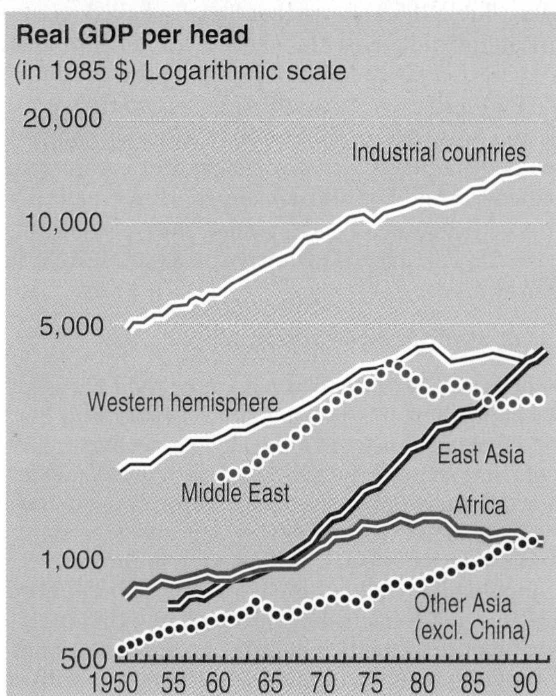

Source: adapted from IMF, *World Economic Outlook*; Summers and Heston.
Figure 105.1 *Growth in real GDP per head*

in 1990 than they were in 1974. On the other hand, in the East Asian countries, with an average growth rate per capita of 5.4 per cent, citizens had more than doubled their income over the period.

Figure 105.1 shows how relative GDP per capita positions have changed since 1950. At the start of the decade, Asia was poorer than Africa. By the mid-1960s, East Asian countries had caught up with Africa and by the early 1990s enjoyed a GDP per capita which was approximately three times as great. Even the other Asian countries, but not including China, starting from a lower GDP per capita, had, by 1993, caught up with African countries. The poor economic performance of the 1980s of the Eastern European countries, the former Soviet Union, countries in the Middle East and those in Africa is shown by flat or declining lines during that period.

At current growth rates, a few of the developing countries will transform themselves into developed countries. Arguably, Hong Kong and Singapore have already achieved this. Japan was a developing country in the 1950s. Some of the oil rich Arab states, like Saudi Arabia or Oman, had GDPs per capita which approached that of the poorer developed countries like Ireland or New Zealand in 1992. South Korea is currently growing so fast that it is difficult not to see it becoming a developed country within the next 20 years. Some Latin American countries, like Chile, Mexico and Venezuela had higher GDPs per capita on a purchasing power parity basis in 1992 than Eastern European countries like the Czech Republic or Poland.

Growth: an inadequate measure

In the 1950s and 1960s, there was an assumption amongst economists that economic growth and economic development were closely linked. High economic growth would lead to fast economic development and vice versa. However, in the 1970s, this assumption was severely questioned. It was correctly pointed out that economic growth only measured growth in a limited number of variables in the economy. It took no account of a large number of other variables in the economy, ranging from health, to the environment, to the distribution of resources within the economy. This is part of the debate which was discussed in units 60 and 101. Michael Todaro, a leading economist in the field of development economics, has put forward three objectives of development which will now be discussed in turn.

The provision of basic needs

Economic growth raises the level of goods available for consumption in an economy. It does not necessarily mean, however, that all will have access to those extra goods. The history of economic development since the Second World War suggests that the benefits of growth are very unevenly spread. For instance, in 1990, 90 per cent of Egyptians had access to safe water. Yet in Peru, a country with a similar GDP per capita, this was true for only 30 per cent of the population. In China, 27 per cent of adults were illiterate in 1990. In Pakistan, again with a similar GDP per capita, the figure was 65 per cent. In 1984, in South Korea, 100 per cent of households had access to electricity in their homes. In Portugal, the figure was only 78 per cent. Further examples can be seen in unit 104 in Tables 104.3-104.5.

Whilst some in Third World countries enjoy incomes which approximate to those in the First World, the majority are much poorer and over a billion people (one-fifth of the world's population) live below the poverty line. Table 105.3 gives a World Bank estimate of the number of people in poverty and their geographical distribution. The region with the highest incidence of poverty is sub-Saharan Africa, where nearly half the population lives below the poverty line.

Table 105.3 *Poverty in the developing world, 1985-2000*

	Percentage of the population below the poverty line			Number of poor (millions)		
Region	1985	1990	2000	1985	1990	2000
All developing countries	30.5	29.7	24.1	1 051	1 133	1 107
South Asia	51.8	49.0	36.9	532	562	511
East Asia	13.2	11.3	4.2	182	169	73
Sub-Saharan Africa	47.6	47.8	49.7	184	216	304
Middle-East and North Africa	30.6	33.1	30.6	60	73	89
Eastern Europe	7.1	7.1	5.8	5	5	4
Latin America and the Caribbean	22.4	25.5	24.9	87	108	126

Source: World Bank, *World Development Report 1992.*

One of the goals of economic development must therefore be the satisfaction of **basic needs** (☞ unit 1) amongst the whole population. Everyone must have access to food and drink and shelter. Good health is a basic need too. Hence, everyone should have access to basic medical care. The eradication of **absolute poverty** (☞ unit 43) in society must therefore be a goal of any development strategy.

Economic systems do not necessarily bring about an increase in welfare for the poor even when fast economic growth is being experienced. In the 1950s and 1960s, it was widely thought that fast increases in income for the better off in society would 'trickle down' to the poor as well. Indeed, this was one of the arguments used by both Ronald Reagan in the United States and Margaret Thatcher in the UK to justify their economic policies which led to sharper inequalities in society. However, the experience has been that there is little or no trickle down effect. **Dual economies** can develop. One half of the economy is growing whilst the other half stagnates.

In development terms, two particular groups can be singled out which are most likely to be in absolute poverty. The first are rural dwellers. Many urban dwellers living in slums in large cities are on the edge of absolute poverty. However, electricity, health care, food and shelter are likely to be more accessible to these than to rural dwellers who may live hundreds of miles away from the nearest town. Moreover, many rural dwellers are engaged in very low productivity subsistence agriculture. Their productivity is even lower than that of many urban slum dwellers.

The second group most at risk is women. In many traditional societies, women have less access to food and education than males. When women find themselves widowed, they have more difficulty surviving than men because female wages are on average lower than male wages. In part this is caused by discrimination. However, it also reflects differences in access to education between genders. Table 105.4 shows that females have less access toeducation than males. In Pakistan, for instance, there are only 52 female children in primary schools compared to 100 male children, and only 41 in secondary education. Table 105.4 also shows differences in life expectancy. In developed countries, females can expect to outlive males by between 5 and 7 years on average. However, this gap is reduced to between 1 and 3 years in many developing countries. In Pakistan, females have the same life expectancy at birth as males.

Table 105.4 *Gender comparisons*

	Life expectancy at birth years		Maternal mortality per 100 000 live births	Females per 100 males in education	
	Female	Male		Primary	Secondary
Ethiopia	50	47	-	64	67
Mozambique	45	43	-	70	61
Tanzania	52	49	342	98	72
Malawi	.45	44	350	82	53
Uganda	44	43	550	-	-
India	62	61	-	71	55
China	71	68	115	86	72
Pakistan	59	59	270	52	41
Peru	67	63	165	-	-
Georgia	76	69	55	-	-
Romania	73	67	-	106	174
Egypt	63	60	-	80	76
Jamaica	76	71	115	99	-
Poland	75	66	-	95	266
Chile	76	69	40	95	115
Brazil	69	64	140	-	-
Thailand	72	67	37	95	97
Mexico	74	67	200	94	92
South Korea	75	67	26	94	87
Saudi Arabia	71	68	-	84	79
South Africa	66	60	-	-	-
Singapore	77	72	10	90	100
Hong Kong	81	75	4	-	-
Switzerland	82	75	-	96	100
United States	80	73	-	95	95

Source: adapted from The World Bank, *World Development Report.*

Raising standards of living

Development is not just about providing basic needs for the whole population. It is also about raising standards of living beyond that of subsistence level. Higher incomes are one sign of rising living standards. A whole range of goods then become affordable, from televisions to meals out to travel.

There are, however, many more aspects to the standard of living of an individual. For instance, improved education not only allows the workforce to become more productive. It also increases the ability of individuals to enjoy and appreciate their culture. Access to work not only provides individuals and their dependents with an income. It also provides self-esteem and a sense of purpose. Access to a clean environment not only contributes to today's standard of living but is also an indication that this standard of living is sustainable for one's children.

Rising living standards are also linked to the ability of citizens to participate in society. The poor are often denied that ability because they do not have the income to be able to buy what is considered to be the 'norm' for that society. A key focus of economic development must then be to reduce sharp inequalities in income.

Expanding the range of economic and social choices

Development is about giving societies and individuals within those societies greater choice. Many Third World countries in the past were colonies of First World countries. Independence brought them greater freedom to decide their own national destiny.

Development is also about giving nations greater freedom to decide on their economic objectives. Many Third World countries are currently subject to economic reform programmes imposed by the IMF (International Monetary Fund ☞ unit 108). Whilst these reform programmes may lead to higher economic growth in the future, they are bitterly resented by the countries concerned because they are seen as limiting the freedom to choose how to operate economic policy by the individual country.

At the individual level, economic development is about allowing people to decide what to buy today, rather than being forced to buy basic necessities only. It is about controlling where one works, which implies that there are jobs available in the economy. It is also about political freedoms, such as the right to free speech, or to choose where to live or who to meet. Some of the East Asian countries with particularly high growth rates, such as China and South Korea, have relatively poor human rights records.

Chile: the response to poverty

The assessment of outside agencies

Mr Gert Rosenthal is the executive secretary of the UN's Economic Commission for Latin America and the Caribbean. He supports the government view that there have been significant improvements in recent years. 'The recuperation that you are seeing in part reflects the fact that when this economy grows, you can pull people out of poverty in a relatively short time,' he says.

'In other countries you can pour a lot of money in, but you are unlikely to see results for a generation. The type of poverty you have here is qualitatively different from that found, for example, in Peru or Bolivia. The levels of education, infant mortality, health and so forth are quite different.

'In Chile the workforce is sufficiently skilled to take up opportunities as they arise. They are trainable. In many other Latin American countries, there comes a point where this is not true,' The creation of jobs is thus the over-riding factor, he says.

Official figures show unemployment continuing to fall sharply. The number of jobless is 4.5 per cent, against 6.5 per cent in 1990 and 20 per cent in 1982. Although some observers question the accuracy of government job statistics, few disagree with Mr Rosenthal's belief that unemployment has 'clearly come down terrifically', nor with his assessment that wages at the lower end of the scale have risen markedly.

According to Prealc, the world employment programme, Chile has bucked the regional trend by creating not only more, but 'better quality' jobs. Since 1985, the proportion of Chileans with low-paid, unstable work has steadily declined. Only 50 per cent of Chileans are self-employed or work for small businesses against 56 per cent in Mexico and 60 per cent in Colombia.

'Real salaries in Chile have shown a sustained recuperation since 1988,' Prealc's report says. 'Despite this, minimum wages are still below those of 1980.' The group estimates real minimum wages at 83.4 per cent of 1980 levels, up from 63.4 per cent in 1985.

Mr Rosenthal says the government has struck the right balance between specific measures aimed at tackling poverty and policies intended to stimulate economic growth and job creation generally. 'If we were asked to grade the government in this are we would give then high marks. They seem to have got it about right.'

Source: adapted in part from the *Financial Times*, 8.12.1993.

Table 105.5 *Poverty in Chile*

	Living below the poverty line		Living in extreme poverty	
	% of total population	number of poor (millions)	% of total population	number (million)
1987	44.4	5.7	16.8	2.2
1990	40.1	5.3	13.8	1.8
1992	32.7	4.4	9.0	1.2
1994	29.0	4.0	-	-

Source: World Bank, *World Development Report.*

The 1993 Presidential election - poverty a high priority

In the December 1993 Presidential election, both the right wing and the left wing presidential candidates put the issue of the country's poor at the top of their agendas. The current President, Mr Eduardo Frei, from the left of Centre Concertacion coalition, claimed that there had already been considerable improvement in the lot of the poor under his presidency. The numbers of people in poverty has declined. Partly this has been due to high economic growth, averaging 6.3 per cent over the period 1989-1993. It has also been helped by the rapid creation of jobs. A variety of measures have been implemented targeted at Chile's poor, including a raising of the minimum wage by 30 per cent in real terms and a large increase in family allowances.

La Pintana

La Pintana is a very poor municipality in south Santiago, the capital city of Chile. It was created by the forcible relocation of some of the city's poor from more prosperous suburbs under the previous military regime. The inhabitants live in cramped, squalid government housing, often overlooking unlit unpaved streets plagued with crime.

La Pintana's 170 000 inhabitants have no hospital and only one secondary school. More than half live below the poverty line. Residents are four times less likely to have regular work than the average in Chile. They are nearly 200 times less likely to own a telephone. Government housing often fails to meet basic standards. Some houses don't even have floors or staircases.

In contrast, in Las Condes, one of Santiago's richest districts, unemployment is low whilst there are well-equipped public health facilities even though most people go to private clinics.

Table 105.6 *Chile, Mexico, Venezuela and Spain, selected development statistics*

	Chile	Mexico	Venezuela	Spain
GDP per capita, $US at PPP rates 1992	8 090	7 490	8 790	13 170
Percentage share of income 1989				
Lowest 20 per cent	3.7	4.1	4.8	8.3
Next 20 per cent	6.8	7.8	9.5	13.7
Growth in GDP, % per annum				
1970-1980	1.8	6.3	3.5	3.5
1980-92	4.8	1.5	1.9	3.2
Life expectancy at birth (years) females				
1970	66	64	68	75
1992	76	74	73	81
Infant mortality rate (per 1000 live births)				
1970	78	72	53	28
1992	17	35	33	8
Low birthweight babies (%) 1990	7	12	9	4
Daily calorie supply				
1965	2 581	2 570	2 266	2 770
1989	2 581	3 052	2 582	3 572
Adult illiteracy, %, 1990				
total	7	13	8	5
females	7	15	17	7
Primary enrolment as % of age group				
1975	94	-	81	100
1991	86	98	61	100
Population with access to clean water (%) 1990	87	81	92	100
Telephone mainlines per 1000 persons 1990	65	66	77	323

Source: World Bank, *World Development Report.*

Write a report for the World Bank on the extent to which Chile has achieved genuine development in the late 1980s and 1990s. In your report:

- **distinguish between development and economic growth;**
- **assess the extent to which Chile has achieved economic development (i) from the data provided about the country and (ii) by comparing it with Mexico, Venezuela and Spain;**
- **discuss what needs to happen if Chile is to become a 'developed' country.**

unit 106 Population, migration and the environment

Applied economics

The population explosion

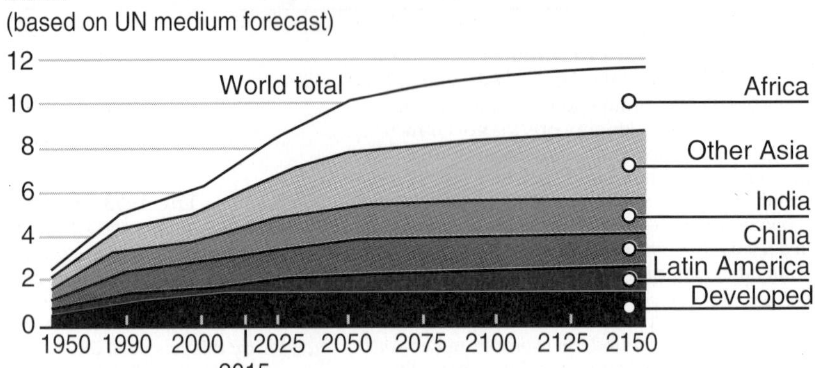

Source: adapted from United Nations.

Figure 106.1 *Population projections by region*

The size of the world's population has exploded in the twentieth century, as Figure 106.1 shows. In 1900, the world's population was an estimated 1.6bn. By 1990, it had grown to 5.3bn. By the year 2000, it is projected to be 6.3bn. The United Nations has predicted that the most likely scenario is that the world's population will stabilise at 12bn in the 21st century.

The population explosion has been caused by the number of births exceeding the number of deaths. Due to better diet, better housing and sanitation, and access to clean water and health care, people are living longer. However, there has been a lagged response of the birth rate to falls in the death rate. In the developed world, birth rates now roughly equal death rates, so that there is little or no population growth as can be seen in Table 106.1. Indeed, the population of some countries, such as the former West Germany, is actually declining. In the developing world, birth rates are still very high, although in some countries they have been falling rapidly in recent years due to a complex mix of factors discussed later in the unit. Until birth rates equal death rates in developing countries, the world's population will continue to grow.

Growth in population varies enormously from country

Table 106.1 *Population structures*

	GDP per capita US$ at PPP rates	Population size (millions)		Hypothetical size of stationary population (millions)	Age structure of the population %						Average annual growth in population %		
					1990			2025					
	1992	1992	2025		0-14	15-64	65+	0-14	15-64	65+	1965 -80	1980 -92	1992 -2000
Ethiopia	340	55	141	370	47.0	50.2	2.8	43.1	54.4	2.5	2.7	3.1	2.6
Mozambique	570	17	40	100	44.1	52.7	3.2	40.4	56.9	2.7	2.5	2.6	2.6
Tanzania	630	26	59	117	46.7	50.3	3.0	40.2	57.2	2.6	2.9	3.0	3.0
Malawi	730	6	21	51	46.7	50.7	2.6	42.3	55.2	2.5	2.9	3.2	2.5
Uganda	1 070	17	45	121	48.7	48.5	2.8	39.7	58.3	2.0	3.0	2.6	3.0
India	1 210	884	1 016	1 370	36.9	58.7	4.4	24.0	68.4	7.6	2.3	2.1	1.7
China	1 910	1 162	1 471	1 680	27.0	67.2	5.8	20.8	66.5	12.7	2.2	1.4	1.0
Pakistan	2 130	119	243	400	44.2	53.0	2.8	30.4	65.1	4.5	3.1	3.1	2.7
Romania	2 750	23	23	23	23.8	65.9	10.3	20.3	64.1	15.6	1.1	0.2	0.0
Peru	3 080	22	36	48	38.0	58.3	3.7	23.9	68.4	7.7	2.8	2.1	1.8
Egypt	3 670	55	86	121	39.2	56.6	4.2	24.4	67.6	12.2	2.1	2.4	1.7
Jamaica	3 770	2	3	4	34.2	59.3	6.5	21.7	67.6	10.7	1.3	1.0	0.6
Poland	4 880	38	42	46	25.1	64.9	10.0	19.9	62.3	17.8	0.8	0.6	0.2
Brazil	5 250	154	224	285	35.4	60.2	4.4	22.8	66.9	10.3	2.4	2.0	1.4
Thailand	5 890	58	81	104	33.9	63.1	3.0	21.9	68.0	10.1	2.9	1.8	1.3
Mexico	7 490	85	136	182	37.3	59.0	3.7	22.9	68.3	12.5	3.1	2.0	1.9
Chile	8 090	14	15	23	30.5	63.6	5.9	21.3	65.7	13.0	1.7	1.7	1.3
South Korea	8 950	44	53	56	25.1	69.4	5.5	18.1	66.0	15.9	2.0	1.1	0.8
Portugal	10 120	10	10	9	20.7	66.3	13.0	16.4	63.5	20.1	0.4	0.1	0.0
Saudi Arabia	11 170	17	43	85	45.5	51.9	2.6	36.3	59.1	4.6	4.6	4.9	3.3
South Africa	11 390	40	69	103	38.2	57.8	4.0	25.6	67.0	7.4	2.4	2.5	2.2
Spain	13 170	39	38	32	19.8	67.0	13.2	15.6	63.4	21.0	1.0	0.4	0.0
New Zealand	14 400	3	4	5	22.7	66.3	11.0	18.7	62.7	18.6	1.3	0.8	0.8
Singapore	16 720	3	4	4	23.6	70.9	5.5	18.1	61.9	20.0	1.6	1.8	1.4
Hong Kong	20 050	6	6	5	21.0	70.2	8.8	15.4	61.4	23.2	2.0	1.0	0.0
Switzerland	22 100	7	7	7	17.0	68.1	14.9	15.8	58.3	25.9	0.5	0.7	0.6
United States	23 120	255	323	348	21.6	66.1	12.3	18.1	61.2	33.0	1.0	1.0	1.0

Source: adapted from the World Bank, *World Development Report*.

to country and continent to continent. Figure 106.1 shows that the largest growth in the world's population is forecast to come from Africa, the world's poorest continent. By the year 2150, one-third of the world's population is predicted to be African. China's population, currently one-fifth that of the world's, will rise by 0.3bn but shrink to 12 per cent of the world's population by 2150.

The size of the population: is it a problem?

Many argue that the planet is already over-populated with 5bn inhabitants. Growth to 12bn will be unsustainable. There are a number of arguments put forward to sustain this proposition.

The food supply and Malthus Malthus was an early nineteenth century British economist who put forward 'the iron law of wages'. He argued that the food supply could only increase arithmetically over time (e.g. 2, 4, 6, 8, 10 ...) whilst the population would grow geometrically (2, 4, 16, 256, ...). The result would inevitably be poverty and starvation with most of the population never getting out of the poverty trap. This was because a rise in wages would lead to more children surviving into adulthood. This would increase the supply of labour, driving down wages, with more children starving to death. In equilibrium, most of the population can only live at subsistence level.

Malthusian economics has proved to be incorrect in the developed world. As was discussed in unit 19, world food supply has more than kept pace with population growth. In the developed world, average daily calorie intake is more than twice what is was 100 years ago. Modern day Malthusians argue that the pace of technological change cannot be kept up. Farmers cannot increase their yields per acre forever by improving the land, applying more fertilizer and developing better strains. There has to be a limit to how much food the planet can grow. Critics of this view say that crop yields in the West have been increasing at about 2½ per cent per annum for 100 years, more than outstripping population growth. Why should this trend not continue? Moreover, the developed countries of the world already have the potential to grow more food than is currently being produced. The objectives of the USA, Canada and the EU are to restrict food production from current levels (☞ unit 34). Food is not a physical problem today, it is a market problem. Starvation occurs because consumers don't have the money to buy food, not because it cannot be produced.

Resource pressures The developed countries of the world are currently growing at about 3 per cent per annum. Yet many developing countries have population growth of 3 per cent per annum. How, then, can developing countries expect to see any increase in income per capita? This is a variant of the Malthusian argument. All of a country's increasing resources resulting from economic growth have to be used simply to keep the average standard of living constant. In Africa in the 1980s, where population growth is high, GDP per capita fell because economic growth did not keep pace with rising population. The average African citizen was poorer in 1990 than in 1980. Critics of this view point out that countries do break out of this cycle. France, Germany and the UK all had high population growth in the nineteenth century. Nearly all developing countries have higher GDP per capita levels today compared to 1950. Some East Asian countries are growing at over 10 per cent per annum at the moment. The African experience of the 1980s is not the norm but the exception.

The environment Even if the growth in food production and in production of all other goods exceeds population growth, this is not environmentally sustainable. Giving every household in the world a refrigerator would do irretrievable damage to the ozone layer when those refrigerators were thrown away. Giving every household a car would lead to global warming on a scale not even predicted today. Constant intensive farm production would lead to permanent degradation of farm lands. Pressure for living space would result in the destruction of countless species of plant and animal, reducing bio-diversity, with unpredictable effects on the environment and on the human species.

For these reasons, economists have attempted to develop a concept of **sustainable development**. The 1987 World Commision on Environment and Development stated that development needed to meet 'the needs of the present generation without compromising the needs of future generations'. In economic terms, this means 'maximising the net welfare of economic activities, while maintaining or increasing the stock of economic, ecological and sociocultural assets over time and providing a safety net to meet basic needs and protect the poor' (Mohan Munasingle in *IMF, Finance and Development*, December 1993). Meeting today's needs should not rob the next generation of ability to grow and develop.

The age structure of the population

Many argue that the planet is already over-populated with 5bn inhabitants. Growth to 12bn inhabitants will bring even greater pressures to bear on the environment. It will require enormous investment in physical and human capital. There is also a question mark about whether the

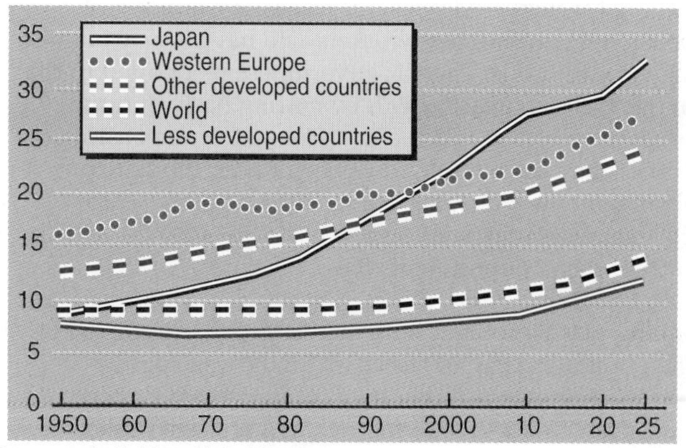

Source: adapted from United Nations.

Figure 106.2 *Population aged 60 and over as a percentage of total population*

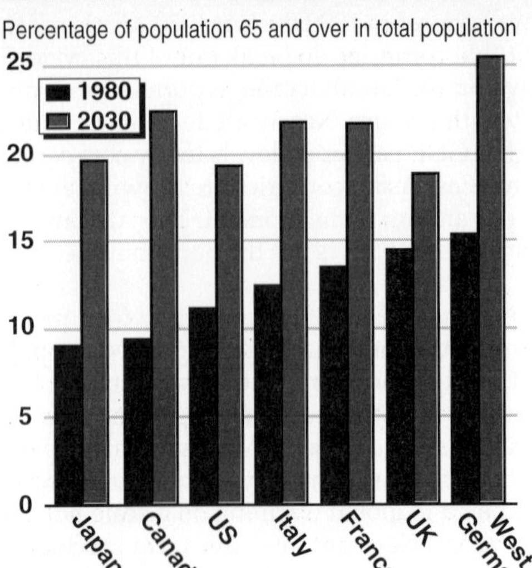

Source: adapted from OECD.

Figure 106.3 *The ageing population of the developed world*

planet will be able to feed 12bn people, discussed below.

However, the process of transition from the 1bn inhabitants in 1900 to 5bn in 1990 to 12bn in 2150 is giving rise to large variations in the age structure of populations of different countries. In First World countries, falling birth rates this century combined with longer life expectancy have led to a gradual increase in the proportion of old people to both the working population and to the total population. Figures 106.2 and 106.3 show that some countries or regions have been worse affected by this trend than others. Increased numbers of old people in the population imply a shift in the structure of production. For instance, there will be a greater demand for health care and residential homes (☞ unit 53). However, there are also major implications for the distribution of income.

Dependency ratios, the number of dependants to the number of workers in the population, are predicted to rise substantially over the next 50 years in the developed world. If pensioners are to share in the growing prosperity of their economies, then there must be a shift in the share of total income being received in favour of the pensioner population and away from the working population. For instance, if pensions are provided by the state, then paying for increased pensions to a larger number of pensioners implies that workers will have to pay higher taxes to fund this. The UK government responded to this in the 1980s and early 1990s by cutting back on future pension commitments (i.e. by making future pensioners poorer than they would have been under the state pension arrangements which existed in 1980). Other western governments may well respond over the next 20 years by cutting their commitments too.

In the Third World, the current problem is not with an ageing population but with the very high proportion of the population that is under 15. Of the developing countries shown in Table 106.1, only the two Eastern European countries had more than 6 per cent of their population over the age of 65. In contrast, all the developing countries had at least 25 per cent of their population under the age of 15 and one-third had between 40 and 50 per cent of their population in this age group. This situation is predicted to improve by the year 2025 for middle income countries, but most low income countries of the world are predicted to remain with over 40 per cent of the population below 15.

There are major problems with having a large proportion of the population below the age of 15. Providing for children will impose a heavy burden on workers. Children need to be clothed and fed. They also need health care and education. There is a close link between poverty and low educational attainment.

- Poor countries cannot afford to provide adequate state education systems.
- Many families cannot afford to send their children to school even if education is free. This is because they need children to work, either on their farms, or as child labourers working for local businesses. Only by securing an income from their children can these families survive.
- Moreover, the local economy often cannot provide jobs suitable for reasonably educated children. There is then little incentive for families to educate their children for the local job market.

As children pass through into adulthood, they then need jobs to survive. However, poor countries have too little physical capital to provide all workers with jobs. Hence, there is widespread unemployment and underemployment. This, particularly in urban settings, can lead to high levels of crime and drug dependency.

Equally, passage to adulthood implies marriage and the setting up of homes. This means that the economy must provide more homes, more sanitation facilities, more clean water, etc. Even if the birth rate is slowing dramatically, it can take 50 to 60 years for the population to stabilise and for the economic effects of children on the economy to reach some sort of equilibrium.

Government policy and the birth rate

It is generally agreed that there is a link between development and the birth rate. As Table 106.1 shows, the poorer the country, the more likely there is to be a high rate of population growth. The link is arguably biological, social and economic.

Development implies better health with fewer children dying. Either for biological or social reasons, or some combination of the two, people react by having fewer children. For instance, if half of all children die before the age of 15, then a family needs on average to have 4 children for two to survive to adulthood. If almost all children survive to adulthood, they only need two.

The higher the level of development, the greater the cost of bringing up children. At low levels of development, children eat little and need little looking after. They can quickly be put out to work and become an economic asset. As levels of development increase, children have to spend time in school, reducing their ability to work. The amount of care taken over children also tends to increase, reducing the amount of time adults can spend working. In a developed country, children have to stay in education for most if not all of their teenage years. There is very little

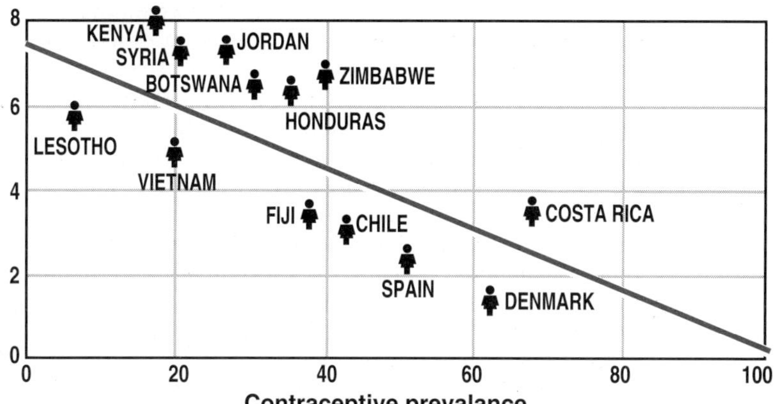

Source: adapted from United Nations.
Figure 106.4 *Fertility and contraception availability*

expectation on the part of parents that the children will contribute any wages to the household. The cost of keeping children in terms of university education, food, clothes, etc. rises as parental incomes rise. The opportunity cost, usually for women, of staying away from work to bring up children also increases as average incomes in the economy rises. From being a financial asset to parents in a poor developing country, they become a large financial burden in developed economies. Not surprisingly, birth rates fall.

Government, however, can play a part in altering the rate of change of the birth rate and influencing the long run equilibrium birth rate in the country.

Education Governments can, through health clinics, schools and the media, try to persuade couples to have fewer children. Studies have shown that this is most effective if aimed at women who have to bear most of the time and health cost of bearing and bringing up children.

Family planning Governments can sponsor family planning programmes. Most developing countries have such programmes, although they differ widely in the amount of resources put into the programme and their effectiveness. In general, as Figure 106.4 shows, the greater the number of women with access to contraceptives, the lower the fertility rate. Family planning can run into cultural objections. As with education, the most effective family planning is achieved with the co-operation of women rather than men. However, women deciding how many children they have can be seen as subverting the domination of men in patriarchal societies. Family planning is also condemned by some religious groups as being immoral.

Incentives and disincentives These have been widely used throughout the developed and developing world. Some are **fiscal** (i.e involve government spending or taxation). France, for instance, which has believed for all of this century that it has too small a population, currently has a generous system of child benefits designed to encourage women to have children. In Singapore, income tax relief is also only given for the first three children. Other incentives and disincentives are physical, legal, administrative or social. In Singapore, again, no account is made of the number of children in a family when allocating public housing. A family with six children will get the same cramped apartment space as a family with one child. In China, the government introduced a widely disliked policy in the early 1980s allowing parents only to have one child. Women had to get the approval of the local neighbourhood committee or council for permission to get pregnant. Approval was usually denied if the parents already had one child unless that child had a disability. Steep fines were imposed on women who had children without permission. Women with two or more children were refused promotion.

It is difficult to evaluate the effectiveness of such programmes because it is impossible to know what the birth rate would have been in the absence of the programme. However, in those cases where incentives are given for men to have vasectomies (as in India in the 1970s), it seems logical the programme must have some impact on the birth rate.

Raising the economic status of women Women are the child-bearers in society. If the state can increase the opportunity cost for women of having children, then the number of children being born can be reduced. This can be achieved mainly through increasing employment opportunities for women. If women can earn a reasonable wage, they will be less likely to marry early. For instance, why should a family marry off a daughter at 14 when she could be put out to work to earn money till she was, say, 18? Women can also leave home and set up independently if they can earn a living wage and make their own choice about when and who to marry. Once married, the opportunity cost of staying at home to look after children rises the greater the wage the women could earn in a paid job. The workplace can also be an important place for education. Government agencies may be able to get access to talk to women in the workplace but not in the home. Women may also support each other against more traditional values through the relationships they build up in the workplace.

Migration

Urbanisation, the shift of the population from the countryside into the towns, has been rapid over the past 40 years as Table 106.2 shows. In the 1950s and 1960s, the widespread migration of people from rural areas into cities was regarded by economists as beneficial. It was argued that workers in rural areas were engaged in low productivity (often agricultural) occupations. In urban areas their labour could be transferred into higher productivity manufacturing and service sector jobs. The growth of secondary and tertiary industries, indeed, demanded a growth in the urban population.

Table 106.2 *Urbanisation*

	Urban population as % of total	
	1970	1992
World	35	42
High income countries	74	78
Middle income countries	46	62
Low income countries	18	27
of which		
Sub-Saharan Africa	19	29
East Asia and Pacific	19	29
South Asia	19	25
Middle East and North Africa	41	55
Latin America and Caribbean	57	73

Source: adapted from the World Bank, *World Development Report.*

In the 1970s and 1980s, however, there has been a reversal of opinion and rural-urban migration has come to be seen as having a negative impact on the development of many countries. This is because migrants often fail to find jobs in the cities. From being low productivity rural workers, they become the zero productivity urban unemployed. Moreover, migrants tend to be young, better educated, rural dwellers. Having received some education, they set off for the city to seek their fortune. This drains rural areas of those individuals who could have played a vital role in increasing the productivity of the rural sector in the economy. In the city, migrants contribute to the already difficult environmental and social pressures, which would not necessarily have been present in the rural area they left.

Rural migrants are often aware that urban unemployment is high and that they may leave a job and family security in the countryside to become unemployed in the town. However, rural migrants base their decisions on **expected income**. For instance, assume that they have a one in two chance of becoming unemployed when going to the city, but if they do get a job, their wages will be four times as high as their present rural wage. Then, the average expected urban wage will be twice that of the rural wage. Potential unemployment is not a deterrent to migration if the potential wage to those who do get jobs is large enough. This theory is called the **Todaro model** after Michael Todaro, the economist who first put it forward in the late 1960s.

Measures which aim to improve the standard of living of urban dwellers relative to rural dwellers will only increase migration and increase unemployment in the country. For instance, an anti-poverty campaign in urban areas, with slum dwellers being given help with housing, access to electricity and sanitation and government work programmes and a higher minimum wage, will increase the expected benefits of being a town dweller. This will then attract further migrants who will create new slums and a new urban poor. There may also be a perverse impact of education programmes on economic development. There is evidence that, as in developed countries, urban employers use qualifications as a rough guide to sorting out applicants for a job. It is the better educated who are most likely to migrate from rural areas into towns. With a fixed number of jobs in the urban job market, employers will be able to increase the educational qualifications of their newest employees by choosing from the now enlarged pool of existing urban workers and the new migrants. Qualification 'inflation' will occur, where success at secondary school level is needed even for quite low productivity jobs. The new workers will be over-qualified for their jobs and the economy will receive a very low rate of return on its investment in education in those individuals. The resources allocated to that investment would have been better used elsewhere to promote development.

The solution to the problem of migration is to improve the economic benefits received by rural dwellers. Prices of agricultural products have often been artificially depressed by governments who have forced farmers to sell part or all their produce to the state. The difference between the price paid to the farmer and the market price then becomes a tax on the farming community. Raising prices to market levels would increase rural incomes and reduce **allocative efficiency** (☞ unit 34) in the economy.

More money could be spent by government on promoting job creation in rural areas. The establishment of labour intensive small scale enterprises would have a number of other benefits, including less of a dependence on the importation of capital-intensive equipment which tends to create a few jobs in city areas. Education policy needs to be changed too. All the evidence suggests that high quality primary education for all children gives a far higher rate of return than primary, secondary and tertiary industry for a few. Investment in primary education in rural areas would give a higher rate of return than, say, investment in secondary schooling in urban areas. It would also reduce education qualification 'inflation' and reduce

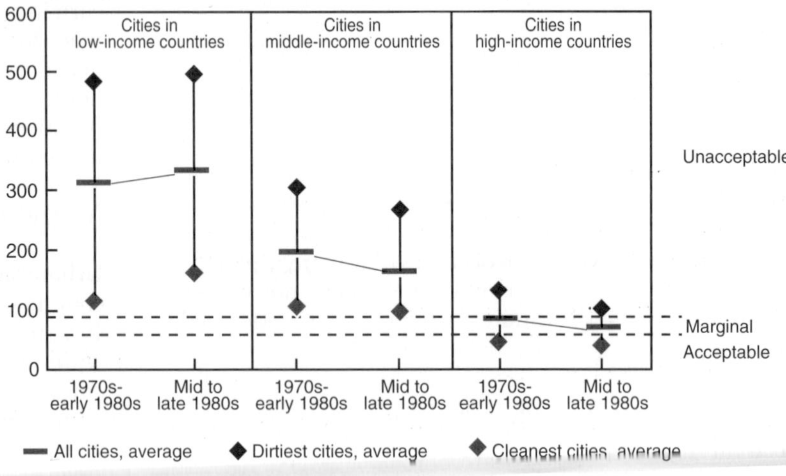

Source: adapted from World Bank, *World Development Report 1992.*
Figure 106.5 *Urban air pollution levels and trends: concentrations of suspended particulate matter across country income groups*

the attractiveness for future parents of migrating to urban areas where their children might receive a better education.

The environmental problem

Environmental problems and government policy responses have already been discussed at length in units 37 and 38. Third World countries face similar problems to First World countries, although the poorest billion inhabitants create special environmental difficulties.

Air pollution In First World countries, industry and the motor car are the main polluters. The same is true in urban areas in the Third World although on a larger scale because environmental controls are laxer. Figure 106.5 shows the extent of the problem in the Third World. Concentrations of suspended particulate matter in cities in low-income countries worsened between the 1970s and the 1980s on average and were unacceptable in most middle-income cities. In rural areas, there is a problem with the burning of biomass fuels, such as manure, straw and wood. When burnt indoors for cooking and heat, these create dangerously high levels of indoor pollution which affect an estimated 400-700 million people, particularly women and children who spend longer indoors. Air pollution is a major cause of respiratory diseases, and results in an estimated 300 000 - 700 000 deaths annually.

Deforestation The cutting down of the tropical rainforests is widely publicised in the West. Deforestation is caused by three main factors. First, forest is cut to create farming land. Second, trees are cut for timber to be sold, for instance, to First World countries. Third, trees are cut for fuel. For the First World, the main problem is that cutting down forests increases the possibility of global warming since trees absorb carbon dioxide. For the Third World, the major problem is degredation of the land and possible desertification. Forests often exist on poor quality land which is unsuited to intensive cultivation. When abandoned after a period of cultivation, the land can become desert or scrub land. Where trees are cut for firewood, the trees can be acting as windbreaks. With fewer trees in an agricultural area, there is the danger of fast erosion of top soil and a consequent loss of productivity of the land.

Soil degradation Deforestation is only one cause of soil degradation. Over-intensive farming caused by too high population densities in a local area is another. Pressure on land supply also forces some farmers to begin to cultivate poor quality non-forest marginal land, which again within a few years leads to soil degradation.

Water scarcity and pollution Lack of water and water pollution are major causes of disease in Third World countries. Table 106.3 shows the numbers affected by four diseases in the Third World and the impact that improved water supplies can have on those diseases. Lack of water also affects the ability of farmers to grow food because of lack of irrigation. Water pollution also affects food crops. For instance, in south China, pollution of rivers is widely thought to have infected local seafood and caused an outbreak of hepatitis A in Shanghai in the 1980s.

Table 106.3 *Impact of inadequate water supply and sanitation facilities, 1990 estimate*

Disease	Millions of people affected by illness	Median reduction attributable to improved water supply and sanitation facilities (%)
Diarrhoea	900	22
Roundworm	900	28
Guinea worm	4	76
Schistosomiasis	200	73

Source: adapted from World Bank, *World Development Report 1992.*

Waste disposal Problems of the disposal of hazardous waste, such as nuclear waste, are familiar in First World countries. In Third World countries, there is hazardous waste too which can have a considerable impact on local communities. However, the more general problem is disposal of everyday garbage. The World Bank estimated in 1992 that about 30 per cent of sold wastes generated in Jakarta, four-fifths of refuse in Dar es Salaam and more than two-thirds of sold wastes in Karachi go uncollected. These pose a serious health hazard, contributing to the spread of disease. Waste also gets into water supplies, leading to problems associated with unclean water.

Reduction of biodiversity Each year, species of plants and animals are becoming extinct. Figure 106.6 shows the estimated number of mammal and bird species lost between 1700 and 1987. This, as explained above, leads to a loss of genetic material which might be of use in agriculture and industry. Many also argue that it is immoral for humans to destroy species.

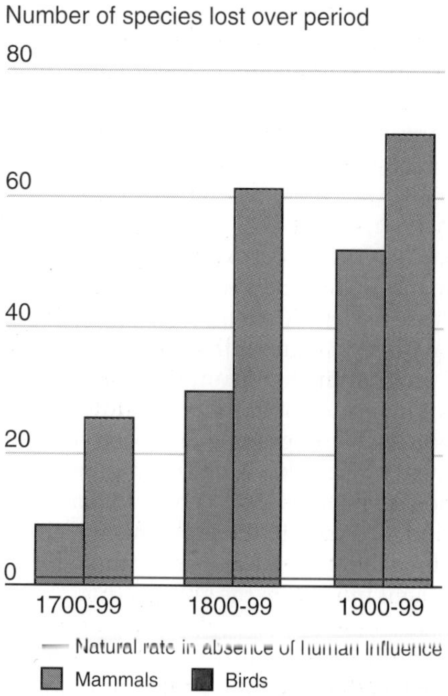

Number of species lost over period

80
60
40
20
0

1700-99 1800-99 1900-99

Natural rate in absence of human influence

Mammals Birds

Source: adapted from World Bank, World Development Report 1992.

Figure 106.6 *Recorded extinctions of mammals and birds, 1700-1987*

Atmospheric change Depletion of the ozone layer and global warming are well known. They could affect Third World countries by increasing skin cancers, increasing the possibility of climatic disasters, and causing a disruption in patterns of food production.

Third World policy responses to the environment

In unit 38, it was explained that governments had a variety of instruments which they could use to reduce pollution externalities. These included:

- banning or imposing quantitative controls on polluting activities;
- extending property rights so that pollution becomes 'owned' and allowing free market forces to act to reduce pollution;
- imposing taxes on pollution;
- subsidising activities which would reduce pollution;
- awarding permits to pollute which become tradeable.

However, many pollution problems arise directly from a lack of development. Increase economic development and many of these environmental problems will disappear. It is no coincidence that in Figure 106.5, urban pollution was greatest in low-income cities and lowest in high-income cities. Reducing pollution by firms through some of the above strategies can only be one part of a much wider strategy. Elements of a successful strategy are also likely to include the following.

Land reform People will be discouraged from investing in their own infrastructure unless they know that they have rights over their property. In urban slums, for instance, where many houses are illegal, giving occupants official ownership will encourage them to put in proper sanitation and running water and fight to have their waste disposed of properly. In rural areas, where many farmers are tenants, giving tenants right of tenure or redistributing the land to them from large landowners will provide them with a long term incentive to adopt agricultural techniques which will ensure the long term survival of their land.

Working with the local community Evidence suggests that government programmes which provide for local communities are far less successful than programmes which work with local communities. For instance, a government programme to replant trees in a local area is likely to result in local people chopping down those trees for fuel as soon as the programme has been completed and government officials have left. A programme where the government persuades local people to plant trees and helps them find solutions to the problems which underlie the initial deforestation of the area is far more likely to have a permanent impact on the area.

Creating economic opportunities for the poor Creating new ways in which the poor can earn their living can have an important environmental impact. For instance, creating low technology labour intensive industries in rural areas will relieve pressure to farm marginal land. It will enable people to purchase more environmentally friendly fuels, rather than resorting to collecting bio-mass fuels such as trees from the local environment. They will have more disposable income to provide their own better water and sanitation facilities. Fewer people will migrate to the cities, relieving pollution problems in urban areas. A vital part of any such economic policy must the creation of economic opportunities for women since they play such a key role cooking, farming, collecting water and dealing with sanitation problems.

Pricing which reflects social costs and benefits Prices in Third World countries often benefit urban elites to the disadvantage of the rest of society. For instance, urban elites, who are most able to pay, may be provided with subsidised water whilst urban slum dwellers and rural dwellers have little or no access to clean water. Properly pricing water, to include the benefits of far better health, should lead governments to aim to provide a basic water supply system for as many as possible rather than a high quality supply for a few.

First World policy responses

The First World could be a major loser from environmental degradation in the Third World. For instance, economic actions in the Third World which increase emissions of greenhouse gases and ozone-depleting gases, or which reduce bio-diversity, could lead to large economic costs in the future for the First World. Therefore, many argue that the First World must adopt appropriate policy responses to deal with the problem.

The most important policy response for First World countries could be to help Third World countries increase their rate of development. People in Third World countries

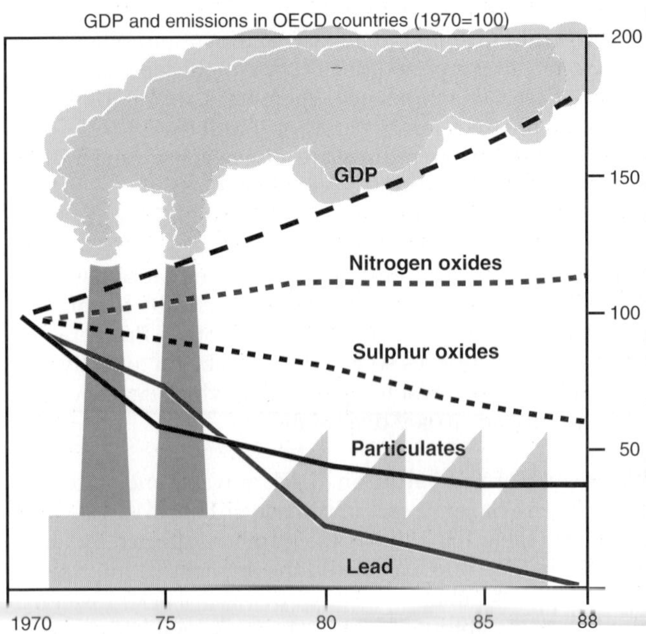

Source: adapted from OECD; US Environmental Protection Agency.

Figure 106.7 *GDP and emissions in OECD countries (1970 = 100)*

do not wish to degrade their soils, use contaminated water or produce greenhouse gases. Figure 106.7, and Figure 106.5 discussed above, show a trend. The higher the level of development, the lower the level of pollution. This is because people place a higher and higher value on the environment as their incomes increase. Consequently, they are prepared to pay higher prices to reduce pollution emissions than when their incomes were lower. As will be discussed in units 107-109, First World countries need to open up their markets more to exports from Third World countries to give those countries greater economic opportunities. They need to forgive debt and increase foreign aid. Inward investment is also vital.

First World countries also need to develop and then disseminate best practice on pollution control. First World countries, with a fraction of the world's population, need further to reduce their own levels of pollution. It would be difficult for First World countries to argue that Third World countries should tackle issues such as global warming when they are the major contributors of greenhouse gas emissions.

There has also been discussion of rewarding Third World countries which comply with environmentally friendly policies. For instance, **debt-for-nature swaps** have been negotiated on a very limited basis, where First World governments forgive debt owed to them by Third World countries if Third World countries comply with a specific conservation programme. Alternatively, it has been suggested that First World countries should pay Third World countries to manage their rain forests. There are a number of problems with these policies. One is that they are difficult to police. Third World governments are likely to receive money from the agreement but it is usually their citizens who are damaging the environment. There is often a lack of political will on the part of the Third World government to stop them doing this. Even if they wanted to, governments often have considerable difficulties enforcing measures. However, the most important drawback is that they can only have a marginal impact on global environmental problems. They are too specific and too small scale to be a significant solution, even though they might attract widespread media publicity in First World countries.

An issue the west ignores at its peril

No issue divides Africa from the First World more strongly than the environment. While the west worries about the endangered black rhino and loss of bio-diversity, most Africans are too exhausted from their daily struggle to find fuel and water to care about the destruction of their environment.

The priorities of each seem irreconcilable, and yet, they need not be. What is needed is a greater awareness in the industrialised world on how its policies exacerbate Africa's environmental crisis. And African governments need to place greater emphasis on combatting the extreme poverty which is a cause, as well as a result, of environmental degradation. There is little time to reverse the damage. At current growth rates, Sub-Saharan Africa's population of 600m will double in 22 years. The World Bank estimates the growth rate will decline from the present 3.1 per cent to 2.5 per cent at the end of the decade, as Aids takes its toll and family planning becomes more widespread. However, even this decline will not be enough to prevent the population doubling early in the next century.

Already, the women in the Sahel and many parts of east Africa walk 15km each day to gather bundles of firewood. In a few years, there will be more mouths to feed and less wood to burn.

Over-cultivation and over-grazing are transforming much of the continent into a vast wasteland: an area twice the size of India, according to the United Nations Environmental Programme (UNEP), is under direct threat of desertification. In addition, Africa is losing 2.7m hectares of woodlands every year. In most countries, forests are disappearing because people need land for farming, not wood to burn.

When famine sweeps across Africa, the west calls it a natural disaster and spends billions of dollars in emergency food relief. But Africa's hunger is not simply a question of crop failure. In 1985, five out of six nations on a United Nations list of famine-afflicted countries were also racked by civil war. In Ethiopia, Chad, Sudan, Mozambique and Angola, it was difficult to distinguish between drought-related famine and war-induced starvation.

Environmental degradation can also add to the pressures from which conflict emerges. 'The next war in our region will be over the waters of the Nile, not the politics,' Mr Boutros Boutros Ghali, now the UN secretary-general, warned in 1985. The Nile basin touches on nine other countries, reaching as far south as Tanzania and Zaire. All upstream nations are keen to extend land under irrigation by tapping Egypt's only source of water.

'Without political imagination,' Mr Boutros Ghali continued, 'Egypt will become a new Bangladesh fraught with drought and famine - but with one difference. This Bangladesh will be on the shores of the Mediterranean, half-an-hour by jet from the rich people in the north.'

Already, according to the UN High Commission for

Refugees, there are 5m displaced people on the continent. To call them refugees would be a misnomer, for most will never be able to return to their homes. Many are fleeing land too degraded to support them. Others seek refuge from civil war, government repression, ethnic conflict, or simply the desperate poverty of rural areas. But up to now, the west has preferred to focus on endangered animals, rather than endangered humans.

The expulsion of Maasai pastoralists from 4,800 square miles of traditional grazing land which became the Serengeti National Park in Tanzania was one of the first important battles fought by western conservationists in Africa. All over the continent, 'experts' imposed the theory that wildlife and people should be separated. This principle is now being challenged. 'It is hard to imagine that 150,000 tourists are not causing greater environmental damage and disturbing wildlife far more than 2,000 Maasai ever did,' says Mr Raymond Bonner, a US journalist and author of *At the Hand of Man: Peril and Hope for Africa's Wildlife*.

New solutions are required which marry the needs of local people to those of the environment. In Luwangwa, Zambia, hunting rights are auctioned among safari companies and the revenues are channelled to the local tribes. As a result, villagers have started supporting the national parks service and set up security committees to prevent poachers entering into their areas. The number of poached carcasses of elephants and black rhinos in Luwangwa fell by 90 per cent between 1985 and 1987.

The lesson to be learned is that Africa needs an economic incentive to protect its wildlife. But western institutions - be they tourist of pharmaceutical companies - are often reluctant to pay the price.

Far more worrying than the endangered black rhino are Africa's disappearing insects and plants - species that could hold the cure for Aids. Already, Africa has destroyed 65 per cent of its original wildlife habitats.

Concerns about the staggering loss of bio-diversity are not exaggerated. A substance discovered in the rosy periwinkle, a species unique to Madagascar, has quadrupled the survival rate for children suffering from Leukemia. Worldwide sales of the rosy periwinkle drug now earn more than $100m a year, but not a cent has accrued to Madagascar in compensation for preserving the plant's habitat.

A growing number of ecologists now argue that the best way of persuading African nations to protect their bio-diversity is by paying them to leave their natural resources intact. What is found in Africa may be needed in Europe and the rest of the developed world.

Paper mills in the US and Japan, for example, are experimenting with an African plant, Kenaf, a relative of jute, which produces five times more pulp than the average tree. After 30 years of investigations, the US Department of Agriculture has singled out Kenaf as the most promising substitute to produce tree-free paper. It is an annual crop, whereas man-made forests require up to 60 years in the northern hemisphere to reach maturity. US newspapers which have tested Kenaf newsprint report that it is brighter, reproduces better pictures, and uses less ink, which does not stain hands.

Africa's environmental problems are often portrayed in doomsday tones. In reality, they are neither insoluble nor insurmountable. What is needed is a radical reassessment of the value the industrialised world places on Africa's environmental health. It is an issue the west ignores at its peril.

Source: the *Financial Times*, 1.9.1993

1. **What environmental problems do Third World countries face? Illustrate your answer with examples from the data.**
2. **(a) A number of solutions to environment problems are identified in the article. Explain these solutions, using diagrams where appropriate. (b) Discuss TWO other policy responses to environmental problem which could be used in Africa.**
3. **To what extent are environmental problems and their solutions in the Third World different from those in the First World?**

Development strategies

Applied economics

Investment and saving

Development economics has a relatively short history. The first major work in this field of economics was done in the 1950s. The most important question which development economists asked themselves to begin with was 'how can an economy grow,' given that the 'problem' with Third World countries was that they were far poorer than First World countries. As explained in unit 105, growth in GDP rather than a more complex measure of development was assumed to be the yardstick by which countries would be measured.

Development economists initially used a widely accepted growth theory of the time called the **Harrod-Domar** growth model, named after the two economists who developed it in the 1930s (shown in Figure 107.1). This theory stated that investment, saving and technological change were the key variables in determining growth. Increased investment in the economy pushes out the **production possibility** frontier of the economy. So too does the introduction of new capital (machines, factories, equipment, offices) where a unit of the new, technologically advanced capital can produce more output than a unit of the old capital. Savings is important because savings approximately equal investment in an economy (☞ units 58 and 99).

This model can be expressed in simple algebraic terms. Savings (S) is a proportion (s) of national income (Y). So $S = sY$. Investment (I) is the change in the capital stock (ΔK). The amount of extra capital (ΔK) needed to produce an extra unit of output (ΔY) is called k, the capital-output ratio and is equal to $\Delta K \div \Delta Y$. As already explained, investment is roughly equal to savings in an economy, and so it can be said that $S = I$.

What then causes economic growth, which is measured by the change in output divided by the original level of output ($\Delta Y \div Y$)? The top of the fraction, ΔY can be found from the definition of the capital output ratio, $k = (\Delta K \div \Delta Y)$. Rearranging this equation gives: $\Delta Y = (\Delta K \div k)$. The bottom of the fraction, Y, can be found from the equation $S = sY$, remembering that $S = I$ and that $I = \Delta K$. This gives us $S = I = \Delta K = sY$. Rearranging the last part of this gives: $Y = \Delta K \div sY$.

ΔK can be found on both the top and bottom of this fraction for the growth rate of the economy and therefore cancel each other out. This leaves us with:

$$\text{The rate of growth} = \frac{\Delta Y}{Y} = \frac{s}{k}$$

Figure 107.1 *The Harrod-Domar model of growth*

The policy implications of the Harrod-Domar model are clear. Increasing the rate of growth is a simple matter of either increasing the savings ratio in the economy which will increase the amount of investment, or it is about technological progress which allows more output to be produced from a single unit of that capital.

The insights of the Harrod-Domar model were used by the first important development economist, an American called Walt W Rostow. He said that economies went through five stages.

1. The traditional society, where barter is common and where agriculture is the most important industry.
2. An economy which has the pre-conditions for take-off into self-sustaining growth. Savings are rising to a level of between 15 and 20 per cent of national income.
3. The take-off stage. The economy begins to grow at a positive rate.
4. The drive to maturity. The economy has broken away from the ranks of economies still in stages 1 and 2 of the development process and is marching towards the status of a developed economy.
5. The age of mass consumption. The economy has finally made it, and its citizens are able to enjoy high consumption levels.

For Rostow, savings was the most important element in getting the economy to stages 3 and 4. The theory also used the insights of the Marshall Plan. This transferred large amounts of resources from the the USA to Europe in the late 1940s to help Europe rebuild its industries. Foreign saving was added to domestic saving to increase the rate of growth of investment in Europe, thus raising European growth rates. Rostow and his followers similarly argued that Third World prosperity could be increased if First World countries gave foreign aid to Third World countries. This would fill a **savings gap**, the difference between the domestic rate of saving and the rate of investment needed for take off and the drive to maturity.

Economists are widely agreed that increasing savings and investment are vital to secure higher growth rates. The economic success stories of East Asia, from Japan to South Korea to Taiwan and Singapore, are built upon investment ratios to national income of 30 per cent or more compared to, say, the 17 per cent ratio currently being achieved by the UK and the 21-22 per cent being achieved by countries such as France and Germany. Figure 107.2 shows this correlation clearly for the high performance Asian economies such as South Korea and Taiwan.

However, these are not a **sufficient** condition for growth. Investment can be wasted. Building a new steel mill in a Third World country might lead to nothing if workers are not able to run the mill, or if there aren't the ports to import iron ore, or roads to transport the finished product. Savings can be exported, with Third World citizens sending their surpluses to Swiss bank accounts or using it to buy shares on the New York stock exchange (the problem of **capital flight**). Foreign aid has too often in the past been diverted into paying for arms rather than being used for investment. Figure 107.2 shows that rates of investment in Sub-Saharan Africa were very similar to those in South Asia in both 1965 and 1990. Yet growth rates differed enormously. Development is, in fact, a far more complex process than that set out in Rostow's stages of growth.

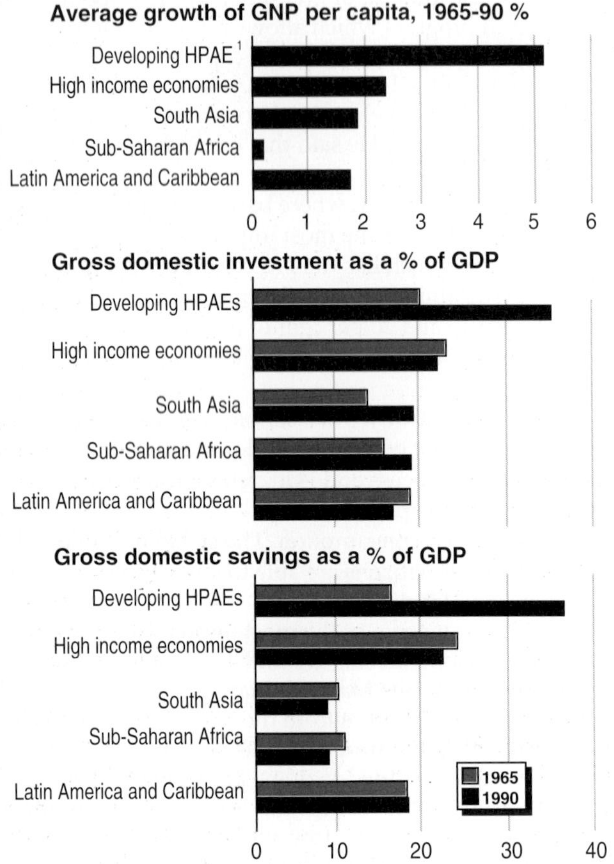

1. High performing Asian economies of South Korea, Taiwan, Singapore, Hong Kong, Malaysia, Indonesia, Thailand.
Source: adapted from World Bank.
Figure 107.2

Structural change models

Another economist, W Arthur Lewis, focused on the role of migration in this process of development. He argued that growth could be sustained by the gradual transfer of workers from low productivity agriculture (the **traditional sector**) to higher productivity urban secondary and tertiary industries (the **modern sector**). The **industrialisation** of the economy, therefore, can be seen as an objective of development. He assumed that marginal workers in rural areas added nothing to the output of the rural economy (i.e. their marginal productivity was zero). Either they genuinely did no work (i.e. they were unemployed) or the work that they did could have been performed by existing workers with no effect on total output (i.e. there was a large amount of underemployment in the rural economy). Workers could gradually be transferred into the urban higher productivity sector. The rate of transfer depended on the rate of capital accumulation in the modern sector of the economy. The greater the investment, the faster the transfer. Eventually, nearly all workers will have been transferred from the traditional sector to the modern sector and the economy will have become developed.

The Lewis model provided key insights into the development process, and was in part used to explain why developed countries with high rural populations, such as France, grew at a faster rate than those with small rural populations, such as the UK in the 1950s and 1960s (☞ unit 99). However, the model proved highly simplistic. For a start, there is considerable evidence that marginal workers in urban slums in the Third World are far more likely to have zero productivity than marginal workers in rural areas. The model also implies that there will be full employment in urban areas, which is certainly not the case. Other key assumptions or conclusions, such as static urban wages during the period of development, also do not fit with development experience. Table 107.1 shows that the change in population from rural to urban has been very similar across all regions of the developing world, and yet, as Figure 107.2 showed, these regions have very differing growth rates in GNP per capita.

Industrialisation in the Third World has also not necessarily led to economic development. Too often, First World Technology has been imported. This has been highly **capital intensive**, requiring little but highly skilled labour. The result has been little job creation in economies where unemployment is very high. In too many cases, highly skilled labour has not been available in the local economy with the result that machinery has been inefficiently used. Economists, such as E.F. Schumacher, have argued that the Third World needs **appropriate technology**, suited to the skills of local workers and which creates jobs. Small scale, rural investment often yields a high rate of return than large scale, urban factory investment. Labour versus capital intensive production is discussed in greater detail in unit 21.

Table 107.1 *Urbanisation*

	% of total population living in urban areas	
	1970	1992
Sub-Saharan Africa	19	29
East Asia and the Pacific	19	29
South Asia	19	25
Middle East and North Africa	41	55
Latin American and Caribbean	57	73
Developed countries	74	78

Source: adapted from World Bank, *World Development Report.*

International-dependence models

In the 1970s, economists began to turn their attention to the links between the First World and the Third World and argue that many of the problems of lack of development were caused by First World countries. In these models, a failure to grow was not caused by conditions inside developed countries, such as low savings ratios, but by external forces.

Part of the failure to grow can be attributed to much of the Third World's colonial past. First World countries exploited their colonies, thus increasing the inequality between themselves and their Third World empires. When the colonies gained independence, they remained tied to First World countries through trade and aid links. Under colonial rule, they had been forced to become exporters of primary commodities. This continues to be true today for many countries. However, the price of commodities has tended to decline over time relative to First World produced industrial goods. Hence, the trade link is continually impoverishing Third World countries. Figure 107.2, however, shows that there is no clear correlation between exports and GNP per capita growth. Whilst East Asia has grown very fast and has a relatively low dependence on commodity exports, South Asia equally has a low dependence and yet has grown at less than half the rate. Growth in the Middle East has been far higher than in Sub-Saharan Africa despite similar proportions of commodity exports.

Another argument put forward by economists of this school is that aid loans to the Third World in the 1960s and 1970s led to the Third World **debt crisis** (☞ unit 109) in the 1980s. This in turn was a major cause of many African and Latin American countries experiencing negative growth rates in that decade as money flowed out of the Third World to pay debts owed to First World banks.

The actions of bodies such as the **IMF** (☞ unit 109) have reinforced dependence of the Third World on the First World. They have consistently given poor advice about how countries should develop and be managed. They have been helped in this by the actions of urban elites in Third World countries. These urban elites have been able, with the help of First World firms, governments and institutions, to enjoy First World living standards. The wealth they enjoy does not 'trickle down' to the rest of society. These urban elites are typically members of the government, the armed forces and key personnel working for or with western companies. Their interests lie with furthering the interests of the First World, not with the Third World people who are their fellow citizens.

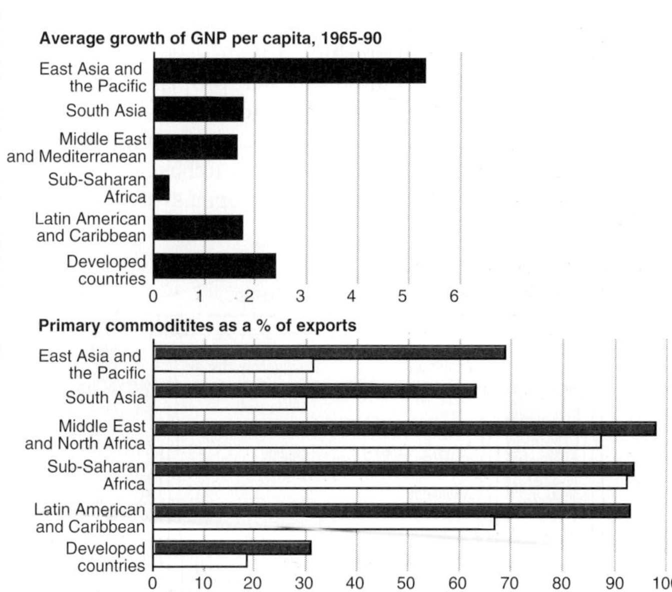

Source: adapted from World Bank, *World Development Report.*

Figure 107.3 *Average growth of GNP and primary commodities as a % of exports*

The neoclassical revolution

During the 1950s, 1960s and 1970s, most Third World governments had built up economic structures which closely resembled the mixed economies of Western Europe. Key industries were often in state hands.

Governments intervened heavily to promote development. For instance, Rostow's ideas that levels of saving were primary in the development process, together with Lewis's two sector model of development, led to the rural poor being taxed far more heavily than urban dwellers. This was often achieved by forcing farmers to sell produce to state agricultural boards at prices far below the market price. The produce could then be sold at market prices overseas or to towns, with the government taking the surplus as revenue which it could then plough back into investment in the economy. Alternatively, part or all of it could be sold to urban dwellers who could then be paid lower wages by employers. This would reduce costs, increase profits and thus increase investment. Even inequality was sometimes considered to be desirable because of the Keynesian view that the savings ratio of high income earners was higher than that of low income earners (☞ unit 79). Redistributing income from the poor to the rich, for instance through taxes, could therefore increase the national savings ratio.

The 1980s saw an economic revolution in ideas in the First World. 'Reaganomics' and 'Thatcherism' were the political names for a movement in economics which argued that growth could be increased by freeing markets from government constraint (☞ unit 69). Reductions in the size of the state, for instance through **privatisation** (☞ unit 45), would increase efficiency because the state was poor at allocating resources. Moreover, private markets should be **deregulated** (☞ unit 46). Government interference, such as state agricultural boards, should be removed. Low growth, so it was argued, was caused by a failure to pursue free market policies.

The new neoclassical approach called, for instance, for a radical change in policies with regard to multinational companies. The traditional view was that the activities of multinational companies in general were harmful to the Third World. They tended to be engaged in the production of primary commodities, such as bananas or copper. They would pay low wages to their Third World workers and had little regard for health and safety at work. Profits were large and these would be repatriated back to the First World. Hence, the multinational contributed little to the Third World country and were run for the benefit of First World shareholders. Not surprisingly, many Third World countries nationalised the operations of multinational companies. However, nationalisation often proved disastrous in the long run. The Third World countries were unable to afford to keep up the investment required in the operations. The nationalised companies were often inefficiently run and productivity fell following nationalisation. With falling output, export earnings fell putting pressure on the balance of payments. In the new climate of the 1980s and 1990s, multinationals have often been reinvited back to Third World countries to resume their activities. There has been a fundamental reappraisal of the balance of benefit between Third World country and multinational.

Neoclassical theory, in fact, suggests that the liberalisation of markets will attract investment from First World countries into the Third World. First World companies will be attracted by cheap land and labour costs to set up factories in Third World countries. Inward investment will increase growth rates. There is little doubt that governments and state organisations were (and many still are) highly inefficient in the Third World. Their policies were a major part of the problem of lack of development. As will be argued in unit 108, all the evidence suggests that openness to international trade is a crucial element in maintaining growth. Therefore, government policies which limit trade and limit the influence of foreign companies on the domestic market are likely to lead to less growth.

Critics of the neoclassical approach point out that growth and development are different. Policies which promote growth, where the benefits go to the better off in society at the expense of the poor, may lead to a backward shift in economic development. Poverty reduction, pro-women programmes, environmental policies all imply government intervening in the market place. Moreover, some of the greatest success stories of recent years, including Japan, South Korea and Singapore, have been economies where there has been heavy state direction of the economy. The creation of genuine free market economies is obviously not a necessary condition for successful development.

Strategies for successful development

The experience of the last 40 years has shown that the causes of economic development are complex. However, a number of important lessons can be learnt. High rates of economic growth and development depended upon the simultaneous achievement of three factors.

Acculumulation The Harrod-Domar growth model is correct in pointing out that savings and investment are vital for high growth. Investment, however, must be balanced. There must be the right mix of investment in private capital, such as machines and factories; in public infrastructure, such as roads, telecommunications and housing; and in people, developing their education and skills.

Allocation Resources must be allocated efficiently. It is pointless investing in new capital equipment if it lies idle for much of the time. It is futile to educate 5 per cent of the population to degree standard if the economy only needs 1 per cent of degree standard workers. Equally, resources must be used in a way which maximises rates of return on those resources. Allocating resources into higher education when greater returns could be achieved by using those resources in primary education will lower the rate of growth of the economy. This is probably the most important insight of neo-classical free market economists.

Productivity change Fast growing economies are ones which are constantly changing their methods of production to incorporate the best and most appropriate technology. Increasing the rate of change of resource inputs, both human and physical, to output will increase economic growth.

These are best achieved, for the most part, in the context of competitive markets. The market, as Adam Smith pointed out, brings together information from large numbers of buyers and sellers. The discipline of the market ensures that resources are allocated efficiently. Being **export-orientated** is essential. Third World countries tend to trade with First World countries rather than between themselves. Selling into First World markets means that the successful export-orientated Third World country has to produce to First World standards. They therefore have to learn to buy and use First World technology. This also encourages the flow of information from First World to Third World. The result is an increase in the rate of change of productivity.

Where competitive markets are inappropriate, allocation of resources should be based on contests between producers. For instance, government may provide **export credits** - loans to foreign buyers who purchase exports from the country. There should be an open system in which

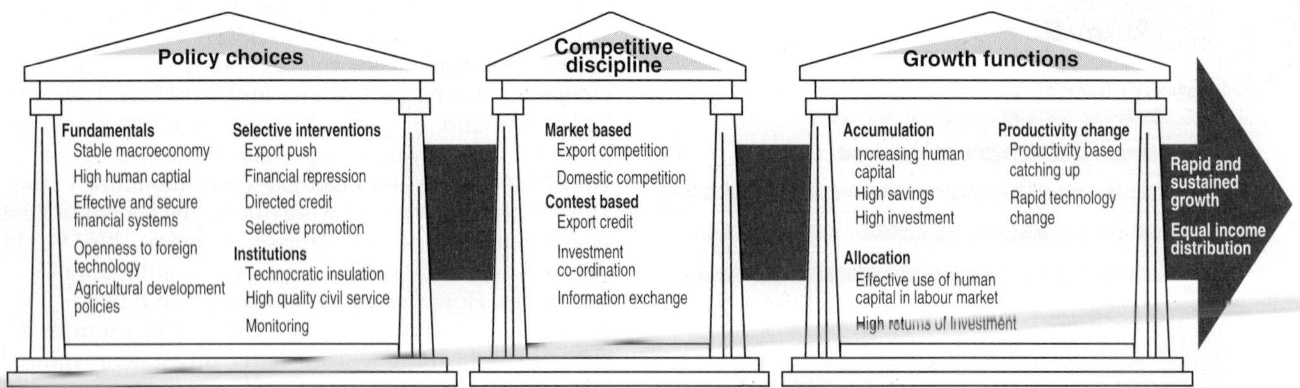

Source: World Bank.

Figure 107.4 *The World Bank theory of growth*

firms are able to compete for the limited number of export credits, with clear rules as to how they are to be allocated.

It should also be remembered that in some markets, market failure is so strong that governments have a duty to restrict competition and organise production itself. In education, for instance, a key to success in economic growth, all high growth countries have developed strong publicly funded systems of primary education.

Having decided what determines growth, and discussed the role that free markets can and cannot play in promoting growth, appropriate growth policies of governments can now be discussed. The World Bank, in Figure 107.4, singles out a number of key areas.

Stable macroeconomy The government must provide a stable macroeconomic climate. This means, for instance, containing inflation, securing a balance between exports and imports, and maintaining sound government finances. Macroeconomic stability encourages firms to invest. It also creates a balanced economy which can grow without having to be adjusted because one or more macroeconomic variables is unsustainable in the long term.

High human capital The importance of human capital in the development process has already been discussed.

Effective and secure financial systems The role of the financial system is crucial. The financial system (including banks) is responsible for gathering the savings of individuals and firms in the economy and allocating some of those to firms for investment. Any country wanting to increasing its savings ratio needs to improve the effectiveness of its financial system.

Limiting price distortions Governments must adopt policies which allow the price signals of the market to allocate resources. Governments, in most cases, are poorer at fixing optimal prices than the market mechanism and hence they should reduce market distortions such as government subsidies.

Openness to foreign technology Governments must encourage domestic firms to use foreign technology. They must also encourage foreign firms to set up in their country, bringing with them technology that can then be copied by domestic firms.

Agricultural development policies With such a large proportion of output and population in the agricultural sector of the economy in the Third World, a failure to develop this sector would lead to lower growth.

Selective intervention The government may choose to intervene to direct the growth of particular industries, for instance by making cheap finance available for investment, or by setting export targets for the industry. Countries such as South Korea and Japan have pursued such intervention in the past. Other equally successful countries, such as Hong Kong, have generally not intervened. So intervention is not a necessary condition of growth.

Institutions A successful economy must have appropriate institutions. For instance, there must be a high quality civil service. Technocrats - those in the civil service, other government agencies and the government itself - must not be open to bribery and must act in the best interests of the nation (the 'technocratic insulation' of Figure 107.4). All economic agents must be monitoring their successes and failures and correcting where necessary.

The International-dependence school of thought are correct in saying that the relationship between the Third World and the First World plays a crucial role in the development process. However, high growth developing countries have tended to use that relationship to import capital and technological knowledge and export goods and services. They have sought to integrate themselves into the world economy. Countries which have had low or negative growth rates have been victims of that relationship, mainly by borrowing money which they had little or no hope of repaying (☞ unit 109). If the world macro-economic framework is hostile to development, it has not been so hostile as to prevent some Third World countries from enjoying spectacular growth rates over the past 20 years.

Comparing development

Table 107.2 *GDP and population*

	Nigeria		Indonesia	
	1965	1992	1965	1992
Population (millions)	60	102	103	184
GDP (US$ millions)	5 380	29 667	5 980	126 363
GNP per capita (US$ at market exchange rates)	90	320	58	670
GNP per capita (US$ at purchasing power parity rates)	-	1 440		2 970

Nigeria and Indonesia

In 1965, Nigeria was regarded as a country with a high potential for growth, whilst Indonesia was being seen as having few prospects. In the 1970s, Nigeria experienced a windfall gain in the form of booming oil prices - Nigeria is a major exporter of oil. It borrowed heavily on the back of oil revenues. The 1980s, with falling oil prices, saw Nigeria getting into difficulties in financing its foreign debt and, in common with many other African countries, Nigeria struggled to grow at all. Indonesia, on the other hand, has grown relatively steadily throughout the period.

Table 107.3 *Distribution and growth of production*

	Percentage of total GDP				Annual percentage growth			
	Nigeria		Indonesia		Nigeria		Indonesia	
	1965	1992	1965	1992	1965-80	1980-1992	1965-80	1980-1992
Agriculture	55	37	51	19	1.7	3.6	4.3	3.1
Industry	12	38	13	40	13.1	0.2	11.9	6.1
of which manufacturing	5	-	8	21	14.6	-	12.0	12.0
Services	33	25	36	40	5.9	3.4	7.3	6.8

Table 107.4 *Structure and growth of demand*

	Percentage of total GDP				Annual percentage growth			
	Nigeria		Indonesia		Nigeria		Indonesia	
	1965	1992	1965	1992	1965-80	1980-1992	1965-80	1980-1992
General government consumption	7	6	5	10	13.9	-3.4	11.4	4.9
Gross domestic investment	15	18	8	35	14.7	-6.6	16.1	6.6
Gross domestic savings	10	23	8	37	-	-	-	-
Exports of goods and services	11	39	5	29	11.1	1.7	9.6	5.6

Table 107.5 *Central government expenditure*

	As a percentage of total government spending			
	Nigeria		Indonesia	
	1972	1992	1972	1992
Defence	40.2	-	18.6	6.8
Education	4.5	-	7.4	9.8
Health	3.6	-	1.4	2.8
Government spending as % of GNP	9.1	-	15.1	19.2

Table 107.6 *Social indicators*

	Nigeria		Indonesia	
	1965	1992	1965	1992
Total fertility rate[1]	6.9	5.9	5.5	2.9
Infant mortality rate	162	84	128	72
Daily calorie supply[2]	2 185	2 312	1 791	2 750
Primary enrolment[3], % of age group	32	71	72	116
of which female	24	62	65	114
Population with access to safe water % of total	-	42	-	51

1. Number of children born per thousand women of child-bearing age.
2. 1965 and 1989.
3. Figures may be more than 100 per cent because some children outside primary school age still attend primary school.

Table 107.7 *Total external debt, debt ratios and inflows of capital ($million)*

	Nigeria		Indonesia	
	1970	1992	1970	1992
Total external debt	452	30 959	2 497	84 835
Total debt service as a % of exports[1]	4.2	28.9	13.9	32.1
Official grants received	40	136	84	180
Net foreign direct investment	205	897	83	1 774

1. Figures are for 1980 and 1992 and not 1970 and 1992.

Source: adapted from World Bank, *World Development Reports.*

1. Compare the change in growth and development of Nigeria and Indonesia over the period 1965 to 1992.

2. (a) Using evidence from the data, suggest what might have caused the difference in development rates between the two countries.

(b) What other evidence would you need to understand fully the differences in development rates?

3. Discuss TWO policies which Nigeria could adopt to improve its growth and development.

Third World trade

Applied economics

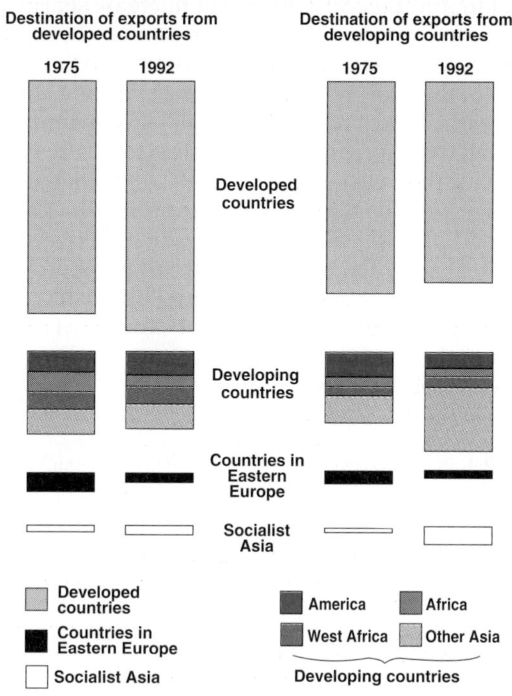

Source: adapted from UNCTAD, *Statistical Pocket Book.*

Figure 108.1 *Direction of trade: exports (1992)*

Patterns of world trade

World trade is as unevenly distributed as world income. Not surprisingly, most world trade occurs between the rich developed countries of the world. As Figure 108.1 shows, in 1992, 74.7 per cent of First World exports went to other First World countries. It might be expected then that, just as developed countries trade mainly amongst themselves, so too would developing countries. However, Figure 108.1 shows that this is not the case. In 1992, 60.5 per cent of Third World exports went to First World countries. Only 31.1 per cent of Third World exports went to other Third World countries.

Composition of world trade

Most world trade is trade in goods rather than services. Figure 108.2 shows the changing pattern of exports of goods of developing countries between 1970 and 1992. In 1970, 72 per cent of Third World exports were of primary commodities. By 1992, Third World countries had considerably reduced their dependence on exports of commodities to 47 per cent. Dependence on food crops, such as coffee and bananas, had approximately halved. The share of manufactured goods, on the other hand, had doubled.

Whilst the developing world in general is moving away from dependence on primary commodity exports, some individual countries are still almost totally reliant on them for export revenues. Table 108.1 gives a breakdown of countries with varying degrees of reliance on non-oil primary commodity exports. These account for between 90-100 per cent of the exports of 19 countries, including some of the world's poorest, such as Ethiopia, Uganda, Burundi, Malawi and Chad.

Table 108.1 *Dependence of developing countries on non-oil primary commodity exports (average 1990-92)*

	Percentage of non-oil primary commodities in total exports					Total
	100-90	90-70	70-50	50-10	10-0	
Population (in millions)	133	263	169	1 922	345	2 832
Number of countries	19	34	27	41	26	147

Source: adapted from UNCTAD, *Statistical Pocket Book.*

On the other hand, a small group of Third World countries have become major exporters of manufactured goods over the past 30 years. Table 108.2 shows these countries, how the value of their manufactured exports has changed over time and the proportion of manufactures in their total exports.

Third World countries have traditionally imported manufactured goods, most of which are not produced in their local economies. This pattern of trade barely changed between 1970 and 1992, with approximately 70 per cent of visible imports being accounted for by manufactures.

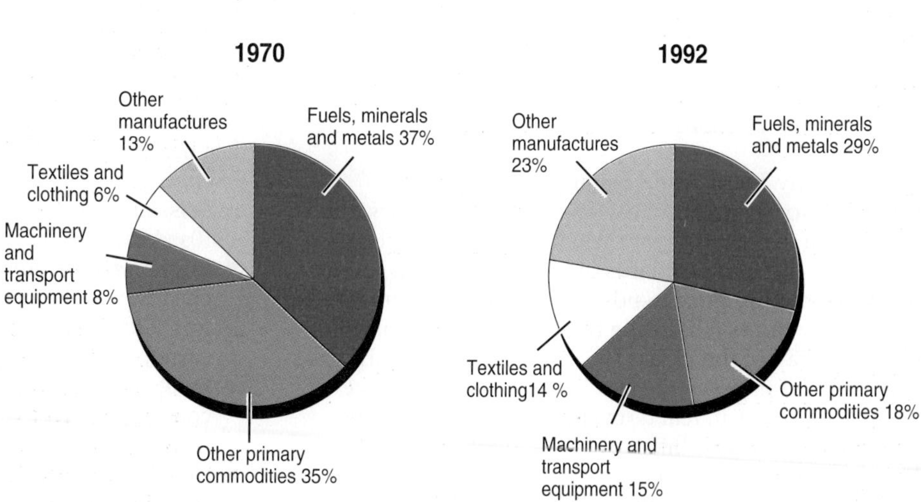

Figure 108.2 *Developing countries: exports*

Table 108.2 *Major manufactures exports*

Country	Total exports of manufactures ($ millions) 1975	1980	1992	Share of manufactures in total exports (%) 1975	1980	1992
Taiwan	4 307	17 429	75 590	81.0	87.9	92.9
Korea	4 126	15 625	70 892	81.4	89.5	92.5
Singapore	2 233	8 344	48 618	41.5	43.1	76.6
Hong Kong	4 464	13 081	28 260	96.8	95.7	93.4
Malaysia	664	2 435	25 935	17.3	18.8	63.7
Thailand	317	1 604	21 113	14.7	25.2	65.6
Brazil	2 192	7 492	20 460	25.3	37.2	56.9
Indonesia	85	499	16 061	1.2	2.3	47.3
India	1 953	4 404	15 137	44.8	58.6	73.2
Mexico	929	1 839	14 227	31.0	11.9	52.3
Turkey	326	782	10 500	23.3	26.9	71.4
Pakistan	560	1 247	5 721	54.3	48.2	78.8
Philippines	259	1 213	4 042	11.7	21.1	41.1
Argentina	722	1 854	3 205	24.4	23.1	26.2
Tunisia	168	798	2 943	19.6	35.7	72.8
China	2 642	8 680	66 807	41.8	47.5	78.7
Total	25 947	113 757	429 511	40.2	44.6	73.9
All developing countries	31 221	105 077	492 154	15.5	18.5	59.0

Source: adapted from UNCTAD, *Statistical Pocket Book.*

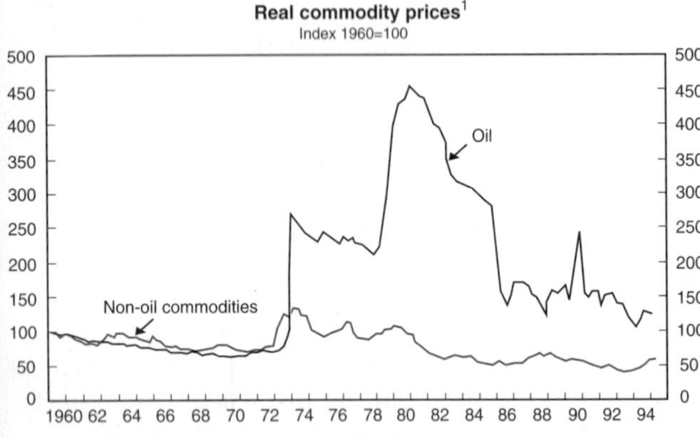

Source: adapted from OECD, *Economic Outlook*, June 1995.

Figure 108.3 *Real commodity prices*

Commodity prices

Because many Third World countries are crucially dependent for their export earnings on commodities, the price which they receive for them has a considerable impact on GDP and standards of living within the country. Broad commodity price trends can be seen in Figure 108.3. Commodity prices fell during the 1960s but rose sharply in the first half of the 1970s. There was a second sharp increase in oil prices in the late 1970s. In general, however, commodity prices in real terms have tended to decline since the mid-1970s. Whilst oil prices today are higher than they were in the 1960s, other commodity prices are only about 50 per cent of their 1960 value. This means that for every tonne of commodity exported in 1960 to the First World, Third World countries now have to export two tonnes to buy the same amount. Not surprisingly, the sharp deterioration in the terms of trade has affected the balance of payments and economic growth rates of developing nations.

Individual commodity prices can fluctuate sharply. It is not unknown for prices to double or halve in the space of 12 months. This is because commodities are relatively inelastic in the short run. If there is a 25 per cent shortfall in this year's coffee crop, First World coffee manufacturers are prepared to pay much higher prices to secure supplies of coffee for their customers. Table 108.3 shows the percentage annual variation in price around the long term mean trend price for selected commodities between 1970 and 1993. Sharply fluctuating prices add more problems to poor Third World countries dependent upon one or two commodities for most of their export earnings. The only way out in the long term is for the country to develop and become less reliant on one industry.

Table 108.3 *Selected primary commodities: instability index*

Commodity		Instability index (Percentage variation) 1970-1979	1980-1989	1990-1993
Tropical beverages		20.0	12.7	7.5
of which	Coffee	23.7	14.5	10.0
	Cocoa	22.5	14.8	9.7
	Tea	13.0	17.2	9.8
Food		30.3	22.2	3.9
of which	Sugar	58.1	50.6	13.4
	Rice	34.4	21.9	7.3
	Bananas	12.0	13.4	18.6
	Wheat	27.8	11.0	10.5
	Pepper	16.3	31.7	19.4
Vegetable oilseeds and oils		19.2	18.5	3.5
of which	Coconut oil	32.2	29.5	19.1
	Sunflower oil	22.1	18.3	6.8
	Groundnut oil	17.9	24.8	14.1
	Copra	34.4	27.7	18.0

Source: adapted from UNCTAD, *Statistical Pocket Book.*

One solution to the problem of fluctuating and yet also falling prices is for developing countries to form **cartels** to stabilize or raise prices. The oil producing cartel, OPEC has been successful to date in raising the real price of oil from its early 1970s price. However, other commodity cartels, such as those for coffee and tin, collapsed in the 1980s. As was explained in unit 12, cartels fail because:

- high prices encourage overproduction and cheating on the part of participant countries;
- it is difficult to persuade all producers to join the cartel;
- most commodity schemes (unlike OPEC) require the commodity to be produced and then stored if there is oversupply at the minimum price - a costly process;
- producers are encouraged to set too high a minimum price, which results in overproduction, and eventually the money to buy up surplus produce runs out.

Trade and development

A reliance on primary commodities for the main source of exports has proved to be disastrous for many developing countries. Not only have real prices fallen over the past 30 years, but there have been very sharp fluctuations in price of commodities. Third World countries therefore need to diversify.

During the 1930s, when the world economy was rocked by the Great Depression in the USA and Europe, many Third World countries, like most First World countries, opted for a policy of **protectionism** (☞ unit 85). It was argued that the best way to protect jobs and promote the growth of domestic industry was to keep foreign goods out. This then led many Third World countries to believe that their own development could best be promoted through a policy of **import substitution**, the deliberate attempt to replace imported goods with domestically produced goods by adopting protectionist measures.

Whilst import substitution policies might create jobs in the short run, as domestic producers replace foreign producers, economic theory would suggest that in the long run output and growth of output will be lower than it would otherwise have been. This is because import substitution denies the country the benefits to be gained from **specialisation**. The theory of comparative advantage (☞ unit 84) shows how countries will gain from trade. Moreover, protectionism leads to dynamic inefficiency. Domestic producers have no incentive from foreign competitors to reduce costs or improve products. Countries which have adopted import substitution strategies have tended to experience lower growth rates than other countries, particularly if they are small countries (the larger the country, the more opportunities there are for specialisation within the country).

The opposite strategy to import substitution is that of **export-led growth**. Rather than becoming less dependent upon world trade, it is argued that growth can be increased by becoming more dependent. Removing trade barriers will force domestic industry either to close or to become as efficient as any world producer. Resources will be reallocated to those industries that produce goods in which the country has a comparative advantage in production. In a developing country, these are likely to be labour intensive, low technology industries. Countries wishing to diversify from exporting commodities can give short term selective assistance to their manufacturing industries. The newly industrialised nations of Brazil and Mexico, and particularly Hong Kong, South Korea and Singapore, have enjoyed above-average growth by adopting such a strategy.

First World protectionism

Export success for Third World countries has not always been easy. Third World countries in general have a comparative advantage in agriculture and low technology, labour intensive manufactured goods. There is no problem in making computer components in China since the computer industry is very young. However, many goods exported from the Third World find themselves in direct competition with goods made in long established industries in the First World. Not surprisingly, these industries respond by pressing their governments for **protection** against these cheaper imports. For instance, agriculture is highly protected in the First World. The EU even exports farm products to the Third World, at hugely subsidised prices, completely going against the principle of comparative advantage. Textiles is another industry which has been fiercely protected by First World countries though to a lesser extent than agriculture.

Despite this protectionism, the volume of trade between First and Third Worlds is growing. The experience of the Tiger economies of East Asia shows that there is a wide range of products which are relatively unprotected by First World countries.

Balance of payments problems

Third World countries are no different from First World countries in experiencing balance of payments problems. However, smaller Third World countries dependent upon

Newly industrialised countries, such as Hong Kong, have enjoyed above-average growth.

Table 108.4 *Selected statistics on tourism*

World total receipts from international tourism[1]		
Years	Value ($ billion)	Average annual growth
1970	17.9	10.1[a]
1980	103.5	19.2[b]
1985	116.0	2.4
1986	140.5	21.1
1987	172.4	22.7
1988	199.3	15.6
1989	214.9	7.9
1990	260.1	21.0
1991	263.2	1.2
1992	297.9	13.2
1993*	304.0	2.1

Percentage share of travel receipts in total exports of services		
Country group	Years 1980	1987
Developed countries	22.1	26.7
Developing countries	30.7	35.4
America	37.3	40.8
Africa	23.7	31.5
West Africa	27.2	33.7
Other Asia	27.8	33.2
Oceania	50.1	48.7
China	-	37.8

Countries specialised in tourism: percentage share of travel receipts in total exports of services in 1992					
Rank	Country	Percent	Rank	Country	Percent
1	Indonesia	90	11	Gambia	70
2	Bahamas	88	12	Namibia	70
3	Saint Kitts and Nevis	84	13	Dominican Republic	69
4	Saint Lucia	83	14	Portugal	66
5	Maldives	79	15	Dominica	63
6	Aruba	76	16	Spain	62
7	Jamaica	75	17	St. Vincent and the Gren.	61
8	Barbados	74	18	Malta	61
9	Grenada	73	19	Thailand	60
10	Antigua and Barbuda	72	20	Uruguay	60

Notes: 1. Includes data for countries not reporting balance-of-payments statistics.
a. 1960-1970.
b. 1970-1980.
Source: World Tourism Organisation and IMF, *Balance of Payments Statistics.*

exports of primary commodities are particularly vulnerable to sharp changes in their **current account** (☞ unit 86) position.

Assume there is a sharp fall in the price of the country's main commodity export. The country is then faced with a dilemma.

- It may predict that the change in price will be short lived and that the price will return to a long term trend price. It decides not to alter its policy position. If, however, the price remains depressed, the country will then be in serious difficulties. Import revenue will be exceeding export revenue. This will be financed either by borrowing from abroad, which increases the country's indebtedness, or by a run down of the country's foreign currency reserves. In the long term, it will need to replenish these. Either way, the country will have been living beyond its means. Harsh deflationary policies combined possibly with a devaluation of the currency will then be needed to bring the current account back into equilibrium (☞ unit 96). Economic growth and development will falter.
- It may decide that the price is the new long term price. It will then have to respond by cutting imports, through deflationary policies and/or a devaluation of the currency. But if prices bounce back, the country will have lost out on economic growth and will have made its citizens suffer unnecessarily.

The success of the Third World countries in Table 108.2 in exporting manufactures, the majority of which go to the First World, has posed its own difficulties on the balance of payments of First World countries. Increased imports and current account deficits have, in some cases, been blamed on 'unfair' competition from cheap labour Third World countries. This has led to calls for protection from workers and firms hit by these Third World imports. However, the Uruguay Round (☞ unit 85) will lead in future to less protection rather than more protection particularly in textiles and clothing. In the future, Third World countries will find it easier rather than harder to export manufactured products to the First World.

Tourism

Third World countries are increasing their exports of services over time. One example of a Third World service industry dependent upon the First World is tourism. Table 108.4 gives a number of statistics relating to the world tourist industry.

- Growth in tourism has been very high since 1970. This is not surprising since tourism has a relatively **high income elasticity of demand** (☞ unit 9).
- Travel receipts account for over a third of all invisible exports for Third World countries, a higher proportion than in the First World. Hence, developing countries are more dependent on the travel industry than First World countries.
- For the top 20 countries which specialise in tourism, the industry accounts for between 60 and 90 per cent of total service exports.

Tourism can be a valuable earner of foreign currency. It is labour intensive and is low technology and is therefore particularly suited to Third World economies. There are criticisms made of the impact of tourism on economic development. It can make local inhabitants feel inferior because they cannot afford the lifestyle on offer in the hotels to First World tourists. It can degrade local people by turning them into characters from a theme park. There may also be a negative impact on the local environment as, for instance, the local shore line is irreparably damaged by the building of hotels. However, on balance, countries which have become tourist destinations have strongly welcomed the opportunity to earn export earnings and diversify their economies.

Tourism

The Mauritian tourist industry

Mauritius, an island in the Indian Ocean, has been one of the success stories of the developing world. In 1965, its GDP per capita was approximately the same as that of Peru or El Salvador. Today, it is over twice their levels with an average per capita growth rate of 3.2 per cent per annum between 1965 and 1995 and 5.5 per cent in the period since 1980. There is full employment on the island and rapidly rising living standards.

Traditionally the island has been heavily dependent on sugar. Then, in the 1960s, the island secured preferential access to the European Union for textiles as part of the Lome Convention (the agreement between the EU and former colonies which reduced tariff and quota barriers into the EU in selected products for those countries). The textiles industry has subsequently boomed, based on cheap labour and good quality products.

The third biggest export earner for the island is tourism. The number of tourists per year has grown from 140 000 in 1984 to 401 000 in 1994. The plan is to allow the industry to grow to a maximum 600 000 tourists per year. Development in the industry has been carefully controlled. The relatively small island, approximately one twentieth the size of Switzerland, has encouraged the growth of up-market holidays. It has limited planning permissions for hotels to prevent its coastline becoming awash with buildings. Charter flights are banned and tourists arriving must come on expensive scheduled flights. The logic is that no one is going to fly 12 hours to come to an overcrowded, overdeveloped tourist resort when they can fly far more quickly and cheaply to Spain or Florida.

What is more, tourism is not always welcomed by local inhabitants. The encroachment of hotels on to beaches which were formally public has become a sore point. And as the Minister for Tourism and Industry, Mr Duval, said: 'We don't want to become a nation of bartenders'. The long term success of the industry must be to provide high quality tourist facilities in relatively unspoilt settings and charge high prices.

Source: adapted from the *Financial Times*, 13.4.1995; and the World Bank, *World Development Report.*

The Caribbean tourist industry

Tourism in the Caribbean is big business. In the resort countries such as Barbados and Antigua, tourism now accounts for one quarter of all export earnings with 22 million stay-over and cruise ships visitors in 1993. The industry provides jobs and incomes, and significant tax revenues. In 1994, for instance, the tax per person on cruise ship visitors landing on an island was set at a minimum of $5, and this rose to $10 in 1995 under an agreement with the cruise line companies.

However, the industry has received a number of set-backs in the 1990s. The Gulf War of 1990 frightened people from flying because of fear of bomb attacks. The recession of 1990-93 in the Western world hit tourist earnings. Well-publicised attacks on tourists, including the killing of two in Jamaica in 1992 and 1993, have discouraged visitors. The rise in the value of the dollar against European currencies in the early 1990s discouraged European tourists, since hotels and other tourist facilities use US dollars as their standard currency. What's more, some US tourists were attracted to holiday in Europe rather than the Caribbean because of the high value of the dollar.

The challenge for the islands in the second half of the 1990s is two-fold. First, the numbers of tourists must be increased. Second, there must be a far greater emphasis placed on developing links from tourism to local industries such as agriculture, services and transportation. Too much of the earnings from a hotel holiday today is spent on imports and too little comes from adding value to existing local goods and services.

Source: adapted from the *Financial Times*, 7.12.1993.

The Indian tourist industry

Indian tourism is relatively underdeveloped. A mere 1.76 million tourists visited the huge country in 1993, accounting for just 0.2 per cent of international tourism and bringing in $1.5bn worth of export revenues. Even so, tourism is India's third-largest foreign exchange earner.

The problem has been been two-fold. First, till the early 1990s, the Indian government has been relatively indifferent to the potential from tourism. The Indian economy has been highly protected, with on emphasis on self-reliance and a discouragement of foreign investment in the country. Second, the industry has offered little for the typical tourist in the way of hotels. Accommodation has tended to be either very expensive five star hotels or very cheap small basic hotels catering for back-packers.

The new pro-market climate of the 1990s is likely to transform the situation. In 1994, the government set itself a target of tripling the number of tourist visitors to 5 million in 5 years. Foreign investment has been positively encouraged, with an estimated $250m coming into the country in 1994 as foreign hotel chains build new hotels catering mainly for the more typical tourist.

Source: adapted from the *Financial Times*, 10.5.1994.

1. **Explain the contribution that tourism can make to a country's (a) balance of payments and (b) national income. Use examples from the data to illustrate your answer.**
2. **To what extent can expansion of the tourist industry increase the level of economic development in Mauritius, India and the Caribbean?**
3. **What are the potential problems for a country which becomes heavily reliant on tourism for its foreign exchange earnings?**

World capital flows

Applied economics

The colonial experience

From the 16th century onwards, European powers acquired colonial empires throughout most of what we call the Third World today, as well as in North America and Australasia. Colonies were acquired for a variety of reasons, but one major factor was economic gain. In the colonial model of the 19th century, European countries supplied capital to their colonies. They built roads, railways and factories, and invested in agriculture. So there were net **capital flows** to the Third World. However, these capital flows were more than outweighed by the repatriation of **interest, profits and dividends** from Third World colonies back to Europe. After all, there was little point in owning a colony if the colonial power had to pay for the privilege of ownership. Hence, colonial powers could be said to have **exploited** their colonies.

In this unit we will consider whether or not world capital flows continue to flow from Third World to First World countries and the impact of differing capital flows on developing countries.

Types of capital flow

There are four main types of capital flow between countries.

- There are **short term loans**. These might, for instance, cover imports and exports of goods and services. A UK firm may buy tea from a Kenyan firm. The British firms would expect to receive credit from (i.e. borrow money from) the Kenyan firm in the short term once the tea had been delivered. Terms for payment might, for instance, be one month from delivery of tea. Alternatively, a Kenyan firm might want to import goods from the UK but the UK suppliers want payment before delivery. The Kenyan company might organise a short term loan with a UK bank to cover the transaction.
- **Long term loans** are used for a variety of purposes. However, a Third World government may borrow money over ten years to finance the building of a power station for instance.
- **Aid** is the giving of money by First World countries to

Table 109.1 *Developing countries: capital flows*[1]

Annual averages in billions of US dollars

		Short term loans	Long term loans	Foreign aid and other exceptional financing	Foreign direct investment	Portfolio investment	Total capital flow
All developing countries	1973-76	- 0.5	17.1	4.0	3.7	- 5.5	18.8
	1977-82	- 12.3	42.0	7.4	11.2	- 10.5	37.8
	1983-89	- 5.5	- 5.7	32.2	13.3	6.5	40.8
	1990-93	37.6	- 7.0	33.2	34.2	26.8	124.8
Africa	1973-76	- 0.2	4.1	0.4	1.1	0.1	5.5
	1977-82	0.5	8.0	1.7	0.8	- 0.2	9.8
	1983-89	- 1.4	0.3	6.1	1.1	- 0.1	6.0
	1990-93	- 3.0	- 3.0	6.6	1.4	0.7	2.7
Asia	1973-76	1.2	4.1	0.6	1.3	0.1	7.3
	1977-82	2.5	10.0	0.3	2.7	0.6	16.1
	1983-89	2.4	7.7	0.3	5.2	1.4	17.0
	1990-93	9.6	10.0	1.9	19.8	7.2	48.5
Middle East and Europe	1973-76	- 3.0	- 0.1	2.1	- 1.0	- 6.0	- 8.0
	1977-82	- 12.5	1.7	1.7	2.5	- 12.5	- 19.1
	1983-89	- 0.5	0.2	0.5	2.6	6.4	9.2
	1990-93	26.1	- 4.0	5.0	1.6	1.3	30.0
Latin America and Caribbean	1973-76	1.5	9.1	0.9	2.2	0.2	13.9
	1977-82	- 2.8	22.2	3.7	5.3	1.6	30.0
	1983-89	- 5.8	- 14.0	25.2	4.4	- 1.2	8.6
	1990-93	5.0	- 9.7	19.7	11.0	17.5	43.5

Source: World Bank, *World Economic Outlook.*

1. The difference between capital coming into developing countries and capital flowing out of developing countries. A minus sign indicates that the developing world lost capital to the developed world.

Third World countries, or is the granting of loans on concessionary terms.

- **Foreign direct investment** and **portfolio equity flows** are monies which flow from country to country and which are used to buy assets in the receiving country. For instance, Coca Cola may set up a plant in Nigeria to manufacture soft drinks. Money sent from the United States to Nigeria to finance this would be an example of foreign direct investment. The purchase by a US pension fund of shares in Chinese companies would be an example of portfolio equity flows.

Table 109.1 shows the relative sizes of these net flows (i.e. the difference between capital flowing into the Third World and capital flowing out) between 1973 and 1993. There has been a considerable change in the structure of these flows over the period. In the 1970s and early 1980s, long term loans were the major component of total net capital flows. This led directly to the debt crisis of the 1980s discussed below. From 1983, foreign aid has assumed a greater role. The 1990s has been the decade of foreign direct investment and portfolio investment.

Within the total, there are significant differences between regions. For instance, political instability in the Middle East led to net flows of capital out of the region in the 1970s and early 1980s. Africa borrowed particularly heavily as a proportion of its total capital flows in the 1970s, which proved disastrous in the 1980s as it was unable to repay its debts. But for foreign aid, Africa would have been a net capital exporter in the decade from 1983. Asia and Latin America have benefited by far the most from foreign direct investment and portfolio investment in the 1990s. Foreign aid has benefited African and Latin America the most over the period. Sizeable amounts of capital have traditionally been sent from developing countries to be invested in bonds and shares in developed countries. This, called **capital flight**, is shown by a negative figure on portfolio investment. Many individuals and businesses in developing countries, particularly those with either high political instability or high inflation, felt that they could earn higher rates of return by investing abroad than by investing in their own countries.

The justification for foreign aid

Following the devastation of the Second World War, the Americans gave Marshall Aid to Europe to help in reconstruction. This became a model for later economic development for the Third World. The argument was persuasive.

- The citizens of Third World countries, because they were so poor, would have a very high propensity to consume and a very low propensity to save. Hence, savings would be likely to be below the level of investment needed to generate high economic growth in the economy. Inflows of foreign capital, for instance supplied through foreign aid programmes, would help fill this **savings gap**.
- Foreign exchange would be extremely scarce. Export revenues would be limited and would be likely to be insufficient to cover imports of machinery and other capital equipment as well as imports of essential raw materials. Foreign aid would help cover this **trade gap**.
- Foreign aid reflects only a fraction of capital flows from the First World to the Third World. However, in the 1970s and 1980s it has at times represented a significant proportion of **net** capital flows (the difference between flows of capital into and out of the developing world). In the 1980s and 1990s, many African countries have become particularly dependent on foreign aid to finance their trade and development.

Types of foreign aid

Foreign aid can take a variety of forms.

Grants The most generous form of aid is a grant. A donor country might, for instance, give a sum of money to a Third World country for a development project, it might offer free technical expertise, or it might offer free university education for foreign students in the donor country.

Loans Aid might take the form of a loan. The loan might be at commercial rates of interest, in which case the donor country is giving little if anything to the Third World borrower. Alternatively, the loan might be a **soft loan**, a loan which carries a lower rate of interest than the commercial rate of interest.

Tied aid Grants or loans might only be available if the recipient country was prepared to purchase goods and services with the money from the donor country. For instance, during the 1980s the UK government devoted some of its aid budget to backing British exports. UK loan aid was available if a Third World country awarded a contract to a British company.

Bilateral and multilateral aid Bilateral aid is given directly from one country to another. A UK loan to Kenya would be an example. Multilateral aid describes the situation when donor countries give money to an international agency, such as UNICEF (the United National Children's Fund), and the agency then disperses the aid. The most important multilateral aid agency is the International Bank for Reconstruction and Development (IBRD), more commonly known as the World Bank. Most bilateral aid is tied in one form or another whilst multilateral aid is generally not tied.

An evaluation of foreign aid

Foreign aid has undoubtedly helped millions in the Third World achieve a better standard of living. However, foreign aid has been increasingly criticised by those in both the First World and in the Third World.

- It is implicitly assumed in the economic argument presented above that Third World governments desire to maximise the economic welfare of their citizens. However, this is not the case in most Third World countries. Governments serve the interests of a narrow range of groups in society, often better-off urban dwellers. Foreign aid monies can be diverted into serving the needs of these groups rather than achieving genuine economic development, particularly for the poor in the Third World.

- 'Fashions' in foreign aid projects change over time. In the 1950s, large scale projects, such as dams and steel mills, were seen as important in economic development. Many of these projects failed to yield a sufficiently high rate of return. Many large scale manufacturing plant projects failed because of lack of infrastructure and lack of skilled workers and management. In the 1990s, aid to help large numbers of small scale enterprises, particularly in rural areas, has been fashionable. Equally, aid projects are likely to have to pass an environmental audit to prevent large scale ecological disasters which have occurred on some previous aid projects. The question that arises is whether Western aid agencies, even now, know what are the best strategies for development.
- Foreign aid which takes the form of subsidised food or consumer goods is likely to be positively harmful to long term Third World development. Food aid in a famine situation can be helpful. However, long term food aid, by increasing the supply of food on the local market, depresses local prices and therefore discourages local production of food. This increases the dependence of the country on imported food, uses up scarce foreign exchange and results in lower living standards for farmers.
- Tied foreign aid, especially in the form of loans, may result in Third World countries getting a worse 'buy' than if they shopped around internationally for the cheapest product.
- Loans need to be repaid with interest. The repayment of loans has resulted in enormous problems for Third World countries, and it is to this issue that we will now turn.

The Third World debt crisis

Aid has not been the only source of financial capital for Third World countries. They have been free to borrow from banks and on First World money markets. In the 1960s and early 1970s, developing countries used commercial sources of finance to some extent. However, the first oil crisis of 1973-74 proved ruinous for most Third World countries.

Non-oil producing countries were faced with sharply increased bills for imports of oil. An easy way to solve the problem in the short run was to borrow the money to finance increased oil prices.

Oil producing countries, on the other hand, were faced with a sudden inflow of foreign currency. In the very short term, there was no way they could spend this money. In the longer term, countries such as Mexico and Nigeria used the extra revenues to finance investment projects. Others, such as Saudi Arabia and Kuwait, have remained net exporters of capital ever since, building up financial assets in the developed world.

In 1974 and subsequent years, large numbers of petro-dollars (dollars used to pay for oil) were deposited by oil producing countries in Western banks. The banks needed to lend these out again if they were to make a profit. First World countries responded to the first oil crisis by deflating their economies, with the aim of squeezing inflation and reducing balance of payments deficits. They didn't want to borrow the money. So banks turned to the Third World. Countries are good risks, it was argued, because governments cannot go bankrupt. Loans to Third World countries were marketed aggressively by the banks in the second half of the 1970s.

The 1980s proved disastrous both for Third World countries and for banks. In 1980, Ronald Reagan was elected President of the United States. Quickly, he cut taxes whilst leaving government spending totals unchanged. The result was a huge increase in the US government budget deficit. To finance the deficit, the government had to issue enormous amounts of new government stock, which sent US interest rates soaring. Sharply increased interest rates then increased the value of the dollar, as foreign investors demanded dollars to invest in the US. This hit Third World countries hard:

- increased interest rates meant that repayments on their debt increased sharply;
- the increased value of the dollar meant that they had to sell far more exports to pay back $1 worth of debt;
- developed countries went into a severe recession; this hit exports from Third World countries in the short term; more seriously, it began the long term decline in commodity prices discussed in unit 108, which hit export revenues hard.

In 1982, Mexico precipitated the Third World debt crisis by **defaulting** (i.e. not paying) on part of its loans. Immediately, First World banks and other lenders stopped lending to countries which they believed would follow Mexico's example. The severity of the **debt crisis** can be measured in a number of ways.

Net capital flows As Table 109.1 shows, net lending to Africa and Latin America dried up immediately after Mexico's default and indeed these continents became net repayers of debt. Between 1977 and 1982, borrowing,

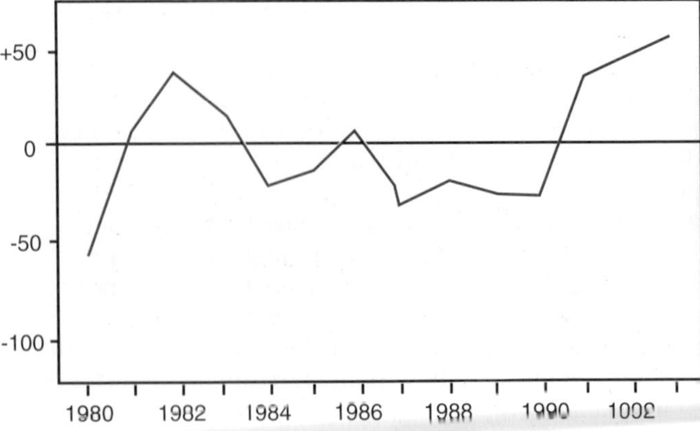

Source: adapted from United Nations, *World Economic and Social Survey, 1994*.

Figure 109.1 *Net transfers to developing countries*

mainly by African governments, averaged approximately $13 for each African citizen. Given that average incomes were only approximately $200, this was a sizeable amount. By the 1990s, African countries were repaying on average $5 a year when average incomes were approximately $300.

Net transfers Table 109.1 does not include repayments of interest on loans. If these are taken into account, the Third World became a net transferee of money to the First World for much of the 1980s as Figure 109.1 shows. What this meant was that the poor in the Third World were sending part of their income to the rich in the First World. Only in the 1990s has the transfer of resources from Third to First World again become favourable to the Third World.

Total Third World debt Third World debt, shown in Table 109.2, increased eighteen fold between 1973 and 1995. Particularly affected were Latin American countries, with Mexico and Brazil having the largest external debts. Africa has suffered badly too because many African countries are amongst the poorest in the world.

Debt-export ratio The ratio of debt to exports is important because, to repay debt, a country has to earn foreign currency (unless of course it takes out new loans to repay the old ones). Exports are the equivalent of wages for a household that has borrowed a large sum to buy a house. Figure 109.2 shows that the value of total debt to exports for one year rose sharply during the first half of the 1980s. Up to 1982, countries were still borrowing. After 1982, many countries defaulted. However, unpaid interest on the loans was added to the total debt by First World banks and other lenders (as is normal commercial practice). So without taking on any more loans, the size of the total debt carried on increasing. One of the effects of the debt crisis was to reduce economic growth rates in developing countries. Lower growth made it even more difficult for them to repay debt. The effect of low or even negative economic growth rates on the debt problem can be seen in the experience of Sub-Saharan Africa whose debt-exports ratio carried on climbing throughout the 1980s and early 1990s. Asian countries, which had borrowed less as a proportion of exports in the first place and had carried on growing strongly throughout the 1980s, saw their debt-export ratios stay roughly constant at around $^3/_4$.

Table 109.2 *External debt of developing countries*

	$bns
1973	97
1982	662
1986	1 032
1990	1 293
1995	1 749
1995	
Africa	250
Asia	615
Middle East and Europe	338
Latin America and Caribbean	546

Source: United Nations, *World Economic Outlook.*

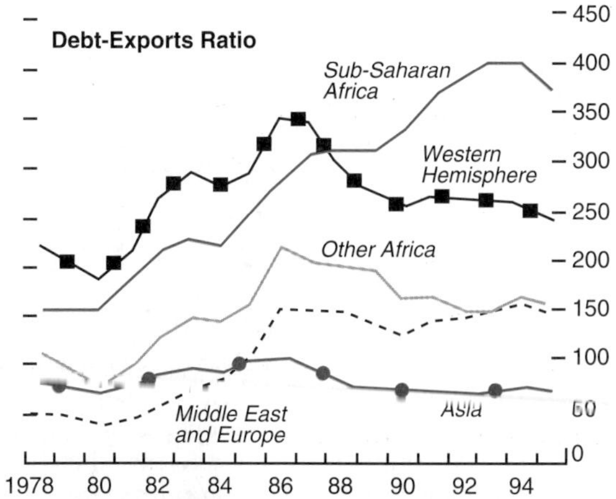

Source: adapted from United Nations, *World Economic Outlook.*

Figure 109.2 *Developing countries: debt to export ratio*

Debt-GDP ratio Table 109.3 gives another measure of indebtedness. It shows the proportion of debt to GDP. The picture is very similar to Figure 109.2, with African countries most indebted and Asian least indebted. For the Third World as a whole, the debt to GDP ratio peaked in 1986 at 39.8 per cent and by 1995, due to less new borrowing and rising GDP, had fallen to 30.8 per cent.

Table 109.3 *Developing countries: ratio of external debt to GDP*

%	1973	1977	1980	1986	1991	1995
Developing countries	13.7	24.9	25.7	39.8	30.8	30.8
of which						
Africa		31.4	26.9	55.5	56.7	62.3
Asia		17.2	16.7	26.6	24.7	24.9
Latin America and Caribbean		29.0	32.2	61.3	39.4	31.2

Source: United Nations, *World Economic Outlook.*

Debt-service to export ratio Figure 109.3 shows the proportion of exports which have been used to repay debt plus interest. Why the crisis started in 1982 in Latin America is clear from the chart. In 1982, Latin American countries used over half their export earnings to repay debt and interest. This is the equivalent of a household paying half its income in mortgage repayments. Since 1982, Latin American countries have reduced the burden of external debt, so that by 1995 the ratio had fallen to 32 per cent. However, the crisis has worsened again in the first half of the 1990s for African countries after an improvement in the second half of the 1980s. Again note the relative success of Asian countries, a mixture of avoiding excessive borrowing and fast growing GDP and exports.

There is a strong parallel between the Third World debt crisis and the mortgage crisis of the early 1990s in the UK. In the late 1980s, many UK households borrowed heavily to buy a house. In the early 1990s, many of those lost their jobs or saw their incomes fall in the recession which followed the Lawson boom. The result was that they failed to keep up repayments on the mortgage. The repayments not made plus continued interest were then added to the size of the original mortgage, so the amount borrowed kept on increasing, making it even more difficult for homeowners to meet the monthly repayment. Homeowners on relatively low incomes who bought at inflated prices in the late 1980s and then lost their jobs were the equivalent of many of the African countries in the 1970s and 1980s. Higher income earners, who borrowed less heavily as a proportion of their income, and who kept on getting pay increases during the 1990-1992 recession, were the equivalent of most of the Asian countries during the period.

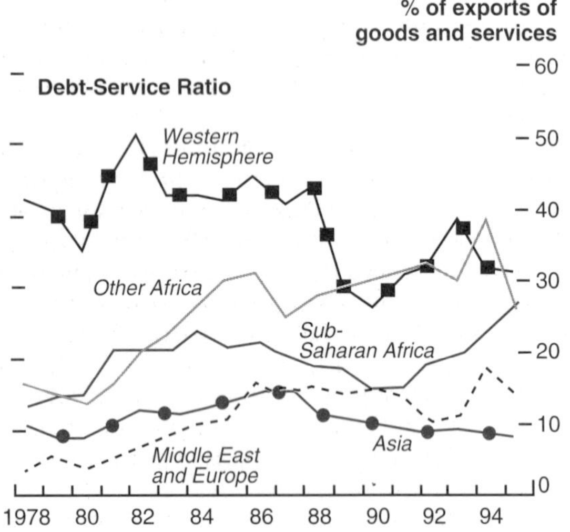

Source: adapted from United Nations, *World Economic Outlook.*

Figure 109.3 *Developing countries: debt-service to export ratio*

Solving the debt crisis

The debt crisis, which erupted in the early 1980s, had been to some extent resolved for most countries by the mid-1990s. The resolution has occurred in a number of ways.

Growing out of the problem Many countries have grown out of the problem. This is like the homeowner who gets into difficulties with a mortgage. If the mortgage repayments are £500 a month and the household income is £600, then the debt is too great. If, however, one of the wage earners gets promotion and pushes up the household income to £1 000, then the mortgage is manageable. Asian countries, for instance, have on the whole seen their GDP and exports rise at a fast enough rate for them to be able to service existing debts and indeed take on new debt.

Debt forgiveness A second solution has been debt forgiveness. Most Third World debt is owed to three main groups: First World governments which have lent money to the Third World as part of their aid programmes; First World banks; multilateral agencies, such as the IBRD, (the International Bank for Reconstruction and Development or World Bank) and the IMF (International Monetary Fund). Third World countries would like all three groups to wipe out some or all of their debts. They argue, correctly, that if their debts were forgiven, they could afford to buy more imports (remember, unless they secure new capital from abroad, debt repayments plus interest have to come from the money earned from exports). If they bought more imports, then they could raise their standard of living now by buying more consumption goods from abroad; or they could increase their growth rate by importing more investment goods such as machinery.

First World governments have, on the whole, been very reluctant to forgive debts. The United States in particular has argued that to forgive debts now would only encourage Third World countries to borrow more money and then plead with the lenders to forgive the debts again. Third World countries tend to owe money to a variety of governments. If the USA refuses to forgive debt to a Third World country, perhaps not surprisingly other governments which are also owed debt by that country become very reluctant to forgive their portion of the debt. However, European countries in particular have forgiven some debt, particularly to poor African countries. There has also been a large amount of **rescheduling** of debt, where the time period for repayment of debt has been considerably extended. This is often combined with forgiveness of interest on the debt for a number of years.

First World banks argue that they cannot forgive debt. The money they lent to Third World countries belongs, in the final outcome, to those who lent money to the First World banks, and the shareholders of the banks. However, banks have had to be realistic. Immediately following the Mexican crisis in 1982, the banks knew that there was a high risk that not all the loans plus interest would be repaid. A large number of countries began to default on some of their loans. By the late 1980s, they knew that the crisis was not a temporary one and that, for a number of countries, the debt was so large that it could never be repaid in full. There was a very real danger that Third World countries would declare themselves effectively bankrupt and simply say they weren't going to repay loans already taken out. So, by the late 1980s the banks were prepared to negotiate seriously on the debt problem. A large number of deals were then made between individual countries and groups of banks. Essentially, the banks agreed to wipe out part of the debt owed. In return, the Third World country had to agree to increase, or at least maintain, existing payments on loans. The banks had to wipe out huge amounts of debt. But the reality was that flows of payments on debt increased.

Structural adjustment International agencies, such as the IMF and the World Bank, have also forgiven debt, but have imposed strict conditions on the forgiveness. The IMF and the World Bank have different roles. The World Bank was set up after the Second World War to provide aid to war torn Europe (hence the 'reconstruction' part of the Bank's full IBRD title). Its main work since then has been to provide loans to Third World countries for development, and more recently to Eastern European countries to aid reconstruction. The World Bank is able to make loans because First World countries have agreed to deposit money with the Bank. It also can make new loans with money which is coming in from repayment of existing loans.

The IMF is not a body which is mainly interested in development. Its role is to help maintain a stable economic international trading environment, particularly by maintaining a stable system of exchange rates. Exchange rates come under pressure when a country's balance of payments gets into the red. So it has funds to lend to countries which get into balance of payments difficulties to help them on a short term basis whilst the country sorts out its difficulties. The debt crisis threatened to destabilise the world trading system and it concerned the balance of payments. Hence, the IMF has been heavily involved in trying to sort out the problem.

When countries have sought debt forgiveness from individual First World countries or from multi-lateral aid agencies like the World Bank, a condition of granting forgiveness has usually been that the country must submit to an IMF **structural adjustment programme**. The IMF is brought in to devise a plan for recovery for the individual Third World country. The main elements of the plan are simple.

- The IMF agrees to lend the country's central bank money to replenish its foreign currency reserves. This then allows the country to carry on importing and exporting.
- The country must increase its exports or reduce its imports to obtain the foreign currency to repay debt. Increased exports are typically achieved by a sharp devaluation of the currency. This also makes imports more expensive, hence cutting them. Foreign investment into the country must also be encouraged, for instance by dismantling curbs on the foreign ownership of firms in the economy.
- The government must increase taxes and cut its spending. This is because the debt is usually owed by the government rather than individuals or firms. Typically, the government funds its debt by printing money, creating inflation and also, in the process, making its exports less competitive in the absence of a corresponding fall in the exchange rate. By increasing taxes and cutting spending, the government will create the resources needed to fund the debt. Of course, the effect of this is to force its citizens to contribute to paying the debt.
- The IMF also insists on a wide package of measures to promote efficiency in the economy. Examples are removing import controls, making the exchange rate fully convertible, privatisation, cutting of subsidies such as food subsidies and deregulation of markets. In the 1980s and 1990s, the IMF has strongly believed that economic growth can only be achieved through a thorough **supply-side** reform (☞ unit 69) of the economy.

Structural adjustment programmes are very unpopular in the Third World. This is hardly surprising since the aim is to increase the country's resources being used to repay debt and reduce those available for domestic consumption and investment. Countries subject to structural adjustment programmes tend to see their growth rate fall immediately, and many experience falls in GDP. Growth rates can then remain low or negative for some time. The IMF usually blames this on a failure to implement the programme fully. The individual country blames the IMF for imposing the wrong policies.

Structural adjustment programmes also hit **economic development** (☞ unit 105) very hard. Reducing food

Reducing food subsidies as part of a structural adjustment programme can increase prices in Third World countries.

subsidies, for instance, increases the price of food. Cutting government spending in general tends to deflate the economy, raising unemployment. Anti-inflation policies which seek to curb wage increases tend to result in falling real wages. All of these help create conditions where the poor eat less, increasing health problems and even leading to malnutrition. Cuts in government spending are also likely to hit education. Without investment in education today, long term growth rates are likely to be reduced. For this reason, programmes have increasingly included new loans from the World Bank designed to allow governments to maintain key health and education programmes.

Opinion is sharply divided about structural adjustment programmes. Critics point out that high economic growth is by far the best way for a country to deal with its debt problem. Structural adjustment programmes, however, in the short term reduce economic growth rates and in the process lead to negative economic development. Advocates say that the alternative of doing nothing would lead to an even worse situation. Past individual structural programmes have made mistakes in not recognising the severity of the downturn in the economy that can be the result of its implementation. Programmes in the 1980s also often coincided with sharp negative shocks for the country, such as dramatic falls in the price of a commodity which was the country's main export earner. The solution is to increase the amount of selective assistance to the country. However, the programme itself will leave the country in a state in which it has the potential to grow in the future.

Direct foreign investment and portfolio capital flows

The debt crisis was caused by large flows of borrowed funds in the 1970s and an inability to repay the borrowings in the 1980s. However, throughout the 1970s, 1980s and 1990s, there has been a build up of a very different type of capital flow: investment capital. Table 109.4 shows the proportion of the two types of net investment capital to net capital flows. Between 1973 and 1976, more financial capital was invested by the Third World in the First World than vice versa. By 1990-93,

Table 109.4 *Developing countries: investment capital as a proportion of total capital flows*

		Foreign direct investment	Portfolio investment	Foreign direct investment plus portfolio investment
All developing countries	1973-76	19.7	- 29.3	- 9.6
	1977-82	29.6	- 27.8	1.8
	1983-89	32.6	15.9	48.5
	1990-93	58.9	46.1	105.0
Africa	1973-76	20.0	1.8	21.8
	1977-82	8.2	- 2.0	6.2
	1983-89	18.3	- 1.7	16.6
	1990-93	51.8	25.9	77.7
Asia	1973-76	17.8	1.4	19.2
	1977-82	10.6	3.7	14.3
	1983-89	30.6	8.2	38.8
	1990-93	40.8	14.9	55.7
Middle East and Europe	1973-76	- 12.5	-75.0	- 87.5
	1977-82	13.1	- 65.4	- 53.1
	1983-89	28.2	69.6	97.8
	1990-93	5.3	4.3	9.6
Latin America and Caribbean	1973-76	15.8	1.4	17.2
	1977-82	17.7	5.3	23.0
	1983-89	51.2	- 14.0	37.2
	1990-93	25.3	40.2	65.5

Source: World Bank, *World Economic Outlook.*

foreign investment represented 105 per cent of net capital inflows. The fast growing Asian economies and Latin American countries secured 91 per cent of all net foreign investment flows in 1990-93. Africa received a mere 3.4 per cent of net world flows. Foreign direct investment is the investment by First World companies in Third World countries. Ford setting up a car manufacturing plant in China would be an example. Portfolio investment is the purchase of shares in firms in Third World countries by First World investors, such as pension funds or unit trusts.

Investment capital is radically different from loan capital.

- A loan has to be repaid even if the investment which is

A Nestlé factory being built in Nigeria. Investment by multinationals can benefit Third World countries.

made with the loan is not successful. A Third World government borrowing money to build a power station has to repay the loan whether the power station is built or not. However, if the power station is built and owned by a First World company, then the First World company takes on the risk of failure. If it fails, the Third World country does not owe any money to the First World.

- Investment capital involves the transfer of some sort ofknowledge from the First World to the Third World. If it is direct investment, then the First World company will almost invariably import some machinery and equipment from the First World. But it will also combine that with locally produced investment capital such as buildings. It will train staff. It will create a climate which ensures commercial success. This has large positive spin-offs for the country. Extra goods for domestic consumption and for export will be produced, increasing GDP. Local workers will be able to absorb First World production techniques, leading probably to the establishment of local competing firms. The First World company will also need suppliers in the local economy. There is therefore a **multiplier effect** on investment and output.
- To counterbalance this, the country will lose some of its sovereignty. It will become dependent to some extent on the activities of foreign firms. However, this is no different from individual countries in the First World. It will also have to allow the repatriation of profits - the equivalent of debt interest. However, profit rates are typically lower than interest rates. What is more, if the investment is relatively unsuccessful, there will be no profit to be repatriated to the First World. The First World firm may also 'exploit' the local economy by setting itself lower safety standards or working its labour force longer hours for lower pay than similar operations in First World countries. However, it should be remembered that one of the main reasons why First World firms are attracted to set up in Third World countries is because of lower costs of production.

The activities of multinationals investing directly in Third World countries differ from those of foreign investors buying shares in Third World firms. As with direct investment, the great advantage of this type of investment is that the risk of failure is transferred from the Third World to the First World. Moreover, First World investors may be a little better at picking investment projects that will be successful than, say Third World governments. There will be a loss of sovereignty and profits will have to flow back to the First World. However, most are agreed that the benefits to the Third World far outweigh the disadvantages. The challenge for the rest of this decade is for more investment capital to be attracted to the poorer countries of the world and particularly Africa. Investment capital could be one way in which Africa could escape from its recent history of low or even negative growth.

Foreign aid

Cuts in foreign aid

The OECD reported in 1995 that developed countries have been cutting their foreign aid budgets. After 20 years of stability, its members had cut their net official development aid sharply from $61bn in 1992 to $56bn in 1993. The organisation said that, faced with difficult economic conditions in their own domestic economies, OECD countries had cut aid budgets as part of wider packages to cut government spending. It noted that the ending of the Cold War had brought no peace dividend for foreign aid. Cuts in defence spending in OECD budgets had been used to increase spending in other areas or had contributed to financing further public spending cuts. The development aid budget is also under pressure from the ever increasing demands of emergency aid relief for disasters, both natural and man-made. Such emergency aid had reached $5bn in 1993.

Increases in net private flows of capital to the Third World were welcomed. However, private lending and investment were no substitute for official aid cuts. This was because 80 per cent of the net private capital flows were going to 20 per cent of developing countries,mainly in East Asia and Latin America. Many of the less popular developing countries with private investors 'could now use more aid, and use it well, because they have been doing so much more to help themselves'.

A consensus was emerging between aid-giving and aid-receiving countries on the need for 'an integrated process of political and economic stability, good governance, popular participation, investing in people, reliance on market forces, concern for the environment and a vigorous private sector'.

Source: adapted from OECD, *Development Co-operation 1994 Report.*

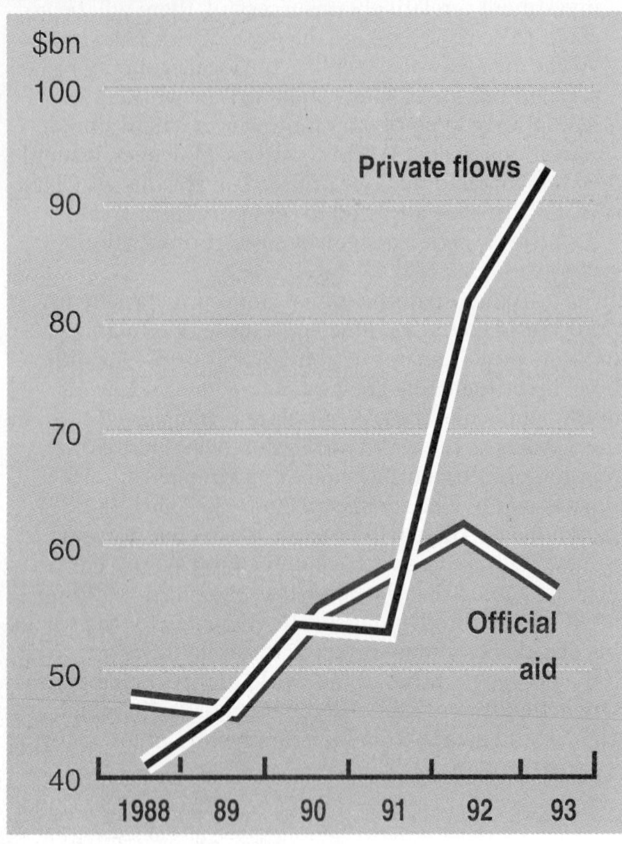

Source: adapted from OECD.
Figure 109.4 *OECD net aid flows*

The role of NGOs

NGOs, Non-Governmental Organisations, are mainly charities. They have come to play an increasingly important role in channelling knowledge and resources from the First World to the Third World. In 1963, there were a few hundred active in the Third World. By 1993, the number had grown to nearly 29 000. Governments have increasingly recognised the value of the work that NGOs do. According to the World Bank, in 1992 official aid agencies, such as governments, gave $2.5bn to NGOs to support their work. The NGOs spent a further $5.9bn themselves. The 30 per cent share of official assistance in 1992 contrasts with a 1.5 per cent share in 1970.

One of the strengths of NGOs which governments have come to appreciate is that they are much better at channelling aid to the poorest in the Third World than themselves. The British government, for instance, has not got the resources to lend a few hundred pounds to a poor Indian family for housing construction. It is interested in giving or lending millions of pounds at a time. However, a charity like Homeless International of Coventry specialises in lending small amounts of money to individuals in the Third World. In India, for instance, it has recently launched a guarantee fund to enable 2 500 families in the Indian states of Andhra Pradesh and Gujarat to borrow roughly £200 each from a local mortgage supplier for housing construction. The charity wants to discourage dependence and encourage people to become economically self-reliant. So to encourage repayment, it has set up a system of peer group pressure in the communities where the borrowers live.

Source: adapted from the *Financial Times*, 13.2.1995.

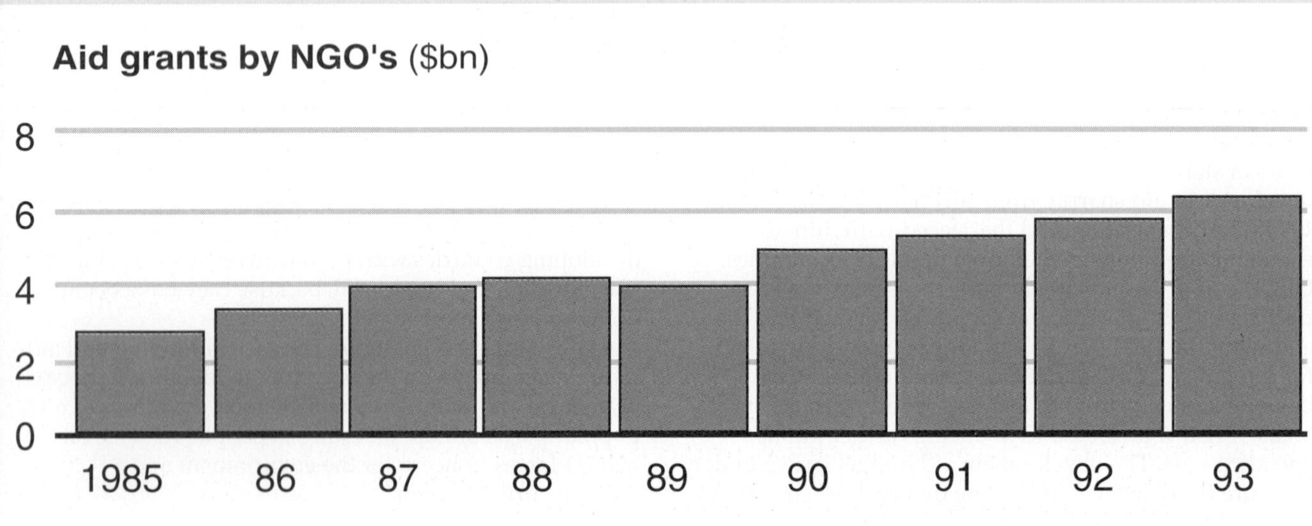

Source: adapted from OECD.
Figure 109.5 *Aid grants by NGOs ($bn)*

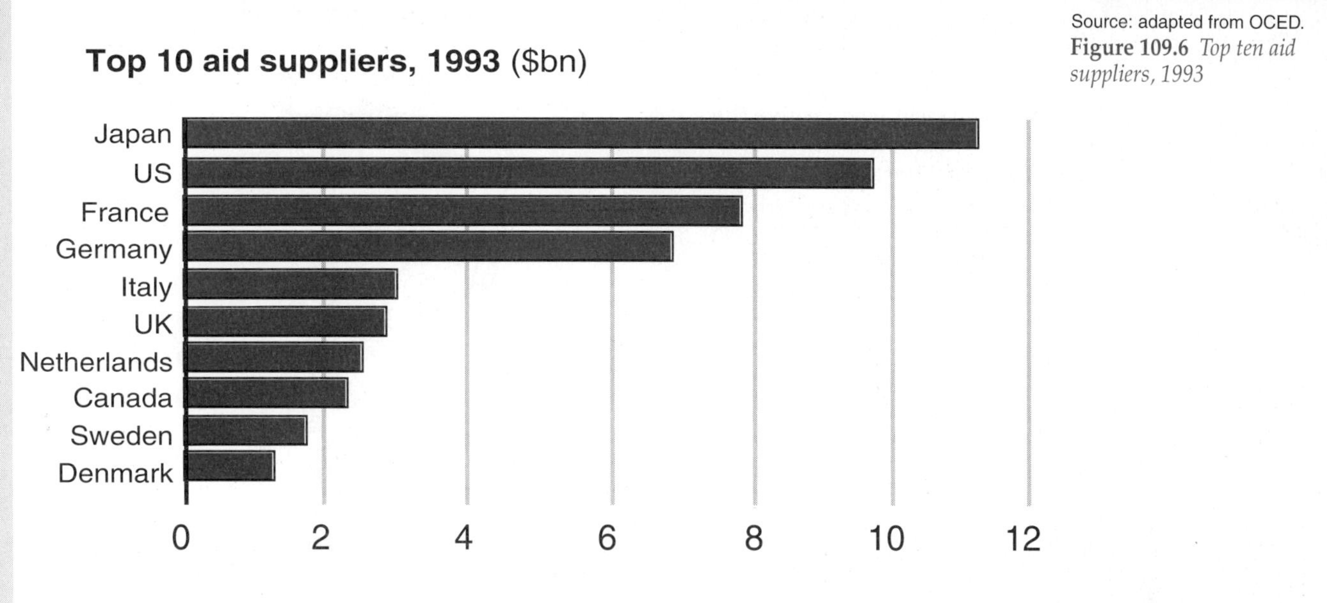

Source: adapted from OCED.
Figure 109.6 *Top ten aid suppliers, 1993*

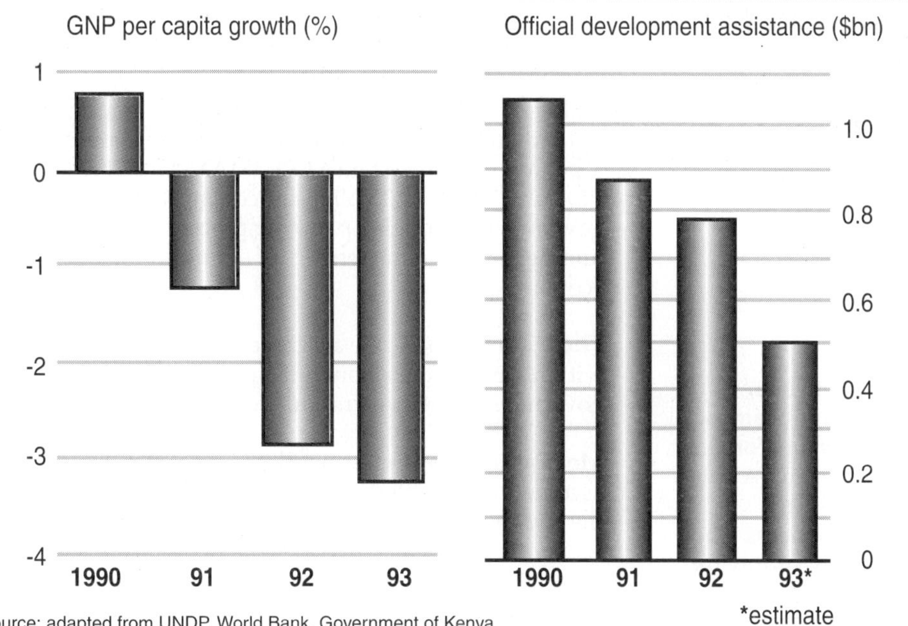

Source: adapted from UNDP, World Bank, Government of Kenya
Figure 109.7 *Kenyan growth and aid: the early 1990s*

The policies of aid in Kenya

In 1991, Kenya's main aid donors cut foreign aid to the country. They were protesting at the country's poor record on human rights, its lack of democracy, the anti-market economic policies being pursued and the widespread corruption in government and para-statal organisations. The aid cuts were one of the causes of the sharp fall in per capita incomes in Kenya in the early 1990s as the economy went into recession. The government reluctantly responded by introducing wide ranging market reforms and allowing opposition parties to be formed.

By 1994, the main aid donors, including the UK and Denmark, were satisfied enough with the reforms to begin to increase aid again but a series of incidents in the first half of 1995, including arrests of opposition MPs and the announcement of the building of a third international airport for the country near the president's home town, made the aid donors reconsider their position.

Source: adapted from the *Financial Times*, 3.5.1995.

1. **Using examples from the data, distinguish between foreign aid and private flows of capital to the Third World.**
2. **How, according to the data, can foreign aid help the development process?**
3. **Discuss whether Third World countries should become dependent on foreign aid as a significant source of foreign capital.**

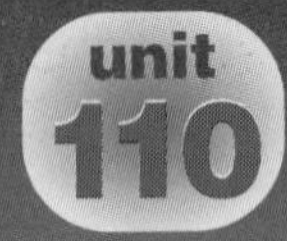

Command economies

Summary

1. The function of any economic system is to resolve the basic economic problem.
2. In a command economy, the state allocates resources through a planning mechanism. Some goods and services are provided free at the point of consumption. Others are sold, although goods may be rationed if the price is below the market clearing price.
3. Command economies have mainly been associated with the former communist regimes of Eastern Europe and the Soviet Union, although Britain during the Second World War was run very much as a command economy.
4. The command economies of Eastern Europe, whilst possibly reducing inequalities in society, had relatively low economic growth rates over the past 20 years. Choice and economic freedom were limited whilst their environmental record was very poor.

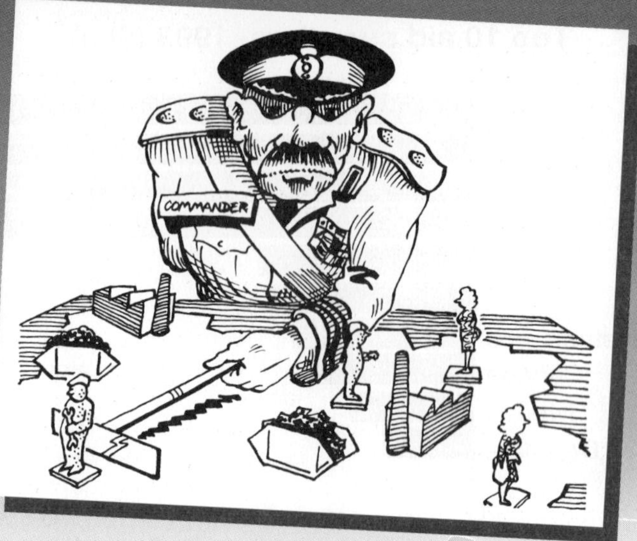

Economic systems

The function of an economy is to resolve the basic **economic problem** - resources are scarce but wants are infinite (☞ unit 1). Resources therefore need to be allocated. This allocation has three dimensions:

- **what** is to be produced;
- **how** is it to be produced;
- **for whom** it is to be produced.

An ECONOMIC SYSTEM is a complex network of individuals, organisations and institutions and their social and legal interrelationships. The function of an economic system is to resolve the basic economic problem. Within an economic system there will be various 'actors'.

- Individuals. They are consumers and producers. They may own factors of production which they supply for production purposes.
- Groups. Firms, trade unions, political parties, families and charities are just some of the groups which might exist in an economic system.
- Government. Government might range from a group of elders in a village, to a local authority to a national or international parliament. One key role of government is to exercise power. It establishes or influences the relationships between groups, for instance through the passing of laws.

Relationships between groups can be regulated by law. In many cases, however, they are regulated by custom - traditional ways of organisation which are accepted by participants within the economic system.

Command economies

In a free market economy (☞ unit 111), economic decision making is decentralised. Millions of economic agents individually make decisions about how resources are allocated. In contrast, in a COMMAND ECONOMY (or PLANNED ECONOMY) resources are allocated by government through a planning process. There are a number of key characteristics of a pure command economy.

The main actors There are three main types of actors within a planned economy- the planners (the government), consumers and workers.

Motivation Consumers, workers and government are all assumed to be selfless, co-operating together to work for the common good. This is in marked contrast with most economic agents in a market economy who are assumed to be motivated only by their own self-interest.

Public ownership All factors of production apart from labour are owned by the state (although labour services can be directed by the state). There is no private property.

Planning Resources are allocated through a planning process. At its most extreme, this means that the state will direct labour into jobs as well as directing consumers what to consume, although it is more likely that they will direct producers what to produce, thus determining the choice of goods available to consumers.

The planning process

Allocating resources through a planning mechanism is a complex operation. Planners have to decide what is to be produced. They have to decide, for instance, how many pairs of shoes, how much alcohol or how many tanks are to be manufactured. They then have to decide how it is to be made. They must decide what techniques of production are to be used and which factors of production are to be employed. Finally decisions about distribution have to be made- which consumers will receive what goods and services.

Planners tend to make use of **input-output analysis** when drawing up their plans. This is a method of charting the flows of resources in an economy. For instance, with a given technology, planners know how many workers, how much iron, how much coal etc. is needed to produce 1 tonne of steel. So they can work out what resources are needed if the economy is to produce, say, 20 million tonnes of steel. Having allocated so many tonnes of coal to steel production, planners now need to work out how many inputs are needed to produce the coal. A complex chart of the economy then arises showing how the factors of production (the inputs) are to be distributed to produce a given quantity of output. Most planned economies have used a mixture of 5, 10 or 15 year plans to outline the growth of their economies in the long term, whilst preparing yearly plans to cover short term planning.

Planning and forecasting is notoriously difficult. Accurate forecasting to produce maximum output assumes that planners know the most efficient way to produce goods and services (i.e. that they have available to them an efficient **production function** for each industry ☞ unit 17). Planners must have accurate statistics about the current state of the economy. There are also many variables which are beyond the control of forecasters. The weather is one important factor which can lead to severe misallocation in the economy.

In practice, planning is so complicated that some choices at least are left to individuals. In all command economies today, workers receive wages. They are then free to choose within limits how to spend this money. Some goods and services, such as education and health care may be provided free of charge to citizens. Others, such as housing, may need to be paid for but there is no free market in the product. Housing is allocated by the state and it is not possible to choose which house to occupy. However, some goods are available for purchase, such as food or clothing.

QUESTION 1 The Belarus tractor factory was a typical example of production in the former Soviet Union. It was allocated supplies of raw materials by the state, and in return manufactured approximately 100 000 tractors a year. It was the sole manufacturer of a particular class of tractor in the country and the sole supplier of these tractors to state farms. Nearly 25 per cent of the factory's output was exported to other Comecon countries. The management estimated that, at current prices, it could sell twice as many tractors as it produced if there was a free market in tractors.

Why was the Belarus tractor factory a 'typical example of production' in a centrally planned economy?

Ideology and the command economy

Command economies have come to be associated with communist (or Marxist) regimes. However, there is no reason why other types of political system should not be associated with a planned economy. Many Third World countries have issued 5 year plans, although they have been to some extent 'indicative' plans because they have relied upon free market forces to deliver much of the output. During the Second World War, the British economy was run very much as a planned economy. Government directed resources and issued output targets to factories. Consumer choice was restricted through a system of rationing.

Moreover, it has been argued that underlying market economies are a complex network of command economies. A firm is a small command economy. With a given number of inputs the firm has to allocate those resources to produce a given quantity of outputs. As in a command economy, firms have to plan how to use those resources and face exactly the same questions of **what** to produce, **how** to produce and **for whom** to produce as a state. The largest firms in the world today, such as General Motors or IBM, have larger outputs than many small developing countries. So even supposedly 'free markets' have an element of planning.

Because communist regimes have tended to organise their economies under command structures, planned economies have tended to be associated with greater equality than under market systems. But again, this need not be the case. Governments could just as well plan to distribute resources in an extremely unequal fashion if they so wished, as is the case in many Third World countries.

The allocation of resources

The planning process determines the allocation of resources within a command economy. However, in practice consumers are given money to spend freely on a limited range of goods and services. There is therefore a type of market mechanism operating in the sale of these products. In a free market, resources are allocated by price. Price rises to the point where demand equals supply. Only those with money can afford to buy the goods. In a planned economy, planners may decide to limit prices so that goods are within the price range of all consumers. For instance, planners may set maximum prices for food or clothing. Experience shows, however, that low prices often result in excess demand. Everyone can afford to buy meat, for instance, but there is insufficient meat in the shops to satisfy consumer demand. There are therefore shortages and resources are usually allocated via a queueing system. When a consignment of goods arrives in a shop, a queue will develop. Those at the front of the queue will be able to buy the goods. Those at the back will be turned away empty-handed.

QUESTION 2 In the 1980s, retail prices were determined centrally in the former Soviet Union. Essentials, such as bread and meat, were very cheap; shop prices of bakery products, sugar and vegetable oil were last changed in 1955. To travel any distance by metro, bus or trolleybus in Moscow cost only 5 kopecs (5p). Housing rent normally cost only 3 per cent of income. Low prices meant long queues and often poor quality goods. This led to large secondary and black markets. Anything more than the essentials of life, such as furniture and many articles of clothing, were very expensive and often in short supply. A typical car owner would, for instance, have saved up for seven to eight years to buy a car. However, the system threw up absurdities. For instance, in1984 the Soviet Union, with a population of 275m, produced 740m pairs of shoes. Yet many of these were unsaleable. There were shortages of shoes in various parts of the Soviet Union and sports shoes and sandals commanded premium prices on the black market.

How are resources allocated in a command economy? Illustrate your answer with examples from the data.

An evaluation of command economies

Choice In a planned economy, individuals have relatively little choice. As workers, they may be allocated jobs in particular occupations or in particular geographical areas. They may be restricted in their ability to change jobs by state requirements. As consumers, they will have little say about what is provided directly by the state, particularly in non-traded services such as education, health, public transport and housing. What is provided for purchase in shops is likely to be limited. There is no mechanism by which firms compete with each other to provide different types of the same good (what would be called **brands** in a free enterprise economy). So consumers are offered only one make of car, one make of cooker, one type of soap powder, etc.

Subsidies on many essential items such as food and clothing are likely to lead to shortages. Queueing is endemic in many planned economies. Moreover, what is available can often be of poor quality. In a planned economy, it is difficult to provide sufficient incentives for enterprises and individual workers to produce good quality products. Production targets are often set in volume terms or in value terms. A factory may be told to produce 10 000 cookers. But it is not penalised if these cookers are of poor quality. They will be delivered to state shops which in turn will receive instructions to sell them to consumers.

Income and growth Economic history suggests that, if a country has a relatively low GNP per head, both planned systems and free market systems will deliver comparable rates of economic growth. However, the experience in the 1970s and 1980s in Eastern Europe was that planned economies have consistently failed to match the growth performance of free enterprise and mixed economies. This was perhaps not surprising. As economies grow, they become more complex. The more complex the economy, the more difficult it is to plan the allocation of resources efficiently. Large firms (remember that a firm in itself is like a planned economy) in free enterprise economies have faced similar problems. They can experience **diseconomies of scale** (☞ unit 20) because their management structures fail to keep production efficient. Many large firms have responded by decentralising decision making. Parts of the business may become 'profit centres', responsible for attaining profit targets set by headquarters. In some firms, individual production units may even compete with each other for business.

It is not only the problems that arise from inadequate planning that can lead to low economic growth in command economies. There is also little individual incentive for enterprise and innovation. If a firm exceeds its targets for this year, its only 'reward' will be an increased target for the following year, which it might find impossible to achieve. If there are very heavy taxes on high incomes, there is little point in individuals working hard within the state sector. If there is no possibility of ownership of the means of production, there is no incentive for individuals to take risks, establishing new enterprises to do something better than existing firms in the market. There is every incentive for individuals to minimise the amount of effort they put into their official work. They are unlikely to lose their jobs, nor will they will lose income (although they may be arrested for anti-state activities - which might act as a deterrent). This contrasts with the considerable energy that the same individuals might put into their jobs in unofficial markets. There might be a thriving black market, for instance. Or the state may allow people to rent small private plots for production of food.

The distribution of income Planners may choose any particular distribution of resources within a planned economy. In practice, command economies have been associated with socialist or Marxist governments committed to a degree of equality of income. Hence planners have set high priorities on providing all citizens with a minimum standard of living. They have achieved this through subsidising essential goods, such as food, and providing other essential services, such as health care free of charge.

Equally, there is considerable evidence to suggest that those in power (e.g. members of the Communist Party) have used the planning system to their own advantage. For instance, special shops have been set up where a privileged few can purchase a much wider variety of goods than is generally available and without queueing. Housing allocation, or placements at university, have been biased in favour of Party members. Indeed, this is what capitalist, neo-classical economists would predict. Those in power are using that power to maximise their own utility. They are not the disinterested, selfless individuals that the model assumes.

Risk Karl Marx dreamt of creating a society in which each would receive according to their need. A family of four would have a bigger house than a family of two. A sick person would receive medical care. Those no longer able to work would still receive an income. So the risks associated with ill health, injury at work, old age and redundancy would be considerably reduced. Communist planned economies, to some extent, achieved this reduction in risk for the individual. However, it can be argued that removing risk also removes incentives to work and create wealth. If, for instance, a worker knows that he will never be made redundant, then there may be little incentive for him to do his job well. If an enterprise knows that it will always be able to sell its produce because consumers have no choice about what to buy, then it has no incentive to produce high quality goods or to be innovative.

The environment One of the problems with a market economy is that individual producers base their production decisions on **private** rather than **social** costs (☞ unit 36), thus creating negative externalities. However, the environmental record of command economies over the past 50 years is arguably worse than those of market economies. The problem is that planners have been far more interested in securing increased output than in reducing damage to the environment. If environmental objectives are not written into plans, then it is inevitable that damage will be caused to the environment by industrial production.

Political and social costs Command economies can only work if there is a centralised bureaucracy devising and implementing plans. They leave little room for individual freedom. Perhaps not surprisingly, the former command economies of Eastern Europe and the economy of China were police states, where the political rights of citizens were, to a very great extent, taken away. Whether a pure command economy could operate within a political democracy is debatable.

QUESTION 3 In the early 1990s, the former Soviet Union was in the throes of an ecological crisis, compared with which most other global pollution problems paled into insignificance. For instance, the huge Aral Sea, once the world's fourth largest inland water, effectively ceased to exist. It had turned into two shrunken salt-poisoned pools in the desert, thanks to the effects of massive and thoughtless irrigation schemes. In Belarus, one-quarter of all the arable land has been destroyed by the fall-out from the Chernobyl nuclear disaster - contaminated with Caesium 137.

'The most serious problem is in fact the economic system', said academician Mr Alexei Yablokov. 'All the decision making comes from the centre - from the government, the ministries, and the Communist Party'. 'The Central committee of the party decides what sort of factory is built where. All the ministries are full of people with the old thinking - more and more production, whatever the price. Their aim is not human happiness, but more production.'

(a) What ecological problems are highlighted in the passage?
(b) Why might such problems be created in a centrally planned economy?

Key terms

Economic system - a complex network of individuals, organisations and institutions and their social and legal interrelationships.
Command or planned economy - an economic system where government, through a planning process, allocates resources in society.

Applied economics

Central planning in the Soviet Union

The Soviet economy from the 1930s to the late 1980s was the country whose economic system perhaps came closest to the model of a command economy. Overall decisions about economic priorities were taken by the highest political body in the Soviet Union, the Politburo, the central committee of the Communist Party. It would decide whether more resources should be devoted to, say, defence, housing or agriculture. Its decisions would then have to be implemented by the Council of Ministers, who would decide how this could be achieved with the help of **Gosplan**, the State Planning Committee. Gosplan is the major planning body. It constructed input-output matrices for the whole of the Soviet economy and worked out production targets for each region and each industry. Over 20 000 products or groups of products needed to be structured into its plan. Yearly plans were made within the context of successive **five year plans**, the first of which was announced by Stalin in 1928. The five year plan was an attempt to plan the economy in the medium term, because a year was really too short for the achievement of longer term goals.

Production plans would then be communicated to 40 different ministries which, working with Regional Planning Commissions in each Republic of the Soviet Union, would send out orders to hundreds of thousands of production units across the country. At each stage, those lower down the hierarchy had the right to challenge the orders sent to it. Almost invariably, they would be challenged if it was felt that the orders could not be fulfilled. If the challenge was accepted, the plan would have to be modified. There was no need for production units to communicate between themselves. If goods were poor quality, for instance, shops would complain not to the manufacturer but to the planners at the next stage in the hierarchy.

The system arguably worked reasonably well in the 1930s and 1940s. It is true that the transition from a market economy in the 1920s to a command economy in the 1930s was marked by political oppression on a scale which possibly even dwarfed the horrors of Nazi Germany, but this was more a political struggle than an economic necessity. However, by the 1960s the Soviet economy was getting far too large to manage centrally and large diseconomies of scale were emerging.

One key factor became apparent. The incentives within the system discouraged efficient production. For those with a job from which they would be unlikely to be sacked because the right to work was guaranteed, there was an incentive to devote little energy to the official job and take a job on the side to supplement earnings. For managers, the key to success was to negotiate for as many raw material and labour inputs as possible and have as low a production target as possible. Hoarding raw materials too was essential in an economy where supplies were variable. That way, production managers could easily reach and even exceed their production targets.

By the 1980s, many in the Soviet Union felt that if their economy was to be dynamic, it should not be planned centrally. Hence, economic reform to transform the economy into a market economy was begun.

The Cuban economy

The Cuban economy

Cuba has been run along socialist lines since a revolution brought Fidel Castro, the country's President, to power in 1958. In 1995, there was free, universal healthcare, education and other social services. All key industries are owned by the state, including the important sugar plantations. Apart from health and education, other essential goods and services are subsidised by the state but they are rationed. For instance, food, clothes and petrol are all rationed.

Black markets

Black markets are now an important feature of Cuban life since the breakdown of trade with the former Soviet Union. Most Cubans say the subsidised food and consumer goods provided by the state rationing system each month do not even come close to feeding an average family. The wide availability of US dollars in Cuba has encouraged the development of black markets in everything from meat to washing powder to repairs.

Unemployment

Cuba has a population of 11 million. Since the 1960s, the State has ensured that there has been no unemployment. However, the restructuring of the economy in the wake of the collapse of trade with the former Soviet Union has put this commitment under immense strain. Under regulations which went into effect from September 1994, workers made redundant should be assigned to other available jobs or to strategic social or economic tasks. If no new job is found immediately, unemployed workers have the right to receive one month's full pay and 60 per cent of their previous salary thereafter.

Self employment was only re-legalised in 1993. In 1994, the government allowed small businesses to be set up in selected parts of the economy such as the restaurant trade. However, it was made illegal for anyone to employ another person unless they were a family member. Potential unemployment has followed in the wake of restructuring, particularly in industries where there has been the introduction of involvement with foreign western investors. In early 1995, for instance, workers were sacked from a well known hotel, the Habana Libre, which is now run by a Spanish company. The head of Cuba's official trade union, the Central de Trabajadores de Cuba, said in a subsequent radio interview that: 'We have to find these people work, because this a socialist country and not a capitalist one.'

The dollar connection

In the 1980s, there was a growing trend for emigré families in the USA to send US dollars to their families back home in Cuba. Dollars could only be used in Cuba in the illegal black market at the time, but families which could get dollars could enjoy a much higher standard of living than those who couldn't. In the wake of the collapse of trade with the former Soviet Union, Cuba legalised the use of dollars in 1993, allowing Cubans to buy food, clothes and consumer items such as televisions at special newly opened state stores with their dollars. These dollar-only stores are not subject to any form of rationing. Any Cuban with dollars can buy as much as his or her dollars will permit. This contrasts with the peso economy where shops ration what Cubans can buy. Dollars are also widely used in black markets.

The Cuban government was forced to open dollar shops for two reasons. First, it needs dollars to finance imports of essentials which are then sold at a subsidised peso price to Cubans. Second, the alternative would have been to use the police to enforce a ban on all black market activity. The government would have received no dollar earnings from this and the GDP of the economy would have fallen, as less was being produced.

The Soviet connection

Following the Revolution in Cuba, the former Soviet Union supported the Cuban economy financially by buying exports from them at preferential prices in the 1960s, 1970s and 1980s. In the late 1980s, 85 per cent of Cuba's exports went to the USSR. The collapse of the Soviet Union in the early 1990s brought this special relationship to an end. Cuba's main export was sugar. Cuba has found it difficult to find alternative export markets for sugar, especially since the USA is still enforcing a trade embargo on the country, first put in place in the 1960s.

The collapse of trade with Russia has had two effects. First, there has been a fall in output and employment in former export industries, which has had to involve some restructuring of the economy. Second, there are now severe shortages of certain previously imported goods. Petrol, for instance, used to be sold to Cuba by the USSR at low prices. There are now shortages of petrol in Cuba because the country is no longer able to afford to buy the quantities that it bought in the 1980s.

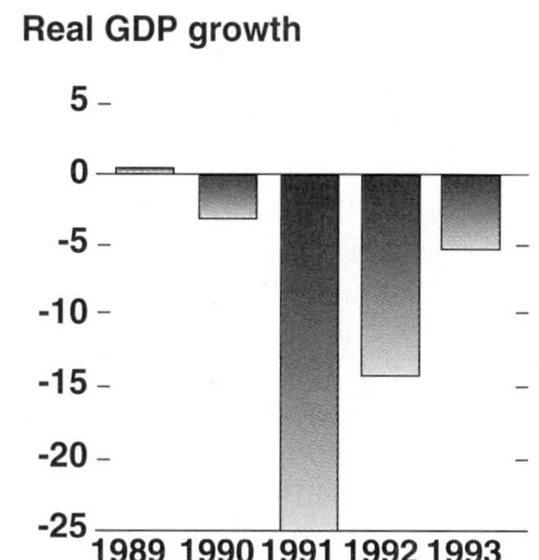

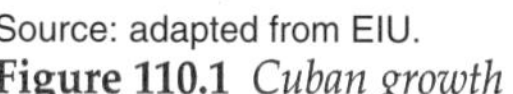
Source: adapted from EIU.
Figure 110.1 *Cuban growth*

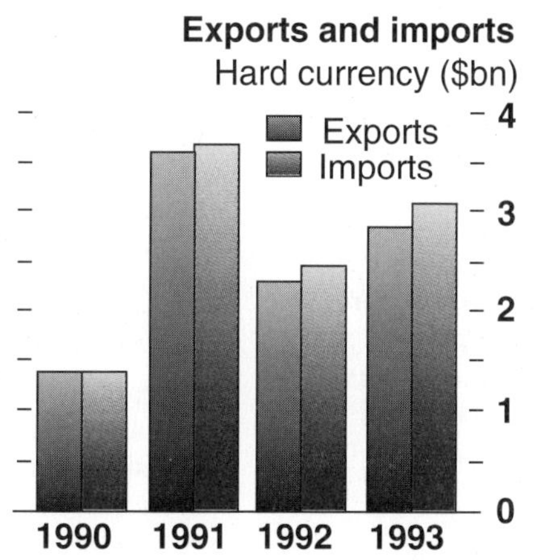

Source: adapted from EIU.
Figure 110.2 *Cuban exports and imports*

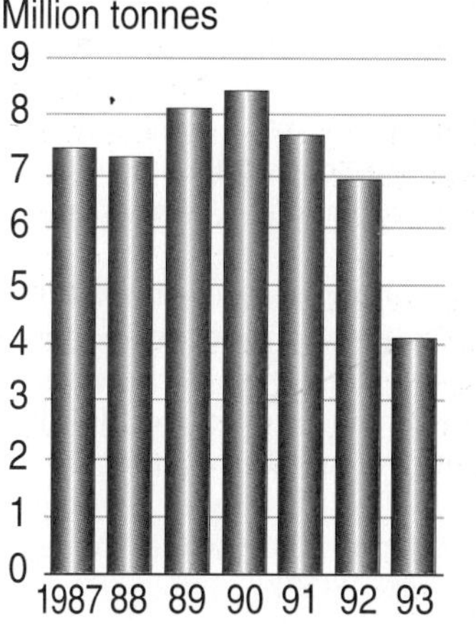

Source: adapted from National Bank of Cuba; State Committee for Statistics.
Figure 110.3 *Cuban sugar production*

Sources: adapted from the *Financial Times*, 16.9.1994, 27.9.1994, 11.11.1994, and 9.5.1995.

1. (a) **What is meant by a 'command economy'?**
   (b) **Why might Cuba in 1995 be described as a command economy? Illustrate your answer with examples from the passages.**
2. **Why would the establishment of a large number of small businesses in the economy owned by individuals move the economy away from the command model?**
3. **Discuss whether a lifting of the US trade embargo on Cuba would make it easier or more difficult for the Cuban government to retain a planning model for its economy.**

unit 111 Market economies

Summary

1. In a free market economy, resources are allocated through the spending decisions of millions of different consumers and producers.
2. Resource allocation occurs through the market mechanism. The market determines what is to be produced, how it is to be produced and for whom production is to take place.
3. Government must exist to supply public goods, maintain a sound currency, provide a legal framework within which markets can operate, and prevent the creation of monopolies in markets.
4. Free markets necessarily involve inequalities in society because incentives are needed to make markets work.
5. Free markets provide choice and there are incentives to innovate and for economies to grow.

Characteristics of the system

A MARKET ECONOMY (also called a FREE ENTERPRISE ECONOMY or a CAPITALIST ECONOMY) is an economic system which resolves the basic economic problem mainly through the market mechanism. There are a number of key characteristics of the system.

The main actors The four main types of actors within the system are consumers, producers, owners of private property (land and capital) and government.

Motivation In a pure market economy, consumers, producers and property owners are motivated by pure self-interest. Their decisions are based upon private gain. Consumers aim to maximise their individual welfare or utility (☞ unit 14). Producers aim to maximise profit (☞ unit 24). The owners of the factors of production aim to maximise their wages, rents, interest and profits (☞ units 48-57).

Government on the other hand is assumed to be motivated by considerations of the good of the community and not by self-interest. It seeks to maximise social welfare (☞ unit 44).

Private ownership Nearly all factors of production within the economy are owned mainly by private individuals and organisations. Government has a duty to uphold the rights of citizens to own property. This it does mainly through the legal system.

Free enterprise Owners of the factors of production as well as producers of goods and services have the right to buy and sell what they own through the market mechanism. Government places few limits on what can be bought and sold. Workers can work for whom they want. Homeowners can sell their houses if they so wish. People are free to set up their own businesses. Consumers are free to use their money to buy whatever is offered for sale. Producers are free to sell whatever they wish to sell.

Competition Competition will exist if economic units are free to allocate their resources as they wish. Producers will have to compete for the spending 'votes' of consumers. Workers will have to compete for the spending 'votes' of their employers. Those wishing to borrow money will have to compete with everyone else who wishes to borrow.

Decentralised decision making Because individual economic agents are free to choose how they wish to allocate resources, decision making within a market economy is decentralised. There is no single body which allocates resources within the economy. Rather, the allocation of resources is the result of countless decisions by individual economic agents. This is Adam Smith's **invisible hand** of the market. He argued that, although economic actors pursued their own self interest, the result would be an allocation of resources in the economy which would be in the interests of society as a whole.

The market mechanism

Any type of economic system must be capable of allocating resources. In particular, it must be able to provide a mechanism for deciding **what, how** and **for whom** production will take place. How are resources allocated under a market mechanism?

What is to be produced? In a pure free market, it is the consumer which determines the allocation of resources. Consumers are **sovereign** (☞ unit 42). Each consumer has a certain amount of money to spend and each £1 is like a spending vote. Consumers cast their spending votes when they purchase goods and services. Firms receive

QUESTION 1 In 1993, Nigel Lawson, a former Chancellor of the Exchequer, gave a speech at the British Association's annual conference. In the speech, he said: 'Throughout the western world ... capitalism has appeared to be in the ascendant and socialism in retreat.' One reason for this was that: 'the rational decisions needed to make a modern economy even halfway efficient can be taken only by a multiplicity of decision-makers armed with the knowledge provided by a myriad of market prices.' A key characteristic of the system is self interest. 'A regard for one's self-interest is a prominent feature in the make-up of almost all mankind. It is not the only feature, but it is a uniquely powerful one. The characteristic of market capitalism is not that it alone is based on the idea of channelling self-interest for the greater good - not that there is anything wrong with that. It is rather that it is a unique mechanism for doing so directly, with the least interposition of government.'

Capitalism also possesses key moral features. 'The family, which looms large in the scheme of market capitalism, is not only the foundation of a stable society, but an important bulwark against tyranny - as is of course the institution of private property, the more widely spread the better. Another key feature of market capitalism is the private sector, non-monopolistic firm. Capitalism is sometimes portrayed as an unattractive competitive jungle, where the values of co-operation are lost in a free-for-all. What this overlooks is that the private sector firm itself provides a model of effective co-operation.'

As for inequality, 'absolute equality, even in the sense in which it is theoretically attainable, must of necessity lead to misery. If there is to be no greater reward for work or saving or effort of any kind than is meted out to those who decline to work or save or make any effort, then remarkably little work, saving or effort will be undertaken. If two people are working at the same job, with equal skill, and one chooses to work overtime while the other does not, failure to pay the former more would be seen as not merely self-defeating but grossly inequitable.' Government has an important role to play here. 'Just as the sensible successful businessman who seeks to help those less fortunate will do so not by changing the way he runs his business but by applying part of his personal wealth to philanthropy, so the wise government will best help the poor not by interfering with the market but by creating a well-designed social security safety net alongside it.'

(a) Identify from the passage the main characteristics of a market economy.
(b) Why, according to Nigel Lawson, does the pursuit of self interest and the existence of inequality in society lead to greater efficiency in the economy?

these spending votes and this in turn enables them to buy the factors of production needed to produce goods and services. How firms cast their spending votes on factors of production in turn will determine how much income each individual consumer has to spend. What happens if consumers want to change the composition of the bundle of goods that they are currently buying? Say, for instance, they decide they want to buy more clothes but buy fewer package holidays. The increase in demand for clothes initially will increase the price of clothes. Clothing manufacturers will consequently earn **abnormal profit** (☞ unit 18), profit over and above what is normal in the industry. They will respond to this by increasing production of clothes. New firms too will set themselves up attracted by the high profit levels. Supply will thus expand as will the degree of competition in the industry. This will force down prices to a level where clothing manufacturers are making a high enough profit to stop some going out of business, but a low enough profit to prevent new suppliers from being attracted into the industry. In the package holiday business, the fall in demand will result in a price war. Profitability will fall. Some firms may even make losses. As a result, firms will scale back the number of the holidays offered and some firms may even go bankrupt. This will continue until package holiday firms once again can earn a sufficiently high level of profit to prevent firms leaving the industry.

Changes in the goods market will then be reflected in the factor markets. Demand for workers, buildings, machines, raw materials etc. will rise in the clothing industry, but fall in the package holiday industry. There will thus be a transfer of resources from one industry to the other.

Notice the key role of profits in this mechanism. Profits act as a signal for what is to be produced. If firms are earning abnormal profits, it is a signal that consumers wish to buy more of a product. If firms are earning insufficient profits or even losses, it must be a signal that consumers wish to see a fall in production in that industry.

How is it to be produced? Producers are in competition with each other. All other things being equal, consumers will buy from the producer which offers the lowest price. So producers must produce at lowest cost if they are to survive in the market place. This then determines how goods are produced. Firms will adopt the lowest cost

QUESTION 2

- The Ford Motor Company launches its new Mondeo car range (1994).
- Sainsbury's, the successful supermarket giant, announces that it is going to set up stores in Northern Ireland (1995).
- Cedric Brown, the Chairman of British Gas, receives a 75 per cent pay rise, increasing his pay to £475 000 a year (1994).
- British Gas closes 160 unprofitable gas showrooms with a loss of an estimated 2 700 jobs (1994).
- The Rowntree Trust says that British society has become less equal since 1979 (1995).

Explain, using the data to illustrate your answer, how resources are allocated in a market economy.

technique of production. Hence, free markets result in **productive efficiency** (☞ unit 34).

For whom? Consumers spend money. The amount of money they can spend is determined by their wealth and by their income. In a free market economy, this is determined by ownership of the factors of production. Workers receive income from sale of their labour, owners of land receive rents, etc. Those with high incomes and wealth are therefore able to buy large amounts of goods and services. Those with low incomes and little wealth can only buy a few goods and services. In a market economy, the wealthy gain a disproportionate share of what is produced. The poor receive relatively little.

The role of government

Government has a number of key roles in a market economy.

- Some goods will not be provided by the market mechanism. Examples are defence, the judiciary and the police force. These are known as **public goods** (☞ unit 44). The government therefore has to provide these and raise taxes to pay for them.
- The government is responsible for the issue of money and for the maintenance of its value. In a market economy, the government has a duty to maintain stable prices.
- The government needs to ensure an adequate legal framework for the allocation and enforcement of property rights. It is pointless having a system based upon individual self-interest if citizens are unable to defend what they have gained. For instance, owners of private property need to be protected from the possibility of theft. There need to be laws about contracts of purchase and sale. It must be illegal to willfully destroy other people's property.
- It is equally important that property rights of any value are allocated to an economic unit in society. If they are not, they will treated as a **free good** (a good unlimited in supply) and consumed to the point where marginal utility is zero (☞ unit 14). The atmosphere is one example of an economic resource which in the past has been owned by no one. Producers and consumers have polluted the atmosphere. This would not be important if it weren't for the fact that we now recognise that such pollution can have an adverse impact upon economic units. At worst, it is predicted that the greenhouse effect and the destruction of the ozone layer will wipe out most life on this planet. Contrast this with the care that people show with their own private property.
- Markets may malfunction for other reasons. In particular, firms or trade unions may seek to gain control over individual markets. Governments therefore need to have powers to break up monopolies, prevent practices which restrict free trade (☞ units 39 to 41) and control the activities of trade unions (☞ unit 51).

The role of government is vital in a market economy. Without government, there would be anarchy. But in a free market economy, the presumption is that government should intervene as little as possible. Government regulation should be the minimum necessary to secure the orderly working of the market economy. Government spending should be confined to the provision of public goods.

QUESTION 3 Political 'democracy' that takes half of personal incomes to spend on welfare, or industrial services which give voters as taxpayers little say and less escape, can be as oppressive as communist socialism. Government cannot be depended on to redress market failure. Its electoral short-termism, its ignorance or indifference to individual preference, its vulnerability to pressure groups and its corruption create government failure that is worse than market failure because it is less corrigible. The common people are best empowered by the market. Government should concentrate on the irreducible minimum of goods and services that cannot be supplied in the market. Optimal size of government is unattainable. But it is better to risk having too little government than too much.

Source: adapted from the *Financial Times*, 19.9.1990.

(a) Explain what, according to the article, should be the role of government in an economy.
(b) What arguments can be put forward to justify this position?

An evaluation of free market economies

Choice In a rich free enterprise economy, consumers will be faced with a wide range of choice. Firms will compete with each other either on price if a good is homogeneous, or on a wider range of factors such as quality if the good is non-homogeneous. However, choice is not available to all. Those with high incomes will have a great deal of choice. Those on low incomes will have little. It matters little to low income families, for instance, if there are 100 types of luxury car on the market, or if it is possible to take cruises on even more luxurious liners. In a planned economy, consumers may find it impossible to spend all their income because goods which are priced within the reach of everyone are not in the shops. In a free enterprise economy, there may be plenty of goods in the shops, but they may be out of the price range of the poorest in society.

Quality and innovation One advantage claimed of a free market economy is that there are strong incentives built into the system to innovate and produce high quality goods. Companies which fail to do both are likely to be driven out of business by more efficient firms. However, this assumes that there is consumer sovereignty in the market. In practice, markets tend to be oligopolistic in structure (☞ units 30-33), dominated by a few large producers which manipulate the market through advertising and other forms of marketing in order to exploit the consumer. So whilst choice and innovation are greater than under planned systems, the advantages of free market economies may not be as great as it might at first seem.

Economic growth In a free market economy, there may be considerable dynamism. However, some free market economies have grown at a considerably faster rate than other free market economies. For instance, Japan has grown much faster than the USA over the past 30 years. Many mixed economies too have grown at comparable if not higher rates to the USA. So free markets are not necessarily the key to high economic growth.

Distribution of income and wealth In a pure free market economy, resources are allocated to those with spending power. Individuals with no source of income can pay the ultimate penalty for their economic failure - they die, perhaps from starvation or cold or disease. This fear of economic failure and its price is a major incentive within the free market system for people to take jobs, however poorly paid. One problem with this mechanism is that there are many groups in society who are likely to have little or no income through no fault of their own. The handicapped, orphaned or abandoned children and old people are examples. Free market economists point out that there is a mechanism by which such people can find support - charity. Individuals who earn money can give freely to charities which then provide for the needs of the least well off in society, or individuals can look after their aged relatives, their neighbours and their children within the local neighbourhood community. In practice, it is unlikely that individuals would give enough to charities, or that the better off would provide accommodation for tramps in their homes to fulfil this role. In a free market economy, there is no link whatsoever between need and the allocation of resources. The unemployed can starve, the sick can die for lack of medical treatment, and the homeless can freeze to death on the streets. Income is allocated to those with wealth, whether it is physical, financial or human wealth.

Risk Individuals take great care to reduce the economic risk which lies at the heart of any free market economy. They can overcome the problem of risk by insuring themselves. They take out health insurance. They buy life insurance contracts which pay out to dependants if they should die. Unemployment and sickness can also be insured against. To cope with the problem of old age, individuals ensure that they have pension contracts.

However, only a percentage of the population have enough foresight or the income to insure themselves adequately. This then means that many in a free market economy become poor, perhaps unable to support themselves or die through lack of medical attention.

QUESTION 4 Socialism captured the imagination because it offered an enticing conception of social and economic progress. It promised not just a great increase in material wealth, but a world where income would not depend primarily on individuals' arbitrary endowments of financial and genetic capital. It also talked sense about freedom - which can be measured only by the choices individuals have the power to exercise. The range of choice is profoundly influenced by a person's economic means.

Capitalism, whilst offering forever increasing economic output, gives no commitment to increased equality. Quite the contrary: incentives are regarded as an essential motor of growth, and they require inequality. But the commitment to inequality means that poverty will never be eradicated. It will be institutionalised. Once a minimum standard of living is attained, people feel poor if they have less than their neighbours. If a trip to the Asteroids becomes a typical weekend jaunt in the 21st or 22nd century, those who cannot afford extra-terrestrial travel will be considered poor. And they will not be comforted by the thought that they are better off than the poor of 1989.

Source: adapted from the *Financial Times*, 9.6.1989.

(a) Assess the criticisms made in the extract of a capitalist economic system.
(b) What are the causes and nature of poverty in a free market economy?

Key terms

Free market economy, or free enterprise economy or capitalist economy - an economic system which resolves the basic economic problem through the market mechanism.

Applied economics

The UK - a free market economy?

In 1979, before the radical government of Margaret Thatcher took power, the UK was quite clearly a mixed economy. Many of the leading industries in the country, such as gas, electricity, telecommunications and the railways were in state control. The government was spending about 45 per cent of the country's income, a very similar proportion to other mixed economies such as France and West Germany. Education and health were both provided by the state along with a wide variety of services from libraries to parks to roads. There was widespread control of the labour market, with minimum wages in many industries and conditions of employment of workers regulated by law.

The changes implemented in the 1980s transformed the shape of the UK economy. The privatisation programme led to large amounts of state assets being sold off to the private sector. The list was long but included car companies (the Rover Group and Jaguar), steel firms (British Steel), energy companies (British Petroleum, British Gas, the electricity companies, British Coal), water companies (the water boards) and telecommunications (BT). The role of the state was cut as public spending programmes axed services. Where the government felt that it could not privatise the service, it attempted to introduce competition into the public sector. For instance, private firms were encouraged to bid for public sector contracts. In the health service, a competitive internal market was established.

Moreover, a wide range of reforms was instituted to reduce regulation and imperfections in markets. In the labour market, trade unions lost powers to act as monopoly suppliers of labour. Rules and regulations in various financial markets were removed to encourage greater competition. In the bus industry, firms were allowed to compete freely on national and local routes.

The spirit of 'Thatcherism' was to release the energies of entrepreneurs in society, to encourage people to work hard and take risks. The successful had to be rewarded and hence marginal rates of income tax were cut, particularly for high earners. On the other hand, those who avoided work should be penalised and hence benefits such as unemployment benefit were cut. The result was an increase in inequality in society.

Some would argue that the UK still remains a mixed economy. Health, for instance, continues to be provided by the state, unlike, say, in the United States. The rest of the welfare state is also larger than in the USA. Others would argue that the gulf between the mixed economies of Europe and that of the UK has become too great for the UK to be seen as a genuine mixed economy. In the mid-1990s, the long term proportion of GDP that is being taken by state spending is around 50 per cent in France, Germany and Italy.

In the UK, it is only 40 per cent. The UK figure is only approximately 5 per cent more than that of the USA or Japan, both free market economies. Those who wish to continue with the Thatcherite revolution would like government spending to fall further, closing the gap between the UK and the USA. In the long term, however, Britain's future lies in Europe. She will find it difficult to resist the pull of increasing the share of income taken by the state to conform with the example being set by her European partners.

The USA economy

Table 111.1 *Income distribution and purchasing power parity estimates of GNP*

	Date of estimate of income distribution	Lowest 20%	Second quintile	Third quintile	Fourth quintile	Highest 20%	Highest 10%	PPP estimates of GNP per capita US$1
United States	1985	4.7	11.0	17.4	25.0	41.9	25.0	23 120
Germany	1988	7.0	11.8	17.1	23.9	40.3	24.4	20 610
France	1989	5.6	11.8	17.2	23.5	41.9	26.1	19 200
Sweden	1981	8.0	13.2	17.4	24.5	36.9	20.8	17 610
United Kingdom	1988	4.6	10.0	16.8	24.3	44.3	27.8	16 730

1 All GNP per capita figures are for 1992.
Source: adapted from the World Bank, *World Development Report.*

Face of America that destroys its Land of the Free myth

Until a year ago, my image of the United Stated was of a wealthy, classless, melting-pot society whose values were embodied in the tough, free-thinking rebel usually portrayed by John Wayne.

That image took a knock during seven days in Arkansas last summer and crumbled this week in Texas.

There is certainly money. In Houston, mirror-glass skyscrapers soar confidently over immaculate parks. In its fabulously wealthy River Oaks suburb, colonnaded million-dollar mansions exceed the dreams of avarice.

But look again and you see another face of America. Shacks and shanty settlements strung out along the highways. Second-hand cars at a half or even a third of British prices. Wal-Mart supermarkets where a pair of jeans costs a fiver.

At first, it strikes you as a land of bargains. Then you talk to ordinary Americans and realise that the prices match the wages and the wages, in many cases, are desperately low.

One of our coach drivers earned a wretched £4,500 a year - below the official poverty level.

The average American family of four earns barely £10,000 and to reach that level, both partners invariably work. In the Land of the Free there is no free lunch. If you can work, you do.

If that sounds fine in theory, what it means in practice is that both our coach drivers in Houston were women, one middle-aged, the other well into her 60s.

It means that a woman hotel executive I met in Brownsville returned to work two weeks after giving birth and thought her employers generous for paying her salary during her absence.

It means that employees accept two weeks' annual holiday as the norm. It means that a word like 'welfare' which has a friendly, benevolent ring to European ears, is regarded in the States at the work of the devil.

Welfare and free health care would sap the American spirit, so the story goes.

The education system is a problem too for Americans. America has recognised the appalling state of its educational system and is making much of its latest drive to improve schools and recruit better teachers.

But there is little talk of producing educated people for their own sake. The motivation, as always, is hard cash and the need to be more competitive against the better-educated Japanese and Europeans.

The campaign for better schools seems to overlook the most important point, that a good education produces thoughtful, innovative people who are prepared to break the mould and try something new.

And maybe that is deliberate. For in its present state of intellectual awareness, America is happy to swallow myths that we Europeans laughed out years ago.

They call it the Land of the Free yet small-town sheriffs and corporate bosses hold powers that feudal lords would have envied.

They boast their classlessness yet have created a society far more formal and unmixed that our own.

And they still foster the belief that any backwoods kid can make it to president, blithely ignoring the fact that every president in living memory has been very wealthy indeed.

You can still make your way to the top in America but it means climbing over rather more backs than Britons might find comfortable.

The woman hotel executive in Brownsville epitomised the thrusting, go-getting face that America likes to project. Back at work a fortnight after childbirth and every inch the liberated ambitious female. How does she do it?

Simple. She has a live-in Mexican maid on £25 a week and God knows how she looks her in the eyes on pay day.

Source: *Express and Star*, 28.4.1989.

Table 111.2 *Real growth of GDP*

Year to year percentage changes

	1960-67	1968-73	1974-79	1980-94
United States	4.5	3.2	2.4	2.3
Japan	10.2	8.7	3.6	3.4
Germany	4.1	4.9	2.3	2.2
France	5.4	5.5	2.8	1.9
United Kingdom	3.0	3.4	1.5	1.0
Italy	5.7	4.5	3.7	2.1
Canada	5.5	5.4	4.2	2.4

Source: adapted from OECD, *Historical Statistics*; *Economic Outlook*.

1. **Using the USA as an example, explain how resources are allocated in a free market economy.**
2. **(a) To what extent are incomes unequal in the USA?**
   (b) Are inequalities in income desirable in a free market economy?
3. **Discuss what might be the advantages and disadvantages to an individual of migrating to work in the USA from the UK.**

unit 112 Mixed economies

Summary

1. In a mixed economy, a significant amount of resources are allocated both by government through the planning mechanism, and by the private sector through the market mechanism.
2. The degree of mixing is a controversial issue. Some economists believe that too much government spending reduces incentives and lowers economic growth, whilst others argue that governments must prevent large inequalities arising in society and that high taxation does not necessarily lead to low growth.

Mixed economies

A MIXED ECONOMY, as the name implies, is a mixture of a planned economy and a free enterprise economy. In practice, no **pure** planned economies or free enterprise economies exist in the world. They are **paradigm models** (☞ unit 115). What we call free enterprise economies are economies where most resources are allocated by the market mechanism. What are called planned economies are economies where most resources are allocated by the planning process. Mixed economies are economies where the balance between allocation by the market mechanism and allocation by the planning process is much more equal.

Characteristics

A mixed economy possesses a number of characteristics.

The main actors The four main types of actor within the system are consumers, producers, factor owners and government.

Motivation In the private sector of the economy, consumers, producers and factor owners are assumed to be motivated by pure self-interest. The public sector, however, is motivated by considerations of the 'good' of the community.

Ownership The factors of production are partly owned by private individuals and organisations, but the state also owns a significant proportion.

Competition In the private sector of the economy there is competition. In the state sector, however, resources will be allocated through the planning mechanism. This implies that consumers are offered choice of goods and services within the private sector of the economy but little or no choice within the public sector.

Government Government has a number of important functions. One is to regulate the economic activities of the private sector of the economy. It needs, for instance, to ensure that competition exists and that property laws are upheld. Another function is to provide not just public goods but also **merit goods** (☞ unit 44), like education and health care. These may be provided directly by the state, or provision may be contracted out to private firms (☞ unit 46) but still paid for out of tax revenues. The state may also choose to own key sectors of the economy, such as the railways, postal services and electricity industries. Many of these will be **natural monopolies** (☞ unit 39).

QUESTION 1 From your knowledge of the UK economy, explain to what extent it possesses the characteristics of a mixed economy.

The degree of mixing

There is considerable controversy about the degree of mixing that should take place in a mixed economy. In Sweden, over 60 per cent of GDP is accounted for by public expenditure, compared to 1995 figures of 49 per cent in Germany, 42 per cent in the UK and 33 per cent in the free market economy of the USA.

In Sweden, there is much greater government spending per capita than, say, in the USA. This means that in Sweden compared to the USA all citizens have access to medical care free at the point of consumption, there are generous state pensions, automatic retraining for those made unemployed and free child care for all working mothers. However, there is a cost. Taxes in Sweden are much higher than in the USA. The fundamental issues concern the following.

- To what extent should the state ensure that all its citizens enjoy a minimum standard of living? For instance, should the state provide insurance for those who become unemployed? Should it in effect guarantee them a job by training longer term unemployed workers until they succeed in obtaining work? Do citizens have a right to free medical care?
- To what extent should there be inequalities in society? The degree of inequality in an economy like Sweden is far less than in the USA. Inequality in the UK increased as public expenditure during the 1980s as a proportion of GDP was cut.
- To what extent should citizens be free to choose how to spend their money? In Sweden, the effective tax burden is 60 per cent, leaving only 40 per cent of income for individuals and companies to choose how to spend. In Sweden, free child care for mothers is provided whether an individual wants it or not.
- To what extent are incentives needed to ensure

continued high growth? Until the late 1980s, the top rate of income tax in Sweden was 72 per cent, with the ordinary worker paying between 40 and 50 per cent. Tax reforms in the late 1980s have switched the burden of tax from income tax, reducing it to 30 per cent for 85 per cent of workers, but extending the 30 per cent VAT rate to a much wider range of goods and services. The marginal rate of income tax is still much higher, though, than in the USA. Supply side economists would argue that higher rates of tax discourage incentives to work and take risks and that this will lead to lower economic growth (☞ unit 69).

- To what extent is government an efficient provider of goods and services compared to the private sector (a debate explored at length in units 44 to 46)?

Mixed economies can be judged on the above issues. They could also be evaluated according to their environmental impact. Mixed economies have a better record on the environment than command economies. Indeed, the Scandinavian mixed economies are in the forefront of implementing measures to protect the environment from industrial activity.

QUESTION 2 Since 1979, the degree of mixing between public and private sectors in the UK has changed. Between 1976 and 1979, government spending accounted for 43 per cent of GDP on OECD estimates. By 1989, it had fallen to 37.5 per cent. After a sharp rise due to the 1990-92 recession, it is forecast to stabilise at 40 per cent in the second half of the 1990s.

Suggest the possible economic consequences of this shift in resources.

Key terms

Mixed economy - an economy where both the free market mechanism and the government planning process allocate significant proportions of total resources.

Applied economics

Sweden

In 1932, the Swedish Democratic Party gained power and created a model of a mixed economy which has been the envy of left wing economists ever since. The Swedish economy lies at one extreme of the mixed economy model, devoting between 60 and 70 per cent of its GDP in the 1980s and 1990s to public expenditure. As Figure 112.1 shows, the proportion of GDP devoted to public expenditure grew considerably in the 1970s, partly because the Swedish government responded to the unemployment pressures caused by external supply side shocks (such as the two oil crises) by increasing demand through extra public spending. Public expenditure as a percentage of GDP fell during the 1980s as the economy grew at over 2 per cent per annum. However, negative growth rates which hit tax revenues combined with a surge in unemployment helped push up public spending from 59.1 per cent as a proportion of GDP in 1990 to 72.6 per cent in 1993. This is forecast to fall by the OECD to 65.7 per cent in 1996 as growth resumes, unemployment falls and tax rates are raised.

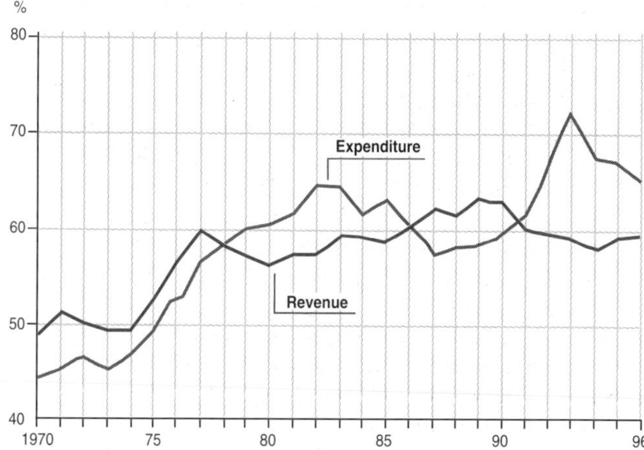

Source: adapted from *Statistics Sweden* and Ministry of Finance.

Figure 112.1 *Public expenditure and revenue as a percentage of GDP*

Sweden provides possibly the most comprehensive welfare state in the world for its citizens with one in three of the workforce employed in the public sector, mainly in education, health or local government.

The Swedish attitude to employment and unemployment is typical of the socialist mentality of the country. Governments have traditionally been prepared to use **demand management techniques** (☞ unit 68) to keep unemployment at very low levels by international standards as shown in Figure 112.2. In 1991, however, a right wing government committed to Thatcher-style market reforms was elected. In response to a recession, it refused to pump prime the economy. It also instituted a number of supply side policies. This led to an increase in productivity in the private sector but at the cost of less employment in the economy. The result was soaring unemployment.

Half of the increase in the ratio of government spending to output between 1991 and 1994 was accounted for by the resulting expenditure on the unemployed. This is because the unemployed in Sweden have traditionally been treated exceptionally well. They receive up to 80 per cent

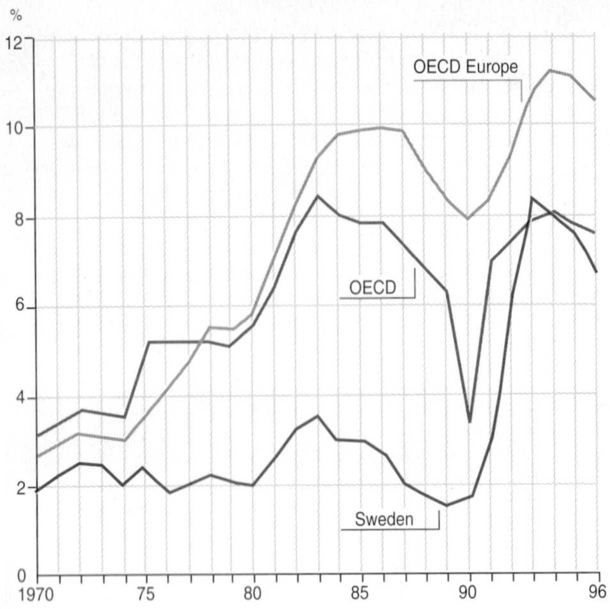

Source: adapted from OECD.

Figure 112.2 *Unemployment in Sweden, OECD countries and European OECD countries*

of their previous after-tax wages in benefits. More importantly, the Swedish employment service goes to every length to ensure that unemployed workers obtain a job or a training place which is suited to their abilities. On the other hand, a worker who refuses an offer of a job or a training place by the state monopoly labour market office will have all his or her benefits removed. In the recession of 1991-93, the Swedish government was forced to increase enormously its training schemes to accommodate the large numbers being forced onto them. Unlike in the UK, however, workers on training schemes are counted as part of the unemployed, and therefore are shown in Figure 112.2.

There is a general recognition amongst the main political parties that the state cannot consume more than 60 per cent of GDP. Government spending must be controlled whilst taxes must be high enough to ensure that the government is able to finance any budget deficit in a non-inflationary way.

There is also a consensus that private industry must grow and become more efficient. Figure 112.3 shows that since 1960, there has been a net increase in public sector employment of 1 million whilst employment in the private sector has fallen by nearly 600 000. The supply side reforms of the early 1990s have been designed to achieve an increase in efficiency and competitiveness in industry. These reforms have included a reduction in the standard rate of income tax from 40-50 per cent to 30 per cent paid for by an increase in VAT, cuts in capital gains taxes, cuts in sickness benefit and privatisation. The cut in sickness benefit was a notable success. Employees were no longer covered for the first day of illness whilst employers rather than the government had to pay for the first two weeks thereafter. The result was a dramatic fall in absenteeism from 30 per cent of the workforce on any one day to 10 per cent. Not surprisingly, firms no longer needed as many workers to produce the same amount of output as before.

Sweden joined the EU in 1995. It sees it as important to secure its European markets and be part of the growing movement towards European union. However, the government also knows that being part of the EU will increase the pressure to maintain financial discipline, for instance by having to conform to the **Maastricht convergence criteria** (☞ unit 98).

Critics of the Swedish model point out that it has seen its GDP per head grow at one of the lowest rates in Europe in the 1970s and 1980s. From having the third highest GDP per capita in the world measured at purchasing power parity rates in 1970, it had slipped to fourteenth by 1995. Like other European countries, it faces a crisis with an aging population in the next century which is likely to further increase the demands on the state. These critics argue that the only way forward is for Sweden to dismantle its welfare state to allow the private sector to become the engine of growth of the economy.

Most Swedes disagree. With a welfare state which provides generous benefits to all in society, ensuring one of the most equal distributions of income in the world, most would lose in any move to a far less equal Thatcher-type economy. Advocates of the Swedish model say that, with more attention being paid to the needs of the private sector, the model can be reformed without breaking the spirit of the consensus that has served the country so well in the past.

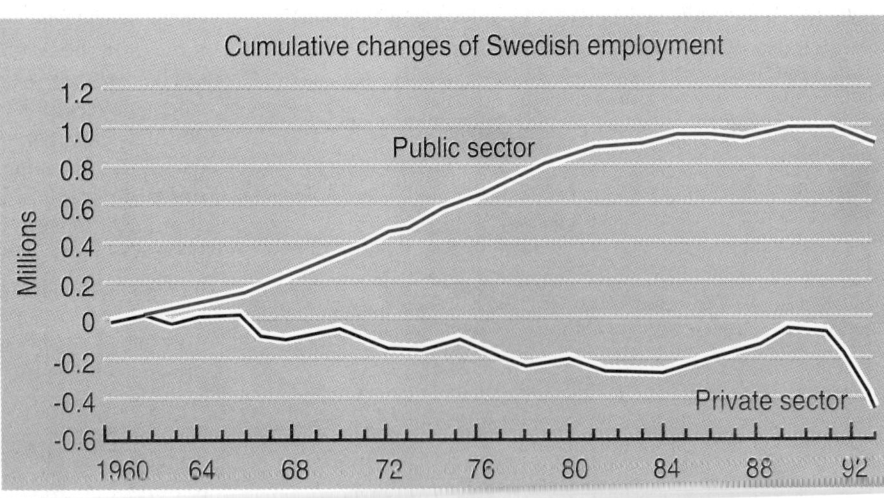

Source: adapted from Henrekson, Jonung and Stymne .

Figure 112.3 *Cumulative changes in Swedish employment (m)*

DATA QUESTION

France

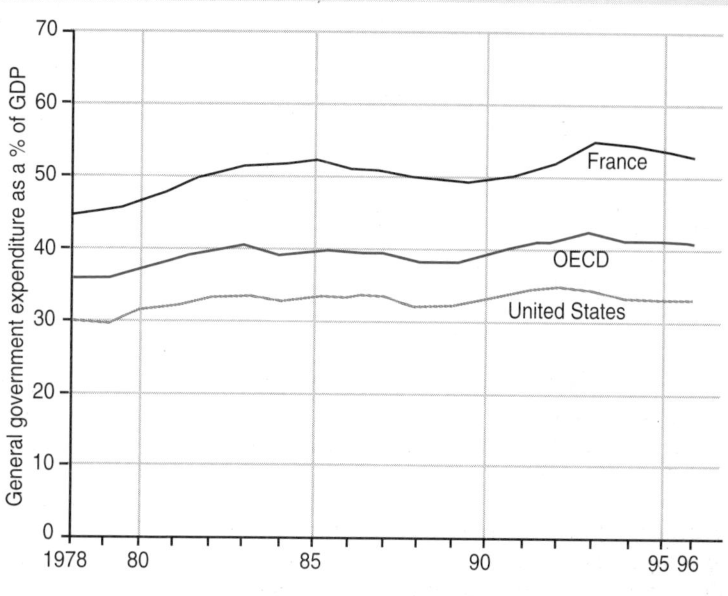

Source: adapted from OECD, *Economic Outlook*.

Figure 112.4 *Government spending as a percentage of GDP: France, USA and the OECD*

The French welfare state

France has a large welfare state. Education, from nursery provision to universities, is paid for by the state. Health care is funded through a complicated system of insurance schemes paid for mainly by employers. However, the state provides a safety net for anyone who is not in an insurance scheme, particularly the poor and the elderly. Local government is a major landlord, offering homes for rent at affordable prices. Home ownership, at less than 50 per cent, is not considered particularly desirable in France.

There is also a state pension scheme which offers pensions of 50 per cent of salary for workers who have paid 37½ years contributions. Critics say it is too generous to meet the demands of a rapidly ageing population. The scheme is a cash management system. This means that contributions by workers today into the scheme are used to pay today's pensions. There are no funds of savings stored up in the scheme to pay future pensioners. In 1995, there were 3.3 workers paying into the scheme for every pensioner. By the year 2005, this will have fallen to 1.9 and in the year 2040 it will be an estimated 1.3. This means that pension contributions will have to rise from their current level of 18.9 per cent of earnings to 35 per cent in 2040. Clearly, this will not be feasible. The alternative is to encourage workers to take out private pension schemes, which would be funded through long term saving and allow the state pension scheme to whittle away as has been the objective of pension reform in the UK in the 1980s.

Privatisation

The French state owns an impressive list of companies, from the electricity industry to gas, water, railways and telecommunications. However, it also owns Air France, Renault cars, the oil company Elf-Aquitaine, the computer company Bull, several banks including Credit Lyonnais, insurance companies such as GAN, the aircraft manufacturer Aerospatiale and the conglomerate Rhone-Poulenc. It plans to privatise many of these. However, the scale of the privatisation programme, the unwillingness to see too great a proportion of the shares fall into foreign hands and the relative smallness of the French stock market could make privatisation a long process.

1. **'France is a mixed economy.' Explain what this means, illustrating your answer with examples from the data.**
2. **To what extent could (a) privatisation and (b) funding of pensions through private pension schemes tilt the French economy towards being a free market economy?**

unit 113

Economic change in Eastern Europe

Applied economics

Table 113.1 *Countries in transition: change in real GDP*

Annual percentage change

	Average 1976-85	1986	1987	1988	1989	1990	1991	1992	1993	1994	1995	1996
Albania	1.0	5.6	-0.8	-1.4	9.8	-10.0	-27.7	-9.7	11.0	-	-	-
Bulgaria	5.8	5.6	5.7	2.4	-0.5	-9.1	-11.7	-5.7	-4.2	0.0	2.0	2.0
Former Czechoslovakia	2.8	2.8	2.1	2.5	4.5	-0.4	-15.9	-8.5	-	-	-	-
Czech Republic	-	-	-	-	-	-	-	-	-0.9	2.6	4.0	5.0
Slovak Republic	-	-	-	-	-	-	-	-	-4.1	4.8	5.0	5.0
Hungary	2.7	1.5	4.1	-0.1	0.7	-3.5	-9.9	-5.1	-0.8	2.5	1.0	3.0
Moldova	-	-	-	-	-	-	-18.1	-20.6	-14.8	-20.0	-	-
Poland	1.8	4.2	2.0	4.1	0.2	-11.6	-7.6	2.6	3.8	5.0	5.5	5.0
Romania	5.2	2.3	0.8	-0.5	-4.3	-7.4	-15.1	-13.5	1.3	3.4	3.0	4.5
Ukraine	-	-	-	-	-	-	-11.9	-17.0	-14.2	-23.0	-	-
Russia	-	-	-	-	-	-	-13.0	-19.0	-12.0	-15.0	-5.0	2.5
Georgia	-	-	-	-	-	-	-20.6	-42.7	-39.1	-35.0	-	-

Source: adapted from UN, Economic Commission for Europe, *Economic Survey of Europe in 1993-94*; OECD, *Economic Outlook*, June 1995.

The basic economic problem

An economic system is a way of resolving the basic economic problem - scarcity of resources in a world of infinite human wants. The Soviet Union had been a command economy since the early 1930s, following collectivisation of agriculture. Eastern European countries became command economies in the late 1940s and early 1950s following communist takeover of their governments. However, the 1990s have seen these economies transforming themselves into market-orientated economies. How can an economy move from being a planned economy to, say, a mixed economy and what costs will be involved in the transition phase?

Output

The process of transformation for most Eastern European countries began in 1990, although Poland and the former Soviet Union began restructuring in the late 1980s. As Table 113.1 shows, the initial result was a sharp fall in GDP. In order to understand the size of this change, it should be remembered that in the 1990-92 recession in the UK, GDP fell by 3.7 per cent. This was considered a deep recession and was enough to double unemployment from 1.6 million to nearly 3 million. For Georgia, which had the misfortune to suffer a civil war in 1992-4 on top of the process of restructuring, GDP fell in 1994 to less than one-fifth of its 1990 value. For every £100 of output in 1989, the country produced a mere £15 in 1994. Poland, on the other hand, saw its GDP fall by only 20 per cent in 1990 and 1991 (remember, this was still five times the size of the fall in the 'deep' recession experienced by the UK in 1990-92) before beginning to record positive growth rates in 1992, 1993 and 1994. By the end of 1994, Poland's GDP was still 10 per cent below its 1990 level.

It is almost inevitable that a transition from a command structure to a market structure will initially reduce output. To understand why, consider how resources are allocated in a command economy. Government planners allocate factors of production between differing production units such as factories or farms. So a food factory might be allocated so much in raw materials, say sugar beet, and a given quantity of new physical capital such as new machines. It then has to supply its output to shops in the country.

The state now attempts to introduce reforms to transform the economy into a market economy. The factory is allowed to sell its final product, sugar, to buyers, state shops or private shops. But equally, it now has to buy its inputs such as sugar beet or machinery. It decides that, in view of the economic uncertainties that it faces, it will not buy any new machines that year. This then has repercussions right through the system. The factory manufacturing machines no longer has a guaranteed market for its product. Faced with the cancellation of the order, it will have to reduce output and lay off workers. It will no longer require as much steel and other inputs from other firms in the economy. They too will lay off workers and reduce output.

On the other hand, the sugar factory may have difficulties obtaining raw materials. State farms, freed from restrictions on what to grow, may decide to grow more wheat and less sugar beet. The sugar factory may also experience problems getting its product to market.

If the sugar is being exported to other countries which are in a transition process, the disruption will be similar. Their factories and shops will be cutting down on imports, uncertain whether they will be able to pay for them. They may also decide now to buy their sugar from a cheaper source in the West, which previously they might have been forbidden to do. The sugar factory may therefore lose all its export orders to that country overnight. There may be little hope that it will ever win back the orders given that the importer now has the whole world to choose from if it wants to start importing again.

The figures in Table 113.1 should be treated with some caution. In the enormous upheaval that transition represents, accurate statistics for production in the official, formal sector of the economy are very difficult to collect.

The fall in output may, in fact, be over estimated. This is because large, informal black economies (☞ unit 60) have emerged in Eastern Europe.

Unemployment

The large falls in output shown in Table 113.1 cannot but have led to sharp rises in unemployment. When Eastern European countries were command economies, one of their strengths was that the economies were managed to ensure almost zero unemployment. The move to a market system led to a large shake-out of labour. First, many enterprises have gone out of business. Factories and plant have been closed and their workers made unemployed. Second, enterprises have been forced to become more efficient, especially if they are now competing in sectors of the economy subject to competition from imports of Western firms. Efficiency is easily gained by shedding labour and making the remaining workforce work harder and more productively.

Table 113.2 shows that some countries have achieved transition at lower costs of unemployment than others. The Czech Republic, for instance, in 1994 had virtually full employment. For other countries, the rise in unemployment has been considerable. However, it should be remembered that unemployment in Western European countries (OECD Europe in Table 113.2) averaged over 10 per cent during the first half of the 1990s. Unemployment in Eastern Europe is not that much greater.

Table 113.2 *Registered unemployment*

Percentage of labour force, end year

	1988	1989	1990	1991	1992	1993	1994	1995*	1996*
Bulgaria	0.0	1.6	1.6	11.7	15.2	16.3	12.0	12.0	12.0
Czechoslovakia	-	-	1.0	6.8	-	-	-	-	-
Czech Republic	-	-	-	-	2.6	3.5	3.2	4.0	4.5
Slovak Republic	-	-	-	-	10.4	14.4	14.8	14.0	13.0
Hungary	0.5	1.6	1.6	7.5	12.3	12.1	10.4	12.0	11.0
Poland	0.3	6.1	6.1	11.5	13.6	15.7	16.2	15.5	15.0
Romania	-	-	-	2.7	8.4	10.2	10.9	12.0	12.5
Russia	-	-	-	-	-	5.7	9.0	12.0	14.0
OECD Europe	9.2	8.5	8.0	8.5	9.5	10.7	11.3	11.0	10.6

*Estimated.
Source: adapted from OECD: *Economic Outlook.*

Inflation

Economic transformation in Eastern Europe has been associated with very high inflation. A rise in prices is almost inevitable if an economy moves towards a free market system. In a command economy, resources are rationed in a number of different ways, but not through price. In the health service, for instance, health care might be rationed according to need, with criteria decided by doctors. In housing, accommodation might be allocated according to age or length of time on a waiting list. In food, citizens might have ration books, or only a very limited range of foods might be available in shops, discouraging shoppers from making too many purchases. Consumer items such as shoes might be available on a

Source: adapted from the *Financial Times*, 12.3.1990.
Figure 113.1 *Price comparisons for state and market prices in Moscow (Roubles per kilogram)*

first come, first served basis.

In a market system, resources are allocated by price. The free market price is inevitably above the old state price if consumers have been rationed in the past. So when a market system is introduced, prices rise until demand equals supply. There is no shortage because some consumers have been priced out of the market.

Figure 113.1 shows the results of a *Financial Times* survey in Moscow in March 1990. State prices for goods were on average less than one-fifth the free market price of the same goods. However, products at state prices, sold through state shops, were either unavailable or were rationed in some way. At market prices, they were freely available from private shops or stalls. But the majority of Muscovites could not have afforded a weekly shop at those market prices. Hence demand for free market produce was relatively low.

Higher prices can spark a wage price spiral. Workers in Eastern Europe have reacted to higher prices by demanding higher wages. If firms give higher wages, then employers will need to pass on those higher costs in the form of higher prices which in turn give rise to further wage demands. For the sort of inflation that was seen in Eastern Europe in the 1980s, it is necessary for the government to **accommodate** those price and wage increases by printing money. If they don't, then firms giving price increases will find that they can't find buyers for their higher priced goods. Lower orders will result in lost production and redundancies. That in turn could mean strikes, riots and civil unrest.

Table 113.3 shows the changes in prices in Eastern European countries in the 1980s and 1990s. When the countries were command economies, inflation tended to be very low, far lower than in Western market economies. The transition period has been marked by large increases in prices. In 1992, Russia saw increases of over 1 300 per cent. This was hyperinflation caused by the Russian central bank issuing huge amounts of money mainly in the form of credits (i.e. loans) to bail out loss making enterprises and prevent them from closing. If these economies are to complete their transition successfully, they must regain control of inflation and ensure stable prices. The danger is that reducing inflation will have a deflationary impact on the economy, further reducing already negative growth rates in GDP. Central banks have to strike the correct short term policy balance between lower inflation but reduced GDP or higher inflation with a higher GDP. This, of course, is the short run Phillips curve trade-off.

Ownership and wealth

In a command economy, land and capital is owned by the state. In a free market economy, most land and capital is owned by the private sector. So the move from one type of economy to the other must involve the sale of state assets to private individuals or companies (what would be called 'privatisation' in a UK context). A number of ways of achieving this have been used in Eastern Europe in recent years.

- The state could give property and capital away to the individuals or companies currently employing them. For instance, tenants of state housing could be given their accommodation. Factories could be given to their workers. One problem with this is that it is a very arbitrary way of sharing out assets. A worker in a factory which produces goods for export to the West would do far better out of this than a worker whose factory was obsolete. This form of privatisation has been widespread throughout Eastern Europe, but has often been done without the official blessing of government authorities. Because the legal systems of Eastern Europe are inadequate to deal with the concept of property ownership, quick-footed factory managers have all too often managed to get enterprises transferred into their names. This has been a particular problem at certain periods in the transition process in Russia and Hungary.
- The state could put all assets which it proposes to sell into a fund, with each citizen receiving a share allocation in the fund. The fund would sell off assets wherever possible, replacing physical assets with cash. Either the cash would be distributed to shareholders in higher dividends or it could be used to invest in the remaining assets of the fund. Shares in the fund would be tradeable, so citizens could choose either to sell the shares and spend the proceeds now or keep them in the hope of earning dividends and making capital gains. This model of privatisation has been pursued in the Czech Republic where it has proved extremely successful. It has ensured a smooth transition of ownership from the public to the private sector which has been seen by its citizens to be equitable.
- The state could sell assets to the highest bidder and use the proceeds to reduce past government debt, pay for increased government spending or reduce current tax levels. Assets could be sold either to domestic individuals or producers, or to foreign companies. This model has been used in most Eastern European countries. In East Germany, for instance, an agency called the Truehand was set up into which was put all of the business assets of the former East German state. Between 1990 and 1995, the Truehand organised the sale of all these assets. Some were sold as existing enterprises to other firms or to their managers. Others were broken up and sold in part lots. Some businesses had to be closed because they were fundamentally unprofitable. In Hungary, some of the most successful enterprises, such as Tungsten lamps, have been sold to foreign buyers who put in the highest bid for the companies.

The speed of privatisation between 1990 and 1995 differed enormously from country to country. In East Germany, almost all the businesses which were to be privatised had been privatised by 1995. In the Czech Republic, the figure was 80 per cent and in Russia over 50 per cent. In contrast, privatisation had barely begun in 1995 in Romania, Bulgaria and many of the members of the Commonwealth of Independent States (CIS - the states apart from Russia which were part of the former Soviet Union).

The distribution of resources

The move from a command economy to a mixed economy has inevitably led to a fundamental shift in the distribution of resources. In free markets, resources are allocated to those with spending power. In turn. those with most spending power are likely to be those whose wealth, whether physical

Table 113.3 *Inflation in Eastern Europe*

Percentage change in consumer prices over previous year

	Average 1976-85	1986	1987	1988	1989	1990	1991	1992	1993	1994	1995*	1996*
Bulgaria	1	3	3	3	6	26	334	80	64	125	60	30
Czechoslovakia	2	1	0	0	5	10	58	-	-	-	-	
Czech Republic	-	-	-	-	-	-	-	10	21	19	27	16
Slovak Republic	-	-	-	-	-	-	-	15	23	13	10	8
Hungary	7	5	9	16	17	28	35	23	22	19	27	16
Poland	19	18	25	60	251	585	70	43	35	32	23	18
Romania	3	1	1	3	19	4	165	210	295	137	45	35
Russia	-	-	-	1	2	5	93	1 350	840	226	102	60
OECD average	10	6	8	9	6	7	6	5	4	4	5	4

* Projected.
Source: adapted from IMF, *World Economic Outlook*; OECD, *Economic Outlook*.

or human, is greatest. As a new wealth owning class emerges in Eastern Europe, the distribution of wealth will become less equal. It will also become less equal as wage inequalities widen. In East Germany, for instance, doctors earned less than coal miners before 1990. This has already been reversed as market forces reward those with high levels of human capital.

The extent to which the distribution of income becomes less equal depends very much on the social security safety nets which are left in place after transition has been accomplished. If the former command economies retain their social security systems relatively intact, then inequalities should resemble those found in, say, West Germany. If they collapse, a distribution more akin to the USA will emerge.

The speed of change

Countries have made or are making the transition at very different speeds. Poland, for instance, one of the first countries to attempt transformation, went through a crash programme of transition in the early 1990s. The effect was severe, with a fall in GDP of over 20 per cent in two years. However, the economy 'quickly' recovered and by 1993 was growing again at a relatively fast rate. GDP in 1995 was still lower than in 1990, but not by very much. The Czech Republic has transformed itself quickly too. A far more sophisticated approach was taken to the process of transformation. Even so, it too lost over 20 per cent of GDP between 1991 and 1992 before growth began to resume again.

At the other extreme, the Ukraine stretched out its transformation process in the first half of the 1990s and was barely nearer becoming a market economy in 1995 than it was in 1990. However, neither did it retain its former command structures. The result was anarchy, with GDP halving between 1991 and 1994. With no command structure, enterprises were not being told which other enterprises were to be 'buying' their product. They therefore had no market for what they were producing from a traditional command viewpoint. At the same time, there was hardly any market system either whereby enterprises could find buyers and sell them their output. Production as a consequence has collapsed. The Ukraine also experienced very high inflation over the period as the central bank printed money to bail out loss making enterprises, rather than allowing them to go bankrupt. A number of enterprises were producing goods which no one wanted to buy and the goods were being put into permanent store, further reducing the amount of goods and services available for consumption and investment. Not surprisingly, Ukranians have suffered harshly. In 1992 and 1993, the real value of wages went down 60 per cent. The Ukraine is widely regarded as an example of how not to manage the process of transformation.

Some countries, such as Bulgaria and Romania, have retained much of their command structures, unlike the Ukraine, and have barely started on the transformation process. They argue that, unlike their more western neighbours like Poland and the Czech Republic, they have little history of western capitalism. Their managers and their workers need much more time to prepare for the transition. Institutions such as stock exchanges and private banks need to be established before the process can be started. In the first half of the 1990s, they have not escaped the fall in GDP experienced by those countries undergoing the transformation process. However, unlike the Ukraine, their economies have not gone into free fall. Much of the decline in GDP was caused by the breakdown of trading relationships with their former Soviet bloc neighbours. This breakdown caused demand for their exports to collapse almost overnight and they have had to find new markets mainly in the West to rebuild their export earnings.

Why was it necessary?

Table 113.1 shows that Eastern European countries were growing at rates very similar to those of their Western European competitors in the 1980s. Unemployment and inflation were low by Western standards. Nevertheless there were two main reasons why change was necessary.

First, the command systems of Eastern Europe were based on repressive political structures. The revolution in Eastern Europe was based on a desire to regain personal political freedom. Command economies can only be run at the expense of personal freedom. They rely on ordering people to take certain actions. To regain personal freedom, individuals had to regain economic freedom. This necessitated a move to a more market-orientated economy.

Second, the figures conceal much of the reality of life in Eastern Europe at the time. Inflation was certainly very low. Prices were kept stable by state enterprises on the orders of the central planning authorities. However, there were enormous inflationary pressures building up in the system in the sense that there was large excess demand in the economy. This was manifested not by rising prices but by lengthening queues. There were long waiting lists for cars and houses. Shops were all too often empty of goods. When there was a delivery of goods, word would get around and a queue would immediately form until the delivery had been completely sold.

Growth of production was satisfactory. However, too much of what was being produced was going into the defence industry, was being used inefficiently in the production process and was therefore being wasted, and was going into investment to provide goods which industry and consumers did not want. Not only production was inefficient. The goods and services that were produced were of poor quality, certainly in comparison with Western goods. The system provided few incentives for any of this to be remedied.

As for low unemployment, a growing proportion of the workforce were gaining second jobs in the black economy. They could afford to work hard at a second, usually illegal, job because they did so little in their official state job. So, in the official sector of the economy, there was huge underemployment of workers - 100 workers being employed, for instance, when 50 could have done the job.

There have been many losers from change. But over time, Eastern European countries want to transform themselves into Western market economies, with comparable standards of living. In the 1980s, they realised that their command structures would never allow them to catch up with the West. Today, Eastern Europeans expect in the long term to achieve their aim.

Poland

Shock therapy

'The objective is to set up a market system akin to the one found in the industrially developed countries. This will have to be achieved quickly, through radical actions ... We are embarking on the reshaping effort under extremely adverse conditions. The economy is in ever more tenuous disequilibrium ... The ecological disaster, the housing crisis, the foreign debt burden, the emigration by the most active part of the young generation - these have been swelling for years. In recent months, additional crisis symptoms surfaced or mounted in force: a rapid price climb linked to a wage explosion, the flight from the zloty, the growing deficit of the state budget and also a drop in output.'

Source: The Polish Government, *The Outline Economic Programme*, 1989.

Institutional restructuring

Poland has seen the creation or restructuring of many of its key economic institutions. A very successful stock exchange has been established. The central bank has been made independent of the government. Private banks have been created whilst state owned banks have shifted their lending policies to encourage new private sector enterprises. Tax reform, such as the introduction of VAT, has broadened the tax base of the government and helped it to reduce its budget deficit.

Liberalisation

In 1989-90, many key prices and markets were liberalised. The result was a widely predicted surge in inflation as excess demand, formerly expressed in the form of rationing, was transformed into higher prices. However, there has subsequently been a very positive response to liberalisation of prices. The Poles have been extremely successful at creating new businesses in response to market signals. The inability of official statistics always to monitor these developments is one reason why some commentators believe that GDP is higher and unemployment lower than officially stated.

Stabilisation

The Polish government has achieved a mixed record on stabilisation during the period of shock therapy in the first half of the 1990s. It has vacillated between controlling the money supply and inflation, and providing enough credit in the economy to prevent enterprises from going bankrupt and workers from suffering too great a cut in real wages. However, there has been an improvement in inflation over the period. The government has managed the Polish exchange rate with perhaps more success than the inflation rate. In 1989 and 1990, it maintained a fixed exchange rate in the belief that this would have a downward bearing effect on inflation. However, it was forced to devalue the zloty because Polish exports were becoming less and less competitive as domestic inflation continued at high rates. Between 1990 and 1995, it adopted a crawling peg system, which has allowed the zloty to decline in value to match high domestic inflation but has also ensured some currency stability.

Privatisation

Poland has been slow at privatising its state owned enterprises. Existing privatisations have been achieved through the state either selling shares in the company to individual private investors, or by selling state owned assets to firms, mostly foreign companies. The pace of privatisation has been sluggish partly because the Polish government has wanted to ensure the continued survival of most of its enterprises. It wanted to avoid the large scale shutdowns that became a feature of privatisation in Eastern Germany. It also was wary of selling too many enterprises to Western companies. There is a strong fear in Poland that its economy could become a satellite economy for Western Europe, prone to large scale shutdowns whenever Western Europe went into recession.

On the other hand, it has been very liberal in allowing new firms to be set up, often in competition with state owned enterprises. The government has forced state companies to maintain strict financial discipline. They have not been allowed to run up substantial losses. Hence, private competition has often led to large increases in productivity in state owned companies.

The establishment of new private firms has been the main reason why the private sector accounted for more than 50 per cent of GDP by 1995.

Source: adapted from the Financial Times. 3.3.1995, 7.3.1995, 28.3.1995.

Table 113.4 *Poland - selected economic indicators*

Annual percentage change

	Average 1976-85	1986	1987	1988	1989	1990	1991	1992	1993	1994	1995*	1996*
Change in GDP	1.8	4.2	2.0	4.1	0.2	-11.6	-7.6	2.6	3.8	5.0	5.5	5.0
Unemployment	-	-	-	0.3	6.1	6.1	11.5	13.6	15.7	16.2	15.5	15.0
Inflation	19	18	25	60	251	585	70	43	35	32	23	18

* Estimates.

Source: adapted from UN, Economic Commission for Europe, *Economic Survey of Europe in 1993-94*; OECD, *Economic Outlook*, June 1995.

1. **Poland moved from being a command economy in the 1980s to a mixed economy in the 1990s. Explain the differences between the two economic systems.**
2. **What difficulties did Poland experience in its transformation?**
3. **Discuss how it could be judged whether Poland was right (a) to make the transition and (b) to do it so quickly through 'shock therapy'.**

Economics - a science?

Summary

1. Economics is generally classified as a social science.
2. It uses the scientific method as the basis of its investigation.
3. Economics is the study of how groups of individuals make decisions about the allocation of scarce resources.
4. Economists build models and theories to explain economic interactions.
5. Positive economics deals with statements of 'fact' which can either be refuted or not refuted. Normative economics deals with value judgements, often in the context of policy recommendations.
6. Models and theories are simplifications of reality.

What is a science?

There are many sciences covering a wide field of knowledge. What links them all is a particular method of work or enquiry called the SCIENTIFIC METHOD. The scientific method at its most basic is relatively easy to understand. A scientist:

- postulates a THEORY - the scientist puts forward a hypothesis which is capable of refutation (e.g. the earth travels round the sun, the earth is flat, a light body will fall at the same speed as a heavy body);
- gathers evidence to either support the theory or refute it - astronomical observation gives evidence to support the theory that the earth travels round the sun; on the other hand, data refutes the idea that the earth is flat; gathering evidence may be done through **controlled experiments**;
- accepts, modifies or refutes the theory - the earth does travel round the sun; a light body will fall at the same speed as a heavy body although it will only do so under certain conditions; the earth is not flat.

Theories which gain universal acceptance are often called LAWS. Hence we have the law of gravity, Boyle's law, and in economics the law of diminishing returns.

QUESTION 1

Table 114.1

Year	Change in consumers' expenditure (£m)	Change in personal disposable income (£m)	Bank base rate (%)	Change in house prices (%)
1988	23 377	20 048	10.9	25.6
1989	10 815	17 427	13.85	20.9
1990	2 121	8 974	14.77	-1.3
1991	-7 612	467	11.70	-1.4
1992	31	10 196	9.56	-4.0
1993	9 327	5 489	6.01	-2.5
1994	9 097	4 597	5.46	2.4

Source: adapted from CSO, *Economic Trends*; *Financial Statistics*; *Social Trends*.

Economists suggest that changes in consumer spending varies with changes in the incomes of consumers (their personal disposable income), interest rates (such as banks; interest rates) and changes in the personal wealth of consumers. Does the evidence in Table 114.1 support or refute this hypothesis?

Economics - the science

Some sciences, such as physics or chemistry, are sometimes called 'hard sciences'. This term doesn't refer to the fact that physics is more difficult than a science such as biology! It refers to the fact that it is relatively easy to apply the scientific method to the study of these subjects. In physics much of the work can take place in laboratories. Observations can be made with some degree of certainty. Control groups can be established. It then becomes relatively easy to accept or refute a particular hypothesis.

This is all much more difficult in social sciences such as economics, sociology, politics and anthropology. In economics it is usually not possible to set up experiments to test hypotheses. It is not possible to establish control groups or to conduct experiments in environments which enable one factor to be varied whilst other factors are kept constant. The economist has to gather data in the ordinary everyday world where many variables are changing over any given time period. It then becomes difficult to decide whether the evidence supports or refutes particular hypotheses. Economists sometimes come to very different conclusions when considering a particular set of data as their interpretations may vary. For example, an unemployment rate of 12 per cent in the North region compared to a national average of 8 per cent may indicate a failure of government policy to help this area. Others may conclude that policy had been a success as unemployment may have been far greater without the use of policy.

It is sometimes argued that economics cannot be a science because it studies human behaviour and human behaviour cannot be reduced to scientific laws. There is an element of truth in this. It is very difficult to understand and predict the behaviour of individuals. However, nearly all economics is based on the study of the behaviour of groups of individuals. The behaviour of groups is often far more predictable than that of individuals. Moreover, we tend to judge a science on its ability to establish laws which are certain and unequivocal. But even in a hard science such as physics, it has become established that some laws can only be stated in terms of probabilities. In economics, much analysis is couched in terms of 'it is likely that' or 'this may possibly happen'. Economists use this type of language because they know they have insufficient data to make firm predictions. In part it is because other variables may change at the same time, altering the course of events. But it is also used because economists know that human behaviour, whilst broadly predictable, is not predictable to the last £1 spent or to the nearest 1 penny of income.

QUESTION 2 An important question in economics is 'What determines how much of a good is bought over a period of time?'. Put forward a hypothesis which might be used to answer this question. Give an indication of how you might attempt to test your hypothesis.

Theories and models

The terms 'theory' and MODEL are often used interchangeably. There is no exact distinction to be made between the two. However, an economic theory is generally expressed in looser terms than a model. For instance, 'consumption is dependent upon income' might be an economic theory. '$C_t = 567 + 0.852Y_t$' where 567 is a constant, C_t is current consumption and Y_t current income would be an economic model. Theories can often be expressed in words. But economic models, because they require greater precision in their specification, are often expressed in mathematical terms.

The purpose of modelling

Why are theories and models so useful in a science? The universe is a complex place. There is an infinite number of interactions happening at any moment in time. Somehow we all have to make sense of what is going on. For instance, we assume that if we put our hand into a flame, we will get burnt. If we see a large hole in the ground in front of us we assume that we will fall into it if we carry on going in that direction.

One of the reasons why we construct theories or models is because we want to know why something is as it is. Some people are fascinated by questions such as 'Why do we fall downwards and not upwards?' or 'Why can birds fly?'. But more importantly we use theories and models all the time in deciding how to act. We keep away from fires to prevent getting burnt. We avoid holes in the ground because we don't want to take a tumble.

QUESTION 3 Make a list of ten questions in economics which you think are important and to which you would hope to have an answer by the time you have finished your course.

Positive and normative models

These two uses of models - to investigate the world as it is and to use the model as a basis for decision making - lead us to distinguish between two types of economic model.

POSITIVE MODELS and positive economics deal with objective or scientific explanations of the economy. For instance, the model of price determination which states that a rise in price will lead to a fall in the quantity demanded is a positive model. It is capable of refutation (☞ unit 115). It is argued by some economists that positive models are value free.

NORMATIVE MODELS and normative economics attempt to describe what ought to be. A normative statement is one which contains a value judgement. A normative model sets a standard by which reality can be judged. For instance, 'The government has a duty to protect the incomes of everybody in society, not just the well-off' would be a normative statement. It contains a value judgement about the role of government.

For some, the study of economics is fascinating in itself. Studying and constructing positive models is reward enough. But most who study economics are principally interested in the subject because of its normative aspects. They want to know how society can be changed - 'Should society help the poor and disadvantaged?', 'How best might pollution be dealt with?'.

Academic economics has a long tradition of the study of positive economics. But 'political economy', the normative study of economics, has an equally long tradition going back to Adam Smith. In fact it is difficult to separate the two. To know how best to help raise the

QUESTION 4 From the Countess of Sandwich.
Sir, I welcome John Major's statement of belief in 'the cascade of wealth between generations' and his desire to abolish inheritance tax for 'the majority of citizenry'. (The FT Interview: 'Ready to fight for his political life', July 1/2). For many people now this statement is both irrelevant and insensitive. This 'majority' is spending its savings on its own old-age care, and the 'cascade of wealth' to which he refers is being dissipated in nursing home fees and means-tested health and social services support.

The cost and efficiency of old-age care is a problem for governments across Europe, not just in the UK. But Major's new manifesto contains no solutions, and his upbeat comments are no sop to those who have - now vainly - worked to pass something on to their children. More importantly, his comments do nothing to advance the discussion on the long-term costs of caring for Europe's ageing population. Instead they ring with the same tired comments on the virtues of 'the enterprise economy' and seem to ignore the distress of many of 'the citizenry' and its professional helpers.
Caroline Sandwich.
Mapperton,
Beaminster, Dorset DT8 3NR

Which are the positive statements and which are the normative statements in this letter?

living standards of the poor (normative economics) we need to know how the economy operates and why people are poor.

Some economists argue that positive economics cannot be distinguished from normative economics because positive economics is subtly value laden. Why, for instance, did economists become so much more interested in the role of the entrepreneur (the risk-taking small businessman) during the 1980s? Much of the answer must be because Margaret Thatcher and Ronald Reagan made such important claims about the benefits of entrepreneurial activity for an economy.

In practice, all economists make value judgements. But many economists argue that 'good' economics distinguishes between positive and normative aspects. Value judgements are exposed so that we can see whether the analysis can lead to different conclusions if different value judgements are made.

Simplification

One criticism made of economics is that economic theories and models are 'unrealistic'. This is true, but it is equally true of Newton's law of gravity, Einstein's Theory of Relativity or any theory or model. This is because any theory or model has to be a simplification of reality if it is to be useful. Imagine, for instance, using a map which described an area perfectly. To do this it would need to be a full scale reproduction of the entire area which would give no practical advantage. Alternatively, drop a feather and a cannon ball from the top of the leaning tower of Pisa. You will find that both don't descend at the same speed, as one law in physics would predict, because that law assumes that factors such as air resistance and friction don't exist.

If a model is to be useful it has to be simple. The extent of simplification depends upon its use. If you wanted to go from London to Tokyo by air, it wouldn't be very helpful to have maps which were on the scale of your local A to Z. On the other hand, if you wanted to visit a friend in a nearby town it wouldn't be very helpful to have a map of the world with you. The local A to Z is very much more detailed (i.e. closer to reality) than a world map but this does not necessarily make it more useful or make it a 'better' model.

Simplification implies that some factors have been included in the model and some have been omitted. It could even be the case that some factors have been distorted to emphasise particular points in a model. For instance, on a road map of the UK, the cartographer will almost certainly not have attempted to name every small hamlet or to show the geological formation of the area. On the other hand, he or she will have marked in roads and motorways which will appear several miles wide according to the scale of the map. There are a number of reasons why this occurs.

- Models are constructed in an attempt to present a clear and simple explanation of reality. Trying to include weather and geological information on a large scale road map would make it much more difficult for the motorist to see how to get from A to B. On the other hand, distorting reality by making roads very wide is extremely helpful to a motorist studying a map because it is much easier to read thick lines than thin lines.
- Models must assume that explanations for much of what is contained in the model lie elsewhere. For instance, a model which explains that consumption varies with income doesn't explain what determines income itself.
- The creator of a model may not be interested in a particular aspect of reality (which is an example of how normative values can be superimposed on supposedly positive models). The cartographer, for instance, preparing an ordinary road map is not interested in the geology of an area.
- The model may be constructed deliberately to distort and mislead. For instance, employers might choose to use a model which predicts that minimum wages always increase unemployment, whilst trade unions might construct a different model which showed that minimum wages increased employment.

Models may also omit variables because the author does not believe them to be of importance. This may be a correct premise. On the other hand, it may be false, leading to the model being poorer than it might otherwise be. For instance, few would criticise a weather model which omits the UK rate of inflation from among its variables. On the other hand, a weather model of the UK which omits wind speed is unlikely to perform well.

In conclusion, all subject disciplines simplify and select from a mass of data. This process seems to cause little concern in sciences such as physics and chemistry. However, it is unfortunate for economists that many critics of the subject seem to think that simplification in economics shows that economists have little or no understanding of economic matters. Nothing could be further from the truth!

QUESTION 5 Take any theory with which you are familiar. Explain what simplifications have been made in the construction of the theory.

Key terms

The scientific method - a method which subjects theories or hypotheses to falsification by empirical evidence.
Theory or model - a hypothesis which is capable of refutation by empirical evidence.
Law - a theory or model which has been verified by empirical evidence.
Positive economics - the scientific or objective study of the allocation of resources.
Normative economics - the study and presentation of policy prescriptions involving value judgements about the way in which scarce resources are allocated.

Applied economics

Positive and normative economics

In an advertisement placed in the *Financial Times* on January 20 1989, the Tobacco Advisory Council (TAC), funded by the British tobacco industry, wrote the following.

'Before the last two Budgets we argued that excessive tax on cigarettes makes no economic sense. We explained that high taxes don't make people smoke less. They simply drive smokers to cheaper, imported brands. (Bad for the balance of payments and bad for British jobs.) We also pointed out that the hefty increases some pressure groups demand would add nearly 1 per cent to the inflation rate.

We're grateful our past warnings were not ignored. But this year there's even more of a case for fiscal restraint. Come 1992, the entire European tobacco market will be up for grabs. To stand a chance, the British Tobacco industry needs to maintain its market base. Higher taxes only undermine its position to the advantage of foreign competition.

There were plenty of sound arguments against excessive tax last year. Does it make sense to pile it on this year, now we're offering you an even better case?'

The article made a number of positive statements which could be tested against economic evidence:

- the quantity of cigarettes smoked is not influenced by the size of the tax on cigarettes;
- an increase in taxes will lead to smokers substituting cheaper brands of cigarettes for the ones they currently smoke;
- these cheaper brands are not manufactured in the UK but are imported;
- these imports lead to a deterioration of the balance of payments position and lead to a loss of jobs, presumably in UK cigarette factories;
- increasing taxes on cigarettes will increase the inflation rate;
- the European Community 1992 programme would increase competition in the European tobacco market;
- companies best placed to survive this increased competition will be those which have a strong domestic market base.

It also made a number of normative statements, such as:

- referring to taxes as 'excessive' and labelling the increases in tax demanded by some pressure groups as 'hefty';
- stating that tax on cigarettes makes 'no economic sense';
- arguing that there was 'even more of a case' in 1989 than in previous years.

Overall, the advertisement could be argued to be normative in tone, using value laden terms even when making positive statements. For instance, instead of talking about a 'loss of British jobs', it says 'bad for British jobs', and the whole argument about the effects of 1992 is peppered with phrases such as 'up for grabs', 'stand a chance' and 'undermine their position'.

What the advertisement did not do is consider any alternative case. For instance, if it believed that a raising of taxes merely leads to substitution by consumers, why did it not argue that taxes on cheaper brands of cigarettes be raised by a greater proportion than an increase on dearer cigarettes? If it was concerned about inflation, the effect of a large increase in tobacco duties could be offset by a fall in duties on other goods such as lead free petrol. Does it matter if jobs are lost in the British tobacco industry if those workers are redeployed to other jobs in the economy? The advertisement also said nothing about the health costs of smoking. It avoided raising this issue by implying that nothing can be done to alter the habits of smokers since raising taxes won't affect the level of demand.

As a piece of economic analysis, it was fundamentally flawed, presenting a one-sided viewpoint in value laden terms and making a number of unsubstantiated assertions. As an advertisement, it was intended to sway opinion. We have no evidence to suggest whether or not it succeeded in this aim.

The housing market

%
50
40
30
20
10
0
10
-20
1964 1970 1980 1990'92

Source: adapted from Nationwide Anglia Index.

Figure 114.1
Inflation in house prices

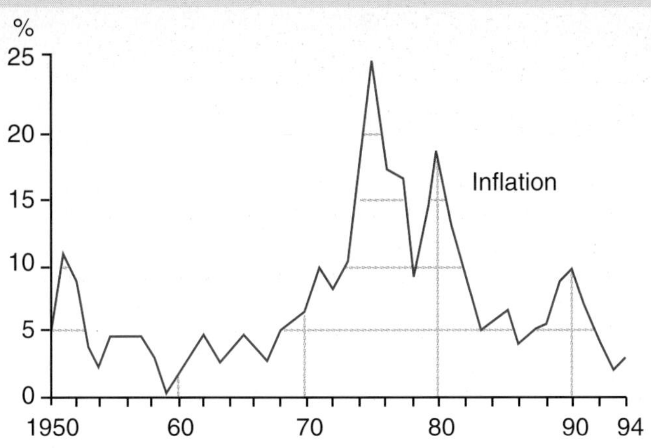

Source: adapted from CSO, *Annual Abstract of Statistics*.

Figure 114.2 *Inflation: change in the Retail Price Index*

1. England and Wales.

Source: adapted from CSO, *Economic Trends Annual Supplement*.

Figure 114.3 *Number of property transactions*[1]

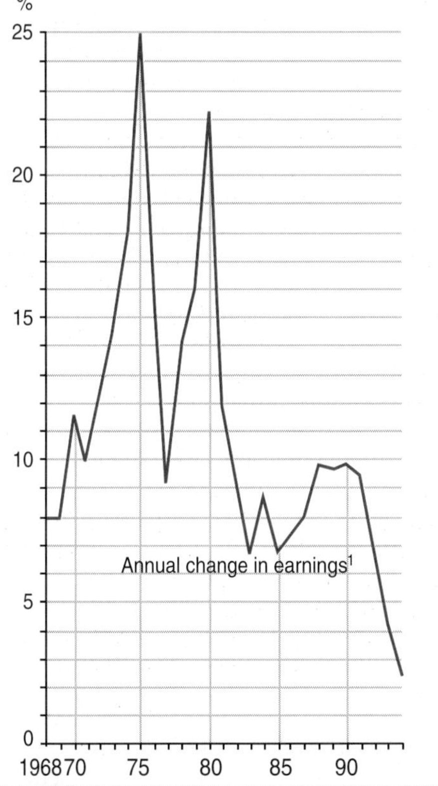

1. Average weekly earnings of full time male employees excluding those whose pay was affected by absence; Great Britain, each year.

Source: adapted from Building Societies Association.

Figure 114.4 *Annual change in earnings*[1]

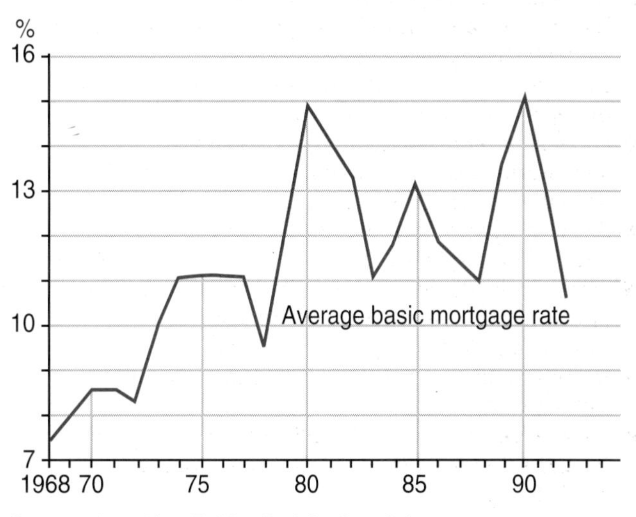

Source: adapted from Building Societies Association.

Figure 114.5 *Average basic mortgage rate*

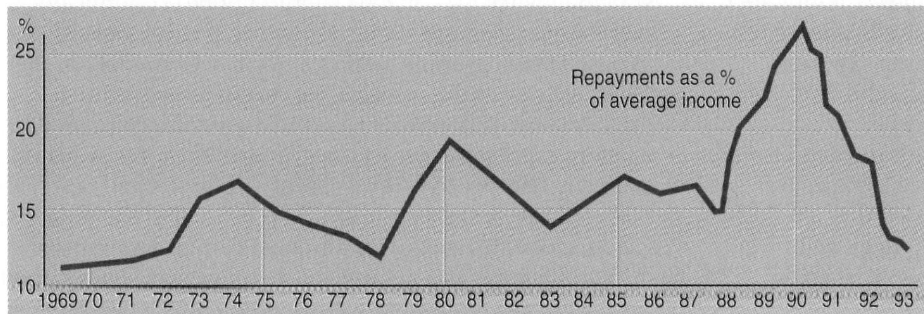

Source: adapted from Council of Mortgage Lenders and Environment Department.

Figure 114.6 *Mortgage repayments as a % of average income*

Figures 114.1 to 114.6 show how house prices and other variables have changed since the late 1960s.

1. **Construct FIVE hypotheses about what determines changes in prices of houses.**
2. **To what extent do the data support or refute your hypotheses?**

unit 115

Economic models

Summary

1. A good model is one which yields powerful conclusions, is elegant and internally consistent.
2. In addition, a good positive model is one which explains past and present events, can predict future events, is universally applicable and has realistic assumptions.
3. A good positive model must be capable of being refuted whilst a good normative model is one which sets out an ideal or paradigm state of affairs.
4. Models can be distinguished according to whether they are static or dynamic models, equilibrium or disequilibrium models, partial or general models, or micro-economic or macro-economic models.

'Good' models

Many of the units in this book are devoted to one economic model or another. Which of these models are 'good' models? A number of criteria can be used to judge a model.

One important criterion by which a positive economic model may be judged is the extent to which it accurately **explains reality**. Reality exists in three different time periods: **the past, the present and the future**. A very powerful model, such as the model of price determination, is able to explain what happened in the past, explain what is happening today and predict what will happen in the future. Price theory provided an explanation of why the rise in oil prices during the 1970s led to a fall in world wide demand for oil. Today it helps us understand why a restriction in the supply of oil by OPEC leads to a price rise. We can predict with confidence that as world oil reserves diminish over the next 300 years the price of oil will rise.

The simple Keynesian theory of income determination, however, is not such a good theory. It explains relatively well the workings of the UK economy in the 1950s and 1960s but only gives a partial insight into how the economy performed in the 1970s and 1980s. This is because the simple Keynesian model ignores both changes in the money supply and supply side shocks - reasonable simplifying assumptions in the 1950s and 1960s but very misleading in the context of economic events in the 1970s and 1980s. It may be that the 1970s and 1980s were an exceptional time period and perhaps in the future the simple Keynesian model will once again prove to be a good one.

Macro-economic computer models of the economy, such as the Treasury model, the London Business School (LBS) model or the National Institute of Economic Research (NIESR) model, are judged mainly on their ability to predict the future. They are specifically called **'forecasting models'**. It could be that the best predictor of next year's rate of inflation is this year's rainfall in the Sahara desert. A model which incorporated this would be a good model if we were solely interested in its ability to forecast but it would be a poor model if we wished to understand the causes of inflation in the UK.

There are a number of economic models which are claimed to be good predictors but are not based on **realistic assumptions**. An example is the neo-classical theory of the firm. In the real world there are virtually no industries which conform to the assumptions of either perfect competition or pure monopoly yet these theories are widely taught and discussed. One justification is that although the assumptions are unrealistic the models provide very powerful and clear predictions about the extremes of behaviour of firms. If we know how firms behave at either end of the spectrum of competition then we can predict how firms will behave between these two extremes. Unfortunately these justifications have no logical or empirical validity. The models of perfect competition and monopoly give us little help in understanding the behaviour of firms in the real world, which is why there are so many alternative theories of the firm.

Positive models must be capable of refutation (☞ unit 114) . A good model will be one where it is possible to gather data and perhaps perform controlled experiments to refute or support the model.

Normative models need to be judged on different criteria. A normative model does not claim to mirror reality. It attempts to provide a guide as to what is desirable or to be recommended. The neo-classical theory of the firm provides such a **paradigm**. By making a number of assumptions, it is possible to show that efficiency will be maximised in an economy where all firms are perfectly competitive (☞ unit 35). Increasing the degree of competition in industry then becomes an ideal or a goal to be aimed for. Monopoly, on the other hand, is shown to diminish welfare. Therefore the policy goal should be to break up monopolies.

Ultimately it is impossible to judge between competing normative theories. It is impossible to prove or disprove a statement such as 'Citizens should not be economically dependent upon the state'. However, it is possible to expose false reasoning within a normative model. In the 1950s, Lipsey and Lancaster, for instance, proved that greater competition might lead to a loss of welfare in the economy if at least one industry in the economy was not perfectly competitive. This 'theory of the second best' rebutted the general assumption prevalent at the time (and indeed still prevalent amongst certain economists and politicians) that greater competition was always good whilst greater monopoly was always bad.

All models need to be judged on the grounds of internal consistency, and elegance. **Internal consistency** simply means that the logic in the argument is correct and that no mistakes have been made with any mathematics used. An **elegant** model is one which is as simple and as lucid as possible.

Finally, models need to be judged on their power. Price theory is a very **powerful** model. With few assumptions and a minimum of logic, it can be used to explain important events across time and between countries. Aggregate demand and aggregate supply analysis similarly is a powerful model which can show the effects of a variety of demand side and supply side shocks on the price level and output.

QUESTION 1

Table 115.1

	Investment[1] (£billion at 1990 prices)	Rate of interest[2] (%)	Change in national income[3] (£billion at 1990 prices)
1987	92.3	9.74	19.6
1988	105.1	10.90	21.9
1989	111.5	13.85	10.5
1990	107.6	14.77	2.7
1991	97.4	11.70	-1.0
1992	96.3	9.56	-2.3
1993	96.6	6.01	9.9
1994	99.7	5.46	18.6

1. Gross domestic fixed capital formation.
2. Bank base rate.
3. Gross domestic product at factor cost.

Source: adapted from CSO, *Economic Trends Annual Supplement.*

To what extent does the data show that (a) the accelerator model and (b) the marginal efficiency of investment model are 'good' models of investment behaviour?

Realism and models

It is often said that some economic models are poor because they are not 'realistic'. However, before coming to this conclusion about any particular theory, it is important to consider what is the purpose of the theory.

- The model may be used to predict **future** events. In this case, it is unimportant if the assumptions or workings of the model are realistic. The value of the model should only be judged in terms of its predictive power.
- The model may be used to analyse the workings of a **group** of individuals. The fact that some individuals behave in a different way to that predicted by the model which attempts to say how groups work on the whole does not make the model unrealistic.
- The model may be used to explain the **workings** of a market or an economy. The detail may be realistic even if the overall predictive power of the model is relatively weak. In this case, the fact that the predictions of the model are unrealistic is not particularly important.
- The model may be **normative**, used to describe what ought to be rather than what is. In this case, realism is obviously not an important criterion.
- The model may be very **simple**. With a few assumptions, the model may come to powerful but simplified conclusions. The fact that predictions are not accurate to the nearest 0.1 per cent does not mean that the model is unrealistic.

Forms of expression

There are a variety of ways in which models can be expressed.

Verbally A model can be expressed in words. 'Consumption increases when disposable income increases' would be an example. The advantage of using words is that models can be made accessible to a wide variety of readers. On the other hand, the use of jargon, such as 'disposable income', can be a barrier to the non-economist. Words can also be imprecise. In the above statement, we don't know the extent to which the increase is proportional.

Algebraically Over the past twenty years there has been an explosion in the use of algebra in academic economics. It enables relationships to be set down very precisely but is often totally incomprehensible to the non-specialist. It

QUESTION 2

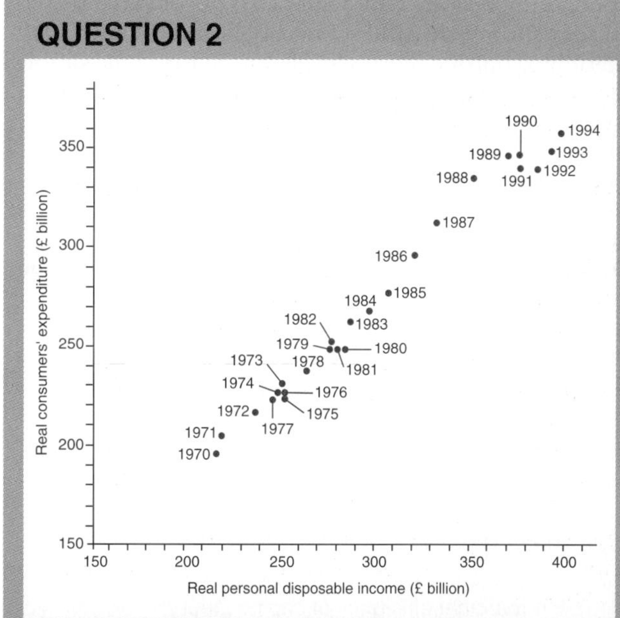

Source: adapted from CSO, *Economic Trends Annual Supplement.*

Figure 115.1 *Real consumers' expenditure and real personal disposable income at 1990 prices*

This is a scatter diagram.
(a) To what extent does it show that there is a positive correlation between consumers' expenditure and their income?
(b) How might you express the relationship between consumers' expenditure and income (i) verbally and (ii) algebraically?

also presumes that economic relationships are precise. Many economists argue the contrary - that economic relationships, whilst consistent, cannot be expressed so accurately.

Graphically The use of graphs has a long history in economics. It provides a convenient shorthand, encapsulating what would otherwise take many words to explain. Graphs, however, have their limitations. For instance, the fact that they can only be used in two dimensions with any ease limits the number of variables that can be used in a model.

Statistically Statistics are essential for economists if they are to verify hypotheses. They encourage precision, but as with algebra, they can be difficult for the non-specialist to understand and can give a misleading impression of accuracy in economics. **Econometrics**, the empirical testing of economic theories using statistical data, is now an important branch of economics.

Exogenous and endogenous variables

Economic models are built with two types of variables. EXOGENOUS VARIABLES are variables whose value is determined outside the model. For instance, in the simple Keynesian model of income determination, investment, government expenditure and exports are exogenous variables. Their values are constant whatever the change in other variables in the model unless it is assumed otherwise. The value of exogenous variables therefore cannot be calculated within the model.

ENDOGENOUS VARIABLES are variables whose value is determined within the model. For instance, in the simple Keynesian model of income determination both consumption and income are endogenous variables. Their value is determined by variables such as income within the consumption function equation. The value of endogenous variables will change if other variables within the model change too.

QUESTION 3 What variables would be exogenous and which would be endogenous in:
(a) the marginal efficiency of capital theory;
(b) the cobweb theorem;
(c) the theory of perfect competition?

Static and dynamic

A DYNAMIC model is one which contains time as one of its variables. A STATIC model is one which contains no time element within the model. Nearly all the models explained in this book are static models. For instance, neither the theory of perfect competition nor the Keynesian theory of income determination contain a time variable. Static models can be used to compare two different situations, a technique called **comparative static analysis**. In the theory of perfect competition, it is common to compare one equilibrium situation with another equilibrium situation. For instance, a short run equilibrium position may be compared to the long run equilibrium position. A time element may even be implicitly assumed within the model - it is assumed that the movement from one equilibrium position to another in perfect competition will take place over a period of time rather than instantly at a point in time. However, the model does not explain the path which the industry or the firm will take in the move from one equilibrium position to another. It merely assumes a 'before' and 'after' situation.

The cobweb theorem and the acccelerator theory are the only two dynamic models explained in this book. The cobweb theorem, for instance, explicitly charts the movement over time of a market in a disequilibrium state.

Dynamic models are in one sense more 'realistic' than static models. Time is a very important variable in the real world. However, as we have already argued, greater realism is not always a desirable characteristic in a model. Dynamic models in economics are more complex and difficult to work with than static models and their predictions are not necessarily more powerful. For instance, if we wish to know how much revenue a government will raise by increasing taxes on beer, all we need is a static price model comparing the equilibrium situation before and after the imposition of the tax. There is no need to know the exact path that the market takes to get from one equilibrium position to another. Dynamic models are not therefore 'better' or 'worse' than static models - that judgement depends upon the use to which a model is to be put.

Equilibrium and disequilibrium models

Equilibrium is a central feature of all the models studied in this book. In economics, EQUILIBRIUM can be described as a point where expectations are being realised and where no plans are being frustrated. For instance, in the Keynesian model of national income determination, equilibrium national income is the point where planned expenditure equals actual income. In neo-classical price theory the cobweb theory is a disequilibrium model because it charts the behaviour of the market as planned demand and supply differ from actual demand and supply. All static models are equilibrium models because they deal with equilibrium positions.

An equilibrium position may be stable. If there is a movement away from equilibrium for some reason, there will be an in-built tendency for equilibrium to be restored. If the equilibrium point is unstable, there will be no tendency to move towards an equilibrium point once disequilibrium has been established.

It is easy to make the incorrect assumption that the market (or whatever is being studied) will always return to an equilibrium position; or that the equilibrium point is somehow the optimal or most desirable position. Neither is necessarily true even if economists tend to believe that knowing where is the equilibrium point is helpful in explaining economic events and in making policy recommendations.

Partial and general models

Just as there is no clear distinction between theories and models, so too there is no clear dividing line between a partial and a general model. A GENERAL MODEL can be said to be one which contains a large number of variables. For instance, a model which includes all markets in the economy is a general model. A PARTIAL MODEL is one which contains relatively few variables. A model of the oil market or the demand for money would be partial models.

A partial model will be one in which most variables are assumed to be in the category of CETERIS PARIBUS. Ceteris paribus is Latin for 'all other things being equal' or 'all other things remaining the same'. It is a very powerful simplifying device which enables economists to explain clearly how an economy works. For instance, in neo-classical price theory ceteris paribus is used constantly. When the effect of a change in price on demand is analysed we assume that incomes, the prices of all other goods, and tastes remain the same. In the Keynesian multiplier model, it is assumed that government spending, exports, the marginal propensity to consume etc. do not change when analysing the effect of a change in investment on national income.

A general model may be realistic because it contains more variables. But again it is not necessarily better than a partial model. If we wish to study the effects of a rise in indirect taxes on the car industry, it is much simpler and easier to use a partial model of price determination than to use a general model. The general model may provide marginally more information but the extra information is unlikely to be worth the time and effort needed to generate it.

Macro-economics and micro-economics

A MACRO-ECONOMIC model is one which models the economy as a whole. It deals with economic relationships at the level of all participants in the economy. A MICRO-ECONOMIC model, on the other hand, deals with the economic behaviour of individuals or groups within society. For instance, the study of the spending decisions of individual consumers or consumers within a particular market such as the market for cars (demand theory) would be micro-economics. The study of consumption patterns for the whole economy (the consumption function) would be an example of macro-economics. The study of the determination of wage rates (wage theory) would be micro-economics. The study of the overall level of wages in the economy (part of national income accounting) would be macro-economics.

QUESTION 4 Consider the following economic models and explain whether they are static or dynamic, equilibrium or disequilibrium, partial or general, and macro-economic or micro-economic models: (a) the Keynesian multiplier model; (b) the accelerator model of investment; (c) the Keynesian consumption function model; (d) the aggregate demand and supply model of income determination; (e) marginal utility theory; (f) the cobweb model; (g) the model of perfect competition; (h) the marginal revenue product theory.

Key terms

Exogenous variables - variables whose value is determined outside the model under consideration.
Endogenous variables - variables whose value is determined within the model being used.
Static and dynamic models - a static model is one where time is not a variable. In a dynamic model, time is a variable explicit in the model.
Equilibrium - the point where what is expected or planned is equal to what is realised or actually happens.
Partial and general models - a partial model is one with few variables whilst a general model has many.
Ceteris paribus - the assumption that all other variables within the model remain constant whilst one change is being considered.
Macro-economics - the study of the economy as a whole.
Micro-economics - the study of the behaviour of individuals or groups within an economy.

Applied economics

Forecasting models

A number of UK macro-economic forecasting models are in current use. They are computer driven, usually relying upon a large number of different relationships to produce predictions about the levels of certain key variables, such as GDP, prices and the balance of payments.

Figure 115.2 shows the main relationships in a version of the Treasury macro-economic model used in the 1970s. The 1994 version of this model used over 500 different equations to describe the relationship between different variables. For instance, the consumption function (☞ units 62 and 79) was specified as the equation below.

$$
\begin{aligned}
\text{LnC} = {} & \text{gLnC} - \underset{(3.0)}{0.17069}\ \text{gLn (C/RLY)} + \underset{(2.4)}{0.012129}\ \text{gLn (100 NFWPE/(PCA RLY)} \\
& + \underset{(1.5)}{0.007192}\ \text{gLn (100000 GPW/(PCA RLY))} - \underset{(2.1)}{0.038861} + (\underset{(4.6)}{0.21265} + 0.16064\text{g} - \underset{(3.3)}{0.14464}\ \text{g}^2)\ (1 - \text{g})\ \text{LnRPDI} \\
& + \underset{(2.7)}{0.027738}\ (1 - \text{g})\ \text{Ln (NFWPE/PCA)} + \underset{(2.9)}{0.081215}\ (1 - \text{g})\ \text{Ln (GPW/PCA)} - \underset{(3.4)}{0.01097}\ (1 - \text{g})\ \text{UNUKP} \\
& - \underset{(2.9)}{0.001806}\ (1 - \text{g})\ \text{RS} + \underset{(3.9)}{0.020091}\ \text{D731} + \underset{(6.9)}{0.036351}\ \text{D792} + \underset{(5.0)}{0.027596}\ \text{D681} - \underset{(3.1)}{0.015498}\ \text{D804} \\
& - \underset{(2.0)}{0.42872}\ \text{g}\ (1 - \text{g})\ \text{(MORT/RPDI)}
\end{aligned}
$$

There are a number of key points which can be picked out from this equation. Consumption is determined by:

- income - the real disposable labour income (RLY - the real incomes of workers after tax and deductions) and, less importantly, real personal disposable income (RPDI);
- wealth - the financial wealth of the personal sector (NFWPE) and the housing wealth of the personal sector (GPW);
- interest rates - the nominal rate of interest (RS);
- unemployment - (UNUKP);
- the amount consumers have to pay in mortgage payments - real mortgage payments (MORT).

The response of consumption to changes in these variables is lagged in different ways. Table 115.2 shows the different elasticities (responses) of consumption to a 1 per cent change in the main variables affecting consumption. For instance, a 1 per cent rise in real disposable labour income (RLY) will lead to a 0.887 rise in consumption in the long run. However, it takes time for this effect to build up. In the first quarter following a 1 per cent rise in RLY, there is no change in consumption at all. By the 5th quarter, there is a 0.467 per cent rise in consumption. By the 13th quarter this has risen to 0.790 per cent.

Real disposable labour income, financial wealth and housing wealth all have a long term effect on consumption. The four other variables in Table 115.2 only have short run effects. For instance, a 1 per cent rise in unemployment will reduce consumption by 0.0109 per cent in the first quarter, 0.0052 per cent in the fifth quarter and a barely significant 0.0012 per cent by the 13th quarter. The model is saying that a 10 per cent rise in unemployment will reduce consumption by 1.09 per cent in the first quarter because it will knock consumer confidence. However, if the unemployment levels stay at that new figure, within five years consumer confidence will have returned and consumption will have returned to its initial level. Notice that the consumption function here is broadly Keynesian. In the long run, 88.9 per cent of any increase in income is spent. Wealth is only a minor determinant of consumption.

The 1994 Treasury model has 135 **exogenous** variables, ranging from indirect taxes to interest rates. Figures for these need to be fed into the model before it can generate estimates of the **endogenous** variables, such as the current balance, total final expenditure, gross domestic product, the Retail Price Index and unemployment. Both real variables, such as the labour force and national income, as well as monetary variables, such as interest rates and money supply aggregates, are included.

The Treasury model, like all the major forecasting models in the UK, is both remarkably accurate in its predictions and yet also highly inaccurate. It is accurate because it succeeds in predicting levels of variables such as GDP, prices, exports, imports and unemployment to within 1 or 2 per cent. It is inaccurate because economists and politicians are not particularly interested in these levels - they are interested in changes in these levels. For instance, there is a 100 per cent difference in a forecast that the economy will grow by 3 per cent this year and that the growth rate will be 1½ per cent. The late 1980s was a particularly difficult time for forecasters. They all tended to underestimate the strength of the Lawson boom. On the other hand, when the economy had slowed down by the end of 1990, only 12 out of the 41 forecasters polled by the

Table 115.2 *Responsiveness of consumption to changes in its determinants*

	Q1	Q5	Q9	Q13	Long-run
Elasticity of C with respect to a 1% increase in:					
Labour income (RLY)	0.0	0.467	0.688	0.790	0.887
Financial wealth (NFWPE)	0.028	0.051	0.061	0.066	0.071
Housing wealth (GPW)	0.081	0.061	0.051	0.046	0.042
Nominal interest rates (RS)	-0.0018	-0.00085	-0.0004	-0.0002	0.0
Real personal disposable income (RPDI)	0.210	0.092	0.044	0.031	0.0
Unemployment rate (UNUKP)	-0.0109	-0.0052	-0.0025	-0.0012	0.0
Real value of mortgages (MORT)	0.0	-0.240	-0.115	-0.055	0.0

Source: The Treasury.

Treasury predicted correctly that there would be a recession in 1991, and all underestimated its depth.

The reasons for these sort of inaccuracies are not difficult to find. The models are built up using past data. So long as economic variables remain relatively constant in level or rates of changes, then the equations built upon past experience will predict with reasonable accuracy. However, shocks to the economy or large changes in an economic variable which had been broadly constant before can lead to sizeable errors in the forecasts. The 1970s, which was not a good decade for forecasters, was rocked by two enormous oil price increases. The outcomes of these were difficult to model. In the UK, the errors of the late 1980s can be mainly attributed to the enormous increase in house prices during the Lawson boom and the subsequent slump in house prices in the recession. The 1994 Treasury model, as explained above, now recognises that house prices affect consumption.

Economists disagree about whether large models like the Treasury model will ever improve their accuracy in forecasting. Some argue that as time goes on, models will become more sophisticated and the effect of sudden shocks will be predicted by the model. Other economists argue that the economy is so complex, the outcome of billions of economic decisions each day, that it will always be impossible accurately to model the economy. More and longer equations in a model won't make the model a better predictor. The debate is about whether economics is an art or a science.

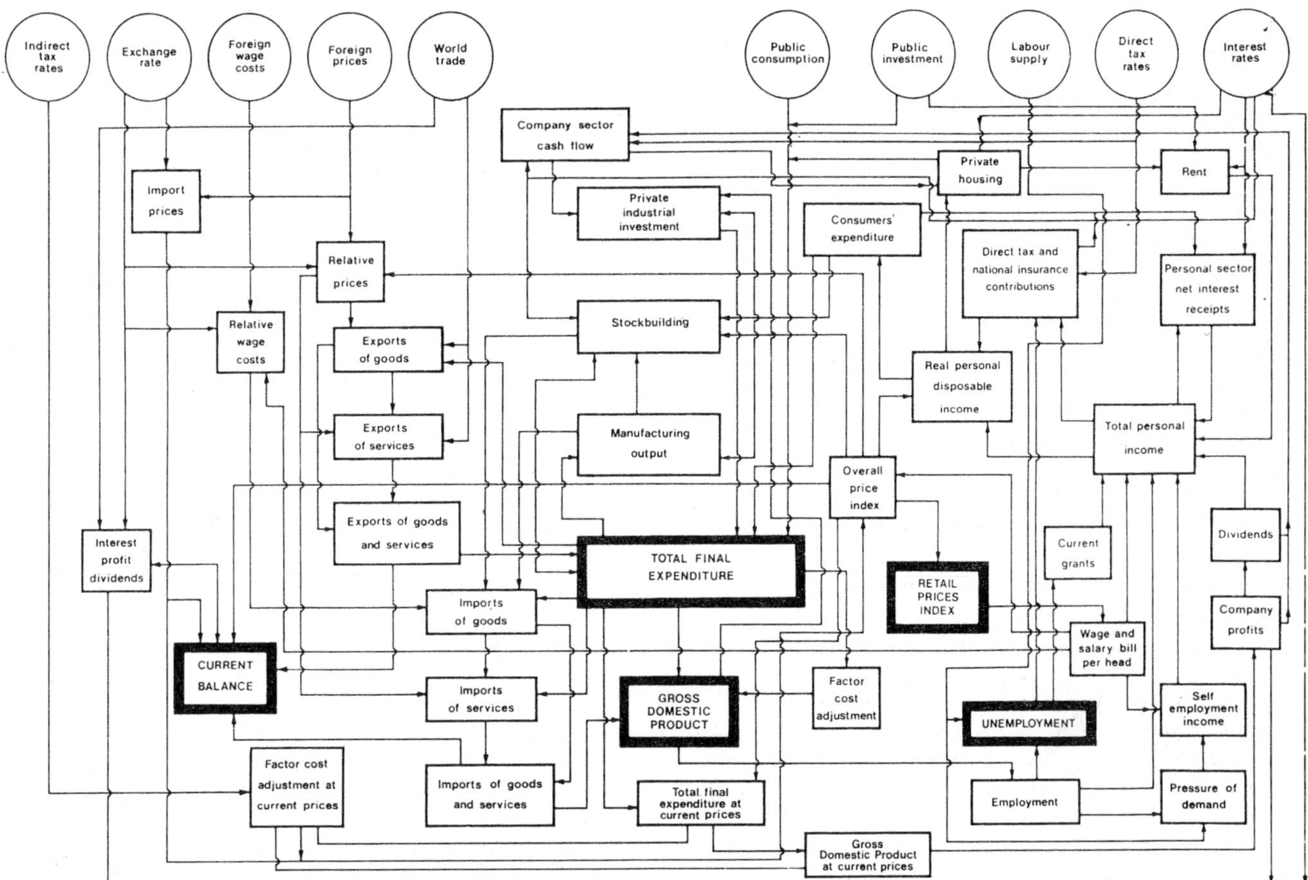

Figure 115.2 *Flow chart of a Treasury macroeconomic model*

Modelling the steel market

Table 115.3 *Steel production, prices and related data, UK*

	Steel output (thousand tonnes)	Steel prices (1990 = 100)	Passenger car output (thousands)	Engineering output (1990 = 100)	GDP at current prices £bn	GDP at 1990 prices £bn
1987Q1	3 989.0	84.31	91.1	81	86.4	108.6
Q2	4 392.0	85.4	93.7	82	89.0	110.1
Q3	4 673.0	86.7	102.9	85	91.6	112.0
Q4	4 672.0	87.7	93.1	87	93.7	113.1
1988Q1	4 751.0	90.3	96.3	88	96.2	114.9
Q2	4 694.0	91.8	102.5	91	98.2	115.5
Q3	4 675.0	94.2	102.7	95	101.9	117.2
Q4	4 727.3	97.6	107.5	95	105.2	118.1
1989Q1	4 854.0	100.0	110.3	95	107.5	118.7
Q2	4 740.6	100.9	108.0	98	108.7	118.9
Q3	4 912.0	101.0	108.6	98	111.5	119.1
Q4	4 282.6	100.3	106.1	100	114.1	119.5
1990Q1	4 539.8	99.1	97.8	102	116.2	120.2
Q2	4 543.9	100.9	101.1	102	119.6	120.6
Q3	4 758.5	100.6	112.3	99	121.7	119.5
Q4	4 075.7	99.3	120.6	97	121.4	118.6
1991Q1	3 912.8	98.6	106.1	96	123.1	117.9
Q2	4 267.5	98.5	109.9	94	123.3	117.3
Q3	4 222.2	97.4	100.8	92	123.6	116.9
Q4	4 101.3	96.3	95.5	92	125.9	117.0
1992Q1	4 134.0	95.8	105.4	91	126.2	116.2
Q2	4 078.1	97.1	110.2	90	128.9	116.2
Q3	4 353.2	97.2	110.0	91	130.1	116.8
Q4	3 650.6	98.2	105.1	92	130.8	117.3
1993Q1	4 028.6	97.8	105.5	92	133.6	117.9
Q2	4 249.6	100.8	120.9	92	135.7	118.5
Q3	4 166.4	102.6	119.4	94	137.7	119.6
Q4	4 126.9	102.1	114.6	93	139.5	120.4
1994Q1	4 065.0	105.5	111.6	99	141.8	121.7
Q2	4 285.6	108.5	121.8	103	143.4	123.4
Q3	4 269.9	111.7	125.4	107	145.4	124.5
Q4	4 722.0	116.6	131.4	109	147.6	125.5
1995Q1	4 384.3	122.4	131.5	112	149.0	126.3

Source: adapted from CSO, *Monthly Digest of Statistics; Economic Trends Annual Supplement.*

1. What is meant by a 'model' in economics?
2. From the data, build a static model of what you think determines steel output in the UK. Your answer to this question should be expressed in three forms: (a) verbally (e.g. steel output is determined by steel prices); (b) algebraically (e.g. $Q_s = 0.75Q_d$); (c) graphically (e.g. as in a demand curve).
3. Now attempt to build a dynamic model of the determination of steel output (e.g. steel output in one quarter is determined by steel prices in the previous quarter).
4. Explain which are the exogenous and which are the endogenous variables in your models.
5. Explain whether you have built a partial model or a general model.
6. What difficulties did you encounter in building your models?

Index

G

T